Printing Anglo-Saxon from Parker to Hickes and Wanley

Library of the Written Word

VOLUME 105

The Handpress World

Editor-in-Chief

Andrew Pettegree (*University of St Andrews*)
Arthur der Weduwen (*University of St Andrews*)

Editorial Board

Trude Dijkstra (*University of Amsterdam*)
Falk Eisermann (*Staatsbibliothek zu Berlin – Preußischer Kulturbesitz*)
Shanti Graheli (*University of Glasgow*)
Katherine Halsey (*Stirling University*)
Earle Havens (*Johns Hopkins University*)
Ian Maclean (*All Souls College, Oxford*)
Angela Nuovo (*University of Milan*)
Malcolm Walsby (ENSSIB, *Lyon*)
Alexander Wilkinson (*University College Dublin*)

VOLUME 84

The titles published in this series are listed at *brill.com/lww*

Printing Anglo-Saxon from Parker to Hickes and Wanley

*With a Catalogue of Early Printed Books
Containing Anglo-Saxon 1566–1705*

By

Peter J. Lucas

BRILL

LEIDEN | BOSTON

Cover illustration: Franciscus Junius of Leiden's Pica Saxon from the Oxford University type specimen of 1693 (also see Illustration 33a).

The Library of Congress Cataloging-in-Publication Data is available online at https://catalog.loc.gov
LC record available at https://lccn.loc.gov/2023047137

Typeface for the Latin, Greek, and Cyrillic scripts: "Brill". See and download: brill.com/brill-typeface.

ISSN 1874-4834
ISBN 978-90-0-451697-7 (hardback)
ISBN 978-90-0-451639-7 (e-book)
DOI 10.1163/9789004516397

Copyright 2024 by Koninklijke Brill BV, Leiden, The Netherlands.
Koninklijke Brill BV incorporates the imprints Brill, Brill Nijhoff, Brill Schöningh, Brill Fink, Brill mentis, Brill Wageningen Academic, Vandenhoeck & Ruprecht, Böhlau and V&R unipress.
All rights reserved. No part of this publication may be reproduced, translated, stored in a retrieval system, or transmitted in any form or by an y means, electronic, mechanical, photocopying, recording or otherwise, without prior written permission from the publisher. Requests for re-use and/or translations must be addressed to Koninklijke Brill BV via brill.com or copyright.com.

This book is printed on acid-free paper and produced in a sustainable manner.

In Memoriam

Sir Henry Spelman
George Hickes
Franciscus Junius
Humfrey Wanley

þa boceras gesawun þa wundru
The learned men saw the marvelous things
Matthew 21.15

∴

*Hu mæg se man wel faran, ðe his mod awent fram
eallum wisum bocum*
How can the man be successful whose mind has strayed
from all books full of wisdom?
ÆLFRIC, *De Novo Testamento*: from **1638.1**, sig. K4^v, cited in **1690.1**, sig. 3C2^r

∴

Contents

Preface and Acknowledgements IX
List of Tables and Figures XVI
Abbreviations XXI

PART 1
Printing Anglo-Saxon with Special Sorts from 1566 to 1705

1 Anglo-Saxon and Its Uses 3

2 The Parkerian Great Primer Anglo-Saxon Type-Design 29

3 The Parkerian and Lambardian Pica Anglo-Saxon Type-Designs 60

4 Anglo-Saxon Type-Designs in the Seventeenth Century to 1705 83

5 Continental Anglo-Saxon Type-Designs 143

6 The Use of Sources, Scholarship and the Social Intellectual Network 176

PART 2
Catalogue of Early Printed Books Containing Anglo-Saxon to 1705

Glossary of Printing, Book-Description and Type-Description Terms 187

List of Type Designs 190

Abbreviations 214

Library Abbreviations 219

Catalogue of Early Printed Books Containing Anglo-Saxon to 1705 236

PART 3
List of Punchcutters and Printers, Bibliography
(*Medieval MSS, Post-Medieval MSS, Printed Books*)

List of Punchcutters   601

List of Printers and Booksellers also Draughtsmen/Engravers   605

Bibliography   631
General Index   695

Preface and Acknowledgements

This book has three parts. Part 1 gives an account of printing Anglo-Saxon with special letter-sorts designed to mimic those found previously in manuscripts. There are eight main type-designs used in England in London, Cambridge and Oxford, all of them originating through the enterprise of scholars and people with influence who knew a good deal about the subject; these take the form AS1, AS2, etc.; brief details of these are given in Table 1. Many books first published in England were published again in modified form on the continent and Anglo-Saxon type-designs were made for them too, seven type-designs in all, these take the form CAS1, etc.; brief details are given in Table 2. These type-designs were made for printers who did not usually have a scholarly Anglo-Saxonist looking over their shoulder; they were made because they were needed to make the new book look like the one it was based on. This study is based on evidence presented in Part 2, which begins with a glossary of terms and some account of the type-designs referred to in the book, focusing on those for Anglo-Saxon. There follows a catalogue of all the early printed books I have found that contain Anglo-Saxon. Each book is given a reference number based on its year of publication, as **1566.1**, so it follows that the books are arranged in chronological order. Basic information is given for each, such as would be found in a bibliography (plus STC, Wing, ESTC or USTC numbers (for books published on the continent up to 1650) as appropriate), the sources of the Anglo-Saxon material in each are enumerated with as much precision as possible (dictionary entries being often so brief that they resist such treatment), and, if the books are printed so as to include special Anglo-Saxon letter-forms or sorts, as a large proportion of them are, details of these are given and discussed. In Part 3 there is an index of punchcutters, the people who actually made the type-designs, and an index of printers and publishers/booksellers, the people who are the link between the type-designs and the books and between the books and the reader. The first part of the Bibliography is a list of manuscripts used for source material in the printed books in the Catalogue, with the reference number for the printed book that made use of each manuscript noted so that it can be seen which manuscripts were used and when; the list of manuscripts is divided into two sections, the first listing medieval manuscripts, the second listing post-medieval manuscripts. The second part of the Bibliography lists books consulted for this study and each entry that relates to a specific printed book is followed by the reference number for that printed book. The book is completed by a general index.

Work first began on this project in 1995 when I was Visiting Fellow at Corpus Christi College Cambridge. Halcyon days. The late Ray Page was librarian of the Parker Library, Tim Graham was on the last year of his stint on the 'Back to the Manuscripts' project, and the sub-librarians were Gill Cannell and Pat Aske before she moved to Pembroke College. The late Catherine Hall was the archivist. Ray had just retired as Elrington and Bosworth Professor of Anglo-Saxon in the university and had been given a room in the attic, which was up so many stairs that he called it 'Paradise'. He even read proofs there. He also greatly enjoyed inviting guests after dinner up to paradise to sample his malt whisky, of which he was a connoisseur: an academic *part des anges*. In this heady atmosphere the present work was hatched.

At the same time in the University Library I attended practical historical printing classes run by Nicholas Smith and Colin Clarkson getting my hands dirty setting type, valuable experience. As a medievalist I also took the bibliography course taught to postgraduates by the late Marie Axton in order to try to bring my skills at describing printed books up to those for describing manuscripts. As will be seen, this book, although primarily aimed at Anglo-Saxonists, combines the study of manuscripts and printed books. In the history of type-design Anglo-Saxon is useful to the historian of print because the special needs that it displayed can produce evidence of punchcutting and typefounding at times when it is otherwise thin or even non-existent because roman, italic or textura designs were well established and available. So this work should also be of interest in relation to the history of the book.

The starting point is encapsulated in the observation by Eric Stanley, first published in 1982: 'We have not even a full list of books using Saxon type, and we have no full and illustrated account of such type' (Stanley, *Collection*, 1987). The approach adopted is to provide in Part 1 an account of the printing of Anglo-Saxon from the beginnings under Archbishop Parker's aegis to the landmark achievement of the *Thesaurus* produced under the direction of Hickes. Part 2 provides a catalogue of all the books found to be relevant for the period 1566 to 1705. Bibliographical method is used to describe these early printed books containing Anglo-Saxon but the focus is on the sources used in the books for the passages containing Anglo-Saxon and where appropriate on the special Anglo-Saxon sorts used in them. I aim to trace the origins of Anglo-Saxon type-designs from manuscript models or already extant printed models where appropriate. Over two hundred and fifty books have been identified. This ground-breaking method shows the history of Anglo-Saxon scholarship and studies from the perspective of the end product, the early printed book. It enables us to pinpoint when a particular manuscript was first used productively to reproduce it or some part of it in authentic print. It shows what interested the early scholars, why the subject was studied, how these interests slowly evolved and who made major contributions. The contributors I consider the most outstanding are remembered in the dedication of the book: George Hickes, Franciscus Junius, Sir Henry Spelman, and Humfrey Wanley. Junius, from Leiden, brought a new linguistic perspective to the subject and bequeathed the fruits of his scholarship and printing materials to Oxford University, where they were used by Hickes and Wanley to produce their magnificent *Thesaurus*. But even in this exalted company Sir Henry Spelman stands out. He saw the need for aids to read manuscripts full of abbreviations, for informing linguistic skills to read Anglo-Saxon with a grammar and a dictionary, for the systematic publication of records, and he put his money where his mouth was by paying for two designs of Anglo-Saxon types and supporting the first lectureship in Anglo-Saxon: at the University of Cambridge. His encouragement of others was notable, his son John, Abraham Wheelock, and William Dugdale amongst others, and his work was revered throughout the rest of the seventeenth century, witness the *Reliquiæ Spelmannianæ* (1698.3). His approach was historical but he saw the need for philological skills as well, skills that were supplied in abundance by Junius a little later.

In pursuing this work I have of course examined many books and manuscripts. By virtue of the fact that I was based in Dublin until 2004 many of these early printed books belong to libraries in Ireland, copies not generally seen by those making standard bibliographies such as STC. Occasionally these copies produce evidence that modifies the account in STC: see especially 1588.1/1588.2/1591.1. The copy of 1683.1 in Armagh is not found in Wing or ESTC. I have also been greatly aided by other resources. The microfiche facsimiles that come with the ASMMF descriptions of Anglo-Saxon manuscripts have sometimes proved invaluable in checking manuscript references. Although somewhat cumbersome to set up they are easy to look through quickly to find the right page or folio. Access to manuscript facsimiles on-line makes checking the details of references much easier than it was when I began, and it will become easier still. Some sites are much more congenial to use, navigate and manipulate than others: the standard set by the Swiss is the goal to aim at: http://www.e-codices.ch. Equally EEBO provides similar reproductions for early English printed books. But it should be stressed that these aids, while invaluable for checking readings, are no substitute for examining the original, which is three-dimensional by comparison with what some have called 'the ghost in the machine'. Another extremely helpful aid has been the Dictionary of Old English Corpus, which enables virtually any Old English quotation to be found. If frustrated the unfound text may well turn out to be 'Elizabethan Old English' such as that concocted by Nowell or Lambarde, which is naturally not included in the Dictionary.

The work has taken a long time, even longer than it should, because I was distracted by other projects, as well as having heavy teaching and administrative responsibilities. I am extremely grateful for the visiting fellowships I enjoyed not only at Corpus Christi College Cambridge but also at Wolfson College Cambridge and Mansfield College Oxford. My gratitude to Wolfson has been increased by the extended welcome it has offered in the form of senior college membership since I retired from Dublin. I am also grateful to Cambridge University Department of Anglo-Saxon Norse and Celtic for welcoming me as an Honorary Research Associate, which has given me access to some convivial occasions and to library resources. I thank also Andrew Pettegree for accepting this book into Brill's Library of the Written Word. It is particularly pleasing that it should be published from Leiden, the very place that nurtured Franciscus Junius, the founding father of Germanic philology.

I have received assistance in various ways from the following, and I thank them from the bottom of my heart: Dr Elizabeth Armstrong (Oxford), Dr Raymond Astbury and Mrs Sheila Astbury (Dublin), Mr Nicolas J. Barker (London), Dr Bruce Barker-Benfield (Oxford), Dr Carole Biggam (Glasgow), Professor Peter Blayney (Toronto), Dr Hans Brandhorst (The Hague), Professor Rolf Bremmer (Leiden), Professor Stefan Brink (Aberdeen), Dr Helen Carron (Cambridge), Professor James Carley (Toronto), Dr Kees Dekker (Groningen), the late Dr Ian Doyle (Durham), Professor David Dumville (Aberdeen), Professor Mordechai Feingold (California), Professor Mirjam Foot (London), the late Professor John L. Flood (London), Professor Timothy Graham (Albuquerque NM), the late Mrs Catherine Hall (Cambridge), Dr Oliver Harris (London), Dr Lotte Hellinga (London), Professor Paul G. Hoftijzer (Leiden), Professor Simon Keynes (Cambridge), Professor Nicolas K. Kiessling (Pullman WA), Mr Daniel Korachi-Alaoui (Canterbury), Dr Peter van der Krogt (Utrecht), Mr John Lane (Leiden), who kindly sent me his notes on Anglo-Saxon types, Dr Elisabeth Leedham-Green (Cambridge), Professor David McKitterick (Cambridge), Ms Jo Maddocks (Oxford), Mr James Mosley (London), Dr Evelyn Mullally (Belfast), the late Ms Robin Myers (Cambridge and London), Dr Colette Nativel (Paris), Dr Ben Outhwaite (Cambridge), the late Professor Ray Page (Cambridge), the late Professor Malcolm Parkes (Oxford), Dr Oliver Pickering (Leeds), Mr Nicholas Rogers (Cambridge), Dr Sophie van Romburgh (Leiden), the late Professor Richard Sharpe (Oxford), Dr Peggy Smith (Reading), the late Professor Eric Stanley (Oxford), Professor Gerald Toomer (Providence, RI), the late Professor Dr Hendrik Vervliet (Antwerp), the late Lord Wardington, Professor Per-Axel Wiktorsson (Uppsala).

For funding support in the earlier stages of part of the work I thank the Bibliographical Society and the Neil Ker Fund at the British Academy. For technical assistance I thank Jennifer Pollard (English Faculty, Cambridge) for help with fonts, Chris Quy (PC-Support, University of Cambridge) for help with Illustrations 46 and 47, and Gavin Lucas (London) for assistance with Illustration 17b.

The following libraries and librarians have offered the use of their collections and facilities with courtesy and helpfulness: The Admiralty Library (Ministry of Defence) formerly at HMG Hydrographic Office Taunton (where I was assisted by Adrian Webb) and now at Portsmouth (from where the Librarian, Jenny Wraight, answered queries), Armagh Public Library (where I was assisted by Lorraine Frazer), Queen's University Library Belfast (where I was assisted by Mary Kelly), Cambridge University Library (where all the staff are wonderfully supportive; I thank Claire Welford-Elkin, Nicola Hudson and William Hale in the Rare Book Room and Anne Taylor in the Map Room in particular, and Rosalind Esche for being helpful beyond the call of duty), Christ's College Cambridge, Corpus Christi College Cambridge, Emmanuel College Cambridge, English Faculty Library Cambridge, King's College Cambridge (where I thank Peter Murray Jones), Magdalene College Cambridge (where I was assisted by the Pepys Librarian, Mrs Aude Fitzsimons), Peterhouse Cambridge (where I thank Roger Lovatt and Scott Mandelbrote), Queen's College Cambridge, St John's College Cambridge (where I thank Kathryn McKee), Sidney Sussex College Cambridge, Trinity College Cambridge, Trinity Hall Cambridge, Canterbury Cathedral Archives and Library (where Sheila Hingley, since moved to Durham, was particularly helpful), Trinity College Dublin (where I thank the late Charles Benson), Archbishop Marsh's Library Dublin (where I thank Muriel McCarthy), Founders' Library Lampeter (where I thank David and Pamela Selwyn), Leeds University Brotherton Library, Leiden Universiteitsbibliotheek (where I was assisted by R. Breugelmans), British Library London (where I was assisted by Philippa Marks), Lambeth Palace Library London, Royal Geographical Society London (who charged a daily consultation fee, but Francis Herbert was very helpful), Chetham's School Library Manchester, Russell Library Maynooth, Bayerische Staatsbibliothek Münich, The National Trust (Blickling Hall, Aylsham, Norfolk (where I was assisted by Yvonne Lewis), University of Newcastle Robinson Library (from where Dr Lesley Gordon answered queries), Bodleian Library Oxford, Balliol College Oxford, English Faculty Library Oxford, Christ Church Oxford (where I was assisted by Steven Archer, Judith Curthoys, Janet McMullin and Cristina Neagu), Exeter College Oxford, Reading University Library (where I was assisted by David Knott).

Figure 41a is reproduced by permission of the Plantin-Moretus Museum, Antwerp. Figures 1, 3a/b. 4, 5, 6a/b, 18a, 19b, 20, 22a/b, 25, 27, 28, 29 are reproduced by permission of the Master and Fellows of Corpus Christi College, Cambridge. Figures 15a/b, 16a/b, 18b, 19a, 21, 24/a/b/c/d, 30, 31, 33a/b, 34a/b, 36, 37, 38, 39, 42, 43, 45, 46, 47, 48, 49 are reproduced by permission of the Syndics of Cambridge University Library. Figure 13 is reproduced by permission of the Fellows of Peterhouse, Cambridge. Figures 23a/b/c are reproduced by permission of the Master and Fellows of Trinity College, Cambridge. Figure 41b is reproduced by permission of the Rijksuniversiteitsbibliothek, Leiden. Figures 2, 26 are reproduced by permission of the British Library Board, London, who charged a fee. Figure 35 is reproduced by permission of the Fellows of Christ Church, Oxford. Figure 14 is reproduced by permission of the Dean and Chapter of Westminster Abbey.

Parts of the text in Part 1, now modified, excerpted and rearranged, have appeared in an earlier form in articles: chapter 2 in 'A Testimonye of Verye Ancient Tyme? Some Manuscript Models for the Parkerian Anglo-Saxon Type-Designs', in *Of the Making of Books: Medieval Manuscripts, their Scribes and Readers: Essays presented to M. B. Parkes*, ed. P. R. Robinson and R. Zim (Aldershot: Ashgate, 1997), pp. 147–88; chapter 3 in 'Parker, Lambarde, and the Provision of Special Sorts for Printing Anglo-Saxon in the Sixteenth Century', *Journal of the Printing Historical Society*, 28 (1999), 41–69; chapter 4 in 'From Politics to Practicalities: Printing Anglo-Saxon in the Context of Seventeenth Century Scholarship', *The Library*, VII.4 (2003), 28–48, and 'Abraham Wheelock and the Presentation of Anglo-Saxon: From Manuscript To Print', in *Beatus Vir: Studies in Early English and Norse Manuscripts in Memory of Phillip Pulsiano*, ed. A. N. Doane and K. Wolf (Tempe AZ:, Arizona Center for Medieval and Renaissance Studies 319, 2006), pp. 383–439; chapter 5 in 'Printing Anglo-Saxon in Holland and John Selden's *Mare Clausum seu de Dominio Maris*', *Quaerendo*, 31 (2001), 120–36, and 'William Camden, Seventeenth-Century Atlases of the British Isles and the Printing of Anglo-Saxon', *Antiquaries Journal*, 98 (2018), 219–44. My thanks to the editors and publishers of these books and journals.

And a big Thank You to the Brill team at Leiden who saw this book through the press: Ivo Romein, who took over from Francis Knikker as managing editor,

Gera van Bedaf the desk editor, and Joshua Hey the copy editor, in particular, and others who worked behind the scenes.

Finally it is difficult to find words to thank my wife Angela, herself a medievalist interested in books as well as texts, and on other occasions co-author with me. Quite simply, without her interest and support this book would not have been written.

> *Peter J. Lucas*
> 27 December 2021
> Feast-day of St John the Evangelist
> Patron of authors, bookbinders, booksellers, compositors, editors, engravers, papermakers, printers, publishers, scholars, typesetters and writers.

Tables and Figures

Tables

1   Anglo-Saxon type-designs and the printers who used them in England and Ireland   xxii
2   Anglo-Saxon type-designs used only on the continent   xxiv
3   Manuscripts used for texts in the first printed book containing AS types   44
4   Other MSS used by those involved in the first AS type designs   45
5   Comparative summary of distinctive features in relevant AS MSS   47
6   Manuscripts from which Wheelock took text for printed books or surviving transcripts   110
7   Other manuscripts for which there is evidence of use by Wheelock   110
8   Other manuscripts for which there is presumed evidence of use by Wheelock   111
9   Summary of occurrence of distinctive/innovatory features in relevant AS MSS   112

Figures

1   Cambridge, Corpus Christi College 100 (s.xvi^2), extracts from the bottom half of p. 280: Transcript of the *Annals of St Neots* in Latin, with *Bede's Death Song* in Old English copied in later and overflowing the space left for it   10
2   London, British Library Cotton Vitellius D.vii, 6: John Joscelyn's transcript of Ælfric's 2nd Letter to Wulfstan in Old English   12
3a   Cambridge, Corpus Christi College 190, 156, lines 7–12: Latin text of Ælfric's 2nd Letter to Wulfstan with Joscelyn's underlining, cross-reference to the Old English text, and triquetra attention-mark   14
3b   Cambridge, Corpus Christi College 190, 342, lines 20–28: English text of Ælfric's 2nd Letter to Wulfstan with Joscelyn's cross-reference to the Latin text   14
4   Readers's Anglo-Saxon type-specimen (AS1) from *A Testimonie of Antiquitie* (1566.2), L7^v (CCC SP.281)   30
5   Reader's Anglo-Saxon type-specimen (AS1) from Lambarde's *Archaionomia* (1568.2), B2^r (CCC Y.7.14)   31
6a   Reader's Anglo-Saxon type-specimen (AS1) from *Ælfredi Regis Res Gestæ* (1574.2), ¶1^v (CCC MS 176)   32

TABLES AND FIGURES   XVII

6b   Anglo-Saxon text (AS1) from Foxe's AS *Gospels* (1571.1), 2G4ᵛ–2H1ʳ, showing
        Lk 6–7 (CCC Y.7.17)   34–35
7   Oxford, Bodleian Library, Junius 121, 80ᵛ, lines 12–23, from a Penitential,
        Bk III, §§1–2   49
8   Oxford, Bodleian Library, Hatton 114, 153ʳ, lines 14–17, Passio Sanctorum
        Martyrum, Alexandri, Eventii & Theodoli, beginning   50
9   Oxford, Bodleian Library, Hatton 113, 56ᵛ, lines 13–15, Sermo in XL,
        beginning   50
10   Oxford, Bodleian Library, Hatton 113, 16ᵛ, lines 15–18, Sermo de baptismate,
        beginning   50
11   Oxford, Bodleian Library, Hatton 113, iᵛ, Anglo-Saxon alphabet by (?)
        Joscelyn   51
12   Oxford, Bodleian Library, Hatton 113, viᵛ, from a Calendar of saints' days   51
13   Reader's Anglo-Saxon type-specimen and text (AS2) from Foxe's *Actes and
        Monuments* (1576.1), ²3G4ᵛ/b (CPH E.11.17)   61
14   Lambarde's handwritten Anglo-Saxon alphabet, Westminster Abbey 30, 2   62
15a   Reader's Anglo-Saxon type-specimen (AS3) from Lambarde's *Perambulation
        of Kent* (1576.2), 2¶3ʳ (CUL Bb*.4.54)   63
15b   Anglo-Saxon text (AS3) from Lambarde's *Perambulation of Kent* (1576.2),
        2Z3ʳ, showing part of the AS Law 'Geþyncðo'   64
16a   Anglo-Saxon text (AS2/3) from Lambarde's *Perambulation of Kent* (1596.2),
        2I7ᵛ–8ʳ, showing part of the AS Law 'Geþyncðo' (CUL Syn.7.59.31). Note that
        Parkerian sorts are used alongside Lambardian sorts.   66–67
16b   Errata page from Lambarde's *Eirenarcha* (1581.1), 2L7ᵛ, showing the
        correction of s/r, þ/p, 3/ʒ, capital/lower-case (CUL Pet.E.6.15)   68
17a   Portion of Illustration 13 enlarged (Parker/Day)   72
17b   Sections from Illustration 15a reassembled and enlarged to allow
        comparisons (Lambarde/Newbery)   73
18a   Reader's Anglo-Saxon type-specimen (AS4) from Spelman's *Concilia*
        (1639.4), *3ᵛ (CCC D.1.5)   90
18b   Anglo-Saxon text from Spelman's *Concilia* (1639.4), P6ᵛ, showing the
        beginning of the Laws of Wihtræd (CUL Ely.a.90)   91
19a   Anglo-Saxon text from Wheelock's edition of Bede's *Historia Ecclesiastica*
        (1643.1), sig. D1ᵛ showing chapter headings set in AS 5 (CUL Pet.A.7.7)   95
19b   Reader's Anglo-Saxon type-specimen of AS5 (excluding square C)
        from Wheelock's edition of Bede's *Historia Ecclesiastica* (1643.1), ¶6ᵛ
        (CCC D.3.22²)   96
20   Cambridge, Corpus Christi College 173, 47ᵛ: Anglo-Saxon Laws
        of Ine 4–5   99

21	Cambridge, University Library Ii.2.4, 90ᵛ, Exeter script of s.xi³/⁴: OE translation of Pope Gregory's *Cura Pastoralis*, ch. 41	115
22a	Cambridge, Corpus Christi College 419, 308: Anglo-Saxon homily 'Larspell' for the 4th Sunday in Lent, beginning	117
22b	Cambridge, Corpus Christi College 419, 73: Anglo-Saxon Homily 'Angelorum nomina', beginning	117
23a	Cambridge, Trinity College B.15.34, 79: Ælfric, Homily 'Dominica III post Pascha', beginning	118
23b	Cambridge, Trinity College B.15.34, 319: Ælfric, *Catholic Homilies* I.xxiv 'Dominica IIII post Pentecosten', beginning	118
23c	Cambridge, Trinity College B.15.34, 376: Ælfric, *Catholic Homilies* II.xxv 'Dominica VIII post Pentecosten', beginning	118
24a	Cambridge University Library Gg.3.28, 44ᵛ: Ælfric, *Catholic Homilies* I.xiv 'Dominica Palmarum', beginning	119
24b	Cambridge University Library Gg.3.28, 131ᵛ: Ælfric, *Catholic Homilies* I.xl 'Dominica II in adventum Domini'	119
24c	Cambridge University Library Gg.3.28, 157ᵛ: Ælfric, *Catholic Homilies* II.ix 'Sancti Gregorii Pape', beginning. Note the cross-reference in Wheelock's hand to 'Serm.51' (CUL Ii.1.33)	120
24d	Cambridge University Library Gg.3.28, 255ʳ: Ælfric, Anglo-Saxon version of *De temporibus anni*, Preamble and §§1.1–4	120
25	Cambridge, Corpus Christi College 201, 190: *Capitula of Theodulf*, ch. xxi, §§ 22–30	121
26	BL Cotton Tiberius C.ii, 75ʳ: Bede, *Historia Ecclesiastica* III.xvi–xvii	122
27	Cambridge, Corpus Christi College 188, 241: Ælfric, *Catholic Homilies* I.xxiv 'Dominica IIII post Pentecosten', beginning	123
28	Cambridge, Corpus Christi College 162, 44: Anglo-Saxon Homily 'Be þam drihtlican sunnandæg folces lar', beginning	123
29	Cambridge, Corpus Christi College 190, 236: from *De Septem Ecclesiasticis Gradibus*, 'De Sacerdotibus, Lectiones de Pentecosten' (= Fehr 1914: 243/7–9)	124
30	Cambridge University Library Ff.1.27, 35: from *Historia Brittonum* (Mommsen 1898: 192a/8–12)	124
31	Reader's Anglo-Saxon type-specimen showing the Junian Pica Anglo-Saxon (AS6) cut by Christoffel van Dijck: Junius & Marshall, *Gothic Gospels* (1665.2), 2*4r (CUL Young 100). The *figura* 'shape' is shown on the left and the *potestas* 'signification' on the right	129
32a	Punches made by Christoffel van Dijck, his Great Primer Italic A–P, at the Museum Enschedé (= Noord-Hollands Archief), Haarlem, Netherlands	130

32b	The AS punches made for Junius, attributable to Christoffel van Dijck, at Oxford University Press Archive	130
33a	Oxford University type-specimen (1695.1), e1r/e2r, showing the range of Junius's types (CUL Broxbourne.d.46)	132–133
33b	Text in Anglo-Saxon and other (Germanic) languages showing the diversity of Junius's types in use: *Gothic Gospels* (1665.2), ²2O3ᵛ (CUL Young 100)	134
34a/b	Text in Anglo-Saxon and other (Germanic) languages showing the display potential of Junius's types: Hickes, *Institutiones Grammaticae* (1689.3), sigs F1ʳ, N4ᵛ (CUL Bb*.2.24(D))	136–137
35	Oxford University type-specimen (1687?.1) showing the Somnerian Pica Anglo-Saxon (Morison/Carter 1967: pl. 11): OXC D.124, fo 9ʳ	139
36	The Oxford University Small Pica Anglo-Saxon (AS8) in 1703/5.1 Booklet 5, †3D1ᵛ, lh col, lower two-thirds: CUL Pet.C.12.24	141
37	Alphabetically arranged Table of special phonetic sorts (CAS1) used by Sir Thomas Smith, *De recta emendata Linguae anglicae scriptione Dialogus* (1568.3), L1 (CUL M*.11.24²(E))	146–147
38	John Selden, *Mare Clausum* (1636.3), T5ᵛ, showing the Dutch 'Boxhornian' English-size Anglo-Saxon (CAS2.1) in an extract from ASC (C) 1052 (CUL Syn.8.63.364)	151
39	John Selden, *Mare Clausum* (1636.1), O8ᵛ, showing the Dutch Elsevierian English-size Anglo-Saxon (CAS2.2) in an extract from ASC (C) 1052 (CUL H.16.48)	153
40	John Selden, Mare Clausum (1636.2), S4ʳ, showing the Dutch Mairian English-size Anglo-Saxon (CAS2.3) in an extract from ASC (C) 1052 (OBL Vet.B2.e.30)	155
41a	The 'Augustyn Engels-Saxische Letteren' = the Blaeu/Voskens Pica Anglo-Saxon (CAS3) shown in the Heirs of Joan Blaeu type-specimen 1695.5, D1 (LUB Letterproeven 744D, no. 33)	158
41b	The Blaeu/Voskens Pica Anglo-Saxon (CAS3) in the Widow Dirck Voskens specimen (1700?.2 (ante1714)), *Proef van Letteren die te bekomen zyn, by de Weduwe van Dirk Voskens* (LUB F.11:24). OE Bede, I.7 (extract), as Miller 1890–98: I.36/33 to 38/2	158
42	The Blaeu/Voskens Pica Anglo-Saxon (CAS3) in 1679.2, 2T3ʳ (p. 333)	160
43	Reader's Anglo-Saxon type-specimen showing the Janssonius English-size Anglo-Saxon (CAS4) in 1646.3, 2*2ʳ (CUL Atlas.3.65.4)	162
44	Joannis Janssonius, *Novus Atlas* (vol. 4; 1646.3), 5Z2ᵛ: ASC(C+F) 189/188 (extracts), showing Anglo-Saxon text embedded in the Latin text (CUL Atlas.3.65.4)	163

45	Joannis Janssonius, *Novus Atlas* (vol. 4; **1646.3**), 6A1ᵛ, showing words with Anglo-Saxon sorts in a head statement set in a Great Primer Roman (CUL Atlas.3.65.4)	163
46	Alphabetical arrangement of assembled Anglo-Saxon sorts found in Janssonius's Atlas (**1646.3**) using CUL Atlas.3.65.4	165
47	Alphabetical arrangement of the Anglo-Saxon sorts (CAS5) found in the Strassburg edition of John Selden's *De iure naturali* (**1665.3**) using CUL C.4.5	167
48	Reader's specimen of the Anglo-Saxon sorts (CAS6) found in Du Cange's *Glossarium* (Paris, **1678.2**), vol. I on sig. ᵖR4ʳ (CUL Aa*.7.5)	169
49	The Du Cangian Pica Anglo-Saxon (CAS6) as it occurs in text in the Frankfurt edition of Du Cange's *Glossarium* (**1681.1**), vol. II, ¶2L4ᵛ–¶2M1ʳ (cols 544–545, re-arranged) (CUL Pet.B.9.5)	171
50	The Wittenberg 'Pica' Anglo-Saxon (CAS7) as found in Selden's *Tituli Honorum* of **1696.1** on sig. ²2Z2ʳ (p. ²365) (OBL Vet. D3 e.118) in a passage from Law II Cnut 71.1–5 (Liebermann I.358)	173

Abbreviations

AS	Anglo-Saxon
ASMMF	Anglo-Saxon Manuscripts in Microfiche Facsimile, ed. †P. Pulsiano, A.N. Doane & M. Hussey, 25+ vols (Binghamton & Tempe AZ, 1994–).
BL	London, British Library
CLA	E.A. Lowe, *Codices Latini Antiquiores*, 11 vols (Oxford, 1934–71)
col	column
ed.	edited by
edn	edition
EEBO	Early English Books On-line
EETS	Early English Text Society
ESTC	English Short Title Catalogue (electronic aid)
fo(s)	folio(s)
introd.	introduced by, introduction
Ker	Ker, N.R., *Catalogue of Manuscripts containing Anglo-Saxon* (Oxford, 1957/1991)
L	Latin
MGH	Monumenta Germaniae Historica
MRTS	Medieval & Renaissance Texts & Studies
MS	manuscript
n.f.	not found (in)
ODNB	*Oxford Dictionary of National Biography*
om.	omitting
SC	Summary Catalogue
STC	*A Short-Title Catalogue of Books printed in England, Scotland, & Ireland and of English Books printed abroad 1475–1640*, by A.W. Pollard & G.R. Redgrave. 2nd edn, 3 vols rev. W.A. Jackson & F.S. Ferguson, completed by K.F. Pantzer (London, 1976–91)
t	translated by, translation
TSF	*Type Specimen Facsimiles*, I ed. John Gustave Dreyfus (London, 1963); II annotated by H.D.L. Vervliet and Harry Carter (London, 1972)
USTC	Universal Short-Title Catalogue (electronic aid)
Wing	*Short-Title Catalogue of Books printed in England, Scotland, Ireland, Wales, and British America and of English Books printed in other countries 1641–1700*, by D.G. Wing. 2nd edn, 4 vols, rev. T.J. Crist, J.J. Morrison, C.W. Nelson & M. Seccombe (New York, 1982–98)

Tables 1 and 2: Anglo-Saxon Type-Designs

TABLE 1 Anglo-Saxon type-designs and the printers who used them in England and Ireland

AS1 (London/Paris?): The Parkerian Great Primer Anglo-Saxon (1566–1646)
Possibly cut by Pierre Haultin, who was in Paris 1565–70 (see ch. 2).
Printers: John Day 1 (1522–84†), John Windet (fl.1584–1610†), William Stansby (fl.1597–1638†), and Richard Bishop (fl.1636–58).

AS2 (London/La Rochelle?): The Parkerian Pica Anglo-Saxon (1576–1640)
Possibly cut by Pierre Haultin (see ch. 3), who went to La Rochelle in 1570.
Printers: John Day 1 (1522–84†), William Stansby (fl.1597–1638†), Richard Bishop (fl.1636–58), William Hall (fl.1598–1614) and John Beale (fl.1611–43†), Eliot's Court Press (fl.1584–1680).

AS3 (London/La Rochelle?): The Lambardian Pica Anglo-Saxon (1576–1670+)
It is not known who cut these designs; possibly Pierre Haultin now in La Rochelle cut this type-design too with contact through his nephew Jérôme in London.
Printers: Henry Bynneman (fl.1566–83†), Henry Middleton (fl.1567–87†), Eliot's Court Press (fl.1584–1680), Melchisidec Bradwood (fl.1602–18) at Eliot's Court Press, Adam Islip (fl.1591–1639†), Felix Kingston (fl.1597–1653†), Humphrey Lownes 1 (fl.1604–30†), Thomas Snodham (*alias* East; fl.1609–25†), John Beale (fl.1611–43†), John Legat 2 (fl.1620–58†), Robert Young (fl.1624–43†), Richard Badger 1 (fl.1629–41), John Grismond 2 (fl.1641–66†), Thomas Warren (fl.1645–59†), William Wilson (fl.1645–65), James Flesher (fl.1649–70†), Evan Tyler (fl.1652–83), John Starkey (fl.1656–89), Alice Warren (fl.1659–65†), Francis and Thomas Warren 2 (fl.1666);
Printers at Oxford: William Turner (fl.1624–43†, Printer to Oxford University 1624–40), Henry Hall 1 (fl.1642–80);
Printers at Cambridge: Roger Daniel (fl.1620–67†, printer to Cambridge University 1632–50), John Hayes (printer to Cambridge University 1669–1705).

AS2/3 The Parkerian and Lambardian Pica Anglo-Saxons mixed (1594–1703)
Printers: Edmund Bollifant (fl.1585–1602) of Eliot's Court Press, John Haviland (fl.1621–38†), partner in Eliot's Court Press, Edward Griffin 2 (fl.1637–52†) at Eliot's Court Press, William Jaggard (fl.1594–1623†), Thomas Wight (fl.1597–1605) in association with Bonham Norton (fl.1594–1635†), William Hall (fl.1598–1614), Thomas Snodham (fl.1609–25†), John Dawson (fl.1613–34?†), Richard Hodgkinson (fl.1624–75†), Thomas Cotes (fl.1627–41†), James Flesher (fl.1649–70†), Thomas Roycroft (fl.1650–77†), Mary Simmons (fl.1656–67) and Samuel Simmons (fl.1666–78), Alice Warren (fl.1659–65†).

TABLE 1   Anglo-Saxon type-designs and the printers who used them in England (*cont.*)

IR1 (London/Paris/La Rochelle?): The Elizabethan English-size Irish (1571–), used for Anglo-Saxon 1622–39)
Who cut the special sorts is not known, but possibly Pierre Haultin, who had connections with England through his typefounder-nephew Jérôme in London.
Printers: Stationers' Society Dublin (fl.1618–41).

AS4 (London): The Spelmannian Great Primer Anglo-Saxon (1639–52)
The punchcutter is moot; the only known person who could have done it is Arthur Nicholls (fl.1632–40).
Printers: Miles Flesher 1 (fl.1617–64†), Robert Young (fl.1624–43†), Richard Cotes (fl.1627–53†), Richard Badger 1 (fl.1629–41), James Flesher (fl. 1649–70†).

AS5 (London): The Wheelockian Great Primer Anglo-Saxon (1641–52)
The only known punchcutter in London at this time is Arthur Nicholls (fl. 1632–40).
Printer: James Flesher (fl. 1649–70†);
Printer at Cambridge: Roger Daniel (fl.1620–67†, Printer to Cambridge University 1632–50).

AS6 (Amsterdam): The Junian Pica Anglo-Saxon (1655–)
Cut by Christoffel van Dijck (c.1603–69) for Franciscus Junius (in Amsterdam) but the punches were subsequently taken to Oxford.
Printers: Christoffel Cunrad (fl. Amsterdam 1650–84), Abraham Subbinck (fl. Breda 1652–66), Hendrick and Johann 1 van Esch (fl. Dordrecht 1659–77);
Printer at Oxford: Sheldonian Theatre (Oxford University Press; fl.1665–).

AS7 (London): The Somnerian Pica Anglo-Saxon (1658–)
Cut by Nicholas Nicholls in anticipation of Somner's *Dictionarium* 1659.1.
Printers: Thomas Roycroft (fl.1650–77†), Robert & William Leybourn (fl.1651–61), William Hall (fl.1657–72), Roger Norton 2 (fl.1658–99), Thomas Newcomb 1 & 2 (1.fl.1648–81†; 2.fl.1673–91†), Evan Tyler (fl.1640–82†) & Ralph Holt (fl.1670–88†), John Darby 1 (fl.1662–1707†), Mary Clarke (fl.1678–1705†), Thomas Braddyll (fl.1679–1704), Elizabeth Holt (fl.1689–1703†) & William Horton (fl.1688–90), Robert Roberts (fl.1676–1701†), Thomas Hodgkin (fl.1676–1724†), Freeman Collins (fl.1679–1713†), William Bowyer 1 (1663–1737).
Printers at Oxford: William Hall 2 (fl.1642–80), Henry Hall 1 (fl.1642–80), Sheldonian Theatre [Oxford University Press] (fl.1665–),

AS8 (Oxford): The Oxford University Small Pica Anglo-Saxon (1701–)
Cut by Peter de Walpergen (fl. Oxford 1676–1703†), punchcutter for the University.
Printer: Sheldonian Theatre (Oxford University Press).

TABLE 2   Anglo-Saxon type-designs used only on the continent

CAS1 (Paris): The Smithian Great Primer Anglo-Saxon Phonetic Special Sorts (1568)
The cutting is of a high standard, possibly by Guillaume 1 Le Bé or Pierre Haultin.
Printer: Robert Estienne 2 (fl.1556–70).

CAS2.1 (Amsterdam or Leiden): The Dutch 'Boxhornian' English-size Anglo-Saxon (1636)
These sorts of low quality may have been cut by an overstretched punchcutter of unknown identity.
Printer: unknown (? Joannis Janssonius).

CAS2.2 (Leiden): The Dutch Elsevierian English-size Anglo-Saxon (1636)
The only known candidate for the punchcutting of these sorts is Arent Corsz[oon] van Hoogenacker (c.1579–1636).
Printers: Bonaventura & Abraham Elzevier (fl. Leiden 1620–53).

CAS2.3 (Leiden): The Dutch Mairian English-size Anglo-Saxon (1636)
The only known candidate for the punchcutting of these sorts is Arent Corsz[oon] van Hoogenacker (c.1579–1636).
Printer: Johan and Theodore (Dirk) Maire (fl. in partnership Leiden 1636).

CAS3 (Amsterdam): The Dutch Blaeu/Voskens Pica Anglo-Saxon (1645—ante1714+)
Probably cut by one of the Voskens half-brothers, Bartholomaeus Voskens the Elder (1613/16–1669) or Reinier/Reinhard Voskens (1621—c.1670).
Printers: Joan Blaeu 1 (1596–1673), Heirs of Joan Blaeu 1 (fl.1679–1703), Hendrick and Dirk 1 Boom (fl.1669–80), widow of Dirk Voskens (Amsterdam, 1647–91).

CAS4 (Amsterdam): The Dutch Janssonian English-size and Great Primer Anglo-Saxon (1646–75)
Cutter unknown.
Printer: Joannis Janssonius (fl. Amsterdam 1613–64).

CAS5 (Strassburg): The Strassburg English-size Anglo-Saxon (Strassburg & Nuremberg 1665)
Cutter unknown.
Printer: probably Georg Andreas Dolhopff (1627–1711; fl. Strassburg 1662–1711).

CAS6 (Paris): The Du Cangian Pica Anglo-Saxon (Paris 1678, Frankfurt-am-Main 1681)
Possibly cut by Guillaume Le Bé 3 (1610?–85).
Printer at Paris: Gabriel Martin (fl.1670–92†);
Printer at Frankfurt-am-Main: Balthasar Christoph Wust 1 (fl.1658–1700).

CAS7 (Wittenberg): The Wittenberg 'Pica' Anglo-Saxon (Wittenberg and Frankfurt-an-der-Oder 1695–6)
Cutter unknown.
Printer: Johann Michael Goderitsch (fl. Wittenberg 1687–1706?).

PART 1

*Printing Anglo-Saxon with Special Sorts
from 1566 to 1705*

∴

CHAPTER 1

Anglo-Saxon and Its Uses

The written word in early England was often recorded in Anglo-Saxon, and this word could carry great authority, especially legal authority. By comparison with Latin Europe, Anglo-Saxon civilization is notable for the amount of literature preserved in contemporary manuscripts in the vernacular language, formerly called 'Anglo-Saxon' but now more usually called 'Old English'.[1] This literature includes laws, a chronicle and many ecclesiastical and liturgical texts, as well as some remarkable poetry. At the end of the Anglo-Saxon period some notable changes occurred in the English language, including the break-down in the twelfth century of the inflexional system inherited from Germanic, and the introduction of much borrowed vocabulary resulting from (a) the settlement of Norse-speakers roughly north and east of a line from London to Liverpool and (b) the influx of French speakers following the Norman Conquest of 1066. Nevertheless charters and writs, including those in the vernacular, continued to be copied. Later on, when the study of earlier records became important, recourse to earlier precedents, especially legal precedents, was often impeded by the difficulties of understanding and authenticating the earlier forms of the English language.[2] Two means of countering these difficulties manifested themselves: glossing and the use of imitative script. These features anticipated what followed in the later sixteenth century: the printing of Anglo-Saxon with special imitative types, a project first authorized and patronized by Matthew

---

1   There is also much vernacular literature in Irish and Norse, but the manuscript evidence is later. I leave Greek out of account.
2   See Antonia Gransden, 'Antiquarian Studies in Fifteenth-Century England', *The Antiquaries Journal*, 60 (1980), pp. 75–97, and on later understanding of earlier forms of English Kathryn A. Lowe, '"As Fre as Thowt"?: Some Medieval Copies and Translations of Old English Wills', *English Manuscript Studies 1100–1700*, 4 (1993), pp. 1–23; Matti Rissanen, 'Middle English Translations of Old English Charters in the *Liber Monasterii de Hyda*: A case of Historical Error Analysis', in *Linguistics across Historical and Geographical Boundaries: in Honour of Jacek Fisiak on the Occasion of his Fiftieth Birthday*, ed. D. Kastovsky & A. Szwedek, 2 vols (Berlin: Mouton de Gruyter, 1986), 1.591–603; Hans Sauer, 'Knowledge of Old English in the Middle English period', in R. Hickey and S. Puppel (eds), *Language History and Linguistic Modelling*, 2 vols (Berlin: Mouton de Gruyter, 1997), 1.791–814; Elizabeth Solopova, 'From Bede to Wyclif: The Knowledge of Old English within the Context of Late Middle English Biblical Translation and Beyond', *RES*, ns 71 (2019), pp. 805–827.

Parker, archbishop of Canterbury (1559–75), and before that Master of Corpus Christi College, Cambridge.[3]

The most notable example of glossing is the so-called Tremulous Hand, the work of a thirteenth-century monk of the Benedictine cathedral priory at Worcester who probably had Parkinson's disease or something similar that caused the shaky appearance of his handwriting.[4] From some of his mistakes, such as *smyltnys* 'mildness' glossed **brihtnesse* 'brightness', it is evident that the Tremulous Hand did not really know Old English, but on the contrary was learning it and may have intended to render it more accessible.[5] He could work out the meaning of Old English words by consulting the Latin sources of Old English translations or by using Ælfric's *Grammar* and *Glossary*, a work which he transcribed for himself (Worcester Cathedral F.174). Furthermore he started to compile an alphabetical Old English—Latin glossary, so his methods verged on the systematic.[6] Although other glossators worked more sporadically they too show the desire to access Old English material from the thirteenth to the fifteenth centuries.

The other method of providing authentic support was to transcribe Anglo-Saxon documents in imitation Anglo-Saxon script.[7] Two examples may be cited.

---

3   For a book-length study of Parker see V.J.K. Brook, *A Life of Archbishop Parker* (Oxford: Clarendon Press, 1962); for a full collection of materials see J. Strype, *The Life and Acts of Matthew Parker* (London: for John Wyat, 1711). For a brief account see Kimberly Van Kampen in W. Baker, W. & K. Womack (eds), *Pre-Nineteenth-Century British Book Collectors and Bibliographers*, Dictionary of Literary Biography 213 (Detroit: Gale, 1999), pp. 251–257.

4   See Christine Frantzen, *The Tremulous Hand of Worcester: A Study of Old English in the Thirteenth Century* (Oxford: Clarendon Press, 1991). For the nature of the 'tremor' see D.E. Thorpe & J.E. Alty, 'What type of tremor did the medieval "Tremulous Hand of Worcester" have?', *Brain*, 138 (2015), pp. 3123–3127.

5   See especially Wendy E. J. Collier, 'A Thirteenth-Century User of Anglo-Saxon Manuscripts', *Bulletin of the John Rylands University Library of Manchester*, 79 (1997), pp. 149–165.

6   See Franzen, *Tremulous Hand*, 119–131.

7   On archaizing hands and 'Bastard Saxon' see Malcolm B. Parkes, 'Archaizing Hands in English Manuscripts', in J.P. Carley & C.G.C. Tite (eds), *Books and Collectors 1200–1700: Essays presented to Andrew Watson* (London: British Library, 1997), pp. 101–141, and Peter J. Lucas, 'Scribal Imitation of Earlier Handwriting: "Bastard Saxon" and its Impact', in M-C. Hubert et al., (eds), *Le Statut du Scripteur au Moyen Age: Actes du XIIe Colloque Scientifique du Comité International de Paléographie Latine (Cluny, 17–20 Juillet 1998)*, Matériaux pour l'Histoire 2 (Paris: l'École des Chartes, 2000), pp. 151–160. For archaizing hands in the twelfth century see Julia Crick, 'Historical Literacy in the Archive: Post-Conquest Imitative Copies of Pre-Conquest Charters and Some French Comparanda', in *The Long Twelfth-Century View of the Anglo-Saxon Past*, ed. M. Brett & D.A. Woodman (Farnham: Ashgate, 2015), pp. 159–190. See also Crick, 'The Art of the Unprinted: transcription and English antiquity in the age of print', in J. Crick & A. Walsham, *The Uses of Script and Print, 1300–1700* (Cambridge: Cambridge University Press, 2004), pp. 116–134.

Thomas Elmham made facsimiles of what he thought were Anglo-Saxon charters sent by King Æthelberht of Kent (560–616) to his abbey of St Augustine's Canterbury (even though they were eleventh-century forgeries), now preserved in what is probably a fair copy in the author's own hand of his incomplete history of St Augustine's (c.1414): Cambridge, Trinity Hall MS 1.[8] They are careful facsimiles where Elmham not only tried to imitate the supposed Anglo-Saxon script but also features of lay-out and display.[9] Another notable example is the cartulary of Holy Trinity Priory in Aldgate, London, written by Thomas de Axbridge 1425–7 and now preserved as Glasgow, University Library Hunter 215 (U.2.6).[10] At the bottom of fo 149ʳ there occurs an Anglo-Saxon charter of King Edward the Confessor written in a plausible Anglo-Saxon minuscule including distinctive Old English letter-forms such as ð, ę (especially in final position), f, ᵹ, p, r, þ 'thorn', ð 'eth', p 'wynn', þ 'that', ⁊ (tironian sign for 'and').[11] In its position in the cartulary this charter authenticates the narrative implicitly endorsing 'the sanctity of the Priory's property and the rents due'.[12] Antiquarian presentation brought with it an authority *ex antiquo verissime probatarum nova iustificatione* 'by a new justification of proofs truly derived from antiquity', to which it was intended others would defer.

The Dissolution of the Monasteries released a flood of documents and archives, cartularies and correspondence that were avidly collected by men whose interests went beyond legal needs to an interest in the past for its own sake and for the contribution it could make to the present. This new breed of antiquaries included John Leland (c.1503–52) and John Bale (1495–1563), whose interests were primarily bibliophilic, but included the hoarding of records.[13] During the 1530s and 1540s Leland travelled throughout England

---

8   Wilhelm Levison, *England and the Continent in the Eighth Century* (Oxford: Clarendon Press, 1946), pp. 174–233. Charles Hardwick, *Historia Monasterii S. Augustini Cantuariensis*, Rolls Series 8 (London: Longman, Green, Longman, and Roberts, 1858).
9   M. Hunter, 'The Facsimiles in Thomas Elmham's History of St. Augustine's, Canterbury', *The Library*, v.28 (1973), pp. 215–20. Cf. Lucas, 'Scribal Imitation', p. 155.
10 See Gerald A.J. Hodgett, *The Cartulary of Holy Trinity Aldgate* (London: London Record Society, 1971). For discussion see Matthew Fisher, *Scribal Authorship and the Writing of History in Medieval England* (Columbus: Ohio State University Press, 2010), pp. 63–68, and his pl. 2 (after p. 150).
11 Sawyer, *AS Charters*, no. 1103, printed by Florence E. Harmer, *Anglo-Saxon Writs* (Manchester: Manchester University Press, 1952), no. 51 on pp. 234–235. The letters 'thorn' and 'eth' had the value of modern 'th', and 'wynn' was the AS letter for 'w'. For convenience I have preferred the traditional (Icelandic) name for the letter 'eth', although the Anglo-Saxon name for it was ðæt 'that'; see Fred C. Robinson, 'Syntactical Glosses in Latin Manuscripts of Anglo-Saxon Provenance', *Speculum*, 48 (1973), pp. 443–475, at p. 451.
12 Fisher, *Scribal Authorship*, p. 67.
13 May McKisack, *Medieval History in the Tudor Age* (Oxford: Clarendon Press, 1971), pp. 1–25.

recording books found and noting those suitable for the royal library, which Henry VIII was keen to augment. While Leland's antiquarian interests were general, among his associates and friends a few showed a more specific interest in Anglo-Saxon sources. The first person known to take a significant interest in Anglo-Saxon materials in the sixteenth century was Robert Talbot (c.1505–58), prebendary of Norwich, noted for his pioneering work on the English part of the Antonine Itineraries, the Roman road-system linking cities.[14] As recorded by Ker, supplemented by Graham, he used (and sometimes owned) several manuscripts containing OE prose: *Anglo-Saxon Chronicle* C (Tiberius B.i, which also contained the OE *Orosius*) and F (Domitian vii), Laws (CCC 383), Laws and Ecclesiastical Institutes (Nero A.i), the OE Bede (CUL Kk.3.18), the OE Heptateuch (Claudius B.iv), Gospels (Bodley 441), Homilies (Vespasian D.xiv), and Ælfric's Grammar (CUL Hh.1.10).[15] He made notes and transcribed passages from some manuscripts, notably parts of Ælfric's Preface to Genesis from Claudius B.iv before it lost its first leaf.[16] This transcript occurs in Talbot's notebook, Cambridge, Corpus Christi College 379 (10^v–12^r), compiled between c.1535 and 1558.[17] A feature of Talbot's transcripts is that while he wrote Old

---

14 T.D. Kendrick, *British Antiquity* (London: Methuen, 1950), pp. 135–136. Talbot's notes on this topic survive in CCC 379, fos 24–65. For Talbot see A.B. Emden, *A Biographical Register of the University of Oxford A.D. 1501 to 1540* (Oxford: Clarendon Press, 1974), p. 555; N.R. Ker, 'Medieval Manuscripts from Norwich Cathedral Priory', *Transactions of the Cambridge Bibliographical Society*, 1.1 (1949), pp. 1–28, esp. p. 3, n. 5, and Pl. IA. As noted by Strype, *Life of Parker*, p. 529, Talbot's books were acquired by Parker after the former's death.

15 N.R. Ker, *Catalogue of Manuscripts containing Anglo-Saxon* (Oxford: Clarendon Press, 1957), p. l, supplemented for the 'Saxonice Bede' by Timothy Graham, 'Robert Talbot's "Old Saxonice Bede": Cambridge University Library, MS Kk.3.18 and the "Alphabetum Norwagicum" of British Library, Cotton MSS, Domitian A.ix', in Carley & Tite, *Books*, pp. 295–316; on the provenance of these manuscripts see p. 315, n. 58.

16 See Richard Marsden, *The Old English Heptateuch and Ælfric's Libellus de Veteri Testamento et Novo*, EETS OS 330 (Oxford: Oxford University Press, 2008), pp. l–li, who collates the readings for his edited text. References to this edition are by page and line. Talbot also transcribed some AS charters in CCC 111, pp. 139–162, and 167–178. Graham ('Saxonice Bede', p. 310, n. 9) identifies these charters by their number in Sawyer's *AS Charters*. For a facsimile of Claudius B.iv see Charles R. Dodwell and Peter Clemoes, *The Old English Illustrated Hexateuch: British Museum Cotton Claudius B. IV*, Early English Manuscripts in Facsimile 18 (Copenhagen: Rosenkilde & Bagger, 1974). For the text see Marsden, *Heptateuch*, pp. 3–7; Talbot transcribes Marsden's lines 1–42, 115–116.

17 The date of Talbot's notebook, using watermark evidence, is discussed by R.I. Page, 'A Sixteenth-Century Runic Manuscript' (1987), repr in Page, *Runes and Runic Inscriptions*, ed. D. Parsons (Woodbridge: Boydell, 1995), pp. 289–94. For discussion see Timothy Graham, 'Early Modern Users of Claudius B.iv: Robert Talbot and William L'Isle', in R. Barnhouse & B.C. Withers (eds), *The Old English Hexateuch*, Medieval Institute Publications (Kalamazoo MI: Western Michigan University, 2000), pp. 287–293, at pp. 275–282, with

English carefully, mostly letter by letter (so avoiding cursive connections and loops), he did not follow the conventional usage in Anglo-Saxon manuscripts of distinguishing Latin and Old English letter-forms, such as Latin/OE d, f, g, r, s or t, his g in particular being distinctive with its descender slanting down to the left and a hook projecting to the right and curling round to the left below, and matching that used in Latin in the heading on fo 10ʳ 'genesis anglice'.[18] But he did reproduce the Old English special letter-forms such as ð, p and ẏ; þ is used sparingly, as at fo 11ᵛ/4 (Marsden 4/28), in imitation of his exemplar (Claudius B.iv). For æ Talbot wrote an a with a hook to the right. The letter e sometimes exhibits a protruding tongue in the Anglo-Saxon manner, especially at line ends. Talbot sometimes used the tironian sign for 'and', as on fo 11ᵛ/12 (Marsden 4/31), alongside sixteenth-century & on fo 11ᵛ/8 (Marsden 4/30). Once, however, Talbot does reproduce Anglo-Saxon s, in 'ꞃæde' on fo 10ᵛ/14 (Marsden 3/17), long ſ being preferred, as no doubt in the exemplar. The tell-tale aberration suggests that he was making a conscious effort to avoid specific Anglo-Saxon forms of familiar letters. If so, he was certainly bucking the trend.

When his contemporary, Robert Recorde (c.1512–58), only seven years younger than Talbot, studied the C version of the *Anglo-Saxon Chronicle* in a manuscript then owned by Talbot (subsequently BL Cotton Tiberius B.i), and decided to copy the beginning of the West Saxon genealogical regnal list in the lower margin of p. 38 in a thirteenth-century chronicle in Cambridge, Corpus Christi College 138, he used Anglo-Saxon letter-forms, d (sometimes), f, g, r, s (with occasional lapses), as well as the Old English special letters æ, þ, ð, p, ẏ.[19] His manner of writing Old English is endorsed in a neat italic script of s.xvi² on the front endleaf (fo [i]ᵛ): 'Robertus Recorde erat qui notauit hunc librum Characterib⟨us⟩ Saxonicis'.[20] The handwriting of this note, with its long descenders turned sharply and fully to the left, and its ascenders turned

---

illustrations of Talbot's handwriting in figs 25–26 on pp. 277–278. Talbot's transcription of parts of Ælfric's Preface to Genesis is edited by Graham, 'Saxonice Bede', at pp. 314–316. For descriptions of manuscripts in the Corpus collection see Montague R. James, *A Descriptive Catalogue of the Manuscripts in the Library of Corpus Christi College Cambridge*, 2 vols (Cambridge: Cambridge University Press, 1912); for MS 379 see II, 226–7. Following the Parker-on-the-Web project all Corpus manuscripts are currently viewable in on-line facsimile.

18 Graham ('Saxonice Bede', p. 296) comments on the distinctiveness of Talbot's g.
19 Timothy Graham, 'The Beginnings of Old English Studies: Evidence from the Manuscripts of Matthew Parker', in S. Sato, *Back to the Manuscripts*, Occasional Papers 1 (Tokyo: Centre for Medieval English Studies, 1997), pp. 29–50, at pp. 31–2 and pls 2–3.
20 CCC 138 contains 'Alexandri Essebiensis epitome historiae Britanniae a Christo nato at annum 1255' annotated by Robert Recorde with OE from the ASC in Tiberius B.i. Noted

curvaciously to the right, resembles that of the annotations in Cambridge, Corpus Christi College 583, 'Matthew Parker's Parchment Roll', an account of the great moments in the archbishop's life, written by an amanuensis but amended with great care in another hand which may well be that of Parker himself; the content is certainly personal and it is difficult to imagine how it could have been written by anyone else unless Parker was standing over him telling him not only the content but where to write the amendments. Although primarily a mathematician, Recorde's method of writing Old English followed the tradition of archaizing script used by earlier scribes such as Thomas Elmham and Thomas de Axbridge.

Whether or not Parker wrote the note in Cambridge, Corpus Christi College 138 it has the tone of authority that bears his stamp, and indicates a complete reversal of policy towards reproducing Anglo-Saxon script from that manifested by Talbot. For under Parker's aegis great care was taken to imitate the distinctive letter-forms to be found in Anglo-Saxon manuscripts. Parker's encouragement of this development can be seen from his letter to Sir William Cecil (later Lord Burghley) dated 24 January 1565/6, in which (to the consternation of modern conservators) Parker is contemplating furnishing a Psalter with a more attractive opening folio to be taken from within the book:

> and methought the leaf going before the xxvith psalm would have been a meet beginning before the whole Psalter, having David sitting with his harp or psaltery, *decachordo vel ogdochordo*, with his ministers with *tubis ductilibus et cymbalis sonoris*, &c., and then the first psalm written on the back side: which I was in mind to have caused Lylye to have counterfeited in antiquity, &c., but that I called to remembrance that ye have a singular artificer to adorn the same, which your honour shall do well to have the monument finished, or else I will cause it to be done and remitted again to your library.[21]

---

by Page, 'Anglo-Saxon Texts in Early Modern Transcripts', *Transactions of the Cambridge Bibliographical Society*, VI.2 (1973), pp. 69–85, at pp. 75–79.

21   John Bruce and Thomas T. Perowne, *Correspondence of Matthew Parker, D.D. Archbishop of Canterbury*, Parker Society (Cambridge: Cambridge University Press, 1853), no. cxc-civ. As stated in *The life off the 70. Archbishopp off Canterbury ... Englished* ([Zürich: C. Froschauer?], 1574; STC 19292a), C1^r, Parker's conservation policy, 'to the ende that these antiquities might last longe and be carefullye kept', was such that 'he caused them beinge broughte into one place to be well bounde and trymly couered'. According to Strype (*Life of Parker*, p. 489) this work was translated by John Stubbs from the 'Vita Parkeri' at the end of the *Historiola* or 'Brief History' of Corpus Christi College, Cambridge, drawn up by Joscelyn presumably on Parker's orders in 1569; for the Latin text see Strype, *Life of Parker*, Appendix, p. 165, also CCC 488, p. 79, or 489, p. 87, and for the *Historiola* (without

Counterfeiting 'Lylye' was Peter Lyly, father of the euphuistic prose writer John Lyly, and Registrar of the Diocesan Consistory Court at Canterbury.[22] Parker endorsed the practice of imitating Anglo-Saxon script when he himself added the 'Tremulous Hand' glosses on a supply leaf in Cambridge, Corpus Christi College 178, p. 31.[23] In the Parkerian household (as well, apparently, as Cecil's) special scribes were employed to 'counterfeit' Anglo-Saxon script 'in antiquity'. Such scribes could be brought in specially to write a passage of Old English in a Latin work. A particularly clear example occurs in Cambridge, Corpus Christi College 100 (s.xvi²). Pp. 261–319 contain the *Annals of St Neots* in Latin, copied from Cambridge, Trinity College R.7.28.[24] *Bede's Death Song* occurs on p. 280 (see Illustration 1) in an imitation Anglo-Saxon minuscule apparently written (in a darker shade of ink) after the scribe had left a space for it, but that space was not sufficient so the last three words were added in the bottom margin together with the Latin paraphrase. The Latin script of this addition shows that the scribe of the Old English was not the same as the main scribe. There is a similar instance (possibly by another scribe, who starts with caroline f and uses caroline a throughout) on p. 29 of the same manuscript, where *Bede's Death Song* in Old English has been added in another hand in space provided by the main scribe; the same hand as wrote the Old English added 'Quod ita latine sonat'. The text in this instance is Symeon of Durham's "Liber de exordio atque procursu Dunelmensis ecclesiae" (pp. 1–122) copied from Durham, Cathedral

---

the 'Vita') see John W. Clark, *Historiola Collegii Corporis Christi by John Josselin*, Octavo Publications XVII (Cambridge: Cambridge Antiquarian Society, 1880). For an account with illustrations of how Parker treated the books in his care see Page, *Matthew Parker and his Books* (Kalamazoo MI: Western Michigan University, 1993).

22 On Peter Lyly see Albert [G.] Feuillerat, *John Lyly* (Cambridge: Cambridge University Press, 1910), pp. 17–20 and 516–520 (his will). The tradition that Lyly personally 'counterfeited' antique writing goes back to Strype, *Life of Parker*, p. 529.

23 Page, *Parker and his Books*, pp. 54, 98, pl. 57; Page thought that the supply leaf was itself written by Parker, but the difference in the shade of the ink between the main text and the glosses (which are paler) indicates that they were written at different times and could therefore very well have been written by different hands, as argued by Graham in 'Beginnings', p. 46, n. 51.

24 See David Dumville and Michael Lapidge, *The Annals of St Neots with Vita Prima Sancti Neoti*, The Anglo-Saxon Chronicle A Collaborative Edition 17 (Cambridge: Brewer, 1985), and my description of TCC R.7.28 in Peter J. Lucas and Jonathan Wilcox, *Manuscripts Relating to Dunstan, Ælfric, and Wulfstan; the "Eadwine Psalter" Group*, ASMMF 16, MRTS 343 (Tempe AZ, 2008), pp. 27–35 (ASMMF no. 82). The text of BDS in CCC 100, p. 280, is not, however, that of R.7.28 (reproduced by Fred C. Robinson and E.G. Stanley, *Old English Verse Texts from many Sources: A Comprehensive Collection*, EEMF xxiii (Copenhagen: Rosenkilde & Bagger, 1991), pl. 3.20). It is very close to that on p. 29, even in details of word-division.

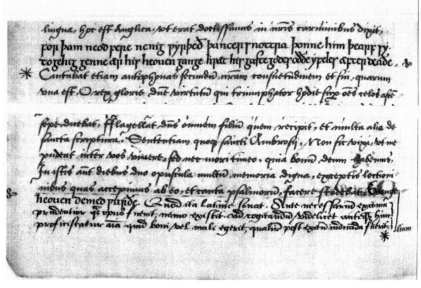

ILLUSTRATION 1   Cambridge, Corpus Christi College 100 (s.xvi²), extracts from the bottom half of p. 280: Transcript of the *Annals of St Neots* in Latin, with *Bede's Death Song* in Old English copied in later and overflowing the space left for it. Reduced: 53% of actual size

Library, A.IV.36 (*olim* Phillipps 9374; s.xii/xiii), given to Parker by Robert Horne, dean of Durham, in 1568.[25] In this manuscript *Bede's Death Song* occurs on fo 25ᵛ, written by the main scribe, who imitates Anglo-Saxon insular letters, but makes the tell-tale mistake of writing 'þancer' with Gothic **r**. It would appear that, since this mistake is taken over in both versions of *Bede's Death Song* in CCC 100, they are both based on the text in this Durham manuscript; presumably someone in Parker's household (rightly) thought it a better text than that in TCC R.7.28, even though neither is Anglo-Saxon in date.

Queen Elizabeth's Privy Council recorded her majesty's 'care and zeale ... for the conservation of such auncient recordes and monuments' as were relevant

---

25   On which see J. Conway Davies, 'A Recovered Manuscript of Symeon of Durham', *Durham University Journal*, 44 (1950–51), pp. 22–28. There is a brief description in David Rollason, *Symeon of Durham: Libellvs de Exordio atqve procvrsv istivs, hoc est Dvnhelmensis, Ecclesie, Tract on the Origins and Progress of this the Church of Durham* (Oxford: Clarendon Press, 2000), pp. xxviii–xxix, and for the text of *Bede's Death Song* in it see pp. 72–3. Ian Doyle, '*Bede's Death Song* in Durham Cathedral Library, MS. A.IV.36', in D. Rollason (ed), *Symeon of Durham* (Stamford: Shaun Tyas, 1998), pp. 157–160, at 158, confirms that the Durham MS provides the exemplar of the text of *BDS* in CCC 100.

to 'both ... the state of ecclesiastical and civil government'.[26] At the same time as Parker was collecting information on religious practice William Cecil (Lord Burghley) was employing Laurence Nowell (the antiquary) and William Lambarde to work on Anglo-Saxon history and legal practices, and Lambarde's *Archaionomia*, a collection of Anglo-Saxon laws (1568.2), appeared in print only two years after Parker's first production, the *Testimonye of Antiquitie* (1566.1).[27] Nowell was tutor to Cecil's son and made a considerable number of transcripts of manuscripts containing Old English before he disappeared on the continent c.1570. His materials passed to Lambarde, who made considerable use of them. Cecil's motivation was parallel to Parker's in that he sought precedents from Anglo-Saxon civil procedures to follow or adapt for the Elizabethan state.[28]

The most important of Parker's associates was John Joscelyn, his Latin secretary (1529–1603).[29] Although not a calligraphic penman, Joscelyn copied Old English frequently and made a dictionary that served as a foundation for that later published by Somner in 1659.[30] His notebook, much damaged by fire in 1731, survives as BL Vitellius D.vii, and contains, *inter alia*, his transcript of Ælfric's second letter to Wulfstan (archbishop of York 1002–23), one of the texts from which excerpts appear in *A Testimonie of Antiquitie* (1566.1, 1566.2).[31]

---

26 C.E. Wright, 'The Dispersal of the Monastic Libraries and the Beginnings of Anglo-Saxon Studies. Matthew Parker and his Circle: A Preliminary Study', *Transactions of the Cambridge Bibliographical Society*, I.3 (1951), pp. 208–237, at pp. 212–213.

27 On Nowell see Carl T. Berkhout, 'Laurence Nowell (1530—ca.1570)', in H. Damico (ed.), *Medieval Scholarship: Vol. 2, Literature and Philology* (New York: Garland, 1998), pp. 3–17.

28 On the cultural appropriation of Anglo-Saxon statecraft into Elizabethan England see Rebecca Brackmann, *The Elizabethan Invention of Anglo-Saxon England: Laurence Nowell, William Lambarde, and the Study of Old English*, Studies in Renaissance Literature 30 (Cambridge: Brewer, 2012), ch. 7.

29 For a brief notice of Joscelyn see Charles H. & Thompson Cooper, *Athenae Cantabrigienses*, 2 vols (Cambridge: Deighton, Bell & Co., 1858–61), II.366–367; for an overview see M. Sue Hetherington, *The Beginnings of Old English Lexicography* (Spicewood TX, privately printed, 1980), pp. 25–51.

30 Somner 1659.1. Joscelyn's manuscript dictionary is BL Titus A.xv–xvi, on which see J.L. Rosier, 'The Sources of John Joscelyn's Old English-Latin Dictionary', *Anglia*, 78 (1960), pp. 28–39. On Joscelyn see also Janet Bately, 'John Joscelyn and the Laws of the Anglo-Saxon Kings', in M. Korhammer et al. (eds), *Words, Texts and Manuscripts: Studies in Anglo-Saxon Culture Presented to Helmut Gneuss on the Occasion of his Sixty-Fifth Birthday* (Cambridge; Cambridge University Press, 1992) pp. 435–466, Angelika Lutz, 'Das Studium der angelsächsischen Chronik im 16. Jahrhundert: Nowell und Joscelyn', *Anglia*, 100 (1982), pp. 301–356, and R.I. Page, 'The Sixteenth-Century Reception of Alfred the Great's Letter to his Bishops', *Anglia* 110 (1992), pp. 36–64, at pp. 47–48, 54.

31 On Joscelyn's notebook see J.S. Gale, *John Joscelyn's Notebook: A Study of the Contents and Sources of B.L., Cotton MS. Vitellius D. vii*, unpubl. M.Phil. thesis, University of Nottingham, 1978. For the text of Ælfric's letters see Bernhard Fehr, *Die Hirtenbriefe Ælfrics*, Bibliothek

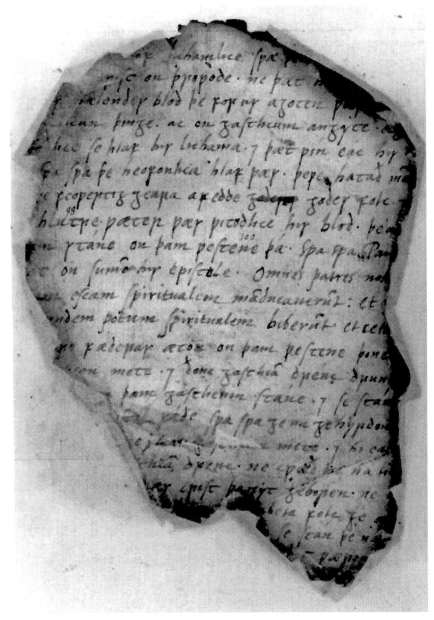

ILLUSTRATION 2 London, British Library Cotton Vitellius D.vii, 6: John Joscelyn's transcript of Ælfric's 2nd Letter to Wulfstan in Old English

The surviving part of his transcript corresponding to that in *A Testimonie* occurs on fos 5ʳ–6ʳ (see Illustration 2). As the reading *of þam gastlicum stane* indicates (Fehr, *Hirtenbriefe Ælfrics*, §105), both derive from Oxford, Bodleian Library, Junius 121, fo 117ᵛ, but since the beginning and end of the passage used for *A Testimonie* are marked in the manuscript with a cross and asterisk respectively, presumably by Joscelyn, it seems likely that the extract for the printed book was made before Joscelyn made his own transcript, which, unlike the extract in *A Testimonie*, does not omit what is §96 in Fehr's edition. Since Joscelyn played a vital role in the editing of *A Testimonie* it is important to examine how he treated Anglo-Saxon script. As can be seen from Illustrations 2, although he did not distinguish **a** or **d**, he did distinguish the following Anglo-Saxon letters: **f, g, r, s** (with occasional ſ), **t**, and the special sorts **þ, ð, ƿ**. As noted above the distinction of OE **t** from Latin **t** is rare in Anglo-Saxon manuscripts, and those cited above were apparently not used by Parker's household, but there is one source in particular where Joscelyn is likely to have seen this distinction. Cambridge, Corpus Christi College 190 contains both the Latin and the Old English text of Ælfric's second letter to Wulfstan, and these texts (on pp. 155/1–156/22 and pp. 341/12–343/12 respectively) were seen by the editors of *A Testimonie*; indeed, a passage erased in Cambridge, Corpus Christi College 265 on p. 177/18–21 has been supplied, with explanatory annotation in the margin by Joscelyn, from Cambridge, Corpus Christi College 190. Pages 341/342 of Cambridge, Corpus Christi College 190 have a membrane tag attached for ease of finding the Old English passage used for the printed book, and on p. 342 there is a cross-reference to p. 156 where the equivalent Latin passage is to be found; p. 156 also has a cross-reference to p. 342 (see Illustration 3a). In the Latin on p. 156 the stem of Latin **t** is often written with a c-stroke that shows above the horizontal bar (e.g., Illustration 3a: pluit, fluxit), whereas on p. 342 (written by a different scribe) OE **t** is a c-stroke that more or less consistently does not go above the line of the horizontal bar (e.g., Illustration 3b: ðæt, luttre). Because these texts were equivalent Joscelyn evidently took special note of the difference in script, even though there is no distinction between Latin and OE **t** on p. 342 itself (cf. Latin 'patres', line 28).[32] The distinction between Latin and OE **t** also occurs in sixteenth-century supply leaves in Cambridge, Corpus Christi College 449 (e.g. fos 1ᵛ, 2ᵛ).

---

der angelsächsischen Prosa 9 (Hamburg: H. Grand, 1914, repr. suppl. P. Clemoes, Darmstadt: Wissenschaftliche Buchgesellschaft, 1966), Brief III. The excerpts in the *Testimonie* correspond to Fehr's §§86–95, 97–109.

32   By contrast, he ignored the distinction between Latin and OE **a**. This distinction was perhaps one that the Elizabethans would have perceived as the difference between roman and italic.

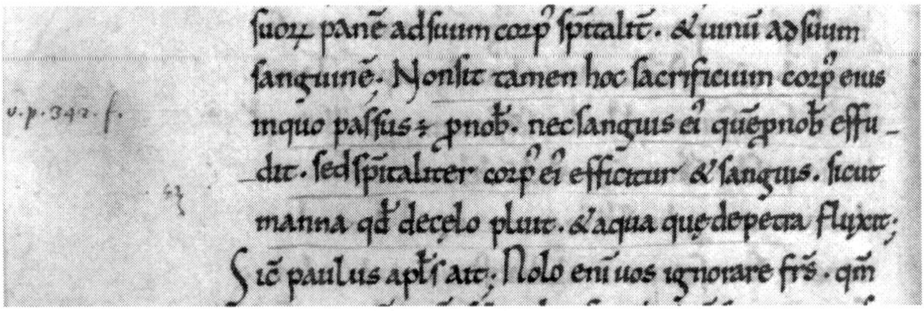

ILLUSTRATION 3A Cambridge, Corpus Christi College 190, 156, lines 7–12: Latin text of Ælfric's 2nd Letter to Wulfstan with Joscelyn's underlining, cross-reference to the Old English text, and triquetra attention--mark. Reduced to 64%

ILLUSTRATION 3B Cambridge, Corpus Christi College 190, 342, lines 20–28: English text of Ælfric's 2nd Letter to Wulfstan with Joscelyn's cross-reference to the Latin text. Reduced to 67%

The process of transferring Anglo-Saxon written material into printed form did not begin until 1566, when the first book with special Anglo-Saxon characters was printed by John Day (1522–84).[33] There were various reasons for this delayed start. First, it was not until the Elizabethan period that there was sufficient revival of interest in Anglo-Saxon materials, particularly, in the first place, for the light that they might shed on the Church in England, which King Henry VIII had separated from Rome.[34] Day worked under the auspices

---

33 On whom see C.L. Oastler, *John Day, the Elizabethan Printer*, Occasional Publications 10 (Oxford: Oxford Bibliographical Society, 1975), and for his earlier career L.P. Fairfield, 'The Mysterious Press of "Michael Wood" (1553–1554)', *The Library*, v.27 (1972), pp. 220–32; see also Elizabeth Evenden, *Patents, Pictures and Patronage: John Day and the Tudor Book Trade* (Aldershot: Ashgate, 2008). For the date of publication (1566?) of *A Testimonie* see the entry for 1566.1 in Part 2 below.

34 Allen Franzen, *Desire for Origins: New Language, Old English, and Teaching the Tradition* (New Brunswick: Rutgers University Press, 1990), pp. 27–47; Jennifer Summit, *Memory's Library: Medieval Books in Early Modern England* (Chicago: University of Chicago Press,

of Matthew Parker, who as archbishop of Canterbury was much concerned to establish older precedents for the liturgy and doctrine being adopted in association with the new Book of Common Prayer and the establishment of the *Ecclesia Anglicana*. This thinking is clearly reflected in the title of Day's first production using Anglo-Saxon types: *A Testimonie of Antiquitie* (1566.1 and 1566.2), which includes text and translation of Ælfric's *Sermo de Sacrificio in die Pascae* probably edited jointly by Parker and Joscelyn.[35]

Secondly, the revolution in written communication brought about by printing was still in progress in the sixteenth century, and brought Englishmen into contact with the continent, because nearly all the tools of the printing trade were imported from there. Up to the 1570s continental craftsmen came to England because they alone could perform some of the more highly skilled tasks.[36] When printing was first introduced into England from the continent the type-designs used were textura or black-letter. Caxton printed Chaucer in such types, for example, the *Canterbury Tales* in 1477 and 1483 (STC 5082/3). Textura types continued in general use for some years. Roman types, which ultimately derived from the letter-forms of the continental caroline minuscule script used at the end of the Anglo-Saxon period, were first used in England in 1509, but textura types were still preferred and the use of roman types, long familiar on the continent (though not in Germany), did not become widespread in England until the middle of the sixteenth century.[37] Pica roman first appeared in 1553.[38] The first book in the English language printed entirely in roman type appeared in 1555.[39] At this juncture, with roman types becoming the preferred option for the main text of an English book, Middle English continued to be printed in textura types, as in Stowe's 1561 edition of Chaucer (STC 5075), and indeed Middle English is found set in textura in several books included in the present study.[40] There was therefore a developing contrast between books containing Middle English set in textura and books containing

---

2008), pp. 101–135. Cf. Brackmann, *Elizabethan Invention*, who rightly notes (p. 8) that Nowell and Lambarde were more focussed on the pursuit of antiquarian knowledge than the search for religious precedents.

35 For a modern edition of Ælfric's text see Malcolm Godden, *Ælfric's Catholic Homilies*, EETS ss 5 (London: Oxford University Press, 1979), pp. 150–160. On the Parkerian edition see John Bromwich, 'The First Book printed in Anglo-Saxon Type', *Transactions of the Cambridge Bibliographical Society*, III.4 (1962), pp. 265–91.

36 See especially Harry Carter, 'Huguenot Typography', *Proceedings of the Huguenot Society of London*, 21 (1970), pp. 532–44.

37 Talbot Baines Reed, *A History of the old English Letter Foundries*, rev. A.F. Johnson (London: Faber & Faber, 1952), p. 40.

38 W. Craig Ferguson, *Pica Roman Type in Elizabethan England* (Aldershot: Scolar, 1989), p. 9.

39 Carter, 'Huguenot Typography', p. 538 and n. 30.

40 As 1635.1, 1679.2, 1696.2, all works by John Selden. In Camden's *Remaines* text from Chaucer is set in Italic: 1605.1, 1614.3, 1623.4, 1629.1, 1636.4, 1657.1, 1674.1.

Latin or English text set in roman. The presence of such a contrast may have influenced what happened in the case of Anglo-Saxon.

Roman type-designs offered the potential to print Anglo-Saxon alongside early Modern English or Latin, but distinctively, if special sorts were made for the specifically Anglo-Saxon characters. The roman letters remained familiar but distinctiveness was provided by special sorts substituted for some of the roman letters. This potential for printing a language which used the roman alphabet but required special sorts was exploited for Irish too, and special sorts were cut for some early spelling reformers, though in this case to match italic founts.[41]

Since the editors of *A Testimonie*, and Joscelyn in particular, were dealing directly with manuscript sources it is inherently likely that some of these manuscripts provided the basis for the models used for the type-designs.[42] It will be convenient to remind ourselves of the characteristics of Anglo-Saxon practice in those manuscripts. Anglo-Saxon scribes used two alphabets, one for writing Latin derived from caroline minuscule, and one for writing Old English derived from Anglo-Saxon square minuscule. They varied 'the forms of a, d, e, f, g, h, r, and s, according to the language they were writing', as, for example, in Oxford, Corpus Christi College 197, art.1 (s. x2), a bilingual copy of the Rule of St Benedict.[43] This manuscript, a relatively early one compared with the majority of bilingual texts that have survived, distinguishes between Latin and Old English particularly scrupulously. 'For example, in Old English only, c and o begin, like e, with a slight projection or horn to the left, the bow of p is open, and the end of the bow of t is often curled up. Another less conspicuous difference is in the form of the shaft of t, which is more curved in Old English than it is in Latin.' In the eleventh century Anglo-Saxon rounded *a* contrasted with Latin caroline a, Anglo-Saxon insular d contrasted with

---

41   For Irish see Dermot McGuinne, *Irish Type Design* (Blackrock, Co. Dublin: Irish Academic Press, 1992, 2nd edn Dublin, 2010), and for Parker's interest in it Bruce Dickins, 'The Irish Broadside of 1571', *Transactions of the Cambridge Bibliographical Society*, I.1 (1949), pp. 48–60. See below, Part 2, List of Type Designs, 1R1. Only slightly later than the first book printed with Anglo-Saxon types, and a little earlier than the first item printed with Irish types, the first book printed in Scottish Gaelic, the Book of Common Order for the Church of Scotland, appeared in 1567, but, although it used a Pica Roman, it did not use special sorts, apart from accents over vowels: see John Carswell, *Foirm Na Nvrrnvidheadh Agas freasdal na Sacramuinteadh* (Edinburgh: Robert Lekpreuik, 1567). For spelling-reformers see Peter J. Lucas, 'Sixteenth-Century English Spelling Reformers and the Printers in Continental Perspective: Sir Thomas Smith and John Hart', *The Library*, VII.1 (2000), pp. 3–21.

42   Although I differ from Geoffrey Wakeman, 'The Design of Day's Saxon', *The Library*, v.22 (1967), pp. 283–298 in many particulars, his pioneering approach was praiseworthy.

43   Ker, *Catalogue*, no.353 and plate 11; quotations from here and p. xxvi.

Latin caroline **d**, Anglo-Saxon horned **e** contrasted with Latin round-backed **e**, Anglo-Saxon long **f** contrasted with Latin caroline tall **f**, Anglo-Saxon insular ᵹ contrasted with Latin caroline **g**, Anglo-Saxon **h** with the right stem or limb turned outwards contrasted with Latin caroline **h** where the stem turns inwards, Anglo-Saxon insular long **r** contrasted with Latin caroline short **r**, and Anglo-Saxon insular long **s** often contrasted with Latin long ſ or round **s**. Later these distinctions were adhered to less strictly. 'In the twelfth century [scribes] usually employ[ed] the caroline form of **a** in Old English texts, and often ma[d]e no distinction in the forms of **e** and **h**, generalizing the forms used in Latin texts'. The letters **d**, **f**, **g**, **r**, and **s**, were generally distinguished. There were also the additional letter symbols, þ, ð, and p, 'thorn', 'eth' and 'wynn'. As for capitals Anglo-Saxon scribes used square capitals or uncials rather than the rustic capitals generally used in Latin texts.[44]

When Anglo-Saxon script is viewed from a later period it is often noted that Anglo-Saxon dotted ẏ is used in a given Old English text. In Anglo-Saxon manuscripts dotted ẏ is used in both Latin and Old English. Sometimes scribes made a distinction, using rounded 𝑦 for Latin, where it is rare but occurs from time to time, and straight-limbed y for Old English, where it is frequent as a vowel-symbol, and this distinction may be observed in BL Tiberius B.i, 35ʳ/14, in 'babylonia' as against 'cynᵹ', but it breaks down in 'þy ylcan' (39ʳ/18) and is hardly a discernible trend.[45] Similarly, the 'undotted ı' of Old English texts viewed with hindsight is a feature of both Latin and Old English in the original manuscripts.

In his preface to his edition of Asser's *Ælfredi regis res gestæ* (1574.2) Archbishop Matthew Parker says that reading texts printed in the Anglo-Saxon types 'will restore for you the memory of the ancient but once familiar language, and will provide no little household furniture for [previously] concealed knowledge.'[46] This statement is anticipated in the address to the reader in John Kearney's translation into Irish of the Catechism, *Abidil Gaoidheilge agus Caiticiosma* (Dublin, [William Kearney], 1571; STC 22.3) that the Irish types 'will open to you that road which leads you to knowledge and which, moreover, has been closed to you formerly'.[47] Besides Irish other living languages were provided with special or modified type-designs to accommodate their particular orthographic features. A notable feature of this activity in providing 'minority' languages with the means of printing them authentically is that most of them sprang from a Protestant ethos. The purpose in these cases was to spread

---

44 Ker, *Catalogue*, p. xxxvi.
45 Dotted ẏ is a feature of Middle English script through to early printed texts; cf. *OED*, s.v. Y.
46 See below.
47 Translated from the Irish in McGuinne, *Irish Type*, p. 10.

the Protestant word of God as widely as possible, amongst south-west French dialect speakers, amongst speakers of Basque, speakers of Scottish Gaelic and speakers of Irish, thus attempting to reach 'beyond the Pale'.[48]

The idea of exploiting the potential of printing technology to aid the printing of languages that required additional symbols to those in the roman alphabet was put into practice on the continent before it occurred in the British Isles. The main centre for promoting this activity seems to have been in south-west France, where Marguerite of Angoulême (1492–1549), queen of Navarre, while remaining a Catholic was much impressed by the Reformation, and protected protestants.[49] Under the influence of her daughter, Jeanne d'Albret, queen of Navarre (1555–72), the Latin psalter of Marot-Bèze was translated into the French vernacular, and then in 1565 printed in the Gascon dialect using modified sorts such as ç, and acute, grave and circumflex accents.[50] She it was who, having imposed Calvinism on Navarre in 1567, protected the Huguenots in La Rochelle, where the punchcutter and printer Pierre Haultin transferred his business from Paris by 1571.[51] The first book he printed in La Rochelle was dedicated to Queen Jeanne: it was the New Testament in Basque, and also utilized modified sorts such as ç, an acute accent, a diaeresis and titulus over vowels, but otherwise it did not use special sorts.[52]

Usage in Navarre probably influenced that in England. Particularly suggestive in this respect is the fact that in 1533, the year of Henry VIII's marriage to Anne Boleyn, and also the year of birth of their daughter, Princess Elizabeth, later Queen Elizabeth I, Marguerite presented to Anne a copy of Marguerite's *Le Miroir de l'Ame Pecheresse*. It was the custom amongst ladies of the French court to take an interest in language appropriate to their maternal

---

48 See List of Type Designs under IR1.
49 For a brief account of Marguerite's activities in the context of orthotypographical reform see Susan Baddeley, *L'Orthographe française au temps de la Réforme* (Geneva: Droz, 1993), pp. 153–154.
50 Jeanne d'Albret was the mother of the later French king Henri IV, who put an end to the Huguenot wars by converting to Catholicism in 1593. On the psalter see Baddeley, *L'Orthographe*, pp. 320–326, and for the text see *Psavmes de David viratz en rhythme gascon per Pey de Garros Laytores* (Toulouse: Jacques 1 Colomiès, 1565). Later there was a version in béarnais dialect: Arnaud de Salette, *Los Psalmes de David metvts en rima bernesa* (Orthez: Louis Rabier, 1583).
51 See Carter, 'Huguenot Typography', p. 536. On the Haultins see Louis Desgraves, *Les Haultin 1571–1623*, L'Imprimerie à La Rochelle 2 (Geneva: Droz, 1960).
52 [Jean Licçarague, t] *Iesvs Christ Gvre Iavnaren Testamentv Berria* (La Rochelle: Pierre Haultin, 1571), on which see Julien Vinson, *Essai d'une Bibliographie de la langue basque*, 2 vols (Paris: J, Maisonneuve, 1891–8), I.5–38, II.522–528.

rôle, and no doubt Marguerite's gift may be seen in this light.[53] For the young Princess Elizabeth translated her work into English in 1544 as 'The Miroir or Glasse of the Synnefull Soule', and, during the reign of her half-sister Mary I, Elizabeth's translation was printed on the continent in 1548 (with a dedication to Elizabeth by John Bale).[54] Moreover, since Elizabeth used the printed edition of Marguerite's *Miroir* that included the first treatise on orthotypography, she must have been aware of the lead given in the practice of printing unusual languages or unusual forms of familiar languages with special sorts during the reign of Marguerite of Navarre, and presumably it would have met with her approval.[55]

53 Baddeley, *L'Orthographe*, p. 154.
54 The manuscript is Oxford, Bodleian Library, Cherry 36 (SC 9810). [Princess Elizabeth], *The Mirror of the Sinful Soul*, facsimile ed. Percy W. Ames (London: Asher, 1897); Marc Shell, *Elizabeth's Glass* (Lincoln NE: University of Nebraska Press, 1993). For the printed book see [Princess Elizabeth] with a dedication to her by John Bale, *A Godly Medytacyon of the Christen soule ... compyled in Frenche by Lady Margarete quene of Nauerre, and aptely translated into Englysh by the ryght vertuouse lady Elyzabeth doughter of our late souerayne Kynge Henri the VIII* [Wesel: Dirik van der Straten], 1548; STC 17320. Bale's dedication and conclusion are included in Shell's edition.
55 Marguerite of Navarre's *Le Miroir*, as published at Paris by Antoine Augereau in December 1533, where it was accompanied by the first treatise on 'orthotypography' *Le Briefue Doctrine pour deuement escripre selon la propriete du langaige froncoys*, and Psalm 6 translated into French verse by Clément Marot, who probably helped with the editing and checking; cf. Baddeley, *L'Orthographe*, pp. 144–146, 159. That this edition (designated E) was the one used is shown by Renja Salminen (ed.), *Marguerite de Navarre, Le Miroir de l'Âme Pécheressse: Edition critique et commentaire suivis de la traduction faite par la princesse Elisabeth future reine d'Angleterre: The Glasse of the Synnefull Soule*, Dissertationes Humanarum Litterarum 22 (Helsinki: Annales Academiae Scientiarum Fennicae, 1979), pp. 253–254; for details of the E edition see pp. 10–13. Anne L. Prescott, in her 'The Pearl of the Valois and Elizabeth I: Marguerite de Navarre's *Miroir* and Tudor England', in M.P. Hannay (ed.), *Silent but for the Word: Tudor Women as Patrons, Translators, and Writers of Religious Works* (Kent OH: Kent State University Press 1985), pp. 61–76, 266–270, at p. 66, plumps for the 1539 Geneva edition printed by Jehan Girard (Salminen's H), but she adduces no supporting evidence, was apparently unaware of Marguerite's gift to Anne Boleyn, and did not see Salminen's work (p. 267, n. 4). On the printer see Jeanne Veyrin-Forrer, 'Antoine Augereau, graveur de lettres et imprimeur Parisien (vers 1485?-1534)', *Paris et Île-de-France, Mémoires de la Fédération des Sociétés historiques et archéologiques de Paris et de l'Ile-de-France* 8 (Paris: Klincksieck, 1957 for 1956), pp. 103–156 (repr. in idem, *La Lettre et Le Texte* (Paris: École normale supérieure de jeunes filles, 1987), pp. 3–50), esp. pp. 126–7, 153 no. 20, and for a reproduction pl. IV facing p. 146; for another reproduction see Nina Catach, *L'Orthographe française à l'époque de la Renaissance* (Geneva: Droz, 1968), p. 51, fig. 11. On the origins of *Le Briefue Doctrine* see Veyrin-Forrer, pp. 119–30, Catach, *L'Orthographe*, pp. 51–70, and Baddeley, *L'Orthographe*, pp. 140–144; for a brief description of its methods see Salminen, *Marguerite de Navarre*, pp. 104–105. For the significance of 1533 as a watershed in the matter of reformed ortho-typography see

Before Marguerite's daughter, Queen Jeanne, was fully in her stride, Parker had already produced or authorized several books printed with the first Anglo-Saxon type-designs, and the use of special sorts combined with a roman (or italic) typeface to print languages that required them was beginning to be undertaken more widely. Only slightly later than the first book printed with Anglo-Saxon types, the first book printed in Scottish Gaelic, the Book of Common Order for the Church of Scotland, appeared in 1567; it utilized accents over vowels, but did not otherwise use special sorts.[56] Also in 1567 there appeared what was apparently the first book to print Welsh in a type-design other than textura; it utilized the punchcutter Robert Granjon's Double Pica Italic.[57] And it provided the lower-case letters ḍ, ḷ and ụ with a subscript dot; since this dot always appears to be in the same position we may presume that special matrices were made for these letters with the subscript dot. But, again, it did not otherwise use special sorts.[58] The other variety of Celtic, however, Irish, was provided with special sorts, the first item to be printed with what came to be known as 'Queen Elizabeth's Irish Types', Pilip Mac Cuinn Chrosaigh's poem *Tuar ferge foighide Dhe* [Dublin, William Kearney], known as the Irish Broadside (STC 19844.5; Sweeney no. 2948) appearing in 1571.[59]

Catach, *L'Orthographe*, p. 147, and for discussion of the issue see Yves Citton and André Wyss, *Les Doctrines Orthographiques du xvie Siècle en France*, Publications Romanes et Françaises 187 (Geneva: Droz, 1989), chs 1–4.

56   See John Carswell, *Foirm Na Nvrrnvidheadh Agas freasdal na Sacramuinteadh* (Edinburgh: Robert Lekpreuik, 1567); STC 16604. Instead of a dot to designate a letter representing an aspirated consonant the letter was followed by an **h**.

57   A.F. Johnson, 'The Italic Types of Robert Granjon', *The Library*, IV.21 (1941), pp. 291–308: type no. 8; H.D.L. Vervliet, *The Type Specimen of The Vatican Press 1628* (Amsterdam: Herzberger, 1967), no.35; and M. Parker et al., 'Typographica Plantiniana: II. Early Inventories of Punches, Matrices, and Moulds, in the Plantin-Moretus Archives', *De Gulden Passer*, 38 (1960), pp. 1–139, MA15 on pp. 21–22.

58   Gruffyd Robert, *Dosparth Byrr Ar Y rhann gyntaf ...* (Milan: attrib. to Vincenzo Girardoni, 1567); STC 21076, and see also A.F. Allison and D.M. Rogers, *The Contemporary Printed Literature of the English Counter-Reformation between 1558 and 1640*, 2 vols (Aldershot: Scolar, 1989–94), II, no. 680. For discussion see A. Crawford and A.P. Jones, 'The Early Typography of Printed Welsh', *The Library*, VI.3 (1981), pp. 217–31, at pp. 219–20 and Pl. III.

59   For the type-design see McGuinne, *Irish Type*, ch. 1. For a catalogue of early printed books produced in Ireland see Tony Sweeney, *Ireland and the Printed Word: A Short Descriptive Catalogue of Early Books ... Printed: 1475–1700* (Dublin: Éamonn de Búrca, 1997). For the Irish Broadside see Dickins, 'Irish Broadside', where Parker's interest in the Irish typeface is indicated. The only surviving copy of the Irish Broadside of 1571 is preserved with Archbishop Parker's books at Corpus Christi College, Cambridge, where it is adorned with an 'ungrammatical' inscription by John Parker, the archbishop's son: 'This irish balade printed in Irelande who belike vse the olde saxon carecte', a reference to the similarities between Irish and Anglo-Saxon, which were both based on insular script—it was

There were 22 special sorts, 10 lower case, and 11 capitals, plus the tironian sign, ⁊, almost as many as those specially cut for the Parkerian Great Primer Anglo-Saxon.[60] This Irish set of type-designs is a considerable achievement, the outstanding instance of providing a living language with special sorts to complement a roman alphabet in the sixteenth century. Who cut the punches for the special sorts is not known, but, like the first Anglo-Saxon special sorts, they were combined with Pierre Haultin's English Roman, perhaps not a coincidence. Haultin had connections with England through his nephew Jérôme who operated as a typefounder in London at least as early as 1568.[61] Queen Elizabeth's Irish Types also appeared in the same year in John Kearney's translation into Irish of the Catechism, *Abidil Gaoidheilge agus Caiticiosma* (Dublin, [William Kearney], 1571; STC 22.3; Sweeney no. 103), where another size of the Irish type-design is also found, a Brevier with a body size of 54.5 mm for twenty lines.[62] This Brevier Irish is found again in the translation by William Daniel (d.1628) of the Book of Common Prayer, *Leabhar na nUrnaightheadh gComhchoidchiond* (Dublin, John Franckton, 1608; STC 16433; Sweeney no. 2436), where the largest portion is on sig. 2L1ʳ.[63] The Elizabethan Irish type designs thus anticipate those authorized for Anglo-Saxon by Archbishop Parker in that they were made in two sizes. Both the Irish and the Anglo-Saxon type-designs were created under the auspices of Archbishop Parker and his innovation and

---

      characteristic of Parker and his household that they could not distinguish scripts by place of origin (or date).

60 See below, List of Type-Designs, IR1.

61 Oastler, *Day,* p. 33 and n. 6; Desgraves, *Les Haultin,* pp. xvii–xviii; Harry Carter, *A View of Early Typography up to about 1600* (Oxford: Clarendon Press, 1969), pp. 86–87.

62 McGuinne, *Irish Type,* pl. 1.6 on p. 10, shows the title page. Here, as also on sigs A3ᵛ, B2ʳ–C3ʳ, E3ᵛ–4ʳ, the Brevier size is found only in a single line, there being no other instances of its use in the book.

63 McGuinne, *Irish Type,* pl. 1.5 on p. 9, shows sig. 2Hh1ᵛ; the body size is taken from measurements in this book (STC 16433). Unfortunately there is insufficient of the Brevier Roman with which the Irish special sorts are combined to identify it, nor are there any other books issued by Kearney (STC, III, 96) or Franckton (STC, III, 66) that use a Brevier Roman. Whoever's it was it could not have been Pierre Haultin's because he did not cut one of this size: see Guillaume Le Bé II, *Sixteenth-Century French Typefounders: The Le Bé Memorandum,* ed. Harry Carter, Documents Typographiques Français III (Paris: for A. Jammes, 1967), pp. 31 and 42, n. 32; cf. also Fred Smeijers, *Counterpunch: Making Type in the Sixteenth Century, Designing Typefaces Now* (London: Hyphen, 1996), pp. 63–67, 133–139. Daniel's translation of the New Testament into Irish, *Tiomna Nuadh* (Dublin: William Kearney, 1595–6?, and John Franckton, 1602; STC 2958), does not contain the Brevier size.

enterprise in providing such a high degree of authenticity for printing them with special sorts is notable.[64]

The power of print to influence in this way was articulated by John Foxe in his *Actes and Monumentes* known as the 'Book of Martyrs':

> In this very tyme so daungerous & desperate, where mans power could do no more, there the blessed wisedome and omnipotēt power of the Lord began to worke for his Churche, not with sworde and tergate to subdue his exalted aduersarie, but with printyng, writing, and readyng, to conuince darkenesse by lyght, errour by truth, ignoraunce by learnyng: So that by this meanes of printyng, the secret operation of God hath heaped vpon that proude kyngdome [of the pope] a double confusion. ... God of his secret iudgement, seyng tyme to helpe hys churche, hath founde a way by this facultie of printyng, not onely to confound his [the pope's] life, and conuersation, ... but also to cast downe the foundation of his standyng, that is, to examine, confute, and detecte his doctrine, lawes, and institution most detestable, in such sorte, that though hys life were neuer so pure: yet his doctrine standyng, as it doth, no man is so blynde, but maye see, þt either the Pope is Antichrist, or els that Antichrist is nere cosine to þe pope: And al this doth, and will hereafter more and more appeare by printyng.
>
> God hath opened the presse to preache, whose voyce the pope is neuer able to stoppe with all þe puissance of his triple crowne. By this printyng, as by the gifte of tongues, & as by the singulare organe of the holy Ghost, þe doctrine of the Gospell soundeth to all nations & countreys vnder heauen: and what God reueleth to one mā, is dispersed to many, and what is knowne in one nation, is opened to all.[65]

This was in the Lutheran tradition, that these older texts were 'a witness preordained by God, so many years before us, for the confirmation of our doctrine'.[66]

---

64   This Irish type-design was later used in books printed in Dublin for quotations from Anglo-Saxon. See below, List of Type-Designs, IR1.

65   Foxe, *Actes and Monumentes* (1570.1), sig. 2D5^r. These thoughts on the power of printing were subsequently published separately in a booklet: John Fox[e], *The Benefit and Invention of Printing ... Extracted out of his Acts and Monuments* (London: T. Sowle, 1704). The papacy had already worked out for itself the power of printing to spread Roman Catholic liturgical usage. This development was subsequently formalized in books printed *typis Propagandæ Fidei*.

66   Quoted by Margaret Aston, 'Lollardy and the Reformation: Survival or Revival?', *History*, 49 (1964), pp. 149–170, at p. 157.

Likewise with Anglo-Saxon the purpose was propagandistic: to present in authentic form older precedents for the liturgy and doctrine being adopted in association with the new Book of Common Prayer and the establishment of the *Ecclesia Anglicana*. The Anglo-Saxon past was used as a tool for the establishment of ecclesiastical pedigree.

This approach was continued in the seventeenth century, and Abraham Wheelock (1593–1653), the first holder of the Anglo-Saxon lectureship at Cambridge, was still arguing about church practice even while civil war was brewing.[67] English churchmen of a Protestant persuasion sought to use Anglo-Saxon evidence to authenticate their theory that Church corruption was instigated by the Norman conquest of 1066.[68] But the main focus of this antiquarian interest shifted somewhat away from ecclesiastical politics towards secular constitutional politics; indeed the trend was already established by the need to resist obsolescence by recording legal documents to support claims and rights.[69] James I and Charles I argued that they had a divine right to rule inherited from their Norman forbears. Since it was felt that Anglo-Saxon materials might provide evidence of 'free' Anglo-Saxon institutions, thereby substantiating the view that the Norman Yoke of dictatorial kingship was a myth, promoting the virtues of the Saxon past had a distinctly political edge in the run-up to the period of the Commonwealth. Despite the obvious dangers, the publication of Anglo-Saxon materials flourished through the later years of Charles I and the Commonwealth period, i.e. 1630–1660, and the twenty-year period from 1639 to 1658 saw the production of the four new sets of punches for Anglo-Saxon type-designs which were the most important of those produced in the seventeenth century.

The process involved in having Anglo-Saxon types made was described by one of the early scholars to carry out such a project, Franciscus Junius (1591–1677).[70] In a letter to John Selden (1584–1654) from Amsterdam Junius wrote on 8 May 1654:

---

67 Michael Murphy, 'Abraham Wheloc's Edition of Bede's *History* in Old English', *Studia Neophilologica*, 39 (1967), pp. 46–59.
68 Christopher Hill, *Puritanism and Revolution: Studies in Interpretation of the English Revolution of the 17th Century* (London: secker & Warburg, 1958), pp. 57–67.
69 Crick, 'Historical Literacy', pp. 160–164.
70 For some account of Junius's life and work see, for example, Keith Aldrich, Philipp Fehl & Raina Fehl, *Franciscus Junius, The Literature of Classical Art*, 2 vols, California Studies in the History of Art 22 (Berkeley: University of California Press, 1991), I.xxvi–xlix; Sophie van Romburg, *"For my worthy freind [sic] Mr. Franciscus Junius": an edition of the correspondence of Francis Junius F.F. (1591–1677)* (Leiden: Brill, 2004); Philippus H. Breuker, 'On the course of Franciscus Junius' Germanic Studies with special Reference to Frisian', in R.H. Bremmer Jr, G. van der Meer & O. Vries (eds), *Aspects of Old Frisian Philology*,

In the meane while have I here Anglo-Saxonick types (I know not whether you call them Punchons) a cutting, and hope they will be matriculated, and cast within the space of seven or eight weeks at the furthest.[71]

Junius's threefold description of his 'types' ('cut ..., matriculated, and cast') in his letter to Selden shows characteristic precision. 'Punchons' were punches, made of steel, at the end of which the required letter pattern was cut by hand. Once the punchcutter had been supplied with handwritten or hand-drawn designs, the image of the character to be cut was transferred in mirror image on to the face of the projected punch, and the inner shape was excavated, or created with a counter-punch, and the outer shape filed away, 'a most exacting occupation requiring the utmost expertness', usually carried out by goldsmiths.[72] The design on the punch could then be checked by means of a soot impression or 'smoke-proof'.[73] To 'matriculate' meant to make matrices by hammering the punch into a small block of copper which then had to be carefully trimmed and filed to size so that it could be used as a mould from which types could be 'cast' in sufficient numbers to make up a fount adequate for the printer's needs.[74] When special sorts were cut to fit with an existing fount there

---

       Amsterdamer Beiträge zur Älteren Germanistik 31/32 (Amsterdam: Rodopi, 1990); Peter J. Lucas, *Franciscus Junius's Cædmonis Monachi Paraphrasis Poetica Genesios*, Early Studies in Germanic Philology 3 (Amsterdam: Rodopi, 2000, re-issued as e-book, Leiden: Brill, 2021), Introduction, §1.

71   Printed by Romburgh, *Franciscus Junius*, p. 848 (Letter 187), and previously by Hickes 1703/5.1: I.xliii (sig. *h*r). A specimen of Junius's types appears in 1693.2: D1–2. See further Peter J. Lucas, 'Junius, his Printers and his Types: An Interim Report', in R.H. Bremmer Jr (ed.), *Franciscus Junius and his Circle* (Amsterdam: Rodopi, 1998), pp. 177–197 and figs 12–16. On Selden see G.J. Toomer, *John Selden: A Life in Scholarship*, 2 vols (Oxford: Oxford University Press, 2009), also Toomer, *Eastern Wisedome and Learning: The Study of Arabic in Seventeenth-Century England* (Oxford: Clarendon Press, 1996), pp. 64–71.

72   For the supply of designs to punchcutters see Carter, *View of Typography*, pp. 25, 43. The quotation is from Stanley Morison, in Charles Enschedé, translated and revised Harry Carter, *Typefoundries in the Netherlands from the Fifteenth to the Nineteenth Century by Charles Enschedé*, ed. Lotte Hellinga (Haarlem: Stiftung Museum Enschedé, 1978), p. 422. On the other hand Smeijers, *Counterpunch*, p. 85, considers making an individual punch relatively easy; see also the discussion of this point by Hendrik D.L. Vervliet in his untitled review of Smeijers's book in *Typography Papers* (Reading), 2 (1997), pp. 133–135.

73   Carter, *View of Typography*, frontispiece; also *Le Bé Memorandum*, pl. [iv] following p. 52.

74   For a reconstruction with photographs of the threefold process of making printing type see A. May, 'Making "Real" Type: Virtue Regained', *Printing Historical Society Bulletin*, 32 (1992), pp. 4–8; see also Phil Baines and Andrew Haslam, *Type & Typography* (London: Laurence King, 2005), pp. 92–93. For an account of the process contemporary with the Parkerian period see Christophe Plantin, *An Account of Calligraphy and Printing in the Sixteenth Century*, t R. Nash, intro. S. Morison (New York: Liturgical Arts Society, 1949),

was a particular challenge (not always met) to design them so that all the new letters were visually coherent with the existing fount and to cut them to fit alongside the next character satisfactorily.

The method of assembling a complete set of types for a language such as Anglo-Saxon was to add special sorts to an existing roman fount. Anglo-Saxon sorts were cut to fit with two (later three) sizes of type, Great Primer (15 point), and Pica (11 point), though it should be noted that differences between type-sizes at this time were more flexible than in modern times. The first Parkerian Anglo-Saxon has the body size of a Great Primer, and it is used in *A Testimonie of Antiquitie* for the main Old English text (1566.1, 1566.2). The second and third sets of Anglo-Saxon type-designs both had a Pica body size. The Parkerian Pica Anglo-Saxon, as I have called it, first occurs in the third edition of Foxe's *Actes and Monumentes* [Book of Martyrs; 1576.1].[75] In the same year the Lambardian Pica Anglo-Saxon was first used for William Lambarde's *A Perambulation of Kent* (1576.2). The third size is English-size (13 point), which comes in between Great Primer and Pica. Size matters. It is a notable feature of all the Parkerian productions containing Anglo-Saxon that where Anglo-Saxon text is used to provide illustration, the Anglo-Saxon is always in a larger type-size than the main text.[76] This differentiation in size might have been accidental but it was certainly appropriate to Parker's conception of the authority that his Anglo-Saxon types conferred on the matter enshrined in them.

Later, however, at times when punchcutters were scarce, or the process of using them would have taken too long or been too expensive, some printers on the continent were forced (or chose) to adopt rudimentary Anglo-Saxon sorts made of wood. Examples include Joannis Janssonius in Amsterdam from 1646 onwards, and Johann Michael Goderitsch in Wittenberg in 1695–6. Using wood for printing is centuries old (from the ninth century in China) and can be successful. Wood is freely available, easily cut, and provides a good surface for accepting ink for printing. From the fifteenth century onwards, in England as on the continent, wood was used for capitals and set alongside metal letter-sorts. During the nineteenth century wood was used for display types, especially for

---

pp. 3–4. On the composition of early typemetal see Herbert Davis and Harry Carter (eds), *Mechanick Exercises on the whole Art of Printing (1683–4) by Joseph Moxon* (London: Oxford University Press, 1962 edn), pp. 379–380.

75 1576.1, II, 3G3^v–6^r (= pp. 1114–1119).

76 This statement is true even of 1576.1, where the main text is in a Small Pica, smaller than the Parkerian Pica Anglo-Saxon used for the passages of Old English.

posters, a technique developed particularly in America.⁷⁷ These types were large, the smallest illustrated by Kelly showing an x-height of 5.5mm. While their quality is remarkable, it is much more difficult to produce smaller type in wood, and setting wooden sorts together with metal ones could be problematic. But it was possible and there was nothing necessarily shameful about it. Later still, in the nineteenth century, no less a scholar than Jacob Grimm had his printer use wooden sorts before special metal sorts could be sourced.⁷⁸ His *Deutsche Grammatik* first appeared in 1819 with no special sorts, using th for þ and ð.⁷⁹ The second edition, which came out in four volumes (1822–37) shows wooden sorts in vol. I (1822, e.g., pp. 63, 252–253), and metal sorts in vol. II (1826, e.g., pp. 110–111), though even here it is evident that þ is a p modified by adding an ascender to the stem. In the *Vorrede* (dated 29 Sept 1818) to the first edition Grimm reports that 'the printing of this book has progressed very slowly and will take over a year'.⁸⁰ He reports further in the second edition.

> After an unsuccessful attempt to have cast sorts that were not available, and in order to avoid further delay, the publishers have had to use individual blocks of wood which strike the eye as unattractive and which simply could not be used at all for some letters; this deplorable state of affairs has been successfully remedied ... thanks to the efforts of a skilled compositor, without which the work would not have been so accurate.⁸¹

This gives some idea of how much preparation time was required to print with special sorts. Even in the nineteenth century, when technology was more

---

77 See Rob R. Kelly, *American Wood Type 1828–1900: Notes on the Evolution of Decorated and Large Types and Comments on Related Trades of the Period* (New York: Da Capo Press, 1969), also James Clough & Chiara Scattolin, *Alphabets of Wood: Luigi Melchiori & the History of Italian Wood Types* (Cornuda: Tipoteca Italiana, 2014), esp. chs 1 & 3.

78 My thanks to John Flood (London) for drawing my attention to this and for indicating where to look.

79 Jacob Grimm (1785–1863), *Deutsche Grammatik*, vol. I (1st edn, Göttingen, 1819); 2nd edn, vol. I (1822), vol. II (1826), vol. III (1831), vol. IV (1837), all published by Dieterichsche Buchhandlung at Göttingen.

80 Grimm, *Deutsche Grammatik*, I (1819), p. xxiv: 'Der Druck dieses Buchs hat sehr langsamen Fortgang und wird über ein volles Jahr dauern'. On p. lxxx he notes that the printers did not have the required special sorts.

81 Grimm, *Deutsche Grammatik*, I (1822), p. xvii: 'Die verlagshandlung hat, nach mislungenem versuch, unvorhandene typen gießen zu laßen, um nicht länger aufzuhalten, zu einzelnen holzstücken greifen müßen, welche unsauber ins auge fallen, für einige buchstaben gar nicht einmahl gebraucht warden konnten; diesen übestand aber riechlich vergolden ... durch verwendung eines tüchtigen setzers, ohne welchen das werk nicht so correct ausgefallen wäre'.

advanced (though punchcutters and typefounders were no doubt thin on the ground), it took Grimm from 1818 to 1826 to get from wanting special sorts to actually obtaining them in metal.[82] As an interim measure he was content with wooden sorts, and indeed on this occasion their quality is reasonably good. Nevertheless they show the work of a meticulous scholar in what is only an adequate presentation. These difficulties and shortcomings experienced in a later century throw into relief the achievements of the creators of Anglo-Saxon type-designs with special sorts in the sixteenth and seventeenth centuries.

In the same year as he wrote to Selden about his Anglo-Saxon type-designs (1654) Junius noted what must have been his considerable expenses in equipping himself with special printing sorts.[83] That the expenditure was sufficiently great to enforce a need to maximise its benefit can be illustrated from the attempt in 1592 to provide Welsh with special sorts of the kind advocated by spelling reformers. Two special letter-forms were designed for Welsh and cut in two sizes.[84] Each size was used with two sizes of both roman and italic, the larger size with a Double Pica and a Great Primer, and the smaller size with a Pica and Long Primer; probably this use with different sizes of roman and italic was achieved by casting the selected special sort on the appropriate body.[85] So each special sort had up to four uses. This economy of investment

---

82 When Othmar Frank (1770–1840) published his *Grammatica Sanskrita* at Würzburg in 1823 the text was reproduced lithographically because no Sanskrit types were available.

83 In Amsterdam Gemeentarchief, Not. Arch. 2435, pp. 37–47, printed by Rolf H. Bremmer Jr and Reina Rácz, 'Junius's Case against William Howard, Viscount Stafford', in Rolf H. Bremmer Jr (ed.), *Franciscus Junius and his Circle* (Amsterdam: Rodopi, 1998), pp. 121–127, esp. 124. The document, which dates from 1654, comprises questions to Junius and his answers for the preparation of a legal case involving Junius and Viscount Stafford, the heir of his former employers the earl and countess of Arundel. Some idea of the costs involved in acquiring punches, etc., may be gauged from a letter from Henri du Tour (= Hendrik van der Keere, Ghent) to Christophe Plantin of 16 January 1576; cf. Max Rooses, *Correspondance de Christophe Plantin*, 9 vols, Uitgaven der Antwerpsche Bibliophilen 12, 15, 26, 29–34 (Antwerp: Buschmann, 1883–1920), V.117–120, at p. 119, where the phrase 'les despens extraordinaires' refers to non-recurring expenses.

84 John Dafydd Rhys, *Cambrobrytannicæ Cymraecæve Linguae Institutiones et Rudimenta* (London: Thomas Orwin, 1592): STC 20966. For discussion and (reduced) illustration see G. von Slagle, 'A Note on Early Welsh Orthography', *The Library*, VI.5 (1983), pp. 254–6; his statement that the special sorts were cut in both roman and italic is erroneous.

85 The larger size is used (a) with Guyot's Double-Pica Italic (H.D.L. Vervliet, *Sixteenth-Century Printing Types of the Low Countries* (Amsterdam: Herzberger, 1968), IT2) but not with an equivalent Roman, and (b) with Haultin's Great Primer Roman (LMA 63 in Parker et al., 'Typographica', 8; Vervliet, *Vatican*, no. 36) and Granjon's Great Primer Italic (TSF II 1567: 23); and the smaller size is used (a) with Haultin's Pica Roman (A. Tinto, 'I Tipi della Stamperia del Popolo Romano', *Gutenberg-Jahrbuch* (1967), pp. 26–38: R.8; Ferguson, *Pica Roman*, pl. 115) and Granjon's 2nd Pica Italic (*pendante*; TSF II, 1567: no.27, Johnson,

to provide the maximum benefit puts Parker's provisions for Anglo-Saxon in perspective. The number of special sorts he had made for Anglo-Saxon is larger than the number made for any of the other languages for which special sorts were provided, although the Irish fount, with the Brevier counted as well as the English size, closely approaches Parker's provisions for both the Great Primer Anglo-Saxon and the Pica Anglo-Saxon. If the spelling-reformer John Hart's estimate of costs for providing special sorts for the extra symbols he wanted to add to the roman alphabet is followed the archbishop could have paid at least £100 to achieve each set of special sorts, i.e. £200 altogether, but this estimate may be high.[86] The Irish fount (or founts) cost less than this, £66 13s. 4d. being paid for them, although Kearney seems to have done it for £22 13s. 4d.[87] The cost of doing it in Dublin may have been less than in London. Possibly Parker paid more than £100. In any case such expenditure would have to be supplemented by the costs incurred by a typefounder or printer in hiring and setting up a workshop. For what Parker was aiming to achieve, the provision of special sorts to enable the authentic printing of Anglo-Saxon, these costs were a measure of his commitment to using them. He may well have calculated that the investment in Anglo-Saxon types for a sizeable project such as the *Testimonie* was worth it and would enable the types to continue to be used for projects that involved using a smaller amount of the special type than was needed for the initial one.

Italic Types, type 7), and (b) with Haultin's Long Primer Roman (LMA 2 in Parker et al., 'Typographica', p. 13, also Tinto, 'Tipi', R.9) and Granjon's Long Primer Italic ('l'immortelle'; Johnson, *Italic Types*, type 11).

86   See Lucas, 'Spelling Reformers', p. 7.
87   McGuinne, *Irish Type*, pp. 5–7. For a more general account of Irish printing activity at this time cf. Raymond Gillespie, 'Irish Printing in the Early Seventeenth Century', *Journal of Irish Economic and Social History*, 15 (1988), pp. 81–88.

CHAPTER 2

The Parkerian Great Primer Anglo-Saxon Type-Design

Three designs of Anglo-Saxon types were produced during the sixteenth century, one during the lifetime of Archbishop Parker (d.1575), and two just after. The first Parkerian Anglo-Saxon has the body size of a Great Primer, and it is used in *A Testimonie of Antiquitie* for the main Old English text (**1566.1** and **1566.2**). The method of assembling a complete set of types for a language such as Anglo-Saxon was to add special sorts to an existing roman fount.

> Of the capitals, eight only ... are distinctively Saxon, the remaining eighteen letters being ordinary roman; while in the lower-case there are twelve Saxon letters as against fifteen of the roman.[1]

This statement applies to the type-specimen set out at the end of *A Testimonie* for the reader's benefit (Illustration 4), which shows twenty-four special sorts. Besides the twelve lower-case ordinary letters there is a lower-case ⁊, the Tironian sign abbreviation for 'and', and the abbreviation þ for 'þæt', and besides the eight upper-case letters, with two sorts for Æ (Æ¹ and Æ² being shown as equivalent to roman and swash italic Æ respectively), making nine special sorts in all, there is an upper-case ⁊, the Tironian sign abbreviation for 'and'. So altogether there were twenty-six special sorts. The two not shown in this specimen appeared a few years later. A *punctus versus* punctuation mark for a mid pause ⸵ (to substitute for the semi-colon utilized in the *Testimonie* specimen) first appears in a specimen in William Lambarde's *Archaionomia* (**1568.2**, also printed by John Day 1: see Illustration 5.[2] The last special sort was a capital X, which first appears in a specimen (on A1ᵛ) in Parker's edition (introd. John Foxe) of the Anglo-Saxon gospels (**1571.1**, also printed by John Day 1). Here it is illustrated in the specimen from Parker's edition of Asser's *Ælfredi regis res gestæ* (**1574.2**), again printed by John Day 1: see Illustration 6; this latter specimen has the benefit of clarity through citing the alphabet in both lower and upper cases in columns. The Anglo-Saxon sorts are combined with Pierre Haultin's English-size Roman, which shows the same x-height, on

---

1 Reed, *Letter Foundries*, p. 91.
2 B2ʳ. The *punctus versus* is not used in the text until sig. H4ᵛ.

> ¶ The Saxon Caracters or letters, that be moste straunge, be here knowen by other common Caracters set ouer them.
>
> d. th. th. f. g. i. r. ſ. t. w.
> ¶ ꝺ. ð. þ. ꝼꝝ. ı. ꝑ. ꞃ. ꞇ. ƿ.
> y. z. and. that.
> ẏ. ȝ. ⁊. ꝥ.
>
> ¶ Æ. Æ. Th. Th. E. H. M.
> ¶ Æ. ſE. Ð. þ. E. Ƿ. M.
> S. W. And.
> S. ƿ. ⁊.
>
> ¶ One pricke signifieth an vnperfect point, this figure ; (which is lyke the Greeke interrogatiue) a full pointe, which in some other olde Saxon bookes, is expressed wyth three prickes, set in triangle wyse thus ∴.

ILLUSTRATION 4
Readers's Anglo-Saxon type-specimen (AS1) from *A Testimonie of Antiquitie* (1566.2), L7^v (CCC SP.281)

a Great Primer body (four lines of Latin set in Roman in *A Testimonie* on I3^r, I5^v and I6^r).[3] The body size is 112mm for twenty lines of printed matter, and the following sizes apply:[4]

Anglo-Saxon:	Body 112	Face 110 × 2.0: 4.3.
Roman:	Body 95	Face 92 × 2.0: 3.

---

3   Haultin's English-size Roman is illustrated in Vervliet, *Vatican*, no. 41, also F. Isaac, 'Elizabethan Roman and Italic Types', *The Library*, IV.14 (1933), pp. 85–100, 212–228, fig.5, and Tinto, 'Tipi', R.7 on p. 28; for discussion see A.F. Johnson, *Selected Essays on Books and Printing*, ed. P.H. Muir (Amsterdam: Van Gendt, 1970), pp. 255–259. See also Parker et al., 'Typographica', p. 8, LMA 63.

4   The convention used follows that explained by Philip Gaskell, *A New Introduction to Bibliography* (Oxford: Clarendon Press, 1972), pp. 12–16. The first figure is the distance from the top

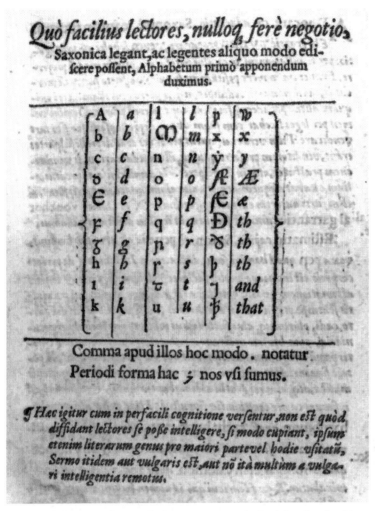

ILLUSTRATION 5   Reader's Anglo-Saxon type-specimen (AS1) from Lambarde's *Archaionomia* (1568.2), B2ʳ (CCC Y.7.14)

Anglo-Saxon 'types' are particularly interesting for the typographical historian because they often offer evidence of punchcutting at a time when most printers were using founts of roman or italic that had been in existence for some time.[5] The punchcutting involved had ideally to be particularly skilful because

> of an ascender to the bottom of a descender multiplied by 20 to obtain the face size corresponding to the body size. The second figure is the x-height of a lower-case letter, and the third figure is the height of a capital letter.

5   Edward Rowe Mores, *A Dissertation upon English Typographical Founders and Founderies* (1778), ed. H. Carter & C. Ricks (Oxford: Oxford Bibliographical Society, 1961), p. lxxii.

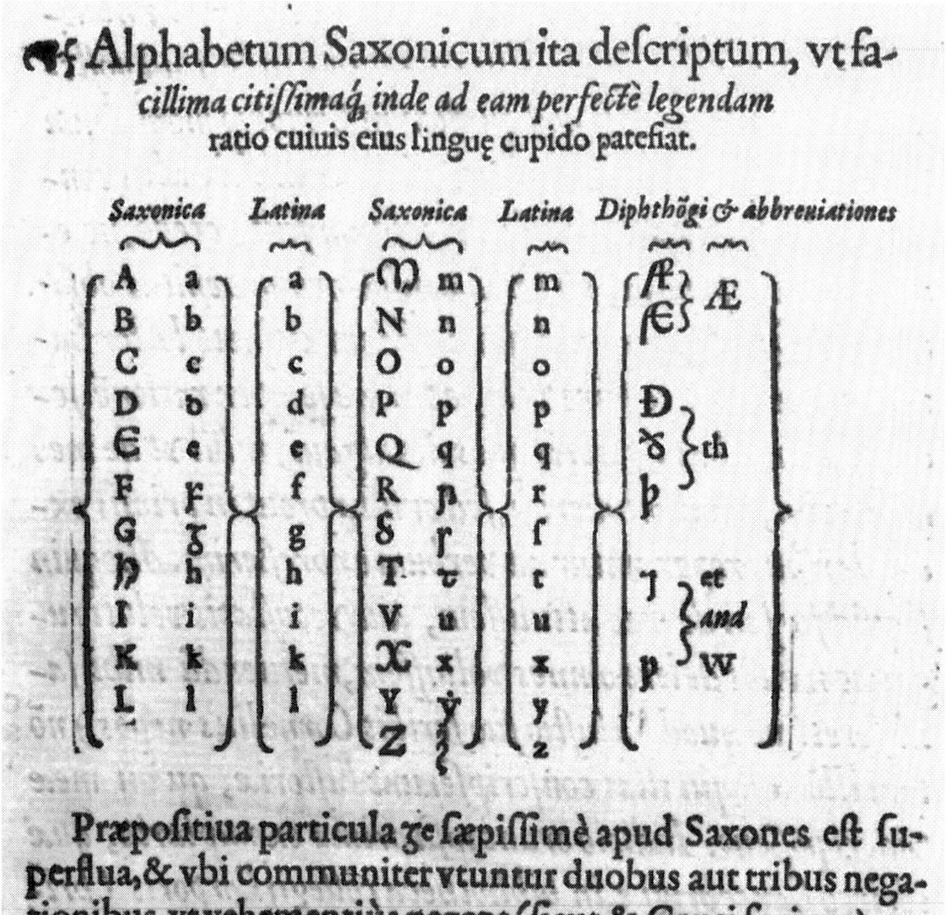

❡ Alphabetum Saxonicum ita defcriptum, vt fa-
cillima citiſſimaq́, inde ad eam perfectè legendam
ratio cuiuis eius linguę cupido patefiat.

Saxonica	Latina	Saxonica	Latina	Diphthŏgi & abbreuiationes
A	a	a	M m	m Æ Æ
B	b	b	N n	n E
C	c	c	O o	o
D	d	d	P p	p Ð
E	e	e	Q q	q ð } th
F	f	f	R r	r
G	g	g	S s	s þ
H	h	h	T t	t ⁊ } et
I	i	i	V u	u } and
K	k	k	X x	x ƿ w
L	l	l	Y y	y
			Z z	

Præpofitiua particula ȝe fæpiſſimè apud Saxones eſt fu-
perflua, & vbi communiter vtuntur duobus aut tribus nega-
tionibus, vt vehementiùs negent (ſicut & Græci faciunt) tamen fecundùm phraſim Anglici ſermonis, vnica tantùm
ſufficit.

ILLUSTRATION 6A   Reader's Anglo-Saxon type-specimen (AS1) from *Ælfredi Regis Res Gestæ* (1574.2),
¶1ᵛ (CCC MS 176)

the special sorts to be cut should match all the qualities of the design of the existing sorts.[6] There has therefore been considerable interest in the statement in the preface to Parker's edition of Asser's *Ælfredi regis res gestæ* (1574.2: A4ʳ):

> For in as much as Day the printer [is the] first (and to my knowledge the only one) [to have] indented these shapes (?moulds) in copper those things that are written in Saxon letters will be easily published in these same types. The reading of which [Anglo-Saxon letters in the new types] indeed will restore for you the memory of the ancient but once familiar language, and will provide no little household furniture for [previously] concealed knowledge. It will be easy to perceive the meaning of utterances and the diversity of words, especially when the similitude of this our language (which we now use) and of the old language is so great.[7]

Two aspects of this important statement require discussion, first, the technical aspect about the making of the first Anglo-Saxon types, and secondly, Parker's attitude to their function.

In the past, as a result of a misreading of this statement in the preface to the Asser, whereby *æri inciderit* is taken to mean 'cut from metal', Day has been credited with cutting the Anglo-Saxon sorts in this fount; he was also credited with the Double Pica Roman and Double Pica Italic found in the Asser.[8] Both

---

6 For a discussion by a modern punch-cutter of what is involved in cutting Anglo-Saxon sorts (lower-case ð, þ, and capital Ð) to match an existing fount see Stan Nelson, 'Cutting Anglo-Saxon Sorts', *Fine Print*, 12 (1986), pp. 228–229.

7 Iam verò cum Dayus Typographus primus (& omnium certè quod sciam solus) has formas æri inciderit: facilè quæ Saxonicis literis perscripta sunt, ijsdem typis diuulgabuntur. Quorum sanè lectio & veteris tibi linguæ, ac quondam domesticæ memoriam renouabit, & haud paruam suppeditabit abstrusæ cognitionis suppellectilem. Facile autem erit vocum vim, & verborum varietatem percipere, præsertim cum tanta sit huius nostræ (qua nunc vtimur) linguæ & illius veteris similitudo.

8 By no less an authority than Reed/Johnson, *Letter Foundries*, pp. 90–93. This error is continued in Carter and Ricks's edition of Mores's *Dissertation*, pp. lxvi–lxviii, and in the title of Wakeman, 'Day's Saxon', and is repeated by McGuinne, *Irish Type*, p. 4. Vervliet, *Printing Types*, says on pp. 26–27 that Parker 'is responsible for the tradition that John Day cut the new Saxon characters', but in fact it was Vervliet's authority for this statement, Talbot Baines Reed, whose misreading of Parker's statement led to the error. For a suggestion leading to the present reading see Bromwich, 'First Book', p. 271, n. 2.

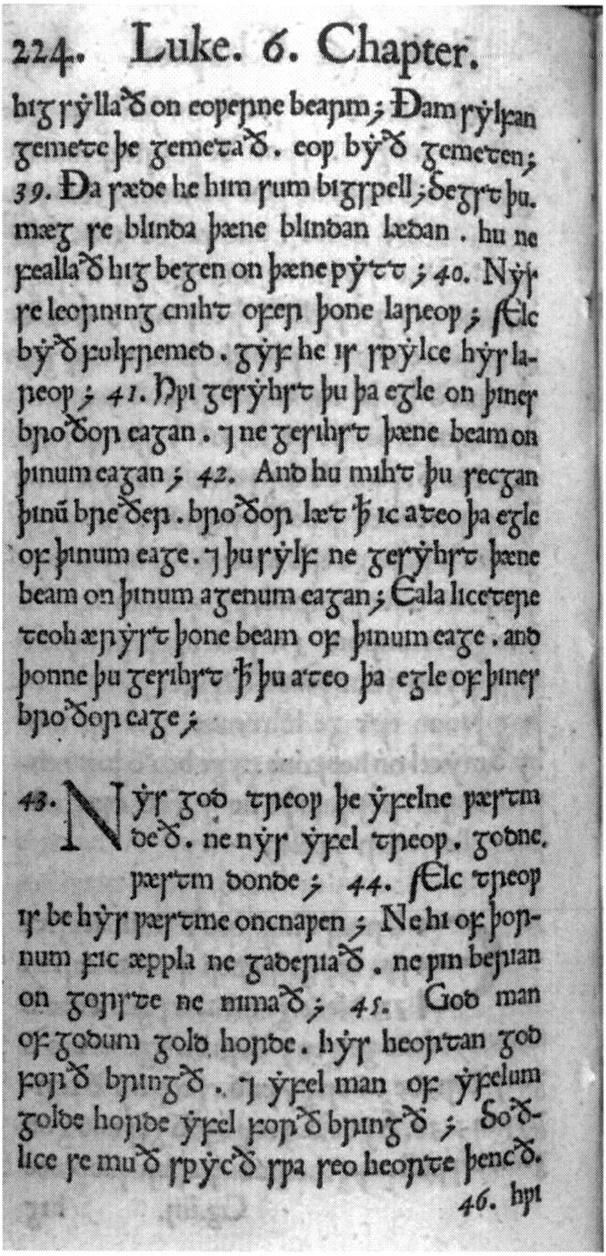

224. Luke. 6. Chapter.

hig syllað on eowerne bearm; Ðam sylfan
gemete þe gemetað. eow byð gemeten;
39. Ða sæde he him sum bigspell; Segst þu.
mæg se blinda þæne blindan lædan. hu ne
feallað hig begen on þæne pytt; 40. Nys
se leorningcniht ofer þone lareow; Ælc
byð fulfremed. gyf he ys swylce hys lareow; 41. Hwi gesyhst þu þa egle on þines
broðor eagan. ⁊ ne gesihst þæne beam on
þinum eagan; 42. And hu miht þu secgan
þinū breðer. broðor læt ꝥ ic ateo þa egle
of þinum eage. ⁊ þu sylf ne gesyhst þæne
beam on þinum agenum eagan; Eala licetere
teoh ærest þone beam of þinum eage. and
þonne þu gesihst ꝥ þu ateo þa egle of þines
broðor eage;

43. Nys god treow þe yfelne wæstm
deð. ne nys yfel treow. godne
wæstm donde; 44. Ælc treow
ys be hys wæstme oncnawen; Ne hi of þor-
num fic æppla ne gaderiað. ne win berian
on gorste ne nimað; 45. God man
of godum gold horde. hys heortan god
forð bringð. ⁊ yfel man of yfelum
golde horde yfel forð bringð; Soð-
lice se muð sprycð swa seo heorte þencð.
46. hwi

ILLUSTRATION 6B Anglo-Saxon text (AS1) from Foxe's AS *Gospels* (1571.1), $2G4^{v}$–$2H1^{r}$, showing Lk 6–7 (CCC Y.7.17). The page has been split to enable reproduction at actual size

Luke. 7. Chapter. 225.

46. hpı clýpıe ȝe me Dꞃıhten. Dꞃıhten. ꞇ ne doð þ ıc eop ꞅecȝe ; 47. Ælc þaꞃa þe to me cýmþ ꞇ mıne ꞅpꞃæca ȝehýꞃþ ꞇ þa deð. ıc hım æꞇýpe hpá he ȝelıc ıꞅ ; 48. He ıꞅ ȝelıc tım-bꞃıendū men hıꞅ huꞅ . ꞅe dealꝼ deopne ꞇ hýꞅ ȝꞃundpeall oꝼeꞃ þæne ꞅtan aꞅette ; Soþlıce ȝeꝼoꞃdenū ꝼlode hıt ꝼleop ınto þam huꞅ. and hıt ne mıhte þ huꞅ aꞅtýꞃıan . hıt ꝼæꞅ oꝼeꞃ þæne ꞅtan ȝetꞃýmed ; 49. Se þe ȝehýꞃð ꞇ ne deð, he ıꞅ ȝelıc þā tımbꞃıendan men hıꞅ huꞅ oꝼeꞃ þa eoꞃþan butan ȝꞃundpealle . ꞇ þ ꝼlod ınꝼleop . ꞇ hꞃædlıce hıt aꝼeoll ꞇ peaꞃð mýcel hꞃýꞃe þæꞅ huꞅeꞅ ;

Cap. 7.

1. Soðlıce þa he ealle hýꞅ ꝼoꞃd ȝe-ꝼýlde on þæꞅ ꝼolceꞅ hlýꞅte . he eode ınto Caꝼaꞃnaum ; 2. Da ꝼæꞅ ꞅumeꞅ hundꞃed maneꞅ þeopa untꞃum. ꞅe pæꞅ ꞅpeltendlıc . ꞅe pæꞅ hým dýꞃe ; 3. And þa he ȝehýꞃde be þam Hæ-lende he ꞅende to hým Iudea ealdꞃaꞅ and bæd þ he come. ꞇ hýꞅ þeop ȝehælde ; 4. Da hı to þam Hælende comun . hı bædon hýne ȝeoꞃnlıce ꞇ þuꞅ cpædon ; He ıꞅ pýꞃðe þ þu hým tılıȝe. 5. pꞃtodlıce he luꝼað uꞃe

Hh.j.   þeode.

of these are attributable to François Guyot.⁹ This older reading caused some difficulty, as Parker's statement might show ignorance of what Day really did.¹⁰ Or it could be interpreted as a form of encouragement, giving Day the credit for what others in no position to object actually did. It is now generally agreed that while Day may have organized the making of the Anglo-Saxon types for Parker, he was a printer, not a punchcutter, nor even a typefounder.¹¹ If, however, *æri inciderit* is taken to mean 'indented in copper', indicating 'made matrices', then the passage makes good sense. Possibly Day made the matrices himself, or he had them made, and he held them, as suggested below. Although there were exceptions, it was quite usual for a printer to hold the matrices and for punchcutters to hold the punches. As far as the punchcutting was concerned, while the Anglo-Saxon sorts may have been cut in England, it is unlikely that they were cut by a native Englishman.¹² It is possible that they were cut abroad.

At about the same time as Parker and his circle were looking to have Anglo-Saxon sorts made, two orthoepists or spelling-reformers also required and had made special sorts for their phonetic orthographic symbols which they wished to add to the roman alphabet for reforming English spelling.¹³ One was Thomas Smith, Doctor of Civil Law, Secretary of State (1548–9, 1572–6) and an associate of Parker's (and of Cecil's, with whom he was imprisoned in the Tower after the fall of Somerset in October 1549), whose *De recta & emendata Linguæ anglicæ scriptione, Dialogus* was printed at Paris by Robert (II) Estienne (**1568.3**).¹⁴ The other orthoepist was John Hart, Chester Herald (1567–74), whose *An Orthographie, conteyning the due order and reason, howe to write or paint*

---

9 Dreyfus in *TSF* I, pl. 1.
10 If *æri* means 'metal', as translated by Reed/Johnson (*Letter Foundries*, p. 90), then its use suggests ignorance, since an informed writer might have been expected to use a more precise word, which would signify the crucial information of what kind of metal was involved; punchcutters had to use steel, which could be relied upon to make an impression when hammered into the (relatively soft) copper of the matrix. If it means 'bronze' or 'brass' its use suggests ignorance of the process of letter-founding.
11 Oastler, *Day*, p. 35.
12 *Pace* Carter and Ricks's introduction to Mores, *Dissertation*, p. lxviii, and Wakeman, 'Day's Saxon', p. 283.
13 See further Lucas, 'Spelling Reformers'.
14 For Smith's relations with Robert (II) Estienne see Elizabeth Armstrong, The Publication of the Royal Edicts and Ordinances under Charles IX: The Destiny of Robert (II) Estienne as King's Printer', *Proceedings of the Huguenot Society*, 19.2 (1953–4), pp. 41–59, at pp. 48–52. For a philological assessment of Smith's work see E.J. Dobson, *English Pronunciation 1500–1700* (Oxford: Clarendon Press, 1968), I.46–62. A life of Smith was compiled by John Strype, the author also of *The Life of Parker* (1711): *The Life of the Learned Sir Thomas Smith Kt. Doctor of the Civil Law* (London: A. Roper, 1698), but see also Mary Dewar, *Sir Thomas Smith A Tudor Intellectual in Office* (London: Athlone Press, 1964).

thimage of mannes voice, most like to the life or nature was printed at London by [?Henry Denham for] William Seres in 1569.[15] His *A Methode or comfortable beginning for all vnlearned, to read English* was printed at London by Henry Denham in 1570.[16] As early as 1551 Hart had advocated making special sorts for his phonetic orthographic symbols, noting the following in his unpublished manuscript 'The opening of the unreasonable writing of our inglish toung'.

> mani will say that it were impossible to frame our commune writen hand ... in souch a iust uniformite, as it mought be easili prynted. ... The cause of theis fayned impossibilities, is ... (for making of new punchons) the lak of the first disbursing of (at most) one hundred pounds.[17]

Success came when, as Chester Herald, Hart was a crown officer in the service of Sir William Cecil. Both Smith and Hart had special sorts made to complement an italic fount. Smith used several Anglo-Saxon letter-forms, viz. f, g, þ, ð, and also undotted ı, and dotted ẏ, made to fit with Claude Garamont's Great Primer Italic.[18] Hart used modifications of roman letter-forms made to fit with two sizes, a Pica Italic for the *Orthographie* in 1569, and a 2-line Great Primer Italic for the *Methode* in 1570, which also utilizes the Pica Italic special sorts; the nearest he came to an Anglo-Saxon letter-form was his symbol for /dʒ/, which was based on the shape of an Anglo-Saxon ᵹ, or, more probably, its Middle English descendant ȝ 'yogh', with the tail looped right round crossing back over itself.[19] As it happens we have contemporary evidence from another spelling-reformer that both had their special sorts made by foreigners. In his *A short Introduction or guiding to print, write, and reade Inglish speech* (London,

---

15   STC 12890. Facsimile, The English Experience no. 40 (Amsterdam: Da Capo Press, 1968); another, English Linguistics 209 (Menston: Scolar, 1969).
16   STC 12889.
17   Bror Danielsson, *John Hart's Works*, Stockholm Studies in English 5 (Stockholm: Almqvist & Wiksell, 1955), quotation on p. 148 from BL Royal 17.C.vii, pp. 168–9; cf. also Danielsson, *Hart's Works*, p. 88. For a philological assessment of Hart's work see Dobson, *Pronunciation*, 1.62–88, with reproduction of the *Orthographie*, fo 54ᵛ, on p. 75.
18   Illustrated in Jeanne Veyrin-Forrer & André Jammes, *Les Premiers Caractères de l'Imprimerie Royale. Étude sur un spécimen inconnu de 1643*, Documents Typographiques Français 11 (Paris: Jammes, 1958), pl. 11, no. 2.
19   The Pica Italic in Hart's *Othographie* is illustrated in Isaac, 'Elizabethan Types', fig. 11. Hart's *Methode* is illustrated in Bror Danielsson, *John Hart's Works on English Orthography and Pronunciation* (Stockholm: Almqvist & Wiksell, 1955), vol. I, fig. 23 on p. 249, but this illustration has been slightly reduced without notice. I follow the size-designation of Carter, *View of Typography*, p. 127.

Henry Denham, 1580), William Bullokar (c.1531–1609) took Smith and Hart to task for employing foreign immigrants to cut their special sorts:[20]

> sir Thomas Smith and M. Chester [i.e. Hart] were driuen to seeke straungers to fashion their figures ... for lack of helpe of skilfull men within the realme at that time ... But now (thanks be to God) the Printer and workmen being Inglish, can aide the Aucthors meaning, in ioining perfect conference of the olde use and new togither, which was not possible to be done by straungers.[21]

If Smith and Hart had to resort to foreign punchcutters it is highly likely that Day (working for Parker) had to do the same. Smith was her majesty's ambassador to France in Paris from 1562 to 1566, and his book was published by a Paris printer in 1568, so probably he had his special sorts cut in Paris, and in this respect he may have been a special case. In England itself two family firms who operated mainly on the continent could have provided the necessary technical expertise for making the Anglo-Saxon special sorts, the Guyot family and the Haultin family. Hart probably used the punchcutting services of both. In the *Methode* (1570) the 2-line Great Primer with which the large special sorts are matched is the bold variety of that size cut by François Guyot.[22] The *Returns of Aliens in London* record 'Fraunces Guyott, a Frenchman, Gabriell, John, Cristofer, and Anne, his children; and James and John his servantes, Dowchemen; they are all printemakers, of the Dowche churche, dwellinge in the howse of John Daye, [Parker's] printer' in 1568, evidence that fits well with the appearance of special sorts matching Guyot's type-design in Hart's

---

20 STC 4086.5, 2nd edn (1581) 4086.7. Facsimile edition by Bror Danielsson and Robin C. Alston, *The Works of William Bullokar vol. I*, Leeds Texts and Monographs n.s. 1 (Leeds: University of Leeds School of English, 1966). Bullokar produced an edition of 'Aesops Fablź in tru ortŏgraphy' in 1585. For a philological assessment of Bullokar's work see Dobson, *Pronunciation*, I.93–117.

21 Quoted from the 1581 edn, p. [21]; similarly the 1580 edn, p. [18]. Bullokar used a Textura (Black Letter) fount and made only minor modifications to existing letter-forms. For a stimulating discussion of extending the roman alphabet with special sorts see David Abercrombie, 'Extending the Roman Alphabet: Some Orthographic Experiments of the Past Four Centuries', in R.E. Asher & J.A. Henderson (eds), *Towards a History of Phonetics* (Edinburgh: Edinburgh University Press, 1981), pp. 206–224.

22 Vervliet, *Printing Types*, IT1. The fullest illustration occurs in C. Axel-Nilsson, *Type Studies: The Norstedt Collection of Matrices in the Typefoundry of the Royal Printing Office, A History and Catalogue* (Stockholm: Norstedts Tryckeri, 1983), NS 174 on p. 116. Also illustrated in Joseph Prijs, *Die Basler Hebraïschen Drucke 1492–1866* (Olten: Bernhard Prijs, 1964), fig. 76. Another example occurs in Bartholomæus Ğurğevíc (= Georgius), *De Turcarum ritu et caeremoniis* (Antwerp: Gregorius Bontius, 1544).

publication of 1570.²³ Perhaps the first visit was on foot of business done earlier, when François Guyot was Christophe Plantin's regular typecaster in Antwerp.²⁴ Later, in 1576, we find 'Gabriell Guyett, frencheman, [second son of François] in Mʳ Dayes hous' again.²⁵ Guyot apparently had associates. One Adrian Tressel, that is Adriaen Karelsz Treseil (schoolmaster), was in London in 1571 with his family including his eldest son Charles 'a graver of letters for prynters', having come 'into this realme for religion about iij yeres past'. Charles is further recorded in 1576 and 1582–3 when, with 'Agata his wife', he is described as 'a carver to the printers'.²⁶ According to J.G.C.A. Briels, Charles probably worked with Gabriel Guyot.²⁷ If Tressel was a punchcutter he could have cut the special sorts for Hart, but there is no evidence that he was in London early enough to have cut special sorts for Day and Parker.

Day was responsible for introducing some of François Guyot's type-designs into England, his Double Pica Roman and Double Pica Italic already mentioned, and in *A Testimonie* the translation facing the Old English text utilizes Guyot's Great Primer Italic.²⁸ Vervliet, not knowing of François Guyot's visit to Day in 1568, asked 'whether this specimen [i.e. example of Anglo-Saxon type-designs] was not originally sent by Guyot to John Day'.²⁹ The only evidence that might apparently confirm this suspicion that Guyot cut the Parkerian Anglo-Saxon type-designs is that of style, but to my eye the evidence looks insufficient.³⁰ In his Double Pica's Guyot apparently pioneered the cutting of a Roman and Italic designed to complement each other.³¹ This idea of complementarity is evident in the use of the Parkerian Great Primer Anglo-Saxon alongside Guyot's Great Primer Italic (he did not cut a Great Primer Roman), but it does not necessarily mean that Guyot cut the Anglo-Saxon sorts.

---

23   Oastler, *Day*, pp. 34 and 78, n. 28, quoting BL Lansdowne 202, fo 19ᵛ. R.E.G. Kirk & Ernest F. Kirk, *Returns of Aliens dwelling in the City and Suburbs of London from the Reign of Henry VIII to that of James I*, 4 vols, Publications of the Huguenot Society of London 10 (Aberdeen: Aberdeen University Press, 1900–8), III.354.
24   Carter, *View of Typography*, p. 95.
25   Ernest J. Worman, *Alien Members of the Book-Trade during the Tudor Period* (London: Blades, East & Blades, 1906), p. 26. Kirk and Kirk, *Returns of Aliens*, II.186.
26   Kirk and Kirk, *Returns of Aliens*, II.174, 248, 269.
27   *Zuidnederlandse Boekdrukkers en Boekverkopers in Republiek der Verenigde Nederlanden omstreeks 1570–1630*, Bibliotheca Bibliographica Neerlandica 6 (Nieuwkoop: De Graaf, 1974), p. 138.
28   *TSF* I, pl. 1; Vervliet, *Printing Types*, IT3.
29   Vervliet, *Printing Types*, pp. 26–27; for the note of Guyot's visit to Day in 1568 as subsequent information see the preface by Harry Carter, p. vii, n. 1.
30   Cf. the remarks about the letters z, H, M below in the List of Type Designs under AS1.
31   Vervliet, *Printing Types*, p. 27, Carter, *View of Typography*, pp. 96–97.

In both Hart's *Orthographie* (1569) and his *Methode* (1570) the Pica Italic with which the special sorts were made to fit was that cut by Pierre Haultin, the Parisian punchcutter who transferred his business to the Huguenot stronghold of La Rochelle in 1571.[32] As far as we know the first foreign typecaster to come to London was Hubert d'Armillier, a former apprentice of Robert Granjon, who probably brought matrices of Granjon's Italics with him when he came to London not later than 1553.[33] Amongst his servants in 1568 was one Jérôme Haultin, the nephew of Pierre.[34] We know that Jérôme in London acquired matrices from his uncle in La Rochelle, for which he paid in 1575–6, and that he cast types to supply to London printers.[35] It seems probable that he was carrying out this work earlier, probably earlier than 1568, as such a supposition provides the most obvious explanation of the occurrence of Haultin type-designs in English books before this date. In the *Testimonie of Antiquitie* the preface is set in Pierre Haultin's Pica Roman.[36] The English Roman with which the Anglo-Saxon sorts are combined is also his. The most obvious candidate for cutting the special sorts in Hart's works to match Haultin's Pica Italic (which Isaac records in England from 1566) is Haultin himself.[37] Is it not possible that the special sorts were cut by Pierre Haultin with Jérôme Haultin acting as the intermediary between Denham and Hart in London and the punchcutter in France?

Similarly with the Anglo-Saxon special sorts: is it not possible that they were cut by Pierre Haultin with Jérôme Haultin acting as the intermediary between Day and the type-designers in London and the punchcutter in France?[38] Like

---

32   On the Haultins see Desgraves, *Les Haultin*. For the identification of the Pica Italic noticed in n. 19 above as Haultin's (Isaac, 'Elizabethan Types', fig. 11) I am indebted to the late Hendrik Vervliet. It occurs in *Biblia Sacra Veteris & Noui Testamenti iuxta Vvlgatam, quam dicvnt, editionem*, ed. Johannes Benedictus (Paris: Heirs of Carola Guillard widow of Claudius Chevallonius, 1558) on sig. *3ᵛ, *4ᵛ, in the Index Testimoniorum (selective table of contents), and at the back of the book the whole of the Index Rerum et Sententiarum is set in it: sigs A⁸ B⁶ C⁶.

33   Carter, *View of Typography*, p. 94.

34   Oastler, *Day*, p. 33 and n. 6.

35   Desgraves, *Les Haultin*, pp. xvii–xviii; Carter, *View of Typography*, pp. 86–87.

36   John A. Lane, 'Identifying Typefaces', *The Library*, VI.14 (1992), pp. 357–65, at p. 362, where the Pica Roman incorrectly attributed to Garamont in Ferguson, *Pica Roman*, is re-assigned to Haultin. Carter (*View of Typography*, p. 86) notes that 'What look like Garamond's faces in our Elizabethan books often turn out on closer acquaintance to be Haultin's'.

37   Isaac, 'Elizabethan Types', fig. 11.

38   However, for the view that Day had the type cut abroad was 'the least likely possibility' see Wynne Jeudwine, *Art and Style in Printed Books: Six Centuries of Typography, Decoration & Illustration* (London: privately printed, 1979), p. 271.

Guyot, Haultin cut a Roman and Italic to complement each other, in this case in Nonpareil size.[39] But he did not cut an Italic larger than Pica.[40] So the pairing of Haultin's English Roman on a Great Primer body with Guyot's Great Primer Italic may have been a practical solution to the problem of finding types of an appropriate size to display the Anglo-Saxon text alongside an early Modern English translation.

When Parker wrote that Day and Day alone 'indented' the new Anglo-Saxon type-designs, however inaccurate his statement about who 'matriculated' them may have been, he did not say and could not have meant that Day was to have exclusive use of them. Two more books containing them appeared within two years of *A Testimonie of Antiquitie*, one written or purportedly written by Parker himself, and one officially sanctioned by him. The second edition of Parker's *A Defence of priestes mariages* (1567.1) was printed at London by Richarde Jugge.[41] The material added in sig. 2O-2? contains four passages in Anglo-Saxon type (on 2Q3^r (p. 288), 2S4^r (p. 306), 2T1^r (p. 308), 2Z4^r (p. 346)) of the same size and design and with the same size and design of roman as in *A Testimonie*. The first edition of the *De antiquitate Cantabrigiensis Academie* (1568.1) by John Caius (1510–73), '[authorized] by my lorde of CANTERBURY' in the year 22 July 1567 to 22 July 1568, was printed at London by Henry Bynneman; it contains passages and marginal glosses in Anglo-Saxon type (on D1^r (p. 49), M3^r (p. 181), M4^r (p. 183), P3^r (p. 229), S8^r (p. 287), S8^v (p. 288), T6^v (p. 300)) of the same size and design and with the same size and design of roman as in *A Testimonie*. Although one printer sometimes did work for another without receiving any credit (as was probably the case with Henry Denham and Hart's *Orthographie*), in these instances it appears more likely that the Anglo-Saxon types, probably the types themselves rather than the matrices, as no great quantity was required, were made available to Jugge and Bynneman, presumably on Parker's instructions, or, at least, with his approval.[42] Parker's statement about 'Dayus ... solus' could therefore mean that Day alone held the matrices

---

39   Illustrated in Christophe Plantin, [*Index sive Specimen characterum C. Plantini*], type-specimen issued from Antwerp, 1567, facsimile intro. D.C. McMurtrie (New York, 1924), sig. D3, nos 1 and 2.
40   On the type-designs cut by Pierre Haultin see H.D.L. Vervliet, 'Printing Types of Pierre Haultin (ca.1510–87)', *Quaerendo*, 30 (2000), pp. 87–129, 173–227.
41   Parker, himself a married man, had a vested interest in this topic: see the Catalogue entry in Part 2 for 1567.1 under Context.
42   As noted long ago by Henry R. Plomer, 'Henry Bynneman, Printer, 1566–83', *The Library*, I.9 (1908), pp. 225–244, at p. 232: 'Here and there a fount of Anglo-Saxon is introduced, which was undoubtedly borrowed from John Day'.

for the Anglo-Saxon type-designs.[43] In this way Parker could control their use through Day.[44]

Parker seems to have regarded Anglo-Saxon types as we regard reproduction furniture, as virtue regained.[45] They would provide a key of remembrance facilitating easier access to the authority of Anglo-Saxon writings. Even more than the archaizing hands that Parker advocated for transcripts, the new types were to be 'emblematic of the past', a past regarded as yielding authoritative guidance for the present and the future.[46] Given this approach, Parker and his associates were bound to look for type-designs that reproduced the shape of letters in the original manuscripts. Since the manuscripts used by Parker and Joscelyn still bear the scars of their usership it is possible to study them with a view to determining where the models for the Parkerian Anglo-Saxon type-designs came from.

---

43 Oastler, *Day*, p. 34, argues that, like his contemporaries Bynneman and Vautrollier, Day stocked matrices.

44 This interpretation is complemented by the observable fact that no other Anglo-Saxon fount was cut in Parker's lifetime, whereas in 1576, one year after his death, two more appeared, both Pica in size, only one of which could have been sanctioned by Parker: AS2 and AS3.

45 In the translation above I have taken the word *supellex* to have its usual meaning of 'household furniture', interpreting the context as indicating something familiar which provides the means of recreating something old and venerable. Possibly Parker was using the word figuratively to indicate 'provisions' (*OED*, s.v. *Furniture*, sense 3) or even 'equipment' or 'accessories' (*OED*, s.v., senses 5 and 6 respectively), but these senses transferred to *supellex* do not seem very satisfactory in this context. 'Furniture' as a technical term in the hand-press period meant the wooden wedges used to hold the blocks of type firmly in the forme, but this usage is not recorded by *OED* until 1683 (Moxon), and could hardly apply in this instance.

46 Parkes, 'Archaizing Hands', p. 123. The phrase is based on Parker's statement in the Preface to the *Ælfredi Regis Res Gestæ* (1574.2) that he is printing the Latin text in Anglo-Saxon characters *ob venerandam ... archetypi antiquitatem* 'for the purpose of revering the antiquity of the original' (A2^r). Since Anglo-Saxon Latin texts did not employ insular script, Parker's use of his Anglo-Saxon types for printing Latin was described by Wakeman, 'Day's Saxon', p. 297, as 'a travesty'. But the inspiration for so doing was probably Irish manuscripts containing Latin texts, such as Lambeth Palace 1370, the 'Gospels of MacDurnan' (s.ix), which Parker owned (see further, next note). Parker and his household could not distinguish scripts by date or place of origin; cf. P.L. Heyworth, *Letters of Humfrey Wanley Palaeographer, Anglo-Saxonist, Librarian 1672–1726* (Oxford: Clarendon Press, 1989), no. 220, also Kenneth Sisam, *Studies in the History of Old English Literature* (Oxford: Clarendon Press, 1953), pp. 271–272. For a description of the 'Gospels of MacDurnan', named after Máel Brigte mac Tornáin, abbot of Armagh (888–927), see Montague R. James, *A Descriptive Catalogue of the Manuscripts in the Library of Lambeth Palace* (Cambridge: Cambridge University Press, 1932), pp. 843–845.

A study of Ker's *Catalogue* yielded a list of some sixty-one manuscripts containing Old English used and/or owned by Parker.[47] The study also yielded a list of some thirty-five manuscripts containing Old English used and/or owned by Joscelyn.[48] Naturally, there is some overlap between these lists, amounting to fourteen manuscripts, so the combined lists give a total of eighty-two manuscripts. Not all these manuscripts were available to Parker and Joscelyn before 1566, when the Anglo-Saxon types were first used. To narrow the list down to manuscripts that must have been in front of Parker and/or Joscelyn when the designs of the new Anglo-Saxon types were being considered, I therefore drew up a list of manuscripts used for the Old English texts and passages quoted in the first book containing Anglo-Saxon types, *A Testimonie of Antiquitie* (1566.1 and 1566.2).[49] In Table 3 the first column on the left gives the institution holding the manuscript, the second the class-mark, the third the date when it was written (in which the forms s.xi^1 and s.xi^3 mean the first and third quarter of the eleventh century, etc.), the fourth the contents (abbreviated), and the fifth the provenance.[50] Even this list of thirteen manuscripts is quite long, reflecting the considerable amount of research that went into the making of *A Testimonie*. There is a notable preponderance in the list for manuscripts dating from the eleventh century.

A few other manuscripts must be added. In BL Nero C.iii, fo 208^r (formerly 191^r), there is a list entitled 'Libri Saxonica Lingua descripti qui ad manus John Gocelin venerunt', which, as far as those actually containing Old English is

---

[47] Ker, *Catalogue*, nos 13–14, 17–21, 23, 29–43, 45–50. 53–73, *84*, *86*, 87–8, *89*, *144*, 269, 312, 325, 338, 346; in the instances italicized the evidence for ownership is through John Parker. With one exception, this list excludes manuscripts queried by Ker. The exception is Lambeth Palace 1370 (formerly 771), mentioned in the previous note, which has Parker's signature in red ochre on the recto of the front flyleaf, gospel chapter numbers added throughout in Parker's hand in red ochre, and a distinctive binding of a characteristic style found amongst several of Parker's books, the perpetrator of which is named after this manuscript: the McDurnan Gospels binder, on whom see Mirjam M. Foot, *The Henry Davis Gift: A Collection of Bookbindings*, 2 vols (London: British Library, 1978–83), I.35–49.

[48] Ker, *Catalogue*, nos 17, 29, 32, 39, 41, 45–9, 53, 65, 67, 116, 140, 153, 155, 157, 163–4, 166, 177, 179, 181, 188, 191–2, 204–5, 207, 209, 240, 324, 331, 338, 343. This list excludes manuscripts queried by Ker.

[49] An earlier list of seven manuscripts by Ker, *Catalogue*, p. liii, item *h*, is incomplete, and its inclusion of CCC 162 is inaccurate. On p. 387 of CCC 162 Parker saw a passage very similar to one printed in the *Testimonie* and noted in the margin 'pag.10', a reference to the text of the first edition of the *Testimonie*, and below this page reference he wrote in red ochre 'in Libello Impresso', i.e. the *Testimonie*.

[50] Following Ker, *Catalogue*, collated with N.R. Ker, *Medieval Libraries of Great Britain: A List of Surviving Books* (London: Royal Historical Society, 1964 edn), and *Supplement*, ed. Andrew G. Watson, 1987.

TABLE 3   Manuscripts used for texts in the first printed book containing AS types

CUL	Hh.1.10	s.xi³/xii	Ælfric, *Grammar*	Exeter
	Ii.2.11	s.xi³	gospels	Exeter
CCC	173	s.ix/x–xi³/⁴	AS Chronicle (A)	Canterbury XCh
	190	s.xi¹/²	ecclesiastical institutes	Exeter
	198	s.xi¹/², xi³/⁴	homilies incl. *In die Pascæ*	Worcester
	265	s.xi^med	Ælfric, letters, etc.	Worcester
ExC	3501	s.x³/⁴	Exeter Book of OE Poetry	Exeter
BL	Cleopatra B xiii	s.xi³	Pater Noster, Creed	Exeter
	Faustina A.ix	s.xii¹/²	homilies incl. *In die Pascæ*	not known
	Nero A.i	s.xi^med	laws, etc.	not known
	Vespasian D.xiv	s.xii^med	homilies	not known
OBL	Junius 121	s.xi³	eccl. institutes, homilies	Worcester
	Laud misc. 636	s.xii¹/², xii^med	AS Chronicle (E)	Peterborough

concerned, is confined to manuscripts of the *Anglo-Saxon Chronicle* known by Joscelyn.[51] The historical orientation of the list is confirmed by what follows on fos 208ᵛ–212ʳ, another list entitled 'Catalogus Aucto⟨rum⟩ qui scripserunt Historiam Anglia quo⟨rum⟩ opera ad manus John Gocelin peruenerunt et vbi extant'.[52] According to Ivor Atkins,[53] who adduces internal evidence, the first list 'dates from before 1567, and probably between 1560 and 1567'. The *Anglo-Saxon Chronicle* manuscripts in this first list must therefore be included amongst those that could have influenced the type-designs. In addition to CCC 173 and Laud misc. 636 already noted they are as in Table 4.

---

51 Printed by C.E. Wright, 'The Dispersal of the Monastic Libraries and the Beginnings of Anglo-Saxon Studies. Matthew Parker and his Circle: A Preliminary Study', *Transactions of the Cambridge Bibliographical Society*, 1.3 (1951), pp. 208–237, at pp. 218–219), who shows that the list owes much to Bale. See also Angelika Lutz, 'Das Studium der angelsächsischen Chronik im 16. Jahrhundert: Nowell und Joscelyn', *Anglia*, 100 (1982), pp. 301–356, at pp. 307–308, and cf. McKisack, *Medieval History*, p. 45.
52 According to Wright, in Francis Wormald and C.E. Wright, *The English Library before 1700* (London: Athlone Press, 1958), p. 157 and n. 24 on p. 173, this second list belongs 'to 1565 or thereabouts', but he does not cite his evidence for so thinking. In London, Lambeth Palace 593, pp. 359–370, there is a list of historians used by Joscelyn, including on p. 370 a list of Anglo-Saxon historical books, but it is not known at what stage these books became available to Joscelyn.
53 'The Origin of the Later Part of the Saxon Chronicle known as D', *English Historical Review*, 55 (1940), pp. 8–26, at p. 25.

TABLE 4   Other MSS used by those involved in the first AS type designs

BL	Otho B.xi	s.x^{med}–xi$^{1/2}$	AS Chronicle (G), etc.	Southwick
	Tiberius A.vi	s.x$^{3/4}$	AS Chronicle (B)	Canterbury StA
	Tiberius B.i	s.xi$^{1/2}$–xi$^{3/4}$	Orosius, AS Chronicle (C)	Abingdon[a]
	Tiberius B.iv	s.xi^{med}–xi$^{3/4}$	AS Chronicle (D)	Worcester[b]

a   The manuscript was at Abingdon when the *Anglo-Saxon Chronicle* annals for 491–1048 were added.
b   But Dorothy Whitelock, *The Peterborough Chronicle (The Bodleian Manuscript Laud Misc. 636)*, EEMF 4 (Copenhagen: Rosenkilde & Bagger, 1954), p. 28, argued that York is also possible.

The manuscripts now in Cambridge were all owned by Parker, but Joscelyn left his mark on all those used for the *Testimonie* except CUL Ii.2.11. Of those now not in Cambridge all, except apparently BL Otho B.xi, were worked on by Joscelyn, but Parker's hand is found only in BL Cleopatra B.xiii and OBL Junius 121 and Laud misc. 636 (the 'Peterborough Chronicle'). As we have seen, BL Tiberius B.i was annotated by Robert Talbot and used by Robert Recorde for his annotations in CCC 138. One manuscript, BL Faustina A.ix, apparently arrived in the Parkerian circle in time to be of use for the second edition only of *A Testimonie* (1566.2).[54] Even though it may not have been in front of Parker and Joscelyn when they (and others) were considering the type-designs, I have included it in Table 3 below in the interests of completeness.[55] As Bromwich demonstrated, the text of the Easter homily in CCC 198 was prepared more carefully (with thin vertical strokes to indicate word-divisions) than that in

---

54   Bromwich, 'First Book', pp. 281 and 284.
55   Wakeman, 'Day's Saxon', mentions twelve manuscripts: CUL Ii.2.11 and Ii.4.6, CCC 140, BL Faustina A.ix, Otho B.xi, Otho C.i(1) and Tiberius B.i, OBL Bodley 441, Hatton 38 and 114, Junius 121 and Laud misc. 482. Five of these are manuscripts of the Anglo-Saxon Gospels (CUL Ii.2.11, CCC 140, Otho C.i, Bodley 441, Hatton 38), only the first of which was used for the *Testimonie*; the others, together with the first, were used for Foxe's edition of the Anglo-Saxon gospels (1571.1), some five years after the *Testimonie*, too late to be sure that they were available when the type-designs were devised (although, of course, they and others could have been). Similarly two others, certainly or possibly, reached Parker too late to be taken into consideration for the type-designs: CUL Ii.4.6 was given to Parker 29 December 1567; Faustina A.ix was apparently first used by Parker when the first edition of the *Testimonie* was already printed. Otho B.xi was used by Lawrence Nowell (in Cecil's household) in 1562, and Laud misc. 482 was used by Joscelyn, so these manuscripts (along with CUL Ii.2.11, Tiberius B.i, Hatton 114 and Junius 121) were potentially available to influence the type-designs, but they show no features not already available in the manuscripts certainly used in the preparation of the *Testimonie* or listed as available to Joscelyn.

Faustina A.ix.⁵⁶ This preparation was probably intended for a copyist to make a transcript that was used by the printer. There is no apparent evidence that these original manuscripts were used in the printer's workshop.

The Parkerian Anglo-Saxon type-designs show particular features that may be related to features in the Anglo-Saxon script(s) on which they were modelled. The following eight features (see Illustrations 4–6) are notable:

1. The descenders of **f**, **r**, **s**, **þ** and **p** are turned to the left at the bottom;
2. The letter **d** is round-backed with a low ascender turned up at the top;
3. The tail of **g** is closed;
4. The letter **ð** shows a long straight ascender (with a cross-bar (rather than a spur) that can be seen on both sides of it) sloping steeply to the left (and slightly turned to the left at the tip), so much so that it requires a space in front of it that looks inappropriate when the letter is medial or final;
5. Capitals are round rather than square in shape, e.g., **Ð**, **Þ**, **P**, **X**;
6. Capital **E**, **H**, and **M** are uncial in shape;
7. Capital **S** is round and the bottom sector is more or less closed.
8. Capital **Æ** shows two designs, **Æ¹** based on an uncial E, and **Æ²** apparently based on bringing together an angular **A** with a tall **e**, or with square E.

For the purpose of trying to identify the probable manuscript models used by the type-designers the shape of the letter **ð** is particularly suggestive. Only in the eleventh century, especially the second half, was this letter so prominent with its long ascender sloping steeply to the left. This feature suggests that the preponderance of eleventh-century manuscripts in the list of manuscripts used by Joscelyn and others is significant. With this and the other features in mind I then examined the thirteen manuscripts used for the compilation of the *Testimonie* (including Faustina A.ix even though it may not have been available early enough) plus the extra four *Anglo-Saxon Chronicle* manuscripts from Joscelyn's list to see whether or not they showed similar features. The results are set out in Table 5. The material condensed here is generally representative of the usage in each manuscript concerned, except that for a few manuscripts there is more than one entry.⁵⁷ Since more than one scribe may have been responsible in any given manuscript, the findings in Table 2 relate as far as possible to the passage(s) used for *A Testimonie*; sometimes the usage recorded for individual capitals indicates existence rather than the norm, so this information might be considered to err on the side of inclusiveness. Although occasional variations from the usage recorded here may be found (and no attempt

---

56 Bromwich, 'First Book', pp. 277–278.
57 E.g., CCC 190: one for Ker, *Catalogue*, art. 17, and one for his art. 3.

TABLE 5 Comparative summary of distinctive features in relevant AS MSS

Source	Feature 1 Descenders turned to left	Feature 2 ð round-backed with low ascender turned up	Feature 3 ȝ closed lower sector	Feature 4 ð long straight ascender steeply sloping to left	Feature 5 round not square capitals	Feature 6 uncial as a secondary display capital Є ᴅ ᴍ	Feature 7 ſ with bottom sector more or less closed	Feature 8 Æ¹ Æ²
MSS								
CUL								
Hh.1.10	√	x	√	x	√	√ √ √	x	√²
Ii.2.11	√	x	√	x	√	√ √ √	x	x
CCC								
173	x	x	x	x	x	√ √ x	x	x
190 (17 + 3)								
pp. 295–308	√	√	√	√	√	x √ x	x	x
pp. 336–49	√	x	√	√	√	√ x x	x	√²
198	x	x	√	√	√	x √ √	x	√²
265	√	√	√	√	√	√ √ x	x	√²
ECL								
3501	√	√	√	√	√	√ x x	x	x
BL								
Cleo.B.xiii	√	x	√	√	√	√ x x	x	x
Faust.A.ix	x	x	x	x	√	x √ x	x	x
Nero A.i	√	x	√	x	√	√ √ x	x	√²
Otho B.xi + Add.								
34652 fo 2	x	x	x	x	√	x x √	x	x
Tib. A.vi	x	x	x	√	√	√ √ -	x	x
Tib. B.i								
fos 3ʳ–32ʳ	x	x	x	x	√	√ √ √	x	√¹
fos 32ᵛ–34ʳ	x	x	x	x	√	√ x x	x	√²
fos 35ʳ–44ᵛ	x	x	x	x	√	√ √ √	x	√¹⁺²
fos 45ᵛ–111ᵛ	x	x	x	√	√	√ √ √	x	√¹
fos 112ʳ–18ᵛ	x	x	√	x	√	√ √ √	x	x
fos 119ʳ–58ʳ	√	x	x	√	√	√ √ √	x	√²
Tib. B.iv								
fos 3ʳ–9ᵛ	x	√	x	x	√	- √ -	x	√²
fos 19ʳ–67ᵛ	x	√	√	√	√	√ √ √	x	-
fos 68ʳ–73ʳ	√	√	√	x	√	√ √ √	x	√²
fos 74ʳ–75ᵛ/21	x	√	x	√	√	- √ √	x	x
fos 76ʳ–90ʳ	√	√	√	x	√	√ √ √	x	x
Vesp.D.xiv	√	x	x	x	√	√ √ √	x	x
Oxford, Bodleian Library								
Junius 121	√	√	√	√	√	√ √ √	√	√¹⁺²
Laud m.636	√	x	x	x	√	√ √ √	x	√²

has been made to record exceptional usages), none are of significance as far as the present argument is concerned.

While some of the features, such as descenders turned to the left, or round rather than square capitals, are quite common in these manuscripts, others, such as capital S, tall with a lower sector more or less closed, and capital Æ based on an uncial E, are rare, while others fall in between. Only one manuscript illustrates all the features indicated: OBL Junius 121. This manuscript was written at Worcester together with two companion volumes in the same hand, Hatton 113 and 114 (olim Junius 99 and 22; SC 5210 and 5134).[58] The secondary display capitals in this trio of manuscripts are particularly fine, utilising colour (green, red and blue, with some silver). They were still at Worcester in 1622/23 when Patrick Young made his catalogue, in which they occur as nos 318 (Hatton 113), 319 (Hatton 114), and 321 (Junius 121).[59] We know that Joscelyn used these manuscripts, because he annotated them and also because he noted in the margins of CCC 198 (the base-text manuscript for the edition of Ælfric's *Sermo in die Pascæ* in the *Testimonie*) where the corresponding texts occur in Hatton 113 and 114.[60] Since the features found in Junius 121 naturally occur also in Hatton 113/114, I looked at these manuscripts too so as to have available the largest possible collection of examples with which to match the features of the first Anglo-Saxon type-designs.

These features may be observed in the Illustrations as follows:

1. The descenders of **f, r, s, þ** and **p** are turned to the left at the tip in ꞅcꞃıꞅꞇ (7.20), ꞅẏðþan (7.20/21), peoꞃoðe (7.23);
2. The letter **d** is round-backed with a low ascender turned up at the tip in unhaðoðe (7.15);
3. The letter **g** has a closed tail in æniʒe (7.23);
4. The letter **ð** shows a long straight ascender (with a bar (rather than a spur) that can be seen on both sides of it) sloping steeply to the left (and slightly turned to the left at the tip) in bıð (7.22);

---

58 A very similar if not identical hand occurs in CUL Kk.3.18, which was also used by Parker and Joscelyn early on. Probably all these manuscripts were written by Hemming, famous for his cartulary (Tiberius A.xiii, part 2), for which see Ker, 'Hemming's Cartulary' in his *Books, Collectors and Libraries* (London: Hambledon Press, 1985), p. 41. Of the manuscripts used for *A Testimonie* CCC 265, another Worcester manuscript, approaches nearest to Junius 121 in showing nearly all the features of the type-designs. In his description in his *Catalogue* Ker compares the script of pp. 222–227 with that of Hatton 113/114.

59 Ivor Atkins and N.R. Ker, '*Catalogus Librorum Manuscriptorum Bibliothecae Wigorniensis*' made in 1622–1623 by Patrick Young, Librarian to King James I (Cambridge: Cambridge University Press, 1944), p. 7.

60 Graham, 'Beginnings', p. 41; cf. also Ker, *Catalogue*, p. 76.

5. Capitals are round rather than square in shape, e.g., Ð, [Ƿ], Þ, X, as in OÐÐE (7.12), ÐROPODE (8.16), SERMO IN XL (9.14);[61]
6. Capital E, H, and M are uncial in shape in GELEAHTROD, MÆSSEPREOST (7.6);
7. Capital S shows a bottom sector that is more or less closed in CRIST-NUNGE (10.17);
8. Capital Æ shows two designs, Æ¹ based on an uncial E, as in MÆSSEPREOST (7.6) and DÆGE (8.16), and Æ² apparently based on bringing together an angular A with a tall lower-case e, or with square E, as in ÐÆRE (10.17).[62]

Of particular interest in Hatton 113 is the occurrence on fo i^v of an Anglo-Saxon alphabet written out across the page in a sixteenth-century hand with the early Modern English equivalents set out in a parallel row below (Illustration 11).

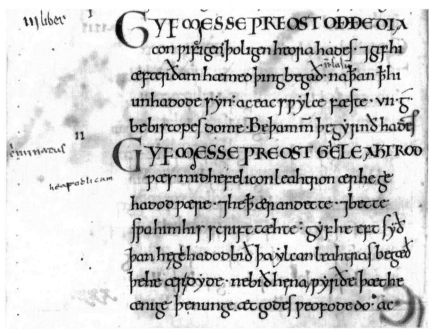

ILLUSTRATION 7   Oxford, Bodleian Library, Junius 121, 80ᵛ, lines 12–23, from a Penitential, Bk III, §§1–2. Reduced to 77%

---

61   Capital Þ is not common in this manuscript, but occurs, e.g., in Þe PAS (71ʳ/8), Þa (145ʳ/21).
62   Æ² occurs in Junius 121 rarely, for example, Æften (113ᵛ/7), and Ælc (119ᵛ/17). Tall e used as a capital occurs in 'Eal' (137ʳ/3).

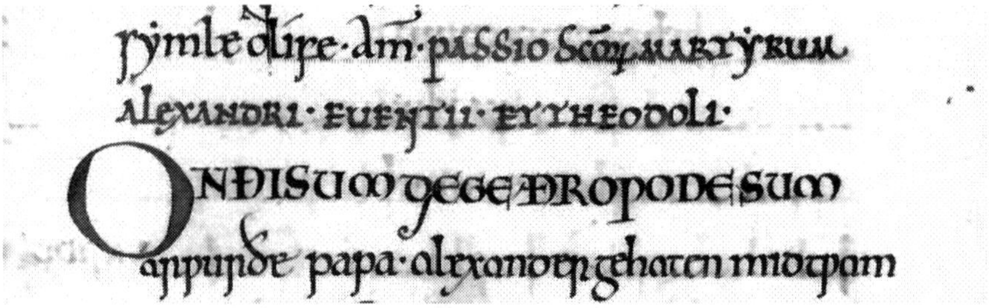

ILLUSTRATION 8   Oxford, Bodleian Library, Hatton 114, 153ʳ, lines 14–17, Passio Sanctorum Martyrum, Alexandri, Eventii & Theodoli, beginning. Reduced to 93%

ILLUSTRATION 9   Oxford, Bodleian Library, Hatton 113, 56ᵛ, lines 13–15, Sermo in XL, beginning

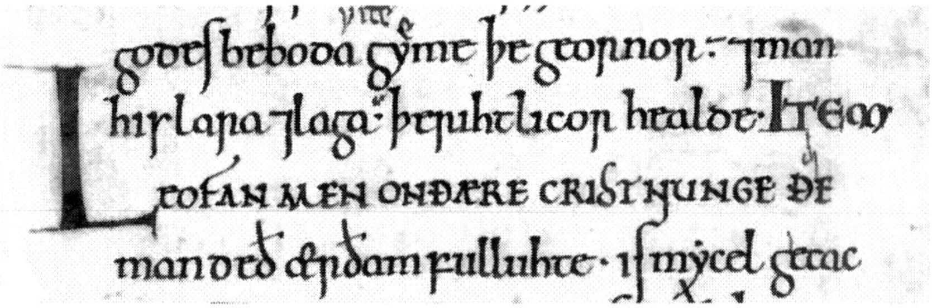

ILLUSTRATION 10   Oxford, Bodleian Library, Hatton 113, 16ᵛ, lines 15–18, Sermo de baptismate, beginning. Reduced to 95%

The various graphs for 'th' are set out separately and also together with the various vowels. This alphabet gives the impression of having been useful for a sixteenth-century reader who was becoming familiar with Old English. At first sight, since Joscelyn was, so far as other evidence indicates, the only sixteenth-century user of the manuscript who was interested in Anglo-Saxon, the most obvious explanation is that the Anglo-Saxon alphabet is by him. As it seems somewhat elementary it was presumably done fairly early in Joscelyn's career as an Anglo-Saxonist.[63] The Anglo-Saxon letters are written somewhat carefully, and even hesitantly, one by one, but some of them match those in the more quickly executed Illustration 2 quite closely, for example a in 'ꞃtane' (line 9), i in 'ȝaꞃtlıcum' (line 4), r in 'ꞃoꝥ' (line 3), s in 'hıꞅ' (line 10). The script of the early Modern English equivalent letters is a curious mixture of secretary and italic forms; for example p and v are secretary forms, while g and l are italic. Nevertheless, it seems to me probable that the alphabet was written by Joscelyn. The identification is made more difficult because, while Joscelyn wrote in different styles of handwriting, he did not, so far as I have discovered, use the letter-forms found in the alphabet together elsewhere. The p with the bowl made by starting at the bottom and writing anti-clockwise turning over into the descender is characteristic of Joscelyn's secretary p in his notebook (Vitellius D.vii, e.g., fos 146–147v) and the 'and' glossing the Tironian sign at the end of the row of Anglo-Saxon letters looks like Joscelyn. While not all the Anglo-Saxon letters in the alphabet are such as one could claim that the type-designs match them, the z included in the Anglo-Saxon row (and simply

ILLUSTRATION 11   Oxford, Bodleian Library, Hatton 113, iv, Anglo-Saxon alphabet by (?) Joscelyn

ILLUSTRATION 12   Oxford, Bodleian Library, Hatton 113, viv, from a Calendar of saints' days

---

63   For examples of Joscelyn's handwriting see Wright, 'Dispersal', p. 234, facsimile (e). I am indebted to Tim Graham for advice on Joscelyn's handwriting.

left out of the early Modern English row, presumably because writing it in would have been mere duplication) is exactly the kind of sixteenth-century z followed by the type-designers.[64] This tell-tale feature suggests that this Anglo-Saxon alphabet could have served as a trial version of some such set of models devised for the type-designs.

Since the crucial manuscripts for influencing the design of the first Anglo-Saxon types have Worcester provenance and show evidence of use by Joscelyn, it follows that Joscelyn probably used them in Worcester. On 4 October 1560 Joscelyn was instituted into the prebend of Gorwall and Overbury in the diocese of Hereford, a position obtained for him by Parker, and which he held until 1577, when he took possession of the living of Hollingbourn, Kent, which Parker bequeathed him.[65] From his base in Hereford diocese Joscelyn found at Worcester one of the finest collections of Anglo-Saxon manuscripts in any of the medieval cathedral libraries.[66] Work on Anglo-Saxon manuscripts continued during the second half of the eleventh century in Worcester, where Wulfstan II (d.1095) was the longest serving Anglo-Saxon bishop after the Norman Conquest. Many of the manuscripts in this collection had been the subject of study much deeper into the Middle English period than in other centres, and perhaps in connection with Wulfstan's canonization in 1203 were glossed by the 'Tremulous Hand' in the early thirteenth century, glosses which Joscelyn and his associates evidently found helpful, and which, as noted above, Parker thought important enough to copy in a transcript himself.[67] Joscelyn's hand is found in twelve Worcester manuscripts, but the only one also to contain Parker's characteristic red ochre crayon is Junius 121. From the fact that Junius 121 is the only manuscript amongst those definitely used early on by Parker and Joscelyn to show all the features indicated above as those characterizing the Parkerian Anglo-Saxon fount it seems reasonable to conclude that this manuscript was probably the main gateway through which the sixteenth-century type-designers passed to acquire the models used by the punchcutters.[68] From the extent of his annotations in it, and from the fact that

---

64 See the notes below on particular letters below in the List of Type-Designs.
65 Bruce and Perowne, *Correspondence*, p. xiii.
66 For a list of Anglo-Saxon manuscripts at Worcester in the Middle Ages see Ker, *Catalogue*, p. xlv, and cf. also p. xlviii; for a list of those written at Worcester see p. lx. As noted by James, *Catalogue Corpus*, p. xxx, Worcester is 'the principal contributor' of Anglo-Saxon manuscripts in the Corpus collection.
67 See Franzen, *Tremulous Hand*; for the continued use of Anglo-Saxon manuscripts in the early Middle English period, see esp. pp. 183–187.
68 This is not to overlook the suggestion above that the distinction between Latin and Old English t was observed by Joscelyn in CCC 190, an Exeter manuscript.

Joscelyn worked on the companion volumes Hatton 113/114, it seems reasonable to conclude that Joscelyn made a contribution to this process, working closely with Parker and perhaps others more calligraphically skilled. In Joscelyn's epitaph there occur the following verses:

> In Learning tryde, whereto he did his mind always incline.
> But others took the Fame and Praise of his deserving Witt,
> And his Inventions, as their owne, to printing did committ.[69]

This statement is usually interpreted as referring to the absence of Joscelyn's name as (co-)author of the *De Antiquitate Britannicæ* (1572.1), taking *Inventions* as 'literary compositions'.[70] It is, however, possible that the reference could be to Joscelyn's type-designs, if such they were, taking *Inventions* as 'something devised ... by the ingenuity of some person, and previously unknown'.[71]

At this point it may be helpful to review the features distinguishing Anglo-Saxon from early Modern English in the lower case of the Parkerian Anglo-Saxon fount as against those distinguishing Anglo-Saxon from Latin in the original manuscripts.

Anglo-Saxon Manuscripts s.x:	a	d	e	f	g	h		r	s	t		æ þ ð ƿ
Anglo-Saxon Manuscripts s.xii:		d		f	g			r	s			æ þ ð ƿ
Parkerian Anglo-Saxon Types:		d		f	g		i	r	s	t	y	æ þ ð ƿ

In the eleventh century, the period from which the majority of surviving Anglo-Saxon manuscripts known in Parker's circle emanated, the usage with regard to **a**, **e**, and **h** was inconsistent. Those in Parker's circle were familiar with the twelfth-century position from manuscripts such as Vespasian D.xiv, where **a**, **e**, and **h** were not distinguished. The pattern established in this first Anglo-Saxon fount was to serve as the model for succeeding founts, and the usage with regard to **t** is particularly notable, as the forms of this letter in Latin and Old English were rarely distinguished in the manuscripts. Whoever was responsible for observing this distinction, and I have suggested above that it was John Joscelyn when he was studying CCC 190, it had considerable repercussions. With regard to **z** the printed form appears to be based on a Textura

---

69 Cooper and Cooper, *Athenae Cantabrigienses*, II.306.
70 For example by McKisack, *Medieval History*, pp. 47–48; though it could equally well have applied to other publications as well. For this interpretation of 'Inventions' see OED, s.v., 7.
71 OED, 'Invention', 9.

z with a hooked terminal such as is found in Textura typefaces. In the 'hierarchy of types' Textura was pre-eminent, being used for the Bible and religious works, notably in Parker's Bishop's Bible.[72] The inclusion of this textura z in the Anglo-Saxon alphabet gives an indication of the kind of impact it was intended to make: it was a prestige type.

With regard to the capitals the Parkerian Anglo-Saxon fount distinguished nine letters, viz. E, H, M, S, X, plus Ð, Þ, Ƿ and two forms of Æ. Apart from the specifically Anglo-Saxon graphs Ð, Þ, Ƿ, there was no systematic distinction in the manuscripts between the forms of these letters used in Latin as opposed to Old English. In the Junius 121 group of manuscripts, for example, the forms of the capitals there employed occur in text in both languages (see Illustrations 8, 10, and 12). The uncial shape of E, H, M, the tall capital S with its bottom sector more or less closed, the curvacious X, and the two forms of Æ, both ornamental in style, all testify to Parker's purpose of producing a prestige type bearing the stamp of antique authority.[73] The fact that some Anglo-Saxon letters occurred in Latin as well would only have added to their *auctoritas* in the eyes of Parker and his circle.[74] Similarly the punctuation, utilizing the point, the *punctus versus*, and the triple point, and the abbreviation mark for 'and', utilizing the Tironian sign rather than the ampersand, are designed to add further verisimilitude to an already convincing display of antique features.

As already indicated Parker regarded these Anglo-Saxon types much as we regard reproduction furniture, providing a new substitute for old authenticity. They differed somewhat in their intended impact from archaizing hands, which were designed to mimic the features of an older script, to produce what McKisack bluntly called 'a fake Old English hand', to 'counterfeit in antiquity', as Parker himself put it.[75] The types were more akin in their impact to some kinds of script that originated on the continent during the Middle Ages. In a period of script reform older models were often resorted to. During the ninth century Lupus of Ferrières supervised the development of a distinctive kind of

---

72 STC 2099; see also T.H. Darlow & H.F. Moule, *Historical Catalogue of Printed Editions of The English Bible 1525–1961*, rev. A.S. Herbert (London: British and Foreign Bible Society, 1968), no. 125.

73 According to Wakeman, 'Day's Saxon', p. 298, these features 'seem to have been based on aesthetic principles'.

74 In the Preface to *A Testimonie* (sig. A3) it is remarked that the homilies found in the original manuscripts 'were not first written in the olde Saxon tounge: but were translated into it ... from the Lattyne', an observation (however incorrect it may be seen to be with the benefit of subsequent scholarship) that could only add to their authority.

75 McKisack, *Medieval History*, p. 47.

caroline minuscule from models in late antique manuscripts.[76] In their search for antique authenticity the fifteenth-century Italian humanists devised a new script based initially on antique models from the tenth or eleventh centuries.[77] *Littera antiqua* evolved and subsequently provided the basis of roman and italic type-design. As stated by Erasmus, it was part of the humanist ethos that what really improved a book was 'an elegant, clear, and readable script which presents Latin words in the Latin alphabet'.[78]

This approach was inherited by Parker, who transferred it to Anglo-Saxon vernacular materials, taking (perhaps coincidentally) as the models for the Anglo-Saxon type-designs made under his direction script of the same period as had originally inspired the humanistic script reformers. The Parkerian designs became established through his authority as archbishop of Canterbury, just as *littera antiqua* became established in Italy through papal authority.[79] And just as the contents of the first book printed with the Parkerian Anglo-Saxon types were *A Testimonie of Antiquitie*, so the mode of presentation employed to communicate those contents was itself a 'testimonye of verye ancient tyme'. Parker's decision to print Anglo-Saxon in this way was to have an influence on the subject that lasted for centuries.

Parker was not interested in providing a service for the publication of Anglo-Saxon materials by all and sundry. He specifically provided for his chosen printer, John Day I, to have exclusive use of the Anglo-Saxon sorts for his first design, the Great Primer Anglo-Saxon. Prestige and exclusivity were associated with this, the first Anglo-Saxon type-design throughout its history. After Parker's death in 1575 John Day used the Parkerian Great Primer Anglo-Saxon only once more, in the fourth edition of Foxe's *Acts and Monuments* (1583.1). After Day's death in 1584 it next appears in the fifth edition of Foxe's *Acts and Monuments* (1596.1) printed by Peter Short, where vol. II, sig. 5G, containing

---

76 Bernhard Bischoff, *Manuscripts and Libraries in the Age of Charlemagne*, t M. Gorman (Cambridge: Cambridge University Press, 1994), p. 126.

77 Bernhard Bischoff, *Latin Palaeography: Antiquity and the Middle Ages*, t D. Ó Cróinín & D. Ganz (Cambridge: Cambridge University Press, 1990), pp. 145–149, and references, esp. B.L. Ullmann, *The Origin and Development of Humanistic Script* (Rome: Edizione de Storia e Letteratura, 1960), also A.C. de la Mare, *The Handwriting of Italian Humanists* (Oxford: for the Association Internationale de Bibliophilie, 1973).

78 elegans, dilucida, distinctaque scriptura, Latinis elementis Latina uerba repraesentatibus: Erasmus, *De recta Latini Graecique sermonis pronuntiatione dialogus*, ed. Johannes Kramer, Beiträge zur Klassischen Philologie 98 (Meisenheim am Glan: Hain, 1978), §924 on p. 52, also t Maurice Pope, in *Collected Works of Erasmus*, ed. J.K. Sowards, vol. 26 (Toronto: University of Toronto Press, 1985), p. 391.

79 For the establishment of *littera antiqua* see Stanley Morison, *Politics and Script*, ed. Nicolas Barker, (Oxford: Clarendon Press, 1972), ch. 6, esp. p. 305.

the Anglo-Saxon textual matter corresponding to that specified from 1576.1 (sig. 3G3ᵛ–6ʳ), was 'farmed out' to another printer, John Windet (fl.1584–1610). The evidence for this comes from differences between the layout of sig. 5G and the other gatherings in the book: it has no catchword at the end (5G4ᵛ), and shows a wider column width (91 rather than 89 mm; 93 mm on 5G2ʳa). There are also differences in typographical features: sig. 5G uses a different Textura, a different Long Primer Roman (on a Small Pica body)—Garamont's (2nd, with a lower x- and capital height) instead of Haultin's Small Pica Roman—different page numbers (mostly italic), different line numbers between the columns, and different numbers in the signatures (arabic as opposed to roman).[80] There can be little doubt that sig. 5G was 'farmed out', and that sig. 5F is only four leaves in anticipation of the material in 5G to be contracted out. This conclusion is also supported by the fact that the printing of the short Old English passage on sig. 5I5ʳ is different from that in sig. 5G in that it is combined with a Great Primer, probably Claude Garamont's, rather than the English-size Roman on a Great Primer body normally used; presumably Short did this himself with a few borrowed special types without being familiar with how it was usually done.

On historical grounds Windet is the only candidate who probably would have had the means to print the Old English in sig. 5G. In 1593 he succeeded to part of the printing material of John Wolfe (fl.1579–1601), becoming his executor in 1601. Wolfe was apprenticed to John Day from 1562 for seven years, the period when the printing of Anglo-Saxon got under way, and an assignee of Day's son Richard, who ceased printing in 1584. Wolfe is the probable conduit through whom the Anglo-Saxon printing materials of John Day reached Windet. The Parkerian Great Primer Anglo-Saxon appears in 1598.2, John Stow's *Survey of London*, where it is used to print a charter of King Edward the Confessor on sig. 2B5v (p. 378). This book was ostensibly printed by John Wolfe, but in fact it was done by John Windet, so this evidence tends to confirm that the printing materials had been acquired by Windet. From Windet they passed to William Stansby (fl.1597–1638), who took over Windet's business in 1609/10. For it is only in books published by Stansby that the Parkerian Great Primer Anglo-Saxon re-emerges, first in the Anglo-Saxon specimen only of John Minsheu's polyglot dictionary, *Ductor in Linguas*, completed by

---

80   The Textura is a Parisian one on Small Pica (Vervliet, *Printing Types*, T41). Garamont's 2nd Long Primer Roman shows Body 72 (on Small Pica); Face 66 x 1.2: 2, and is illustrated/described in TSF II c.1599: no.9; Parker et al, 'Typographical', MA 47a on p. 62; Isaac, 'Elizabethan Types', fig. 14. Haultin's Long Primer Roman shows Body 72; Face 66 x 1.5: 2.5, and is illustrated in TSF II 1567: no. 29 (Dr/1); Vervliet, *Vatican*, no. 54; Tinto, 'Tipi', R.9.

Stansby (1617.1).[81] Perhaps imitating Day, Stansby specialised in books of substance for which larger sizes of type were appropriate: John Selden's *Eadmeri Monachi Cantuariensis Historiæ Novorum* (1623.3); Selden's *Titles of Honor* (2nd edn 1631.1); and Selden's *Mare Clausum seu de Dominio Maris* (1635.1).[82] Later, Stansby's business passed to Richard Bishop, who used the Parkerian Great Primer Anglo-Saxon for the last time in 1646.6. It had lasted some 80 years. It was always exclusive to those who had it, Day, Wolfe (who apparently did not use it), Windet, Stansby and Bishop.[83]

A notable feature of the books containing the Parkerian Great Primer Anglo-Saxon in the seventeenth century is that, with the exception of the specimen to John Minsheu's polyglot dictionary, *Ductor in Linguas* (1617.1), completed by Stansby, they are all by John Selden (1584–1654): his *Eadmeri Monachi Cantuariensis Historiæ Novorum* (1623.3); his *Titles of Honor* (2nd edn 1631.1); his *Mare Clausum seu de Dominio Maris* (1635.1); and both his *De Iure Naturali et Gentium* (1640.4) and his *Uxor Ebraica seu De Nuptiis & Divortiis ex Iure Civili* (1646.6) published by Stansby's successor, Richard Bishop.[84] Selden was one 'of the giants in early seventeenth-century scholarship' with 'an incisive legal

---

81 The main text is in Long Primer, but the AS specimen (sig. πA6ᵛ) uses a larger size than that used in the text. On this work see Peter J. Lucas, 'John Minsheu, Polymath and Poseur: Old English in an Early Seventeenth-Century Dictionary', in K. Lenz & R. Möhlig (eds), *Of Dyuersitie & Chaunge of Langage: Essays presented to Manfred Görlach on the occasion of his 65th birthday* (Heidelberg: Winter, 2002), pp. 144–156.

82 Mark Bland, 'William Stansby and the Production of *The Workes of Beniamin Jonson*, 1615–16', *The Library*, VI.20 (1998), pp. 1–33 (at pp. 4–6) compares Stansby's operation with that of Christophe Plantin in Antwerp, but it is also notable that Stansby used the same English-size Roman (Haultin's) and Pica Roman (also Haultin's) as Day in combination with the Parkerian Anglo-Saxon type-designs.

83 As noted above it was also used by Richard Jugge and Henry Bynneman, both of whom did work for Parker, but in very small quantities.

84 Minsheu's *Ductor in Linguas* shows the main text is in Long Primer, but the AS specimen (sig. πA6ᵛ) uses a larger size than that used in the text. For an affectionate portrait of Selden and his career see A.L. Rowse, *Four Caroline Portraits* (London: Duckworth, 1993), pp. 125–155; see also *ODNB*, s.n., and J.N.L. Myres (introd.), *The Bodleian Library in the Seventeenth Century: Guide to an Exhibition held during the Festival of Britain 1951* (Oxford: Bodleian Library, 1951), pp. 43–47, also Sandra Naiman in Baker & Womack *British Book Collectors*, pp. 297–306. On his scholarly methods see F. Smith Fussner, *The Historical Revolution: English Historical Writing and Thought 1580–1640* (London: Routledge & Paul, 1962), ch. 11. For his historical approach see Harold D. Hazeltine, 'Selden as Legal Historian: A Comment in Criticism and Appreciation', in *Festschrift Heinrich Brunner zum siebzigsten Geburtstag* (Weimar: Böhlau, 1910), pp. 579–630. Cf. also Toomer, *Eastern Wisedome*, pp. 64–71. The following year, 1647, Miles Flesher I (fl.1617–64†) printed another book of Selden's containing Anglo-Saxon, the *Fleta seu Commentarius Juris Anglicani* (1647.2), for which another Anglo-Saxon fount was used: see below.

mind'.[85] 'He knew Hebrew and Arabic [also Persian and Aramaic] as well as the classical and [European] "learned modern" languages'.[86] He was 'jurist, statesman, orientalist, [and] historian', a man of deep learning and broad historical vision who believed that the study of the past could illuminate the present.[87] His collection of some 8,000 books is one of the most important ever received by the Bodleian Library.[88] By using Stansby as his printer he not only availed of Stansby's penchant for books of substance, for which, as noted by Bland, larger sizes of type were appropriate ('Stansby', 4–6), but he also ensured privileged access to the Parkerian Great Primer Anglo-Saxon type-design. Selden never printed an Old English text, but he cited short passages from his reading of Anglo-Saxon texts to corroborate his arguments. Here we encounter the power of special sorts to corroborate and enhance an author's arguments with all the prestige and authority that went with the use of these types designed to convey the authenticity of the antique and venerable. Selden believed in going back to the oldest authority he could find, and when this was Anglo-Saxon he cited the original along with a Latin translation.[89] A good example of this practice is his *Mare Clausum*. Without special types he could not properly demonstrate the full authority of his scholarship. In Selden's books, however, the passages in Anglo-Saxon occur in the same size of type as the surrounding text (not larger as with Parker's books), or even in a size smaller than that of the main text.[90] This practice probably mirrors Selden's thinking, in so far as he 'avoided

---

85   There is a comprehensive intellectual biography of Selden in Toomer, *Life*. On his use of antiquarian material see Graham Parry, *The Trophies of Time: English Antiquarians of the Seventeenth Century* (Oxford: Oxford University Press, 1995), ch. 4. For a contemporary pen-portrait (by Clarendon) see D. Nichol Smith, *Characters from the Histories & Memoirs of the Seventeenth Century* (Oxford: Clarendon Press, 1918), pp. 167–168.

86   Henry A. Cronne, 'Charter Scholarship in England', *University of Birmingham Historical Journal*, 8 (1962), pp. 26–61, at p. 45.

87   Hazeltine, 'Selden', p. 579 and passim.

88   On Selden's library and its fate see D.M. Barratt, 'The Library of John Selden and its Later History', *Bodleian Library Record*, 3 (1950–51), pp. 128–142, 208–213, 256–274, and Toomer, *Life*, II.793–799.

89   Selden explains his policy in this regard in *The Historie of Tithes* (1618.1), 2B2ᵛ (p. 196), at the beginning of ch. 8, cited by Hazeltine, 'Selden', p. 600, n. 1.

90   In the *Mare Clausum* the main text is printed in a Great Primer, whereas the Anglo-Saxon quotations are printed with the Anglo-Saxon sorts combined with an English-size Roman, albeit on a Great Primer body. For this book and its impact see Peter J. Lucas, 'Printing Anglo-Saxon in Holland and John Selden's *Mare Clausum seu de Dominio Maris*', *Quaerendo*, 31 (2001), pp. 120–136.

the elevation of the Anglo-Saxon period in importance' in the development of English law.[91]

John Selden was virtually the only author to have availed of the Parkerian Great Primer Anglo-Saxon type-designs, occurring as they do in just the five books already mentioned in the seventeenth century, all by Selden.[92] He was also virtually the only author to have availed through Stansby of the Parkerian Pica Anglo-Saxon type-designs, a smaller set of designs based on those of the Great Primer, which first appeared in 1576 (AS2).[93] This set of designs was used (without admixture from any other set of designs) for the first edition of Selden's *Titles of Honor* (1614.4), and for his *Historie of Tithes* (1618.1), both earlier than the other books with the larger type-design. This apparent virtual exclusivity in the use of the Parkerian Anglo-Saxon type-designs (probably the result of Selden being virtually the only author who wanted to use them), which Selden enjoyed through Stansby, shows one side of how printing politics could work. However, after Stansby's death the Parkerian Pica Anglo-Saxon makes a further appearance (a partial one) in Sir John Spelman's *Psalterium Davidis Latino-Saxonicum Vetus* (1640.3), where sig. B was printed by Stansby's successor, Richard Bishop, before the book was taken over by Richard Badger I, who printed the rest using a different Anglo-Saxon fount. Apparently Bishop was the Spelmans' first choice, but when his compositor left him by 31 Aug 1638 and he 'dalied and delaied', the business was transferred to Badger by 5 Sept 1638, the dates of Henry Spelman's letters to Wheelock.[94]

---

91   D.R. Woolf, *The Idea of History in Early Stuart England* (Toronto: University of Toronto Press, 1990), p. 211.
92   As noted above the Parkerian Great Primer Anglo-Saxon also occurs in the specimen at the beginning of John Minsheu's dictionary, *Ductor in Linguas* (1617.1), printed by Stansby, but not in the text.
93   The Parkerian Pica Anglo-Saxon also occurs in Minsheu's *Ductor in Linguas* (1617.1), sigs T–2Z.
94   CUL, Dd.3.12, fos 28ʳ, 29ʳ. First noted by John C.T. Oates, *Abraham Whelock (1593–1653) Orientalist: Anglo-Saxonist, & University Librarian*, unpubl. Sandars Lectures in Bibliography (Cambridge, 1966), p. 28. Oates published his observations in *Cambridge University Library: A History. From the Beginnings to the Copyright Act of Queen Anne* (Cambridge: Cambridge University Press, 1986), p. 201.

CHAPTER 3

The Parkerian and Lambardian Pica Anglo-Saxon Type-Designs

After Parker's death in 1575 Day printed Anglo-Saxon in another (smaller) size, Pica, which appeared in 1576. This Pica Anglo-Saxon first occurs in the third edition of Foxe's *Book of Martyrs* (**1576.1**) on pp. 1114–19. This readers' specimen is somewhat incomplete and potentially misleading. When the specimen and the text are taken together twenty-four special sorts are shown, twelve lower-case letters

d, f, g, i, r, s, t, y, z;   þ, ð, p

together with ꝫ, the tironian sign for 'and', þ, the abbreviation for 'þæt', and ꝫ, the punctus versus, making a total of fifteen sorts so far, and nine capitals

Æ¹ and Æ², E, H, M, S;   Þ, Ð, P

There is no capital X. These Pica Anglo-Saxon special sorts are used by Day in conjunction with Pierre Haultin's Pica Roman (formerly attributed to Claude Garamont), the same punchcutter with whose design of English Roman the Parkerian Great Primer Anglo-Saxon was combined.[1] This Pica Roman (Body 83: Face 80 × 1.7: 2.5) was the one regularly used by Day during the period 1566–84. Although this Pica Anglo-Saxon first appeared after Parker's death it is probable that the archbishop authorized it and, to distinguish it from the other Pica Anglo-Saxon, I refer to it as the Parkerian Pica Anglo-Saxon.

In the same year another Pica Anglo-Saxon was used for William Lambarde's *A Perambulation of Kent* printed by Henry Middleton (fl.1567–87) for Ralph Newbery (fl.1560–1604): **1576.2**.[2] Newbery is probably the more

---

[1] For the attribution of this Pica Roman (still erroneously attributed to Garamont in Ferguson, *Pica Roman*) to Haultin see Lane, 'Identifying Typefaces', p. 362. On Haultin as a punchcutter see Smeijers, *Counterpunch*, pp. 63–67, 133–139.

[2] Middleton was later in the forefront of using the new spelling conventions to distinguish i/j and u/v: see Immanuel Tremellius and Franciscus Junius [father of Junius the Anglo-Saxonist] (eds), *Testamenti veteris Biblia sacra sive libri canonici, … Latini recens ex Hebraeo facti* (London: Henry Middleton, 1579–80; STC 2056), and for discussion, R.B. McKerrow, 'Some

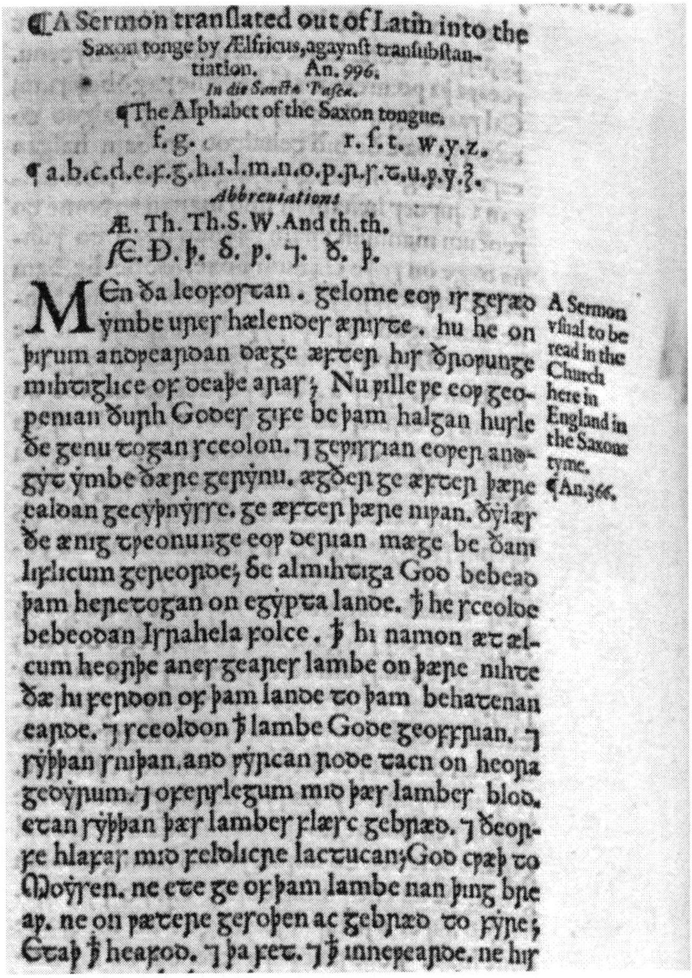

ILLUSTRATION 13 Reader's Anglo-Saxon type-specimen and text (AS2) from Foxe's *Actes and Monuments* (1576.1), ²3G4ᵛ/b (CPH E.11.17)

important of the two men because it was he who transferred the rights on to the Stationers' Company in 1584, and because he was associated with other books by Lambarde containing small amounts of this same Pica Anglo-Saxon.[3]

Notes on the Letters i, j, u, and v in Sixteenth Century Printing', *The Library*, III.1 (1910), pp. 239–259, at pp. 258–259.

3 For the transfer of rights see Edward Arber, *A Transcript of the Register of the Company of Stationers of London 1554–1640*, 5 vols (London: Arber, 1875–7, vol. 5, Birmingham: Arber,

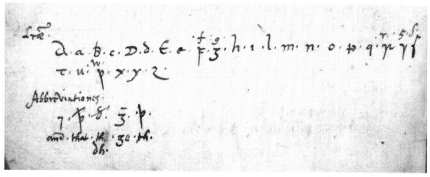

ILLUSTRATION 14   Lambarde's handwritten Anglo-Saxon alphabet, Westminster Abbey 30, 2. Reduced to 78%

The specimen (Illustration 15a) reflects features of Lambarde's handwritten Anglo-Saxon alphabet (Illustration 14) and shows many similarities with, and some differences from, the Parkerian Pica Anglo-Saxon special sorts used by Day. Altogether, in this Lambardian Pica Anglo-Saxon, as I call it to distinguish it from the Parkerian one, there are twenty-two special sorts, including twelve lower-case letters (and one capital misused as a lower-case letter),

d, [S], e, f, g, h, r, s, t, y;   þ, ð, p

together with ⁊, the tironian sign for 'and', þ, the abbreviation for 'þæt', and ׃, the punctus versus, making a total of sixteen sorts so far, and five capitals,

Æ¹ and Æ², E, M;   Þ, Ð.

Notable absentees are i and z amongst the lower-case letters, and upper-case P, capital 'Wynn', also X and upper-case ⁊. The specimen does not show lower-case þ, but it occurs in the text, e.g., in 'oþper' at sig. 2Q2ʳ/17. A notable additional feature is the inclusion of an Anglo-Saxon lower-case e. In the

---

1894), II.789. Lambarde's *Eirenarcha* was first published by Newbery (1581.1) and subsequently appeared in several further editions under his imprint (1582.1, 1588.1, 1591.1, 1592.1, 1594.1. The Pica Anglo-Saxon sorts appear in a short extract from the *Laws of Ine* (as ed. Liebermann, *Gesetze*, 13,1) and are combined with different romans in the various editions, some of them too small for a good fit: in 1581.1 and 1582.1 the Anglo-Saxon sorts are combined with Granjon's 1st Pica Roman, but in 1588.1, 1591.1, 1592.1 and 1594.1 they are combined with a smaller type-size, Garamond's (second) Long Primer Roman.

THE PARKERIAN AND LAMBARDIAN PICA ANGLO-SAXON TYPE-DESIGNS 63

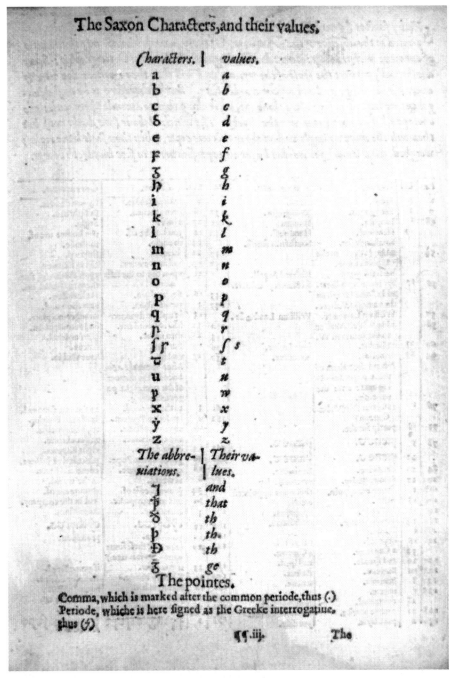

ILLUSTRATION 15A Reader's Anglo-Saxon type-specimen (AS3) from Lambarde's *Perambulation of Kent* (1576.2), 2¶3ʳ (CUL Bb*.4.54)

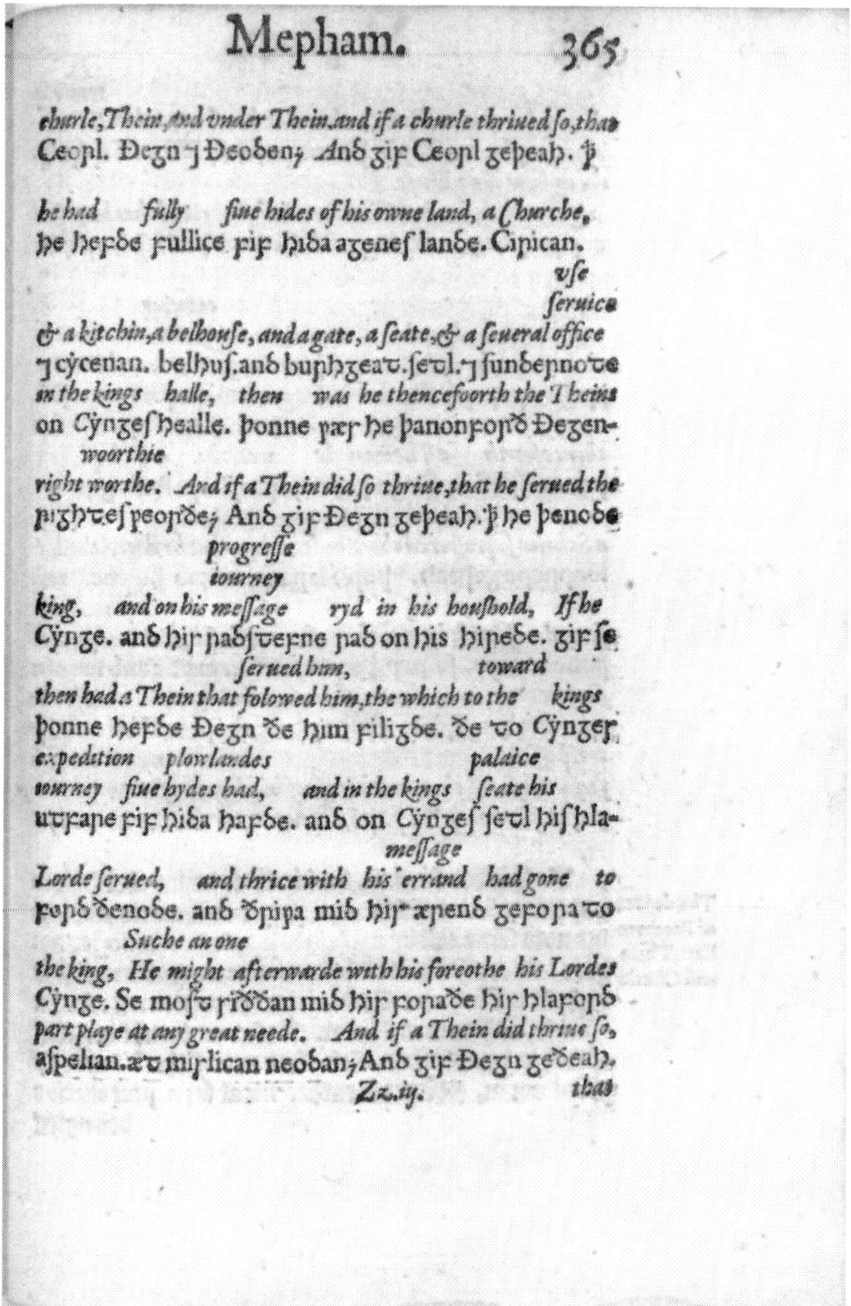

Mepham. 365

churle, Thein, And vnder Thein, and if a churle thriued so, that
Ceorl. Ðegn ⁊ Ðeoden; And gif Ceorl geþeah. ꝥ
he had fully fiue hides of his owne land, a Churche,
he hefde fullice fif hida agenes lande. Cirican.
vse / seruice
& a kitchin, a belhouse, and a gate, a seate, & a seueral office
⁊ cycenan. belhus. and burhgeat. setl. ⁊ sundernote
in the kings halle, then was he thencefoorth the Theins
on Cynges healle. þonne wæs he þanonforð Ðegen-
woorthie
right worthe. And if a Thein did so thriue, that he serued the
rihtes weorðe; And gif Ðegn geþeah. ꝥ he þenode
progresse / iourney
king, and on his message ryd in his houshold, If he
Cynge. and his radstefne rad on his hirede. gif se
serued him, toward
then had a Thein that folowed him, the which to the kings
þonne hefde Ðegn ðe him filigde. ðe to Cynges
expedition / iourney fiue hydes had, and in the kings palaice / seate his
utfare fif hida hafde. and on Cynges setl his hla-
message
Lorde serued, and thrice with his errand had gone to
forð ðenode. and ðriwa mid his ærend gefora to
Suche an one
the king, He might afterwarde with his foreothe his Lordes
Cynge. Se most syððan mid his forade his hlafords
part playe at any great neede. And if a Thein did thriue so,
aspelian. æt myclican neodan; And gif Ðegn gedeah.
Zz.iij. *that*

ILLUSTRATION 15B Anglo-Saxon text (AS3) from Lambarde's *Perambulation of Kent* (1576.2), 2Z3r, showing part of the AS Law 'Geþyncðo'

1576.2 edition of the *Perambulation* the 22 special sorts are used in conjunction with Robert Granjon's Pica Roman.[4] The measurements are: Body 83: Face 80 × 1.6: 2.9. In the specimen (Illustration 15a), and almost always throughout the Old English passages printed, the special sort used for Anglo-Saxon lower-case d is in fact capital S, the design of which, with its closed bottom sector, made it particularly susceptible to being mistaken for lower-case d, but the expected round-backed lower-case d occurs sporadically, e.g., on sigs C3ᵛ (p. 22), and X4ʳ (p. 175) in pealð. The correct use of lower-case d and capital S in the second edition (1596.2) confirms the mistaken usage in the first edition; cf. Illustration 16a.

These two Pica Anglo-Saxon fonts of 1576 are very similar; the design of the lower-case letters f, g, r, s, t, y, þ, ð, p, also the signs ꝥ, ꝧ, ꝓ, and the capitals Æ¹, Æ², E, M, Ð at first sight look very alike; d and S (mostly used for d in 1576.1) also more or less correspond. Particularly close, to the point of being indistinguishable, are the lower-case thorns and the abbreviation sign þ. Some apparent differences turn out to be superficial. Lambarde/Middleton's h, used as a lower-case letter, more or less corresponds to Parker/Day's capital H, though ironically Lambarde/Middeton's h is slightly larger than Parker/Day's H. This failure on Middleton[/Newbery]'s part to distinguish lower and upper case letters extends to þ/Þ and later to p/P as well. By 1581 Henry Bynneman printing for Newbery had a special sort for upper-case P in addition to the other special sorts, bringing the total of special sorts to twenty-three. In the first edition of Lambarde's *Eirenarcha* (1581.1) Bynneman used both capital and lower-case thorns as lower-case letters: the confusion is particularly clear on the errata page (2L7ᵛ) in 'Monþ & Monþon' (Illustration 16b). Bynneman does not use the Anglo-Saxon undotted i, nor does he show Anglo-Saxon z, essentially, as noted by a character in Shakespeare, an 'unnecessary letter', particularly for Anglo-Saxon, and its absence in Lambarde's *Archaionomia* (1568.2), printed by Day (Illustration 5), suggests that the author had a view on the matter similar to that of Shakespeare's character, a view presumably not shared by Parker, even though Lambarde and Parker were on good terms and collaborated in a friendly manner from about 1565 onwards.[5]

An even more significant difference between Lambarde and Parker concerns Lambarde's provision of a special sort for Anglo-Saxon lower-case e. As we have seen, Parker's Great Primer Anglo-Saxon was designed on the basis of

---

4 For the attribution to Granjon see H.D.L. Vervliet, 'Roman Types by Robert Granjon', *De Gulden Passer*, 76–77 (1998–9), pp. 5–76, no.2 on pp. 11–13.

5 On the friendship between Lambarde and Parker see Retha M. Warnicke, *William Lambarde, Elizabethan Antiquary 1536–1601* (Chichester: Phillimore, 1973), pp. 32–33.

500   **Mepham.**

placed in diuers old copies of the Saxon lawes, after the end of all, as a note or aduertisement.

It was sometime in the English lawes, that the people and
hit þeꞃ hpilum on Englalagum þ leod and lagum
       dignitie
the lawes were in reputation: And then were the wisest of the
ꞃoꞃ begeþincðum; And þa ꞃæꞃon leod piſan peopðo-
       woorshipfull
people woorship woorthie, euery one after his degree: Earle, and
ſciper pyꞃða.   ælc be hiꞃ mæðe.   Eoꞃl and

churle, Thein, and vnder Thein. And if a churle thriued so, that
Ceoꞃl. Ðegn and Ðeoden; And gif Ceoꞃl geþeah. þ

he had fully fiue hides of his owne lande, a Churche,
he heꞃde ꞃullice ꞃif hida ageneꞃ lande.   Ciꞃican.
                                              vse
                                            seruice
and a kitchin, a belhouse, and a gate, a seate, and a seuerall office
⁊ cycenan. belhuꞃ. and buꞃhgeaꞇ. seꞇl. ⁊ sundeꞃnoꞇe

in the kings halle, then was he thenceforth the Theins
on Cyngeꞃ healle. þonne þæꞃ he þanonꞃoꞃð Ðegn-
       woorthie
right woorthe. And if a Thein did so thriue, that he serued the
ꞃihꞇeꞃ peopðe; And gif Ðegn geþeah. þ he þenode

       progresse
       iourney
king, and on his message   ryd in his housholde, If he
Cynge. and hiꞃ ꞃadſeꞃne ꞃad on hiꞃ hineðe. gif ſe
       serued him,   *toward*
then had a Thein that followed him, the which to the kings
youꞃne heꞃde Ðegn ðe him ꞃiligðe. ðe ꞇo Cyngeꞃ
                                                        expedition

ILLUSTRATION 16A   Anglo-Saxon text (AS2/3) from Lambarde's *Perambulation of Kent* (1596.2), 2I7ᵛ–8ʳ, showing part of the AS Law 'Geþyncðo' (CUL Syn.7.59.31). Note that Parkerian sorts are used alongside Lambardian sorts.

> Mepham. 501
>
> *expedition plowlandes   palaice*
> *iourney fiue hides had,   and in the kings seate his*
> utfane fif hida hafde, and on Cyngef setl hir hla-
>   *messages*
> *Lorde serued,   and thrice with his errande had gone to*
> fopð ðenode. and ðpipa mið hir ærend gefona to
>   *Such an one*
> *the king, He might afterwarde with his foreothe his Lordes*
> Cynge. ðe most riððan mið hir fonaðe hir hlafond
>
> *par' plaꝩo at any great neede.   And if a Thein did thriue so,*
> afpelian.æt mirlican neoðan; And gif Ðegn geðeah.
>   *woorthy*
> *that he became an Earle, then was he afterwarde an Earles*
> ꝥ he peande to Eople. þonne ꝥ he rið an Eorlriht.
> *the rightes of an Earle.*
>   *right woorthy. And if a Merchant so thriued that he passed*
> ter peopðe;   And gif Mafrene gefeah, ꝥ he fende
>   *cunning*
>   *broad*   *science*
> *thrice ouer the wide Seas, of his   owne   craste,   he was*
> hpige ofer pið sæ.   be hir agenum cræfte. se þer
> *thenceforth   a Theine right   woorthy.   And if*
> þonne syððan Ðegn rihter peopðe;   And gif
>   *thriued*
> *a Scholar so prospered thorowe learning, that he degree had, and*
> leopnene gefeah. þurh lane. ꝥ he had hæfde. and
>   *priuilege*
> *serued Christ, he was then afterwarde of dignitie and peace*
> henoðe xpe.   se þær þonne riððan mæðe and munde
>
> *so   muche   woorthy, as therunto belonged : vnlesse he*
> spa micelne pyrðe.   spa þærto gefyrede. but on he
> *trespassed   might not vse*
> *forfaited for that he the vse of his degree vse ne might,*
> fonfonhte. ꝥ he þær had note notian ne moste;
>   Bp

manuscript models, primarily eleventh-century ones, and the design of both the Parkerian and the Lambardian Pica Anglo-Saxons is essentially the same. In Anglo-Saxon manuscripts Anglo-Saxon ligatured *e* with an extended tongue was used throughout the tenth century and into the early eleventh century but became less common with the advance of caroline minuscule script.[6] Nevertheless it is still found sporadically, for example, in Junius 121, especially

---

6 Ker, *Catalogue*, pp. xxxii–xxxiii.

> **These Faultes, that haue escaped, may be thus amended.**
>
> | Pag. | Line. | Faulte. | Amendment. |
> |---|---|---|---|
> | 10 | 19 | ɼɪpɪʊʀoɪðr̃ | ɼɪpɪʊɾɪʊr |
> | 100 | 27 | being one of: | being our of. |
> | 158 | 26 | priuate armye: | priuate arme. |
> | 182 | 28 | þeoꝼaꞃ: | þeoꝼaꞃ. |
> | | 29 | ꞇaþ: | ꞇaþ. |
> | | Ibid. | ꞃꞃam: | ꞃꞃam. |
> | | Ibid. | hloþ: | hloþ. |
> | 183 | 1 | þɲɪꞇꞇɪȝ: | þɲɪꞇꞇɪȝ. |
> | 212 | 24 | Moꞃþ:& Moꞃþoꞃ | Moꞃþ & Moꞃþoꞃ. |
> | 218 | 1 | belly is: | belly,the doer is |
> | 221 | 22 | perhappes they had: | perhaps Bourglars had. |
> | | 23 | name, or rather: | name, whiche rather. |
> | 247 | Laſt. | ouunonuga | ouunonuga |
> | 260 | 24 | gainſt him, then: | gainſt him, ſo that he eſcape thereby, then. |
> | 301 | 24.25 | if he be preſent. | if he be not preſent. |
> | 306 | Laſt. | (at the moſte) | or two (at the moſte) |
> | 422 | 1.2 | Countie, and there | Countie, there. |
> | 470 | 10 | complaint. | Complainant. |
> | 481 | 24 | receiue. | retaine. |
> | | Ibid. | holden, at about. | holden, about. |

ILLUSTRATION 16B   Errata page from Lambarde's *Eirenarcha* (1581.1), 2L7ᵛ, showing the correction of s/r, þ/p, 3/ȝ, capital/lower-case (CUL Pet.E.6.15)

at the end of lines.[7] The Lambardian Pica Anglo-Saxon lower-case e looks as though it was based on the tongued *e* found in Anglo-Saxon manuscripts, so it

---

7   See above, Illustration 7, line 7 ge-, line 8 bette, and Ker, *Catalogue*, pl. IV, line 10 errore. Ker's statement on p. xxxiii that ligatured *e* does not occur in the set script of mid eleventh century manuscripts from Exeter and Worcester seems to be an overstated generalization, since Junius 121 is a Worcester manuscript, and an extremely important one as far as the Anglo-Saxon sixteenth-century type-designs were concerned: see above, ch. 2. On fo 4ʳ there is an annotation by Parker ('sub Lanfra⟨n⟩co', i.e Lanfranc, archbishop of Canterbury 1070–89) which suggest that he had Junius 121 available for close study, probably in Lambeth, where it could conveniently have been utilized for the design of the first Anglo-Saxon types; Parker then returned the manuscript to Worcester, as he did others (Hatton 42, for example), and others still to Exeter: see Peter J. Lucas & Jonathan Wilcox, *Manuscripts Relating to Dunstan*,

is apparently consistent in its design philosophy with the other letters. Why in this one particular what was approved by Lambarde was presumably not commended by Parker is probably connected with the initiation of spelling reform practices on the continent.

In Italy, in his *Epistola de le lettere nuovamente aggiunte ne la lingua italiana* published in 1524, Gian Giorgio Trissino (1475–1550) used a tongued *e* in final position to distinguish stressed close /e/ from unstressed /ɛ/.[8] Trissino's works were published by Lodovico degli Arrighi da Vicenza (fl.1510–27), who designed two or more Italics, as distinguished by Barker, revising the earlier work of Morison, and following Casamassima and Osley.[9] Arrighi's punchcutter was Lautizio Perugino, apparently the same person as the goldsmith praised by Cellini, Lautizio de Bartolomeo dei Rotelli, who included a tongued *e* in both varieties of Arrighi's first italic.[10] In France tongued *e* was normally used

---

Ælfric, and Wulfstan; the "Eadwine Psalter" Group, ASMMF 16 (Tempe AZ: MRTS, 2008), p. 94, and Timothy Graham, 'A Parkerian Transcript of the List of Bishop Leofric's Procurements for Exeter Cathedral: Matthew Parker, The Exeter Book, and Cambridge University Library MS Ii.2.11', *Transactions of the Cambridge Bibliographical Society*, x.4 (1994), pp. 421–459.

8 For Trissino see Giovanni Giorgio Trissino, *Scritti Linguistici*, ed. Alberto Castelvecchi (Rome: Salerno, 1986). For Trissino's *Epistola* and the debate which it provoked see Brian Richardson (ed.), *Trattati sull' Ortografia del Volgare 1524–1526* (Exeter: University of Exeter, 1984). Cf. also Brian Richardson, *Print Culture in Renaissance Italy* (Cambridge: Cambridge University Press, 1994), pp. 87 and 215, n. 31.

9 Trissino, *Canzone* (Rome: Arrighi, 1524), *Coryciana*, ed. Blosius Palladius (Rome: Arrighi, 1524), *La Sophonisba del Trissino* (Rome: Arrighi, 1524). For Arrighi see E. Casamassima, 'I Disegni di Caratteri di Ludovico degli Arrighi Vicentino (notizie 1510–1527)', *Gutenberg-Jahrbuch* 1963, pp. 24–36, and 'Ancora su Ludovico degli Arrighi Vicentino (notizie 1510–1527) Risulati di una "Recognitio"', *Gutenberg-Jahrbuch* 1965, pp. 35–42, who distinguished five type-designs, but A.S. Osley, 'The Origins of Italic Type', in A.S. Osley (ed.), *Calligraphy and Palaeography: Essays presented to Alfred Fairbank on his 70th Birthday* (London: Faber & Faber, 1965), pp. 107–120, and Stanley Morison, *Early Italian Writing-Books Renaissance to Baroque*, ed. N. Barker (London: British Library, 1990), I.4 and II.4, have shown that there are basically two designs with variants. For earlier work on Arrighi see A.F. Johnson and Stanley Morison, 'The Chancery Types of Italy and France', *The Fleuron*, 3 (1924), pp. 23–51, fig. 1 on p. 24 (= Casamassima, Type Ib), and fig. 3 on p. 28 (= Casamassima, Type II); for a convenient reproduction of these two type-designs side by side see Morison, *Type Designs of the Past and Present* (London: Fleuron, 1926), p. 17, also Morison, *On Type Designs* (London: Benn, 1962), pp. 36–37. These illustrations show the two type-designs used for printing Latin text; for convenient reproductions of Arrighi's first Italic used for Italian (= Casamassima, Type Ia) see Johnson, *Type Designs* (1966 edn), fig. 26 (and for discussion pp. 99–102), and Gaskell, *Bibliography*, fig. 11b on p. 24. For a list of books in Arrighi's Italics see Casamassima, 'Ancora', pp. 38–42, which includes the books listed in the previous note. See also Luigi Balsamo & Alberto Tinto, *Origini del Corsivo nella Tipografia Italiana del Cinquecento*, Documenti sulle Arti del Libro 6 (Milan: Edizioni Il Polifilio, 1967), pp. 127–147.

10 Illustrated in Casamassima, 'Disegni', p. 26, figs 1–2.

for a final -*e* that required to be pronounced, e 'long qu'on dict masculin', as in Latin *pietate*, as opposed to 'e petit fœminin'. The first printer to use a special sort for this tongued *e* was Conrad Neobar in Guillaume de Branteghem's gospel harmony *La Vie de Nostre Seigneur Iesus Christ par figures* (Paris, 1540).[11] In the following years a number of printers used such special sorts, for example, Jean 1 de Tournes, who utilized tongued *e* in Pasquier de Louhans's translation of Plutarch's minor works (Lyon, 1546). In Antwerp Christophe Plantin had matrices of Claude Garamont's (first) Long Primer Roman with special sorts that included one for tongued *e*.[12] Similarly with Garamont's Great Primer Roman.[13] The fact that tongued *e* was employed quite widely on the continent may explain why its use in Anglo-Saxon texts was potentially controversial. Parker and his immediate associates were probably familiar with the Italian usage at least through their Cambridge contacts.[14] If tongued *e* was known to signify a particular pronunciation in Latin, its use could have been considered misleading for Anglo-Saxon. On the other hand Lambarde apparently took a different view and did employ a tongued *e* in his Anglo-Saxon typeface.

Although the Parkerian and Lambardian Anglo-Saxon Picas look alike they are in fact different, as a detailed examination of them reveals; to facilitate such examination I provide enlargements (Illustrations 17a–b). Apart from the differences already noticed the following may be noted:[15]

---

[11] Philippe Renouard (founder editor), *Imprimeurs & Libraires Parisiens du XVIᵉ siècle*, V (Paris: Service des travaux historiques de la ville de Paris, 1991), p. 110, no. 91, illustrated on p. 108, from where the quotations are taken, also in Pl. B(IV) 23.

[12] *TSF* II 1567: 31, and see Parker et al., 'Typographical', MA 48 on pp. 7–8.

[13] *TSF* II 1567: no. 22; and c.1599: no. 15; Parker et al., 'Typographical', MA 20a on p. 22. For the use of this design incorporating tongued (and hooked) *e* see Louis Meigret, *Defęnses de Louís Meigręt touchant son Orthographíe Françoęze, conre lęs çęnsures ę calōnies de Glaumalis du Vezelet, ę de sęs adherans* (Paris: Wechel, 1550), repr. in European Linguistics 1480–1700 No. 8 (Menston: Scolar, 1969), e.g. sig. A2ʳ line 25, C4ᵛ line 15. For an alphabetic reproduction of this design including special sorts see Catach, *L'Orthographe*, p. 213, fig. 14.

[14] Cf. Alred Fairbank & Bruce Dickins, *The Italic Hand in Tudor Cambridge*, Cambridge Bibliographical Society Monograph 5 (London: Bowes & Bowes, 1962), p. 2 and plates, esp. 9, 10b, 12b.

[15] I use the terminology given by Philip Gaskell, 'A Nomenclature for the Letter-forms of Roman Type', *The Library*, v.29 (1974), pp. 42–51, except for the addition of a few terms necessary for the description of a non-roman type-design.

	Parker/Day	Lambarde/Middleton/Bynneman
d		Terminal on ascender turned up more sharply
f		Terminal and bar extend further to right; bar higher
g	Link projects further leftwards	
r	Serif to right stem blunt	Serif to right stem tapered up
s		Terminal extends further to right
t		Hooked terminal extends upwards further; bar longer
ð	Bar shorter, especially to left	Bar longer, especially to left; ascender slopes slightly more steeply to left
p		Squarer bowl; upper left serif tapered
y		Longer terminal
Æ[1]	Short, virtually non-existent lower arm, short middle arm, left diagonal of A joins upper arm of E smoothly	Lower and middle arms longer, left diagonal of A joins upper arm of E on a slightly lower projectory, left diagonal has more pronounced serif
Æ[2]	Left diagonal of A joins upper arm of Ꞓ smoothly	Left diagonal of A joins upper arm of Ꞓ on a slightly lower projectory
H	Left and right stems same depth	Right stem has more severely twitched terminal and extends deeper than left stem
M	Right shoulder lower than left	Right and left shoulders same height, right stroke more rounded outwards
S	Upper stroke extends further to right	
Ð	Bowl stroke slightly splayed inwards at upper and lower parts	Bowl stroke straight and horizontal at upper and lower parts
Ꞃ	Shorter bar, short tail, with slightly angled terminal	Longer bar, with longer tail sharply angled

⁋A Sermon tranſlated out of Latin into the
Saxon tonge by Ælfricus, agaynſt tranſubſtan-
tiation.   An. 996.
In die Sancta 'Paſca.
⁋The Alphabet of the Saxon tongue.
f. g.   r. ſ. t. w. y. z.
⁋ a. b. c. d. e. ꝼ. ᵹ. h. ı. l. m. n. o. p. ꞃ. ꞅ. u. p. y. ?.
Abbreuiations
Æ. Th. Th. S. W. And th. th.
Æ. Ð. þ. ꞅ. p. ⁊. ð. þ.

Men ða leoꝼoꞃtan . ᵹelome eoꞃ iꞅ ᵹeꞅæð
ymbe uꞃeꞅ hælenðeꞅ æꞃiꞅte . hu he on
þiꞃum anðpeaꞃðan ðæᵹe æꝼteꞃ hiꞅ ðꞃoꞃunᵹe

ILLUSTRATION 17A   Portion of Illustration 13 enlarged 164% (Parker/Day)

These differences show that the two type-designs are to be distinguished from each other. In general terms the Lambardian Pica, with its wider set of letters like s and t, which often occur together, gives a different appearance on the page, as these letters take up excessive width in relation to other pairs of letters. Nevertheless, some letters, particularly þ and þ, are so similar that they raise the possibility that the Parkerian and Lambardian designs may derive from the same punch, with perhaps one matrix being supplied to Parker and another to Lambarde, but such a possibility depends on one punchcutter being responsible for both designs, and is improbable. In general the two type-designs are so similar that they were probably based on the same models, and this general similarity in relation to the models used is more important than the close resemblance of some letters between the two sets of designs. What they both resemble most closely is the Parkerian Great Primer Anglo-Saxon used by Day. Apart from the lower-case *e* in the Lambardian Pica Anglo-Saxon, it is hardly necessary to look any further to find the models on which they were based.

The punchcutting for Anglo-Saxon 'types' had to be particularly skilful because the special sorts to be cut should ideally match all the qualities of the design of the existing sorts; some were, some were not.[16] Since Day acquired

---

16   For a discussion by a modern punchcutter of what is involved in cutting Anglo-Saxon sorts (lower-case ð, þ, and capital Ð) to match an existing fount see Nelson, 'Cutting'.

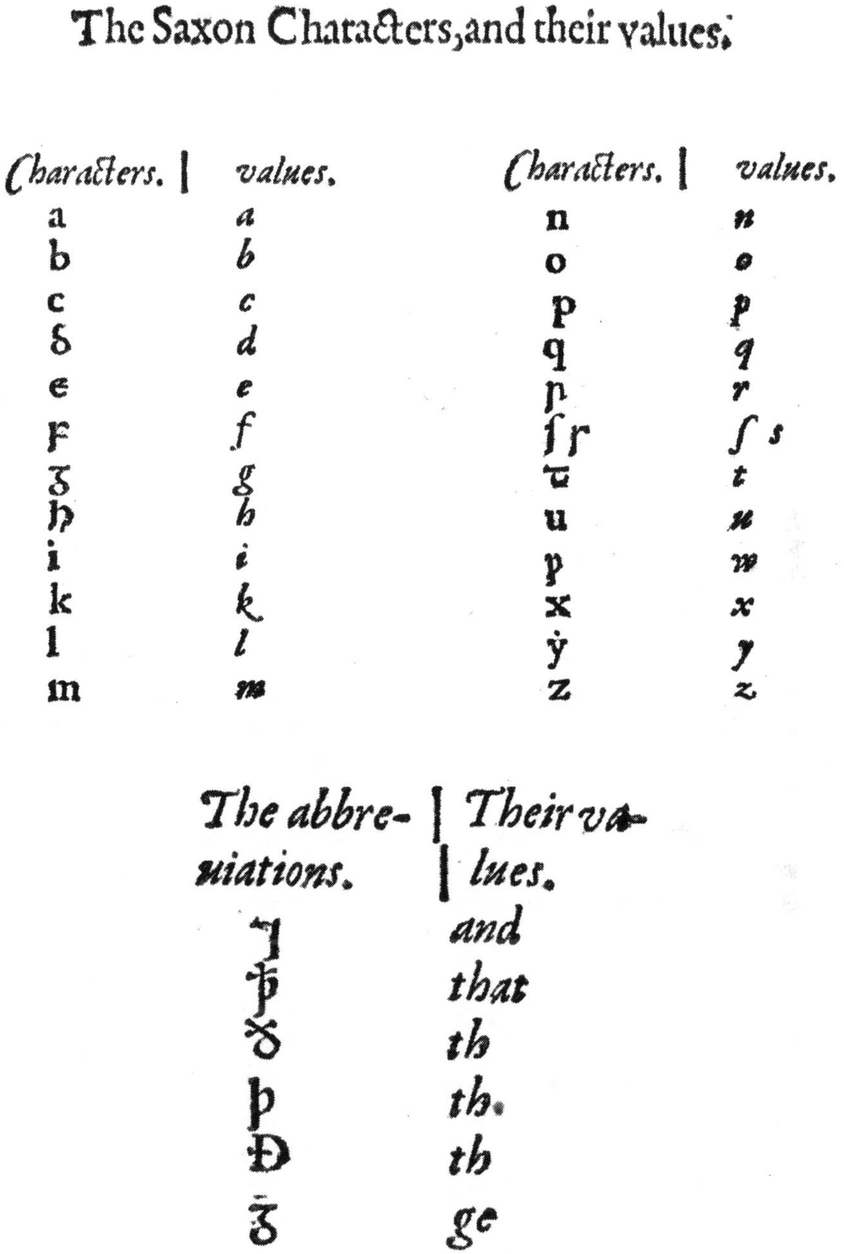

The Saxon Characters, and their values.

Characters.	values.	Characters.	values.
a	a	n	n
b	b	o	o
c	c	p	p
ð	d	q	q
e	e	r	r
f	f	ſr	ſ s
ʒ	g	t	t
h	h	u	u
i	i	p	w
k	k	x	x
l	l	ẏ	y
m	m	z	z

The abbreviations.	Their values.
⁊	and
þ	that
ð	th
þ	th.
Ð	th
ʒ̄	ge

ILLUSTRATION 17B   Sections from Illustration 15a reassembled and enlarged 200% to allow comparisons (Lambarde/Newbery)

the Parkerian Great Primer Anglo-Saxon types under the archbishop's auspices it is highly probable that Day was also the printer for whom the Parkerian Pica Anglo-Saxon designs were made, and indeed that they were probably made to fit with the Pica Roman that he used at this time, that by Pierre Haultin. Parker stated that Day alone possessed his Great Primer Anglo-Saxon, which I take to mean that Day alone held the matrices. Consequently, perhaps on foot of the archbishop's death in 1575, Lambarde decided to commission Anglo-Saxon special sorts for use by the printer(s) working for him, but less attention was paid to how the Anglo-Saxon and Roman sorts would fit together. Moreover, from the use of the Pica Anglo-Saxon types in Middleton and Bynneman's books for Newbery it is evident that they were less familiar with how to use them than Day; the misuse of capitals as lower-case letters (H for h, S for ð, and later Ᵽ for þ) is enough in itself to suggest that the attention to fit between the ordinary roman and the special sorts lacked finesse.

So the sixteenth century produced three Anglo-Saxon sets of type-designs in two sizes, one Great Primer Anglo-Saxon (Parkerian) with twenty-six special sorts, used by John Day (and others), and two Pica Anglo-Saxons, one (Parkerian) with twenty-four special sorts used by Day, and one (Lambardian) with twenty-two (later increased to twenty-three) special sorts used by Henry Middleton and Henry Bynneman printing for Ralph Newbery. All of them continued in use well into the seventeenth century, no new set of designs appearing in England until 1639. Indeed the level of activity in the use of the Pica designs was heavier in the first third of the seventeenth century than in the last third of the sixteenth, 44 books using them, including five in one year (1610), as opposed to 27 in the earlier period. So the history of their use is interesting in itself.[17] Sometimes they appear in passages of Old English text and sometimes in words only, always in combination with a Roman type-design that is usually of the same type-size.

After the two books issued in 1576, Foxe's *Book of Martyrs* using the Parkerian Pica Anglo-Saxon (**1576.1**), and Lambard's *Perambulation of Kent* using the Lambardian Pica Anglo-Saxon (**1576.2**), only two more books using the Pica Anglo-Saxon type-designs appeared before Day's death in 1584. The first two editions of Lambarde's *Eirenarcha* (**1581.1** and **1582.1**) were printed by Henry Bynneman for Ralph Newbery utilizing the Lambardian Pica.[18] Presumably Newbery oversaw the supply of the Anglo-Saxon types formerly used by

---

17   The contribution in this area by Richard W. Clement, 'The Beginnings of Printing in Anglo-Saxon, 1565–1630', *Publications of the Bibliographical Society of America*, 91 (1997), pp. 192–244, requires amendment in several particulars.

18   1581.1: sig. N3^v–4^r; 1582.1: sig. N4^r.

Middleton to Bynneman. Newbery seems to have operated as a publisher, supplying his printers with wood-blocks for printer's devices, so it would have been perfectly feasible for him to have supplied specialist types as well.[19] Following the death of Henry Bynneman in 1583 much of his printing materials went to the newly formed printing group known as Eliot's Court Press, with whom Newbery was associated.[20] This press was to be of considerable importance in the printing of Anglo-Saxon for the next sixty years or so.

On Day's death the Parkerian Pica apparently went to Eliot's Court Press printing for Ralph Newbery, who proceeded to use it instead of the Lambardian Pica, which disappeared for fifteen years. For Ralph Newbery the Eliot's Court Press printed the first two editions of William Camden's *Britannia* (1586.1 and 1587.1), both utilizing the Parkerian Pica Anglo-Saxon for supposed Anglo-Saxon place-name etymologies.[21] Eliot's Court Press also printed the third edition (1590.1) for George Bishop, which also used the Parkerian Pica Anglo-Saxon. Meanwhile, the Eliot's Court Press printed for Ralph Newbery the third edition of Lambarde's *Eirenarcha* (1588.1), and then an altered version of the third edition (1591.1), in the following year the fourth edition (1592.1), and then the fifth edition (1594.1), all utilizing the Parkerian Pica Anglo-Saxon.[22]

Also in 1594, the appearance of the fourth edition of Camden's *Britannia* (1594.2), printed by Eliot's Court Press for George Bishop, signals a change in the usage of the two Pica Anglo-Saxons: they appear mixed together.[23] Presumably the Press had already acquired the Lambardian Pica Anglo-Saxon stock of Henry Bynneman (d.1583) supplied by Ralph Newbery (d.1604). This mixed Parkerian-Lambardian fount appears again in the fifth edition of Camden's *Britannia* (1600.1) printed at Eliot's Court Press probably by Edmund Bollifant (*alias* Carpenter) for George Bishop.[24] In the second edition of Lambarde's *Perambulation of Kent* (1596.2), printed by Edmund Bollifant (*alias* Carpenter) at Eliot's Court Press, the only Parkerian sort that appears is

---

19   For example, R.B. McKerrow, *Printers'& Publishers'Devices in England & Scotland 1485–1640*, Illustrated Monographs xvi (London: Bibliographical Society, 1949), nos 153, 240.

20   On the Eliot's Court Press see Henry R. Plomer, 'The Eliot's Court Printing House, 1584–1674', *The Library*, IV.2 (1922), pp. 175–84, and 'Eliot's Court Press: Decorative Blocks and Initials', *The Library*, IV.3 (1923), pp. 194–209.

21   Cf. V. Watts, 'English Place-Names in the Sixteenth Century: The Search for Identity', in A.J. Piesse (ed.), *Sixteenth-Century Identities* (Manchester: Manchester University Press, 2001), pp. 46–48.

22   1588.1: sig. O1^r; 1591.1: O1^r; 1592.1: M7^v; 1594.1: M7^v.

23   Particularly clear examples of Parkerian and Lambardian lower-case letters used together occur with f on sig. 2O3^v in Taðencliffe, and with s on sig. Q1^r in Cirrancearten.

24   Parkerian and Lambardian lower-case s both occur on sig. V1^v; Parkerian g occurs on G3^v as against Lambardian g on H6^r, etc.

s, so this book will be discussed further below.[25] Meanwhile the mixed fount appeared under the imprint of Thomas Wight and Bonham Norton in the sixth edition of Lambarde's *Eirenarcha* (1599.1).[26] The mixed fount also occurs under the imprint of Thomas Wight in the seventh edition (1602.1).[27] This mixed fount occurs again in sigs A-S of John Minsheu's polyglot dictionary, *Ductor in Linguas*, printed by Melchisidec Bradwood at Eliot's Court Press (1617.1).[28] And it occurs yet again in the revised edition, *Minshæi Emendatio*, printed by John Haviland [of Eliot's Court Press] (1625.1 and 1626.2).[29] It occurs too in the Anglo-Saxon specimen (but not the text) on a cancel in the revised re-issue of Lisle's *Saxon Treatise* under the title of *Divers Ancient Monuments in the Saxon Tongue* printed by Edward Griffin 2 [at Eliot's Court Press] (1638.1).[30]

Crucially, for their longevity of survival, the combined Parkerian and Lambardian Pica Anglo-Saxon type-designs appeared in all the editions of John Speed's *Theatre of the Empire of Great Britaine* during the seventeenth century, starting with 1611.1, printed by William Hall (fl.1598–1614), the bookseller/publishers being John Sudbury (fl.1610–15) and his nephew, George Humble (fl.1611–32).[31] Humble was granted privilege to print this work for 21 years on 29 April 1608.[32] Speed's book came with maps engraved by Jodocus Hondius (Joost de Hondt, 1563–1612), the premier engraver of his time. The second imprint, by John Beale (fl.1611–43†), who was Hall's associate in printing Speed's *Historie* in 1611–12, occurred three years later (1614.1). Like the first edition of 1611–12 it too used a combination of the two Pica Anglo-Saxon

---

25 On 2I4ᵛ/17 Parkerian s in mancẏɼ, Lambardian s in ʒolðeɼ.
26 Anglo-Saxon occurs on M7ᵛ (text) and Q6ʳ (words): Lambardian f and Parkerian s in Ðeoɼaɼ, Parkerian f and Lambardian s in ɼeoɼan; there is no Lambardian e.
27 Anglo-Saxon occurs on L7ᵛ (text) and O7ᵛ (words): Lambardian e, also f in fɼam against Parkerian f and s in Ðeoɼaɼ.
28 Up to and including sig. S the mixed Parkerian and Lambardian Pica Anglo-Saxon is found, with Parkerian and Lambardian g both occurring, e.g., on S5ʳ s.v. Gauelkind, and on S3ʳ, s.v. Furlong, AS fÐaɲle shows Lambardian f and Parkerian H and r. Lambardian e last occurs on S3ʳ, s.v. *a* Gable, in AS ʒeʙel.
29 The specimen on p2ᵛ shows mainly Lambardian sorts (without e) but some sorts are Parkerian, e.g., M. In the text Parkerian g in ʒaſt, s.v Ghost, occurs beside Lambardian g in ʒẏɼt, s.v. Gift, both on O5ᵛ (col 331), and Parkerian r occurs in pɲæc, s.v. Wreake, on 2I3ᵛ beside Lambardian r in cnaɲa, s.v. knaue, on R5ᵛ.
30 The AS specimen occurs on p2ʳ: Lambardian Pica Anglo-Saxon mixed with a number of Parkerian Pica Anglo-Saxon sorts, viz. d, t, y; þ, ð, Ƿ (=uc); Æ¹, Æ².
31 For this topic see further Peter J. Lucas, 'William Camden, Seventeenth-Century Atlases of the British Isles and the Printing of Anglo-Saxon', *The Antiquaries Journal*, 98 (2018), pp. 219–244.
32 W.W. Greg, *A Companion to Arber* (Oxford: Clarendon Press, 1967), p. 51.

type-designs, the Parkerian and the Lambardian. Evidently they were passed from Hall to Beale, no doubt under the watchful eye of publisher George Humble, who presided over the plates for the maps. In the Latin edition (1616.1) again there appears a combination of the Parkerian and the Lambardian Pica Anglo-Saxon designs. The printer was Thomas Snodham (fl.1609–25†) and the publisher was George Humble together with his uncle John Sudbury. The next edition of Speed's *Theatre* (1627.1, re-issued with some leaves and maps newly printed as 1632.1) was printed by John Dawson (fl.1613–34?†), and the publisher again was George Humble. Here too we find the same combination of Pica Anglo-Saxon types as before, and the common link again is George Humble the publisher. When George Humble died in 1640 his rights to Speed's *Theatre* etc., and the plates, and evidently the Anglo-Saxon types, were inherited by his eldest son William Humble (fl.1640–59). He did nothing with them, but in 1659, when he ceased business, he sold them to one William Garrett. He in turn did nothing with them, but transferred them to Roger Rea the Elder (1665†) and Roger Rea the Younger (fl.1650–62–?1668). They were the publishers of the next edition of Speed's *Theatre* (1650/?1665.1), which came out in 1650 according to the title page, but in reality it was later, probably 1665, printed by Mary Simmons (fl.1656–67) and Samuel Simmons (fl.1665–78). Once again the same combination of Anglo-Saxon type-designs is used.

The most obvious explanation of this successive use of the same Anglo-Saxon type-designs in combination is that they were passed down together with the plates for the maps made by the engraver Hondius. The last edition to use Anglo-Saxon types is 1676.1, which came out under the aegis of the publishers Thomas Basset (fl.1658–96), and Richard Chiswell (fl.1667–1711), who had acquired the plates from Roger Rea the Younger. Presumably they acquired the Anglo-Saxon types as well, as again the same combination of the Parkerian Pica and Lambardian Pica appears, now almost a century since they were first used. In this 1676 edition both these Elizabethan type-designs make an appearance considerably later than the last occurrence of the Parkerian Pica Anglo-Saxon in 1640, and later than the last occurrence of the Lambardian Pica Anglo-Saxon in 1670. It seems reasonable to suppose that they were held by the successors to George Humble, even through the Great Fire of London in 1666. Here is a remarkable story of a combination of specialist type-designs first found in 1594, and still found in 1676, mainly by virtue of their use in successive printings of one book. And this story complements the story of the plates engraved by Hondius in the first decade of the seventeenth century. Acquired by Humble after 1608 they went through a succession of owners and were used in a succession of editions of the same book up to 1676. Indeed they were used longer after that, until 1795,[33] the need for such plates exercising a conservative influence on map-making. As far as I know the Parkerian/Lambardian Pica Anglo-Saxon type-designs used in combination did not last as long as that, but they do make what may be their last appearance in 1703.2, the second edition of Somner's *Antiquities of Canterbury*, revised by Nicolas Battely. Its publisher, Robert Knaplock (fl.1696–1737†), was the brother of Ralph Knaplock, who was partner of Jacob Tonson in 1697, and who was freed by Thomas Bassett in 1678.[34] Basset was one of the publishers of **1676.1**. This tenuous connection is a possible explanation of how Knaplock and his printer came to have the use of these special type-designs, which had not been used for twenty-seven years.

Because of the succession of editions of Speed's *Theatre* we have been taken forward. Back in 1607 another change took place. Since there is no evidence that the Lambardian Pica Anglo-Saxon fount in its pure form (without admixture of Parkerian letter-sorts) was used between 1582 and 1607 this change probably reflects the casting of a new set of types from the matrices for Eliot's Court Press. The Lambardian Pica Anglo-Saxon designs occur exclusively (without any admixture of Parkerian designs) in the sixth edition of Camden's *Britannia* printed by Eliot's Court Press for George Bishop and John Norton 1 (**1607.2**), and in the sixth edition of Foxe's *Acts and Monuments of Martyrs* printed by [Humphrey Lownes 1] for the Stationers' Company (**1610.3**).[35] It also occurs exclusively in the seventh edition of Camden's *Britannia* printed by [Eliot's Court Press] for George Bishop and John Norton 1 (**1610.5**), followed by Michael Drayton's *Poly-Olbion* printed by [Humphrey Lownes 1] for Matthew Lownes, John Browne 1, John Helme, and John Busby 2 (**1612.1**).[36] After a gap of fourteen years the Lambardian Pica Anglo-Saxon was next used for Henry Spelman's *Archæologus*, printed by John Beale (**1626.1**). In **1631.2** it was used in James Ussher's *Discourse of the Religion Anciently Professed by the Irish and*

---

33   Helen Wallis (ed.), *Historians' Guide to Early British Maps*, Guides and Handbooks 18 (London: Royal Historical Society, 1994), p. 6.

34   *Register of Company of Stationers*, III (1917), 475.

35   Anglo-Saxon occurs on 5G2^v–4^v and 5I5^r. Clement, 'Beginnings', p. 231, n. 102, reports on the authority of Peter Blayney that sigs 5G, 5H, and 5I, the first and last of which contain the Anglo-Saxon, were 'farmed out', but does not say to whom, and cites no evidence; probably only sig. 5G was contracted out, as Dr Blayney has kindly confirmed to me (private communication dated 25 Jan 1999). It has no catchword at the end, a wider column width (88 mm on 5G2–4 rather than 86.5 mm), different, more widely spaced, page numbers, different line numbers between the columns, and shows variant forms of the running title *K.Hen.8* (e.g., *King Henry.8*). Eliot's Court Press is the most obvious candidate for printing it. Lownes probably printed the small amount of Anglo-Saxon on sig. 5I5^r using borrowed type.

36   Anglo-Saxon occurs in text on 2D1^v, and in words on C5^v, M3^v, R2^r, R3^r, S1^r.

Brittish, printed by Robert Young (item 4).[37] In the same year it was used in volume II of the seventh edition of Foxe's *Acts and Monuments of Martyrs* printed by Adam Islip, Felix Kingston and Robert Young (1631.3).[38] In 1639.4 the Lambardian Pica Anglo-Saxon was used in a few words in Spelman's *Concilia* printed by Richard Badger 1, even though the main Anglo-Saxon text shows another design which appears for the first time in this year, and the following year (though it was perhaps printed first) it does supply the main Anglo-Saxon text in Sir John Spelman's edition of the *Psalterium Davidis*, also printed by Badger (1640.3), and was used for passages in William Somner's *Antiquities of Canterbury* printed by John Legat 2 (1640.1).[39] In Abraham Wheelock's edition of Lambarde's *Archaionomia* printed by Roger Daniel, printer to Cambridge University 1632–50 (1644.2), where, again, the main Old English text is in a new design, the Lambardian Pica Anglo-Saxon is used in the 'Glossarium' on 2E1ʳ–4ʳ. Some years later Somner used it once more in the supplement on Old English words in Meric Casaubon's *De Quatuor Linguis Commentationis*, which appeared under the imprint of James Flesher (1650.1). In 1655.3 Sir William Dugdale began using it in the first volume of his *Monasticon Anglicanum*, which was printed by Richard Hodgkinson, and in the second by Alice Warren (1661.1), and he used it too in *The History of St Pauls Cathedral*, printed by Thomas Warren (1658.1), and in *Origines Juridiciales*, printed by Francis and Thomas Warren (1666.1). Meanwhile it had appeared in Silas Taylor's *The History of Gavelkind* printed by William Wilson in (1663.1), but by this time there was apparently a shortage of d's, as beside ordinary Anglo-Saxon d there occurs another sort, which is capital S with the upper stroke broken off.[40] Finally this type-design bows out in 1670.1 in Robert Sheringham's *De Anglorum Gentis Origine Disceptatio*, printed at Cambridge by John Hayes for Edward Story.

This Lambardian Pica Anglo-Saxon also appeared with Parkerian s, which occurs in conjunction with Lambardian s. The apparent anticipation of this conjunction by the Eliot Court Press production of Lambarde's second edition of his *Perambulation of Kent* (1596.2) was mentioned above. Here the printer's frequent use of Roman tall ſ perhaps suggests a need to conserve the types for Anglo-Saxon long s.[41] Apart from that usage Lambardian Pica Anglo-Saxon

---

37 Anglo-Saxon occurs in a marginal note on D6ᵛ.
38 Anglo-Saxon occurs on 5G2ᵛ–4ᵛ, 5I5ʳ.
39 Anglo-Saxon occurs in text on 2Z2ᵛ, 2Z3ʳ.
40 Anglo-Saxon occurs in text on G4ʳ, K3ᵛ, Q4, T3ᵛ, T4ʳ.
41 Lambarde went to some trouble to revise this work, and his copy of the first edition (1576.2) with his amendments for the second edition (1596.2) is preserved in the Bodleian Library, Oxford, shelf-mark 4⁰ Rawl.263. Possibly the use of his own Lambardian fount

with occasional Parkerian s appears first in the printing of the eighth edition of Lambarde's *Eirenarcha* by Adam Islip for the Stationers' Company (**1607.1**), and then in **1608.1**, when it is found in Robert Glover's *Nobilitas Politica vel Civilis*, [ed. Thomas Milles, Glover's nephew], printed by William Jaggard, and again in Thomas Milles's *The Catalogue of Honor*, also printed by Jaggard (**1610.4**), and yet again in Milles's *Treasurie of Auncient and Moderne Times* printed by Jaggard (**1619.2**).[42] It seems reasonable to suppose that Islip and Jaggard were supplied with this fount by Eliot's Court Press or one of its printers. Of all the special sorts used s would have been the one most frequently called on.[43] Perhaps the occasional Parkerian s's were thrown in from old stock. Back at Eliot's Court Press the Lambardian Pica Anglo-Saxon with occasional Parkerian s was retained and appeared subsequently in William Lisle's *Saxon Treatise concerning the Old and New Testament* printed by John Haviland [at Eliot's Court Press] for Henry Seile (**1623.1**), the re-issue entitled *Divers Ancient Monuments in the Saxon Tongue*, in the text on the cancel (O2v) printed by Edward Griffin II [at Eliot's Court Press] (**1638.1**), the third edition of William Lambarde's *Perambulation of Kent* printed by Richard Hodgkinson for Daniel Pakeman (**1640?.1**, re-issued **1656.1** with new title page), Sir Roger Twysden's *Historiæ Anglicanæ Scriptores X*, ed. John Selden, printed by James Flesher in (**1652.1**), with glossary by Somner, and finally, in **1664.1**, the Lambardian Anglo-Saxon Pica with Parkerian s occurs, again with some broken-S-type d's, in Sir Henry Spelman's *Glossarium Archaiologicum*, edited by Dugdale, and printed by Alice Warren.[44] Some admixture of founts is indicated by the fact that both Flesher and the Warrens print some books with the Lambardian

---

with Parkerian s emanated from his own instructions, in which case what happened in 1607 could be seen as authentic.

42 In **1607.1** Anglo-Saxon occurs on M5ʳ (text) and P7ʳ words). Parkerian s occurs, e.g., on M5ʳ in ꞃýððan (cp. ꞃıꝼ, erron. for ꝼıꞃ). In **1608.1** Anglo-Saxon occurs in text on N1ᵛ–3ʳ; Parkerian s occurs, e.g., on N1ᵛ line 16 in ꞃunðeꞃnoꞇe. In **1610.4** Anglo-Saxon occurs in text on G6ᵛ–H1ʳ; Parkerian s occurs, e.g., on G6ᵛ in aȝeneꞃ. In **1619.2** Anglo-Saxon occurs in text on 2Y2; Parkerian s occurs, e.g., on 2Y2ʳ in ꞃeꞇl.

43 The letter e is not so frequent in Old English as in Modern English, and sometimes the special sort for it was not employed even when the main design being used was the Lambardian Pica.

44 In **1623.1** Anglo-Saxon occurs in the main text on A1ᵛ–L3ᵛ; Parkerian s occurs, e.g., on M4ᵛ/7 in mæꞃꞃeppeoꞃꞇaꞃ (2nd and 3rd s). In **1638.1** Parkerian and Lambardian s occur side by side in ȝecýþnýꞃꞃe (O2ᵛ/8). In **1640?.1** Parkerian s can be seen, e.g., at 2D2ʳ/24 Æpeꞃꞇ. In **1652.1** Anglo-Saxon in this design occurs on B4ᵛ (p. 8), E3ᵛ (col. 76) and in the glossary by Somner on 2X3ʳ–²2D7ᵛ. On ²X4ʳ Parkerian s occurs in unꞃcýlðıȝ (bottom line) and Lambardian s in ꞃpıpıȝe (penultimate line). In **1644.1** Lambardian Pica Anglo-Saxon with occasional Parkerian s occurs, e.g., on D3ᵛ, s.v. **Agild**, and in **1664.1**, e.g., on H1ʳ, Parkerian s in ꝼæꞃꞇen, Lambardian s in aðaꞃ.

Pica Anglo-Saxon unadulterated (Flesher: 1650.1; Warren: 1655.3, 1661.1, 1658.1, 1666.1) and others with the Lambardian Pica Anglo-Saxon with Parkerian s (Flesher: 1652.1; Warren: 1664.1).

Some books, the ninth edition of Lambarde's *Eirenarcha* printed by [Adam Islip] for the Stationers' Company (1610.1), and John Selden's *Jani Anglorum* printed by Thomas Snodham (*alias* East) for John Helme (1610.2), have only a small amount of Old English text, so it is difficult to be sure that the absence of a Parkerian s is significant.[45] The same reservation would apply to the tenth and eleventh editions of Lambarde's *Eirenarcha*, both 1614.2 and 1619.1 printed by [Adam Islip] for the Stationers' Company.[46] These books could belong with the group that used the Lambardian Pica Anglo-Saxon exclusively, or they could belong with the group that used the Lambardian Pica Anglo-Saxon with occasional Parkerian s.

In 1614 John Selden began his partnership with William Stansby, who printed all his subsequent books containing Anglo-Saxon published during Selden's lifetime. In his *Titles of Honor* (1614.4) the Old English passages are printed exclusively in the Parkerian Pica Anglo-Saxon combined with Pierre Haultin's Pica Roman, the same combination as used by Day in 1576.[47] Likewise, Selden's *Historie of Tithes* (1618.1, 1618.2, 1618.3, 1618.4) was printed by [Stansby] using this type. In the meantime these types were used for sig. T–2Z of Minsheu's polyglot dictionary, *Ductor in Linguas*, printed by [Stansby] (1617.1).[48] These were the only three books to appear with the Parkerian Pica Anglo-Saxon in this period (1614–18). As with the Parkerian Great Primer Anglo-Saxon Stansby was the only printer to use these materials ultimately inherited from Day, and they were not used again.[49]

The Parkerian and Lambardian Pica Anglo-Saxons performed great service over a considerable period, the Lambardian designs being extensively used and lasting some ninety-five years, and the two designs in combination lasting for over a hundred years. But already there were signs of a need to supplement, or perhaps a desire to modernise, in 1634. In Oxford the expanded edition of Sir Thomas Ridley's *A View of the Civile and Ecclesiasticall Law* by John Gregory printed by William Turner (1634.1) used the Lambardian Pica

---

45 In 1610.1 Anglo-Saxon occurs on M5ʳ (text) and P8ʳ (words). In 1610.2 Anglo-Saxon occurs on B6ʳ (one word), C8ʳ (one word), G2ᵛ–3ʳ (words only).
46 In 1614.2 Anglo-Saxon occurs on M5ʳ (text) and P8ʳ (words). In 1619.1 Anglo-Saxon occurs on M5ʳ (text) and P8ʳ (words).
47 Anglo-Saxon occurs in text on I3ʳ, R2ᵛ, 2G1ʳ, 2G1ᵛ, 2K4ʳ, 2M2, 2N1ʳ, 2V3ʳ.
48 The Parkerian Pica Anglo-Saxon appears unadulterated from sig. T, e.g., on T3ᵛ, s.v. Greue, f, g, r in ʒeneɼa.
49 Stansby's business passed to Richard Bishop in 1636.

Anglo-Saxon with occasional Parkerian s.⁵⁰ But it includes also a newly cut s with a shorter terminal extending to the right and a sharply angled serif to the stem (first on T2ʳ, e.g. line 32 ælmeſſſeoh). It appears again in the revised edition of Ridley's book (**1639.1**), also printed by [Turner] but with preliminaries by John Dawson 2.⁵¹ The new s is similar to that ultimately adopted in the set of designs cut by Nicholas Nicholls for William Somner for use in his Dictionary of **1659.1**.⁵² The only known punchcutter who could have cut these new punches is Arthur Nicholls, who was active from 1632 (or possibly earlier) to about 1640 (or possibly later).⁵³ If it was him, he was ahead of the trend, for between 1639 and 1659 four new sets of type-designs based on new punches appeared, including that by Nicholas Nicholls (Arthur's son) for Somner (AS7).

---

50   Anglo-Saxon occurs in text on L3ʳ, T1ᵛ–2ᵛ, 2A1ᵛ, 2A4ᵛ, 2C1ʳ–2ʳ, 2C2ᵛ.
51   Anglo-Saxon occurs in text on L3ʳ only (see line 33 'ʒeopnſulneſſe').
52   For a reproduction of a type-specimen attributable to Nicholas Nicholls (**1665?.1**) which includes this design see Mores, *Dissertation*, p. lxxv.
53   See Mores, *Dissertation*, pp. lxxi–lxxii, and John A. Lane, 'Arthur Nicholls and his Greek Type for the King's Printing House', *The Library*, VI.13 (1991), pp. 297–322, at pp. 302–307.

CHAPTER 4

Anglo-Saxon Type-Designs in the Seventeenth Century to 1705

Altogether there are about 180 items printed in the seventeenth century that include Anglo-Saxon types. Sometimes these types appear in passages of Old English text, or even whole editions of texts, and sometimes in words only, always in combination with a Roman type-design which is usually (but not always) of the same type-size. Two type-designs dominate the century in terms of the frequency of their occurrence. The first is the sixteenth-century Lambardian Pica Anglo-Saxon that made its debut in Lambarde's *Perambulation of Kent* (1576.2) and is last found in its pure form in 1670.1, the historian Robert Sheringham's *De Anglorum Gentis Origine Disceptatio*.[1] The second is the Somnerian Pica Anglo-Saxon apparently cut in anticipation of the publication of 1659.1, the first Anglo-Saxon dictionary, William Somner's *Dictionarium Saxonico-Latino-Anglicum*. I have found this set of type-designs in over 40 books from the seventeenth century and it was still being used in the eighteenth. With both these more frequently used Anglo-Saxon type-designs a different approach to the necessity of controlling access to them is shown. In the case of the Lambardian designs these were in the possession of the group of London printers known as the Eliot's Court Press.

While the Eliot's Court Press or individual printers in the syndicate presumably held matrices they apparently allowed small amounts of type to be set by other printers from their cases; they may also have allowed their cases to be borrowed or they may have allowed a duplicate set of types to be made for another London printer, William Jaggard (fl.1594–1623), for example.[2] Presumably commercial considerations were uppermost here, rather than the desire for political control; certainly the Eliot's Court Press syndicate remained in business for some 69 years, from 1584 to 1652. The Somnerian Pica Anglo-Saxon was probably cut by the punchcutter Nicholas Nicholls, who probably retained the punches, but matrices or supplies of type (Nicholls was a type-founder) may have been supplied to several printers, including the nascent Oxford University Press, which used the types extensively. It is notable that this set of type designs occurs in 1658, one year before Somner's *Dictionarium*, in William Burton's

---

1 See above, chapter 3.
2 Jaggard printed Anglo-Saxon in 1608.1, 1610.4 and 1619.2.

Commentary on Antoninus his Itinerary printed by the London printer Thomas Roycroft (**1658.2**).³ Altogether the Somnerian Pica Anglo-Saxon occurs in the work of at least fifteen printers in the seventeenth century.⁴ Presumably again commercial considerations were uppermost, although some printers may have helped colleagues with whom there was a family connection.

At this point it may be helpful to provide a brief review of the kinds of evidence available for this investigation. The evidence is of three kinds: (1) that of material bibliography, the printed books where the various type-designs used can be noted and analysed; (2) the records of the printers and their associates, including type-specimens, together with the archives of those responsible for regulating them; and (3) the surviving printing materials, especially punches and matrices. For the sixteenth-century printing of Anglo-Saxon nearly all the evidence to survive belongs to the first category, it being supplemented only by some statements by Parker in his prefaces and by information gleaned from correspondence, which would come in the second category. No punches or matrices for Anglo-Saxon types survive from the sixteenth century, so there is no evidence at all under the third category.

For the seventeenth century the evidence is more full. Gerard Langbaine the elder (1609–58), Provost of Queen's College, Oxford, was much interested in antiquarian studies. A letter of his to Archbishop Ussher from 21 June 1650 shows a fascination with how the style of Anglo-Saxon letter-forms resembles that of Irish script.⁵ Ussher would have been aware of this resemblance as he had used the Elizabethan Irish types (IR1) to print Anglo-Saxon in his *Veterum Epistolarum Hibernicarum Sylloge* (**1632.3**) and his *Britannicarum Ecclesiarum Antiquitates* (**1639.2**).⁶ Langbaine was anxious to promote Anglo-Saxon studies through print and the Oxford University Archives preserve negotiations

---

3 Ten years later Roycroft sold Oxford University a printing press: Martyn Ould, *Printing at the University Press, Oxford 1660–1780*, 2 vols (Seaton: Old School Press, 2016–18), II.20–21.
4 Thomas Braddyll (fl.1679–1704), Mary Clarke (fl.1678–1705†), Freeman Collins (fl.1679–1713†), John Darby 1 (fl.1662–1707†), (probably) Elizabeth Flesher (fl.1671–89, stepmother of Miles Flesher 2), William Hall 2 (fl. Oxford 1657–72, Printer to Oxford University 1662, called William 1 by Wing IV.415–6), Thomas Hodgkin (fl.1676–1724†), Elizabeth Holt (fl.1689–1703†) business partner of William Horton (fl.1684–1702†), Robert and William Leybourn (fl. in partnership 1651–61), Thomas Newcomb 1 (fl.1648–81†), Thomas Newcomb 2 (fl.1672–91†), Roger Norton 2 (fl.1658–99), Robert Roberts (fl.1676–1701†), Samuel Roycroft (fl.1678–1717†), Thomas Roycroft (fl.1650–77†), Sheldonian Theatre [= nascent Oxford University Press] (fl.1665–).
5 Elizabethanne Boran, *The Correspondence of James Ussher 1600–1656*, 3 vols (Dublin: Irish Manuscripts Commission, 2015), III.976, Letter 561.
6 Langbaine also sends Ussher a likeness of an Anglo-Saxon runic alphabet from the Welsh manuscript OBL Auct.F.4.32, fo 20^r, later reproduced in **1703/5.1** after p. 168.

dating from 1651–2 between him, acting on behalf of the University, and Nicholas Nicholls, 'Letter-founder', for the supply of a Hebrew fount.[7] From correspondence we know too that Langbaine was negotiating in his capacity as Keeper of the University Archives to acquire the Somnerian Anglo-Saxon design (AS7) in 1653.

> I spoke with Mr Vice-chan: about a Saxon letter, he is not unwilling and I doubt not of effecting that part. [in an addendum] I have spoken to the bearer Mr Robinson to enquire & inform me about a Saxon l⟨ett⟩re for wch I shall pay.[8]

The fount, which shows twenty-seven special sorts, was received by the University from Nicholls in 1656 and the sum of £23 7s 2d was paid for it.[9] In the University Archives there are three specimen pages of text printed with it (**1656.2**).[10] According to Hart, Oxford University Press still possessed ten matrices for the fount at the end of the nineteenth century, but this statement is erroneous.[11] My visit to the Oxford University Press Archive on 14 March 2000 confirmed this finding.[12] Since the design appears on a type-specimen attributed to Nicholls of c.1665 he evidently marketed it (**1665?.1**), as the number of printers who used it confirms.[13] The University Archives also preserve a bond dated 22 Aug 1657 with William Hall II, the printer (fl. Oxford 1657–72, Printer to Oxford University 1662), 'for restoring ... 177 pound weight of Saxon Letters', i.e. types (not the matrices), which were lent to Hall for printing 'of a new Saxon Lexicon composed by William Somner' and recording that Hall paid £45 on deposit for the privilege, nearly twice as much, incidentally, as

---

7   Oxford, Bodleian Library, University Archives, SEP.P17b(4).
8   Oxford, Bodleian Library, MS Ashmole 854, fo 297^r, letter from Langbaine to Sir William Dugdale, printed in Thomas Hearne, *Chronicon, sive Annales Prioratus de Dunstaple, una cum excerptis e chartulario ejusdem prioratus* (Oxford: Sheldonian Theatre, 1733), II.726 (sig. 4Z1^v); the letter is dated 6 Dec, and the addendum 16 Dec 1653.
9   Oxford University Archives, WPb/21/4 (= Vice-Chancellors' Accounts 1650–64), fo 152^r/6: 'For a font of Saxon Letters. to Mr Nichols Letter founder [£]023 . 07[s] . 02[d]'.
10 Oxford University Archives, SEP.P17b(4a), sheets 2, 3, 6. The specimens are noticed by W. Turner Berry & A.F. Johnson, *Catalogue of Specimens of Printing Types by English and Scottish Printers and Founders 1665–1830* (London: Oxford University Press, 1935), p. 2.
11 Horace Hart, *Notes on a Century of Typography at the University Press Oxford 1693–1794*, ed. H. Carter (Oxford: Clarendon Press, 1970), p. 34, rebutted by John Simmons in Stanley Morison & Harry Carter, *John Fell—The University Press and the Fell Types* (Oxford: Clarendon Press, 1967), p. 243, n. 2.
12 I am grateful to the archivist, Dr Martin Maw, for his assistance.
13 BL, Bagford Collection, Harley 5977, no. 200, reproduced in Mores, *Dissertation*, p. lxxv.

the University paid for them.¹⁴ The term 'restoring' is interesting and could mean that the University had matrices from which the Saxon Letters were recast. When the University received the 'font of Saxon Letters' possibly what they received was a set of matrices rather than or in addition to a fount. Here another dimension of printing politics is revealed. While the punchcutter held the punches, the purchaser of a set of matrices or types, Oxford University, held them, and lent the type at a price to their chosen printer. William Hall the printer may in turn have held on to the type (or he may have re-borrowed it), as he used it again in 1662.1, the fourth edition of Sir Thomas Ridley's *A View of The Civile and Ecclesiasticall Law*. In 1675.1 it was used again for the fifth edition printed by Henry Hall (fl. Oxford 1642–80), namesake and possible kinsman of William Hall 11. Apparently access to printing Anglo-Saxon was seen as a privilege worth guarding, or at least as an expense that any others who might have wanted it would have to afford for themselves.¹⁵

This finding can be set against the University's (and Langbaine's) experience with Arabic types.¹⁶ In 1637 the London bookseller Samuel Browne, brother of one of the Oxford University proctors for that year, had negotiated on behalf of the University the purchase of type, matrices and punches from the estate of the punchcutter Arent Corsz[oon] van Hoogenacker of Leiden.¹⁷ Amongst this stock there was a set of Arabic sorts described as English-size. The designs are closely modelled on the earlier Arabic of Thomas Erpenius (made about 1615).¹⁸ Early in 1647 John Greaves, then Savilian Professor of Astronomy at the University, persuaded Gerald Langbaine as Keeper of the Archives to lend him the Arabic matrices, which he promptly took to London, where Nicholas

14 Oxford University Archives, SEP.P17b(3), fo 44, summarized in Falconer Madan, *Oxford Books. A Bibliography of Printed Works Relating to the University and City of Oxford or Printed or Published There*, 3 vols (Oxford: Clarendon Press, 1895–1931), II.xxix, n. 1.
15 Ould, *Printing*, II.24, suggests that the strictness of the conditions may simply reflect a distrust of printers.
16 For this story see Toomer, *Eastern Wisedome*, pp. 170–172. See also Geoffrey Roper, 'Arabic Printing and Publishing in England before 1820', *British Society for Middle Eastern Studies Bulletin*, 12 (1985), pp. 12–32, at p. 16.
17 Harry Carter, *A History of the Oxford University Press Volume 1 ... to the year 1780* (Oxford, 1975), pp. 33–34; Morison and Carter, *John Fell*, pp. 233–43; John A. Lane, 'Arent Corsz Hogenacker (ca. 1579–1636): An Account of his Typefoundry and a Note on his Types', *Quaerendo* 25 (1995), pp. 83–113, 163–191, at pp. 109–10. The specimen broadside is preserved in Oxford University Archives, SEP.P17b(4); see H. C[arter] & J.S.G. S[immons, *A Specimen of Types cast at the University Press, Oxford, in matrices believed to have been bought at Leyden in 1637* (Oxford: Oxford University Press, 1957), which includes specimen reproductions (there is a copy of this rare item at the St Bride Printing Library, London). On Browne see STC III.30.
18 Carter & Simmons, *Specimen*.

Nicholls cast types for him that were used by the printer Miles Flesher 1 in Greaves's book *A Discovrse of the Romane Foot and Denarivs* (London: Miles Flesher 1 for William Lee, 1647; Wing G1800).[19] Langbaine considered himself deceived by Greaves who allegedly borrowed the matrices on the pretext of examining them to see how they might be improved.[20] The story perhaps illustrates one honourable academic's innocence in the world of business.[21] It would not be surprising if the security surrounding materials owned by the University printing house was subsequently increased and such measures would have included the Anglo-Saxon types.

So far we have considered three sets of type-designs from the sixteenth century: (1) the Parkerian Great Primer Anglo-Saxon (AS1) and (2) the Parkerian Pica Anglo-Saxon (AS2), which in the seventeenth century were both exclusive to the printer William Stansby (and his successor, Richard Bishop) and were used almost exclusively by John Selden; and (3) the Lambardian Pica Anglo-Saxon (AS3), which was widely available to a number of printers probably supplied in the seventeenth century by the Eliot's Court Press. We have also seen that later in the seventeenth century the Somnerian Pica Anglo-Saxon, though no doubt cut with a specific book in mind, was also widely available. Before Somner, however, there were other scholars in seventeenth-century England who had sets of Anglo-Saxon type-designs made for them: Spelman, Wheelock, and Junius, and it will now be appropriate to treat each in turn.

1 The Spelmanian Great Primer Anglo-Saxon Type-Design

Sir Henry Spelman (1563/4–1641) studied law and became a political adviser to the king on legal/constitutional matters. Beginning as an assistant to the privy councillors appointed members of a commission set up by James I in 1622 to investigate the fees taken in civil and ecclesiastical courts, he became a full commissioner in 1623, attending many meetings and writing several reports. But at heart he was a country gentleman from Norfolk with antiquarian interests, a remarkable scholar who became 'one of the earliest pioneers in

---

19 Arabic types occur on sig. I2.
20 John Johnson & Strickland Gibson, *Print and Privilege at Oxford to the year 1700*, Oxford Bibliographical Society 7 (Oxford: Oxford University Press, 1946), p. 27, n. 2. Johnson and Gibson record the date of Greaves's receipt for the matrices as January 1648, which in modern reckoning means January 1649. Greaves did in fact facilitate the improvement of the matrices.
21 Greaves was formally expelled from his professorship and from the university on 30 Oct 1648.

historical method'.[22] His methodology was painstaking. To deal with the problems he had in reading medieval documents he compiled a list of abbreviations and contractions found in Latin manuscripts, the *Archaismus graphicus ab Henrico Spelman in uso filiorum conscriptus*, anticipating Capelli by three hundred years.[23] He presided over the earliest surviving modern Anglo-Saxon grammar.[24] In 1626 he published his *Archaeologus in modum Glossarii* (**1626.1**), a glossary of law terms compiled because of the difficulties he experienced in his early research with Anglo-Saxon and Latin legal vocabulary, covering the letters A—G. Only the first part was published by Spelman himself, and the work had to be completed in print by Sir William Dugdale's edition of 1664, over twenty years after Spelman's death (**1664.1**). The 1626 edition was printed using the Lambardian Pica Anglo-Saxon, and so also was the 1664 edition (with the admixture of occasional Parkerian Pica Anglo-Saxon s). Spelman's greatest work was his *Concilia, Decreta, Leges, Constitutiones, in re Ecclesiarum Orbis Britannici*, the Councils, Decrees, Laws and Constitutions of the English Church, 'the first attempt to deal in a systematic way with the early documents concerning the church, and [it] practically inaugurated a new historical study', the first volume of which (up to 1066) took seven years to compile and was printed by Richard Badger 1 (**1639.4**).[25] For this book a new Great Primer Anglo-Saxon was cut, presumably to Spelman's specification, the first attempt in England at a new set of Anglo-Saxon type-designs since 1576; see Illustration 18. It shows 25 special sorts.[26] It is used in conjunction with a Great Primer Roman that shows some resemblance to that of Ameet Tavernier, a Dutch punch-cutter of the sixteenth century.[27] Badger was not the only printer to use this Spelmanian Great Primer Anglo-Saxon. It occurs in words in Matthew Paris's

---

22 Cronne, 'Charter Scholarship', p. 44.
23 Copies of Spelman's work on abbreviations include Cambridge, Corpus Christi College 238, a fair copy given by Spelman to the college, Cambridge Gonville and Caius College 189, 415 (the former a copy by John Walden of the second), given by Charles Spelman, Sir Henry's grandson, Cambridge University Library Mm.5.25, Dorchester, Dorset Record Office, Fox-Strangways (Ilchester) Archive D.124, Edinburgh University Library La.III.565, London, BL Harley 3929, 6353, Lansdowne 207 (e), 785, Sloane 1059, Stowe 1059 (made for Charles I when Prince of Wales), Society of Antiquaries 65–6, Oxford, Bodleian Library Douce 251 (SC 21825), 289 (SC 21863), Eng.misc.f.419 (SC45925), Rawlinson B.462, C.155, New Haven, Yale University, Beinecke Library, MS Osborn Fb 1 (dated 1606), Edinburgh University Library, La.III.565, and London, Society of Antiquaries, MSS 65–6. Adriano Capelli, *Dizionario de Abbreviature Latine et Italiane* (Milan: Hoepli, 1961).
24 See Peter J. Lucas, 'The Earliest Modern Anglo-Saxon Grammar: Sir Henry Spelman, Abraham Wheelock and William Retchford', *Anglo-Saxon England*, 45 (2016), pp. 379–417.
25 Quotation from *DNB*, s.n., art. by W. Carr.
26 It occurs in the catalogue of the James foundry as no. 52: see Mores, *Dissertation*, pp. [14] and 111.
27 Vervliet, *Printing Types*, R20.

Vitæ Duorum Offarum sive Offanorum, Merciorum Regum (**1639.3**), edited by William Watts, who had helped Spelman earlier with his *Archaeologus*, and published by Miles Flesher 1 (fl.1617–64†), and it occurs again in Spelman's *De Sepultura* (**1641.1**). Two more works by Spelman also printed by Flesher show it: Spelman's *Tithes too Hot to be Touched* (**1646.2**) and Spelman's *Larger Treatise concerning Tithes* (**1647.1**). It appears again in two more works: the second edition of John Gregory's *Notes and Observations upon some Passages of Scripture*, printed by Richard Cotes (**1650.2**), and Sir Roger Twysden's *Historiæ Anglicanæ Scriptores X*, printed by James Flesher (fl.1649–70†), the son of Miles Flesher 1 (**1652.1**).

In **1647.2** Miles Flesher 1 also used the Spelmanian Great Primer Anglo-Saxon for printing the *Fleta seu Commentarius Juris Anglicani*, with a 'Dissertatio' by John Selden. Selden's participation in this book was apparently induced by the publisher rather than coming of his own volition. At the beginning of his 'Dissertatio ad Fletam' (sigs 3N1^r–4B3^r) Selden explains that he had nothing to do with the editing or printing of the *Fleta*, but that after it was printed the publishers asked him to add '& Titulum & de Libro, Autore, Nomine aliquid', which he did in the form of his 'Dissertatio'.[28] Despite these apparent special reasons for Selden's use of a London printer other than Richard Bishop (who had exclusive use of the Parkerian Great Primer Anglo-Saxon), Selden effectively transferred at this time to Flesher as his printer. His *De Synedriis & Præfecturis Iuridicis Veterum Ebræorum Liber Primus* (**1650.3**) was printed by Flesher and shows the Spelmanian Great Primer Anglo-Saxon on sigs 2N3^r (p. 277), 2O2^r (p. 283), 2R3^r (p. 309), and 4H2^v–3^v (pp. 604–6). The remaining two volumes of *De Synedriis* were also printed by Flesher, volume III after Selden's death (**1655.4**).[29] A possible reason for Selden staying with Flesher as his printer was Flesher's acquisition, mentioned above, of the Arabic types 'pirated' from Oxford by Greaves, as these were superior to those used by Bishop (which first appeared in 1635), even though Selden himself probably paid for them.[30] Another reason may be that Bishop's business was tailing off, as is suggested by the decreasing number of books bearing his imprint as the

---

28 See sig. 3N1^v (p. 454). See also David Ogg (ed.), *Ioannis Seldeni: Ad Fletam Dissertatio* (Cambridge: Cambridge University Press, 1925).

29 I have found no Anglo-Saxon in vol. II (1653; Wing S2425A). Vol. III (**1655.4**) shows the Lambardian Pica Anglo-Saxon in words on sig. 2D3^r (p. 205).

30 Hart, *Notes*, p. 182; Toomer, *Eastern Wisedome*, p. 71. Abraham Wheelock's posthumous edition of the Persian Gospels was also printed by a Flesher (James, son of Miles 1): *Quatuor Evangeliorum Domini Nostri Jesu Christi Versio Persica Syriacum & Arabicum suavissimè redolens* (London: James Flesher, 1657); Wing B2796A. See Geoffrey Roper, 'Persian Printing and Publishing in England in the 17th Century', in K. Eslami (ed.), *Iran and Iranian Studies: Essays in Honor of Iraj Afshar* (Princeton NJ: Zagros, 1998), pp. 316–28, at p. 319.

Alphabetum Anglo-Saxonicum hìc apponimus : non integrum illud vetus, cujus multi desiderantur characteres, sed quo Latinis intermixto literis, ipsi Saxones nostri recentiores usi sunt, & nos plerunque in hoc opere retinuimus.

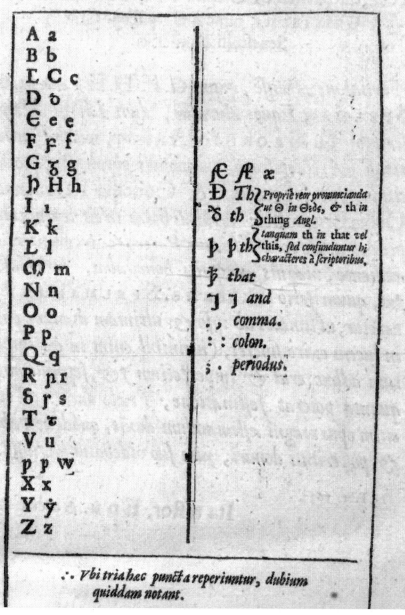

ILLUSTRATION 18A   Reader's Anglo-Saxon type-specimen (AS4) from Spelman's *Concilia* (1639.4), *3ᵛ (CCC D.1.5)

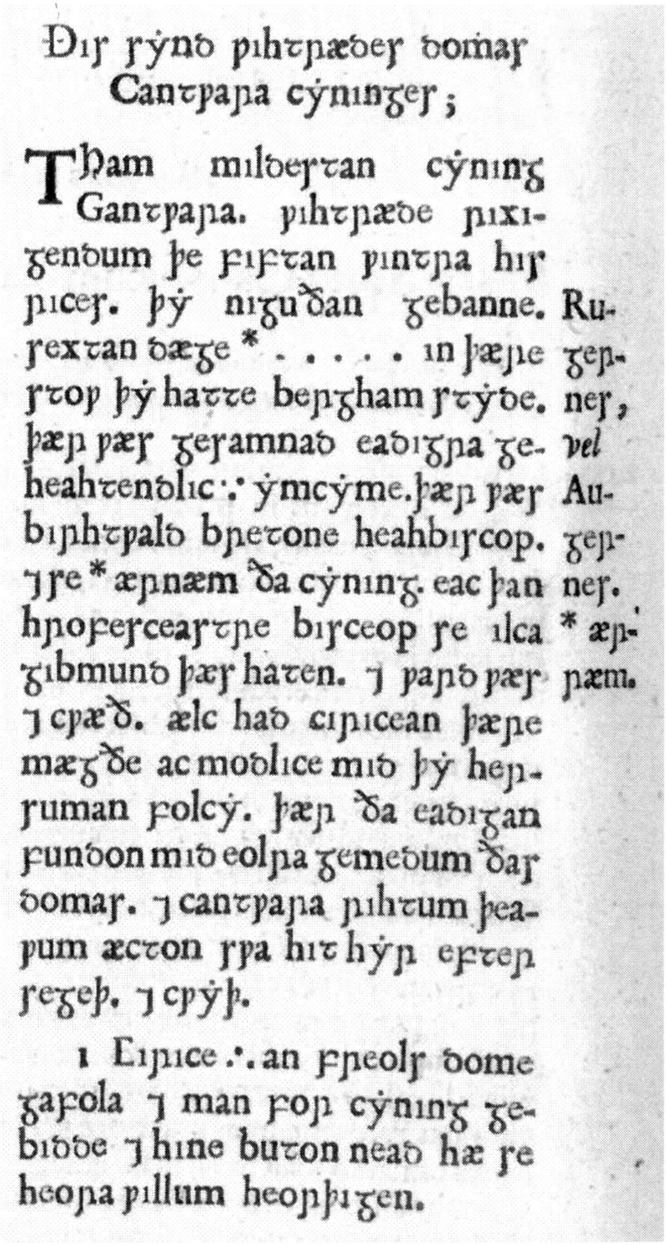

Ðis synð pihtrædes domas
Cantwara cyninges;

Þam mildestan cyning Cantwara. pihtræde pixigendum þe fistan pintra his rices. þy nigudan gebanne. Rustextan dæge * . . . . . in þære gesstop þy hatte bergham stybe. þær pæs geramnað eadigra geheahtendlic∴ ymcyme.þær pær biphtrpald bretone heahbiscop. sse * æpnæm ða cyning. eac þan hposerceastre bisceop se ilca gibmund þæs haten. ¬ pand pæs ¬ cpæð. ælc had ciricean þære mægðe ac modlice mid þy heyruman polcy. þær ða eadigan pundon mid eolra gemedum ðas domas. ¬ cantwara pihtum þeapum æcton spa hit hyr ester sesseþ. ¬ cpyþ.

Runes, vel Ausesnes. * æsræm.

1 Ciruce∴ an sreols dome gasola ¬ man sor cyning gebidde ¬ hine buton nead hæ se heora pillum heorþisen.

ILLUSTRATION 18B Anglo-Saxon text from Spelman's *Concilia* (1639.4), P6ᵛ, showing the beginning of the Laws of Wihtræd (CUL Ely.a.90)

1650s progressed, and that authors found him slow to respond, as is suggested by the Spelmans' experience mentioned above.[31]

So altogether there are nine books showing the Spelmanian set of Anglo-Saxon type-designs. The type-design lasted just fourteen years (1639–52). Despite Spelman's familiarity and facility with manuscripts the Spelmanian Great Primer Anglo-Saxon type-design (AS4) is closely modelled on the Parkerian Great Primer Anglo-Saxon (AS1), but the following differences in the Spelmanian design are notable:

Æ¹	middle and lower arms extend more to right
Æ²	left stem descends lower with serif angled more to left
C	square C not in AS1
ð	terminal of ascender hooked over further to the right
e	tongued e not in AS1
∈	middle arm slightly lower
f	longer terminal and bar, more pronounced upper serif
ȝ	upper arm slightly higher at right than left and has more pronounced terminals
h	upper serif more sheared, lower left serif angled more to left, lower right serif more hooked
m	left stem has terminal turned more to the right, right stem has hooked serif more sharply angled
n	left stem has upper serif more sheared and lower serif angled more to left, right stem has lower right serif extending further on both sides of the stem
r	right diagonal parts from stem slightly lower, stem has lower left serif angled more to left
s	upper left stroke leans more to the left
t	terminal hooked up slightly less
þ	longer serifs
ƿ	longer serifs
ð	slightly shorter ascender
Ð	longer serifs
p/P	capital similar to AS1 lower-case but bowl slightly higher than stem
ꝩ	lower serif angled more to left
ꝫ	upper and lower serifs and spur more pronounced

---

31   For a list of Bishop's imprints see Wing IV.102.

2   The Wheelockian Great Primer Anglo-Saxon

Spelman, being greatly interested in Anglo-Saxon antiquities, and much impressed by the richness of their preservation in Cambridge, decided to establish an Anglo-Saxon lectureship in Cambridge University, to which Abraham Wheelock (1593–1653) was appointed from 1638 until his death in 1653. Wheelock was a Shropshire lad who went up to Cambridge in 1611, where he was resident at Trinity College, graduating BA in 1614, and MA in 1618. He then went to Clare College, as a Fellow from 1619 until his marriage in 1632, being ordained a deacon in 1619 and a priest in 1622, when he became vicar of St Sepulchre's church in Cambridge, and graduated BD in 1624.[32] In 1629 he was appointed University Librarian, a post not sufficiently lucrative at that time to be the sole means of support for someone in Wheelock's position.[33] Spurred on by this stimulus Wheelock took up Spelman's invitation to become his Anglo-Saxon assistant in Cambridge in 1637. As part of the arrangements pertaining to his Anglo-Saxon lectureship he became Vicar of Middleton (Norfolk) in 1638, which was in Spelman's patronage.[34] His character was that of a 'humble and affable man', a conscientious scholar, willing to please and in need of regular reassurance from his patrons, constantly (over)-anxious about money, modest and somewhat nervous of political instability.[35] He was notably reluctant to travel. In a letter to Sir Symonds D'Ewes of 26 January 1640,

---

32   There is a good account of Wheelock by Oates, *Cambridge University Library*, chs 7–8. These chapters were based on the Sandars Lectures in Bibliography which Oates delivered at Cambridge University in 1966. For the spelling of Wheelock's name I have preferred that which he and Spelman used in almost all instances in English. Cf. Toomer, *Eastern Wisedome*, p. 86, n. 151.

33   Oates calculates that Wheelock's income from this post would have been about £17.00 per year (*Cambridge University Library*, p. 184). The basic stipend was £3 6s 8d. At the same time the remuneration for the library keeper of Trinity College Dublin was £3: see Vincent Kinane & Anne Walsh (eds), *Essays on the History of Trinity College Library, Dublin* (Dublin: Four Courts Press, 2000), pp. 26–27.

34   On the church and parish, including Wheelock's incumbency, see F. Blomefield & C. Parkin, *An Essay towards a Topographical History of the County of Norfolk*, 11 vols (London: W. Bulmer for W. Miller, 1805–10), IX.30–32. On Wheelock's death the parish position was separated from the lectureship, which was taken up by William Somner: see James Ingram, *An Inaugural Lecture on the Utility of Anglo-Saxon Literature* (Oxford: Oxford University Press, 1807), pp. 39–41.

35   The quotation is from a brief memorial character-sketch recorded by Thomas Baker (1656–1740) in CUL, Mm.1.44, p. 476, as being supplied by Wheelock's daughter from an unknown author. W. Sclater, *The Crowne of Righteousnes* (London: John Grismond for John Clarke 1, 1654: Wing S916) includes an encomium on the occasion of his funeral: see pp. 27–34.

Wheelock assures D'Ewes that he would come to see him if he were not so busy in Cambridge with his Arabic and his Anglo-Saxon work; and just seventeen days later, in a letter to Sir Henry Spelman of 12 February 1640, Wheelock assures Spelman, who had recently had a fall, that he would have come to see him in the Barbican (London) if his wife had not been ill.[36] Nearly all his extant letters were written from Cambridge.[37] He was a productive scholar. Only six years after his recruitment by Spelman he produced his edition of Bede's *Historia Ecclesiastica* (**1643.1**), for which he is deservedly famous, to which Wheelock added an edition of the *Anglo-Saxon Chronicle*, and a re-edition of the Anglo-Saxon *Laws* (**1644.1**; the *Archaionomia*, previously edited by William Lambarde (**1568.2**)); the two (**1643.1** and **1644.1**) were then combined in a single publication (**1644.2**). These books were printed by Roger Daniel (1593?–1667), bookseller and printer in London 1620?–29?, 1650–66, and Printer to Cambridge University 1632–50.[38]

To provide the contents with what was considered to be the appropriate style and authenticity of appearance a new Great Primer Anglo-Saxon for the appropriate special sorts was cut to Wheelock's specification (see Illustration 19a). It shows 30 special sorts (including the raised point used for punctuation), with an exceptionally large number of capitals (see Illustration 19b).[39] This set of designs was being cut in London by early 1640, as indicated by a letter from Wheelock to Sir Symonds D'Ewes dated 30 March 1640:

---

36   The letter from 26 Jan 1640 is in BL Harley 374, fo 129ʳ. For Wheelock's work on Arabic see Toomer, *Eastern Wisedome*, pp. 86–93. The letter from 12 Feb 1640 is in BL Add. 34600, fo 209ᵛ.

37   MSS containing Wheelock's letters are to be found in BL Additional 34600, 34601, CUL Dd.3.64, OBL Tanner 67, 70 (to Spelman), BL Harley 374 (to D'Ewes), and CUL Dd.3.12 (Spelman to Wheelock). BL Harley 7041 contains transcripts by Thomas Baker (s.xviii¹) of the letters in CUL Dd.3.12; it was from that manuscript (Harley 7041) that the selected letters printed by Henry Ellis, *Original Letters of Eminent Literary Men of the Sixteenth, Seventeenth, and Eighteenth Centuries*, Camden Soc. 1.23 (London: J.B. Nichols, 1843), were taken. A further (later) series of transcripts survives in CUL Additional 7596. One letter, not present in CUL Dd.3.12, survives in Harley 7041. See Peter J. Lucas, 'Abraham Whelock and the Presentation of Anglo-Saxon: From Manuscript To Print', in A.N. Doane & Kirsten Wolf (eds), *Beatus Vir: Studies in Early English and Norse Manuscripts in Memory of Phillip Pulsiano* (Tempe AZ: MRTS, 2006), pp. 383–439, at pp. 431–439. For a conspectus of Spelman's letters see Peter J. Lucas, 'A Conspectus of Letters to and from Sir Henry Spelman (1563/4–1641)', *The Antiquaries Journal*, 202 (2022), 370–388 + on-line supplement: doi:10.1017/S0003581522000026.

38   David J. McKitterick, *A History of Cambridge University Press, Volume I, Printing and the Book Trade in Cambridge 1534–1698* (Cambridge: Cambridge University Press, 1992), pp. 168–193, 296–306.

39   It occurs in the catalogue of the James foundry as no. 51: see Mores, *Dissertation*, pp. [14] and 111.

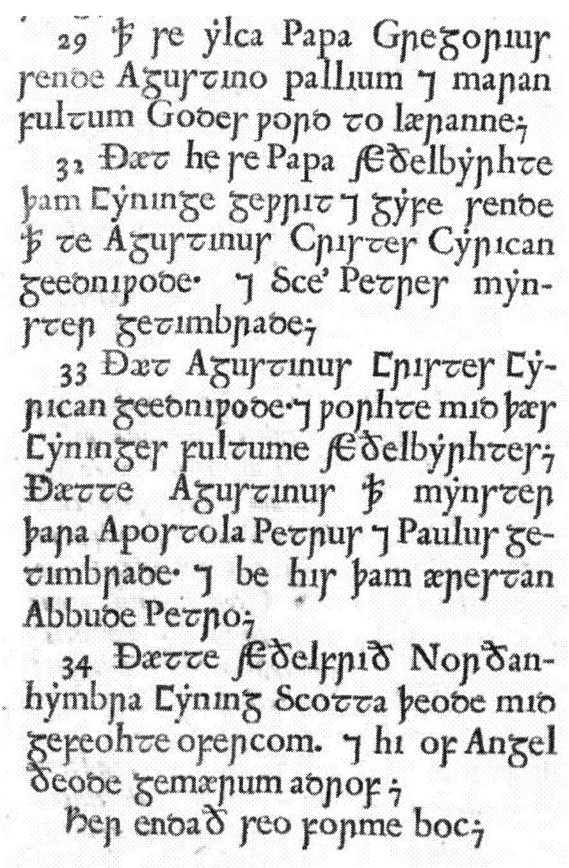

29 ꝥ ſe ylca Papa Gregoriuſ
ꞅenꝺe Aguꞅtino pallium ⁊ manan
ꝼultum Goꝺeꞅ poꝺ to lænanne;

31 Ðæt he ſe Papa Æðelbyꞃhte
þam Cyninge geꞃꝛit ⁊ gyꞃe ꞅenꝺe
ꝥ te Aguꞅtinuꞅ Cꞃiꞅteꞅ Cyꞃican
geeꝺniꝺoꝺe· ⁊ Sce' Petꞃeꞅ mynꞅteꞃ getimbꞃaꝺe;

33 Ðæt Aguꞅtinuꞅ Cꞃiꞅteꞅ Cyꞃican geeꝺniꝺoꝺe·⁊ ꝺoꞃhte miꝺ þæꞅ
Cyningeꞅ ꝼultume Æðelbyꞃhteꞅ;
Ðætte Aguꞅtinuꞅ ꝥ mynꞅteꞃ
þaꝺa Apoꞅtola Petꞃuꞅ ⁊ Pauluꞅ ge-
timbꞃaꝺe· ⁊ be hiꞅ þam æꞅeꞅtan
Abbuꝺe Petꞃo;

34 Ðætte Æðelꝼꞃiꝺ Noꞃðan-
hymbꞃa Cyning Scotta þeoꝺe miꝺ
geꞃeohte oꝼeꞃcom. ⁊ hi oꝼ Angel
ꝺeoꝺe gemæꞃum aꝺꞃoꝼ;

Heꞃ enꝺað ꞅeo ꝼoꞃme boc;

ILLUSTRATION 19A   Anglo-Saxon text from Wheelock's edition of
Bede's *Historia Ecclesiastica* (1643.1), sig. D1ᵛ
showing chapter headings set in AS 5 (CUL
Pet.A.7.7)

Our printer, Roger Daniel, is now actively working on printing the Saxon records. The characters are being fitted out now in London, as I hope, and are being fashioned or are in preparation.[40]

---

40   Typographus noster \Rogerus Daniel/ ... iam nauiter adlaborat monumentis Saxonicis imprimendis. Characteres iam Londini, et politi, ut spero, aut ornantur, aut in ornatu sunt: BL, Harley 374, fo 143ʳ, printed in John Nichols, *Bibliotheca Topographica Britannica*, 8 vols (London: John Nichols, 1780–90), VI.ii.78.

Alphabetum Anglo-Saxonicum.

A a	N n	Æ æ	
B b	O o	Ð Th	*Proprie reor pronuncianda ut Θ in Θιός, & th in thing Anglicè.*
C c	P p	ð th	
Ð ð	Q q		
Ɛ E e	R ꞃ r	Þ th	*tanquam th in that vel this, sed confunduntur hi charatteres à scriptoribus.*
F ꝼ f	S ꞅ ſ		
Ᵹ G ᵹ g	Ꞇ τ t	ꝥ that.	
Ƕ H h	V Ʋ u	⁊ and	
J i	Ƿ p w	· comma	
K k	X x	; periodus.	
L l	Y ẏ		
ᛘ m	Z z		

ILLUSTRATION 19B Reader's Anglo-Saxon type-specimen of AS5 (excluding square C) from Wheelock's edition of Bede's *Historia Ecclesiastica* (1643.1), ¶6ᵛ (CCC D.3.22²)

On 29 April 1641 Wheelock wrote to Spelman:

> Most honored Sir, had not Mʳ Daniel oᵘʳ printer two seueral times returned to London without my knowlege, on whose courtesie for the deliuerie of my Letters, I wholie depended, I had written a month before. I vnderstand by Mʳ Daniel, what paines yoᵘʳ w⟨o⟩r⟨shi⟩p hath taken about the Saxon types, in instructing the grauener, for w⟨hi⟩ᶜh I am much bound to giue youʳ w⟨o⟩r⟨shi⟩p thankes.[41]

Evidently Sir Henry Spelman was the source of funds to pay for this new set of type-designs, 'instructing' the punchcutter ('grauener').[42] The only known

---

41 BL, Additional 34601, fo 46ʳ.
42 *OED*, s.v. instruct, v., sense 3: 'To furnish with authoritative directions as to actions ... ; to direct, command', recorded from 1557. Oates, *Cambridge University Library*, p. 204, says that Spelman 'assisted in their design', but I know of no evidence for this interpretation; the error is taken over by Parry, *Trophies*, p. 181, n. 34. The identification of Spelman as the paymaster of the Anglo-Saxon type partly answers the puzzlement of McKitterick, *History*, pp. 191–192, as to 'how the Bede was financed: its Saxon type alone was a considerable investment, for which Daniel was never to find further use.'

punchcutter in London at that time is Arthur Nicholls (father of Nicholas), who was active 1632–53, being one of the four typefounders named in the Star Chamber Decree of 1637.[43] To ascertain the possibility that Nicholls may have cut the Wheelockian Great Primer Anglo-Saxon it is necessary to go forwards in time and work backwards. In the sale catalogue of the typefoundry of John James printed in 1782 the Wheelockian Great Primer Anglo-Saxon is one of four Anglo-Saxon founts shown; the other three are the Spelmanian Great Primer (AS4, used for Spelman's *Concilia*, 1639.4), the Somnerian Pica (AS7, used for Somner's *Dictionarium*, 1659.1), and the Oxford University Small Pica (AS8, first used for Benson's *Vocabularium*, 1701.1).[44] According to Edward Rowe Mores a Great Primer Anglo-Saxon and a Pica Anglo-Saxon came to James from the Grover foundry.[45] Thomas Grover, having worked as an apprentice ('servant') for Nicholas Nicholls (son of Arthur), probably succeeded to Nicholls's business.[46] The Pica is the Somnerian Pica (AS7), delivered to Oxford University by Nicholas Nicholls in 1656. The identity of the Great Primer that Grover passed on to the James foundry is not clear: it could be either the Spelmanian or the Wheelockian set of designs; Lane assumes it is the Wheelockian, but there is no evidence either way.[47] In fact Arthur Nicholls is the only known candidate as punchcutter for both, unless his son Nicholas was a punchcutter by this time. Although this evidence 'is hardly proof that [Arthur] Nicholls himself was responsible for the type used by Daniel in 1643', it is suggestive.[48]

Like the set of Anglo-Saxon type-designs designed for Spelman's *Concilia* (AS4), the Wheelockian Great Primer Anglo-Saxon is used in combination with a Great Primer Roman. It first occurs in two verse compositions in what purports to be Anglo-Saxon (one by Wheelock) offered as contributions to a book of verses published on behalf of Cambridge University to celebrate Charles I's return from Scotland in November 1641 (1641.3).[49] It then occurs in the Bede (1643.1) and the re-edition of Lambarde's *Archaionomia* (1644.1), which were then combined in one book in 1644.2. Apart from this flurry of activity in Cambridge the Wheelockian set of type-designs occurs only in Marchamont

---

43   Star Chamber 1637: G4^v. On Nicholls see Lane, 'Arthur Nicholls', pp. 297–322.
44   Mores, *Dissertation*, facsimile between pp. 104/105, E1^v (= p. [14]), no. 51 on p. 111.
45   Mores, *Dissertation*, pp. 44–45.
46   Michael Treadwell, 'The Grover Typefoundry', *Journal of the Printing Historical Society*, 15 (1980/81), pp. 36–53, at pp. 37–38.
47   Lane, 'Arthur Nicholls', p. 305.
48   Quotation from David McKitterick, *Four Hundred Years of University Printing and Publishing in Cambridge 1584–1984. Catalogue of the Exhibition in The University Library Cambridge* (Cambridge: Cambridge University Press, 1984), p. 54, item 45; cf. also idem, *History*, p. 190.
49   1641.3: A4^r, G4^r.

Nedham's (or Needham's) English translation of Selden's *Mare Clausum*, entitled *Of the Dominion, or, Ownership of the Sea*, printed by William Du-Gard in London (1652.1); presumably Du-Gard acquired these types (perhaps not the matrices) from Roger Daniel after the latter moved his business to London in 1650, so a commercial transaction was probably involved. After this publication the Wheelockian set of type-designs disappears from view, apart from a reissue of Du-Gard's printing in 1663.2.[50] The life-span of this type-design was just twelve years (1641–52). To judge from the number of books showing these two Anglo-Saxon founts Spelman and his printer seem to have guarded them carefully, and perhaps Wheelock too until Daniel moved to London. A curiosity occurs in 1678.1, the posthumous publication of Sir John Spelman's *Ælfredi Magni Anglorum Regis Invictissimi Vita*, ed. Obadiah Walker (aided by Christopher Wase), published in Oxford at the Sheldonian Theatre: the Anglo-Saxon type-design used was the Somnerian Pica acquired by the nascent Oxford University Press, but three instances of the Wheelockian Great Primer Anglo-Saxon capital E occur amongst the Somnerian Pica types on sigs 2P2^r, 2Q1^v, 2Q2.

Combined with the Great Primer Roman that it accompanies (see Illustration 19a) the body size of the Wheelockian Great Primer Anglo-Saxon is 118 mm for twenty lines: face 116 × 2.3: 3.5 (varies for different capitals). The following special sorts are shown: 12 (lower case) d, e, f, g, i, r, s, t, y; þ, ð, p; + 14 (upper case) Æ², C, D, E, F, G, H, I, M, S, T, U, Ð, P; + 4 (others) Þ, ꞇ, ɟ, · (raised point) = 30 sorts. All are shown in the reader's specimen on Illustration 19b, including the raised point (called a 'comma'), except square C, which can be seen in the text of Bede along with many other sorts (including Roman C) on Illustration 19a, where the use of the raised point is also illustrated.

The earlier, sixteenth-century, designs for Anglo-Saxon types exerted a profound influence on later designs, but some seventeenth-century founts show additional special sorts, and here the influence of continuing contact with manuscripts can potentially be traced. These additional special sorts tend to be capitals. Square C was first used in the Spelmanian set of designs of 1639 (AS4), where it is the only new sort in that fount, created somewhat crudely by taking a roman E and breaking off the middle arm. Square G first occurs in the Wheelockian set of designs in 1643 (AS5). Both occur in Anglo-Saxon manuscripts as secondary display capitals in, for example, CCC 173, containing the A-version of the *Anglo-Saxon Chronicle* and some Laws (see Illustration 20), a manuscript certainly used by Wheelock, and possibly by Spelman. Wheelock, Junius and the Somnerian fount use both square C and square G. In the

---

50   The main parts (sigs e–k, B–3R) constitute the re-issue.

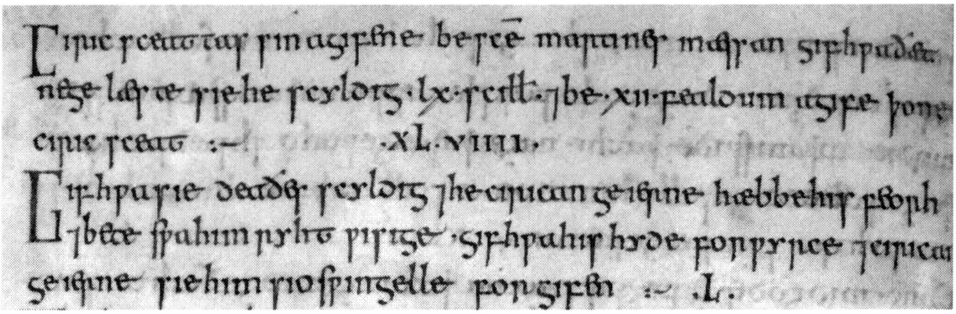

ILLUSTRATION 20   Cambridge, Corpus Christi College 173, 47ᵛ: Anglo-Saxon Laws of Ine 4–5.
Reduced to 75%

Wheelockian fount there are more special sort capitals than in any of these others. The presence of these extra specially designed letters creates the presumption that Wheelock was sensitive to the graphic form of script letters. In what follows, on the basis that correspondences can be observed between Wheelock's usage and that of the relevant manuscripts, I shall try to characterize the distinctive features of the Wheelockian Great Primer Anglo-Saxon with a view to defining which features show manuscript influence. As will be evident my concern is with what Michael Twyman called the intrinsic (as opposed to the extrinsic) features of verbal graphic language: the range of characters, the fount, the style of letter-forms, and the size of letter-forms.[51]

In describing the features of the type-design I follow as far as possible the terminology given for roman type in Gaskell, 'Nomenclature', which is invaluable. According to Gaskell roman letter-forms show stems, diagonals, bowls, counters, strokes, shoulders, arms, tails, spurs, ears, terminals and serifs. In his 'Glossary of terms', but not in his diagrammatic descriptions of the letters, he also uses the terms ascenders and descenders, which are part of the palaeographer's armoury, and certainly essential. Gaskell recognized that his nomenclature would require modification for dealing with type-faces other than roman, e.g., italic, and this limitation applies particularly to Anglo-Saxon,

---

51 Michael Twyman, 'The Graphic Presentation of Language', *Information Design Journal*, 3 (1982), pp. 2–22, at pp. 11–14. His distinction between intrinsic and extrinsic features of verbal graphic language has the merit of being non-judgemental. Scholars interested in the *mise en texte*, the disposition of text in relation to space on the page (i.e., extrinsic features), have referred to *la forme des signes graphiques, ce qui caractérise en réalité la page* as constituting *en quelque sorte le substrat*, but this seems to me to be special pleading (cf. Carla Bozzolo et al., 'Page Savante, Page Vulgaire: Étude Comparative de la Mise en Page des Livres en Latin et en Français écrits ou imprimés en France au xvᵉ Siècle', in E. Baumgartner & N. Boulestreau (eds), *La Présentation du Livre* (Paris x—Nanterre: Centre de Recherches du Département de Français, 1987), pp. 122–133, at p. 131.

since some of the letters are not roman. Gaskell's nomenclature, moreover, was not intended to describe the transition from script to print. Where writing is fluid, produced by the movement of the nib on smooth membrane or paper, type is fixed, the product of sculpting in metal. One of the main differences between humanistic script (of the period just before the development of roman type) and roman type is that, where letters written with the quill show a hooked terminal, either where the nib is led into the stroke, or where the nib is drawn away and lifted from the stroke, letters in roman type show serifs.[52] When a serif was made with a quill it required a separate stroke crossing the main stroke which it introduces or terminates, and the nib had to be held at a different angle.[53] Gaskell's term 'hooked terminal' is valuable in that it gives a separate name for the part of the stroke that in type is the equivalent of the written approach-stroke or termination-stroke. But it lacks the precision of palaeographical usage, which refers, for example, to descenders turned to the left, a description which, besides indicating that the terminal is hooked, states in which direction it is hooked. With these caveats in mind we can proceed.

Given the precedents from previous founts, the Parkerian Great Primer (AS1), the Parkerian Pica (AS2), the Lambardian Pica (AS3 which also appears in Wheelock's edition of the Anglo-Saxon Laws (1644.1) in the *Glossarium* on 2E1ʳ–4ʳ), and the Spelmanian Great Primer (AS4), there is nothing remarkable about the range of sorts selected for representation in the Wheelockian lower case; as in the Lambardian Pica tongued *e* is included. But the visual impact made by the fount as a whole is distinctive. From the Anglo-Saxon letters there is a general impression of sinuosity (see Illustration 19). In addition to the expected curves in the bowls, shoulders and tails of the relevant letters, there are a number of hooked terminals, as to **d** (ascender), **g** (approach stroke to upper arm), **t** (approach stroke to upper arm), all to the right, and to the left, **f** (descender), **r** (descender), **s** (descender, and upper stroke rolled right over), and **p** (descender). Hooked terminals in such numbers are more characteristic of script than type-design. There is a suggestion of attention to detail in the mimicking of a particular script feature in the way the ascender of **ð** is tagged to the left. Studies of early type-design have shown that 'the correct imitation

---

52   Cf. Carter, *View of Typography*, p. 48; Juliet S. Twomey, 'Whence Jenson. A Search for the Origins of Roman Type', *Fine Print*, 15 (1989), pp. 134–141.

53   When it was done it was often done sporadically to begin with (cf. Geoffrey D. Hargreaves, 'Florentine Script, Paduan Script, and Roman Type', *Gutenberg-Jahrbuch*, 67 (1992), pp. 15–34, at p. 17 re. Florence), although more thoroughly subsequently (Hargreaves, 'Florentine Script', p. 26 re. Padua).

of the best writing was the commonly understood goal', and there is every reason to suppose that the same approach applies in Wheelock's case.[54]

In the development of roman type-design the upper-case letters were based on classical Latin inscriptional forms with serifs at the terminals.[55] The lower-case letters were then modified to conform to this style so that where before there were hooked terminals, now wherever possible there were serifs.[56] The Wheelockian Great Primer Anglo-Saxon shows the opposite process. Having chosen so many sinuous forms for the lower case, he then proceeded to choose complimentary shapes for as many capitals as possible, so that their style matched that of the small letters.

The Wheelockian upper case shows a much larger number of sorts (14) than in the other design sets. The Parkerian Great Primer showed nine (Æ^1, Æ^2, E, H, M, S; Þ, Ð, Ƿ), but Wheelock has eliminated the duplication of two sorts of Æ (keeping the more curvacious one), and excluded Ƿ, presumably on the grounds that Ð will serve in all appropriate instances. He has therefore added seven more capitals, nearly all consonants: square C, D, F, square G, I, T, U. Apart from the square letters C and G (on which see further below), these all add to the overriding impression of sinuosity. The D is a round-backed form with a short ascender ending in a hooked terminal. F is similar to the lower-case form, showing a hooked approach stroke at the top of the stem, and a bowed upper arm with the terminal rolled over. Even I shows a hooked terminal to its tail. T is the insular form, similar to the lower-case, but with the stroke terminal scrolled. In the U the left part of the stroke is curved like a swan's neck, and the right stem has a hooked terminal at the base. Of the letters also found in earlier founts Wheelock's E takes the Greek form, as is to be expected, but both the upper and lower arms show scrolled terminals, creating a design suggestive of wrought-iron work. H takes the expected uncial form

---

54   Quotation from Nicolas Barker, *Aldus Manutius and the Development of Greek Script & Type in the Fifteenth Century* (New York: Fordham University Press, 1992), p. 69.

55   See, for example, Felice Feliciano (c.1460), *Alphabetum Romanum*, ed. G. Mardersteig, t R.H. Boothroyd (Verona: Officina Bodoni, 1960). Feliciano recommended that the height of the letter should be ten times the maximum thickness of the stroke: see his comments on the letter A on fo 1r (t p. 125) and the illustration on p. 58; he was followed in this respect by Moyllus (Moille), Dürer, and Tory, through whom ideas such as Feliciano's may have filtered through to the sixteenth-century French type-designers: see Matthew Carter, 'Theories of Letterform Construction. Part 1', *Printing History* 14 (1992), pp. 3–16. On constructed capital letters cf. Donald M. Anderson, *The Art of Written Forms: The Theory and Practice of Calligraphy* (New York: Dover, 1969), pp. 125–133; for a modern treatment see David L. Goines, *A Constructed Roman Alphabet: A Geometric Analysis of the Greek and Roman Capitals and of the Arabic Numerals* (Boston: D.R. Godine, 1982).

56   Carter, *View of Typography*; Twomey, 'Whence Jensen'; Hargreaves, 'Florentine Script'.

with the right stem curved inwards, but an added feature is the ornamental miniature loop attached to the shoulder-side of the upper stem. M also takes the expected uncial form and S follows the Parkerian S in showing the lower part of the stroke closing right back round on to the middle part of the stroke. P shows a hooked terminal to the descender and a rounded bowl. Of the other special sorts ⁊, the Tironian sign for 'and', also shows a hooked approach stroke and terminal to the descender.

In view of the general preference for sinuous shapes square C and square G are aberrations (see Illustrations 19a–19b). However, the square forms are often not used, and square C is not found at all in Wheelock's second book, his re-edition of the Anglo-Saxon Laws (1644.2). On this evidence it is reasonable to conclude that Wheelock himself was less than wholehearted in his enthusiasm for these square forms, since they do not contribute to the overall impression of sinuosity created by his Anglo-Saxon type-designs when considered as a set.[57]

There are, then, a number of innovations and distinctive features in the Wheelockian Great Primer Anglo-Saxon fount which may be tabulated as follows:

1. A general preference for sinuous shapes (apart from square C and G), shown particularly by numerous hooked terminals. This feature is correspondingly more important than the following ones, because it applies to a number of letter-forms.
2. Lower-case ð shows the ascender tagged to the left.
3. Upper-case square C.
4. Round-backed D, with a short ascender ending in a terminal gently hooked upwards.
5. E, with both the upper and the lower arms showing scrolled terminals.
6. F, showing a hooked approach stroke at the top of the stem, and a bowed upper arm with the terminal rolled over.
7. Square G.
8. H in uncial form with an ornamental miniature loop attached to the shoulder-side of the upper stem.
9. I, with a hooked terminal at the base of the stem.
10. T, similar to the lower-case, but with the stroke terminal scrolled.
11. U, with the left part of the stroke curved like a swan's neck, and the right stem showing a hooked terminal at the base.
12. P is rounded, not 'square' or sharply angled.

---

57 Alternatively the paucity of square Cs and Gs is the result of some technical problem with the supply of type.

In order to try to ascertain where Wheelock may have found inspiration for his innovations and preferences it is necessary to be sure which manuscripts he used. Only then can we examine the manuscripts to see whether or not they show the features with which those identified as characterizing his fount can be matched.

Work on the models for early roman type-designs in Italy has argued on the basis of what the Italians call a *coincidenza*.[58] The style of writing exhibited in manuscripts being written at a particular time and place (Padua in the 1460s) provided the model for the type produced at the same time in the same place (Padua 1470). Because of the contiguity of script and type-design there was a transference of letter shapes from one medium to the other: a *coincidenza*. For his Canon Roman (*TSF II*: 1567.16) and English-size Roman type designs (*TSF II*: 1567.22) Claude Garamond followed the design of some letters (**a, c, e, m, n, o, u**) from the sorts cut by Francesco Griffo for Pietro Bembo in his *De Ætna* (Aldus Manutius, 1495), and Giovanni Mardersteig showed that Garamond must have used a copy of the *De Ætna*, which Nicolas Barker suggests was brought back from Italy by Geofroy Tory.[59] An even stronger form of argument is possible. In the analysis above of the Parkerian Great Primer Anglo-Saxon, the first Anglo-Saxon type-design, I was able to show that the models for the designs were to be found amongst the manuscripts demonstrably used by Parker and his household, who then instructed the punchcutter. This form of argument is even more compelling than argument by *coincidenza*, and it applies to Wheelock's designs too.

As a reluctant traveller Wheelock apparently never went outside Cambridge to see a manuscript. Consequently nearly all the manuscripts he used were in Cambridge, and still are.[60] This scenario creates a situation analogous to the

---

58   Twomey, 'Whence Jensen'; Hargreaves, 'Florentine Script'.
59   Giovanni Mardersteig, 'Aldo Manuzio e i Caratteri di Francesco Griffo da Bologna', in *Studi di Bibliografia e di Storia in onore di Tamaro de Marinis*, 4 vols ([Verona], 1964), III.105–147, at pp. 133–134, to which attention was drawn by Nicolas Barker, 'The Aldine Roman in Paris, 1530–1534', *The Library*, v.29 (1974), pp. 5–20, at p. 11. Barker says that the relevant letters in three of Garamond's early designs were based on the Aldine model, of which it is sufficient to specify two here: the third he names as 'a *gros texte* for display'. For discussion of Barker's argument in relation to other work on French Old-Style Romans see Kay Amert, 'Origins of the French Old-Style: The Roman and Italic Types of Simon de Colines', *Printing History*, 14 (1992), pp. 17–40, at pp. 18–20.
60   The manuscripts used by Wheelock are approached from a different point of view by Hetherington, *OE Lexicography*, pp. 84–85 and 261–264. Her analysis is based on texts cited in an Anglo-Saxon Lexicon compiled by Wheelock (and others?) which survives in Harley 761, fos 2–86. Nearly all the items that she cites occur in my lists below, but exceptions will be dealt with in notes. Difficulty is caused by the fact that entries were put in

country-house detective novel: the potential suspects are circumscribed. As we shall see, they number about forty. On 27 December 1639 Wheelock wrote from Cambridge to Spelman in London as follows:

> I am at leasure fitting Bede his historie (by the help of six aunciet MS. Three in Lat. & three in Sax.) for the preſſe; I shall craue all convenient helps yo⟨ur⟩ worship may afford, w⟨i⟩th the iust acknowlegem⟨en⟩t of soe great hono⟨ur⟩ to that worke: a work fit to be reviewed since it lays out the first plantation, & progreſſe o[f] the Saxon church, & somwhat of consequence of the Britan⟨n⟩s, & since (by yo⟨ur⟩ worships Leaue,) I desire to reade this authour, & to compare him w⟨i⟩th Gildas in the most remarkeable paſſages of storie, & Doctrine, Ecclesiastical, & political: Dr Ward hath borrowed for me Sr Thom: Cottons aunciet Latin MS. I meane Bede his hist. &[c.] & I find both it, & the other two Latin MS. agree w⟨i⟩th all other new copies concerninge Augustines death before the death of my oulde neighbors the Monckes of Bangor-Eiscoid.'[61]

The only manuscripts from outside Cambridge that Wheelock saw were two borrowed from Sir Thomas Cotton, who had inherited the great collection put together by his father, Sir Robert. One was Otho B.xi (since severely damaged in the 1731 fire), containing the Anglo-Saxon version of Bede's *Historia Ecclesiastica* and the *Anglo-Saxon Chronicle* (G), used for collation for the Bede and as the main text for the *Chronicle* in Wheelock's 1643.1 edition.[62] The other was a Latin Bede, probably Tiberius C.ii, borrowed through the good offices of Samuel Ward, Master of Sidney Sussex College. On 31 March 1640 Wheelock wrote to Sir Thomas asking to be able to keep 'these pretious Monuments [in margin:] Bede his Hist. Lat. et Sax.', i.e., one Latin Bede and one Anglo-Saxon Bede, somewhat longer than originally projected, and he evidently did so.[63]

---

at different times, and it is by no means certain that Wheelock was responsible for all the entries in the Lexicon, though he was certainly the last to work on it. The present analysis is on firmer ground, although Hetherington's work provides useful corroboration for most of the manuscripts used.

61 BL Additional 34600, fo 195. The allusion at the end is predicated on Wheelock's Shropshire origins.

62 Where the A-version in CCC 173 was used for purposes of collation; cf. Angelika Lutz, 'The Study of the Anglo-Saxon Chronicle in the Seventeenth Century and the Establishment of Old English Studies in the Universities', in Timothy Graham (ed.), *The Recovery of Old English: Anglo-Saxon Studies in the Sixteenth and Seventeenth Centuries* (Kalamazoo MI: Western Michigan University, 2000), pp. 1–82, at pp. 34–40.

63 The lettter is in BL Julius F.vi, fo 123, and is printed in Ellis, *Original Letters of Eminent Literary Men*, p. 160, no. lviii. In a note Ellis thinks that both manuscripts were Latin

For the text of the Anglo-Saxon translation of Bede's *Historia Ecclesiastica* he followed CUL Kk.3.18, collated with CCC 41 and Cotton Otho B.xi.[64] For the Latin text of Bede he collated three manuscripts: TCC R.5.22 (s. xiv), CSS 102 (*olim* D.5.17; s. xv), and the Cotton manuscript, probably Tiberius C.ii.[65]

The texts used by Wheelock for the West Saxon Genealogical Regnal List require special comment. The work occurs in the 1643.1 edition of Bede between the preface and the list of chapter headings, as only in Kk.3.18 amongst the manuscripts, which Wheelock followed as his main text.[66] He collated it with two other versions, his B and C. B is CCC 173, fo 1^r.[67] C is not Otho B.xi, from which the relevant leaf, now BL Additional 34652, fo 2, was removed in the early modern period; suggestions for the 'culprit' include Sir Robert Cotton himself, and William L'Isle, but the deed was probably done earlier, in the sixteenth century.[68] C is Tiberius A.iii, fo 178, which was itself removed from Tiberius A.vi, fos 1–35, possibly, as Sisam suggested (with different reasoning),

---

Bedes, but Wheelock only claims to have used one Latin Bede borrowed from Cotton via Ward, and of the two manuscripts mentioned in the letter one has to be Otho B.xi. The other manuscript mentioned by Ellis is Tiberius A.xiv, also an eighth-century Latin Bede (Lowe, CLA, Suppl., no. 1703); it is possible that Wheelock used this manuscript rather than Tiberius C.ii. In the unlikely event that he did so the tenor of the present argument is not affected. Tiberius C.ii also contains glosses: see P. Vaciago, 'Old English Glosses to Latin Texts: A Bibliographical Handlist', *Medioevo e Rinascimento*, 4 (1993), pp. 1–67, at p. 16, no. 64. The Latin Bede 'bound with my armes' had been borrowed by Ward from Sir Robert Cotton's library earlier (BL Harley 6018, fo 159^v), and when he lent it to Ussher he wrote (1624) 'I will expect the book from you, when you have done with it, for that I would keep it till Sir Robert restore a book of mine', quoted by James P. Carley, 'Books seen by Samuel Ward 'in Bibliotheca Regia', circa 1614', *British Library Journal*, 16 (1990), pp. 89–98, at p. 92, from Charles R. Elrington, *The Whole Works of the most Rev. James Ussher*, 17 vols (Dublin: Hodges, Smith & Co., 1847–64), xv.229. Presumably Wheelock restored the manuscript to Sir Thomas after Ward's death in 1642.

64 CCC 41 was borrowed from Corpus by Wheelock: Graham, 'Wheelock's Use', pp. 13–15.

65 Bede's *Historia Ecclesiastica* in TCC R.5.22 comprises Part I, fos 1–43. Part III, fos 72–158, is an eleventh-century copy of the Alfredian translation of Pope Gregory's *Cura Pastoralis*, which must be included amongst the Anglo-Saxon manuscripts possibly studied by Wheelock. As noted by Oates, *Cambridge University Library*, p. 204, he also used SJC 27, a fourteenth-century Latin Bede, but it was not a significant influence.

66 See David Dumville, 'The West Saxon Genealogical Regnal List: Manuscripts and Text', *Anglia*, 104 (1986), pp. 1–32. For a diplomatic edition of the some of the texts available to Wheelock (CCC 173, CCC 383, Tiberius A.iii, fo 178, and also extracts copied by Robert Recorde s.xvi in CCC 138) see Bruce Dickins, *The Genealogical Preface to the Anglo-Saxon Chronicle*, Occasional Papers 2 (Cambridge: Department of Anglo-Saxon, 1952).

67 Wheelock also had access to the Genealogical List in CCC 383, fo 108^v/3–26, but there is no evidence that he made any use of it.

68 Cotton as the culprit was first suggested by Sisam, *Studies*, p. 334, n. 1. Sisam notes that Cotton was working on a genealogy of James I, tracing it back to Alfred: PRO SP 14/1/3

by Cotton.[69] These findings are confirmed by the reading at the end of the first paragraph in Dumville's edition: Wheelock reads 'winter', a reading that must come from Tiberius A.iii, fo 178, because all other witnesses have *gear* 'year'.[70] Presumably Wheelock was supplied by Sir Thomas Cotton with Tiberius A.iii, fo 178, as well as, or together with, Otho B.xi (which lacked what is now Add. 34652, fo 2).[71]

Wheelock's appointment to the Lectureship in Anglo-Saxon at Cambridge was encouraged by Archbishop Ussher of Armagh. Thus counselled Wheelock inherited the Parkerian view of Anglo-Saxon materials as useful for bolstering the doctrine and practice of the Church of England.[72] This approach, spelt out in the dedication to Cambridge University, is heralded in his letter to Spelman dated 13 June 1638:

    'A discourse of ye discent of the K's Majesty from the Saxons' 26 March 1603. For the suggestion that L'Isle was the culprit see Ker, *Catalogue*, no. 180 on p. 234.

69 The identification of Tiberius A.iii, fo 178, as C was noted previously by Dorothy Whitelock, 'The Old English Bede', *Proceedings of the British Academy*, 48 (1962), pp. 57–90, at p. 60, and nn. 23–4 on p. 81. For a zincograph facsimile of fo 178ʳ see Benjamin Thorpe, *The Anglo-Saxon Chronicle according to the several original authorities*, 2 vols, RS 23 (London: Longman, Green, Longman & Roberts, 1861), I, pl. vii. Tiberius A.vi, fos 1–35, contains ASC B, for which see S. Taylor, *The Anglo-Saxon Chronicle: A Collaborative Edition, Volume 4, MS B* (Cambridge: Brewer, 1983), pp. xvi–xvii.

70 Dumville, 'Regnal List', p. 22, textual note 47. The text in Tiberius A.iii, fo 178, was copied (1) by Laurence Nowell the antiquary (at Sir William Cecil's house in 1562) on fos 5–6ʳ of BL, Additional 43703, in which there follows a transcript of the OE version of Bede's *Historia Ecclesiastica* (from Otho B.xi) which lacks the Genealogical Regnal List from what is now Add. 34652, fo 2 (presumably already removed from Otho B.xi), and (2) by a Parkerian scribe in OBL Laud misc.661, fos 44–5, where it follows a transcript of the *Anglo-Saxon Chronicle* (B) from Tiberius A.vi, to which it originally belonged, and presumably still belonged in Parker's time. Nowell's transcript in Add. 43703 is preceded by the list of popes who sent pallia to Canterbury, a copy evidently taken from Tiberius A.vi, fo 35ᵛ, in which manuscript the list of popes also immediately preceded the Genealogical Regnal List (before that was removed). This evidence suggests that the Genealogical Regnal List (i.e. Add. 34652, fo 2) was removed from Otho B.xi before Cotton's time, and that the Genealogical Regnal List (i.e. Tiberius A.iii, fo 178) was removed from Tiberius A.vi at a later time, possibly (by Cotton?) to supply the gap in Otho B.xi (to which there is no objection as regards the relative sizes of the manuscripts, as Otho was originally larger than Tiberius (244 × 177mm as opposed to 228 × 158mm).

71 When Franciscus Junius (1591–1677) made his transcript of the List (OBL Junius 66 (SC 5177), pp. 19–20) from what is now Tiberius A.iii, fo 178, it was already part of this codex, as he refers to it as coming from the same codex as contained Ælfric's Colloquy, viz. Tiberius A.iii, fos 60ᵛ–64ᵛ. On the assumption that Wheelock borrowed what is now Tiberius A.iii, fo 178 (together with Otho B.xi) and did not go to London to see it, perhaps it joined Tiberius A.iii on return from him; some such explanation is required to account for its incorporation in Tiberius A.iii.

72 Cf. Murphy, 'Wheloc's Edition', pp. 46–59.

> I am now readinge of Beda, with King Alured his translation. which[,] I see, will correct many thinges, ... but the maine busines which possesseth my thoughts, is, the discovery (out of Bede, & others, especiallie in manuscripts) of the Apostolical doctrine, by comparinge our present church with the aunciaent church here in England: which work will most properlie suite with your reader [i.e. Wheelock himself], because he is to be a searcher of truthes out of the fountaines themselues.[73]

Wheelock used his edition of Bede as a vehicle to communicate what he thought of as supporting evidence from other texts, mainly homilies; for full details see the entry for **1643.1** in Part 2 below. According to my analysis Wheelock cites passages from 84 separate homilies, and he prints in full two of Ælfric's Catholic Homilies, second series: on sigs 3C4^v–3E2^v 'in dedicatione ecclesiae', and on sigs 3O3^v–3Q2^r 'in die Pascae'.[74] Cambridge manuscripts from which he took this illustrative material include CUL Gg.3.28, Ii.1.33, Ii.4.6, CCC 162, 191, 198, 419, TCC B.15.34, and R.4.26 (containing Middle English, but the extracts printed by Wheelock utilize his Anglo-Saxon types).[75]

Wheelock also made transcripts of Old English texts for Sir Henry Spelman, which the latter used for his *Concilia* of **1639.4**. For these Wheelock certainly used CCC 201 and 383.[76] In his *Cambridge University Library* Oates suggests that Wheelock also made transcripts of Latin texts for Spelman from Corpus 190 and 279, and from CTH 1, but while the suggestion is eminently plausible,

---

[73] BL Add. 25384, fo 29^v.

[74] Respectively Godden, *Catholic Homilies*, XL, 335–345 and Godden, *Catholic Homilies*, XV, 150–160. For the latter Wheelock collated the text printed in L'Isle (**1623.1**: O2^v–R3^v) with that in CUL Gg.3.28, as can be seen in Wheelock's own copy of **1623.1** (CUL Adv.d.48.10).

[75] Ii.4.6 is annotated by Wheelock, e.g. on fos 258^v–259^r. From CCC 162, p. 563, Wheelock also transcribed the end of Ælfric, CH, I.xl, in CUL Gg.3.28, fo 134 top margin, to supply the text missing from this homily (Dominica II in adventu Domini; Peter Clemoes, *Ælfric's Catholic Homilies: The First Series: Text*, Early English Text Society, Supplementary Series 17 (Oxford: Oxford University Press, 1997), pp. 530/185–8) as a consequence of fo 133 being lost. With regard to CCC 191 Wheelock borrowed it from Corpus: see Timothy Graham, 'Abraham Wheelock's Use of CCCC MS 41 (Old English Bede) and the Borrowing of Manuscripts from the Library of Corpus Christi College', *Cambridge Bibliographical Society Newsletter* (Summer 1997), pp. 10–16, at p. 14. A transcript of it made for Wheelock survives as BL Harley 440. Corpus 419 contains Wheelock's embryonic index at fos i–ii^r, pp. 368–370. TCC R.4.26 contains Wheelock's embryonic index at fos a–d, 164–165.

[76] Wheelock borrowed CCC 201 from Corpus: see Graham, 'Wheelock's Use', p. 14. His transcript of the Canons of Edgar (dated 25 Oct 1637) from CCC 201 survives in BL Add. 35333, art. 5. In the *Concilia* Spelman claims CCC 383 (fos 57^v/23–58^v/4) as his source for the Law *Be wifmannes beweddunge* (Liebermann, *Gesetze*, I.442–444) on sig. 2M2^r.

there are apparently no surviving transcripts to confirm the supposition.[77] Wheelock also transcribed on eight leaves of paper the beginning of Ælfric's homily on the Assumption of the Virgin Mary (CH, I.xxx) from CCC 188, pp. 318/1–326/19, in order to make good the textual lacuna in CUL Gg.3.28, where they are bound in between fos 94/97.[78] Other manuscripts consulted by Wheelock include CCC 138 (from which Wheelock transcribed an unwanted extract for Spelman), 140 (which Spelman asked Wheelock to compare a reading from in his letter of 5 September 1638), and 318, from which the Latin life of Bede, art. 4 (pp. 356–62), was taken to preface the *Historia Ecclesiastica*.[79] He also consulted CUL Ff.1.27 (with twelve leaves of index notes by Wheelock), Ff.1.28 (annotated by Wheelock, e.g., fos 78^v, 88^v, 138^v, 235^r), Hh.1.10 (with an embryonic index by Wheelock on fos iii–vi), Ii.2.4 (in which Wheelock noted on the inside of the front cover that he read it between 3 September 1638 and 17 July 1639), and Ii.2.11 (which Spelman asked Wheelock to compare a reading from in his letter of 5 September 1638).[80] Wheelock must also have seen

---

77   Spelman certainly used CCC 190 and 279, but whether he had transcripts of them is moot. The 'Capitula libri poenitentialis Theodori archiepiscopi' on sig. M5 of the *Concilia*, the 'Capitula de Sacerdotali jure Egberti Archiepiscopi' on sig. Y6^v–Z1^r and the 'Capitula de libro Scintillarum' on sig. Z1^v are from CCC 190, pp. vi—x, as acknowledged for the latter two by Spelman on sig. Y6^v and Z1^v. The 'Synodus S. Patricii' on sigs D1^v–2^v is from CCC 279, pp. 1–10, as acknowledged by Spelman on sig. D2^v. Likewise Spelman certainly used CTH 1. The 'De fundatione primarum ecclesiarum' on sigs I1^v–K1^v (pp. 112–24) is from CTH 1 (as ed. Hardwick 1858: pp. 77/1–90/11, 109/27–110/26, 111/29–113/3, 114/4–116/15, 119/16–124/20), as acknowledged by Spelman on I1^v; so also is the 'Epitaphium Sancti Gregorii' on E3^v (p. 68; as ed. Hardwick 1858: 124–125). The transcript of CTH 1 in BL Harley 686 is not by Wheelock. The suggestion was made by Oates in his *Cambridge University Library*, p. 199. His suggestion that Wheelock made a transcript from CUL Ff.1.27 for Spelman seems improbable since Spelman borrowed the manuscript himself (Oates, *Cambridge University Library*, p. 200, and n. 19).

78   Wheelock notes on his paper transcript (fo 2^v) that he took the transcript from 'Col. Ben. Cantabr. vol. 3. p. 318', a reference to Parker's third book of homilies, now CCC 188. The transcribed text corresponds to Clemoes, *Catholic Homilies*, pp. 429/4–434/150 eadige. Wheelock's embryonic index occurs in CCC 188 at pp. ii–vii.

79   On CCC 138: Spelman to Wheelock 22 September 1637 in CUL Dd.3.12, fo 10. Cf. Oates, *Cambridge University Library*, p. 198; Spelman thought the extract of little use, and it has apparently not survived. Spelman to Wheelock about CCC 140: CUL Dd.3.12, fo 31.

80   With reference to CUL Ff.1.27 the 'Synodus apud Acleam' on sig. 2B2^r (p. 305) is excerpted from Richard of Hexham on p. 230a/17–25, as acknowledged by Spelman; for the subject-matter see A.W. Haddan & W. Stubbs, *Councils and Ecclesiastical Documents*, 3 vols (Oxford: Clarendon Press, 1869–73), II.464. In the manuscript there is a mark (and three others on pp. 228, 230) beside this passage in the margin. The mark is somewhat like an H with the two stems consisting of upright spears linked by a double cross-bar tilted down from left to right with a small o between the cross-bars in the centre. It was presumably made by Spelman (not Wheelock). On the manuscript see David N. Dumville,

CUL Ff.1.23 and TCC R.17.1 (the Eadwine or Canterbury Psalter), both of which Spelman borrowed through Wheelock's good offices so that his son John could work on them for his edition of the Anglo-Saxon Psalter (1640.3).[81] Wheelock also presumably saw TCC R.5.16, another manuscript borrowed (on two separate occasions) by Spelman.[82] This information about the manuscripts used by Wheelock is summarized in Tables 1–3, where the first column on the left gives the institution holding the manuscript, the second the class-mark, the third

'The Sixteenth-Century History of Two Cambridge Books from Sawley', *Transactions of the Cambridge Bibliographical Society*, 7:4 (1980), pp. 427–44, at pp. 433–437. There is a transcript of CUL Hh.1.10 (Ælfric's Grammar) made for Sir Symonds D'Ewes (who borrowed it from Cambridge) in BL Harley 8, fos 5ʳ–72ʳ; the transcript is annotated in the margins by D'Ewes for the purposes of extrapolating words for use in his Dictionary. Hetherington, *OE Lexicography*, p. 263, claims that Wheelock also knew BL Faustina A.x (Ælfric's Grammar; siglum F), citing as evidence the alleged occurrence in the margin of 'corr. F.' beside the entry for 'Laupenbeam, Laurus'; this entry occurs on fo 49ʳ, but I could find no sign of the marginal note. I have found no evidence that Wheelock used Faustina A.x. In Ii.2.4 Wheelock wrote on fo 3ʳ 'Sum Bibliotheca publicæ Cantabrigiensis', presumably as a reminder to anyone who borrowed it (including himself!) of where it belonged. There are notes by Wheelock on fo 150ʳ. Regarding Ii.2.11 Hetherington, *OE Lexicography*, pp. 85, 264, claims that Wheelock used BL Royal 1.A.xiv (AS Gospels), but she cites no evidence. In Harley 761, on fo 88ʳ, there occurs what purports to be a list of sources which read (before it was amended) 'Euang: Sax. impressa in Bib: pub. Cant. 2. MS v in Coll. Regal.i.', which I interpret as saying that Foxe's Anglo-Saxon Gospels (1571.1) used as a source occur in CUL Ii.2.11 with variants taken from Royal 1.A.xiv; Hetherington's misreading of MS 'in' as 'M.' and her failure to note what was written first and what was written later, *OE Lexicography*, p. 261, n. 82, has resulted in her misunderstanding. I have found no evidence that Wheelock used Royal 1.A.xiv.

81 With regard to CUL Ff.1.23 David N. Dumville, 'On the Dating of Some Late Anglo-Saxon Liturgical Manuscripts', *Transactions of the Cambridge Bibliographical Society*, 10 (1991), pp. 40–57, at pp. 40–41, dates it earlier in the eleventh century than has traditionally been the case. For a reduced monochrome facsimile of TCC R.17.1 see Montague R. James, *The Canterbury Psalter* (London: P. Lund, Humphries & Co., 1935). Folios 164ʳ–70ᵛ are reproduced in full-size colour facsimile in Fred C. Robinson and E.G. Stanley, *Old English Verse Texts from many Sources: A Comprehensive Collection*, EEMF xxiii (Copenhagen: Rosenkilde & Bagger, 1991), no. 30. On the manuscript see Margaret Gibson et al. (eds), *The Eadwine Psalter: Text, Image, and Monastic Culture in Twelfth-Century Canterbury* (London: Modern Humanities Research Association, 1992), with many illustrations, and especially Teresa Webber on the script of the Anglo-Saxon gloss on pp. 18–21, with which compare Phil Pulsiano, 'The Scribes and Old English Gloss of the Eadwine's Canterbury Psalter', in *Proceedings of the Patristic, Mediaeval and Renaissance Conference* (Villanova University, Augustinian Historical Institute), 14 (1989), pp. 223–60. See also Vaciago, 'OE Glosses', p. 9, no. 31. For the borrowing of the TCC manuscript by Spelman cf. Oates, *Cambridge University Library*, pp. 200–203, and David McKitterick in Gibson et al., *Eadwine Psalter*, pp. 198–199. It was returned together with CUL Ff.1.23 (Spelman to Wheelock 17 September 1639, as recorded in CUL Dd.3.12, fo 49).

82 As is evident from Spelman's letter to Wheelock of 8 December 1637 (CUL Dd.3.12, fo 15).

TABLE 6   Manuscripts from which Wheelock took text for printed books or surviving transcripts

Institution	Shelf-mark	Date	Contents	Provenance
CUL	Gg.3.28	s.x/xi	Ælfric, homilies	Durham
	Ii.1.33	s.xii^2	homilies, saints' lives	Exeter
	Ii.4.6	s.xi^{med}	homilies	Tavistock (Devon)
	Kk.3.18	s.xi$^{3/4}$	AS Bede	Worcester
CCC	41	s.xi^1	AS Bede, homilies	Exeter
	162	s.xi^{in}	homilies	South East: Rochester, or Canterbury St Augustine's
	173	s.ix/x—xi^2	AS Chronicle (A)	Canterbury Christ Church
	188	s.xi^1	homilies	not known
	191	s.xi$^{3/4}$	Rule of Chrodegang	Exeter
	198	s.xi^1, xi^2	homilies	Worcester
	201 (pp. 1–178)	s.xi^{in}/xi^{med}	homilies, laws, etc.	not known
	201 (pp. 179–272)	s.xi^{med}	Capitula of Theodulf, etc.	Exeter
	318	s.xiii	Latin Life of Bede, etc.	Rochester
	383	s.xi/xii	laws	London St Paul's
	419	s.xi^1	homilies	Canterbury/Exeter
CSJ	27	s.xiv	Latin Bede	Pleshey College (Essex)
CSS	102 (olim D.5.17)	s.xv	Latin Bede	Bury St Edmunds
TCC	B.15.34	s.xi^{med}	homilies	Canterbury?
	R.4.26	s.xiv^2	ME verse Chronicle attrib. 'Robert of Gloucester'	not known
	R.5.22 (fos 1–43)	s.xiv	Latin Bede	not known
	(fos 44–71)	s.xii	Latin Saints' Lives	not known
	(fos 72–158)	s.x/xi	OE Pastoral Care	Sherborne
BL Cotton	Otho B xi	s.x^{med}/xi^1	AS Bede, ASC (G), laws	Winchester, Southwick
	Tiberius A.iii, fo 178	s.x^2	WS Geneal. Regnal List	Abingdon, Canterbury St Augustine's
	Tiberius C.ii	s.viii^{ex}	Latin Bede	Lindisfarne

TABLE 7   Other manuscripts for which there is evidence of use by Wheelock

Institution	Shelf-mark	Date	Contents	Provenance
CUL	Ff.1.27 (pp. 1–40, 73–252)	s.xii^2/xiii^1	Gildas, Nennius, etc.	Sawley (Yorks)
	Ff.1.27 (pp. 253–642, 41–72)	s.xii^2/xiv	Gerald of Wales, etc.	Bury St Edmunds
	Ff.1.28	s.xv	Richard of Cirencester	not known
	Hh.1.10	s.xi$^{3/4}$/xii	Ælfric, Grammar	Exeter
	Ii.2.4	s.xi$^{3/4}$	OE Pastoral Care	Exeter
	Ii.2.11	s.xi$^{3/4}$	gospels	Exeter
CCC	138	s.xiv	Chronica varia	Norwich
	140	s.xi^1/xii	gospels, etc.	Bath

TABLE 8   Other manuscripts for which there is presumed evidence of use by Wheelock

Institution	Shelf-mark	Date	Contents	Provenance
CUL	Ff.1.23	s.xi^{med}	Glossed Psalter	(?) Canterbury St Augustine's
CCC	173, fos 59–83	s.viii^2	Sedulius	Winchester, Canterbury
	190 (A)	s.xi^1	Penitentials	Exeter
	190 (B)	s.xi^{med}	ecclesiastical institutes	Exeter
	279	s.ix/x	Synodus Patricii, Canones	Worcester
TCC	R.5.16	s.xiv	Johannes Glastoniensis	Glastonbury
	R.17.1	s.xii^{med}	Glossed Psalter	Canterbury Christ Church
CTH	1	s.xv	Thomas of Elmham	Canterbury St Augustine's

the date when it was written (in which the form s.xi$^{3/4}$ means the third quarter of the eleventh century), the fourth the contents (abbreviated), and the fifth the provenance.[83] Of course, as University Librarian, Wheelock had access to all the manuscripts in the University Library, and, no doubt, to any he wished to see in the Colleges.

Of the twelve features identified above as distinctive or innovatory in Wheelock's Great Primer Anglo-Saxon, lower-case ð with a prominent ascender tagged to the left is characteristic of manuscripts from the second half of the eleventh century.[84] It is probably no coincidence that so many of the manuscripts in the list of those used by Wheelock are from the middle or second half of the eleventh century. However, there are also a number of later medieval manuscripts, and two considerably earlier ones, from the end of the eighth century. So, with the twelve features in mind, I returned to the manuscripts listed in Table 6–8 to see whether or not they showed similar features. Since hooked terminals are so numerous in Wheelock's type-designs I have limited the search in the manuscripts to descenders turned to the left. The results are set out in Table 9 and includes not only Anglo-Saxon manuscripts but also later medieval manuscripts, which cannot be expected to show those features that are exclusively Anglo-Saxon. The material condensed into this Table is generally representative of the usage in each manuscript concerned, but occasionally the usage recorded for individual capitals indicates existence rather than the norm. In CUL Ii.2.11, for example, round-backed D is marked as present, but I found it only on fo 118^v in 'Duo'. Although occasional variations

---

83 Following Ker, *Catalogue*, collated with Ker/Watson, *Medieval Libraries*.
84 Ker, *Catalogue*, p. xxxi.

TABLE 9   Summary of occwurrence of distinctive/innovatory features in relevant AS MSS

	1	2	3/7		4	5	6	8	9	10	11	12
	Hooked descender terminals	ð with ascender tagged to left	L	L̵	D square backed	Є with scrolled arms	F with bowed upper arm	Ꝺ with miniature loop	I with hooked terminal	T with stroke terminal scrolled	U with curved left stroke	ꝑ round-backed
MSS												
Cambridge University Library												
Gg.3.28	x	x	√	√	√	x	√	x	√	x	√	√
Ii.1.33	√	x	x	x	x	x	x	x	√	x	x	√
Ii.4.6	x	x	x	√	√	x	√	x	x	x	√	√
Kk.3.18	x	x	x	x	x	x	x	x	x	x	√	√
Ff.1.27												
(pp. 1–40, 73–252)	-	-	-	-	√	x	-	x	-	√	√	-
(pp. 253–642)	-	-	-	-	√	x	-	x	-	x	√	-
Ff.1.28	-	-	-	-	-	x	-	x	-	x	x	-
Hh.1.10	√	x	x	x		x	x	x	x	x	√	√
Ii.2.4	√	√	x	x	x	x	x	x	x	x	x	√
Ii.2.11	√	√	x	x	√	x	x	x	x	x	√	√
Ff.1.23F	x	√	√	√	√	x	x	x	x	x	√	-
Cambridge, Corpus Christi College												
41	x	x	x	√	x	x	x	x	x	x	x	√
162	x	x	√	√	x	x	-	x?	x	x	-	√
173	x	x	√	√	x	x	x	x	√	x	x	x
173 (fos 59–83)	x	-	x	x	√	x	√	x	√	x	√	-
188	√	x	x	x	√	x	√	x	√	x	√	√
191	√	√	x	√	√	x	x	x	x	x	√	√
198	√	x	x	x	x	x	x	x	x	x	√	√
201 (pp. 1–178)	x	x	x	√	√	x	x	x	√	x	√	√
(pp. 179–272)	√	√	x	x	√	x	x	x	x	x	√	√
318	-	-	-	-	-	x	-	x	-	x	-	-
383	√	x	x	x	x	x	x	x	x	x	√	√
419	√	√	x	x	x	x	x	x	x	x	√	√
138	-	-	-	-	-	x	-	x	-	x	-	-
140	x	√	x	√	√	x	x	x	√	x	√	√
190 (A)	x	√	x	x	√	x	x	x	√	√	√	x

ANGLO-SAXON TYPE-DESIGNS IN THE 17TH CENTURY TO 1705   113

	1	2	3/7		4	5	6	8	9	10	11	12
	Hooked	ð	L	Ŀ	D	Ꞓ	F	Þ	I	T	U	Þ
	descender with terminals	with ascender tagged to left	square		round-backed	with scrolled arms	with bowed upper arm	with miniature loop	with hooked terminal	with stroke terminal scrolled	with curved left stroke	round-backed
190 (B)	√	√	x	x	x	x	x	x	x	x	√	√
279	x	-	√	x	√	x	√	x	x	x	√	-
Cambridge, St John's College												
27	-	-	-	-	-	x	-	x	-	x	-	-
Cambridge, Sidney Sussex College												
102	-	-	-	-	-	x	-	x	-	x	-	-
Cambridge, Trinity College												
B.15.34	x	√	√	√	√	x	x	x	x	x	√	√
R.4.26	-	-	-	-	-	x	-	x	-	x	-	-
R.5.22												
(fos 1–43)	-	-	-	-	-	x	-	x	-	x	-	-
(fos 44–71)	x	-	-	-	√	x	x	x	x	x	√	-
(fos 72–158)	x	x	√	√	√	x	√	x	x	x	√	√
R.5.16	-	-	-	-	-	x	-	x	-	x	x	-
R.17.1	√	x	√	x	√	x	x	x	√	x	√	√
Cambridge, Trinity Hall												
1	-	-	-	-	-	x	-	x	-	√	-	-
British Library, Cotton MSS												
Otho B.xi[a]	x	x	x	x	x	x	√	x	x	x	x	√
Tiberius A.iii, fo 178	x	x	x	x	x	x	x	x	x	x	x	x
Tiberius C.ii	x	-	√	x	√	x	√	x	√	x	√	-

Note: Some manuscripts marked as not showing insular capital T with the stroke terminally scrolled do, nevertheless, show insular-shaped capital T (with a curve but no scroll): viz. CUL Gg.3.28 (fos 28ᵛ, 34ᵛ, etc.), CCC 140 (Scribe 3, fo 102ᵛ), CCC 188 (p. 447), CCC 201 (p. 4), CCC 279 (p. 126), TCC R.17.1 (fo 195ᵛ, with illuminated example on fo 221ʳ), Otho B.xi (fo 30ᵛ), Tiberius C.ii (fo 60ᵛ), and also CUL Ff.1.27 (pp. 253–642, e.g., at p. 286, with round-backed D at p. 303), and Ff.1.28 (fo 135ʳ; this manuscript also shows capital I with a curved terminal on fo 79ᵛ and U with a curved left stroke (but closed at the top) on fo 10ʳ).

[a] Otho B.xi was seriously damaged by the 1731 fire, so for the purposes of characterizing elements of script I have also examined the leaf detached from it before the fire, Additional 34652, fo 2, even though there is every indication that Wheelock did not see it.

from the usage recorded here may be found, none are of significance as far as the present argument is concerned.[85]

In Anglo-Saxon manuscripts there was as in other manuscripts a hierarchy of scripts.[86] To state the matter somewhat simplistically with manuscripts from the tenth century onwards in mind: first, at the top of the hierarchy, were illuminated display capitals, secondly there were secondary display capitals, and thirdly the minuscule of the text. For the capitals that were appropriate to have provided models for the Wheelockian type-designs we should look particularly at the secondary display capitals, since these were made by scribes using the nib to make letter-strokes without ornamentation. These Anglo-Saxon secondary display capitals show a mixture of square, rustic and uncial forms.[87] Such forms were often used by a single scribe, not systematically as in Carolingian manuscripts from Tours, but in conjunction with each other without apparent differentiation.[88] For example, in all relevant manuscripts square C, G, S and P are nearly always accompanied in the same hand by rustic (round) C, G, S and P. Uncial D and M appear side by side rustic D and M, and uncial E, F, H and T occur side by side square E, F, H and T.

While some features, such as curvacious U and rounded P, are relatively common in the manuscripts, others, such as uncial T with the stroke terminal scrolled, are rare, and some, such as uncial E with scrolled arms, do not occur at all. Some of the post-Anglo-Saxon manuscripts show nothing of relevance to Wheelock's type-designs. Of the Anglo-Saxon ones no one manuscript provides the models for all the design features of Wheelock's Anglo-Saxon sorts.

---

85   Some manuscripts are written by more than one scribe. For example, CUL Ii.1.33 is written (probably) in two hands, the first of which rarely shows hooked terminals, while the second shows them more frequently. In this case, in the interests of inclusiveness, I have indicated the presence of hooked terminals in the manuscript. Similarly in CCC 198 the main scribes 2 and 4 show hooked terminals, whereas scribes 1 and 3 do not, so I have indicated them as present. In CCC 162 Scribe 2 (p. 565 only) shows ð with the ascender tagged to the left, but, since Scribe 1 does not show the feature, I have marked it as lacking in the manuscript. On the other hand in CCC 190(A) Anglo-Saxon is present only in additions made by various scribes, so the presence of ð with the ascender tagged to the left on p. 246 gains an indication of its occurrence in this part of the manuscript. CCC 140 has each gospel written by a separate scribe, of whom only the Matthew scribe sometimes shows hooked terminals, so I have indicated them as absent, since this is the predominant impression given by the manuscript. Fragmentary manuscripts, such as Tiberius A.iii, fo 178, have insufficient text to show the features of capitals.

86   The classic statement of this concept is by B.L. Ullman, *Ancient Writing and its Influence* (London: Harrap, 1932), p. 113.

87   For a convenient account of the development of these forms see E.M. Thompson, *An Introduction to Greek and Latin Palaeography* (Oxford: Clarendon Press, 1912), pp. 272–297.

88   The usage at Tours is noted by Ullman, *Ancient Writing*, p. 113.

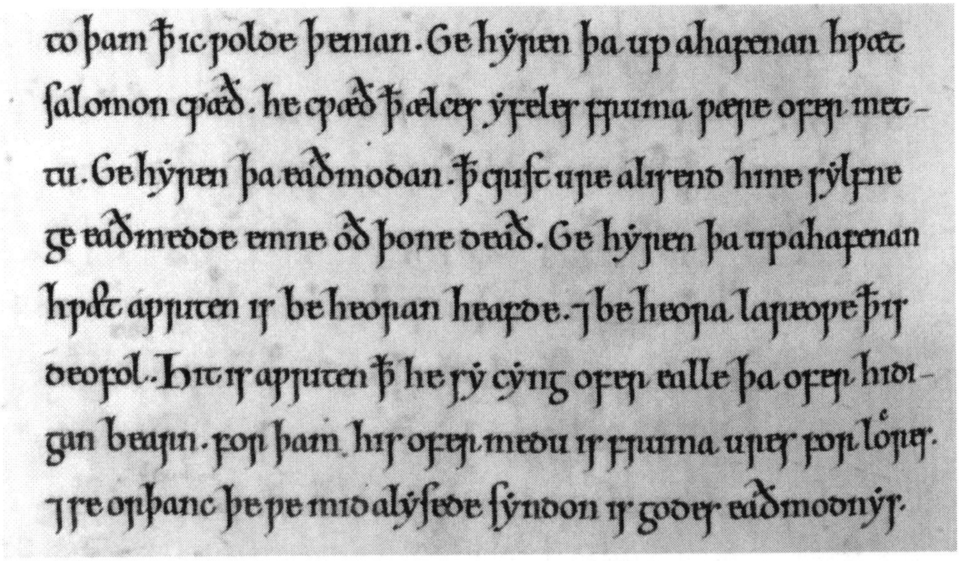

ILLUSTRATION 21   Cambridge, University Library Ii.2.4, 90ᵛ, Exeter script of s.xi³/⁴: OE translation of Pope Gregory's *Cura Pastoralis*, ch. 41. Reduced to 75%

In so far as Wheelock formed his designs on manuscript models he presumably allowed continual reading over a period to stimulate the gradual formulation of a repertoire of suitable designs.

Of the features listed the first, letters with hooked descender terminals, is of greater importance than the rest, because it relates to a large number of letter-forms affecting the overall impact made by looking at Wheelock's Anglo-Saxon text on the page.[89] Sinuosity of style is particularly marked in CUL Ii.2.4 (Illustration 21), which shows elegant curvacious letter-forms, 'a stately upright script' according to Ker in his *Catalogue*. Originating from Exeter in the third quarter of the eleventh century, it was written by one of the scribes identified with the scriptorium of Leofric, bishop of Exeter (1046–72).[90] Descenders are regularly turned to the left, and the ascender of ð is tagged

---

[89] For this reason the manuscript that shows the largest number of features imitated (as enumerated here), viz. CUL Gg.3.28, is not as influential as a primary model as might appear, since it does not present an overall sinuosity of style. For individual letter-forms it was no doubt notably influential.

[90] There is a list of Exeter manuscripts produced before the twelfth century in Patrick W. Conner, *Anglo-Saxon Exeter: A Tenth-Century Cultural History* (Woodbridge: Boydell, 1993), pp. 3–11. He draws upon the work of Elaine Drage, 'Bishop Leofric and the Exeter Cathedral Chapter, 1050–1072: A Reassessment of the Evidence', Unpubl. D.Phil. thesis, Oxford University, 1978.

to the left. As he records on the inside of the front cover, Wheelock read this manuscript between 3 September 1638 and 17 July 1639, an extended formative period in his Anglo-Saxon studies.[91] The script is taller than his type-designs, and shows split ascenders (not taken over in the type-designs), but the similarity in sinuosity is strong. Other manuscripts in the group used by Wheelock also show Exeter script of this period, e.g., CCC 190, pp. 351–9 (Ker's items 20–21) and pp. 295–308 (Ker's item 17), where similar features are shown. In fact, nearly a quarter of the manuscripts (or parts of manuscripts) listed (10 out of 41) were in Exeter in the eleventh century, and most of them were produced there, including those produced in Bishop Leofric's scriptorium: CUL Hh.1.10, Ii.2.11, CCC 190 (B), 191, and 201 (pp. 179–272). This Exeter script of the third quarter of the eleventh century from Bishop Leofric's scriptorium differentiates well between Latin and vernacular forms.[92] It is this script, particularly that in CUL Ii.2.4 (Illustration 21), that apparently provided the foundation for the overall style of Wheelock's Anglo-Saxon type-designs. To this base he then presumably added the other distinctive letter-forms that he found in various manuscripts as he read them. For some features he apparently took his models from Anglo-Saxon usage in Latin texts; it is unlikely that Wheelock would have made a distinction between Anglo-Saxon and Latin script features, and in any case early Anglo-Saxon manuscripts did not make such a distinction.

The relevant features in the manuscripts with which the corresponding features in his type-designs may be matched are noted in the illustrations as follows:

1. Hooked terminals. Descenders turned to the left are evident in CUL Ii.2.4 (Illustration 21), e.g., ſe oþþanc (line 8 = bottom line). They may also be seen in other manuscripts, as CCC 419, p. 308 (Illustration 22a, line 6), in 'ſpɲecan' etc.

2. Lower-case ð shows the ascender tagged to the left, as in CUL Ii.2.4 (Illustration 21, line 2 in cpæð), CCC 419, p. 308 (Illustration 22a, line 2 in luɼiað), TCC B.15.34, p. 79 (Illustration 23a, line 3 in ða), p. 319 (Illustration 23b, line 4 in ɼæʒð).

3. Upper-case square C. This feature occurs in CUL Gg.3.28, fo 44ᵛ 'CRISTES' (Illustration 24a, line 3), TCC B.15.34, p. 376 'MARCUS' (Illustration 23c,

---

91 As noted above, Wheelock was recruited by Spelman in 1637. By the end of that year Spelman regarded him as an equal partner in Anglo-Saxon scholarship (Oates, *Cambridge University Library*, p. 198).

92 As noted by T.A.M. Bishop, *English Caroline Minuscule* (Oxford: Clarendon Press, 1971), p. 24, commentary to pl. 28 (CCC 191).

ANGLO-SAXON TYPE-DESIGNS IN THE 17TH CENTURY TO 1705 117

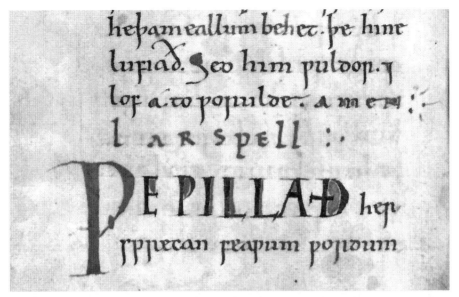

ILLUSTRATION 22A Cambridge, Corpus Christi College 419, 308: Anglo-Saxon homily 'Larspell' for the 4th Sunday in Lent, beginning

ILLUSTRATION 22B Cambridge, Corpus Christi College 419, 73: Anglo-Saxon Homily 'Angelorum nomina', beginning

ILLUSTRATION 23A Cambridge, Trinity College B.15.34, 79: Ælfric, Homily 'Dominica III post Pascha', beginning. Reduced to 86%

ILLUSTRATION 23B Cambridge, Trinity College B.15.34, 319: Ælfric, *Catholic Homilies* I.xxiv 'Dominica IIII post Pentecosten', beginning. Reduced to 83%

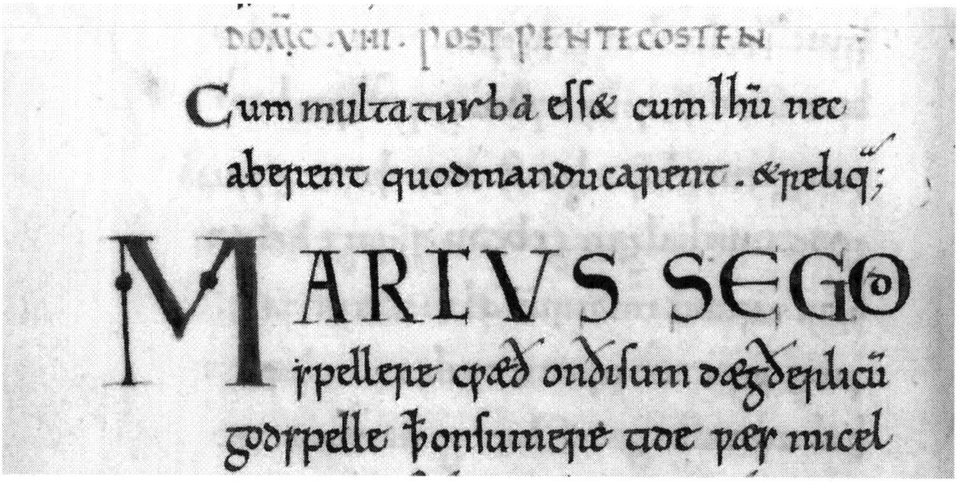

ILLUSTRATION 23C Cambridge, Trinity College B.15.34, 376: Ælfric, *Catholic Homilies* II.xxv 'Dominica VIII post Pentecosten', beginning. Reduced to 85%

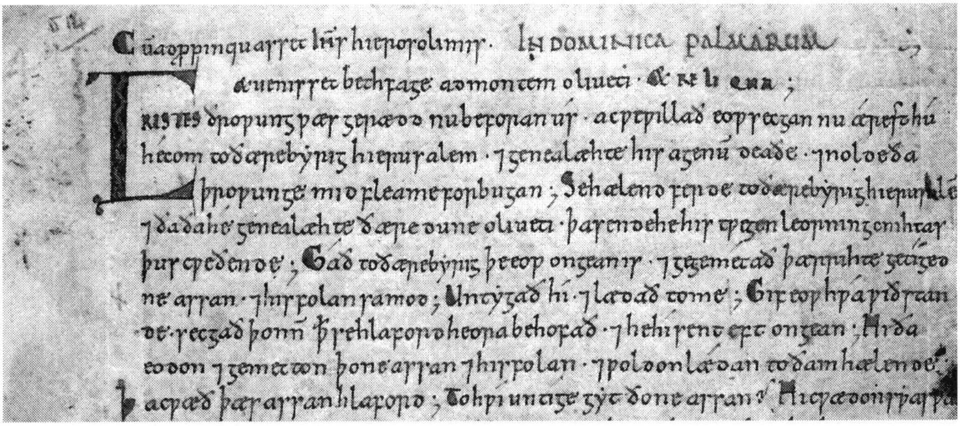

ILLUSTRATION 24A Cambridge University Library Gg.3.28, 44ᵛ: Ælfric, *Catholic Homilies* I.xiv 'Dominica Palmarum', beginning. Reduced to 66%

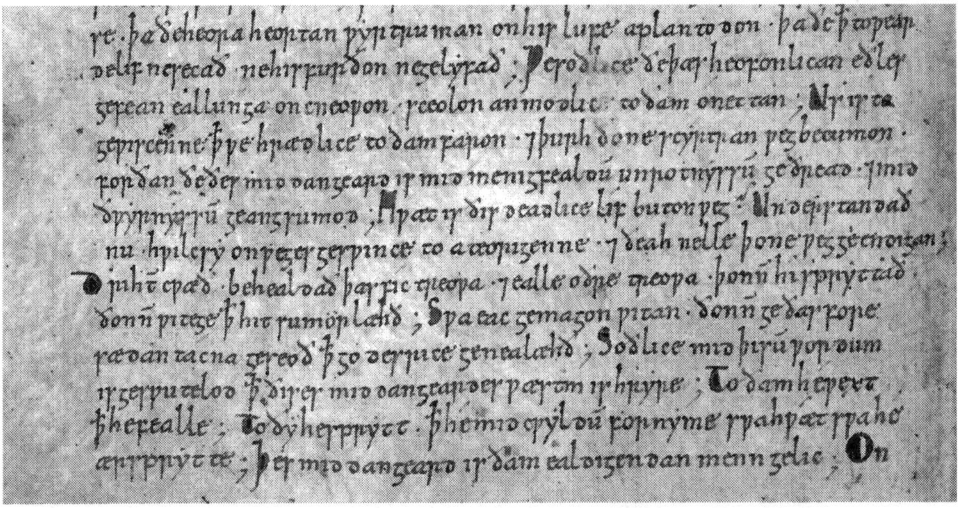

ILLUSTRATION 24B Cambridge University Library Gg.3.28, 131ᵛ: Ælfric, *Catholic Homilies* I.xl 'Dominica II in adventum Domini'. Reduced to 66%

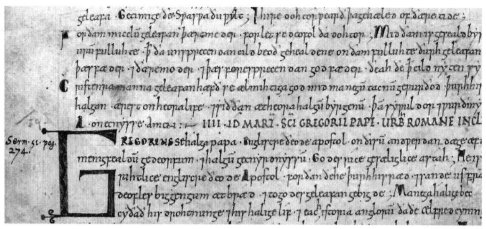

ILLUSTRATION 24C Cambridge University Library Gg.3.28, 157ᵛ: Ælfric, *Catholic Homilies* II.ix 'Sancti Gregorii Pape', beginning. Note the cross-reference in Wheelock's hand to 'Serm.51' (CUL Ii.1.33). Reduced to 66%

ILLUSTRATION 24D Cambridge University Library Gg.3.28, 255ʳ: Ælfric, Anglo-Saxon version of *De temporibus anni*, Preamble and §§1.1–4. Reduced to 66%

line 4), and together with square G (feature 7) in CCC 173, fo 47ᵛ 'ᴌɪᴘɪᴄ' (Illustration 20, line 1).

4. Round-backed D, with a short ascender ending in a terminal gently hooked upwards, as in TCC B.15.34, p. 319 'ɢᴏᴅ' (Illustration 23b, line 3). Cf. CUL Gg.3.28, fo 131ᵛ 'Driht⟨en⟩' (Illustration 24b, line 7), CCC 201, p. 190 'Dolum' (Illustration 25, line 2), also Tiberius C.ii (s.viii), fo 75ʳ, 'Deniq:' (Illustration 26, line 1).

5. E, with both the upper and the lower arms showing scrolled terminals. Unless transferred from scrolled T this feature does not occur in manuscripts, although it is certainly authentically Anglo-Saxon, for example, in its resemblance to the design of wrist-bands known as Class A. The

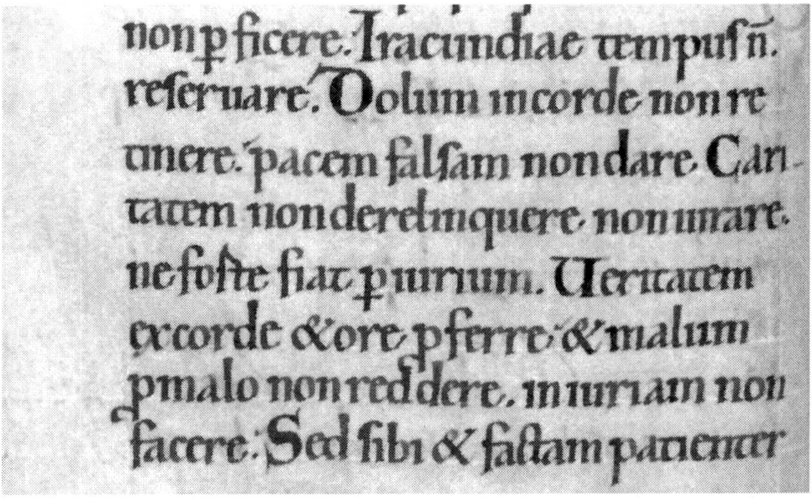

> nonpficere. Iracindiae tempuſñ.
> reſeruare. Oolum incorde non re
> tinere. pacem falſam non dare Cari-
> tatem non derelinquere non iurare·
> ne foſte fiat piuriuri. Veritatem
> ex corde & ore pferre & malum
> pmalo non reddere. iniuriam non
> facere. Sed ſibi & faſtam patientir

ILLUSTRATION 25   Cambridge, Corpus Christi College 201, 190: *Capitula of Theodulf*, ch. xxi, §§ 22–30. Reduced to 92%

wrist-band illustrated by John Hines, *The Scandinavian Character of Anglian England in the Pre-Viking Period*, British series 124 (London: British Archaeological Records, 1984), p. 382, fig. 2.5, is from Holywell Row (nr Mildenhall, Suffolk).[93] Since this particular wrist-band was excavated by the archaeologist T.C. Lethbridge at some time between 1929 and 1948 it was not available to Wheelock, but he may have seen something similar, which served to inspire his design for Anglo-Saxon capital E. Another possible source of inspiration is uncial E with the spaces between the arms shaded to indicate prominence; the shading with metallic ink was applied with a circular motion to provide a ball of colour, as in CCC 188, p. 241 'Erant' (Illustration 27, line 5).

6. F, showing a hooked approach stroke at the top of the stem, and a bowed upper arm with the terminal rolled over, as in CUL Gg.3.28, fo 157ᵛ 'Fon' (Illustration 24c, line 2), also Tiberius C.ii (s.viii), fo 75ʳ 'Fentun' (Illustration 26, line 6).

---

[93] I am most grateful to Jean Somerville, Project Director for the Cambridge Museum of Archaeology and Anthropology, for her helpfulness in locating this item (no. Z7112B) so that I could examine the original.

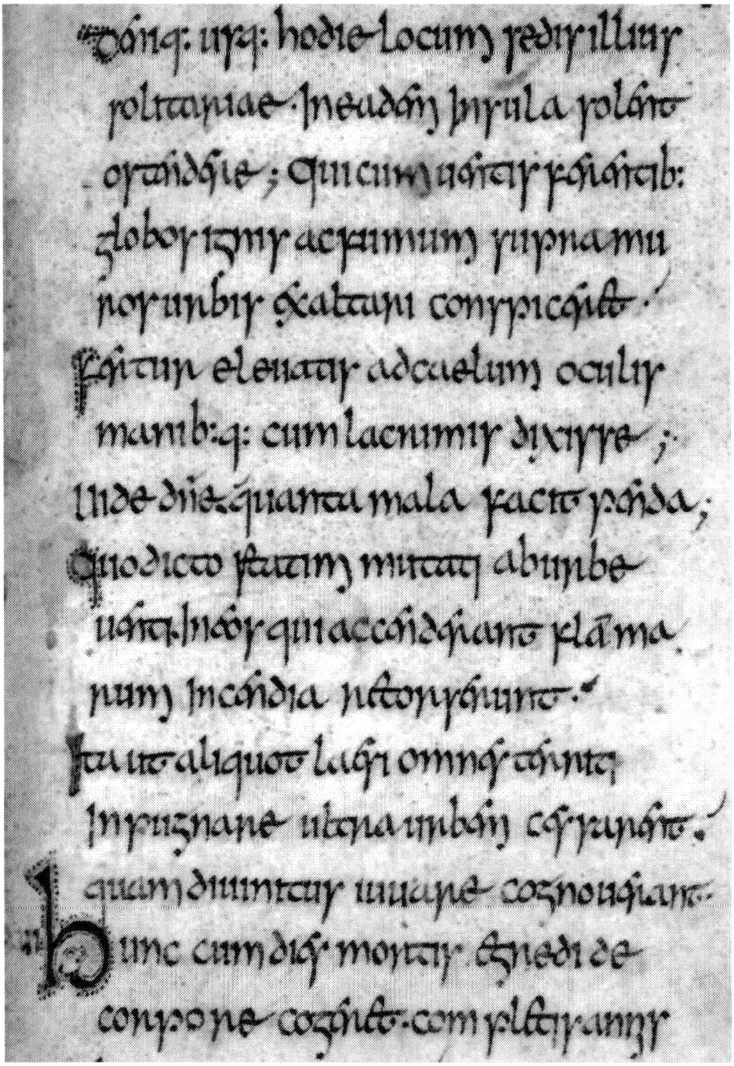

ILLUSTRATION 26 BL Cotton Tiberius C.ii, 75ʳ: Bede, *Historia Ecclesiastica* III.xvi–xvii

7. Upper-case square G, as in CUL Gg.3.28, fo 157ᵛ 'ᴳREGORIUS' (Illustration 24c, line 8), TCC B.15.34, p. 319 '\HA/LIGE' (Illustration 23b, line 3), and together with square C (feature 3) in CCC 173, fo 47ᵛ 'ᴳɪꝼ' (Illustration 20, line 4).

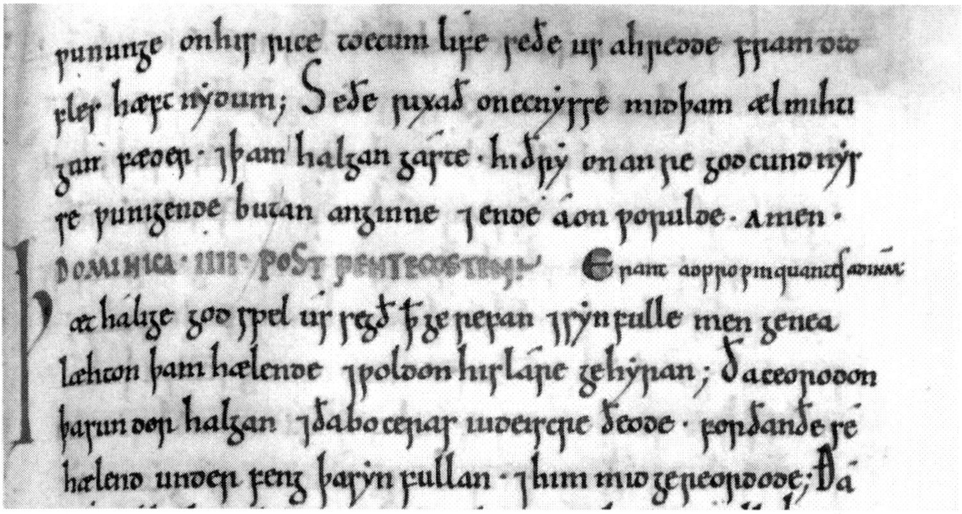

ILLUSTRATION 27   Cambridge, Corpus Christi College 188, 241: Ælfric, *Catholic Homilies* I.xxiv 'Dominica IIII post Pentecosten', beginning. Reduced to 83%

ILLUSTRATION 28   Cambridge, Corpus Christi College 162, 44: Anglo-Saxon Homily 'Be þam drihtlican sunnandæg folces lar', beginning. Reduced to 81%

8. H in uncial form with an ornamental miniature loop attached to the shoulder-side of the upper stem. This feature does not occur in manuscripts. It may have been inspired by **h** with a bar across the ascender in 'DRIÐTLICAN' on CCC 162, p. 44 (Illustration 28, line 2). Although this **h** is undoubtedly an error—'drih' with a bar across the ascender of **h** is an abbreviation for OE *drihten* 'lord', as in the same manuscript, p. 252/10—it may still have provided the idea for the ornamentation in the printed sort. Another possible influence is uncial capital Ð with an ornamental motif on the ascender, as in CCC 419, p. 73 'ÐER' (Illustration 22b, line 3); cf. also Tiberius C.ii (s.viii), fo 75ʳ, 'Ðunc' (Illustration 26, line 15).

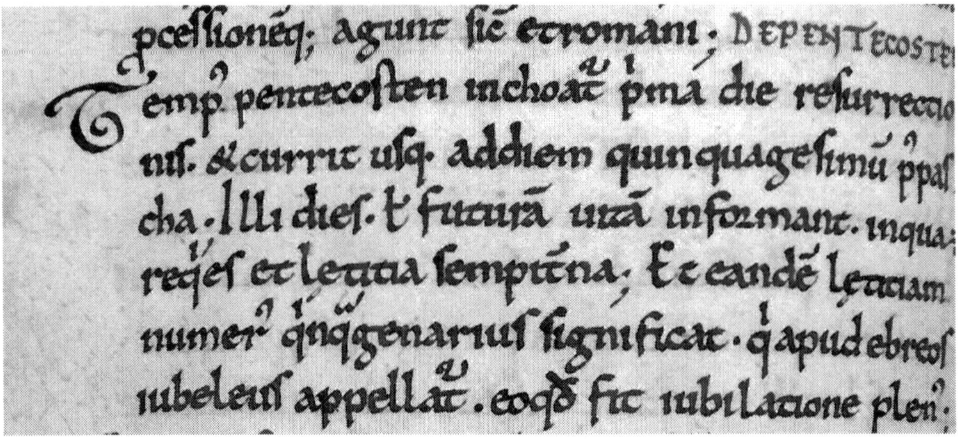

ILLUSTRATION 29 Cambridge, Corpus Christi College 190, 236: from *De Septem Ecclesiasticis Gradibus*, 'De Sacerdotibus, Lectiones de Pentecosten' (= Fehr 1914: 243/7–9). Reduced to 89%

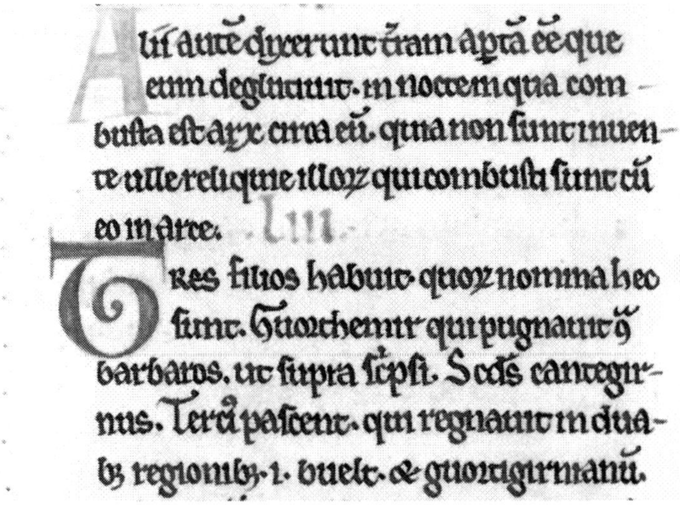

ILLUSTRATION 30 Cambridge University Library Ff.1.27, 35: from *Historia Brittonum* (Mommsen 1898: 192a/8–12)

9. I, with a hooked terminal at the base of the stem, as in CUL Gg.3.28, fo 255ʳ 'Ic' (Illustration 24d, line 2), also Tiberius C.ii (s.viii), fo 75ʳ, 'IN' (Illustration 26, line 19).
10. T, similar to the lower-case, but with the stroke terminal scrolled.[94] This feature occurs rarely in the manuscripts. An outstanding example is that in CCC 190, p. 236 'Temp⟨us⟩' (Illustration 29, line 2), and Wheelock would have seen others in later manuscripts, such as CUL Ff.1.27, p. 35 (Illustration 30, line 2), and CTH 1. For such a T with a curl but not a scroll see CUL Gg.3.28, fo 44ᵛ 'To hwi' (Illustration 24a, line 11), fo 131ᵛ 'To ðam', 'To ðy' (Illustration 24b, lines 10, 11).
11. U, with the left part of the stroke curved like a swan's neck, and the right stem showing a hooked terminal at the base, as in CCC 201, p. 190 'Ueritatem' (Illustration 25, line 5), TCC B.15.34, p. 79 'URE' (Illustration 23a, line 2). Cf. also CUL Gg.3.28, fo 44ᵛ 'Unτyʒað' (Illustration 24a, line 8), fo 131ᵛ 'Unðepɼτanðað' (Illustration 24b, line 5), 'Uɼ' (Illustration 24b, line 2).
12. Þ is rounded, not 'square' or sharply angled. This feature is common in the manuscripts, e.g., CUL Gg.3.28, fo 131ᵛ 'Þeρoðlice' (Illustration 24b, line 1), fo 255ʳ 'Þιτoðlice' (Illustration 24d, line 4), CCC 419, p. 308 'ÞE ÞILLAÐ' (Illustration 22b, line 5).

Early type-designs sought to mimic the best models that could be found in manuscript usage. Roman typefaces triumphed 'over the various national letter styles in much of Europe after 1530', e.g., 'Black Letter' (Textura) in England, because of 'the prestige of their manuscript origins and the prestige of the Latin texts for which they seemed a natural means of expression'.[95] It was the essence of this triumph that Archbishop Parker effectively recreated when he had his own Anglo-Saxon types made, probably through the auspices of his Latin Secretary, John Joscelyn. Through the choice of authentic letter-forms and the prestige of the ancient English texts printed with them, Parker's Great Primer Anglo-Saxon was a typeface that echoed this prestige. The predominant influence on Parker's type-designs was Worcester manuscripts, and Junius 121 in particular. Despite Wheelock's familiarity with this kind of script in CUL Kk.3.18, which he used as his base text for the Anglo-Saxon Bede, he has apparently re-thought the process through, using as his model Exeter script from

---

94 Some manuscripts show small t with the stroke curled to distinguish it from Latin, e.g., OCC 197, illustrated in Ker, *Catalogue*, pl. II.
95 Henri-Jean Martin, *The History and Power of Writing*, t L.G. Cochrane (Chicago: University of Chicago Press, 1995), p. 304.

Leofric's scriptorium of the third quarter of the eleventh century. Wheelock's Great Primer Anglo-Saxon is combined with a Great Primer Roman. One of the great advantages of Roman type is that the presence of serifs increases readability, the gelling of words on the page.[96] Wheelock's Anglo-Saxon type in practice retained serifs in letters that were not provided with Anglo-Saxon special sorts, but in other letters where special sorts were provided, serifs were generally dispensed with in favour of sinuosity of shape provided especially by hooked terminals to descenders. Whereas Exeter script from Leofric's scriptorium (Illustration 21) shows an evenness of sinuous approach, this consistency is not evident in Wheelock's text (Illustration 19) because it is an amalgam of standard roman and special Anglo-Saxon sorts. Wheelock's re-thinking of the process went so far as to re-model the same lower-case letters as were used in previous Anglo-Saxon founts, and to extend the number of upper-case special sorts. His decision not to repeat Parker's second Æ, or þ, suggests that expense may have been a consideration. Certainly it would have been much more expensive to design special sorts for every letter of the alphabet.[97]

From a graphic-aesthetic point of view the combination of Wheelock's Great Primer Anglo-Saxon, which is modelled on script, and the accompanying Great Primer Roman, which is, of course, modelled on earlier designs of roman type, was not a marriage made in heaven. But it was a good working partnership that clothed Wheelock's scholarship in graceful attire, sufficiently attractive and interesting still to be talked about today. In a different context Matthew Carter used the phrase 'nostalgic pastiche' to describe a type-design that looks back to various earlier models without thinking through the new design's contemporary purpose.[98] Wheelock's Anglo-Saxon type-designs are not a pastiche, because they look to a consistent model to inform them: Exeter script from Leofric's scriptorium. They are nostalgic in the sense that they were a deliberate attempt to re-create typographically the style and impact of handwriting in authentic manuscripts. This style has even been extended to some letters that do not show such features in the manuscripts: the most notable instance is the E with its 'wrought-iron curlyhues' possibly taken over from T. However, the adopted mode of presentation was not just a matter of taste, still less of acceding to the preferences of readers, but rather an attempt to enshrine

---

96   As opposed to legibility, which is the distinguishability of individual letters, a distinction made by Walter Tracy in R. McLean (ed), *Typographers on Type: An Illustrated Anthology from William Morris to the Present Day* (London: Lund Humphries, 1995), pp. 170–171.

97   For some remarks on the costs of creating a (partial) Anglo-Saxon fount see above, ch. 1. Compare Sir Henry Spelman's remark (about a different matter) in his letter of 05/10/38: 'my mynde & purse be not of like dimension'.

98   McLean, *Typographers*, p. 184.

authority in elegance, the elegance of authenticity. Wheelock established himself securely in the tradition begun by Parker of presenting Anglo-Saxon with as much authenticity as possible. He alone amongst all Parker's successors to date went back to the manuscripts and re-invented Anglo-Saxon type-design.

3   The Junian Pica Anglo-Saxon Type-Design

Unlike Selden, Spelman, and even Wheelock and Somner, who had good Old English, Franciscus Junius was a scholar of Germanic, and knew Frisian, Gothic, Old High German, Old Icelandic and Old Saxon, as well as Old English. His set of Anglo-Saxon type-designs first appeared in Amsterdam in 1655, a small amount in the *Observationes in Willerami Abbatis Francicam Paraphrasin Cantici Canticorum* (1655.1), and the whole text of the four poems from OBL Junius 11, *Genesis, Exodus, Daniel*, and *Christ and Satan*, in the *Cædmonis Monachi Paraphrasis Poetica* (1655.2).

Franciscus Junius (1591–1677), or François du Jon, was born at Heidelberg. To distinguish him from his father, also Franciscus Junius (1545–1602), a protestant theologian of considerable distinction, Junius added the letters F.F. (= Francisci Filius) to his name. His grandfather and father were French and the latter had worked primarily in Heidelberg for nearly twenty years before the younger Junius's birth, but after that event his mother died, and in 1592 his father took up a professorship at the University of Leiden, so his upbringing was in the Netherlands. Leiden University, founded in 1575, was a centre for the study of the Reformed Religion and attracted many scholars of the Calvinist school. Amongst Junius's father's colleagues was Joseph Justus Scaliger (1540–1609), who helped to make Leiden a European centre of philology. His father's pupils included Hugo Grotius (1583–1645) and Gerardus Joannes Vossius (1577–1649), who married Junius's sister Elisabeth in 1607, and who, as rector of Dordrecht Latin school, became responsible for Junius's education after his father's death of the plague in 1602. At school Junius was taught Latin and Greek grammar and literature, and Christian doctrine. At Leiden University, beginning in 1608, he studied mathematics and theology. Following a dispute in the Dutch Reformed Church concerning the doctrine of predestination in which Junius and Vossius were caught up, Junius was displaced and went to France, and then on to England in 1621 to become librarian to the earl of Arundel, Thomas Howard (1585–1646), and tutor to his son. He was based at Arundel House in London. Howard, whose wife Aletheia Talbot was heiress to the earl of Shrewsbury, was a collector of *objets d'art* and books on a scale unprecedented in England outside the royal family, so much so that he was dubbed the 'Father of Vertu in England'.[99] Junius remained in England for much of his life, spending many years studying in Oxford.[100] Although his Pica Anglo-Saxon type-designs were cut in Amsterdam, Junius brought them to England and left the 'utensils' to Oxford University.[101] The university used them extensively, so for historical convenience I have included the designs with the English rather than with the continental ones. They were used on the continent only in books published by Junius himself or his close associates.

Junius belonged to an intellectual élite in which he was reared to be a scholar who passed on the benefits of humanistic enquiry to the leaders of nations. Already at the age of seventeen he was editing his father's work for publication in collaboration with his half-brother, Joannes Casimirus Junius (1582–1624), the two sons dedicating the 1608 edition of the *Animadversiones* by Franciscus Junius Sr to James I, king of England. Junius's early concern for the presentation and appearance of his books emerges in a letter written 1 April 1635 to Vossius, in which he was discussing the arrangements for the publication of the *De Pictura Veterum* (1637), to be dedicated to James's successor, Charles I, and to be seen through the press in Amsterdam by Vossius while Junius was in London.[102] He wrote: 'But the thought occurred to the mind that the typographer can be deceived in choosing the form of the book and the kind of type.'[103] Here is open testimony of Junius's careful attention not only to the content and the layout of a book, but even to the shape of the letters with which it was to be printed.

His Pica Anglo-Saxon is evidently modelled on the Parkerian designs, particularly the Parkerian Pica. In both sets of designs, for example, the ð shows its ascender leaning over heavily to the left, and all the other letters are closely modelled on the Parkerian design. Junius adds square C, previously used in the Spelmanian and Wheelockian Great Primers, and square G, also previously used in the Wheelockian Great Primer. These Junian designs show a high quality of cutting, almost certainly by Christoffel van Dijck (c.1603–69), the foremost punchcutter of the century, whose type-designs were to be in great

---

99 Seymour de Ricci, *English Collectors of Books and Manuscripts 1530–1930 and their Marks of Ownership* (Cambridge: Cambridge University Press, 1930), pp. 25–26.

100 For a summary of Junius's life see Lucas, *Junius's Cædmon*, pp. ix–xii. For full details based on his extensive correspondence see von Romburgh, *Franciscus Junius*.

101 As noted by Ould, *Printing*, II.84–88.

102 On this work see Aldrich, Fehl and Fehl, *Franciscus Junius*, and Colette Nativel, *Franciscus Junius, De Pictura Veterum libri tres (Roterodami, 1694): Édition, traduction et commentaire du livre I*, Travaux du Grand Siècle 3 (Geneva: Droz, 1996).

103 'sed subibat animum cogitatio, posse Typographum falli, in voluminis forma, ac Typorum modo eligendi': Paulus Colomesius, *Gerardi Joan. Vossii et Clarorum Virorum ad eum Epistolae* (Augsburg: L. Kronigerus, 1691), II. no. 217, on p. 157.

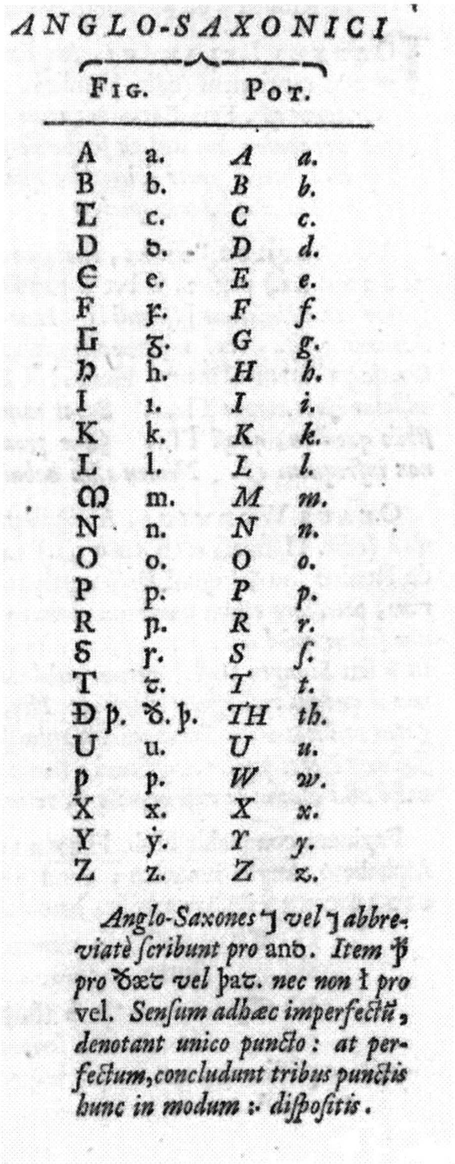

ANGLO-SAXONICI

Fig.		Pot.	
A	a.	*A*	*a.*
B	b.	*B*	*b.*
C	c.	*C*	*c.*
D	ð.	*D*	*d.*
E	e.	*E*	*e.*
F	f.	*F*	*f.*
G	ᵹ.	*G*	*g.*
H	h.	*H*	*h.*
I	i.	*I*	*i.*
K	k.	*K*	*k.*
L	l.	*L*	*l.*
M	m.	*M*	*m.*
N	n.	*N*	*n.*
O	o.	*O*	*o.*
P	p.	*P*	*p.*
R	r.	*R*	*r.*
S	ſ.	*S*	*ſ.*
T	t.	*T*	*t.*
Ð þ.	ð. þ.	*TH*	*th.*
U	u.	*U*	*u.*
ƿ	p.	*W*	*w.*
X	x.	*X*	*x.*
Y	ẏ.	*Y*	*y.*
Z	z.	*Z*	*z.*

Anglo-Saxones ⁊ vel ⁊ abbreviatè ſcribunt pro and. *Item* ꝥ *pro* ðæt *vel* þæt. *nec non* ɫ *pro* vel. *Senſum adhæc imperfectū, denotant unico puncto : at perfectum, concludunt tribus punctis hunc in modum :· diſpoſitis.*

ILLUSTRATION 31
Reader's Anglo-Saxon type-specimen showing the Junian Pica Anglo-Saxon (AS6) cut by Christoffel van Dijck: Junius & Marshall, *Gothic Gospels* (1665.2), 2*4r (CUL Young 100). The *figura* 'shape' is shown on the left and the *potestas* 'signification' on the right

ILLUSTRATION 32A   Punches made by Christoffel van Dijck, his Great Primer Italic A–P, at the Museum Enschedé (= Noord-Hollands Archief), Haarlem, Netherlands
PHOTO: JOHN LANE

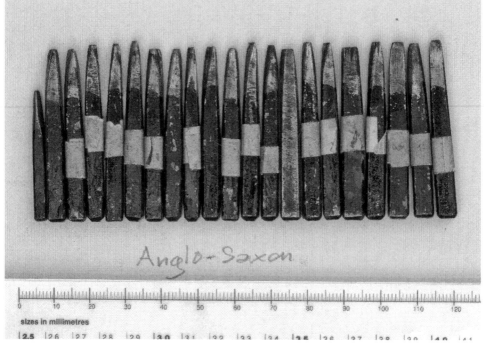

ILLUSTRATION 32B   The AS punches made for Junius, attributable to Christoffel van Dijck, at Oxford University Press Archive
PHOTO: JOHN LANE

demand for the nascent Oxford University Press. Van Dijck was the only skilled punchcutter in Holland between c.1652 and c.1668, as the Voskens brothers (on whom see below) left Amsterdam for Frankfurt soon after 1651.[104]

The most compelling evidence in support of identifying van Dijck as the punchcutter comes from the physical shape of the punches. When the work of different punchcutters is viewed side by side there is a noticeable difference between the shapes of the punches produced by each one.[105] In this light the similarity between those definitely made by van Dijck and those left by Junius to Oxford University is remarkable; their identification was confirmed by Lane 1993; see Illustration 32.[106] Further confirmation is provided by the fact that the Pica Roman used by Junius in combination with his Pica Anglo-Saxon is also by van Dijck, attributed to him in the type-specimen issued by Anna van Beerninck, the widow of Daniel Elsevier about 1681.[107] The excellent fit between the roman and the special Anglo-Saxon sorts, both cut by the same highly skilled punchcutter, contributes to the attractiveness of their overall appearance.

Junius's type-designs are also notable for reflecting their instigator's linguistic expertise and philological flair, in that, as well as for Old English, Junius had special sorts made for Gothic and Runic, and he resurrected an older Schwabacher fount for Icelandic, and another for Danish, all in Pica size. His pupil and fellow-scholar Jan van Vliet (1620–66) recalls Junius as 'having at his own expense had cut very exquisite punches and matrices of the Gothic, Runic, Anglo-Saxon, ancient German, Danish and many other languages (all of which I give an example of here)'.[108] The punches for the new designs were acquired by Junius, who thus kept complete control of their use; his 'printing utensils' were bequeathed to Oxford University, and punches and matrices for

---

104 For a brief account of van Dijck's life and career see John A. Lane, *The Diaspora of Armenian Printing 1512–2012* (Amsterdam and Yerevan: University of Amsterdam, 2012), pp. 72–75.
105 The work of several punchcutters, including one of Junius's Pica Anglo-Saxon punches, is shown side by side in Morison & Carter, *John Fell*, pl. 18, where the Junius Pica Anglo-Saxon punch is no. 14.
106 See John A. Lane, *The Enschedé Type Specimens of 1768 & 1773: A Facsimile with an Introduction and Notes* (Haarlem: Stichting Museum Enschedé, 1993), p. 57, commentary on *Kleine Text Curcyf no.2*. Cf. Peter J. Lucas, 'Junius, his Printers and his Types: An Interim Report', in R.H. Bremmer Jr (ed.), *Franciscus Junius and his Circle* (Amsterdam: Rodopi, 1998), pp. 177–197, at pp. 190–195. Of course the punches produced by a single punchcutter do vary somewhat, especially in relation to the size of the letter cut at the end.
107 TSF 1963: no. 12; Davis & Carter, *Mechanick Exercises*, 2nd endplate.
108 hebbende op sijn eijgen kosten seer keurlijcke stempels en moeder-vormen van de Gotse, Runisse, Engel-Saxe, oude Duijtse, Deense en meer andere talen doen steecken (van alle welcke ick hier een staeltje geve): **1664.2**: a1ᵛ.

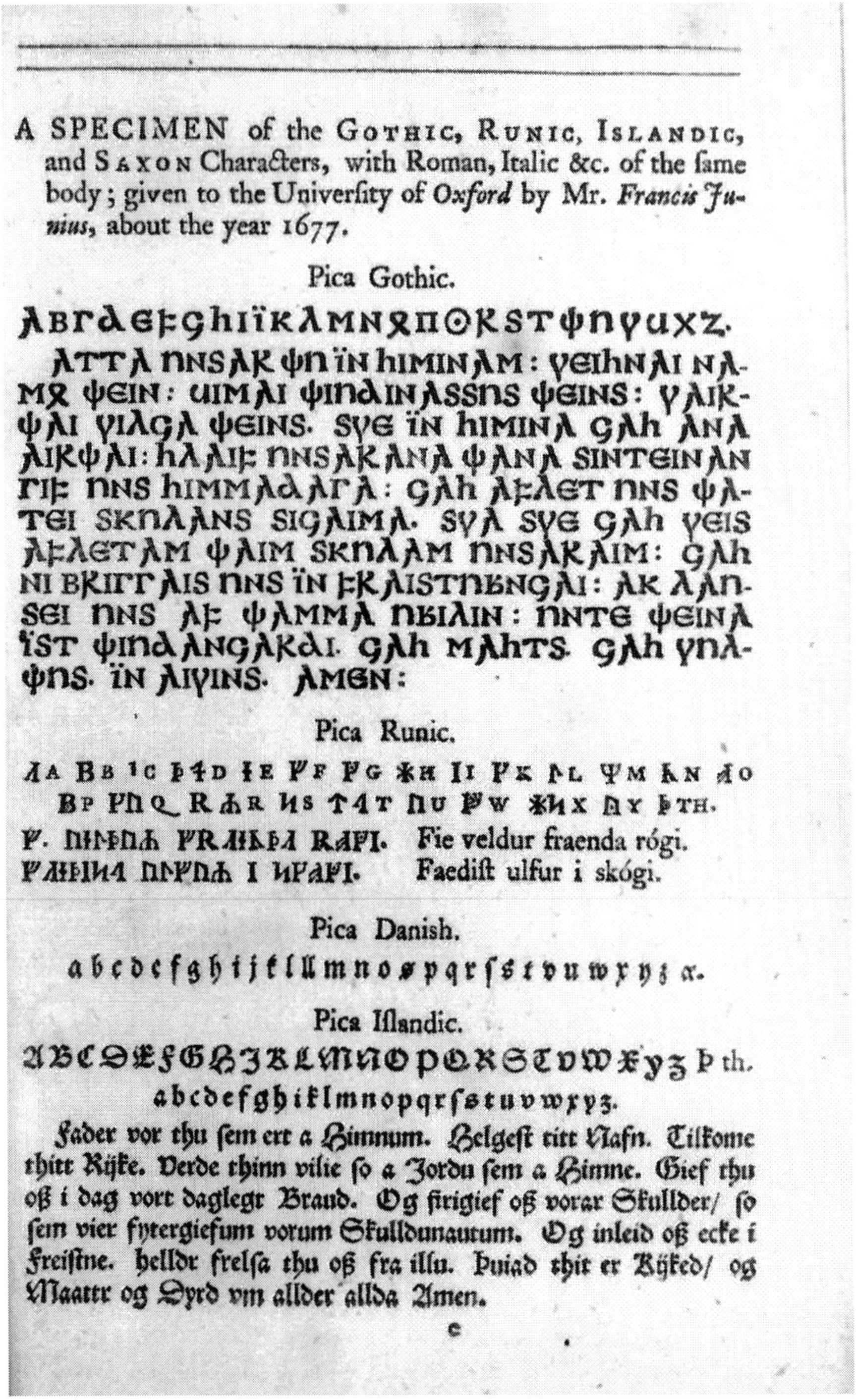

A SPECIMEN of the GOTHIC, RUNIC, ISLANDIC, and SAXON Characters, with Roman, Italic &c. of the same body; given to the University of *Oxford* by Mr. *Francis Junius*, about the year 1677.

Pica Gothic.

ABΓΔEϜGhiïKΛMNℜΠΟΚSTΦΠΥUXZ.

ATTA ΠNSAR ΦΠ ïN hIMINAM: ΨEIhNAI NA-
MR ΨEIN: UIMAI ΦINAINASSNS ΨGINS: ΥAIR-
ΦAI ΥIΛGA ΨEINS. SΥG ïN hIMINA GAh ANA
AIRΦAI: hA AIϜ ΠNSARANA ΦANA SINTEINAN
ΓΙϜ ΠNS hIMMAΔAΓA: GAh AϜΛGT ΠNS ΦA-
TEI SRΠΛANS SIGAIMA. SΥA SΥG GAh ΨEIS
AϜΛGTAM ΦAIM SRΠΛAM ΠNSARAIM: GAh
NI BRIΓΓAIS ΠNS ïN ϜRAISTNBNGAI: AR AΠ-
SEI ΠNS AϜ ΦAMMA ΠBIΛIN: ΠNTE ΨGINA
ïST ΦINAANGARΔΙ. GAh MAhTS. GAh ΥNA-
ΦNS. ïN AIΥINS. AMGN:

Pica Runic.

ᛆA Bᛒ ᛐC ᛑ᛭D ᛂE ᚠF ᛄG ᛪH Iı ᛔK ᛙL ᛦM ᚿN ᚮO
Bᛔ ᛕᚿQ Rᛅᚱ ᚻS ᛏᛐT ᚿU ᛒᚢW ᛪᛡX ᚤY ᛓTH.

ᚠ. ᚿᛁᛐᛂᚿᛆ ᛔRᛅᛅᛒᛆ RᛆᛔI. Fie veldur fraenda rógi.
ᚠᛆᛂᛓIᛙᛆ ᚿᛁᛔᚿᛆ I ᛙᛔᛆᛔI. Faedist ulfur i skógi.

Pica Danish.

abcdefghijklmnopqrſstvuwxyz æ.

Pica Islandic.

𝔄𝔅ℭ𝔇𝔈𝔉𝔊ℌ𝔍𝔎𝔏𝔐𝔑𝔒𝔓𝔔ℜ𝔖𝔗𝔘𝔙𝔚𝔛𝔜𝔷 Þ th.
abcdefghiklmnopqrſstuvwxyz.

Fader vor thu sem ert a Himnum. Helgest titt Nafn. Tilkome
thitt Rijke. Verde thinn vilie so a Jordu sem a Himne. Gief thu
oß i dag vort daglegt Braud. Og firigief oß vorar Skullder/ so
sem vier fytergiefum vorum Skulldunautum. Og inleid oß ecke i
Freistne. helldr frelsa thu oß fra illu. Þuiad thit er Rijked/ og
Maattr og Dyrd vm allder allda Amen.

ILLUSTRATION 33A Oxford University type-specimen (1695.1), e1r/e2r, showing the range of Junius's types (CUL Broxbourne.d.46)

Pica Saxon.

ABCDEFGhIKLMNOPRSTÐUpXYZ.
abcdefghiklmnopprtðþupxẏz·ʒ.

Fæðeɲ uɲe þu þe eaɲt on heoꝼenum. Sı þın nama ʒehalʒod:.
To-becume þın ɲıce:. Ɣepuɲðe þın pılla on eoɲðan. ꞃpa ꞃpa on
heoꝼenum:. Uɲne dæʒhpamlıcan hlaꝼ ꞃẏle uꞃ to dæʒ;. And
ꝼoꞃʒẏꝼ uꞃ uɲe ʒẏltaꞃ. ꞃpa ꞃpa pe ꝼoꞃʒıꝼað uɲum ʒẏltendum:.
And ne ʒelædde þu uꞃ on coꞃtnunʒe. ac alẏꞃ uꞃ oꝼ ẏꝼele:.
Soðlıce:.

Pica Greek.

Πάτηϱ ἡμῶν ὁ ἐν τοῖς οὐϱανοῖς &c.

Pica Roman.

A Æ B C D E F G H I J K L M N O P Q R S T V U W X Y Z.

A Æ B C D E F G H I J K L M N O P Q R S T V U W X Y Z.

Pater noſter qui es in cœlis, ſanctificetur nomen tuum. Veniat
regnum tuum: fiat voluntas tua, ſicut in cœlo, ita etiam in terra.
Panem noſtrum quotidianum da nobis hodie. Et remitte nobis
debita noſtra, ſicut & remittimus debitoribus noſtris. Et ne nos
inducas in tentationem, ſed libera nos ab illo malo. Quia tuum
eſt regnum, & potentia, & gloria in ſecula, Amen.

Pica Italick.

A Æ B C D E F G H I J K L M N O P Q R S T V U W X Y Z.

Pater noſter qui es in cœlis, ſanctificetur nomen tuum. Veniat re-
gnum tuum: fiat voluntas tua, ſicut in cœlo, ita etiam in terra.
Panem noſtrum quotidianum da nobis hodie. Et remitte nobis debita
noſtra, ſicut & remittimus debitoribus noſtris. Et ne nos inducas in
tentationem, ſed libera nos ab illo malo. Quia tuum eſt regnum, &
potentia, & gloria in ſecula, Amen.

Pica English.

𝔄𝔅ℭ𝔇𝔈𝔉𝔊ℌ𝔍𝔎𝔏𝔐𝔑𝔒𝔓𝔔𝔕𝔖𝔗𝔘𝔙𝔚𝔛𝔜𝔝

Our Father, which art in heaven; Hallowed be thy
Name. Thy kingdom come. Thy will be done in earth,
as it is in heaven. Give us this day our daily bread. And
forgive us our treſpaſſes, as we forgive them that treſ-
paſs against us. And lead us not into temptation; But
deliver us from evil. Amen.

294 S I.

Ælfrici grammaticâ cap. 5; Bonus, ꞅod. Melior, beꞇeꞃe. Optimus, ꞃeloꞃꞇ. *quamquam & ꞃeloꞃe dicebant pro* beꞇeꞃe, *ut videre est Matth.* 6: 25 & 26. *Etiam* ꞃel *hoc sensu occurrit*. no ðꝩ ꞃel bꝩde, Non eo melius se gessit; *Cædmon* 85, 20. me ꞃel ꞃæꞃ, Mihi melius erat; *Beda* v, 3 & 5. ꞃpa ꞃe man ꞃpꝩðeꞃ bꝩð aꞃan-dod. ꞃpa he ꞃelpa bꝩð :- Quanto validius probatur homo, tanto melior erit; *Albinus vel Alcuinus resp.* x L. ða Eʒipꞇiꞃcean ꞃeloꞃꞇ cunnon on pimcꞃæꞃꞇe:- Ægyptii optime versati sunt in fastis, i. *ratione supputandi tempora* ; *Æqu. vernum* xv. ꞃeleꞃꞇa Theophiluꞃ, Optime Theophile; *Luc.* 1:3. ꞃeleꞃꞇe pin, Falernum; *gl R*, 32. *Ab hoc interim* ꞃel *videtur Anglosaxonibus* Bona commodi temporis oportunitas ꞃel & ꞃæl *dici*. *unde* ʒeꞃælan, Provenire, accidere, *in bonam plerumque partem*. *inde* ꞃælba & ʒeꞃælða *sunt* Res prosperæ. ꞃæliʒ. ʒe-ꞃæliʒ, Felix, beatus. &c. Runico quoque lexico 𐌸𐌰𐌹𐍂𐌷𐌰𐌹𐍄𐌰 *dicuntur* Qui sub bono rege beate vivunt. *Alamannis*, *Danis*, *Belgis* 𝔰𝔞𝔩𝔦𝔤 *est* Beatus. *Vide annotata nostra in Tatiani* IV, 6.

SI, Hæc, illa; *i. Luc.*1:29. *Marc.*6:24. SI, Hæc; ἀυτη. *Luc.*7:44, 45. SI SIAꞂꞀ, Ipsa; αυτη. *Luc.*7:12.

SIB, Pax. *Anglosax.* ꞃibb. *Alam.* ſibba. *Vocabulum Gothis olim fuisse in usu*, *discimus ex illo* 𐌲𐌰𐍃𐌹𐌱𐌾𐍉𐌽, Reconciliari, *quod occurrit Matth.* 5:24. *item ex illo* 𐌿𐌽𐍃𐌹𐌱𐌾𐌰, Iniquus, improbus, *quod est Marc.* 15:28. & *de quo agimus suo loco*. *De origine vocabuli* ſibba *fuse egimus in annotatis ad Tatiani* v 1, 3.

SIBUN, Septem. *Cambrobritannis* saith. *Anglosaxonibus* ꞅeoꝼon. *Alamannis* ſibun. *Cimbris* 𐍅𐌹𐌰𐌽. *Danis* ſiuff. *Islandis* ſio. *Anglis & Belgis* ſeben. *Græcis* ἑπτά. *Vide Vossii etymologicum Latinum in* Septem. SIBUN 𐌷𐌻𐌰𐌹𐌱𐌰𐌽𐍃, Septem panes; *Marc.*8, 5, 6, 20. SIBUN SPꝔKGI-ÐANS: Septem sportas; *Marc.*8:8, 20. SIBUN 𐌱𐍂𐍉𐌸𐍂𐌰𐌷𐌰𐌽𐍃: Septem fratres; *Marc.*12:20. *pro quo* SIBUN 𐌱𐍂𐍉𐌸𐍂𐌲𐌽𐍃 *est Luc.*20:29. 𐌿𐌽𐌷𐌿𐌻𐌸𐍉𐌽𐍃 SIBUN: Dæmonia septem; *Luc.* 8:2. 𐌻𐌹𐌱𐌰𐌽𐌳𐌴𐌹 𐌼𐌹𐌸 𐌰𐌱𐌹𐌽 𐌲𐌴𐍂𐌰 SIBUN: Vivens cum marito annis septem; *Luc.*2:36. SIBUNTIGUNS, Septuaginta; *Luc.*11:1, 17. SIBUNSINϕAM, Septies; *Luc.*17:4.

SIGAN. 𐌲𐌰𐍃𐌹𐌲𐌰𐌽, Delabi, deorsum ferri, subsidere, occidere. ϕAN 𐌲𐌰𐍃𐌰𐌲 𐌵𐌽 SA 𐌽𐌹𐌻: Cùm occidisset jam Sol; *Marc.*1:32. *pro quo Lucæ* 4:40 *legimus* 𐌼𐌹𐌸 ϕ𐌰𐌽𐌴𐌹 ϕ𐌰𐌽 𐍃𐌰𐌿𐌽 𐍃𐌿𐌽𐌽𐍉: *Benedicti regulæ Anglosaxonice interlineatæ*, *cap.*4 ; æꞃ nꝩðeꞃꞃiʒe *vel* nꝩðeꞃʒanʒe, Ante occasum. *Boëth.* xxv; þeah ꞃeo ꞃunne oꞃeꞃ midne dæʒ onꞃiʒe and luꞇe ꞇo ðæꞃe eoꞃðan. Licet Sol inclinato jam in postmeridianum tempus die subsidat
& ver-

ILLUSTRATION 33B   Text in Anglo-Saxon and other (Germanic) languages showing the diversity of Junius's types in use: *Gothic Gospels* (1665.2), [2]203[v] (CUL Young 100). Reduced to 80%

Anglo-Saxon, Gothic and Runic are still in the Oxford University Press archive, twenty-one Anglo-Saxon punches and two sets of matrices, one of twenty and the other of eighteen.[109] For a specimen see Illustration 32a. When these various sets of designs are used together, as in the edition of the Anglo-Saxon and Gothic Gospels prepared by Junius and his pupil and friend Thomas Marshall (1665.2), the visual effect is striking compared with anything that had gone before (Illustration 33). Drawing on his breadth of knowledge and depth of understanding Junius produced a remarkable tool for scholarly publication. It is no wonder that when George Hickes prepared his Anglo-Saxon and Gothic grammar (1689.3) for the press he chose to have it printed with the Junian types, and several books emanating from the group of Oxford scholars associated with Hickes used the Junian Pica Anglo-Saxon set of type-designs as well (Illustration 34).[110] The century began with one great scholar, John Selden, using an existing Anglo-Saxon fount, already designed for Archbishop Parker in the previous century. Now, at the end of the century, we see another great scholar, George Hickes, also using an existing Anglo-Saxon fount, that designed for Franciscus Junius, teacher, friend and collaborator of Marshall, who taught Hickes. When the punches were rediscovered in Bodley's Librarian's study in 1697 no doubt new matrices were made, and new types for the flurry of scholarly Anglo-Saxon publications emanating from the Sheldonian Theatre at the end of the seventeenth-century and beginning of the next century.[111] And the Junian types continued to be used well into the eighteenth century.

---

109   The types and punches are described in Hart, *Notes*, pp. 38–40. OUP Archives hold 9 lower-case letters + 8 capitals + 4 others = 21 punches: d, f, g, r, s, t; þ, ð, p; C, E, G, H, M, S, Ꝑ, Ð; þ, ꝛ, Ꝛ, ∴. OUP Archives, Case D, Box 33, hold 9 lower-case letters + 8 capitals + 3 others = 20 matrices: d, f, g, r, s, t; þ, ð, p; C, E, G, H, M, S, Ꝑ, Ð; þ, ꝛ, Ꝛ; plus another set of 10 lower-case letters + 8 capitals + 0 others = 18 matrices: d, f, g, i, r, s, t; þ, ð, p (on a smaller body and so attached to another to make it the same length as the others); C, E, G, H, M, S, Ð, Ƿ (of greater length and thickness). This capital Ƿ 'Wynn' was cut by Peter van Walpergen, who worked as a punchcutter for Fell's Oxford University Press (fl.1676–1702); it is a square capital modelled on the Somnerian capital Ƿ-design.
110   E.g., Edmund Gibson, 1691.4, 1692.1; Edward Thwaites, 1698.1; Christopher Rawlinson, 1698.2; William Elstob, 1699.1; (corporate) University of Oxford, 1700.2. The punches were rediscovered in the study of Thomas Hyde (Bodley's Librarian) in 1697 (Morison & Carter, *John Fell*, p. 244).
111   For the rediscovery of Junius's punches see Carter, *History of OUP*, pp. 125–126.

MOESO-GOTHICA. 41

Sixtyne, *sexdecim*. *Ang*. ſixteen. R. ᚺᛁᛆᛪᚢᛏᛆᛕ, *ſiaxtan*.
Seoxontyne, *septemdecim*. *Ang*. ſebenteen. R. ᚺᛁᛆᚢᛏᛆᛕ, *ſiautan*.
Eahtatyne, *octodecim*. *Ang*. eighteen. R. ᛆᛏᚱᛏᛆᛕ, *atrtan*.
Nixontyne, *novemdecim*. *Ang*. nineteen. R. ᚴᛁᚾᛆᛏᛆᛕ, *niuntan*.
Tpentix, *viginti*. *Ang*. twenty. R. ᛏᛁᛌᛪᛒ, *tiuhu*.
An, ꝺ tpentix, *viginti*, & *unum*.
Dpittix, *triginta*. G. ΘΚΙΝSΤΙΓΝΝS. *Ang*. thirty. R. ᛏᛪᚱᛁᛆᛏᛁ-
ᛪᛁ, *thriatihi*.
Feopentix, *quadraginta*. G. ᚺᛁᛆᚢᚱᛪᛏᛁΓΝΝS. *Ang*. forty. Run.
ᚠᛁᛆᚢᚱᛆᛏᛁᛪᛁ, *ſiauratihi*.
Fiptix, *quinquaginta*. G. ᚺᛁᛗᚠᛏᛁΓΝΝS. *Ang*. fifty. R. ᚠᛁᚤᛏᛁᛪᛁ,
femtihi.
Sixtix, *ſexaginta*. *Ang*. ſixty. R. ᚺᛁᛆᛪᚢᛏᛁᛪᛁ, *ſiahſtihi*.
* ᚻUNDreoxontix, *ſeptuaginta*. G. SΙᛒΝΝΤΙΓΝΝS. *Ang*. ſebenty. * *Hic notan-*
R. ᚺᛁᛆᛒᛆᛏᛁᛪᛁ, *ſiavatihi*. *dum quòd ab*
ᚻUNDeahtatix, *octoginta*. G. ᛆᚺᛏᛆNᛏᚴᚺᚾᚾᛆ. *Ang*. eighty. *hoc Numero*
R. ᛆᛏᛏᛁᛏᛁᛪᛁ, *attitihi*. 70, ᚻUND
ᚻUNDnixontix, *nonaginta*. G. NINNᛏᚴᚺᚾᚾᛆ. *Ang*. ninety. ιN *apud Anglo-*
NINNᛏᚴᚺᚾᚾᛆ ᛆS ᚷᛆ NINNᚴ Γᛆᚴᛆᛁᚺᛏᛆᛁᛉᚴ, *ſuper Nona-* *ſaxones præ-*
ginta novem juſtis, Luc. 15. 7. R. ᚴᛁᛆᛏᛁᛪᛁ, *niutihi*. *ponitur uſque*
ᚻUNDteontix, *centum*. G. ᚺᚾᚾᛆ, *Joh*. 6. 7. Luc. 7. 41. Marc. 14. 5. *ad* ᚻUND-
Item ᛏᛆᛁᚺᚾᚾᛏᛆᛁᚺᚾᚾᛆ, vel ᛏᛆᛁᚺᚾᚾᛏᚴᚺᚾᚾᛆ, q. d. *decem* tpelptix,
decies, Luc. 16. 6, 7. 15. 4. Sed (inquit *Gloſſographus* ſagaciſſimus) quoti- 120.
diani ſermonis uſus difficilem *polyſyllabicæ* vocis pronuntiationem averſatus,
poſtremam longioris appellationis partem retinuit. Valdè quoque ſuſpicor
poſterioris ævi ſcribas, non obſervatâ hujus reduplicationis cauſâ, corruptè
ſcripſiſſe ᛏᛆᛁᚺᚾᚾᛏᛆᛁ ᚺᚾᚾᛆ, vel ᛏᛆᛁᚺᚾᚾᛏᚴ ᚺᚾᚾᛆ, pro ᛏᛆᛁ-
ᚺᚾᚾᛏᛆᛁᚺᚾᚾᛆ, vel ᛏᛆᛁᚺᚾᚾᛏᚴᚺᚾᚾᛆ. Ac ſimiliter ᛆᚺᛏᛆN-
ᛏᚴᚺᚾᚾᛆ, vel NINNᛏᚴᚺᚾᚾᛆ *diviſim* ſcripſiſſe ᛆᚺᛏᛆNᛏᚴ
ᚺᚾᚾᛆ, & NINNᛏᚴ ᚺᚾᚾᛆ, atque adeò ex hâc *Gothicorum* librario-
rum depravatâ ſcripturâ credo etiam *Angloſaxones* [quum non viderint quor-
ſum *Gothi* poſtponerent ᚺᚾᚾᛆ perperàm ab integrâ Cardinalis Numeri
denominatione reſectum] illud ᚺᚾᚾᛆ potiùs præpoſuiſſe majoribus numeris Cardinalibus, necnon ipſi quoque Centenario ᚺᚾᚾᛆteontix. Nam
utut teontix per ſe denotet *denadecies*, i. e. *centum*, præpoſuerunt tamen ei
veluti ex ſupervacuo illud ᚺᚾᚾᛆ, quod per *Gothicorum Amanuenſium* oſ-
citantiam à numeris Cardinalibus avulſum poſtponebatur. *Centum*, Ang.
an ᚻundred. R. ᛪᚾᛆᛕᚱᛆᛏᛆ, *Hundrata*.
ᚻUNDenluxontix, *centum*, & *decem*.
ᚻUNDtpelptix, *centum*, & *viginti*.
Tpahund, *ducentum*. *Ang*. twohundred.
Dpeohund, *tercentum*. *Ang*. threehundred.
Duꝼand, *mille*. G. ΘNSNNᛆ, per multiplicem contractionem, ut con-
jecturat *Gloſſator*, factum ex ᛏᛆᛁᚺNNS, vel ᛏᛁΓᛉS ᚺᚾᚾᛆ. *Ang*. a
Thouſand. R. ᛏᛪᚾᚢᛁᛆᛏᛁ, *Thuſinti*. Tpa puꝼendo, *bis mille*, Marc. 5. 13.
G. ᛏᚤᛉS ΘNSNNᛆᚷᛉS. ᛏᛆᛁᚺNN ΘNSNNᛆᚷᛉM, ᛏᚤᛆM-
F ᛏᛁΓNM

ILLUSTRATION 34A/B   Text in Anglo-Saxon and other (Germanic) languages showing the display potential of Junius's types: Hickes, *Institutiones Grammaticae* (1689.3), sigs F1r, N4v (CUL Bb*.2.24(D)). Reduced to 80%

CAP. XVIII.

In quo, inſtitutis quibuſdam parallelifmis, Linguæ Angloſaxonica, & Mœſo-Gothica cum Iſlandica, ſive Scandia-Gothica conferuntur.

A TQUE hìc quidem tantùm non laſſato, & ſuſcepto operi finem imponere volenti ecce mihi allata eſt multum deſiderata Grammatica ISLANDICA *Runolphi Jonæ*, quam *Hafniâ* petitam pro humanitate ſua mihi tranſmiſit Reverendus & Ornatiſſimus Vir *Johan. Meckenius*, Illuſtriſſimo *Georgio, Daniæ* & *Norwegiæ* Principi hæreditario, à ſacris domeſticis. Avidè perlegi *Iſlandicæ* linguæ rudimenta, utpote in quibus, & quæ erudirent, & delectarent curioſos Lectores me inventurum ſperarem. Neque res multum aliter, atque expectavi, evenit. Nam aurea multa & quæ præſertim oſtendunt propinquitatem *Angloſaxonicæ*, & *Mœſo-Gothicæ*, cum veteri *Cimbro-Gothicâ* inter legendum ſe obtulere, quam inſtitutis certis quibuſdam parallelifmis, ſive collationibus, linguarum & antiquitatum Arctoarum ſtudioſis non gravabor in peculiari Capite ob oculos ponere.

I.

Collatio prima, quæ eſt Articulorum.

Art. *Angloſax.* Se, ꞃeo, þæꞇ.
Art. *Mœſo-Goth.* SA, SR, ΨATA.
Art. *Iſlandicus,* Sa, ſu, það.

Num. Sing.			Num. Plur.		
nom. Sa.	Su.	Thað.	nom. Their.	Thair.	Thaug.
gen. theſs.	theirrar.	theſs.	gen. theirra.	theirra.	theirra.
dat. theim.	theirre.	thui.	dat. theim.	theim.	theim.
acc. thann.	tha.	thað.	acc. thaa.	thær.	thaug.
abl. theim.	theirre.	thui.	abl. theim.	theim.	theim.

Docet *Runolphus* Articulos *Iſlandicos* (inter quos enumerat pronomen ſecundæ perſonæ, quod præponitur vocativis) ex pronominum promptuario eſſe ſumptos. Nos vero obſervavimus Articulos *Angloſax.* & *Mœſo-Goth.* quum Demonſtrativi, tum Relativi pronominis vim, & uſum obtinere, & diſcentibus in idem redit utraque præceptio.

Collatio

4 The Somnerian Pica Anglo-Saxon Type-Design Called 'English'-Size

As we have seen above the Somnerian Pica Anglo-Saxon (1658–) was probably cut by Nicholas Nicholls, and supplies of type (possibly matrices) were provided to the nascent Oxford University Press, which used them for Somner's Anglo-Saxon dictionary (1659.1). The range of special sorts shown by this fount follows the usage of earlier ones, particularly the Parkerian models and Junius. Lower-case letters include d, e (without tongue), f, g, i, r, s, t, y, þ, ð, p. The top bar of the g is rather long. Capitals include A, Æ¹ and Æ², square C, E, square G, H, K, M, S, Ð, P, W, of which A, K and W are additions to previous founts, K appearing in the earliest specimen as both lower-case and upper-case (1656.2); see Illustration 35. K and W are not regularly used in Old English spelling, as c was regularly used for /k/ and p 'wynn' for /w/, although k for /k/ is found from time to time. After the Conquest of 1066, however, Norman scribes favoured k for /k/ because they used c for /s/ (hence PresE *ice* /aɪs/ for OE *is* /ɪːs/), and they introduced the graph w. The influence on these forms, therefore, must be post-Conquest, and the only manuscript text that frequently employs *W* as well as K is the *Peterborough Chronicle*, now OBL Laud misc. 636, a manuscript widely used from Parker's time onwards.¹¹² The Copy Annals and First Continuation are written in one hand of the second quarter of the twelfth century, and the Second Continuation in another hand from the middle of the twelfth century. Capital K occurs, e.g., on fo 24ᵛ, where its form is somewhat like an enlarged lower-case k without the bow closed. The Somnerian type-designer may have added the hooked descender, or this feature may come from another manuscript. Capital *W* occurs, e.g., on fo 35ʳ, and has the form of two Vs intersecting. At the beginning of the first annal on fo 1ᵛ there is a secondary display capital A, which may have inspired the Somnerian A; although it is the only such capital A in the manuscript with a bar across the top, its position at the beginning of the text would have given it greater prominence. Additional sorts shown include þ, ⁊, ⸵ (punctus elevatus), ⁊̇ (punctus versus); Somner is the first to include the punctus elevatus in a set of Anglo-Saxon type-designs. Again, as indicated above, this design was widely employed by several printers and it continued to be used in the eighteenth century.

---

112 Facsimile ed. Whitelock, *Peterborough Chronicle*: for discussion of the script see pp. 14–18.

Long Primer English.

Ur Father, which art in heaven, Hallowed be thy Name; Thy kingdom come. Thy will be done in earth, as it is in heaven. Give us this day our daily bread. And forgive us our trespasses, as we forgive them that trespass against us. And lead us not into temptation; But deliver us from evil. For thine is the kingdom, the power, and the glory, for ever and ever. Amen.

A B C D E F G H I K L M N O P Q R S T U W X Y Z

Brevier Roman.

Pater noster qui es in cœlis, sanctificetur nomen tuum. Veniat regnum tuum: fiat voluntas tua, sicut in cœlo, ita etiam in terra. Panem nostrum quotidianum da nobis hodie. Et remitte nobis debita nostra, sicut & remittimus debitoribus nostris. Et ne nos inducas in tentationem, sed libera nos ab illo malo. Quia tuum est regnum, & potentia, & gloria in secula, Amen.

A B C D E F G H I K L M N O P Q R S T V U W X Y Z J Æ

Brevier Ital.

Pater noster qui es in cœlis, sanctificetur nomen tuum. Veniat regnum tuum: fiat voluntas tua, sicut in cœlo, ita etiam in terra. Panem nostrum quotidianum da nobis hodie. Et remitte nobis debita nostra, sicut & remittimus debitoribus nostris. Et ne nos inducas in tentationem, sed libera nos ab illo malo. Quia tuum est regnum, & potentia, & gloria in secula, Amen.

A B C D E F G H I K L M N O P Q R S T V W X Y Z Æ

Non-pariel Roman.

Pater noster qui es in cœlis, sanctificetur nomen tuum. Veniat regnum tuum; fiat voluntas tua, sicut in cœlo, ita etiam in terra. Panem nostrum quotidianum da nobis hodie. Et remitte nobis debita nostra, sicut & remittimus debitoribus nostris. Et ne nos inducas in tentationem, sed libera nos ab illo malo. Quia tuum est regnum, & potentia, & gloria in secula, Amen.

A B C D E F G H I K L M N O P Q R S T V U W X Y Z J Æ

Pica Saxon.

A B C D E F G h I k L M N O P R S T Ð U W X Y Z &:·
a b c ð e f ʒ h i k l m n o p p ꞃ ꞅ t ð u p x ẏ z ᛫ ꝥ

Fæðeꞃ uꞃe þu þe eaꞃt on heoꝼenum. Si þin nama ʒehalʒod:· To-becume þin ꞃice:· Ʒepupðe þin ꝥilla on eoꝛþan. ꞅpa ꞅpa on heoꝼenum:· Upne ðæʒhpamhcan hlaꝼ ꞅẏle uꞅ to ðæʒ:· And ꝼoꞃʒẏꝼ uꞅ uꞃe ʒẏltaꞅ. ꞅpa ꞅpa pe ꝼoꞃʒiꝼað upum ʒẏlten- ðum:· And ne ʒelæðþe þu uꞅ on coꞅtnunʒe. ac alẏꞅ uꞅ oꝼ ẏꝼele:· So ðlice:·

ILLUSTRATION 35   Oxford University type-specimen (1687?.1) showing the Somnerian Pica Anglo-Saxon (Morison/Carter 1967: pl. 11): OXC D.124, fo 9ʳ

5   The Oxford University Press Small Pica Anglo-Saxon Type-Design

The person probably responsible for drawing the designs of this Small Pica Anglo-Saxon (AS8: Face 66 x 1.5: 2.4) was Humfrey Wanley (1672–1726), the outstanding palaeographer, and credit for their implementation belongs to Edward Thwaites (1671–1711), the distinguished Old English scholar. The design was cut by Peter de Walpergen (fl. Oxford 1676–1703†) who was punchcutter for the university press.[113] Whether it was made for the book it first appeared in, Benson's *Vocabularium Anglo-Saxonicum* (1701.1), is doubtful, as the previously issued prospectuses for this book, 1690.2 (printed but not published) and 1699.2, used the Junian Anglo-Saxon Pica (AS6). In 1701.1 AS8 is combined with Christoffel van Dijck's Small Pica Roman (Body 69), with Latin glosses in van Dijck's Small Pica Italic (Face 66 x 1.3: 2.00).[114] The special sorts shown are all lower-case, eleven of them: ð, f, ʒ, ı, p, ſ, τ, ẏ; þ, ð, ρ.

In Hickes's *Thesaurus* of 1703/5.1 it is found in Booklet 5, 2D1ᵛ–4I1ʳ (Wanley's catalogue of AS manuscripts after Oxford, which is in the larger Pica), where it is combined with the same Small Pica Roman interspersed with the same Small Pica Italic as in Benson's *Vocabularium* (1701.1), both by van Dijck. The same lower-case special sorts are used with the addition of ʒ, which may have been available earlier but was not needed in a word-list. In 1701.1 no Anglo-Saxon capitals are used even at the price of using Th- and W- for some words, and that is also the case in Booklet 5 of 1703/5.1 up to sig. 2V, where Th- is used instead of Ð, and W- instead of Ƿ. After the libraries in Oxford and Cambridge have been dealt with, the section on other libraries (starting with those in the Royal collection) begins on sig. 2X1ᵛ, where Ƿ makes its first appearance, and Ð first appears on sig. 2X2ʳ. The abbreviation þ also makes its first appearance on sig. 2X2ᵛ. Small capital ᴆ first appears on sig. 3A1ᵛ in the name ÆÐELWERD, and is rarely used. The first three of these extra sorts also appear in Booklet 6, Index VI, sigs G1ʳ–M1ᵛ (Wanley's index to authors and works cited in Booklet 5), Ð notably in lemma on sig. L2 and Ƿ notably in lemma on sig. M1; see Illustration 36. It seems probable that the four extra sorts became available during the printing of Booklet 5, i.e. Walpergen was making new punches as the printing of the book progressed. Since Walpergen died in 1703, it is possible

---

113   Morison & Carter, *John Fell*, pp. 70–72; Hart, *Notes*, p. 72; Ould, *Printing*, II.66–83.
114   For van Dijck's Small Pica Roman see David J. McKitterick, 'A Type-Specimen of Christoffel van Dijck?', *Quaerendo*, 7 (1977), pp. 66–75, at p. 70, no. 225 Descendiaen Romeyn. For van Dijck's Small Pica Italic see Hart, *Notes*, p. 26.

5. fol. 94, b. Her Cyðon Hv Seoc Man Mot His Fæsten Alysan.

Incip. Mon mæᵹ aneſ dæᵹeſ fæſtan alyſan mid anum peniᵹe. Eac man mæᵹ alyſan aneſ dæᵹeſ fæſten mid twam hund ſealma. ⁊ xx. ſealma.

6. *Ibid.* *Modus confitendi peccata.*

Incip. Ðonne man to hiſ ſcriſte ᵹanᵹe. þænne ſceal he mid ſpiðe micelan ᵹodeſ eᵹe. and mid micelſe eadmodnyſſe beforan him hine ſelfne aþenian. and hine biddan ſepenðſe ſteſne.

Expl. Seo tƿelſte iſ maniciphad ſſa þam ſceaðam ſeaſð æt cſiſteſ þroſunᵹa.

LI. fol. 95. Incipivnt Monasteriales Indicia.

Incip. Ðiſ ſindon þa tacna þe mon on mynſtſe healdan ſceal. þæſ mon æſteſ neᵹoleſ beboðe ſpiᵹan haldan pile. and ᵹeoſnelice mið ᵹoðeſ fultume beᵹyman ſceal.

Expl. to ðon oðſum on bindan tacne. Explicivnt Monasteriales Indicia.

LII. fol. 98, b. Her Onᵹind Embe Tƿelf Derƿyrðan Stanas ⁊ Gimmas Ðe Ƿe Leornvdan In Pocalipsis Ðære Bec.

Incip. Ðæt æſeſte ᵹim cynn iſ þ blac and ᵹſene ⁊ þa hiſ ſyndon buto to ᵹædeſe ᵹemencᵹede ⁊ ſindon on naman Gearſiſ haten.

Expl. Tƿelſta iſ Caſbunculuſ haten ſe iſ byſnende ᵹlede ᵹelic.

LIII. *Ibid. De Adamante, Magnete, lapide Asbesto, Selenite Alexandrio, Stircite, Catholico, Mocrito,* &c.

Init. Sum ſtan iſ ðe Adamanſ hatte. nele hine iſeſn ne ſtyle ne aſiht heaſdeſ ᵹnetan.

Expl. Se mæᵹ pið æᵹhƿylcum attſe and duſte.

LIV. fol. 99. *Praecepta quædam, ex libro (ut videtur) Proverbiorum Salomonis, aut Ecclesiastici Syracidis desumpta.*

Incip. Ƿaſna þe pið þa pyſðmynſaſ þe þu butan ᵹylce heldan ne miht healicnyſ pyſðmynſa iſ leahtſa micelnyſ. On maſan pice ſe maſa bið ᵹecpylmeð.

Expl. ne fopſoᵹa æniſe. nanne foplæt þu ᵹelæſne fſam þe. nan unſot ᵹeſice fſam þe. nan fſam þe ᵹeſcind ᵹehſoſſe. Ealle ᵹemæne. Eallum ſyle. ⁊ callum ᵹeeaſca.

ILLUSTRATION 36
The Oxford University Small Pica Anglo-Saxon (AS8) in 1703/5.1 Booklet 5, †3D1ᵛ, lh col, lower two-thirds: CUL Pet.C.12.24

that he was still working on this fount when he died. According to Morison & Carter, *John Fell*, p. 250, Oxford University Press retains fifteen matrices

Đ, ᴅ, ð, ꝼ, ȝ, ꝑ, ꞃ, ꞇ, p, ẏ, þ, ð, þ, ∴, ƿ,

and the four corresponding punches, Đ, ᴅ, ƿ, þ are distinctively those of Walpergen. It is notable that the punches are for letters apparently added later: Đ, ƿ, ᴅ and þ.

There is an explanation for this set of circumstances. In his diary for 6 Oct 1705 Thomas Hearne (1678–1735) noted that 'M^r. Wanley writ the Preface to the Catalogue of Septentrional MSS. in English, wch was afterwards translated into Latin by M^r. Thwaites, or else his Pupils, who supervis'd and corrected the whole Catalogue, & order'd it as he [Thwaites] pleas'd'.[115] While this remark applies to Booklet 5, and sigs †a1^r–†d1^v in particular, Thwaites's letters indicate that his role was indeed supervisory, as Hearne stated.[116] Thwaites's letter to Wanley of 3 July 1702 asks Wanley to send more copy (presumably of Booklet 5) and wants to know if Wanley has sent the specimen drawings of letters to Peter de Walpergen so that he can get on with cutting them.[117] It seems probable that the letter-drawings referred to are for these extra sorts for AS8, which altogether shows sixteen sorts. Probably Thwaites, with Wanley's collaboration, was the chief instigator of this fount, or at least of developing it further. The design is based on Junius's except for the square capital ƿ, which comes from the Somnerian fount (AS7). According to Morison & Carter, *John Fell* (p. 250), Oxford University Press retains fifteen matrices and four corresponding punches, which are distinctively those of Walpergen. It is notable that the punches are for the letters apparently added later: Đ, ƿ, ᴅ and þ.

---

115 Thomas Hearne, *Remarks and Collections of Thomas Hearne*, vol. I, ed. C.E. Doble, Oxford Historical Society Publications II (Oxford: Clarendon Press, 1885), p. 52.
116 R.L. Harris, *A Chorus of Grammars: The Correspondence of George Hickes and his Collaborators on* Thesaurus linguarum septentrionalium, Publications of the Dictionary of Old English 4 (Toronto: Pontifical Institute of Medieval Studies, 1992), pp. 68–69.
117 Harris, *Chorus*, p. 372. An Anglo-Saxon alphabet by Wanley is preserved in OBL Eng.bibl.c.3 (SC 33184), p. 29, which the designs in the type-fount strongly resemble.

CHAPTER 5

Continental Anglo-Saxon Type-Designs

Until recently it has been thought that 'continental printers did not possess a special fount for printing Anglo-Saxon'.[1] The first one noticed here (CAS1, 1568), the Great Primer Anglo-Saxon phonetic special sorts made for Elizabeth I's ambassador to Paris, Sir Thomas Smith (1513–77), did not constitute an Anglo-Saxon fount as such, rather it provided phonetic symbols some of which were based on Anglo-Saxon models, as Smith was interested in spelling-reform rather than Anglo-Saxon. But in the seventeenth century there were several continental Anglo-Saxon founts. They are evidently the result of continental printers wishing to reproduce the works of four outstanding English scholars who used Anglo-Saxon in their work: William Camden, Sir Henry Spelman, John Selden, and William Somner. In mimicking or trying to mimic the Anglo-Saxon letter-forms they were acting professionally in doing what was needed in a context where there was usually no controlling presence making sure that the Anglo-Saxon was produced authentically; an exception is Joan Blaeu's *Cinqvième Volvme de la Geographie Blaviane, contenant L'Angleterre* (= Atlas Maior, vol. V **1662.3**), which shows signs of well-informed revision. The quality of these continental founts is therefore mixed.

The first attempts on the continent to print passages of Anglo-Saxon occur in 1636 (CAS2.1, 2.2, 2.3) and were produced in haste to meet a political situation brought about by Charles I's desire to use Selden's *Mare Clausum* (**1635.1**) as a propagandist tool against the Dutch argument for open seas. In the 1635 edition these passages appear in the Parkerian Great Primer Anglo-Saxon (AS1). Apart from this type-design, there were in 1635, the year of publication of Selden's *Mare Clausum*, only two other Anglo-Saxon type-designs in existence, the Parkerian Pica Anglo-Saxon (AS2) and the Lambardian Pica Anglo-Saxon (AS3). Both of these made their debut in 1576, both were of Pica size, smaller than the Parkerian Great Primer, and both originated in London. No-one since Parker's and Lambarde's time had created a set of special sorts for printing Anglo-Saxon, and no-one had used such special sorts outside London.[2]

---

1 E.G. Stanley, *A Collection of Papers with emphasis on Old English Literature*, Publications of the Dictionary of Old English 3 (Toronto: Pontifical Institute of Medieval Studies, 1987), p. 51. This article provides an historical survey of continental interest in Anglo-Saxon.
2 Woodcuts were used in the type-specimen in William Camden, *Anglica, Normannica, Hibernica, Cambrica, a Veteribus scripta* (Frankfurt am Main: Johann Aubry 1, 1602; USTC 2052453),

Whereas in London there was an established tradition of printing Anglo-Saxon going back nearly 70 years, in Holland innovation or ingenuity were required, or both in combination. When three unauthorised pirate editions of this book were produced in Leiden (or in one case possibly Amsterdam) the Dutch printers were faced with a considerable challenge in copying the Anglo-Saxon sorts, and any crudeness in their appearance should be related to the lack of local precedents and the lack of local expertise in Anglo-Saxon, as well as to the speed with which the work had to be done in the circumstances.[3] The third and fourth Anglo-Saxon type-designs (CAS3 and CAS4) were also produced in Holland, this time for the parts of the text of Camden's *Britannia*, to accompany the British volumes of the great atlases produced by the firms of Blaeu and Janssonius. The fifth and seventh sets of Anglo-Saxon type-designs (CAS5 and CAS7) were produced in Germany all involving the works of John Selden, and the sixth set (CAS6), like the first, in Paris, because Du Cange's great Latin dictionary (**1678.1**) drew on Spelman's *Archaeologus* (**1626.1** and **1664.1**) and Somner's *Dictionarium* (**1659.1**).

1   The Smithian Great Primer Anglo-Saxon Phonetic Special Sorts

Sir Thomas Smith (1513–77) held a Cambridge DCL obtained by incorporation of one acquired by studying in Padua from 1540 to 1542. He was Secretary of State (1548–9, 1572–6), and English ambassador to the French court in Paris from 1562 to 1566. A man of impeccable educational pedigree with a continental perspective, his *De recta & emendata Linguæ anglicæ scriptione, Dialogus* was printed at Paris by Robert Estienne II as **1568.3**.[4] Smith's proposals were well summarized in **1605.1** by William Camden:

---

on sig. 3*4ᵛ, also (1603), on sig. 3*6ᵛ, but there are no special sorts in the text of the prose and verse Prefaces to the *Alfredian Pastoral Care* on sigs C1ʳ–2ʳ.

3   For full details see Peter J. Lucas, 'Printing Anglo-Saxon in Holland and John Selden's *Mare Clausum seu de Dominio Maris*', *Quaerendo*, 31 (2001), pp. 120–136.

4   USTC 140541. For Smith's relations with Robert Estienne II see Elizabeth Armstrong, 'The Publication of the Royal Edicts and Ordinances under Charles IX: The Destiny of Robert (II) Estienne as King's Printer', *Proceedings of the Huguenot Society*, XIX.2 (1953–4), 41–59, esp. 48–52. Smith was also the author of *De recta & emendata lingvæ Græcæ pronvnciatione*, written in the form of a letter to Stephen Gardiner, bishop of Winchester, dated (M4ʳ) 12 August 1542, but published together with the book on English from Paris in 1568. A life of Smith was compiled by John Strype: *The Life of the Learned Sir Thomas Smith Kt. Doctor of the Civil Law* (London: for A. Roper, 1698; Wing S6023), but see now Mary Dewar, *Sir Thomas Smith A Tudor Intellectual in Office* (London: Athlone Press, 1964).

Sir Thomas Smith her Maiesties secretarie not long since, a man of great learning and iudgement, occasioned by som vncertainty of our Orthographie, though it seeme grounded vpon *Sound, Reason,* and *Custome,* laboured to reduce it to certaine heads; Seeing that whereas of Necessity there must be so many letters in every tongue, as there are simple and single sounds, that the Latine letters were not sufficient to expresse all our simple sounds. Therefore he wished that we should have A short, and A long, bicause *a* in Man and in *Mân* of horse hath different sounds; E long as in *Mên* moderate, and *e* short as in Men, and an English e as in wée, thee, he, me: I long, and I short, as in Bi, *per,* and Bî, *emere* ['buy']: O short, and O long, as in smŏk of a woman, and smôk of the fire: V long, as in Bût, *Ocrea* ['boot'], and V short, as in Bŭt, *Sed:* and v or y *Greeke,* as slu, nu, tru ['sly', 'nigh', 'try']. For consonants he would have C be never vsed but for Ch, as it was among the olde English, and K in all other words; for Th, he would have the *Saxon* letter *Thorne,* which was a D with a dash through the head, or þ; for I consonant the *Saxon* ȝ, as ȝet, not Ieat for ȝeat-stone, ȝay for Iay: *Q,* if he were king of the A, B, C, should be putte to the horne, and banished; and *Ku* in his place, as *Kuik,* not *quik, Kuarel,* not *quarel: Z;* he would have vsed for the softer S, or eth, and es, as *dîz* for dieth, *lîz* for lies, and the same z inverted for *sh,* as *zal* for *shall, flez* for *flesh.* This briefly I have set you downe his devise, which albeit *Sound* and *Reason* seemed to countenance, yet that Tyranne *Custome* hath so confronted, that it will never be admitted.[5]

Smith had special sorts made to complement an italic fount, his resulting English alphabet having 34 letters. As he was making proposals, not advocating a finalized system, some of his special symbols are alternatives, Δ 'delta' and ð 'eth', for example, both indicating /ð/, θ 'theta' and þ 'thorn' both indicating /θ/. Special sorts for phonetic symbols come from two sources of inspiration. Several are explicitly based on an Anglo-Saxon model: Anglo-Saxon ꝼ for /v/, Anglo-Saxon ð for /ð/, Anglo-Saxon þ for /θ/, Anglo-Saxon dotted ẏ for /y/, Anglo-Saxon Ð for /ð/; and others which were probably inspired by an Anglo-Saxon model include ȝ for /dȝ/, undotted ı for /i/ and p for /u:/. Tongued *e* for /ɛ/ could be from Anglo-Saxon ligatured *e* with an extended tongue, though it was not used in the Parkerian Great Primer Anglo-Saxon

---

5 Camden 1605.1, p. 24. Regarding the remark about 'D with a dash through the head' Camden is treating capital Ð 'Eth' as if it were capital Þ 'Thorn'. In the modern edition of Camden's *Remains concerning Britain* by Robert D. Dunn (Toronto: University of Toronto Press, 1984) see esp. p. 33.

LING. ANG. SCRIPT.   41

ALPHABETVM ANGLICVM.

		vir	galerus	corrumpere
A a	a breuis	man	hat	mar
		iuba	odiſſe	equa
Aˆ ä a-	a longa	mân	hät	ma-r
		apis	lectus	iubere	latus
B b b	be	bed	bid	ſid
		ceraſum	vultus	ſcindere
C c c	ce	ceri	cër	cop
		columba	charus	malus
D d d	de	dou	dër	bad
		tu	ibi	balneare
Δ ð Δ Đ	Δe	Δou	Δër	baðˍ
		ductus	natus	infernus
E e	e breuis	led	bred	hel
		plūbum	panis	ſanare
Eˆ ë ẽ e-	e longa	lëd	brêd	he-l
		genus	naſci	calcaneum
Ƒ ë̇	ë Anglica	lëd	brëd	hel
		lima	tibia Alemãnica,	certamen
F f f	ef	fil	fil	ſtrïf
		vile	quinque	certare
Ѵ ѵ ƒ	eѵ	vï-l	fi-ѵ	ſtriѵ
		elegans	gignere	lignum
G g	ge	gai	get	log
		graculus	gagates,	hoſpitio excipere
Ȝ ȝ ȝ	Ȝe	Ȝai	ȝet	loȝ
		habuit	caput	ſuſpirati
H h h	ha	had	hed	ſih
		occultum	iube	per
I i y	i breuis	hid	bid	bi
		occultare	manere	emere
Iˆ ï ï̃ i-	i longa	hïd	bi-d	bĩ
		catus	præhende	dorſum
K k k	ka	kat	kac	bak

l.i.

ILLUSTRATION 37   Alphabetically arranged Table of special phonetic sorts (CAS1) used by Sir Thomas Smith, *De recta emendata Linguae anglicae scriptione Dialogus* (1568.3), L1 (CUL M*.11.24²(E))

DE RECTA ET EMEND.

			ferò	ductus	imple
L	*l l*	el	lät	led	fil
			ſtorea	lac	obſcurum
M	*m m*	em	mat	milk	dim
			non	collum	ſpelunca
N	*n n*	en	nay	nek	den
			ſalire	equus	offa
O	*o o*	o breuis	hop	hors	ſop
			ſpes	raucus	ſapo
*O*ˆ *õ ö o-*		o longa	höp	hörs	ſop
			olla	emaciare	ſinus
P	*p p*	pe	pot	pïn	lap
			liberatus	penna	cotoneũ malũ
Q	*q q*	quu	quit	quil	quins
			forex	aries	vectis
R	*r r*	er	rat	ram	bar
			locationis charta,	pediculi	aleæ
S	*ſ s*	es	lës	lis	dis
			paſcua	mendacia	moritur
Z	*ʒ z*	eʒed	leʒ	liʒ	di-ʒ
			ternio canũ,	piſcis	diſcus, lanx
Σ	*ς ς*	eς	leς	fiς	diς
			plũbũ albũ	ſtuppa	fouea
T	*t t*	te	tin	töu	pit
			tenue	degelaſcere	medulla ar-
T Θ θ þ		þe	θin	þou	piþ boris
			dama mas	plenus	limus
V U u u		u breuis	buk	ful	mud
			liber	ſtultus	ira, vel affectº
*V*ᴬ *p ũ w̃*		v-u löga, bük	fül	mwd
			verus	ruta	ceruleũ, nouũ
Y	*υ ÿ*	ϋ Græca	trυ	rυ	blυ nÿ
			ſecuris	vulpes	ſex
X	*χ x*	ex	ax	fox	ſix.

In hoc Catalogo literæ ſunt xxxiiii.

type-design, but, as noted above, it might also be from Italian or French usage, both of which are manifestly plausible influences in Smith's case.[6] Smith also used Greek letter-forms, as capital *Δ* 'delta' in two forms, one slanted to the right (as for italic usage) and one straight upright Δ, both indicating /ð/; upside down 'delta' in its straight form ∇ for /f/; capital and lower-case 'theta', Θ (upper-case), θ (lower-case), both indicating /θ/; and ʊ 'upsilon' for /y/. All these special sorts were designed to fit with Claude Garamont's Great Primer Italic, and were presumably made in Paris.[7] The cutting is of a high standard and may have been done by Guillaume Le Bé.[8] There were up to seventeen special sorts, plus the use of suprascript diaeresis, tilde and double acute accent marks.[9]

2   The Dutch Anglo-Saxon Type-Designs Produced for Selden's *Mare Clausum*

Selden's book sparked a nerve in Holland, at that time the 'bookshop of the world', where it spawned three 'pirate' editions in one year, 1636.[10] Importation of these foreign pirated editions of the *Mare Clausum* was forbidden by proclamation of King Charles I (STC 9060). All of these Dutch editions were smaller in format than the English 1635 edition, which was in folio. One (**1636.3**), in octavo, was printed in Amsterdam (or possibly Leiden) by an unidentified printer 'iuxta exemplar'.[11] Added to it is a treatise by the Leiden historian and

---

6   Tongued *e* does not occur in an Anglo-Saxon type-design until the Lambardian Pica Anglo-Saxon of **1576.2**; see above, Chapter 3.
7   Illustrated in Veyrin-Forrer and Jammes, *Les Premiers Caractères*, pl. 11, no. 2, and in *TSF* II, c. 1599, no. 22. As noted by H.D.L. Vervliet, *French Renaissance Printing Types: A Conspectus* (London: Bibliographical Society and Printing Historical Society, 2010), p. 326, the type-design (It 115) is first found in a Paris imprint of 1562.
8   On whom see Carter (ed.), *Le Bé Memorandum*.
9   Some of the special sorts, e.g., ȝ and inverted z, occur in more than one size.
10 For the 'bookshop of the world' see Andrew Pettegree & Arthur der Weduwen, *The Bookshop of the World: Making and Trading Books in the Dutch Golden Age* (London: Yale University Press, 2019).
11 STC 22176; USTC 3018464, 1016382. On sigs. b3ʳ (end of *Apologia*) and d7ʳ (end of *Tractatus*) there is an ornamental tailpiece 22 × 25 mm, showing a garlanded (?)ox's head with a crab-shaped tassle hanging from a yoke, which might enable the printer to be identified, but this tailpiece does not occur among the 'marques typographiques' illustrated in *Bibliotheca Belgica*, IV.60–203, nor has it been found in P. van Huisstede and J.P.J. Brandhorst, *Dutch Printer's Devices 15th–17th Century: A Catalogue* (Nieuwkoop: De Graaf, 1999); I am grateful to Hans Brandhorst for his assistance.

philologist Marcus Zuerius Boxhorn (1602–53), *Apologia pro Navigationibus Hollandorum*, dedicated to William Bontius (Willem de Bondt), Professor of Law at Leiden University (†1646).[12] This treatise was previously published with two 1633 editions of Grotius's *Mare Liberum*, to which Selden's book was a riposte.[13] Probably the Boxhorn edition was the first of the three Dutch editions to be published, and on 15 April 1636 Charles I issued his proclamation

> By the king. A proclamation to forbid importing, buying, selling, or publishing any forraine edition of Mare clausum,[14]

Another (**1636.1**), in duodecimo, was printed by Bonaventura and Abraham 1 Elzevier in Leiden 'iuxta exemplar Londinense'.[15] The third (**1636.2**), in quarto, was printed by Joannes and Dirk Maire, also in Leiden.[16]

2.1 The Dutch 'Boxhornian' English-Size Anglo-Saxon

The printer of this unauthorised pirate 'Boxhorn' edition of Selden's *Mare Clausum* (**1636.3**), so called because of the appended work by Boxhorn, has not been identified, but he must have been based in Amsterdam or Leiden. This edition shows the most obvious indication of haste in its composition. The main text in Pierre Haultin's Pica Roman is interspersed with Robert Granjon's second and third Pica Italics (*Cicero pendante* and *Cicero currens*) alternating between batches of gatherings until the last two when the alternation is between parts of the gatherings.[17] Presumably there were two compositors in

---

12 On Boxhorn see Kees Dekker, *The Origins of Old Germanic Studies in the Low Countries* (Leiden: Brill, 1999), pp. 209–218.
13 Hugo Grotius, *De Mari Libero* (Leiden: Bonaventura and Abraham 1 Elzevier, 1633), one in 16°, and the other in 24°: H.B. Copinger, *The Elzevier Press* (London: Grafton, 1927), nos 1998–1999; USTC 1027876, 1027877.
14 STC 9060: BL C.112.h.3, fo 54.
15 Copinger, *Elzevier Press*, no. 4287. STC 22175.3; USTC 3018465, 1027917.
16 STC 22175.7; USTC 3018463, 3018453, 1511072.
17 For Haultin's Pica Roman see Vervliet, *French Printing Types*, no. 72 on p. 142. For Granjon's second and third Pica Italics see Vervliet, *French Printing Types*, nos 272 and 274 on pp. 304 and 306. Granjon's second Pica Italic (Vervliet, no. 272) occurs in sigs A–D, G–H, L–M, X, Z–2A, 2C, 2E. 2H1–4, 2I3–4, and his third Pica Italic (Vervliet, no. 274) occurs in sigs E–F, I–K, N–V, Y, 2B, 2D, 2F–2G, 2H5–2I2.

one shop working in tandem, one with a case of the *pendante* and one with a case of the *currens*. For the Anglo-Saxon passages sixteen special sorts are shown (see Illustration 38): d, f, g, H, i, r, s, t; þ, ð; Æ², E, S, Ð; þ, ⁊. They are combined with Haultin's Pica Roman, but whereas the Pica Roman on its own has a body size of 84 mm per 20 lines, when combined with the Anglo-Saxon special sorts the body size is 96 mm, i.e. English-size. Even then there is overlap between lines, as on sig. T5ᵛ (p. 298), lines 10–11 (Illustration 38), where g and s in cẏnᵹ and aſteaðe overlap þ (twice) in þꞃitꞇiᵹoþan below; presumably some letters at least were cast on a smaller body allowing ascenders and descenders to be kerned, overlapping the edge of the body, a practice frequently followed with Hebrew and Greek sorts to facilitate the compositor in adding accents; for example, Guillaume Le Bé's Pica Hebrew 'sans points' is English-size 'avec les points'.[18] Under Parker's auspices it was usual to print Anglo-Saxon larger than the surrounding text, but here it is not in imitation of the lay-out in Selden's book, and in general appearance looks crude. There are at least two reasons for this crude appearance. While some letters, g, þ, ð (Illustration 38, line 11, þam niᵹon, ð not shown), and all the capitals except S (Illustration 38, lines 10, 9, Æþelꝛeð, Eaðꝛapð) are Great Primer in size (presumably modelled on the Parkerian set of designs), other letters, such as f and r (Illustration 38, lines 12, hæꝛðe, ᵹeaꝛe) are of a size in keeping with the Pica with which they are combined. Another reason for this crudeness of appearance arises from the fact that some letters are not Anglo-Saxon at all but perceived near-equivalents from other founts.

For lower-case p 'wynn' a Roman p is used (Illustration 38, line 11, pæꝛ erron. for pæꝛ 'was'). For t an upside-down number 2 is used: 2 for t (Illustration 38, line 12, hehꞇ). The capital H (used in lower-case position) and lower-case d (Illustration 38, line 10, ðeꝛeᵹẏlð) match that from a German seventeenth-century Pica Fraktur design found on a type-specimen issued by Johann Erasmus Luther (1642–83) at Frankfurt in 1678, and which survives in the Norstedt collection in Stockholm.[19]

The lower-case s (Illustration 38, line 12, þæꝛ) matches a final-position 'tzade' and the tironian sign (Illustration 38, line 11) matches a final-position 'caph' from a square Hebrew fount. This Hebrew fount is apparently the same as the Mediaen Hebreus shown in the type-specimen (A4ᵛ no.2) of

---

18   *TSF* II: c. 1599, nos 28–29.
19   For the Luther specimen see Gustav Mori, *Frankfurter Schriftproben aus dem 16. bis 18. Jahrhundert* (Frankfurt-am-Main, 1955), plate 9, where it is labelled 'Cicero Fractur'. See also C. Axel-Nilsson, *Type Studies: The Norstedt Collection of Matrices in the Typefoundry of the Royal Printing Office, A History and Catalogue* (Stockholm: Norstedts Tryckeri, 1983), no. NS 332.

298   Mare Clavsvm, sev

a Ms. in in anno sequente collocant Annales aliquot
Bibliot. Anglo-Saxonici ᵃ adeoque annos 39. ab ini-
Cotto-
niana. tiis tributi hujus (quod & Hepeʒylð seu He-
Compacti regildum id est tributum Militare seu Navale ap-
cum
Guil. pellant) ad illam Edvvardi Regis abolitio-
Gisbur- nem intercessisse testantur; idem interea cum
nensis
annali- Ingulpho & Hovedenio, quantum ad ini-
bus. tia attinet, asserentes. In anno scilicet ML.II;
Aleðe Eaðpaɾð cynʒ (sic Annales illi) þ
Hepeʒylð þ Æþelɾeð cynʒ æɾ aɾɾealðe,
þ pæɾ on þam niʒon ⁊ þɾizziʒoþan
ʒeaɾe þæɾ þe hehz on ʒannon hæɾðe, id
est, Abolevit Edvvardus Rex Tributum illud milita-
b Ms. pe- re, seu Heregildum quod antea indixerat Æthel-
nes Ca- redus Rex; anno nimirum XXXIX à tempore quo
mera-
rios incæpit. At verò apud autorem ᵇ Dialogi de
Scac- Scaccario sub Henrico Rege II conscripti
carii,
c.27.Idē (eum fuisse Gervasium Tilburiensem vulgo
habetur putatur) legitur solutum esse quotannis us-
dialo-
gus etiā que ad tempora Guilielmi Regis primi seu
in Codice Normannorum adventum. Nempe per qua-
Rubro
penes tuordecim annos integros, qui abolitionem
Reme- illam proximè secuti sunt. Nam tamdiu re-
morato-
rē Regis. gnavit Edvvardus Rex quem excepit Guilielmus ille. Verba autoris sunt; *Circumadjacentium insularum prædones, irruptione facta, maritima depopulantes, aurū, argentū & quæque pretiosa tollebant. Verum cùm Rex & indigenæ bellicis ap-*

para-

ILLUSTRATION 38   John Selden, *Mare Clausum* (1636.3), T5ᵛ, showing
the Dutch 'Boxhornian' English-size Anglo-Saxon
(CAS2.1) in an extract from ASC (C) 1052
(CUL Syn.8.63.364)

Joannes Janssonius, *Verkoopinge van een Oude en Welgesorteerde Druckerie en Lettergieterie* (Amsterdam: J. Janssonius, 1666), preserved at Oxford, Bodleian Library, Marshall 148; Janssonius had matrices for this fount (C1^r) but not punches (C1^v). The edition (e.g., on sig. C3^r) also uses the Augustijn Arabisch shown in the Janssonius specimen (A4^v, no. 5). This apparent identification raises the possibility that the printer of the 'Boxhorn' edition is indeed Janssonius. As we shall see when his large atlases are considered below, haste and improvisation were characteristic of his work. The Hebrew fount occurs in the book with these two characters, e.g., on sigs C5^r–8^r, with a mem-height of 2.5 mm (i.e. the height of the normal letters without ascenders or descenders), where it is cast on a Pica body (84) to match the Roman. However, if the fount were cast on a body without the ascenders or descenders overlapping the edge of the body, the Hebrew letters tzade and caph would fit on an English-size body without overlap, so, for convenience, it is useful to consider this design as English-size, and this size-attribution fits the body-size of the Anglo-Saxon text.

2.2   *The Dutch Elsevierian English-Size Anglo-Saxon*

The Elzevier edition (1636.1) has its main text set in Pierre Haultin's Small Pica Roman (Body 72).[20] The passages in Anglo-Saxon show 19 special sorts combined with a Pica Roman (?Haultin's: see Illustration 39): **d, f, g, H, i, r, s, t, y; þ, ð, p; Æ¹, Æ², E, S, Ð, þ, ꝫ**. Because some letters are so large the body size of the Anglo-Saxon passages is 104 mm for 20 lines, probably achieved by judicious leading where the body-size is 72; in Illustration 39, line 16, the left shoulder of *M* in *Mili-* has been filed away to make room for the **g** in ƀeɼeȝylð above. They are uneven in the quality of their cutting. Anglo-Saxon lower-case **s, þ,** and **p** are reasonably good (Illustration 39, lines 24, 25, pæɼ, þam), especially **s** and **p**, **r** and **ð** are appropriate in size (Illustration 39, line 26, ȝeaɲe; **ð** not shown), and **i** and **y** are the Roman letters respectively without and with a dot. But other letters are less good: **f, t** and **g** (Illustration 39, lines 26–27, hehꞇ onȝannon hæɼðe) are Great Primer in size (presumably modelled on the Parkerian design, which they resemble closely) with **g** showing such a long tail that it is set high alongside the other letters; it was the **g** that caused the problem just noted in the word below ƀeɼeȝylð. **d** looks as though it is the same as **ð** with the ascender broken off immediately below the cross-stroke. All the capitals are on the tall side.

---

20   Vervliet, *French Printing Types*, no. 54 on p. 124.

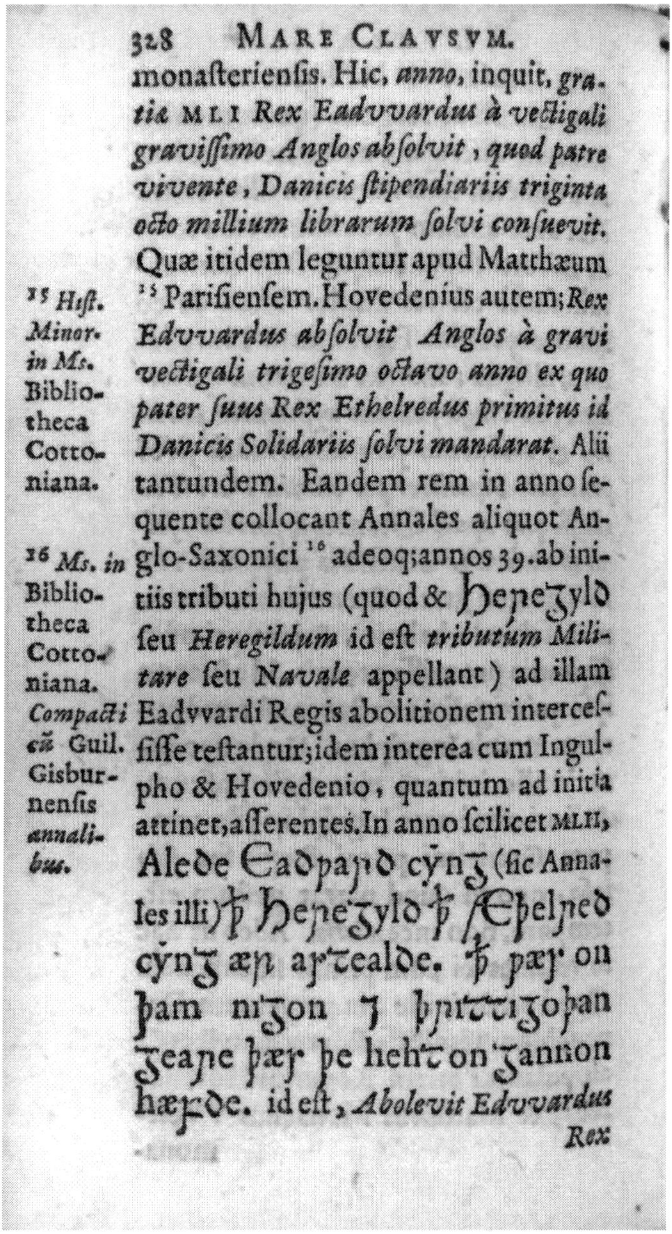

328   MARE CLAVSVM.
monafterienfis. Hic, *anno*, inquit, *gra-tia* MLI *Rex Eadvvardus à vectigali graviſſimo Anglos abſolvit, quod patre vivente, Danicis ſtipendiariis triginta octo millium librarum ſolvi conſuevit.* Quæ itidem leguntur apud Matthæum [15] Parifienfem. Hovedenius autem; *Rex Edvvardus abſolvit Anglos à gravi vectigali trigeſimo octavo anno ex quo pater ſuus Rex Ethelredus primitus id Danicis Solidariis ſolvi mandarat.* Alii tantundem. Eandem rem in anno ſequente collocant Annales aliquot Anglo-Saxonici [16] adeoq;annos 39. ab initiis tributi hujus (quod & heregyld feu *Heregildum* id eſt *tributum Militare* feu *Navale* appellant) ad illam Eadvvardi Regis abolitionem interceſſiſſe teſtantur;idem interea cum Ingulpho & Hovedenio, quantum ad initia attinet,aſſerentes.In anno ſcilicet MLII, Aleðe Eaðpaɲð cynʒ (ſic Annales illi) þ heɲeʒylð þ Æþelɲeð cynʒ æɲ aɲtealðe. þ pæɾ on þam nıʒon ʒ bɲıttıʒoþan ʒeaɲe pæɾ þe heht on ʒannon hæɾðe. id eſt, *Abolevit Edvvardus Rex*

[15] *Hiſt. Minor. in Ms. Bibliotheca Cottoniana.*

[16] *Ms. in Bibliotheca Cottoniana. Compacti cū Guil. Gisburnenſis annalibus.*

ILLUSTRATION 39   John Selden, *Mare Clausum* (1636.1), O8ᵛ, showing the Dutch Elsevierian English-size Anglo-Saxon (CAS2.2) in an extract from ASC (C) 1052 (CUL H.16.48)

2.3 *The Dutch Mairian English-Size Anglo-Saxon*

The Maire edition (1636.2) has its main text set in another Pica Roman (Body 83) interspersed with Granjon's third Pica Italic, the *Cicero currens*.[21] The passages in Anglo-Saxon show 17 special sorts combined with the Pica Roman: **d, f, g, H, r, s, t, y; þ, ð, p; Æ¹, E, S, Ð; þ, ꞃ**; there is no Anglo-Saxon dotless **i** and only the one form of capital **Æ**. Although the size of most of the Anglo-Saxon sorts is English-size, the body size of the Anglo-Saxon passages matches that of the Pica Roman, the only one of the three Dutch editions of which this can be said. However, as with the Elzevier edition, the Anglo-Saxon characters are uneven in the quality of their cutting. Anglo-Saxon lower-case **s, þ**, and **p** are reasonably good (Illustration 40, line 18, pæꞃ, þam), especially **s** and **p, r** and **ð** are appropriate in size (Illustration 40, line 18, ꞇeaꞅe; **ð** not shown), and **y** is the Roman letter with a dot. But other letters are less good: **f, t** and **g** (Illustration 40, lines 18–19, hehꞇ onᵹannon hæꝼðe) are Great Primer in size (presumably modelled on the Parkerian design, which they resemble closely), **g** having such a long tail that it is set high alongside the other letters. **d** looks as though it is the same as **ð** with the upper stem broken off immediately below the bar. All the capitals are on the tall side. These problems of excess height (the tension between English-size letters and a Pica-size text body) are particularly noticeable where there is an overlap between lines, as, for example, in Illustration 40, lines 17/18, where the tail of **g** in cẏnᵹ (1st) falls below the ascender of **þ**; in the same lines cf. also Æþelꞃeð above þꞃiꞇꞩᵹoþan and aꞅꞇeal- above hehꞇ.

2.4 *Evidence for Punchcutting from These Dutch Editions of Mare Clausum*

When the attention that was evidently given to overcoming these problems is taken into account, the similarity of this Dutch Mairian English-size Anglo-Saxon fount to that in the Elzevier edition is even more noticeable. As far as most of the characters are concerned they are similar to the point of identity. One wonders whether some letters were cut for a Great Primer size (as in Selden's English edition) and then it was realized that the special sorts had to be combined with a Pica, so the rest were cut with an x-height more in accordance with this size, and there was no time (or resources) to do the oversized letters again. Only two characters show difference. **H** in the Elzevier edition has the upper left serif right across the top of the left stem, whereas **H**

---

21 Vervliet, *French Printing Types*, no. 274 on p. 306.

De Dominio Maris, Lib. II.   143

ipso, quo id quod narrat gestum est, tempore, non incelebris. Adeò ut hac in re fides ei cum primis sit habenda. Quod verò ait ille, in perpetuum Danegeldum remisisse Edwardum Regem; astipulantur etiam Rogerius Hovedenius, & Matthæus Monachus Westmonasteriensis; Hic, *anno,* inquit, *gratiæ* ML I *Rex Eadvvardus à vectigali gravissimo Anglos absolvit, quod patre vivente, Danicis stipendiariis triginta octo millium librarum solvi consuevit.* Quæ itidem leguntur apud Matthæum *a* Parisiensem. Hovedenius autem; *Rex Edvvardus absolvit Anglos à gravi vectigali trigesimo octavo anno ex quo pater suus Rex Ethelredus primitus id Danicis Solidariis solvi mandarat.* Alii tantundem. Eandem rem in anno sequente collocant Annales aliquot Anglo-Saxonici *b* adeoque annos 39. ab initiis tributi hujus (quod & heregylð seu *Heregildum,* id est, *tributum Militare* seu *Navale* appellant) ad illam Eadwardi Regis abolitionem intercessisse testantur; idem interea cum Ingulpho & Hovedenio, quantum ad initia attinet, asserentes. In anno scilicet ML II; Aleðe Eaðparð cynᵹ (sic Annales *b* illi) þ heregylð þ Æþelneð cynᵹ æp arðealðe. þ pæꞅ on þam niᵹon ꞅ þꞃittiᵹoþan ᵹeape þæꞅ þe heht on ᵹannon hæꞅðe, id est, *Abolevit Edvvardus Rex Tributum illud militare, seu* Heregildum, *quod antea indixerat Æthelredus Rex; anno nimirum* XXXIX *à tempore quo incepit.* At verò apud autorem Dialogi de Scaccario sub Henrico Rege II conscripti (eum fuisse Gervasium Tilburiensem vulgo putatur) legitur solutum esse quotannis usque ad tempora Guilielmi Regis primi seu Normannorum adventum. Nempe per quatuordecim annos integros, qui abolitionem illam proximè secuti sunt. Nam tamdiu regnavit Edvvardus Rex quem excepit Guilielmus ille. Verba autoris *c* sunt; *Circumadjacentium insularum prædones, irruptione facta, maritima depopulantes, aurum, argentum & quæque pretiosa tollebant. Verùm cùm Rex & indigenæ bellicis apparatibus instructi, in suæ gentis defensionem, instarent, illi fugas adgrediebantur æquoreas. Inter hos itaque penè præcipua & semper pronior ad nocendum erat bellicosa illa & populosa Gens Danorum; qui præter communem raptorum avaritiam acriùs instabant, quia aliquid sibi de antiquo jure, in eiusdem regni dominatione, vendicabant, sicut Britonum pleniùs narrat historia. Ad hos igitur arcendos, à Regibus Anglicis statutum, ut de singulis Hidis Regni, jure quodam perpetuo, duo solidi argentei solverentur in usus virorum fortium, qui perlustrantes & jugiter excubantes maritima, impetum hostium reprimerent. Quia igitur principaliter pro Danis institutus est hic reditus,* Danegeldum, *vel* Danegeldus, *dicitur. Hic igitur annua lege, sicut dictum est,*

sub

ILLUSTRATION 40   John Selden, Mare Clausum (1636.2), S4ʳ, showing the Dutch Mairian English-size Anglo-Saxon (CAS2.3) in an extract from ASC (C) 1052 (OBL Vet.B2.e.30).

in the Maire edition has the upper left serif only to the left of the stem; and the right stem has a longer tail in the Maire edition. And ꝛ in the Elsevier edition has a longer stem; this difference may result from using different Hebrew characters, perhaps final-position 'caph' in the Elzevier edition as opposed to 'daleth' (or 'resh'?) in the Maire edition.[22] There are also two characters in the Elzevier set not in the Maire set: dotless i and Æ[2] (Illustration 40, lines 23, 25, Æþelneð, nıȝon) Whatever the explanation for the differences there is no escaping the conclusion that one punchcutter lies behind at least the bulk of the Anglo-Saxon characters in both the Elzevier and Maire editions. He may have been commissioned separately by both printers, one of whom was more demanding than the other—hence the additional symbols and more elegant H (with a shorter tail) in the Elzevier edition. Because of the political situation that led to the printing, two commissions could easily have come in at the same time. The punchcutter could then have supplied both customers with matrices; it was common for punchcutters to hold the punches unless the customer specifically required them.

From this evidence we seem to have the work of two punchcutters operating in Holland, at least one of them, responsible for the designs in the Elzevier and Maire editions, almost certainly in Leiden. Although it is possible in theory that the two designs, one for the Elzevier and Maire editions, and one for the Boxhorn edition, were cut by the same punchcutter, the relative crudeness of the Anglo-Saxon sorts in the Boxhorn edition suggest an attempt by someone who was at best an amateurish or hard-pressed punchcutter who took short cuts by borrowing similar-looking sorts from other founts. Leiden was a thriving printing town at the time; in addition to the Elzeviers and Maires, Gruys and Wolf record fifteen printers active there in 1636, just over half the number in Amsterdam.[23] But the evidence for punchcutters in the period around 1636 is thin. In Leiden, however, there lived, until his death in late 1636, the punchcutter Arent Corsz[oon] van Hoogenacker (c.1579–1636).[24] In 1637 the London

---

22 On the Elzeviers and Maires' printing of Hebrew see L. Fuks and R.G. Fuks-Mansfeld, *Hebrew Typography in the Northern Netherlands 1585–1815*, 2 vols (Leiden: Brill, 1984–7): I.32–45. The mem-height of the Hebrew in both the Maire edition and the Elzevier edition is 1.5 mm, but they are not identical. Maire used the one called 'Maire squ.3' in Fuks and Fuks-Mansfeld, *Hebrew Typography*, I.36. The Elzevier one corresponds to [Typi] Hebraici & Chaldaici no. 5 in *Specimen Typorum Johannis Elsevirii* (Leiden: Johan Elzevier, 1658).

23 J.A. Gruys & C. de Wolf, *Thesaurus 1473–1800: Dutch Printers and Booksellers With places and years of activity*, Bibliotheca Bibliographica Neerlandica 28 (Nieuwkoop: De Graaf, 1989), pp. 206–207.

24 On van Hoogenacker see John A. Lane, 'Arent Corsz Hogenacker (ca. 1579–1636): An Account of his Typefoundry and a Note on his Types', *Quaerendo* 25 (1995), pp. 83–113,

bookseller Samuel Browne, brother of one of the Oxford University proctors for that year, negotiated on behalf of Oxford University the purchase of type, matrices and punches from van Hoogenacker's estate.[25]

Here is the only known candidate for the requisite punchcutting in Leiden, especially as we know that Joannes Maire used van Hoogenacker's Arabic and Hebrew.[26] Although not particularly distinguished these Anglo-Saxon sorts in the Elzevier and Maire pirate editions of Selden's *Mare Clausum* constituted the first attempt to cut a set of Anglo-Saxon special sorts in the seventeenth century. In the twenty or so years to follow, at least four new sets were designed, three in England, and the other, again, in Holland in 1655, almost certainly cut by Christoffel van Dijck, for Franciscus Junius. That was a major achievement, but the attempts in 1636 were a remarkable precursor of what was to come. Selden's book caused not only a political stir, but also occasioned a notable typographical stir, providing evidence of new punchcutting at a time when other evidence is thin.

3 The Blaeu/Voskens Pica Anglo-Saxon

Like Camden's *Britannia* and Speed's *Theatre* Blaeu's atlases show Anglo-Saxon types in 'etymological' place-names and one passage of Anglo-Saxon. This Blaeu Anglo-Saxon was not imported from England. At this time Dutch punch-cutters led the world. Indeed, as we have seen from the Dutch pirate editions of Selden's *Mare Clausum*, the first Anglo-Saxon type-designs produced in the seventeenth century were actually Dutch, unfortunately in response to a political situation, so they were not as well planned or executed as they might have been. Alongside Cristoffel van Dijck, who was the punchcutter of the century, there were others who were also outstanding. In particular there were the half-brothers, Bartholomeus Voskens (the elder; 1613/16–1669) and Reinier/Reinhard Voskens (1621–c.1670).[27] One of them is the probable

---

163–191.

25   Carter, *History of OUP*, pp. 33–34; Morison and Carter, *John Fell*, pp. 233–243; Lane, 'Hogenacher', pp. 109–110. The specimen broadside is preserved in Oxford University Archives, SEP.P17b(4); see C[arter] and S[immons], *Specimen*, which includes specimen reproductions. Van Hoogenacker's stock was eventually sold 14 April 1672, but it is not clear what became of it; see Enschedé, *Typefoundries*, p. 67. On Browne see STC: III.30.

26   Morison and Carter, *John Fell*, pp. 242, 238.

27   For a genealogical tree of the Voskens family in the seventeenth century see John A. Lane, *Early Type Speciments in the Plantin-Moretus Museum* (London: British Library, 2004), p. 50.

> Auguftyn Engels-Saxifche Letteren, 4 pond.
> ЄⱮXſEÆÐ þȜꞇƦꞀꝨЄꞪoÞꝚȝƿƀ

ILLUSTRATION 41A
The 'Augustyn Engels-Saxische Letteren' = the Blaeu/Voskens Pica Anglo-Saxon (CAS3) shown in the Heirs of Joan Blaeu type-specimen 1695.5, D1 (LUB Letterproeven 744D, no. 33)

> Mediaan Engels Sax.
> Ða he ða mið ȝꞁimmum ꞅꝑinȝlum ꞃ ꞇinꞇꝥe-
> ȝum pæceð pæꞃ. ꞃ he calle þa piꞇu ðe him
> man oyðe ȝeþyloelice ꞃ ȝeꝥeonðe ꞃoꞃ oꞃi-
> ꞇne abæꞃ aꞃæꞃnðe. þa ꞃe ðema þ ða oncneoꞃ.

ILLUSTRATION 41B
The Blaeu/Voskens Pica Anglo-Saxon (CAS3) in the Widow Dirck Voskens specimen (1700?.2 (ante1714)), *Proef van Letteren die te bekomen zyn, by de Weduwe van Dirk Voskens* (LUB F.11:24). OE Bede, I.7 (extract), as Miller 1890–98: 1.36/33 to 38/2

cutter of this Blaeu Anglo-Saxon. First appearing in the atlas 1645.1 it occurs fifty years later in the Heirs of Joan Blaeu type-specimen 1695.5 as 'Augustyn Engels-Saxische Letteren' on sig. D1; that is to say it claims (misleadingly) to be English-size.[28] The letters are shown in a single line, beginning with capitals. However exactly the same design in the same size also occurs as 'Anglo-Saxon Mediaan' in the one of the Widow of Dirk Voskens & Sons type-specimens 1700?.2 (ante1714); that is to say it is described as a Pica.[29] Since the body-size can be estimated from the four lines printed in the Widow Voskens specimen as 80, the dimensions are Body 80, Face 80 x 1.6: 2.5; so it has to be a Pica. It seems reasonable to conclude that it was cut by one of the Voskens half-brothers,

---

28 Lane, *Plantin-Moretus*, no. 138. There is no published facsimile of this specimen, but I am grateful to the late Hendrik Vervliet (Antwerp) for supplying me with a copy of the relevant page.

29 Lane, *Plantin Moretus*, no. 11. A facsimile may be seen in Wytze Gs. Hellinga, *Copy and Print in the Netherlands: An Atlas of Historical Bibliography* (Amsterdam: Federatie der Werkgeversorganisatiën in het Boekdrukkersbedrijf, 1962), II. pl. 160. Blaeu's atlas 1645.1 is USTC 1512949.

Bartholomeus and Reinier, as they were the two punchcutting members of the family who were active in the early 1640s.

It shows 12 lower-case letters, d, e, f, g, h, i (in the Widow Voskens specimen only) r, s, t, þ, ð, p, seven capitals, Æ (two designs), E, M, S (assuming this letter, which occurs at the end after the lower-case letters, is a capital, for in the Widow Voskens specimen it is used as lower-case d), Ð, X, and two others, the abbreviation ƀ, and the Tironian sign ⁊. There is notably no special Anglo-Saxon lower-case y (used as a vowel in Old English) in these specimens.[30] The predominant model for them is undoubtedly the Lambardian Pica Anglo-Saxon found in the 1607.2 edition of Camden's *Britannia*. Features recalling the Lambardian Pica Anglo-Saxon are (1) the letters e and h, which do not occur in the other sixteenth-century designs (though the Lambardian h is very similar to the Parkerian capital H), (2) the long arm of letters f and s, (3) the broader bar of letters t and Ð, (4) g with the link not projecting very far leftwards, (5) capital M with left and right shoulder the same height, and (6) the use of capital S for lower-case d. However, one feature recalls the Parkerian Great Primer Anglo-Saxon: the capital X, which occurs only in this design. And another feature recalls either the Parkerian Great Primer Anglo-Saxon or the Parkerian Pica Anglo-Saxon: the letter i with no dot is exclusive to these Parkerian designs. Evidently the designs for the Blaeu Pica Anglo-Saxon were based primarily on the Lambardian Pica Anglo-Saxon with two features probably from the Parkerian Great Primer Anglo-Saxon. These English sixteenth-century models were used in the printed books by Camden, Speed, Lambarde and Parker. There is no distinctive trace of influence from the Anglo-Saxon type-designs made for seventeenth-century English books. After the last of the Blaeu atlases containing Anglo-Saxon was printed in 1662, this design makes another appearance in some passages of Anglo-Saxon in the edition of John Selden's *De Synedriis*, 1679.2 (Illustration 42), printed in Amsterdam by Hendrick and Dirk 1 Boom (fl.1669–80), and the widow of Joannes van Someren (fl.1678–1703).

---

30   It would appear that the failure to make an Anglo-Saxon y was recognized as a mistake, as in the *Atlas* text (1645.1) an Anglo-Saxon y is improvised by using the standard Great Primer y and adding a superscript quotation-mark or acute accent over the right upright. It should have been a dot over the centre of the y.

Cap. 14. *Veterum Ebræorum.* 333

propter senectutem, cum quidam adolescentes essent, sed propter sapientiam. Hinc Duces, Comites, Reguli, principes, ac primates provinciarum, urbium, oppidorum, variatim apud Majores nostros sic dicti, quod liquet maximè ex Annalibus aliisque scriptis Anglosaxonicis cum Latinis Bedæ, Florentii, Huntingdoniensis, Hovedenii, ejusmodi aliorum annalibus collatis. hunðꝛeð Ealðoꞃ ᵐ erat *Centurio* seu *Centuriæ præfectus*, ðu þꞃeaxna Ealðoꞃman *Comes Australium Saxonum.* Item Ealðoꞃbuꞃh *metropolis*, ut Græca ealðoꞃbuꞃh *Constantinopolis.* Et cum Georgius Cappadox qui sancti nomine fruitur, Comes Cappadociæ apud veteres nuncupetur, Alfricus ⁿ in ejus vita Anglosaxonica Ealðoꞃman on þæꞃ ꞃcyꞃe Cappaðocia eum vocat. Hinc Alfwinus sub Eadgaro Rege *Aldermannus*° *Angliæ* dictus seu Principis locum per Angliam sustinens. Nam & ubi Beda habet ᵖ anno 640 de Earconberto Cantuariorum Rege, eum idola destrui & jejunium quadragesimalè observari per totum regnum suum *Principali autoritate* præcepisse, Anglosaxonica versione substituitur mið hiꞃ Ealðoꞃlicneꞃꞃe quasi diceres *Senioralis*, seu *Senioratus sui* autoritate. Atque ut ylðꞃan ylðꞃum in Euangeliis Saxonicis ita etiam & Ealðꞃum & Ealðꞃaꞃ pariter & Ealðoꞃmannum pro Senioribus & Viris principibus ex usu jam ostenso, adhibita esse palam est. *Seniores, Scribæ & Principes Sacerdotum* apud Matthæum vertuntur ᵠ ylðꞃum ꞇ bocꞃum ꞇ ealðoꞃmannum þæꞃa ꞃaceꞃða. Et *Principes Sacerdotum* ʳ *& Seniores populi* þæꞃa ꞃaceꞃða ealðꞃaꞃ anð þæꞃ ꝼolceꞃ ealðꞃaꞃ sæpius; ubi Seniores & Principes planè velut synonyma. Etiam in eodem capite ˢ non semel pro *Principibus Sacerdotum & Senioribus* Anglosaxo þæꞃa ꞃaceꞃða Ealðꞃaꞃ ꞇ þa hlaꝼoꞃðaꞃ ubi pro Senioribus *lhafordas* quod postmodum in 𝕷𝖆𝖛𝖊𝖗𝖉𝖘 & dein in 𝕷𝖔𝖗𝖉𝖘 pro *Senioribus* seu *Seigneurs* aut *Dominis* expressim substitutum. Alibi autem in eadem versione ᵗ heah ꞃaceꞃðum pro *principibus Sacerdotum* & Ealðoꞃmannum pro *Senioribus*. In Luca autem ubi dicitur *quia* ᵘ *oportet filium hominis multa pati & reprobari a Senioribus & principibus Sacerdotum & scribis* Ealðꞃum pro *Senioribus* & Ealðoꞃmannum pro *Principibus Sacerdotum* adhibetur, uti etiam alibi ˣ in ejusdem Euangelio ubi pro *ad Principes Sacerdotum magistratus templi & Seniores* habetur ꞇo þam ealðoꞃmannum anð ꞇo þam pꞃꞇum anð þæꞃ ꞇempleꞃ ealðꞃum. *Seniores* heic pꞃꞇum redduntur seu *sapientes* & magistratus etiam ealðꞃum seu *Seniores.* Paulo post etiam ibi ʸ & ꝼolceꞃ ylðꞃan pro *Senioribus populi*, & ꞃaceꞃða ealðeꞃmenn pro *Principibus Sacerdotum*; quemadmodum etiam in sacro sermone זקני הכהן *Seniores de Sacerdotibus* pro primariis seu principibus Sacerdotum subinde ᶻ usurpatur. Transit postmodum Saxo-

Tt 3

ILLUSTRATION 42 The Blaeu/Voskens Pica Anglo-Saxon (CAS3) in 1679.2, 2T3ʳ (p. 333)

4 The Janssonius English-Size and Great Primer Anglo-Saxon

Blaeu had a competitor, and the competition was so intense that his father, Willem Janszoon, adopted his grandfather's nickname 'Blaeu' ('blaewe Willem') to distinguish his firm from that competition.[31] The competitor was Jan Janszoon (usually anglicized as Jansson; 1588–1664), better known under the Latinized form of his name used in his publications Joannis Janssonius (fl. Amsterdam, 1613–64). Janssonius was the son-in-law of the map-engraver Jodocus Hondius (Joost de Hondt, 1563–1612) by virtue of his marriage to Elisabeth de Hondt (d.1627), and had already been involved in producing atlases with Jodocus's son Henricus Hondius.[32] Janssonius's first atlas of the British Isles combined with Camden's Latin text, including the supposed Anglo-Saxon place-name etymologies and a passage of Anglo-Saxon, appeared a year after Blaeu's: 1646.3.[33] After Janssonius died in 1664 the business was carried on by his son-in-law, Johannes Janssonius van Waesbergen.

Janssonius was a very busy man, an international entrepreneur with outposts of his business in Berlin, Copenhagen, Danzig, Frankfurt, Geneva, Königsberg and Lyon; in particular he was summoned to Stockholm by Queen Christina of Sweden around this time.[34] So it is probably no surprise that Janssonius's *Novus Atlas*, vol. IV (**1646.3**), shows several signs of haste in production, as noted generally by Skelton.[35] There are instances of changing type-size in mid-column, and there is the use of different English-size Italics in conjunction with the main text set in an English-size Roman. Mostly Robert Granjon's 3rd English-size Italic is used, but another Italic is used on sigs 5I–5P, and yet another on sigs 5Q–5T, suggesting that different typesetters

---

31 For some account of the competition see Cornelis Koeman et al., 'Commercial Cartography & Map Production in the Low Countries 1500–ca.1672', in David Woodward (ed.), *The History of Cartography*, III.2 (Chicago: University of Chicago Press, 2007), pp. 1296–1383, esp. pp. 1324–1330, also Andrew Pettegree & Arthur der Weduwen, *The Bookshop of the World: Making and Trading Books in the Dutch Golden Age* (London: Yale University Press, 2019), pp. 110–115.

32 R.A. Skelton, *County Atlases of the British Isles 1579–1850: A Bibliography* (London: Carta, 1970), pp. 221–226.

33 USTC 1513713 (= 1649 re-issue).

34 Cornelis Koeman, *Atlantes Neerlandici: Bibliography of Terrestrial, Maritime and Celestial Atlases and Pilot Books, published in the Netherlands up to 1880*, 5 vols (Amsterdam: Theatrum Orbis Terrarum, 1967–71), II.158–161; F.B. de Marez Oyens, 'Jan Janssen as Counterfeiter and Pirate', *Quaerendo*, 9 (1979), 350–352; H. Pummer, 'Johannes Janssonius. Buchdrucker und Buchhändler der Königin', *Nordisk Tidskrift för Bok- und Biblioteksväsen*, 69 (1982), pp. 33–48.

35 Skelton, *County Atlases*, p. 81.

ALPHABETUM ANGLO-SAXONICUM

hîc apponendum curavimus, ut Saxonica nomina quæ paſſim in libro occurrunt, facilius legantur.

A	a	h	b	ꞃ	r	ẏ	y
b	b	i	i	ꞅ	s	Æ	Æ
c	c	l	l	ꞃ	ſ	Æ	æ
ð	d	ꝏ	m	t	t	Đ	Th
E	E	n	n	u	u	ð	th
e	e	o	o	ƿ	vv	þ	th
f	f	p	p	ꚛ	X	⁊	and
ᵹ	g	q	q	x	x	ꝥ	that

ILLUSTRATION 43 Reader's Anglo-Saxon type-specimen showing the Janssonius English-size Anglo-Saxon (CAS4) in 1646.3, 2*2^r (CUL Atlas.3.65.4). Heading reduced

with different cases of type were at work simultaneously towards the end, thus maximising speed of completion, but with insufficient attention to aesthetic homogeneity. The same stricture of too much haste in production applies to the Anglo-Saxon types used by Janssonius, which were evidently the result of insufficient forethought and preparation, and are of much lower quality than the Blaeu Pica Anglo-Saxon; ambition seems to have outstripped achievement. Unfortunately they are not found in any type-specimen, not even Janssonius's own (posthumous) type-specimen of 1666.[36]

Each Janssonius atlas has an Anglo-Saxon specimen (on sig. 2*2^r in 1646.3), showing 20 sorts altogether, 11 lower-case letters, d, e, f, g, r, s, t, y, þ, ð, p, 8 capitals, Æ¹, Æ², E, H, M, S, Đ, X, and 1 other, ⁊: see Illustration 43. This specimen does not, however, show all the sorts shown in the text, though it does show some capital sorts that are not found in the text at all. On sig. 5Z2^v there are two short passages of Anglo-Saxon in column a (Illustration 44), but the Anglo-Saxon sorts are found in combination with text set in two sizes. For the most part they are combined with Haultin's English-size Roman in the main text set out

---

[36] Joannes Janssonius, *Verkoopinge van een Oude en Welgesorteerde Druckerie en Lettergieterie* (Amsterdam: J. Janssonius, 1666): OBL, Marshall 148. As far as I know this type-specimen has not been issued in a facsimile.

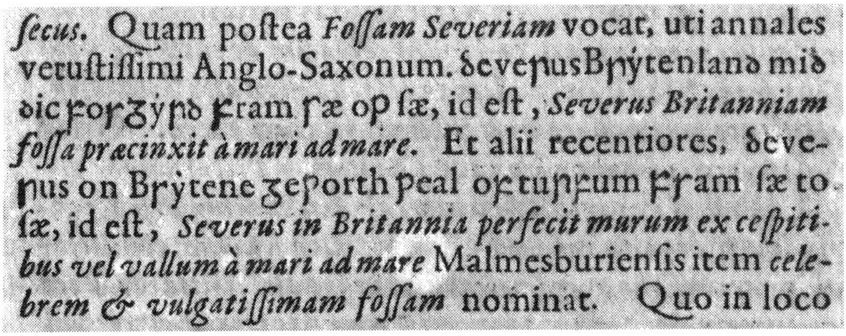

secus. Quam poſtea *Foſſam Severiam* vocat, uti annales vetuſtiſſimi Anglo-Saxonum. ðeveꝑusBꞃýtenlanð miððic ꝼoꞃʒýꝑð ꝼram ꝼæ oꝓ ꝼæ, id eſt, *Severus Britanniam foſſa præcinxit à mari ad mare.* Et alii recentiores, ðeveꝑus on Bꞃýtene ʒeꝓorth ꝑeal oꝼ tuꝑꞃum ꝼꞃam ꝼæ to ꝼæ, id eſt, *Severus in Britannia perfecit murum ex ceſpitibus vel vallum à mari ad mare* Malmesburienſis item *celebrem & vulgatiſſimam foſſam* nominat. Quo in loco

ILLUSTRATION 44   Joannis Janssonius, *Novus Atlas* (vol. 4; 1646.3), 5Z2ᵛ: ASC(C+F) 189/188 (extracts), showing Anglo-Saxon text embedded in the Latin text (CUL Atlas.3.65.4)

qua hæc nomina exoleverant, & regiones omnes quæ tra xonico nomine Noꝛþan-ƕumbꞃa-ꞃic, *id eſt,* Norda *men nomen in reliquis agris nunc obliteratum, in una No*

N O R T H - H V

Orthumbria , Saxonice Noꝛþan-ƕumbeꞃ-lonð , & vulgo *North-umber-land.* Trianguli ſed non æquilateri figura quodammodo incluſa

ILLUSTRATION 45   Joannis Janssonius, *Novus Atlas* (vol. 4; 1646.3), 6A1ᵛ, showing words with Anglo-Saxon sorts in a head statement set in a Great Primer Roman (CUL Atlas.3.65.4)

in double columns (listed in the entry for 1646.3 under **Type**). But on several pages they are combined with a Great Primer Roman in head-statements set in François Guyot's Great Primer Italic.[37] It would appear that Janssonius wanted Anglo-Saxon letters in two sizes, English-size and Great Primer. This desire may be reflected in particular on sig. 6A1ᵛ, where Anglo-Saxon words are contained

---

37   The Great Primer Roman is no. 2 in the Janssonius 1666 speciment, sig. A2ᵛ. Guyot's Great Primer Italic showing Body 117, is no. 1 in the Janssonius 1666 specimen, sig. A2ᵛ; found in 1646.3, e.g., on sigs Y1ʳ, 2P2ᵛ, 3N1ʳ, 5G1ᵛ and 6A1ᵛ.

in a head-statement in Great Primer that uses the full width of the page, and two columns of English-size text below, in the a-column of which Anglo-Saxon words also occur (Illustration 45). The Great Primer þ in the head-statement is noticeably larger than the English-size one in column a.[38] There are also at least two designs of the Anglo-Saxon letters **f** (e.g. on sig. 2G2ᵛ/a), **g** (e.g. on sigs X1ᵛ, 2L1ʳ/b), **H** (e.g. on sigs 2G1ʳ/a, 2I1ʳ), **r** (e.g. on sigs N2ʳ, 3Q2ᵛ/b, 3R2ᵛ/b), **s** (e.g. on sig. 2X2ᵛ), **p**, **M** (e.g. on sig. 3L2ʳ/b), **S**. Short cuts are shown by the use of **S** with the upper shoulder broken off for **d**, and by using inverted **2** for **t** (more than one variety, e.g. on sigs 3R2ᵛ/b, 4N2ᵛ/b), a ruse used previously by one of the Dutch printers of Selden's *Mare Clausum*. It is necessary to reconstruct the full repertoire by amalgamating images of the various letters on different pages into one alphabetical arrangement (Illustration 46). The majority of the sorts are English-size and combine well from the point of view of size with Haultin's English-size Roman used for the main text. As far as the larger Anglo-Saxon sorts are concerned it seems reasonable to suppose that the seven lower-case larger sorts, which are Great Primer in size, were presumably made to fit with the Great Primer Roman. This ambitious plan, if such it was, did not work out well in practice, because the two sizes of Anglo-Saxon sorts are mixed up in use.

When the images of the various sorts are examined together it is, however, evident that the shapes of some letters and the varying thickness of the stems in particular show greater variation than the above account allows for. The following features may be noted:

d   Very small, with the ascender showing variable length; created by breaking off the upper part of the stroke of capital S (which shows a closed lower sector), and even used where unbroken S would be appropriate, as in Weaʀꞇ-ðeaxan-pıc on sig. 2X2ᵛ;

f   Rather large, sometimes with stem tapered to the left at the top, and sheared with a serif to the left at the base, sometimes without these refinements. The length of the bar varies;

g   This letter shows considerable variation. The letter occurs twice side by side in Gpenꞇbpıᵹᵹ-ꞅcýpe on sig. 3R2ᵛ/a, the second being noticeably larger. In neither does the tail close right round to make a counter. Similarly on sig. X1ᵛ/a, and again on sig. 5Z2ᵛ/a there are two letters **g**, one with the tail closed round and one where it does not do so. On sig. N2ʳ it is larger again and set like a capital in the middle of the name Peᵹpeopn; this time too the tail does close right round.

---

38   Unless they are capital and lower-case, though not so distinguished in use. Two þ-sorts also occur on sig. 2O2ᵛ/a.

Individual Special Sorts alphabetically arranged and re-assembled from **1646.3**, Janssonnius's *Novus Atlas* (vol. 4) with abridged translation of text from Camden's *Britannia* (**1607.2**). Many letter-forms do not match each other, and some letters show what looks like an attempt at two sizes, notably g, h, t and þ.

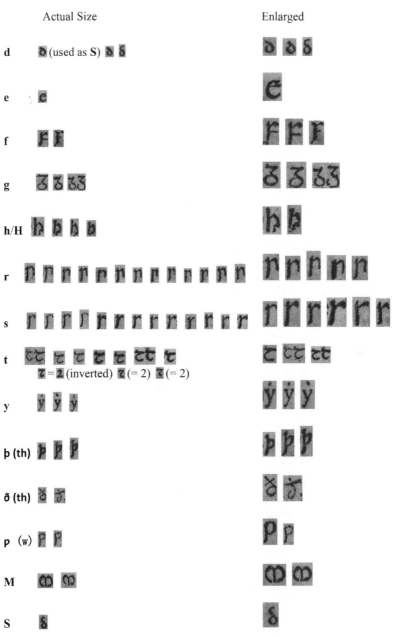

ILLUSTRATION 46   Alphabetical arrangement of assembled Anglo-Saxon sorts found in Janssonius's Atlas (**1646.3**) using CUL Atlas.3.65.4

h   Rather large, as also in AS3, but probably borrowed from another (Textura?) fount; two h's occur in one name Sheoverham on sig. 2G1ʳ/a and do not look the same;

r   Another letter that shows variation, in the straightness or slight curvature of the stem, in the thickness of the strokes, and in the angle or straightness of the right arm;

s   Some s's are good, showing a straight stem sheared at the top and turned to the left at the base. On sig. X1ᵛ/a two instances occur side by side and the second looks relatively crude;

t   Uses inverted 2 for t, not always the same sort, as, for example, on sig. 4N2ᵛ/b, in the name Vttok-cester;

y   English-size Roman y surmounted by a dot;

þ   This letter can be seen in two sizes on sig. 2O2ᵛ/a in the names Baþancercep and Baþan, both reasonably well shaped and proportioned;

ð   This letter occurs twice on sig. 3Q2ᵛ/b in the names Gaþ-muð and Iieþ-muð, the first looking firm in outline with a cross-bar angled across the ascender, but that to the right of it has a smaller counter and the cross-bar is too long and too thick;

p   On sig. 2B1ʳ/a in the name Meþropape there is a decently cut p with a sheared top to the stem and a terminal at the base hooked to the left; it is set rather high on the line. On sig. Z1ʳ/b in the name Meðpeaʒerton there is another p with a larger counter. On sig. 5K2ᵛ/a an italic *p* is used for p;

Æ   Two forms of Æ, no doubt ultimately inherited from the Parkerian design, are shown in the specimen, but I have not found them in the text;

E   Greek-style E is shown in the specimen and in the text;

M   Round-shouldered M no doubt from another fount; on sig. 3L2r/b two different M's occur in Maleðune and Mealðune, one of which matches that found in CAS3;

S   This letter, with a closed tail making a small counter, is shown twice on sig. 5Z2ᵛ/a in the same Severus. As noted above, when the upper part of the stroke is broken off it is used for d;

Ð   This letter shows a slightly wide counter; evidently it is the D of the main text with a cross-bar through the stem;

X   Shown in the specimen but not found in the text; again inherited from AS1;

þ   Probably a modified p, seen only in the specimen;

ɼ   Shown in the specimen but not found in the text;

The Dutch edition of 1647.4 shows even more signs of haste, notably capital M used sideways for E (sig. V1ᵛ). Evidently Janssonius had some metal special Anglo-Saxon sorts, but in his quest for speed in a competitive situation he probably supplemented them with wooden sorts that do not exactly match

Images of individual Special Sorts alphabetically arranged and re-assembled from **1665.3**, the Strassburg edition of Selden's *De iure naturali*.

Lower-case letters:    d f g i r s t y þ ð p
                                                 th th w

Capitals: 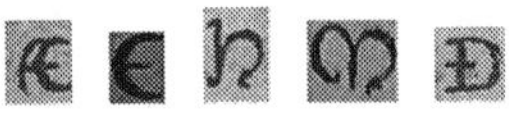   Æ E H M Ð

Others: 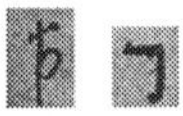   þ ⁊ (= &)

ILLUSTRATION 47   Alphabetical arrangement of the Anglo-Saxon sorts (CAS5) found in the Strassburg edition of John Selden's *De iure naturali* (1665.3) using CUL C.4.5

each other and detract from the professional appearance of his text. His priorities were speed and quantity rather than quality.

5   The Strassburg English-Size Anglo-Saxon

As indicated above John Selden's books published in his lifetime were mostly printed by William Stansby, who used the Parkerian Great Primer Anglo-Saxon type-design (AS1). When continental printers came to reprint Selden's works they were almost inevitably faced with Anglo-Saxon passages printed in the Parkerian design (AS1). Consequently this is the model that they followed, as is the case with the Strassburg edition (**1665.3**) of Selden's *De iure naturale* (**1640.4**). The 18 special sorts are of moderately good quality.
   The following features are notable:
d   Quite a large counter, with a distinctively long ascender sloping up to the left, the end of which is hooked over to the right;
f   Quite a long shoulder; the stem slants very slightly down towards the right, and shows minimal serifs;
g   At the left of the top bar there is a minimal terminal hooked upwards, the link is long and the tail goes right round to make a small counter;
i   This occurs once only, on sig. 5T2^v, and is probably a small numeral 1;
r   The space between the left stem and the right arm is relatively narrow; the stem has a minimal serif at the top and a terminal hooked to the left at the bottom;

s   This letter shows a bulbous terminal to the shoulder and no serifs; the top of the stem is sheared down from the top right;
t   The bar is very long and turned up at the left end;
y   A dot has been attached to a y from another fount;
þ   The stem shows no serifs;
ð   The ascender is relatively upright and the cross-stroke relatively long angled slightly up at the left and slightly down at the right;
p   The stem shows a minimal serif at the top and none at the bottom; the bowl is angled down from the right towards the stem;
Æ² Notably lacks a tail to the left stem;
E   This occurs on sig. 3N1ʳ. There is a stroke like a left bracket and a bar across the centre, but no serifs or terminals;
H   Very similar to the Parkerian and Lambardian H, with a serif at the top of the stem, a terminal hooked to the left at the base of the stem, and a terminal hooked to the right at the base of the arm;
M   This occurs on sig. 3N1ᵛ. Very similar to the Parkerian M, with the base of the left stem hooked round to the right, and the base of the right arm ending in a bulbous dot with a thin terminal hooked downwards from it;
Ð   Very similar to the Parkerian and Lambardian Ð;
Þ   Shaped like the þ, but the base of the stem shows a serif, and the cross-bar is turned down both to the left and the right;
ꝸ   Very upright, with a relatively long bar showing a serif at the left end, and the tail showing a terminal.

Although the printer of the second edition of John Selden's *De Iure Naturali* (1665.3) is not stated, it was almost certainly Georg Andreas Dolhopff (1627–1711; fl. Strassburg 1662–1711). He married a daughter of the Strassburg publisher Johann Andreas Zetzner, whom he served as a printer from 1662, and the two jointly published this book together with the Endters of Nuremberg and the Societas Strassburg. From 1668 to 1671 Balthasar Joachim Endter worked for Dolhopff and Zetzner, and the contact between the two businesses (Dolhopff/Zetzner in Strassburg, and Endter in Nuremberg) probably gave rise to the Endter's interest in the book. Evidence of punchcutters or typefounders at this time in this location or nearby has proved elusive. From 1740 there is the study of the art of printing and typefounding by Christian Friedrich Gessner, which includes an *Alphabetum Saxonicum vetus* or *vetustissimum* 'Old/Ancient Saxon Alphabet', probably continental Old Saxon, printed from an engraved plate, and the forms are continental rather than insular, notably **f, g, r, y, z**.[39]

---

39   Christian F. Gessner, *Die so nöthig als nütliche Buchdruckerkunst und Schriftgiesserey*, 2 vols (Leipzig: Gessner, 1740), II.163 and fig. XXVI (p. 162).

Supplementary to Gessner's book is the *Orationis Dominicae Versiones*, which includes versions of the Lord's Prayer in *Saxonica Antiqua* 'continental Old Saxon' printed in a Fractur and another version *Anglo-Saxonica* 'Old English' printed in an Italic, to which the editor has added the comment *Characterem litterarum invenire haud potuimus* 'We could not at all find [appropriate] letter sorts' to print it properly.[40] Things were apparently no better in Nuremberg, where the Endters published a type-specimen catalogue, but again it does not contain any designs for Anglo-Saxon (though it does include Gothic and Runic).[41] In Konstanz the punchcutter Balthasar Köblin cut non-Latin types c.1654—c.1680.[42] But although he was active at the right time, whether a printer in Strassburg would have gone to a punchcutter in Konstanz for special sorts is moot. In this light Dolhopff's achievement in printing Anglo-Saxon with special sorts looks more remarkable.

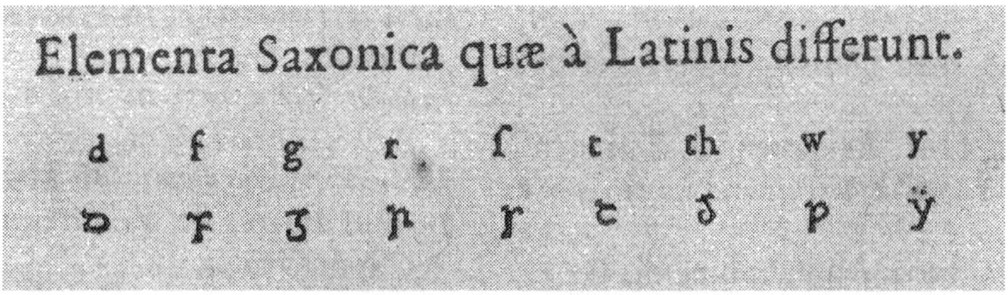

ILLUSTRATION 48 Reader's specimen of the Anglo-Saxon sorts (CAS6) found in Du Cange's *Glossarium* (Paris, 1678.2), vol. I on sig. πR4ʳ (CUL Aa*.7.5)

6 The Paris Du Cangian Pica Anglo-Saxon

Du Cange's famous Latin dictionary, which included some Anglo-Saxon word-forms, was printed *typis* of Gabriel Martin, (fl. Paris, 1670–92†), and published *impensis* of Louis Billaine (fl. Paris, 1652–81†): 1678.2. It shows Anglo-Saxon in nine lower-case sorts, ð, ꞙ, ȝ, ꝑ, ꞃ, ꞇ, ẏ; đ, ꝑ, capitals not being needed for a dictionary where the headwords were all Latin. These Anglo-Saxon sorts have not been located elsewhere (other than in the second edition produced at Frankfurt, for which see below), nor have I found them in any type-specimen.

---

40 Gessner, *Buchdruckerkunst*, supplement to vol. II *Orationis Dominicae Versiones* C4ʳ and C4ᵛ (pp. 39–40) printed *litteris Takkianis* 'with the printing sorts of Johann Tacke', Leipzig: Gessner, 1740.

41 J.H.G. Ernesti, *Die wol-eingerichtete Buchdruckerey* [of the Endters at Nuremberg] (Nuremberg: Johann Andrea Endters seel. Sohn und Erben, 1721).

42 *Ex informatione* John Lane (personal communication).

Martin owned an important printing-shop, which may have included provision for typefounding.[43] But it is unlikely that he was a punchcutter (see below).

The following features of the design may be noted.

d   The counter is large and the bowl very wide with the ascender just an upward hook at the upper left of the bowl;

f   The shoulder has a terminal pointing diagonally up to the left, and it shows a downward hook. There is a terminal at the base going to the left. There is a marked difference from the s, on which f was often based by the addition of a bar;

g   There is a flat bar at the top and the link does not project very far to the left; the tail is open;

r   The space between the left stem and the right arm is slightly wide; hooked terminals to the left at the top and bottom of the stem;

s   Very similar to the Lambardian Pica Anglo-Saxon s;

t   The top bar is turned up at the left;

y   Indistinguishable from that used in the Lambardian fount. Probably it is the same roman y with a dot fixed above;

ð   This letter shows a small counter and the ascender is relatively upright; the cross-bar shows no serifs;

p   This letter shows a terminal hooked to the left at the top of the stem, but a short descender with no terminal. The bowl is angled down towards the stem at the left.

Overall the design may have been modelled on the Lambardian Pica Anglo-Saxon type-design (AS3) but it shows some idiosyncracies. The cutting is of a moderate standard, the ð being notably poor. There were not many punchcutters or typefounders in Paris at that time, as there was little demand. Writing in 1742 Pierre Simon Fournier, le jeune (1712–68), reported that after the death of Jacques de Sanlecque II (1612–59) there followed a period of about 60 years in which it was difficult to find anyone even to cut the new letters J (consonant) and U (vowel) when this usage was introduced into French printing.[44] At the time that the Anglo-Saxon sorts were made for 1678.2 there are very few known men who might have made them. One possibility is Mathieu Malherbe Des Portes (c.1659–c.1726), a cutter of punches and dies for coins and medals who turned his hand to occasional punchcutting for typefounders; he is best known

---

43   Philippe Renouard, 'Les Fondeurs de Caractères Parisiens et leur Clientèle de Province à la fin du xviie siècle', *Bulletin du Bibliophile* (1900), pp. 3–16, 79–86, at p. 12.

44   Pierre Simon Fournier le jeune, *Modèles des Caracteres de l'Imprimerie* (Paris: Fournier, 1742), B1r.

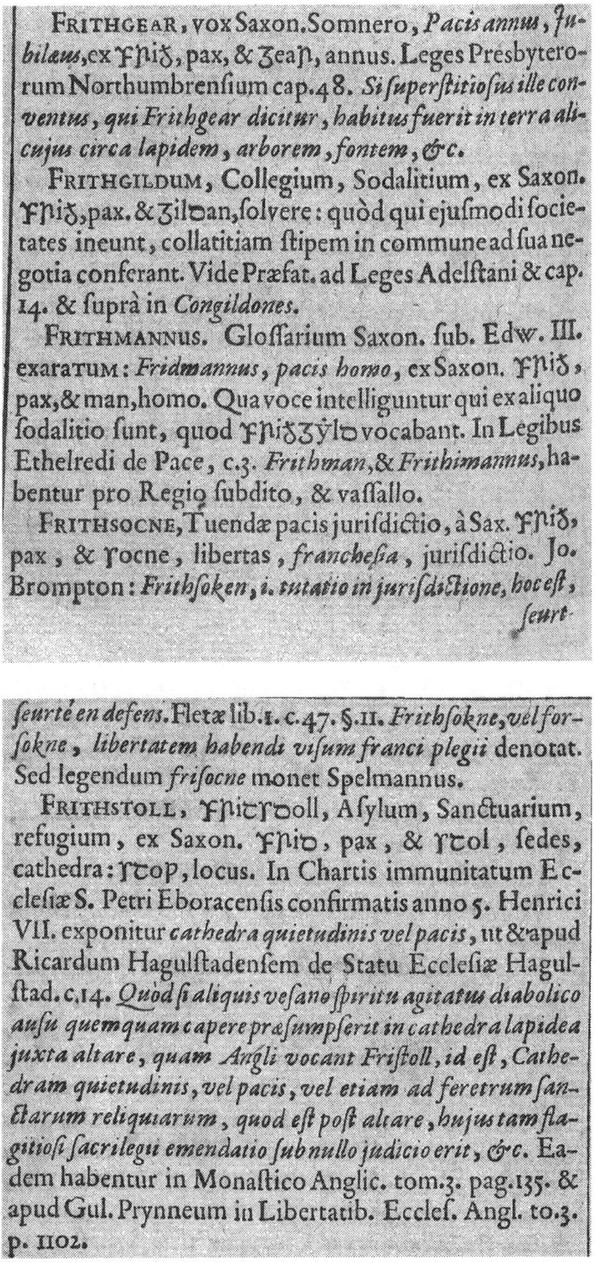

FRITHGEAR, vox Saxon. Somnero, *Pacis annus, Jubilæus,* ex ᚠᚱᛁᚦ, pax, & ᚷᛠᚾ, annus. Leges Presbyterorum Northumbrensium cap. 48. *Si superstitiosus ille conventus, qui Frithgear dicitur, habitus fuerit in terra alicujus circa lapidem, arborem, fontem, &c.*

FRITHGILDUM, Collegium, Sodalitium, ex Saxon. ᚠᚱᛁᚦ, pax. & ᚷᛁᛚᛞan, solvere: quòd qui ejusmodi societates ineunt, collatitiam stipem in commune ad sua negotia conferant. Vide Præfat. ad Leges Adelstani & cap. 14. & suprà in *Congildones.*

FRITHMANNUS. Glossarium Saxon. sub. Edw. III. exaratum: *Fridmannus, pacis homo,* ex Saxon. ᚠᚱᛁᚦ, pax, & man, homo. Qua voce intelliguntur qui ex aliquo sodalitio sunt, quod ᚠᚱᛁᚦᚷᚣᛚᛞ vocabant. In Legibus Ethelredi de Pace, c. 3. *Frithman,* & *Frithimannus,* habentur pro Regio subdito, & vassallo.

FRITHSOCNE, Tuendæ pacis jurisdictio, à Sax. ᚠᚱᛁᚦ, pax, & ᚱocne, libertas, *franchesia*, jurisdictio. Jo. Brompton: *Frithsoken, i. tutatio in jurisdictione, hoc est, seurt-*

seurté en defens. Fletæ lib. 1. c. 47. §. 11. *Frithsokne, vel forsokne, libertatem habendi visum franci plegii* denotat. Sed legendum *frisocne* monet Spelmannus.

FRITHSTOLL, ᚠᚱᛁᚦᛋᛏoll, Asylum, Sanctuarium, refugium, ex Saxon. ᚠᚱᛁᚦ, pax, & ᛋᛏol, sedes, cathedra: ᛋᛏop, locus. In Chartis immunitatum Ecclesiæ S. Petri Eboracensis confirmatis anno 5. Henrici VII. exponitur *cathedra quietudinis vel pacis,* ut & apud Ricardum Hagulstadensem de Statu Ecclesiæ Hagulstad. c. 14. *Quòd si aliquis vesano spiritu agitatus diabolico ausu quemquam capere præsumpserit in cathedra lapidea juxta altare, quam Angli vocant Fristoll, id est, Cathedram quietudinis, vel pacis, vel etiam ad feretrum sanctarum reliquiarum, quod est post altare, hujus tam flagitiosi sacrilegii emendatio sub nullo judicio erit, &c.* Eadem habentur in Monastico Anglic. tom. 3. pag. 135. & apud Gul. Prynneum in Libertatib. Ecclef. Angl. to. 3. p. 1102.

ILLUSTRATION 49   The Du Cangian Pica Anglo-Saxon (CAS6) as it occurs in text in the Frankfurt edition of Du Cange's *Glossarium* (1681.1), vol. II, ¶2L4ᵛ–¶2M1ʳ (cols 544–545, re-arranged) (CUL Pet.B.9.5)

for the 'Cicero la Police' cut for the typefounder Pierre Cot c.1700.[45] If he did make these Anglo-Saxon sorts he would have been a very young man, with limited experience. Alternatively, and probably more likely, they might have been cut by Guillaume Le Bé III (1610?–85), who, while principally a typefounder, also sometimes turned his hand to punchcutting.[46]

The same sorts in the same design re-appear in the second edition, a slavish reprint of the first produced at Frankfurt-am-Main, where it was printed *typis* of Balthasar Christoph Wust I (fl. 1658–1700) and the bookseller was Johann David Zunner II (fl. 1666–1700): **1681.1**. Presumably types or possibly matrices were sent from Paris to Frankfurt, where the publisher probably paid for them. Evidence of trade in type between Paris and the provinces is provided by Renouard and includes one transaction *outremer* to Lisbon.[47] So there is nothing out of the ordinary about the presumed sale of a relatively small amount of printing material to Frankfurt, which in any case was famous for its book fair.

7   The Wittenberg 'Pica' Anglo-Saxon

All three books that show these somewhat makeshift Anglo-Saxon sorts are by Selden, his *De iure naturali* (**1695.4**), *Tituli Honorum* (**1696.1**) and *De Synedriis* (**1696.2**). They were printed by Johann Michael Goderitsch (fl. Wittenberg 1687–1706?) for the bookseller Jeremias Schrey at Frankfurt-an-der-Oder. A previous attempt by Schrey to publish a work by Selden that contained Anglo-Saxon, his *Uxor Ebraica* (**1673.3**), simply omitted the two Anglo-Saxon passages in the **1640.4** edition. Again the primary model Anglo-Saxon type-design used for the Wittenberg printings was the Parkerian Great Primer (AS1), used in the editions of Selden's works published in his

---

45   Jeanne Veyrin-Forrer, 'Le "Cicero la Police" et Mathieu Malherbe Des Portes', *Bulletin de la Librairie Ancienne et Moderne*, 51 (1971), pp. 207–214, repr. in idem, *La Lettre et le Texte* (Paris: École normale supérieure de jeunes filles, 1987), pp. 81–87, at p. 85; Nicolas de La Mare, *Traité de la Police*, I (Paris: Jean et Pierre Cot, 1705).

46   E. Howe, 'The Le Bé Family: Typefounders, Printers, Paper Merchants, Engravers and Writing Masters, 1525–1730', *Signature*, 8 (1938), pp. 1–27, at pp. 17–21. Philippe Renouard, *Répertoire des Imprimeurs Parisiens Libraires et Fondeurs de Caractères en exercice à Paris au XVIIe siècle* (Nogent le Roi: Libr. des Arts et Métiers-Éditions, 1995; facsimile reprint of Renouard's corrected proofs 1898), describes Guillaume Le Bé 3 as both a 'fondeur' and a 'graveur'. There are very few other possibilities: Jean Cot (d.1708) established his business as 'fondeur de caractères' in 1683, too late for 1678, and there is no evidence that he was a punchcutter. Another typefounder, Jacques Cottin, died in 1682, but was inactive after 1670.

47   Renouard, 'Fondeurs', pp. 14–16, 79–86.

Cap. 5. *Tituli Honorum.* 365

(innuit, exiſtimo, verbum *tinnio*) *quaſi* Tinnello, *cio e picciol ſuono the coſi ſi dice in quella lingva il ſuono de metalli per cioche alſono d' una piciola campana (come ognium ſia) ſi corre a Tinello, il quale e un luogo (perche non lo ſapeſſe) dove in commune ſi va a mangiare da Cortigiani come al refettorio da frati. Et era all' hora di tanto honore il mangiare in Tinello quanto e hoggi riputato coſa vile & dishorrevole.* In legibus vero præcipientibus, quantum *Taini* ſolvere debeant poſt mortem ſuam, diſtinctionem eorundem reperimus in varios ordines, & quidem juxta tenuras ſuas, ut videtur, & poſſeſſiones. Sybban Cyning ðeðenes hereðeaƿa ſa him nihƿƿe ƿingon (verba Legum *Canuti* Regis cap. 69.) IV. horƿ ƿpa ðeraðoloðe, anð ƿpa unðeraðoloðe. anð ƿpa ƿpahð. & IV. ƿperƿa & ƿpa ƿeala ƿcylða & helm & byrƿnnan & ƿrðið mancuƿ ðolðer. Ænð Meðmeƿa Deðna horƿ & hiƿ ðereƿan & hiƿ pæpen opƿe halƿ. Fanðe on peƿ ƿeaxan & on Myƿcan ƿpa punð, a & Cynin ðeƿ Deðeneƿ hereðeaƿa mine miððenum ðe hiƿ ƿocne hæbbe IV. Punðƿ anð ðiƿ he ƿo þa Cyninð Foƿhðon cyððe hæbbe ƿpa horƿ an ðeraðoloðe & oþen unðeraðoloðe anð I. ƿpunð & ƿpa ƿperƿa & ƿpa ƿcylðaƿ & ƿiƿƿið mancoƿ ðolðer. anð ƿe ðe larƿe hæbbe & larƿe maðeƿy II. punð. id eſt, Relevium ſeu *Relevatio* (juxta verſionem antiquam.) *Thani a rege proximi ſolvitur IV. equis, duobus ſtratis, duobus non ſtratis, duobus gladiis, IV. haſtis, totidem ſcutis, una galea, una lorica, & quinquaginta Marcis auri.* Meðmeƿa Deðn (ſeu ut vocat b verſio latina antiqua, *Mediocris homo, quam Angli dicunt* Leƿƿe- þeðn, quod corrupte profertur *Lespegend*. In Conſtitutionibus Foreſtaruram *Canuti* editis §. 1. & 2. nec non in verſionibus Hiſtoriæ *Brumtoni* vocatur *Mediocris Thaynus*) *Relevatio eſt equus ejus & apparatus, arma, vel juxta morem Weſt Saxonum Halfange ſuum & in Mercia dua libra, & in Anglia orientali dua libra. Regis Tainus ſuo gaudens ſoco ex Danorum lege ſoluit IV. libras. Si vero Regi propior ſit, duos equos, ſtratum unum & alterum non ſtratum, gladium, duas haſtas, duo ſcuta, ac quinquaginta Marcas auri: atque ſi minus habeat, minusque dives ſit, duas libras.* Sic videmus Relevationem *Thainorum* varie redimendam juxta leges *Weſt Saxonum, Anglorum orientalium, Mercia & Danorum*. Fuerunt præterea & diviſiones aliæ teſte libro *Domesday* in conſtitutionibus *Bercheriæ, & Nottinghamia & Eboraci* quæ utut ad Ærarium
Z z 2 redie-

ILLUSTRATION 50   The Wittenberg 'Pica' Anglo-Saxon (CAS7) as found in Selden's *Tituli Honorum* of 1696.1 on sig. ²2Z2ʳ (p. ²365) (OBL Vet. D3 e.118) in a passage from Law II Cnut 71.1–5 (Liebermann I.358)

lifetime, although **1695.4** is based on the Strassburg edition of *De iure naturali* (**1665.3**), which used the Strassburg imitation of AS1, and **1696.2** is based on the Amsterdam edition of *De Synedriis* (**1679.2**) which used the Blaeu/Voskens design (CAS3), which in turn were based on the Lambardian Pica Anglo-Saxon (AS3).

The following features of the design may be noted.

d   This letter is consistently oversized with a large counter, tall ascender sloping slightly to the left and turned to the right at the top. It is set low so that the bowl is below the line. The shape of all the letters is very similar rather than identical, the height of the ascender and the extent to which it is turned at the top being variable. It is difficult to avoid the conclusion that these sorts were made of wood. Capital S is much the same;

e   Larger than the e of the Pica Roman used for the main text and the point where the bar meets the bowl at the right is generally indistinct. Probably from another roman fount;

f   A vertical stroke with a diagonal going upwards to the right and a bar joined at the point of intersection, this bar appearing at the text base-line, making the letter oversized. The length of the strokes varies somewhat, thus leading to the conclusion that these sorts were made of wood;

g   These vary considerably, as on sig. 2A4^v, particularly with regard to the size of the counter enclosed by the tail, and are all oversized. The variation leads to the conclusion that these sorts are made of wood;

i   A small numeral 1 borrowed from another fount;

r   Displays considerable variation in the thickness of the strokes, the length of the terminal at the top of the stem; it is sometimes set correctly on the line, but often not. Again the variation leads to the conclusion that these sorts are made of wood;

s   A vertical stroke with a diagonal going upwards to the right, the length of the strokes being slightly variable and there is also variation in the point on the vertical that the diagonal is joined to. Again the variation leads to the conclusion that these sorts are made of wood;

t   Grossly oversized with the angle at which the stroke leaves the top bar variable. The variation, seen particularly at the top of sig. 3G3^v, leads to the conclusion that these sorts are made of wood;

y   When provided with a suprascript dot the shape and the angle of setting varies, suggesting that these sorts are made of wood. This shows great laziness as it was relatively easy to attach a dot to a y, but a punch was required to do it properly, so presumably no typefounder was available. On the other hand other letters suggest that some new punchcutting was attempted.

þ   This sort shows a stem with no serifs, and is apparently metal;
p   This sort shows a stem with a serif at the top but none at the bottom. It is apparently metal and may be a **p** borrowed from another fount;
E   A Greek-style **E** from another fount;
H   A Textura **H** from another fount;
S   The same as **d**, showing a notable weakness of effort and thought;
ꝥ   Used once on sig. 3G3ʳ instead of **þ**, it may well be the same sort with a bar across the ascender;
⅂   Simply a Roman capital L turned upside down.

This fount was clearly a makeshift amalgam of various solutions, showing a great deal of printers' expediency, and I have not found it anywhere else.

CHAPTER 6

The Use of Sources, Scholarship and the Social Intellectual Network

As can be seen from the entries in the Catalogue under *Sources of Passages in OE utilizing AS Type*, a relatively small number of authors quote Old English from a primary source, i.e. a manuscript. In the first few years of printing Anglo-Saxon with special sorts there was no alternative, so for the *Testimonie of Antiquitie* (1566.1), the *Defence of Priestes Mariages* (1567.1), *The Gospels* (1571.1), the *De Antiquitate Britannicæ Ecclesiæ* (1572.1), and the *Ælfredi Regis Res Gestæ* (1574.2), Parker, Joscelyn and their associates used manuscripts containing Old English (or sometimes later transcripts often in imitative script). So especially did Lambarde for his *Archaionomia* (1568.2) and for his *Perambulation of Kent* (1576.2); Caius did so too for his *De Antiquitate Cantabrigiensis Academiæ* (1568.1). Access to research facilities in the sixteenth and seventeenth centuries were generally difficult, so that 'only the most gifted [and well-connected] could succeed'.[1] Those who did stand out.

William Camden enjoyed very high standing as a scholar for his *Britannia* (1607.2), the first edition (without many maps) having been published in 1586, and his *Remaines* (1605.1) largely comprised material not included in the main work. Much of the *Britannia* was based on field-work, but Camden used documentary sources too. His position at the prestigious Westminster School, second master from 1575, and headmaster from 1593 to 1597, followed by his appointment as Clarenceaux king of arms, a senior position at the College of Arms, as well as his membership of the Elizabethan Society of Antiquaries, would have opened doors to libraries holding books he wished to consult. From his *Britannia* he had a considerable reputation on the continent and corresponded with many the leading scholars who were his contemporaries.[2]

Born in Dublin of well-to-do parents in 1581 James Ussher studied at Trinity College Dublin and quickly established himself as a scholar and church politician, dubbed a prodigy of industry and learning. He was an avid

---

1 J. Butt, 'The Facilities for Antiquarian Study in the Seventeenth Century', *Essays and Studies*, 24 (1938[1939]), pp. 64–79, at p. 79. See also F.M. Powicke, 'Sir Henry Spelman and the *Concilia*', *Proceedings of the British Academy*, 16 (1930), pp. 345–79, at p. 379.
2 See Henry Ellis, *Original Letters of Eminent Literary Men of the Sixteenth, Seventeenth, and Eighteenth Centuries*, Camden Soc. I.23 (London: J.B. Nichols, 1843).

bibliophile.³ The only Irish-born bishop appointed under James I, in 1625 he became archbishop of Armagh, the most senior churchman in the Church of Ireland, and corresponded with all the leading scholars and personalities of the day, often offering trenchant advice.⁴ His letter on the *Religion Anciently Professed by the Irish* was published as a supplement to Sir Christopher Sibthorp's *Friendly Advertisement* (1622.2), arguing that the doctrine and practice of the early church in Ireland was in line with contemporary Protestant usage, and he published also his *Veterum Epistolarum Hibernicarum Sylloge* (1632.3), and his *Britannicarum Ecclesiarum Antiquitates* (1639.2), which drew on a vast range of printed and manuscript sources. His religious views reflected the puritan background that characterised his education, and his advice to Wheelock in particular, taken seriously, to mine Anglo-Saxon texts for information supportive of the Church of England, is very much in the Parkerian tradition. He strongly encouraged Spelman to establish his Lectureship in Anglo-Saxon at Cambridge University.

Sir Henry Spelman was a founding member of the Society of Antiquaries in its earliest form;⁵ from his record and contribution he could be considered the doyen of English antiquaries. Born at Congham, near King's Lynn, Norfolk,⁶ he came of good family, one that had a strong association with the law. While studying that subject at Furnival's Inn, and then Lincoln's Inn, which he entered in 1586, he became interested in the history and antiquities of England. Through his wife's inheritance Spelman secured the wardship of Hamon L'Estrange, son of Sir Nicholas L'Estrange (d. 1591/2), his wife's cousin. This allowed him to reside at the L'Estrange property of Hunstanton, Norfolk, where, living as a country gentleman, he wrote several works on subjects such as armorials and the pros and cons of political union. Knighted in 1604 he served as sheriff of Norfolk from November 1604 until February 1606 and as justice of the peace until 1616. His acknowledged expertise on the historical records of Norfolk (and Suffolk) was such that he wrote the description of Norfolk

---

3 See William O'Sullivan, 'Ussher as a Collector of Manuscripts', *Hermathena*, 88 (1956), pp. 34–58.
4 See Elizabethanne Boran, with (Latin and Greek translations by) David Money, *The Correspondence of James Ussher 1600–1656*, 3 vols (Dublin: Irish Manuscripts Commission, 2015).
5 There is a list of members of the Elizabethan Society of Antiquaries in Norwich, Norfolk Record Office, MS 7198 (formerly Gurney XXII(1)), fo 65.
6 For a pedigree of the Spelman family see H. St George, *The Visitation of London anno 1633, 1634, and 1635* (London: Harleian Soc 17, 1883), p. 257. For a pedigree of the Spelman family of Congham and Holme beginning with Sir Henry see E. Bysshe, *The Visitation of Norfolk, anno Domini 1664* (London: Norfolk Record Soc iv–v, 1934), p. 204. For a pedigree of the Spelman family beginning with Sir John Spelman (d.1546), see J. H. Baker, *The Reports of Sir John Spelman*, 2 vols (London: Selden Soc. 93–94, 1977–78), I.xvi.

printed in John Speed's *Theatre of the Empire of Great Britain* (1611).[7] In 1612, when Hamon L'Estrange's minority had ended, Spelman moved his permanent residence to Tothill Street in London. There, while busy working on commissions in the service of the king, he made a substantial contribution to scholarship through his many publications, particularly his *Glossarium/Archæologus* (1626.1), his monumental *Concilia* (1639.4), and, together with his son John, the *Psalterium Latino-Saxonicum* (1640.3). His reputation was such that works continued to appear posthumously: as the *Ælfredi Vita* (1678.1), and the *Reliquiæ* (1698.3). Spelman was avid in his hunt for sources, particularly at Cambridge, where through his association with Abraham Wheelock, who as well as being University Librarian held the Lectureship in Anglo-Saxon funded by Spelman, he was able to borrow manuscripts from the university and college libraries. On one occasion he repaired a manuscript borrowed from Trinity College without prior consultation, providing it with a clasp, and incurred the wrath of the fellows, but defended his action vigorously as in the interests of conserving the manuscript. His correspondence reveals much of his thinking as he progressed, especially that with Jeremy Stephens who assisted him with the *Concilia*, and that with Olé Worm in Copenhagen reveals the warm and friendly relations between two scholars working on cognate material in different places.[8]

As Spelman's Lecturer in Anglo-Saxon at Cambridge Abraham Wheelock helped Spelman greatly, providing many transcripts of texts from manuscripts to which he had ready access. Wheelock took his duties seriously and studied manuscripts containing Old English closely. Only six years after his recruitment by Spelman he produced his great work, for which he is justly remembered, his edition of Bede's *Historia Ecclesiastica* (1643.1), in which he not only edited Bede's text but, with Ussher's exhortations in mind, annotated it with ample quotations from Ælfric's homilies. To this he added an edition of the *Anglo-Saxon Chronicle*, and a year later his re-edition of the Anglo-Saxon laws (the *Archaionomia* previously edited by William Lambarde in 1568) appeared with the Bede and the *Chronicle* in one impressive volume (1644.1). As we have seen, Wheelock used his close scrutiny of manuscripts to design his own English-size Anglo-Saxon type-design.

---

7 See Peter J. Lucas, 'William Camden, Seventeenth-Century Atlases of the British Isles and the Printing of Anglo-Saxon', *Antiquaries Journal*, 98 (2018), at pp. 225–227. All other English county descriptions in Speed's work were derived from Camden's *Britannia* (1607), or from the English translation of 1610.

8 See Peter J. Lucas, 'A Conspectus of Letters to and from Sir Henry Spelman (1563/4–1641)', *Antiquaries Journal*, 102 (2022), 370–388 + on-line supplement: doi:10.1017/S0003581522000026.

John Selden trained as a lawyer but his historical scholarship was adorned with considerable linguistic expertise, citing in his works not only Latin and Greek, but Hebrew, Chaldean, Samaritan, Aramaic, Arabic, Persian and Ethiopic, as well as French, German, Spanish, Italian, and Old English. Anglo-Saxon was not therefore a special interest of Selden's, but simply a valuable source of information providing historical support for his arguments where appropriate. He was a friend of Sir Robert Cotton and spent a great deal of time in his library. And he was himself an avid bibliophile. His scholarly output was prodigious, making him one of the outstanding scholars of his time. Books citing Old English include his *Historie of Tithes* (1618.1), the life of *Eadmer* (1623.3), his study of the *Titles of Honor* (1631.1), *Mare Clausum* (1635.1), *De Iure Naturali* (1640.4), and *De Synedriis* (1650.3).

The historical approach grounded in sound philology adopted by Spelman was continued by Sir Roger Twysden, 2nd baronet Twysden of Roydon Hall, whose devotion to legal propriety led to him having a somewhat troubled time during the Civil War. In the 1650s he settled down to scholarship, reading extensively in original sources, and drawing on Anglo-Saxon for part of his *Historiæ Anglicanæ Scriptores X* (1652.1). Among his friends he counted Sir Henry Spelman himself, Sir Simonds D'Ewes, John Selden and Sir William Dugdale. Dugdale also continued in the Spelmanian tradition, having met the great man when still young. Dugdale edited and completed Spelman's *Glossarium Archaeologicum* (1664.1) and published historical works that abound in citations of original sources: the *Monasticon Anglicanum* I (1655.3), the *History of St Pauls* (1658.1), *Monasticon Anglicanum* II (1661.1), and his *Origines Juridiciales* (1666.1), all of which include Old English.

Although primarily a historian with a legal training Spelman saw the importance of philology and encouraged it. This encouragement bore fruit in the decades following his death. After Wheelock's death the honorarium for the Lectureship in Anglo-Saxon went to William Somner, who was registrar to the ecclesiastical court of Canterbury. Known for his *Antiquities of Canterbury* (1640.1), Somner contributed the Old English glossary in Sir Roger Twysden's *Historiæ Anglicanæ Scriptores X* (1652.1). Having scoured all available sources of Old English he then produced what he is justly famous for, his *Dictionarium Saxonico-Latino-Anglicum* (1659.1), the first published Anglo-Saxon dictionary, for which a new Pica Anglo-Saxon type-design was made. Later he cited Old English in his *Treatise of Gavelkind* (1660.1), and in his *Roman Ports and Forts* (1693.1).

Somner was not the only philological contributor at this time. Brought up and trained in Leiden, Franciscus Junius, son of a distinguished biblical scholar, came to England in 1621 as librarian to Thomas Howard, earl of Arundel, where he had access to the wealth of materials in Arundel's large collection. Junius became the first great Germanic philologist, studying Old English within its historical linguistic context alongside cognate Germanic languages. His Germanic credentials appear clearly in his *Willeram* (1655.1) but in the same year his *Cædmon* (1655.2) furnished what was the first edition of Old English poetry, containing the biblical poems in MS Junius 11, *Genesis, Exodus, Daniel,* and *Christ and Satan*, pioneering work indeed, 160 years before the first edition of *Beowulf*. Then with Thomas Marshall, later to become Rector of Lincoln College, Oxford, he produced the *AS/Gothic Gospels* (1665.2) where the texts of the Gospels in Gothic and Old English are printed side by side, with annotations. To provide for the printing of these works Junius accumulated or had made sets of type-designs for Gothic, Runic, Old English and Old Norse texts. These he left to Oxford University, where they provided the means of publishing a series of books on Old English by several authors who became known as the Oxford Saxonists. While Junius may not have founded a school he did the next best thing of establishing a base on which one could and did grow. The principal among the Oxford Saxonists was George Hickes, whose *Institutiones Grammaticæ Anglo-Saxonicæ* (1689.3) provided the grammar to complement Somner's dictionary. Among Hickes's cohort were Edward Thwaites, whose most notable achievement was his *Heptateuchus* (1698.1), but who did a great deal of 'backroom' work helping others, especially Hickes, with their publications. Another of the Oxford Saxonists was Edmund Gibson, famous for his *Chronicon Saxonicum* (1692.1), an edition of the *Anglo-Saxon Chronicle* that surpassed Wheelock's but still left room for improvement. Others in the Hickes coterie were Christopher Rawlinson, who produced an edition of the Alfredian Boethius: *Boethi Consolationis Philosophiæ Libri V* (1698.2), where Old English verse was set out in half-lines for the first time, and William Elstob, who is notable for his edition of Wulfstan's *Sermo Lupi* (1701.2) and co-authored with Hickes *Several Letters* (1705.1). And last but certainly not least Humfrey Wanley, the great palaeographer, virtually co-authored with Hickes the monumental *Thesaurus* (1703/5.1), a work that brought together virtually everything that was known about Old English and cognate languages with a description of every manuscript containing Old English then known.

Historical knowledge constituted authority, and the transcribing and printing of Anglo-Saxon documents provided what Julia Crick has called a 'view [of] English royal government arrayed in its pristine state',[9] enough to give authentication to political desire. In the other books we see much repetition of the same material, so that perhaps the most cited book, coming early in the

---

9 See Crick, 'Art of the Unprinted', quotation at p. 126.

sequence of events and containing much Anglo-Saxon material, is Lambarde's *Archaionomia* (1568.2). This repetition confirms the importance of the material to the books' readers.

One of the features of the work on Anglo-Saxon in the seventeenth century is that the scholars involved knew, encouraged, influenced and collaborated with each other; they formed a social intellectual network.[10] Before it was effectively suppressed by James I, William Camden, Richard Carew, Sir Robert Cotton, William Lambarde, John Stow, Sir Henry Spelman and Francis Thynne were all members of the Elizabethan Society of Antiquaries, which met regularly.[11] When Junius was librarian to the earl of Arundel from 1621 onwards, although his primary interest then was art-historical, he would have been aware of the use being made of what is now BL Arundel 60, a Latin psalter glossed throughout in Old English, which happened to be an ideal manuscript for someone such as Junius, who had a thorough Latin and theological training, to learn Old English from. By the summer of 1622 William Lisle had completed his collation of this manuscript with his base manuscript, the Eadwine Psalter (TCC R.17.1), for the edition of the Old English Psalter that is contained in his workbook, OBL Laud misc. 201, a project that remained unpublished.[12] If Junius was not aware of Lisle's work he would certainly have known of the collation of the manuscript for Sir John Spelman's *Psalterium Davidis Latino-Saxonicum Vetus*, based on the manuscript owned by his father, Sir Henry, now BL Stowe 2.[13] Junius later owned a copy of the book.[14] When Sir Roger Twysden compiled his *Historiæ Anglicanæ Scriptores X* for publication in 1652 it was edited by John Selden and had a glossary by William Somner, so we have here in this great book an example of collaboration involving two of the outstanding scholars of the period who dealt with Anglo-Saxon: Selden and Somner. Somner

---

10 For some account of social network theory, involving zones, density and multiplexity see Jeremy Boissevain, *Friends of Friends: Networks, Manipulators and Coalitions* (Oxford: Blackwell, 1974), esp. pp. 24–48.

11 See McKisack, *Medieval History*; Linda Van Norden, 'Sir Henry Spelman on the Chronology of the Elizabethan College of Antiquaries', *Huntington Library Quarterly*, 13 (1949–50), pp. 131–160.

12 See P. Pulsiano, 'William L'Isle and the Editing of Old English', in Graham, *Recovery*, pp. 173–206; also Timothy Graham, 'William L'Isle's Letters to Sir Robert Cotton', in Elaine Treharne and Susan Rosser (eds), *Early Medieval English Texts and Interpretations* (Tempe AZ: MRTS, 2002), pp. 353–376.

13 London: Richard Badger 1 1640; STC 2369.

14 Now MS Junius 33 (SC5145), which he adorned by collating it with the Junius Psalter (now MS Junius 27; SC5139). On Junius's books and manuscripts in the Bodleian see E.G. Stanley, 'The Sources of Junius's Learning as revealed in the Junius Manuscripts in the Bodleian Library', in Bremmer, *Junius and his Circle*, pp. 159–176.

dedicated his *Dictionarium* to Sir Henry's nephew, Roger Spelman. For his edition of the Pseudo-Ælfric Vocabulary printed in his *Dictionarium* Somner followed Junius's transcript. When Junius in Holland wanted to know how his type-designs 'will be liked' in England he wrote to Selden about it.[15] These are just a few examples of the interconnection between the scholars in this field.[16]

There was a social network of patrons too. Particularly notable are the sisters and co-heiresses of the earl of Shrewsbury. Lady Alethia Talbot was married to Thomas Howard, earl of Arundel, famous for his marbles, and patron of Junius. Lady Elizabeth Talbot married Henry Gray, earl of Kent, and she patronized John Selden. Lady Mary Talbot married William Herbert, earl of Pembroke, to whom the First Folio of Shakespeare was dedicated, and to whom Selden presented a copy of his *Eadmer* (**1623.3**).[17]

Not only was there a social intellectual network supporting antiquarian publication but also a small business network. Speed's ambitious project to produce the *Theatre of the Empire* needed trade support and he received it from the bookseller George Humble, who had a shop in Popes-head Alley. On 29 April 1608 Humble was granted a privilege to print Speed's work for 21 years.[18] Humble seems to have enjoyed a virtual monopoly of map-publication in London until his death in 1640.[19] From the subsequent history of the editions it is evident that Humble must have held the plates, and almost certainly the Anglo-Saxon types as well. The amount required was small, so probably they were types, rather than matrices or punches. Humble it probably was who acquired these mixed special sorts from Elliot's Court Press, the printers of Camden's 1594 and 1600 *Britannia*, and passed them on to Speed's printer William Hall (fl.1598–1614).

The social intellectual network extended to the continent. Camden and Spelman had an extensive range of continental correspondents.[20] Junius, of course, was Dutch, but he was Holland's gift to English scholarship. English scholarship was much appreciated on the continent.[21] Hugo Grotius, whose

---

15 A continuation of the letter cited above in ch 1 and printed by Romburgh, *Franciscus Junius*, p. 848, also Hickes 1703/5.1: I.xliii.
16 Cf. Toomer, *Life*, I.311–319, and II.822–824.
17 David S. Berkowitz, *John Selden's Formative Years: Politics and Society in Early Seventeenth-Century England* (Washington DC: Folger Shakespeare Library, 1988), p. 303, n. 53.
18 Greg, *Companion*, p. 154.
19 Skelton, *County Atlases*, p. 234.
20 See, for example, Linda Van Norden, 'Peiresc and the English Scholars', *Huntington Library Quarterly*, 12 (1948–9), pp. 369–89. For Camden's correspondence see Thomas Smith, *Camdeni Epistolae* (London: for Richard Chiswell, 1691; Wing C361). For Spelman's correspondence see Lucas, 'Conspectus'.
21 Cf. Stanley, 'Continental Contribution', pp. 49–52.

work on the freedom of the seas was criticised by Selden, nevertheless called Selden 'the glory of the English nation'.[22] Selden collaborated with Daniel Heinsius in Leiden on the publication of continental editions of some of his works. Several of Selden's works were reprinted on the continent. Spelman's *Archæologus* and Somner's *Dictionarium* are much cited in Du Cange's great Latin dictionary: **1678.2**. Indeed Spelman was reportedly known in France as 'Varro Anglicanus', after the most learned Roman.[23] Perhaps even more notably Camden's *Britannia* (**1607.2**), complete with (inaccurate) Anglo-Saxon place-name etymologies and an excerpt from the *Anglo-Saxon Chronicle*, was used as the textual accompaniment to the Great Britain and Ireland volumes of the great world atlases produced by the rival Amsterdam publishing houses of Blaeu and Janssonius.[24]

This book is about printing Anglo-Saxon, in particular with special sorts. But none of it would have happened without the impetus provided by scholars. To begin with scholars such as Matthew Parker and his colleagues in the archdiocese of Canterbury were looking for evidence to support their point of view regarding the establishment of the Church of England, particularly in relation to the taking of communion in both kinds (bread and wine) as opposed to the Catholic practice of offering the congregation bread only. At the same time as Parker was collecting information on religious practice William Cecil (Lord Burghley), Elizabeth I's Treasurer and effective head of government, was employing Laurence Nowell (the antiquary) and William Lambarde to work on Anglo-Saxon history and laws to provide precedents for Elizabethan governmental practices, and Lambarde's *Archaionomia* (**1568.2**) appeared only two years after Parker's first production, the *Testimonye of Antiquitie* (**1566.1**). In the next century Sir Henry Spelman developed a more thorough scholarly approach. He wrote works of reference to help readers decipher ancient manuscripts, namely his *Archæologus in Modum Glossarii* (**1626.1**), his unprinted *Archaismus Graphicus* and his unprinted Anglo-Saxon grammar, and he produced a major work on the texts recording church councils (**1639.4**). He founded a lectureship in Anglo-Saxon at Cambridge University that was held by another serious scholar, Abraham Wheelock, who produced an edition of Bede's *Historia Ecclesiastica* together with the *Anglo-Saxon Chronicle* (**1643.1**) and a re-edition of Lambarde's *Archaionomia* (**1644.1**). So far all of

---

22 Anthony à. Wood, *Athenae Oxonienses*, ed. P. Bliss, 3 vols (London: F.C. & J. Rivington, 1813–17), III.366.
23 Extract from a letter sent by John Spelman in Angers to Sir Henry, BL Add 34599, fo 108ᵛ.
24 For bibliographical descriptions of these books see Koeman, *Atlantes Neerlandici*, rev. Peter van der Krogt, *Koeman's Atlantes Neerlandici*, 7 vols ('t Goy-Houten: HES, 1997–2010).

this work is focussed on history, but 1655 marks a significant shift towards a more all-encompassing approach. The historical approach is confirmed with even greater detail in referencing historical records, especially charters, by Sir William Dugdale in his *Monasticon Anglicanum* (**1655.3**). But in the same year the books by Franciscus Junius, dubbed 'the oracle of the Northern tongues', showed a deep interest in the philology of English as part of the Germanic family of languages, as his *Willeram* (**1655.1**), and they showed a literary dimension in the first edition ever of Old English poetry in his *Cædmon* (**1655.2**).[25] By leaving all his books, papers (including transcripts) and printing utensils to Oxford University Junius laid the foundations for the development of Anglo-Saxon as a subject with ample resources to draw on. Building on this base George Hickes produced the first published modern Anglo-Saxon grammar (**1689.3**) and later with Humfrey Wanley and others his *Thesaurus* (**1703/5.1**), a work of immense scope showing a great breadth of knowledge on matters English and Germanic, and including a volume cataloguing all the then known Anglo-Saxon manuscripts, which is still an important reference work today.

---

25   Junius was dubbed 'the oracle of the northern tongues' by White Kennett in **1693.1**, h5ʳ.

PART 2

*Catalogue of Early Printed Books Containing
Anglo-Saxon to 1705*

Glossary of Printing, Book-Description and Type-Description Terms

arm	a horizontal letter-stroke
ascender	letter-stroke that goes up above the top-line of the body of the letter
bar	a horizontal stroke that crosses a vertical one, as in **t**
bifolium	two conjoint leaves made from folding a sheet of paper or membrane
body	the size of a piece of type from front to back measured in millimetres over twenty lines of text
bow	a curved stroke that does not enclose an area
bowl	a curved stroke enclosing an area
capitals	the larger letters of the alphabet, otherwise called upper-case
collation	the formal description of the make-up of a book in gatherings with indications of foliation and/or pagination
conjugate leaf	a leaf joined to another as a result of folding a sheet of paper and then included in a gathering (or quire)
contraction	a symbol or mark used to indicate letters that have not been spelt out
counter	the area of a letter that is enclosed, as in **o** or **A**
descender	letter-stroke that goes down below the bottom-line of the body of a letter
duodecimo	used to describe the format of a (small) book made up of sheets folded to make twelve leaves
ear	a small stroke such as that to the right of the bowl of a **g**
edition	a bibliographical entity: a particular work produced in a number of copies, all basically identical
English-size	typesize 20 lines 96mm
face	the top level surface of a piece of type used for printing
foliation	the numbering of the leaves of a book
folio	1. a leaf in a book 2. used to describe the (relatively large) format of a book composed of sheets folded once into two leaves
font	a full set of type-designs
fount	a complete set of type-letters as used by a printer

gathering	a set of leaves made up of sheets folded one inside the other to constitute a unit in a printed book. Cp. quire
Great Primer	typesize 20 lines 122mm
kern	an overhang formed by casting a letter (usually Greek or Hebrew) on a thinner body than usual to allow combination with accents
leaf	two pages back to back
ligature	two (or more) letters linked to each other, often cast as one sort
Long Primer	type-size, 20 lines 67mm
lower-case	the small letters of the alphabet
matrix	a mould, usually made of copper, into which a punch has been driven, and from which the face of the letter is cast to make type
octavo	used to describe the (relatively small) format of a book made up of sheets folded three times into eight leaves
page	one side of a leaf
Pica	typesize 20 lines 86mm
punch	a small rod of steel with a letter engraved at the end and used to drive into a matrix
punctus elevatus	punctuation mark indicating a mid pause, similar in function to a modern comma or semi-colon
punctus versus	punctuation mark indicating a heavier pause, similar in function to a modern full stop
quarto	used to describe the (medium-size) format of a book composed of sheets folded twice into four leaves
quire	a set of leaves made up of sheets folded one inside the other to constitute a unit in a manuscript. Cp. gathering
recto	the right-hand page in a book opening
sansserif	without serifs
sheet	a piece of paper usually printed flat and then folded one inside another to make up a gathering; various sheet sizes were used
serif	a small stroke at the end of a main stroke, single (one side or the other) or double (on both sides)
shoulder	the curved stroke emanating from the stem of letters such as **f, h, r**
Small Pica	typesize 20 lines 76mm
sort	each variety of letter in a fount, a piece of type
spur	a small projection from a stroke or terminal

GLOSSARY OF PRINTING

stem	a vertical stroke
tagged	the way a horizontal stroke intersects with a vertical stroke in script
tail	the parts below the base-line of **g, y, J, Q** etc.
terminal	the ending of a stroke (other than a serif), often hooked or sheared
type	a piece of metal or wood having on its face a letter or character for use in printing
typeface	the design of the letter-forms in a font
type-design	the distinctive letter-forms of a fount (or partial fount) resulting from the creation of a set of punches
upper-case	the larger letters of the alphabet, capitals
verso	the left-hand page in a book opening
x-height	the height between the base-line and the top-line of the body of a letter

Symbols Used in Collation Formulae

π	unsigned preliminary gathering
πA	signed preliminary gathering that uses a signature letter also used in the main sequence of signatures
χ	unsigned leaves inserted in a gathering

Old English (Anglo-Saxon) Special Letters

æ	'ash', a separate letter in the OE alphabet
þ	'thorn', representing a sound similar to MnE 'th'
ð	'eth', representing a sound similar to MnE 'th'
ƿ	'wynn', the OE letter for 'w'

List of Type Designs

This list sets out all the type-designs representing Anglo-Saxon identified in this book, together with the size of the Roman (and occasionally other) type-designs used in conjunction with them.

Types are listed giving
(1) their name and size,
(2) their measurements, Body + x-height + capital height
(3) where they are illustrated, preferably on a type-specimen, and
(4) the books in which they occur, designated by the date number assigned in the Catalogue below, e.g. 1566.1.

The following abbreviations are used for type-designs:

AS   Anglo-Saxon (used in England, but may have been cut on the continent (AS1, 2, 3, and certainly AS6)
CAS Continental Anglo-Saxon (made and used in France, Germany or Holland)
IR   Irish

After the Anglo-Saxon and Irish type-designs some account of the Roman, Italic and Textura type-designs found in the books is set out. This list is not exhaustive. Some standard designs were re-founded but no attempt is made to distinguish 'editions' or possible 're-modelling' of these designs. Some printers were job-printers and used different type-designs mixed together.

The methodology used to identify types as belonging to a particular design was to lay an image of certain examples of letter-forms printed on a cellulose sheet over the example to be identified and examine it closely, if necessary under a magnifying glass. If the basic framework or skeleton of each letter is always consistent, and the relative positions and weights of the strokes remain constant, then, no matter how poor the press-work or how over-inked the impression may be, these features are taken to indicate that the letter-forms were cast in matrices deriving from the same punches, and form further instances of the relevant type-design. Sometimes enlargement of the letter-forms was required, as in the comparison of AS2 and AS3. For a more elaborate method of analysing type, more suited to Roman types especially, see Olocco 2020: esp. 217; for unevenness in printing see pp. 203–14.

Anglo-Saxon (Listed in Chronological Order)

AS1 (London/Paris?): The Parkerian Great Primer Anglo-Saxon (1566–1646)

This design shows 26 special sorts altogether, 11 lower-case, ð, ꝼ, ʒ, ı, ꝑ, ſ, τ, ẏ; þ, ð̵, p; 10 capitals, Æ¹, Æ², Є, Ꝺ, Ꟁ, ꝸ, X; Ꝑ, Đ, Ᵽ; and 4 others, þ, ꞃ, ꞁ, ꞇ.

Possibly cut by Pierre Haultin (see Part 1, Chapter 2), who was in Paris 1565–70 before transferring to the Protestant stronghold of La Rochelle. Acquired by Day and combined with Haultin's English-size Roman on a Great Primer Body: Body 112 × 2.0: 4.3.

Printed by John Day I (1522–84†): 1566.1, 1566.2, 1567.1, 1568.1, 1568.2, 1570.1, 1571.1, 1572.1, 1574.1, 1574.2, 1583.1;

Printed by John Windet (fl.1584–1610†), who succeeded to part of the printing materials of John Day I via Day's son Richard and John Wolfe (fl.1579–1601): 1596.1, 1598.2;

Printed by William Stansby (fl.1597–1638†), who took over the business of John Windet: 1617.1 (specimen), 1623.3, 1631.1, 1635.1;

Printed by Richard Bishop (fl.1636–58), who succeeded to the printing business of William Stansby: 1640.4, 1646.6.

Some notes on particular letters:

Lower-case Letters

i undotted. As noted by Wakeman (1967: 286) on the authority of Oastler the Anglo-Saxon undotted i is the same as the roman i without the dot. The two can be seen and measured side by side in 1566.2, sig. I5ᵛ/I6ʳ.

ð. The choice of this form, with its long ascender sloping steeply to the left, led to considerable problems in setting the Old English in 1566.1/1566.2, and there is evidence of the substitution of þ for ð in medial and final positions in the revision of the setting between the first and second editions, e.g. 1566.1 M3ᵛ/18 oðer > oþer 1566.2 H5ᵛ/18. This problem was solved by recasting the type from the matrix in such a way that it would fit snugly against the preceding letter. The recast variety is first seen in 1571.1 between sigs 2G and 2H. Up to 2G4ᵛ/26 'þencð' the ð shows a space in front of it which distances it from the letter it follows. From 2H1ʳ/2 'doð' the ð fits snugly against its preceding letter.

z. This form is matched by the z in the Parkerian Anglo-Saxon alphabet in Hatton 113 (Illustration 11), but not, as far as I have been able to observe, by anything authentic in Anglo-Saxon manuscripts, where the usual form of z is roughly similar to the modern printed form. The Parkerian written z resembles a Secretary-script z of the period,[1] and the printed version appears to be

---

[1] See, e.g., A. Heal, *The English Writing-Masters and their Copy-Books 1570–1800: A Biographical Dictionary & a Bibliography* (Cambridge: Cambridge University Press, 1931), pl. xxv (no. 2), from John de Beauchesne and John Baildon, *A Booke containing Divers Sortes of Hands* (London: Thomas Vautrollier 1570: STC 6445.5), the earliest writing book published in England,

based on a Textura z with a hooked terminal such as is found in Marshe's Small Pica Textura (sometimes called 'Black Letter' or 'English')[2] used, for example, for 1567.1, or in the Pica Textura tentatively attributed to Guyot,[3] or in the *lettres de forme*, *lettre bastarde*, and *lettres tourneures* of Geofroy Tory.[4] Another possibility is that the use of a sixteenth-century Secretary-script or Textura z was inspired by the shape of z sometimes found in Irish manuscripts. In Lambeth Palace MS 1370 (the 'Gospels of MacDurnan' of s.ix)[5] z sometimes occurs with the lower arm turned down and round to form a tail, e.g. in 'nazarenum' on 209^v/10 at Jn 18.7, although, unlike sixteenth-century z, the diagonal extends beyond the juncture with the lower arm.

Capitals

Size. In 1566.1 Roman capitals are very occasionally from a Great Primer fount, e.g. Great Primer F on sig. F2^v/18 beside English-size F on sig. E3^v/12. This practice is commoner in 1571.1, e.g. on sig. 2D2^v Great Primer D and G (line 2) beside English-size D (line 18) and G (line 3).

Æ. In 1566.2, but not in subsequent specimens, Æ^1 and Æ^2 are shown as equivalent to Roman and swash italic Æ respectively. Æ^1 in particular is quite rare in the manuscripts, but, besides the Junius 121 group, is found notably in Tiberius B.i, throughout the Orosius (fos 3–111), as a full display capital, but also as a secondary display capital, for example, on fo 70^r, lines 1, 2, and 8;[6] here Æ^1 is used side by side angular capital Æ on an alternating basis, and this usage may have been influential in the decision to cut two capital Æ shapes.

H, M. Both these uncial-shaped capitals have not so much a hooked terminal as an attention-seeking twitch at the base of their lower right stem. This feature too is compatible with a Textura face, such as Marshe's Small Pica Textura, and it occurs also in the cadeaulx (i.e. 'quadreaulx', display capitals a quarter of the height higher than those following them) of Geofroy Tory.[7] However, the feature may derive from manuscript usage. Twitched M, for example, occurs

---

also A.G. Petti, *English Literary Hands from Chaucer to Dryden* (London: Edward Arnold, 1977), fig. 23 on p. 18, and G.E. Dawson & L. Kennedy-Skipton, *Elizabethan Handwriting 1500–1650* (London: Faber, 1968, re-issued Chichester: Phillimore, 1981), pl. 2A.

2 See Type Index, p. 213.
3 Vervliet, *Printing Types*, T34.
4 Geofroy Tory, *Champ Fleury* (Paris: Giles Gourmont 1529), O2v, O3rv, t and annot. G.B. Ives (New York: Grolier Club, 1927), pp. 176–178.
5 See above, Part 1, p. 42, note 46.
6 See Lucas 1997: 183, pl. 30.
7 *Champ Fleury* (1529), O2r, t Ives (1927), p. 175. For uncials used in print cf. Vervliet, *Printing Types*, 208–215.

in Hatton 113, vi^v (see Illustration 12), and quite frequently in Tiberius B.i, e.g., 63^r/9. Twitched H occurs for example in Faustina A.ix, 132^v/22.

X. Although it occurred rarely in proper names, as 'Xersis' in Tiberius B.i, 37^r/6, 14, a special sort for this letter was probably cut because of its frequency in the manuscripts as an abbreviation for 'Christ'. A good example, which might have served as a model, occurs in Hatton 113, 56^v (Fig. 9, where it is a numeral); for others that are similar cf. CCC 265, p. 157/15, and Vespasian D.xiv, 27^v/5. But in the event this form of abbreviation was not used in print, and so the special sort was to all effects and purposes redundant.

Punctuation
ꝛ. Before the punctus versus became available a (?Pica) Roman semi-colon was used, as in the 1566.2 specimen (Illustration 4).

CAS1 (Paris): The Smithian Great Primer Anglo-Saxon Phonetic Special Sorts (1568)

The Smithian phonetic special sorts on Anglo-Saxon models designed to fit with a Great Primer Italic and found only in Sir Thomas Smith's *De recta & emendata Linguae Anglicae Scriptione, Dialogus* printed by Robert Estienne the Younger (USTC 140541). The cutting is of a high standard and may have been done by Guillaume I Le Bé (1523/4–98). Pierre Haultin is also a possibility.

Special sorts for phonetic symbols include several explicitly based on an Anglo-Saxon model: ꝼ, ð, þ, ẏ, Ð; and others which may have been inspired by an Anglo-Saxon model: ҽ, ẏ, ı.

Contemporary interest in Paris in Anglo-Saxon script is shown by the calligraphic imitator Pierre Hamon (Armstrong 1963: 548–51), but he used a 'Bastard Saxon' model (i.e. an early MnE archaizing hand), which is unlikely to have been that behind the design of Smith's special sorts. Probably the designs were supplied by Smith himself.

Printed by Robert Estienne the Younger (fl.1556–70): **1568.3**.

AS2 (London/La Rochelle?): The Parkerian Pica Anglo-Saxon (1576–1640)

This design shows 24 special sorts, 12 lower-case, ƀ, ꝼ, ȝ, ı, ꞃ, ꞅ, ꞇ, ẏ, z; þ, ð, p; 9 capitals, Æ¹, Æ², Ꞓ, Ð, Ꝺ, 8; Þ, Ð, P, together with 3 others, ⁊, the tironian sign for 'and', ꝥ, the abbreviation for 'þæt', and ꝛ, the punctus versus.

Possibly cut by Pierre Haultin (see Part 1, Chapter 3), who was in Paris 1565–70.

Used by John Day in combination with a Pica Roman; the lower-case AS sorts are slightly higher, and the capitals notably so: Body 82 × 1.7: 2.6

Printed by John Day I (1522–84†): **1576.1, 1614.4**;
Printed by William Stansby (fl.1597–1638†): **1618.1**;

Printed by Richard Bishop (fl.1636–58): **1640.3** (sig. B).

With an English-size Roman (R92; Vervliet 2010: no. 98): Body 92 × 2: 3.1
Printed by William Hall (fl.1598–1614) and John Beale (fl.1611–43†) for John Sudbury (fl.1610–15) and George Humble (fl.1611–32): **1611.2**;

Used by Ralph Newbery and others combined with a Long Primer Roman:
Printed by Eliot's Court Press (fl.1584–1680) for Ralph Newbery (fl.1560–1604†): **1586.1, 1587.1, 1588.1, 1591.1, 1592.1, 1594.1**;
Printed by Eliot's Court Press for George Bishop (fl.1566–1611): **1590.1**;
Printed by William Stansby (fl.1597–1638†): **1617.1** (sigs T–2Z).

AS3 (London/La Rochelle?): The Lambardian Pica Anglo-Saxon (1576–1670)

This design shows 22 special sorts, 12 + 1 lower-case (including one capital misused as a lower-case letter), ð, [ʃ], e, ꝼ, ȝ, h, ꞃ, ꞅ, ꞇ, ẏ; þ, ð, p; 6 capitals, Æ^1 and Æ^2, Є, Ϻ; Ᵽ, Đ; together with 3 others, ⁊, the tironian sign for 'and', þ, the abbreviation for 'þæt', and ˑj, the punctus versus.

It is not known who cut these designs. It is not impossible that Pierre Haultin cut this type-design too with Lambarde (and Newbery) using a similar arrangement to that used by Day for AS1 and AS2. With Pierre Haultin now in La Rochelle the contact may have been his nephew Jérôme in London. The cost may have been borne by Cecil (Lord Burleigh), but I have found no evidence to support this possibility.

With a Long Primer Roman: Body 65 × 1.2: 2
Printed by Melchisidec Bradwood (fl.1602–18) at Eliot's Court Press (fl.1584–1680) for John Brown 2 (fl.1612–34): **1617.1** (sigs A–S).

Used by Ralph Newbery and others combined with a Pica Roman: Face 82 × 1.6: 2.9
Printed by Henry Middleton (fl.1567–87†) for Ralph Newbery (fl.1560–1604†): **1576.2**;
Printed by Henry Bynneman (fl.1566–83†) and [for] Ralph Newbery: **1581.1, 1582.1**;

With a Pica Roman:
Printed by an unidentified printer for the Stationers' Co.: **1610.3**.
Printed by Eliot's Court Press (fl.1584–1680) for George Bishop (fl.1566–1611) and John Norton (fl.1586–1612) *impensis*: **1607.2, 1610.5**;
Printed by [Adam Islip] (fl.1591–1639†) for the Stationers' Co.: **1610.1, 1614.2**, and (combined with various sizes) **1619.1**;
Printed by Adam Islip, Felix Kingston (fl.1597–1653†) and Robert Young (fl.1624–43†): **1631.3**;
Printed by [Humphrey Lownes I] (fl. as bookseller 1590–1603 and printer 1604–30†) for Matthew Lownes (fl.1595–1625†), John Browne 1 (fl.1598–1622†), John Helme (fl.1607–16†), and John Busby II (fl.1607–31†): **1612.1**.

LIST OF TYPE DESIGNS

Printed by John Beale (fl.1611–43†): **1626.1**;
Printed by Richard Badger I (fl.1629–41) for Philemon Stephens I (fl.1622–65†; brother of Jeremiah) in partnership with Christopher Meredith (fl.1625–53†) *impensis*: **1639.4** (sigs a1^v, and 3C5^v, 3D3^v in catchwords), **1640.3**;
Printed at Oxford by William Turner (fl.1624–43†, Printer to Oxford University 1624–40): **1634.1** (with some new sorts);
Printed at Cambridge by Roger Daniel (fl.1620–67†, printer to Cambridge University 1632–50) for Cornelius Bee (fl.1634–72): **1644.1** (sigs 2E1^r–4^r);
Printed by Thomas Warren (fl.1645–59†): **1658.1**;
Printed by William Wilson (fl.1645–65) for John Starkey (fl.1656–89): **1663.1**;
Printed by Thomas Snodham (*alias* East; fl.1609–25†) for John Helme (fl.1607–16†): **1610.2**;
Printed by Robert Young (fl.1624–43†): **1631.2**;
Printed by Felix Kingston (fl.1597–1653†), John Legat II (fl.1620–58†) and Robert Young (fl.1624–43†) for Andrew Hebb (fl.1625–48†)/ Joyce Norton (widow of John Norton I, fl.1632–8) and Richard Whitaker (fl.1619–48†)/ Andrew Crooke (fl.1632–74†)/ William Apsley (fl.1599–1640)/ George Latham (fl.1620–58†): **1637.1**;
Printed by John Legat II (fl.1620–58†) for Richard Thrale (fl.1625–67): **1640.1**;
Printed by James Flesher (fl.1649–70†) for Richard Mynne (fl.1624–50) *sumptibus*: **1650.1**;
Printed by James Flesher for Cornelius Bee (fl.1634–72†), father-in-law of James Flesher, **1655.4** (words on sig 2D3^r);
Printed by James Flesher for Richard Royston (fl.1629–86, also had a shop in Oxford), and Nathaniel Brookes (fl.1646–77): **1665.1** (phrase);
Printed by Francis and Thomas Warren II (fl.1666): **1666.1**;
Printed at Oxford by Henry Hall I (fl.1642–80) for Edward Forrest II (fl.1646–85): **1646.1** (words);
Printed (no printer stated) for the Stationers' Co.: **1641.2** (sigs 2P1^v–4^r);
Printed by John Grismond II (fl.1641–66†) for John Crooke I (fl.1637–†1669) and Thomas Heath (fl.1651–69): **1654.1** (words on sig D4^r);
Printed by Evan Tyler (fl.1652–83) for John Crook I (fl.1648–1669†): **1658.3**;
Printed by Alice Warren (fl.1659–65†): **1661.1**;
Printed at Cambridge by John Hayes (printer to Cambridge University 1669–1705) for Edward Story (Cambridge fl.1653–77, †1692/3): **1670.1**.

With an English-size Roman: Body 92 × 2: 3.1
Printed by John Beale (fl.1611–43†) for George Humble (fl.1611–32): **1623.2** (word), **1627.2** (word).

Letters only (AS ȝ, þ later corrupted to p): **1605.1, 1614.3, 1623.4, 1629.1, 1636.4, 1657.1, 1674.1**.

AS2/3:
1. The Parkerian and Lambardian Pica Anglo-Saxons mixed together (1594–1703)
    With a Long Primer Roman:
Printed by [Eliot's Court Press for] George Bishop (fl.1566–1611): **1594.2**;
Printed by Thomas Wight (fl.1597–1605) in association with Bonham Norton (fl.1594–1635†): **1599.1**;
Printed by John Haviland (fl.1621–38†), partner in Eliot's Court Press: **1625.1**.
    With a Pica Roman:
Printed by [(?)Edmund Bollifant (fl.1585–1602) at Eliot's Court Press for] George Bishop (fl.1566–1611): **1600.1**;
Printed by James Flesher: **1650.1** for Richard Mynne (fl.1624–50) *sumptibus*, **1652.1** for Cornelius Bee (fl.1634–72†) *sumptibus*;
Printer not stated, for Robert Knaplock (fl.1696–1737†): **1703.2**.
    With various sizes (English-size, Pica and Long Primer, also (in **1616.1**) Brevier):
Printed by William Hall (fl.1598–1614) for John Sudbury (fl.1610–15) and George Humble (fl.1611–32): **1611.1, 1614.1** (part printed by Thomas Snodham);
Printed by Thomas Snodham (fl.1609–25†) for John Sudbury (fl.1610–15) and George Humble (fl.1611–32): **1616.1**;
Printed by John Dawson (fl.1613–34?†) for George Humble (fl.1611–32): **1627.1**;
Printed by Mary Simmons (fl.1656–67) and Samuel Simmons (fl.1666–78) for Roger Rea the Elder (1665†) and Roger the Younger (fl.1650–62–?1668): **1650/?1665.1**;
No printer stated, for Thomas Basset (fl.1658–96) and Richard Chiswell (fl.1667–1711): **1676.1**.
    With an English-size Roman: Body 92 × 2: **3.1**
Printed by Edmund Bollifant (fl.1585–1602) of Eliot's Court Press: **1596.2**;
Printed by John Dawson (fl.1613–34?†), also Thomas Cotes (fl.1627–41†), for George Humble (fl.1611–32): **1632.2**.

2. The Lambardian Pica Anglo-Saxon with Parkerian s (1602–58)
    With a Long Primer Roman: **1639.1**.
    With a Pica Roman:
Printed by Thomas Wight (fl.1597–1605): **1602.1**;
Printed by [Adam Islip (fl.1591–1639†)] for the Stationers' Company: **1607.1**;
Printed by John Haviland (fl.1621–38†) [at Eliot's Court Press] for Henry Seile I (fl.1619–61†): **1623.1**;
Printed by Edward Griffin II (fl.1637–52†) [at Eliot's Court Press] for Francis Eglesfield (fl.1637–88): **1638.1** (O2^v),

Printed by William Jaggard (fl.1594–1623†) *typis*: **1608.1, 1610.4**;
Printed by James Flesher (fl. 1649–70†, son of Miles Flesher I for Cornelius Bee (fl.1634–72†) *sumptibus*: **1652.1**;
Printed by Richard Hodgkinson: **1655.3**;
Printed by Alice Warren (fl.1659–65†): **1664.1**;
Printed by William Jaggard (fl.1594–1623†): **1619.2**;
Printed by James Flesher (fl.1649–70†), son of Miles Flesher I, who features in the will of John Haviland (of Eliot's Court Press) for Richard Mynne (fl.1624–50) *sumptibus*: **1650.1**;
Printed by Richard Hodgkinson (fl.1624–75†) for Daniel Pakeman (fl.1631–64†): **1640?.1**.
With an English-size Roman (Body 92), mixed with AS7
Printed by Thomas Roycroft (fl.1650–77†) for Henry Twyford (fl.1640–89) and Timothy Twyford (fl.1657–70): **1658.2**.

IR1 (London/Paris/La Rochelle?): The Elizabethan English-size Irish (first appearance Dublin, 1571, used for Anglo-Saxon 1622–39)

Queen Elizabeth's Irish type-design came about thanks to Archbishop Parker's wish to spread the uses of the *Ecclesia Anglicana* beyond the Pale, where Irish was spoken more than English.

The first item to be printed with it appeared in 1571: Pilip Mac Cuinn Chrosaigh's poem *Tuar ferge foighide Dhe* [Dublin, William Kearney], known as the Irish Broadside (STC 19844.5; Sweeney no. 2948; O'Cuiv 1994: 191–212; Sharpe & Hoyne 2020: no. 4), discussed by Dickins 1949: 48–60 & pls V–VI. The only surviving copy of the Irish Broadside of 1571 is preserved with Archbishop Parker's books at Corpus Christi College, Cambridge, where it is adorned with an 'ungrammatical' inscription by John Parker, the archbishop's son: 'This irish balade printed in Irelande who belike vse the olde saxon carecte', a reference to the perceived similarities between Irish and Anglo-Saxon script. On this type-design see McGuinne 1992: ch. 1 & pls 1.3, 1.5; Pollard 2000: 543–544.

There were 22 special sorts, 10 lower case, and 11 capitals, plus the tironian sign, ꝉ, almost as many as those specially cut for the Parkerian Great Primer Anglo-Saxon (AS1).

    10 lower-case sorts: a ƌ e ꝼ ᵹ i p ꝑ s t;
    11 capitals: A B Ð E Ꝼ Ᵹ I M N T U

Who cut the special sorts is not known, but, like the first Anglo-Saxon special sorts, they were combined with Pierre Haultin's English Roman, perhaps not a coincidence; with the Irish special sorts the body size is 95.5 mm. Haultin had connections with England through his nephew Jérôme who operated as a typefounder in London at least as early as 1568 (Oastler 1975: 33 and n. 6; Desgraves 1960: xvii–xviii; Carter 1969: 86–87). Queen Elizabeth's Irish Types also appeared in the same year in John Kearney's translation into Irish of the Catechism, *Abidil Gaoidheilge agus Caiticiosma* (Dublin: [William Kearney] 1571; STC 22.3; Sweeney no. 103; Sharpe & Hoyne 2020: no. 5).

Used for Anglo-Saxon by the Stationers' Society Dublin (fl.1618–41), where it is combined with Pierre Haultin's English-size Roman:

1622.2, 1632.3, 1639.2.

CAS2.1 (Amsterdam or Leiden): The Dutch 'Boxhornian' English-size Anglo-Saxon (Body 96, but many letters oversized) used by an unknown printer in combination with a Pica Roman (1636)

These sorts of low quality may have been cut by an amateur punchcutter of unknown identity.

For the Anglo-Saxon passages 16 special sorts are shown, 10 lower-case, 4 capitals and 2 others: ð, ꝼ, ᵹ, ƿ, ı, ꝥ, ꞃ, ꞇ; þ, ð; Æ², Ɛ, 8, Ð; þ, ꝫ. See Part 1, Chapter 5 and Illustration 38.

1636.3.

CAS2.2 (Leiden): The Dutch Elsevierian English-size Anglo-Saxon (Body 104, but many letters oversized) used by the Elseviers in combination with a Pica Roman (1636)

The only known candidate for the punchcutting of these sorts is Arent Corsz[oon] van Hoogenacker (c.1579–1636).

The passages in Anglo-Saxon show 19 special sorts, 12 lower-case, 5 capitals and 2 others: ð, ꝼ, ᵹ, ƿ, ı, ꝥ, ꞃ, ꞇ, ẏ; þ, ð, p; Æ¹, Æ², Ɛ, 8, Ð, þ, ꝫ. See Part 1, chapter 5 and Illustration 39.

1636.1.

CAS2.3 (Leiden): The Dutch Mairian English-size Anglo-Saxon (Body 83, but many letters oversized) used by the Maires in combination with a Pica Roman (1636)

The only known candidate for the punchcutting of these sorts is Arent Corsz[oon] van Hoogenacker (c.1579–1636).

The passages in Anglo-Saxon show 17 special sorts combined with the Pica Roman, 11 lower-case, 4 capitals and 2 others: ð, ꝼ, ᵹ, ƿ, ꝥ, ꞃ, ꞇ, ẏ; þ, ð, p; Æ¹, Ɛ, 8, Ð; þ, ꝫ. See Part 1, chapter 5 and Illustration 40.

1636.2.

AS4 (London): The Spelmannian Great Primer Anglo-Saxon (1639–52)
No doubt cut specially for Spelman's *Concilia* **1639.4**, and modelled on AS1 with the addition of square C and tongued *e*; some 25 special sorts are shown, 12 lower case, 10 capitals and 3 others: ð, e, ꝼ, ȝ, ı, ꝑ, ꞃ, τ, ẏ; þ, ð, p; Æ¹, Æ², Ⲗ, Ⲉ, Ⱨ, Ⲙ, Ⴝ, Ᵽ, Đ, Ᵽ; ꝗ, ꝗ, þ. See Part 1, chapter 4 and Illustration 18.

The punch-cutter is moot, but may have been Arthur Nicholls (fl.1632–40); this supposition is on the basis that there is no other obvious person who could have done it. See further below under AS5.

James no. 52 (see Mores *Dissertation*: [14] and 111).

With an English-size Roman:
Printed by Robert Young (fl.1624–43†) for Matthew Walbancke (fl.1618–67) and William Cooke (fl.1632–42): **1641.1**;
Printed by [Miles Flesher I] (fl.1617–64†) for Philemon Stephens (fl.1622–65†): **1646.2** (words), **1647.1** (= re-issue of prec.);
Printed by Miles Flesher I (fl.1617–64†) for William Lee II (fl.1620–58?+), Daniel Pakeman (fl.1631–64†) and Matthew Walbancke (fl.1618–60): **1647.2**;
Printed by James Flesher (fl. 1649–70†, son of Miles Flesher I, for Cornelius Bee (fl.1634–72†, father-in-law of James Flesher): **1650.3**.

With a Great Primer Roman: Body 118, Face 110 × 2.1: 3.2/4 (varies for different capitals):
Printed by Miles Flesher I (fl.1617–64†, brother-in-law of Richard Bishop) *typis*, for Cornelius Bee (fl.1634–72†), and Laurence Sadler (fl.1631–64): **1639.3**;
Printed by Richard Badger I (fl.1629–41) for Philemon Stephens I (fl.1622–65†) in partnership with Christopher Meredith (fl.1625–53†) *impensis*: **1639.4**;
Printed by Richard Cotes (fl.1627–53†) for Richard Royston (fl.1627–86†): **1650.2** (words);
Printed by James Flesher (fl. 1649–70†, son of Miles Flesher I) for Cornelius Bee (fl.1634–72†) *sumptibus*: **1652.1**.

AS5 (London): The Wheelockian Great Primer Anglo-Saxon (1641–52)
This design was made for Wheelock's edition of Bede (**1643.1**). It was cut in London by early 1640, as indicated by a letter from Wheelock to Sir Symonds D'Ewes dated 30 Mar 1640:

> Typographus noster \Rogerus Daniel/ ... iam nauiter adlaborat monumentis Saxonicis imprimendis. Characteres iam Londini, et politi, ut spero, aut ornantur, aut in ornatu sunt.

> Our printer, Roger Daniel, is now actively working on printing the Saxon records. The characters are being fitted out now in London, as I hope, and are being got ready or are in preparation.
>
> BL Harley 374, 143ʳ, printed in Nichols 1780–90: VI.ii.78

The only known punchcutter in London at that time is Arthur Nicholls, who was active 1632–40; he was in prison in 1640. On 18 June 1641 Johannes de Laet reported in a letter to Sir William Boswell (d.1650), English ambassador at The Hague, that Sir Henry Spelman *ostendit mihi nuper typos anglosaxonos novos ad impressionem Historiae Bedae*, 'showed me the new Anglo-Saxon types for the printing of Bede's *Historia*' (BL Add 6395, p. 121). One of these Great Primer Anglo-Saxons (AS4 or AS5, or possibly both?) came to James from the Grover foundry (Mores, *Dissertation*, ed. Carter and Ricks, 44–45), Thomas Grover having worked for Nicholas Nicholls (son of Arthur), to whose business he probably succeeded (Treadwell 1980/81: 38). Lane 1991: 305 assumes that the fount that came was AS5. See Part 1, Chapter 4.

Thirty special sorts are shown: 12 lower case, ð, e, ꝼ, ȝ, ı, ꞃ, ꞅ, ꞇ, ẏ; þ, ð, ꝑ; 14 capitals, Æ², Ꞇ, D, Ꝫ, F, Ᵹ, Ƕ, I, ꟽ, S, T, U, Ð, Ꝑ; + 4 others, þ, ꝯ, ꝫ, · (raised point). All are shown in the reader's specimen on Illustration 19B, including the raised point (called a 'comma'), except square C.

James no. 51 (see Mores *Dissertation*: [14] and 111).

With a Great Primer Roman: Body 118 × 2.2: 3.5 (varies for different capitals): **1641.3, 1643.1, 1644.1, 1644.2, 1652.2** (re-issued as **1663.2**), **1678.1** (E only).

CAS3 (Amsterdam): The Dutch Blaeu/Voskens Pica Anglo-Saxon (1645–ante1714+)
No doubt made for the atlases of the British Isles in the series of great atlases put out by Joan Blaeu (1645–62). Probably cut by one of the Voskens half-brothers, Bartholomaeus Voskens the Elder (1613/16–1669) or Reinier/Reinhard Voskens (1621–c.1670), as they were the two punchcutting members of the family who were active in the early 1640s; since Dirk Voskens took over the Blaeu business in 1678 it is not, however, absolutely impossible that he inherited this work from another punchcutter (Enschedé 1978: 115). This Anglo-Saxon fount occurs in the Heirs of Joan Blaeu specimen of **1695.5** (where it is unhelpfully described as 'Auguſtyn Engels-Saxiſche', i.e. English-size), also on the Widow (of Dirk) Voskens specimen **1700?.2(ante1714)**, where it is correctly described as Mediaan Engels Sax, i.e. Pica. For the mislabeling by size in the earlier specimen cf. AS7.

It shows 21 special sorts, 12 lower-case, ð, e, ꝼ, ȝ, h, ı (in the Widow Voskens specimen only) ꞃ, ꞅ, ꞇ, þ, ð, ꝑ; 7 capitals, Æ (two designs), Ꝫ, ꟽ, S (assuming

LIST OF TYPE DESIGNS 201

this letter, which occurs at the end after the lower-case letters, is a capital, for in the Widow Voskens specimen it is used as lower-case d), Ð, X; and 2 others, the abbreviation þ, and the Tironian sign ⁊. The predominant model for them is undoubtedly AS3, the Lambardian Pica Anglo-Saxon found in the 1607.2 edition of Camden's *Britannia*. See Part 1, Chapter 5.

Combined with a Great Primer Roman: Body 80 × 1.6: 2.5:

1645.1, 1645.2, 1646.5, 1647.5, 1648.1, 1648.2, 1659.3, 1662.2, 1662.3, 1662.4, 1679.2 (printed in Amsterdam by Hendrick and Dirk I Boom (fl.1669–80), and the widow of Joannes van Someren (fl.1678–1703)), **1695.5** (specimen), **1700?.2** (specimen **ante1714**).

CAS4 (Amsterdam): The Dutch Janssonian English-size and Great Primer Anglo-Saxon (1646–75)
Evidently made for the atlases of the British Isles in the series of great atlases put out by Joannis Janssonius in rivalry with those of Blaeu. These designs were evidently the result of insufficient forethought and preparation, and are of much lower quality than the Blaeu Pica Anglo-Saxon (CAS3); ambition seems to have outstripped achievement. They are not found in any type-specimen, not even Janssonius's own (posthumous) type-specimen of 1666 (OBL Marshall 148[18]). It is not known who cut them. Evidently Janssonius had some metal special Anglo-Saxon sorts, but he probably supplemented them with wooden sorts that do not exactly match each other and detract from the professional appearance of his text.

The Anglo-Saxon specimen in each atlas shows 20 sorts, 11 lower-case, ð, ℯ, ꝼ, ȝ, ꞃ, ꞅ, ꞇ, ẏ, þ, ð, p; 8 capitals, Æ¹, Æ², Є, Ꜥ, Ⰽ, 8, Ð, X; and 1 other, ⁊: see Illustration 43. This specimen shows some capital sorts that are not found in the text at all, but fails to show all the sorts found in the text. Most sorts are used by Janssonius in combination with an English-size Roman, but it would appear that Janssonius wanted Anglo-Saxon letters in two sizes, English-size and Great Primer, so that they could be used not only in the main text but also in header statements. Unfortunately the two sizes got mixed up in practice: see Illustrations 45–46. There are 7 lower-case sorts in the larger Great Primer size: ð, ꝼ, ȝ, ꞃ, ꞅ, þ, p.

Found with an English-size Roman and occasionally a Great Primer Roman: 1646.3, 1646.4, 1647.3, 1647.4, 1659.2, 1659.4, 1675.2.

AS6 (Amsterdam): The Junian Pica Anglo-Saxon cut by Christoffel van Dijck for Franciscus Junius (in Amsterdam) but subsequently taken to Oxford (1655–)
Note: the capital $\bar{V}$ used by OUP was cut by Peter van Walpergen (fl.1676–1703).

Christoffel van Dijck (c.1603–69) was the foremost punchcutter of the century, whose type-designs were to be in great demand for the nascent Oxford University Press. The attribution to van Dijck depends for certainty on the shape of the punches being identified as characteristic of his work (see Illustration 32B); this identification was confirmed by Lane 1993: 57 (*Kleine Text Curcyf no.2*). The Junian Pica Anglo-Saxon is combined by Junius and his associates with van Dijck's Pica Roman (Body 83), so providing an exceedingly good fit that contributes to the attractiveness of the overall appearance of Anglo-Saxon text. The design was no doubt modelled on the Parkerian Pica (AS2).

Altogether 25 special sorts are shown in print: 11 lower-case, ð, ꞃ, ȝ, ı, ꝥ, ſ, τ, ẏ; þ, ð, p; 9 capitals, Ꞓ, Є, Ᵹ, Ꞩ, ꟽ, S, Þ, Ð, Ꝥ; and 5 others, þ, ꞏ, ꞏ, ꞏ, ∶. See Illustration 33A.

Note: The punctus versus, ꞏ, is found only in 1703/5.1.

OUP Archives hold 9 + 8 + 4 = 21 punches:

ð, ꞃ, ȝ, ꝥ, ſ, τ; þ, ð, p; Ꞓ, Є, Ᵹ, Ꞩ, ꟽ, S, Þ, Ð; þ, ꞏ, ꞏ, ÷ .

OUP Archives, Case D, Box 33, hold 9 + 8 + 3 = 20 matrices: ð, ꞃ, ȝ, ꝥ, ſ, τ; þ, ð, p; Ꞓ, Є, Ᵹ, Ꞩ, ꟽ, S, Þ, Ð; þ, ꞏ, ꞏ; plus another set of 10 + 8 + 0 = 18 matrices: ð, ꞃ, ȝ, ı, ꝥ, ſ, τ; þ, ð, p (on a smaller body and so attached to another to make it the same length as the others); Ꞓ, Є, Ᵹ, Ꞩ, ꟽ, S, Þ, Ỹ (Walpergen's, of greater length and thickness).

When the punches were rediscovered in Bodley's Librarian's study in 1697 (OBL Ballard 4, fo 102; Morison/Carter 1967: 244, Carter 1975: 125–126) no doubt new matrices were made (hence the second set of matrices), and also new types that were used for the flurry of scholarly Anglo-Saxon publications emanating from the Sheldonian Theatre at the end of the seventeenth-century onwards.

With the Junian Pica Roman (by van Dijck): Body 83 × 1.8: 2.9:

1655.1, 1655.2, 1664.2 (re-issued as 1666.2), 1665.2 (re-issued as 1684.3), 1679.1, 1689.3, 1690.2, 1691.4, 1692.1, 1693.2 (type-specimen), 1695.1 (type-specimen), 1698.1, 1698.2, 1699.1, 1699.2, 1700?.1, 1701.2, 1703/5.1.

With Arthur Nicholls's Pica Roman: Body 81.5 × 1.7: 2.7 (Lane 1991: 315): 1700.2.

AS7 (London): The Somnerian Pica Anglo-Saxon called 'English'-size (1658–)
This design was cut by Nicholas Nicholls in anticipation of Somner's *Dictionarium* 1659.1. Presumably Nicholls retained the punches, as supplies of type (Nicholls was a typefounder) were provided for numerous printers including the nascent Oxford University Press. At least fifteen printers used them, and it is notable that they appeared in 1658.2, printed by Thomas Roycroft, before the publication of Somner's *Dictionarium*. Whereas the Junian Pica

LIST OF TYPE DESIGNS

Anglo-Saxon (AS6) is almost always combined with Junius's Pica Roman the variety of printers using AS7 means that it is used with a variety of Roman designs, whichever was to hand for the printer concerned, although from the books produced by or for the nascent OUP and others it is clear that the preferred Roman was Arthur Nicholls's.

The range of special sorts shown by this fount follows the usage of earlier ones, particularly Junius's, as Nicholls says that is what the design of the fount was based on. Some 31 special sorts are shown altogether (Body 80 × 1.7: 2.7), 12 lower-case, ð, *e*, ꝼ, ᵹ, ı, ꝥ, ꞃ, ꞇ, ẏ; þ, ð, p; 14 capitals, A, Æ¹, Æ², Ꞇ, Ꞓ, Ᵹ, Ƕ, K, Ꟁ, Ꞅ, Ꝥ, Ð, Ƿ (Walpergen's), W; and 4 others, þ, ꞃ, ꞃ,ꞃ (1659.1, 1682.1, 1685.1), : (1678.1, also uses a raised dot), Ꞓ, Ꞓ([Gk E with a stroke like a left-hand round bracket closing off the openings on its right] (1685.1, 1687?.1). See Illustration 35.

Note 1: A, K and W are additions to previous founts;

Note 2: Some books show an improvised punctus versus, as 1676.2 (semi-colon) and 1687.1 (the number 7 with a suprascript dot).

James no. 53 (Mores, *Dissertation*, ed. Carter/Ricks, 111), described by Carter as 'a creditable piece of work with a bigger range of sorts than the [Anglo-]Saxon of Junius'. The James specimen shows another sort for y without the suprascript dot, the larger ꞃ but not the smaller one, and includes the Ꞓ closed off to the right with a stroke like a left-hand round bracket.

Specimens:

1656.2: Specimen texts in OBL, University Archives, SEP.P17b(4a), separate item, contains 3 specimen pages, 2 of parts of the AS law 'Geþyncðo' from Lambarde 1576.2, pp. 364–366 (or later edn), 1 from Alfred's Boethius 1698.2, ch. 30, §2. K appears as both lower-case and capital.

1665?1: Printer's specimen in BL, Bagford Collection, Harley 5977 no. 200.

1687?.1, 1693.2 and 1695.1: OUP Printer's specimens.

Matrices:

It is possible that Oxford University possessed matrices supplied by Nicholls (see above, Part 1, Chapter 4).

Supposed Matrices:

According to Hart (1970: 34, where AS7 *e* is not shown) 10 matrices survived in OUP Archive including two of Ƿ, but when I visited the Archive on 14 Mar 2000 they could not be found; Case D, Box 33 (containing Junius's matrices for Saxon, Gothic and Runic) has a note to say that it also contains the Nicholls Pica Anglo-Saxon, but it does not. Hart was mistaken. Morison/Carter 1967: 243, n.2, state that the 10 matrices were made for adapting Junius's Pica Anglo-Saxon to Small Pica body-size, probably by Vincent Figgins c.1790–1800.

Purchase:

As recorded in OU Archives WPb/21/4, fo 152ʳ/6: 'For a font of Saxon Letters. to Mʳ Nichols Letter founder [£]023 . 07[s] . 02[d]'. Cf. also Madan 1895–1931: III.106–7, no. 2458 (re.**1659.1**), where he notes that the types would have been kept in the Domus Typographica, on which see Madan 1895–1931: III.409.

There is a letter from Gerald Langbaine (who evidently paid for the fount) to William Dugdale dated 6 Dec 1653 in OBL Ashmole 854, fo 297ʳ:

> I desire you present my service to Mr Somner, since I received yours I spoke with Mr Vice-chan: about a Saxon letter, he is not unwilling and I doubt not of effecting that part. But whether wee shall obteyne any thing considerable for Mr Somner (I can promise for none but my self) I cannot tell. I will be most willing to further and promote any motion in his behalf wch carryes probability of successe. And I hope I may be able to procure him 40li for the copy of his lexicon if it be ready. [in an addenda dated 16 Dec and written sideways on the lh margin] 'I have spoken to the bearer Mr Robinson to enquire & inform me about a Saxon l⟨ett⟩re for wch I shall pay—'; printed in *Chronica Prioratus de Dunstable*, ed. T. Hearne.
>
> Oxford: Sheldonian Theatre, 1733, II.726

Contract between OU and Hall the printer:

OBL, OU Archives, SEP.P17b(3), fo 44, 'A bond for restoring ... 177 pound weight of Saxon Letters from Will' Hall', dated 22 Aug 1657, shows that the university may have lent matrices to Hall to make types for the printing 'of a new Saxon Lexicon composed by William Somner' (i.e. **1659.1**) and that Hall paid £45 on deposit for the privilege.

With an English-size Roman:
1685.2;
With Arthur Nicholls's Pica Roman:
1659.1, **1662.1** (set within text in Long Primer Roman), **1671.1** (words), **1676.2**, **1678.1**, **1682.1** (re-issued as **1683.1**), **1685.1**, **1687.3** (phrase), **1689.1** (some letters re-cut), **1703.1**;
With a Pica Roman
1658.2 (words within main text in English-size Roman), **1660.1**, **1671.3**, **1672.1**, **1673.1** (re-issued as **1683.2**), **1675.1**, **1680.1**, **1682.2** (re-issued as **1689.2**), **1682.3** (re-issued as **1683.3**), **1684.1** (words), **1684.2**, **1684.4**, **1684.5** (set within text in Long Primer Roman), **1686.1** (Latin), **1687.1**, **1687.2**, **1689.3** (tp), **1690.1**, **1691.1**, **1691.2**, **1691.3**, **1692.1** (tp), **1692.2**, **1693.1**, **1695.2**, **1695.3** (some sorts apparently modified by filing at the top), **1698.3**, **1700.1**, **1702.1** (some modified sorts), **1705.1**;

With a Long Primer Roman:
1671.2 (re-issued as 1680.2).

CAS5 (Strassburg): The Strassburg English-size Anglo-Saxon (Strassburg and Nuremberg 1665)
When continental printers came to reprint John Selden's works (mostly printed by William Stansby), they were almost inevitably faced with Anglo-Saxon passages printed in the Parkerian design (AS1). Consequently this is the model that they followed, as is the case with the Strassburg edition (1665.3) of Selden's *De iure naturale* (1640.4). The special sorts are of moderately good quality, 18 being shown: 11 lower-case, ð, ꝼ, ȝ, ı, ꞃ, ſ, ꞇ, ẏ; þ, ð, p; 5 capitals, Æ², Ɛ, Ð, Ꝥ, Đ; and 2 others, þ, ꞇ. See Part 1, Chapter 5, and Illustration 47.

Although the printer of 1665.3 is not stated, it was almost certainly Georg Andreas Dolhopff (1627–1711; fl. Strassburg 1662–1711). He married a daughter of the Strassburg publisher Johann Andreas Zetzner, whom he served as a printer from 1662, and the two jointly published this book together with the Endters of Nuremberg and the Societas Strassburg. From 1668 to 1671 Balthasar Joachim Endter worked for Dolhopff and Zetzner, and the contact between the two businesses (Dolhopff/Zetzner in Strassburg, and Endter in Nuremberg) probably gave rise to the Endter's interest in the book. Evidence of punchcutters or typefounders at this time in this location or nearby has proved elusive. From 1740 there is the study of the art of printing and typefounding by Christian Friedrich Gessner, which includes an *Alphabetum Saxonicum vetus* or *vetustissimum* 'Old/Ancient Saxon Alphabet', probably continental Old Saxon, printed from an engraved plate, and the forms are continental rather than insular, notably ꝼ, ȝ, ꞃ, ẏ, z. Supplementary to this book is the *Orationis Dominicae Versiones*, which includes versions of the Lord's Prayer in *Saxonica Antiqua* 'continental Old Saxon' printed in a Fractur and another version *Anglo-Saxonica* 'Old English' printed in an Italic, to which the editor has added the comment *Characterem litterarum invenire haud potuimus* 'We could not at all find [appropriate] letter sorts' to print it properly. In Konstanz the punchcutter Balthasar Köblin cut non-Latin types c.1654–c.1680, so he was active at the right time, but whether a printer in Strassburg would have gone to a punchcutter in Konstanz for special sorts is moot.

CAS6 (Paris): The Du Cangian Pica Anglo-Saxon (Paris 1678, Frankfurt-am-Main 1681)
Du Cange's famous Latin dictionary was printed *typis* of Gabriel Martin, (fl. Paris, 1670–92†), and published *impensis* of Louis Billaine (fl. Paris, 1652–81†):

1678.2. It shows Anglo-Saxon in nine lower-case sorts, ð, ꝼ, ȝ, þ, ſ, τ, ẏ; ð, p, capitals not being needed for a dictionary where the headwords were all Latin. These Anglo-Saxon sorts have not been found in any type-specimen. Martin owned an important printing-shop, which may have included provision for typefounding, but it is unlikely that he was a punchcutter. See Part 1, Chapter 5, and Illustration 48.

Overall the design may have been modelled on the Lambardian Pica Anglo-Saxon type-design (AS3) but it shows some idiosyncracies. The cutting is of a moderate standard, the ð being notably poor. There were not many punchcutters or typefounders in Paris at that time, as there was little demand. Writing in 1742 Pierre Simon Fournier, le jeune (1712–68), reported that after the death of Jacques de Sanlecque II (1612–59) there followed a period of about 60 years in which it was difficult to find anyone even to cut the new letters J (consonant) and U (vowel) when this usage was introduced into French printing. At the time that the Anglo-Saxon sorts were made for **1678.2** there are very few known men who might have made them. One possibility is Mathieu Malherbe Des Portes (c.1659–c.1726), a cutter of punches and dies for coins and medals who turned his hand to occasional punchcutting for typefounders; he is best known for the 'Cicero la Police' cut for the typefounder Pierre Cot c.1700. If he did make these Anglo-Saxon sorts he would have been a very young man, with limited experience. Alternatively, and probably more likely, they might have been cut by Guillaume Le Bé III (1610?–85), who, while principally a typefounder, also sometimes turned his hand to punchcutting.

The same sorts in the same design re-appear in the second edition, a slavish reprint produced at Frankfurt-am-Main, where it was printed *typis* of Balthasar Christoph Wust I (fl. 1658–1700) and the bookseller was Johann David Zunner II (fl. 1666–1700): **1681.1**. Presumably types or possibly matrices were sent from Paris to Frankfurt, where the publisher probably paid for them. Evidence of trade in type between Paris and the provinces is provided by Renouard (1900: 14–16, 79–86) and includes one transaction *outremer* to Lisbon, so there is nothing out of the ordinary about the presumed sale of a relatively small amount of printing material to Frankfurt, which through its famous fair was a centre of exchange in the booktrade.

CAS7 (Wittenberg): The Wittenberg 'Pica' Anglo-Saxon (Wittenberg and Frankfurt-an-der-Oder 1695-6)
All three books that show these somewhat makeshift Anglo-Saxon sorts are by Selden, his *De iure naturali* (**1695.4**), *Tituli Honorum* (**1696.1**) and *De Synedriis* (**1696.2**). They were printed by Johann Michael Goderitsch (fl. Wittenberg 1687–1706?) for the bookseller Jeremias Schrey at Frankfurt-an-der-Oder. A

previous attempt by Schrey to publish a work by Selden that contained Anglo-Saxon, his *Uxor Ebraica* (1673.3), simply omitted the two Anglo-Saxon passages present in the 1640.4 edition. Again the primary model Anglo-Saxon type-design used for the Wittenberg printings was the Parkerian Great Primer (AS1), used in the editions of Selden's works published in his lifetime, although 1695.4 is based on the Strassburg edition of *De iure naturali* (1665.3), which used the Strassburg imitation of AS1 (CAS5), and 1696.2 is based on the Amsterdam edition of *De Synedriis* (1679.2) which used the Blaeu/Voskens design (CAS3), which in turn were based on the Lambardian Pica Anglo-Saxon (AS3).

The special sorts shown total 15 (+2) sorts, including 8 (+1) lower-case, ð, ꝼ, ȝ, ꝥ, ſ, ꞇ; þ, ð, p (= Fraktur p); 5 (+1) capitals, Ɛ (from another fount), H (Ð + Fraktur H), ꟿ, Ȿ, Ð; and 2 others, þ, ꝺ. See Part 1, chapter 5, and Illustration 50. A notable feature of the design is that some sorts show variations that are inconsistent with metal sorts made from a matrix. It is difficult to avoid the conclusion that these sorts were made of wood. Some sorts were evidently borrowed from other founts. This fount was clearly a makeshift amalgam of various solutions, many of them showing thoughtlessness and laziness, and I have not found it anywhere else.

AS8 (Oxford): The Oxford University Press Small Pica Anglo-Saxon cut by Peter van Walpergen (1701–).

This Small Pica Anglo-Saxon (Face 66 × 1.5: 2.4) was cut by Peter van Walpergen (fl. Oxford 1676–1703†) who was punchcutter for the university press (Ould 2018: II.66–83). Whether it was made for the book it first appeared in, 1701.1, Benson's *Vocabularium Anglo-Saxonicum*, is doubtful, as the prospectuses for this book, 1690.2 (printed but not published) and 1699.2, used the Junian Anglo-Saxon Pica (AS6). In 1701.1 AS8 is combined with Christoffel van Dijk's Small Pica Roman (Body 69), with Latin glosses in van Dijck's Small Pica Italic. The special sorts shown are all lower-case, 11 of them: ð, ꝼ, ȝ, ı, ꝥ, ſ, ꞇ, ẏ; þ, ð, p. In 1703/5.1 it is found in Booklet 5, †2D1ᵛ–†4I1ʳ (Wanley's catalogue of AS manuscripts after the ones at Oxford, which are in the larger Pica), where it is combined with the same Small Pica Roman interspersed with the same Small Pica Italic, both by van Dijck; the same lower-case special sorts are used with the addition of ꝺ, which may have been available earlier but was not needed in a wordlist; see Illustration 36. In 1701.1 no Anglo-Saxon capitals are used even at the price of using Th- and W- for some words, and that is also the case in Booklet 5 of 1703/5.1 up to sig. †2V, where Th- is used instead of Ð, and W- instead of Ᵹ. After the libraries in Oxford and Cambridge have been dealt with, the section on other libraries (starting with those in the Royal collection) begins on †2X1ᵛ, where Ᵹ makes its first appearance, and Ð first appears on

†2X2ʳ. The abbreviation þ also makes its first appearance on †2X2ᵛ. Small capital ᴅ first appears on †2Z1ᵛ in the name ÆÐELSTAN, and small capital ᚹ first appears on †3A1ᵛ in the name ÆÐELᚹERD; neither is heavily used. The first three of these extra sorts also appear in Booklet 6, Index VI, G1ʳ–M1ᵛ (Wanley's index to authors and works cited in Booklet 5), Ð notably in lemma on L2 and ᚹ notably in lemma on M1. It seems probable that the five extra sorts became available during the printing of Booklet 5, i.e. Walpergen was making new punches as the printing of the book progressed. Since Walpergen died in 1703, it is possible that he was still working on this fount up to his death.

There is an explanation for this set of circumstances. In his diary for 6 Oct 1705 Thomas Hearne (1678–1735) noted that 'Mʳ. Wanley writ the Preface to the Catalogue of Septentrional MSS. in English, wᶜʰ was afterwards translated into Latin by Mʳ. Thwaites, or else his Pupils, who supervis'd and corrected the whole Catalogue, & order'd it as he pleas'd'. While this remark applies to Booklet 5, and sigs †a1ʳ–†d1ᵛ in particular, Thwaites's letters indicate that his roll was indeed supervisory (Harris 1992: 68–69), as Hearne stated. Thwaites's letter to Wanley of 3 July 1702 asks Wanley to send more copy (presumably of Booklet 5) and wants to know if Wanley has sent the specimen drawings of letters to Peter van Walpergen so that he can get on with cutting them. It seems probable that the letter-drawings referred to are for these extra sorts for AS8, which altogether shows seventeen sorts. Probably Thwaites, with Wanley's collaboration, was the chief instigator of this fount, or at least of developing it further. The design is based on Junius's except for the square capital P, which is copied from that in the Somnerian fount (AS7). According to Morison & Carter (1967: 250), Oxford University Press retains fifteen matrices

Ð, ᴅ, ð, ꝼ, ᵹ, ꝑ, ꞃ, ꞇ, p, ẏ, þ, ð, þ, ∴, ᚹ,

and the four corresponding punches, Ð, ᴅ, ᚹ, þ are distinctively those of Walpergen. It is notable that the punches are for letters apparently added later: Ð, ᚹ, ᴅ and þ.

Specimen: Oxford University 1706 (Hart 1970: 72), showing this 'Small Pica Saxon' with 11 lower-case sorts, two small capitals, ᴅ and ᚹ, two others, ꞈ and þ, plus two full capitals, Ð and Þ, the latter 'Thorn' being an 'intruder' here because it was cut by Walpergen to accompany Junius's 'Pica Islandic' and appears with that fount in the 1693 specimen (Hart 1970: 39). The curious 'n'-sort with a comma-like addition to the right stem must also be an 'intruder'. Capital ᚹ is lacking in this specimen, probably because the Þ 'Thorn' was confused with ᚹ 'Wynn'.

Roman, Italic and Other Type-Designs Referred to in the Catalogue

In descending order of size

Roman

François Guyot's Double Pica Roman
   Body 142   Face 140 × 2.7: 5
TSF I: pl.1; Vervliet 1968: R17

Claude Garamont's Great Primer Roman
   Body 112   Face 110 × 2.0: 3.5
Isaac 1933: fig. 2; TSF I, 3 (Romain Gros Text de Garamond); Plantin 1567: sig. C1 (no. 2) = TSF II, 1567.22; Veyrin-Forrer & Jammes 1958: pl. 11, no. 1

Ameet Tavernier's Great Primer Roman
   Body 118   Face 116 × 2.3: 3.5
Vervliet 1968: R20; Isaac 1933: fig. 3

Pierre Haultin's Great Primer Roman
   Body 118   Face 110 × 2.3: 3.5
LMA 63 in Parker et al. 'Early Inventories' (1960), p. 8; Vervliet 1967: no. 36

Nicholas Nicholls's Great Primer Roman
   Body 116   Face 108 × 2.0: 3.8
Mores *Dissertation*: lxxv = **1665?.1**: Hart 1970: 138 and note on p. 190

Pierre Haultin's English-size Roman:
   Body 95.   Face 92 × 2.0: 3.3.
TSF I: pl. 14 (fragment 396); Isaac 1933: fig. 5; Vervliet 1967: no. 41; for discussion see also Johnson 1970: 255–259

Arthur Nicholls's English-size Roman
   Body 95   Face 94 × 2.0: 3.2
Lane 1991: fig. 10

François Guyot's Pica Roman
   Body 82   Face 78 × 1.5: 2.5
TSF I, 1; Vervliet 1968: R27

Claude Garamont's Pica Roman: Plantin's *Mediane Garamont Romain*:
   Body 83.   Face 80 × 1.7: 2.5
TSF I: pl. 2; TSF II, 1567: 26 [= Plantin 1567: sig. C3 (no.2)]

Pierre Haultin's Pica Roman,
   Body 83.   Face 80 × 1.7: 2.5
TSF I: pl. 14 (fragment 393); Tinto R8; Vervliet 2010: no. 72
For the attribution to Haultin (not Garamont) see Lane 1992: 360. Lane (1992: 364) notes that this design comes with two lower cases, 1. (?*ante*)1567, 2. (?)1570ff. Vervliet 1999/2000 separates them as R82A/R82B

Robert Granjon's 1st Pica Roman, called Lyon(b) by Ferguson 1989: 9–11.
   Body 83/86   Face 82 × 1.6: 2.9
Vervliet 1998–9: no. 2, pp. 11–13; Vervliet 2010: no. 75

Arthur Nicholls's Pica Roman
   Body 81.5.   Face 80 × 1.7: 2.7
Lane 1991: 315

The Junian Pica Roman—attributable to Christoffel van Dijck and left by Franciscus Junius to Oxford University
   Body 83   Face 80 × 1.8: 3.0
The presence of this design on the Widow Elsevier specimen of 1681 creates the presumption that it could be the work of van Dijck. The fact that Junius used it in conjunction with van Dijck's AS sorts strengthens the case for it being van Dijck's.
TSF I: pl. 12 Mediaen Romeyn no.1; **1693.2** d2^r simulated in Hart 1970: 40. Lucas 1998: 192–193

Pierre Haultin's Small Pica Roman
   Body 70/72   Face 66 × 1.5: 2.5
TSF II 1567 29 (Dr/1); Vervliet 1967: no. 54; Tinto R.9; Vervliet 2010: no. 54

Christoffel van Dijck's Small Pica Roman
   Body 69   Face 66 × 1.5: 2.4
McKitterick 1977: 70, no. 225 Descendiaen Romeyn; Hart 1970: 26 and note on p. 180

Claude Garamont's (first) Long Primer Roman
　　Body 67　　Face 64 × 1.5: 2
TSF II, 1567, no. 31; Parker et al.1960: MA48; Vervliet 2010: no. 39

Claude Garamont's (second) Long Primer Roman
　　Body 68　　Face 66 × 1.2: 2
TSF I, pls 2, 3; TSF II, c.1599, no. 9; Parker et al 1960: 62, MA 47a; Isaac 1933, fig. 14; Vervliet 2010: no. 43

Pierre Haultin's Long Primer Roman
　　Body 67　　Face 66 × 1.3: 2.1
LMA2 in Parker et al. 'Early inventories' (1960), p. 13; Tinto R.9; Vervliet 2010: no. 44

　　Italic
François Guyot's Double Pica Italic
　　Body 144　　Face 140 × 2.8: 4.6
TSF I: pl. 1; Vervliet 1968: IT2.

Claude Garamont's 4th Great Primer Italic
　　Body 118　　Face 116 × 2.1: 3.3
Veyrin-Forrer & Jammes 1958: pl. 11, no. 2; TSF II, c.1599: 22; Vervliet 1999: 35–40; Vervliet 2010: no. 294.

François Guyot's Great Primer Italic
　　Body 112　　Face 110 × 2.4: 3.5
TSF I.1, 6, 9; Vervliet 1968: IT3

Robert Granjon's 3rd Great Primer Italic
　　Body 117.5　　Face 115 × 2: 3.1
TSF I: pls 2, 3, 4; TSF II, 1567: 23 (with ampersand from Granjon's 2nd Great Primer Italic = Johnson 1941: type 6); Vervliet 2010: no. 293

Robert Granjon's 3rd English-size Italic
　　Body 95.　　Face 93 × 2: 2.5.
Veyrin-Forrer & Jammes 1958: pl.11, no.4; Dreyfus 1963: pl. 2; TSF II, c.1585: 27; Johnson 1941: type 13 on fig. 12; Vervliet 1967: no.44; Vervliet 1999: fig. 19; Vervliet 2010: no. 282

Arthur Nicholls's English-size Italic
   Body 95   Face 94 × 2.0: 2.7
Lane 1991: fig. 10

Robert Granjon's 2nd Pica Italic, the *Cicero pendante*
   Body 83.5   Face 82 × 1.7: 2.6
Plantin 1567: sig. C4 (no. 1) = TSF II, 1567: 27; TSF I.2 (with different ampersand); Johnson 1941: type 7; Gaskell 1972: fig. 12(a) on p. 25; Vervliet 2010: no. 272

Robert Granjon's third Pica Italic, the *Cicero currens*
   Body 83   Face 82 × 1.8: 2.1.
TSF II, 1567: 28; Johnson 1941: type 12; Vervliet 2010: no. 274

Ameet Tavernier's Pica Italic
   Body 82.   Face 80 × 1.7: 2.7.
Isaac 1933: 214, and fig.18; Vervliet 1968: IT8. According to Isaac 1936: 42 and pl. 73a (= 1933: fig. 18) 'Day's first Elizabethan italic'

François Guyot's Pica Italic
   Body 84.   Face 77 × 1.5: 2.4
TSF I: pl. 1; Vervliet 1968: IT10

The Junian Pica Italic—attributable to Christoffel van Dijck and left by Franciscus Junius to Oxford University
   Body 83   Face 80 × 1.5: 2.8
The presence of this design on the Widow Elsevier specimen of 1681 creates the presumption that it could be the work of van Dijck. The fact that Junius used it in conjunction with van Dijck's AS sorts strengthens the case for it being van Dijck's. Attributed to van Dijck on stylistic grounds by Lane 1993: 58 (*Mediaan Curcyf no.2*)
TSF I: pl. 12 Mediaen Cursijf no. 2; **1693.2** d2^r simulated in Hart 1970: 40, and note on p. 183; Lucas 1998: 192–193; McKitterick 1977: no. 197

Christoffel van Dijck's Small Pica Italic
   Body 69   Face 66 × 1.4: 2.1
Hart 1970: 26 and note on pp. 180–181

Robert Granjon's 1st Long Primer Italic, known as 'Garamonde Cursive premiere'
   Body 68.   Face 66 × 1.3: 2.
TSF II, 1567, no. 32; Isaac 1933: fig. 24; Johnson 1941: type 2; Vervliet 2010: no. 238

Robert Granjon's 5th Long Primer Italic, known as 'l'immortelle'
    Body 66   Face 65 × 1.5: 1.8
TSF I: pl. 2; Johnson 1941: type 11; Vervliet 2010: no. 250

Robert Granjon's 6th Long Primer Italic, known as 'Italique Valentine'
    Body 68.   Face 65 × 1.5: 1.8
TSF II, c.1585, no. 54, Veyrin-Forrer & Jammes 1958: pl. 12, no. 4; Vervliet 2010: no. 251

Textura (Sometimes Called 'Black Letter' or 'English')

Peter van Walpergen's Pica Textura
    Body 82.5.   Face 80 × 2.2: 3.1
1693.2 c2ʳ 'New Engliſh Engliſh' and d2ʳ 'Pica Engliſh', simulated in Hart 1970: 28; see also Morison/Carter 1967: 114–115

Marshe's Small Pica Textura
    Body 76.   Face 74 × 2.2: 3.1
Isaac 1936: pl. 54; it appears as 'Pica Engliſh' on the type-specimen attributed to Nicholas Nicholls (1665?.1), reproduced in Mores, *Dissertaion*, lxxv, and as 'Pique Engliſh' in the Oxford University Specimen 1693.2, sig. c2ʳ, simulated in Hart 1970: 28 (with note on p. 182), but the attribution to Nicholls is rightly doubted by Mosley (1984: no. 168) as the design appears before Nicholls was born.

Long Primer and Brevier Texturas are also found.

Abbreviations

abp	archbishop
Adams	*Catalogue of Books printed on the Continent of Europe, 1501–1600, in Cambridge Libraries,* by H.M. Adams, 2 vols (Cambridge: Cambridge University Press, 1967).
Ang	Anglesey
approx	approximately
AS	Anglo-Saxon
ASMMF	Anglo-Saxon Manuscripts in Microfiche Facsimile, ed. †P. Pulsiano, A.N. Doane & M. Hussey, 25+ vols (Binghamton, & Tempe, AZ: MRTS, 1994–).
BBA	Bibliotheca Bibliographica Aureliana = *Répertoire bibliographique des livres imprimés en France au XVIIe siècle* (Baden-Baden: Koerner, 1978–), cited by number in series and item number
Bd	Bedfordshire
Bk	Buckinghamshire
BLG	*Catalogue of Books Printed in the German-Speaking Countries and of German Books printed in other Countries from 1601 to 1700 now in the British Library,* 5 vols (London: British Library, 1994).
BME	*British Map Engravers,* by Laurence Worms & Ashley Baynton-Williams (London: Rare Book Society, 2011), cited by page number
bp	bishop
Brc	Breconshire
Brk	Berkshire
BSL	Bible Society Library (currently in CUL)
C	Cambridgeshire
Ch	Cheshire
CLA	E.A. Lowe, *Codices Latini Antiquiores,* 11 vols (Oxford: Clarendon Press, 1934–71)
cm	centimetre(s)
Co	Cornwall
col	column
coll.	collated by/with
Crd	Cardiganshire
Crm	Carmarthenshire
Crn	Caernarvonshire

Cu	Cumberland
D	Devon
Db	Derbyshire
Dict. 1641–67	*A Dictionary of the Printers and Booksellers who were at work in England Scotland and Ireland from 1641 to 1667*, by Henry R. Plomer (London: Bibliographical Society, 1907)
Dict. 1668–1725	*A Dictionary of the Printers and Booksellers who were at work in England Scotland and Ireland from 1668 to 1725*, by Henry R. Plomer et al. (London: Bibliographical Society, 1922)
DLB	*The British Literary Book Trade, 1475–1700*, ed. James K. Bracken and Joel Silver = Dictionary of Literary Biography 170
DMH	*Historical Catalogue of Printed Editions of The English Bible 1525–1961*, ed. T.H. Darlow and H.F. Moule, rev. A.S. Herbert (London: British and Foreign Bible Society, 1968)
Dnb	Denbighshire
Do	Dorset
DOE	*Dictionary of Old English*, ed. Antonette diPaolo Healey *et al.*, in progress (Toronto: Toronto University Press, 1986–), available on-line
Du	Durham/Dunelmensis
e	earl
E	Essex
ed.	edited by
edn	edition
ELN	*English Language Notes*
ESTC	English Short Title Catalogue (electronic aid, hosted by British Library)
fo(s)	folio(s)
F	French
Flt	Flintshire
Gl	Gloucestershire
Glm	Glamorgan
Gneuss	Gneuss, Helmut, and Michael Lapidge, *Anglo-Saxon Manuscripts: A Bibliographical Handlist to 1100* (Toronto: Toronto University Press, 2014)
GR	*A Bibliography of Publications on Old English Literature to the end of 1972*, ed. Stanley B. Greenfield and Fred C. Robinson (Toronto: Toronto University Press, 1980)

Ha	Hampshire
He	Herefordshire
HE	Historia Ecclesiastica
HLQ	*Huntington Library Quarterly*
Hrt	Hertfordshire
Hu	Huntingdonshire
IMEV	*Index of Middle English Verse*, ed. Carleton Brown & Russell H. Robbins (New York: Columbia University Press, 1943) re-ed. Julia Boffey & Anthony S.G. Edwards (London: British Library, 2005)
introd.	introduced by, introduction
IoM	Isle of Man
IoW	Isle of Wight
Irl	Ireland
K	Kent
Ker	Ker, Neil R., *Catalogue of Manuscripts containing Anglo-Saxon* (Oxford: Clarendon Press, 1957/1991).
Kg	King
L	Latin
La	Lancashire
Lei	Leicestershire
Li	Lincolnshire
Me	Merionethshire
Mellot	Jean-dominique Mellot, *Répertoire d'imprimeurs/libraires (vers 1500 –vers 1810)* (Paris: BN, 2004)
MGH	Monumenta Germaniae Historica
mm	milimetre(s)
Mon	Monmouthshire
MR	Master of the Rolls
MRTS	Medieval & Renaissance Texts & Studies
MS	manuscript
Mtg	Montgomeryshire
Mx	Middlesex
Nb	Northumberland
n.f.	not found (in)
Nf	Norfolk

Nt	Nottinghamshire
Nth	Northamptonshire
NW	North Wales
O	Oxfordshire
ODNB	*Oxford Dictionary of National Biography*
om.	omitting
OU	Oxford University
PBSA	*Papers of the Bibliographical Society of America*
PCP	Alfredian Preface to Pope Gregory's *Cura Pastoralis*
Pelteret	Pelteret, David A.E., *Catalogue of English Post-Conquest Vernacular Documents* (Woodbridge: Boydell, 1990). Cited by item number
Pmb	Pembrokeshire
PO	Private Owner
Qn	Queen
R	Rutland
Rch	Richmondshire
Rdn	Radnorshire
S	Scotland
Sa	Shropshire
Sawyer	Sawyer, Peter H., *Anglo-Saxon Charters: An Annotated List and Bibliography* (London: Royal Historical Society, 1968). Cited by item number
SC	Summary Catalogue
Sf	Suffolk
So	Somerset
Sr	Surrey
St	Staffordshire
STC	*A Short-Title Catalogue of Books printed in England, Scotland, & Ireland and of English Books printed abroad 1475–1640*, by Alfred W. Pollard & Gilbert R. Redgrave. 2nd edn, 3 vols rev. W.A. Jackson & F.S. Ferguson, completed by Katharine F. Pantzer (London: Bibliographical Society, 1976–91)
SW	South Wales
Sx	Sussex

t	translated by, translation
TSF	*Type Specimen Facsimiles*, I ed. John Gustave Dreyfus, II annotated by Hendrik D.L. Vervliet and Harry Carter (London: Bowes & Bowes, 1963/1972)
UP	University Press
vc	vice-chancellor
VD17	*Das Verzeichnis der im deutschen Sprachraum erschienenen Drucke des 17. Jahrhunderts*, online at http://www.vd17.de/
W	Wiltshire
Wa	Warwickshire
We	Westmorland
Wing	*Short-Title Catalogue of Books printed in England, Scotland, Ireland, Wales, and British America and of English Books printed in other countries 1641–1700*, by Donald G. Wing. 1st edn, 3 vols (New York: Modern Language Association of America, 1945–51); 2nd edn, 4 vols, rev. T.J. Crist, J.J. Morrison, C.W. Nelson & M. Seccombe (New York: Modern Language Association of America, 1982–98)
Wo	Worcestershire
Y	Yorkshire
YE	Yorkshire East Riding
YN	Yorkshire North Riding
YW	Yorkshire West Riding

Library Abbreviations

AAS	American Antiquarian Society Library, Worcester MA
ABH	Aylsham (Nf), Blickling Hall (National Trust)
ABM	Aix-en-Provence, Bibliothèque Méjanes
ACA	American Congregational Association Library, Boston MA
ACRC	A Coruña, Real Consulado, Biblioteca
ACU	Australian Catholic University, Aquinas campus, Ballarat, Victoria
ADL	Auckland, Dalberton Library
AHC	Australian High Court Library, Canberra
AKNA	Amsterdam, Koninklijke Nederlandse Adademie van Wetenschappen
AML	Auckland Museum Library
AMM	Albi, Médiathèque Municipale Pierre Amalric
AntUB	Antwerp Universiteitsbibliotheek
ANU	Australian National University Library, Canberra
ANZ	Auckland Public Library, New Zealand
APL	Armagh Public Library (Bishop Robinson Collection)
APM	Antwerp, Plantin-Moretus Museum
APS	American Philosophical Society Library, Philadelphia PA
ARA	Alkmaar, Regionaal Archief
ARG	Antwerp, Ruusbroecgenootschap
ASB	Antwerp, Stadsbibliotheek Hendrik Conscience
ASP	Adelaide, Collegiate School of St Peter, Australia
ATL	Alexander Turnbull Library, National Library of New Zealand, Wellington
AUB	Amsterdam Universiteitsbibliotheek
AUL	Aberdeen University Library
AUNZ	Auckland University Library, New Zealand
AVUB	Amsterdam Universiteitsbibliotheek, Vrije Universiteit
AZU	Arizona State University, USA
BA	Boston Athenaeum, Boston MA
BAL	British Architectural Library, at the Royal Institute of British Architects, London
BAV	Biblioteca Apostolica Vaticana
BBC	Biella, Italy, Biblioteca Civica
BBIR	Bologna, Biblioteche scientifiche degli Istituti ortopedici Rizzoli
BBM	Besançon, Bibliothèque Municipale
BBP	Barcelona, Biblioteca Publica Episcopal del Seminario de Barcelona

BBR	Brussels, Bibliothèque Royale, aka Koninklijke Bibliotheek
BBU	Bologna, Biblioteca Universitaria
BCB	Bowdoin College Library, Brunswick ME
BCCH	Boston College, Chesnut Hill MA
BCL	Birmingham Central Libraries
BCLNI	Belfast Central Library, Northern Ireland
BCLW	Bangor Cathedral Library, Wales
BEC	Buffalo and Erie County Public Library, Buffalo NY
BGS	Bruges, Grootseminarie
BHCL	Birkenhead Central Library
BJH	Baltimore, John Hopkins University Library
BL	London, British Library
BLC	Bristol Central Library
BLH	Belfast, Linen Hall Library
BMC	Bryn Mawr College Library, PA
BMM	Bayeux, Médiathèque Municipale Centre Guillaume le Conquérant
BNA	Barbados National Archives
BNL	Budapest, National Széchényi Library
BPH	Berwick-on-Tweed, Paxton House
BPL	Boston Parish Library, Lincolnshire
BPM	Boston Public Main Library
BrCaL	Bristol Cathedral Library
BrCL	Bradford Central Library
BriCL	Brighton Central Library
BromCL	Bromley Central Library
BrPL	Bridgenorth Parochial Library
BrSB	Bruges, Stadsbibliotheek
BSA	Bückeburg Staatsarchiv, Schaumburg-Lippische Hofbibliothek
BSB	Berlin, Staatsbibliothek Preußischer Kulturbesitz
BSE	Bury St Edmunds Cathedral Library
BSEC	Bury St Edmunds Central Library
BSL	Bible Society Library (currently in CUL)
BSO	Birmingham, Selly Oak Colleges
BUB	Bremen, Staats- und Universitätsbibliothek
BUG	Bibliotheek van de Universiteit Gent
BUL	Bristol University Library
BUN	Biblioteca Universitaria, Naples
BUT	Belfast, Union Theological College Library
BUW	Bangor University Library, North Wales
BxBM	Bordeaux, Bibliothèque Municipale

CaCL	Carlisle Cathedral Library
CBM	Châlons-en-Champagne Bibliothèque Municipale
CBS	Cremona, Biblioteca Statale
CBU	Cagliari, Biblioteca Universitaria
CCA	Canterbury, Cathedral Archives and Library
CCC	Cambridge, Corpus Christi College, Parker Library
CCL	Cambridge, Clare College Library
CCPL	Christchurch Public Library, New Zealand
CDC	Cambridge, Downing College Library
CDLS	Canterbury District Law Society, New Zealand
CEC	Colchester, Essex County Library
CfCL	Chelmsford Cathedral Library
CFM	Cambridge, Fitzwilliam Museum Library
CGC	Cambridge, Gonville and Caius College Library
ChC	Cambridge, Christ's College Library
ChCL	Chichester Cathedral Library
ChestC	Chester Cathedral Library
CHPL	Public Library of Cincinatti and Hamilton County, USA
CINU	University of Cincinnati Library
CJL	Cambridge, Jesus College Library
CKB	Copenhagen, Kongelige Bibliotek
CLB	Coburg Landesbibliothek
CLL	Central Library, Leeds
CLM	Countway Library of Medicine, Boston MA
CLN	Central Library, Norwich
CLS	Central Library, Sheffield
CMC	Cambridge, Magdalene College Library
CME	Cambridge, Murray Edwards College, Rosemary Murray Library
CML	Canterbury Museum Library, New Zealand
CMN	Cassino, Biblioteca Statale del Monumento Nazionale di Montecassino
CNC	Cambridge, Newnham College Library
CPC	Cambridge, Pembroke College Library
CPH	Cambridge, Peterhouse, Perne Library
CPL	Cleveland Public Library, Cleveland OH
CRDS	Colgate Rochester Divinity School, Rochester NY
CRH	Cambridge, Ridley Hall Theological College
CQC	Cambridge, Queen's College, Old Library
CSC	Cambridge, St Catharine's College Library
CSel	Cambridge, Selwyn College Library
CSJ	Cambridge, St John's College Library

CSL	Charterhouse School Library, Godalming, Surrey
CSS	Cambridge, Sidney Sussex College Library (Muniment Room)
CTCM	Mannix Library, Catholic Theological College, East Melbourne, Australia
CTH	Cambridge, Trinity Hall, Old Library
CUA	Cambridge University Archives, University Library
CUB	Cologne Universitäts- und Stadtbibliothek (Köln)
CUD	Cambridge University, Faculty of Divinity Library
CUI	Cornell University Library, Ithaca
CUK	Canterbury, University of Kent Library
CUL	Cambridge University Library
CUofA	Catholic University of America
CUW	Cardiff University Library, Wales
CUZ	Cambridge University, Department of Zoology
CWC	Cambridge, Westminster College, Cambridge Theological Federation
CWR	Case Western Reserve University, Cleveland OH
DAL	Downside Abbey Library, Somerset
DC	Dulwich College Library
DCL	Durham Cathedral Library
DCLI	Dublin City Libraries
DCoL	Derbyshire County Library, Matlock
DDUL	Durham USA, Duke University Library
DenPL	Denver Public Library, USA
DEWL	Dublin, Edward Worth Library
DGA	Duffel, Gemeentearchief
DKC	Dunedin, Knox College, Hewitson Library, New Zealand
DKI	Dublin, Honorable Society of King's Inn
DML	Dublin, Archbishop Marsh's Library
DOL	Dublin, Oireachtas Library (Irish Parliament Library)
DPL	Doddington Parochial Library, Kent
DPLNZ	Dunedin Public Library, New Zealand
DRCS	Dublin, Royal College of Surgeons Library
DRD	Derry and Raphoe Diocesan Library
DSU	Dresden, Sächsische Landesbibliothek / Staats- und Universitätsbibliothek
DUB	Düsseldorf Universitätsbibliothek
DUL	Durham University Library, including the collections of Ushaw College
DWL	Dr Williams's Library, London

EAL	Edinburgh, Advocates Library
ECC	Cambridge, Emmanuel College Library
ECL	Exeter Cathedral Library
EdCL	Edinburgh Central Library
EdUL	Edinburgh University Library
EmU	Emory University Library
ERCP	Edinburgh, Royal College of Physicians Library
Eton	Eton College Library
EUL	Exeter University Library
FBB	Florence, Biblioteca Berenson
FBC	Faenza, Biblioteca Comunale Manfrediana
FBN	Florence, Biblioteca Nazionale Centrale
FHB	Fulda Hochschul- und Landesbibliothek
FSL	Folger Shakespeare Library
FUL	Flinders University Library, Adelaide, Australia
GBAB	Ghent, Bisdom Archief en Bibliotheek
GBC	Universidad de Granada, Biblioteca Central
GBCG	Genoa, Biblioteca de Dipartimento di Cultura Giuridica
GBR	Groningen, Bibliotheek der Rijksuniversiteit
GC	Getty Center, Los Angeles
GCB	Ghent, Centrale Bibliotheek van de Universiteit Gent
GCC	Girton College, Cambridge
GCL	Goucher College Library, Baltimore MD
GETS	Garrett-Evangelical Theological Seminary, Evanston IL, adjacent NWU
GFB	Gotha Forschungsbibliothek
GlCL	Gloucester Cathedral Library
GML	Glasgow, Mitchell Library
GNM	Greenwich, National Maritime Museum
GOK	Ghent, Ongeschoeide Karmelieten
GRCP	Glasgow, Royal College of Physicians and Surgeons
GRUB	Greifswald Universitätsbibliothek
GSM	Gouda Streekarchief Midden-Holland
GSU	Georgia Southern University Libray, Statesboro GA
GTS	General Theological Seminary (Episcopal), New York
GUB	Göttingen, Niedersächsische Staats- und Universitätsbibliothek
GUC	Getafe, Spain, Universidad Carlos III, Biblioteca de Ciencias Sociales y Juridicas

GUL	Glasgow University Library
GUW	Georgetown University Library, Washington DC
GWU	George Washington University, Washington DC
HBV	Den Haag, Bibliotheek Vredespaleis 'Peace Palace'
HCC	Hamilton College, Clinton NY
HCL	Hereford Cathedral Library
HCLM	Countway Library of Medicine (Harvard), Boston MA
HCP	Haverford College Library, PA
HFL	Hammersmith and Fulham Libraries
HHC	Hurd Library, Hartlebury Castle, Worcs.
HHL	Henry E. Huntington Library, San Marino CA
HKB	Den Haag, Koninklijke Bibliotheek
HLB	Halle Universitäts- und Landesbibliothek
HLC	Honnold Library, Claremont CA
HNLB	Hannover, Niedersächsische Landesbibliothek
HnSB	Hannover Stadtbibliothek
HOL	House of Lords Library, London
HRC	Harrogate, Ripley Castle Library
HSA	Hispanic Society of America, New York
HSB	Haalem Stadsbibliotheek
HSUB	Hamburg, Staats- und Universitätsbibliothek
HU	Hull University Library
HUB	Heidelberg Universitätsbibliothek
HUC	Hebrew Union College, Jewish Institute of Religion, New York, Los Angeles and Cincinnati
HUL	Harvard University, Houghton and other Libraries
IBUL	Indiana University Library Bloomington
ICS	Institute of Classical Studies, London
ILF	Igoe Library Foundation, Charleston, South Carolina
ILP	Innerpeffrey Library, Perthshire
IMC	Isle of Man Cathedral of St German, Peel, Isle of Man
IPL	Inverness Public Library
ISU	Indiana State University, Terre Haute
IUL	Illinois University Library, Urbana IL
JCB	John Carter Brown Library, Brown University, also John Hay Library
JUB	Jena Universitätsbibliothek
JUT	University of Tokyo Library, Japan

KBG	Kew, Royal Botanical Gardens, Library and Archives
KBJ	Kraków, Biblioteka Jagiellonska
KCC	Cambridge, King's College Library
KCL	Kent County Library, Maidstone
KLL	King's Lynn Library
KNA	Kew, National Archives
KSC	Kilkenny, St Canice's Cathedral Library, currently at MRL
KSRL	University of Kansas, Kenneth Spencer Research Library, Lawrence KS
KSU	Kennesaw State University GA, Bentley Rare Book Gallery
KUB	Kiel Universitätsbibliothek
KUL	Keele University Library
LBC	Louvain-la-Neuve, Bibliothèque Centrale
LBCL	London, Birkbeck College Library
LBL	Leeds University, Brotherton Library (including Ripon Cathedral Library)
LBM	Lyon, Bibliothèque Municipale
LBR	Leiden, Bibliotheek der Redactie van het Woordenboek der Nederlandsche Taal
LBS	Lucca, Biblioteca Statale
LBU	Liège, Bibliothèque Universitaire
LCL	Lincoln Cathedral Library
LCLP	Lafayette College Library, Easton PA
LCP	Library Company of Philadelphia
LDC	London, Dutch Church Library (Austin Friars)
LFL	Lampeter, St David's College, University of Wales, Founders' Library (the Founders being Thomas Burgess (1756–1837), bp of St Davids, Thomas Bowdler (1754–1825), and Thomas Phillips (1760–1851)): books are cited by shelfmark (not book number)
LGI	London, Gray's Inn Library
LGL	London, Guildhall Library
LGS	Lewisham Grammar School Library
LHL	Longleat House Library
LHU	Liverpool, Hope University, Sheppard-Worlock Library
LiCL	Litchfield Cathedral Library
LIL	Lincoln's Inn Library, London
LIT	London, Inner Temple Library
LJM	Liverpool, John Moores University Library
LKC	London, King's College Library
LKFG	Leeuwarden, Koninklijk Fries Genootschap

LKU	Leuven, Katholieke universiteit Central Bibliotheek
LL	The London Library
LlCL	Llandaff Cathedral Library
LLS	London, Law Society Library
LMT	London, Middle Temple Library
LPB	Leeuwarden, Provinciale Bibliotheek van Friesland, now Fries Historisch en Letterkundig Centrum TRESOAR
LPL	London, Lambeth Palace Library (including Sion House Library)
LQL	London, Library of the Religious Society of Friends (Quakers)
LRCO	London, Royal College of Obstetricians and Gynaecologists
LRCS	London, Royal College of Surgeons of England Library
LRS	London, Royal Society Library
LSA	London, Society of Antiquaries of London
LSE	London School of Economics Library
LSH	London, Senate House Library
LSJ	Leuven, Bibliothèque de la Société des Jésuites
LSU	Louisiana State University Shreveport LA
LTC	London, Trinity College Library
LU	Leicester University Library
LUB	Leiden Universiteitsbibliothek
LUBS	Lund Universitetsbiblioteket, Sweden
LUL	Liverpool University Library
LWI	London, Warburg Institute Library
MA	Moravian Archives, Bethlehem PA
MAB	Maredsous, Abbaye Bénédictine
MAS	Milan, Archivio Storico Civico e Biblioteca Trivulziana
MBC	Milan, Biblioteca comunale
MBFZ	Madrid, Biblioteca de Francisco Zabálburu
MBN	Madrid, Biblioteca Nacional de España
MBP	Madrid, Biblioteca de Palacio Real
MBS	Munich, Bayerische Staatsbibliothek
MBU	Modena, Biblioteca Estense Universitaria
MCL	Manchester Central Library
MCRS	Massachusetts Center for Renaissance Studies, Amherst MA
MCS	Manchester, Chetham's School Library
MHC	Mount Holyoke College, South Hadley MA
MJRUL	Manchester, John Rylands University Library
MMC	Montpellier, Médiathèque centrale d'agglomération Emile Zola

MMN	Madrid, Museo Naval, Biblioteca
MMU	University Library, Hamilton, Canada
MMUL	Montréal, McGill University Library
MOL	Museum of London, Barbican
MonUL	Monash University Library, Australia
MPHL	Moscow, State Public Historical Library
MRA	Madrid, Real Academia de Jurisprudencia y Legislación
MRAH	Madrid, Real Academia de la Historia
MRL	Maynooth, Russell Library, Ireland
	Maynooth University and St Patrick's College Maynooth, Co. Kildare
MSA	Mechelin, Stadsarchief, Belgium
MSL	Medical Society of London
MTC	Moore Theological College, Newtown NSW
MTP	Maldon, Essex, Thomas Plume's Library
MUB	Munich Universitätsbibliothek
MUC	Madrid, Biblioteca Universidad Complutense
MUL	Minnesota University Library
MULNZ	Massey University Library, New Zealand
MUM	McGill University Library, Montréal QC
NAL	National Art Library, Victoria & Albert Museum
NBM	Nancy, Bibliothèque Municipale
NBN	Naples, Biblioteca Nazionale Vittorio Emanuele III
NBND	Namur, Bibliothèque des Facultés Notre Dame de la Paix
NBU	Namur, Bubliothèque Universitaire Moretus Plantin
NCCL	Newcastle Cathedral Library
NCL	Norwich Cathedral Library
NCM	Norwich Castle Museum Library
NewCL	Newcastle Central Library
NHM	Natural History Museum, London
NIA	Northern Ireland Assembly Library
NLA	National Library of Australia, Canberra
NLC	Newberry Library, Chicago
NLE	National Library of Estonia, Talinn
NLI	National Library of Ireland, Dublin
NLM	US National Library of Medicine, Bethesda MD
NLO	St Mark's Church, Niagara-on-the-Lake, Ontario
NLPS	Newcastle-upon-Tyne, Literary and Philosphical Society
NLS	National Library of Scotland, Edinburgh

NLW	National Library of Wales, Aberystwyth
NMS	National Museums of Scotland, Edinburgh
NMU	New Mexico State University, USA
NPG	National Portrait Gallery, London, Heinz Archive & Library
NRL	University of Newcastle upon Tyne, Robinson Library
NSW	State Library of New South Wales, Mitchell Library
NT	Libraries of The National Trust
NU	Northumbria University Library, Newcastle upon Tyne
NUB	Nijmegen Universiteitsbibliotheek
NUIG	National University of Ireland Galway
NUL	Nottingham University Library
NWU	Northwestern University Library, Evanston IL, adjacent GETS
NYAM	New York, Academy of Medicine
NYCC	New York, City College, University of New York
NYCU	New York, Columbia University Library
NYFU	New York, Fordham University Library
NYHS	New York Historical Society Library
NYPL	New York Public Library
NYPM	New York, Pierpont Morgan Library
NYS	New York State Library
NYU	New York University Library
OAM	Oxford, Ashmolean Museum Library
OAS	Oxford, All Souls College, Codrington Library
OBC	Oxford, Balliol College Library
OBF	Oxford, Blackfriars Library
OBFC	Osimo, Italy, Biblioteca Comunale Francesco Cini
OBL	Oxford, Bodleian Library
OBrC	Oxford, Brasenose College Library
OCC	Oxford, Corpus Christi College Library
OEC	Oxford, Exeter College Library
OEF	Oxford, English Faculty Library
OGF	Oxford, Greyfriars, Franciscan House of Studies Library
OHA	Oxford University, Department of the History of Art
OHC	Oxford, Hertford College Library
OHF	Oxford University History Faculty Library
OHM	Oxford, Harris Manchester College Library
OJC	Oxford, Jesus College Library
OKC	Oxford, Keble College Library

OLC	Oxford, Lincoln College Library
OLMH	Oxford, Lady Margaret Hall
OLS	Otago District Law Society Library, Dunedin, New Zealand
OMaC	Oxford, Magdalen College Library
OMaCS	Oxford, Magdalen College School Library
OMC	Oxford, Merton College Library
OMFC	Oxford, Mansfield College Library
OMHS	Oxford University Museum of the History of Science
OMM	Orléans, Mediathèque Municipale
ONC	Oxford, New College Library
ONuC	Oxford, Nuffield College Library
OOC	Oxford, Oriel College Library
OPH	Oxford, Pusey House Library
OQC	Oxford, Queen's College Library
ORP	Oxford, Regent's Park College Library
ORS	Oxford, Radcliffe Science Library
OSA	Oxford, St Anne's College Library
OSC	Oxford, Somerville College Library
OSG	Oxford University, School of Geography
OSH	Oxford, St Hilda's College Library
OxHC	Oxfordshire History Centre
OStC	Oxford, St Catharine's College Library
OStE	Oxford, St Edmund Hall Library
OStH	Oxford, St Hugh's College Library
OSJ	Oxford, St John's College Library
OSL	Oxford University, Sackler Library
OSP	Oxford, St Peter's College Library
OSU	Ohio State University Library
OTI	Oxford, Taylor Institution Library
OTC	Oxford, Trinity College Library
OU	Open University Library, Milton Keynes
OUC	Oxford, University College Library
OUL	Otago University Library
OUP	Oxford University Press Archives
OUS	Oxford Union Society Library
OWmC	Oxford, Wadham College Library
OWoC	Oxford, Worcester College Library
OXC	Oxford, Christ Church Library

PAL	Portsmouth, Admiralty Library (Ministry of Defence); the books in this library were seen when housed in the Hydrographic Office at Taunton
PBA	Paris, Bibliothèque de l'Arsenal
PBC	Palermo, Biblioteca Centrale della Regione Siciliana Alberto Bombace
PBL	Perth, A. K. Bell Library
PBM	Paris, Bibliothèque Mazarine
PBN	Paris, Bibliothèque Nationale
PBS	Paris, Bibliothèque de la Sorbonne
PBU	Pisa, Biblioteca Universitaria
PBSG	Paris, Bibliothèque St Geneviève
PFL	Free Library of Philadelphia
PHS	Historical Society of Pennsylvania, Philadelphia PA
PMAG	Peterborough Museum and Art Gallery
PML	Penzance, Morrab Library
PNL	Prague, Czech National Library
PPL	Providence Public Library, Rhode Island, USA
PrPL	Prees Parochial Library, Shropshire
PrTS	Princeton Theological Seminary, Princeton NJ
PSL	Pacific School of Religion, Berkeley CA, Flora Lamson Hewlett Library
PST	School of Theology, Southern Methodist University, Dallas TX
PTS	Pittsburgh Theological Seminary
PUL	Pennsylvania University Libraries, Philadelphia
PUS	Paris, Université de Paris, Bibliothèque Universitaire de la Sorbonne
PUY	Petyt Library, University of York
QBN	Bibliothèque Nationale de Quebec, Canada
QCL	Queen's College, Dalton McCaughey Library, Parkville, Victoria, Australia
QML	Queensland Museum Library, South Bank, Australia
QMU	Queen Mary University, London
QSC	Supreme Court, Brisbane, Queensland, Australia
QSL	State Library of Queensland, Australia
QUB	Belfast, Queen's University Library
QUK	Kingston, Ontario, Queen's University Library
QUL	Queensland University Library, St Lucia Campus, Brisbane
RBA	Rome, Biblioteca Universitaria Alessandrina
RBC	Ravenna, Biblioteca Comunale Classense
RBCas	Rome, Biblioteca Casanatense

RBG	Rome, Biblioteca Giorgio del Vecchio dei Dipartimento di Scienze Giuridiche
RBM	Rouen, Bibliothèque Municipale
RBN	Rome, Biblioteca Nationale Centrale Vittorio Emanuele II
RBP	Rieti, Biblioteca Comunale Paroniana
RBS	Rare Book School, Charlottesville VA
RCB	Representative Church Body Library, Churchtown, Co. Dublin, Ireland
RCL	Rochester Cathedral Library
RGS	London, Royal Geographical Society
RIA	Royal Irish Academy Library, Dublin
RKA	Rochester, Strood Medway Archives and Local Studies Centre, Kent County Archives
RLV	Richmond VA, Library of Virginia
RLW	Rectors Library, Whitchurch, Salop
RmBM	Reims, Bibliothèque Municipale
RNJ	Rutgers State University, New Brunswick, NJ
RNL	National Library of Russia, St Petersburg
RRH	Rothamsted Research Library, Harpenden
RSL	Russian State Library, Moscow
RUB	Rostock Universitätsbibliothek
RUH	Rice University, Houston TX
RUL	Reading University Library
SAC	St Asaph's Cathedral Library
SACL	St Albans Cathedral Library
SAN	Somerset Archaeological and Natural History Society, Taunton
SBP	St Bride Printing Library, London
SBPU	Strasbourg, Bibliothèque Publique et Universitaire
SBT	Shakespeare Birthplace Trust Library
SBU	Salamanca, Biblioteca Universitaria
SCI	Sydney, Catholic Institute, Veech Library
SCL	Salisbury Cathedral Library
SCN	Smith College Library, Northampton MA
SDC	St David's Cathedral Library, Wales
SDL	St Deiniol's Library, Hawarden
SfUL	Stanford University Library, CA
SHC	Surrey Heritage Centre, Woking
ShCL	Sheffield Central Library
SHU	Sheffield Hallam University Library

SIU	Southern Illinois University, Morris Library, Carbondale IL
SJS	Sir John Soane Museum, London
SJTC	St John's and Trinity Colleges, Kinder Library, Auckland, New Zealand
SKB	Stockholm, Kungliga Biblioteket
SKS	Starr King School for the Ministry, Wilbur Collection, Berkeley CA
SLB	Speyer Landesbibliothek
SLC	Sutro Library, California State Library
SLP	St Louis Public Library, St Louis MO
SLU	St Louis University, St Louis MO
SLWU	Washington University, St Louis MO, Olin Library
SML	Southwell Minster Library
SMU	Southern Methodist University, Dallas TX
SMUL	Sydney, Macquarie University Library, Australia
SOG	Society of Genealogists, London
SoUL	Southampton University Library
SPC	St Paul's Cathedral Library, London
SRO	Suffolk Record Office, Ipswich
SSA	State Library of South Australia
SSL	Shrewsbury School Library
StA	St Andrews University Library
StCL	Stonyhurst College Library
SUB	Sussex University Library, Brighton
SUL	Sheffield University Library
SUNY	State University of New York, Stony Brook NY
SUW	Swansea University Library, Wales
SvBU	Seville, Spain, Biblioteca Universitaria
SWCL	Southwark Cathedral Library
TBA	Turin, Biblioteca dell'Accademia delle Scienze
TBC	Turin, Biblioteca Civica Centrale
TBU	Turin, Biblioteca interdipartimentale Gioele Solari dell'Università degli Studi di Torino
TCC	Cambridge, Trinity College, Wren Library
TCD	Dublin, Trinity College Library
TCH	Trinity College, Hartford CT, Watkinson Library
TCL	Truro Cathedral Library
TCU	Texas Christian University, Fort Worth TX
TFM	Toledo, Biblioteca de la Provincia Franciscana de Castilla-La Mancha
TML	Taranaki Museum Library, New Zealand

LIBRARY ABBREVIATIONS 233

TMM	Toulouse, Médiathèque Municipale José Cabanis
TMT	Troyes, Médiathèque de l'Agglomération Troyenne
TNO	Tullane University, New Orleans LA
TPL	Tong Parochial Library, Shrewsbury, Shropshire Archives
TRR	Toronto, Library of Center for Reformation & Renaissance Studies
TSC	The Supreme Court Library, Tallahassee FL
TUB	Tilburg Universiteitsbibliotheek
TUL	Toronto University Library
UAB	University of Akron OH, Bierce Library
UAF	University of Arkansas, Fayetteville AR
UAL	University of Adelaide, Barr Smith Library
UAZ	University of Arizona, Tucson AZ
UBC	University of British Columbia Library, Vancouver
UBL	University of Birmingham Library
UCBL	University of California Berkeley Library
UCC	University of Calgary Library, Canada
UCDL	University of California Davis Library
UCH	University of Chicago Library
UCIL	University of California Irvine Library
UCL	University College London Library
UCLA	University of California Los Angeles Library
UCRL	University of California Riverside Library
UCSB	University of California Santa Barbara Library
UCSC	University of California Santa Cruz Library
UCSD	University of California San Diego Library
UCSR	University of California, Southern Regional Library Facility, Los Angeles
UDN	University of Delaware, Newark, DE
UIL	University of Iowa Library
ULim	University of Limerick, Bolton Library and Glucksman Library
UMI	University of Michigan Library
UML	University of Melbourne, Baillieu Library
UNC	University of North Carolina Library, Chapel Hill NC
UND	University of Notre Dame, IA
UNSW	University of New South Wales, Australia
UOC	University of Colorado Library
UPL	University of Princeton Library
URNY	University of Rochester NY

USL	University of Sydney, Fisher Library
USLC	United States Library of Congress
USMA	United States Military Academy, West Point NY
USNA	United States Naval Academy, Nimitz Library, Annapolis MD
UTA	University of Texas at Austin Library
UTK	University of Tennessee Knoxville Library
UTL	University of Tasmania, Morris Miller Library
UTS	Union Theological Seminary, New York
UTUB	Utrecht Universiteitsbibliotheek
UUB	Uppsala, Universitetsbibliotek
UUM	Ulster University, Magee Campus, Derry, Co. Londonderry
UVC	University of Victoria Library, Canada
UVL	University of Virginia Library
UW	University of Waterloo, Ontario, Canada
UWA	University of Western Australia, Reid Library, Crawley WA
UWJ	University of Witwatersrand, Johannesburg, South Africa
UWL	University of Waikato Library, Hamilton, New Zealand
UWO	University of Western Ontario, London, Ontario, Canada
UWS	University of Washington, Seattle
VBD	Viterbo, Biblioteca Diocesana
VBN	Venice, Biblioteca Nazionale Marciana
VBS	Veroli, Italy, Biblioteca Statale de Monumento Nazionale di Casamari
VBU	València, Biblioteca Universitaria
VBV	València, Biblioteca Valenciana
VCL	Vassar College Library, Poughkeepsie NY
VCU	Virginia Commonwealth University, Richmond VA
VIP	Vicenza, Instituzione Pubblica Culturale Biblioteca Civica Bertoliana
VON	Vienna, Österreichische Nationalbibliothek
VPL	Library of the Parliament of Victoria, Melbourne, Australia
VSC	Supreme Court of Victoria Library, Melbourne, Australia
VSL	Victoria State Library, Australia
VUB	Universidad de Valladolid, Spain, Biblioteca Histórica de Santa Cruz
VUW	Victoria University of Wellington Library, New Zealand
WAAB	Weimar Herzogin Anna Amalia Bibliothek
WAL	Westminster Abbey Library
WBO	Warsaw, Biblioteka Ossolineum
WBU	Waco TX, Baylor University Library

WCAI	Williamstown MA, Sterling and Francine Clark Art Institute
WCC	Windsor Castle, St George's Chapter Library
WCF	Winchester College Fellows Library
WCL	Wells Cathedral Library
WCM	Wellesley College Library, Wellesley MA
WCS	Whanganui Collegiate School, Whanganui, New Zealand
WCW	Williams College, Chapin Library, Williamstown MA
WFM	Wisbech and Fenland Museum, Wisbech.
WHAB	Wolfenbüttel Herzog August Bibliothek
WiCL	Winchester Cathedral Library
Wigan	Wigan Central Library
WIHM	Wellcome Institute for the History of Medicine Library, London
WoCL	Worcester Cathedral Library
WMil	University of Wisconsin-Milwaukee Library
WMUL	University of Wisconsin-Madison Memorial Library
WMW	William and Mary College, Williamstown MA
WRL	Windsor Castle, Royal Library
WSL	Westminster School Library
WSS	William Salt Library, Stafford
WUL	University of Warwick Library, Coventry
WUM	Wesleyan University Library, Middletown CT
XCU	Canterbury University, Christ Church, New Zealand
YML	York Minster Library
YUB	Yale University, Beinecke Library, Sterling Memorial and other Libraries
YUC	York University Library, Toronto, Canada
YUL	York University Library
ZBD	Zamora, Biblioteca Diocesana
ZBP	Zamora, Biblioteca Publica del Estado
ZBS	Zaragoza, Biblioteca del Seminario de San Carlos
ZZB	Zürich, Zentralbibliothek

Catalogue of Early Printed Books Containing Anglo-Saxon to 1705

For each entry identified by the date-number of the book, the basic bibliographical information (author, title, place of publication, printer, publisher, date of publication, format, collation and pagination) is given with reference to STC, Wing, Adams, USTC, ESTC, as appropriate. Two points of interest are treated as fully as possible.

(1) The manuscript or printed source(s) of the Anglo-Saxon material used in each book. Often there may be an intermediary transcript between the original Anglo-Saxon manuscript and the printed version. While every attempt has been made to track these transcripts down some may have eluded me.

(2) The type-designs found in each book, concentrating first on the Anglo-Saxon type-designs, and then, as far as possible, the other type-designs used in conjunction with them. Types are listed under (1) their name and size, (2) their measurements, Body + (Face +) x-height + capital height. In describing the features of letter-design I use the terminology given by Gaskell, 'Nomenclature', except for the addition of a few terms necessary for the description of a non-roman type-design. See the *Glossary* above. Where books show a large number of instances of small amounts of Anglo-Saxon type, as Camden, **1586.1** etc and atlases using his text, as **1645.1** etc, and du Cange **1678.2**, it has been deemed necessary to save space by listing these by page number only.

Collations, with format and pagination are provided, sometimes more briefly when the book shows minor use of Anglo-Saxon. When a book is more complicated in structure than usual (as **1572.1**, **1618.1**, **1703/5.1**, not atlases) the collation is given with discreet blocks of printed material described as booklets (a term borrowed from manuscript description) so that the structure of the whole book can be made clearer. Notes on date or context are added when these are of particular interest. To help interested readers a list of where available copies of each book can be found is provided, but may not be exhaustive. Many books are available in on-line facsimile via ESTC, USTC or EEBO. Notes are provided on copies seen as appropriate.

The bibliographies at the end of each book entry are selective and the majority of entries relate to the material book rather than the contents. In the interests of brevity reference is by surname and year of publication.

1503.1: Arnold, Richard (–1521?), [*Chronicle*] beginning *The names of þe baylifs custos mairs and sherefs of þe cite of London from the tyme of king Richard* *the first*. [Antwerp: Adriaen van Berghen, 1503?]. STC 782; ESTC S104099; USTC 410041.

    Collation: 2⁰ in 6s: A⁴ ²A⁸ B⁴ C–E⁸ F–Q⁶ R⁸ S–T⁶ V⁶(-V6); [12], xvii–cxviii, [1] leaves.

Writ of William I (not in Anglo-Saxon types)
Source of Passage utilizing Anglo-Saxon Types: none, see **Type** below.
Type:
Main text in an English-size Textura: Body 98.
B4r   From unidentified MS: Writ of William I (Pelteret 8) in same Textura type as the main text.

    Copy seen: CCC SP.318.

    Copies also at: BL, CUL, CMC, TCC, LGL, MOL, MJRUL, OBL, OCC; USLC, NYPM, FSL, HHL, HUL, IUL, NLC, UTA, WCW, WMUL; SSA.

1555.1: Gessner, Conrad, *Mithridates: De differentiis linguarum tum veterum quae hodie apud diversas nationes in toto orbe terrarum usu sunt*. Zürich: Christoph Froschouer, 1555. USTC 305141; Adams G550. 2nd edn Zürich: Johann Wolph, 1610.

    Collation: 8⁰: A–K⁸ fos [2] + 78 + 1 tab.
No AS, but the Lord's Prayer in OHG, Old Dutch, and Icelandic, is printed in a Pica Schwabacher: see E7ʳ, F1ʳ, and the fold-out leaf after K8.

    Copy seen: CUL M*.12.4(F).

    Copies also at: BL, GUL, OBL, NLW, DML, PBSG, PUS, BBM, MBS, CBS, FBN, MBN, SBU, KBJ, BNL, RNL; NYPL, NYCU, BJH, DDUL, PUL, UTA, TRR.

Bibliography: Sharpe & Hoyne 2020: no.2 on pp 50–51.
Facsimile: Aalen: Scientia-Verlag, 1974.

1566.1: [Parker, Matthew, & John Joscelyn, eds], *A Testimonie of Antiquitie*. 1st edn. London: John Day, [1566]. STC 159; ESTC S124446; GR 5276. AS1.
Excerpts from Ælfric, ASC (E), Laws, Lord's Prayer, etc.

    Date: prob 1566, as stated by Strype 1711: 237–238. A narrow range of possible dates is arrived at from the signatories of the bishop's statement (¶1ʳ–¶2ᵛ): publication must have been after 20 October 1566, when Nicholas Robinson, bp of Bangor, was consecrated, and before 26 June 1568, when Thomas Young, abp of York, died. Arber's index (v.56, no. 1025), misleadingly entitled the 'London Book Trade Directory', records the book as for sale from John Day in 1566 (not just 17 Nov to 31 Dec as misstated by Adams 1917: 23, n. 4, and much repeated subsequently), but this date, while probably correct, has no authority. For a rehearsal of the known evidence see Keleman 1997.

Collation: 8⁰ in 4s: ¶†⁴ ¶∗⁴ ¶*⁴ ¶∴⁴ A² B–P⁴ ¶² Q–S⁴ [$4 signed (-¶†1.4, ¶*4, ¶*4, ¶∴3,4, B1, P4, Q1.4, R4, S3,4)] 88 leaves, foliated [i–xviii], 1–56, 57–70.

SOURCES OF PASSAGES UTILIZING ANGLO-SAXON TYPES:
1. Preface

1.1   ¶†3ᵛ   Ælfric's 'Excusatio Dictantis' (opening statement) at the end of his homily *Depositio S. Martin* (Godden 1979: XXXIV) from CCC 198, 385ᵛ/5–9;

1.2   ¶†4   Ælfric's *Grammar*, opening statement from AS Preface presumably quoted from CUL Hh.1.10, 1ᵛ/4–7, beside which there is an annotation by Joscelyn (cf. Zupitza 1880: 2);

1.3   ¶*2ᵛ–3ʳ   (*in Pica Italic*) Ælfric's *Grammar*, Latin Preface, quoted from Hh.1.10, 1ʳ/12–18, where the reading *scolis uenerabilis apelwoldi presulis* is distinctive (cf. Zupitza 1880: 1);

1.4   ¶*4ʳ   Ælfric's *Letter to Sigeferth* preceding the homily for the second Sunday after Epiphany presumably from Vespasian D.xiv, 6ᵛ/15–21 (Assmann 1889: 13); cf. Tite 2003: 183;

1.5   ¶*4   List of Books given by Leofric to Exeter Cathedral from ECL 3501, 1ʳ/1–4, 19–22, 1ᵛ/14–20, where the place of resumption on 1ᵛ/14 has been marked with a vertical line and a cross in the margin, presumably by Joscelyn; not from CCC 101 (transcript s.xvi²) as the reading *deorwurþ* is closer to ECL 3501 *deorwurðe* than CCC 101 *deorwurde* (cf. Pelteret 91);

1.6   ¶∴1ᵛ   L quotation of scribal statement from OBL Junius 121, 101ʳ/15–18;

1.7   ¶∴3ʳ   Story about wife retention from ASC E 1129, OBL Laud misc. 636, 87ʳ/22–24 (Clark 1954: 51), the same source page also used in 1567.1.

2. Text

2.1   B1ᵛ–M1ᵛ   Ælfric's *Sermo de Sacrificio in die Pascae* (Godden 1979: no.XV) from CCC 198, 218ʳ/1–226ʳ/4, with some readings from Faustina A ix, 131ʳ/5–139ʳ/20; distinctive readings from CCC 198 (Godden's E) include *heardlice* (20), *tacnie* (37), *swa eac* (66), *hlaf* (75), *sume* (150), *ælcum* (152), *oðære* (159), *ungesewenlice* (194), *he na* (210), *ðe sylf* (216), *efenlæcað* (307–8), *hyrdnysse* (311), *modes* (315); readings taken over from Faustina A.ix (Godden's N) include *race* (34), TAU (54), *manegum* (81), *gehwilcum* (90), *ac* (107), *ðone ylcan* (186), *husel* (225), *ne* (246), *gewistfullian* (267), *mistlicum* (284), *swa* (295), *he* (315), *unscæððigan* (331), *andweardum* (332); CUL Ii.4.6, where this sermon occurs as Ker's art. 20, was given to Parker 29 Dec 1567, too late to be taken into account for this printed version (and the text contains no distinctive readings from it), even though the earliest state of four pages of the book have been bound into it after fo 156;

2.2   M3ᵛ–N1ᵛ   Ælfric's letter to Wulfsige III (bp of Sherborne 992–1002) extracts (Fehr 1914: §§133–142) from Junius 121, 109ᵛ/23–110ᵛ/5, where the readings *mus oððe nytenu* (§134), *gymene* (§135), *xiiii niht* (§136), *halgan* (§141), and *to his gastlican blode* (§142) are distinctive, and where the end of the passage used has been marked by Parker in the text, with his triquetra mark in the margin to call attention to it; the editors also saw CCC 190, pp. 305/20–306/17;

2.3   N2ᵛ–O4ᵛ Ælfric's second letter to Wulfstan (abp of York 1002–23) extracts (Fehr 1914: §§86–95, 97–109) from Junius 121, 116ʳ/8–118ʳ/7, where the readings *gefyllað* (§86), *doð unwislice* (§87), *bebead* (§92), *of þam gastlicum stane* (§105), *þa þæt Israhela* (§107), *þeah he* (§108) are distinctive, and where the beginning and end of the passage used are marked with a cross and asterisk respectively, presumably by Joscelyn; also saw CCC 190, pp. 341/12–343/12. Joscelyn's transcript of this passage from Junius 121 occurs in Vitellius D.vii, 5ʳ–6ʳ (damaged by fire);

2.4   P2ᵛ–4ʳ   Latin text (in Pica Roman type) of Ælfric's second letter to Wulfstan from CCC 265, pp. 176/17–178/4 (where the beginning of the passage quoted has been underlined, with Joscelyn's triquetra in the margin), collated with CCC 190, pp. 155/1–156/22, from which a passage erased in CCC 265 on p. 177/18–21 has been supplied, with explanatory annotation in the margin by Joscelyn; the readings *est [enim] sanguis* (P3ʳ/23) and *qui [pro vobis et] pro multis* (P3ʳ/2425) are distinctive against CCC 190, which includes the words in square brackets, although in CCC 265 the words *vobis et pro* have been supplied above the line by Joscelyn, only to be ignored (assuming they were already there) for the printed text.

3. Editorial statement

3.1   Q2ʳ   Ælfric's letter to Wulfsige, extract (Fehr 1914: §§61–62) from Junius 121, 105ᵛ/10–16, where the readings *on sunnan dagum* and *andgyt* are distinctive, and where the beginning of the passage has been underlined, with Joscelyn's triquetra in the margin;

3.2   Q2ᵛ–3ʳ   AS Laws I Cnut 21–22.1 (Liebermann 1903: I, 302) from Nero A.i (Loyn 1971), 13ᵛ/10–14ʳ/8, where the readings *inweardre, smeagan oft, huru cunne* are distinctive; the reading *geleafan 7 ariht* is correct despite Liebermann's indication that '7' comes from CCC 383; in the reading *smeagan oft* the words '7 spyrian', written by Joscelyn, are indicated for insertion before *oft*, but evidently this collation was done after 1566 (between 1568 and 1580, according to Loyn 1971: 39).

4. Supplementary text

4.1a Q4   AS text of Mt.6.7–9 (preceding Lord's Prayer, Liuzza 1994: 12) from CUL Ii.2.11, 9ᵛ/19–10ʳ/1, where the readings *nellon* (2x) are distinctive; also distinctive against CCC MS 140 are the spellings *gebiddan* (not *-on*), *fæla* (not *fela*), *heora mænig-* (not *hyra menig-*), and *Eornost-* (not *Eornust-*);

4.1b Q4ᵛ–R1ᵛ AS text of Lord's Prayer from Cleopatra B.xiii, 58ʳ/15–22, but the reading *þin wylla on eorðan swa swa on heofenũ* is apparently from CUL Ii.2.11 (Cleopatra has *Sy þin willa swa swa onheofenum swa eac on eorðan*), and *cume þin rice* may also be from the same source, since that MS has *to me be cume* with *to me be* underlined (for omission?) though *ge* has been added above *be* (?s.xvi²) to give Cleopatra's reading *ge cume*; the text may have been collated with the preparatory material for 1571.1: D1ᵛ–2ʳ; cf. Tite 2003: 211;

4.2 R1ᵛ–3ʳ AS text of Creed from Cleopatra B.xiii, 58ʳ/23–58ᵛ/11;

4.3 R3ʳ Prologue to Ten Commandments from Ælfric's second (OE) letter to Wulfstan (Fehr, §121), from CCC 190, p. 344/8–11, collated with Junius 121, 118ᵛ/22–119ʳ/2; the reading *of þam munte* is a conflation with *of* (not *on*) from Junius 121 and omission of *ylcan* from CCC 190;

4.4 R3ᵛ–S1ʳ Ten Commandments (1st nine only, cf. Liebermann I, 26–29) from CCC 173, 36ʳ/1–17, where the readings *londe 7 of hiora* (prol.), *noman* (2), *gehalgige*, *sint* (3), *medder* (4), *dearnenga* (6) are distinctive, but the reading *sealde ðe* (4), which is not in the surviving MSS, appears also in Lambarde's *Archaionomia* [1568.2], G4ᵛ/4; Nero A.i (Loyn 1971) was collated by Joscelyn with readings from CCC 173, so that the collated text on fos 51ʳ/1–51ᵛ/3 could have been the basis of this printed text, but only if the collation was done early enough.

TYPE:

AS1: main AS text in the Parkerian Great Primer Anglo-Saxon acquired by Day (Body 112). The Anglo-Saxon sorts are combined with Pierre Haultin's English-size Roman (Body 95), which shows the same x-height, on a Great Primer body (four lines of Latin set in Roman on O1ʳ, O3ᵛ and O4ʳ):

The specimen on S3ᵛ shows 24 special sorts, omitting X and any punctuation markers.

Special sorts shown: 11 lower-case   ð, f, ʒ, ı, p, ſ, t, ẏ;   þ, ð, p;
                     9 capitals   Æ¹, Æ², Є, b, ꟽ, 8;   Þ, Ð, P;
                     3 others   þ, ꜩ, ꜩ
            Total: 24 sorts.

François Guyot's Great Primer Italic (Body 112) is used for the facing translation. Haultin's Pica Roman (Body 82.5) is used for the preface.

Robert Granjon's second Pica Italic (of three), the *Cicero pendante* (Body 82.5) is used throughout, except on P3ᵛ: on the title page (¶†1ʳ), in the preface (¶†2ʳ, ¶†4ʳ, ¶*2–3, ¶*4ᵛ–¶*2ᵛ, ¶*3ᵛ, ¶∴1ᵛ–3ᵛ), on the Sermon title page (B1ʳ), in quotations in the translation (C2ʳ–3ʳ, I2ʳ), in the running titles (¶†2ᵛ–M2ʳ), for marginal comments to the Sermon translation, in the colophon to the sermon (M2ᵛ), in the editorial introduction to the letter to Wulfsige (M3ʳ), in

the editorial link-statement between the letter to Wulfsige and the letter to Wulfstan (N1^v–2^r), for editorial statements (P1^v–2^r), the bishops' statement (¶1^r–2^v), in the editorial introduction to the Lord's Prayer, etc. (Q1^v–3^v), in the closing editorial statement (S1^r–3^r), in the statement of specimen Saxon sorts (S3^v), and in the printer's colophon (S4^r).
Ameet Tavernier's Pica Italic (Body 80; Isaac 1933: 214 and fig. 18; Vervliet 1968: IT8) is used in the marginal comment (P3^v).

>Copies seen: *Preliminary*: four pages of an earlier state of the AS sermon and facing-page translation made prior to the 1st edition survives in CUL MS Ii.4.6 (Ker 21), bound in between fos 156/157. The watermark over the fold indicates that it is a single half-sheet, imposed on one side only in the following pattern, with arrows pointing to the top of the page for reading:
>
>| AS text, p. 4, i.e. 4^v ⇒ | ⇐ Trans. sig. Av, i.e. 5^r |
>| Trans. sig. Aiij, i.e. 3^r ⇒ | ⇐ AS text, p. 1, i.e. 1^v |
>
>This pattern conforms to no practical arrangement for imposition and must have been experimental (cf. Bromwich 1962: 286–287). Many changes in the text and especially the translation are noted by Bromwich.
>*Provisional*: BL Add. MS 18160 is like the 1st edition except that, after P4^v (blank), instead of ¶², it has four unprinted leaves foliated 77–80 with the handwritten statement 'As the writing⟨es⟩ of ...' followed by the personal signatures of the bishops numbered 1–20 (18–20 blank), followed on fo 80^v by the handwritten statement 'hii patres precedentes subscripserunt manib⟨us⟩ suis propriis in hoc Libellulo'. ¶*3^v, 4^r (re. the marriage of priests: cf. 1567.1), ¶∵2^r, 3^r, 4^v, A1^r and Q2^r have marginal annotations by Joscelyn and there are annotations by Parker on ¶*1^r and ¶*2^r. B1^v is marked 'fol.218.a', a reference to CCC MS 198. ¶*3^r and I2^r have a smudge of printer's ink.
>*1st edition*: OBL Douce A 384; CCA W2/X.4.44 (shows ¶² after A2); Somner's copy with his annotations; previously belonged to John Ludd (d.1649), Somner's headmaster at King's School, Canterbury. BL C.53.h.34 has ¶² between A2 and B1; CSJ U.20.46 (Thomas Baker's copy) lacks S4; LPL 1567.4 lacks M3, 4, N–P4, ¶²; BL C.37.a.47 has only Q–S4, lacking S4; OBL Gough Sax.Lit.127 (binding by MacDurnan Gospels binder; *Fine Bindings* 1968: no.75; Nixon 1970: 254 no.7) has S4 blank followed by χ² with the errata on χ1^r; 8⁰.T.28.Seld.Th. has S4 blank then ¶² (i.e. not between gatherings P and Q) stuck along the inner edge to χ1 containing the errata on χ1^r.
>Copies also at: NCL, NLS, OCC, WAL; FSL, NYPM, HUL, LCP, PFL, UCH, YUB.

Bibliography: Bately 1992: 439; Bromwich 1962; Clement 1997: 208–211; Fehr 1914: xxix–xxxi; Kelemen 1997; Lucas 1997; Niles 2015: 57–60.

1566.2: [Parker, Matthew, & John Joscelyn, editors], *A Testimonie of Antiquitie*. 2nd edn of **1566.1**. London: John Day, [1566]. STC 159.5; ESTC 122220; GR 5276. AS1.

    Collation: 8⁰: A–L⁸ [$4 signed (-A1,4, B4, L4)] 88 leaves, foliated 1–75, 76–89 (25 misnumbered 24, 49 omitted, 52 misnumbered 32, 65 misnumbered 64).

SOURCES OF PASSAGES UTILIZING ANGLO-SAXON TYPES:
As **1566.1** with sig. references modified as indicated below

1. Preface

1.1	A3^v	As 1566.1	¶†3^v;
1.2	A4	As 1566.1	¶†4;
1.3	A6^v–7^r	As 1566.1	¶*2^v–3^r;
1.4	A8^r	As 1566.1	¶*4^r;
1.5	B4	As 1566.1	¶*4;
1.6	B5^v	As 1566.1	¶∴1^v;
1.7	B7^r	As 1566.1	¶∴3^r.

2. Text

2.1	C3^v–H3^v	As 1566.1	B1^v–M1^v;
2.2	H5^v–H7^v	As 1566.1	M3^v–N1^v;
2.3	H8^v–I6^v	As 1566.1	N2^v–O4^v;
2.4	I8^v–K2^r	As 1566.1	P2^v–4^r;

3. Editorial statement

3.1	K6^r	As 1566.1	Q2^r;
3.2	K6^v–K7^r	As 1566.1	Q2^v–3^r;

4. Supplementary text

4.1a	K8	As 1566.1	Q4;
4.1b	K8^v–L1^v	As 1566.1	Q4^v–R1^v;
4.2	L1^v–L3^r	As 1566.1	R1^v–3^r;
4.3	L3^r	As 1566.1	R3^r;
4.4	L3^v–L5^r	As 1566.1	R3^v–S1^r;

TYPE:

AS1: main AS text in the Parkerian Great Primer Anglo-Saxon acquired by Day (Body 112). The Anglo-Saxon sorts are combined with Pierre Haultin's English-size Roman (Body 95), which shows the same x-height, on a Great Primer body (four lines of Latin set in Roman on I3^r, I5^v and I6^r).

The specimen on L7^v shows 24 special sorts, as **1566.1**, lacking X and ⁊ (punctus versus).

Special sorts shown:	12 lower-case letters	ð, f, ȝ, ı, p, r, τ, ẏ, z; þ, ð, ƿ;
	9 capitals	Æ¹, Æ², Є, Ꝼ, Ꟃ, 8; Þ, Ð, Ƿ;
	3 others	þ, ⁊, ⁊
Total:	24 sorts.	

François Guyot's Great Primer Italic (Body 112) is used for the facing translation. Haultin's Pica Roman (Body 82.5) is used for the preface. Robert Granjon's second Pica Italic (of three), the *Cicero pendante* (Body 82.5) is used on the title page (A1^r), in the preface (A2^r, A4^r, A6–7, A8^v–B2^v, B3^v, B5^v–7^v), on the Sermon title page (C3^r), in quotations in the translation (C8^r–D1^r, F8^r), in the running titles (A2^v–H4^r), in the colophon to the sermon (H4^v), in the editorial introduction to the letter to Wulfsige (H5^r), in the editorial link-statement between the letter to Wulfsige and the letter to Wulfstan (H7^v–8^r), in the closing editorial statement (L5^r–7^r), in the statement of specimen Saxon sorts (L7^v), and in the printer's colophon (L8^r).

In the 1st edn all Pica italics were set in this type, except for Tavernier's Pica Italic in the marginal comment (P3^v = 2nd edn K1^v), but the following were changed in this 2nd edn:

Ameet Tavernier's Pica Italic (Body 80) is used for marginal comments to the Sermon translation, for editorial statements (I7^v–8^r), the bishops' statement (K3^r–K4^v), in the editorial introduction to the Lord's Prayer, etc. (K5^v–7^v); another design of v and w occurs mixed in with Tavernier's. Curiously, the alteration seems to have been a retrograde one, as Tavernier's Pica Italic was 'Day's *first* Elizabethan italic' (Isaac 1936: 42, emphasis mine).

Copies seen:
With title page statement of royal privilege with *Maiəſtatis*: CCC SP.281, CSJ Ee.13.42, ECC S12.5.24 and S12.5.50, TCD MM.0.80, BL 695.a.31, OBL Vet.A1.f.58. DML T3.5.61 (bequest of Bp Steark 1745) lacks L8. TCC C.7.80 shows K1 missigned 'L.i.' and G7 misbound between G2 and G3.

With title page statement of royal privilege with *Maieſtatis*: BL 695.a.30 lacks D8; G19698 lacks F7.

Lacking title page statement of royal privilege: CUL Syn.8.56.93, KCC C.66.46. CUL Syn.8.56.89 lacks A1, L8; Pet F.5.3 lacks L8.

Imperf.: OBL Wood 134^3 lacks A1–C2, L7–8 (formerly owned by Gerald Langbaine: Kiessling 2002: no. 22).

Copies also at: BUL, CPH, DWL, EdUL, GUL, LCL, LHL, LPL, NT, OAS, OBC, OEC, OEF, OQC, OXC, SCL, UBL; FSL, GTS, NYPM, UTS, HHL, IUL, KSRL, NLC, OSU, PFL, TUL.

Bibliography: as 1566.1; Hill 1966: 195 (re. CCC SP.281).
Facsimile: The English Experience 214, Amsterdam, 1970, from KCC C.66.46.

1567.1: [Parker, Matthew, compiler], *A Defence of Priestes Mariages*. London: 1st edn Richard Jugge & John Kingston, 2nd edn Richard Jugge, 1567. STC 17518 and 17519; ESTC S112324 and S112350. AS1.

Excerpts from ASC (E), Rule of Chrodegang

Note: The second edition is the same as the first until gathering 2O, where the change is signalled on 2O1.4 by a change of fount used for the running titles, but 2O2.3 are still the same half-sheet as used for the first edition. Gatherings 2P–2? are all new to the second edition, except that the matter of 2Ƶ2ᵛ–2?2ᵛ constitutes an expanded version of the first edition sig.2P1ʳ–2P4ʳ.

Date: According to Strype (1711: 504) this book, presumably the first edition, was published in 1562. Arber (I.339) records from the Register of the Stationers' Company Jugge's payment of xiid for the licence to print this book 'intituled *a defence of preestes maryges stablesshed by the imperiall lawes of this Realme of Englonde*' in the year 22 July 1566 to 22 July 1567, presumably a reference to the second edition. Arber's index records the book as for sale from Richard Jugge in 1567 (Arber V.61, no.1165). Whether the two editions were separated by five years or not is a matter for conjecture, but on the evidence of the watermark it would appear that they were produced close together. The watermark is a hand throughout (Briquet 'Main' III), including the preliminaries and last two gatherings with apparently add-on signatures, sim. to Briquet 11365 (assigned to Vlaadingen 1557) with the letters RB, but incorporating a 3-shaped design as well, as, e.g., in Briquet 11377–79 and elsewhere.

Collation:

1st edition: 4⁰: π⁴ *² A–2O⁴ [$3 signed (-*2, I3, 2K3; 2N3 missigned N3)] 158 leaves, foliated [i–vi], 1–21 (13 misnumbered 3), then paginated 22–282, *283* (133/134 misnumbered 125/126, 137/138 misnumbered 129/130, 191 misnumbered 189, 192 misnumbered 190, 239 unnumbered, 240/241 omitted, 275–282 misnumbered 267–274).

2nd edition: 4⁰: Ƶ⁴ *² A–2Z⁴ 2Ƶ⁴ 2?⁶ [$3 signed (-*2, I3, 2K3, 2X3, 2Y3, 2Z3, 2Ƶ2,3; 2?2; 2N3 missigned N3)] 200 leaves, foliated [i–vi], 1–21 (13 misnumbered 3), then paginated 22–359 (133/134 misnumbered 125/126, 137/138 misnumbered 129/130, 191 misnumbered 189, 192 misnumbered 190, 239 unnumbered, 240/241 omitted), 360–367.

Context: The topic of this book was highly controversial. Following Philipp Melanchthon's *A very godly defense, full of lerning, defending the mariage of preistes,* t Lewis Beuchame [i.e. G. Joye] (Lipse: U. Hoff [i.e. Antwerp: widow of C. Ruremond], 1541) [STC 17798; cf. also 21804; USTC 410407; cf. also 700915], and John Poynet's *A defence for mariage of priestes, by Scripture and aunciente wryters* (London: Reyner Wolff, 1549) [STC 20176], Thomas Martin published *A Traictise declaryng and plainly prouyng, that the pretensed marriage of Priestes, and professed persones, is no mariage* (London: Robert Caly, 1554) [STC 17517].

The present book was compiled in reply. According to Strype (1711: 504–505) the reply was initially composed either by Sir Richard Morison or more probably by John Poynet, by now former bishop of Winchester (1551–3; d.1556), who certainly wrote *An Apologie fvlly avnsvveringe by Scriptures and aunceant Doctors a blasphemose Book gatherid by D Steph. Gardiner* [bp of Winchester 1531–51, 1553–5] *of late Lord Chauncelar D. Smyth of Oxford Pighius and other Papists as by ther books appeareth and of late set furth vnder the name of Tomas Martin Doctor of the Ciuile lawes* (*as of himself he saieth*) *against the godly mariadge of priests,* no place of publication or printer given, but the colophon says 'The end of the first bok of answer to Martin and other of that hereticall sect. 1556' [STC 20175]. However, CCC MS 583, 'Parker's MS parchment roll', written by an amanuensis, but containing amendments in a neat italic script that may well be Parker's own hand, states under the entry for 26 October 1554 (up to 6 August 1557), printed by Bruce and Perowne, *Correspondence of Parker* (1853), p. 483, t p.ix: 'Et scripsi defensione⟨m⟩ conjugii sacerdotu⟨m⟩ cont[ra] Thom[am] Martin'. In Trinity College Dublin, MS 248 is a series of notes taken from authorities on the subject with annotations by Parker (e.g., fos i^v–ii^r, 37^r; description in Colker 1991: I, 438–439), so Parker had this material to draw on. It was presumably the book he wrote in 1554 (which drew on the earlier materials) that was resurrected by Parker, who made the additions found in the second edition. Strype says

his Son in his *Memorial Book* speaks in some Places of his Fathers Book, *Of the Lawfulness of Priests Mariage*. It may be worthy noting, that in some of these Books, towards the Conclusion are Inlargements consisting of ten whole Sheets, about 76 Pages: For this Amplification is but in some few of the Books, and left out in the Rest; that the Book, I suppose, might be easier for Sale; and those few that were inlarged might be for the Archbishop's own Use, to present to his Friends.

1711: 505

John Parker's 'Memorial Book' is presumably Lambeth Palace MS 737 (see Strongman 1977), but a careful (though not exhaustive) check through it failed to locate any such reference. Whether Strype had this item in mind as his authority when he claimed that the augmented edition was for presentation to friends is not clear, but his inclusion of 'I suppose' suggests that he was making his own deduction. Whether relying on an authority or not Strype seems to be mistaken, since copies of the 2nd edition are now more numerous than the 1st.

SOURCES OF PASSAGES UTILIZING ANGLO-SAXON TYPES:

2Q3ʳ (p. 288)   From Laud misc. 636, 82ᵛ/16–17: ASC (E), annal for 1123 (Clark 1954: 44);

2S4ʳ (p. 306)   From Laud misc 636, 81ᵛ/29–82ʳ/4: ASC (E), annal for 1123 (Clark 1954: 43);

2T1ʳ (p. 308)   From Laud misc. 636, 87ʳ/19–24: ASC (E), annal for 1129 (Clark 1954: 51), the same source page as also used in 1566.1;

2Z4ʳ (p. 346)   From CCC MS 191, p. 127/3–7: *Rule of Chrodegang*, ch.lxii (Napier 1916: 77/6–8; Langefeld 2003: 301/15–17). In the printing of this passage the word-elements 'ʒehealðon ꝼẏn' at the end of the second line of OE should occur at the beginning of the line. Parker thought (erroneously) that this work was by Theodore (abp of Canterbury 668–90) t Ælfric, as evidenced by a note of the MS contents in his hand on fo [ii]v. The passage was included in a short extract copied by Joscelyn in Vitellius D.vii, 12ʳ.

There are also extracts (in Pica Roman type) from AS Latin manuscripts:

2Z2ᵛ–3ʳ (pp. 343–4)   From CCC 190, p. 197/1–4, via TCD 248, 46ʳ: Ælfric's First Latin Letter to Wulfstan (abp of York 1002–23) extracts (Fehr 1914: 48, §§111–112); also in CCC 265, p. 169/9–12; the printed text has 'dicimus' against MSS 'diximus';

2Z3ᵛ (p. 345)   From CCC 279, p. 3/7–14, via TCD 248, 46ʳ: Synodus Patricii, extract (Haddan and Stubbs 1869–73: II.328, §6); the printed text has 'contemnantur' against CCC 279 'contempnentur'.

Note: All these passages are marked in the MSS: for those in Laud misc. 636 marked with red ochre crayon see Whitelock 1954: 23; that in CCC 191 has the Latin text entered above the OE in Joscelyn's hand from p. 125 (where it is underlined in brown ink); that in CCC 190 has the text underlined in brown ink; that in CCC 265 has the text underlined in red crayon, with a red crayon pointing hand drawing attention to it and Joscelyn's triquetra-like mark in brown ink in the margin; that in CCC 279 has the text underlined in red crayon. Cf. also Page 1993: 89–92.

TYPE:

Main text in a Pica Textura (sometimes called 'Black Letter' or 'English') illustrated in Isaac 1936: pl. 54; it appears as 'Pica Englifh' on the type-specimen attributed to Nicholas Nicholls (1665?.1), and as 'Pique Englifh' in the Oxford University Specimen 1693, sig. C2, simulated by Hart 1970: 28, but the attribution of the type-design to Nicholls is rightly doubted by Mosley 1984: no. 168. Body 82. Face 75 × 2.4: 3.2.

AS1: The Parkerian Great Primer Anglo-Saxon acquired by Day (Body 112) occurs in the text as follows: 2Q3ʳ (p. 288), 2S4ʳ (p. 306), 2T1ʳ (p. 308), 2Z4ʳ (p. 346).

The Anglo-Saxon sorts are combined with Pierre Haultin's English-size Roman (Body 95), which shows the same x-height, on a Great Primer body.
Special sorts shown: 11 lower-case letters ð, f, ʒ, ı, p, ſ, t, ẏ; þ, ð, ƿ;
4 capitals E; Þ, Ð, Ƿ;
2 others ⁊, þ
Total: 17 sorts.

Copies seen: 1st edition: BL C.37.f.14; ECC 332.5.112, OBL Ashmole 1190 and A.11.5.Linc show ±2G1,4, and Ashmole 1190 lacks 2K3.

Copies also at: OAS, OJC, OSJ, Wigan, YML, TCD, ULim; FSL, HHL, HUL, YUB.

Copies seen: 2nd edition: BL 697.g.13 (the gift of Richard Rawlinson to Thomas Baker), G.12040, CCC SP.41, CUL SSS.22.9; CUL Syn.7.56.46 has 2S3 before 2S2; CUL B*.8.17 has 2O3 before 2O2 and lacks π, *, 2Ĩ, 2?; CCC Y.7.5, CSJ Gg.3.39, KCC A.6.88, DML G2.5.42 and OBL 4⁰ U 21 Jur. show ±2G1,4; TCD BB.kk.22 and GG.kk.47 show ±2G1.(?)4; QCC Q.4.16 lacks 2G1; CCC Y.7.5 and TCD BB.kk.22 lacks 2K3.

BL 697.g.13 and DML G2.5.42 include Martin's tract of 1554.

Copies also at: LBL, LPL, MJRUL, OBC, OCC, OMC, ONC, OQC, OXC, StA; FSL, HHL, HUL, MUL, UCBL, UTS.

Bibliography: Adams 1910; Arber 1875–94: I.339, V.61, no. 1165; Crawford 1910: I.2228; Kleist 2006 and 2008; Page 1993: pls 48–51; Sanders 1983: 537–538; Stanley 1995: 169; Strype 1711: 504–505.

1568.1: [Caius, John], *De Antiquitate Cantabrigiensis Academiæ*. London: Henry Bynneman, 1568. STC 4344; ESTC S107131. AS1.

Extracts from OE **Bede, Alfredian** PC, **Ælfric's Grammar,** ASC **(D)**

Collation: 8⁰: A–X⁸ Y⁸ (Y2 + χ1.2) Z–2A⁸ [$5 signed (-A1, Z5; Y2 χ1.2 both signed Y2)] 194 leaves, pp. 1–360 [the additional leaves Y2(χ1.2) are numbered '340.*b*', '340.*c*', '340.*d*', '340.*e*'], *361–384*. Supplemented by 8⁰ in 4s: ²A–E⁴ [$4 signed (-²C4, ²D4, ²E3,4; ²D3 signed C3)] 20 leaves, unpaginated.

Context: Written in response to Thomas Caius of Oxford's *Assertio antiquitatis Oxoniensis Academiae*, which is included in the present book as a supplement and which Strype (1711: 257–258) claims Parker showed Caius in manuscript. Parker is said by Strype to have vetted Caius's own text before approving its publication.

SOURCES OF PASSAGES UTILIZING ANGLO-SAXON TYPES:

M4ʳ OE Version of Bede's *Historia Ecclesiastica*, III.18, from CCC 41, p. 166/3–8, where the form of the text can only be from this MS (cf. Schipper 1899: 273, Miller 1890–8: I.1, 208, II.1, 226); note that the words 'ær on cent nam . ⁊ he him lareowas gesett æfter' have been inserted in CCC 41 by Joscelyn from collation with CUL Kk.3.18, 41ʳ/5–6 (Joscelyn's contribution to CCC 41, p. 66, noted by Ker 1990: 43).

S8ʳ King Alfred's Version of Gregory's *Pastoral Care*, Preface, from CCC 12, 3ʳ/23–6, where the forms *bisceop, rice, fiftigum* (with *ig*), *moncessa* are distinctive against OBL Hatton 20, 2ᵛ/3–4, (Ker 1956) and CUL Ii.2.4, 6ᵛ/7–8, but reference to Bishop Wærferth of Worcester on S7ᵛ indicates knowledge of Hatton 20 as well, perhaps via Joscelyn (cf. Page 1992: 47–8); note on Z8ʳ in the errata, 'moneceſſa' on S8ʳ (p. 287, line 9) is corrected to 'monceſſa', but not in AS type.

S8ʳᵛ Ælfric's *Grammar*, concluding sentence, from CUL Hh.1.10, 93ᵛ/6–7, where the forms *gemacigað, scillinge, xxx*, and *mancs* are distinctive (cf. Zupitza 1880: 296); alternatively the source could be Royal 15.B.xxii, 71ʳ/11–12, a supply leaf copied s.xvi² from Hh.1.10 and containing Parker's annotation in red ochre 'finis' to mark the end of the manuscript text.

T6ᵛ *Anglo-Saxon Chronicle* (D), Annal 885, from Tiberius B.iv, 37ᵛ/4–8, where the reading *westseaxna cyninges* is distinctive (cf. Thorpe 1861: I, 154–7); the name 'Marinus' has been underlined and Joscelyn's triquetra attention-mark occurs in the margin (the manuscript was part-owned and annotated by Joscelyn). Nowell's transcript, BL Add 43704, based on the E version, has a different version on fo 17ʳ.

X1ᵛ *Anglo-Saxon Chronicle* (D), Annal 877, from Tiberius B.iv, 35ᵛ/4–6, where the reading *herfæste* is distinctive (cf. Thorpe 1861: I, 146–147); in the manuscript there are suprascript collational amendments apparently from the A-version in the hand of Joscelyn, probably added later, since none are adopted here. Nowell's transcript, Add 43704, is based on the E version, and omits this passage, which should be on fo 17ʳ.

TYPE:

Main text in Robert Granjon's second Pica italic (of three), the *Cicero pendante* of 1562 (Dreyfus 1963: pl. 2; Gaskell 1972: fig. 12(a) on p. 25).

Body 82.5. Face 80 × 1.5: 2.5. Bynneman's use of this type in England is early.

AS1: The Parkerian Great Primer Anglo-Saxon occurs as follows:

D1ʳ	(p. 49)	text of Latin verses (includes several Roman capitals)
M3ʳ	(p. 181)	rh margin
M4ʳ	(p. 183)	text + rh margin
P3ʳ	(p. 229)	rh margin
S8ʳ	(p. 287)	text1 + rh margin + text2 + catchword
S8ᵛ	(p. 288)	text2 (cont.)
T6ᵛ	(p. 300)	text

The Anglo-Saxon sorts are combined with an English-size Roman, Granjon's *Gros* Cicero (Dreyfus 1963: pl. 4), which shows the same x-height, on a Great Primer body:

Special sorts shown: 12 lower-case letters: ð, ꝼ, ȝ, ı, ƞ, ꞃ, ꞇ, ẏ, ʒ; þ, ð, ꝑ;
4 capitals: Æ¹, Є, Ꝺ, Ᵽ;
3 others: ꝥ, ꝫ, ꝭ.
Total: 19 sorts.

Copies seen: ABH 5861 (with Y2χ1.2 loose in place), CUL Syn.8.56.74, Syn.8.56.97, CUA (formerly Registry) copy, CCC Y.7.1 lack ²E4; TCC VI.1.82 has Y2χ1.2 misbound with Y2 + Y2χ1 and Y6 + Y2χ2; CUL Cam.e.568.1, Pet D.1.59, CCC SP.417, ECC 338.8.49, TCC VI.1.88, DML 01.7.67, TCD II.n.32 (signed 'Edw: Wan[...]', 'Joh Worth'), RR.0.53 (signed 'Claud. Gilbert', 'John Oliver'), LPL 1568.01 lack Y2χ1.2; TCC VI.1.91 (gift of Samuel Sandars 1873) has B4.5 outside B3.6, and lacks Y2χ1.2, ²E4; BL G.12261 (with armorial stamp of Thomas Grenville inside front cover) lacks Y2χ1.2, Y4.5; KCC IX.3.10 lacks N4.5, Y2χ1.2, ²E4.

Copies also at: CGC, ChC, CJL, CMC, CPH, CSJ, LHL, LHU, LRCS, LSH, NLS, NT, OEF, OQC, OSJ, OTI, OUC, OXC, SDL, WIHM, YML, DML, GUB; FSL, DDUL, HHL, HUL, KSRL, LCP, NLC, UMI, UCBL, UPL, USLC, UTA, YUB; UAL, UML.

Bibliography: Arber 1875–94: I.382, v.64, no. 1226; Brooke 1985: 74–75; Bruce-Perowne 1853: 298–300; Eccles 1957; McKisack 1971: 70–71; Madan 1895–1931: II.16–18; Page 1992: 40–41; Plomer 1908: 232; Roberts 1912; Strype 1711: 257–258; Tite 2003: 106–107.

1568.2: Lambarde, William (drawing on materials supplied by Laurence Nowell the antiquary (1530–c.1570; ODNB), as stated on A3ʳ), *Archaionomia*. London: John Day, 1568. STC 15142; ESTC 122075. GR 6281. AS1.

Note: Lambarde's note in CCA MS Lit.E.2, 33ʳ, refers to the printing of I–II Cnut '3 Septemb. 1568'.

Laws

Collation: 4⁰: πA–D⁴ πE² C–Y⁴ 2A–2Q⁴ [$4 signed (-πA1,2 πB2 πD4 πE2 C1.4 D4 M2 O3 2M3 2O3; 2E4 and 2G4 missigned 'Ee.iij.' and 'Gg.iij.' respectively)] 162 leaves, foliated [i–xviii], 0, 1–140 (fos 19, 45, 47, 57, 73, 77, 82, 94 unnumbered; 74 misnumbered 72, 75 misnumbered 74, 86 misnumbered 85, 87 misnumbered 86, 100 misnumbered 10, 112 misnumbered 121, 113 misnumbered 13-), *141–143*.
Different states shown by textual variants on sig. I3ʳ (fo 26).

State 1: | State 2:

reddendum, neq; enim alio quocunq; iudiciali libro opus fuerit: hoc folum meminerit qui fedet in alios Iudex, nolle fe aliam de alijs proferre fentētiam, quam de fe ipfe latam irí voluerit. Vbi vero propagato dei euangelio plurimæ nationes verbo dei fidē adiunxerant, nonnulli tam in Anglia, quā alijs in regionibus epifcoporū aliorūqȝ clariſſimorū fapientū conuentus agebāntur, atq; hij diuina edoci miferatione cuiq; iā primū peccāti pœnā imperabāt pecuniariā, eiufqȝ (abfq; omni diuinæ offenſionis cōcitatione) exigēdæ munus magiftratibus (data prius venia) deferebāt.... | *eſſe reddenduμ, neq; enim alio quocūq; iudiciali libro opus fuerit: hoc foluμ meminerit qui fedet in alios Iudex, nolle fe aliā de alijs proferre fentētiam, quā de fe ipfe latā irí voluerit. Vbi vero propagato dei euangelio plurimæ nationes atqȝ adeò Angli verbo dei fidē adiunxeraμt, nōnulli per orbē terrarū cōciones, atq; etiā in Anglia, epifcoporū aliorūqȝ clariſſimorū fapiētū conuētus agebātur, atq; hij diuina edo ci miferatione cuiq; iā primū peccāti pœnā impera bāt pecuniariā, eiufqȝ (abfq; omni diuinæ offenſionis cōcitatioμe) exigēdæ munus magiftratibus (data prius venia) deferebāt: ...*

State 3 differs from State 2 in having *cœtus* instead of *cōciones* in line 6.

SOURCES OF PASSAGES UTILIZING ANGLO-SAXON TYPES:

(1) C1v–G3r   From a MS now presumed lost, which contained readings affiliated with those in BL Add. 43703 (Nowell), BL (Dept of Printed Books) Henry Davis Gift M30 (Nowell), Nero A.i, CCA Lit.B.2 (Nowell), CCC 383 (item 3, 23r/5–30v/19), and a Quadripartitus MS: Laws of Ine, coll. Liebermann I, 89–123. [Wormald 1997: 262–274]

(2) G3v–O1r   From Nero A.i (probably); a transcript by Nowell survives in CCA Lit.B.1, 245r–69v: Laws of Alfred, coll. Liebermann I, 26–89.

(3) O1v–3r   From CCC 383, item 19, 57r/17–57v/23: Prologue to Laws of Alfred and Guthrum, coll. Liebermann I, 1268. [Wormald 1997: 251–254]

(4) O3v–P4r   From CCC 383, items 14–15, 52v/9–54v/2: Laws I and II Eadweard, coll. Liebermann I, 138–44. [Wormald 1997: 251–254]

(5) P4v–R1r   From CCC 383, item 9, 13r/1–14v/24: Laws of Alfred and Guthrum, coll. Liebermann I, 128–134. [Wormald 1997: 251–254]

(6) R1v–R3r   Prob taken from the 'Elizabethan Anglo-Saxon' translation by Nowell from the Latin 'Quadripartitus', using the version in CCC 70, pp. 19/27–20/14, a s.xiv[1] copy of Claudius D ii: Laws I Æthelstan, coll. Liebermann I, 146–9, with Titus A xxvii. [Sisam 1953: 232–258; Wormald 1997: 240]

(7) R3v–V1r   From a MS now lost, which contained readings affiliated with those in BL Add. 43703 (Nowell), CCA Lit.B.2 (Nowell), CCC 383 (item 10, 14v/24–15v/26), and a Quadripartitus MS: Laws II Æthelstan 1, coll. Liebermann I, 150–166. [Wormald 1997: 256–262]

(8) V1v–V4r/7   From a MS, not now extant, with readings affiliated to the MSS itemised in (7), as Add 43703, 265r–266r: Laws V Æthelstan, coll. Liebermann I,

166–169. Now extant in an AS MS only in RKA DRc/R1 (= Textus Roffensis, but this was not known by Lambarde until 1573: see 1576.2).

(9) V3ᵛ/7–X1ʳ/11   Prob taken from the 'Elizabethan Anglo-Saxon' translation by Nowell from the Latin 'Quadripartitus', using the version in CCC 70, pp. 23/47–24/15 (lacks Liebermann's §30 as does 1568.2), a s.xiv¹ copy of Claudius D ii: 'Norðleoda laga', coll. Liebermann I, 458–461. Now known to be extant in CCC 201 and RKA DRc/R1, but Lambarde did not know these MSS by 1568. [Sisam 1953: 232–258; Wormald 1997: 240]

(10) V4ᵛ/9–X1ʳ   Prob taken from the 'Elizabethan Anglo-Saxon' translation by Nowell from the Latin 'Quadripartitus', using the version in CCC 70, p. 24/16–30, a s.xiv¹ version of Claudius D.ii (Wormald 1994: 121): 'Mircna laga', coll. Liebermann I 462–465. Now known to be extant in CCC 201 and RKA DRc/R1, but Lambarde did not know these MSS by 1568. [Sisam 1953: 232–258; Wormald 1997: 240]

(11) X1ᵛ–Y1ʳ   From CCC 383, items 1617, 54ᵛ/4–56ʳ/11: Laws I and II Eadmund, coll. Liebermann I, 184–90. [Wormald 1997: 251–254]

(12) Y1ᵛ–2A2ʳ   From Nero A.i: Laws II and III Edgar, coll. Liebermann I, 194–205; derivation from Nero A.i, fo 41ff., is shown by readings such as *mynstre*, *his sulh gega* (II.1,1), *he* (II.1,2), *ðonne* (II.2,1), *deoror* (III.8,2). [Wormald 1997: 254–255]

(13) 2A2ᵛ–2B1ʳ   From CCC 383, item 7, 11ʳ/10–12ʳ/20: Laws I Æthelred, coll. Liebermann I, 216–20. [Wormald 1997: 251–254]

(14) 2B1ᵛ–2C2ʳ   From CCC 383, item 24, 59ᵛ/17–62ʳ/2: Laws II Æthelred, coll. Liebermann I, 220–226. [Wormald 1997: 251–254]

(15) 2C2ᵛ–2D2ʳ   From CCC 383, item 25, 62ʳ/3–63ʳ/26: Agreement re. Welsh Marches, coll. Liebermann I, 374–378. [Wormald 1997: 251–254]

(16) 2D2ᵛ–2M1ʳ   From Nowell's 'composite' version in CCA Lit.E.2 (annotated by Lambarde), with marks of printer's ink and thumb-prints (particularly marked on fos 27ᵛ–28ʳ), and on fo 33ʳ 'excusum [*printed*] 3 Septemb. 1568'), based on Harley 55, with collations from CCC 383, items 12–13, 38ʳ/1–52ᵛ/1, and possibly Nero A.i: Laws I and II Cnut, coll. Liebermann I, 278–371. [Wormald 1997: 241–250, also Dammery 1994]

The following three items make up the 'Tripartita' [Wormald 1997: 250–251]:

(17) 2M1ᵛ–2M3ʳ   From CCC 70, pp. 53/10–55/9, collated with a Tripartita MS (Liebermann I, xli), probably a copy by Nowell (now lost), of which a fair copy survives as Huntington HM 26341: Laws of William I, coll. Liebermann I, 486–491.

(18) 2M3ᵛ–2Q2ʳ   From CCC 70, pp. 55/10–72/46 (= 2P4 bottom), but matter on 2Q1–2Q2ʳ/10 not in CCC 70, so probably from Nowell's copy of the Tripartita

in the antecedent of Huntington HM 26341: Laws of Edward the Confessor (= Retractatus), coll. Liebermann I, 627–670.

(19) 2Q2ʳ/11–2Q2ᵛ   From CCC 70, pp. 72/47–74/27, probably supplemented by Nowell's copy of the Tripartita in the antecedent of Huntington HM 26341: On the Dukes of Normandy (not in Liebermann).

TYPE:

AS1: Main OE text in the Parkerian Great Primer Anglo-Saxon. The Anglo-Saxon sorts are combined with Pierre Haultin's English Roman on a Great Primer body (some words of Latin set in Roman on ᵖE2ᵛ). The specimen on B2ʳ shows 19 special sorts:

    11 lower-case letters   ð, ꝼ, ȝ, ı, ꝑ, ſ, τ, ẏ; þ, ð, ƿ;
    5 capitals   Æ¹, Æ², Є, Ꝏ, Ð;
    3 others   þ, ꝫ, ꝯ

Total: 19 sorts.

It omits lower case ȝ, upper case Ꝺ ẞ Ꝑ Ꝟ X and ꝯ. The punctus versus appears for the first time in this specimen, but is not used in the text until H4ᵛ.

Special sorts shown in the text:

    11 lower-case letters   ð, ꝼ, ȝ, ı, ꝑ, ſ, τ, ẏ; þ, ð, ƿ;
    9 capitals   Æ¹, Æ², Є, Ꝺ, Ꝏ, ẞ; Ꝑ, Ð, Ƿ (on S2ᵛ);
    4 others   þ, ꝫ, ꝫ, ꝯ

Total: 24 sorts.

The facing Latin translation up to 2D2ʳ utilizes François Guyot's Great Primer Italic.

The facing Latin translation from 2D3ʳ to 2M1ʳ utilizes Pierre Haultin's Pica Roman (Body 82.5). From 2M1ᵛ to 2Q2ʳ the same fount is utilized for the Latin text.

The dedicatory letter (A2ʳ–B1ᵛ) utilizes Guyot's Double Pica Italic.

The Pica Italic on ᵖB2–ᵖE1, T2ʳ (where it has been leaded), 2B3ʳ, 2C3ʳ, 2M2ʳ–3ʳ, 2O4ʳ–2P4ᵛ is Robert Granjon's second Pica Italic, the *Cicero pendante* (Body 82.5).

Granjon's Long Primer Italic, known as 'l'immortelle' is utilized on E1ᵛ (bottom), O3ʳ, 2M1ʳ, and 2Q2–4.

Copies seen:

State 1 with undefective catchword at P4ᵛ: CSJ C.11.31 (one of Lambarde's own copies with corrections and annotations in his hand (including glosses, partly continuous, on C1ᵛ–D3ᵛ, perhaps for Thomas Potter, to whom Lambarde apparently gave the book), subsequently owned by Geoffrey Toller 1638 and Thomas Baker, from whom it came to St John's); TCD DD.ii.22;

State 2 with undefective catchword at P4^v: CCC Y.7.13; KCC M.71.9^1 (the gift of Richard Day 1576; cf. Munby 1948: 228–9); OBL 4º.L.5.Jur.Seld. (Selden's copy with updated readings and annotations in Lambarde's own hand);

State 3: DML H.8.45 (signed 'Ralphe Rokebye' 1581, also 'John Cressie' on B2^r);

State 3 with undefective catchword at P4^v: CCC Y.7.14, CTH D*.7.16; OBL Gough Sax.lit.151 (signed John Marshall 1583, John Grene 1585, both of Lincoln's Inn).

State 1/2: CQC E.1.4 (signed 'Thomas Waaklyn' and 'R. Bryan. 1671') is unusual in showing State 1 on I2^r but State 2 on I3^r; it shows the defective catchword on P4^v, and the misnumbering of fos 74, 112.

BL Add 11750 is Sir Symonds D'Ewes's copy with his annotations.

Copies also at: CCA, ChC, ChCL, CJC, CPC, CPH, TCC, DRD, ECL, LGI, LPL, LSH, NLS, OAS, OBC, OCC, OEC, OEF, OLC, OQC, OSA, OTI, YML, BSB, GUB; FSL, NYPL, BMC, DDUL, GCL, HUL, IUL, KSRL, NLC, NWU, UCLA. HHL, RB 62136 shows Lambarde's annotations (Berkhout 2000: 419).

Bibliography: Arber 1875–94: v.65, no. 1240; Bately 1992; Berkhout 2000: 419; Binns 1990: 359–360; Brackmann 2012: 196–200; Catto 1981: 372–374; Clement 1997: 212–213; Grant 1996; Keynes 2014: 151 (on the map on πD4^v); Niles 2015: 62–65; Sisam 1953: 232–258; Warnicke 1973: 22–26; Wormald 1994; Wormald 1997.

1568.3: Smith, Sir Thomas, *De recta & Emendata Linguae Anglicae Scriptione, Dialogus*. Paris: Robert Estienne the Younger 1568. USTC 140541; STC 22856.5; ESTC S4906. CAS1.

Letter-symbols.

Collation: 4º: *² a–l⁴ [$3 signed (-*1)] 46 leaves, foliated [i–ii], 1–44.

TYPE:

Main text in Claude Garamont's Great Primer Roman (Body 118) interspersed with Garamont's 4th Great Primer Italic.

CAS1: Special sorts for phonetic symbols include several explicitly based on an Anglo-Saxon model: ꝼ, þ, ẏ; Ð; and others which may have been inspired by an Anglo-Saxon model: *e*, ȝ, ı. They are of Italic slant designed to fit with Garamont's 4th Great Primer Italic. The cutting is of a high standard and may have been done by Guillaume I Le Bé (1525–98). Contemporary interest in Paris in Anglo-Saxon script is shown by the calligraphic imitator Pierre Hamon (Armstrong 1963: 548–51), but he used a 'Bastard Saxon' model that is unlikely to have been that behind the design of Smith's special sorts.

Copies seen: CUL Aa*.3.26² (D), M*.11.24 (E); ECC FB 11¹ (*2 occurs after l4; given by the author to Walter Mildmay, founder of EC, 3 Dec 1568; contemporary gold-tooled vellum binding); S5.3.17² (Abp Sancroft's copy, lacks *2).

Copies also at: BL, CCA, CCC, CMC, CPH, TCC, LCL, NT, OBL, OAS, OEC, OQC, OSJ, OTC, OWoC, OXC, SSL, DEWL, DML, ABM, PBN, GUB, VON; BPM, NLC, IUL, YUB.

Note: According to Berkhout (2000: 418–419), the copy in University of Virginia, Alderman Library, Dept of Special Collections, Atcheson L. Hench Collection, *DA358 L3 S4 1568, has annotations by Lambarde.

Bibliography: Armstrong 1953–4: 48–52; Le Bé [1967]; Dewar 1964; Dobson 1968: I, 46–62; Howe 1938 (on Le Bé); Hughes 2014; Lucas 2000; Schreiber 1982: no. 238.

Facsimile: English Linguistics 1500–1800, no. 109 (Menston: Scolar, 1968), from BL C.46.g.2^1.

Danielsson, Bror, *Sir Thomas Smith Literary and Linguistic Works* [*1542, 1549, 1568*], Part III (Stockholm: Almqvist & Wiksell, 1983). Facsimile with facing MnE translation.

1570.1: Foxe, John, *Actes and Monuments*. 2nd edition. London: John Day, 1570. STC 11223; ESTC S113108. GR5277. AS1.

Extracts from 1566.2, 1567.1

Collation (cf. Dunkin 1947–48: 160) vol. II, bks 7 and 8 only:

2^0 in 6s: π^1 2Aa–2Yy^6 3A–3R^6 3S^6 (3S4 + χ1) 3T–3Z^6 3&^{6} 3*^{4} [$4 signed (-3*4)]. 282 leaves, paginated 923–1481, *1482* (p. 938 unnumbered; pp. 1093, 1095 misnumbered 1083, 1085, pp. 1371, 1374 misnumbered 1355, 1366, p. 1449 misnumbered 1440).

SOURCES OF PASSAGES UTILIZING ANGLO-SAXON TYPES:

3K4^v/a /49–53 (p. 1302a) From **1566.2**, A3^v, Ælfric's 'Excusatio Dictantis' (opening statement) at the end of his homily *Depositio S. Martin* (Godden 1979: XXXIV);

3K4^v/a /60–3 (p. 1302a) From **1566.2**, A4, Ælfric's *Grammar*, opening statement from OE Preface (cf. Zupitza 1880: 2);

3K4^v/b/13–32 (p. 1302b) From **1566.2**, H5^v–H7^v, Ælfric's letter to Wulfsige III (bp of Sherborne 992–1002) extracts (Fehr 1914: §§133–142) omitting H5^v/1–14 (Fehr 1914: §§133–134);

3K4^v/b/64–3K5^r/b/19 (pp. 1302b–1303b) From **1566.2**, H8^v–6^v, Ælfric's second letter to Wulfstan (abp of York 1002–23) extracts (Fehr 1914: §§86–95, 97–109);

3K5^v/b/52–3L1^v/b/7 (pp. 1304b–1308b) From **1566.2** (as shown by the text followed at G6^v/G7^v), C3^v–H3^v, Ælfric's *Sermo de Sacrificio in die Pascae* (Godden 1979: XV), with substantive omissions on pp. 1306/7 comprising E5^v/16–E7^v/17 (Godden: 157–73), and F6^v/1–5 (Godden: 222–4), generally faithful, but ꞃpa omitted p. 1305b/13 and sporadic interchange of ð/þ, ⁊/anð, -e/-Ø;

3N3^r/a/19–23 (p. 1335a) From **1567.1**, 2T1^r, *ASC* (E), annal for 1129 (Clark 1954: 51), the same manuscript source page (but a shorter extract) also used in **1566.1**, B7^r.

TYPE:

Main text in a Pica Textura (Body 82; Face 78 × 2: 2.8).

Pierre Haultin's Pica Roman occurs occasionally, the longest passage being 11 lines on 3N1ʳ/b. A Small Pica Roman (Body 72) occurs on 3X2ʳ–5ʳ, and a Long Primer Roman (Body 68) on 3X6.

Robert Granjon's 2nd Pica Italic (*pendante*) occurs passim, e.g. 2Aa5ᵛ–6ʳ/a.

Ameet Tavernier's Pica Italic occurs in a secondary capacity (presumably when the Granjon was all used up in setting), e.g. on 2A6ʳ/a–6ᵛ/a, 2K6ᵛ–2Llr, 2M5ᵛ–2N1ʳ.

Robert Granjon's Long Primer Italic, known as 'l'immortelle', occurs occasionally, e.g. on 2R1ᵛ/a, 2V1ʳ/a, 2V4, 3I2ʳ–5ʳ, and it is used to gloss the AS lower-case letters in the AS specimen on 3K5ᵛ.

AS1: The Parkerian Great Primer Anglo-Saxon is shown in the specimen on 3K5ᵛ/b (p. 1304) with the following special sorts:

    12 lower-case letters: ð, ꝼ, ȝ, ı, ꞃ, ſ, τ, ẏ, 3 (= z); þ, ð, ƿ;
    5 capitals: Æ², ꞅ, Þ, Ð, Ƿ;
    1 other: ⁊

  Total: 18 sorts;

omitting Æ¹, Є, Ⱶ, Ϻ, X, lower-case ⁊, þ, j (the latter sort not being used at all despite its earlier appearance in 1568.2).

AS text occurs in the Parkerian Great Primer Anglo-Saxon (Body 112) as indicated above. The Anglo-Saxon sorts are combined with Pierre Haultin's English Roman (Body 95), which shows the same x-height, on a Great Primer body (three lines of Latin set in Roman on 3K5ʳ/b/3–5 (p. 1303b)).

Special sorts shown: 11 lower-case letters: ð, ꝼ, ȝ, ı, ꞃ, ſ, τ, ẏ; þ, ð, ƿ;
    7 capitals: Æ¹, Æ², Є, Ⱶ, Є, ꞅ, Ð;
    3 others: þ, ⁊, ⁊.

    Total: 21 sorts.

Not found: z; X; Þ, Ƿ; j.

Total AS sorts shown overall: 13 + 9 + 3 = 25.

> **Copy seen:** CUL K*.7.16 (contemporary gold-tooled binding probably by John de Planche (cf. Foot 1978–83, II, 79–80, no. 47, also Foot 1993: 187–189, Nixon 1970: 243–253), tp on membrane, illustrations hand-coloured).
>
> **Copies also at:** AUL, BL, BSE, CCA, TCC, DWL, HCL, LPL, LUL, OBL, OBrC, OHC, OLC, OMaC, ONC, OOC, OSJ, YML; FSL, HCP, HHL, HUL, LCP, NLC, UCH, UCLA, YUB.

Bibliography: Arber V.73, no. 1435; Clement 1997: 214–215; Dunkin 1947–48; Evenden & Freeman 2011; Haller 1967: ch. IV; King 2006; Newcombe 1997; Oliver 1946–47.

1571.1: [Parker, Matthew (gen. ed.), John Joscelyn (prob ed.) and] John Foxe (intr.), *The Gospels of the Fower Evangelistes.* London: John Day, 1571. STC 2961; ESTC S102559; DMH 131; GR 5860. AS1.

Collation: 4⁰: A⁴ ¶² B–Y⁴ Aa–Yy⁴ AA–HH⁴ [$4 signed (-A1, Q4; Cc1–4 missigned C1–4)] 210 leaves, paginated [i–xii], 1–408 (1, 120, 193 unnumbered)].

State 1 shows Dd1,3 missigned D1,3; State 2 shows Dd1,3 correctly signed.

SOURCES OF PASSAGES UTILIZING ANGLO-SAXON TYPES:

AS text of the four gospels (ed. Liuzza 1994) from Bodley 441, 1ʳ–55ʳ (Mt), 57ʳ–90ʳ (Mk), 91ʳ–150ʳ (Lk), 151ʳ–94ᵛ (Jn), which is followed almost slavishly, with introductory headings and the statements of appropriate days for using texts as readings in the liturgy from CUL Ii.2.11 (Liuzza's A). Some passages in Bodley 441 (Liuzza's B) are on supply leaves of s.xvi² with the text copied from CCC 140 (Liuzza's Cp): Mk 1.1–4.37, Mk 16.14–20, Lk 16.14–17.1 (but a few readings differ, esp. 16.30 *ferde* = Cp *færð*), Lk 24.51–53, Jn 21.9 *gewrit* to 21.25 AMEN, distinctive readings against A being 20.14 *se hælend wæs*, 20.31 *habbað*, 21.7 *on his tunecan*, 21.7 *innan sæ*, 21.9 *on fyr*, 21.20 *se ðe*, but 20.19 *dura* (with A), and 21.24 *gewitnys* (with CA) not Cp's erron. *gewit*, the latter two quite possibly editorial amendments.

Distinctive readings from B (of which there are more in Mt and Mk because C (Otho C.i1) does not survive for Mt or much of Mk) include:

Mt 3.7 *gerihtwisendra*, 3.14 *cymsðu*, 4.10 *geeaðmestð*, 5.32 *forlegnysse*, 6.3 *swyre*, 6.31 *ymhydige*, 7.16 *cwysþu*, 8.24 *þæræ*, 9.17 *ealdæ*, 9.38 *wyryhtan*, 10.11 *þere*, 11.8 *cynega*, 14.32 *he wæron on þam scipe*, 15.19 *hyfele geþancas, utrihthæmedu*, 16.28 *cumendne*, 18.1 *wensþu*, 18.18 *heofenan* (1st), 19.9 *se þe þæt forlætene*, 21.7 *fola*, 21.41 *hyfelan*, 22.7 *cinc* (cp. 22.2, 11), 23.5 *healsbec*, 23.9 *heofenon*, 23.39 *sycgon*, 24.26 *westynne*, 24.42 *Wacigað*, 27.15 *mannan*, 27.20 *hælynd*, 27.29 *bysmredon*;

Mk 5.8 *eala þu unclæna*, 5.10 *dydde*, 5.25 *blodes ryre*, 6.31, 32 *stowæ*, 6.50 *wundor*, 7.5 *gesetednyssa*, 12.43 *mæstπ*, 13.8 *aristþ*, 14.72 *crewe*;

Lk 1.62 *woldo*, 9.53 *onfeng*, 12.43 *dondne* BC, 18.18 *godne* BA, 18.33 *swigað*, 22.61 *crewe* BC, 22.56 *sittendne*, 23.11 *his hirede*, 23.21 B's *aho\. / hine aho\./ hine* becomes *ahoh hyne ahoh hyne* not as Cp *ahoð hine ahoð hine*, so it has been 'corrected' erron;

Jn 4.17 *næft* BC, 4.52 *gyrsandæg* BC, 5.14 *geworde*, 5.43 *underfoð*, 8.15 *flæsc*, 12.19 *betwux* BCR, 12.19 *ne fremað*, 12.35 *habbon* BCA, 17.10 *7 mine synt þine*, 17.14 *ne om* BCR but *ne eom* as Cp in 17.16, 18.15 *hælend*, 18.16 *þærut* BC, 19.11 *næfðest*, 19.24 *ure* BCA.

There is very little evidence of MS collation, and what there is suggests that, apart from rubrics and headings, Cp was the only MS used for this purpose.

In Mt there is no evidence, unless 8.17 *þæt gecweden* as Cp (not B *þæt þe gecweden*); 22.2, 11, 27.42 *cyning(e)* as Cp for B *cing(e)*; 26.25 *Cwyst þu* as Cp for

B *cwystu*; 26.53 *Wenst þu* as Cp for B *Wenstu*, are evidence of use of Cp, but such alterations (or omissions) were well within the capability of Parker's team. [In Mt 24.27, 31, 38, *oð* is miswritten *ot* in B, corrected only at 24.31. All are correct in 1571.1, as in Cp.]

In Mk 6.22 *cyning* (as A) for B *cincg* could be editorial. Mk 6.29 has Cp's *lic namon* not B's *lic'h'amon namon*, 9.21 has Cp's *Ac gyf* not B's erron. *Aagif*, 11.31 has MSS's *ge* not B's omission of same, 14.12 has Cp MSS's *wylt þu* not B's *wyltu*. Lk 4.34 has ACp's *nadzarenisca* against B's *nadzarenisa*, 8.13 has Cp's *costnunge* not B's *costunge*, 11.4 has A's *costnunge* against BCp's *costunge* (pres. an erron. correction); in Lk 19.29 Cp's *genemned* (A *nemned*) is followed in preference to B's *genem*; 20.15 ACp's *ofslegene* is followed in preference to B's *ofslege*; 22.46 has A's *costnunge* instead of BCp's *costunge*; 23.5 has *folc* as in other MSS against B's erron. *floc*. These alterations too could be editorial.

In Jn 1.1 ON FRVMAN *wæs*, lacking in B, is supplied from A (whence also the rubric) where Cp has ON FRYMÐE WÆS; Jn 3.21 has *cymð* from Cp *cymþ* not B's *cymd*; 7.43 has Cp's *ungeþwærnes* not B's *ungehwærnes*, again 10.19; 8.43 omits an extra portion of text with Cp (and Bp's Bible) against BCRH, 13.5 has ACp's *þwoh* against BC *hwoh*, at 14.21 B's erron *Seð* corr. to *Se þe*, 15.13 has Cp's *mara* against BCAR *maran*, 15.21 has Cp's *forþam* against BC *for þe*, 16.20 has Cp's *heofiað* against BCRH *heofað*.

TYPE:

AS1: The main AS text is in the Parkerian Great Primer Anglo-Saxon. The Anglo-Saxon sorts are combined with Pierre Haultin's English Roman, which shows the same x-height, on a Great Primer body.

The specimen on A1ᵛ shows 25 special sorts, omitting upper-case ɪ:

    12 lower-case letters: ð, f, ᵹ, ı, ꝑ, ſ, τ, ẏ, ȝ (= z); þ, ð, ƿ;
    10 capitals: Æ¹, Æ², Є, Ꝺ, ꟽ, Ꞩ, X; Þ, Ð, Ƿ;
    3 others: þ, ɪ, ꞌ.

Total: 25.

Special sorts shown in the text:

    12 lower-case letters: ð, f, ᵹ, ı, ꝑ, ſ, τ, ẏ, ȝ (=z); þ, ð, ƿ;
    9 capitals: Æ¹, Æ², Є, Ꝺ, ꟽ, Ꞩ; Þ, Ð, Ƿ;
    4 others: þ, ɪ, ɪ, ꞌ.

Total: 25.

Total special sorts shown in the specimen and the text: 12 + 10 + 4 = 26.

A change in the casting of the special sort ð occurs between sig. Gg and Hh. Up to Gg4ᵛ/26 'þencð' the ð shows a space in front of it that distances it from the letter it follows. From Hh1ʳ/2 'ðoð' the ð fits snugly up to its preceding letter.

The text of the Bishop's Bible on the outer side of the main AS text is in a Brevier Textura (sometimes called 'Black Letter' or 'English'; Body 54 mm).

The statements of appropriate days for using texts as readings in the liturgy are set in Robert Granjon's Long Primer Italic, known as 'l'immortelle'.

The arabesque ornament on A1, Q4^r, 2C4^v, 2H4^v is attributed to Granjon (Dreyfus 1963: pl. 2; it also appears in Plantin 1567).

Note: Wood-cut large initials (somewhat crude) are provided for Є, Þ, Ð, Ƿ.

Copies seen: CCA W/I.4.21 (State 2 with Dd.1, 3 correctly signed); CUL I.24.9 (sel.c) (signed gift of Matthew Parker 1574), I.24.10 (sel.c) (signed by Thomas Knyvett = McKitterick 1978: no. 295), Young 140; BSL 200B71; CCC Y.7.17 (acquired 1928); ECC S1.4.19 (gift of Abp Sancroft); CPH N.4.31 (gift of Andrew Perne); TCD A.f.3; BL C.10.a.4 (signed 'Geo. Davenport. 1658.'); OBL 4°.G.24.Th.Seld. (John Selden's copy signed on A1^r and in s.xvii binding), Douce E.239, Gough Sax.Lit.146 (signed by John Stury and Wm Bohun on A1^r). State 1 with variant signings in sig. Dd: KCC M.71.9^2 (formerly A.14.16, bound with copy of 1568.2, the gift of Richard Day in 1576; cf. Munby 1948: 228–229), and M.34.52; LPL **E130 (with armorial stamp of (?) Thomas Sackville KG, earl of Dorset (d.1608) on cover); LPL 1571.3 (with armorial stamp of Abp Whitgift on cover); OBL MS Laud misc.476 (with armorial stamp of Abp Laud on cover, and his signature on sig. A1^v; some Latin glosses to the AS in hand of s.xvii). LPL 1571.31 (with armorial stamp of Abp Laud on cover, and his signature on sig. B1^r) has the text of the Bishop's Bible amended throughout in hand of (?)s.xvii and references to CCC MS 140, with which the book seems to have been compared.

CSS T.5.50 (gift of Robert Legard, s.xvii) lacks sig. Dd (blank leaves supplied in lieu); ECC 328.2.101 (signed Joseph Holand 1586) lacks F2.3, sig. H I K L, Tt2.3, AA2.3.

Copies also at: CMC, CQC, LCL, NLS, NT, OAS, OBC, OBrC, OCC, OEC, OEF, OLC, OMaC, OOC, OQC, OSJ, OUC, OWmC, RCL, WAL; FSL, NYCU, NYPL, NYPM, BPM, GTS, HCP, HHL, HUL, IUL, KSRL, UCBL, UCLA, YUB; ATL.

Bibliography: Clement 1997: 215–216; Haller 1967: ch. IV; Munby 1948; Murphy 1968; Niles 2015: 60–62; Tite 2003: 152–153 (Otho C.i owned by (?)Joscelyn).

1572.1: Parker, Matthew [assisted by John Joscelyn], *De Antiquitate Britannicæ Ecclesiæ*. London: John Day, 1572. STC 19292; ESTC S102901. AS1.

Note: The statement that the book was printed by Day is found only in some copies: viz. CUL Sel.3.229, LUB Thys.915.

Extracts from Wulfstan, Sermo Lupi; Charter of Henry I (1100)

Collation: 2° in 4s:

No two copies of this book are made up exactly alike. The basic structure of the book consists of a number of blocks of gatherings, which for convenience and clarity may be called booklets. To this basic structure a number of sub-booklets are sometimes added, which may occur in various positions.

Booklet 1: De vetustate Britannicæ Ecclesiæ testimonia.

π^2 ¶^{4} (±¶4) A^4 B^4 (±B4+χ1.2) C–E^4 F–G^2. [\$4 signed (-¶4, G2); B4(χ1) signed B5] 32 leaves, paginated [xii] + 1–45, [46–48] (B4 numbered 15a–b, B4(χ1.2) numbered 16a–d; 10 misnumbered 15).

Sub-booklet 1A: 'Augustinus' (in triple columns)

^{1}A–^{1}C^4. [\$4 signed] 12 leaves, paginated [1], 2–24.

Sub-booklet 1.1: English/Welsh bishops, arms of 1572 incumbents, list, index.

^{2}¶^{2}. [^{2}¶2 signed]. 2 leaves, unnumbered.

Sub-booklet 1.2: Chronological list of bishops by king's reign.

[☞]^2. [\$2 signed]. 2 leaves, unnumbered.

Booklet 2: Archbishops of Canterbury, Augustine to Reginald Pole.

^{2}A–^{2}G^4 H^4 I^6 K–O^4 P^4 (P3+χ1–4) Q–Y^4 Aa–Mm^4 Nn^4 (±Nn2) Oo^4 Pp^4 (±Pp1+χ1) Qq–Yy^4 AA–HH^4 II^2. [\$4 signed (-^{2}A4, Gg4, Hh4, Kk4, Ll4, Mm4, Nn4, Oo4, Pp4, Qq4, Rr4, Ss4; ±^{2}A2 signed 'A*.ij', ^{2}A2(χ1.2) both signed 'A.iij.', P(χ1,2) signed 'P.iiij.', 'P.v.')] 219 leaves, paginated 1–424 (92 unnumbered (blank), 255, 315, 348 misnumbered 254, 351, 346 respectively, A2(χ1.2) numbered 4a–d, P3(χ1–4) numbered 122a–h, Pp(χ1) numbered 294a–b).

Booklet 3: 'Matthæus' (Archbishop Parker).

χ–2χ^4 3χ^6. 14 leaves, paginated 1–18, (17) (3χ2^v unnumbered (blank), 19–22, [23], 3χ5^v–3χ6 unnumbered (blank). In OBL 4^0.Rawl.593 another booklet occurs here: see below under Copies.

Booklet 4: Index.

^{2}⁂2 *–3*^{2}. [\$2 signed (-3*2)] 8 leaves, unnumbered.

Sub-booklet 4.1: Errata.

4χ^2. [Unsigned] 2 leaves, unnumbered.

Booklet 5: [Supplement] Materia academiæ Cantebrigiensis.

$^2\pi^4$ [a]–[f]^2 [g]^2 (-[g]2) [h]–[n]^2. [Unsigned] 30 leaves, paginated [i–viii], 1–23, [24–26], 27–47, [48–50] ([g]2 discounted from the number series). [a] = pp. 1–4, [b] = pp. 5–8, [c] = pp. 9–12, [d] = pp. 13–16, [e] = pp. 17–20, [f] = pp. 21–3, [24], [g]1 = pp. [25–26], [g]2 blank, [h] = pp. 27–30, [i] = pp. 31–4, [k] = pp. 35–8, [l] = pp. 39–42, [m] = pp. 43–6, [n] = pp. 47, [48–50].

Sub-booklet 5.1: List of bishops 1500–71.

5χ^2. [Unsigned] 2 leaves, unnumbered.

Sub-booklet 5.2A: Extension of list of documents in possession of Cambridge U. + De Scholarum Collegioriumque in Academia Cantebrigiensis (= re-setting of [h]).

❋^{2}. [1 signed]. 2 leaves, unnumbered.

Sub-booklet 5.2B: Scholarum publicarum extructio.

2✱2. [1 signed]. 2 leaves, unnumbered.

SOURCES OF PASSAGES UTILIZING ANGLO-SAXON TYPES:

H4ʳ   Wulfstan, *Sermo Lupi ad Anglos*, opening lines (Whitelock 1952: 33/4–7; Bethurum 1957: 267/7–10). Omission of the words *for folces synnan* between *nyde* and *ær* establishes that the source was one of three MSS: C = CCC 201, p. 82/4–6; B = CCC 419, pp. 95/13–96/3; H = Bodley 343 143ᵛ/13–14; almost certainly C, as the readings *world, worlde aswalenge, wirse, swiðe* indicate. Some misreadings, t for c in *getwawað, nealætð*, e (final) for c in *aswalenge*, suggest that the text was based on that of an unpractised transcriber; the cursive approach-stroke to the two c's was presumably misinterpreted as the bar of a τ.

N2ʳ   Diploma of King Henry I (Sept 1100 × July 1101) from an unknown MS; Latin text only in LPL 1212, 14ʳ/1–5 (*olim* p. 25), ends 'Id⟨e⟩m in Anglico ibid⟨e⟩m', but it is not there. L and OE texts handwritten by John Parker occur in LPL 959 (=1572.1) 116ᵛ = L4ᵛ. Ed. Rymer 1816–30: I.i.12 in L and OE (from 1572.1). (Pelteret 44; Davis, Johnson and Cronne 1956: no. 532)

TYPE:

Main text in Robert Granjon's 3rd English-size Italic (Vervliet 1999: fig. 19a).

Pierre Haultin's English-size Roman is used for the preface (¶1–4), and for verse quotations on 2Y2ʳ and 2F4ᵛ.

AS1: The Parkerian Great Primer Anglo-Saxon acquired by Day combined with Haultin's English-size Roman occurs in text on H4ʳ (p. 63) and N2ʳ (p. 103), and in words on Booklet 1, D3ʳ (p. 29), F1ᵛ (p. 42), Booklet 2, 2A2ʳ (p. 3), 2A2(χ2)r (p. 4c), 2A3ᵛ (p. 6), I3ʳ (p. 69), K1ʳ–2ʳ (p. 77–9), Booklet 4.1, 4χ1ʳ (errata).

Special sorts shown: 11 lower-case letters: ð, f, ȝ, ı, ꝑ, ſ, τ, ẏ; þ, ð, p;
                        5 capitals: Æ¹, Є, Ꝺ, 8; Ᵽ;
                        2 others: þ, ꝫ.
                        Total: 18 sorts.

The ð shown is the one that fits snugly to the preceding letter, as found in 1571.1, sig. 2H to the end.

Robert Granjon's second Pica Italic (of three), the *Cicero pendante*, occurs on P3(χ3ᵛ–4ʳ).

Copies seen:

BL C.24.b.8 (Parker's presentation copy to Queen Elizabeth I, with embroidered velvet binding (Davenport 1896: 40–43 & fig. 10) and membrane tp and sub-tp, hand-coloured at appropriate places) shows Booklets 1 (-G2), 1.1, 1.2, 2, 4, 5 (²π2ʳᵛ blank) with 5.1 between [d] and [e], and 5.2A between [f] and [g], and 5.2B between [g] and [h], and 4.1; it lacks Sub-booklet 1A and Booklet 3.

BL C.24.b.7 (Parker's presentation copy to Richard FitzAlan, earl of Arundel, with blind-stamped binding and Arundel arms in gold at the centre, with 'Arundell' and 'Lumley' at foot of title page = Jayne & Johnson 1956: no. 1089), and hand-colouring at appropriate places (not the tp)) shows Booklets 1 (-π2, G2), 1.1, 1.2, 2, 4, 5 (lacks ^{2}π2–4, [g]) with 5.1 between [d] and [e] and 5.2A/B in place of [g]; it lacks Sub-booklet 1A, Booklet 3, and Sub-booklet 4.1.

BL G11757 shows Booklets 1 (-π2, G2), 1.1, 1.2, 2, 3, 5.2, 5 (cancel [g] only), 4; it lacks Sub-booklets 1A, 4.1, all of Booklet 5 except cancel sig.[g], and Sub-booklet 5.2B.

CUL Sel.3.217 shows Booklets 1 (-π2, G2), 1.1, 1.2, 2, 3, 4, 4.1 (-4χ2), 5 (-^{2}π4, [n]2) with 5.1 between [d] and [e] and 5.2A (❋1) in place of [g] followed by cancel [g]; it lacks Sub-booklet 1A.

CUL Sel.3.229 (Parker's presentation copy to Lord Burleigh in a Lambeth binding; Nixon 1970: 265 no. 1; Nixon & Foot 1992: 40) has membrane tp (i.e. ±π) and sub-tp (i.e. ±^{2}π1) and is hand-coloured at appropriate places, as the title page, ¶1^r (initial), A1^r (initials), etc.; the pages are frame-ruled as for a manuscript production. It shows Booklets 1 (-G2), 1.1, 1.2, 2, 4, 5, lacking 1A, 3, 4.1, 5.1, 5.2A/B. In Booklet 2 sig. A shows ±A2 + χ1.2 with +A2 signed 'A*.ij' paginated 2, 3, and A2(χ1.2) paginated 4a–4d. Booklet 1.1 is represented by a hand-coloured membrane leaf (=^{2}¶1) which occurs after Booklet 1, while ^{2}¶2 occurs at the end after Booklet 5. Booklet 5 shows ^{2}π3 after [g]1; it lacks ^{2}π2,4.

CCC Y.8.3 (gift of Thomas Baker) shows Booklet 1 (lacking π, but with the title written out by Baker on a substitute leaf, with Booklet 1.1 wrapped around sig.¶ to give the order ^{2}¶1, ¶1–4, ^{2}¶2), 2, 3 (with 3χ^{12} consisting of pp. 17–18, (17) + blank, 7 stubs, 19–20, 21–22, 23 + blank), 4 (lacking 3*2), 5 (with [a]–[d] followed by two blank leaves, then Sub-booklet 5.1 (both leaves), [e]–[h], then cancel [g], and [i]–[n]1, lacks [n]2); it lacks Sub-booklets 1A, 5.2, 5.3.

CPH K.8.12 (gift of Andrew Perne) shows Sub-booklet 1.1 wrapped around 1.2, Booklet 1 (lacks π2, ¶4, G2), Booklet 2 (±^{2}F1 (?), Ii2.3 blank, no evidence of ±Nn2), Booklet 3, Booklet 4; Booklet 5 is incomplete but contains some additional material, lacking ^{2}π2,4, but ^{2}π3 is followed by ^{2}❋3,4, then [a]–[f], then ^{2}❋1, ❋2–3, ^{2}❋2, and ^{2}❋3,4 repeated (i.e. sub-booklet 5.3 enclosing the central leaves of sub-booklet 5.2), and [h]–[n] are lacking. It lacks sub-booklets 1A, 4.1, 5.1. The missing pages from Booklets 1 and 2 are supplied in photocopy in a folder inside the back cover.

LPL MS 959 (2 vols) is this book much annotated by John Parker and others and complemented by many additional manuscript items; it requires a separate study. This account focusses on the printed book. Vol. I contains: fos 1–17 handwritten leaves; fos 18–29 Sub-booklet 1A; fos 36–65 Booklet 1 (lacks π2, G2) with title page lacking text of title and verse; fos 66–7 Sub-booklet 1.1; fos 68–69 Sub-booklet 1.2; fo 70 single printed leaf unsigned and unnumbered, with Latin verse on the recto side only headed 'Cantiæ ſtatus ab aduentu Cæſaris.' and initialed at the bottom B.C. (= Bartholomew Clerk, (later) dean of the Arches); fos 71–177A Booklet 2 sig. A–Bb3 with handwritten inserted leaves fos 128, 130–1, 153 (1st), 163, 172–3, 176 (1st), 177 (1st), 178. Vol. II contains: fos 178A–294 Booklet 2 (cont.) sig. Bb4–II2, including an additional printed leaf (fo 186) headed 'Prouisiones & Emptiones', and more handwritten inserted leaves fos 299–317, 319–321, 323, 324 (1st), 328, 332–334; fos 340–341 Sub-booklet 5.2 ❋2–3; fo 342 Sub-booklet 4.1 (lacks 4χ2); fos 343–352 Booklet 4 with handwritten inserted leaves fos 348–349; fos 353–389 Booklet 5 consisting of $^2\pi$ with $^2\pi 2(+\chi)$ being an additional leaf 'area scholaris' but headed 'Sigilii Academiæ' [a]–[d], sub-booklet 5.1, [e]–[f], sub-booklet 5.2 ❋1, [h]–[n] with handwritten inserted leaves fos 359, 375, 376 (1st, misnumbered 396), 380–1A; fos 390–395 handwritten leaves.

OBL A.19.9.Th. (gift of John Parker to Richard Cosin) shows Booklet 1 (lacks π, but in the equivalent position has $^2\P 1$ from Sub-booklet 1.1 printed on the recto sides of two separate leaves; lacks $^2\P 2$), 2 (with ±^{2}F1), 3, 1.2, 4 (with 4χ1 from Sub-booklet 4.1 pasted on to a binding strip between 3*1 and 3*2), 5 (lacks $^2\pi 2,4$, [h], but has [g]1 followed by sub-booklet 5.2 (i.e. ❋2, ^{2}❋1, then ❋1, then in place of [h] ^{2}❋2 with another variant printing on separate leaves of $^2\pi 1^v$ and $^2\pi 3^r$ (from 1574.1) between ❋2 and ^{2}❋1, and sub-booklet 5.1 between [d] and [e] in Booklet 5; it lacks Sub-booklet 1A.

OBL 4^0.Rawl.593 shows Booklet 1 (±π1) preceded by copperplate etching of Parker pasted on to a flyleaf, 1.1, 1.2 with 5.1 (-5χ2), 2, 3 (-3χ6), 1A, 4, 4.1, 5 (-$^2\pi 2,4$, [h]-[n]) with 5.2A in place of [g] and 5.2B in place of [h].

Copies also at: CTH, MJRUL, OMaC, OMC, OXC, TCD; FSL.

Bibliography: Crawford 1910: III, 6859–6861; Martin 1834: 1–10; Willis and Clark 1886: III, 14–19 (on Schools Quadrangle).

Manuscripts: A draft for the Introduction (Booklet 1: A1–G1 De vetustate Britannicæ Ecclesiæ testimonia) by Joscelyn survives in Vitellius D.vii, 54^r–59^v, and drafts for Booklet 2 (2A1–2G4, H1–2I2 abps of Canterbury) by Joscelyn survive in Vitellius D.vii, 61^r–89^v, and Vitellius E.xiv, 270^r–379^r.

1574.1: Caius, John, *De Antiquitate Cantabrigiensis Academiæ*. 2nd edn of 1568.1. London: John Day, 1574. STC 4345; ESTC S107133. AS1.

Extracts from King Alfred's Will, Laws of Alfred, Alfredian PC, ASC (D), OE Bede, Will of Ealdorman Æthelmær, Ælfric's Grammar

Collation: 4^0: A–Y^4 2A–2O^4 [$3 signed (-A1, 2M3, 2O3; +A4, B4, C4, D4, E4, F4, G4, H4, I4, L4, M4, Q4, R4, T4, V4, 2E4)] 144 leaves, paginated *1–3*, 4–268, *269–88* (110 misnumbered 111, 111 misnumbered 110, 210 misnumbered 202, 211 misnumbered 203, 214 misnumbered 206, 215 misnumbered 207).

SOURCES OF PASSAGES UTILIZING ANGLO-SAXON TYPES:

R4^v From 1568.1 M4^r: OE Version of Bede's *Historia Ecclesiastica*, III.18;

X4ᵛ–Y1ʳ   From BL Add 82931 (*olim* Earl of Macclesfield MS 24.g.9), 'Liber de Hyda', 10b/21: King Alfred's will (Sawyer 1507), 2nd part (Edwards 1866: 62), opening statement. Use of this MS is suggested by the forms *Alfred* and *gife*, against *Ælfred* and *gyfe* in the Hyde Register (BL Stowe 944, 30ᵛ/14–15, facs Keynes 1996, ed. Harmer 1914: 17), as well as by its certain use at sig. 2E1ᵛ. Alternatively, the source could be the transcript in BL Lansdowne 717 by John Stow (1572), 23ᵛ/32, but this MS does not contain the source for 2E1ᵛ. MS 'Westseaxena', 'cinge mid' misprinted as 'Wetseaxena', 'cnige vnd'.

The passage has been expanded from the corresponding one in 1568.1 P3ʳ. Cf. 2I2ᵛ below.

2D4ᵛ–2E1ʳ   From 1568.1 S8ʳ: King Alfred's Version of Gregory's *Pastoral Care*, Preface;

The word 'moneceffa' on S8ʳ (p. 287, line 9) has been corrected to 'monceffa', as indicated in 1568.1 on Z8ʳ in the errata (but not in AS type).

2E1ʳ   From 1568.1 S8ʳᵛ: Ælfric's *Grammar*, concluding sentence;

An erroneous word-division has been introduced whereby:

1568.1 gemacigað ænne → 1574.1 gemaciga ðænne [cf. **Type** below].

2E1ᵛ   From the Liber de Hyda, 35d/51–36a/4: Extracts in AS from the Will of Æthelmær (Sawyer 1498; Whitelock 1930: 24–27, 125–128; cf. also Edwards 1866: 254–255). John Stow's partial transcript of the Liber de Hyda in BL Lansdowne 717 contains this will only in ME and Latin (not AS) on 46ʳ–47ʳ. This passage is part of an insertion added to the corresponding passage in 1568.1 S8ᵛ.

2F3ʳ   From 1568.1 T6ᵛ: *Anglo-Saxon Chronicle* (D), Annal 885;

2H2ʳ   From 1568.1 X1ᵛ: *Anglo-Saxon Chronicle* (D), Annal 877;

An erroneous expansion of a contraction has occurred whereby:

    1568.1 gedældo → 1574.1 gedældom

2I2ᵛ   From 1568.2 I3ᵛ/12–13, or possibly from a MS, e.g., CCC 173, 40ʳ/8–9: Preface to the Laws of Alfred 49.10 (Liebermann I, 46–47). Only five words: *Ic ða Ælfred Westseaxna cynnig* [recte *cyning*].

This passage is part of an insertion added to the corresponding passage in 1568.1 Y1ʳ.

TYPE:

Main text in Robert Granjon's 3rd English-size Italic.

AS1: The Parkerian Great Primer Anglo-Saxon combined with Pierre Haultin's English Roman occurs as follows:

E2ᵛ	(p. 36)	text of Latin verses (includes several Roman capitals, but initial Q is from another fount)

R4ʳ	(p. 135)	rh margin
R4ᵛ	(p. 136)	text + lh margin
X4ᵛ–Y1ʳ	(pp. 168–169)	text + lh margin + catchword
2D4ᵛ–2E1ʳ	(pp. 208–209)	text1 + lh margin +catchword + text2
2F3ʳ	(p. 221)	text

Special sorts shown: 11 lower-case letters: ð, ꝼ, ȝ, ı, ƿ, ſ, ꞇ, ẏ; þ, ð, p;
4 capitals: Æ¹, Є, Ꝺ, Ᵽ;
2 others: þ, ⁊
Total: 17 sorts.

AS ð is the older casting prior to 1571.1 (sig. 2H to end), the one that does not fit snugly against the preceding letter.

Marginal rubrics are set in Granjon's Long Primer Italic, known as 'l'immortelle'.

Copies seen:

With 'duobus' title page: KCC H.15.6 (gift of Richard Day 1576; cf. Munby 1948: 229); CCC B.7.56 (gift of John Parker).

With 'aliquot' title page: CCA W/T.7.51 (Somner's copy, previously owned by William Watts 1631, acquired for 4s); BL C.32.h.15 (formerly 731.i.1, gift of Matthew Parker, signed Arundell, Lumley = Jayne and Johnson 1956: no. 1252), 672.d.12 (signed 'Matthæus Cantuar: 1574.'), Henry Davis Gift 61 (gift of Parker to Sir Thomas Smyth (1513–77), with inscription on *De Pronunciatione* C4ᵛ and Lambeth binding (Nixon 1970: 265 no. 5; Foot 1978–83: II, 86–88, no. 54), later owned by Sir Thomas Wilson (1560–1629), whose signature occurs on the front flyleaf; lacks *Historia*); OBL 40.A.35.Art. (±A1), Broxb.106.28 (±A1), Wood 480 (±A1); BL C.24.a.27 (gift of John Parker to James I in Lambeth binding; Nixon 1970: 265 no. 4) shows ±A1 (Plomer 1927: 259–260), with the editorial statement from A1ᵛ pasted on a blank flyleaf before the substitute title-page. CCC Y.7.2 (Parker's copy with his archiepiscopal coat of arms on the Lambeth binding (reprod. Burlington 1891: pl. lxxviib; Nixon 1970: 265 no. 6) and a note of his costs in producing it written by John Parker on the verso of the front flyleaf, reprod. Plomer 1927: pl. 1) lacks A1, I2, shows ±T2, but includes the errata leaf after 2O3.

Copies also at: BCL, CFM, ChC, CGC, CNC, CPC, CPH, CQC, CSJ, CTH, TCC, EdUL, LHL, OBC, OCC, OEC, OMC, OOC, OQC, OSJ, OUC, OWoC, OxC, StA, WCC, DML, TCD, GUB; FSL, HHL, USLC, HCLM, HUL, KSRL, NWU, SCN, YUB; UML.

Bibliography: Arber 1875–94: V.91, no. 1865; Brooke 1985: 74–75; Hind 1952–64: 81–84 (on Lyne's map); Plomer 1927; McKisack 1971: 70–71; Roberts 1912; Shirley 1991: no. 106, pl 46 (Lyne's map).

1574.2: Asser: *Ælfredi Regis Res Gestæ*. London: John Day, 1574. STC 863; ESTC S118080; GR 5494. AS1.
Asser: Life of King Alfred, King Alfred's Will (Latin), Prose PCP, Verse PCP

Date: On 23 Nov 1574 Parker sent a copy of the book with his letter to Lord Burghley (Bruce and Perowne 1853: no. ccclxiii). Normally bound with *Historia Breuis Thomae Walsingham* (London: Henry Bynneman, 1574; STC 25004) and *Ypodigma Neustriæ vel Normanniæ per Thomam de Walsingham* (London: John Day 1, 1574; STC 25005). On F4^v there is a reference to 1574.1, sig. 2D4^v (p. 208), a reference taken over from CUL Ii.2.4, 4^v, marginal annotation in Parker's hand beside lines 4–5 (Page 1992: 49, n. 18).

Collation: 2⁰ in 4s: A^4 ¶^{2} A–F^4 [$4 signed (-A1, A1; A3 missigned '¶.iij', D3 missigned 'D.iiij')] 29 leaves, paginated [i–x], 1–40 (36–37 unnumbered), *41–48*.

SOURCES OF PASSAGES UTILIZING ANGLO-SAXON TYPES:

A1^r–E2^r From (presumably) BL Otho A.xii, 1–55, destroyed in the 1731 fire; some transcripts survive (Stevenson 1959: §§28–32) of which the most important is CCC 100, pp. 325–62 (s.xvi^2): Latin text of Asser's *Life of Alfred*. In the Preface (¶1^r) Parker says 'hoc te scire volo ... in omnibus iis libris quos divulgavi, nihil ut de meo adiecerim, aut diminuerim', which is strictly true in the sense that he added nothing of his own composition, but in this book interpolations were made from other works, notably the *Annals of St Neots* (which Parker thought were also by Asser) and Matthew Paris's *Chronica majora* (Stevenson 1959: text §§50b–d, 53b–c, 54b, 106b–c); on Parker as editor of historical texts cf. McKisack 1971: 40–44. Cf. Tite 2003: 149.

E2^v–4^v From BL Add 82931 (*olim* Earl of Macclesfield MS 24.g.9), 'Liber de Hyda' (s.xv), 9b/57–10a/4, 11c/3–12a/38: Latin version of King Alfred's will (Sawyer 1507; as Edwards 1866: 57–60, 71–5). BL Lansdowne 717, 22^r/1–23^r/15 and 26^r/6–27^v/6, by John Stow (1572) contains a transcript of the text from the Liber de Hyda, but two additions by Stow do not appear in Parker's print: E2^v/27 quod [ipse] de; E3^r/15 rex [ante me] viam. The will in AS, dating from 873–88 (Stevenson 1959: lxvii), ed. Harmer 1914: 15–19, was copied in the Liber de Hyda from the Hyde Register, i.e. the Liber Vitæ of New Minster, Winchester, BL Stowe 944, 29^v–33^r (facs in Keynes 1996, also Ordnance Survey 1878–84: III.22), and translated into ME and Latin, the two versions sharing some errors (Harmer 1914: 92). Parker's printed text shows the following substantive variations from the MS (none shown by Stow): E2^v/5 salute] MS paupertate; E3^r/29 aut] MS an; E4^r/33 cognationi] MS manui; also AS names have been changed to more authentic AS forms.

F1^r–2^r From CUL Ii.2.4, 5^r/1–6^v/14: AS prose preface to the Alfredian translation of Pope Gregory's *Pastoral Care* (as Sweet 1871–2: 2–9); the rubric and the readings *Wulfsige* (3/1), *mæniu* (5/11), *æfterspyrigean* (5/16), *þi*, *æryst* (5/25), *hit* (7/2, 2nd), MS *hie* with the bar of e erased), *agenge* (7/2, 7/4, 7/5), *hic* (7/3, MS *hie* with the bar of e erased), *gemong* (7/17), *minõ* (7/21, MS *minon*) are distinctive. However, at 5/24 *forlætõ* for MS *forlæten* suggests correction against another MS (cf. 1568.1 S8ʳ). Two divergent readings are presumably errors: *gretung* for MS *gretan* (3/1), and *þemed* for MS *þe nied* (7/7), while *Thamise* for MS *temese* (3.18) is presumably an editorial 'improvement'.

F2ᵛ From CUL Ii.2.4, 6ᵛ/15–7ʳ/2: AS verse preface to the Alfredian *Pastoral Care* (as Dobbie 1942: 110); the readings *æryndgewrit* (1), *egbugendum* (3), *gestrinde* (8), *mærða* (10), *forþam he, swilcra* (13), *bysyne, biscopum* (14) are distinctive, but the addition by a hand of s.xvi² (? the translator) of \n/ in *adiht\n/ode* (4) and of *Gregorius* (6) in the margin, both taken over in this printed book, suggests collation with TCC MS R.5.22, 72ʳ.

F3ʳ–4ᵛ From supply leaves (s.xvi2) in CUL Ii.2.4, 3ᵛ/1–4ᵛ/9: Latin translation of AS prose preface to the *Pastoral Care*.

F4ᵛ From supply leaf (s.xvi²) in CUL Ii.2.4, 4ᵛ/10–21: Latin translation of AS verse preface to the *Pastoral Care*. The reference to 1574.1 is from CUL Ii.2.4, where it occurs twice, once in the margin of the Latin translation on 4ᵛ/4–5, where the addition is in the hand of Matthew Parker (Page 1992: 49, n. 18), and once in the margin beside the AS text on 6ᵛ/8.

TYPE:

AS1: the main text (including Latin) is in the Parkerian Great Primer Anglo-Saxon combined with Pierre Haultin's English Roman.

Special sorts shown: 11 small letters: ð, ꝼ, ʒ, ı, ꝺ, ꞃ, ꞇ, ẏ; þ, ð, p;
                              8 capitals: Æ¹, Æ², Ɛ, Ꝺ, ꟽ, Ꞅ, Ꝧ, Ð;
                              3 others: þ, ꝯ, ꝵ;
             Total: 22 sorts.

On F1ʳ–2ᵛ AS ð is the later casting that first appears in 1571.1 (sig. 2H to end), the one that fits snugly against the preceding letter.

The specimen on ¶1ᵛ shows 20 special sorts, omitting ı, þ, p, þ, ꝯ and ꝵ.

                          9 small letters: ð, ꝼ, ʒ, ꝺ, ꞃ, ꞇ, ẏ, z; ð;
                          10 capitals: Æ¹, Æ², Ɛ, Ꝺ, ꟽ, Ꞅ, X; Ꝧ, Ð, Ᵽ;
                          1 other: ꝵ;
             Total: 20 sorts.

Total sorts overall: 12 + 10 + 3 = 25.

According to Parker's statement in the Preface he printed the Latin text in Anglo-Saxon characters *ob venerandam ... archetypi antiquitatem* 'for the purpose of revering the antiquity of the exemplar' (A2ʳ). Since later Anglo-Saxon Latin texts did not employ insular script, Parker's use of his Anglo-Saxon types for printing Latin was described by Wakeman (1967: 297) as 'a travesty'. But, as stated in the Preface (A3ᵛ–A4ʳ) the inspiration for so doing was Irish manuscripts containing Latin texts, a good example being Lambeth Palace Library,

MS 1370 (Ker 284), the 'Gospels of MacDurnan' (s.ix), which Parker almost certainly owned; alternatively Parker and his team could have been inspired by earlier AS manuscripts, such as the eighth-century Sedulius in CCC 173 (part 2), or by later medieval imitations of AS script (Lucas 2000b). Parker and his household's inability to distinguish scripts by place of origin is confirmed by the inscription by John Parker, the archbishop's son, on the Irish Broadside of 1571 (in CCC; cf. Dickins 1949, also McGuinne 1992: 11), which utilizes the Elizabethan Irish types: 'This irish balade printed in Irelande who belike vse the olde saxon carecte.'.

François Guyot's Double Pica Italic is used for the preface ($A2^r$–$¶1^r$), and Guyot's Double Pica Roman for the Latin translation of the prose preface to the *Pastoral Care* ($F3^r$–4^v); Robert Granjon's Long Primer Italic, known as 'l'immortelle' is used for the suprascript translation/gloss of the prose and verse prefaces to the *Pastoral Care* ($F1^r$–2^v).

Note: Woodcut large initials for Є and ꟽ appear (cf. 1571.1).

> Copies seen: With ¶2 intact: CCC MS 176, CTH L.6.22 (contemporary binding shows armorial stamp with an upright key surmounted by a six-pointed star having the letters M C either side of the key, i.e. 'Mattheus Cantuariensis', Matthew Parker, abp of Canterbury); with ¶2 as a stub: CCC Y.8.4, CUL Syn.4.57.2 (Roger Twysden's copy), CUL Syn.4.57.9, TCC VI.3.34, CSJ C.4.32; with ¶1 pasted to a stub: BL 192.a.5, LPL 1574.01 (binding shows armorial stamp of Sir Christopher Hatton). Lacking ¶2: ABH 1781 (lacks $A1$); ECC 309.4.65 (in contemporary binding), KCC G.30.5, CSS L.4.37, TCD P.b.10 (lacks $A1$), RR.e.38 (*ex libris* 'Claud Gilbert', with $A1$ mounted on blank leaf), BL C.80.d.16 (with 'Arundell' and 'Lumley' at foot of title page = Jayne & Johnson 1956: no.945; then with the class-mark 9505.g.13), G5639 (with armorial stamp of Thomas Grenville on front cover).
>
> CPH M.1.3 (gift of Andrew Perne) shows ±$A1$ as part of a bifolium with the second leaf blank, so that A4 has its stub reversed and is wrapped around the singleton ¶1.
>
> OBL C.1.9.Med.Seld. (Selden's copy) shows ¶2 as a stub reversed on its hinge so as to appear before A2 and ±$A1$ attached to the stub.
>
> KCC G.30.5 ('Donum Iohannis Day Typographi'; cf. Munby 1948: 225–7) shows ±$A1$; the title page on limp membrane is that of 1572.1 (the same woodcut frame) with traces of paper slips, presumably cut out from the appropriate title-page, that were pasted over the title and verse windows;
>
> CSJ C.4.32 (Thomas Baker's copy) and TCD P.b.10 have the present work bound at the end instead of the usual position at the beginning; CUL Syn.4.57.9 has the four-leaf preface of the *Historia Breuis Thomæ Walsingham* misbound between

A1 and A2; CCC Y.8.4 lacks F⁴; TCC Grylls:10:235 lacks A2–4, ¶², E2.3; TCD RR.e.38 has no accompanying works.

BL C.80.d.16, CUL Broxbourne b.51, CCC MS 176, CPH M.1.3, CTH L*.6.22 and TCC Grylls:10:235 have the variant catchword at F3ᵛ.

CUL Broxbourne b.51 has the name 'Matthew Parker' written at the top of A1ʳ, but inked over; it also occurs in red ink (?signature) at the top of A1ʳ in the *Historia Breuis Thomæ Walsingham*, with which the book is usually bound.

Copies also at: CGC, EAL, EdUL, GML, LSH, OCC, OEC, OEF, ONC, OOC, OUC, OUP, OWmC, OXC, UCL, WCF, WIHM, WRL, BSB, GUB; FSL, NYPL, NYPM, UTS, HHL, HUL, IUL, KSRL, LCP, NWU, OSU, USLC, UTA, UVL; NSW.

Bibliography: Arber 1875–94: v.91, no. 1864; Binns 1990: 190; Clement 1997: 216–218; Edwards 1866 (King Alfred's will); Hagedorn 1989; Munby 1948: 225–227; Niles 2015: 65–70; Stevenson 1959: §4.

1576.1: Foxe, John (ed.), *The Second Volume of the Ecclesiastical History, conteyning the Actes and Monumentes of Martyrs.* 3rd edn of 1570.1 (= 2nd edn). London: John Day, 1576. STC 11224; ESTC S121348. AS2.

Extracts from 1566.1, 1567.1

Collation (vol. II only): 2⁰ in 6s: π¹ A⁶ 3B–3Y⁶ ²3A–3M⁶ ²3N⁶ (²3N6 +χ1) ²3O–3R⁶ ²3S–3T⁴ [$4 signed (3L4 missigned 'KKk.iiij.', ²3T2 missigned 'TTT.iiij.')] 244 leaves, paginated [i–iv], 773–1256 (799 misnumbered 899, 898–899 misnumbered 886–887, 995 misnumbered 965, 1002 misnumbered 1011, 1011 misnumbered 1002, 1038 misnumbered 1047, 1047 misnumbered 1038, 1112 misnumbered 1084, 1117 misnumbered 1073, 1130 misnumbered 1120, 1140 misnumbered 1104, 1194 misnumbered 1294, 1231 misnumbered 1230).

SOURCES OF PASSAGES UTILIZING ANGLO-SAXON TYPES:

²3G3ᵛ/a/68–73 (p. 1114a)   From 1570.1, 3K4ᵛ/a/49–53 (p. 1302a), Ælfric's 'Excusatio Dictantis' (opening statement) at the end of his homily *Depositio S. Martin* (Godden 1979: XXXIV), with no spelling deviations except mıcelnıʃʃe for 1570.1 mıcelnẏʃʃe;

²3G3ᵛ/a/79–82 (p. 1114a)   From 1570.1, 3K4ᵛ/a/60–3 (p. 1302a), Ælfric's *Grammar*, opening statement from OE Preface (cf. Zupitza 1880: 2), with erroneous ða for 1570.1 ðaʃ (lıꞇclan);

²3G3ᵛ/b/16–35 (p. 1114b) From 1570.1, 3K4ᵛ/b/13–32 (p. 1302b), Ælfric's letter to Wulfsige III (bp of Sherborne 992–1002) extracts (Fehr 1914: §§135–42), with erroneous ðpıȝhꞇen for 1570.1 ðpıhꞇen;

²3G3ᵛ/b/66–4ʳ/b/3 (pp. 1114b–15b)   From 1570.1, 3K4ᵛ/b/64–5ʳ/b/19 (pp. 1302b–3b), Ælfric's second letter to Wulfstan (abp of York 1002–23) extracts (Fehr 1914: §§86–95, 97–109) with erroneous ðæȝe peꞇꞇan for 1570.1 ðæȝe ʃeꞇꞇan, and ʃacpıꝼıcıum for 1570.1 ʃumeþe ʃacpıꝼıcıum;

²3G4ᵛ/b/11–6ʳ/b/16 (pp. 1116b–19b) From 1570.1, 3K5ᵛ/b/52–3L1ᵛ/b/7 (pp. 1304b–8b), Ælfric's *Sermo de Sacrificio in die Pascae* (same omissions as in 1570.1; Godden 1979: xv), with retention of erroneous þıꞃne . hlaꞅ . (²3G5ʳ/a/40, with unwanted point between the words), and new errors bebeað þam (²3G4ᵛ/b/20–1) for 1570.1 bebeað ᛗoýꞅeꞅ þam, eꞃend (²3G5ʳ/b/61) for 1570.1 aꞃenð, pæðeꞃ oꞅ (²3G5ᵛ/a/17) for 1570.1 pæðeꞃ þa oꞅ, ꞇeꞃmeaȝēne (²3G5ᵛ/b/5) for 1570.1 ꞇoꞃmeaȝenne, etc.; there are also many minor alterations, notably sporadic interchange of ð/þ, ⁊/and, -Ø/-e;

²3I3ᵛ/b/32–6 (p. 1138b) From 1570.1, 3N3ʳ/a/19–23 (p. 1335a), ASC (E), annal for 1129 (Clark 1954: 51), with no spelling deviations except þa for ða.

TYPE:
Main text in Long Primer/Bourgeois Textura   Body 61   Face 58 × 1.5: 2.2
Pierre Haultin's Long Primer Roman (passim)   Body 62   Face 60 × 1.4: 2
AS2: The Parkerian Pica Anglo-Saxon occurs on 23G3ᵛ–6ʳ (pp. 1114–19), 1113ᵛ (p. 1138) combined with Pierre Haultin's Pica Roman.
The specimen on ²3G4ᵛ shows 17 special sorts:

    11 lower-case letters: ꞅ, ȝ, ı, ꞃ, ꞅ, ꞇ, ẏ, z; þ, ð, ꝥ;
    5 capitals: Æ², Ꞅ, Þ, Ð, Ꝥ;
    1 other: ⁊.
  Total: 17.

Special sorts shown in the text:
    12 lower-case letters: ð, ꞅ, ȝ, ı, ꞃ, ꞅ, ꞇ, ẏ, z; þ, ð, ꝥ;
    8 capitals: Æ¹, Æ², Ɛ, Ꟶ, ᛗ, Ꞅ, Þ, Ð;
    3 others: þ, ⁊, ȷ.
  Total: 23.

Total special sorts shown in the specimen and the text: 12 + 9 + 3 = 24.
Note: There is only one size of the Tironian sign for 'and' (width 1.5 mm), which, according to my count, occurs 116 times.

Copy seen: CPH E.11.17 (in contemporary blind-tooled binding; gift of Andrew Perne).

Copies also at: BL, BPL, CMC, CQC, CUW, DWL, LPL, LSH, NT, NUL, OBL, OBC, OBrC, OWmC, OXC, QUB, StCL, WoCL; FSL, NYPL, HHL, HCP, UCBL, UCH, UTA, UVL, WMUL; UAL.

Bibliography: Arber, v.99, no. 2098; Clement 1997: 219–221; Keynes 2014: 156 (map of AS heptarchy); Shirley 1991: no. 115a.

1576.2: Lambarde, William, *A Perambulation of Kent*. London: Henry Middleton for Ralph Newbery, 1576. STC 15175 & 15175.5; ESTC S108236 & S124785. GR 6282. AS3.

Extracts from Charters, Laws, Wills

Collation: 4⁰: ¶⁴ 2¶⁴ (2¶4 + χ1) A–G⁴ H⁴ (±H1 + χ1) I–3H⁴ 3I². [$3 signed (+B4, H4, K4, L4, M4, N4, O4, P4, S4; -¶1, 2R2, 3I2; N3 missigned M3, 2L3 missigned 2K2, 2S2 missigned S2; H1(χ1) signed 'H.ii.')] 227 leaves, paginated [i–ix], *1*, 2–435, *436* (13 misnumbered 12, 16 misnumbered 15, 50 misnumbered 51, 51 misnumbered 50, H1(χ1) misnumbered 58, 59, 65 misnumbered 33, 68–69 misnumbered 36–37, 72 misnumbered 40, 85 misnumbered 88, 88 misnumbered 85, 161–168 misnumbered 169–176, 212–213 misnumbered 112–113).

Note: An earlier state is shown in gatherings 2¶ and X: 2¶1 is unsigned and 2¶3 is missigned 2¶2; X1ᵛ and X2ʳ are misnumbered 172 and 169.

SOURCES OF PASSAGES UTILIZING ANGLO-SAXON TYPES:

Note: The second and fourth of these passages are supplied with a double-decker translation, literal above the text and interpretative above the literal; the fourth occasionally has a triple-decker translation, with two interpretative versions above the literal.

B4ᵛ (p. 15)   *Laȝamon's Brut* (Brook and Leslie 1963: 1.370, lines 7141/7152) slightly adapted from Caligula A.ix, 84ʳ/ᵛ, citing the formula þær hæile hlaroþð cynyngȝ and the response ðrinc hæile. *Laȝamon's Brut* was presumably considered no different from OE; the form hlaroþð has apparently been archaized.

2Q2ʳ–4ʳ (pp. 307–311)   AS Charter listing estates liable for work on Rochester Bridge (Birch 1885–93: no. 1322; Robertson 1939: no. 52) from the unique MS source, RKA, DRc/R1 (Textus Roffensis), 166ᵛ/1–7ʳ/18. Robertson (1939: 106/108) notes some of Lambarde's transcriptional errors.

2X3ᵛ (p. 350)   William I: London Charter in AS (Liebermann 1903–16: 1.486, Robertson 1925: 230; Pelteret 8), extract from §1, but the text does not match the sole AS witness, so it is probably Elizabethan AS, translated from a later Latin version (printed by Liebermann) based on the AS. Text (not noticed by Liebermann or Robertson): pılliam cẏng ȝreıt pılliam bıſceop. ȝ ȝoðpe-|ȝer poþ tȝeþeran. ȝ ealle þa buþhpaþen þe on lun-|ðen beonȝ

2Y3ʳ–2Z1ᵛ (pp. 357–362)   Will of Byrhtric (Birch 1885–93: no. 1132; Whitelock 1930: no. 11; Campbell 1973: no. 35) from the unique MS source, RKA, DRc/R1 (Textus Roffensis), 144ʳ/5–5ʳ/24. Sawyer 1511.

2Z2ᵛ–3ᵛ (pp. 364–366)   AS Law 'Geþyncðo' (om. end of §3 and §§4, 8: Liebermann 1903–16: 1.456–458) from RKA, DRc/R1 (Textus Roffensis), 93ʳ/17–93ᵛ/23, as is shown by the opening passage hıt þær hpılum on Enȝla laȝum.

3H1ᵛ (p. 434)   Neȝhe fyþe felðe, anð neȝ he fyþ ȝelðe: anð rır | ponð roþ þe þeþe. er he bicome healðeþ: apparently a false Anglo-Saxonisation of the later 'verse' given on 3E1ᵛ (p. 402):

Neg he fyth feald and Neg he fyth geld.
And fiue pound for the were, er he become healder,

translated 'Hathe he not since any thing giuen? nor hathe he not sence any thing payd? Then let him pay fiue pound for his were, before he become tenant, or holder againe'.
But some copies [i.e. exemplars] have the first verse thus:
Nigond sithe seld, and nigon sithe gelde',   (p. 403)
† 'Let him nine times pay, and nine times repay'.
TYPE:
Main text in a Pica Textura (Body 83.5).
The Pica Roman (Body 83; Face 80 × 1.6: 2.9) used from time to time (larger portions on 2E4ᵛ, 2F1ʳ, 3B2ᵛ) is Robert Granjon's 1st Pica Roman; it is used for the AS passages as well, where the Body cannot be measured because of the interlined translation, but the Face measures 80 × 1.6: 2.9 as for the Roman.
AS3: The Lambardian Pica Anglo-Saxon combined with Granjon's 1st Pica Roman.
The specimen on 2¶3ʳ shows the following special sorts:

11 lower-case letters:	ẟ (for ð), *e*, f, ȝ, ƕ (for h), ꞃ, ſ, τ, ẏ; ð, p;
2 capitals:	Þ, Ð;
4 others:	þ, ꝫ, ẋ, j̇.
Total:	17.

AS types occur in text on B4ᵛ, 2Q2ʳ–4ʳ, 2X3ᵛ, 2Y3ʳ–2Z1ᵛ, 2Z2ᵛ–3ᵛ, 3E3ʳ, 3H1ᵛ, and in words/names on C3, K3ᵛ, L4ʳ, M1ᵛ, O1ʳ, O4ᵛ, P3ʳ, P4ʳ, R4ᵛ, S3ʳ, V2ᵛ, V4ᵛ (combined with an English-size Roman), X1ᵛ, X2ᵛ, X3ʳ, Y2ᵛ, Y3ᵛ, Y4ᵛ, Z2ᵛ, Z3ʳ, 2A3ᵛ, 2A4ʳ, 2B2ʳ, 2B3, 2B4ᵛ, 2C1ᵛ, 2C3ʳ, 2C4ʳ, 2D3ʳ, 2E1ʳ, 2F2ʳ, 2F3ᵛ, 2F4ʳ, 2O1ᵛ, 2O3ʳ, 2R2ʳ, 2R3ʳ, 2S1ʳ, 2S3ʳ, 2S4ʳ, 2T3ʳ, 2T4ᵛ, 2V3ᵛ, 2V4ʳ, 2X1, 2X3ʳ, 2X4ᵛ, 2Y1ᵛ, 2Z2ʳ, 2Z4ʳ, 3A1ᵛ, 3A3ᵛ, 3C3ʳ.
Special sorts shown:

14 lower-case letters:	ð, ẟ (for ð), *e*, f, ȝ, ƕ (for h), ꞃ, ſ, τ, ẏ;
	þ (in oþꞃeſ on 2Q2ʳ/17), Þ (for þ), ð, p;
5 capitals:	Æ¹, Æ², Є, ꟽ, Ð;
3 others:	þ, ꝫ, j̇.
Total:	22.

The specimen shows capital ẟ as lower-case ð, and this is normal in text, but lower-case ð does occur correctly used on C3ᵛ (p. 22), the first occasion in the text that AS ð is called for, also in pealð on X4ʳ (p. 175), in Meðpœȝ on Y4ᵛ (p. 176), in Moð and ðene on 2F3ᵛ (p. 230), in ſꞃeonðerbyꞃiȝ and ſꞃinonðerbyriȝ (roman r used 2x) on 2O1ᵛ (p. 290), in Stꞃoȝð on 2R2ʳ (p. 315). Roman d is used in Єȝeleſſond on 2S1ʳ. AS capital ẟ is not used for capital ẟ, only as lower-case ð.

AS *e* not used where appropriate on C3, K3ʳ, M1ᵛ, O4ᵛ, P3ʳ, R4ᵛ, S3ʳ, V2ᵛ, X1ᵛ, X3ʳ, X4ʳ, Y2ᵛ, Y3ᵛ, Y4ᵛ, Z2ᵛ, Z3ʳ, 2A3ᵛ, 2B2ʳ, 2B3ᵛ; it first appears on 2C1ᵛ (p. 202), and then regularly until not used on 2D3ʳ, 2E1ʳ, 2F2ʳ, 2F3ᵛ, 2O1ᵛ, 2O3ʳ, then in a passage on 2Q2ʳ–4ʳ, but it is not used on 2S1ʳ, 2S3ʳ, used on 2S4ʳ, 2T3ʳ, 2T4ᵛ, 2V3ᵛ, 2V4ʳ, 2X1, 2X3ʳ, 2X3ᵛ, 2X4ᵛ, 2Y1ᵛ, and in a passage on 2Y3ʳ–2Z1ᵛ, 2Z2ʳ, 2Z4ʳ, 3C3ʳ, and passages on 3E3ʳ, 3H2ᵛ.

AS ẏ is not used where appropriate on S3ʳ, Z2ᵛ, 2F2ʳ, 2O1ᵛ.

The specimen does not show lower-case þ. It is used occasionally in words occurring in text, but in AS text passages capital Þ is generally preferred.

AS p is shown straight and tilted (top left to bottom right) in the errata on 2¶3ᵛ. Italic *p* (= Granjon's 2nd Pica Italic) is used for 'wynn' in Cyʃpiƿe on Z2ᵛ, and in Cātpaƿabẏƿiȝ on 2F4ʳ.

Total special sorts shown in the specimen and the text (allowing capitals to stand as capitals even when only used as lower-case): 11 + 8 + 4 = 23.

Granjon's second Pica Italic (of three), the *Cicero pendante*, is used for quotations throughout, and also for the above-the-line translations of OE on 2Qr–4ʳ, 2Y3ʳ–2Z1ᵛ, 2Z2ᵛ–3ᵛ.

Copies seen: Issue 1 (lacks Middleton's name in colophon):

With earlier state of 2¶ and X: CUL Syn.7.57.65;

With later state of 2¶ and X: CUL Bb*.4.54; OBL Gough Kent 60.

Issue 2: With later state of 2¶ and X: OBL Douce L.197, 4º Rawl.587 (Lambarde's gift to Sir Henry Sidney (1529–86) with dedication in Lambarde's own hand and map on 2¶4(χ1) hand-coloured, also gold-tooled binding with the initials HS); CUL Pet.F.1.56 lacks H1 and H1(χ1), LPL 1576.2 lacks 2¶4(χ1) (= map).

OBL 4º.Rawl.263 lacks ¶1 (= tp), 2R2 and 3H4–3I2 (including printer's colophon) but contains amendments in Lambarde's own hand, being the title page, dedication, and index amongst other annotations, preparatory for the 2nd edition (= 1596.2). It shows the earlier state of sig. X, but the later state of 2¶; the map on 2¶4(χ1) is hand-coloured.

Copies also at: Issue 1, BL, CCA, EAL, GlCL, GUL, LiCL, LSH, NT, OCC, OEC, SUL, WRL, YML, DKI; FSL, USLC, NYPL, HHL, HUL, IUL, LCP, NLC, UCLA, UVL;

Issue 2, AUL, TCC, ORS, RGS, UBL, DEWL; YUB.

Bibliography: Arber 1875–94: v.100, no. 2145; Brackmann 2012: 136–147; Clement 1997: 222–224; Keynes 2014: 156 (on the map at 2¶4(χ1) and its exposition); Liebermann 1898: §§12, 27, 28; Lucas 1999: 52–62; Mendyk 1989: 47–49; Moore 1992: 32, pls 46–47; Shirley 1991: no. 116; Stanley 1995: 437; Warnicke 1973: 29–35.

Manuscripts:

BL Add 20033, dated 31 Jan 1570 (2ʳ), fair copy in Lambarde's hand, incomplete at the end, dedicated to Thomas Wotton (1521–87), with ?16c gold-tooled binding showing the initials FW (possibly a relation);
RKA, U47/48 Z1; 'fair' copy in Lambarde's hand dated 1570.
Edition:
Lambarde, William, *A Perambulation of Kent: conteining the Description, Hystorie, and Customes of That Shire* (Chatham: W. Burrill, 1826), repr. in facsimile intr. R. Church (Bath: Adams & Dart, 1970).

1576.3: Gilbert, Sir Humphrey, *A Discourse of a Discoverie for a New Passage to Cataia.* London: Henry Middleton for Richard Jones, 1576. STC 11881; ESTC S105732.
    Collation: 4^0: ¶–3¶⁴ 4¶² B–H4¹². [88] p.
    No AS, but translation (probably by Nowell) of the passage about Ohtere's voyage from the OE *Orosius* on B4 based on Tiberius B.i (Brewer 1952–3: 206–7). Tiberius B.i was owned by Robert Talbot (Tite 2003: 106). See also 1589.1, 1598.1.
    Copies: BL, TCC, GUL, WAL, DML; FSL, USLC, HHL, JCB, PFL, YUB.

1577.1: Holinshed, Raphael (c.1525–80), *The Laste Volume of the Chronicles of England, Scotlande, and Irelande, with their descriptions from William Conquerour untill this present tyme. Faithfully gathered and compiled by Raphaell Holinshed.* 2 vols. London: [Henry Bynneman] for John Harrison, 1577. STC 13568. ESTC S93012. Vol II only.
Writ of William I (in Roman)
    Collation: 2^0 (vol II only): ¶2 t⁸ (-t1) v–z⁸ A–K⁸ L⁸ (±L7) M–4D⁸ 4E⁸ (4E4+χ1) 4F–4N⁸ 4O⁸ (±4O3) 4P–4U⁸ 4X⁸ (±4X1) 4Y⁸ 4Z² ²A–M⁴ N² ()²; [4], 291–659, 700–981, 990–1593, [1], 1593–1876, [104] p.
SOURCES OF PASSAGES UTILIZING ANGLO-SAXON TYPE: none, see Type below.
TYPE:
Main text in Pica Textura: Body 86.
v6v (p. 316 misnumbered 332)   From unidentified MS: Writ of William I (Pelteret 8) printed in Pica Roman (text riddled with errors) with the Latin below in Pica Italic.
    Copy seen: CUL Young 227.
    Copies also at: BCLNI, BL, CUL, GML, MCS, NCL, NIA, NLS, OXC; NLI; FSL, NYPL, NLC, ILF, WCW, YUB; ATL.

1581.1: Lambarde, William, *EIRENARCHA: or of The Office of the Justices of Peace, in two Bookes*. London: Henry Bynneman [for] Ralph Newbery, 1581. STC 15163; ESTC S109320. AS3.

Laws of Ine (extract)

    Collation: 8⁰: A⁴ B–2L⁸. [\$5 signed (-A1,3,4; 2D5 missigned D5] 268 leaves, paginated [i–viii], 1–511, *512–28* (257–259 misnumbered 157, 158, 159 respectively, 463 misnumbered 453, 465 misnumbered 399).

SOURCE OF PASSAGE UTILIZING ANGLO-SAXON TYPES:

N3ᵛ–4ʳ Extract from the Laws of Ine 13,1 (as Liebermann I, 94–5) probably from 1568.2 (C4ᵛ/6–8) or possibly from CCC 383, item 3, 24ᵛ/1–3, where the words '7 syððan' have been added s.xvi before 'here', and other MSS read 'siððan bið here'.

TYPE:

Main text in Pica Textura: Body 86; Face 80 × 2: 2.8.

Robert Granjon's Pica Roman (Body 86), e.g., on L2ᵛ–3ʳ (pp. 148–9).

Granjon's second Pica Italic, the *Cicero pendante* (Body 82.5).

AS3: Lambardian Pica Anglo-Saxon (with cap 𝔖 for ð) on N3ᵛ–4ʳ (pp. 182–3; text), P2ᵛ (p. 212; words), 2L7ᵛ (errata): combined with Granjon's Pica Roman.

Special sorts shown:

    11 lower-case: ð (= cap 𝔖), *e*, ꝼ, ȝ (= no. 3 in text, corrected in errata), ꝺ, ꞃ, ſ/ſ, ꞇ; þ, ð, p. Note confusion of ꞃ and ſ. Roman not AS y.

    1 capital: Ᵽ confused with lower-case þ, as in Morþor on P2ᵛ/2L7ᵛ and on N3ᵛ–4ʳ catchword/text, corrected in errata). On P2ᵛ rom cap M not AS, also in errata.

    Others: 7 (number) used for Ᵹ; : (colon) used for punctus versus;

    Total: 12 sorts.

Anglo-Saxon glossed suprascript on P2ᵛ (p. 212) in a Long Primer Italic.

    Copies seen: State 1 (with defective f in catchword at 2A7ᵛ: 𝔍f): CUL Pet D.4.44, Q*.12.38 (with errata page pasted on to 2L7ᵛ);

    State 2 (with normal f in catchword at 2A7ᵛ: 𝔍f): CUL Pet. E.6.15; BL 1381.b.24; OBL 35.c.51.

    Copies also at: BUL, EdUL, MCL; FSL, NYCU, HHL, BPM, HUL, IUL, NWU, UMI.

Bibliography: Clement 1997: 224; Putnam 1926; Warnicke 1973: esp. 71–72.

Facsimile (of CUL Q*.12.38): English Experience 273 (Amsterdam, Da Capo, 1970).

Manuscript: BL Add 41137: author's 'holograph draft' dated 1579, apparently used as the author's master copy, to which amendments were added up to 1600 for subsequent editions; there are no signs of it having been used as the printer's copy. The AS passage (in the printed book on N3ᵛ–4ʳ) occurs on fo 39ʳ/1–3 and reads: þeoꝼaꞃ þe haꞇaþ oððe ꞃeo|ꞃon men. ꝼꞃam ꞃeoꝼon hloþ oþ ꝼɩꝼ ⁊ þꞃɩꞇɩᵹ. | ⁊ ꞃẏþþan heꝺe.

1582.1: Lambarde, William, *EIRENARCHA: or of The Office of the Justices of Peace, in two Bookes.* 2nd edn of **1581.1**. London: Henry Bynneman [for] Ralph Newbery, 1582. STC 15164; STC 15164a, with substitute preliminary gathering. ESTC 108154 & 108156. AS3.
Law of Ine (extract)
  Collation: 8⁰: A⁴ B–2L⁸. [$5 signed (-A1,3,4)] 268 leaves, paginated [i–viii], 1–511, *512–528* (115 misnumbered 511).
  Note: BL 1381.b.26 contains after sig. A another gathering: ²A⁸ ($4 signed).
SOURCE OF PASSAGE UTILIZING ANGLO-SAXON TYPES:
N4ʳ (p. 183)   From 1581.1 N3ᵛ–4ʳ   Extract from Laws of Ine 13,1
                                           (ed. Liebermann, I, 94–5)
TYPE:
Main text in a Pica Textura   Body 86.   Face 80 × 2: 2.8.
Robert Granjon's Pica Roman, e.g., on L2ᵛ–3ʳ (pp. 148–149).
                                 Body 86.   Face 80 × 1.6: 2.8.
Granjon's second Pica Italic, the *Cicero pendante*
                                 Body 82.5. Face 80 × 1.5: 2.5.
AS3: Lambardian Pica Anglo-Saxon (with cap ẟ for ð) used in conjunction with Granjon's Pica Roman on N4ʳ (p. 183; text) and P2ᵛ (p. 212; words).
Special sorts shown:
  11 lower-case sorts: ð (= cap ẟ), *e*, ꝼ, ᵹ, ꝅ, ꞃ, ꞅ/ſ, ꞇ, þ (usually cap Þ), ð, ꝺ.
  Two sizes of þ seem to be used both as lower case: cap Þ appears in þeofas (where its capital status is appropriate) and everywhere else except in oþ, which has a lower case þ.
  Total: 12 sorts.
AS 1, ẏ not used; no caps used distinctively as upper case letters; roman colon used not AS punctus versus; uses 7 (number) for ⁊; on P2ᵛ rom cap **M** is used not AS ⱮⱭ.
Anglo-Saxon glossed suprascript on P2ᵛ (p. 212) in a Long Primer Italic.
  Copies seen:
    STC 15164: BL 1381.b.26 (lacks sig.2L; bound with Lambarde's *Duties of Constables* 1584 (STC 15147); OBL Dep.f.42 (lacks 2L8).
    STC 15164a: KCC A.5.106 (gift of George Chawner 1914) lacks 2L8 (STC wrongly designates 15164); BL 6283.aa.4 (owned by Thomas Ruddocke); OBL Vet.A.1.f.72(1).
    Copies also at: STC 15164, CEC; FSL, HHL, HUL, IUL, MUL, UCBL.

STC 15164a, CEC, LSH, LUL, OTC; FSL, USLC, NYCU, BMC, HHL, HUL, MUL, NLC, UTA.

Bibliography: see 1581.1.

1583.1: Foxe, John (ed.), *The Second Volume of the Ecclesiastical Historie, conteining the Acts and Monuments of Martyrs*. 4th edn of 1570.1 (= 2nd edn; 3rd edn 1576.1). London: John Day, 1583. STC 11225; ESTC S122167. AS1.

Extracts from 1566.1, 1567.1 taken from 1576.1

Collation vol. II, bks 7 and 8 only:

2⁰: 2Aa–2Yy⁶ 3A–3N⁶ 3O⁶ (3O1 + χ1) 3P–3S⁶ 3T–3V⁴ [$4 signed (-2Aa1, 2Pp3, 3T4, 3V4), 2Nn2 missigned 'NN.ij'] 249 leaves, paginated *797–798*, 799–1293 (omitting no. 1222; 3Oχ1 unnumbered, pp. 802, 803 misnumbered 798, 799, 843 misnumbered 841, 845 misnumbered 849, 897 misnumbered 881, 918 misnumbered 927, 927 misnumbered 918, 1149 misnumbered 1152, 1152 misnumbered 1149, 1194 misnumbered 1203, 1203 misnumbered 1194, 1278 misnumbered 1286, 1285 misnumbered 1293).

SOURCES OF PASSAGES UTILIZING ANGLO-SAXON TYPES:

3G4ʳ/b/76–81 From 1576.1, 23G3ᵛ/a/68–73 (p. 1114a), Ælfric's 'Excusatio Dictantis' (opening statement) at the end of his homily *Depositio S. Martin* (Godden 1979: XXXIV);

3G4ᵛ/a /4–7 From 1576.1, 23G3ᵛ/a/79–82 (p. 1114a), Ælfric's *Grammar*, opening statement from OE Preface (cf. Zupitza 1880: 2), with þa for 1576.1 ða for 1570.1 ðaꞅ (lıꞅtlan);

3G4ᵛ/a/26–44 From 1576.1, 23G3ᵛ/b/16–35 (p. 1114b), Ælfric's letter to Wulfsige III (bp of Sherborne 992–1002) extracts (Fehr 1914: §§135–142), with ðꞃıȝhten for 1570.1 ðꞃıhten, and a new error bletꞃah for 1576.1 bletꞃaþ;

3G4ᵛ/b/1 to 3G5ʳ/a/7 From 1576.1, 23G3ᵛ/b/66–4ʳ/b/3 (pp. 1114b–15b), Ælfric's second letter to Wulfstan (abp of York 1002–23) extracts (Fehr 1914: §§86–95, 97–109), with ðæȝe peꞇꞇan for 1570.1 ðæȝe ꞅeꞇꞇan, and ꞅacꞃıꞅıcıum for 1570.1 ꞅumeꞅe ꞅacꞃıꞅıcıum;

3G5ᵛ/a/12 to 3G6ᵛ/b/57 From 1576.1, 23G4ᵛ/b/11–6ʳ/b/16 (pp. 1116b–19b), Ælfric's *Sermo de Sacrificio in die Pascae* (same omissions as 1570.1; Godden 1979: XV), with bebeað þam (3G5ᵛ/a/20) for 1570.1 bebeað Ꝥoyꞅeꞅ þam, eꞃenð (3G6ʳ/a/52) for 1570.1 aꞃenð, pæðeꞃ oꞃ (3G5ʳ/b/13) for 1570.1 pæðeꞃ þa oꞃ, ꞇeꞃmeaȝēne (3G6ᵛ/a/2) for 1570.1 ꞇoꞃmeaȝenne, etc.

3I6ʳ/b/1–5 From 1576.1, 23I3ᵛ/b/32–6 (p. 1138b), ASC (E), annal for 1129 (Clark 1954: 51).

TYPE:

Main text in Small Pica Textura	Body 72	Face 70 × 2: 3
Small Pica Roman e.g. on 2Qq2ʳ–3ᵛ	Body 72	Face 70 × 1.5: 2.2

AS1: The Parkerian Great Primer Anglo-Saxon acquired by Day occurs on 2G4ʳ–6ᵛ and 3I6ʳ in combination with an English-size Roman Body 117   Face 100 × 2: 4. Special sorts shown:

In the specimen on 3G5ᵛ/a: 12 lower-case sorts: ð, ꝼ, ȝ, ı, ꝑ, ſ, τ, ẏ, 3; þ, đ, ꝑ;
                               5 capitals: Æ¹, S, Ƿ, Ð, Ꝑ;
                               1 other: ⁊;
                    Total: 18 sorts;
In the text: 11 lower-case sorts: ð, ꝼ, ȝ, ı, ꝑ, ſ, τ, ẏ; þ, đ, ꝑ;
                               6 capitals: Æ¹, Є, Ð, ꟽ, Ꞩ, Ꝑ;
                               3 others: ⁊, þ̇, ⁊̇;
           Overall total: 23 sorts.

AS đ is the later casting that first appears in 1571.1 (sig. 2H to end), the one that fits snugly against the preceding letter. An aberration appears to be 'segð' on 2G4ᵛ/b/24.

   Copy seen: CUL Young 199–200 (in gold-tooled binding probably by John Bateman, successor to the MacDurnan Gospels binder; cf. Foot 1978–83: II, pl. to no. 53).
   Copies also at: AUL, BL, BLC, CGC, CRH, KCC, DWL, HCL, NLS, OAS, OBL, OBrC, MJRUL, LPL, NT, UBL, WCL; FSL, HHL, HUL, IUL, SCN, UCBL, YUB;
Bibliography: Arber V.129, no. 2964.

1586.1: Camden, William, *Britannia sive Florentissimorvm Regnorvm, Angliæ, Scotiæ, Hiberniæ, et Insvlarvm adiacentium ex intima antiquitate Chorographica Descriptio*. London: [Eliot's Court Press] per Ralph Newbery, 1586. STC 4503; ESTC S107379 . AS2.

OE Proper Names

   Context: Following a proposal originally put forward by John Leland (summarized by Levine 1987: 81) and published by John Bale in 1549 (STC 15445), Camden provided a chorographical description of Britain, starting from the records of Roman Britain and the Antonine Itinerary (cf. 1658.2). He used the Roman description of the tribes in Britain as a framework for the divisions of Britain, into which the various counties were grouped. The study of topography necessitated a knowledge of place-names, for which Anglo-Saxon was required. For this purpose Camden undoubtedly used the manuscript of Nowell/Lambarde's *Dictionarium Angliae topographicum* (Cotton Titus A.xiii, subsequently published as Lambarde 1730). Not knowing this Powicke (1948: 75) described Camden's philology as 'pitiful', but Camden's recognition, drawing on Lambarde's lead, of the importance of the historical study of linguistic forms helped to establish Anglo-Saxon as a necessary ingredient for the study of the past in England (cf. Watts 2001: 46–48). His approach was in the continental tradition, and the book was frequently reprinted on the continent, as well as going through several editions in England, becoming the occasion for several new Anglo-Saxon type-designs, or the re-casting of existing ones.

Collation: 8⁰: A–2N⁸ O⁴ [$4 signed (-A1, 2I4, 2O3,4; 2D1,2,3 missigned D1,2,3). 292 leaves, paginated [i–xvi], 1–556, 557–568 (pp. 486–488 unnumbered, pp. 187 misnumbered 117, 213 misnumbered 113, 245 misnumbered 145). Note: State 2 shown by 2D1 and 2D3 signed correctly.

Types:
Main text in Claude Garamont's (second) Long Primer Roman
    Body 68   Face 66 × 1.2: 2

AS2: The Parkerian Pica Anglo-Saxon occurs badly fitted with Garamond's Long Primer Roman in words on pp. 33, 48, 57, 59–60, 63, 71, 80, 83, 89, 92–93, 98–99, 101, 106, 109, 113, 115–117, 121–122, 126, 129, 138–139, 141, 143, 148, 151–152, 154–156, 158, 161, 163, 166, 168–169, 171–172, 174, 177, 181, 185, 188, 190–191, 193–194, 197–198, 200, 204–205, 210, 212, 218–219, 226, 237, 239, 241, 246–248, 252–254, 256, 261, 263, 266, 271–272, 276, 280, 284, 294, 297, 299, 306–308, 312–313, 320, 322, 324, 327–329, 333, 336, 339, 341–342, 351, 391, 399–400, 402–5, 407, 417, 419, 428, 435, 441, 445, 467, 469, 471, 526–527, 551.

Special sorts shown:

    10 lower-case sorts: ð, f, ʒ, p, r, t, ẏ; þ, ð, p (straight, with left branching serif at foot);

    5 capitals: E, Ð (used correctly), M, S (used correctly), Ð (p. 261; 2.8 mm).
    Total: 15 sorts.

Anomalies: r used erron. for p on pp. 48, 60; AS *e* and 1 not used, nor æ/Æ (cf. P2ᵛ Aeʒlerbunʒe, 2F7ʳ Gaetrheueð); on p. 163 p used erron for p (wynn), and considerable ignorance of OE shown by the form Cantʒpanlantð. Error on p. 551 with Roman y for AS ẏ: Seolrey (correct on p. 156).

    Copies seen:

    State 1, with 2D1 and 2D3 missigned: CUL Pet.C.4.36; DML I.5.28.

    State 2, with 2D1 and 2D3 signed correctly: CUL Syn.8.58.3 (gift of George I, 1715).
    Copies also at: BL, BUL, CPC, CSJ, TCC, CUW, MJRUL, LHL, LSH, MTP, NLS, OJC, OMaCS, OQC, OWoC, OXC, SAC, SBT, UCL, DML, GUB; FSL, USLC, NYPL, HHL, DDUL, GTS, HUL, NLC, UTA.

Bibliography:
Arber V.142, no. 3313; Boon 1987; Clement 1997: 224–225; Collinson 1998; Edwards 1998; Fussner 1962: ch. 9; Herendeen 2007: ch. 5; Kendrick 1950: ch. 8; Kunst 1995; Levine 1987: 93–95; Levy 1964; Levy 1967: 148–154; McKitterick 1997; Mendyk 1989: 49–54; Parry 1995: ch. 1; Piggott 1951; Powicke 1948: esp. 74–78; Rockett 1990 and 1995; Taylor 1934: 9–12, no. 257; Watts 2001: 46–48.

Editions:
Gibson, Edmund (2 vols) 1722; Gough, Richard (3 vols) 1789, 2nd edn (4 vols) 1806, repr. in facsimile as vol. 73 of the series *Anglistica et Americana*, Hildesheim, 1974.
On-line: L text of 1586.1 together with Philemon Holland's English t (1610.5) at <www.philological.bham.ac.uk/cambrit>

1587.1: Camden, William, *Britannia sive Florentissimorvm Regnorvm, Angliæ, Scotiæ, Hiberniæ, et Insvlarvm adiacentium ex intima antiquitate Chorographica Descriptio*. 2nd edn of 1586.1. London: [Eliot's Court Press] per Ralph Newbery, 1587. STC 4504; ESTC S107382. AS2.

OE Proper Names

Collation: 8⁰: A–2V⁸ [$4 signed (-A1, 2O1). 354 leaves, paginated [i–xvi], 1–648, 649–672 (pp. 560–562 and 613 unnumbered, pp. 225 misnumbered 125, 428 misnumbered 328, 481 misnumbered 482, 502 misnumbered 452, 529 misnumbered 526).

Types:
Main text in Claude Garamond's (second) Long Primer Roman
    Body 68   Face 66 × 1.2: 2
Long quotations (e.g. on B4ʳ) in a Long Primer Italic
    Body 68   Face 62 × 1.2: 1.9

AS2: Parkerian Pica AS shown on specimen on A8ᵛ, and badly fitted with Garamond's Long Primer Roman in words on pp. 44, 62, 76–78, 80, 88, 90, 98, 102, 108, 111–112), 114, 117, 119, 121, 128, 131, 134–139, 143, 145, 149–150, 153, 162–163, 165, 168, 173–174, 177–178, 181–183, 185, 187–188, 190–191, 194, 197–199, 201, 203, 206, 210, 214, 218, 221–222, 225–226, 229–230, 232, 237, 243–245, 252–253, 262–263, 275, 277, 280, 285–287, 292–294, 297, 302, 304, 307, 312, 314, 318, 322–323, 328, 340, 343, 346, 353–356, 360–361, 369, 372, 374, 377, 379, 384, 388, 393, 395–396, 406, 451, 462–463, 465–468, 470, 482, 484, 499, 503–504, 506, 514, 538, 541, 543, 545, 606–607, 639.

Special sorts shown in specimen:
    12 lower-case sorts: ð, ꝼ, ᵹ, ꝟ (=h), ı, p, ꞅ, τ, ẏ; þ, ð, p (straight, with straight descender);
    7 capitals: Æ¹, Æ², Є, ᗰ, S, X, Ð;
    2 others: ꝥ, þ.
    Total: 21 sorts.
Special sorts shown in text:
    10 lower-case sorts: ð, ꝼ, ᵹ, p, ꞅ, τ, ẏ; þ, ð, p (straight, but slopes top left to bottom right on pp. 153, 163 2x, 185; top right to bottom left on p. 230),

p: Form with descender with outward (leftward) splay from bow down (not left branching foot) occurs on pp. 168, 194 and generally, but tilted one has no splay. Straight descender with no splay or serif on pp. 197, 201, 206, 287. Straight with left-branching serif at foot on p. 253.

Anomalies: AS *e* and ı not used pp. 80, 90; ſ erron. for p on p. 88 (taken over from 1586.1 p. 71), ꝼat Bapan (hot Bath) on p. 128 with p erron for þ and H for h (?).

5 capital sorts: Є, Ꝺ (used correctly e.g Ꝺantersyp pp. 145, 188, 287, ?incorrect p. 128), Ϻ, Ꞅ (pp. 108, 112, 173, 183 Ꞅealſey, 185, 206, 262, but AS Ꞅ not used pp. 73, 138), Đ (p. 302);

Anomalies: Woðeneꞃðic with no cap wynn on p. 134 (cp. pintancerten p. 150), Minꞃten on p. 137 with roman capital M, Bꞃiȝhthealmeꞃtun p. 185

On p. 191 (1586.1 p. 163) considerable ignorance of OE is shown by the form Cantȝuaplantð, but 1586.1 p used erron for p (wynn) has been 'corrected' to u, also 1586.1 Ꝺapepic (R4ᵛ) has been corrected to 1587.1 Ꝺapepic (T8ʳ).

On V7ᵛ (p. 302) Đeotꞃopð is an improvement on 1586.1 Đeotꞃopð S3ʳ (p. 261); conversely 1586.1 Nopthuic (S4ʳ) ➝ 1587.1 Norchuic (V8ᵛ).

AS æ/Æ not used, (cf. R3ʳ Aeȝleꞃbunȝe, 2K4ᵛ Gaetꞃheueð), as 1586.1.

    Copies seen: CUL Syn.8.58.11; QUB Percy 221.

    Copies also at: BL, BCL, BPL, CPC, CUW, IPL, MJRUL, LSH, NewCL, NT, NUL, OAM, OBL, OQC, OTC, OXC, NLI, BNL; FSL, HHL, HUL, KSRL, LCP, MRCS, NLC, PUL, UTA, UTK, YUB.

Bibliography: Harris 2015: 280–283; Vine 2014. See also **1586.1**

1588.1: Lambarde, William, *EIRENARCHA: or of The Office of the Justices of Peace, in foure Bookes*. 3rd edn of **1581.1**. London: [(?)Eliot's Court Press for] Ralph Newbery, 1588. STC 15165; ESTC S108197. AS2.

Laws of Ine (extract)

    Collation: 8⁰: π¹ A² B–2Z⁸. [$4 signed (-Q2, 2S3,4, 2Z4)] 363 leaves, paginated [i–vi], 1–627, 628–720 (pp. 220–221, 226–227 unnumbered as printed sideways).

SOURCE OF PASSAGE UTILIZING ANGLO-SAXON TYPES:

O1ʳ (p. 193)   From (?)**1581.1** N3ᵛ–4ʳ: Laws of Ine 13,1 (extract, as Liebermann I.94–5).

TYPE:

Main text in Pica Textura	Body 82.	Face 78 × 2: 3.
Pierre Haultin's 2nd Pica Roman (e.g. L8ᵛ)	Body 82.5.	Face 80 × 1.8: 2.9.
Robert Granjon's second Pica Italic (of three), the *Cicero pendante*	Body 82.5.	Face 80 × 1.5: 2.5.

AS2: Parkerian Pica Anglo-Saxon on O1ʳ (p. 193, text) and Q7ʳ (p. 239, words) combined with a Long Primer Roman of which the only dimension available here is the x-height 1.4.

Special sorts shown:
  10 lower-case sorts: f, ȝ, ƕ (uc used lc), ꝑ, ꞃ, ꞇ, ẏ; þ, ð, p;
  2 capitals: Ꟁ, Ð;
  2 others: ꝿ, ʝ.

Anomalies: No *e*, 1 (i.e. these are ordinary roman); ð does not occur, nor do other capitals.

  Total: 14 sorts.

  Copies seen: TCC VI.2.7; ECC 326.5.53 (lacks preliminaries and 2Z8); BL 959.a.18 (lacks 2Z8; signed Paul Aylworth, s.xvii), 1485.w.4 (signed by Robert Rudd 1668).

  Copies also at: CGC, CSJ, EdUL, NewCL, NT, OBL, MBS; FSL, HHL, HUL, IUL, KSRL, NWU, NYS.

Anoher edition (not distinguished by STC, which observes the relevant features only in 1591.1): **Copy seen:** TCD EE.mm.29 (lacks 2Z8).

1588.2: The same as 1588.1, except for sigs D and E, revised versions of which have been substituted. 1588.2 can be distinguished from 1588.1 by noting features on D4ʳ:

1588.1   D4 signed;   D4ʳ begins *anno*, ends *in-*, catchword *uenerint*;
1588.2   D4 unsigned;   D4ʳ begins *vim*, ends *vel*, catchword *qua*.

Bibliography: see 1581.1.

1589.1: Hakluyt, Richard, *The Principall Navigations, Voiages and Discoveries of the English Nation*. London: [for] George Bishop and Ralph Newbery, deputies to Christopher Barker, 1589. STC 12625; ESTC S106735. Facsimile intr. Stephen B. Quinn and Raleigh A. Skelton (Cambridge: Cambridge University Press, 1965).

  Collation: 2⁰: *⁸ A–T⁶ U–X⁴, 2A–2V⁶ 2X–2Y⁶ (-2X5–2Y6+'2Y6'), 3A–3L⁶ 3M¹² 3N–3Y⁶, 4A–4E⁶ 4F⁴. [16], 242, [2], 243–501, [1], 506–643, [12], 644–825, [12] p.

No AS, but translation (probably by Nowell) of the passage about Ohtere's voyage from the *Orosius* on 3H5ᵛ (p. 599) via 1576.3 based on Tiberius B.i [Brewer 1952–3: 207–209]. Cf. **1576.3**.

  Copies: BL, CUL, ChC, CPC, TCC, ERCP, LMT, LUL, OBL, OAS, ONC, OWmC, OWoC, OXC, UCL; FSL, USLC, HHL, NYPL, NYPM, HUL, AAS, JCB, NLC, UCBL, UVL; ATL, NSW, SSA.

1590.1: Camden, William, *Britannia sive Florentissimorvm Regnorvm, Angliæ, Scotiæ, Hiberniæ, et Insvlarvm adiacentium ex intima antiquitate Chorographica*

Descriptio. 3rd edn of **1586.1**; 2nd edn **1587.1**. London: [Eliot's Court Press for] George Bishop, 1590. STC 4505; ESTC S107384. AS2.

OE **Proper Names**

Collation: 8⁰: A–3D⁸ [$4 signed (-A1,3 2N4 2X1)] 400 leaves, paginated [i–xvi], 1–762, *763–784* (pp. 405, 672–674 unnumbered; pp. 90 misnumbered 89, 321 misnumbered 221, 342 misnumbered 326, 404 misnumbered 304).

Variant state shown by turning of 6 in page number 644 so that it looks like 944 in CUL Pet.C.10.23.

TYPE:

Main text set in a Pica Roman   Body 82   Face 78 × 1.5: 2.5
Granjon's 2nd Pica Italic used for long quotations, e.g. on F8ʳ–G4ᵛ.
AS specimen on A8ʳ = AS2 Parkerian Pica, showing the following special sorts:

11 lower-case sorts: ð, ꝼ, ᵹ, ı, p, ꞃ, ꞇ, ẏ; þ, ð, p;
8 capitals: Æ¹, Æ², Є, Ꝺ, ꟽ, S, X; Ð;
2 others: ꝫ, þ.

Total: 23 sorts.

AS2: Parkerian Pica AS poorly fitted with Claude Garamond's (second) Long Primer Roman shown in words on pp. 25, 54, 74, 101, 103, 106, 113, 116, 118, 126, 132, 141, 145, 147–149, 152, 154, 156–157, 165, 169, 173–174, 176–177, 179, 184, 186, 191–192, 195, 204–206, 209, 211, 217–218, 223–224, 226, 228–229, 231–232, 234, 236, 238–239, 242, 246–248, 250–251, 254, 256, 262, 266, 271, 274–275, 279–80, 284–288, 293, 300–303, 313, 322–323, 336–337, 339, 342, 349, 351, 356–359, 362, 369, 371, 374, 382–383, 389, 393–394, 400, 417, 420, 423, 432–433, 435, 440–441, 451, 455, 457, 461–463, 469, 474, 480–481, 483, 496, 524, 546, 555, 557, 560–562, 564, 566–567, 581, 585, 603, 608–609, 611, 621, 648, 650, 653–655, 722–723, 751.
Special sorts shown in text:

10 lower-case sorts: ð, ꝼ, ᵹ, p, ꞃ, ꞇ, ẏ; þ, ð, p (straight on p. 116, tilted top left to bottom right on p. 106); Roman medial h on pp. 118, 169, 176, 186 (ꝺanꞇeꞃchẏp erron., cf. 1587.1 ꝺanꞇeꞃhẏp);
6 capitals: Є, Ꝺ, ꟽ, S; Ð, P. Capital P and lower-case p used correctly on p. 451 in Paꞃꞃẏnᵹ-pẏc; lower-case p used initially for a capital on pp. 211, 286, and on p. 313 (2x) for capital P used correctly in 1587.1 p. 253; capital P used for lower-case in ЄalnePic 2T8ʳ (p. 655); capital W (not 'wynn') used on pp. 173, 206; capital Æ not used on p. 302 in Aeᵹleꞃbuꞃᵹe, lower-case æ not used on p. 609 in Gaeꞇꞃheueð.

Anomalies: On p. 239 (1587.1 p. 191; 1586.1 p. 163) considerable ignorance of OE is shown by the form Canꞇᵹuapɩanꞇð. The use of AS type breaks down on p. 311 (cp. p. 337), where we find 'Saxonicè Ligean' for 1587.1 'Saxonicè Liᵹeā' (p. 252);

on p. 411 Deoraby for 1587.1 Deoþbẏ (p. 361). Another name-word has been newly Anglo-Saxonized on p. 441: Noþth-woþthig, where only the rs are AS. Note: For the forms of AS proper names Camden drew on the manuscript of Lambarde's *Dictionarium Angliae topographicum*; see 1586.1 under Context.

    Copies seen: CUL Syn.7.59.24; LFL 1C (signed on tp by Thomas St Aubyn (1578–1637) of Clowance, Cornwall, who made numerous annotations, partly cropped when the book was bound later in s.xvii).

    Copies also at: BL, BCL, CGC, ChC, CUW, DUL, LSH, NLS, NT, OBL, OAM, ONC, OQC, OXC, StA, UCL, YML, GUB; FSL, USLC, NYCU, HHL, HUL, IUL, MCRS, YUB.

Bibliography: see 1586.1.

1590.2: Camden, William, *Britannia sive Florentissimorvm Regnorvm, Angliæ, Scotiæ, Hiberniæ, et Insvlarvm adiacentivm ex intima antiquitate Chorographica Descriptio.* Frankfurt-am-Main: Johann Wechel, impensis Peter Fischer, hæredum Henricus Tacquius, 1590. USTC 617285; Adams C408.

    Collation: 8^0: A–3D^8 [16], 762, [22] p.

    AS names appear within square brackets in Italic with no special sorts, e.g., L4^v (p. 152).

    Copy seen: CUL Hhh.807 (owned by Nathaniel Harris 1593, bound in brown calf, blind-stamped ornament front and back).

    Copies also at: OBL, OXC, StA, TMT, BUG, CLB, CUB, DUB, FHB, GFB, HLB, HUB, JUB, MBS, MUB, VON, ZZB, FBN, MBC, PBU, RBA, RBC, VBD, MBN, SBU, VBU, RSL, BNL.

1591.1: Lambarde, William, EIRENARCHA: *or of The Office of the Justices of Peace, in foure Bookes.* Re-issue of 1588.2 (3rd edn rev) with replacement preliminaries). London: [(?)Eliot's Court Press for] Ralph Newbery, 1591. STC 15166; ESTC S113604. AS2.

    Note: STC's claim that this item is a modification of 1588.1 with new sigs D and E is superseded by the observation of the relevant features in 1588.2, which now needs to be recognized as a separate item with its own distinguishing number, presumably 15165.5.

Laws of Ine (extract)

    Collation: 8^0: π^4 A^{1+1} B–2Z^8. [$4 signed (-D4, Q2, 2S3,4, 2Z4)] 366 leaves, paginated [i–x], 1–627, 628–720 (pp. 220–221, 226–227 not numbered as printed sideways).

    Copies seen: CPC 12.15.31 (gift of Swithun Butterfield (d.1611) whose initials in the form of a monogram are on the cover and in the left-hand blank shield at the bottom of the title-page border; lacks 2Z8); BL 1607/387 bound with Lambarde's *Duties of Constables* (1587; STC 15148); OBL 35.c.41(1) lacks sigs π, except for π1

(=tp), A, and 2Z8, and bound with Lambarde's *Duties of Constables* (1601; STC 15153).

Copies also at: MJRUL, OAS; FSL, HHL, HUL, MUL.

Bibliography: see 1581.1.

1592.1: Lambarde, William, *EIRENARCHA: or of The Office of the Justices of Peace, in foure Bookes.* 4th edn of 1581.1, re-set from 1591.1. London: [(?)Eliot's Court Press for] Ralph Newbery, 1592. STC 15167; ESTC S108199. AS2.

Laws of Ine (extract)

    Collation: 8⁰: A–2V⁸. [$4 signed (-A1, O4, 2I4, 2Q3)] 344 leaves, paginated [i–ii], 1–600, 601–686 (212–213, 218–219 unnumbered, 239 misnumbered 293, 362, 363, 366 misnumbered 342, 343, 346 respectively, 575 misnumbered 576; '7' in 47 partly turned on side).

SOURCE OF PASSAGE UTILIZING ANGLO-SAXON TYPES:

M7ᵛ (p. 188)   From 1581.1 N3ᵛ–4ʳ: Extract from Laws of Ine 13,1 (Liebermann, I, 94–5).

TYPE:

Main text in a Pica Textura (Body 82; the same as in 1588.1) interspersed with Pierre Haultin's 2nd Pica Roman (Body 82.5), e.g. L5ʳ (p. 167), and Robert Granjon's second Pica Italic (of three; Body 82.5), the *Cicero pendante*, e.g. L6ʳ (p. 169).

AS2: The Parkerian Pica Anglo-Saxon occurs on M7ᵛ (p. 188, text) and P5ʳ (p. 231, words) combined with Haultin's Long Primer Roman (R66; Vervliet 2010: no.42) as used for Precedents, e.g. on 2T3ʳ.

    Body 68   Face 66 × 1.4: 2

Special sorts shown:

        9 lower-case sorts: ꝼ, ȝ, ꝑ, ſ, ꞇ, ẏ; þ, ð, ꝓ;
        4 capitals: Ƕ (used lc), Ꝥ, Þ (used lc in ƕɑꞇɑÞ), Ð;
        2 others: ꝫ, ꝯ.

Total: 15 sorts

No ꝺ in the passage; other capitals also do not occur.

Copies seen: TCD DD.o.71; OBL Vet.A1.e.82 (contemporary gold-tooled white vellum binding with the initials HM).

Copies also at: BL, MJRUL, SBT, SUL; FSL, NYCU, HHL, HUL, KSRL, MUL, TSC, UVL, WMUL. (E)STC report a copy in Downing College, Cambridge, but it was not found there.

Bibliography: see 1581.1.

1593.1: Megiser, Hieronymus, *Specimen Quadraginta diversarum atque inter se differentium linguarum & dialectorum, Oratio Dominica, totidem linguis expressa*. Frankfurt-am-Main: Johann Spies 1593. Adams M1038; another edn 1603 = USTC 2052717. Facsimile, *Das Vaterunser in vierzig Sprachen [von] Hieronymus Megiser*, ed. Branko Berčič, Litterae Slovenicae 4 (Munich: R. Trofenik, 1968).

Collation: 8⁰: A–C⁸ [56] p.

No AS, but on B6ʳ no. xxv offers a version of the Lord's Prayer described as 'ANGLOSAXONICÈ seu linguâ Vallicâ, & vetere Britannicâ', which is in fact Welsh; it is printed in a Paragon Roman.

Copy seen: CUL F159.e.1.6.

1594.1: Lambarde, William, *EIRENARCHA: or of The office of the Iustices of Peace in foure Bookes*. 5th edn of 1581.1 re-set from 4th edn 1592.1. London: [(?)Eliot's Court Press for] Ralph Newbery, 1594. STC 15168; ESTC S108200. AS2.

Laws of Ine (extract)

Collation: 8⁰: A–2V⁸ 2X⁴ [$4 signed (-A1, O3, 2X4)] 348 leaves, paginated [i–ii], 1–606, *607–694* (pp. 214–215, 220–221 unnumbered as printed sideways; 1st '4' of p. 494 inverted).

SOURCE OF PASSAGE UTILIZING ANGLO-SAXON TYPES:

M7ᵛ   From **1581.1** N3ᵛ–4ʳ: Extract from Laws of Ine 13,1 (Liebermann, I.94–95)

TYPE:

Main text in a Pica Textura	Body 82	Face 76 × 1.9: 2.8
Pica Roman (as on I8ʳ = p. 141)	Body 82	Face 80 × 1.7: 2.7
Pica Italic (as on R6ʳ = p. 153)	Body 83	Face 80 × 1.5: 2.2

AS2: The Parkerian Pica Anglo-Saxon occurs on M7ᵛ (p. 188, text) and P6ʳ (p. 233, words) combined with Claude Garamond's (second) Long Primer Roman, as used for Precedents e.g. 2V3ᵛ.   Body 68   Face 66 × 1.4: 2

Special sorts used: 9 + 1 lower-case sorts: f, ᵹ, ƀ, p, ſ, t, ẏ; þ, ð, ꝑ;
                      2 capitals: Ꟁ (on P6ʳ), Ð;
                      2 others: ꝉ, j̇.
            Total: 14 sorts

Note: No ð occurs in the text.

Copies seen: TCC VI.7.20¹ (bound with STC 15146; gift of Dr James Duport (Dean of Peterborough, Vice-Master TCC); OBL 35.c.47¹ (bound with STC 15151).

Copies also at: BL, MJRUL, LL, NT; FSL, NYCU, NYHS, HHL, HUL, IUL; NSW.

Bibliography: see 1581.1.

1594.2: Camden, William, *Britannia sive Florentissimorvm Regnorvm, Angliæ, Scotiæ, Hiberniæ, et Insvlarvm adiacentium ex intima antiquitate Chorographica Descriptio.* 4th edn of 1586.1. London: [Eliot's Court Press for] George Bishop, 1594. STC 4506; ESTC S107385. AS2/3.

OE proper names

    Collation: 8⁰: A–3A⁸ 3B⁴ [$4 signed (-A1 3B3,4)] 380 leaves, paginated [i–xvi], 1–717, *718–744* (pp. 317 misnumbered 217, 366 misnumbered 368).

TYPE:

Main text in Pica Roman   Body 82   Face 78 × 1.5: 2.5

Granjon's 2nd Pica Italic used for long quotations, e.g. on G3ʳ–8ʳ.

AS2: Specimen on A8ʳ = Parkerian Pica Anglo-Saxon: identical to that in 1590.1, A8ʳ.

AS2/3: The Parkerian Pica Anglo-Saxon with admixture of letters from the Lambardian Pica Anglo-Saxon badly fitted with a Long Primer Roman is shown in words on pp. 62, 81, 105, 107, 110, 112, 118, 121–122, 131, 136–137, 145, 149–53, 156, 158, 161–162, 169, 173, 177–80, 186, 188, 192–193, 196, 204–205, 208, 210, 214–216, 221–222, 224–226, 228–229, 231–233, 235–236, 238, 243, 245, 247–248, 250, 253, 257, 261, 265, 267–268, 270, 272–273, 277–281, 285, 291–293, 295, 301–303, 312–314, 328, 330, 333, 340–341, 346–348, 352, 359, 361, 364, 371–372, 378–379, 382, 389, 404, 407, 410, 418–419, 421, 425–427, 436, 439, 442, 445–457, 453, 457–458, 463–465, 477, 492, 502, 521, 529–530, 533–535, 537, 539, 551, 554, 566, 571, 576–578, 588, 611–612, 614, 617–618, 681–682, 706.

Special sorts shown in text:

    11 lower-case sorts: ð, e (pp. 445, 457, 492, 571, 576, 617, 681–2, 706), f, ᵹ, h (also roman lc h), n, ſ, t, ẏ; þ, ð (p. 161), p (upright with serif to left of foot on pp. 112, 205, 210, no serif p. 173);

    6 capitals: E, h (p. 169), M, S, Ð (pp. 359, 418), P (p. 588);

Clear examples of Parkerian and Lambardian 1576 Lambardian/Parkerian Pica AS:

AS lower-case letters used together are ſ on Q1ʳ (p. 225) in Ciſſanceaſtep 'Chichester', also p. 529; f on 2O3ᵛ in p. 566 Taðencliffe; ᵹ, Parkerian on H8ᵛ (p. 112), Lambardian on H5ʳ (pp. 105, 436); þ, Parkerian on 2R2ʳ (p. 611), Lambardian on 2R2ᵛ (p. 612).

Note: AS used for a catchword on X5ʳ.

Slavish copying at 1590.1 Deoρbiſ-ſcẏpe p. 440 ⟩ idem 1594.2 p. 425; the hyphen comes from 1586.1 p. 312, taken over in 1587.1 p. 360.

Some attempt to improve/correct the AS letters or ramp up their impact between editions is observable as follows:

    1590.1 pealh p. 113 ⟩ 1594.2 pealſh p. 118 (sim. 118 ⟩ 122);

1590.1 Oxenꝼoꞃðꞃcy̌ꝑe p. 284 ⟩ 1594.2 Oxenꝼoꞃðꞃchy̌ꝑe p. 277;

1590.1 Deuenꞃhiꝑe p. 126 ⟩ 1594.2 Deuenꞃchiꝑe p. 131;

1590.1 Suðꞃex p. 226 ⟩ 1594.2 Suðꞃex p. 224;

1590.1 Þe enim articulum effe Saxonicum credo, pro quo The nunc vtimur p. 311 ⟩ 1594.2 Þe enim articulum effe Saxonicum credo, pro quo The nunc vtimur p. 302

1590.1 peoᵹaꝑe-ceaꞃceꝑ, peᵹeoꝑna-ceaꞃceꝑ, & piꝑeceaꞃceꝑ p. 457 ⟩ 1594.2 Peoᵹaꝑe-ceaꞃceꝑ, Peᵹeoꝑna-ceaꞃceꝑ, & Piꝑeceaꞃceꝑ p. 442;

1590.1 Kiꝑꝑby p. 561 ⟩ 1594.2 Kiꝑkby̌ [near Pontefract] p. 534;

1590.1 Ealneƿic p. 655 ⟩ 1594.2 Ealnꝑic p. 618.

Heavier use of AS type is indicated as follows:

1590.1 pinbuꝑnham ⟩ 1594.2 py̌nbuꝑnÞam p. 152;

1590.1 Sheoueꞃham ⟩ 1594.2 SÞeoueꞃÞam p. 204;

1590.1 Wanacinᵹ ⟩ 1594.2 ƿanacinᵹ p. 205;

1590.1 Scoꝑeham ⟩ 1594.2 ScoꝑeÞam p. 228;

1590.1 Bꞃiᵹhthealmeꞃcun ⟩ 1594.2 BꞃiᵹhtÞealmeꞃcun p. 229;

1590.1 Deoꝑham ⟩ 1594.2 DeoꝑÞam p. 272;

1590.1 Saxonicè Liᵹean ⟩ 1594.2 Saxonicè Liᵹean p. 301;

1590.1 ꝼullonham ⟩ 1594.2 ꝼullonÞam p. 313;

1590.1 pealðham ⟩ 1594.2 pealðÞam p. 328;

1590.1 Noꞃthuy̌c ⟩ Noꞃðꝑy̌c 1594.2 p. 361;

1590.1 Eliᵹ ⟩ Ely̌ᵹ 1594.2 p. 378, 1590.1 Eliᵹe p. 390 ⟩ Ely̌ᵹ 1594.2 p. 379;

1590.1 Eaxanholme p. 433 ⟩ 1594.2 EaxanÞolme p. 419;

1590.1 Noꞃth-woꝑthig (newly with AS) p. 441 ⟩ 1594.2 NoꞃtÞ-poꝑtÞiᵹ p. 427;

1590.1 Auᵹuꞃcy̌neꞃ ac p. 461 ⟩ 1594.2 Auᵹuꞃcy̌neꞃ ak p. 445;

1590.1 Pƿeken-ceaꞃceꝑ p. 474 ⟩ 1594.2 Pƿeken-ceaꞃceꝑ p. 457;

1590.1 Scꝑobbeſbiꝑiᵹ p. 475 ⟩ 1594.2 Scꝑobbeꞃby̌ꝑiᵹ p. 458;

1590.1 Dunſeꞇꞇan p. 512 ⟩ 1594.2 Dunꞃeꞇꞇan p. 492;

1590.1 Taðenclıꝼꝼe p. 597 ⟩ 1594.2 Taðencliꝼꝼe p. 566;

1590.1 peoꝑ p. 603 ⟩ 1594.2 peoꝑ p. 571;

1590.1 Lanᵹceaꞃceꝑ p. 608 ⟩ 1594.2 Lanᵹceaꞃceꝑ p. 576;

1590.1 Tunnanceꞃceꝑ p. 653 ⟩ 1594.2 Tunnanceꞃceꝑ p. 617;

1590.1 ꟽoneᵹe p. 722 ⟩ 1594.2 ꟽoneᵹe p. 681;

1590.1 Enᵹleꞃea p. 723 ⟩ 1594.2 Enᵹleꞃea p. 682,

1590.1 Þanceꞃchy̌ꝑ ⟩ 1594.2 Þanceꞃhy̌ꝑ p. 188, as 1587.1, both erron. for -scyr. On p. 236 (1590.1 p. 239, 1587.1 p. 191, 1586 p. 163) considerable ignorance of OE shown by the form Cantᵹuaꝑlantð.

AS lost between editions: 1590.1 Giᵹhtꞃlepe 'Islip' p. 293 omitted in 1594.2 when the item was moved to T4ᵛ (p. 280).

Note: For the forms of AS proper names Camden drew on the manuscript of Lambarde's *Dictionarium Angliae topographicum*; see 1586.1 under Context.

    Copies seen: CUL Syn.6.59.10 (signed Louisa Julia Manners, Goadby Hall, 1832), Pet.B.2.35 (signed Wh[ite] Kennet).

    Copies also at: BL, BCL, BCLW, CMC, SCJ, CUW, DWL, ECL, EdUL, HRC, MJRUL, LGL, NLS, NT, OBL, OAS, OEF, OQC, OXC, SUL, UBL, UCL, BSB, GUB; FSL, HHL, HUL, IUL, MCRS, NLC, PUL, UPL, UTA, UTK, YUB

Bibliography: see 1586.1.

1596.1: Foxe, John (ed.), *The [Seconde] Volume of the Ecclesiastical Historie, conteyning the Acts and Monuments of Martyrs.* 5th edn of 1570.1 (= 2nd edn), vol. II, bks 7 and 8 only. London: Peter Short, 1596; sig. 5G printed by [John Windet]. STC 11226; 2nd issue (1597) 11226a. ESTC S122169 & S122170. AS1.

    Note: Sig. 5G was contracted out. It has no catchword at the end, a wider column width (91 rather than 89 mm; 93 mm on 5G2^{r}a), different page numbers, different line numbers between the columns, and uses arabic rather than roman numbers in the signature; see also under Type below. Sigs 5F–5G are made up of four leaves rather than the usual six. On historical grounds Windet is just about the only candidate who could have had the means of printing this amount of Old English, having succeeded to part of the printing materials of John Wolfe (fl.1579–1601), who was an apprentice to John Day I when the printing of Anglo-Saxon first got under way and who was an assignee of Day's son Richard, who ceased printing in 1584.

Extracts from 1566.1, 1567.1 taken from 1583.1

    Collation (vol. II, books 7 and 8 only): 2⁰: 4A⁶ (-4A1) 4B–4V⁶ 5A–5E⁶ 5F–5G⁴ 5H–5M⁶ 5N⁶ (5N4 + χ1) 5O–5S⁶ 5T1 (end of Book 8) [$3 signed (-4A1, 5F3, 5G3), 5G2 missigned 4G2] 225 leaves, paginated 731–1177 (pp. 761 misnumbered 751, 920 misnumbered 620, 1119 misnumbered 1179, 1166 misnumbered 1116). Different states shown by pp. 761, 1119 and 1166 being correctly numbered.

    Note 1: Sig. 4A1, originally the tp for vol. II, has been removed to provide the tp to vol. I.

    Note 2: The collation suggests that separate provision was made for Gatherings 5F–5G where it was anticipated the main Old English text would occur (in fact it is found in sig. 5G); the OE text in sig. 5I is set differently.

SOURCES OF PASSAGES UTILIZING ANGLO-SAXON TYPES:

5G2^v/b/24–7 (p. 1040) From **1583.1**, 3G4^r/b/76–81, Ælfric's 'Excusatio Dictantis' (opening statement) at the end of his homily *Depositio S. Martin* (Godden 1979: XXXIV), with no spelling deviations;

5G2ᵛ/b/33–6 (p. 1040)   From 1583.1, 3G4ᵛ/a/4–7, Ælfric's *Grammar*, opening statement from OE Preface (cf. Zupitza 1880: 2), with no spelling deviations and retention of erroneous þa (before lıꞅtlan) introduced in 1576.1 ða for 1570.1 ðaꞅ;

5G2ᵛ/b/53–67 (p. 1040)   From 1583.1, 3G4ᵛ/a/26–44, Ælfric's letter to Wulfsige III (bp of Sherborne 992–1002) extracts (Fehr 1914: §§135–142), with retention of erroneous ðpıȝhten and bleꞅꞃah;

5G3ʳ/a/12–b/4 (p. 1041)   From 1583.1, 3G4ᵛ/b/1 to 3G5ʳ/a/7, Ælfric's second letter to Wulfstan (abp of York 1002–23) extracts (Fehr 1914: §§86–95, 97–109), with retention of erroneous ðæȝe peꞇꞇan (for 1570.1 ðæȝe ꞅeꞇꞇan), but 1583.1 (and 1576.1) erroneous ꞅacpıꞃıcıum has been corrected to 1570.1 ꞅumeþe ꞅacpıꞃıcıum; new errors include poenıðeꞇꞇalē for 1583.1 poenıꞇenꞇıalem, ðıȝan for 1583.1 ðıcȝan, ꞅpa cpæꞇe for 1583.1 ꞅpa cpæðe; many abbreviations, especially nasal tituli, have been introduced;

5G3ᵛ/a/54 to 5G4ᵛ/b/61 (pp. 1042–1044)   From 1583.1, 3G5ᵛ/a/12 to 3G6ᵛ/b/57, Ælfric's *Sermo de Sacrificio in die Pascae* (same omissions as 1570.1; Godden 1979: XV), keeping exactly the same lineation, with retention of erroneous bebeað þam (5G3ᵛ/a/63) omitting ꟿoýꞅeꞅ, eþenð (5G4ʳ/b/7), pæðeþ oꞃ (5G4ʳ/b/25) omitting þa, ꞇeþmeaȝēne (5G4ᵛ/a/10), etc.; new errors include ꞇocnapan (5G4ʳ/a/44) for ꞇocnapaþ, mæþon for næþon (5G4ʳ/b/51); spellings are generally not altered (e.g. ð/þ are kept exactly as in 1583.1), but e for æ and d for t sometimes occur.

5I5ʳ/a/72–6 (p. 1065)   From 1583.1, 3I6ʳ/b/1–5, *ASC* (E), annal for 1129 (Clark 1954: 51), with no spelling deviations.

TYPE:

Main text set in a Small Pica Textura   Body 72   Face 70 × 2: 3
Pierre Haultin's Small Pica Roman, as on 5A2ᵛ–4ʳ   Body 72   Face 70 × 1.5: 2.5
However sig. 5G (which contains most of the OE in the book) uses a different Textura (Parisian Textura on Small Pica: Vervliet 1968 T41), and, instead of Haultin's Small Pica Roman, Garamond's (2nd) Long Primer Roman (with a lower x- and capital height) on a Small Pica body.

AS1: The Parkerian Great Primer Anglo-Saxon occurs on 5G2ᵛ–4ᵛ (pp. 1040–1044) with the full range of special sorts combined with Haultin's English Roman, Body 116.

Special sorts shown in the specimen (p. 1042):

      12 lower-case sorts: ð, ꞃ, ȝ, ı, þ, ꞅ, ꞇ, ẏ, ȝ; þ, ð, p;
      5 capitals: Æ¹, 8; Þ, Ð, P.

Special sorts shown in the text:

      11 lower-case sorts: ð, ꞃ, ȝ, ı, þ, ꞅ, ꞇ, ẏ; þ, ð, p;

	7 capitals:	Æ¹, Є, Ꭰ, Ϻ, &, Ð, Ƿ;
	3 others:	þ, ꞽ, j̇;
Total:	21 sorts.	Overall total: 23 sorts.

AS ð is the later casting that first appears in 1571.1 (sig. Hh to end), the one that fits snugly against the preceding letter.

On sig. 5I5ʳ (p. 1065) the Parkerian Great Primer Anglo–Saxon has been combined with a Great Primer of the following dimensions:

Body size (estimated) 115   Face not available × 2: 3.5.

This Great Primer is probably Claude Garamond's, but there are only a few features on which to base the identification: **b**, **p**, and the dimensions. The Great Primer **æ** and **i** have been used in place of AS **æ** and **i**. The small amount of OE printed here shows inexperience manifested by combining it with the 'wrong' Roman.

Copies seen:

First Issue: CUL Syn.1.59.2–3 (the 2 vols as bound divide between 5E5 and 5E6).

Second issue [STC 11226a]: Identical except that the title page to vol. II (sig. 4A1) remains in its correct sequence, but with 'ſeconde' in place of overprinted 'firſt' and '1597' in place of '1596', new preliminaries having been provided for vol. I, and pp. 761, 1166 are correctly numbered; p. 1119 is correctly numbered in CSJ R.1.19, but not in OBL S.3.19.Th., which has a blind-tooled binding in brown calf with metal bosses and the name and date in gold 'ROBERT HVCKLE | 1642', and gold initials 'R H' either side of the central metal boss.

Copies also at: STC 11226, BL, BUL, CCA, CSJ, HHC, MJRUL, LBL, LPL LSH, NAL, OBrC, OMC, OWoC, RCL, RLW, SAC, WAL, WoCL; FSL, HHL, GTS, JCB, NYU, PST, PUL, UCH, UTA; ANZ, VSL.

STC 11226a, BCLNI, CCA, CLN, OBrC, SAC, UBL, WCF; FSL, HHL, SMU, UCBL, WCM.

Bibliography: Arber V.185, no. 4236; Yamada 1989: 34; Clement 1997: 221; Lucas 1999.

1596.2: Lambarde, William, *A Perambulation of Kent.* 2nd edn of 1576.2, of which the printer's copy for this edition survives as OBL 40.Rawl.263 (illus. Moore 1992: pls 46–47). London: Edmund Bollifant (*alias* Carpenter) [at Eliot's Court Press], 1596. STC 15176; ESTC S108239. AS2/3.

Extracts from Charters, Laws, Wills

Collation: 4⁰ in 8s: A–D⁸ E⁸ (E8 + χ1) F–2O⁸ 2P⁶ [$4 signed (-A1, D2)] 303 leaves, paginated [i–x], 1–588, *589–94*; E8(χ1)r paginated 71 (as also is F1ʳ)

SOURCES OF PASSAGES UTILIZING ANGLO-SAXON TYPES:

Note: The second and fourth of these passages are supplied with a double-decker translation, literal above the text and interpretative above the literal; the fourth occasionally has a triple-decker translation, with two interpretative versions above the literal.

B8ʳ (p. 21)　　　　　From 1576.2 B4ᵛ: Citations from Laȝamon's Brut;
2B6ᵛ–8ʳ (pp. 386–9)　From 1576.2 2Q2ʳ–4ʳ: AS Charter listing estates liable for work on Rochester Bridge (Robertson 52);
2H7ᵛ (p. 484)　　　　From 1576.2 2X3ᵛ: William I: London Charter in AS (Pelteret 8), §1, extract;
2I3ᵛ–6ʳ (pp. 492–7)　From 1576.2 2Y3ʳ–2Z1ᵛ: Will of Byrhtric;
2I7ᵛ–8ʳ (pp. 500–1)　From 1576.2 2Z2ᵛ–3ᵛ: AS Law 'Geþyncðo', §§1–7;
2P1ʳ (p. 583)　　　　From 1576.2 3H1ᵛ: Dubious AS 'verse' Neȝƕeeſyþe

TYPE: The main text is set in an English-size Textura (Body 93); Pierre Haultin's English-size Roman (Body 94) is used for specific passages, e.g. Q4ʳ, including the equivalent passages set in Pica Roman in 1576.2; Robert Granjon's English Italic (Body 94) is used for specific passages, e.g. Q3ᵛ, including the equivalent passages set in Pica Italic in 1576.2.

Robert Granjon's second Pica Italic, the *Cicero pendante* is used for the above-the-line translation, and also for the Index.

AS3: The Lambardian Pica Anglo-Saxon is shown in the AS specimen on A5ʳ, re-set from 1576.2.

Special sorts shown:　12 lower-case sorts:　　ð, e, f, ȝ, ƕ, ꝑ, ſ, τ, ẏ; þ, ð, p;
　　　　　　　　　　1 capital:　　　　　　　Ð;
　　　　　　　　　　3 others:　　　　　　　þ, ꝧ, ꝥ
　　　　　Total: 16 sorts.

AS2/3: In the text the Lambardian Pica Anglo-Saxon, mixed with occasional sorts from AS2 the Parkerian Pica Anglo-Saxon, occurs especially on 2B6ᵛ–8ʳ, 2H7ᵛ, 2I3ᵛ–6ʳ, 2I7ᵛ–8ʳ, 2P1ʳ, but also on very many other pages where OE words or phrases are cited. Normally it is combined with Robert Granjon's Pica Roman (which occurs on A5ʳ with the AS specimen), but on B8ʳ it is combined with a Long Primer Roman in short phrases.

Special sorts shown:　11 lower-case letters: ð, e, f, ȝ, ƕ (used as a small letter), ꝑ, ſ
　　　　　　　　　　　(including Parkerian ſ in e.g. hiſ on 2I4ʳ/10), τ, ẏ; þ
　　　　　　　　　　　(including Parkerian AS2 þ in ȝelaþian on C2ᵛ), ð, p;
　　　　　　　　　　7 capitals: Æ¹ (Parkerian), Æ² (Parkerian), E
　　　　　　　　　　　(Parkerian), ꟽ (Parkerian), S, Ð;
　　　　　　　　　　3 others: þ, ꝧ, ꝥ
　　　　　Total: 21 mixed sorts.

Parkerian and Lambardian s occur alongside each other on 2I4ᵛ/17 (p. 494): Parkerian s in mancẏꞅ, Lambardian s in ʓolðeꞅ. For the Parkerian capitals see especially 2B8ʳ (p. 389), 2I3ᵛ (p. 492), 2I5ᵛ (p. 496)
No capital Þ or capital þ is shown.

> **Copies seen:** ABH 1247; CCA W2/B.2.2; DML H.8.16; OBL 4⁰.L.16.Art; CUL Syn.7.59.31 has 2P6 with bottom third cut out. TCD RR.l.14 (*ex libris* 'Claud. Gilbert') lacks E8(χ)1; TCD GG.kk.66 (signed 'W. Palliser') lacks A1, E8(χ)1, 2P2–6 (text supplied in handwritten copy).
>
> **Copies also at:** BL, CGC, CJC, CMC, CSJ, GUL, MJRUL, LCL, LGL, LPL, LSH, MTP, NLS, NT, OAS, OHC, OJC, OMaC, OQC, OSJ, OTC, OUP, SAC, SBT, SPC, UBL, UCL, WCF, WRL, MBS; FSL, NYCU, AAS, BMC, EmU, FSL, HHL, HUL, IUL, KSRL, MCRS, NWU, UCBL, UCLA, UCSD, UMI, UVL, YUB, QUK, UVC.

Bibliography:
Keynes 2014: 156 (on map at A5ᵛ and its exposition); Plomer 1922: 178; Shirley 1991: no. 190.

Edition:
Lambarde, William, *A Perambulation of Kent: conteining the Description, Hystorie, and Customes of That Shire* (Chatham: W. Burrill, 1826), repr. in facsimile introd. Richard Church (Bath: Adams & Dart, 1970).

Note: There are MS notes on Kent ('ex vetusto lib. Eccl⟨es⟩iæ Xpi Cantuariensis, que⟨m⟩ habet Will' Louelace [now TCC O.9.26, s.xiv], seruiens ad lege⟨m⟩ 1576') by Lambarde in Vespasian A.v, 81ᵛ–89ᵛ (Ramsay 1995: 377, n. 171).

1596.3: Savile, Sir Henry, *Rerum Anglicarum Scriptores post Bedam praecipui, ex vetustissimis codicibus manuscriptis nunc primum in lucem editi*. London: George Bishop, Ralph Newbery & Robert Barker, 1596. STC 21783; ESTC S121919.

> **Collation:** 2⁰: ¶² A–R⁶ S⁸ T–2D⁶ 2E⁴ 2F–4R⁶ 4S⁴, *–2*⁴ 3*⁶, 2A–H². Fos [2], 520, [30]
>
> Contains Æthelweard's (L) *Chronicle* 4K5ʳ–4M3ᵛ, and the *Historia Croylandensis* attributed to Ingulf (d.1109) 4M4ʳ–4S4ʳ, but really a 14c forgery. AS names appear in the Roman or Italic of the main text. No AS special sorts.
>
> **Copies:** BL, CUL, OBL, APL, BPL, BrPL, BUL, CCA, CCC, ECC, CGC, CJC, KCC, CNC, CTH, TCC, DCL, DRD, EAL, ECL, EdUL, Eton, GlCL, CUL, HCL, LCL, LPL, NCL, NT, OAS, OBC, OBrC, OCC, OEF, OHM, OJC, OKC, OMaC, OMC, ONC, OQC, OSC, OSH, OSJ, OTC, OTI, OWmC, OWoC, OXC, RLW, SoUL, SPC, SUL, WAL, WCC, WCL, WoCL, YML, DEWL, DML, TCD; FSL, USLC, NYPL, HHL, HUL, CUofA, KSRL, LCP, NLC, UTA; NLA, UML, VSL.

1597.1: Jordan, Raimon, ed. Bonaventura Vulcanius (de Smet), *De Literis & Lingua Getarum, siue Gothorum, ... quibus accesserunt Specimina variarum Linguarum*. Leiden: Officina Plantiniana, apud Franciscus Raphelengius, 1597. Adams J321, V1024. USTC 423877; STC 24893.3; ESTC S1742.

    Collation: 8°: *⁸ a–g⁸ (g8 blank). [16] 109 [3] p.

Prose Preface to the Alfredian Pastoral Care on e5^r–8^v (pp. 73–80) from 1574.2: F1^r–2^r, taking over several distinctive readings; the Parkerian Great Primer AS type-design (AS1) is mentioned on e4^v, but here AS appears in a Great Primer Roman with no special sorts.

    Copies: BL, CCA, CUL, ECC, TCC, DUL, EdUL, GUL, LCL, NLS, NLW, OBL, OCC, OEC, OLC, OTI, OWoC; PBN, PBA, PBM, AMM, BBM, BMM, MMC, NBM, RmBM, TMT, AntUB, APM, ASB, BrSB, GCB, AKNA, AUB, GSM, HKB, LPB, LUB, TUB, CKB, SKB, BSB, GUB, HLB, RUB, WHAB, WBO, BBU, FBN, RBA, RBC, RBCas, RBN, TBC, ZBD, RNL, RSL; NYPL, HHL, HUL, NLC, UNC, UTA, YUB.

1598.1: Hakluyt, Richard, *The Principall Navigations, Voiages and Discoveries of the English Nation deuided into three seuerall volumes*. London: [for] George Bishop, Ralph Newbery, and Christopher Barker, 1598. 2nd edn of **1589.1**. STC 12626; ESTC S106744.

    Collation: (vol. I) 2°: *–2*⁶ A–3E⁶ 3F⁴. [24], 619, [1] p.

No AS, but translation (probably by Nowell) of the passage about Ohtere's and Wulfstan's voyages from the OE *Orosius* on A2^v–3^v (pp. 4–6) based on Tiberius B.i [Brewer 1952–3: 207–209].

    Copy seen: CUL RCS.Case.b.104.

    Copies also at: BL, ChC, KCC, CMC, CPC, TCC, EdUL, ERCP, GlCL, LCL, LGL, LMT, LPC, NLS, NT, OBL, OBC, OMaC, OSJ, OTC, OWoC, SAC, SUL, WCF, YML, DML, TCD; FSL, USLC, NYPL, NYPM, HHL, HCC, HUL, IUL, LCP, NLC, UCBL, UTA, UVL, YUB.

1598.2: Stow, John, *A Survay of London. Contayning the Originall, Antiquity, Increase, Moderne estate, and description of that Citie*. London: [John Windet for] John Wolfe, 1598. STC 23341. ESTC 117887. AS1.
Writ of Edward the Confessor

    Collation: 4o in 8s: A⁴ B–2G⁸ 2H¹⁰; [8], 450, 467–480, 465–483, [1] p.

SOURCE OF PASSAGE UTILIZING ANGLO-SAXON TYPE:

2B5v (p. 378)   From (prob) Cotton Faustina A.iii (s.xiii), fos 110^v–11^r: Writ of Edward the Confessor granting freedom in use of their lands to St Peter of Westminster 1051 × 1066 (Sawyer 1149), opening statement.

Type:

Main text in a Pica Textura (Body 82)
AS1: The Parkerian Great Primer Anglo-Saxon appears in text cited above.
Special sorts shown: 8 lower-case sorts: ð, f, ȝ, i, ſ, ꞇ; þ, ð;
                                 3 capitals: Ɛ, δ, Ᵽ;
                                 2 others: ꝫ, ꝥ.
                     Total: 13 sorts

Note: Long ſ is used instead of Anglo-Saxon s.

    Copies seen: CUL Pet.B.4.32, Hanson d.84.

    Copies also at: BL, CTC, GUL, HHC, LGL, MJRUL, MOL, OBL, ONC, OXC, SBT, UCL, WIHM; TCD; FSL, HHL, HUL, NYPL, BMC, GC, UCLA, UTA, UVC, YUB.

Bibliography: Harmer 1952: no. 105.

1599.1: Lambarde, William, *EIRENARCHA: or of The Office of the Iustices of Peace, in foure Bookes*. 6th edn of **1581.1**, re-set from 5th edn **1594.1**, in which on M7ᵛ the OE word ꝥataꝥ has the second a barely visible, so it is not reproduced in **1599.1**. London: Thomas Wight and Bonham Norton, 1599. STC 15169. AS2/3.

Laws of Ine (extract)

    Collation: 8⁰: A–N⁸ O⁴ P–2X⁸ 2Y⁴ [$4 signed (-A1, O4, 2Y4)] 352 leaves, paginated [i–ii], 1–206, *206a–h*, 207–606, *607–694* (p. 165 numbered '165t', p. 186 misnumbered 185, pp. 214–215 and 220–221 unnumbered).

SOURCE OF PASSAGE UTILIZING ANGLO-SAXON TYPES:

M7ᵛ   From **1581.1** N3ᵛ–4ʳ: Extract from Laws of Ine 13,1 (Liebermann, I, 94–5). Notable errors introduced in this edition are omission of second a in ꝥataꝥ, ſiſ for fiſ and a space in þꞃiꞇ ꞇiȝ.

TYPE:

Main text in Pica Textura	Body 83	Face 76 × 2: 3
Pica Roman (as on L5ʳ)	Body 83	Face 80 × 1.8: 2.7
Granjon's 2nd Pica Italic (as on L5ᵛ)	Body 83.5	Face 80 × 1.3: 2.6

AS2/3: Mixed Parkerian and Lambardian Pica Anglo-Saxon on M7ᵛ (p. 188, text) and Q6ʳ (p. 233, words) combined with Claude Garamond's (second) Long Primer Roman, as used for Precedents, e.g. on 2V4ʳ   Body 68   Face 66 × 1.4: 2

Special sorts used: 10 lower-case sorts: f, ȝ, h, ꝥ, ſ, ꞇ, ẏ; þ, ð, p;
                                 2 capitals: Ꟁ (on Q6ʳ), Đ;
                                 2 others: ꝫ, j̇
                     Total: 14 sorts

    Copies seen: CUL Pet.D.4.45, CTH D*.5.28 (with paper patch stuck over the bottom third of 2G6ʳ); OBL 35.c.38(1).

    Copies also at: BL, CNC, OBrC, StA; FSL, USLC, NYCU, HUL, NLC, YUB.

Bibliography: see **1581.1**.

1599.2: Kiliaan (van Kiel), Cornelis, *Etymologicum Teutonicae Linguae sive Dictionarium Teutonico-Latinum*, 3rd edn. Antwerp: Joannes Moretus, 1599. USTC 402476. Facsimile ed. Frans Claes SJ, *Kiliaans Etymologicum van 1599*, Monumenta Lexicographica Neerlandica, ser. II, vol. 3 (The Hague: Mouton, 1972).

    Collation: 8°:*⁸ A–Z⁸ a–z⁸ Aa–Bb⁸. [8] 794 [=764] [4] p.
Words in AS and other appropriate languages appear in Textura with no special sorts.

    Copies: BL, MJRUL, OLC, UCL; DML, PBN, SBPU, AntUB, APM, ARG, ASB, BBR, BGS, GBAB, GCB, GOK, LBC, LKU, LSJ, MAB, NBND, NBU, DGA, GBR, LBR, LKFG, LPB, LUB, GUB, HKB, HNLB, HSUB, JUB, MBS, WHAB, RBP, MBN, MBP, MUC, ZBP, RNL; FSL, USLC, NYCU, NYPM, DDUL, HUL, IUL, NLC, PUL, UCH, YUB.

1600.1: Camden, William, *Britannia sive Florentissimorvm Regnorvm, Angliæ, Scotiæ, Hiberniæ, et Insvlarvm adiacentium ex intima antiquitate Chorographica Descriptio*. 5th edn of 1586.1 re-set from 4th edn 1594.2. The present edition is the first to treat of coins. London: [(?)Edmund Bollifant at Eliot's Court Press for] George Bishop, 1594. STC 4507; ESTC S107386. AS2/3.

OE proper names

    Collation: 4⁰ in 8s: A–F⁸ G⁸ (G1+χ1.2) H⁸ (H5+χ1.2) I–3H⁸ 3I–3N⁴ [$4 signed (-A1,3, 2Y2, 3I–3N3,4; 3A missigned 'Aa')] 456 leaves, paginated [i–xvi], 1–831, *832–858*, 1–30, *31–32* (p. nos.325–326, 643–644 omitted; pp. 132 misnumbered 142, 242 misnumbered 342, 377 misnumbered 277, 637 misnumbered 647, 725 misnumbered 735). State 2 shows sig. 3A correctly signed.

TYPE:

Main text in François Guyot's Pica Roman (used by Edmund Bollifant 1600–2 according to Ferguson 1989, who calls it EC2):   Body 82.
Robert Granjon's second Pica Italic (of three), the *Cicero pendante* (as on H8ʳ–I4ʳ):   Body 81
AS2/3: The Parkerian and Lambardian Pica Anglo-Saxons combined with Guyot's Pica Roman.
The specimen on A7ʳ shows primarily Parkerian special sorts with Lambardian e and H:

    13 lower-case sorts: ð, *e*, ꝼ, ȝ, ƕ (used as l.c., e.g., T2ʳ, T3ʳ, but also as capital on M1ᵛ, V1ᵛ) ı, ꞃ, ſ, τ, ẏ; þ, ð̄, ꝑ (ꝑ straight descender, serif, good fit; used in initial capital position Q3ʳ, R5ʳ, R8ʳ, Y3ᵛ, 2A1ᵛ, but W used R2ʳ);
    6 (+1) capitals: Æ¹, Æ², Є, Ꮖ, ꞅ, Ð; (+ ƕ)
    2 others: ꞁ, þ;
    Total: 21 special sorts.

In addition to these the text shows ꝫ (punctus versus) on 2A7ʳ (p. 367), 2F8ᵛ (p. 450).

The text does not show i, Æ¹, Æ², nor ᚷ, þ, as OE occurs in words only. On L3ᵛ (p. 150) Parkerian capital Ƿ and ƿ are used in lower-case position. Sometimes AS type is not used where it would be appropriate, e.g., P2ᵛ no ᛗ in Minꞅtep, N8ᵛ no ẏ in Glaꞅtney + S7ʳ Sealꞅey.

AS2/3, the Parkerian/Lambardian Pica AS is shown in words on: pp. 29, 86, 107, 132, 135, 138, 141, 147, 150–151, 160–161, 166–167, 175, 178–183, 186, 188, 191–192, 200, 204, 208, 210–212, 214, 221, 223, 228–229, 232, 241–243, 246, 249, 255–257, 262, 264, 266, 268–269, 273, 275, 277–278, 280–281, 283, 287–290, 292, 294, 296, 299, 303, 307, 311, 313–314, 317–320, 324, 327–330, 337, 342, 344–346, 353–354, 356, 365, 367, 383–384, 386, 389–390, 397–398, 404–406, 410, 417, 420, 423, 430, 432, 437–438, 442, 450, 468, 471, 474, 484, 486, 488–489, 493–495, 505, 509, 511, 514–517, 521, 523, 528, 530, 534, 536, 538, 554, 570, 582, 601, 610–611, 616–617, 619, 623–624, 635, 639, 641–642, 657, 664, 670, 672, 682, 718, 720–721, 725–728, 794–795, 819.

Suspect OE occurs in: R8ʳ Geȝuẏꞅiꞅ (Bede Gewissae HE III.7), T5ʳ Cantȝuaplantꝺ, X5ʳ Þeocꞅbuꝵẏ, X7ʳ Beoꝵkenlau.

Heavier use of AS type:	1594.2 p. 81 Enȝlelonꝺ > 1600.1 p. 107 Enȝlelonꝺ,
	1594.2 p. 105 Cẏninȝe > 1600.1 p. 132 Cẏninȝe,
	1594.2 p. 107 Ealdoꝵman > 1600.1 p. 135 Ealdoꝵman,
	1594.2 p. 112 piꞇꞇena-ȝemoꞇ > 1600.1 p. 141 piꞇꞇena-ȝemoꞇ,
	1594.2 p. 131 Deuenꞅchiꝵe > 1600.1 p. 160 Deuenꞅchiꝵe,
	1594.2 p. 571 Þeozteu > 1600.1 p. 664 Heoꝵtu,
Expansion of AS material:	1594.2 p. 285 Saxonicè Buꝵenceaꞅteꝵ præterfluit > 1600.1 p. 337 Saxonicè Buꝵenceaꞅteꝵ & Beꝵnaceaꞅteꝵ præterfluit

But lighter use of AS type also shown:

1594.2 p. 253 Sonꝺẏc > 1600.1 p. 299 Sonꝺꝵyc,

1594.2 p. 427 Noꝵtꝭ-poꝵtꝭiȝ > 1600.1 p. 495 Noꝵtꝭ-woꝵtꝭiȝ,

1594.2 p. 436 Ƿaꝵꝵẏnȝ pẏc > 1600.1 p. 505 Waꝵꝵẏnȝ wẏc.

Note: For the forms of AS proper names Camden drew on the manuscript of Lambarde's *Dictionarium Angliae topographicum*; see **1586.1** under Context.

Copies seen: State 1: CUL Hunt.53.4 (with Hχ1.2 after H5), Syn.7.60.164 (A1,2 misbound after A6, lacks F3, Gχ1.2, Hχ1.2), Pet.B.2.36 (lacks Gχ1.2, Hχ1.2 (torn stub)); TCD K.l.22 (lacks P6);

State 2 (with sig. 3A correctly signed): CUL Syn.7.60.163 (with portrait of Camden added after A7, Hχ1.2 after H5). Note also OBL C.8.1.Art (author's presentation copy to OU).

Copies also at: BL, KCC, CSJ, TCC, CUW, EdUL, HCL, HHC, LHL, LSH, NLS, NT, NUL, OAM, OAS, OBrC, OCC, OHM, ONC. ONuC, OPC, OSJ, OUC, OWmC, SBT, SDC, UBL, UCL, WAL, WCC, WCL, YML, DML; FSL, USLC, NYHS, NYPL, HHL, HUL, BMC, JCB, IUL, KSRL, LCP, NLC, NWU, UTA, UVL, YUB, QUK; ATL, OUL.

Bibliography: Keynes 2014: 156–8 (maps); and see **1586.1**.

1601.1: Savile, Sir Henry, *Rerum Anglicarum Scriptores post Bedam praecipui, ex vetustissimis codicibus manuscriptis nunc primum in lucem editi*. Frankfurt-am-Main: Claude de Marne and heirs of Johann Aubry I, typis Johann Wechel, 1601. USTC 2134610.

Collation: 2°: A–4F⁶ 4G⁸ a–g⁶ h⁴. 916, [92] p.

Repr. of **1596.3**. Contains Æthelweard's (L) *Chronicle* 4A1ᵛ–4B4ᵛ, and the *Historia Croylandensis* attributed to Ingulf (d.1109) 4B4ᵛ–4G8ᵛ, but really a 14c forgery. AS names appear in the Roman or Italic of the main text. No AS special sorts.

Copies seen: CUL R.2.9, L*.8.3(A).

Copies also at: MJRUL, DSU, GFB, GUB, HnSB, HLB, RUB; MMUL.

1602.1: Lambarde, William, *EIRENARCHA: or of The Office of the Iustices of Peace, in foure Bookes*. 7th edn of **1581.1** re-set from 6th edn **1599.1**. London: Thomas Wight, 1602. STC 15170; ESTC S108202. AS3 (with AS2 s).

Laws of Ine (extract)

Collation: 8°: A–2S⁸ [$4 signed (-A1, O2, 2N4; 2P1–4 missigned 2O1–4, 2Q4 missigned 'Q4.')] 328 leaves, paginated [i–ii], *1*, 2–589, *590–674* (nos 202–221 not used; p. 88 unnumbered, pp. 228–229 unnumbered (printed sideways); pp. 22 misnumbered 24, 25 misnumbered 26, 29 misnumbered 31, 81 misnumbered 91, 85 misnumbered 77, 100 misnumbered 110, 106 misnumbered 160, 202–206 misnumbered 222–226, 470 misnumbered 472, 472 misnumbered 473, 474–475 misnumbered 476–477, 478–479 misnumbered 480–481, 482 misnumbered 484, 499 misnumbered 599).

SOURCE OF PASSAGE UTILIZING ANGLO-SAXON TYPES:

L7ᵛ (p. 172) From **1581.1** N3ᵛ–4ʳ: Extract from Laws of Ine 13,1 (Liebermann, I, 94–95).

All three errors introduced in **1599.1** (q.v.) are taken over.

TYPE:

Main text in Pica Textura   Body 82.5   Face 78 × 2: 3
Robert Granjon's 1st Pica Roman, e.g. on K6ʳ (p. 153)
                           Body 83   Face 80 × 1.3: 3
Robert Granjon's second Pica Italic (of three), the *Cicero pendante* (e.g. on K6ᵛ
= p. 154)   Body 83   Face 80 × 1.5: 2.5.
AS3 Lambardian Pica Anglo-Saxon with Parkerian s on L7ᵛ (p. 172, text) and O7ᵛ
(p. 240, words) combined with Granjon's 1st Pica Roman.
Special sorts shown: 10 + 1 lower-case sorts: e, ꝼ, ᵹ, ꝺ, ꞃ, ſ, ꞇ, ẏ; þ, ð, ƿ;
                        1 capital: Ð;
                        2 others: ꝺ, j̇.
          Total: 14 sorts
No **d** in text; and on O7ᵛ roman capital **M** (not AS) is used.
The Parkerian sorts include **s** in ꞃeoꞃan.
   Copies seen: CUL Syn.8.60.59; OBL 8⁰.L.4.Jur.
   Copies also at: BL, OQC, OWoC, SHC; FSL, NYCU, HHL, DDUL, HUL, IUL, MCRS.
Bibliography: see 1581.1.

1602.2: Camden, William, *Anglica, Hibernica, Normannica, Cambrica, a veteribus scripta*. Frankfurt-am-Main: Johann Aubry I, impensis Claude de Marne and heirs 1602. USTC 2052453; BLG C116.
   Collation: 2°: 3*⁶ A–4H⁶ 4I⁴. [8], 898, [34] p.
Shows AS specimen on 3*4ᵛ (modelled on 1574.2 but with **t** and **Ð** back to front) but the special sorts are produced from woodcuts. At sig. C1ʳ–2ʳ is shown the text of the OE prose preface to the Alfredian translation of Pope Gregory's *Pastoral Care* (ed. Sweet 1871–2: 2–9) and the text of the OE verse preface to the Alfredian *Pastoral Care* (ed. Dobbie 1942: 110), both from 1574.2, and both in Roman without AS special sorts.
   Copies: BL, OBL, DUL, GUL, NLS, PBSG, CBM, LUB, DSU, GFB, GUB, HUB, RUB, WHAB; IBUL, IUL.

1603.1: Camden, William, *Anglica, Hibernica, Normannica, Cambrica, a veteribus scripta*. Frankfurt-am-Main: Johann Aubry I, impensis Claude de Marne and heirs 1602. USTC 2135819; BLG C117. Re-issue of 1602.2 except for the preliminaries being expanded to include Camden's preface.
   Collation: 2°: 3*⁶ A–4H⁶ 4I⁴. [12], 898, [34] p.
Shows AS specimen on 3*6ᵛ (as 1602.2 3*4ᵛ). OE texts the same as 1602.2. No AS special sorts in the texts.
   Copies seen: CUL Acton.a.25.178, R.2.10, L*.8.4(B).

Copies also at: BL, DUL, EdUL, MJRUL, OBL, APL, DML, BN, ABM, CBM, OMM, PBSG, RBM, SBPU, TMM, BUG, HKB, LUB, BSB, DSU, GFB, MBS, WAAB, WHAB, BAV; IBUL, IUL, UBC.

1605.1: Camden, William, *Remaines of a Greater Worke, Concerning Britaine, the Inhabitants thereof, their Languages, Names, Surnames, Empreses, Wise Speeches, Poësies, and Epitaphes*. London: George Eld for Simon Waterson 1605. STC 4521; ESTC S107408. Individual sorts only: AS3 ȝ, þ.

Lord's Prayer, Letter-symbols

Collation: 4^0: [Booklet 1] A–2G^4 2H^2 [Booklet 2] a–g^4 h^2 [$3 signed (-A1,2; +b-g4)] 152 leaves, paginated [i–viii], 1–235, *236*, 1–59, *60* (Booklet 1: pp. 67 misnumbered 76, 98 misnumbered 92, 99 misnumbered 83, 102 misnumbered 96, 103 misnumbered 93, 158 misnumbered 851; Booklet 2: pp. 18–19, 22–23 unnumbered). State 2 shows pp. 98, 99, 102, 103 numbered correctly.

SOURCES OF PASSAGES UTILIZING ANGLO-SAXON TYPES:

C4 (pp. 15–16)   From Nero D.iv (Lindisfarne Gospels, then owned by Robert Bowyer), 37^r/21–37^v/12: Lord's Prayer (Mt. 6.9–13; gloss somewhat garbled), facsimile ed. Kendrick et al. 1956, text ed. Skeat 1871–87: 55;

C4^v From 1566.2 §4.1b K8^v–L1^v (including variants): Lord's Prayer; cf. Thorpe 1844–6: II.596/5–10;

Note: There are several other later historical versions of the Lord's Prayer cited as illustration of the changing English Language (cf. Berkhout 2000: 417).

TYPE:

Main text in Pierre Haultin's Pica Roman interspersed with Robert Granjon's 2nd Pica Italic *pendante*.

C4: Lord's Prayer in OE twice: no special sorts, but æ is correct in the second version; suprascript translation in Granjon's 2nd Pica Italic.

AS3: The Lambardian Pica Anglo-Saxon (individual special sorts only) occurs on D4^v (p. 24) in a report on the spelling reform practices advocated by Smith in 1568.3: ȝ, þ.

Note: A passage from Chaucer's *Nun's Priest's Tale* is printed on a4 in Granjon's 2nd Pica Italic with no special sorts.

Copies seen: State 1: CUL Pet.A.3.31 (H2/H3 in reverse order); State 2: ABH 1289, CUL Syn.7.60.59.

Copies also at: BL, BCL, KCC, CNC, CSJ, TCC, CUW, Eton, GUL, LCL, LPL, LSH, NAL, NCL, OBL, OEC, OEF, OWoC, SAC, SBT, UCL, YML, TCD; FSL, HHL, HUL, IUL, NLC, UCH, UTA, YUB.

Bibliography: Clement 1997: 229; Dunn 1984: xliv; Parry 1995: 45–48; Piggott 1951: 202–206; Tite 2003: 137; GR 530.

Edition: W. Camden, *Remains concerning Britaine*, introd. Thomas Moule (London: John Russell Smith, 1870), based on **1674.1**, facsimile repr. Anglistica & Americana 74 (Hildesheim: Georg Olms, 1970), and repr. with new introd. by Leslie Dunkling (Wakefield: EP Publishing, 1974).

1605.2: Parker, Matthew, *De Antiquitate Britannicæ Ecclesiæ*. Hannover: 'Typis' Andreas Wechel, 'apud' Claude de Marne and the heirs of Johann Aubry I, 1605. USTC 2027163; BLG P138. Another edn of **1572.1**.
    Collation: 2^0:)(^{4} A–2G^6 2H^8. [8], 359, [16] p.
    Shows woodcut blocks of AS text on H3^r (= **1572.1** ^{2}H4^r Wulfstan, *Sermo Lupi*, opening lines, as Whitelock 1939: 47/4–7), and on K5^v (= **1572.1** ^{2}N2^r: Diploma of King Henry I (Sept. 1100 × July 1101), as Rymer 1816–30: I.i.12 (Pelteret 44); the blocks follow the lineation of the AS text in **1572.1** exactly.
    Copies seen: CUL R.8.13, Pet.O.6.9.
    Copies also at: BL, AUL, DUL, EdUL, MJRUL, OBL, DML, AUB, CBM, DSU, GUB, LBM, OMM, PBSG, SBPU, SKB, TMM, WHAB; IBUL.

1605.3: Verstegan, Richard, *A Restitution of Decayed Intelligence in Antiquities*. Antwerp: Robert Bruney for John Norton I and John Bill I in London, 1605. STC 21361; ESTC S116255; USTC 3002102.
    Collation: 4^0: †–3†^{4} A–2X^4. [24], 338, [14] p.
    Words in AS (Glossary at end with 900 entries) and other Germanic languages appear in Textura with no AS special sorts.
    Copies seen: CUL SSS.44.13, Adams.7.60.4, Syn.7.60.220.
Bibliography: Bremmer 2000.
Facsimiles: English Experience 952 (Amsterdam: Theatrum Orbis Terrarum, 1979) using OBL Wood 598; English Recusant Literature 323 (Ilkley: Scolar, 1976) using ECC copy.
    Copies also at: BL, BUL, ChC, CCL, CJL, CMC, CSJ, ECC, KCC, TCC, CCA, ECL, EUL, DAL, LSH, LPL, LTC, LWI, NLS, NUL, OBL, OBC, OCC, OEF, OLC, ONC, OQC, OStE, OTC, OWmC, SBT, SDL, SUL, YML, DRD, DML, NLI; EmU, FSL, HHL, HUL, IUL, LCP, MUL, NLC, NYPL, NWU, UCh, UCLA, UIL, USL, UTA, UTS, UVL, YUB; ANZ, ATL, NSW, UML.

1605.4: Kiliaan (van Kiel), Cornelis, *Etymologicum Teutonicae Linguae sive Dictionarium Teutonico-Latinum*, 4th edn. Alkmaar: Jacob de Meester for Cornelis Claesz. (Amsterdam), 1605. USTC 1010165.
    Collation: 8^0: *^{8} A–Z^8, a–z^8, 2A–2C^8 2D^4. 789 p.

Words in AS and other appropriate languages appear in Italic with no special sorts.

Copies: BL, TCC, GUL, OTI, PBN, ARA, AUB, LUB; TRR.

1605.5: Serarius, Nicolaus, *Epistolæ S. Bonifacii Martyris, Primi Moguntini Archiepiscopi, Germanorum Apostoli, pluriumque Pontificum, Regum, & aliorum, nunc primùm è Cæsaree Maiestatis Viennensi Bibliothecâ luce, notisque donatæ*. Mainz: Balthasar Lippius, 1605. USTC 2040045.

Collation: 4⁰: [8], 351, [4] p.

OE verse *Proverb from Winfred's Time* (Dobbie 1942: 57; facsimile Robinson & Stanley 1991: pl. 1 from Vienna, Nationalbibliothek lat.751 (Theol.259), 34ʳ/5–6 (sole witness), in Epistola lxi on K1ʳ (p. 73) in English-size Italic (with no AS special sorts) quoted as prose in a Latin prose letter itself printed in English-size Roman.

Copies: OBL, PBN, RBM, SBPU, BSB, DSU, MBS, RUB, WAAB, WHAB.

1607.1: Lambarde, William, *EIRENARCHA: or of The Office of the Justices of Peace, in foure Bookes*. 8th edn of 1581.1 re-set from 7th edn 1602.1. London: [Adam Islip] for the Stationers' Co., 1607. STC 15171; ESTC S105029. AS3 (with AS2 s).

Laws of Ine (extract)

Collation: 8⁰: A–2X⁸. [$4 signed (-A1); 2D3 signed D3] 352 leaves, paginated [i–ii], 1–621, 622–702 (pp. 222–223 unnumbered (printed sideways); pp. 315, 317 misnumbered 215, 217 respectively).

SOURCE OF PASSAGE UTILIZING ANGLO-SAXON TYPES:

M5ʳ (p. 183)   From 1602.1 L7ᵛ: Extract from Laws of Ine 13,1 (Liebermann, I, 94–95).

All three errors first introduced in 1599.1 (q.v.) are taken over from 1602.1.

TYPE:

Main text in Pica Textura   Body 82   Face 80 × 2: 2.9
Granjon's 1st Pica Roman (e.g. L3ʳ)   Body 83   Face 80 × 1.6: 2.8
Pica Italic, Robert Granjon's second, the *Cicero pendante* (e.g. C3ʳ–5ʳ)
                                   Body 83   Face 80 × 1.5: 2.5.

AS3: The Lambardian Pica Anglo-Saxon occurs on P7ʳ (p. 235, words) and with Parkerian s on M5ʳ (p. 183, text) set with Granjon's Pica Roman.

Special sorts shown: 11 lower-case sorts: e, ꝼ, ȝ, ꝺ, ꝑ, ſ, ꞇ, ẏ;   þ, ð, p;
                       1 capital: Ð;
                       2 others: ꝫ, ꞃ.
              Total: 14 sorts.

Note: No d occurs in the text; and on P7^r roman (not AS) capital **M** is used.

Copies seen:

TCD HH.nn.67 signed 'W. Palliser' has tp stuck on blank; BL 1608/1470 (owned by Hugh Cecil, e of Lonsdale); OBL Douce L.73¹.

Copies also at: CCA, EAL, GUL, NLW; FSL, NYCU, HUL, IUL, MUL.

Bibliography: see 1581.1.

1607.2: Camden, William, *Britannia sive Florentissimorvm Regnorvm, Angliæ, Scotiæ, Hiberniæ, et Insvlarvm adiacentium ex intima antiquitate Chorographica Descriptio.* 6th edn of 1586.1 expanded from 5th edn 1600.1. London: [Eliot's Court Press for] George Bishop and John Norton 1, 1607. STC 4508; ESTC S122157. AS3.

ASC (C) and (F), OE proper names

Collation: 2⁰ in 6s: ✢–2✢⁴⁺² (+2✢χ1.2) A–L⁶ M⁴⁺¹ (+M1χ1.2) N⁴⁺¹ (+N1χ1.2) O⁴⁺² (+O1χ1.2, +O4χ1.2) P⁶ Q³⁺¹ (+Q2χ1.2) R⁵⁺¹ (+R5χ1.2) S⁶ T⁵⁺¹ (+T1χ1.2) V³⁺¹ (+V1χ1.2) X⁵⁺¹ (+X2χ1.2) Y³⁺¹ (+Y2χ1.2) Z⁶ 2A⁵⁺¹ (+2A3χ1.2) 2B⁵⁺¹ (+2B3χ1.2) 2C² 2D³⁺¹ (+2D2χ1.2) 2E¹⁺¹ (+2E1χ1.2) 2F³⁺¹ (+2F2χ1.2) 2G² 2H³⁺¹ (+2H2χ1.2) 2I⁴ 2K³⁺¹ (+2K2χ1.2) 2L⁴ 2M³⁺¹ (+2M2χ1.2) 2N² 2O³⁺¹ (+2O2χ1.2) 2P² 2Q³⁺¹ (+2Q2χ1.2) 2R² 2S¹⁺¹ (+2S1χ1.2) 2T² 2V¹⁺¹ (+2V1χ1.2) 2X–2Y² 2Z¹⁺¹ (+2Z1χ1.2) 3A²⁺¹ (+3A2χ1) 3B²⁺¹ (+3B2χ1.2) 3C–3D² 3E¹⁺¹ (+3E1χ1.2) 3F³⁺¹ (+3F2χ1.2) 3G³⁺¹ (+3G2χ1.2) 3H² 3I¹⁺¹ (+3I1χ1.2) 3K⁵⁺¹ (+3K3χ1.2) 3L¹⁺¹ (+3L1χ1.2) 3M² 3N³⁺¹ (+3N2χ1.2) 3O–3P² 3Q¹⁺¹ (+3Q1χ1.2) 3R² 3S¹⁺¹ (+3S1χ1.2) 3T¹⁺¹ (+3T1χ1.2) 3V¹⁺¹ (+3V1χ1.2) 3X² 3Y³⁺¹ (+3Y2χ1.2) 3Z³⁺¹ (+3Z2χ1.2) 4A¹⁺¹ (+4A1χ1.2) 4B² 4C¹⁺¹ (+4C1χ1.2) 4D³⁺¹ (+4D2χ1.2) 4E¹⁺¹ (+4E1χ1.2) 4F¹⁺¹ (+4F1χ1.2) 4G³⁺¹ (+4G2χ1.2) 4H¹⁺¹ (+4H1χ1.2) 4I³⁺¹ (+4I2χ1.2) 4K⁵⁺¹ (+4K3χ1.2) 4L⁴ 4M¹⁺¹ (+4M1χ1.2) 4N⁵⁺¹ (+4N3χ1.2) 4O⁴ 4P¹⁺¹ (+4P1χ1.2) 4Q² 4R³⁺¹ (+4R2χ1.2) 4S⁴ 4T¹⁺¹ (+4T1χ1.2) 4V³⁺¹ (+4V2χ1.2) 4X⁶ 4Y⁴ 4Z³⁺¹ (+4Z2χ1.2) 5A⁶ 5B⁵⁺¹ (+5B3χ1.2) 5C–5E⁶ 5F³⁺¹ (+5F2χ1.2) 5G–5R⁶ 5S–5V⁴ [$3 signed (+O4, X4; -✢1,3, 2✢3, O3, Q3, R3, V3, Y3, 2C2, 2D3, 2F3, 2G2, 2H3, 2I3, 2K3, 2L3, 2M3, 2N2, 2O3, 2Q3, 2R2, 2T2, 2X2, 2Y2, 3A2, 3C2, 3D2, 3F3, 3G3, 3H2, 3M2, 3N3, 3O2, 3R2, 3X2, 3Y3, 3Z3, 4B2, 4D3, 4G3, 4I3, 4L3, 4O3, 4Q2, 4R3, 4S3, 4V3, 4Y3, 4Z3, 5F3, 5S3, 5T3, 5V3; O4 missigned O3, R5 missigned R3, X4 missigned X3, 4H1 missigned 4G2)] 406 + 55 leaves, paginated [i–xvi], 1–860, *861–84* (pp. nos 347–8 used twice; the following are not included in the numerical series: M1^v.Mχ1^r, N1^v.N1χ1^r, O1^v.O1χ1^r, O4^v.O4χ1^r, Q2^v.Q2χ1^r, R51^v.R5χ1^r, T1^v.T1χ1^r, V1^v.V1χ1^r, X2^v.X2χ1^r, Y2^v.Y2χ1^r, 3G2^v.3G2χ1^r, 3I1^v.3I1χ1^r, 3K3^v.3K3χ1^r; the following are not numbered: pp. 250–251, 262–263, 276–277, 282–283, 288–289, 300–301, 316–317, 332–333, 343–345, 353–355, 364–365, 372–373, 383–385, 391–392, 395–397, 410–411, 416–417, 444–445, 454–455, 468–469, 475–477, 493–495, 502–503, 506–509, 515–517, 520, 522–523, 526–529, 532–533, 537–539, 542–545, 549–551, 559–561, 576–577,

597–599, 608–609, 621–623, 628–629, 654, 656–657, 676, 678–679, 723–725; pp. 193 misnumbered 139, 223 misnumbered 221, 226 misnumbered 218, 348 misnumbered 338, 442 misnumbered 444, 471 misnumbered 461, 496 misnumbered 494, 511 misnumbered 510, 579–582 misnumbered 577–580, 605 misnumbered 601, 645–646 misnumbered 643–644, 648 misnumbered 649, 649 misnumbered 648, 686 misnumbered 682, 827 misnumbered 837, 833 misnumbered 823). State 2 shown by pp. 223, 226 correctly numbered.

SOURCES OF PASSAGES UTILIZING ANGLO-SAXON TYPES:

The following extracts of OE text do not occur in previous editions:

4Y4ʳ (p. 651) From (probably) Tiberius B.i [acquired by Cotton from Robert Bowyer in 1606 (Wormald and Wright 1958: 202 and 212, n. 68, citing Harley 6018, 154ᵛ)], 117ʳ: ASC(C) 189 (extract); this first passage could also be from MS B (Tiberius A.vi); note erron. ꝼoꞃꝼȳꝺ for MS ꝼoꞃ-;

From Domitian A.viii, 34ʳ/15–18: ASC(F) 188 (extract), both as Thorpe 1861: I.14–15; in the second extract (facs. Dumville 1995, as Baker 2000: 12) the phrase oꝼ ᴄuꞃꝼum is distinctive; Domitian A.viii was in Camden's possession before it went to Cotton (Ker 1957: 187–188, Baker 2000: xiii, Lucas 2001, Harrison 2007; Tite 2003: 205).

TYPE:

Main text in Haultin's English-size Roman (Body 95) interspersed with Granjon's 3rd English-size Italic (e.g. on 5M3ᵛ–5P6ᵛ);

AS3: The Lambardian Pica Anglo-Saxon occurs in the specimen on 2✱4ʳ.

Special sorts shown: 11 lower-case sorts: ð, e, ꝼ, ȝ, ꞃ, ꞅ, ᴄ, ẏ; þ, ð, ꝑ;
                          7 capitals: Æ¹, Æ², Є, Ꜧ, Ꝏ, Ꞅ, Ð;
                          2 others: þ, ⁊.
            Total: 20 sorts.

AS3: The Lambardian Pica Anglo-Saxon combined with Haultin's Pica Roman (as used on 2✱2ᵛ–3ʳ) occurs in the text in words on pp. 19, 84 (showing erron. ꝑ for 1600.1 þ), 99, 114–115, 118, 120, 128, 133, 136, 144, 147, 153, 155–158, 161–162), 164, 170, 173, 176–180, 185, 187, 189–190, 192 (showing erron. Ꝏẏnꞅꝺeꞃ for 1600.1 mẏnꞅᴄeꞃ), 197, 202–203, 205, 207, 211–212, 216, 219–220, 223, 225–226, 228–229, 231–232, 234–237, 239, 241–242, 246–247, 252–256, 258, 264, 266–267, 278–279, 291–292, 302–303, 315, 318, 322, 325, 330, 334, 337, 346–347, 348bis, 356, 361, 366, 374, 389, 393, 398, 401, 407–408, 412, 418, 425, 432–436, 438, 442, 446, 449–450, 456–458, 460, 471–472, 492, 511, 547, 562, 565–567, 570–571, 579, 582, 584–585, 594, 602, 605–606, 610, 618, 655, 658, 664–665, 668–670, 838, 853;

Special sorts shown: 13 lower-case sorts: ð, *e*, ꝼ, ȝ, Ꜧ, 1 (on R1ᵛ), ꞃ, ꞅ, ᴄ, ẏ; þ, ð, ꝑ;
                        4 capitals: Є, Ꝏ, Ꞅ, Ð (on 2O2χ1ᵛ);
                        1 other: ⁊ (punctus versus 1st on 2H3ʳ).

Total: 18 sorts.

ꝺ is used regularly as a lc letter, occasionally initially (R5ʳ), but that does not necessarily signify that it was perceived as a capital, as f, p also occur lc initially; roman H is used in an AS name-element Heoptu on 4Q1ᵛ. Note ꝺextolꝺerꝺam on 5A3ʳ (p. 665).

AS capitals also used with roman ones in a Latin inscription on 3B3ᵛ.

Note: For the forms of AS proper names Camden drew on the manuscript of Lambarde's *Dictionarium Angliae topographicum*; see 1586.1 under Context.

Copies seen: State 1: TCD DD.dd.36 (lacks Y2.Y2χ1; shows map belonging after 2❋4 after I1; gift of William Drury);

State 2 (with pp. 223, 226 correctly numbered): BL Maps C.7.b.1 (with ❋2 after ❋3); CUL R.8.26 (with hand-coloured maps and ornaments, and contemporary gold-tooled binding showing the initials EP), L*.8.30(B) (lacks 3Q, shows 3A2χ1 misbound after 3Z3; with hand-coloured maps and ornaments, and contemporary gold-tooled binding); ECC 306.4.13 (O3 misplaced after O6, with some maps hand-coloured); TCD DD.dd.25 (lacks tp); OBL MS Smith 1 (SC 15608) with notes by the author, subsequently owned by Cotton and later by Hearne; lacks O1), C.8.1 Art (presented by Camden to OBL with some hand-written amendments). OBL C 1.4 Art.Seld is Selden's copy with his annotations.

Copies also at: BPL, CCC, CCL, CGC, ChC, KCC, CMC, CPC, CSC, CSS, TCC, DAL, DCL, Eton, GNM, HHC, LCL, LDC, LiCL, LPL, NIA, NSL, NT, NUL, OAM, OAS, OBC, OCC, OJC, OMC, OMaC, OQC, OSJ, OWmC, OXC, RRH, SCL, SoUL, SPC, StA, UBL, WAL, WCF, WCL, WiCL, WoCL, YML, DML, FBB; FSL, HHL, HUL, BMC, DDUL, IUL, LCP, NLC, UCLA, UTA.

Bibliography: Ellis 1843: 104–106 (letter accompanying presentation copy); Harris 2015; Harrison 2007; Hind 1952–64: II.31–32 and pl. 6d (maps), II.327 (tplate); Keynes 2014: 158–159 (map of AS heptarchy); Levy 1967: 154–159; Lucas 2001; Lucas 2018; Shirley 1991: nos 279–280; Skelton 1970: no. 5; Taylor 1934: 11–12, no. 755.

Facsimile (reduced): Anglistica et Americana 57 (Hildesheim, Olms, 1970). Based on the copy at the Universitäts Münster (Englisches Seminar), XVII 5031/1. Shows variant tp (with 'Tabulis' for 'Chartis').

1607.3: Cowell, John, *The Interpreter: or Booke containing the Signification of Words, Wherein is set forth the true meaning of all, or the most part of such words and Termes, as are mentioned in the Law Writers, or Statutes of this ... Kingdome, requiring any Exposition or Interpretation.* Cambridge: John Legat 1, 1607. STC 5900; ESTC S108959. 'Suppressed' by royal proclamation 1610, as noted in Camden's copy (Westminster Abbey, Muniment Room, CB.95) on 4C4ᵛ and the following page.

Collation: 4⁰: *⁴ A–4C⁴. [584] p.

Words in AS appear in Italic with no special sorts.
Facsimile: English Linguistics 1500–1800 318 (Menston: Scolar, 1972) using OBL Douce C 276.

Copy seen: WAL CB.95.

Copies also at: BL, BCL, BUL, CCA, CUL, ECC, CGC, KCC, CTH, TCC, LHL, LPL, LSH, NLS, OBC, OQC, OStE, OSJ, OWmC, OWoC, YML, TCD; FSL, USLC, NYCU, HHL, HUL, DDUL, NLC, NWU, UTS, WMUL, YUB.

1608.1: Glover, Robert, [ed. Thomas Milles, Glover's nephew], *Nobilitas Politica vel Civilis*. London: William Jaggard, 1608. STC 11922; ESTC S111376. AS3 (with occasional AS2 s).

AS Law 'Geþyncðo'

Collation: 2° in 6s: A⁴ B–Q⁶ R⁶ (R6 + χ1) [$4 signed (-A1,2,4, G1,3, H1, I3, L2, R3)] 101 leaves, paginated [i–viii], 1–190, *191–2* (L2 not included in the pagination series; pp. 62, 66, 74, 82, 90, 96, 127–128, 183–184 not numbered; pp. 26 misnumbered 29, 129 misnumbered 117, 155 misnumbered 156, 156 misnumbered 166, 168 misnumbered 163, 185 misnumbered 187).

SOURCE OF PASSAGE UTILIZING ANGLO-SAXON TYPES:

N1ᵛ–3ʳ (pp. 132–135)   From 1596.2 2I7ᵛ–8ʳ: AS Law 'Geþyncðo' 1–7 (Liebermann I.456–458).

TYPE:

Main text in Pierre Haultin's Great Primer Roman (Body 118) interspersed with a Great Primer Italic.

AS3 with some AS2 s: Lambardian Pica Anglo-Saxon with occasional Parkerian s (e.g. on N1ᵛ/16 in ſunðeꞃnoꞇe) occurs in combination with Haultin's Pica Roman (small portion on G6ᵛ at bottom) in text on N1ᵛ–3ʳ (pp. 132–135). Special sorts shown:

12 lower-case sorts: ð, *e*, ꝼ, ᵹ, ꞕ, ꞃ, ſ, ꞇ, p, ẏ; þ, ð;

3 capitals: Є, ᛘ, Ð;

3 others: þ, ꟩, ꞌj;

Total: 18 sorts

Copies seen: CUL L*.9.3(B) (with updated errata slip pasted over on R6ᵛ), R.8.21 (signed Thomas Knyvett 20 Nov 1609, with contemporary gold-tooled binding of brown calf).

Copies also at: BL, CJC, CSJ, TCC, KNA, LGL, LHL, LSH, NPG, NLS, NT, OBL, OJC, OLC, ONC, OQC, OSJ, OWmC, SBT, SPC, UBL, UCL, WoCL, WRL, TCD, BSB, GUB; FSL, USLC, HHL, HUL, NLC, YUB.

Bibliography: Clement 1997: 230–231; Selwyn 1997 (Glover's books).

1609.1: Freher, Marquard, *Orationis Dominicæ et Symboli Apostolici Alamannica Versio Vetustissima*. [Heidelberg: Gotthard Vögelin] 1609. USTC 2014995; BLG L1076.

    Collation: 4⁰: A–B⁴ [$3 signed (-A1, B3)] 8 leaves, unnumbered.

    The Lord's Prayer and Creed in Old High German, the notes to which include comparative AS forms (e.g., A3ʳ, B1ʳ), printed in Robert Granjon's Paragon Italic (Body 129) with no AS special sorts.

    Copies at: BL, NLS, GFB, GUB, RUB, SLB, WAAB, WHAB

1610.1: Lambarde, William, EIRENARCHA: *or of The Office of the Justices of Peace, in foure Bookes*. 9th edn of 1581.1 re-set from 8th edn 1607.1. London: [Adam Islip] for the Stationers' Co., 1610. STC 15172; ESTC S108210. AS3.
Laws of Ine (extract)

    Collation: 8⁰: A–2Y⁸ [$4 signed (-A1; 2V4 missigned 'V4')] 360 leaves, paginated [i–ii], 1–634, *635–718* (p. 350 misnumbered 351, pp. 224–225 unnumbered (printed sideways)).

SOURCE OF PASSAGE UTILIZING ANGLO-SAXON TYPES:

M5ʳ (p. 183)   From 1607.1 M5ʳ: Extract from Laws of Ine 13,1 (Liebermann, I, 94–5).

All three errors first introduced in 1599.1 (q.v.) are taken over plus wrong word-division resulting in þoððe ꝺþric, and ꝺeꝼe is printed for 1607.1 ꝺeꝼe; and it uses an inverted italic exclamation mark instead of the punctus versus used in 1607.1.

TYPE:

Main text in Pica Textura   Body 83   Face 78 × 2 : 3
Pierre Haultin's Pica Roman   Body 84   Face 80 × 1.9: 3
Robert Granjon's Pica Italic (no. 2), the *Cicero pendante*, e.g. on C3ʳ–5ᵛ
                      Body 82.5   Face 80 × 1.5: 2.5

AS3: The Lambardian Pica Anglo-Saxon is combined with Haultin's Pica Roman in text as indicated above under Contents and in words on P8ʳ (p. 237).

Special sorts shown: 11 lower-case sorts: e, ꝼ, ȝ, h, ꝺ, ꝼ, t, ẏ; þ, ð, ꝑ;
                    1 capital: Ð;
                    1 other: ꝺ;
        Total: 13 sorts.

Note 1: d not used in the passage, and on p. 237 roman (not AS) capital **M** is used.

Note 2: Uses a semi-colon and an inverted italic exclamation mark for the punctus versus.

    Copies seen: CUL J.12.20; BL 1607/1631 (owned by A.A. Arnold).

Copies also at: BCL, MCL, NCL, NLW, OBrC, OStH, TPL, UBL, WAL; FSL, HHL, HUL, BMC, IUL, LSU, UCH.
Bibliography: see 1581.1.

1610.2: Selden, John, *Jani Anglorvm: Facies Altera.* London: Thomas Snodham (*alias* East) for John Helme, 1610. STC 22174; ESTC S121883. AS3.
OE Words + Laws of Ine (extract) in Textura
   Collation: 12⁰: A–G¹² [$5 signed (-A1,2, F3 missigned E3)] 84 leaves, paginated [i–xxiv], 1–133, *134–44* (p. 60 not numbered).
TYPE:
Main text in a Long Primer Roman (Body 67; Face 66 × 1.4: 2), interspersed with a Long Primer Italic (Body 67; Face 65 × 1.2: 1.8).
AS3: The Lambardian Pica Anglo-Saxon occurs in combination with a Pica Roman on B6ʳ (one word; p. 11), C2ʳ (one word; p. 47), G2ᵛ–3ʳ (words only, pp. 124–5) showing the following six sorts: ð, e, ʒ, þ, ſ, ꝳ, ꝼ (used as ð); Roman i and W are preferred where AS sorts could have been used appropriately; on C2ʳ the word peŋʒıð occurs but initial lower-case p is not wynn but an italic *p*.
Note: An extract from the beginning of the Laws of Ine (as Liebermann I.88–) occurs in Textura on G2ᵛ.
   Copies seen: CUL X.16.26, Rel.e.61.3 (lacks A1; gift of Frances Jenkinson); ECC S2.5.92; TCC VI.6.39; DML K4.5.23² (lacks A1; owned by Thomas Madden).
   Copies also at: BL, BCL, LCL, OBL, OJC, OQC, OSJ, GUB; FSL, USLC, NYCU, HHL, HUL, IUL.
Bibliography: Christianson 1984: 272–283; Clement 1997: 235 and n. 110; Parry 1995: 98–107; Toomer 2009: I.88–102.

1610.3: Foxe, John (ed.), *The Second Volume of the Ecclesiastical Historie, containing the Acts and Monuments of Martyrs.* 6th edn of 1570.1 (= 2nd edn) reset from 5th edn 1596.1. London: [Humphrey Lownes 1] for the Stationers' Co., 1610. STC 11227; ESTC S123056. AS3.
   Note: Sig. 5G was contracted out: it has no catchword at the end, a wider column width (88 mm on 5G2–4 rather than 86.5 mm), different more widely spaced page numbers, different line numbers between the columns, and shows variant forms of the running title *K.Hen.8* (e.g., *King Henry.8*); and was printed by [(?)Eliot's Court Press].
Extracts from 1566.1, 1567.1 taken from 1596.1
   Collation: (vol. II, books 7 and 8 only; cf. 1596.1): 2⁰: 4A–4V⁶ 5A–5E⁶ 5F–5G⁴ 5H–5M⁶ 5N⁶ (5N4 + χ1) 5O–5S⁶ 5T1 (end of Book 8) [$3 signed (-4A1, 5F3, 5G3)] 226 leaves, paginated [729–31], 732–1177 (pp. 968 misnumbered 986, 1025

misnumbered 1015, 1033/1034 misnumbered 1023/1024, 1040 misnumbered 1310, 1058 misnumbered 1158, 1059 misnumbered 1509, 1075 misnumbered 1076, 1119 misnumbered 1179, 1124 misnumbered 1224).

SOURCES OF PASSAGES UTILIZING ANGLO-SAXON TYPES:

5G2ᵛ/b/72–5 (p. 1040) From 1596.1, 5G2ᵛ/b/24–7, Ælfric's 'Excusatio Dictantis' (opening statement) at the end of his homily *Depositio S. Martin* (Godden 1979: XXXIV), with the same lineation, and the only spelling deviation being roman y for AS ẏ in ꞅẏ;

5G2ᵛ/b/82–4 (p. 1040)   From 1596.1, 5G2ᵛ/b/33–6, Ælfric's *Grammar*, opening statement from OE Preface (cf. Zupitza 1880: 2), with no spelling deviations except ʒꞃāmaτıca for 1596.1 ʒꞃammτıca (*sic*) and retention of erroneous þa (before lıꞃτlan) introduced in 1576.1 ða for 1570.1 ðaꞅ;

5G3ʳ/a/17–32 (p. 1041) From 1596.1, 5G2ᵛ/b/53–67, Ælfric's letter to Wulfsige III (bp of Sherborne 992–1002) extracts (Fehr 1914: §§135–42), with erroneous halʒam for 1596.1 halʒā, and retention of erroneous ðꞃıʒhτen and bleτꞅah;

5G3ʳ/a/62–b/40 (p. 1041)   From 1596.1, 5G3ʳ/a/12–b/4, Ælfric's second letter to Wulfstan (abp of York 1002–23) extracts (Fehr 1914: §§86–95, 97–109), with erroneous unτꞃnmū for 1596.1 unτꞃumū with 2nd u inverted, retention of erroneous poenıðenτıalē for 1596.1 poenıðeτıalē (1583.1 poenıτenτıalem), ðæʒe peττan (for 1570.1 ðæʒe ꞅeττan), ðıʒan (1583.1 ðıcʒan), ꞅpa cpæτe (1583.1 ꞅpa cpæðe); new errors include apoꞃτ. for 1596.1 apoꞃτolū., chıꞅτ for 1596.1 cꞃıꞅτ;

5G3ᵛ/b/31 to 5G4ᵛ/b/63 (pp. 1042–1044)   From 1596.1, 5G3ᵛ/a/54 to 5G4ᵛ/v/61, Ælfric's *Sermo de Sacrificio in die Pascae* (same omissions as 1570.1; Godden 1979: XV), keeping exactly the same lineation, with retention of erroneous bebeað þam (5G3ᵛ/a/63) omitting ꟽoẏꞅeꞅ, eꞃenð (5G4ʳ/b/7), pæðeꞃ oꞅ (5G4ʳ/b/25) omitting þa, τeꞃmeaʒēne (5G4ᵛ/a/10), etc.; new errors include τocnaꞃan (5G4ʳ/a/44) for τocnaꞃaþ, mæꞃon for næꞃon (5G4ʳ/b/51); spellings are generally not altered (e.g. ð/þ are kept exactly as in 1583.1), but e for æ and d for t sometimes occur.

5I5ʳ/a/72–5 (p. 1065)   From 1596.1, 5I5ʳ/a/72–6, ASC (E), annal for 1129 (Clark 1954: 51), with no spelling deviations other than the substitution of the nasal titulus for -m, -n-.

TYPE:

Main text in Small Pica Textura	Body 72	Face 70 × 2: 3
Small Pica Roman, e.g. on 5A2ᵛ–4ʳ,	Body 71	Face 70 × 1.7: 2.5

AS3: The Lambardian Pica Anglo-Saxon (Body 84) combined with Granjon's Pica Roman (with a relatively high x-height) occurs on 5G2ᵛ–4ᵛ (pp. 1040–1044) and 5I5ʳ (p. 1065) without AS *e*, the lack of which is probably due to its lack in

the 1596.1 edition used as the copytext (where the OE is set in AS1, which never shows AS *e*) rather than lack of availability; probably for the same reason (use of 1596.1 as the exemplar) AS ƕ is used only as a capital not lower-case as is usual in AS3; AS i is shown regularly *pace* Clement (1997: 231).

The specimen on 5G3ᵛ shows tailed z (i.e. not the form that resembles ʒ 'yogh').

Special sorts shown in text: 11 lower-case sort: ð, f, ʒ, ı, p, ſ, t, ẏ; þ, ð, p;
                          7 capitals: Æ¹, Æ², E, ƕ, ɱ, S, Ð;
                          3 others: ɉ, þ, j̇;
                 Total: 21 sorts.

Note: Lower-case þ is not shown, as capital Þ is used in place of it.

    Copies seen: CUL K*.7.2(A) (with contemporary gold-tooled binding); ECC 309.1.33; TCD F.a.2; OBL Douce F.subt.5 (with 17c binding in brown calf with gold-tooled central ornament showing the initials 'sw', and hand-coloured illustrations and MS-style ruling pattern throughout in red ink).

    Copies also at: BL, APL, BCL, BUT, CCA, ChestC, EdUL, GML, HCL, LHU, LPL, MTP, NLS, NT, OBrC, OCC, ORP, OUC, OWmC, YML; FSL, USLC, NYHS, UTS, HHL, HUL, EmU, GUW, HCP, MCRS, NLC, PST, QUK, UVC; ATL.

Bibliography: Clement 1997: 231–233.

1610.4: Milles, Thomas, *The Catalogue of Honor* [includes translation of 1608.1]. London: William Jaggard, 1610. STC 17926; ESTC S114605. AS3 (with occasional AS2 s).

AS Law 'Geþyncðo'

    Collation: 1st part only (A1–K6): 2⁰ in 6s: A–K⁶ [$ signed (-E2, G1)] 60 leaves, paginated [i–xii], 1–99, 100–108 (p. 61 not numbered; pp. 89 misnumbered 84, 99 misnumbered 97);

    State 2 of sig. I shown by the correct number at p. 89: State 2 of sig. K shown by corrections made—see below under **Copies seen**.

SOURCES OF PASSAGES UTILIZING ANGLO-SAXON TYPES:

G6ᵛ–H1ʳ (pp. 72–73) From 1608.1 N1ᵛ–3ʳ: AS Law 'Geþyncðo' 1–7 (Liebermann I.456–458).

TYPE:

Main text in Pierre Haultin's English-size Roman (Body 96);

AS3 with AS2 s: Lambardian Pica Anglo-Saxon with occasional Parkerian s (e.g. G6ᵛ aʒeneſ) occurs in combination with Haultin's Pica Roman (small portion on F3ʳ) in text on G6ᵛ–H1ʳ. Special sorts shown:

                12 lower-case sorts: ð, e, f, ʒ, ƕ, p, ſ, t, ẏ; þ, ð, p;
                3 capitals: E, ɱ, Ð;
                3 others: þ, ɉ, j̇.
       Total: 18 sorts.

Copies seen:

Sig. I State 1: CUL L*.9.2(B) (lacks A1, G5); State 2 (with p. 89 numbered correctly): CUL Adv.a.18.1; ECC 310.2.56.

Sig. K State 1: CUL Adv.a18.1; State 2: CUL L*.9.2(B); ECC 310.2.56.

CUL Adv.a18.1 contains a proof-sheet of K1ᵛ.6ʳ corrected in Jaggard's printing-house (Blayney 1982: 235–238), and some of the corrections appear in other copies, e.g.:

K1ᵛ/11 (p. 98)   Bohemia, Hungary.   →   Bohemia, and Hungary.
K6ʳ/9 (p. 107)   fucceffiue.   →   Succeffiue.

Copies also at: BL, APL, BCL, ChC, CGC, CMC, CNC, CUW, ECL, EdUL, GML, LCL, LHL, LiCL, LPL, LSH, LUL, NLS, NT, OBL, OBC, OBrC, OCC, OEC, OMC, OQC, OSJ, SCL, UBL, UCL, WCC, YML, DML, TCD; FSL, USLC, NYPL, HHL, HUL, IUL, KSRL, NLC, NWU, SLP, UCBL, UTA, WMil, YUB, QUK, TUL; UML.

Bibliography: Blayney 1982: 235–238; Clement 1997: 231; Moore 1992: 67.

1610.5: Camden, William, *Britain, or A Chorographicall Description of the most Flourishing Kingdomes, England, Scotland, and Ireland, and the Ilands adjoyning.* English t of 1607.2 by Philemon Holland. London: [Eliot's Court Press, for] George Bishop and John Norton I, 1610. STC 4509; ESTC S107167. AS3.
OE proper names

Note: Camden assisted Holland with the translated edition (Vine 2010: 80–81, n. 3); corrections notified by others incorporated (Vine 2010: 93–98).

Collation: 2^0 in 6s: ❊⁸ A–G⁶ H⁸ I–L⁶ (+L1χ1.2) K–P⁶ (+P5χ1.2) Q–R⁶ (+R1χ1.2) S⁶ (+S1χ1.2, S6χ1.2) T–V⁶ (+V5χ1.2) X–Y⁶ (+Y1χ1.2) Z⁶ (+Z6χ1.2) 2A–2B⁶ (+2B1χ1.2) 2C⁶ (+2C1χ1.2) 2D⁶ (+2D3χ1.2) 2E–2F⁶ 2G⁶ (+2G4χ1.2) 2H⁶ (+2H4χ1.2) 2I–2K⁶ (+2K2χ1.2, 2K5χ1.2) 2L⁶ (+2L2χ1.2) 2M⁶ (+2M3χ1.2) 2N–2O⁶ (+2O1χ1.2) 2P⁶ (+2P5χ1.2) 2Q⁶ (+2Q5χ1.2) 2R⁶ (+2R6χ1.2) 2S⁶ (+2S6χ1.2) 2T⁶ (+2T4χ1.2) 2V⁶ (+2V4χ1.2) 2X⁶ (+2X2χ1.2, 2X4χ1.2) 2Y–2Z⁶ (+2Z1χ1.2, 2Z4χ1.2) 3A⁶ (+3A2χ1.2) 3B⁶ (+3B2χ1.2, 3B6χ1.2) 3C⁶ (+3C4χ1.2) 3D⁶ (+3D4χ1.2) 3E⁶ (+3E6χ1.2) 3F⁶ (+3F3χ1.2, 3F5χ1.2) 3G⁶ (+3G1χ1.2, 3G6χ1.2) 3H⁶ (+3H4χ1.2, 3H5χ1.2) 3I⁶ (+3I2χ1.2, 3I4χ1.2, 3I6χ1.2) 3K⁶ (+3K1χ1.2, 3K3χ1.2, 3K5χ1.2) 3L⁶ (+3L1χ1.2, 3L6χ1.2) 3M–3N⁶ (+3N5χ1.2) 3O⁶ (+3O2χ1.2) 3P⁶ (+3P1χ1.2, 3P5χ1.2) 3Q⁶ (+3Q4χ1.2) 3R⁶ (+3R5χ1.2) 3S⁶ (+3S2χ1.2) 3T–3X⁶ (+3X1χ1.2) 3Y⁸ (+3Y8χ1.2) 4A–4E⁶ (+4E6χ1.2) 4F–4V⁶ 4X–5I² [\$3 signed (+❊4, H4, 3Y4; -❊1, 4A1, 4V3, 4X2, 4Y2, 4Z2, 5A2, 5B2, 5C2, 5D2, 5E2, 5F2, 5G2, 5H2, 5I2; 2L2 missigned L2)] 564 leaves, paginated [i–xvi], 1–822, 823–4, ²1–233, ²234–88 (pp. nos 207–208 used twice; pp. nos 300–301 not used; p. 56 misnumbered 58, 277 misnumbered 276, 287 misnumbered 278, 299 misnumbered 287, 369 misnumbered 269, 498 misnumbered 510, 507 misnumbered 519, 609 misnumbered 600, 662 misnumbered 650, 787 misnumbered 794, 794 misnumbered 787, ²43 misnumbered 34, ²123–130 misnumbered 111–118; p. 429 has 2 inverted; the following pages are not numbered: 322, 356, 404, 438, 484, 496, 528, 546, 552,

572, 580, 600, 626, 629, 648, 664, 674, 678, 708, 716, 764, 798, ²2, ²56). State 2 shown by p. 277 correctly numbered.

TYPE:

Main text in Pierre Haultin's English-size Roman (Body 95) interspersed with Robert Granjon's 3rd English-size Italic (e.g. D6ᵛ–F1ʳ).

AS3: The Lambardian Pica Anglo-Saxon occurs in the specimen on ✻8ʳ. Special sorts shown:

    11 lower-case sorts: ð, e, ꝼ, ȝ, ƿ, ꞃ, ꞇ, ẏ; þ, ð, p;
    7 capitals: Æ¹, Æ², Ꮛ, Ꭸ, ᛞ, S, Ð;
    2 others: þ, ꝫ.
    Total: 20 sorts.

AS3: The Lambardian Pica Anglo-Saxon combined with Haultin's Pica Roman (as on ✻6ᵛ–7ʳ) occurs in the text in words on pp. 26, 117 (showing erron. p as 1607.2 for 1600.1 þ), 138 (with erron. -lonð for 1607.2 -lonð), 163–164, 166, 177, 184, 187–188, 199, 204, 209, 212–214, 216, 220, 222, 225, 233, 237, 241, 243–244, 246–247, 255, 258, 261–262, 265 (showing erron. Mynꞃðeꝼ for erron. Mynꞃðeꝧ for 1600.1 mynꞃꞇeꝧ), 279, 281, 284, 286, 292, 294, 300, 303, 306–308, 313, 315–317, 321, 323, 325, 328, 330–332, 335–336, 339, 342 (with erron. Sonꞇþẏc for 1607.2 Sonðþẏc), 344, 350–351, 357, 359–360 (with erron. Tðeocꞃbuꝧẏ and Olenaȝ for 1607.2 Tðeocꞃbuꝧẏ and Oleneaȝ), 362, 364, 366, 373 (with erron. Oxenpoꝧð- for 1607.2 Oxenꞃoꝧð-), 375, 377, 393 (with erron. Clẏꞇeꝧn for 1607.2 Cẏlꞇeꝧn), 395, 406, 408, 419, 421, 439, 441, 446, 450–451, 458 (with erron. -ꝧẏꞇ for 1607.2 -ꝧẏc), 459–460, 463, 471, 473, 476, 485–486, 492, 497, 505, 525, 529, 533, 542, 544, 547, 553–554, 562, 573, 575 (with -ceaꞃꞇeꝧ corrected from 1607.2 -ceaꞃꞇeꝼ), 578, 581–582, 587, 589, 593, 595, 601–602, 604, 614, 619, 640, 653, 677, 689–690, 693–694, 696 (with erron. Gueꞃꝧ for 1607.2 Gueꝧꝼ), 700–701, 711, 714, 717–718, 731, 738, 742–743, 745, 755, 797, 799, 806–807, 811–813, 2203, 2223.

Special sorts shown:

    12 lower-case sorts: ð, e, ꝼ, ȝ, Ꭸ, ƿ, ꞃ, ꞇ, ẏ; þ, ð, p;
    4 capitals: Ꮛ, Ꭸ, S (also used for ð, e.g., on S5ᵛ), Ð;
    3 others: ꝫ (on 2B6ʳ), þ (on 4T4ʳ), ꝫ (1st on 2T1ʳ).
    Total: 19 sorts.

Note 1: AS undotted i does not appear.
Note 2: Ꭸ is used regularly as a lc letter, occasionally initially as a capital, e.g. ꝧanꞇeꞃcðẏꝧ on Y2ᵛ.
Note 3: ð and S (for ð) used side by side in 'Maleðune, and MealSune' on 205ᵛ (p. 446).
Note 4: AS capitals also used with roman ones in a Latin inscription on 2X6ᵛ.

Copies seen: State 1: CUL Pet.B.5.15 (lacks map after 3P5);

State 2 (with p. 277 correctly numbered): CCA W/G.5.16 (with ❋3 and ❋1 interchanged; Somner's copy, acquired for 25s. 1641 ❋3ʳ); CUL Syn.3.61.25 (lacks ❋3); LFL 2G (with ❋3 and ❋1 interchanged).

Copies also at: BL, BCL, BCLNI, BPH, BUT, ChC, CSS, CTH, TCC, CLL, CUW, EdUL, GUL, HCL, HRC, MJRUL, LGI, LGL, LMT, MOL, NIA, NLS, NT, NUL, OBL, OMaCS, OOCOSH, OXC, SAC, SBT, SCL, WIHM, YML, DML, ULim; FSL, NYPL, NYCU, HHL, HUL, IUL, MRCS, NLC, UCH, UOC, UVL, QUK; ACU, ATL, NLA, SSA, USL.

Bibliography: Boon 1987: 10–11; Harris 2015; Nurse 1993; Rice 1966; Shirley 1991: nos 307–308; Skelton 1970: no. 6.
Facsimile: vol. 1 (of 3) introd. Robert J. Mayhew (Bristol: Thoemmes, 2003).
On-line: L text of **1586.1** together with Philemon Holland's English t (**1610.5**) at <www.philological.bham.ac.uk/cambrit>

1610.6: Freher, Marquard, *Decalogi, Orationis, Symboli Saxonica Versio Vetustissima*. Heidelberg: Gotthard Vögelin, 1610. USTC 2080667; BLG T160.

    Collation: 4⁰: A–B⁴ C². Fos [10]

OE text of the Ten Commandments, the Lord's Prayer, and the Creed in a 2-line English-size Roman (Body 186) with no AS special sorts, **th** being used for þ, **d** for ð, **vv** for p.

    Copy seen: CUL G.13.22⁴

    Copies also at: BL, DUL, OBL, NLS, DML, BN, PBSG, BUB, GFB, GUB, SLB, WAAB, WHAB, BAV.

1611.1: Speed, John, *The Theatre of the Empire of Great Britaine Presenting an Exact Geography of the Kingdomes of England, Scotland, Ireland, and the Iles adioyning, with the Shires, Hundreds, Cities and Shire Townes, within yᵉ Kingdome of England*. London: William Hall for John Sudbury and George Humble, 1611/1612. Humble was granted privilege to print this work for 21 years 29 April 1608 (Greg 1967: 51). STC 23041; ESTC S117917. AS2/3.

OE Proper Names

    Collation: 2 sheets of 2⁰ quired (irregularly) in order of pagination, except that sigs ¶, 2F and ✳ show 3 sheets: ¶⁶, A–2E⁴, 2F⁶, 2G–2L⁴, 2M–2N², ✳⁵ (leaf 6 probably used as P1 in **1611.2**) [$2 signed (+¶3, 2F5; -2M, 2N (2nd sheet not present); Z2 missigned Z3, 2F3 missigned 2F1, 2F5 missigned 2F2, 2K1 missigned 2K2)]. 149 leaves, foliated (always on the text side) [i–vi], 1–146 (nos 115–116 used twice), *147–151* (fos 98 misnumbered 97, 112 misnumbered 102, 126 misnumbered 124; fos 95–96, 127–128 and 133–134 not numbered).

    Note 1: Each folded sheet, consisting of two leaves, is signed as a single leaf, so A⁴ consists of two sheets folded, the first signed A (here designated as A1–2), the second signed A2 (here designated as A3–4). The sheets are grouped so that two sheets bearing a particular letter (or multiple of it) sandwich the second sheet bearing the previous letter.

Note 2: The text, abridged from Camden, *Britannia* 1607.2, is printed back to back with the maps, and the map pages, being always a double-page opening on the reverse side of text pages, receive no numbers.

TYPE:

Main text mainly in Pierre Haultin's English-size Roman
         Body 93   Face 90 × 2: 3

but sometimes the type-size is reduced so that the textual material fits on the reverse side of maps, as:

Pierre Haultin's 2nd Pica Roman (Vervliet R82B) on T1^r–X1^r (fos 73–81), Z1^r (fo 89), 2A1^v (fo 92), 2H1^r (fo 123), 2L1 (fos 137–138), 2K2^r (fo 141), 2N1^r (fo 145):
         Body 82   Face 78 × 1.8: 2.5

Pierre Haultin's Long Primer Roman (Vervliet R67) on 2B1 (fos 99–100), 2L2^r (fo 139):   Body 67   Face 64 × 1.4: 2.0

Italics of the same size are used in the course of the main text to highlight names, etc.

Two Anglo-Saxon Pica designs are used mixed together in county names. Normally they occur with the English-size main text, but they are also found with main text in Pica (T1^r = fo 73, Z1^r = fo 89) and Long Primer (P1^r = fo 57).

AS2: The Parkerian Pica Anglo-Saxon.
Special sorts shown: ð, ꝼ, ƿ, ſ, ꞇ, ẏ; ð, p; Æ.   8 + 1

AS3: The Lambardian Pica Anglo-Saxon.
Special sorts shown: e, ᵹ, ᚦ, ƿ, ſ, ꞇ; þ (= ƿ), p; S (= ð). 8 + 1

Note: Anglo-Saxon i is not used. The setting is prone to errors, as s for r, p for þ and even p.

 Copy seen: CUL L*.7.8(AA) lacks 2D3–4 (fos 113–114).

 Copies also at: BL, CCL, EEC, CGC, CJC, KCC, CPH, TCC, ECL, GlCL, GML, LPL, NAL, NLS, OBL, OMaC, ONC, OQC, OSJ, OStE, OXC, TCD, ULim; USLC, NYPL, BA, GUW, HHL, IUL; QUL, SSA.

Bibliography: Keynes 2014: 159–160 (on map of AS heptarchy); Lucas 2018; Shirley 1991: nos 316–318; Skelton 1970: no. 7, pp. 30–44.

Facsimile: John Arlott, *John Speed's England: A coloured facsimile of the maps and text from the Theatre of the Empire of Great Britaine, first ed. 1611*, 4 vols (London, 1953–4).

1611.2: Speed, John, *The History of Great Britaine under the Conquests of ye Romans, Saxons, Danes and Normans, their Originals, Manners, Warres, Coines*

& Seales, with y*e* Successions, Lives, acts & Issues of the English Monarchs from Iulius Cæsar, to our most gracious Soueraigne King Iames*. London: William Hall for John Sudbury and George Humble 1611. STC 23045; ESTC 117937. AS2.

>Note: The signatures and pagination are continuous with Speed's *Theatre of the Empire* 1611.1.

Word

>Collation: 2 sheets of 2⁰ quired (irregularly) in order of pagination, except that sigs 6C and 6D show 3 and 4 sheets respectively: P² (lacks 2 torn out), 2M², 2O–6B⁴ (4Z and 5Z not used), 6C⁶, 6D⁸, 6E–6Y⁴ [$2 signed (+ 3K3, 6C3, 6D3–4, 2M1 signed 2M2, 3X2 signed 2X)] 404 leaves, paginated 151–786, then foliated 787–802, then paginated 803–94, *895–946*.

>Note: The signatures and pagination are continuous with Speed's *The Theatre of the Empire of Great Britaine* (STC 23041). Each folded sheet, consisting of two leaves, is signed as a single leaf, so A⁴ consists of two sheets folded, the first signed A (here designated as A1–2), the second signed A2 (here designated as A3–4). The sheets are grouped so that two sheets bearing a particular letter (or multiple of it) sandwich the second sheet bearing the previous letter.

>Another issue shows (a) in place of P1 ¶6 [¶2 signed 1, ¶4 signed 2, ¶5 signed 3], and (b) after 6X4ᵛ ✶6 (lacks 6 presumably blank) [✶1 signed, ✶3 signed 2].

TYPE:

Main text in Pierre Haultin's English Roman   Body 93   Face 90 × 2: 3
An English Italic is used to highlight speeches, names, etc., as on 6F3ʳ–4ʳ (pp. 812–13).   Body 93   Face 90 × 2: 2.5
AS2: Parkerian Pica AS used in one word on 2P1ʳ/b (p. 159) Bꝥıðꞃ. Compare 3H3ᵛ (p. 292), where the names of the AS kings are in Italic.
Special sorts shown: 4 lower-case sorts: ð, ı, ꝥ, ꞃ.

>Copies seen: CUL L*.7.9(AA). Another issue (1614, STC 23046) CUL CCA.20.3, Bury 18.1 (lacks ¶4–6 and ✶1–6).

>Copies also at: BL, BCL, CJC, KCC, CPH, CSJ, TCC, CUW, ChCL, EUL, ClCL, LiCL, LPL, NLS, NT, NUL, OBL, OBrC, OEF, OMaC, ONC, OQC, OSJ, OXC, UBL; NLI, TCD; FSL, USLC, NYCU, HHL, HUL, NLC, USNA; QUL.

Bibliography: Parry 1995: 75.

1612.1: Drayton, Michael, ed. John Selden, *Poly-Olbion.* [*or A Chorographicall Description of Tracts, Rivers, Mountaines, Forests, and other Parts of this renowned Isle of Great Britaine, With intermixture of the most Remarquable Stories, Antiquities, Wonders, Rarityes, Pleasures, and Commodities of the same: Digested in a Poem.*] London: [Humphrey Lownes I] for Matthew Lownes, John Browne I, John Helme, and John Busby II, 1612. STC 7226; ESTC S121629. AS3.
Laws of Ine (extract), words

Collation: 2⁰: π⁴ A⁴ B–2C⁶ 2D² [$3 signed (-2D2)]. 160 leaves, paginated [i–xvi], 1–303, *304* (pp. 258 misnumbered 285, 276 misnumbered 266). There are eighteen 2-leaf folding maps inserted between leaves A4/B1, C5/6, E1/2, F3/4, H1/2, I1/2, K2/3, L1/2, M6/N1, O6/P1, Q1/2, S1/2, T4/5, V4/5, X4/5, Y2/3, Z2/3, 2B3/4; in all cases the recto of the 1st leaf and the verso of the 2nd leaf are blank.

SOURCE OF PASSAGE UTILIZING ANGLO-SAXON TYPES:
2D1ᵛ (p. 302)   Extract from the Laws of Ine 3 (Liebermann I, 90–91) prob from 1568.2 C2ᵛ (*om.* mon *in* ðeowmon)

TYPE:
Main text (Songs) in Pierre Haultin's English-size Roman: Body 94.
Illustrations (commentary by Selden) in Pierre Haultin's 2nd Pica Roman (Vervliet R82B): Body 82.
AS3: The Lambardian Pica Anglo-Saxon combined with Haultin's 2nd Pica Roman in text of the commentary on 2D1ᵛ (p. 302), and in words on C5ᵛ (p. 22), M3ᵛ (p. 126), R2ʳ (p. 183), R3ʳ (p. 185), S1ʳ (p. 193).
Special sorts shown:
        9 lower-case sorts: ð, ꝼ, ᵹ, ı, p, ſ, τ, ẏ; ꝑ;
        3 capitals: Є, Ƨ (also = ð), Þ;
        1 other: ꝗ;
Total: 13 sorts.
Note: AS *e*, Ꭰ and ꟺ are not used despite opportunities to do so.

Copies seen: CUL Keynes H.4.17 (A2,3 misbound after 2D1); OBL Wood 403 (Kiessling 2002: no. 2304: lacks portrait; not seen).
Copies also at: BL, ChC, CMC, TCC, CUW, GML, HHC, ILP, LSH, LUL, NT, ONC, OWmC, QUB, SUL, UBL, WCF, WCL; FSL, USLC, NYPL, HHL, HUL, BMC, HCP, IUL, LCP, NWU, UCBL, UTA, WMUL, UTA, TUL, UVC.

Bibliography: Christianson 1984: 283–286; Clement 1997: 235; Hind 1952–64: II.330–331 and pls 207b–208 (tp and maps), II.321–322, 405 (portrait of Henry, Prince of Wales); Helgerson 1992: 117–124, 128–130, 139–147; Juel-Jensen 1961: 297–300; Parry 1995: 108–113; Skelton 1970: no. 8; Toomer 2009: I.108–124.

1612.2: Mylius (van der Mijle), Abraham, *Lingua Belgica: sive de lingua illius communitate tum cum plerisque alijs, tum præsertim cum Latina Graeca Persica; deque communitatis illius causis; tum de linguae illius origine et latissima per nationes quamplurimas diffusione; ut et de ejus preſstantia*. Leiden: Uldrick Cornelissz Honthorst and Joris Abrahamsz van der Marsce 'pro bibliopolio Commeliniano', 1612. USTC 1027670.

Collation: 4⁰: a–c⁴ A–2L⁴ (2L4 blank). [24] 259 [8] p.
No AS, but includes the Lord's Prayer in Icelandic printed in a Pica Schwabacher from 1555.1 on 2K1 (pp. 255–256).

Copies: BL, CUL, MJRUL, OTI, DML, PBN, PBM, SPBU, GCB, LKU, AUB, HKB, HSB, LUB, NUB, UTUB, RUB, WHAB.

1613.1: Drayton, Michael, ed. John Selden, *Poly-Olbion. or A Chorographicall Description of Tracts, Rivers, Mountaines, Forests, and other Parts of this renowned Isle of Great Britaine, With intermixture of the most Remarquable Stories, Antiquities, Wonders, Rarityes, Pleasures, and Commodities of the same: Digested in a Poem.* London: Humphrey Lownes I for Matthew Lownes, John Browne I, John Helme, and John Busby II, 1613. STC 7227; ESTC S121632. Re-issue of 1612.1 with additional tp and table.
Laws of Ine (extract), words
   Collation: Identical with 1612.1 except for $+\chi_1$ between π_2 and π_3 (= tp), and + ❀⁴ (= table).
   Copies seen: CUL Syn.4.61.11 (lacks tp), TCD TT.d.44 (*ex libris* Claud Gilbert).
   Copies also at: BL, BCL, CCA, CMC, TCC, EAL, EdUL, GlCL, GML, CUL, LHL, NLS, OBL, OBrC, OEC, OHC, OQC, OSJ, OTC, OWoC, SBT, SPC, UBL; FSL, NYPL, NYSL, CCNY, HHL, HUL, UCBL, UCH, UTA, UVL, TUL; ANZ, USL.
Bibliography: Juel-Jensen 1961: 300–302; Skelton 1970: no. 9.

1613.2: Kiliaan (van Kiel), Cornelis, *Etymologicum Teutonicae Linguae sive Dictionarium Teutonico-Latinum*, 4th edn. Alkmaar: Jacob de Meester, 1613, (a) for Jan Evertsz. Cloppenhurgh I (Amsterdam) = USTC 1026581 (b) for Hendrik Laurensz. (Amsterdam) = USTC 1012418, also re-issued without the printer's name 1620 = USTC 1030509, (c) for Dirk Pietersz. Pers (Amsterdam), not found in USTC, (d) for Symon Moulert (Middelburg) = USTC 1035387, also re-issued without the printer's name 1620 = USTC 1018257. Re-issue of **1605.3**.
   Collation: 8^0: *⁸ A–Z⁸ a–z⁸ 2A–2C⁸ 2D⁴. Fos 404.
   Words in AS and other appropriate languages appear in Italic with no AS special sorts, e.g., s.v. Seyl on H1^r (p. 481).
   Copies: BL, OBL, BBR, AUB, HKB, LUB.

1613.3: Verstegan, Richard, *Nederlantsche Antiquiteyten met de bekeeringhe van eenighe der selue landen tot het kersten ghelooue, devr S. Willibrordvs.* Antwerp: Gaspar Bellerus, 1613. USTC 1001870.
   Collation: 8^0: +⁴ A–G⁸. 60 leaves, paginated [i–viii] 1–112.
   OE text of the Lord's Prayer, the Hail Mary, and the beginning of St John's Gospel printed in a Long Primer Textura with no special sorts on C3^r–4^v.
   Copies: BL, ASB, ARG, GCB, LKU, AUB, LUB.

CATALOGUE OF EARLY PRINTED BOOKS CONTAINING ANGLO-SAXON 317

1614.1: Speed, John, *The Theatre of the Empire of Great Britaine Presenting an Exact Geography of the Kingdomes of England, Scotland, Ireland, and the Iles adioyning, with the Shires, Hundreds, Cities and Shire Townes, within y^e Kingdome of England*. London: William Hall for John Sudbury and George Humble, 1614 (but Bks II–IV printed by Thomas Snodham, 1616). 2nd edn of 1611.1. STC 23041.4; ESTC S112623. AS2/3.

OE proper names

Collation: 2o: A–4H² [$1 signed (+ A2, B2, 3F2, 3X2, 3Z2, 4F2, 4G2; -A1, 3F1, 3X1, 3Z1 (all tps)] 152 leaves, foliated (always on the text side) [i–viii], 1–94, 99–126, [131–132], 137–146, *147–154* (fo nos 19–20 not used), paginated 95–98, 127–130, 133–136 (95–96, 127–128, 130, 133–134 not numbered).

Note: The text is printed back to back with the maps, and the map pages, being always a double-page opening on the reverse side of text pages, receive no numbers.

TYPE:
The size varies according to the amount of text in relation to the amount of space available.
The preferred type is Pierre Haultin's English-size Roman (as on I1^r)
                          Body 92   Face 90 × 2: 3.0
but the following also occur:
Pierre Haultin's 2nd Pica Roman (Vervliet R82B), as on L1^r:
                          Body 82.5   Face 78 × 1.8: 2.5
Pierre Haultin's Long Primer Roman (Vervliet R67), as on Y1^r:
                          Body 66   Face 64 × 1.4: 2.0
Italics of the same size as the main text are used to highlight names, etc.
Two Anglo-Saxon Pica designs are used mixed together in county names. They occur with main text in English-size (as on I1^r), with Pica (as on L1^r), and with Long Primer (as on Y1^r and 2K1^r).

AS2: The Parkerian Pica Anglo-Saxon.
Special sorts shown: 9 lower-case sorts: ð, f, ȝ, p, ſ, τ, ẏ; þ, ð;
                             2 capitals: Æ, S.
               Total: 11 sorts.

AS3: The Lambardian Pica Anglo-Saxon.
Special sorts shown: 3 lower-case sorts: *e*, h (=ƕ), τ;
                             1 capital: S.
               Total: 4 sorts.

Note: Anglo-Saxon **i** is not used. The setting is prone to errors, as **s** for **r**, **ð** for **d**, **þ** for **p**.

Copy seen: ChC K.14.21 (binding in brown calf with name of John Watkin, alumnus and donor (s.xvii), in gold leaf as part of the cover design; lacks sig. 3Y).
Copies also at: BL, BCL, CSS, CUW, NT, OMC, OStE, TCD; FSL IUL.
Bibliography: Shirley 1991: nos 343–345; Skelton 1970: no. 10.

1614.2: Lambarde, William, EIRENARCHA: or of The Office of the Justices of Peace, in foure Bookes. 10th edn of 1581.1 re-set from 9th edn 1610.1. London: [Adam Islip] for the Stationers' Co., 1614. STC 15173; ESTC S108212. AS3.
Laws of Ine (extract)
Collation: 8^0: A–2Y^8. [$4 signed (-A1); 2V3,4 missigned V3,4] 360 leaves, paginated [i–ii], 1–634, 635–718 (pp. 224–225 unnumbered as printed sideways; pp. 233 misnumbered 227, 239 misnumbered 205, 251 misnumbered 25, 308 misnumbered 207, 318 misnumbered 218, 319 misnumbered 316, 325 misnumbered 323, 350 misnumbered 351, 365 misnumbered 395, 368 misnumbered 336, 499 misnumbered 404, 521 misnumbered 523).
SOURCE OF PASSAGE UTILIZING ANGLO-SAXON TYPES:
M5^r (p. 183)   From 1610.1 M5^r: Extract from Laws of Ine 13,1 (Liebermann, I, 94–95).
All three errors first introduced in 1599.1 (q.v.) are taken over plus wrong word-division resulting in þoððe ⁊þric first introduced in 1607.1 (q.v.), and ꞅeꝼe first introduced in 1610.1 (q.v).
TYPE:
Main text in Pica Texura   Body 83.5   Face 78 × 2: 3
Pierre Haultin's Pica Roman (e.g. on L3^r = p. 163)   Body 84   Face 80 × 1.8: 3
Robert Granjon's Pica Italic (no.2), the *Cicero pendante* (e.g. on L4^r = p. 165)
                                                               Body 84   Face 80 × 1.5: 2.5
AS3: Lambardian Pica Anglo-Saxon on M5^r (p. 183, text) and P8^r (p. 237, words) combined with Haultin's Pica Roman.
Special sorts shown: 11 lower-case sorts: e, ꝼ, ȝ, ꞅ, p, ꞅ, ꞇ, ẏ; þ, ð, ƿ;
                       1 capital: Ð;
                       1 other: ⁊;
           Total: 13 sorts.
Note 1: No d in text; and on p. 237 roman (not AS) capital M is used.
Note 2: Uses semi-colon and inverted exclamation mark for the punctus versus.
Copies seen: TCC VI.9.104 (gift of Henry Puckering alias Newton); DML H.8.5; BL 883.b.4; OBL 35.b.35.
Copies also at: BUL, CMC, CSJ, KNA, LGL, LSH, NLW, OBF, OOC, OXC; FSL, NYCU, UTS, HHL, HUL, IUL, JCB, KSRL; UWA, VSC.
Bibliography: see 1581.1.

1614.3: Camden, William, *Remaines, concerning Britaine: but especially England, and the Inhabitants thereof: their Languages. Empreses. Names. Apparell. Surnames. Artillarie. Allusions. Wise Speeches. Anagrammes. Prouerbs. Armories. Poesïes. Monies. Epitaphes.* 2nd edn of **1605.2**. London: John Legat 1 for Simon Waterson, 1614. STC 4522; ESTC S107394. Individual sorts only: AS3 ȝ and þ.
Lord's Prayer; Letter-symbols
>   Collation: 4⁰: A² B–3B⁴ 3C² [$3 signed (-A1, 3C2)]. 192 leaves, paginated [i–iv], 1–386 (pp. nos 182–189 not used; pp. 58/59 misnumbered 60/57, 333 misnumbered 338); State 2 shows pp. 58/59 numbered correctly.

SOURCES OF PASSAGES UTILIZING ANGLO-SAXON TYPES:
D4ʳ (p. 23)   From **1605.2** C4: Lord's Prayer;
D4 (pp. 23–4)   From **1605.2** C4ᵛ: Lord's Prayer (with marginal variants from another version).

TYPE:
Main text in Pierre Haultin's Pica Roman (Body 83) interspersed with Robert Granjon's 2nd Pica Italic *pendante*.
D4 (pp. 23–4): Lord's Prayer in OE (?) twice: no special sorts, but æ is correct in the 2nd one; suprascript translation to 1st version in Granjon's 2nd Pica Italic.
AS3: The Lambardian Pica Anglo-Saxon (individual special sorts only) occurs on E4ᵛ (p. 32) in a report on the spelling reform practices advocated by Smith in **1568.3**: ȝ, þ.
Note: A passage from Chaucer's *Nun's Priest's Tale* is printed in Granjon's 2nd Pica Italic with no special sorts on 2S1ᵛ–2ʳ.
>   **Copies:** State 1: CUL Syn.7.61.45 (lacks 3C2); State 2: CUL Adams.7.61.1 (lacks 3C2).
>   **Copies also at:** BL, BUL, CCC, CCL, ChC, KCC, CMC, CSJ, TCC, CUW, DWL, ECL, EdUL, Eton, LGL, LSH, NLS, NT, OCC, OEC, OJC, OMaCS, OMC, ONC, ORP, OSA, OSC, OWmC, UBL, UCL, WCF, WCR, DML, GCB, BSB; FSL, USLC, NYCU, UTS, HHL, HUL, DDUL, GTS, LCP, NLC, UCH, UTA, UTK, UVL, WUM, YUB; QSL.

Bibliography: Dunn 1984: xliv–xlv.

1614.4: Selden, John, *Titles of Honor*. London: William Stansby for John Helme. STC 22177; ESTC S117085. AS2.
Laws (extracts)
>   **Context:** Modelled on Jean du Tillet the elder (Sieur de la Bussière), *Receuil des Rangs de Grands de France*, included as part of his *Receuil des Roys de France*, sigs 3A–4o in the edition printed at Paris by Pierre Ramier for Jean Houzé (1606 for 1607); on du Tillet see Kelley 1970: esp. 226–233.
>   **Collation:** 4⁰: a–d⁴ A²(+χ1) B–3I⁴ 3K² [$3 signed (+3G4; -a1, 2Q3, 2X–3E3, 3F2, 3K2 not present)] 237 leaves, paginated [i–xxxviii], 1–391, *392–436* (pp. 193

misnumbered 194, 201 misnumbered 101, 202/203 misnumbered 206/207, 206/207 misnumbered 202/203).

SOURCES OF PASSAGES UTILIZING ANGLO-SAXON TYPES:

I3ʳ (p. 61) From 1568.2 G3ᵛ: AS Law Alfred El.Prol. (extract; Liebermann I.26); Note: Selden's incomplete grasp of OE grammar is illustrated by Dpihcen pæʃ ʃpɲæcen ðæʃ popðʃ co Ɯoẏce;

R2ᵛ (p. 124) From 1596.2 2I7ᵛ: AS Law 'Geþyncðo' 1 (extract; Liebermann I.456), and from 1568.2 2E2ᵛ: AS Law Cnut I 6,2a (Liebermann I.290);

2D2ᵛ (p. 204) From 1568.2 V3ᵛ: AS Law Norðleoda 2–3 (extract; Liebermann I.460); and 2K1ᵛ: AS Law II Cnut 58,2 (extract; Liebermann I.350);

2G1ʳ (p. 225) From 1568.2 2K1ᵛ: AS Law II Cnut 58.2 (extract; Liebermann I.350);

2G1ᵛ (p. 226) From 1568.2 C1ᵛ: AS Law Ine prologue (extract; Liebermann I.88–9);

2K4ʳ (p. 255) From 1568.2 2B3ᵛ: AS Law II Æthelred 6 (extract; Liebermann I.222);

2M2 (pp. 267–268) From 1568.2 2K4ᵛ: AS Laws II Cnut 71 (words and phrases; Liebermann I.358); and from 1596.2 2I7ᵛ: AS Law 'Geþyncðo' 1–2 (words and phrases; Liebermann I.456);

2N1ʳ (p. 273) From 1568.2 2K4ᵛ: AS Law II Cnut 71.1 (extract; Liebermann I.358);

2V3ʳ (p. 333) From 1574.1 R4ᵛ: OE Bede III.18 (extract; Miller 1890–8: II.226).

TYPE:

Main text in Pierre Haultin's Pica Roman (Body 83) mixed with Robert Granjon's second Pica Italic.

AS2: Parkerian Pica Anglo-Saxon combined with Haultin's Pica Roman occurs in text on I3ʳ, R2ᵛ, 2G1ʳ, 2G1ᵛ, 2K4ʳ, 2M2, 2N1ʳ, 2V3ʳ, and in words on G3ᵛ (p. 46), 2M2ʳ (p. 267), 2M4ᵛ (p. 272), 2N4ʳ (p. 279), 3D4ʳ (p. 391).

Special sorts shown: 10 lower-case sorts: ð, ꝼ, ȝ, p, ʃ, c, ẏ; þ, ð, ƿ;
                           1 capital: Ꝺ (used for ð) on 2N1ʳ (once only);
                           2 others: þ, ꝫ.
              Total: 13 sorts.

Note: Errors in setting include s for ʃ, p for ꝼ, and þ for þ (corrected on 3D4ʳ).

Copies seen: (lacking 3K2) CUL Syn.7.61.226; OBL Douce S.208, Vet.A2.e.344 (with indentation of bottom two lines on a3ᵛ).

Copies also at: BL, BCL, CCL, CGC, KCC, CMC, CPC, CLL, DAL, DWL, EdUL, GML, IPL, LCL, LHL, LSH, NLS, PML, OEF, SAC, WAL, DML, TCD; FSL, USLC, NYCU, NYHS, NYPL, HHL, HUL, BMC, CUofA, NLC, NWU, UCLA, UPL, UTA, WMUL, YUB.

Bibliography: Christianson 1984: 286–295; Clement 1997: 236; Crick 2004: 130–131; Parry 1995: 113–114; Toomer 2009: I.126–158; Woolf 1990: 213–215.

1615.1: Speed, John, *Theatre of the Empire*. Composite volume comprising maps that anticipate 1627.1 with text from 1614.1 cut and pasted around them and the reverse side blank. London: Thomas Snodham for John Sudbury and George Humble, 1615. STC 23041.2; ESTC S519. No AS.
    Copy seen: OBL MAP RES 81/C17 b.1 (lacks Wales, Scotland and Ireland).
    Copy also at: LSA.

1616.1: Speed, John, *Theatrum Imperii Magnae Britanniae Exactam Regnorum Angliæ Scotiæ Hiberniæ et Insularum adiacentium Geographiam ob oculos ap[ro]ponens, vna cum Comitatibus, Centurijs, Urbibus et primarijs Comitatuum Oppidis, intra Regnum Angliæ divisis et descriptis*. Latin translation of 1611.1 by Philemon Holland. London: [Thomas Snodham] for John Sudbury and George Humble 1616. STC 23044; ESTC S107575. AS2/3.
OE Proper Names
    Collation: 2^0: A–4H² [$1 signed (+ A2, B2, C2, D2, 3F2, 3X2, 3Z2, 4F2, 4G2; -A1, 3F1, 3X1, 3Z1 (all tps)] 154 leaves, foliated (always on the text side) [i–viii], 1–94, 99–126, 131–132, 137–146, *147*–52 (fo 35 misnumbered 36), paginated 95–98, 127–130, 133–136 (95–96, 127–128, 130, 133–134, 136 not numbered).
    Note: The text is printed back to back with the maps, and the map pages, being always a double-page opening on the reverse side of text pages, receive no numbers.
TYPE:
The size varies according to the amount of text in relation to the amount of space available.
The preferred type is Pierre Haultin's English-size Roman (as on K1^r)
                      Body 93   Face 90 × 2: 3.0
but the following also occur:
Pierre Haultin's 2nd Pica Roman (Vervliet R82B), as on I1^r:
                      Body 82.5   Face 78 × 1.8: 2.5
Pierre Haultin's Long Primer Roman (Vervliet R67), as on L1^r:
                      Body 67   Face 64 × 1.4: 2.0
Italics of the same size are used in the course of the main text to highlight names, etc.
A Brevier Roman occurs on Y1^r and 2K1^r.
Two Anglo-Saxon Pica designs are used mixed together in county names. They occur with main text in English-size (K1^r = fo 11, M1^r = fo 15, 2C1^r = fo 43, 2G1^r =

fo 51, 2O1ʳ = fo 65, 2P1ʳ = fo 67, 2Q1ʳ = fo 69, 2R1ʳ = fo 71), with Long Primer (L1ʳ = fo 13, X1ʳ = fo 33, 2E1ʳ = fo 47, 2S1ʳ = fo 73), and Brevier (Y1ʳ = fo 35, 2K1ʳ = fo 57).
AS2: The Parkerian Pica Anglo-Saxon.
Special sorts shown: ð, ꝼ, ȝ, ꝥ, ꞃ, ꞇ, ẏ; ð; Æ.   8 + 1
AS3: The Lambardian Pica Anglo-Saxon.
Special sorts shown: e, ꝼ, h (=ᛑ); ꝼ; þ.   3 + 1 + 1
Note: Anglo-Saxon i is not used. Only a few setting errors, as r for s, þ for þ, each once.

    Copy seen: CUL Atlas 4.61.1.
    Copies also at: BL, AUL, CGC, LBL, LHL, LSH, OBL, OCC, GUB; FSL, USLC, IUL.
Bibliography: Shirley 1991: nos 352–354; Skelton 1970: no. 11, pp. 48–49.

1616.2: Camden, William, *Britannia sive Florentissimorvm Regnorvm, Angliæ, Scotiæ, Hiberniæ, & Insularum adiacentium ex intima antiquitate Chorographica Descriptio*. Frankfurt-am-Main: Peter Ruland, typis Johan Bringer 1616. USTC 2108347; BLG C119.

    Collation: 8⁰: 523, [24], 3, [4], 762, [22] p.
    AS names appear in Italic with no special sorts, e.g., M7ʳ (p. 173).
    Copies at: GUL, MJRUL, OBL, DML, BN, PBM, PBSG, LBM, OMM, SBPU, MBS, WHAB; IUL; OUL

1617.1: Minsheu, John, *ΗΓΕΜΩΝ ΕΙΣ ΤΆΣ ΓΑΩΣΣΑΣ* [HEGEMON EIS TAS GLOSSAS], id eft, Ducor in Linguas, *The Gvide Into Tongves. Cum illarum harmonia, & Etymologijs, Originationibus, Rationibus, & Deriuationibus in omnibus his vndecim Linguis*. London: [Eliot's Court Press, completed by William Stansby, sigs A–S printed by Melchisidec Bradwood at ECP, sigs T–2Z printed by Stansby, probably after 1615 (he took over the business of John Windet 1609/10), subsidiary sig.2A–N printed by another (unidentified), and all finished by Stansby, who added the preliminaries] for John Brown II 1617. STC 17944; ESTC S121927. Sigs A–S show AS2/3; sigs T–2Z show AS2; specimen shows AS1.

    Date: 1617. Licence to print granted 20 Feb 1610/11 for 21 years (Greg 1967: calendar no. 159 on p. 51, document no. 23 on p. 157) and the printing probably took some years.

Words and Phrases
    Note: Almost certainly the first English book to be sold by subscription, on which see Clapp, Feather, Pollard & Ehrman under Bibliography below. A prospectus dated 8 Dec 1610 was issued with a view to attracting subscribers (see Feather 1984: J.Pros.1 (fiche D1–4)), but the sample entries do not contain Anglo-Saxon.

Collation: 2⁰: π² πA⁶ A–2Y⁶ 2Z² [$3 signed (-2Z2)] 280 leaves, paginated [i–xvi], 1–543, 544 (pp. 51 misnumbered 52, 77 misnumbered 97, 183 misnumbered 184, 201 misnumbered 101, 261 misnumbered 259, 263 misnumbered 261, 360 misnumbered 350, 397/399 misnumbered 437/439).

Subsidiary (STC 17949): ²π² ²A–P⁶ ²Q² (+χ1) [$3 signed (+²A4, ²B4; -²Q2] 94 + 1 leaves, unnumbered.

Note: p. 263 misnumbered 261 in DML K3.1.20, ECC 313.1.70, but correctly numbered 263 in CUL Bb*.1.13, CCC L.2.15 and LFL Case A4.

TYPE:

Main text in Long Primer Roman and Italic

Claude Garamond's (second) Long Primer Roman   Body 68 Face 66 × 1.2: 2.

The change in Italic and in the AS sorts used from sig. S to sig. T indicates a change of printer: up to sig. S it was Melchisidec Bradwood, and from sig. T it was William Stansby.

Two Long Primer Italics are used, one up to and including sig. S, another from sig. T:

(1) Robert Granjon's Long Primer Italic, known as 'Garamonde Cursive premiere'
   Body 67   Face 64 × 1.5: 2.

(2) Robert Granjon's Long Primer Italic, known as 'Italique Valentine'
   Body 68   Face 65 × 1.5: 1.8.

AS1: Specimen (supplied by Stansby) on A6ᵛ shows the Parkerian Great Primer AS.

Text: Pica Anglo-Saxon combined with Claude Garamond's (second) Long Primer Roman

(1) AS2/3 mixed up to sig. S, e.g., on S5ʳ s.v. 𝕲auelkind ʒ is found in AS2 and AS3 forms, on S3ʳ s.v. 𝕱urlong (b) AS ꝼhaꝑle shows AS3 f and AS2 H and r. This mixture includes AS3 *e*, which last occurs on S3ʳ s.v. *a* 𝕲able in AS ʒ*e*bel.
Special sorts shown:

   AS2: ð,   ʒ, ƕ, ꝑ, ꝼ, ꞇ, ẏ;   p;   Æ², Є, ꟁ, ꟅƔ;
   AS3: ð, *e*, ꝼ, ʒ, ꝑ, ꝼ;   ꟁ.

(2) AS2 unadulterated from sig. T, e.g., on T3ᵛ s.v. 𝕲reue AS2 f, g, r in ʒeꝛeꝼa.
AS sorts found (incl. capitals used as l.c.) Æ¹, ð, є, ꝼ, ʒ, ƕ, ꟁ, ꝛ, s, ꞇ, þ (p. 438 in Seeke, p. 489 in Though, p. 490 in Throte), ð̄ (p. 487 in Thanke, etc.), p, Ᵽ (p. 479 in Swathe), ẏ.

   Capitals: Æ¹, Є, ꟁ, Ʂ.

No AS i, X nor æ (cf. Haye-boote, but æ occurs s.v. Craft, Crane, in Cnæðen s.v. Knead), spræce s.v. Speech, ꝼpæꞇe s.v. Sweete, Tæʒl s.v. Taile, etc., ae in Maen s.v. Moone, æ in Offlætan s.v. Offering.

Letters used wrongly, e.g. Hoary, Horse, Knaue, New.

But often AS letters are not used where they would be appropriate: e.g. on M5ᵛ, s.v. Ðie, 'Sax: ſtepuen'. AS sorts often alternate with roman where AS would be appropriate, esp. e, y.

A feature of its use is the inclusion of capitals where lower-case letters would be appropriate, e.g. on A2ʳ s.v. Abstaine (Æ), I5ᵛ s.v. Cramme (M), L2ʳ s.v. Friday (H), 2R6ʳ s.v. Swathe (Þ).

 Copies seen: CCC L.2.15 (contains also STC 17944a, names of recipients of book, the last name being 'Mr. Andrewes'); CUL Bb*.1.13(A) (lacks STC 17944a); ECC 313.1.70 (contains also, inserted after πA5, STC 17944a, names of recipients of book, the last name being '*Sir Iohn Franckline* Knight'; binding shows gold-tooled diamond lozenge on front); TCD EE.aa.13 (contains also, inserted between π1 and π2, STC 17944a, names of recipients of book, the last name being 'Mr. *Welles*'); DML K3.1.20 (lacks STC 17944a and ²Q2(χ1)); LFL Case A4 (contains also, inserted between π1 and π2, STC 17944a, names of recipients of book); OBL B.6.10.Art (contains also, inserted between π1 and π2, STC 17944a, names of recipients of book, the last name being '*Sir Thomas Metham* Knight'), with contemporary gold-tooled binding; Douce M.subt.21 (contains also, inserted after π2, STC 17944a, names of recipients of book, the last name being '*Sir Iohn Franckline* Knight'), with contemporary binding; Broxb.82.1 (contains also, inserted after πA6, STC 17944a, names of recipients of book, the last name being 'Mr. *Welles*'), in contemporary binding.

 Note: two states shown by the catchword at Y1ʳ.

 State 1: DML K3.1.20; OBL B.6.10.Art.

 State 2: CUL Bb*1.13(A); CCC L.2.15; ECC 313.1.70; TCD EE.aa.13; LFL Case A4; OBL Douce M.subt.21, Broxb.82.1.

 Copies also at: BL, BPL, BUL, CCA, ChC, CGC, CJC, KCC, CMC, CPC, CSJ, CSS, CTH, TCC, CSL, CUW, DUL, EdUL, Eton, HCL, LCL, LGL, LHL, LiCL, LPL, LRCS, LSH, NAL, NCCL, NCL, NLS, NUL, OAS, ABC, OBrC, OCC, OEC, OEF, OHC, OJC, OLC, OMaC, OMC, ONC, OOC, OQC, OSJ, OTC, OTI, OUP, OWmC, OWoC, SJS, UBL, WAL, WCC, WIHM, WoCL, YML, ULim; FSL, USLC, NYPL, HHL, HUL, JCB, KSRL, NLC, NWU, PUL, SLC, SLU, UCBL, UCLA, UVL, QUK.

Bibliography: Clapp 1931–2: 209–216; Clement 1997: 233–234; Feather 1984: 26–28 & facs.1; Joan 1962; Kerling 1979: 312–319; Lucas 2002; Mores (ed. Carter/Ricks) 1961: 8; Pollard & Ehrman 1965: 180–181; Rosier 1961; Schäfer 1973; Steiner 1970: 52–54; Williams 1948.

1617.2: Camden, William, *Guilielmi Camdeni, Viri Clarissimi Britannia*, ed. Regnerus Vitellius Zirizæus (Reinier Telle of Zierikzee). Amsterdam: Willem Jansz. Blaeu 1617. USTC 1012786.

Collation: 8⁰: §⁸ A–2Y⁸ 2Z¹⁰. [3] [10] 714 [22] p.
AS names appear in Italic with no special sorts, e.g., O4ᵛ (p. 216).
Copy seen: BL 577.a.2.
Copies also at: AUL, DUL, OBL, OUC, PBN, ABM, OMM, AUB, GRUB, WHAB, GBC, PNL.

1618.1: Selden, John, *The Historie of Tithes.* [London: William Stansby] 1618. STC 22172, 22172.3, 22172.5, 22172.7 = ESTC S123284, S117046, S123286, S123423. AS 2.
Extracts from ASC, Laws, Canon of Edgar *Be Dædbetan*
  Context: This book, arguing that there was no divine right to tithes, but only the right of common practice, proved extremely controversial, and Selden was forced to apologise for the publication of his book, although he did not recant his findings: see especially Woolf 1990: 230–235.
  Collation: 4⁰: a–e⁴ A–3K⁴ ²a–f⁴ [$3 signed (-a1,3)] 268 leaves, paginated [i–vi], I–XXXIV, 1–491, *492–496*.
  Note 1: pp. 249, 252 misnumbered 149, 152, as indicated below;
  Note 2: **1618.4** shows e1 missigned 'c'.
  Editions: The book may be divided into three booklets: the preliminaries, sig.a–e; the main text, sig. A–3K; the supplementals, sig. ²a–f. There are 4 editions of the preliminaries and the main text, and 3 editions of the supplementals. Subsequent editions after the first have been re-set so expertly that details have to be used to distinguish them.
  (1) **1618.1** [STC 22172]
  Sig.a2ʳ lines 3/4 shows 'of *Connington* | Kight and Baronet.'; 2D3ʳ line 6 cẏnınᵹ; 2E4ʳ line 21/end eal; 2I1ʳ pp. 249, 252 misnumbered 149, 152, line 1 'litle'; ²a2ʳ line 5 begins 'of a firſt borne' (no hyphen): OBL Vet.A2.e.288 (bookplate of Richard Corbet); CUL H.11.35 (signed Thomas Knyvett), but has a–e from (2) with tp IGNAVIA in red; OBL Vet.A2.e.313 with tp IGNAVIA in black, but has 2I1ʳ from (2).
  (2) **1618.2** [STC 22172.3]
  Sig.a2ʳ lines 3/4 shows 'of *Connington.* | Knight and Baronet.', 3 lines from bottom '*be*'; 2D3ʳ line 6 cẏnınᵹ with ᵹ inverted; 2E4ʳ line 21/end ea; 2I1ʳ p. 249, 252 misnumbered 149, 152, line 1 'little'; ²a–f same setting as (1): OBL 4⁰.S.25.Th.Seld.
  (3) **1618.3** [STC 22172.5]
  Sig.a2ʳ lines 3/4 shows 'of *Connington* | Knight and Baronet.'; H4ᵛ p. 64 misnumbered 56; 2D3ʳ line 11 ᵹeryllaþ (undotted y); 2E4ʳ line 21/end eal; 2I1ʳ p. 249, 252 correctly numbered; ²a2ʳ line 5 begins 'of a firſt-borne' (with hyphen), line 2 begins 'in Works': CUL Pet.G.6.3; LFL 2B (signed by Thomas King of Grays Inn 1742); OBL 4⁰.S.44.Th.; PO 1618.3.
  (4) **1618.4** [STC 22172.7]

Sig.a2ʳ lines 3/4 shows 'of *Connington*. | Knight and Baronet.', 3 lines from bottom '*bee*'; 2I1ʳ p. 249 misnumbered 146, p. 252 correctly numbered; ²a2ʳ line 5 begins 'of a firſt-borne' (with hyphen), line 2 begins 'in Workes': CUL Q*.10.66, Ely.d.556; OBL Vet.A2.e.286 shows 2I1ʳ as in (3).

For another edition see 1680.1.

SOURCES OF PASSAGES UTILIZING ANGLO-SAXON TYPES:

2C2ʳ (p. 203) From 1568.2 Q2ᵛ: AS Law Edward and Guthrum 6 (Liebermann I.130); with reference to Lambarde's edn;

2C2ᵛ (p. 204) From 1568.2 P4ᵛ: AS Law Edward and Guthrum Prol. (Liebermann I.128); the reading 'sealf' is distinctive of Lambarde;

2C3ᵛ (p. 206) From ASC 855, as Thorpe 1861: I.124–125
The textual evidence is insufficient to determine which MS was used. Selden lists 3 MSS (BCE) on 2f3ᵛ with reference to this page. He borrowed MSS from Cotton as recorded in Harley 4018, a list of borrowings from Cotton's library: see Tite 2003.

2D3ʳ (p. 213) From 1568.2 R1ᵛ: AS Law I Æthelstan Prol. (Liebermann I.146–147 makes clear the distinctiveness of Lambarde's text) with L version from Quadripartitus; but the OE text has been collated with Nero A.i, 87ʳ/1–3, from which some additional words are added in the margin;

2D4ʳ (p. 215) From 1568.2 X1ᵛ: AS Law I Edmund 2 (Liebermann I.184–185) with L version of Quadripartitus; Lambarde cited as source and the readings teoþungum and nylle are distinctive;

2E1ᵛ–2ʳ (pp. 218–19) From 1568.2 Y1ᵛ–2ᵛ: AS Law II Edgar 1,1–3,1 (Liebermann I.196–199) with L version of Quadripartitus; Lambarde's reading hlaford is distinctive, but collation with Nero A.i, 42ᵛ/13, is revealed by the additional reading landhlaford in the margin;

2E3ᵛ (p. 222) From Nero A.i, 90ᵛ/7–10: AS Law V Æthelred 11,1 (Liebermann I.240) not in 1568.2, but cf. next;

2E4ʳ (p. 223) From 1568.2 2E2ᵛ–3ᵛ: AS Law I Cnut 8 (Liebermann I.290–3) with L version of Quadripartitus; Lambarde's readings gegoðe and nælle are distinctive.

Also refers to MS for Latin Quadripartitus '*In historia Iornalensi fol.71b* MS Bibl Cotton, sed optimum harum legum ex exemplar. extat in Bibliotheca Sereniss. Principis Magnæ Brit. ad *D.Iacobi.*': Text begins [Et] reddantur Deo debitæ rectitudines annis singulis: hoc est elemosina carrucarum xv diebus post Pascha ...

2F1 (pp. 225–6) From Tiberius A.iii, 96ʳ/1: 'Directions for a Confessor' (formerly 'Canon of Edgar') *Be Dædbetan* 'Of Penitents' no. 15 (extract), as Thorpe 1840: II.282/22–23, coll. Fowler 1965: 29/374; the source is deduced from Selden's statement that he took the text 'a *Recens Ms, apud ... Rob. Cotton*', as, despite the adjective 'recens', I have not discovered it amongst any early modern transcripts (it is not in Joscelyn's notebook, Vitellius D.vii, for example), and Tiberius A.iii is the only Cottonian MS to contain it (for other MSS see Fowler 1965): the extract occurs as the first words on fo 96^r, where it is particularly noticeable;

2I3^r (p. 253)   From Otho B.xi (damaged by fire), Bede *HE*, I.16, as Miller 1890–8: 1.64/6–8);

2L4^v (p. 272)   From a spurious Charter of Æthelstan in an unidentified Cotton
MS   ða forne ðraue by heuen cyng
                    Of ilc a plou of Estreding [East Riding]

= Hart 1975: no. 120a on pp. 118–119 [original] stated to be lost. Sawyer 451 cites several late sources. The text here does not match Dugdale II 129–130 or Thorpe 1865: 180 (lines 21–22), both of which are from Lansdowne 269, fo 213. Nor does it match Cotton Ch.iv.18 as printed by Birch 1339, nor Dodsworth 10, fo 43^v.

Note 1: Toomer 2009: I.285–286 offers an 'abbreviated listing' of the sources Selden used; for Selden's own list see ^{2}f2^v–^{2}f4^v. MSS consulted included Claudius A.vi, Claudius B.vi, Cleopatra D.ii, Domitian iii, Domitian x, Faustina A.iv, Faustina B.ii, Nero D.ii, Otho B.xiii, Tiberius A.ix, Tiberius E.vi, Vitellius E.xv, but none of them contains Anglo-Saxon.

Note 2: At 2C4^v–2D1^r (pp. 208–9) Selden cites L text of Sawyer Charter 302 from Claudius B.vi, fo 12^v (Tite 2003: 124). At 2E2^v–3^v (pp. 220–222) Selden cites Claudius A.iii, fos 32–33 (Tite 2003: 121). At 2M2^v (p. 276) Selden cites Faustina A.v, fo 37^v (Tite 2003: 218)

TYPE:

Main text in Pierre Haultin's English-size Roman (Body 100);

AS2: The Parkerian Pica Anglo-Saxon combined with a Pica Roman occurs in text as indicated above and in words on e1^v, e2^r, 2D3^v (p. 214), 2E1^r (p. 217), 2E2^v (p. 220), 2K1^v (p. 258), 2K2^r (p. 259), 2M2^v (p. 276), 3F2^v (p. 412).

Special sorts shown: 11 lower-case sorts: ð, ꝼ, ʒ, ı, p, ſ, t, ẏ; þ, ð, p;
                       3 capitals: Æ², ꟽ, 8;
                       4 others: ꝫ, ꝫ, þ, ꝫ.
          Total: 18 sorts.

Note: On 2C2^v there is a capital U from another fount.

   Copies seen: see above under Editions.
   Copies also at: 1618.1 BL, CGC, CMC, CNC, CSJ, ChestC, DRD, ECL, EdUL, GUL, HCL, LGL, LiCL, LPL, MTP, NT, NUL, OBC, OKC, OLC, OSJ, OStE, SAC, SDC, SUL, WAL, WCC, TCD, ULim; FSL, HHL, HUL, IUL, NWU, PTS, UCBL, UCDL.

1618.2 CUL, KCC, TCC, DPL, EdUL, Eton, GUL, LCL, LHL, NLS, IEF, OHM, OJC, OKC, ONC, OSJ, SCL, UBL, UCL, YML, DEWL; NYCU, UTS, HHL, HUL DDUL, GETS, IUL, MUL, NWU, UMI, UTA, TUL; ATL, UWL.

1618.3 BL, BPL, CCA, CTH, TCC, MJRUL, LPL, LSH, NT, OEF, OQC, OWmC, OXC, TCD; FSL, NYPL, BMC, HHL, HUL UCH, UCLA, UMI, UPL, UTA; VUW.

1618.4 BL, BCL, DCL, GML, LPL, LSH, NLS, NT, OMFC, ONC, OUC, OXC, SBT, UBL, WiCL, TCD; FSL, USLC, NYCU, HHL, HUL, BMC, LCP, MCRS, NWU, UAB, UCBL, UCDL, UCH, UCLA, UCRL, UCSC, UCSD, UMI.

Bibliography: Berkowitz 1988: 35–39; Butt 1938: 77; Christianson 1984: 299–307; Clement 1997: 236; Fussner 1962: 278–298; Parry 1995: 118–124; Toomer 2002, passim but esp. 357–360; Toomer 2009: I.257–310; Woolf 1990: 216–235.
Facsimile: The English Experience 147 (Amsterdam: Da Capo, 1968).
Manuscript: OBL Bodley 305 (SC27681), fos 77–121, contains notes used for this work in Spelman's own hand.

1618.5: La Bigne, Margarinus de, *Magna Bibliotheca Veterum Patrum, ex Antiquorum Scriptorum ecclesiasticorum*. Cologne: Anton Hierat (sumptibus), 1618. USTC 2156028; BLG L4.

> **Collation:** 2⁰: π² A–2R⁶ 2S⁴. [2], 592 p.
>
> Vol. VIII includes a reprint of 1605.4: Nicolaus Serarius, *Epistolæ S. Bonifacii* at F4ʳ–N4ᵛ, where the OE verse *Proverb from Winfred's Time* (Dobbie 1942: 57) occurs in Epistola lxi on K1ʳ (p. 73). It is taken over here on H3ʳ (p. 89) in a Pica Italic (with no special AS sorts) quoted as prose in a Latin prose letter itself printed in Pica Roman.
>
> **Copy seen:** CUL 3.14.8 (lacks 2S4).
> **Other copies:** BL. USTC reports one copy of no fixed abode.

1619.1: Lambarde, William, EIRENARCHA: *or of The Office of the Justices of Peace, in foure Bookes*. 11th and final edn of 1581.1 re-set page for page from 10th edn 1614.1. London: [prob. Adam Islip] for the Stationers' Co., 1619. STC 15174; ESTC S108213. AS3.

Laws of Ine (extract)

> **Collation:** 8⁰: A–2Y⁸ [$4 signed (-A1, P2]. 360 leaves, paginated [i–ii], 1–634, *635–718* (pp. 224–225, 376 unnumbered; pp. 12 misnumbered 13, 101 misnumbered 85, 153 misnumbered 155, 213, 215 misnumbered 113, 115 respectively, 239 misnumbered 205, 304, 308 misnumbered 204, 207 respectively, 350 misnumbered 351, 365 misnumbered 395, 368 misnumbered 336, 499 misnumbered 404, 521 misnumbered 523).
> SOURCE OF PASSAGE UTILIZING ANGLO-SAXON TYPES:

M5ʳ (p. 183)   From 1614.1 M5ʳ: Extract from Laws of Ine 13,1 (Liebermann, I, 94–95).

All three errors first introduced in 1599.1 (q.v.) are taken over plus wrong word-division resulting in þoðð̄e ᛝþriꞇ first introduced in 1607.1 (q.v.), and ƕeꞅe first introduced in 1610.1 (q.v.).

TYPE:

Main text in a Pica Texura   Body 83   Face 80 × 2: 3
A Pica Roman (e.g. on T6ᵛ–7ʳ = pp. 298–9) Body 84   Face 80 × 1.8: 3 (same as 1614.1)
Granjon's Pica Italic (no. 2), the *Cicero pendante* (e.g. on C3ʳ–5ʳ = pp. 35–9)
                                   Body 83.5   Face 80 × 1.5: 2.5

AS2/3: The Lambardian Pica Anglo-Saxon with some Parkerian Pica Anglo-Saxon sorts on M5ʳ (p. 183, text) and P8ʳ (p. 237, words) combined with the Pica Roman.

Special sorts shown: 11 lower-case sorts: e, ꞅ, ᵹ, ƕ, ꝑ, ꞃ, ꞇ, ẏ;   þ, ð, ꝑ;
                     1 capital: Ð;
                     1 other: ᛝ;
           Total: 13 sorts.

Note 1: No d in text; and on p. 237 roman (not AS) capital M is used.
Note 2: Uses a semi-colon and an inverted exclamation mark for the punctus versus.

    Copies seen: CUL J.12.11; OBL Crynes 521(1).

    Copies also at: BL, CSJ, TCC, GUL, LSE, OAS, UBL, YML, DKI; FSL, NYCU, HHL, HUL, DDUL, IUL, JCB, NWU, UCH, TUL; MonUL, UML, VSC.

    Note: The copy reported by (E)STC in TCD could not be found there.

Bibliography: as 1581.1.

1619.2: Milles, Thomas, *The Treasurie of Aunicent and Moderne Times* [vol. 2] Αρχηιοα~πλουτοσ. Containing, ten following bookes to the former. [Bk 5 includes translation of 1608.1 as found in 1610.4] London: William Jaggard, 1619. STC 17936.5; ESTC S114956. AS3 (with occasional AS2 s).

Law 'Geþyncðo' (extract)

    Collation: Book 5 only (2Q–3A): 2⁰: 2Q–3A⁶ [$3 signed (-2X3, 2Y1)] 54 leaves, paginated 445–552 (pp. 508–509, 517 not numbered; pp. 490–491 misnumbered 450–451).

SOURCE OF PASSAGE UTILIZING ANGLO-SAXON TYPES:

2Y2 (pp. 519–20)   From 1610.4, G6ᵛ–H1ʳ: AS Law 'Geþyncðo' 1–7 (Liebermann I.456–458); re-set line by line with erroneous þæꞅ for pæꞅ in line 4 taken over (correct in 1608.1).

TYPE:

Main text in Pierre Haultin's English-size Roman (Body 95);
AS3 with AS2 s: The Lambardian Pica Anglo-Saxon with occasional Parkerian s
(e.g. 2Y2ᵛ/25 moɼce) occurs in combination with a Pica Roman in text on 2Y2.
Special sorts shown: 12 lower-case sorts: ð, e, f, ȝ, Ð, ɲ, ɼ, τ, ẏ; þ, ð, p;
                      3 capitals: E, Ϻ, Ð;
                      3 others: þ, ꝫ, ꝫ̇.
       Total: 18 sorts.

Copies seen: APL EE.II.46; CUL Syn.3.61.24 (lacks tp, 2R3.4); TCC VI.4.13 (gift of John Laughton).

Copies also at: BL, BUL, ECC, CPH, CUW, EdCL, EdUL, HCL, IPL, LSH, MTP, NLS, NT, OBL, OAS, OBrC, OEF, OLC, OOC, OUC, OWmC, OWoC, SBT, SUL, UBL, KSC, TCD; FSL, USLC, NYHS, NYPL, HHL, HUL, CLM, NLC, SCN, UTA, UVL; ANZ, ATL.

Bibliography: see 1608.1.

1621.1: Gil, Alexander, *Logonomia Anglica. Quâ gentis sermo faciliùs addiscitur. Secundò edita, paulò correctior, sed ad vsum communem accommodatior.* London: John Beale, 1621. STC 11874, 2nd edn of 11873 (1619); ESTC S103107. AS3
Ælfric's *Letter to Sigeferth* (extract)
Letter-symbols.
    Collation: 4⁰: πA–B⁴ A–T⁴. 84 leaves, paginated [i–xvi], 1–152.
SOURCE OF PASSAGE SHOWING ANGLO-SAXON WITHOUT UTILIZING ANGLO-SAXON TYPES:
†B1ʳ   From 1566.1 ¶*4ʳ or 1566.2 A8ʳ: Ælfric's *Letter to Sigeferth*, opening sentence printed in a Small Pica with no special AS sorts except for an œ-ligature for AS 'ash'; *th* used for *þ/ð*.
TYPE:
AS3: The Lambardian Pica Anglo-Saxon is used for phonetic symbols.
Special sorts shown: 2 lower-case sorts: ȝ, ð (on B2ᵛ, etc);
                      1 capital: Ð (on B2ᵛ).
For use with an English-size Roman another larger ð has been improvised, apparently by adding what looks like a dagger tilted leftwards from the upper left-hand part of the bowl of an o, as on †B4ᵛ, R2ʳ.
    Copy seen: CUL Bb*.5.20(E).
    Copies also at: BL, CCA, CCL, ECC, KCC, CMC, CSJ, TCC, GUL, LRS, OBL, OBrC, OEF, YML, TCD, GUB; FSL, NYCU, HHL, HUL, NLC, UMI; XCU.
Bibliography: Alston I.4; Dobson 1968: I.131–155.
Facsimile: English Linguistics 1500–1800, no. 68 (Menston: Scolar, 1968), from a copy in the Folger Shakespeare Library.
Edition: Otto L. Jiriczek, *Alexander Gill's Logonomia Anglica* (Strassburg: Trübner, 1903).

1622.1: Drayton, Michael, *A Chorographicall Description of all the Tracts, Riuers, Mountains, Forests, and other Parts of this Renowned Ifle of Great Britain.* London: Augustine Mathewes, 1622. STC 7228; ESTC S121639. Identical to **1613.1** with new tp.

Laws of Ine (extract), words

Collation: Identical with **1613.1** except for +χ1 between π2 and π3 (= tp).

Copies seen: CCA W/L.7.19 (Somner's copy, acquired for 7s 6d 1641 π2^r); CUL Williams 425; ECC 313.5.55.

Copies also at: BL, CNC, CSJ, TCC, EAL, MJRUL, LPL, OBL, OXC, DEWL, DML, TCD, GUB; FSL, USLC, HHL, HUL IUL, KSRL, NLC, SIU, UCLA, UTA, WMUL, YUB; ATL.

Bibliography: Juel-Jensen 1961: 302; Skelton 1970: no. 13.

1622.2: Sibthorp, Sir Christopher, *A Friendly Advertisement to the Pretended Catholickes of Ireland*, with supplementary letter by James Ussher on the *Religion Anciently Professed by the Irish*. Dublin: Stationers' Society, 1622. STC 22522; ESTC S102408. IR1.

Alfredian Preface to the Pastoral Care **(extract)**

Collation: 4° (in 8s): a^4 b–c^8 A^4 B–2D^8 2E–2R^4 [a–2D $4 signed (-a1.4, A4); 2E–2R $3 signed] 284 leaves, paginated [i–xlviii], 1–418, 1–100, *101–102* (pp. 176 misnumbered 170, 378 misnumbered 367).

Note: Variant state shown by p. 378 misnumbered 368.

SOURCES OF PASSAGE UTILIZING ANGLO-SAXON TYPES:

2I3^r From (?)Tiberius B.xi (now destroyed; cf. Hatton 20, 2^r/22–2^v/1): *Preface to the Alfredian Pastoral Care*, 3-word extract (Sweet 1871: I.6/22); there is insufficient text to determine which manuscript was used, but it is likely that Ussher used Cotton's library.

TYPE:

Main text of Ussher's Letter set in Pierre Haultin's English-size Roman (Body 93); IR1: Elizabethan English-size Irish combined with Haultin's English Roman on 2I3^r.

Special sorts shown: ɑ, ı, p, ꝑ, s, ꞇ.

Copies seen: State 1 CUL Hib.7.62.3, Hib.7.62.23^1; State 2 (with p. 378 numbered 368) OBL B.3.4.Linc.;

Issue 2 (with tp dated 1623) CUL Hib.7.62.19^1.

Copies also at: BL, ECC, CSJ, EdUL, GUL, LMT, LPL, NLI, TCD; FSL, GTS, PFL.

Bibliography: Baker & Womack 1999: 357–366 (art. on Ussher by S.M. Towers); Dickins 1949: 54; Ford 2007: 123–132; Parry 1995: 134–138; Sayle 1916: nos 12 and 13; Sharpe & Hoyne 2020: no. 21 on pp. 96–97.

1623.1: Lisle, William, *A Saxon Treatise concerning the Old and New Testament. written about the time of King Edgar (700 yeares agoe) by Ælfricus Abbas, thought to be the same that was afterward Archbishop of Canterburie. Whereby appeares what was the Canon of Holy Scripture here then received, and that the Church of England had it so long agoe in her Mother-tongue.* London: John Haviland [of Eliot's Court Press] for Henry Seile, 1623. STC 160; ESTC S100438. AS3 (with occasional AS2 s).

Ælfric, Letter to Sigeweard, Easter Homily (et al. from 1566.1), Bede, *HE* (extracts)

Collation: 4⁰: π² ¶⁴ a–f⁴ A–V⁴ [$3 signed (-G2, K3, L3, M1, O2)] 110 leaves, unpaginated but numbers for openings 12–43 are supplied on D1ʳ–L4ʳ, and 1–14 on O2ᵛ–R4ʳ.

SOURCES OF PASSAGES UTILIZING ANGLO-SAXON TYPES:
1. Preface
1.1   C1ᵛ   OE version of Bede's *Historia Ecclesiastica*, extract from the end of Book II, ch.2 (Miller 1890–8: I.104/8–11, II.91) probably from Otho B xi (largely destroyed in the 1731 fire), which Lisle borrowed from Cotton (Harley 6018, 148ᵛ);
1.2   C2ʳ   OE version of Bede's *Historia Ecclesiastica*, extract from the beginning of Book II, ch.3 (Miller 1890–8: I.104/12–13, II.91) probably from Otho B xi.
1.3   f3ʳ   Unidentified (attrib. Alfred): Sif [*recte* Gif] on þeos gesælig doend gesihþe godes, &c.

2. Ælfric's Letter to Sigeweard on the Old and New Testaments
2.1   A1ᵛ–F3ᵛ   On the Old Testament (Crawford 1969: 15–51) from Laud misc. 509 (borrowed by Lisle from Cotton: Harley 6018, 53ʳ and 148ᵛ), 120ᵛ/2–131ᵛ/21.
2.2   F3ᵛ–L3ᵛ   On the New Testament (Crawford 1969: 51–75) from Laud misc. 509, 131ᵛ/22–141ᵛ/21.

3. Preface to Ælfric's *Sermo de Sacrificio in die Pascae* from 1566.1
3.1   M2ᵛ   From 1566.1 A3ᵛ, Ælfric's 'Excusatio Dictantis' (opening statement) at the end of his homily *Depositio S. Martin* (Godden 1979: XXXIV);
3.2   M3ʳ   From 1566.1 A4, Ælfric's *Grammar*, opening statement from OE Preface (Zupitza 1880: 2);
3.3   M4ᵛ   From 1566.1 A8ʳ, Ælfric's *Letter to Sigeferth* preceding homily for 2nd Sunday after Epiphany (Assmann 1889: 13);
3.4   N2ʳ   From 1566.1 B4, List of Books given by Leofric to Exeter Cathedral;

3.5	N2ᵛ	From 1566.1 B5ᵛ, L quotation of scribal statement;
3.6	N3ʳ	From 1566.1 B7ʳ, Story about wife retention from ASC E 1129 (Clark 1954: 51).

4. Text of Ælfric's *Sermo de Sacrificio in die Pascae* (Godden 1979: xv) from 1566.1

O2ᵛ–R3ᵛ		From 1566.1 C3ᵛ–H3ᵛ (English translation also taken over).

5. Other Texts from 1566.1

5.1	S1ᵛ–2ʳ	From 1566.1 H5ᵛ–H7ᵛ, Ælfric's letter to Wulfsige III extracts (Fehr 1914: §§133–142) with English translation also taken over;
5.2	S2ᵛ–T1ʳ	From 1566.1 H8ᵛ–I6ᵛ, Ælfric's second letter to Wulfstan extracts (Fehr 1914: §§86–95, 97–109) with English translation also taken over;

6. Editorial statement preceding supplementary texts from 1566.1

6.1	T3ᵛ	From 1566.1 K6ʳ, Ælfric's letter to Wulfsige, extract (Fehr 1914: §§61–62);
6.2	T4ʳ	From 1566.1 K6ᵛ–K7ʳ, AS Laws I Cnut 21–22.1 (Liebermann 1903: I, 302);

7. Supplementary texts from 1566.1

7.1a	V1ʳ	From 1566.1 K8, OE text of Mt.6.7–9 (preceding Lord's Prayer, Liuzza 1994: 12);
7.1b	V1ʳ	From 1566.1 K8ᵛ–L1ᵛ, OE text of Lord's Prayer;
7.2	V1ᵛ	From 1566.1 L1ᵛ–L3ʳ, OE text of Creed;
7.3	V2ʳ	From 1566.1 L3ʳ, Prologue to Ten Commandments from Ælfric's second (OE) letter to Wulfstan (Fehr, §121);
7.4	V2	From 1566.1 L3ᵛ–L5ʳ, Ten Commandments (1st nine only, cf. Liebermann 1903: I, 26–29).

TYPE:

Main text (Prefaces etc.) in Pierre Haultin's English-size Roman (Body 94);
Quotations in Robert Granjon's 3rd English-size Italic (Body 95);
English translations and Latin text on T2 in Granjon's 3rd Great Primer Italic (Body 116);
AS3: Specimen on π2ʳ shows exclusively Lambardian Pica Anglo-Saxon (AS i not used). Special sorts shown: 11 lower-case sorts: ð, f, ȝ, ƕ, p, ſ, t, ẏ; þ, ð, ƿ;
                        8 capitals: Æ¹, Æ², E, M, 8; Þ, Ð, Ƿ;
                        2 others: ⁊, þ;
              Total: 19 sorts (see note).

Note: þ and ƿ are shown twice both as lower-case and capital. Provision is made for AS i, z, and H but the sorts are roman.
AS3 with occasional AS2 s: Text shows Lambardian Pica Anglo-Saxon with occasional Parkerian s (e.g. c1ᵛ/20 ſe, A1ʳ/6 ſpricð, M4ᵛ/7 mæſſeppeoſtaſ 2nd and 3rd s) combined with Robert Granjon's 1st Pica Roman (shown on S1ʳ) on

b4ᵛ, c1ᵛ, c2ʳ, c3ʳ (words), f2ᵛ (words), f3ʳ (source unidentified), f3ᵛ (names of laws), A1ᵛ–L3ᵛ, M2ᵛ, M3ʳ, M4ᵛ, N2ʳ, N2ᵛ, N3ʳ, O2ᵛ–R3ᵛ, S1ᵛ⁻²ʳ, S2ᵛ–T1ʳ, T3ᵛ, T4ʳ, V1ʳ, V1ᵛ, V2.

Special sorts shown: 12 lower-case sorts: ð, ę, ꝼ, ʒ, ƕ, ꞃ, ꞅ, ꞇ, ẏ; þ, ð, ƿ;
                        5 capitals: Æ², Ǣ, ꝳ, ẟ, Ð;
                        3 others: þ, ꝯ, ꝥ.
                        Total: 20 sorts.

Copies seen: CCA W/R.3.12² (Somner's copy with annotation in his hand on fo 2ᵛ); CUL Adv.d.48.10 (with copious annotations by Abraham Wheelock collating the text with MS Gg.3.28; binding in brown calf gold-tooled by a 'Cambridge' binder—Hobson 1929: type A, pl. 41, tools 15, 39); CCC Y.7.15; ECC S1.4.26¹ (tp imperf, lacks V4; abp Sancroft's copy bound with 1655.2).

Copies also at: BL, CGC, CJC, CMC, CSJ, ChCL, DWL, EdUL, GUL, HHC, LCL, LSH, MTP, NLS, OBL, OAS, OBC, OBF, OCC, OEF, OQC, ORP, OTC, OWoC, StA, UBL, UCL, WoCL, YML, DML, TCD, GUB; FSL, NYPL, HHL, HUL, BMC, GCL, IULM KSRL, NLC, NWU, PUL, UCH.

Bibliography: Clement 1997: 236–239; Graham 2000a: 271–316, esp. 287–93; Niles 2015: 110–113, 135–139; Tite 2003: 151–152 (re. Otho B.xi). GR 5227.

1623.2: Speed, John, *The Historie of Great Britaine under the Conquests of yᵉ Romans, Saxons, Danes and Normans, their Originals, Manners, Warres, Coines & Seales, with the Successions, Lives, Acts & Issues of the English Monarchs from Iulius Cæsar to our most gracious Soueraigne King Iames.* London: John Beale for George Humble, 1623. 2nd edn of **1611.2**. STC 23046.3; ESTC S121976. AS3.

OE Proper Name

Collation: 2⁰: π⁴⁺¹ A⁸ B–2H⁶ 2I⁴ 2K–4S⁶ 4T⁴ 4V–4Y⁶ 4Y*bis*⁶ 4Z⁸ 4Z*bis*¹⁰ 4Z*ter*² 5A–5T⁶ 5V⁴ [$3 signed (+A4, B4, E4, F4, 2K4, 2L4, 2M4, 2O4, 2P4, 2Q4, 2R4, 2S4, 2T4, 2V4, 2Y4, 2Z4, 3A4, 3B4, 3C4, 3D4, 3E4, 3F4, 3G4, 3H4, 3I4, 3K4, 3L4, 3M4, 3N4, 4Z4, 4Z*bis*4–5; -2I3, 4T3, 4Z*ter*2, 5V3; B1 missigned C, G2 missigned G3, R2 missigned S, 4Y*bis*2 missigned 4Q2, 4Z*bis*3 missigned 4Z*bis*2, 5C3 missigned 4C3, 5D3 missigned 5E3)]. 679 leaves, paginated [i–xx], 1–246, nos 247–248 not used, 249–308, 309–362 not used, 363–430, nos 391–430 used twice, 431–1058, then foliated 1059–1101, no. 1096 used twice, nos 1102–1106 not used, then paginated again 1107–1258, *1259–1342* (pp. 9 misnumbered 19, 16 misnumbered 10, 54 misnumbered 53, 65 misnumbered 58, 104–113 misnumbered 132–141, 119 misnumbered 129, 122 misnumbered 132, 187, 193, 197 misnumbered 587, 593, 597, 240–241 misnumbered 242–243, 246 misnumbered 248, 248 misnumbered 329, 294 misnumbered 286, 754 misnumbered 759, 931 misnumbered 929, 1061–1062 misnumbered 1060/1101, 1084 misnumbered 1076, fo 1101 misnumbered 1001, 1165 misnumbered 1145, 1211 misnumbered 1201; pp. 196, 213, 219, 224, 233, 239, 251 not numbered (all showing a diagram of a genealogical tree).

Note 1: π^{4+1} shows a single leaf signed ¶3 added after π1.

Note 2: The anomalies in the collation, e.g. at 2I4|2K1, evidently reflect the way the book was divided into sections for printing purposes.

Note 3: Two issues are shown by minor variants, as Issue 1 shows p. 932 misnumbered 930, and p. 1241 misnumbered 243, whereas Issue 2 shows the correct number 932, and 243 'corrected' to 1243.

TYPE:

Main text in Pierre Haultin's English Roman Body 94 Face 90 × 2:3

An English Italic is used to highlight speeches, names, etc., as on 4P3^v–4^r (pp. 1008–9). Body 94 Face 90 × 2:2.5

AS3: The Lambardian Pica AS occurs in Bρıðſ on B1^v (p. 8).

Special sorts shown: 3 lower-case sorts: ð, ρ, ſ, but the 1 looks like a small numeral 1.

Total: 3 sorts.

Copies seen: Issue 1: CUL CCA.48.27 (lacks sig.2O; bookplate of Sir William Nigel Gresley 1806–47).

Issue 2: Pet P.3.2 (shows 3K1 and 3K6 twice, and so lacks 3K2, 3K5; binding shows spine strengthened with MS strip from a 15c choirbook).

Copies also at: APL, AUL, BSE, CCA, TCC, ChCL, DWL, GlCL, GUL, LMT, NT, OBL, OCC, OMC OStE, OSH, OTC, PBL, SoUL, UBL, WAL, YML; FSL, HHL, BA, IUL, MCRS, NWU, PSL, UCBL, UCH, UTK, YUB; SSA.

Bibliography: see 1611.2.

1623.3: Selden, John, *Eadmeri Monachi Cantvariensis Historiæ Novorvm.* London: William Stansby for Richard Meighen and Thomas Dewe, 1623. STC 7438; ESTC S121437. STC 7438.2; ESTC S121439 is a variant omitting the names of the booksellers on tp. AS1.

Regularis Concordia (extracts), Laws, Prognostication

Collation: 2⁰ in 4s: +⁴ 2+⁶ A² B–2E⁴ 2F² [\$2 signed (+ 2+3; -A2, 2F2; +2 missigned +3, 2+3 missigned A3)]. 122 leaves, paginated [i–viii], I–XVI, 1–218, *219–220* (p. 59 misnumbered 49).

State 2 shows +2 correctly signed.

SOURCES OF PASSAGES UTILIZING ANGLO-SAXON TYPES:

V1^r–4^v (pp. 145–152) From Faustina B.iii, 159^r–162^v: Prohemium Regularis Concordiae (Kornexl 1993: 1–19), glossing the L text;

X1 (pp. 153–4)   From Tiberius A.iii (dismembered from Faustina B.iii by Cotton), 177ʳ/v, last part of ch. 12 of the Regularis Concordia (Kornexl 1993: 145–7) glossing the L text;

Y3ᵛ (p. 166)   From 1568.2, Y4ᵛ: AS Law III Edgar 5.1–2 (Liebermann I.202); the inclusion of mon after hæbbe is distinctive of Lambarde;

Z1ᵛ (p. 170)   From Tiberius A.iii, 42ᵛ: Be eacenum wife (extract) begins ȝẏf heo nẏmð Lilian (Cockayne 1864–6: III.144; Liuzza 2011: T18.2 on p. 212);

2E4ʳ (p. 215)   From Tiberius A.vi or B.i: ASC (B/C) 596 (Thorpe 1861: I.34/35; cp. Tite 2003: 106;

2F1ᵛ (p. 218)   From 1568.2, S3ᵛ: AS Law II Æthelstan 14 (Liebermann I.158); the inclusion of þe cpæþon is distinctive of Lambarde.

Note: The Latin text is based on BL Titus A.ix (as noted in Wormald and Wright 1958: 203); Selden lists the manuscripts he consulted at the end of 1618.1, q.v.

TYPE: Main text in Pierre Haultin's English-size Roman (Body 94).

AS1: The Parkerian Great Primer Anglo-Saxon occurs in combination with Haultin's English-size Roman (on a Great Primer body) on 2+5ᵛ, V1ʳ–4ᵛ, X1, Y3ᵛ, Z1ᵛ, 2E4ʳ, 2F1ᵛ.

Special sorts shown: 11 lower-case sorts: ð, f, ȝ, ı, p, ſ, t, ẏ; þ, ð, p;
                      6 capitals: Æ¹, Є, Ꝺ, ꟽ, ⁊, Ð;
                      1 other: ꟼ;
             Total: 18 sorts.

Copies seen: State 1: APL EE.II.38; CUL R.8.41 (lacks +1, 2F2); ECC S12.3.11¹ (abp Sancroft's copy).

State 2 (with +2 correctly signed): CCA W/I.6.23 (lacks 2F2; Somner's copy with his annotations).

Copies also at: BL, AUL, BCL, BUL, CaCL, CGC, ChC, KCC, CMC, CPC, CPH, CSJ, TCC, ChCL, DUL, EAL, ECL, EdUL, EUL, GML, HHC, LCL, LGI, LHL, LMT, LPL, LSH, MTP, NCL, NLS, NT, OBL, OAS, OBD, OBF, OEC, OEF, OJC, OMaC, OMC, ONC, OOC, OPC, OQC, OSJ, OTC, OTI, OUC, OWmC, OWoC, SCL, SPC, SUL, WAL, WCC, WoCL, YML, DEWL, DML, KSC, TCD, ULim, BSB; FSL, USLC, NYPL, NYPM, UTS, HHL, HUL, IUL, KSRL, LCP, NLC, NWU, OSU, SLP, UCBL, UTA, YUB.

Bibliography: Binns 1990: 192–193; Clement 1997: 236; Pohl 2019; Tite 2003: 103–104; Toomer 2009: I.334–345.

Text:

Edition: M. Rule, *Eadmeri Historia Novorum in Anglia*, RS 81, London, Longman, 1884.
Translation: G. Bosanquet, *History of Recent Events in England—Historia Novorum in Anglia*, intr. R.W. Southern (London, 1964).

1623.4: Camden, William, *Remaines, Concerning Britaine: but especially England, and the Inhabitants thereof. their Languages. Empreses. Names. Apparell. Surnames. Artillarie. Alluſions. Wiſe Speeches. Anagrammes. Prouerbs. Armories. Poeſies. Monies. Epitaphes*. London: Nicholas Okes for Simon Waterson, 1623. 3rd edn of **1605.2**. STC 4523; ESTC S107501. Individual sorts only: AS3 ȝ and þ.
Lord's Prayer; Letter-symbols
  Collation: 4⁰ in 8s: A–X⁸ Y⁸ + χ1 Z⁴ [$4 signed (-A1,2,4, Z4; A3 missigned A2, S2 missigned S3)] 180 leaves, paginated [i–vi], 1–350, *351–352* (pp. nos 9–10 used twice, pp. 7 and 262 not numbered; pp. 41 misnumbered 31, 43 misnumbered 32, 68 misnumbered 86, 78/79 misnumbered 76/77, 84/85 misnumbered 48/58, 120 misnumbered 102, 124 misnumbered 123, 130 misnumbered 103, 152 misnumbered 512, 185 misnumbered 181, 206 misnumbered 306, 216 misnumbered 219, 244 misnumbered 218, 253 misnumbered 254, 281 misnumbered 276);
  State 2 shown by A3 signed correctly and by p. 85 correctly numbered.
SOURCES OF PASSAGES UTILIZING ANGLO-SAXON TYPES:
B6ʳ/ᵛ (pp. 19–20)   From **1614.2** D4ʳ: Lord's Prayer;
B6ᵛ (p. 20)   From **1614.2** D4ʳ/v: Lord's Prayer (with marginal variants from another version).
TYPE:
Main text in Pierre Haultin's Pica Roman (Body 82) interspersed with Robert Granjon's 2nd Pica Italic *pendante*.
B6 (pp. 19–20): no special sorts, but æ is correct in the second version of the Lord's Prayer in OE; suprascript translation to the first version in Granjon's 2nd Pica Italic.
AS3: The Lambardian Pica Anglo-Saxon (individual special sorts only) occurs on C2ᵛ (p. 28) in a report on the spelling reform practices advocated by Smith in **1568.3**: ȝ, þ.
Note: A passage from Chaucer's *Nun's Priest's Tale* is printed in Granjon's 2nd Pica Italic with no special sorts on T4ᵛ–5ʳ.
  Copies: State 1: CUL Syn.7.62.89; State 2: CUL Acton.d.25.83, Keynes P.3.3, SSS.30.12.
  Copies also at: BL, APL, BCL, BUL, ChC, ECC, CGC, CUW, DPL, MJRUL, OBL, SBT, UCL; FSL, NYHS, GTS, HHL, HUL, DDUL, IUL, NLC, UCL, TUL; UWA.

Bibliography: Dunn 1984: xlv–xlvi.

1623.5: Speed, John, *The History of Great Britaine under the Conquests of y*^{e} *Romans, Saxons, Danes and Normans, their Originals, Manners, Warres, Coines & Seales, with the Successions, Lives, Acts & Issues of the English Monarchs from Iulius Cæsar to our most gracious Soueraigne King Iames.* London: [John Beale] for George Humble, 1623. 2nd edn of **1611.2**, variant of **1623.2**. STC 23047; ESTC S120483. AS2.

OE Proper Name

Collation: 2⁰: ¶⁴ A–2H⁴ 2K–4M⁴ 4N⁶ 4O–4Q⁴ 4q⁴ 4R⁶ 4r⁸ 4S–5M⁴ [$2 signed (+ 2D3, 2L3, 2M3, 2N3, 4N3, 4R3, 4r3–4; -¶1, 2D2, 2I2)]. 434 leaves, paginated [i–xii], 155–798, then foliated 799–828, then paginated 829–924, *925–972* (the p. nos 395–402 used twice; pp. 285, 301, 304, 310, 320, 325, 922, 924, and fo 801 not numbered; pp. 222 misnumbered 216, 284 misnumbered 282, 319 misnumbered 329, 597 misnumbered 596, 898 misnumbered 899, and fo 816 misnumbered 817).

Note: The pagination is continuous with Speed's *The Theatre of the Empire of Great Britaine* (**1611.1**, or **1614.1**).

TYPE:

Main text set in Pierre Haultin's English-size Roman

                                           Body 94   Face 90 × 2: 3.0

An English-size Italic is used for speeches, etc., as on 4L1^r (p. 771).

                                           Body 94   Face 90 × 2: 2.5

AS2: The Parkerian Pica AS used in one word on B1^r/b (p. 159) Bꝥıꞅꞃ, with 8 used erroneously for ð.

Special sorts shown: ı, ꝥ, ꞅ, 8.

Copy seen: ChC K.14.20 (binding in brown calf with name of John Watkin, 17c alumnus and donor; lacks 5M4).

Copies also at: BL, BrCL, CUL, LGL, MCL, OMC, OStE, OTC, WAL; VCL.

Bibliography: see **1611.2**.

1623.6: Kiliaan (van Kiel), Cornelis, *Etymologicum Teutonicae Linguae sive Dictionarium Teutonico-Latinum*, 4th edn. Utrecht: Herman van Borculo I, 1623 = USTC 1028259, also (b) for Jan Everdsen van Doorn. Re-issue of **1605.3** with additions.

Collation: 8⁰: π⁸ A–3G⁸. 392 leaves.

Words in AS and other appropriate languages appear in Italic with no special sorts.

Copies at: ILP, BN, GBR, HKB, LPB, NCB, UTUB, NBN.

1624.1: Guild, William, *Three Rare Monuments of Antiquitie ... of the Bodie and Blood of Christ* [t from Ratramnus, Ælfric, and Hrabanus Magnentius]. Aberdeen: Edward Raban for David Melvill, 1624. STC 12492; ESTC S103528.

   Collation: 8⁰: A–I⁸ K⁴. 150, [2] p.
   Contains no AS, translation only.
   Copies at: BL, CMC, GUL, NLS, OBL, StA; FSL, HHL.

1625.1: Minsheu, John, *Minshœi Emendatio, vel à mendis Expurgatio, seu Augmentatio sui Ductoris in Linguas, The Gvide Into Tongves. Cum illarum Harmonia, & Etymologijs, Originationibus, Rationibus, & Deriuationibus in omnibus his novem Linguis*. 2nd edn of **1617.1**. London: John Haviland [of Eliot's Court Press], 1625. STC 17945, 17945.5; ESTC S 121891, S120933. AS2/3.
Words and Phrases
   Collation: 2⁰ in 6s: π² A–2H⁶ 2I⁴ [$3 signed (-2I3)] 192 leaves, A1–2I4 numbered in columns 1–760 (cols 721–724 misnumbered 719–722, 729–736 misnumbered 727–734, 741–744 misnumbered 739–742, 749–750 misnumbered 747–748).
   Note: STC 17945.5 shows ±π1 and cols 747–748 misnumbered 745–746.
TYPE:
Main text in Claude Garamond's (second) Long Primer Roman (Body 68) interspersed with Robert Granjon's Long Primer Italic 'Valentine'.
AS2/3: specimen on π2ᵛ shows mainly AS3 (without e) but some sorts are AS2, e.g., ꟽ.

Special sorts shown: 10 lower-case sorts: ð, ꝼ, ȝ, ꝑ, ſ, ꞇ, ẏ; þ, ð, p;
                      6 capitals: Æ¹, Æ², Є, ꟽ, S, Ð;
                      2 others: ꞇ, þ.
         Total: 18 sorts.
In text combined with Garamond's Long Primer Roman:
AS2 ȝ in ȝaſt s.v **Ghost**, AS3 ȝ in ȝẏꝼꞇ s.v. **Gift**, both on O5ᵛ (col. 331);
AS2 p in ppæc s.v. **Wreake** on 2I3ᵛ (col. 756); AS3 p in cnapa s.v. **knaue** on R5ᵛ (col. 404).

   Copies seen:
   STC 17945: CSS E.1.21; OBL Antiq.b.E.1625.1.
   STC 17945.5: APL II.I.22 (with ?18c binding in brown calf showing gold-tooled royal arms on front cover); MCS 5600(I.1.8; acquired 21 May 1656); sim. copies of **1627.3**.
   Copies also at: BL, CPH, LSH, NLS, NLW, NRL, NT, OSJ, OTI, SAC, SoUL, GUB; FSL, HHL, HUL IUL, BPL, UVL.
Bibliography: see **1617.1**.

1626.1: Spelman, Henry, *Archæologus in Modum Glossarii ad Rem Antiquam Posteriorem.* London: John Beale, 1626. STC 23065, 23065.5; ESTC S123508, 117517. AS3.

Note: According to Cronne (1956: 79) ten years after publication the greater part of the edition was unsold when two booksellers took it off Spelman's hands.

ASC, Charters, Gospels, Laws, Martyrology, Psalter, Will of Mantat

Collation: 2⁰ in 6s: π³ A–2O⁶ 2P⁴ [$4 signed (-2N1, S–2E4, 2I–2K4, 2M–2N4, 2P3,4; 2D2 missigned D2, 2E1 missigned 2E2, 2O3 missigned 2L3) 229 leaves, paginated [i–vi], 1–452 (pp. nos 157–168 not used, pp. nos 193–194 and 241–250 used twice; pp. 53–56 misnumbered 51–54, 94 misnumbered 96, 95 misnumbered 93, 99 misnumbered 199, 105 misnumbered 104, 106 misnumbered 108, 134 misnumbered 135, 143 misnumbered 142, 173–176 misnumbered 107–110, 178 misnumbered 112, 235 misnumbered 233, 241–242 misnumbered 231–232, 246 misnumbered 247, 247–248 misnumbered 237–238, 256 misnumbered 254, 257 misnumbered 158, 273 misnumbered 279, 288 misnumbered 287, 318–319 misnumbered 316–317, 401 misnumbered 205, 404 misnumbered 208, 410 misnumbered 418, 419 misnumbered 411; p. 407 not numbered).

Note: Some copies (not confined to Issue 2) show ±A1, and many copies show ±E2.

SOURCES OF PASSAGES UTILIZING ANGLO-SAXON TYPES:

(In the 'Clavis' on π3ᵛ Spelman describes the book as not so much a Glossary, although it takes that form, as a collection of general commentaries, an Encyclopaedia. In view of this uncertainty, the following source references include only longer passages. Except where otherwise stated Spelman's own L version accompanies AS Law extracts.)

A3ʳ (p. 5)   From 1568.2 Q3ᵛ, 2H2ᵛ: AS Laws Edward and Guthrum 11 (Liebermann I.134; phrase with abere for Lambarde æbere MSS æbære), and II Cnut 26 (Liebermann I 328; phrase with ebere for Lambarde æbere);

A6ʳ (p. 11)   From 1568.2 2K1ᵛ: AS Law II Cnut 58.1 (Liebermann I.350) with reference to Lambarde's L version which is quoted but also to the Quadripartitus L version which is also quoted (no doubt from MJRUL Lat. 420, formerly used by Spelman (Liebermann 1892: 66, §99) before passing through the Gurney family of Keswick Hall, Norwich, to Manchester);

Note: Spelman made notes on Lat. 420 when it was owned by Francis Tate (1560–1616; *ODNB*): they occupy fos 273–276 of Norwich, Norfolk Record Office, MS 7197, as noted by Beadle 2016: 47 and n. 30.

C2ᵛ (p. 28)   From 1571.1 L3ᵛ: Mt.20:25 (with ðeodo for þeoda);

C6ᵛ (p. 36)   From 1568.2 O1ᵛ: Prologue to Laws of Alfred and Guthrum (Liebermann I.126);

E5ʳ (p. 57), From 1568.2 Q3ᵛ: AS Law Edward and Guthrum 9 (Liebermann I.132);

G1ʳ (p. 73) From (?)CUL Add. MS 3020, 18ʳ/20–23 (Red Book of Thorney) (only other surviving MS is BL Add 5937): Will of Mantat during reign of Cnut leaving land at Twywell (Nth) to Thorney Abbey, C (extract); Sawyer 1523, as Whitelock 1930: no. 23, Hart 1966: 204–205; the phrase hıre allen halʒan is apparently taken over verbatim;

H5ᵛ (p. 94) From 1568.2 2F3ᵛ: AS Law I Cnut 26 (Liebermann I.304);

I1ʳ (p. 97) From 1571.1 I2ᵛ: Mt.15.27 (with eatað for etað);

I2ʳ (p. 99) From 1571.1 N1ʳ, 2L3ᵛ: Mt.23.4 (not 11.4 as stated), Lk 11.46;

I2ᵛ (p. 100) From 1571.1 2E3ᵛ: Jn.15.2 (with we for þe);

K1ᵛ (p. 110) From 1568.2 K1ᵛ: AS Law Alfred 3 (Liebermann I.5051) with distinctive reading boꝧh bꞃece; L version is that of Quadripartitus;

K3ʳ (p. 113) William I: London Charter in AS (Pelteret 8; pr. Liebermann 1903–16: I.486, Robertson 1925: 230), extract from §1, but the text does not match the sole AS witness, so it is probably Spelmanian AS, translated from a later Latin version (printed by Liebermann) based on the AS. Text (variant version in 1576.2 (2X3ᵛ), neither noticed by Liebermann or Robertson): Williem king grets williem bisceop & Godfred portrefan & ealle ða burghwarn binnan London.

From Laud misc.636, 57ᵛ/12–14: *ASC* E 1066 (Thorpe I.337/8–9); the passage is unique to this MS;

P6ʳ (p. 191) From 1568.2 C2ᵛ: AS Law Ine 3 (Liebermann I.90) with the distinctive reading ðolıʒ (Lambarde Þolıʒe);

V2ʳ (p. 241) From 1568.2 V3ᵛ: AS Law 'Norðleoda' (Liebermann I, 460–461) in Lambarde's distinctive Elizabethan Anglo-Saxon version;

V6ʳ (p. 249) From 1568.2 E4ᵛ: AS Law Ine 49 (Liebermann I.110), with the distinctive readings ꝼẏx and pẏpð and taking over the number '50' (for 49) from Lambarde;

X4ʳ (p. 247bis) From 1568.2 X2ᵛ–3ᵛ: AS Law II Edmund Prol.2–§1 (Liebermann I.186) with distinctive reading cpæðon;

From 1568.2 X4ᵛ: AS Law II Edmund 7 (Liebermann I.188) with the distinctive readings ꞅeꞇꞇan, ꞅoꞃꞅpꞃæcan;

From 1568.2 2N2ʳ: AS Law Edward confessor 12 (extract; Liebermann I.638–639);

X5ʳ (p. 249bis) From Claudius A.iii, 4ᵛ/21: the word ꝼınð-ꝼæꝥelðe (just this word) from AS Charter Æthelred to Christ Church Canterbury (Sawyer 914, Hart 1966: p. 62, no. 84, as Kemble 1839–48: no. 715, at III.350/10;

Z5ᵛ (p. 274) From 1568.2 2K3ᵛ: Laws II Cnut 69.1 (phrases; Liebermann I.356);

From 1571.1 T3ᵛ: Mk.6.21;

Z6ʳ (p. 276) From 1568.2 I4ᵛ: Laws Alfred 2 (Liebermann I.48); omission of hpelcne after hama is distinctive of Lambarde;

2A3ʳ (p. 281) From 1571.1 C4ᵛ, 2R2ᵛ: Mt.5.40, Lk.22.24;

From BL Stowe 2 (formerly owned by Spelman), 122ᵛ: Citation from Ps 106.40 (Kimmens 1979: 212), later ed. J. Spelman 1640.3, 2L2ᵛ;

2C2ᵛ (p. 304) From 1571.1 O2ᵛ–O3ʳ (i/y, þ/ð only changes): Mt.25.27 (extract);

2C5ʳ (p. 309) From 1568.2 2F1ᵛ: AS Law I Cnut 20 (Liebermann I 300) with distinctive reading pæpaꞃ for Lambarde's pæpā against MSS ꞃæpan;

2C6ᵛ (p. 312) From 1568.2 C2ᵛ: AS Law Ine 6,3 (Liebermann I.92–93) with Lambarde's distinctive reading ᵹeꞃolᵹӯlðen huꞃ; the reference to 'Reg.MSS' is obscure;

2D2ʳ (p. 315) From 1568.2 Y4ᵛ: AS Law III Edgar 5 (Liebermann I.202–203); Lambarde's mis-reading ꞃcıpeᵹemoꞇe bıꞃceop is distinctive;

2D3ʳ (p. 317) From Tiberius B.i, 160ʳ: ASC C 1065 (Thorpe I.332/10): the phrase hıꞃ ᵹæpꞃumā namon is unique to this MS;

2D6ʳ (p. 323) From 1568.2 2K2ᵛ: Law II Cnut 61 (Liebermann I 350–351);

2E5ʳ (p. 333) From 1566.1 C4ᵛ: Ælfric, Easter Day Sermon (Godden 1979: 150/9–10);

From 1568.2 Y2ᵛ: AS Law II Edgar 4 (Liebermann I.198);

2E6ʳ (p. 335) From 1568.2 2I1ᵛ: AS Law II Cnut 35 (Liebermann I.336–338) with Lambarde's distinctive reading abıð(e), and L version of Quadripartitus;

2E6ᵛ (p. 336) From 1568.2 2F1ᵛ: AS Law I Cnut 20 (Liebermann I.300);

2H1ʳ (p. 361) From 1568.2 2O2ʳ: Law Edward Confessor 23 (Liebermann I.648);

2H2ᵛ (p. 364) From 1568.2 N3ᵛ: AS Law Alfred 61 (Liebermann I.82) with Lambarde's L translation;

2L1ᵛ (p. 398) From 1568.2 2C3ᵛ: AS Law Dunsæte 3,2 (Liebermann I.376); cf. 2N1ᵛ;

2M1ʳ (p. 410) From 1572.1 N2ʳ: Diploma of King Henry I (Pelteret 44);

2N1ᵛ (p. 422) From 1568.2 2C3ᵛ: AS Law Dunsæte 3,2 (Liebermann I.376); cf. 2L1ᵛ;

2N5ʳ (p. 429) From CCC 196, p. 30: OE Martyrology (extract; Rauer 2013: §94b; the reading anð ða pınðaꞃ beoð ðonne ꞃmӯlꞇe is distinctive); p. 30 has annotations 'Junius' and 'se ærra lıða' from the text, probably emanating from Spelman. Spelman notes that the book was called 'Spell-boc', a title on the former cover as also reported later by Wanley (Ker, p. 75).

TYPE:

Main text in Pierre Haultin's Pica Roman (Body 83) interspersed with Robert Granjon's second Pica Italic.

AS3: The Lambardian Pica Anglo-Saxon combined with Haultin's Pica Roman occurs mostly in words and short extracts (but on pp. 73, 83, 95–102, 113,

partly combined with Haultin's English-size Roman) on pp. 5, 8–12, 24, 26–31, 33, 35–37, 44, 48–50, 53–54, 65–66, 70, 73 (Gt Primer), 81, 83, 93–102, 112–113, 153–154, 172–173, 181, 183, 191, 193–194, 208, 217, 239, 241, 246bis, 247bis, 249–250bis, 251–252, 255–256, 264, 274, 280–284, 291–292, 294, 296–298, 300, 304, 306, 308–310, 313–317, 319–329, 333–336, 346–350, 352, 361, 364, 369, 371–372, 379, 398, 410, 422–423, 428.
Special sorts shown:
   12 lower-case sorts: S (= ð), *e*, f, ȝ, Ð, p, ſ, t, ẏ (often not used);
           þ, ð, p (leans top left/bottom right);
   6 capitals: Æ¹, Æ², Є, Ϻ, S (used correctly on P1^r), Ð;
   2 others: ⁊, ɉ;
 Total: 19 sorts.
Note 1: No AS i; þ caused some problems and on I2^r a p is used (inked to thorn in TCC VI.12.8, CUL Syn.4.62.43 and OBL O.2.18.Art.Seld)
Note 2: Uses the number 7 for the Tironian sign; but on 2N5^r has correct Tironian sign ⁊.
Note 3: Clement (1997: 241) claims this AS3 is 'more calligraphic, particularly in the long ſ, e, and ⁊', but this claim is illusory: long ſ is the usual Roman sort, and the ⁊ is a no. 7 except on 2N5^r. AS3 combines well with the Pica Roman which, characteristically of Haultin, has quite a wide set.
Note 4: Used for Irish names on P4^v, P5^v (p. 190).
Copies seen: With ±E2:
Issue 1: TCC VI.12.8 (with ±A1), CUL Pet.P.4.3 (lacks D2,3,5, showing 2D2 (missigned D2), 2D3,5 in their place); Issue 2: CUL Bury 26.2, Syn.4.62.43; ECC S5.2.30; OBL O.2.18.Art.Seld (Selden's copy).
Without ±E2: Issue 2: CUL M*.8.13(B) ('ex dono Authoris' 28 Dec 1627, owned by Henry Lucas 1655); LFL 5H (with ±A1).
Copies also at: BL, CPH, CSJ, CTH, ChCL, DAL, ECL, GlCL, HHC, IPL, MJRUL, KNA, LPL, LSH, MTP, NLS, NT, NUL, OAS, OBC, OMC, OSJ, OStC, OWoC, OXC, RLW, SAC, UBL, UCL, WAL, YML; FSL, USLC, NYCU, HHL, HUL, GCL, KSRL, NLC, StUL, UCBL, UCLA, UMI, UTA, UTK, UVL; OUL
Bibliography: Clement 1997: 241; Moore 1992: 17, 32; Norden 1948–9: 382; Parry 1995: 173–177; Pococke 1987: 93–103, 107–116. GR 6283.
Manuscript: recorded sold to Harrop, 6 May 1999 (*EMS*, 9 (2000), 293).
As a supplementary 'supportation of a passage touching them in his Glossarie', s.v. feodum 'fief', Spelman wrote in English a longer work 'Of the Original of Feuds in England', completed 30 July 1639, the autograph of which survives as Harvard Law School MS 2062 (Gurney sale 1936, lot 198), on which see Baker 1990: no. 699: see **1698.3**.

Manuscript (Printer's Copy): OBL Tanner 288 (SC 10115), 23ʳ–25ᵛ (sigs Q5ʳ/b/51–Q6ʳ/a/21).
Note: OBL MS e Mus.48 (SC 3733), 5ʳ–250ᵛ (lacks π3, E2) is a copy of **1626.1** used as a printer's copy for **1664.1** sigs A1ʳ–3B2ʳ. It goes to the letter R.
Manuscript Index: LPL 783, 339ʳ–350ʳ: index by Franciscus Junius used by Jan van Vliet (Dekker 1998: 131).

1626.2: Minsheu, John, *Minshœi Emendatio, vel à mendis Expurgatio, seu Augmentatio sui Ductoris in Linguas, The Gvide Into Tongves. Cum illarum Harmonia, & Etymologijs, Originationibus, Rationibus, & Deriuationibus in omnibus his novem Linguis*. London: John Haviland [of Eliot's Court Press], 1626. STC 17946; ESTC S114544.
Words and Phrases
Identical with **1625.1**.
> **Copies seen:** CUL Adams 2.62.1 (with cols misnumbered as in STC 17945 =**1625.1**); OBL L.1.10.Art.Seld.
> **Copies also at:** BL, KNA, LGI, OOC, WSL; HSA, IUL, LCP, UCLA, UPL, UTA.

1626.3: Camden, William, *The abridgment of Camden's Britañia With The Maps of the seuerall Shires of England and Wales*. London: John Bill I, 1626. STC 4527; ESTC S107395.
> **Collation:** 4⁰: π² a–c⁴ [A–E]⁴ F–N⁴. [132] p. maps.

Place-names that might have contained AS letter-forms are printed in italic with no special sorts, as *Berrocſcyre* (B3ᵛ) or *Suthfolc* (F3ᵛ).
> **Copy seen:** CUL Syn.7.62.57.
> **Copies also at:** APL, BL, BCL, ChC, ECC, CGC, CUW, DPL, MJRUL, LSH, OBL, SBT; FSL, NYHS, GTS, HHL, HUL, IUL, NLC, UVL, TUL; UWA.

1627.1: Speed, John, *The Theatre of the Empire of Great Britaine Presenting an Exact Geography of the Kingdomes of England, Scotland, Ireland, and the Iles adioyning, with the Shires, Hundreds, Cities and Shire Townes, within yᵉ Kingdome of England*. London: John Dawson for George Humble, 1627. 3rd edn (1st) of **1611.1**. STC 23042; ESTC S520. AS2/3.
OE Proper Names
> **Collation:** 2⁰: A–4H² [$1 signed (+ B2, C2, D2, 3F2, 3X2, 3Z2, 4F2; -3F1, 3X1, 3Z1)] 154 leaves [incl. 2 for sig. A], foliated [i–viii], 1–94, 99–126, 131–132, 137–146, *147–152*, paginated 95–98, 127–130, 133–136 (pp. 95–96, 127–128, 130, 133–134 not numbered).

Note: The text is printed back to back with the maps, and the map pages, being always a double-page opening on the reverse side of text pages, receive no numbers.

TYPE:

The size varies according to the amount of text in relation to the amount of space available.

The preferred type is Pierre Haultin's English-size Roman (as on I1^r)

      Body 93   Face 90 × 2: 3.0

but the following also occur:

Pierre Haultin's 2nd Pica Roman (Vervliet R82B), as on L1^r:

      Body 82   Face 78 × 1.8: 2.5

Pierre Haultin's Long Primer Roman (Vervliet R67), as on Y1^r:

      Body 67   Face 64 × 1.4: 2.0

Italics of the same size as the main text are used to highlight names, etc.

Two Anglo-Saxon Pica designs are used mixed together in county names. They occur with main text in English-size (as on I1^r), with Pica (as on L1^r), and with Long Primer (as on Y1^r and 2K1^r).

AS2: The Parkerian Pica Anglo-Saxon.

Special sorts shown: ð, ȝ, ı, ꝑ, ꞅ, ẏ; þ, ð, p; Æ, &. 9 + 2

AS3: The Lambardian Pica Anglo-Saxon.

Special sorts shown: e, ꞅ, h (=ð), ꝑ, ꞇ. 5

Note: The setting is prone to errors, as d upside down, f for r, s for r, ð for d, p for þ.

 Copies seen: CMC H.10.5 (lacks A2, Z, 3G, 4H2); Pepys 2910 (but Bks II, III and IV dated 1631; lacks 4H2; 3X1 and 3X2 reversed, 3A1^r|3A2^v blank).

 Copies also at: CCA, CUL, GML, TCD; HUL.

Bibliography: Skelton 1970: no. 16.

1627.2: Speed, John, *The History of Great Britaine under the Conquests of ye Romans, Saxons, Danes and Normans, their Originals, Manners, Warres, Coines & Seales, with the Successions, Lives, Acts & Issues of the English Monarchs from Julius Cæsar to our most gracious Soveraigne King James*. London: [John Beale] for George Humble, 1627. 2nd edn (2nd) of **1611.2**, variant of **1623.2**. STC 23048; ESTC S124203. AS3.

OE Proper Name

 Collation: 2⁰ in 4's: ¶⁴ A–2H⁴ 2I² 2K–4M⁴ 4N⁶ 4O–4Q⁴ 4Q*bis*⁴ 4R⁶ 4R*bis*⁸ 4S–5M⁴ [$2 signed (+ 2D3, 2L3, 2M3, 2N3, 2O3, 4N3, 4R3, 4R*bis*3–4; -¶1 (title), 2D2, 2I2)].

 434 leaves, paginated [i–xii], 155–402, 395–798 (i.e. 395–402 used twice), then foliated 799–828, then paginated again 829–924, *925–972* (pp. 284 misnumbered

282, 286 misnumbered 289, 319 misnumbered 329, 556 misnumbered 558, 561 misnumbered 551, 586 misnumbered 585, 597 misnumbered 596, [fo] 816 misnumbered 817, 835/836 misnumbered 837/838, 898 misnumbered 899; pp. 285, 296, 301, 304, 310, 314, 320, 325 not numbered (all showing a diagram of a genealogical tree), also not numbered fo 801, pp. 922, 924).

Note: The main text beginning at A3^r starts as a slavish re-setting of **1611.2** retaining page numbers (155–) and catchwords (but with slight variations as **1627.2** G2^r differs from **1611.2** 2S4^r, K2^r differs from 2Z2^r K3 differs from 2Z3, M3^v–4^v differs from 3B3^v–4^v, R1^r differs from 3E3^r), and this method is followed to S4^v when the addition of supplementary material (first at R3^v–4^r) makes it impractical to continue such slavish re-setting.

TYPE:

Main text in Pierre Haultin's English Roman   Body 95   Face 92 × 2: 3
Robert Granjon's 3rd English-size Italic is used to highlight speeches, names, etc., as on sig. 4L1^r (p. 771)   Body 95   Face 90 × 2: 2.5
AS3: Lambardian Pica AS in Bpıðr on B1^r (p. 159).
Special sorts shown: ð, þ, ſ + 1 (= small no. 1?).   3

 Copies seen: CUL Ely.a.189; CUL R.1.20 (lacks 5M4; K2^r shows a crease in the paper when printed); CUL Pet P.5.8 (lacks tp, 2X2–3, 5M4).

 Copies also at: BCLW, CGC, CTH, CUW, DCL, EAL, GML, LGL, LHL, LSH, OAS, OBC, OOC, OWoC, SJS, WCC, TCD, BSB; HHL, BMC, IUL, LSU, MUL, UPL, YUB; ANZ, UML.

Bibliography: Shirley 1991: nos 398–400, and see **1611.2**.

1627.3: Minsheu, John, *Minshæi Emendatio, vel à mendis Expurgatio, seu Augmentatio sui Ductoris in Linguas, The Gvide Into Tongves. Cum illarum Harmonia, & Etymologijs, Originationibus, Rationibus, & Deriuationibus in omnibus his novem Linguis.* London: John Haviland [of Eliot's Court Press], 1627. STC 17947; ESTC S. Identical with **1625.1** except for the title-page.

 Copies seen: CCA W/B.5.1 (with cols misnumbered as in STC 17945 = **1625.1**; Somner's interleaved copy with a draft version of his dictionary = **1659.1**); CUL Bb*.1.14 (with cols misnumbered as in STC 17945 =**1625.1**), Ely a.253 (with cols misnumbered as in STC 17945 = **1625.1**), Hunt.20.11 (with cols misnumbered as in STC 17945 = **1625.1**), Pet.M.6.10 (with cols misnumbered as in STC 17945 = **1625.1**); ECC 313.1.71; TCD EE.aa.12 (with cols 747–748 misnumbered 745–746 as in STC 17945.5 = **1625.1**); DML K3.1.1 (with cols 747–748 misnumbered 745–746 as in STC 17945.5 = **1625.1**); OBL Douce M.subt.20 (with cols 747–748 misnumbered 745–746 as in STC 17945.5 = **1625.1**); QUB Percy 711 (with cols 747–748 misnumbered 745–746 as in STC 17945.5 = **1625.1**).

Copies also at: BL, BCL, BSE, BUL, ChC, ECC, CGC, CPC, CPH, CSJ, TCC, DUL, EdUL, GML, ILP, LHL, LPL, LSH, LUL, NCL, NLS, NT, OBC, OCC, OEF, OLC, ONC, OQC, OSA, OTC, OTI, OXC, PBL, PML, RLW, SBT, SPC, SUL, UBL, WiCL, WIHM, YML, NLI; FSL, USLC, HHL, HUL, CLM, GCL, KSRL, LCP, NLC, NWU, SLC, SCN, UCBL, UCDL, UCLA, UTA UVL, WUM, YUB; ATL, MonUL, NLA, SSA, UAL, UML, USL.

1628.1: Verstegan, Richard, *A Restitution of Decayed Intelligence in Antiquities.* Re-issue of 1605.3. London: John Bill I, 1628. STC 21362; ESTC S116256.
Copies at: BL, BPL, CCA, CUL, CMC, CNC, CTH, DAL, EdCL, EdUL, Eton, GML, LKC, LPL, LQL, LSH, MTP, NCL, NLS, OBL, OBrC, OEC, OEF, OLC, OOC, OSJ, OUC SPC, UBL, UCL, WAL, WCC, WIHM, WRL, TCD; FSL, UTS, HHL, HUL, KSRL, LCP, NLC, UTA, YUB, TUL; OUL, SSA.

1629.1: Camden, William, *Remaines, Concerning Brittaine: but especially England, and the Inhabitants thereof: their Languages. Names. Syrnames. Allusions. Anagrammes. Armories. Moneys. Empresses. Apparell. Artillarie. Wise Speeches. Prouerbs. Poesïes. Epitaphs.* London: A[dam] I[slip] for Simon Waterson, 1623. 4th edn of 1605.2 re-set from 3rd edn 1623.4. STC 4524; ESTC S107502. Individual sorts only: AS3 ȝ and þ.
Lord's Prayer, Letter-symbols
Collation: 4⁰ in 8s: A–Y⁸ [$4 signed (-A1)] 176 leaves, paginated [i–iv], 1–346 (pp. nos 8–9 used twice; p. 258 not numbered; pp. 74 misnumbered 54, 287 misnumbered 987, 315 misnumbered 215, 321 misnumbered 221).
TYPE:
Main text in a Pica Roman (Body 83) interspersed with Robert Granjon's 2nd Pica Italic *pendante*.
B5 (pp. 19–20): no special sorts, but æ is correct in the second version of the Lord's Prayer in OE; suprascript translation to the first version in Granjon's 2nd Pica Italic.
AS3: The Lambardian Pica Anglo-Saxon (individual special sorts only) occurs on C1ᵛ (p. 28) in a report on the spelling reform practices advocated by Smith in 1568.3: ȝ, þ.
Note: A passage from Chaucer's *Nun's Priest's Tale* is printed in Granjon's 2nd Pica Italic with no special sorts on T1ᵛ–2ʳ.
Copies seen: ABH 1254; CUL Syn.7.62.19.
Copies also at: BL, BCL, BPL, CCA, ECC, CPC, CSJ, TCC, DAL, EdUL, Eton, GML, LGI LHL, LMT, LSH, OBL, OAS, OBC, OMaC, OOC, OUP, SoUL, UBL, UCL, WAL,

WIHM, TCD, MBS; FSL, NYPL, HHL, HUL, IUL, BMC, EmU, MRCS, NLC, UCBL, UCH, UTA, WMUL, TUL; BNA; QSL, UWA.

Bibliography: see 1605.1.

1631.1: Selden, John, *Titles of Honor.* 2nd edn, completely rewritten (with augmented use of manuscript sources), of **1614.3**. London: William Stansby for Richard Whitaker, 1631. STC 22178; ESTC S117044. AS1.

ASC, AS Laws (extracts), Ælfric, OE Bede, Charters, OE Martyrology

Collation: 2⁰ in 4s: †⁴ §⁴ ¶⁴ A⁶ B–5Y⁴ 5Z⁶ [$2 signed (+ A3, L3, 5Z3; -†1, L2)] 476 leaves, paginated [i–xxxvi], 1–67, 98–942, *943–944* (pp. nos 68–97 not used, pp. nos 101–102 used twice, p. 39 misnumbered 37, 58 misnumbered 46, 313 misnumbered 213, 355 misnumbered 375, 473 misnumbered 437, 499 misnumbered 497, 519 misnumbered 513, 592 misnumbered 992, 700 misnumbered 690, 891 misnumbered 893, 895/896 misnumbered 847/848).

State 2 shown by <u>LONDON,</u> in red on tp and by pp. 355, 895/896 correctly numbered, but p. 894 misnumbered 994.

SOURCES OF PASSAGES UTILIZING ANGLO-SAXON TYPES:

O2ʳ (p. 127)   From 1568.2 C1ᵛ; AS Law Ine Prol. (extract; Liebermann I.88);

4D3ʳ (p. 601) From (prob) Otho B.xi (since damaged by fire): OE Bede II.14 (Miller I.1/138/16–17);

4D4 (pp. 603–4) From **1614.3** 2D2ᵛ and **1568.2** V3ᵛ: AS Law Norðleoda 2–5 (Liebermann I.460); and **1568.2** 2K1ᵛ (also **1614.3** 2G1ʳ): AS Law II Cnut 58,1–2 (Liebermann I.350);

4E1ʳ (p. 605) From (prob) Tiberius A.xiii, 77ᵛ (others possible): A Charter assigning lease of land by Oswald bp of Worcester (Sawyer 1332; Robertson 1939: 114/3–4, no. 55, but nos 42, 46, 56–8 also possible). Cp. Tite 2003: 105.

From (prob) Vespasian A.i, 63ᵛ: Extract from glossed Ps 67.27;

4E1ᵛ (p. 606) From (prob) Julius E.vii, 70ᵛ/5–6: Ælfric, Life of St George (Skeat 1881: I.308, lines 5–7 abridged);

4E2ᵛ (p. 608) From (prob) Otho B.xi: OE Bede V.4 (Miller I.2/394/14–16), also III.2 (Miller 158/7–8), also v.5 (Miller I.1/22/12) and others, incl. II.10 (Miller I.1/134/26–7);

4E3ʳ (p. 609) From (prob) Otho B.xi: OE Bede III.14 (Miller I.1/194/4–5); From (prob) Tiberius B.iv, 33ᵛ: ASC 870 (Thorpe 1861: I.138/17–20); the readings are not distinctive;

4E3ᵛ (p. 610)	From Augustus ii, no.25: Diploma of William I supporting the rights of Baldwin abbot of Bury St Edmunds 31 May 1081, extract (Pelteret 28, as Douglas 1932: 50–5, no. 7) Willelm Engla Kyng & Eorle ofer Normandie & ofer þa Mans ic sende greting Ærcebiscopan & leodbiscopan Æbbodan & Eorlan & eallum geleaffullum mannum, also Odo Eorl ofer Cent
4E4ʳ (p. 611)	From (prob) Otho B.xi (now damaged by fire): OE Bede [HE BkIV ch. 22,] 11.9 (Miller I.1/122/19), cyninges Ðegn, cyninges Ðegn him se holdesta
4E4 (pp. 611–12)	From Tiberius B.iv, 43ᵛ, 64ʳ: ASC 897, 1013 (Thorpe 1861: I.175/29–32, 270/41); the reading ða peſtpæna ðeᵹenaſ is distinctive; From (prob) Julius C.vii, 198ᵛ: Writ of Edward the Confessor 1042 × 1066 to St Paul's, London (Sawyer 1104; Gibbs 1939: 9; Harmer 1989: no. 54);
4F1ʳ (p. 613)	From Tiberius B.iv, 45ʳ: ASC 905 (Thorpe 1861: I.181/35–6); the spelling Sulſ is distinctive;
4F2ʳ (p. 615)	From (prob) Tiberius B.iv, 37ᵛ: ASC 886 (Thorpe 1861: I.157/16–18);
4G1ʳ (p. 621)	From 1614.3 2N1ʳ and 1568.2 2K3ᵛ–4ᵛ: AS Law II Cnut 71–1a (Liebermann I.356–8); From 1596.2 2I7ᵛ (cf. 1614.3 R2ᵛ): AS Law 'Geþyncðo' 2 (Liebermann I.456);
4G2 (pp. 623–4)	From 1568.2 2K4ᵛ also 1614.3 2N1ʳ: AS Law II Cnut 71.1–5 (Liebermann I.358); Lambarde's reading ðeᵹeneſ heneᵹeate is distinctive;
4H2ʳ (p. 631)	From Laud misc.636, 57ʳ/8: ASC 1064 (Thorpe 1861: I.331/5–6); this reading is exclusive to this MS. This MS belonged to William L'Isle apparently until his death in 1637, acquired by Laud 1638.
4H2ᵛ (p. 632)	From 1568.2 C1ᵛ (cf. also 1614.3 2G1ᵛ): AS Law Ine Prol. (extract; Liebermann I.88–89);
5A2ʳ (p. 759)	From 1568.2 C3ᵛ: AS Law Ine 10 (extract; Liebermann I.94);
5B3ʳ (p. 769)	From 1623.1 L1ᵛ/2–3: Ælfric, On the New Testament (extract; Marsden 2008: 228/877);
5G4ᵛ (p. 812)	From CCC 196, pp. 12–13: OE Martyrology re St George (Rauer 2013: §67/1–4, 6–13; distinctive readings include mapτýpeſ (2), æſτep þam (4), mancpealm (9), ſτope anð ſ

	ꝼeceðnýꞅꞅe (12); cited by Selden as no. 36, its number in the catalogue by T. James (1600).
5H1ʳ (p. 813)	From (prob) Julius E.vii, 70ᵛ/5–6: Ælfric, Life of St George (Skeat 1881: 1.308, lines 28–9);
5Z3ᵛ (p. 938)	From an unidentified MS of Ælfric's Glossary: Extract 'Comes Ealddormann oþþe gerefa' (Zupitza 1880: 300/15; Wright/Wülcker 1883–4: no. 10): '(so is it written in the the copie I use, and over it in as old a hand is vel gerefa with stroke draawne through it): Grammatica Ms penes Lamb. Moreton Eq. Aurat.'.

TYPE:
Main text in Pierre Haultin's English-size Roman (Body 94) interspersed with Granjon's English-size Italic.

AS1: Parkerian Great Primer Anglo-Saxon combined with Haultin's English-size Roman (but some Great Primer sorts are used) occurs on N1ʳ (p. 117), T4ᵛ (p. 172), 4D2ᵛ (p. 600), 4D3ʳ (p. 601), 4E1–4 (pp. 605–612), 4F1ʳ (p. 613), 4F2ʳ (p. 615), 4G1ʳ (p. 621), 4G2 (pp. 623–624), 4G3ʳ (p. 625), 4G4ʳ (p. 627), 4H2ʳ (p. 631), 4H3ᵛ (p. 634), 4H4ʳ (p. 635), 4P2ʳ (p. 687), 4Q2ʳ (p. 695), 5A2ʳ (p. 759), 5B3ʳ (p. 769), 5G4ᵛ (p. 812), 5H1ʳ (p. 813).

Special sorts shown:	11 lower-case sorts:	ð, ꝼ, ᵹ, ı, ꝑ, ꞅ, ꞇ, ẏ; þ, ð, ƿ;
	7 capitals:	Æ¹, Æ², Є, Ⱶ, ⱮⱮ, Ꞅ, Ð;
	3 others:	þ, ꝗ, ꝗ.
	Total:	21 sorts.

Note 1: No capital thorn or wynn found.
Note 2: Æ¹ often has the top right shoulder broken.

Copies seen: ECC 313.5.65; OBL Douce S.306a (lacks 5Z6), T.1.10.Jur.Seld. (lacks unattributed engraved illustrations on 4O3ʳ, 4Z1ᵛ and 5A4ᵛ); State 2: CUL O.3.8.
Copies also at: BL, BCL, BPL, BUL, CCA, CPH, CSJ, TCC, CaCL, ChCL, CLL, DCL, ECL, Eton, ILP, LHL, LKC, LPL, MTP, NAL, NLS, NT, OAS, OBC, OEC, OEF, ONC, OOC, OQC, OSJ, OTC, OWoC, SML, StA, UBL, WCL, DML, KSC, TCD, ULim; FSL, USLC, NYCU, UTS, HHL, HUL, IUL, MCRS, MUL, NWU, UCH, UMI, UTA, UTK, UVL; ANZ, OUL, SSA, UAL, UWL, XCU.

Bibliography: Crick 2004: 131–132; McKenzie & Bell 2005: 1.369 (1654/5); Shirley 1991: no. 435a; Tite 2003: 172; Toomer 2009: 1.158–168; Woolf 1990: 213–215, 236–238.

1631.2: Ussher, James, *A Discourse of the Religion Anciently Professed by the Irish and Brittish.* 2nd edn of the same item in **1622.2**. London: Robert Young for the

Stationers' Co., Partners of the Irish Stock, 1631. STC 24549 (usually found as item 4 in 24544 and 24544.5); ESTC S118950. AS3.

Alfredian Preface to the Pastoral Care (extract)

Collation: 4⁰ in 8s: A⁴ B–I⁸ K⁴ *⁴ [$4 signed (-A1, A4, K3, K4, *4; B2 missigned A2)] 76 leaves, paginated [i–viii], 1–133, *134–144* (pp. 90 misnumbered 80, 91 misnumbered 77, 93 misnumbered 63).

SOURCE OF PASSAGE UTILIZING ANGLO-SAXON TYPES:

D6ᵛ (p. 44) From 1622.2 2I3ʳ: *Preface* to the Alfredian *Pastoral Care*, 3-word extract (Sweet 1871: 1.6/22); the source is indicated by the taking over of mjnū with Irish 'i'.

TYPE:

Main text in Pierre Haultin's English-size Roman (Body 93);

AS3: The Lambardian Pica Anglo-Saxon in combination with a Pica Roman (not otherwise attested in this volume) occurs in a marginal note on D6ᵛ. Special sorts shown: 4 lower-case sorts: e, $þ$, $ſ$, $ꞇ$.

Copies seen: STC 24544: CUL Pet.G.6.534; OBL MS Ashmole 1250, Viner 475; (lacking *4) CUL Ely.d.516²; OBL Antiq.e.E.1631.2 and 4⁰.V11.Th.Seld.

STC 24544.5: OBL Vet.A2.e.217.

Copies also at: APL, BL, BCLNI, BUT, NLS, NT, OAS, OJC, OLC, OMC, OMFC, OQC, ORP, OSJ, OTC, OXC, SRO, UBL, WoCL, DML, DOL, NLI, RIA, TCD, ULim, GUB; FSL, NYPL, HHL, HUL, DSRL, NLC, NWU, PTS, UCDL, UCH; VSL.

Bibliography: see 1622.2.

1631.3: Foxe, John (ed.), *The Second Volume of the Ecclesiasticall Historie, containing the Acts and Monuments of Martyrs*. 7th edn of **1570.1** (= 2nd edn) reset from 6th edn **1610.3**. London: Adam Islip, Felix Kingston and Robert Young, 1631 (vol. I dated 1632). STC 11228; ESTC S123057. AS3.

Extracts from 1566.1, 1567.1 taken from 1610.3

Collation: (vol. II, books 7 and 8 only): 2⁰: A–I⁶ K⁸ L–3H⁶ [$3 signed (G2 missigned C2, K4 missigned K3, 3B2 missigned 2B2)] 326 leaves, paginated [1–4], 5–650 (pp. nos 112–113 used twice; pp. 183, 297 not numbered; pp. 176 misnumbered 166, 236–237 misnumbered 230–231, 244 misnumbered 242, 262 misnumbered 226 (with 2nd 2 inverted), 269 misnumbered 279, 352 misnumbered 350, 353 misnumbered 358, 402 misnumbered 400, 424 misnumbered 426, 452–453 misnumbered 552–553, 459 misnumbered 458, 484 misnumbered 448, 493 misnumbered 491, 494 misnumbered 449, 520 misnumbered 522, 588 misnumbered 586; 624 has 2 inverted).

SOURCES OF PASSAGES UTILIZING ANGLO-SAXON TYPES:

These passages are re-set from 1610.3 but the format is smaller, with narrower columns, so it was not possible to re-set line by line.

2P1ʳ/b (p. 447)   From 1610.3 5G2ᵛ/b/72–5, Ælfric's 'Excusatio Dictantis' (opening statement) at the end of his homily *Depositio S. Martin* (Godden 1979: XXXIV), but without AS sorts, and printed in the Small Pica Roman used with the main text;

2P1ʳ/b (p. 447)   From 1610.3 5G2ᵛ/b/82–4, Ælfric's *Grammar*, opening statement from OE Preface (cf. Zupitza 1880: 2), but without AS sorts, and printed in the Small Pica Roman used with the main text;

2P1ᵛ/a (p. 448)   From 1610.3 5G3ʳ/a/17–32, Ælfric's letter to Wulfsige III (bp of Sherborne 992–1002) extracts (Fehr 1914: §§135–142), but with spasmodic AS sorts;

2P1ᵛ/b/1–2ʳ/a/6 (pp. 448–449)   From 1610.3 5G3ʳ/a/62–b/40, Ælfric's second letter to Wulfstan (abp of York 1002–23) extracts (Fehr 1914: §§86–95, 97–109), but with spasmodic AS sorts;

2P2ᵛ/a/64–4ʳ/b/31 (pp. 450–453)   From 1610.3 5G3ᵛ/b/31 to 5G4ᵛ/b/63, Ælfric's *Sermo de Sacrificio in die Pascae* (same omissions as 1570.1; Godden 1979: XV), but with spasmodic AS sorts;

2S1ᵛ/a/47–51 (p. 484)   From 1610.3 5I5ʳ/a/72–5, ASC (E), annal for 1129 (Clark 1954: 51), but with no AS sorts, and printed in the Small Pica Roman used with the main text.

TYPE:

The main text is set in a Small Pica Textura (Body 72) interspersed with a Small Pica Roman and a Small Pica Italic.

AS3: The Lambardian Pica Anglo-Saxon is combined (showing very poor use of the special sorts) with Haultin's Pica Roman (Body 83) on 2P1ᵛ–4ʳ.

Special sorts shown in the AS specimen on 2P2ᵛ:

10 lower-case sorts:	ð, f, ȝ, ƿ, ſ, t, ẏ; þ, ð, p;
3 capitals:	Æ¹, S, Ð;
1 other:	ꝺ;

Special sorts shown in the text:

10 lower-case sorts:	ð, *e*, f, ȝ, ƿ, ſ, t, ẏ; þ, ð;
7 capitals:	Æ¹, Æ², E, Ð, ꟽ, S, Ð;
3 others:	ꝺ, þ, j̇.

Total: 20 sorts.

Overall total: 21 sorts.

Note 1: No special *e* in the specimen, and no p used in the text.

Note 2: OE passages on 2P1ʳ/b and 2S1ᵛ/a are set in the Small Pica Roman used with the main text.

Copy seen: OBL Mason F.146 (= vol. II of 3).

Copies also at: BL, BCL, BUT, CCA, CUL, CCL, CPC, CSJ, CSS, DUL, EdUL, GUL, ILP, IPL, LPL, LQL, LSH, NewCL, NLS, NT, OBrC, OEC, OJC, ORP, OTC, OXC, RUL, SCL, YML, TCD; FSL, USLC, NYPL, HHL, HUL, IUL, KSRL, NLC, WSL, YUB.

Bibliography: see 1570.1.

1631.4: Weever, John, *Ancient Funerall Monuments within the united monarchie of Great Britaine, Ireland, and the Ilands adiacent.* London: Thomas Harper for Laurence Sadler, 1631. STC 25223; ESTC S118104.

Collation: 2^0: π^4 A^4 B–Z^6 2A–2Z^6 3A–3Z^6 4A–4D^6 4E^4 a–b^4. [20], 871, [17] p.
Prints L text of AS charter (Sawyer 1246) in Italic on 3E6^v (p. 600). Contains no AS.

Copies seen: CUL R.8.20, Pet.R.4.7, Keynes.D.6.16.

Copies also at: APL, BL, BCL, BUL, CCA, CCL, ECC, CGC, CJC, KCC, CMC, CSJ, CSS, CTH, TCC, CaCL, ChestC, ChCL, CLL, DCL, ECL, EdUL, Eton, GML, MJRUL, LCL, LGL, LHL, LSH, MTP, NPG, NCL, NLS, NMS, NT, NUL, OBL, OAM, OAS, OBC, OBrC, OCC, OEC, OEF, OHA, OHC, OHM, OKC, OLC, OLMH, OMFaC, OMC, ONC, OQC, OStC, OSJ, OTC, RCL, SACL, SBT, SML, SOG, SoUL, UEA, WAL, WCC, WIHM, WoCL, YML, DML, MRL, TCD; FSL, USLC, NYPL, NYCU, UTS, HHL, HUL, IUL, BMC, CUofA, EmU, GETS, GUW, KSRL, LCP, MCRS, NWU, UCBL, UCLA, UCH, UIL, UTA, UTK, MMU, QUK; ATL.

1632.1: Speed, John, *The Theatre of the Empire of Great Britaine Presenting an Exact Geography of the Kingdomes of England, Scotland, Ireland, and the Iles adioyning, with the Shires, Hundreds, Cities and Shire Townes, within ye Kingdome of England.* London: John Dawson, 1632. 2nd impression of 1627.1, 3rd edn of 1611.1. STC 23043; ESTC S122267. AS2/3.
Date: 1632. The date is inferred from the date '1632' on the map of England G1^v–G2^r. Part of this edition could be re-used surplus from 1627.1, as in the BL copy (Maps c.7c.6(2)) this is the date printed on the title page, and in the CCC copy (EP.W.10(2)) this is the date printed on the title-page of Bk II (3F1^r), i.e. before Speed's death in 1629; the BL copy shows '1631' on this page. Bks II and III show the date '1631' on sigs 3X1^r and 3Z1^r respectively.

OE Proper Names

Collation: 2^0: [A^2], B–4H^2 [$1 signed (+ B2, C2, D2, 3F2, 3X2, 3Z2, 4F2; - 3F1, 3X1, 3Z1)] 154 leaves [incl. 2 for sig. A], foliated [i–viii], 1–94, 99–126, 131–132, 137–146, 147–152, paginated 95–98, 127–130, 133–136 (pp. 95–96, 127–128, 130, 133–134, 136 not numbered).

Note: The text is printed back to back with the maps, and the map pages, being always a double-page opening on the reverse side of text pages, receive no numbers.

TYPE:

The size varies according to the amount of text in relation to the amount of space available.
The preferred type is Pierre Haultin's English-size Roman (as on I1ʳ)
                    Body 92   Face 90 × 2: 3.0
but the following also occur:
Pierre Haultin's 2nd Pica Roman (Vervliet R82B), as on L1ʳ:
                    Body 82   Face 78 × 1.8: 2.5
Pierre Haultin's Long Primer Roman (Vervliet R67), as on Y1ʳ:
                    Body 66   Face 64 × 1.4: 2.0
Italics of the same size as the main text are used to highlight names, etc.
AS2 + AS3: Two Anglo-Saxon Pica designs are used mixed together in county names. They occur with main text in English-size (as on I1ʳ), in Pica (as on L1ʳ), and in Long Primer (as on Y1ʳ and 2K1ʳ).
AS2: The Parkerian Pica Anglo-Saxon.
Special sorts shown: ð, ȝ, p, ꞃ, ẏ; þ, ð, p; Æ.   8 + 1
AS3: The Lambardian Pica Anglo-Saxon.
Special sorts shown: e, ꞃ, h (=b), τ; ð.   5
Note 1: AS i is not shown. The setting is prone to errors, as f for r, s for r, ð for d, p for þ.
Note 2: Skelton's remark in relation to 1627.1 that 'the text has been re-set throughout in slightly larger type' (1970: 62) is misleading and should be discounted.
   Copies seen: BL Maps c.7c.6(2) (lacks 4H2), CCC EP.W.10(2) (lacks sig. A, 4H2).
   Copies also at: CUL, OBL, OStE, UCL, TCD; FSL, NYCU, HHL, HUL.
Bibliography: Shirley 1991: nos 432–434; Skelton 1970, no. 18.

1632.2: Speed, John, *The Historie of Great Britaine under the Conquests of the Romans, Saxons, Danes and Normans, their Originals, Manners, Warres, Coines & Seales, with the Successions, Lives, Acts & Issues of the English Monarchs from Julius Cæsar unto the Raigne of King James, of famous Memorie.* London: John Dawson [supplemented by Thomas Cotes] for George Humble, 1632. 3rd edn of 1611.2. STC 23049, variant of 23048.5. ESTC S997. AS2/3.
OE **Proper Name**
   Collation: 2⁰ in 6's: ¶⁶ A–2H⁶ 2I⁴ 2K–4S⁶ 4T⁴ 4V–4Z⁶ 5A⁸ 5B–5Y⁶ 5Z⁸ [$3 signed (+ A4, B4, E4, F4, 2K4, 2L4, 2M4, 2O4, 2P4, 2Q4, 2R4, 2S4, 2T4, 2V4, 2Y4, 2Z4, 3A4, 3B4, 3C4, 3D4, 3E4, 3F4, 3G4, 3H4, 3I4, 3K4, 3L4, 3M4, 3N4, 4A4, 5A4, 5B4, 5C4; -¶1–2, 2I3, 4T3, 5Z3; 5R1–3 missigned 5O1–3)]. 692 leaves, paginated [i–xxii], 1–1042, then foliated 1043–1086, then paginated again 1087–1237, *1238–1324* (pp. 86 misnumbered 66, 111/112 misnumbered 101/102, 181 misnumbered 18,

251 misnumbered 252, 306 misnumbered 206, 463 misnumbered 467, 509 misnumbered 519, 777 misnumbered 778, [fo] 1067 misnumbered 1085, pp. 1183 misnumbered 1283, 1218 misnumbered 1216; pp. 196, 213, 224, 233, 239, 249, 257 not numbered (all showing a diagram of a genealogical tree)).

TYPE:
Main text in Pierre Haultin's English Roman   Body 94   Face 90 × 2:3
Robert Granjon's 3rd English-size Italic is used to highlight speeches, names, etc., as on sigs 3X3ᵛ and 4P3ᵛ–4ʳ (pp. 992–993)   Body 95   Face 90 × 2: 2.5
AS2 + AS3: Parkerian and Lambardian Pica AS mixed in Bɲıðꝼ on B1ᵛ (p. 8).
Special sorts shown:
Parkerian: ꝏ (erron. used for ð), ·j (punctus versus erron. used for 1)   2
Lambardian: ꝑ, ꝼ   2

    Copy seen: CUL Adams.3.63.1 (annotated by hand with a dotted triquetra-mark with tail beside passages apparently important to the reader).
    Copies also at: BL, BCL, CCA, CCC, CFM, KCC, CMC, CNC, CPC, CSJ, TCC, CUW, ECL, EdUL, GML, HHC, IPL, LGL, LSH, NCL, NT, OBL, OAS, OBrC, OHC, OJC, OLC, OLMH, OPC, OUC, OWmC, OWoC, OXC, PML, SBT, SML, SOG, SUL, SWCL, WoCL, YML, NLI, ULim; FSL, USLC, NYCU, HHL, AAS, BPM, EmU, HCP, LCP, MCRS, NLC, PFL, SCN, SLP, SLU, UTA, UVL.

Bibliography: see 1611.2.

1632.3: Ussher, James, *Veterum Epistolarum Hibernicarum Sylloge*. Dublin: Stationers' Society, 1632. STC 24557; ESTC S119083. IR1.

Words

    Collation: 4⁰: ¶⁴ 2¶² 2A–2X⁴ (subsequent issue(s) show 2P4+χ1, 2X3+χ1) [$3 signed (-¶1, 2¶2, 2X3); 2S2 missigned 2S1; 2P4(χ1) signed *†] 90 leaves (+2 in subsequent issue(s)), paginated [i–xii], 1–165, *166–168* (2P4(χ1) when present numbered 121–122 (i.e. *bis*), 2X3ᵛ when with text numbered 166, and 2X3(χ1) when present numbered 167–168).

SOURCES OF PASSAGES UTILIZING ANGLO-SAXON/IRISH TYPES:
2E4ʳ (p. 39)   From Salisbury Cathedral Library MS 38, fo 2, as deduced from the variants to the L text given by Ehwald: the words 'tunning tat fridh' in Letter 5 of Aldhelm of Malmesbury to Eahfrid (= (?)Heahfrith: cf. Lapidge and Herren 1979: 145), ed. Ehwald 1919: 488–494, esp. 490/16. Ehwald reports that the words are not written in AS script, but the 'dh' here must be an attempt to render ð in Irish type, using the device of h after a consonant to indicate difference (in Irish it indicates aspiration); the words are conjectured to be for 'cunning Tatfrið', i.e. Tatfrith's experience, but for an alternative reading

see Lapidge and Herren 1979: 201, n. 30. For Ussher's use of Salisbury MSS cf. Ker 1985: 181–183.

2P4(χ1)v (p. 122) From an unidentified MS: L Charter of King Edgar to St Mary's Abbey, Worcester, abridged (Sawyer 731, as Kemble 1839–48: no. 514 at VI.237–242). OE occurs in one name only.
TYPE:
Main text in Pierre Haultin's Pica Roman (Body 83)
IR1: Used in combination with Haultin's Pica Roman for AS on 2E4^r (3 words) and on 2P4(χ1)v for the word Gleawceastre (except that the w is a larger size). Also used for Irish on 2S1^r.

> Copies seen: APL KC.VIII.19; CUL F.5.1^4, J.11.56, Hib.7.63.5^2, Hib.7.63.10^2, Hib.7.63.13, Hib.7.63.14, Hib.7.63.15 (lacks 2X4), Hib.7.63.16 (lacks 2X4), Hib.7.63.38 (lacks 2X2, 2X4 bound in its place; given by Gordon Duff), Hib.7.63.43^1; OBL 4^0.V27Art.Seld. (Selden's copy), Douce ww.78, Byw.I.4.11, Byw.I.4.12^1 (lacks sig.2¶; Thomas Baker's copy).
>
> Copies also at: BL, BSEC, BUT, ECC, CGC, CSJ, CSS, TCC, DRD, EdUL, Eton, GUL, LCL, LHU, LPL, LSH, NLS, NT, OBC, OCC, OGF, OHC, OMaC, OMC, ONC, OQC, OSJ OTC OUC, RLW, SPC SRO, UBL, UCL, WCC, WoCL, YML, DML, MRL, NLI, NUI, RIA, BSB; FSL, HHL, HUL, LCP, NLC, PFL, PUL, UCBL, YUB.

Bibliography: Baker & Womack 1999: 357–366 (art. on Ussher by S.M. Towers); Parry 1995: 138–139; Sayle 1916: nos 29–31.

1632.4: Kiliaan (van Kiel), Cornelis, *Etymologicum Teutonicae Linguae sive Dictionarium Teutonico-Latinum*, 4th edn. Utrecht: Herman van Borculo 1, 1632, also (b) for Jan Everdsen van Doorn, (c) for Jan Evertsz. Cloppenburgh 1 (Amsterdam) = USTC 1012175, (d) for Hendrik Laurensz. (Amsterdam). As **1623.4** = re-issue of **1605.3** with additions.

> **Collation:** 8^0: 3*^{8} A–3F^8. Fos [976]
>
> Words in AS and other appropriate languages appear in Italic with no special sorts.
>
> **Copy seen:** CUL Aa.22.34.
>
> **Copies also at:** BL, OBL, TCC, BUG, AUB, HSB, LUB, PNL; IUL.

1634.1: Ridley, Sir Thomas, expanded edn by John Gregory, *A View of The Civile and Ecclesiasticall Law*. Oxford: William Turner, 1634. STC 21055, 21055.5, 2nd edn of 21054. ESTC S123262. AS3 with some new sorts.
Laws, Will of Byrhtric

> **Collation:** 4^0: *^{4} 2*^{2} B–2Q^4. [$3 signed (-*1, S3)] 158 leaves, paginated [i–xii], *1*, 2–277, *278–304*.

Note: Different states indicated by 2K2 (normal) being missigned 2C2 (variant) in some copies.

SOURCES OF PASSAGES UTILIZING ANGLO-SAXON TYPES:

L3ʳ (p. 77) From 1568.2, sigs 2E4ᵛ and 2I3ᵛ: Extracts from Laws I Cnut 16, 17 (Liebermann I.296), and II Cnut 46.1 (Liebermann I.344).

T1ᵛ–2ᵛ (pp. 138–40) From 1568.2, sig. C2ᵛ, R1ᵛ–2ᵛ, X1ᵛ, Y1ᵛ–2ᵛ, 2E2ᵛ–3ᵛ: Extracts from Laws Ine 4 (Liebermann I.90), I Æthelstan Prol. (Liebermann I.146), I Edmund Prol., 2 (Liebermann I.184), II Eadgar 1, 4 (Liebermann I.196–8), I Cnut 8 (Liebermann I.290–2). A distinctive reading from Lambarde 1568.2 2E3ᵛ/1 occurs at T2ᵛ line 28 [to] þam mẏnꞅꞇeꞃ.

2A1ᵛ (p. 178) From 1568.2, sig. 2D3ᵛ, 2E3ᵛ: Extracts from Laws I Cnut 3 (Liebermann I.282), I Cnut 11 (Liebermann I.294) with reference to the same law at II Edgar 2 (Liebermann I.196), where the form eoꞃþe is from 1568.2, sig. Y1ᵛ. On this page there is a reference to Lambarde's 1568.2.

2A4ᵛ (p. 184) From 1568.2 sig. 2E1ᵛ–2ᵛ: Extract from Law I Cnut 6 (Liebermann I.288–290).

2C1ʳ (p. 193) From 1568.2 sig. K1ᵛ–2ᵛ: Extracts from Law Ælfred 5 (Liebermann I.50).

2C1ᵛ–2ʳ (pp. 194–5) From 1596.2 sig. 2I5, as indicated by the form Sꞇꞃeꞇꞇune against 1576.2 Sꞇꞃæꞇꞇune on sig. 2Y4ᵛ: Extract from Will of Byrhtric (Birch 1132; Whitelock 1930: no. 11; Campbell 1973: no. 35; Sawyer 1511).

2C2ᵛ (p. 196) From 1568.2 sig. K3ᵛ: Extract from Law Ælfred 8 (Liebermann I.54).

TYPE:

Main text in Pierre Haultin's Pica Roman (Body 81);

AS quotations occur in the 'Notes' by Gregory, which are set in Claude Garamond's (second) Long Primer Roman (Body 66);

AS3: The Lambardian Pica Anglo-Saxon combined with Haultin's Pica Roman, with Parkerian as well as Lambardian s, but also with a new sort for s showing a shorter terminal extending to the right (dropping down at the end) and a sharply angled serif to the stem (first on T2ʳ, e.g. line 32 ælmeꞅꞅꞃeoh), possibly attributable to Arthur Nicholls (on whom see Lane 1991).

Special sorts shown include

    12 + 1 lower-case sorts: ð (but δ used for ð on T2ᵛ), e, f, ᵹ, ı (1st on T1ᵛ), ꞃ, ꞅ, ꞇ, ẏ; þ (on 2A4ᵛ/17), ꝥ (as lc), ð (1st on T1ᵛ), p;

    4 capitals: Æ¹ (1st on 2C1ᵛ), Æ² (1st on T1ᵛ), Є (1st on T2ʳ), Ꞅ (1st on T1ᵛ);

    3 others: þ, ꝫ, ꝫ̇ (1st on 2A1ᵛ).

Total: 20 sorts.

Note: The new s was probably a prototype for AS7 s which differs only in respect of the terminal to the right not dropping down at the tip.

    Copies seen: OBC 585.b.16 (copy of George Coningsby 18c) has 2K2 missigned 2C2, and lacks 2Q4; ECC 331.4.108 (lacks 2Q4); OBL 4⁰.R.2.Jur.Seld. (lacks 2Q4); CUL H.11.60 (lacks 2Q4); with 2K2 missigned 2C2: OBL 4⁰.R.11(1)Jur. (lacks 2Q4), OBC 585.b.15 (lacks 2Q4).

    Copies also at: CJC, KCC, CPC, CSJ, CSS, TCC, DRD, LCL, LGI, OEC, RLW; HHL, KSRL, LCP.

Bibliography: Madan 1895–1931: I.180.

1634.2: Verstegan, Richard, *A Restitution of Decayed Intelligence in Antiquities*. Re-issue of 1628.1, 1st edn R1605.2. London: John Norton II for Joyce Norton and Richard Whitaker, 1634. STC 21363; ESTC S116259.

    Copies: BL, BCL, BPL, CCA, CUL, ECC, CFM, CGC, CSJ, CTH, TCC, DAL, GUL, LGL, LSH, NAL, NewCL, NLS, NMS, NPG, NT, OBL, OAS, OBC, OLMH, OQC, OTC, OUC, OWmC, SAC, SBT, SUL, UBL, WAL, YML, TCD, ULim, GCB; FSL, NYCU, NYPL, HHL, HUL, BMC, EmU, LCP, MCRS, NLC, NWU, PUL, SLU, UCBL, UCLA, UMI, UTA, UTK, UVL, WMUL, YUB.

1635.1: Selden, John, *Mare Clausum seu de Dominio Maris Libri Duo*. London: William Stansby for Richard Meighen, 1635. STC 22175; ESTC S117048. AS1.

    Date: Written by 1618 (Barratt 1964), but published in 1635. Entered to Stansby 18 Sept 1635 (Arber IV.348).

ASC (extracts)

    Context: For the political circumstances in which this book was written see Lucas 2000 and Toomer 2009: I.388–395. Although Selden's work is usually seen as the antidote to Hugo Grotius's *Mare Liberum sive de iure quod Batavis competit ad indicana commercia dissertatio* (Leiden: Louis Elzevier, 1609; USTC 1028212) [*The Freedom of the Seas*, t R.V.D. Magoffin (New York, 1916)], it is more directly opposed to the views of Fernando Vázquez de Menchaca, *Controversiarum Illustrium, aliarumque usu frequentium libri tres* (Frankfurt-am-Main: Georg Rab for Sigmund Feyerabend *impensis*, 1572 (USTC 626421); first published 1559), for which see Cromartie 1995: 39–40. Selden later sought to justify his publication in his *Vindiciæ ... Maris Clausi* (London: for Cornelius Bee, 1653; Wing S2444; ESTC S207189). See also Berkowitz 1988: 54–55 and 308–309, notes 8–10.

    Collation: 2⁰ in 4s: π^2 $^2\pi^2$ b⁴ A⁶ B–2S⁴ [\$2 signed (+A3)]. 174 leaves, paginated [i–xxviii], 1–304, *305–320*.

SOURCES OF PASSAGES UTILIZING ANGLO-SAXON TYPES:

Y2ᵛ (p. 164)   From Tiberius B.i, 135ʳ: ASC (C) 897 (as Thorpe 1861: I.175/37–177/5); the readings onᵹen, ꞃullneah are distinctive;

Y4ᵛ (p. 168)   From Tiberius B.i, 146ᵛ: ASC (C) 1008 (as Thorpe 1861: I.258/26–30); the reading oꝼ þꞃim hunꟈ hiꟈum is distinctive;

Z2ʳ (p. 171)   From Tiberius B.i, 154ʳ: ASC (C) 1012 (as Thorpe 1861: I.268/38–270/4); the reading aꞃpoꝼene pæꞃon is distinctive;

Z3ʳ (p. 173)   From Tiberius B.iv, 73ʳ: ASC (D) 1052 (as Thorpe 1861: I.312/12–15); this passage is distinctive;

Z4ʳ (p. 175)   From Tiberius B.i, 154ᵛ: ASC (C) 1014 (as Thorpe 1861: I.274/27–28); the reading Ᵹꞃenapic læiᵹ is distinctive.

Note: Middle English also occurs in this book printed in a Great Primer Textura:

2L3 (pp. 261–2)   From Vitellius E.x (since damaged by fire): *Libelle of Englyshe Policye*, lines 1–28, 34–5, 998–1001 (Warner 1926: 1–3, 50). [IMEV 3491] Selden says the MS used was in the Cotton library, so Vitellius E.x is the only candidate.

TYPE:

Main text in a Great Primer Roman, probably a mixed fount as two sorts of **g** are shown on p. 29, interspersed with a Great Primer Italic:

          Body 112   Face 102 × 2.5: 3.6

AS1: The Parkerian English-size Anglo-Saxon is combined with an English-size Roman on a Great Primer body as listed above.

Special sorts shown: 11 lower-case sorts: ꟈ, ꝼ, ᵹ, ı, ꝺ, ꞃ, ꞇ, ẏ; þ, ð, ꝥ;
        7 capitals: Æ¹, Æ², Ꞓ, Ꟈ, Ꞅ, Þ, Ð;
        3 others: þ, ꝗ, ꝗ (large);
    Total: 21 sorts.

Note 1: Both sorts of ð occur, the one that fits snugly to the preceding letter (e.g. on Y2ᵛ in oðꝛe 1st), and the (earlier) one that doesn't (e.g. on Y2ᵛ in oðꝛe 2nd).

Note 2: Middle English on 2L3 is printed in a Great Primer Textura (Body 116).

Copies seen: CUL J.3.51; ECC S8.3.16; OBL D.2.8.Art.Seld., MS Add.C 262 (lacks π and ²π; annotations c.1639 by Charles, 2nd baron Stanhope of Harrington).

Copies also at: BL, CCC, KCC, CMC, CPH, CJS, CTH, TCC, EAL, ECL, EdUL, GUL, LMT, LPL, LSH, MTP, NAL, NLS, NT, OCC, OJC, OLC, ONC, OQC, OSJ, OUC, OWoC, OXC, SML, SPC, UBL, WAL, WoCL, YML, DEWL, DML, TCD, BSB, GUB, MUC; FSL, USLC, NYPL, NYCU, UTS, HHL, HUL, BMC, LCP, NLC, NWU, SLU, UCBL, UCLA, UTA, UVL, YUB, QUK, TUL; ANL, AUNZ, UML, UTL.

Bibliography: Barratt 1964; Berkowitz 1988: 51–54; Cromartie 1995: 39–40; Korsten 2001: 132; Lucas 2001; Seaton 1935: 267–270; Toomer 1996: 71 (Arabic types); Toomer 2009: I.388–437.

1635.2: Fox, Luke, *North-West Fox*. London: Bernard Alsop and Thomas Fawcet for Michael Sparke, 1635. STC 11221; ESTC S105645.

    Collation: 4⁰: A⁴ a² B–T⁴ V⁴ (V2+'u3'.'u2') x–2I⁴ 2K². [12], 79, 100–171, [1], 169–269, [3] p., folded plate.

    Translation of the passage about Ohtere's voyage from Orosius on B1^v–2^r (pp. 2–3), prob. taken from Hakluyt 1589.1. No AS. [Brewer 1952–3: 209].

    Copy seen: CUL Syn.7.63.134.

    Copies also at: BL, CCA, CMC, Eton, GUL, OBL, OAS, OHC, OSJ, OXC, DML, BSB; FSL, USLC, NYCU, NYHS, HHL, HUL, AAS, NLC, SLU, UCBL, UTA, YUB, TUL.

1636.1: Selden, John, *Mare Clausum seu de Dominio Maris Libri Duo* (forbidden Dutch import). [Leiden: Bonaventura and Abraham Elzevier], 1636. Unauthorised edn of **1635.1**. STC 22175.3; ESTC S117098; USTC 3018465 & 1027917. CAS 2.2.

    Note: Importation of these foreign pirated editions of Selden's *Mare Clausum* was forbidden by proclamation of King Charles I (STC 9060).

    Context: For the political circumstances in which this book was published see Lucas 2000.

ASC (extracts)

    Collation: 12⁰: *⁸ 2*⁴ A–Z¹² 2A⁸ [$5 signed (-2*4)] 296 leaves, paginated [i–xxiv], 1–567, 568.

    Note: Maps (lacking in some copies) have been inserted between M5 and M6, and between T8 and T9.

SOURCES OF PASSAGES UTILIZING ANGLO-SAXON TYPES:

N12^r (p. 311)	From **1635.1** Y2^v: ASC 897 (Thorpe 1861: I.175/37–177/5); note error in sþa for **1635.1** ſpa.
O3^r (p. 318)	From **1635.1** Y4^v: ASC 1008 (Thorpe 1861: I.258/26–30);
O6^v (p. 324)	From **1635.1** Z2^r: ASC 1012 (Thorpe 1861: I.268/38–270/4);
O8^v (p. 328)	From **1635.1** Z3^r: ASC 1052 (Thorpe 1861: I.312/12–15);
O10^v (p. 332)	From **1635.1** Z4^r: ASC 1014 (Thorpe 1861: I.274/27–28).

TYPE:

Main text in Pierre Haultin's Small Pica Roman interspersed with a Small Pica Italic;

CAS 2.2: The Dutch Elseverian English-size Anglo-Saxon (but many letters oversized) used by the Elsevier's (Body 104) is combined with a Pica Roman on N12 (pp. 311–12), O3^r (p. 318), O6^v (p. 324), O7^r (p. 325).

Special sorts shown:	12 lower-case sorts:	ð, ꝼ, ʒ, Ð, ı, ꝑ, ſ, ꞇ, ẏ; þ, ð, p;
	5 capitals:	Æ¹, Æ², Є, 8, Ð;
	2 others:	ꝶ, þ
Total:	19 sorts.	

Note: These sorts look crude and fit badly with the main text: on O8ᵛ (p. 328) the left shoulder of **M** in *Mili-* has been filed away to make room for the **g** in ƀeneʒẏlð above.

> Copies seen: TCC VI.6.55, Grylls.5.25; CUL H.16.48 (lacks maps); OBL Vet.B3.f.232.
> Copies also at: BL, DUL, EAL, EdUL, Eton, MJRUL, KCL, LHL, NLS, UCL, PBA, ABM, LBM, HBV, HKB, HSB, NUB, BSB, WHAB, NLE; FSL, USLC, NYPL, HHL, HUL, CUI, ISU, LCP, MUL, UPL, UTA; QUL.

Bibliography: Copinger 1927: no. 4287; Lucas 2000: 130–131, 133–134.

1636.2: Selden, John, *Mare Clausum seu de Dominio Maris Libri Duo* (forbidden Dutch import). [Leiden]: Johan and Theodore Maire, 1636. Unauthorised edn of **1635.1**. STC 22175.7; ESTC S1345; USTC 3018463, 3018453 & 1511072. CAS2.3.
ASC **(extracts)**

> Collation: 4⁰: (?)⁴ (!)² A–2G⁴ 2H² [$3 signed (-(?)1)] 128 leaves, paginated [i–xii], 1–244.

SOURCES OF PASSAGES UTILIZING ANGLO-SAXON TYPES:

R4ᵛ (p. 136)	From **1635.1** Y2ᵛ: ASC 897 (Thorpe 1861: I.175/37–177/5); note lack of error of sþa in **1636.1** for **1635.1** ſpa;
S2ʳ (p. 139)	From **1635.1** Y4ᵛ: ASC 1008 (Thorpe 1861: I.258/26–30);
S3ʳ (p. 141)	From **1635.1** Z2ʳ: ASC 1012 (Thorpe 1861: I.268/38–270/4);
S4ʳ (p. 143)	From **1635.1** Z3ʳ: ASC 1052 (Thorpe 1861: I.312/12–15);
S4ᵛ (p. 144)	From **1635.1** Z4ʳ: ASC 1014 (Thorpe 1861: I.274/27–28).

TYPE:
Main text in Pierre Haultin's Pica Roman (Body 83) interspersed with Robert Granjon's 3rd Pica Italic, the *Cicero currens*.
CAS2.3: The Dutch Mairian Pica Anglo-Saxon (Body 82) combined with Haultin's Pica Roman occurs as listed above.

Special sorts shown: 11 lower-case sorts: ð, f, ʒ, ƕ, p, ſ, τ, ẏ; þ, ð, ꝑ;
                  4 capitals: Æ¹, Є, 8, Ð;
                  2 others: þ, ꝺ.
          Total: 17 sorts.

Note 1: AS i is not shown.
Note 2: These sorts look crude.
Note 3: Hebrew is printed occasionally, e.g., on C1ᵛ–2ʳ.

> Copies seen: ECC 331.4.8 (lacks sig. (!)); OBL Vet.B2.e.30.
> Copies also at: BL, EAL, OBC, OMC, OWmC, DML, PBN, PBA, PBSG, RBM, GCB, AUB, AVUB, HBV, HKB, LUB, BSB, KUB, RUB, WHAB, GUC, MMN, MRA, MUC, VUB, ZBS; USLC, NYPL, NYCU, HHL, HUL, MUL, UPL.

Bibliography: Fuks and Fuks-Mansfeld 1984–7: I.32–33 (on Joannes Maire as printer of Hebrew), Harms 1979: no. 27 on pp. 70–71 (added map); Lucas 2000: 131–134; Shirley 1991: nos 457a–b and 468a–b (added maps).

1636.3: Selden, John, *Mare Clausum seu de Dominio Maris Libri Duo* (forbidden Dutch import). [?Amsterdam or Leiden:] printer not identified (?Joannes Janssonius), 1636. Unauthorised edn of **1635.1**. STC 22176; ESTC S123287; USTC 3018464 & 1016382. CAS2.1.

AS (extracts)

    Collation: 8⁰: *⁸ 2*⁴ A–2H⁸ 2I⁴ a–d⁸ [$5 signed (-*1, 2*4, G3, Q4, 2C2, 2I4, a1, b4)] 296 leaves, paginated [i–xxiv], 1–504, ²1–61, ²62–64 (pp. 101, 208, 247, 403, ²1, ²22–24 unnumbered; p. 244 misnumbered 344, 317 misnumbered 217).

SOURCES OF PASSAGES UTILIZING ANGLO-SAXON TYPES:

S6ᵛ (p. 284)	From **1635.1** Y2ᵛ: ASC 897 (Thorpe 1861: I.175/37–177/5);
T1 (pp. 289–90)	From **1635.1** Y4ᵛ: ASC 1008 (Thorpe 1861: I.258/26–30);
T3ᵛ (p. 294)	From **1635.1** Z2ʳ: ASC 1012 (Thorpe 1861: I.268/38–270/4);
T5ᵛ (p. 298)	From **1635.1** Z3ʳ: ASC 1052 (Thorpe 1861: I.312/12–15);
T6ᵛ–T7ʳ (pp. 300–1)	From **1635.1** Z4ʳ: ASC 1014 (Thorpe 1861: I.274/27–8).

TYPE:

Main text in Pierre Haultin's Pica Roman (Body 84) interspersed with Granjon's 2nd (sigs A–D, G–H, L–M, X, Z–2A, 2C, 2E. 2H1–4, 2I3–4) and 3rd (sigs E–F, I–K, N–V, Y, 2B, 2D, 2F–2G, 2H5–2I2) Pica Italic; presumably there were two printers working in one shop.

CAS2.1: The Dutch 'Boxhornian' English-size Anglo-Saxon (Body 96) used with Haultin's Pica Roman (Body 84) but the size of the Anglo-Saxon sorts is greater, and they are crude. They occur on S6ᵛ, S7ʳ, T1, T3ᵛ, T5ᵛ, T6ᵛ–T7ʳ.

Special sorts shown:	9 lower-case sorts:	ð, ꝼ, ᵹ, ƕ, ꞃ, ſ, ꞇ; þ, ð;
	4 capitals:	Æ², Є, 8, Ð;
	2 others:	þ, ꞅ;
Total:	15 sorts (see Note 2 below).	

Note 1: These crude-looking sorts are probably modelled on those in **1635.1** = AS1, hence they are larger than the Pica Roman they are combined with.

Note 2: Roman **i** with the dot filed off is used for AS i, making 15 + 1 sorts.

Note 3: Roman **p** is used for p (wynn).

Note 4: d is probably a Textura ð, but not one that is found amongst the Textura types elsewhere in the book.

Note 5: H is probably a Textura 𝔥 of ?English-size (not found amongst the Textura types elsewhere in the book), but very similar to the Textura 𝔥 used in **1636.1**.

Note 6: **s** is a Hebrew sort (seen in Hebrew on C5ᵛ).
>Copies seen: CUL Syn.8.63.364, ECC S2.5.66 (a–d⁸ after 2*4; Sancroft's copy); OBL 8⁰.S2.Art.Seld. (Selden's copy; a–d⁸ after 2*4).
>Copies also at: BL, CCA, EAL, MTP, NLS, OCC, OWoC, OXC, SUL, TCD, GCB, HBV, LUB, UUB, BSB, RBN, RBG, BBC, CBU, FBN, GBCG, NBN, PBC, TBA, TBU, VBN, VBS; FSL, USLC, NYPL, NYCU, HHL, HUL, IUL, USNA, NTA, YUB; QSC.

Bibliography: Lucas 2000: 128–30.

1636.4: Camden, William, expanded edn by John Philipot (Somerset Herald), *Remaines, Concerning Britaine, but especially England, and the Inhabitants thereof, their Languages. Names. Surnames. Allusions. Anagrammes. Armories. Monies. Empreses. Apparell. Artillarie. Wise Speeches. Prouerbs. Poesïes. Epitaphs.* London: Thomas Harper for Simon Waterson, 1636. 5th edn of 1605.2 enlarged from 4th edn 1629.1. STC 4525, 4526. Individual sorts only: AS3 ȝ and þ.
Lord's Prayer; letter-symbols
>Collation: 4⁰: A–3H⁴ [$3 signed (-A1,2, 2X3)] 216 leaves, paginated [i–viii], 1–420, *421–424* (pp. 20 misnumbered 10, 291 misnumbered 29).

SOURCES OF PASSAGES UTILIZING ANGLO-SAXON TYPES:

D4ʳ (p. 23)   From 1629.1 B5ʳ: Lord's Prayer, with no (*for* 1623.2 do) at line 7;
D4 (pp. 23–24)   From 1629.1 B5: Lord's Prayer (with marginal variants from another version) with fwa fwa (*for* fwa, fua) at line 3, and coftnung (*for* erron. cuftnung) at line 7.

TYPE:

Main text in Pierre Haultin's Pica Roman (Body 82) interspersed with Robert Granjon's 2nd Pica Italic *pendante*.

D4 (pp. 23–24): no special sorts, but æ is correct in the second version of the Lord's Prayer in OE; suprascript translation to the first version in Granjon's 2nd Pica Italic.

AS3: The Lambardian Pica Anglo-Saxon (individual special sorts only) occurs on E4ᵛ (p. 32) in a report on the spelling reform practices advocated by Smith in 1568.3: ȝ, þ.

Note: A passage from Chaucer's *Nun's Priest's Tale* is printed in Granjon's 2nd Pica Italic with no special sorts on 2S3ʳ–4ʳ.

>Copies seen: STC 4525: CUL Syn.7.63.110 (with ±A1, lacking portrait).
>STC 4526: CUL Syn.7.63.103 (interleaved).
>Copies also at: BL, BCL, CaCL, CGC, KCC, CMC, TCC, CUW, DUL, EdUL, GML, GUL, MJRUL, LGL, LPL, LSH, MTP, NAL, NCL, NLS, NT, NUL, OBL, OSJ, OWoC, OXC, SBT, UCL, WRL, DEWL, GUB, MBS; FSL, USLC, NYPL, NYCU, HHL, HUL, IUL, BMC, EmU, JCB, LCP, PUL, UCBL, UCH, UPL, UTA, YUB, TUL, UVC; ATL, SSA, UAL, USL, UWA.

Bibliography:
Reprinted by J.R. Smith, London, 1870, with a memoir of Camden by T. Moule, and some notes by M.A. Lower. See also 1605.2.

1637.1: Camden, William, t Philemon Holland, *Britain, or A Chorographicall Description of the most Flourishing Kingdomes, England, Scotland, and Ireland, and the Islands adjoyning, out of the Depth of Antiquitie.* 2nd edn slavish re-setting of 1610.5. London: Felix Kingston, John Legat II and Robert Young for Andrew Hebb/ Joyce Norton and Richard Whitaker/ Andrew Crooke/ William Apsley/ George Latham, 1637. STC 4510, 4510.2, 4510.4, 4510.6, 4510.8 = ESTC S122164, S1529, S121328, S2550, S115671. AS3.

ASC, OE proper names

Collation: 2^0 in 6s: ¶⁸ A–3X⁶ 3Y⁸ 4A–4T⁶ 4V–4X⁴ 4Y–5B⁶ [\$3 signed (+¶4, 3Y4; -¶1,3, H3, 3O2, 4V2.3, 4X3; 4Y1,2,3 missigned 5Y, 4X2, 5Y3 respectively)] 564 leaves, paginated [i–xvi], 1–822, *1–2*, 3–233, *234–294* (pp. nos 207–208 used twice; pp. nos 89–92, 301–302 not used; pp. 95, 372, 572, 580, 626, 630, 648, 664, 674, 678, 708, 716, 764, 798, ²56 not numbered; pp. 287 misnumbered 278, 298 misnumbered 290, 299 misnumbered 287, 300 misnumbered 299, 363 misnumbered 375, 369 misnumbered 269, ²123–132 misnumbered ²111–120, ²221 misnumbered ²121).

Some of these errors, e.g., p. 287 misnumbered 278, are taken over from 1610.5.

Illustrations (by William Kip unless otherwise stated) on the two pages of one opening, additional to the above collation, occur as follows:

After P5 (Co), R1 (D), S2 (Do), T1 (So), V5 (W), Y2 (Ha by Hole), Z6 (Brk by Hole), 2B2 (Sr), 2C1 (Sx), 2D4 (K), 2G2 (Gl by Hole), 2H4 (O by Hole), 2K2 (Bk by Hole), 2K5 (Bd), 2L2 (Hrt), 2M3 (Mx by John Norden), 2O1 (E), 2P5 (Sf), 2Q5 (Nf), 2R6 (C), 2S6 (Hu), 2T4 (Nth), 2V4 (Lei), 2X2 (R), 2X4 (L), 2Z1 (Nt), 2Z4 (Db by Hole), 3A2 (Wa), 3B2 (Wo by Hole), 3B6 (St), 3C4 (Sa by Hole), 3D4 (Ch by Hole), 3E6 (He by Hole), 3F3 (Rdn), 3F5 (Brc by Robert Vaughan), 3G1 (Mon by Hole), 3G6 (Glm by Hole), 3H4 (Crm), 3H5 (Pmb), 3I2 (Crd), 3I4 (Mtg), 3I6 (Me), 3K1 (Crn by Hole), 3K3 (Ang, single leaf), 3K5 (Dnb), 3L1 (Flt), 3L6 (YW by Hole), 3N4 (YE by Hole), 3O2 (YN by Hole), 3P5 (bishopric of Du), 3Q4 (La by Hole), 3R5 (We), 3S2 (Cu), 3X1 (Nb by Hole), 3Y8 (S by Hole), 4E5 (Irl by Hole).

SOURCES OF PASSAGES UTILIZING ANGLO-SAXON TYPES:

3V4ʳ (p. 791) From 1610.5 3V4ʳ: ASC(C+F) 189/188 (extracts), both as Thorpe 1861: I.14–15;

TYPE:

Main text in Pierre Haultin's English-size Roman (Body 95) interspersed with Robert Granjon's 3rd English-size Italic (e.g. on D6ᵛ–F1ʳ)

AS3: The Lambardian Pica Anglo-Saxon occurs in combination with a Pica Roman in the reader's specimen on ¶8ᵛ and in the text in words as in 1610.5.

Special sorts shown
(1) in the specimen: 12 lower-case sorts: ð, *e*, ꝼ, ᵹ, ƕ, ꝑ, ſ, τ, ẏ; Ƿ [=uc], ð, p;
                       6 capitals: Æ¹, Æ², Є, ᛗ, ᛋ, Đ;
                       2 others: þ, ⁊.
                Total: 20 sorts.
(2) in the text: 12 lower-case sorts: ð, *e*, ꝼ, ᵹ, ƕ, ꝑ, ſ, τ, ẏ; Ƿ [=uc], ð, p;
                       4 capitals: Є, ᛗ, ᛋ (also used for d, e.g., on T4ʳ), Đ;
                       3 others: ⁊ (on 2B6ʳ), þ (on 4T3ʳ), ⁊ (on 3Y2ᵛ).
                Total: 19 sorts.
                Overall total: 21 sorts.

Note 1: AS undotted i does not appear.

Note 2: ð and ᛋ (for ð) are used side by side, as in 'ᛗaleðune, and ᛗealᛋune' on 2O5ᵛ (p. 446).

Note 3: ƕ is used regularly as a lower-case letter, occasionally initially, e.g. ƕanτerƈƕẏꝑ on Y2ᵛ. There is a new capital H (crude) used on 2T1ʳ.

Note 4: AS capitals are also used with roman ones in a Latin inscription on 2X6ᵛ.

 Copies seen: STC 4510: CUL Syn.2.63.1;

 STC 4510.2: CSJ C.3.17 (lacks ¶1, 5B6; ¶2/3 reversed, ¶6/7 reversed; shows ¶8χ1ᵛ–2ʳ copperplate map of Anglo-Saxon England by Hole; lacks maps after 2B2, 2S6; those after S2, Y2 misplaced after I5, N5 respectively); DML M1.4.60 (lacks ¶3,6–7, 5B5–6; shows ¶5χ1ᵛ–2ʳ copperplate map of Anglo-Saxon England by Hole);

 STC 4510.4: CUL Adams.3.63.7 (with contemporary gold-tooled binding of brown calf);

 STC 4510.6: NRL Folio PI.914.2-CAM [not seen, *ex informatione* Dr Lesley Gordon];

 STC 4510.8: OEF YJ.38.50.Bri (lacks 5B6, sig.¶ shows the order 13824567).

 Copies also at: STC 4510: BL, BCL, BrCaL, BrPL, KCC, TCC, CaCL, DRD, GUL LCL, LGH, LHL, NLS, OBL, OBC, OEC, OPC, OStC, OStE, SoUL, StA, WoCL, DML, TCD; NYPL, HHL, BA, NCL, YUB;

 STC 4510.2: ILP, LPL, MCS, NLS, OMaC, OSG, OxHC; UTS, HHL, HUL, NWU, SCN, UTA, UVL, WMUL;

 STC 4510.4: TCC, MTP, OXC, PBL; FSL;

 STC 4510.6: BCL, SUL; FSL, NYSL, HUL, CUI, SCN, SfUL;

 STC 4510.8: BCLNI, EUL, GML, LSH, NUL, SBT, UCL, NLI; HUL, IUL.

Bibliography: Skelton 1970: no. 23; Shirley 1991: nos 473–474 (maps of Britannia and AS heptarchy).

1638.1: Lisle, William, *Divers Ancient Monuments in the Saxon Tongue*. London: Edward Griffin II [of Eliot's Court Press] for Francis Eglesfield, 1638. Re-issue of 1623.1 with cancels in place of π2 M1 and O2. STC 160.5; ESTC S108569. Cancels: AS2/3 in specimen; AS3 with occasional AS2 s in text.

OE texts as 1623.1

TYPE: As 1623.1 except for AS specimen on π2^r and OE text on O2^v.

AS2 + AS3: Specimen shows the Lambardian Pica Anglo-Saxon mixed with a number of Parkerian Pica Anglo-Saxon sorts, viz. ð, τ, ẏ; þ, ð, Ᵽ (=uc); Æ¹, Æ².

AS3 with occasional AS2 s: Text on O2^v shows Lambardian Pica Anglo-Saxon with occasional Parkerian s.

Special sorts shown: 12 lower-case sorts: ð, e, f, ᵹ, ƕ, p, r, τ, ẏ; þ, ð, p;
                2 capitals: E, ᛗ;
                3 others: ⁊, þ, ȝ.
        Total: 17 sorts.

AS2 s and AS3 s occur in close proximity in ſẏþþan ſnıþan (O2^v/15).

Copies seen: CUL F.10.60 (with cancels bound as printed in a single gathering); APL LL.VI.4 (lacks V4, but with original sub-tp at M1); ECC 325.4.72; PO 1638.1 (with M1 and O2 interchanged).

Copies also at: BL, BUL, CCC, CJC, TCC, CCA, DUL, ECL, EdUL, LGL, LPL, LSH, LUL, MTP, NLS, NT, OBL, OEC, OEF, OJC, OLC, OOC, OQC, OSA, OTC, OUC, OWmC, SoUL, SPC, UBL, UCL, WAL, TCD, GUB; FSL, NYPL, UTS, HHL, HUL, BMC, GCL, KSRL, NLC, NWU, UCBL, UTA, UVL, TUL; DPLNZ.

Bibliography: Dickins 1947–8: 53–55.

1639.1: Ridley, Sir Thomas, expanded edn by J. Gregory, *A View of The Civile and Ecclesiasticall Law*. Revised edn of 1634.1 up to sig. S with Gregory's expansions cut out later in the book. London: John Dawson II [but all except the preliminaries Oxford: William Turner], 1639. STC 21056; ESTC S94904. AS3 with AS2 s, and another s.

Laws Cnut (extracts)

Collation: 4⁰: *-2*² B–2N⁴. [$3 signed (-*1, 2G3); 2M2 missigned '*Nn* 2'] 144 leaves, paginated [i–viii], *1*, 2–254, *255–280* (pp. 227 misnumbered 217, 230–231 misnumbered 224, 221).

SOURCE OF PASSAGES UTILIZING ANGLO-SAXON TYPES:

L3^r (p. 77)   From 1634.1 L3^r: Extracts from AS Laws I Cnut 16, 17 and II Cnut 46.1.

TYPE:

Set using the same type- and block-designs as 1634.1, the layout copied extremely closely up to sig. S, after which the additional material added in the 2nd edn is cut except for that in Part III, ch.2, §3, which is retained.

Main text in Pierre Haultin's Pica Roman (Body 80);
AS quotations occur in the 'Notes' by Gregory, which are set in Claude Garamond's (second) Long Primer Roman (Body 66);
AS3: Lambardian Pica Anglo-Saxon on L3ʳ only with Parkerian as well as Lambardian s, but with also a new sort for s showing a shorter terminal extending to the right and a sharply angled serif to the stem (see line 33 'ʒeoꝧnꞅulneꞅꞅe') combined with Haultin's Pica Roman.
AS sorts include: ð, ꝼ, ʒ, ꝧ, ꞅ, τ, ẏ; Ꝥ (as lc), p; þ, ꞇ. Altogether 11 sorts. Compare 1634.1.
   Copies seen: CSJ I.9.42 (lacks 2N4; gift of Peter Gunning, bp of Ely, 1684); OBL Vet.A2.e.324.
   Copies also at: CGC, LSH, OQC, UCL; FSL, HUL, MUL, UCH, UVL.
Bibliography: as 1634.1.

1639.2: Ussher, James, *Britannicarum Ecclesiarum Antiquitates*. Dublin: Stationers' Society 1639. STC 24548a; ESTC S119082. IR1.
   Context: This project was originally to be undertaken by Sir Robert Cotton at the request of King James I (Wormald and Wright 1958: 196).
ASC, **prose Guthlac, Martyrology, Saints (resting place)**
   Collation: 4⁰: ¶⁴ π A² a⁴ A–6F⁴ 6G⁴ (6G2+χ1.2) 6H–6P⁴ 6R⁴ (-6R4) 6S–7M⁴ [$3 signed (-¶1)] 611 leaves, paginated [i–xx], 1–1196, *1197–1198* (p. 1192 misnumbered 1132); 6G2(c1.2) not included in the numerical series.
   Note 1: 6R4, present in Hib.7.63.33, is a cancel;
   Note 2: Some gatherings were set twice indicating two states:

	State 1	State 2
3B has 3B1ʳ catchword	fa (Douce, Seld)	evagari (Bywater)
3M has 3M1 line 1	*ranarum* (Douce, Seld)	*ranarū* (Bywater)
5N has 5N2 signed	5N (Douce, Seld)	5N2 (Bywater)
5N3ʳ catchword	*tibus* (Douce, Seld)	*tutibus* (Bywater)
5N4ʳ catchword	*anfractibus*, (Douce, Seld)	*anfracti-* (Bywater)
5N4ᵛ catchword	mesburienſem (Douce, Seld)	mesbu-. (Bywater)

   In State 1 sig. 5N occurs with the sheets in reverse order: 2, 1, 4, 3.
SOURCES OF PASSAGES UTILIZING ANGLO-SAXON/IRISH TYPES:
E2ᵛ (p. 36)   From Domitian A.viii, 34ʳ/5–6: ASC (F) 167, as Thorpe 1861: I.15, Baker 2000: 11; the wording beginning on ðẏꞅan ẏlcan ʒeaꝧe ꞅenðe luciuꞅ is distinctive;
H3ʳ (p. 61)   From Vespasian D.xxi, 21ᵛ: OE prose Life of St Guthlac (Gonser 1909: 113, ch. 3, line 2/3), featuring the names ʒꞃaꝧτe ea, ʒꞃaꝧτe ceaꞅτeꝧ; cp. Tite 2013: 184;

3C4ʳ (p. 391) From (?) Otho B.xi (subsequently damaged by fire), and OBL Laud misc.636, 7ʳ: Contrasting the forms Geatum/Iotum 'Jutes' between OE Bede I.15 (Miller 1890: I.1.52/4) and ASC(E) 449 (Thorpe 1861: I.21/14);

4Z2ᵛ (p. 732) From (?) Vitellius D.vii, 131ᵛ/132ʳ (copied from CCC 196, where it is now lacking, by Joscelyn s.xvi): OE Martyrology at 17 Mar (Rauer 2013: §44/2);

5V3ʳ (p. 893) From CCC 201, p. 150/24–5: re. the resting place of ss Aidan and Patrick at Glastonbury (Liebermann, *Heiligen*, 1889: II.37 on p. 17);

5X2ʳ (p. 899) From OBL Laud misc.636, 6ᵛ: ASC(E) 430, as Thorpe 1861: I.19; the wording is distinctive.

TYPE:

Main text in Pierre Haultin's Pica Roman (Body 83) with many passages in Robert Granjon's second Pica Italic (Body 83). Haultin's English-size Roman (Body 95) occurs on 2L4ᵛ–2M4ᵛ, 3A4ᵛ–3B2ʳ, 3Q3ᵛ–3S2ʳ, etc.

IR1: English-size Elizabethan Irish used in combination with Haultin's Pica Roman mixed with his English-size (esp. h) for AS on E2ᵛ (p. 36), H3ʳ (p. 61), 3C4ʳ (p. 391), 5V3ʳ (p. 893), 5X2ʳ (p. 899).

Special sorts: a (= italic a), ƀ, *e* at end of passage, ꝼ, ʒ, ı, p, ꝑ, s, ꞇ, ẏ; ð = d with an acute accent over it; A; ꝺ. (14 sorts)

Note: the occasional use of IR1 for Irish (as on 5R1ᵛ, 5T4ʳ, 6O3ʳ) is not included in the analysis here.

Copies seen (see above under Collation): State 1:

With tp in black: APL B.VII.36 (7M1–3 torn at the top; lacks 7M4); CUL K*12.46; LFL2C-1 (but the leaves in sig. 5N are in the correct order).

With tp in black and red: CUL Hib.7.63.33 (binding of brown calf showing a frame enclosing a heraldic device in gold front and back, inside the front cover the bookplate of Thomas Bramston of Skreens); LFL 2C-2; OBL 4⁰.v.7.Th.Seld. (Selden's copy), Douce v.200;

State 2: OBL Byw.T.8.23 lacks πA² and 6G2(c1.2).

Copies also at: BL, BCLNI, BUL, BUT, CCA, CCC, ECC, CGC, CJC, CPH, CSJ, CSS, CTH, CaCL, CUW, DCL, EdUL, Eton, GML, GUL, HCL, MJRUL, LCL, LHL, LMT, NCL, NLS, NMS, NT, OAS, OBC, OBrC, OCC, OGF, OHM, OLC, ONC, OOC, OSJ, OTC, OWmC, OWoC, RLW, SPC, SRO, StA, UBL, WAL, WiCL, YML, DML, KSC, NLI, RCB, RIA, BSB, GUB, MBS; FSL, USLC, UTS, HHL, HUL, CUofA, DDUL, GUW, KSRL, NLC, UCBL, UCLA, UTA YUB, QUK.

Bibliography: Baker & Womack 1999: 357–366 (art. on Ussher by S.M. Towers); Dickins 1949: 54; Ford 2007: 210–220; McGuinne 1992: 4–22; Parry 1995: 139–141; Sayle 1916: nos 51–52; Sharpe & Hoyne 2020: no. 26 on pp. 108–110.

1639.3: Paris, Matthew, ed. William Watts aided by John Selden, *Vitæ Duorum Offarum sive Offanorum, Merciorum Regum*. London: Miles Flesher for Cornelius Bee and Laurence Sadler, 1639. STC 19210, 2nd part. This 2nd part of STC 19210 also appears with Wing P358, another edition of Matthew Paris's *Historia Major* printed by Richard Hodgkinson in 1640–1 (BL 678.h.1–2). AS 4.
Words
> Collation: 2^0: *6 A–R6 S8 T–Y6 y6 2y6 3y6 4y4 Z8 [$3 signed (+*4, S4, -N3, 4y3; Z2 missigned Z3)] 170 leaves, paginated [i–xiv], 1–310, *311–326* (pp. 34, 146–148, 218, 266 unnumbered).
>
> Note: variant states shown by p. 220: State 1: misnumbered 120; State 2: numbered correctly.

TYPE:

AS sorts occur only in the Glossary, which, to judge from the signatures (y–4y, between Y and Z), was apparently an afterthought. Remarks are therefore confined to this part of the book.

Main text in Pierre Haultin's Pica Roman interspersed with Granjon's 2nd Pica Italic.

AS4: The Spelmanian Great Primer Anglo-Saxon occurs in words on y4 (pp. 273–274), 4y1ᵛ (p. 304), and 4y4 (pp. 309–310).

Special sorts shown: ð, *e*, ȝ, ı, ꝑ, τ, ẏ; ꟽ, ꝸ.   7 + 2 + 0 = 9 sorts

> Copies seen: State 1 (p. 220 numbered 120): BL 195.g.11 (lacks Z8), 678.h.1 (lacks Z7,8), 9510.I.1 (lacks Z7,8); CCA W/E.6.15 (lacks Z8); OBL Gough Gen.top.232; Douce P.30 (with gold-tooled coat of arms on front; lacks Z8); fol.BS.294 (on very large paper);
>
> State 2 (p. 220 numbered correctly): BL G4834 (on larger paper, Z7 mounted on another leaf, lacks Z8); ECC S12.1.31 (on larger paper, shows Z7 before Z1 and lacks Z8; Sancroft's copy, with 17c gold-tooled binding showing his coat of arms added); TCD v.dd.5 (lacks Z8).
>
> Copies also at: BCLW, CUL,CGC, KCC, CMC, CPH, CSJ, CTH, TCC, CaCL, ChestC, DC, DRD, DUL, DWL, EdUL, LCL, LHL, LPL, LSH, NCL, NT, OBC, OCC, OHC, OJC, OLC, ONC, OOC, OPH, OTC, OUS, OXC, SoUL, SPC StA, UBL, WAL, WCF, WiCL, WoCL, WRL, DEWL, DML, ULim, GUB; FSL, USLC, NYPL, HHL, HUL, DDUL, LCP, MCRS, NLC, StUL, UCBL, UCLA, UTA, UVL, YUB, QUK; ACU, SSA.

Bibliography: Stanley 1987: 441; Toomer 2009: I.345–349.

1639.4: Spelman, Sir Henry [assisted by Jeremiah Stephens; their correspondence (1630–41) preserved in BL, Add 34599, fos 113–167, 34600, fos 2–167, 34601, fos 41, 44, Harley 7001, fos 70, 83, Harley 7003, fo 376, Oxford, Queen's College 280, fos 280–282; see Lucas 2022], *Concilia, Decreta, Leges, Constitvtiones, in re Ecclesiarum Orbis Britannici* (from the coming of Christianity to the Norman Conquest). London: Richard Badger 1 for Philemon Stephens 1 (brother of Jeremiah) and Christopher Meredith, 1639. STC 23066; ESTC S121742. AS4 + AS3.

    Date: 1639. Entered to Ph. Stephens and Meredith at the Stationers' Co. 10 Aug 1637 (Arber IV.391). Attestatio by Edmund Scott, domestic seneschal to Abp Bray, dated 13 Feb 1633 ([*]3^r), also in Add 34600, 5^r. Summa approbationis by William Bray, abp of Canterbury, dated 27 Oct 1637. Imprimatur by William Bray, abp of Canterbury, dated 23 Jan 1638, to MS dedication in OBL Tanner 288 (SC 10115), 36^v. A draft tp, dated 1638, occurs in Add 34600, 5^v.

Laws, Charters, Theodulfi Capitula

    Collation: 2⁰ in 6s: §⁶ [*]⁴ ¶⁴ A⁸ a⁸ B⁴ C–3F⁶ 3G–3I⁴ [$4 signed (-§1,2, [*]3, ¶3,4, B4, 2T1, 3G4, 3H4, 3I4)] 346 leaves, paginated [i–iv], 1–V, *VI–XXIV*, 1–637, *638–662* (sig. a8 not included in the numbering; pp. 96 misnumbered 99, 176 misnumbered 167, 211–212 misnumbered 209–210, 213–214 both misnumbered 212, 250 misnumbered 256, 252 misnumbered 258, 257 misnumbered 264, 261 misnumbered 265, 397 misnumbered 398, 456 misnumbered 459).

SOURCES OF PASSAGES UTILIZING ANGLO-SAXON TYPES:

K3 (pp. 127–8)   From RKA, DRc/R1 (Textus Roffensis, *olim* Rochester Cathedral Library MS A.3.5), 1^r/1–10: Laws Æthelbert, Inscr. 1–3 (Liebermann I.3);

N3^r–5^v (pp. 163–168)   From Laud misc.636, 17^v/15–19^r/10 (where the passage is marked off, with an annotation probably emanating from Spelman on fo 17^v lh margin, and 'Amen' added on fo 19^r rh margin): ASC(E) 675 (Thorpe I.58–59);

O6^v–P2^v (pp. 182–186)   From 1568.2 C1^v–G2^v: Laws Ine Prol. 1–6,5, 13, 23, 45, 61, 76–76,3 (Liebermann I.88–122); Lambarde's L translation is also taken over;

P6^v–Q2^r (pp. 194–197)   From RKA, DRc/R1 (Textus Roffensis, *olim* RCL MS A.3.5), 5^r/13–6^v/23: Laws Wihtræd, complete (Liebermann I.12–14); MS sole witness, and the L t is Spelman's own;

Q6^v–R1^r (pp. 206–207)   From RKA, DRc/R1 (Textus Roffensis, *olim* RCL MS A.3.5), 7^r/1–7^v/10: Laws Hadbot (Liebermann I.464–468); the version followed is clearly that of this MS (see esp. 9,1–10), and the L t is Spelman's;

2C6^v (p. 326)	Sole witness now is Tiberius A.xiii, 22^v/1–23^r/17, but the text here, somewhat abbreviated, shows many deviations (e.g. 'Herefordensem Ecclesiam spectabant' for 'Herfordensem æcclesiam præstita fuerunt') and the variant form of the witness list on 2D1^r is what corresponds with Tiberius A.xiii, 23^r/15–17: Record of an agreement (attributed to the synod of 'Clofeshoh' 803) between Deneberht (bp of Worcester) and Wulfheard (bp of Hereford) = Sawyer 1431, Finberg 1961: no. 52 (Birch no. 309); L with AS names;
2D4^v–5^v (pp. 334–336)	From Tiberius A.xiii, 47^r/1–48^r/6: Settlement of a dispute (attributed to the synod of 'Clofeshoh' 824) between Heaberht (bp of Worcester) and the familia of Berkeley = Sawyer 1433, Finberg 1961: no. 62 (Birch no. 379); L with some AS;
2F2^v–2G1^r (pp. 354–363)	From 1568.2 G3^v–I3^v: Laws Alfred preface (Liebermann I.26–46); Lambarde's L translation is also taken over;
2G1^v–5^r (pp. 364–371)	From 1568.2 G3^v–N1^v: Laws Alfred 1–3, 5–6,1, 8–8,3, 10–11,5, 15, 18, 20–1, 25–26, 33, 38–38,1, 40–1, 43 (Liebermann I.46–78); Lambarde's L translation is also taken over;
2I2^v–5^r (pp. 390–395)	From 1568.2 P4^v–Q4^v: Laws Edward and Guthrum Prol., 1–4,1, 5–12 (Liebermann I.128–134); Lambarde's L translation is also taken over;
2I5^v–2K2^r (pp. 396–401)	From 1568.2 R1^v–T4^v: Laws I Æthelstan, II Æthelstan Prol., 1–2, 5–6,3, 14–14,2, 23–26,1, Epil. (Liebermann I.148–166); Lambarde's L translation is also taken over;
2L5^r–2M1^r (pp. 419–423)	From 1568.2 X1^v–4^v: Laws I Edmund, II Edmund Prol., 1–5 (Liebermann I.184–188); Lambarde's L translation is also taken over; Spelman also had Wheelock's transcript of I Edmund (Add 35333, fo 45) from CCC 201, pp. 96–97;
2M2^r–3^r (pp. 425–427)	From CCC 383, 57^v/23–58^v/4 via a transcript by Wheelock (Oates 1986: 199): Law *Be wifmannes beweddunge* (Liebermann I.442–444); Spelman claims this MS as his source on 2M2^r, confirmed in Spelman's letter to Wheelock 12 Oct 1637; the L translation is Spelman's own;

2N1r–4v (pp. 435–442)	From BL Add 82931 (*olim* Earl of Macclesfield MS 24.g.9), 'Liber de Hyda' (s.xiv/xv), 27v–29r: Charter of King Edgar 966 to New Minster, Winchester (= Hyde), ed. Edwards 1866: 192–202 = Sawyer 745, Finberg 1964: no. 100, Birch no. 1190, L with AS names on 2N4v; the source MS is shown by the variant 'animaque' (not 'namque'), the second word in ch. 2;
2N5r–6r (pp. 443–445)	From 1568.2 Y1v–2v: Laws II Edgar Prol., 1–5,1 (Liebermann I.194–198);
2O1r–2O5v (pp. 447–456)	From BL Add 35333 (*olim* Phillipps 21538), art. 5, 45v/15–51r/15 (Wheelock's transcript of CCC 201, pp. 97/3–101/23), used as printer's copy with page-signatures and -numbers in the margin (Oates 1986: 199): Canons of Edgar, as Fowler 1972: 2–18, also Thorpe 1840: II.244–258; Spelman cites CCC 201 as his source on 2O1r;
2O5v–2P1v (pp. 456–460)	From Add 35333, art. 5, 51v/16–54v/2, 56r/1–10 (Wheelock's transcript of CCC 201, pp. 115/14–117/2 [annotations by (?)Wheelock occur on pp. 114 (bottom) and 117 (top)]): 'Directions for a Confessor' (*olim* Canons of Edgar), *De Confessione*, ed. Thorpe 1840: II.260–264; §§2–3 + next item §§1–2a (correct arrangement) ed. Fowler 1965: 19/82–20/112;
2P1v–5v (pp. 460–468)	From Add 35333, art. 5, 56r/11–62r/23 (Wheelock's transcript of CCC 201, pp. 117/9–121/10): 'Directions for a Confessor' (*olim* Canons of Edgar), *Modus Imponendi Poenitentiam*, as Thorpe 1840: II.266–276; §§2b–46 (correct arrangement) as Fowler 1965: 20/113–26/303;
2P5v–2Q2v (pp. 468–474)	From Add 35333, art. 5, 62v/1–67r/21 (Wheelock's transcript of CCC 201, pp. 121/11–124/8): 'Directions for a Confessor' (*olim* Canons of Edgar), *Be Dædbetan*, as Fowler 1965: 26/304–32/432, also Thorpe 1840: II.278–86;
2Q2v–3v (pp. 474–476)	From Add 35333, art. 5, 67v/1–68v/20 (Wheelock's transcript of CCC 201, pp. 124/8–125/9): 'Directions for a Confessor' (*olim* Canons of Edgar), *Be*

	mihtigum mannum, as Fowler 1965: 32/433–34/478, also Thorpe 1840: II.286–288;
2R6ʳ (p. 493)	From (prob) Tiberius A.vi, 34ʳ/14–21 or possibly Tiberius B.i, 143ʳ/21–143ᵛ/1 (Tiberius B.i shows Siðemann with double-n and erron. hıſ æt abbanðune for ıſ æt abbanðune): ASC 977, as Thorpe 1861: I.230; Tiberius B.i shows an annotation by Robert Talbot (16c) identifying Kẏptlıngtune as Kidlington (O) but Spelman's note fails to identify the place where Sideman, bp of Crediton, died;
2S1ʳ–4ᵛ (pp. 495–502)	From CCC 201, pp. 43/11–46/15: Law *Norðhymbra preosta* (Liebermann I.380–385);
2S5ᵛ–2T1ᵛ (pp. 504–508)	From Claudius A.iii, 4ʳ/1–5ᵛ/24: (?spurious) Charter of King Æthelred to Christ Church Canterbury 1006 for 1001, as Kemble 1839–48: III.no. 715, Wilkins 1737: I.282–284 = Sawyer 914, Hart 1966: no. 84; see also below, 3B3ᵛ.
2T2ᵛ–3ʳ (pp. 510–511)	From Claudius A.iii, 31ᵛ (sole witness): Metrical inscription *Halgungboc* printed as prose with end tapering to point (Dobbie, ASPR VI, 97; Ronalds and Ross 2001);
2T4ʳ–2V4ʳ (pp. 513–525)	From Claudius A.iii, 35ᵛ–8ᵛ (sole witness), prob via a transcript made for Spelman s.xvii in KSRL, MS E107, fos 207–210, apparently marked by the printer: AS Laws VI Æthelred, complete (Liebermann I.246–258);
2V6ʳ (p. 529)	From 1568.2 X1ᵛ: Law I Edmund Prol. (extract, coll Liebermann I.184);
2X5ʳ–2Y5ʳ (pp. 539–551)	From 1568.2 2D2ᵛ–2F4ᵛ, with ch. nos collated with (?)Harley 55: AS Laws I Cnut, complete (Liebermann I.278–306);
2Y5ᵛ–2Z3ᵛ (pp. 552–560)	From 1568.2 2F4ᵛ–2L4ᵛ: AS Laws II Cnut Prol., 1–6, 38–56,1, 66–7, 84–84,6 (Liebermann I.308–370);
3A3ᵛ–3B2ᵛ (pp. 572–582)	From CUL Gg.3.28, 264ʳ/19–266ᵛ/30 prob. via a transcript by Wheelock (cf. Oates 1986: 199): Ælfric's Letter to Wulfsige, bp of Sherborne 992–1001/2, as Fehr 1914:1–24, §§1–108; use of CCC 190, pp. 295–308 claimed on 3A3ᵛ, but Fehr's §§53, 73, 105–108 (ending imperf.) (= **1639.4** §§21, 27, 35) follow Gg.3.28;

3B3^r (p. 583)   From CUL Gg.3.28, 1^v/10–15 (sole witness): Ælfric, Preface to CH1 (Clemoes 1996: 174/44–50);

3B3^v (p. 584)   From above 2T1^r (= Claudius A.iii, 5^v/17): (?spurious) Charter of King Æthelred to Christ Church Canterbury 1006 for 1001 (extract from witness list), as Kemble 1839–48: III.no. 715, p. 351; see above 2S5^v–2T1^v.

3B4^r–3E2^r (pp. 585–617)   From CCC 201, pp. 231/1–269/6 and 179–222: OE and L versions of the Capitula of Theodulf of Orléans (c.760–821), OE and L as Sauer 1978: 304–403 (There is a draft of this section, heavily revised, in KSRL, MS E107, fos 38–54, apparently marked by the printer);

3E2^v (p. 618)   From (prob) CUL Hh.1.10, 1^v/26–2^r/6: Ælfric's Grammar, Preface (extract), as Zupitza 1891 coll. as U: 3/9–16.

Note: The 'Synodus alia S. Patricii' on sig. D3^r–5^r is from a transcript supplied by Ussher (now BL Add 25384, 17^r–20^r), as also acknowledged by Spelman on sig. D5^r.

TYPE:

Main text in Pierre Haultin's English-size Roman (Body 93) interspersed with Granjon's 3rd English-size Italic

AS4: The Spelmanian Great Primer Anglo-Saxon combined with a Great Primer Roman (mixed sorts) occurs in the specimen on [*]3^v, in text as indicated above, and in words on T6^r (p. 241), 2K3^r (p. 403), 2M1^v (p. 424), 2T3^v (p. 512).

Specimen: special sorts shown: 11 lower-case sorts: ð, f, ȝ, ı, ƿ, ꞃ, ꞇ, ẏ; þ, ð, p;
10 capitals: Æ^1, Æ^2, Ɫ, Ɛ, Ꝺ, Ꞃ, Ꞅ, Þ, Ð, Ꝑ;
2 others: ꝫ, þ.
Total: 23 sorts.

Failure to show AS e may be an error as Roman e occurs twice, the first probably in place of AS e, which was not perhaps ready, or the distinctiveness of which was not appreciated by the printer, as it does not appear in the text until O6^v. Contrast C, which is not heavily used (Roman C being preferred), but AS Ɫ occurs on K3^r, the first page of OE text.

Text: special sorts shown: all plus e (1st on O6^v).   12 + 10 + 2 = 24 sorts.

AS3: Lambardian Pica Anglo-Saxon combined with Pierre Haultin's Pica Roman (which occurs normally on I6ᵛ) occurs in words on a1ᵛ, and in catchwords on 3C5ᵛ, 3D3ᵛ;

Special sorts shown: ð, e, ꝼ, ȝ, ı, þ, ꞃ, ꞇ; p; Є, Ꝼ, Ꝺ. 9 + 3 + 0 = 12 sorts.

Copies seen: CCA W/R.8.24 (Somner's copy with his annotations); CUL B*.3.22(B) (lacks [*]4); LFL 5H (lacks [*]4); MBS Res/2⁰Conc.c.58; OBL S1.1.Th.Seld. (Selden's copy);

(lacking [*]4 and a8) CUL R.13.18 (lacks §1), Ely.a.190; OBL L.2.12.Art. [with annotations by Somner, owned by William Elstob 1700 (who collated the text of the AS Law *Be wifmannes beweddunge* with that in the Textus Roffensis), Richard Rawlinson s.xviii];

BL 7.f.4 (complete with variant printing of lectori at a8); (lacking [*]4 and a8): BL 494.l.1 (with [*]3–4 before [*]1–2, lacks a8; red morocco binding gold-tooled for Charles II); CUL Pet.P.4.4 (given by Thomas Woolsey, archdeacon of Northampton, 1708); CCC D.1.5 (given by the author, with his handwritten corrections on, e.g., §5ᵛ, O4ᵛ–P3ᵛ, 2O5ᵛ; gold-tooled contemporary binding of brown calf); OBL Gough Eccl.top.74 (with annotations by W. Kennet). Corrections to 1639.4 by Somner and Ussher are to be found in OBL MS Jones 13 (SC 8920), and OBL MS Add. C.301 respectively.

Copies also at: APL, BPL, BUT, ChC, ECC, CGC, CJC, KCC, CMC, CNC, CPC, CPH, CSJ, CSS, TCC, CaCL, ChCL, DAL, DCL, DWL, ECL, Eton, EUL, GUL, HCL, IMC, LCL, LGL, LHL, LHU, LlCL, LMT, LSH, NCCL, NLS, NT, OAS, OBrC, OCC, OJC, OKC, OLC, OMaC, OMC, ONC, OOC, OPH, OQC, ORP, OSJ, OStE, OUC, OWoC, SAC, SCL, SRO, WAL, WCC, WCL, WiCL, YML, DKI, DML, KSC, TCD, ULim, BSB; FSL, USLC, NYPL, NYCU, UTS, HHL, HUL IUL, CUofA, EmU, KSRL, NLC, SLU, UCBL, UTK, UVL, YUB; UTL.

Bibliography: Clement 1989: 12; Moore 1992: 17, 42, pl. 48; Parry 1995: 168–173; Powicke 1930. GR 6284.

Manuscript: BL Add 34600, 139ʳ–144ᵛ, contains several drafts of the dedication to Charles I (§3ʳ–6ʳ), the first with amendments by Ussher. OBL e Mus.49 is the original MS copy of vol. 2.

Manuscript (Printer's Copy): OBL Tanner 288 (SC 10115), 27ʳ–36ᵛ (sig. §3ʳ–6ʳ). KSRL E107 contains what is apparently printer's copy of items at 2T4ʳ–2V4ʳ and 3B4ʳ–3E2ʳ (see above).

Note: Vol 2 (from the Norman Conquest to Henry VIII), ed. William Dugdale (London: Alice Warren 1664; Wing S4920) contains no Anglo-Saxon.

1639.5: Camden, William, *Guili. Camdeni Viri Clarissimi Britannia*, the abridged edn by Reyner V. Zierikzee (**1617.2**). Amsterdam: Willem Jansz. Blaeu, 1639. USTC 1032364.

    Collation: 12⁰: A–T¹² V⁶ 234 leaves.

AS names appear in Italic with no special sorts, e.g., D6ᵛ (p. 84).

    Copy seen: CUL Yorke.e.9.

    Copies also at: BL, AUL, TCC, DUL, NLS, OBL, OXC, PBN, OMM, SBPU, AUB, HKB, GRUB, WHAB, SKB, PNL, RBN, MAS, MBFZ, ACRC; NYPL, IUL.

1640.1: Somner, William, *The Antiquities of Canterbury*. London: John Legat II for Richard Thrale, 1640. STC 22918; ESTC S121902. AS3.
Legal Agreement

    Collation: 4⁰: *⁴ 2*⁴ A–3T⁴ 3V⁴ (+χ1) [$3 signed (-*1,3)] 273 leaves, paginated [i–xvi], 1–516, *517–530*.

    Note: Illustrations have been inserted between sig. 2*4ᵛ and A1ʳ, between F3ᵛ and F4ʳ, and between Z2ᵛ and Z3ʳ.

SOURCES OF PASSAGES UTILIZING ANGLO-SAXON TYPES:

2Z2ᵛ (p. 364)   From BL Stowe Charter 30: Property sale agreement (968), extract from §2: Sawyer 1215, Birch 1885–99: III.491, no. 1212;

2Z3ʳ (p. 365)   From a lost MS: Agreement between Christ Church and the Merchant Guild, Canterbury (Pelteret 90). Ed. Urry 1967: 385 from **1640.1**.

TYPE:

Main text in Pierre Haultin's English-size Roman (Body 93) interspersed with Robert Granjon's first English-size Italic.

AS3: The Lambardian Pica Anglo-Saxon (Body 80) is combined with a Pica Roman (small amount on the 2 pages with AS text; Face 78 x 1.7: 2.8) and occurs in text on 2Z2ᵛ, 2Z3ʳ, and in words on A1ᵛ (p. 2), T3ʳ (p. 149).

Special sorts shown: 12 lower-case sorts: ð, *e*, ꝼ, ᵹ, 1, ꝑ, ꞃ, ꞇ, ẏ; þ, ð̄, ƿ;
                    5 capitals: Æ², Є, Ꝥ, 8, Ð;
                      1 other: ꞃ.
                    Total: 18 sorts.

Note 1: AS Ꝥ used in text once only in the name Ꝥloðpiᵹ on 2S2ᵛ.
Note 2: Є, Ꝥ occur in Latin on N3ᵛ (p. 102).

    Copies seen: CCA W2/B.4.11 (interleaved copy with corrections added in Somner's hand); OBL 4⁰.S.41.Art.Seld. (Without errata leaf): CUL L*.10.47(D), Lib.6.64.1, Acton.c.25.703; OBL Douce ss.162, Gough Kent 13 (with copy of letter from Somner to Meric Casaubon and other notes), Wood 388 (uncropped).

Copies also at: BL, BAL, CJC, CMC, CPC, CTH, TCC, CaCL, CUK, MJRUL, LCL, LGL, LHL, LPL, LSH, MTP, NLS, NUL, OCC, OEC, OEF, OJC, OLC, OOC, OQC, OTC OUC, OWmC, OXC, LRS, SACL, SCL, SPC, UCL, WCC, WCL, WIHM, TCD, BSB; FSL, NYCU, HHL, HUL, IUL, AAS, CUofA, DDUL, HCP, JCB, KSRL, NLC, NWU, TCH, UTA, YUB, QUK; ATL.

Note: A large-paper edition presented to Charles II on his Restoration is now HHL 60681 (Urry 1997: xiv).

Bibliography: Parry 1995: 182–185; Parry 1997; Urry 1967: 385; Urry 1977: ix, xvii.

1640.2: Jonson, Ben [ed. Sir Kenelm Digby], *The English Grammar*, in *Workes of Benjamin Jonson. The Second Volume.* London: [John Dawson 2] for [Thomas Walkley and] Richard Meighen, 1640. STC 14754; USTC S111824, booklet 5. Italic þ; woodblock ð.

Note 1: Since vol. I was printed by Richard Bishop, who possessed AS1, the lack of such sorts and the resort to crude substitutes is notable; co-operation between the printers of vols I and II was evidently nil in this respect.

Note 2: Ben Jonson borrowed a manuscript containing 'Alfricus Grammar Saxon' (prob Julius A.ii) from Cotton's library (MS Harley 6018, 149^v). He owned copies of 1571.1, 1610.2 (ex dono auctoris), 1614.3, 1622.1, 1623.3 (ex dono editoris); see McPherson 1974.

OE letter symbols

Collation (Booklet 5 only): 2°: A–K^4 L^2 M–R^4 [$2 signed (-A1)] 70 leaves, paginated 1–132 (pp. 30–33 unnumbered).

TYPE:
Latin text in Robert Granjon's English-size Italic (Body 95);
English text in Pierre Haultin's English-size Roman (Body 93);
Italic þ (two designs) made to fit with this (or slightly larger?) on G1^v–2^r.
Very crude ð of rather large proportions also shown.

Copies seen: CUL Syn.4.64.14 (used by Percy Simpson); OBL Gibson 520, Vet.A2. d.73, and Don.d.66 (with sig. L between K2 and K3); CCA W2/A.2.12 (Somner's copy acquired 1646 for 9s inscribed on tp); CUL Syn.4.64.15 (gift of Percy Simpson).

Copies also at: BL, BCL, ChC, CGC, KCC, CNC, TCC, DUL, EdUL, MJRUL, LCL, MTP, NCL, OAS, OBrC, OCC, OHM, OQC, OWmC, SCL, StA, UBL, UCL, DML, BSB; FLS, USLC, NYPL, NYCU, HHL, HUL, IUL, BJH, BPM, DDUL, KSRL, NWU, PUL, SLC, TCU, UCBL, UCLA, UMI, UVL; ANZ, ATL.

Bibliography: Greg 1939–57: III.1079–1081; Alston I.no. 8; Dobson 1968: I.324–327; Funke 1940; Herford & Simpson 1925–52: II.416–435.

Facsimile: English Linguistics 1500–1800, no. 349 (Menston: Scolar, 1972).

1640.3: 'put forth by' Spelman, Sir John, under the direction of his father Sir Henry Spelman (quotation from CUL Dd.3.12, 49r: H. Spelman to Wheelock 17 Sept 1639), *Psalterium Davidis Latino-Saxonicum Vetus*. London: Richard Badger 1 for Philemon Stephens and Christopher Meredith, 1640 (sig. B by Richard Bishop). STC 2369; ESTC S102229. AS3, but AS2 in sig. B.

> Note: Apparently Bishop was the Spelmans' first choice of printer, but when his compositor left him by 31 Aug 1638 and he 'dalied and delaied' (as first noted by Oates 1966: 28), the business was transferred to Badger by 5 Sept 1638, the dates of H. Spelman's letters to Wheelock (CUL MS Dd.3.12, 28^r, 29^r). The imprimatur for this edition dated 17 May 1638 occurs in BL MS Stowe 2, 180^v, along with the name of Sir Henry Spelman, who owned this MS, which was used as the basis of the edition.

Stowe Psalter

> Collation: 4^0: A–2Y^4 2Z^2 [$3 signed (-A1,3, B1, 2Z2)] 182 leaves, unnumbered. State 2 of sig. B shown by B1 signed.

SOURCES OF PASSAGES UTILIZING ANGLO-SAXON TYPES:

B1^r–2Z2^r From BL Stowe 2, 1^r–168^v, collated with CUL Ff.1.23, TCC R.17.1, and BL Arundel 60: L Psalter with OE glosses, as Kimmens 1979.

Type: Sig. B was set by Bishop, the rest by Badger.

(1) Sig. B: main Latin Psalter text in a Great Primer Italic (with 3.5 mm capitals); AS2: The Parkerian Pica Anglo-Saxon combined with a Pica Roman is used for the AS text interlined above the Latin.

Special sorts shown: ð, ꝼ, ᵹ, ı, ꝥ, ꞃ, ꞇ, ẏ; þ, ð, p; þ, ꝧ, ꝗ.   11 + 0 + 3 = 14 sorts.

(2) All except sig. B: main Latin Psalter text in a Great Primer Italic.

AS3: The Lambardian Pica Anglo-Saxon occurs in the specimen on A4^v and is combined with Pierre Haultin's 2nd Pica Roman (which occurs independently on A4^v) used for the AS text interlined above the Latin.

Special sorts shown:

(1) in the specimen

ð, e, ꝼ, ᵹ, ı, ꝥ, ꞃ, ꞇ, ẏ; þ, ð, p; Є, Ꜩ, Ꝡ, Ꞅ, Ð; þ, ꝧ.   12 + 5 + 2 = 19 sorts.

(2) in the text

ð, e, ꝼ, ᵹ, ı, ꝥ, ꞃ, ꞇ, ẏ; þ, ð, p;   þ, ꝧ, ꝗ.   12 + 0 + 3 = 15 sorts.

Total = 20 sorts.

Manuscript: Draft 'Lectori' by Sir Henry Spelman in BL Add 34600, 124^r, followed on 125^r by a collation of the matter following the Psalter in the three manuscripts used, and then by notes sent by Johannes de Laet with his letter of 30 Oct 1638, pr. Bremmer 2008: 173–174.

> **Copies seen:** with B1 unsigned: CUL Syn.5.64.15; TCC A.8.78 (with contemporary gold-tooled binding), C.28.2 (lacks 2A–2Y); OBL 4^0.P.23.Th.Seld., MS Junius 33 (SC 5145) with collations in Junius's hand from MS V[esp.A.i] = Vespasian Psalter

(ed. Sweet 1885, facs. ed. Wright 1967), Ps.Anglo-Sax.d.2 (with tags for Psalm nos and annotations by Joseph Bosworth); with B1 signed: BL 1008.b.6; CCA W/B.2.23; CUL Syn.5.64.16; CCC Y.2.10; ECC S10.2.13 (Abp Sancroft's copy); TCC Adv.c.18.68 (W. Aldis Wright's copy with his textual corrections preparatory to the partial edition by Harsley 1889); OBL Douce BB.161, Gough Sax.lit.194, MM.2.Th.².

Copies also at: BSEC, CCA, CGC, CJC, KCC, CPC, CSJ, CaCL, DUL, ECL, LCL, MTP, NLS, NUL, OAS, OBC, OBrC, OEF, OHC, OLC, OMaC, OOC, OQC, OSA, OSJ, OUC, OWoC, SPC, SRO, UCL, WCC, WoCL, DKI, DML, TCD, GUB; FSL, HHL, HUL, IUL, KSRL, PST, UTA, UVL, YUB.

Bibliography: Kimmens 1979; Hombergen 1983; McKitterick 1992: 198–199; Oates 1966: 28; Oates 1986: 201–202; Pulsiano 1994: 65–68 (description of MS Stowe 2); Temple 1976: no. 99 (MS Stowe 2); Vaciago 1993: no. 99 (MS Stowe 2). GR 5936.

1640.4: Selden, John, *De Iure Naturali & Gentium, iuxta Disciplinam Ebræorum.* London: Richard Bishop, 1640. STC 22168; ESTC S117078. AS1.

OE Gospels, Orosius, Law of Alfred (extracts)

   Collation: 2^0 in 4s: π⁴ b–d⁴ A–5P⁴ [$2 signed (+S3)] 444 leaves, paginated [i–xl], 1–847, *848*.

SOURCES OF PASSAGES UTILIZING ANGLO-SAXON TYPES:

4D4ʳ (p. 575)   From 1571.1 C4ʳ, D2ᵛ, D3ʳ, 2L2ᵛ, V3ʳ, 2V4ʳ, 2O2ʳ, L1ʳ: OE Gospels: Mt.5.31, Lk.1.28, 42, 11.27, Mk.7.26, Jn.4.7, Lk.16.18, Mt.19.10;

   From Tiberius B.i, 106ʳ/13: OE Orosius VI.xxx, two words hıſ pıſ for L 'concubina'; over OE cıeſeſe (mostly erased) a later hand (but Selden says 'nec manu recenti') has written 'wife' (Bately 1980: 148/9n.); for the Latin see PL 31: 1124; for the OE and Latin side by side, Sweet 1883: 282–283.

5O4ʳ (p. 839)   From 1568.2 I2ᵛ: Preface to Law of Alfred 49.5 (extract), as Liebermann I.44; the form eope is distinctive.

TYPE:

Main text in Arthur Nicholls's English-size Roman (Body 94 on 3C2ᵛ, otherwise leaded) interspersed with his English-size Italic, and with other exotic fonts.

AS1: The Parkerian Great Primer Anglo-Saxon acquired by Day occurs in combination with a Pica Roman in text as indicated under Contents above and in words on 3L4ʳ, 3M2ᵛ.

Special sorts shown:	11 lower-case sorts:	ð, f, ȝ, ı, ƿ, ſ, τ, ẏ; þ, ð, ꝑ;
	5 capitals:	Æ², Є, Ꝺ, Ꝏ, Đ;
	4 others:	þ, ꝫ, ꝫ (large), ȷ.
	Total:	20 sorts.

Note: Both ð's are shown on 4D4ʳ, the one that fits snugly to the previous letter (e.g. ꞅꝛemað) and the (earlier) one that does not (e.g. ꞅoðlıce).

  Copies seen: APL RR.III.26; CUL C.8.47 (gift of George I, 1715), Q*.9.28(C), Hunt.23.7 (lacks π1, 4X4, and sigs 4Y–5P), CCC M.2.15.

  Copies also at: BL, ChC, ECC KCC, CPC, CSJ, TCC, CaCL, CUW, DWL, EAL, ECL, Eton, GML, GUL, LiCL, LMT, LPL, LSH, NLS, NT, OBL, OBC, OLMH, ONC, OPC, OQC, OTC, OWoC, OXC, SPC, StA, WiCL, WoCL, YML, DML, TCD, GCB, BSB; FSL, USLC, NYSL, NYCU, HHL, HUL, IUL, UCH, UCLA, YUB.

Bibliography: Toomer 2009: II.490–562.

1640?.1: Lambarde, William, *A Perambulation of Kent.* 3rd edn of 1576.2, re-set from 2nd edn 1596.1. London: Richard Hodgkinson for Daniel Pakeman, (?)1640. STC 15176.5; ESTC S124362. AS3 with AS2 s.

Extracts from Charters, Laws, Wills

  Collation: 8⁰: A–C⁸ ²C⁸ D–2T⁸ 2U⁴. [$4 signed (-A1, 2U4); C2–4 missigned B2–4] 398 leaves, paginated [i–xvi], 1–656, 657–680.

SOURCES OF PASSAGES UTILIZING ANGLO-SAXON TYPES:

  Note: The first and third of these passages are supplied with a double-decker translation, literal above the text and interpretative above the literal; the fourth occasionally has a triple-decker translation, with two interpretative versions above the literal.

2D2ʳ–4ᵛ	From 1596.2 2B6ᵛ–8ʳ: AS Charter listing estates liable for work on Rochester Bridge;
2L2ᵛ	From 1596.2 2H7ᵛ: William I: London Charter in AS, §1, extract;
2L6ᵛ–2M2ᵛ	From 1596.2 2I3ᵛ–6ʳ: Will of Byrhtric;
2M4ʳ–5ᵛ	From 1596.2 2I7ᵛ–8ʳ: AS Law 'Geþyncðo', §§1–7;
2S5ᵛ	From 1596.2 2P1ʳ: Dubious AS 'verse' Neȝheeꞅyþe.

TYPE:

Main text in Arthur Nicholls's Pica Roman interspersed with Robert Granjon's second Pica Italic (*pendante*), to be seen especially on T6–7, Y3, Y6, 2O6ᵛ, 2T1ʳ–2V3ᵛ.

AS3: The Lambardian Pica Anglo-Saxon occurs in combination with Nicholls's Pica Roman throughout but especially on 2D2ʳ–4ᵛ, 2L2ᵛ, 2L6ᵛ–2M2ᵛ, 2M4ʳ–5ᵛ, 2S5ᵛ; it occurs in a catchword on 2M3ʳ.

The full range of sorts occurs (but ƿ is lacking):

    13 lower-case sorts: ð, e, ꞅ, ȝ, h, ı, ꞃ, ꞅ, τ, ẏ; þ, ð, p;
    7 capitals: Æ¹, Æ², E, M, S, Ð, P;
    3 others: þ, ꞇ, ꞌ;
  Total: 23 sorts.

Note 1: There are two sorts for s, one as normal in AS3, and one as found in AS2, of Parkerian design; the Parkerian one can be seen, e.g., at 2D2R/24 Æpeʀt.
Note 2: Lower-case and upper-case p can be seen side by side at 2L2ᵛ/9.
Granjon's 2nd Pica Italic is used for the translation above the AS passages.

    Copies seen: CUL R.6.6[1] lacks E2(c1) (beginning of catchword on ²C8ᵛ not inked; K6ᵛ has first letter too high 'ᵗt'); OBL Crynes 522 (2T1–3 misbound at the end) lacks E2(c1), OBL Gough Kent 68 (2T1–3 misbound at the end) lacks E2(c1).

    Copies also at: APL, BL, NT, WAL; KSRL.

Bibliography: see 1576.2.

1641.1: Spelman, Sir Henry, *De Sepultura*. London: Robert Young for Matthew Walbancke and William Cooke, 1641. Wing S4924; ESTC R14887. AS4.

Laws I Cnut (extract)

    Collation: A–E⁴ F² [$2 signed (+A3; -A1–2, F2)] 22 leaves, paginated [i–iv], 1–38, *39–40*.

SOURCES OF PASSAGE UTILIZING ANGLO-SAXON TYPES:

E4ᵛ (p. 36)   From 1568.2 2E3ᵛ: AS Law I Cnut 13 (Liebermann I.294); the text apparently reflects Lambarde's readings pihtæʀt, -hpæpe.

TYPE:

Main text in Pierre Haultin's English-size Roman (Body 92);

AS4: Spelmanian Great Primer Anglo-Saxon (Body 117.5) combined with Haultin's English-size Roman (except for a Paragon œ-ligature used for OE æ), occurs on E4ᵛ, and in one word only on F1ʳ;

Special sorts shown: 9 lower-case sorts: ð, e, ȝ, ı, p, ſ, t, ẏ; ð, p;

                        2 others: þ, ꝥ;

                        Total: 11 sorts.

    Copies seen: APL KE.V.16A[11]; CUL Dd.*2.16[10](D), ECC 327.5.93[10]; OBL 4⁰.B.96[4]; OBL Gough Lond. 165[5], Radcl.e.53[9], and TCD ss.n.87[3] (Claudius Gilbert's copy) lack A1; CUL G.11.45 and OBL C.13.11[8].Linc. lack F2; CUL R.10.18[8] and OBL Pamph.C.43[6] lack A1 and F2; TCD P.ff.12 lacks A1, F1.2.

    2nd state (records on sig. F1ᵛ that the work was written in 1630): CUL sss.57.1; TCD FF.hh.16².

    Copies also at: BL, BCL, CSJ, TCC, CLL, DWL, EdUL, Eton, GML, HOL, MJRUL, LCL, LHL, LWI, MTP, NLS, NT, OBC, OCC, OEC, OJC, OMaC, OSJ, OWoC, SoUL, SUL, UCL, YML; FSL, USLC, NYPL, UTS, HHL, HUL, IUL, KSRL, NLC, NLM, NWU, PFL, SLC, UCLA, UOC, UTA, UVL, YUB; MonUL, UWA.

Manuscripts:

CUL Dd.3.40 (Baker and Ringrose 1996: 12–13), apparently a fair copy, s.xvii[1], some slight differences of word order, ends incomplete at 1641.1 E2ʳ/10, so there is no AS text copied.

TCD 733 (G.4.11), art. 1, is another fair copy, s.xvii, with unnumbered leaves, but it does not include the AS text.
Bibliography: Parry 1995: 165–166.

1641.2: Foxe, John (ed.), *The Second Volume of the Ecclesiasticall History, containing the Acts and Monuments of Martyrs*. 8th edn (vol. II, bks 7 and 8 only) of 1570.1 (= 2nd edn) reset from 7th edn 1631.3. London: no printer stated, for the Stationers' Co., 1641. Wing F2035; ESTC R29862. AS3.
Extracts from 1566.1, 1567.1 taken from 1631.3
  Collation (vol. II, including preliminaries, books 7 and 8 only): 2⁰ in 6s: πA⁸ πB⁶ 2πA⁴ 2πB⁴ *4 2*4 3*4 A⁴ B–I⁶ K⁸ L–3H⁶ [$3 signed (+ πA4; -πA1,2; πA1,2 signed A3,4, ²πB3 missigned B2, G2 missigned C2)] 356 leaves, paginated [i–xliv], *1–22, *23–24, [5], 6–650 (pp. nos 112–113 used twice; pp. 122 misnumbered 121, 176 misnumbered 166, 257 misnumbered 258, 262 misnumbered 226, 269 misnumbered 279, 352 misnumbered 350, 402 misnumbered 400, 409 misnumbered 309, 424 misnumbered 426, 452–453 misnumbered 552–553, 459 misnumbered 458, 490 misnumbered 492, 494 misnumbered 449, 515 misnumbered 513, 520 misnumbered 522, 588 misnumbered 586).
SOURCES OF PASSAGES UTILIZING ANGLO-SAXON TYPES:
These passages are from 1631.3 re-set page by page without AS sorts:
2P1ʳ/b (p. 447)   From 1631.3 2P1ʳ/b, Ælfric's 'Excusatio Dictantis' (opening statement) at the end of his homily *Depositio S. Martin* (Godden 1979: XXXIV);
2P1ʳ/b (p. 447)   From 1631.3 2P1ʳ/b, Ælfric's *Grammar*, opening statement from OE Preface (cf. Zupitza 1880: 2);
These passages are from 1631.3 re-set line by line with spasmodic AS sorts:
2P1ᵛ/a/18–36 (p. 448)   From 1631.3 2P1ᵛ/a/18–36, Ælfric's letter to Wulfsige III (bp of Sherborne 992–1002) extracts (Fehr 1914: §§135–142);
2P1ᵛ/b/1–2P2ʳ/a/6 (pp. 448–9)   From 1631.3 2P1ᵛ/b/1–2P2ʳ/a/6, Ælfric's second letter to Wulfstan (abp of York 1002–23) extracts (Fehr 1914: §§86–95, 97–109);
2P2ᵛ/a/64–2P4ʳ/b/31 (pp. 450–3)   From 1631.3 2P2ᵛ/a/64–2P4ʳ/b/31, Ælfric's *Sermo de Sacrificio in die Pascae* (same omissions as 1570.1; Godden 1979: XV);
This passage is from 1631.3 re-set page by page without AS sorts:
2S1ᵛ/a/47–51 (p. 484)   From 1631.3 2S1ᵛ/a/47–51, ASC (E), annal for 1129 (Clark 1954: 51).
TYPE:
Main text in a Small Pica Textura (Body 71.5) interspersed with a Small Pica Roman.

AS3: The Lambardian Pica Anglo-Saxon is combined (with very poor use of the special sorts) with Arthur Nicholls's Pica Roman (Body 81) on 2P1ᵛ–4ʳ:
AS specimen on 2P2ᵛ shows the following special sorts (not all the sorts used, but including p, which is not used in the text):

        11 lower-case sorts: ð, e, f, ʒ, ƿ, ſ, τ, ẏ; þ, ð, p;
        3 capitals: Æ², S, Ð;
        1 other: ꝫ;
  Total: 15 sorts.

Special sorts shown in the text:
        10 lower-case sorts: ð, e, f, ʒ, ƿ, ſ, τ, ẏ; þ, ð;
        7 capitals: Æ¹, Æ², E, Ꝺ, Ꟃ, S, Ð;
        3 others: þ, ꝫ, ꝫ;
  Total: 20 sorts.

Overall total 11 + 7 + 3 = 21 sorts.
Note. OE passages on 2P1ʳ/b and 2S1ᵛ/a are set in the Small Pica Roman (without AS sorts) used for the main text.

Copies seen: CUL P.1.11 (= vol. II); ECC 314.1.42 (= vol. II); LFL 12H; OBL D.1.2.Th.Seld. (= vol. II) lacks A1,2 (Selden's copy, binding with gold tooled ornament), Douce F subt.7 (= vol. II) lacks 3*4, A1,2.

Copies also at: BL, BCLW, BPL, BrCaL, BUW, BUT, CCA, CCC, CJC, KCC, CMC, CUW, DWL, EAL, EdUL, GML GUL, LBL, LGL, LiCL, LMT, LQL, LSH, NAL, NLS, NLW, NT, NUL, OBrC, OHM, OQC, ORP, OSP, OXC, RCL, SAC, SDC, SoUL, SUL, UBL, WAL, WCC, WoCL, DML, NLI, TCD; FSL, USLC, NYPM, UTS, HHL, HUL, BMC, CUofA, KSRL, LCP, NLC, NWU, PSL, PTS, SIU, TCH, UCBL, UCH, UCLA, UTA, YUB; MonUL, SSA.

Bibliography: see 1570.1.

1641.3: Holdsworth, Richard (ed., for Cambridge University), *Irenodia Cantabrigiensis ob Paciferum Serenissimi Regis Caroli è Scotia Reditum* (verses celebrating the return of Charles I from his visit to Scotland, whose allegiance he secured against the English parliament). Cambridge: Roger Daniel, 1641. Wing C340; ESTC R10511. AS5.
17c verse compositions using OE words by William Retchford and Abraham Wheelock
    Collation: 4⁰: ¶⁴ A–K⁴ L² [$3 signed (-¶1, L2)] 46 leaves, unnumbered.
SOURCES OF PASSAGES UTILIZING ANGLO-SAXON TYPES:
A4ʳ Verse translation *Anglo-& Scoto-Saxonicè* by Wheelock of his own Hebrew composition (A3ᵛ), beginning 'SCotland buton feohte';
G4ʳ Verse composition by William Retchford, beginning 'EAla ðu Garsecges lond'.

Note: These verse compositions may have been partly inspired by reading the ME *Metrical Chronicle* attributed to 'Robert of Gloucester' in TCC R.4.26, cited by Wheelock in 1643.1, where brief extracts are printed in Anglo-Saxon type.

TYPE:

Main text in Pierre Haultin's English-size Roman (Body 94).

AS5: The Wheelockian Great Primer Anglo-Saxon combined with a Great Primer Roman occurs in text on A4ʳ and G4ʳ.

Special sorts shown: 12 lower-case sorts: ð, *e*, f, ȝ, ı, ꝑ, ꞃ, ꞇ, ẏ; þ, ð, ƿ;
                         9 capitals: D, Ɛ, F, Ꞅ, I, S, Ð, U, Ƿ;
                         1 other: ȷ̇;
                Total: 22 sorts.

Copies seen: CUL Cam.c.641.1, SSS.32.26, SSS.37.9;

BL, Bagford Collection, Harley 5929, item no. 435, preserves sig. A4 cut down to 158 × 108 mm and pasted (with the recto side uppermost) in a scrap-book anthology.

Copies also at: BL, BCL, CCC, CCL, KCC, DWL, DUL Eton, GUL, LCL, LiCL, LPL, MJRUL, MTP NLS, NT, OBL, OAS, OBC, OBrC, OLC, OQC, PUY, UBL, WCF, YML; FSL, HHL, HUL, IUL, MUL, NLC, NWU, UCLA, UTA, YUB.

Bibliography: Forster 1982: 157; Murphy 1982: 27–28; Oates 1986: 204; Utley 1942.

1642.1: Kiliaan (van Kiel), Cornelis, *Kilianus Auctus seu Dictionarium Teutonico-Latino-Gallicum*, 5th edn of **1599.2** (= 3rd edn). Amsterdam: Jan and Jodocus Janssonius 1642. USTC 1013692 & 1030494.

    Collation: 8⁰: *⁴ A–Z⁸ 3A⁴ (lacks 3A4, blank?). Fos [392]

Words in AS and other appropriate languages appear in Italic with no special sorts.

    Copy seen: BL 965.c.17.

    Copies also at: NLS, OBL, OJC, OTI, OUC, DML, PBN, PBSG, GCB, AUB, HKB, LUB, NUB, UTUB, LUBS, MRA.

1643.1: Bede, ed. Abraham Wheelock, *Historiæ Ecclesiasticæ Gentis Anglorum Libri V a Venerabili Beda Presbytero scripti*; *Chronologia Anglo-Saxonica* [= ASC]. Cambridge: Roger Daniel, 1643. Wing B1661; ESTC R2636. AS5.

    Date: 1643/4. The *Ad Lectorem* (B1ʳ) refers to the death of Samuel Ward (7 Sept 1643; ODNB); cf. Oates 1986: 205, n. 29. The tp of the subsidiary on 3T3ʳ carries the date 1644.

    Collation: 2⁰ in 4s: A⁴ B–4E⁴ 4F² [$3 signed (-A1, 3T3, 4F2; P1 apparently signed 'P' with 'O' overprinted)] 298 leaves, paginated [i–xvi], 1–570, *571–580* (pp. nos 464–467 not used; pp. nos 487–490 used twice; pp. 20, 160, 500–502 not numbered; pp. 485–486 misnumbered 481–482).

Note 1: Paste-on cancels are supplied on (1) B2ʳ, (2) L2ʳ, (3) 2E4ʳ, (4) 2Q1ᵛ, (5) 3S4ʳ, (6) 4E2ʳ, (7) 4E3ʳ, but are not always present; sometimes corrections (1) and (5) are supplied in ink; (8) deletion of part of a marginal note at 3F1ᵛ also occurs.

Note 2: There are two variants of 3T3, one, the original, showing a dedication to Sir Simonds D'Ewes, which is presumably the one usually cut out, and another (substituted) showing a sub-title-page for the *Anglo-Saxon Chronicle* dated 1644.

Bede, *Historia Ecclesiastica* (Old English and Latin); *Anglo-Saxon Chronicle* (Old English and Latin); Ælfric, extracts from *CH*, *LS*, etc.; Wulfstan, anonymous homilies, etc.

Context: Wheelock was appointed to the Lectureship in Anglo-Saxon at Cambridge University established by Sir Henry Spelman with the encouragement of James Ussher, archbishop of Armagh. Counselled by Ussher, Wheelock inherited the Parkerian view of Anglo-Saxon materials as useful for bolstering the doctrine and practice of the Church of England (even in the midst of a civil war that drew encouragement on the parliamentary side from what were believed to be 'free' Anglo-Saxon constitutional arrangements); cf. Murphy 1967. This approach, spelt out in the dedication to Cambridge University, is heralded in his letter to Spelman dated 13 June 1638:

I am now readinge of Beda, with King Alured his translation. which[,] I see, will correct many thinges, ... but the maine busines which possesseth my thoughtes, is, the discovery (out of Bede, & others, especiallie in manuscripts) of the Apostolical doctrine, by comparinge our present church with the auncient church here in England: which work will most properlie suite with your reader [i.e. Wheelock himself], because he is to be a searcher of truthes out of the fountaines themselues (BL Add 25384, 29ᵛ).

SOURCES OF PASSAGES UTILIZING ANGLO-SAXON TYPES:

B1ʳ   From CUL Gg.3.28, 157ᵛ/16–18: Ælfric, CH2, Sancti Gregorii Pape (extract), as Godden 1979: IX, 72/heading, 6–8;

C1ʳ–3T2ʳ (pp. 1–499)   From CUL Kk.3.18, collated with CCC 41 and Otho B.xi (+ leaves in Otho B.x; damaged by fire but copied before the fire by Nowell in BL Add 43703): OE version of Bede's *Historia Ecclesiastica*, as Miller 1890–8, with the WS Genealogical Regnal List interpolated between the Preface and the *Capitula* (as only in Kk.3.18);

Note: In a letter to Sir Thomas Cotton dated 31 Mar 1640 (Julius F.vi, 128ʳ) Wheelock thanks Sir Thomas for the loan of 'Beda his hist. Lat. et Sax.' (i.e. Otho B.xi, which also includes ASC); pr. Ellis 1843: 160.

C3ʳ–4ʳ (pp. 5–7)   From Kk.3.18, 3ᵛ–4ʳ, collated with CCC 173, 1ʳ, and Tiberius A.iii, fo 178 (originally belonged with Tiberius A.vi, fos 1–35): WS Genealogical Regnal List, with parallel L t in rh column, as Dumville 1986: 21–25, Miller 1890–8: I.486–488;

F1ʳ (p. 25)   From TCC R.4.26, 5ᵛ/18–22, 10ʳ/7: ME *Metrical Chronicle* attrib. 'Robert of Gloucester', as Wright 1887, I.15, 37, lines 211–215, 505; this manuscript has an embryonic index by Wheelock divided between front and back;

H1ʳ–I1ᵛ (pp. 41–50)   From Gg.3.28, 60ʳ/13–63ᵛ/11: Ælfric, CH1, Feria IIII de fide Catholica (almost entire), as Clemoes 1997: no. XX, 335/2–3, 335/17–343/248;

K3 (pp. 61–62)   From Gg.3.28, 185ʳ/16–27: Ælfric, CH2, de Passione Domini (extract), as Godden 1979: no. XIV, 148/313–327;

K3ᵛ (p. 62)   From Gg.3.28, 4ᵛ/6–12: Ælfric, CH1, de Initio Creaturæ (extract), as Clemoes 1997: no. I, 182/110–117;

K3ᵛ (p. 62)   From Gg.3.28, 135ʳ/4–7: Ælfric, CH2, de Natale Domini (extract), as Godden 1979: no. I, 3/13–17;

K3ᵛ–4ʳ (pp. 62–63)   From Gg.3.28, 5ʳ/15–5ᵛ/2: Ælfric, CH1, de Initio Creaturæ (extract), as Clemoes 1997: no. I, 184/155–175;

K4 (pp. 63–64)   From CUL Ii.4.6, 286ʳ/12–286ᵛ/18: Ælfric, Homily Dominica I post Pentecosten (extract), as Pope 1967–8: I.484/118–485/138;

K4ᵛ–L2ʳ (pp. 64–67)   From Gg.3.28, 24ᵛ/9–25ᵛ/12: Ælfric, CH1, in Epiphania Domini (extract), as Clemoes 1997: no. VII, 236/127–238/200;

L2ʳ–3ʳ (pp. 67–69)   From Ii.4.6, 141ʳ/9–142ᵛ/15, 143ᵛ/10–144ʳ/7: Ælfric, CH1, in Dominica Palmarum (extracts), as Clemoes 1997: no. XIV, 291/42–293/85, 294/111–121;

O4ᵛ (p. 96)   From Otho B.xi, art. 10, 'p. 353, line 6' (now extant only in Nowell's transcript in BL Add 43703, 258ᵛ/4–9): verse *Seasons for Fasting* 87–94 printed as prose, as Dobbie 1942: 100, also Holthausen 1952–3: 194–195, and see Grant 1972;

P1ʳ (p. 97)   From Ii.4.6, 37ʳ/2–14: Ælfric, CH2, Dominica in Sexagesima (extract), as Godden 1979: VI, 57/136–146;

R1ᵛ (p. 114)   From TCC R.4.26, 82ʳ/32–4, 82ᵛ/5–7: ME *Metrical Chronicle* attrib. 'Robert of Gloucester', as Wright 1887, I.339–340, lines 4812–4814, 4819–4821;

S3ʳ (p. 125)   From Gg.3.28, 143ʳ/24–25: Ælfric, CH2, in Epiphania Domini (extract), as Godden 1979: no. III, 26/1–2;

S4ʳ (p. 127)   From **1639.4** N4ʳ, §6: ASC(E) 675 (extracts);

S4ᵛ (p. 128)   From Gg.3.28, 83ᵛ/17–18: Ælfric, CH1, Passio Petri et Pauli (extract), as Clemoes 1997: no. XXVI, 398/270–271;

T4ʳ (p. 135)   From Gg.3.28, 97ʳ/15–16: Ælfric, CH1, Assumptio Sanctae Mariae Virginis (extract), as Clemoes 1997: XXX, 434/167–435/169;

X4ʳ (p. 151)   From Ii.4.6, 259ʳ/4–13: Ælfric, Homily Dominica post Ascensionem Domini (extract), as Pope 1967–8: I.380/48–381/53;

Y1ʳ (p. 153)   From Gg.3.28, 157ᵛ/13–16: Ælfric, CH2, Sancti Gregorii Pape (extract), as Godden 1979: no. IX, 72/1–6;

Y1ᵛ–2ʳ (pp. 154–155)   From Gg.3.28, 239ᵛ/26–240ʳ/18: Ælfric, CH2, in Natale unius Confessoris (extract), as Godden 1979: no. XXXV, 301/63–302/90;

Y2 (pp. 155–156)   From Gg.3.28, 228ᵛ/28–229ʳ/5: Ælfric, CH2, in Natale Sancti Mathei (extract), as Godden 1979: XXXII, 274/70–9;

Y2ᵛ (p. 156)   From Ii.4.6, 279ʳ/13–279ᵛ/16: Ælfric, Homily Dominica Pentecosten (extract), as Pope 1967–8: I.400/100–401/119;

Z3ʳ (p. 165)   From CUL Ii.1.33, 161ᵛ/6–10: Ælfric, LS Oswald (extract), as Skeat 1881–1900: II.XXVI.126/17–20 (prints þone norðe for MS ane norðe);

From Ii.4.6, 127ʳ/19–127ᵛ/3: Ælfric, CH2, Dominica V in Quadragesima, as Godden 1979: XIII, 136/290–293;

From above T4ᵛ: Bede, HE II.12 (= 9);

From Gg.3.28, 194ᵛ/22–28: Ælfric, CH2, Inventio Sanctae Crucis, as Godden 1979: XVIII, 175/53–176/61;

Z4 (pp. 167–168)   From Gg.3.28, 197ʳ/10–17: Ælfric, CH2, Feria II Letania Maiore (extract), as Godden 1979: XIX, 183/93–104;

Z4ᵛ (p. 168)   From Gg.3.28, 52ᵛ/6–10, 12–13, 25–30: Ælfric, CH1, Dominica II post Pasca (extracts), as Clemoes 1997: XVII, 313/18–314/24, 314/26–27, 41–46;

2A2ᵛ (p. 172)   From Gg.3.28, 129ᵛ/30–130ʳ/2: Ælfric, CH1, Dominica I in Adventu (extract), as Clemoes 1997: XXXIX, 522/75–79;

2A2ᵛ–3ʳ (pp. 172–3)   From Gg.3.28, 223ʳ/15–25: Ælfric, CH2, Assumptio Sanctae Mariae Virginis (extract), as Godden 1979: XXIX, 259/119–33;

2A3ʳ (p. 173)   From Gg.3.28, 246ʳ/6–10: Ælfric, CH2, in Natale unius Confessoris (extract), as Godden 1979: XXXVIII, 320/54–9;

2A3 (pp. 173–174)   From Ii.1.33, 212ᵛ/15–213ʳ/18: OE translation of Alcuin's *De virtutibus et vitiis* (§ De scripturarum lectione), as Warner 1917: 94/1–26;

2B2ʳ (p. 179)   From Gg.3.28, 141ᵛ/16–22, 143ʳ/1–26, 143ᵛ/6–15, 143ᵛ/24–144ʳ/7: Ælfric, CH2, in Epiphania Domini (extracts), as Godden 1979: III, 21–2/91–8, 25/195–26/230, 26/245–257, 27/270–290;

2D2ʳ–3ʳ (pp. 195–7)   From Gg.3.28, 250ᵛ/11–12, 14–16, 250ᵛ/18–251ʳ/5, 251ʳ/13–21: Ælfric, CH2, in natale Sanctarum Virginum (extracts), as Godden 1979: XXXIX, 332/167–8, 171–4, 332/176–333/198, 334/208–19;

2F4ʳ (p. 215)   From Gg.3.28, 199ᵛ/25–6: Ælfric, CH2, In Letania maiore Feria III (extract), as Godden 1979: XX, 190/14–15;

From Gg.3.28, 203ᵛ/14–15, 202ʳ/21–2: Ælfric, CH2, in Letania Maiore Feria III (extract), as Godden 1979: XX, 197/248–50, 196/218–220;

2F4ᵛ (p. 216)   From **1639.4** 2O6ʳ (p. 457), §2: Canon of Edgar *De Confessione* (extract);

From TCC B.15.34, pp. 146/10–13, 153/12–15: Ælfric, CH2, Feria III de Dominica Oratione (extracts), as Clemoes 1997: XIX, 329/120–2, 332/204–6;

From TCC B.15.34, pp. 260/7–11, 271/10–15: Ælfric, Sermo ad populum in octavis Pentecosten dicendus (extract), as Pope 1967–8: XI, I.425/195–198, 437/396–399;

2G2^v (p. 220)   From Gg.3.28, 65^v/4–6: Ælfric, CH1, in Ascensione Domini (extract), as Clemoes 1997: XXI, 348/99–101;

From Ii.4.6, 252^v/1–6, 252^v/18–253^r/3: Ælfric, CH1, in Ascensione Domini (extract), as Clemoes 1997: 350/137–139, 146–148;

2G2^v–3^r (pp. 220–1)   From 1623.1 H1^v/1–25: Ælfric on the New Testament (extract, some omissions) ed. Lisle, as Crawford 1923: 57/952–58/973;

2H2^v (p. 228)   From Ii.4.6, 47^v/1–10: Ælfric, LS Ash Wednesday (extract), as Skeat 1881–1900: I.XII.260/3–10;

2H2^v–3^r (pp. 228–9)   From Ii.4.6, 111^v/3–112^r/11: Ælfric, LS de Oratione Moysi (extract), as Skeat 1881–1900: I.XIII.288/89–290/115;

2I2^v–3^r (pp. 236–7)   From Gg.3.28, 211^v/28–212^r/14: Ælfric, CH2, in Festivitate Sancti Petri Apostoli de Sancto Petro (extract), as Godden 1979: XXIV, 226/154–175;

2I3^r–4^r (pp. 237–9)   From Gg.3.28, 80^v/16–81^r/19: Ælfric, CH1, Passio Petri et Pauli (extract), as Clemoes 1997: XXVI, 390/60–391/96;

2K2 (pp. 243–4)   From Gg.3.28, 174^v/28–175^r/5, and Ii.4.6, 99^v/2–14: Ælfric, CH2, Dominica in media Quadragesime (extract), as Godden 1979: XII, 118/300–8;

2K2^v (p. 244)   From CCC 198, 190^v/2–8, 13–17 (a passage slightly longer than the first here is marked in the MS by a pointing hand and cross-signs at beginning and end in the margin): Homily in Sabbato Sancto (extracts), as Evans 1981: 138/134–138, 138/142–144;

From 1639.4 3C6^r: Capitula of Theodulf of Orléans (extract), as Sauer 1978: 337/23–27;

From Ii.4.6, 64^r/9–13: Ælfric, CH1, Dominica I in Quadragessima (extract), as Clemoes 1997: XI, 273/209–274/211;

2K2^v–3^v (pp. 244–6)   From Ii.4.6, 65^r/15–19, 65^v/4–14: Ælfric, CH2, Dominica I in Quadragesima (extract), as Godden 1979: VII, 60/11–14, 60/18–61/25;

2K3 (pp. 245–246)   From Ii.4.6, 66^r/10–66^v/5, 66^v/15–20, 67^r/9–67^v/18: Ælfric, CH2, Dominica I in Quadragesima (extract), as Godden 1979: VII, 61/35–46, 62/54–8, 62/64–63/85;

2M1 (pp. 257–258)   From TCC B.15.34, pp. 355/11–357/7: Ælfric, Homily Dominica VI post Pentecosten (extract), as Pope 1967–8: II.519/81–520/114; the MS has been annotated by Wheelock on p. 355;

2N2^v (p. 268)　　　From Gg.3.28, 129^v/9–10: Ælfric, CH1, Dominica I in Adventu Domini (extract), as Clemoes 1997: XXXIX, 521/50–52;

2N2^v–3^r (pp. 268–9)　From Gg.3.28, 196^v/13–16: Ælfric, CH2, Feria II Letania Maiore (extract), as Godden 1979: XIX, 181/54–182/59;

2N3^r (p. 269)　　　From TCC B.15.34, pp. 257/20–258/1: Ælfric, Sermo ad populum in octavis Pentecosten dicendus (extract), as Pope 1967–8: I.422/150–152;

　　　From TCC B.15.34, pp. 408/2–409/1: Ælfric, Homily Dominica X post Pentecosten (extract), as Pope 1967–8: II.554/168–84;

2P1^v–2^r (pp. 282–3)　From TCC B.15.34, p. 260/13–21: Ælfric, Sermo ad populum in octavis Pentecosten dicendus (extract), as Pope 1967–8: I.425/200–7;

2P2^r (p. 283)　　　From Gg.3.28, 37^v/5–25: Ælfric, CH1, Dominica I in Quadragessima (extract), as Clemoes 1997: XI, 270/108–26;

2P2 (pp. 283–4)　　From Ii.4.6, 73^r/2–3, 73^r/11–73^v/3: Ælfric, CH2, Dominica II in Quadragesima (extract), as Godden 1979: VIII, 68/51–52, 69/58–65;

2P2^v (p. 284)　　　From Ii.4.6, 209^v/18–19, 214^r/6–12: Ælfric, Homily Dominica V post Pascha (extract), as Pope 1967–8: I.359/56–7, 366/208–12

From Gg.3.28, 57^r/4–10: Ælfric, CH1, Feria III de Dominica Oratione (extract), as Clemoes 1997: XIX, 326/26–33;

2P3^v–4^r (pp. 284–5)　From Gg.3.28, 60^r/13–15: Ælfric, CH1, Feria IIII de Fide Catholica (extract), as Clemoes 1997: XX, 335/1–2;

2Q1^r (p. 289)　　　From Gg.3.28, 239^r/17–19: Ælfric, CH2, in Natale unius Apostoli (extract), as Godden 1979: XXXV, 299/10–13;

　　　From Gg.3.28, 247^v/11–15: Ælfric, CH2, in Natale unius Confessoris (extract), as Godden 1979: XXXVIII, 324/180–4;

2S3 (pp. 309–10)　　From Ii.4.6, 109^v/20–111^r/3, 111^v/1–5, 114^v/17–20: Ælfric, LS de oratione Moysi (extract), as Skeat 1881–1900: I.XIII.284/28–288/68, 288/87–90, 298/216–8;

2S4^v (p. 312)　　　From Ii.1.33, 34^v/13–35^r/3: Ælfric, LS Æthelthryth (extract), as Skeat 1881–1900: I.XX.432/1–19;

2T1 (pp. 313–314)　　From Gg.3.28, 116^v/13–14, 16–20, 28–30, 118^r/5–10, 20–28: Ælfric, CH1, Kalende Novembris Natale omnium Sanctorum (extract), as Clemoes 1997: XXXVI, 486/16–17, 486/19–487/24, 487/34–7, 490/116–123, 490/137–491/146;

2T1^v (p. 314)　　　From Gg.3.28, 120^r/15–21: Ælfric, CH1, in Natale omnium Sanctorum (extract), as Clemoes, XXXVI, 495/284–496/291;

2T4^r (p. 319)　　　From Gg.3.28, 204^v/12–27, 205^r/10–12: Ælfric, CH2, Alia Visio, de Efficacia Sanctae Missae (extract), as Godden 1979: XXI, 204/140–159, 205/176–180;

2X2 (pp. 331–2)   From CCC 191, pp. 88/15–23, 89/13–90/3: Rule of Chrodegang, §48, as Napier 1916: 56/30–35, 57/12–25;

Note. Wheelock's transcript of CCC 191 (copied by William Retchford) survives as Harley 440 (later owned by Hickes), but this transcript would presumably have been supplied to H. Spelman before it could be used for 1643.1;

2X2^v–3^r (pp. 332–3)   From 1623.1 S1^v: Ælfric's Letter to Wulfsige, ed. Lisle from 1566.1, as Fehr 1914: 29–31, §§133–142;

2X3^r–4^r (pp. 333–5)   From 1623.1 S2^v–4^v: Ælfric's 2nd Letter to Wulfstan, ed. Lisle from 1566.1, as Fehr 1914: 178–86, §§86–109;

2Y2^v–2Z1^r (pp. 340–345)   From Ii.1.33, 217^r/7–219^v/19: OE translation of Alcuin's *De virtutibus et vitiis* (§§ de compunctione cordis, de confessione peccatorum, de penitentia), as Assmann 1889: 382–386 (less full), and Warner 1917: 99/20–102/33;

3A1^v (p. 354)   From (prob) Gg.3.28, 163^v/3–5: Ælfric, CH2, xiii kalendas Aprilis Depositio Sancti Cuthberhti episcopi (extract), as Godden 1979: X, 88/239–242;

From 1568.2 T4^v: Law II Æthelstan, Epilogue, as Liebermann I.166; unique to Lambarde;

From 1639.4 2L5^r: Law I Edmund, Prologue (beginning), as Liebermann I.184;

3A3^r (p. 357)   From 1568.2 H4^v: Laws of Alfred, Prologue §38, as Liebermann I.40; the reference is to Lambarde by folio and line;

3A3 (pp. 357–358)   From 1639.4 3D4^v: Theodulfi Capitula XXXV, as Sauer 1978: 373–375; parts of the setting match that in 1639.4 line by line;

3A3^v (pp. 358)   From CCC 191, pp. 135/21–136/5: Rule of Chrodegang, §73, as Napier 1916: 82/7–14;

From 1639.4 3A6^v, §24: Ælfric's Letter to Wulfsige, as Fehr 1914: §68;

3B2^r (p. 363)   From Gg.3.28, 160^v/16–29: Ælfric, CH2, XIII kalendas Aprilis Depositio Sancti Cuthberhti Episcopi (extract), as Godden 1979: X, 81/1–19;

3B2^v (p. 364)   From CCC 191, pp. 79/1–80/1: Rule of Chrodegang, §43 (part), as Napier 1916: 51/15–34;

3C2 (pp. 371–2)   From Gg.3.28, 205^r/30–205^v/2, 205^v/5–18: Ælfric, CH2, in Letania Maiore feria IIII (extract), as Godden 1979: XXII, 206/25–207/27, 207/31–49;

3C2^v–3^r (pp. 372–3)   From Gg.3.28, 26^v/24–26, 26^v/28–27^r/2, 27^r/21–26: Ælfric, CH1, Dominica III post Epiphania Domini (extract), as Clemoes 1997: VIII, 241/22–242/25, 242/27–31, 243/54–60;

3C4^v–3E2^v (pp. 376–388)   From Gg.3.28, 251^r/22–255^r/13: Ælfric, CH2, in Dedicatione Ecclesiae (in full), as Godden 1979: XL, 335/1–345/317;

3F2ʳ (p. 395)   From Ii.4.6, 132ʳ/11–15, 130ᵛ/17–131ʳ/2: Ælfric, CH2, Dominica Palmarum de Passione Domini (extracts), as Godden 1979: XIV, 142/139–142, 140/99–141/103;

3F2ᵛ (p. 396)   From Ii.4.6, 178ʳ/13–18, 178ᵛ/3–12: Ælfric, CH2, Alius Sermo de die Paschae, as Godden 1979: XVI, 166/173–176, 179–184;
From Ii.4.6, 131ʳ/9–16: Ælfric, CH2, Dominica Palmarum de Passione Domini (extract), as Godden 1979: XIV, 141/107–13;

3F2ᵛ–3ʳ (pp. 396–397)   From Gg.3.28, 69ʳ/7–13, or Ii.4.6, 268ᵛ/19–269ʳ/11: Ælfric, CH1, in die Sancto Pentecosten (extract), as Clemoes 1997: XXII, 358/98–105;

3F3ʳ (p. 397)   From Gg.3.28, 55ᵛ/20–56ʳ/2: Ælfric, CH1, in Letania Maiore (extract), as Clemoes 1997: XVIII, 322/153–323/166;

3F3 (pp. 397–398)   From TCC B.15.34, p. 74/5–16: Ælfric, CH1, Dominica II post Pasca (extract from additional passage), as Clemoes 1997: XVII (Appendix B) 541/191–197;

3F3ᵛ (p. 398)   From Ii.4.6, 29ᵛ/13–15, 30ʳ/4–12: Ælfric, CH2, Dominica in Septuagesima (extract), as Godden 1979: V, 49/219–21, 226–32;
From TCC B.15.34, p. 275/11–20: Ælfric, Sermo ad Populum in octavis Pentecosten dicendus (extract), as Pope 1967–8: I.440/441–441/472;

3G2ᵛ (p. 404)   From Gg.3.28, 113ʳ/11–17: Ælfric, CH1, Dominica XXI post Pentecosten (extract), as Clemoes 1997: XXXV, 477/40–46;
From Gg.3.28, 144ᵛ/4–9, 14–15: Ælfric, CH2, Dominica II post Epiphania (extract), as Godden 1979: IV, 30/29–36, 42–43;

3G2ᵛ–3ʳ (pp. 404–405)   From Gg.3.28, 51ʳ/22–4: Ælfric, CH1, Dominica I post Pasca (extract), as Clemoes 1997: XVI, 309/73–310/92;

3H2ʳ (p. 411)   From Gg.3.28, 166ᵛ/10–16: Ælfric, CH2, XII kalendas Aprilis Sancti Benedicti Abbatis (extract), as Godden 1979: XI, 97/171–178;

3I2ᵛ–3ᵛ (pp. 420–422)   From CCC 162, pp. 43/6–44/17: Ælfric, CH1, Feria IIII de Fide Catholica, as Clemoes 1997: XX, 343/248–344/277;

3I3ᵛ–3K1ᵛ (pp. 422–426)   From Gg.3.28, 262ᵛ/9–263ᵛ/29: Homily in XL de penitentia, as Thorpe 1844–6: II.602–608;

3K2ᵛ (p. 426)   From TCC B.15.34, pp. 365/21–366/7, 366/9–11, 375/16–376/5: Ælfric, Homily Dominica VII post Pentecosten (extract), as Pope 1967–8: II.532/39–533/48, 541/222–230;

3K4ᵛ (p. 432)   From CCC 191, pp. 57/18–58/11: Rule of Chrodegang, §29, as Napier 1916: 38/2–19;

3L2ʳ (p. 435)   From Ii.1.33, 205ʳ/5–14: Ælfric, LS Exaltation of the Cross (extract), as Skeat 1881–1900: II.XXVII.150/115–152/124;

From Gg.3.28, 194ʳ/13–14, 194ᵛ/11–15: Ælfric, CH2, v Non. Mai Inventio Sanctae Crucis (extract), as Godden 1979: XVIII, 174/1–2, 175/39–44;

3M4ᵛ (p. 448)   From Gg.3.28, 227ᵛ/24–228ʳ/2: Ælfric, CH2, Dominica XVI post Pentecosten: De Sancta Maria (extract), as Godden 1979: XXXI, 271/1–10;

From Gg.3.28, 43ʳ/10–22: Ælfric, CH1, VIII kalendas Aprilis Adnuntiatio Sancte Mariæ (extract), as Clemoes 1997: XIII, 285/125–286/1;

3N1ʳ (p. 449)   From Gg.3.28, 97ʳ/12–30: Ælfric, CH1, XVIII kalendas Septembris Assumptio Sancteç Marieç Virginis (extract), as Clemoes 1997: XXX, 434/163–435/184;

3N1ᵛ (p. 450)   From Gg.3.28, 240ʳ/29–240ᵛ/4: Ælfric, CH2, in Natale unius Apostoli (extract), as Godden 1979: XXXV, 302/105–112;

From Gg.3.28, 79ᵛ/26–9: Ælfric, CH1, VIII kalendas Iulii Nativitas Sancti Iohannis Baptistae (extract), as Clemoes 1997: XXV, 387/223–226;

3O2–3ʳ (pp. 460–461)   From CCC 419, pp. 38/3–39/7, 44/14–19, 48/16–49/1: Homily Sunnandæges spell (extracts), as Napier 1883: XLIII, 205/5–14, 207/4–6, 208/9–11;

From CCC 419, pp. 76/12–14, 76/16–77/2, 78/1–7, 87/12–19, 86/2–8: Sermo angelorum nomina (extracts), as Napier 1883: XLV, 227/7–11, 20–23, 230/8–11, 229/27–30;

From CCC 419, pp. 64/10–65/6 (the beginning of this passage is marked with a triple point): Homily Sunnandæges spell (extract), as Napier 1883: XLIII, 212/25–32;

3O3ᵛ (p. 462)   From CCC 419, p. 116/12–18: Wulfstan, Sermo de Baptismate (extract), as Napier 1883: V, 34/3–5, Bethurum 1957: VIIIc, 177/36–8;

3O3ᵛ–3Q2ʳ (pp. 462–79)   From Gg.3.28, 185ᵛ/19–189ᵛ/22: Ælfric, CH2, in die Pascae (in full), as Godden 1979: XV, 150/1–160/337; Wheelock collated this MS with the printed text in his copy of 1623.1 (CUL Adv.d.48.10);

3R1ʳ–4ᵛ (pp. 485–2488)   From CCC 419, pp. 161/8–182/9: Wulfstan, Homily de Fide Catholica (in full), as Napier 1883: III, 20–29, Bethurum 1957: VII, 157–65;

3S4ʳ (p. 495)   From CCC 419, p. 1/1–6, 16/160–18/1 (the beginning of this passage is marked with a triple point): Homily de Temporibus Anticristi, as Napier 1883: XLII, 191/25–192/1, 197/14–198/1;

3S4ʳ–3T1ᵛ (pp. 495–8)   From Gg.3.28, 261ᵛ/13–262ᵛ/8: Prayers, as Thorpe 1844–6: II.596–600;

3T4ʳ–4D3ᵛ   From Otho B.xi, art. 3 (= G), collated with CCC 173 (= A): *Anglo-Saxon Chronicle* to 1001, then 1005–70 from A, as Thorpe 1861; MS G was severely damaged in the Cotton library fire of 1731, but a transcript by Nowell, BL Add 43703, fos 200–232, survives, on the relation of which to G see Campbell 1938: App.1 (re. *Brunanburh*).

TYPE:
Main OE text in AS5: The Wheelockian Great Primer Anglo-Saxon combined with a Great Primer Roman (Body 118);
Main Latin text in Haultin's English-size Roman (Body 94);
Latin text of chapter list on C4ʳ–E2ʳ and elsewhere in Granjon's first English-size Italic (Body 94).
AS5 Specimen, special sorts shown: ð, ꝼ, ᵹ, ꝑ, ſ, ꞇ, ẏ; þ, ð, ꝑ; Ð; þ, ꞇ.
$\qquad\qquad\qquad\qquad\qquad\qquad\qquad\qquad\qquad\qquad$ 10 + 1 + 2 = 13 sorts.
AS5 Text, special sorts shown: ð, *e*, ꝼ, ᵹ, 1, ꝑ, ſ, ꞇ, ẏ; þ, ð, ꝑ; Æ², Ł, Ꝺ, Ꞓ, Ꝼ, Ᵹ, Ꝥ, I, Ꞁ, S, Ꞇ, U, Ð, Ꝥ; þ, ꞇ, ꞌ, also uses raised point. $\qquad$ 12 + 14 + 4 = 30 sorts.
Note 1: Square C and G often not used, standard Roman G being the preferred usage.
Note 2: Capital Ꝥ not found.

   Copies seen: BL 490.k.2 (lacks 3T3; elaborate blind-stamped binding); CUL Rel.a.64.2 (all paste-on corrections present; lacks 3T3; with elaborate contemporary gold-tooled binding on brown goatskin by John Houlden of Cambridge, matching that of OBL S.Seld.c.21), Cam.a.643.1 (lacks 3T3; shows Wheelock's presentation inscription to Joshua Hoyle dated 22 Mar 1643 (i.e. 1644), with gold-tooled binding on brown calf); Pet.A.7.7 (lacks 3T3); CCC D.3.22¹ (lacks 3T3); CQC I.12.18 (lacks 3T3; with contemporary binding of brown calf with gold-tooled motif in the centre, inscribed by Wheelock to the College inside the front cover); TCC E.10.7 (lacks 3T3; with contemporary binding of brown calf with gold-tooled motif in the centre flanked by the initials AW); OBL MS Junius 10¹ (SC 5122, showing ±3T3, B4 + χ1.2 = 1644.1 ¶6χ1.2 with map of Anglo-Saxon England by William Hole; with additions, collations and annotations in Junius's hand); S.Seld.c.21 (lacks 3T3; binding matches that of CUL Rel.a.64.2; given to Selden by Henry Rich (†1649), e of Holland, chancellor of CU; *Fine Bindings* 1968: no. 156).
   With 3T3 showing the dedication to Sir Simonds D'Ewes: CUL Cam.a.643.3 (3T3 partially cut off).
Bibliography: Lutz 1977; McKitterick 1984: 54, item 45; McKitterick 1992: 187–192; Niles 2015: 113–116; Nixon and Foot 1992: 58 and pl. 47 (bindings of CUL Rel.a.64.2, OBL S.Seld.c.21); Shackleton 1968: no. 156 and pl. xxxvii (as prec.); Oates 1986: 204–209; Whitelock 1962: 60–61, 81, also 1974 (re. *capitula*).
GR 5546.

1644.1: Lambarde, William, ed. Abraham Wheelock, *Archaionomia, sive de Priscis Anglorum Legibus libri*. Cambridge, Roger Daniel for Cornelius Bee (London), 1644. Wing A3605. AS5.

Laws

    Collation: 2^0 in 4s: ¶⁶ (¶6 + χ1.2) A–2C⁴ 2D–2E⁶ 2G⁴ [\$3 signed (+¶4, 2D4; -¶1, V1; 2E2,3 missigned 2F2,3)] 128 leaves, paginated [i–xvi], 1–226, *227–236* (sig. V1 not included in the numbering; pp. nos 157–158 used twice; p. 174 not numbered).

SOURCES OF PASSAGES UTILIZING ANGLO-SAXON TYPES:

From **1568.2**:

(1) A1ʳ–B3ᵛ   Laws of Ine (**1568.2** C1ᵛ–G3ʳ; Liebermann I.89–123);

(2) B4ʳ–E2ʳ   Laws of Alfred (**1568.2** G3ᵛ–O1ʳ; Liebermann I.26–89: **AfEl, Af**);

(3) E2ᵛ–3ʳ   Laws of Alfred and Guthrum (**1568.2** O1ᵛ–3ʳ; Liebermann I.126–128: **AGu**);

(4) E3ᵛ–F1ʳ   Laws I and II Edward the Elder (**1568.2** O3ᵛ–P4ʳ; Liebermann I.138–144: **I–II Ew**);

(5) F1ʳ–2ᵛ   Laws of Alfred and Guthrum (**1568.2** P4ᵛ–R1ʳ; Liebermann I.128–134: **EGu**);

(6) F3   Law I Æthelstan (**1568.2** R1ᵛ–R3ʳ; Liebermann I.146–149: **I As and As Alm**);

(7) F3ᵛ–G3ʳ   Laws II Æthelstan (**1568.2** R3ᵛ–V1ʳ; Liebermann I.150–166: **II As**);

(8) G3ʳ–4ʳ/9   Laws V Æthelstan (**1568.2** V1ᵛ–V4ʳ/7; Liebermann I.166–169: **V As**);

(9) G4ʳ/10–4ᵛ/2   'Norðleoda laga' (**1568.2** V3ᵛ/7–X1ʳ/11; Liebermann I.458–461: **Norðl**);

(10) G4ᵛ/3–24   'Mircna laga' (**1568.2** V4ᵛ/9–X1ʳ; Liebermann I.462–465: **Mirc, Að**);

(11) H1ʳ–2ᵛ/6   Laws I and II Edmund (**1568.2** X1ᵛ–Y1ʳ; Liebermann I.184–190: **I–II Em**).

From **1639.4**; the L translation is Spelman's, and the same errors occur, e.g. *þæt* at the end of §1 taken over into §2:

(11a) H2ᵛ/7–3ʳ   Law 'Be wifmannes beweddunge' (**1639.4** 2M2ʳ–3ʳ; Liebermann I.442–444); = **1639.4** (pp. 425–427).

From **1568.2**:

(12) H3ᵛ–I1ʳ/16   Laws II and III Edgar (**1568.2** Y1ᵛ–2A2ʳ; Liebermann I.194–205: **II–III Eg**).

From **1639.4**; Spelman's note about a lacuna in the MS is taken over verbatim on I4ᵛ from **1639.4** 2O5ᵛ:

(12a) I1ʳ/18–4ᵛ   Canons of Edgar (**1639.4** 2O1ʳ–2O5ᵛ; Thorpe 1840: II.244–258);

(12b) I4ᵛ–K2ʳ   Canons of Edgar, 'De Confessione' (**1639.4** 2O5ᵛ–2P1ᵛ; Thorpe 1840: II.260–264);

(12c) K2ʳ–L1ᵛ Canons of Edgar, 'Modus Imponendi Poenitentiam' (1639.4 2P1ᵛ–5ᵛ; as Thorpe 1840: II.266–276; §§2b–46 (correct arrangement) as Fowler 1965: 20/113–26/303);

(12d) L1ᵛ–3ᵛ Canons of Edgar, 'Be Dædbetan' (1639.4 2P5ᵛ–2Q2ᵛ; Thorpe 1840: II.278–286);

(12e) L4 Canons of Edgar, 'Be mihtigum mannum' (1639.4 2Q2ᵛ–3ᵛ; Thorpe 1840: II.286–288).

From 1568.2:

(13) L4ᵛ–M1ᵛ Laws I Æthelred (1568.2 2A2ᵛ–2B1ʳ; Liebermann I.216–220: **I Atr**);

(14) M1ᵛ–4ᵛ Laws II Æthelred (1568.2 2B1ᵛ–2C2ʳ; Liebermann I.220–226: **II Atr**);

(15) M3ᵛ–N1ʳ Agreement re. Welsh Marches (1568.2 2C2ᵛ–2D2ʳ; Liebermann I.374–378: **Duns**);

(16.1) N1ʳ–O2ʳ Laws I Cnut (1568.2 2D2ᵛ–2F4ʳ; Liebermann I.278–306: **I Cn**);

(16.2) O2ʳ–Q3ᵛ Laws II Cnut (1568.2 2F3ᵛ–2M1ʳ; Liebermann I.308–371: **II Cn**);

From 1639.4:

(16a) Q4ʳ–R4ʳ Ælfric's Letter to Wulfsige, bp of Sherborne 992–1001/2 (1639.4 3A3ᵛ–3B2ᵛ; as Fehr 1914: 1–24, §§1–108).

From 1568.2:

(17) R4ᵛ–S1ʳ Laws of William I (1568.2 2M1ᵛ–3ʳ; Liebermann I.486–491; **WlArt**);

(18) S1ᵛ–T4ʳ Laws of Edward the Confessor = Retractatus (1568.2 2M3ᵛ–2Q2ʳ; Liebermann I, 627–670: **ECf**);

(19) T4ᵛ On the Dukes of Normandy (1568.2 2Q2ʳ/11–2Q2ᵛ).

TYPE:

Main OE text in AS5: The Wheelockian Great Primer Anglo-Saxon is combined with a Great Primer Roman (Body 118);

Main Latin text in Haultin's English-size Roman (Body 94) interspersed from R4ᵛ onwards with Granjon's first English-size Italic;

AS specimen on ¶6ᵛ shows:

    12 lower-case sorts: ð, *e*, f, ᵹ, 1, p, ſ, t, ẏ; þ, ð, ƿ;
    13 capitals: D, Є, F, L, Ð, I, ᘉ, S, T, U; Æ², Ð, Ƿ;
    4 others: ⁊, þ, · (raised point), j̇.
  Total: 29 sorts.

Note: Square C not shown.

Special sorts shown in text: 12 lower-case sorts: ð, *e*, f, ᵹ, 1, p, ſ, t, ẏ; þ, ð, ƿ;
    13 capitals: D, Є, F, L, Ð, I, ᘉ, S, T, U; Æ², Ð, Ƿ;
    3 others: ⁊, þ, j̇.
  Total: 28 sorts.

Note: Square C and the raised point not found.

Glossarium on 2E1ʳ–4ʳ:

Main text in Robert Granjon's second Pica Italic (Body 82) interspersed with Pierre Haultin's Pica Roman;

AS3: The Lambardian Pica Anglo-Saxon is combined with Haultin's Pica Roman in words only:

Special sorts shown: 10 lower-case sorts: ð, ꝼ, ȝ, ƿ, ꞃ, ꞇ, ẏ; þ, ð, p;
                       3 capitals: E, Ꝥ, Ð.
                         Total: 13 sorts.

Note: No letters *e*, ı, ƿ and ꝸ found, although there are places where they could have been used.

> **Copies seen:** (with tp in black and red): BL 17.d.3 (with the arms of George III stamped in gold on the front and back covers), 507.i.10; CCA W/H.6.12 (Somner's copy, with annotations to Laws of Henry I); CUL I.8.25; CCC M.1.30; (with tp in black only): BL MS Harley 307 (untrimmed, with annotations to Laws II Edgar and I–II Cnut by Junius); CUL Cam.a.643.2 (lacks ¶6χ1.2); CCC D.3.22²; OBL MS Junius 102 (SC 5122, with additions, collations and annotations in Junius's hand; lacks ¶6χ1.2, which is bound in 1643.1 = B4χ1.2). See also **1644.2**.
>
> **Copies also at:** APL, BCLW, BUT, BUW, ChC, CCL, CGC, KCC, CMC, CPC, CPH, CSJ, CSS, CTH, TCC, ECL, LHL, NewCL, NLS, OAS, OJC, OSA, OXC, SACL, DML, NLI, TCD; HHL, HUL, IUL, APS, BPM, LCP, NLC, PrTS, SCN, UCLA, YUB; OUL.

Bibliography: Keynes 2014: 159 (map); McKitterick 1992: 191; Shirley 1991: no. 538a.

1644.2: Bede, ed. Abraham Wheelock, *Historiæ Ecclesiasticæ Gentis Anglorum Libri V a Venerabili Beda Presbytero scripti*; *Chronologia Anglo-Saxonica* [= ASC]; Lambarde, William, ed. Abraham Wheelock, *Archaionomia, sive de Priscis Anglorum Legibus libri*. Cambridge: Roger Daniel for Cornelius Bee (London), 1644. Wing B1662; ESTC R11643. Combines **1643.1** and **1644.1** with new title. AS5. Bede, *Ecclesiastical History*; *Anglo-Saxon Chronicle*; Laws

> **Collation:** 2⁰ in 4s: [Part 1] π² A⁴ (±A1) [as **1643.1**] B⁴ (B4 + χ1.2) C–4E⁴ 4F² [\$3 signed (-A1, 3T3, 4F2; P1 apparently signed 'O' with 'P' overprinted)], [Part 2 as **1644.1**] ¶⁶ A–2C⁴ 2D–2E⁶ 2G⁴ [\$3 signed (+¶4, 2D4; -¶1, V1; 2E2,3 missigned 2F2,3)] 302 + 126 leaves, paginated as **1643.1** and **1644.1**.

SOURCES OF PASSAGES UTILIZING ANGLO-SAXON TYPES:

As **1643.1** and **1644.1**.

TYPE: As **1643.1** and **1644.1**.

> **Copies seen:** CCA W/E.6.20 (Somner's copy with annotations in his hand, e.g. B2ᵛ, 4C3ʳ, Laws Henry I); CUL K*.8.24; ECC S8.1.38 (Abp Sancroft's copy, with

his coat-of-arms gold-tooled on the covers); CUL R.8.9 (tp of Part 2 shows inverted triangular ornament; with etched map of AS England by Hole = 1644.1 ¶6c1ᵛ–¶6c2ʳ inserted in Part 1 after A4), Cam.a.644.2 (A2.3 appear between π1 and π2; shows A4 bound in reverse order with recto on verso and vice-versa; flyleaf signed 'George Hickes' and there are annotations in Part 2, e.g. G4ᵛ and H2ᵛ); Cam.a.643.2 (between π1 and π2 there occurs 3T3 detached from its rightful place, followed by 1643.1 sig. A⁴, followed by A1, lacks A2–4 being identical with 1643.1; with the etched map of AS England by Hole = 1644.1 ¶6χ1ᵛ–¶6χ2ʳ inserted after π2); OBL A.14.13.Th. (owned by (?)George Hickes, Richard Rawlinson e18c), Douce B subt.76 (lacks ¶⁶ in Part 2), Vet.A3.c.196 (shows ±A1 bound in reverse order with the consecration on ±A1ʳ and ±A1ᵛ blank, with annotations by Richard Taylor e19c).

Note: QUB Percy MS 8 has as its foundation the Chronologia part but is much augmented by notes in the hand of Edward Lye.

Copies also at: BL, BUL, ChC, KCC, CMC, CUD, DCL, DUL, GML, LCL, LSH, MTP, NLS, NLW, NT, OAS, OBC, OCC, OEF, OHM, OJC, OLC, OQC, OTC, OWoC, OXC, SCL, SDC, SoUL, SPC, SUL, UBL, WAL, WCC, WiCL, WoCL, TCD, PBN, GUB; FSL, NYCU, HUL, IUL, ACA, KSRL, LCP, NLC, UCH, UCLA, UVL, YUB; VUW.

Bibliography: see 1643.1, 1644.1.

1644.3: La Bigne, Margarinus de, *Magna Bibliotheca Veterum Patrum, ex Antiquorum Scriptorum Ecclesiasticorum*. Paris: Giles Morell (sumptibus), 1644. USTC 6042397.

Collation: 2^0 in 6s: ã² A–4F⁶ 4G⁴. [4], 830, [62] p.

Vol. XVI includes a reprint of 1618.2 including Nicolaus Serarius's *Epistolæ S. Bonifacii*, where the OE verse *Proverb from Winfred's Time* (Dobbie 1942: 57) occurs in Epistola lxi. It is taken over here on F6ʳ (p. 71) in a Pica Italic (with no special sorts) quoted as prose in a Latin prose letter itself printed in Pica Roman.

Copy seen: CUL 3.13.16.
Copy also at: PBN.

1644.4: Coke, Sir Edward, *The Fourth Part of the Institutes of the Laws of England*. London: Miles Flesher for William Lee II & Daniel Pakeman, 1644. Wing C4929; ESTC R1842.

Collation: 2^0: [A]⁶ B–3A⁴ + χ1. [16], 364, [2] p

Prints AS charter texts (L), as Sawyer 731 in Italic on pp. 359–360, but no AS sorts.

Copies: BL, CCA, LIT, LMT, LQL, NLS, NT, NUL, OBL, OJC, OQC, OSJ, PBN; FSL USLC, NYCU, HHL, HUL, BA, BMC, BPM, NWU, PUL, YUB; MonUL.

1644.5: Paris, Matthew, ed. William Watts, *Vitæ Duorum Offarum sive Offanorum, Merciorum Regum.* 2nd part. Paris: 'apud' widow of Guillaume Pelé [= Marguerite Vallée], 1644. Cf. **1639.3**

Collation: 2^0: †^{6} a–s^6 t^4. [12], 215, [9] p.

AS words taken over at, e.g., p6^v (p. 180, col. 1, line 8), in Roman type with approximated letters (as 'o' for 'ð') and no special sorts.

Copy seen: CSJ A/G.24.25.

1645.1: Blaeu, Joan, *Theatrum Orbis Terrarum ſive Atlas Novus, Pars Qvarta.* (= Camden's *Britannia*, as in **1607.2**, from which it is set (note erron. page-heading YORKE-SHIRE (6S1^r) taken over from 1607.2 404^r)). Amsterdam: Joan Blaeu I, 1645. USTC 1512949. CAS3.

ASC (C) and (F) extracts, OE proper names

Collation: 2^0: π^1 *^{1} 2*^{2} (2*2 + c2) A–Y^2 (Y2 + c1.2) Z–2N^2 2O^1 2P–2T^2 2V^1 2X–2Z^2 3A^1 3B–3E^2 3F^1 3G–3K^2 3L^1 3M–3N^2 3O^1 3P–3Q^2 3R^1 3S–3X^2 3Y^1 3Z–4K^2 (4K2 + c1.2) 4L–4M^2 4N^1 4O^2 4P^1 4Q–4S^2 4T^1 4V–5A^2 5B^1 5C^2 5D^1 5E–5N^2 5O^1 (5O1 + c1.2) 5P^2 5Q^1 5R–5T^2 5V^1 5X^2 5Y^1 5Z–6C^2 6D^1 6E^2 6F^1 6G^2 6H^1 6I–6N^2 6O^1 6P–6X^2 6Y^1 6Z^2 7A^1 7B–7L^2 7M^1 7N–7P^2 [7Q]^1 [$2 signed (-2*2, S2, 2D2, 2G2, 2I2, 2L2, 2P2, 2S2, 2X2, 2Y2, 3B2, 3D2, 3G2, 3M2, 3P2, 3S2, 3V2, 3Z2, 4C2, 4F2, 4I2, 4L2, 4O2, 4Q2, 4S2, 4V2, 4X2, 5A2, 5C2, 5E2, 5H2, 5K2, 5M2, 5P2, 5R2, 5S2, 5T2, 5X2, 5Z2, 6B2, 6C2, 6E2, 6G2, 6I2, 6K2, 6N2, 6P2, 6S2, 6V2, 6Z2, 7B2, 7F2, 7K2, 7N2, 7O2); 7G2 missigned 6G2]; 287 + 8 leaves, paginated [i–viii], 1–460, 461–462 (with pages showing maps not included in the pagination, except for 2D1^v–2^r, 7K2^r).

Note: Because this is a large atlas all the leaves are mounted on guards.

SOURCE OF PASSAGE UTILIZING ANGLO-SAXON TYPES:

7E2^r (p. 427)   From 1607.2 4Y4^r: ASC(C + F) 188/189 (extracts), as Thorpe 1861: 14–15, including erron. ſæ oþ ſæ with p for þ, and note the use of AS ſ (as opposed to Roman long ſ) in only the first of 4 instances of ſæ; ꝼoꞃᵹẏnð is also from 1607.2.

TYPE:

Main text in Pierre Haultin's Great Primer Roman (Body 115) interspersed with a Great Primer Italic in two columns.

CAS3: The Blaeu English-size Anglo-Saxon probably cut by one of the Voskens half-brothers occurs in the specimen on 2*2^r and is used in combination with Haultin's Great Primer Roman in the text in words on pp. 15, 63, 75, 88, 90, 92, 98, 103, 107, 114, 116, 121–125, 127–128, 130, 134, 136, 139–140, 141–142 (with erron. Tꞃuþabꞃıᵹ (*recte* Tꞃ-) from 1607.2), 146, 148, 150, 152 (showing erron. ꟽẏnſðeꞃ (for mynꞅtep) from 1607.2), 159, 160 (with τ inverted), 162–163, 166–167, 170, 173–174, 176, 177–178 (with erron. Haꝛðınᵹa- for 1607.2 Haꞅtınᵹa-), 180, 181 (with 2nd τ inverted), 182, 183–184 (with τ inverted on p. 184), 185, 187, 189–191, 194 (with erron. o for ꞅc), 195, 197 (with erron. –ꞅcꝺẏꞅe from 1607.2), 198–202, 205–207, 213 (with τ inverted), 215, 221–222 (with τ inverted 2x on p. 222), 228–229, 238–239, 242, 244, 248, 251 (with erron. Ꝺeaᵹleᵹe for 1607.2 Ꝺeaðleᵹe), 256–257, 259, 264, 268, 271, 275, 284, 286, 288, 290, 295–6 (with τ inverted on p. 295), 298, 301, 306, 311–312, 313–314 (with τ inverted on p. 314), 315, 318, 320, 322–323, 327–330, 336, 347, 354, 368, 373, 375–377, 379, 385, 387–388, 394, 400, 402, 404, 409, 431, 434–435, 437–438 (with τ inverted on p. 437), 444, 454;

Special sorts shown in specimen on 2*2ʳ:

    11 lower-case sorts: ð, *e*, ꝼ, ᵹ, ꝑ, ꞅ, τ, ẏ; þ, ð, p;
    8 capitals: Æ¹, Æ², Є, Ꝺ, Ꟁ, Ꞅ, Ð, X;
    2 others: þ, ꝛ.
Total: 21 sorts.

Special sorts shown in text:

    11 lower-case sorts: ð, *e*, ꝼ, ᵹ, ꝑ, ꞅ, τ, ẏ (looks like GP y with dot added slightly to right of centre); þ, ð, p;
    5 capitals: Є, Ꝺ (used lc on Z1ᵛ etc., cap on 2R2ᵛ), Ꟁ, Ꞅ (used for d on V1ʳ, cap on 3A1ᵛ), Ð;
    1 other: ꝛ (on Z1ᵛ, 4A1ʳ, oversized, made up of a subscript number 7 surmounted by a dot to the left of centre, but occasionally to the right of centre, e.g., 7K1ᵛ, a fact which suggests two castings).
Total: 17 sorts.

Overall total 11 + 8 + 3 = 22 sorts.

Note 1: Ꝺ is used regularly as a lc letter, occasionally initially, but that does not necessarily signify that it was perceived as a capital, as ꝼ, p also occur lc initially; roman H is used in an AS name-element Heopτu on 6T1ᵛ. Note Ꝺex-τolðerꟁam on 7H1ʳ (p. 435).

Note 2: AS capitals are also used with Roman ones in a Latin inscription on 4Y1ʳ.

Note 3: There are apparently two sorts for **s**, e.g. on 3A1ᵛ (p. 166), 3M1ʳ (p. 197); the one with the top stroke going up at a steep angle is probably a miscasting.

    Copy seen: BL Maps C.5.d.3 (Shirley T.BLA-1h).
    Copies also at: OXC, BBP, TFM, VUB; UBC.

Bibliography: Keuning 1959: 84–85; Koeman 1967–71: Bl.43A; Koeman 1970: 36–39; Lucas 2018: 229–233; Shirley 1991: nos 548–550; Skelton 1970: no. 28; Vervey 1981: 13–14.

1645.2: Blaeu, Joan, *Le Theatre du Monde, ou Nouvel Atlas, mis en lumiere par Guillaume et Iean Blaeu. Quatriesme Partie* (= French translation of Camden's *Britannia*, as in 1607.2, based on 1645.1). Amsterdam: Joan Blaeu I, 1645. USTC 1015077. Re-issued 1646, 1648, with the date changed. CAS3.

ASC (C) and (F) extracts, OE proper names

Collation: 2⁰: π² *3 (*3 + χ1.2) A–K² L¹ M–P² Q¹ R–V² X² (X1 + χ1.2) Y–2B² 2C¹ 2D–2M² 2N¹ 2O–2S² 2T¹ 2V–3H² 3I¹ 3K–3S² 3T¹ 3V–3Y² 3Z² (3Z2 + χ1.2) 4A–4I² 4K¹ 4L–4T² 4V² (4V2 + χ1.2) 4X² 4Y¹ 4Z–5B² 5C¹ 5D–5E² 5F¹ 5G–5I² 5K¹ 5L² 5M¹ 5N–5P² 5Q¹ 5R–5T² 5V¹ 5X² 5Y¹ 5Z² 6A¹ 6B–6N² [$2 signed (-*2, *3, A2, R2, 2A2, 2D2, 2F2, 2H2, 2L2, 2O2, 2Q2, 2R2, 2V2, 2Y2, 3A2, 3D2, 3E2, 3G2, 3K2, 3M2, 3O2, 3R2, 3V1 (but entered by hand), 3V2, 3Y2, 4A2, 4C2, 4D2, 4F2, 4G2, 4H2, 4L2, 4M2, 4N2, 4Q2, 4R2, 4T2, 4X2, 4Z2, 5A2, 5B2, 5D2. 5E2, 5G2, 5H2, 5I2, 5L2, 5N2, 5O2, 5R2, 5S2, 5X2, 5Y2, 5Z2, 6B2, 6C2, 6G2, 6I2, 6L2, 6M2, 6N2); T2 missigned T3, 2D missigned D, 2S2 missigned S2] 244 + 8 leaves, paginated [i–x], 1–380, *381–382* (pp. nos 111–116 used twice, pp. nos 51–60, 285–290 not used, pp. 66 misnumbered 50, 80–85 misnumbered 70–75, 93 misnumbered 87, 165 misnumbered 164, 207 misnumbered 107, 251–252 misnumbered 245–246, 253–256 misnumbered 153–156, 263 misnumbered 167, 280 misnumbered 268, pp. 222, 372 not numbered, with pages showing maps not included in the pagination, except for 6K1ᵛ).

Note 1: Because this is a large atlas all the leaves are mounted on guards.

Note 2: The running title on 3N2ʳ is erron. 'OXFORD-SHIRE' but should be 'HERFORD-SHIRE'.

SOURCE OF PASSAGE UTILIZING ANGLO-SAXON TYPES:

6F1ᵛ (p. 358)   From **1645.1** 7E2ʳ: ASC(C + F) 188/189 (extracts), as Thorpe 1861: 14–15, including erron. ſæ op ſæ with p for þ, and note the use of AS ſ (as opposed to Roman long ſ) in only the first of 4 instances of ſæ; erron. ꝼoꞃᵹẏnð is also taken over.

TYPE:

Main text in Pierre Haultin's English-size Roman (but with some different capitals, e.g., C, S; Body 96) interspersed with Robert Granjon's 3rd English-size Italic, e.g., on 2T1ʳ, in two columns.

Sigs M–N (on numismatic matters) are set in Haultin's Great Primer (but with some different capitals, e.g., C, M; Body 115). This larger type is also used for the tribe-headings and historical resumés, and in some of these the English-size AS is used in words, where it is ill-fitting, e.g. on 2F1ʳ, 2T1ᵛ.

CAS3: The Voskens/Blaeu English-size Anglo-Saxon occurs in the specimen on *3ʳ and is used in the text in combination with the English-size Roman on p. 358 and in words on pp. 13, 65, 75, 85, 87–88, 93, 97, 99, 105, 107, (¹111–114, ¹116, ²111, ²112, ²116), 118, 121, 122 (with erron. Tꞃuþabꞃıᵹ), 123, 127, 129–131, 132 (showing erron. neꝥan Ɱynꞅðeꝥ), 136, 138, 139 (with 2x erron. –ꝥoꝥð for -ꞃopð), 140–141, 144–145, 147–148, 150, 153–154, 156–63, 165, 168 (with erron. Ⅽ)eꞃꞃcþaꞃe for 1607.2 Ⅽ)eꞃꞃc-paꞃe), 170 (with erron. -ꞃchýꞃe for -ꞃchýꞃe), 171–174, 177, 178 (with erron. Baenꞃbýꞃıꝺ, *recte* Baneꞃ-), 179, 185–186, 191, 199, 207, 210, 212, 213 (with erron. Ꝺaꞃe-þıc for *recte* Ꝺaꞃeꞃıc), 215–216, 218, 222–224, 228, 231, 233 (with erron. Ꝺunðeðune- for *recte* Ꝺunceðune-), 236, 243–244, 246–247, 251–252, 253, 255, 259, 262 (with erron. Ⅵne-ceaꞃ-ven-ꞃcýꝺe for *recte* Ⅵꞃeceaꞃ-ꞃeꞃcýꞃe), 263, 265–266, 268, 270–272, 275–277, 280, 283, 298, 304, 311, 314, 319 (with *recte* Ꝺueꞃꞃıc), 329–330, 335, 338, 340–341, 344;

AS forms that would be included in a completely faithful rendering of Camden's text are rendered in Italic on 4P1ᵛ (p. 264), 5P1 (pp. 321–2), 5P1ʳ (p. 323), 5R2ᵛ (p. 328), 6F2ᵛ (p. 360), 6H1ᵛ (p. 364), 6H2ᵛ (p. 366), 6I2ᵛ (p. 370), 6M1ʳ (p. 377). Special sorts shown in specimen on *3ʳ:

    11 lower-case sorts: ð, *e*, ꞃ, ꝺ, ꞃ, ꞃ, c, ẏ; þ, ð, p;
    8 capitals: Æ¹, Æ², Ꝼ, Ꝺ, Ⅽ), S, X; Ð;
    2 others: þ, ꞽ.
  Total: 21 sorts.

Note 1: Ꝺ is glossed '*h*', so it may have been perceived as lc, but as Æ¹ amd M are glossed '*æ*' and '*m*' respectively nothing decisive can be deduced from this observation. See also Note 5 below.

Note 2: Lower-case y is surmounted by a dot, slightly to the left of centre. See also Note 4 below.

Special sorts shown in the text:

    11 lower-case sorts: ð, *e*, ꞃ, ꝺ, ꞃ, ꞃ, c, ẏ; þ, ð, p;
    8 capitals: Ꝼ, Ꝺ (used uc and lc on 2O1ʳ), Ⅽ), S; Ð;
    1 other: ꞽ (e.g., X1ʳ)
  Total: 17 sorts.
  Overall total: 11 + 8 + 3 = 22 sorts.

Note 3: Two s-sorts, one with a short top-stroke hooked downwards, can be seen together on, e.g., 4T1ʳ (p. 275).

Note 4: The y-sort on 2G1ʳ is a Pica y surmounted by a dot, also on 2O1ʳ. On 2M1ʳ English-size y occurs twice, but while the first has a central dot, the dot is slightly to the right of centre in the second. On 3V1ʳ a Great Primer y is surmounted by an acute accent.

Note 5: Roman H occurs initially in Heoꞃcu (5X2ᵛ).

Note 6: The opportunity to use a distinctive AS Æ is avoided on 3K2ᵛ in Æꝺleꞃbuꞃꝺe.

Note 7: AS capitals are also used with Roman ones in a Latin inscription on 4I1ʳ.

    Copy seen: OBL 2027.a.46 (Map Res 31 = 1648 re-issue, with contemporary Dutch binding in white vellum with gold tooling, and with hand-coloured maps and illustrations; this volume of the set lacks tp, also the map of England which belongs in sig. x (but no text lost); 6N2 (*indice des cartes*) has been detached and re-inserted after π2).

Copy also at: AUB.

Bibliography: Koeman 1967–71: Bl.42A; Shirley 1991: nos 551–553; Skelton 1970: no. 29;

1646 re-issue: Koeman 1967–71: Bl.42B; Shirley 1991: nos 568–570; Skelton 1970: no. 31;

1648 re-issue: Koeman 1967–71: Bl.42C; Shirley 1991: nos 619–621; Skelton 1970: no. 43;

Lucas 2018: 228–233.

1645.3: Vossius, Gerardus Joannes, *De Vitiis Sermonis, et Glossematis Latino-Barbaris, Libri Quatuor*. Amsterdam: Louis Elzevier, 1645. USTC 1032615.

  Collation: 4^0: ?⁴ *–3*⁴ A–5X⁴ [5Y]¹. 488 leaves.

Words in AS and other Germanic languages appear in Textura with no special sorts, e.g., $2H4^v$ (p. 248).

Note: The AS sorts of **1636.1** are not shown.

  Copy seen: CUL Aa*.10.20.

  Copies also at: BL, TCC, DUL, GUL, OBL, OBC, OTC, UCL, PBN, PBM, PBSG, BxBM, LBM, OMM, RmBM, SBPU, GCB, AUB, HKB, LUB, GCB, GRUB, KUB, WHAB, SKB, FBC, FBN, MAS, NBN, OBFC, RBN, VIP, SvBU; NYPL, HUL, IUL, IBUL; OUL.

1646.1: Gregory, John, *Notes and Observations upon some Passages of Scripture*. Oxford: Henry Hall for Edward Forrest I, 1646. Wing G1920; ESTC R200932. AS3. **Words**

  Collation: 4^0: A⁴ ¶⁴ *⁴ B–Z⁴ [$3 signed (-A1, F3, L3)] 100 leaves, paginated [i–xxiv], 1–176.

TYPE:

Main text in a Pica Roman (g has a shoulder link pointing down).

AS3: The Lambardian Pica Anglo-Saxon occurs in the 'words' 'ȝunȝal Whiteȝan' (with ꞇ for t, i.e 'white star') on $V3^v$ (p. 150) combined with the Pica Roman; Special sorts used: 1 lower-case: ȝ, and 1 other: ꞇ. Total: 2.

Note: Special sorts are used for astrological symbols on $*4^r$ and $V4^v$.

  Copies: CUL 8.24.13²; LFL T312³; OBL 4^0.A.1⁷.Th.Seld (Selden's copy).

  Copies also at: BL, CQC, TCC, GUL, NT, OAS, OCC, OQC, OStE, OXC, TPL, WAL, DML, TCD; HHL, IUL, AAS, SCL, UCLA, UTA, YUB.

Bibliography: Madan 1895–1931: II, 426, no. 1879.

1646.2: Spelman, Sir Henry, ed. Jeremiah Stephens, *Tithes too Hot to be Touched*. London: [Miles Flesher] for Philemon Stephens (brother of editor), 1646 (main parts re-issued 1647.1). Wing S4931; ESTC R19648. AS4.

> **Date:** [1646]. Apparently written by 1613, as implied by Spelman in his *De Non Temerandis Ecclesiis* (London: John Beale, 1613; STC 23067.4), B2^r–3^v.

Words

> **Collation:** 4⁰: A⁸ a–d⁴ B–2A⁴ 2B² [$3 signed (+ A6 missigned A4; -A1, 2B2; d2 signed A2, B2 signed A2)] 118 leaves, paginated [i–l], 1–189, *190* (p. 188 misnumbered 288; pp. nos 113–114 used twice; pp. nos 61–66, 137–138 not used).

TYPE:

Main text in Pierre Haultin's English-size Roman (Body 93);
AS4: The Spelmanian Great Primer Anglo-Saxon combined with Haultin's English-size Roman occurs in words on K1^r (p. 67);
Special sorts shown: 5 lower-case sorts: e, ı, ſ, τ; ð.

> **Copies seen:** ECC 330.4.62¹ (sig. A2 from 1647.1 inserted after A8); TCD HH.gg.29¹ (sig. A2 from 1647.1 inserted after A1), NN.m.37¹ (Claudius Gilbert's copy; sig. A2 from 1647.1 inserted after A1); OBL Wood B.32.

> **Copies also at:** BL, BPL, BSO, CUL, CSJ, CaCL, DWL, GUL, LHL, LSH, NAL, NCL, NLS, NLW, OAS, OBC, OCC, OSJ, OXC, SUL, UBL, UCL; FSL, NYCU, UTS, HHL, HUL, IUL, CPL, MCRS, UCBL, YUB, TUL; JUT.

Bibliography: Parry 1995: 163–164; Woolf 1990: 223.

1646.3: Janssonius, Joannes, *Novus Atlas, sive Theatrum Orbis Terrarum*, vol. IV (= Camden's *Britannia*, as in 1607.2 with some rearrangement in the order of counties and additional passages marking the introduction of S. and N. Wales and Yorkshire, and a new description of the Fens). Amsterdam: Joannes Janssonius, 1646. Re-issued 1649 with only the date changed = USTC 1513713. CAS4.

ASC (C) and (F) extracts, OE proper names

> **Collation:** 2⁰: *–2*² A–2A² 2B¹ 2C–2E² 2F¹ 2G–2Q² 2R¹ 2S–3F² 3G¹ 3H–3L² 3M¹ 3N–3O² 3P¹ 3Q–3S² 3T¹ 3V–4E² 4F¹ 4G–4H² 4I¹ 4K–4L² 4M¹ 4N–4O² 4P¹ 4Q–4T² 4V¹ 4X–5E² 5F–5G¹ 5H–5K² 5L¹ 5M² 5N¹ 5O–5Z² 6A¹ 6B–6I² 2A–P² 2Q¹ 2R² 2S¹ [$2 signed (-*1, A2, D2, P2, T2, Y2, 2C2, 2E2, 2G2, 2L2, 2N2, 2S2, 2V2, 2Y2, 3B2, 3D2, 3F2, 3K2, 3N2, 3Q2, 3S2, 3V2, 3Y2, 3Z2, 4B2, 4D2, 4G2, 4H2, 4K2, 4N2, 4Q2, 4S2, 4T2, 4X2, 4Z2, 5B2, 5C2, 5D2, 5H2, 5I2, 5K2, 5M2, 5O2, 5Q2, 5S2, 5V2, 6B2, 6E2, 6H2, ²A2, ²B2, ²I2, ²K2, ²M2, ²N2, ²O2, ²P2)] 268 leaves, paginated [i–viii], 1–364, ²1–50, ²*51–52* (p. 210 not numbered; pp. 199 misnumbered 196, 219 misnumbered 119, 236 misnumbered 136, 270 misnumbered 170, 342–343 misnumbered 442

and 243, ²29–30 misnumbered 25–26; 55 double-page openings with illustrative maps are not included in the pagination).

SOURCE OF PASSAGE UTILIZING ANGLO-SAXON TYPES:

5Z2ᵛ (p. 336)   From 1607.2 4Y4ʳ: *ASC*(C + F) 189/188 (extracts), both as Thorpe 1861: I.14–15;

TYPE:

Main text in Pierre Haultin's English-size Roman (Body 94, in the Janssonius 1666 specimen, A3ʳ) interspersed with Robert Granjon's 3rd English-size Italic (the one shown in the Janssonius 1666 specimen, A3ʳ), but another on sig. 5I–5P, and yet another on sig. 5Q–5T.

CAS 4: The Dutch Janssonian English-size imitation of the Lambardian Pica Anglo-Saxon occurs in the specimen on 2*2ʳ showing the following special sorts (Illustration 43):

    11 lower-case sorts: ð, *e*, ꝼ, ȝ (= yogh of roman fount), ꝥ, ꞃ, ꞇ, ẏ; þ, ð, p;
    8 capitals: Æ¹, Æ², Є, Ꞅ, Ꝁ, S, Ð, X;
    2 others: ꝯ, þ.

Total: 21 sorts.

CAS 4: The Dutch Janssonian English-size Anglo-Saxon combined with Haultin's English-size Roman occurs in the text in words on pp. 11, 47 (retaining erron. p from 1607.2 for 1600.1 þ; shows 2 sorts for ꝥ and large ȝ), 56 (S for d), 66–67, 69, 73, 74 (showing 3 beside AS ȝ; d looks better than in specimen), 77, 78 (with inverted t), 79–84, 87 (good p), 89–90, 92–93, 95, 97–98, 99 (d used for S; 2 sorts for h/H used lc), 100, 101 (good d), 102, 105 (good small t), 107, 108 (retaining from 1607.2 erron. Mẏnꞃðeꝥ for 1600.1 mẏnꞃꞇeꝥ), 112–114, 117, 119, 121, 124 (with 2 t's and 2 þ's), 125, 128–132, 134, 138, 140, 144 (with d for S, and 2 s's), 145–148, 154–157, 161–162, 167, 172, 180–181, 183 (with 2 sorts for cap M), 185, 187–188, 190, 194 (with inverted 2 for t), 195, 196 (with two r's), 200 (with 2 r's and two different inverted 2's for t), 203, 205 (with S for d), 211, 219, 221, 223–224, 228, 230 (with d for S once but correct S twice), 233, 237, 241–244, 246 (with two sorts for t), 248, 250, 253–255, 258, 263, 274, 286, 290–291, 294, 296–297, 298 (with erron. þ and italic p for p), 302–304, 310 (with S for d, and large ꝼ), 313 (with italic p for W), 315, 317, 321, 338 (with italic p for p erron for þ), 342–344, 350, 352.

AS words also occur combined with a Great Primer Roman (no. 2 in the Janssonius 1666 specimen, A2ᵛ) in head-notes set in François Guyot's Great Primer Italic (Body 117; no. 1 in the Janssonius 1666 specimen, A2ᵛ), e.g. Y1ʳ (p. 77), 2P2ᵛ (p. 128), 3N1ʳ (p. 187), 5G1ᵛ (p. 290), 6A1ᵛ/ab (p. 338 best e.g. of use and contrast with setting in English-size, see Illustration 45), for which some larger sorts were presumably designed, though the sizes are mixed up in use. Large (i.e. Great Primer) sorts occur for f (both sizes on 2G2ᵛ/a), g (on N2ʳ/b), r (both on 3R2ᵛ/b), s (both on 2X2ᵛ), t (both on 4N2ᵛ/b), þ (both on 2O2ᵛ/a),

p (small on 2B1ʳ/a, large on Z1ʳ/b). Perhaps this explanation also accounts for the two h/H's? Apparently also two sizes of S were made, but the smaller one (as on 2A1ᵛ/a) was mistakenly used for d, as on 3V1ʳ/a, and this mistake later became prevalent in 1659.2.
Special sorts used in text:

12 (+ 7) lower-case sorts (fgrstþp 2x):	ð, e (1st on 2H1ʳ/a), ꝼ (x 2), ȝ (x 2), ꝺ, ꞃ (x 2), ſ (x 2), ꞇ (x 2), ẏ; þ (x 2), ð, p (x 2);
5 (+ 1) capitals:	Є, Ꝺ, Ꝿ, Ꞅ (x 2), Ð;
1 other:	˙ɟ (punctus versus);

Total: 12 + 5 + 1 = 18 (+8) sorts.
Note 1: Also uses the ȝ 'yogh' of the English-size Roman, e.g. on 2L1ʳ/b.
Note 2: The two different h/H sorts can be seen side by side on 2I1ʳ (p. 105).
Note 3: Inverted 2 (two designs) is often used for t, as on 3R2ᵛ/b.
Note 4: AS capitals are also used with Roman ones in a Latin inscription on 4D2ᵛ.

Copies seen: BL Maps C.6.b.1 (Shirley T.JAN-3a) with hand-coloured tp, maps and illustrations; CUL Atlas.3.65.4.
Copy also at: BUN (= 1649 re-issue).
Bibliography: Keuning 1951: 78–79; Krogt 1997: 1:403.4I; Lucas 2018: 233–239; Moreland and Bannister 1989: 110–111, 303–305; Shirley 1991: nos 575–577; Skelton 1970: no. 34.
Facsimile: Mais 1951 (tp, 2*1ᵛ, and 34 maps only, reduced).

1646.4: Janssonius, Joannes, *Le Nouvel Atlas ou Theatre du Monde, auquel est representée La Grande Bretagne, contenant les Royaumes d'Angleterre, d'Escosse & d'Irlande*, vol. IV (= French translation of **1646.3** based on Camden's *Britannia*, as in **1607.2**). Amsterdam: Joannes Janssonius, 1646. USTC 1513106. Re-issued 1647, 1658 with the date changed. CAS4.

ASC (C) and (F) extracts, OE proper names

Collation: [main text in 2 booklets, A-6O, ²A-Q (Scotland and Ireland)]: 2⁰: *-2*² A-L² M¹ N-Q² R¹ S-X² Y¹ Z-2I² 2K¹ 2L-2M² 2N¹ 2O-2R² 2S¹ 2T-3G² 3H¹ 3I-3K² 3L¹ 3M² 3N¹ 3O-3R² 3S¹ 3T-3V² 3X¹ 3Y-4G² 4H¹ 4I-4O² 4P¹ 4Q-4R² 4S¹ 4T-4V² 4X¹ 4Y-5B² 5C¹ 5D-5F² 5G¹ 5H-5M² 5N¹ 5O-5Q² 5R¹ 5S-5V² 5X¹ 5Y² 5Z¹ 6A² 6B¹ 6C-6E² 6F¹ 6G-6O² ²A-G² ²H¹ ²I-Q² [$2 signed (-*1, A2, E2, Z2, 2G2, 2I2, 2L2, 2Q2, 2T2, 2Y2, 3A2, 3C2, 3E2, 3I2, 3M2, 3O2, 3T2, 3Y2, 4A2, 4C2, 4E2, 4F2, 4G2, 4I2, 4L2, 4N2, 4O2, 4Q2, 4T2, 4Y2, 5A2, 5B2, 5D2, 5F2, 5H2, 5I2, 5K2, 5O2, 5P2, 5S2, 5T2, 5Y2, 6A2, 6C2, 6H2, 6L2, 6N2, ²A2, ²C2, ²I2, ²K2, ²M2, ²N2, ²O2, ²P2)] 270 leaves, paginated [i–viii], 1–374, ²1–46 (pp. 63–66 misnumbered 73–76, 235–236 misnumbered 233–234, 270 misnumbered 268, 369–374 misnumbered

375–380; 56 double-page openings with illustrative maps are not included in the pagination).

SOURCE OF PASSAGE UTILIZING ANGLO-SAXON TYPES:

6G1ᵛ (p. 350)   From 1646.3 5Z2ᵛ: ASC(C + F) 189/188 (extracts), both as Thorpe 1861: I.14–15;

TYPE:

Main text in an English-size Roman (Body 93) interspersed with an English-size Italic (e.g., on 2N1ʳ), another from S-3X.

CAS4: The Dutch Janssonian English-size imitation of the Lambardian Pica Anglo-Saxon occurs in the specimen on 2*2ᵛ showing the following special sorts:

    11 lower-case sorts: ð, e, f, ᵹ, p, r, t, ẏ; þ, ð, p;
    8 capitals: Æ¹, Æ², E, Ð, M, S, Ð, X;
    2 others: þ, ȝ.
  Total: 21 sorts.

The Dutch Janssonian English-size Anglo-Saxon combined with the English-size Roman occurs in the text in words on pp. 13, 55–56 (retaining erron. p from 1607.2 for 1600.1 þ), 65, 75 (shows 2 sorts for p, small þ), 77–78, 83 (showing 3 beside AS ᵹ, and 2 s-sorts), 87 (with 2 sorts of inverted 2 for t), 88 (with 2 for t, large þ), 89, 90, (with 2 e and s sorts), 92 (with 2 r sorts), 94 (with 2 sorts of inverted 2 for t, ?non-AS d), 95 (d smaller than on p. 94), 98–101, 104–105, 107, 109–111, 2L2ᵛ/a (p. '99'), 113 (small ?non-AS d), 114–115, 119, 121, 123 (retaining (as 1646.3) from 1607.2 erron. Mẏnrðep for 1600.1 mẏnrtep), 127–128, 129 (with Hebrew final-position 'tzade' for r), 135, 137, 141 (with 2 þ's), 143, 144 (with 2 s's, one not AS), 145–148, 150, 152, 156, 158, 163–167, 173–174, 175 (with erron. þ for p), 176, 182–183, 188, 194 (with erron. d for S), 195, 203–4, 206 (with crude cap M), 208–209, 211–212, 214 (with *recte* heaðleᵹe for 1646.3 heaᵹleᵹe), 218–220, 224, 227, 229, 233 (with ȝ erron. for y), 240–241, 243–244, 248, 250, 252, 256, 259–263, 265–266, 268, 271–272, 274, 276, 281, 292, 303, 308 (with S (= modified 8) for d), 309, 321–322, 327 (with S for ð, and p for r), 330–333, 336 (with italic þ for p), 357, 363, 365 (with 2 sizes of ᵹ and Hebrew final-position 'tzade' for r).

Special sorts shown in the text (which, as far as the AS is concerned, is poorly set, and inverted 2 for t is prevalent):

Lower-case sorts: ð (x 2, used for S on 3Q1ᵛ/a), e (x 2), f, ᵹ (x 2, both, e.g., on 4D2ʳ/ab), p (x 2), r (x 2), t (e.g., 4C2ᵛ, but frequently inverted 2), ẏ (1st on 2M1ᵛ/b); þ (x 2, one italic), ð, p (x 2, (1) roman, clear example on 4B1ʳ/a, (2) italic on 3Q2ʳ/a);

Capitals: E (2 sorts, both, e.g., on 4D2ʳ/ab), Ð (used lc Q1ʳ/b; 2 sorts, both on 4O2ᵛ/b), M (with variant from another fount, e.g., 2R1ʳ/a), S (2 sorts, (1)

e.g., on 4T1ʳ/a, (2) larger variant on 4L2ᵛ/b, which on 4V1ᵛ/a looks like 8 with the top right corner broken off), Ð;
Other: ȷ̇.
There are three sorts of ẏ, (1) with grave accent to right of centre (e.g., 2M1ᵛ/b), (2) with grave accent to left of centre (e.g., 2M2ʳ/b), and (3) with a dot, e.g. on 2R1ʳ/b; smaller y on 3E1ʳ/a.
Total sorts: 11 (degrsyþp 2x, y x3) + 5 (EHMS x2) + 1 (Ð) = 17 (+ 15).
Note 1: Some other sorts are also imported, such as Hebrew final-position 'tzade' for ſ.
Note 2: AS capitals are also used with roman ones in a Latin inscription on 4L2ᵛ.
Note 3: Towards the end of the book the Anglo-Saxon is omitted on pp. 313–316, 320, 352, 356, 358.

>Copies seen: BL C.6.b.2 (= 1647 re-issue; Shirley T.JAN-3e); CUL Atlas 3.65.10 (re-issue dated 1652; Latin title, lacks main text).

>Copies also at: PBN, LBS, MBU, PNL.

Bibliography: Krogt 1997: I.1:414.4I; Shirley 1991: nos 579–582; Skelton 1970: no. 35;

1647 re-issue: Krogt 1997: I.1:415.4J; Shirley 1991: nos 603–606; Skelton 1970: no. 39;

1658 re-issue: Krogt 1997: I.1:417.4L; Skelton 1970: no. 52;

Lucas 2018: 233–239.

1646.5: Blaeu, Joan, Novus Atlas, *Das ist Welt-beschreibung mit schönen newen auszführlichen Land-Taffeln in Kupffer gestochen und an den Tag gegeben*, vol. IV (= German translation of Camden's *Britannia*, as in **1607.2** based on **1645.1**). Amsterdam, Joan Blaeu I, 1646. Re-issued 1647, 1648 (based on maps of **1648.1**) = USTC 1513612, with the date changed, and (?)1652 with new tp and additional maps (BL Maps 9 Tab.21). CAS3.

Alphabetical Specimen

>Collation: 2⁰: [8] 488 [i.e. 448] [1] [54] [4] p

TYPE:

Main text in an English-size Fraktur (Body 95).

CAS5: The Blaeu/Voskens English-size Anglo-Saxon shown in the specimen on 2*.*1ʳ:

Special sorts shown:	10 lower-case sorts:	ð, e, f, ȝ, Ƕ, p, ſ, t; þ, ð, p;
	8 capitals:	Æ¹, Æ², Є, Ϣ, S, Ð, X;
	2 others:	þ, ȷ.
	Total:	20 sorts.

Note: Anglo-Saxon capital Ƕ is indicated as a lower-case letter. Anglo-Saxon ẏ is not shown.

Copy seen: LBL Whitaker 31 (1648 re-issue) with hand-coloured maps and 'Blaeu' binding of white vellum on boards with gold-tooled ornament. Ex libris Fridericus Müller â Löwenstein; stamp of Herzoglicher S. Meiningischer Bibliothek.
Copy also at: PNL (1648 re-issue).
Bibliography: Koeman 1967–71: Bl.47A/B/C/D; Shirley 1991: nos 571–573 and 622–624 (1648 re-issue); Skelton 1970: 32, 33, 44.

1646.6: Selden, John, *Uxor Ebraica Seu De Nuptiis & Divortiis Ex Iure Civili, id est, Divino & Talmudico, Veterum Ebræorum, Libri Tres*. London: Richard Bishop, 1646. Wing S2443; ESTC R4001. AS1.

Laws (extracts)

    Collation: 4⁰: a⁴ (±a1, -a2) b⁴ A–4L⁴ [sigs a–b, A–Z $3 signed (-a1, b3; a3 missigned b3); sigs 2A–4L $2 signed] 327 leaves, paginated [i–xxii], 1–630, *631–632*.

SOURCES OF PASSAGES UTILIZING ANGLO-SAXON TYPES:

2N4ᵛ (p. 280)   From **1644.1** Q2ʳ: Law II Cnut §70.1 (Liebermann I.356); the reading æhte confirms the use of Lambarde's text;

2R4ʳ (p. 311)   From **1639.4** 2M2ᵛ–3ʳ or **1644.1** H3ʳ: Law *Be wifmannes beweddunge* §§ 6 (extract) and 8 (Liebermann I.442); Selden gives both references, referring to **1644.1** as Lambarde, *Archaionomia*, but the reference to p. 60 can only be to **1644.1** not **1568.2**.

TYPE:

Main text in Pierre Haultin's English-size Roman (Body 100).

AS1: The Parkerian Great Primer Anglo-Saxon occurs combined with Haultin's English-size Roman in text as indicated above.

Special sorts shown:	10 lower-case sorts:	ð, f, ʒ, ı, ꝑ, ſ, ꞇ; þ, ð, ꝑ;
	1 capital:	Æ²;
	1 other:	ꝑ.
Total:	12 sorts	

Note 1: Roman y is used for Anglo-Saxon ẏ;

Note 2: On 2O3ʳ (p. 285) Selden quotes Chaucer CT A.459–60 in a Paragon Textura.

Translation: J.R. Siskind, *John Selden on Jewish Marriage Law* (Leiden: Brill, 1991).

    Copies: CUL Q*.5.29(E) (lacks a2), Bensly.5.b.76 (lacks a2; signed by I. Carpenter and William Booth), C.5.8 (lacks a2; sigs b and A in reverse order).

    Copies also at: APL, BL, BUT, CCC, TCC, DUL, ECL, MTP, NLS, NT, OBL, OJC, OQC, OSJ, OXC, SDC, WiCL, WoCL, YML, DML, PBN, PBM, BSB, MUC; FSL, USLC, NYPL, NYCU, HHL, HUL, IUL, BMC, PrTS, UCLA, QUK.

Bibliography: McKenzie & Bell 2005: I.528; Toomer 2009: II.643–691.

1646.7: Verstegan, Richard, *Nederlantsche Antiquiteyten met de bekeeringhe van eenighe der selve Landen tot het Kersten gheloove, door S. Willibrordvs*. Brussels: Govaerdt Schoevaerdts, 1646. USTC 1513131. Reprint of **1613.3**.
    Collation: 8⁰: A–O⁸. 112 p.
OE text of the Lord's Prayer, the Hail Mary, and the beginning of St John's Gospel printed in a Long Primer Textura with no special sorts on C3ʳ–4ᵛ.
    Copy seen: BL 4685.a.4.
    Copy also at: AUB.

1647.1: Spelman, Sir Henry, ed. Jeremiah Stephens, *The Larger Treatise concerning Tithes*. London: M[iles] F[lesher] for Philemon Stephens (brother of editor) 1647. Wing S4928. (Mostly) reissue of **1646.2**. AS4.
Words
    Collation: 4⁰: A² a–d⁴ B–2A⁴ 2B² [a]–[c]⁴ [d]² [$3 signed (-A1, 2B2; d2 signed A2, d3 signed A3, B2 signed A2)] 126 leaves, paginated [i–xl], 1–189, *190*, ²1–27, ²28 (pp. nos 113–114 used twice; pp. nos 61–66, 137–138 not used).
Type: as **1646.2**.
    Copies seen: CCA W/L.1.48 (Somner's copy, gift of Sir Roger Twysden; also contains Spelman's *Apology of the Treatise De non temerandis Ecclesiis* [Wing S4917] inserted before the *Answer*); ECC 328.2.31;
    Lacking sigs.[a–d]: APL AA.IV.32; OBL 4⁰.L.6⁴.Th.BS.
    Copies also at: BL, BCL, BrPL, CUL, TCC, CaCL, DUL, DWL, EAL, ECL, Eton, LCL, LPL, LSE, LSH, MCS, NLS, NT, OBC, OEC, ONC, OQC, OXC, SPC, UBL, YML, DEWL, DML, KSC, PBN; FSL, UTS, HHL, HUL, IUL, NLC, UCLA, UMI, QUK; NLA.
Bibliography: see **1646.2**.

1647.2 Selden, John (ed.), *Fleta seu Commentarius Juris Anglicani*. London: Miles Flesher for William Lee II, Matthew Walbancke and Daniel Pakeman, 1647. Wing F1290, F1290A = ESTC R15006, R2001. AS4.
ASC **(extract)**
    Collation: 2⁰ in 4s: A–4B⁴ [$3 signed (-A1, Q3, V3, X3, Y3, Z3, 2A3, 2B3, 2C3, 2D3, 2E3, 4B3)] 284 leaves, paginated [i–viii], 1–553, *554–556* (pp. nos 63–64 used twice; after p. 552 there are two blank pages unnumbered; pp. 82 misnumbered 28, 158 misnumbered 160, 228 misnumbered 28). Wing F1290 shows ±A1.
    Variant states shown by M3 unsigned and p. 158 correctly numbered: p. 158 correct in LFL 4A; both correct in CUL J.14.22.
SOURCE OF PASSAGE UTILIZING ANGLO-SAXON TYPES:
3Q2ᵛ (p. 480)   From **1643.1** 3V2ʳ, cited as p. 507: *Anglo-Saxon Chronicle* 435, recte 409 (opening statement), as Thorpe 1861: I.16/27–30.

Note: The L text is based on Julius B.viii, as noted by Wormald and Wright 1958: 203.

TYPE:

Main text of Dissertatio in Pierre Haultin's English-size Roman (Body 92) interspersed with Robert Granjon's 3rd English-size Italic.

AS4: The Spelmannian Great Primer Anglo-Saxon occurs in text as indicated above under Contents combined with Haultin's English-size Roman.

Special sorts shown: 8 lower-case sorts: ð, e, ꝼ, ı, ꝓ, ſ, τ; þ;
                             1 other: ȝ.
                    Total: 9 sorts.

Copies seen: Wing F1290: CUL J.14.22. Wing F1290A: CUL J.10.24 (gift of John Hacket, bp of Lichfield, 1670); LFL 4A (p. 158 correctly numbered); PO 1647.2 (M3 unsigned).

Copies also at: Wing F1290: BL, CJC, CNC, CSel, CSJ, CTH, NT, NUL, OBL, OAS, OCC, OXC, SPC, YML, DML, TCD, BSB; USLC NYCU, NYFU, HUL, IUL, JCB, PUL, UCLA, YUB; OLS.

Wing F1290A: BL, DWL, OBL, OBrC, OHF, OQC, SCL, YML, DEWL, DKI, GUB; USLC, HHL, HUL, PUL; VSL.

Bibliography: Denholm-Young 1969: ch. 10; Ogg 1925; Toomer 2009: I.196–210.

1647.3: Janssonius, Joannes, *Novus Atlas, oder Welt-Beschreibung, in welcher ausführlich abgebildet Die Königreiche Engelland, Schotland und Irland. Das Vierdte Theil.* (= German translation of Camden's *Britannia*, based on 1607.2). Amsterdam: Joannes Janssonius, 1647. USTC 1122346. CAS4.

Alphabetical Specimen

     Collation: 2^0: *–2*² A–7G² a–x². [8] 452 62 [2] p. 56 maps.

TYPE:

Main text in an English-size Fraktur (Body 93), with Anglo-Saxon printed in Roman (without special sorts) interspersed as appropriate.

AS in specimen on 2*2ᵛ, showing the following special sorts (looking somewhat worn):

                 10 lower-case sorts: ð, ꝼ, ȝ, ꝓ, ſ, τ, ẏ; þ, ð, p;
                 8 capitals: Æ¹, Æ², Є, Ð, Ϻ, S, Ð, X;
                 2 other: þ, ȝ.
     Total: 21 sorts.

Note: The **e**-sort may be a special one, but it is not possible to distinguish it from standard **e**.

     Copy seen: BL Maps 9.Tab.4 (with maps, tp, and illustrations hand-coloured).

     Note: There are copies of both the 1652 and the 1658 re-issues in GNM (not seen); see *National Maritime Museum Catalogue of the Library*, introd. Michael Sanderson, 5 vols (London, HMSO, 1968–), III.1, nos 102–103.

Bibliography: Koeman/Krogt 1997: I.1:425.4J; Shirley 1991: nos 607–610; Skelton 1970: nos 40 and 46. For the 1652 re-issue (vol. 5 of six) see Krogt 1997: I.1:427.5; Skelton 1970: no. 53; for the 1658 re-issue in two volumes, vols 7–8 of the *Novus Atlas Absolutissimus*, see Krogt 1997: I.1:428.7–8 (Skelton 1970: no. 68).

1647.4: Janssonius, Joannes, *Nieuwen Atlas, ofte Werelt-Beschrijvinghe vertonende Groot Britannien, vervattende de Koninghrijcken van Engelandt Schotlandt ende Yrlandt. Het Vierde Deel.* (= Dutch translation of Camden's *Britannia*, based on 1607.2, but with some re-arrangement and the text on the Pictish Wall (including the quotations from the AS *Chronicle*) is omitted). Amsterdam: Joannes Janssonius, 1647. Not found in USTC. Re-issued 1649, 1652, 1653, 1658/9, 1659. CAS 4.

OE proper names

Collation: [Several individual signatures are bifolia and these are indicated by sig. + χ1]

π^1 ❖^{2} A–Q^2 R^1 S–X^2 Y–Z^1 2A–2C^2 2D^1 2E–2L^2 2M^2 (2M2 + χ1) 2N^2 (2N1 + χ1, 2N2 + χ1) 2O–2Q^2 2R^1 2S^4 (2S1 + χ1, 2S2 + χ1) 2T–2Y^2 2Z^4 (2Z1 + χ1, 2Z2 + χ1, 2Z3 + χ1, 2Z4 + χ1) 3A^2 3B^2 (3B2 + χ1) 3C–3E^2 3F^1 3G^2 3H^1 3I^3 (3I1 + χ1, 3I2 + χ1, 3I3 + χ1) 3K^2 (3K1 + χ1, 3K2 + χ1) 3L^2 (3L1 + χ1, 3L2 + χ1) 3M–3N^2 3O^6 (3O1 + χ1, 3O2 + χ1, 3O3 + χ1, 3O4 + χ1, 3O5 + χ1, 3O6 + χ1) 3P^2 3Q^1 3R–3S^2 3T^1 3V–3Y^2 3Z^4 (3Z1 + χ1, 3Z2 + χ1, 3Z3 + χ1) 4A^3 (4A1 + χ1, 4A2 + χ1) 4B–4C^2 4D^1 4E–4K^2 [4L]^1 [\$2 signed (+ 2S3, 2Z3, 2Z4, 3I3, 3O3, 3O4, 3O5, 3O6, 3Z3, 3Z4, 4A3; -@2, A2, S2, 2E2, 2F2, 2G2, 2H2, 2I2, 2K2, 2L2, 2O2, 2P2, 2Q2, 2T2, 2W2, 2X2, 2Y2, 3A2, 3C2, 3D2, 3E2, 3G2, 3M2, 3N2, 3P2, 3R2, 3S2, 3V2, 3Y2, 4B2, 4C2, 4E2, 4F2, 4G2, 4H2, 4I2, 4K2; 3L1 missigned 'Zll', 3Y1 missigned 'Zyy')] 194 leaves, paginated [i–vi], 1–200, *203–210* (of which the following are not numbered: pp. ^{1}97–108, ^{1}109–114, ^{1}119–120, 121–126, 129–130, 133–134, ^{1}135–140, ^{2}139–140, 141–142, ^{1}143–144, 153–158, ^{1}159–172, ^{2}163–166, ^{1}179–194, ^{2}191–196, ^{1}199–202, ^{1}201–202, ^{2}201–202; so the following pp. nos are counted twice: 101–114, 121–126, 135–140, 143–144, 159–162, 167–172, 189–192, 195–202; and pp. nos 163–166 and 193–194 are counted three times; p. ^{2}190 misnumbered 186, ^{1}197–198 misnumbered 187–188; pages showing maps are not included in the pagination).

Note 1: W is used as a signature letter under 2W.

Note 2: On sig. 2D1^v/b the bottom of the column has a slip pasted over containing the last three lines of print plus the (correct) catchword. Presumably the following section 'Het koninckrijck Engelandt', which is not from Camden, was an afterthought; although there is no disruption in the series of gathering signatures until 2M, this is the point (2E) where the page numbering begins to go awry. The catchwords also suggest that the structure of the book was being decided as it was made up.

Note 3: Because this is a large atlas all the leaves are mounted on guards.
TYPE:
Main text in an English-size Textura (Body 93.5 = Augustyn Duyts no.1 on Ploos van Amstel specimen 1767) interspersed with an English-size Roman Body 93.5 (more than one fount appears to be used, apparently corresponding to the Augustijn Romeyn nos 1 and 2 in the Janssonius 1666 specimen), e.g., ❖1ᵛ, V1ʳ, 2X2ᵛ. Sometimes a smaller size of Textura, a Pica (Body 83 = Mediaan Duits no. 2 on Ploos van Amstel specimen 1767) is used, e.g., for the whole of Nf on 2Y, but more often towards the bottom half of the b-column on the verso side (in order to fit material in on the page), e.g on ❖2ᵛ, 3L2ᵛ, 3O2c1ᵛ, 3O4c1ᵛ. At other times a larger size, a Great Primer (Body 115), is used, e.g., for the whole of the Fens on 2Z3 (bifolium), the whole of Nt on 3C, and the whole of Crd on 3L, but only the first page of La (3O6ʳ), so that the textual material fills out the two pages allowed for text on the reverse of the map.

CAS4: The special sorts made for the Janssonius atlases combined with the appropriate English-size Roman occurs in words in the text on pp. 14, 57, 59, 72, 83–84, 86, 94, ²103, ²105–106, ¹109, ¹121–122, ¹124, ²121–122, 127, ¹135, ¹139, ²137, ²139, ²144, 147, 149, ²163, ²166, ²169, ²172, 174.

The typesetter evidently had some difficulty with Anglo-Saxon, as is shown by the form 'ʒpeŋc-bpɪz-ycyŋe' on 2Z1ʳ, presumably for Ᵹpentbpɪʒrcẏpe. From 3D1ʳ onwards there is a tendency to print AS forms in Roman without special sorts.

Special sorts shown:

    11 lower-case sorts: ð, f, ʒ, Ꝺ (used lc on Q1ʳ), ꝧ, ſ, τ (often upside-down 2), ẏ (Small Pica y (?), surmounted by a dot, as on 2A1ᵛ); þ, ð, p (= (Pica) Italic *p*, as on P2ʳ);

    5 capitals: Є (as on 2A2ᵛ), Ꝺ (on 2Z1ʳ, different from the one used lc), ꝳ (as on 2C2ᵛ, used sideways for E on V1ᵛ), ẟ (used for lc d beside ð on 2S3ᵛ), Đ;

    1 other: ꝉ (just 7 on 2Z2ʳ).

    Total: 17 sorts.

Note 1: There are two sorts for ʒ, as on 2A1ʳ, 2S2c1ᵛ, and two sorts for ſ, as on P2ʳ, 2C2ᵛ.

Note 2: The opportunity to use capital Æ is not taken in Aeʒleſbuŋʒe on 2S2c1ᵛ.

    Copy seen (1652 re-issue): Portsmouth, MOD, Admiralty Library Vc.10 (with maps and tp hand-coloured; white vellum gold-tooled contemporary Dutch binding).

Bibliography:
1647/4 and 1649 re-issue: Shirley 1991: nos 607–610; Skelton 1970: nos 41, 47; Koeman/Krogt 1997: 1:434.4J&L;
1652/3 re-issues: Skelton 1970: nos 54, 56; Koeman/Krogt 1997: 1:435.4L;

1658/9 re-issues: Skelton 1970: no. 67; Koeman/Krogt 1997: 1:436.4V; Lucas 2018: 233–239.

1647.5: Blaeu, Joan, *Toonneel des Aerdrycx, oft Nievwe Atlas, uytgegeven door Wilhelm en Johan Blaev. Vierde Deel.* (= Dutch translation of Camden's *Britannia*, as in 1607.2, based on 1645.1). Amsterdam: Joan Blaeu I, 1647. USTC 1515259. CAS3.

ASC (C, F) extracts, OE proper names

Collation: 2⁰: π¹ *² 2*¹ A–Q² R¹ S–X² Y¹ Z–2H² 2I¹ 2K–2Y² 2Z¹ 3A–3D² 3E¹ 3F–3O² 3P¹ 3Q–4D² 4E¹ 4F–4N² 4O¹ 4P² 4Q¹ 4R–4Y² 4Z¹ 5A–5V² 5X¹ 5Y–5Z² 6A¹ 6B–6F² 6G¹ 6H–6L² 6M¹ 6N–6P² 6Q¹ 6R–7F² [$2 signed (-*1, A2, S2, Z2, 2E2, 2G2, 2K2, 2M2, 2P2, 2S2, 2V2, 2X2, 3A2, 3C2, 3F2, 3K2, 3N2, 3Q2, 3S2, 3V2, 3Z2, 4C2, 4F2, 4G2, 4I2, 4L2, 4M2, 4P2, 4R2, 4S2, 4X2, 4Y2, 5A2, 5D2, 5E2, 5G2, 5K2, 5L2, 5M2, 5N2, 5O2, 5Q2, 5R2, 5T2, 5V2, 5Y2, 5Z2, 6B2, 6C2, 6F2, 6H2, 6L2, 6N2, 6P2, 6R2, 6X2, 7D2, 7E2; D2 missigned D3, L2 missigned L3)] 275 leaves, paginated [i–viii], 1–422, *423–424* (pp. nos 395–398 used twice; pp. 199–200 misnumbered 191–192, 311–312 misnumbered 301–302, 356 misnumbered 556, 418 misnumbered 318; p. 410 not numbered; with the exception of p. 410 the pages showing maps are not included in the pagination). Because this is a large atlas all the leaves are mounted on guards.

SOURCE OF PASSAGE UTILIZING ANGLO-SAXON TYPES:

6V1ᵛ (p. 396)   From **1645.1** 7E2ʳ: ASC(C + F) 188/189 (extracts), as Thorpe 1861: 14–15, including erron. ꞅoꞃᵹẏpð. Ultimately from **1607.2** 4Y4ʳ, including erron. ꞅæ oꞃ ꞅæ with p for þ, but note the use of AS ꞅ in all 4 instances of ꞅæ, as opposed to only the first in **1645.1**.

TYPE:

Main text in Pierre Haultin's English-size Roman (but with different capitals; Body 96) interspersed with Robert Granjon's 3rd English-size Italic, e.g., on 2Z1. CAS3: The Voskens/Blaeu English-size AS occurs in a specimen on 2*1ʳ and is used in the text in combination with the English-size Roman on pp. 14, 59, 72, 83–84, 86–87, 94, 98, 100, 106, 108, 113, 115, 118–119, 121, 124, 126, 129, 131 (with erron. Tꞃuþabꞃnıᵹ (*recte* Tꞃ-) from **1645.1**), 132, 136, 138, 140–141, 145, 148–149, 151–152, 155–156, 159, 161–162, 164, 166 (with Haꞃtınᵹa- from **1645.1**), 167, 169–75, 177–178 (with erron. Sonðpẏc), 179, 182, 184–189, 192, 194, 201, 203–204, 208–209, 214–215, 224–225, 228, 230, 234, 237 (with erron. Ðeaᵹleᵹe for **1607.2** Ðeaðleᵹe), 241–242, 244, 248, 252, 254, 258, 267, 269, 271, 273, 275, 277–278, 280, 283, 288, 292–293, 295–296, 299–300, 303, 306–307, 309, 315, 325, 331, 342, 347, 349, 351 (with erron. Gueꞅꞅ for Guepꞅ), 352 (with erron. Ðꞃıppum 'Ripon'), 358–359, 361, 368, 371, 373, 375, 380 (with erron. Wınþaðꞃe-meꞃ for Wınpaðꞃe-meꞃ), 395,

399, 402 (with erron. Ɛaln-þic for Ɛaln-pic), 409 (with final y instead of the punctus versus), 418.

Special sorts shown in the specimen on 2*1ʳ:

11 lower-case sorts:	ð, *e*, ꝼ, ȝ, p, ꞃ, τ, ẏ; þ, ð, p;
8 capitals:	Æ¹, Æ², Ɛ, Ꝼ, Ꟙ, S, Ð, X;
2 others:	þ, ⁊.
Total:	21 sorts.

Note: Both H and M are provided with lower-case equivalents, though with the latter there is no doubting its upper-case status.

Special sorts shown in the text:

11 lower-case sorts:	ð, *e*, ꝼ, ȝ, p, ꞃ, τ, ẏ; þ, ð, p;
5 capitals:	Ɛ, Ꝼ, Ꟙ, S (1st uc on 3A1ʳ, used for lc d on, e.g., V1ᵛ, 2T1ʳ, 5L1ʳ), Ð;
1 other:	⁊.
Total:	17 sorts.

Note 1: Two s-sorts shown, e.g., side by side on 2C2ᵛ/a (p. 94); they look like different cuts.

Note 2: The main y-sort appears to be an English-size y surmounted by a dot (e.g., on 2E2ᵛ, 2Q1ᵛ). But the first one used is a Pica y, also surmounted by a dot, e.g., on 2A1ᵛ, again on 5E2ᵛ. Variant y-sorts with the dot in central position or to the right of centre may be seen on 3F1ʳ. A y-sort provided with an acute accent to the right of centre occurs on 4T2ʳ, 5C2ᵛ, 5G2ᵛ, 5L1ʳ.

Note 3: Ꝼ is used regularly as a lc letter (e.g., on Q1ʳ), occasionally initially (e.g., on 2N2ᵛ), but that does not necessarily signify that it was perceived as a capital, as ꝼ, p also occur lc initially; roman H is used in an AS name-element Heoꞃτu on 6L1ʳ. Note Ꟙanτeꞃcꟙẏp on 2R2ᵛ.

Note 5: The English-size Anglo-Saxon is also used in combination with Haultin's Great Primer Roman (interspersed with Granjon's Great Primer Italic D) on 2K1ʳ, 3A1ʳ, 3F1ʳ, 4C2ᵛ, but the AS sorts are too small to fit well; on 4C2ᵛ there occurs a dotted Great Primer y.

Note 6: Opportunities to use capital Æ are not taken, e.g., Aeȝleꞃbuꞃȝe on 3F1ʳ.

Note 7: Roman d is used side by side AS ð (in error, corrected in 1648.2) on 4T2ʳ/a.

Note 8: AS capitals are also used with Roman ones in a Latin inscription on 4S2ᵛ.

> Copy seen: RGS 1.C.218 (with hand-coloured tp (dated 1648), maps and occasionally illustrations, e.g., 2R1ʳ, 3N1ʳ; 'Blaeu' binding of white vellum on boards with gold-tooled ornament and the initials I.R.P. in the central lozenge on the front).

Bibliography: Koeman 1967–71: Bl.45A; Lucas 2018: 229–233; Shirley 1991: nos 596–598; Skelton 1970: no. 38.

1648.1 Blaeu, Joan, *Theatrum Orbis Terrarum ſive Atlas Novus, Pars Qvarta.* (= Camden's *Britannia*, as in 1607.2). 2nd edn of 1645.1 (sigs 1ᵛ–2*2ᵛ re-set slavishly). Amsterdam: Joan Blaeu I, 1648. USTC 1014299. CAS3.
ASC (C) and (F) extracts, OE proper names

Collation: 2⁰: π¹ *1 2*² (2*2 + χ2) A–2B² 2C¹ 2D–2O² 2P¹ 2Q–2S² 2T¹ 2V² 2X¹ 2Y–2Z² 3A¹ 3B–3I² 3K¹ 3L–3T² 3V¹ 3X–3Y² 3Z¹ 4A–4F² 4G¹ 4H–4K² 4L¹ 4M–4R² 4S¹ 4T–4V² 4X¹ 4Y² 4Z¹ 5A–5I² 5K¹ 5L² 5M¹ 5N² 5O¹ 5P–5R² 5S¹ 5T² 5V¹ 5X–5Z² 6A¹ 6B² 6C¹ 6D–6G² 6H¹ 6I–6K² 6L¹ 6M–7B² [$2 signed (-2*2, A2, Q2, V2, 2A2, 2D2, 2F2, 2H2, 2L2, 2N2, 2P2, 2Q2, 2R2, 2V2, 2Y2, 3B2, 3F2, 3H2, 3L2, 3N2, 3P2, 3S2, 3V2, 3X2, 4A2, 4B2, 4D2, 4F2, 4H2, 4K2, 4M2, 4N2, 4Q2, 4R2, 4T2, 4Y2, 5A2, 5C2, 5E2, 5F2, 5G2, 5H2, 5I2, 5l2, 5N2, 5P2, 5Q2, 5R2, 5T2, 5X2, 5Y2, 6B2, 6D2, 6G2, 6I2, 6M2, 6N2, 6R2, 6X1, 6Z2, 7A2, 7B2)] 262 leaves, paginated [i–viii], 1–394, *395–396* (pp. nos 355–360 used twice, p. 381 not numbered, and the pages showing maps are not included in the pagination).

Note 1: The page heading on 2Z1ʳ is erron. 'BARK-SHIRE' instead of 'SUSSEX'.

Note 2: Because this is a large atlas all the leaves are mounted on guards.

SOURCE OF PASSAGE UTILIZING ANGLO-SAXON TYPES:

6Q1ᵛ (p. 364)   From 1645.1 7E2ʳ: ASC(C + F) 188/189 (extracts), as Thorpe 1861: 14–15, including erron. ꝼoꞃȝẏꝺ. Ultimately from 1607.2 4Y4ʳ, including erron. ꝼæ oꝼ ꝼæ with p for þ, but note the use of AS ſ (as opposed to Roman long ſ) in only the first of four instances of ꝼæ, a feature taken over from 1645.1.

TYPE:

Main text in Pierre Haultin's Great Primer Roman (Body 114) interspersed with a Great Primer Italic [the same as in 1645.1] (e.g. S2ʳ–T1ᵛ) in two columns.

CAS3: The Blaeu/Voskens English-size Anglo-Saxon occurs in the specimen on 2*2ʳ and is used in combination with Haultin's Great Primer Roman in the text in words on pp. 13, 52, 63, 74, 76–77, 83, 87, 89, 95, 97, 101–104, 106–107, 109, 112, 114, 116–117, 118 (with erron. Tꞃuþabꞃiȝ (*recte* Tꝥ-) from 1607.2), 119, 122–123, 125–127, 131, 133–134, 136–137, 139–140, 143, 145–146, 148–161, 164 (with erron. ꟽeꝛ ꝼoꝛaꝛe for 1607.2 ꟽeꝛſc-paꝛe), 166–170, 173–175, 181–182, 188, 194–195, 203–204, 207–209, 211–212, 214 (with erron. Ꝺeaȝleȝe for 1607.2 Ꝺeaꝺleȝe), 219–221, 226, 230, 232, 236, 245, 247, 249, 251, 253, 255–256, 258, 261, 265, 269–273, 276–277, 279–280, 283–284, 286, 291, 300, 307, 317, 321, 324–325, 327, 332–333, 335, 342, 345, 347–348, 349 (with 7 instead of the punctus versus ⁊), 354, 367, 371, 373–374 (with 7 instead of ⁊ x2), 380 (with 7 instead of ⁊), 389.

Note: When the Blaeu Anglo-Saxon is used in combination with Haultin's English-size Roman (Body 96), as on 5D2ᵛ, the appearance is much improved. An English-size Roman y has been provided with a superscript dot for printing in this size.

Special sorts shown in the specimen on 2*2ʳ:
    11 lower-case sorts: ð, *e*, ꝼ, ȝ, ꝑ, ſ, ꞇ, ẏ; þ, ð, ƿ;
    8 capitals: Æ¹, Æ², Ꝫ, Ꝺ, ꝳ, Ƨ, Ð, X;
    2 others: þ, ꝲ.
  Total: 21 sorts.
Special sorts shown in the text:
    11 lower-case sorts: ð, *e*, ꝼ, ȝ, ꝑ, ſ, ꞇ, ẏ (a GP y with a dot added slightly to the right of the centre); þ, ð, ƿ;
    5 capitals: Ꝫ, Ꝺ (see below), ꝳ, Ƨ (used for ð on V1ʳ, cap on 3A1ᵛ), Ð;
    1 other: ꝲ (on Z1ᵛ, 4A1ʳ, oversized, made up of a subscript number 7 surmounted by a dot to the left of centre, but occasionally to the right of centre, e.g., 7K1ᵛ, a fact which suggests two castings).
  Total: 17 sorts.
  Overall total 11 + 8 + 3 = 22 sorts.
Note 1: Two ꝼ-sorts are shown on 2A1ʳ (p. 87); they look like different cuts.
Note 2: Two ẏ-sorts shown on 2G1ʳ (p. 103); one has an acute accent instead of a dot.
Note 3: Ꝺ is used regularly as a lc letter (e.g., on Z1ᵛ), occasionally initially (e.g., on 2R2ᵛ), but that does not necessarily signify that it was perceived as a capital, as ꝼ, ƿ also occur lc initially; Roman H is used in an AS name-element Heoꝑꞇu on 6G1ʳ. Note ꝺexꞇolðeꝼꝺam on 6S2ʳ.
Note 4: AS capitals are also used with roman ones in a Latin inscription on 4Y1ʳ.
    Copy seen: BL Maps C.5.d.2 (Shirley T.BLA-1k; with tp and maps hand-coloured).
    Copies also at: AUB, LUB, BSA, BBIR, BUN, FBN, LBS, MRAH.
Bibliography: Koeman 1967–71: Bl.56; Koeman 1970: 36–39; Lucas 2018: 229–233; Shirley 1991: nos 616–618; Skelton 1970: no. 42; Vervey 1981: 13–14.

1648.2 Blaeu, Joan, *Vierde Stvck der Aerdrycks-Beschryving, welck vervat Engelandt.* (= Dutch translation of Camden's *Britannia*, as in 1607.2). 2nd edn of 1647.5. Amsterdam: Joan Blaeu I, 1648. Not found in USTC. CAS3.
  ASC (C, F) extracts, OE proper names
    Collation: 2⁰: π¹ *² 2*¹ A–2A² 2B¹ 2C–2E² 2F¹ 2G–2O² 2P¹ 2Q–2R² (2R2 + χ1.2) 2S–3E² 3F¹ 3G–3P² 3Q¹ 3R–3V² 3X¹ 3Y–4G² 4H¹ 4I–4K² 4L¹ 4M–4N² 4O¹ 4P² 4Q¹ 4R² 4S¹ 4T–5B² 5C¹ 5D² 5E¹ 5F–5H² 5I¹ 5K–5L² 5M¹ 5N–5Q² 5R¹ 5S–5T² 5V¹ 5X² 5Y¹ 5Z–6E² 6F¹ 6G–6N² 6O¹ [$1 signed (+*2; -*1)] 242 +2 leaves, paginated [i–viii], 1–364 (the pages showing maps are not included in the pagination).
    Note: Because this is a large atlas all the leaves are mounted on guards.

SOURCE OF PASSAGE UTILIZING ANGLO-SAXON TYPES:
6E2ᵛ (p. 338)   From 1645.1 7E2ʳ: ASC(C + F) 188/189 (extracts), as Thorpe 1861: 14–15, including erron. ꝼoꞃᵹẏꝥð. Ultimately from 1607.2 4Y4ʳ, including erron. ꞃæ oꝥ ꞃæ with ꝥ for þ, but note the use of AS ꞃ in all 4 instances of ꞃæ, as opposed to only the first in 1645.1 and 1648.1.

TYPE:
Main text in Pierre Haultin's English-size Roman (but with different capitals; Body 97) interspersed with Robert Granjon's English-size Italic, e.g., on 2R1ᵛ–2ʳ. CAS3: The Blaeu/Voskens English-size Anglo-Saxon occurs in the specimen on 2*1ʳ and it is used in the text in combination with the Roman on pp. 12, 50, 61, 71, 73–74, 79, 83, 85–86, 90, 92, 96–97, 98 (Sceaτeꞃbyꝥnᵹ), 101–103, 107–108, 110, 111 (with erron. Tꞃuþabꝥıᵹ (recte Tꝥ-) from 1647.5), 112, 115, 117, 119–120, 123, 126–129, 131–132, 134–135, 137–138, 140, 141–142 (with Haꞃτınᵹa- from 1647.5), 143–148, 149–150 (with erron. Sonðꝥẏc from 1647.5), 151, 154, 156–60, 163–165, 171–172, 177–178, 183–184, 192–193, 195, 197, 200–201, 203 (with erron. Ꝺeaᵹleᵹe from 1647.5), 207–9, 213, 216, 218, 221, 228, 230–232, 235–237, 239, 241, 245, 248–252, 254, 256, 258, 261–263, 269, 278, 284, 293, 297, 299, 300 (with recte Gueꞃꝼ for erron. Gueꞃꞃ in 1647.5), 302 (with recte Ꝺꝥıppun for erron. Ꝺꝥıppum 'Ripon' in 1647.5), 306–308, 314, 317, 319, 321, 325 (with erron. Wınþaðꝥe-meꝥ for Wınpaðꝥe-meꝥ from 1647.5), 341, 344, 347 (with erron. Ꝫaln-þıc (over line division) for Ꝫaln-pıc from 1647.5), 351 (with final y instead of the punctus versus from 1647.5), 360.

Special sorts shown in the specimen on 2*1ʳ:

10 lower-case sorts:	ð, e, ꝼ, ᵹ, ꝥ, ꞃ, τ; þ, ð, p;
8 capitals:	Æ¹, Æ², Ꝫ, Ꝺ, Ꟁ, S, Ð, X;
2 others:	þ, ꝫ.
Total:	20 sorts.

Note 1A: the y in the specimen has no dot or accent over it, and so is not treated as AS.

Special sorts shown in the text:

10 lower-case sorts:	ð (1st on 2E1ʳ), ꝼ (1st on 2K2ᵛ used erron. for ꞃ), ᵹ, ꝥ, ꞃ, τ, ẏ; þ, ð (1st on 2R2ᵛ), p;
5 capitals:	Ꝫ, Ꝺ, Ꟁ, S (1st as uc on 2P1ᵛ; used for ð on R1ʳ, Y1ʳ, 2N1ᵛ), Ð;
1 other:	ꝫ.
Total:	16 sorts.

Note 1B: The y-sort appears to be a Pica y and is surmounted by a dot, e.g., 2K1ʳ, but on 4O1ᵛ (p. 252) there appears a y with an acute accent to its right.
Note 2: Two ꞃ-sorts are shown on V1ʳ (p. 71); they look like different cuts.

Note 3: Ꝺ is used regularly as a lower-case letter (e.g., on N2ᵛ), occasionally initially (e.g., on 3Z2ᵛ), but that does not necessarily signify that it was perceived as a capital, as ꝼ, p also occur lc initially; roman H is used in an AS name-element Heoptu on 5X1ʳ. Note ꝺantercꝶyp on 2M1ʳ.

Note 4: AS capitals are also used with Roman ones in a Latin inscription on 4F2ᵛ.

>Copies seen: BL Maps C.4.b.5, C.4.d.1 (Shirley T.BLA-1j and T.BLA-1r), both with tp and maps hand-coloured; RGS 1.B.73 (lacks π1, so there is no indication of whether it is 1648.2 or the re-issue; with hand-coloured maps; 'Blaeu' binding of white vellum on boards with gold-tooled ornament; gift of Lord Northbrook 1879).

>Note: Skelton 1970: no. 77 lists BL C.4.d.1 as dating from 1664, the '3rd' Dutch edn, with the date 1648 retained on the tp, but the typesetting is the same as in BL C.4.b.5, including the preliminaries.

Bibliography: Koeman 1967–71: Bl.46; Lucas 2018: 229–233; Skelton 1970: no. 45; Vervey 1981: 13–14.

1664 re-issue (as part of the *Grooten Atlas*): Koeman 1967–71: Bl.57 ('identical with the edition of ... 1648'); Shirley 1991: nos 619–621; Skelton 1970: no. 77.

1650.1: Casaubon, Meric, *De Quatuor Linguis Commentationis, Pars Prior: Quæ, De Lingua Hebraica: Et, De Lingua Saxonica*, with supplement on OE words by William Somner. London: James Flesher for Richard Mynne *sumptibus*, 1650. Wing C801; ESTC R10985. AS3 with AS2 s.

Words

>**Collation**: 8⁰: A⁴ B–2I⁸ 2K⁴ [$4 signed (-A1.4, C4, 2E2, 2K4)] 256 leaves, paginated [i–viii], 1–418, *419–420*, ²1–72, ²*73–84* (p. ²64 has '64' inverted).

>Note: State 1 shown by p. 173 having '17' on its side in CCA W2/X.3.12, OBL 8⁰.C.37.Art.Seld.

TYPE:

Main text in a Pica Roman (Body 80; Face 78 x 1.7: 2.6).

AS3: The Lambardian Pica Anglo-Saxon combined with the Pica Roman occurs in words throughout the supplement by Somner (2E3ʳ–2I6ᵛ);

Special sorts shown on the specimen on 2E2ᵛ:

>13 lower-case sorts: ð, *e*, ꝼ, ʒ, Ꝺ, ı, p, ꞃ, τ, ẏ; þ, ð, p;
>6 capitals: Æ¹, Æ², Є, ᛘ, 8, Đ;
>3 others: ꝭ, þ, ȷ.

>Total: 22 sorts. This is also the overall total, as no extra sorts are shown in the text.

Special sorts shown in words in the text:
   13 lower-case sorts: ð, *e*, f, ʒ, ƕ, ı, p, ſ, τ, ẏ; þ, ð, p;
   4 capitals: Æ¹, Æ², S, Ð;
   1 other: ȷ.
Total: 18 sorts.

Copies seen: State 1 (showing p. 173 with '17' on its side): CCA W2/X.3.12 (Somner's copy with his annotations). OBL 8⁰.C.37.Art.Seld.;
State 2 (with p. 173 printed normally): ABH 7892; CUL Z.12.22; ECC S5.5.54 (Abp Sancroft's copy); OBL Douce C.405.

Copies also at: BL, CCC, CGC, KCC, CMC, CPC, CSJ, TCC, CaCL, DRD, DWL, ECL, GUL, LCL, LHL, LSH, MJRUL, MTP, NLS, NLW, NUL, OBC, OCC, OLC, OQC, OSJ, OWoC, OXC, RCL, SPC, StA, WAL,WCC, YML, DML, NLI, TCD, ULim, PBN, GCB, BSB, GUB, MBS; FSL, NYPL, HHL, HUL, IUL, DDUL, KSRL, LCP, NLC, UCBL, UCLA, UPL, UTA, WMUL, YUB.

Bibliography: Eros 1976; Hetherington 1980: 131–135. GR 53.

1650.2: Gregory, John, *Notes and Observations upon some Passages of Scripture*. London: Richard Cotes for Richard Royston, 1650. Wing G1921; ESTC R32462. 2nd edn of **1646.1**. AS4
Words
  Collation: 4⁰: A⁴ ¶⁴ *⁴ B–Z⁴ [$3 signed (-A1, Z3)] 100 leaves, paginated [i–xxiv], 1–175, *176*.
TYPE:
Main text in Arthur Nicholls's Pica Roman (Body 84), interspersed with his Pica Italic.
AS4: The Spelmannian Great Primer Anglo-Saxon occurs in two words on V4ʳ (p. 151) in combination with a Great Primer Roman;
Special sorts used: ʒ, ȷ.
Other special sorts are used for astrological symbols on *4ʳ and X1ʳ.
  Copies seen: CUL Syn.7.61.106² (signed Timothy Earle); ECC 332.5.101⁴; TCD FF.kk.36 (signed William Palliser (Fellow 1668; abp of Cashel 1694–1727)); another issue with additional tp: CUL Ely.d.99.
  Copies also at: BL, TCC, CUW, CaCL, ChestC, DCC, DRD, DWL, ECL, LHL, LPL, LUL, NLS, NLW, OBL, OBC, OGF, OJC, OKC, ONC, OSJ, OXC, RLW, SAC, SCL, UBL, WAL, WiCL, WoCL, YML, KSC; NYSL, GTS, HUL, IUL, NLC, UPL, YUB, TUL; NLA.

Bibliography: see **1646.1**.

1650.3: Selden, John, *De Synedriis & Præfecturis Iuridicis Veterum Ebræorum Liber Primus*, vol. I. For vol. III see **1655.4** (vol. II (1653) shows no Anglo-Saxon). London: James Flesher for Cornelius Bee, 1650. Wing S2425; ESTC R4091. AS4.

Ælfric, Gospels (extracts)

Collation: 4⁰: A⁴ a–b⁴ B-4O⁴ 4P² [$3 signed (-A1,2, 4P2)] 342 leaves, paginated [1–4, i], ii–xii, *xiii–xx*, 1–656, *657–660*.

SOURCES OF PASSAGES UTILIZING ANGLO-SAXON TYPES:

2N3ʳ (p. 277)   From 1643.1 2I3ʳ: Ælfric, CH2.xxiv, in Festivitate Sancti Petri Apostoli de Sancto Petro (extract), as Godden 1979: 226/162;

From 1571.1 K3ᵛ: Mt 18.17 (extract), as Liuzza 1994: 37;

2O2ʳ (p. 283)   From 1571.1 K3ᵛ: Mt 18.17 (extract), as Liuzza 1994: 37;

2R3ʳ (p. 309)   From 1643.1 2G4ᵛ/3: Bede, *Hist. Eccl.* III.22 (word amanꞃumoðe), as Miller 1890–98: I.228/11; other forms, as Amanꞃumnunᵹe, Amanꞃumiᵹe, Amanꞃum, presumably reconstructed from it, as the first and third do not feature in surviving OE;

3V3ʳ (p. 517)   From 1639.4 2P3ᵛ: Phrase beᵹeonðan 8æ extracted from 'Directions for a Confessor' (*olim* Canons of Edgar), as Fowler 1965: 20/113;

4H3ʳ (p. 605)   From OBL Selden supra 63 (SC 3451), 42ʳ: Laurence Nowell (the antiquary), *Vocabularium Saxonicum*, svv. Ealdor, Ealdorman, Ealdorburh (Marckwardt 1952: 59–60); cf. also 1626.1 V2ᵛ, s.v. Eorla; Nowell is confirmed as the source by the absence of his phrase 'Suþseaxna Ealdorman' in surviving OE;

From 1631.1 4E1ᵛ: re: S. George Ealðoꞃman in Cappadocia;

From 1643.1 2B3ᵛ/5: Bede, *Hist. Eccl.* III.8 (phrase miðˌ hiꞃ Ealðoꝑlicneꞃꞃe), as Miller 1890–8: I.172/8;

From 1639.4 2O1ʳ: Wulfstan's Canons of Edgar 2 (extrapolated phrase ẏlðꝑan ⁊ ẏlðꝑum), as Fowler 1972: 2; other phrases (Ealðꝑum ⁊ Ealðꝑaꞃ; Ealðoꝑmannum) not traced;

From 1571.1 I4ᵛ: Mt.16.21 (phrase), as Liuzza 1994: 34;

From 1571.1 Y2ᵛ: Mk 10.33 (phrases, adapted), as Liuzza 1994: 83;

From 1571.1 P4: Mt 27.12, 20 (phrase), as Liuzza 1994: 58, 59;

4H3ᵛ (p. 606)   From 1571.1 X1ʳ, 2A1ʳ, 2B4ʳ: Mk 8.31, 11.27, 14.43 (phrases), as Liuzza 1994: 79, 86, 92;

From 1571.1 2R3ᵛ: Lk 22.52 (phrase), as Liuzza 1994: 150;

From 1571.1 2R4ᵛ: Lk 22.66 (phrases), as Liuzza 1994: 151.

TYPE:

Main text in Pierre Haultin's English-size Roman (Body 93) interspersed with Robert Granjon's 3rd English-size Italic (e.g. 3Q2) with quotations in Arabic, Greek, Hebrew, Syriac and Textura types.

AS4: The Spelmanian Great Primer Anglo-Saxon occurs in combination with Haultin's English-size Roman in text as indicated above under Contents, and in words on 2N2ᵛ, 4H2ᵛ.

On all the pages on which it appears the AS type occasions a wider space between lines presumably resulting from it being cast on a Great Primer body. Special sorts shown:

        11 lower-case sorts: ð, *e*, ꝼ, ȝ, ı, ꞃ, ſ, τ, ẏ; þ, ƿ;
        3 capitals: Є, Ð, 8;
        2 others: ƀ (used erroneously for þ), ꝗ.
Total: 16 sorts.

Note: An opportunity to use square C is not taken on 2N3ʳ.

Copies seen: CUL Q*.5.55(E), C.5.59 (lacks A1).

Copies also at: CPH, CSJ, TCC, EdUL, LHL, LiCL, LPL, MCS, OBL, OAS, OLC, OQC, OTC, OXC, SDC, SML, SPC, WAL, WoCL, TCD, PBN, BSB, GUB, MSB; USLC, UTS, HHL, HUL, IUL, DDUL, HUC, UCLA, YUB.

Bibliography: Toomer 2009: II.693–724.

1650.4: Vredius (de Wree), Olivarius, *Historiæ Comitum Flandriæ Liber Prodromus Alter. Flandria Vetus Sive Ethnica Dicta Prima Francia*. Bruges: Lucas van den Kerckove, 1650. USTC 1003158.

    Collation: 2⁰: ã⁶ A–I⁶ K⁴ (K4 blank); +6 A–2Z⁶ 3A–3S⁴ a–n⁴ (with 1 folding plate). 470 leaves, paginated [12] 110 [3] [3 blank]; [12] 692 [1 blank] [2] [1 blank] LXXX [24]

An OE extract from Bede, HE v.12 (from 1643.1) appears in an English-size Italic with no special sorts on sig. i4ᵛ–k1ʳ (pp. lxxii–lxxiii).

    Copy seen: CUL X.9.1–2.

    Copies also at: BL, NLS, OBL, DML, CBM, LBM, SBPU, AntUB, ASB, MSA, AUB, LUB, JUB, WHAB, SKB, CMN, VBV; IUL.

1650.5: Boxhorn, Marcus Zuerius, *Prima Religionis Christianæ Rudimenta, Antiquissima Saxonum & Alemanorum Lingua scripta*. Leiden: Johannes van Sambix, 1650. USTC 1028439.

    Collation: 12⁰: a¹² b¹⁰. 22 leaves

Contains Decalogue, Lord's Prayer, Creed in OE, printed in a Pica Roman, plus some AS Laws of Alfred printed in a Pica Italic, but no special AS sorts are shown.

    Copy seen: CUL Ely.e.125.

    Copies also at: AUB, HKB.

1650/?1665.1: Speed, John, *The Theatre of the Empire of Great Britaine Presenting an Exact Geography of the Kingdomes of England, Scotland, Ireland, and the Iles adioyning, with the Shires, Hundreds, Cities and Shire Townes, within ye Kingdome of England*. London: Mary and Samuel Simmons for Roger Rea the Elder and Roger Rea the Younger, 1650 (as stated). 4th edn of **1611.1**. Wing S4885; ESTC R219672. AS2/3.

>Note 1: George Humble's rights to Speed's *Theatre* etc., and the plates, were inherited by his eldest son William Humble (fl.1640–59), who sold them in 1659 to William Garrett, who in turn transferred them to Rea.

>Note 2: While the stated date is 1650 the actual date is probably (?)1665. The title pages of Bks II (3F1ʳ), III (3X1ʳ) and IV (3Z1ʳ) all say 1662, the same year as the publication of Speed's *Prospect* (Wing S4883), which precedes the present book. The date 1662 has also been added to some of the maps (Skelton 1970: 124). But it might have been even later. The next owners of the plates etc. were Thomas Bassett and Richard Chiswell, publishers of the next edition, **1676.1**, and they put an advertisement in the Term Catalogue for 1675 noting that the book had been out of print for 7 years, which could put the present edition as late even as 1669 (Skelton 1970: 124–125).

OE **proper names**

>**Collation:** 2⁰: Leaves mounted on guards. ¶¹ A–D¹ [3*² ⁺ ¹] E–3E² 3F¹ 3G–3V² 3X¹ 3Y² 3Z¹ 4A–4G² 4H¹ [$1 signed (+ 3*2 4F2 4G2)] 150 leaves (including insertion), foliated [i–viii], 1–94, 99–126, 131–132, 137–146, *147–151* (fo 106 misnumbered 116), nos 95–96, 127–128, 133–134 unnumbered but presumably paginated in theory, pp. nos 97–98, 129–130, 135–136 having no leaf to be used on.

>Note 1: The text is printed back to back with the maps, and the map pages, being always a double-page opening on the reverse side of text pages, receive no numbers.

>Note 2: This edition is a slavish reprint of **1627.1**.

TYPE:

The size varies according to the amount of text in relation to the amount of space available.
The preferred type is Arthur Nicholl's English-size Roman, as on I1ʳ:
                        Body 95   Face 90 x 2: 3.0
but the following also occur:
Pierre Haultin's 2nd Pica Roman (Vervliet R82B), as on L1ʳ:
                        Body 81   Face 78 x 1.8: 2.5
Pierre Haultin's Long Primer Roman (Vervliet R67), as on Y1ʳ and 2K1ʳ:
                        Body 67   Face 64 x 1.4: 2.0
Italics of the same size as the main text are used to highlight names, etc.

AS2/AS3: Two Anglo-Saxon Pica designs are used mixed together in county names. They occur with main text in English-size (as on I1ʳ), with Pica (as on L1ʳ), and with Long Primer (as on Y1ʳ and 2K1ʳ).
AS2: The Parkerian Pica Anglo-Saxon.
Special sorts shown: 8 lower-case sorts: ð, ꝼ, ȝ, ꝑ, ꞃ; þ, ð, p;
                       1 capital: Æ.
AS3: The Lambardian Pica Anglo-Saxon.
Special sorts shown: 4 lower-case sorts: e, h (= ƕ), τ, ẏ.
Note 1: AS i is not shown.
Note 2: The setting is prone to errors, as d for t, f for r, s for r, ð for d, p for þ.
Note 3: Skelton's remark in relation to a previous edition that the text 'has been reset in smaller type' (1970: 124) is misleading and should be discounted.

>   **Copy seen:** BL 118.e.8. This book is very rare. If it were published before the Great Fire of London in 1666 many copies could have been burnt, and such an occurrence would go a long way towards explaining its present great rarity. The copy listed by Wing and ESTC at CMC was not found there.
>   **Copies also at:** KLL, LGS, OXC; BPM, UMI, YUB.

Bibliography: Shirley 1991: nos 667–669; Skelton 1970: no. 81.

1652.1: Twysden, Sir Roger, ed. John Selden, *Historiæ Anglicanæ Scriptores X*, with glossary by William Somner. London: James Flesher for Cornelius Bee *sumptibus* and Johan and Daniel Elsevier at Leiden 1652. Wing H2094(aA); ESTC R5810 & R216920. AS4 + AS3 with AS2 s.

BDS, *Durham*, **Dictionary Citations**

>   **Collation:** 2⁰ in 6s: π A⁶ a–f⁴ g² A⁴ B–5B⁶ 5C–5F⁴ 5G² 2A–²2M⁶ ²2N⁴ [\$3 signed (+ ²2D4; -πA1,2, a3, b3, c3, d3, g2, A3, Q2, 2I3, 5C3, 5D3, 5E3, ²A1, ²E1,2, ²2N2)] 828 leaves, paginated then in columns, pp. [i–xii], 1–L, L1–LII, [A1–8], 1–8, cols 9–2768, *2769–3170* (col. nos 2297–2306 not used; cols 83–84, 282–284, 333–336, 423–424, 425–428, 1285–1288, 1753–1756, 2307–2310 not numbered; cols 181–182 misnumbered 179, 180).
>   Note 1: Evidently printed in two booklets, with too much space being allowed for the first booklet, with the result that col. nos 2297–2306 are not used. Sigs ²A- are signed [A], etc, but I have preferred ²A etc as being clearer.
>   Note 2: Sig. g2 is included in the collation, although it is not present in any of the copies seen, and the catchword on g1ᵛ anticipates A1ʳ.

SOURCES OF PASSAGES UTILIZING ANGLO-SAXON TYPES:

a4ᵛ (p. VIII)   From **1643.1** 3V4ʳ: ASC(A) 565 (extract), as Thorpe 1861: I.32;
b1ʳ (p. IX)   From **1643.1** Z4ʳ: OE Bede, *HE* 3.3, as Miller 1890: 160/2–4;

b1ᵛ (p. x)   From 1643.1 Z4ʳ: OE Bede, *HE* 3.3, as Miller 1890: 158/31–160/2;
b2ᵛ (p. XII)   From 1643.13 Q4ʳ: OE Bede, *HE* 5.23, as Miller 1890: 478/27–29;
d1ᵛ (p. XXVI)   From Nero D.iv, 259ʳ/25–45: Colophon to Lindisfarne Gospels, facs. Kendrick et al. 1956, as Harmer 1914: 36/7–20 (XXII.ii), Millar 1923: 3 (facs. pl. xxxvi);
B4ᵛ (p. 8)   From Faustina A.v, 43ʳ/7–11: *Bede's Death Song* (WS version, as Dobbie 1942: 108, cf. also Arnold 1882–5: 44), sole MS as stated on 2V3ʳ (= 'Liber S. Mariæ de Fontibus') under p. 8.col.2.l.10, and as indicated by the textual variants ʒehıȝȝene (3), hpet, ẏuelef (4); for the 'Symeon' group see Dobbie 1937: 83–87; cf. Tite 2003: 218;
E3ᵛ (col. 76)   From CUL Ff.1.27, p. 202, as stated on 2V3ʳ (= MS 'ex Bibliotheca Publica *Cantabrigiensi*'): *Durham* (as Dobbie 1942: 27), as indicated by the errors taken over in lines 14 ꝥðelpolð (recte Æðelpolð), 17 pıf (recte hıf) and 20 ðe (recte ðæn); not from Harley 533 (= transcript of Ff.1.27) as this MS shows additional errors, e.g. line 5 ʒemopıʒe (recte ʒemonıʒe); see also 22D8ᵛ below.

²X3ʳ–²2D7ᵛ Glossary by William Somner: frequent citations from 1568.2, 1571.1, 1639.4; other citations include:

²Y2ᵛ s.v. Bucellus: From RKA, DRc/R1 (Textus Roffensis, *olim* RCL A.3.5), 90ᵛ/1–2: Law VI Æthelstan 8,1 (extract), as Liebermann I.178;
²Z6ʳ s.v. Fidelis   From RKA, DRc/R1 (Textus Roffensis, *olim* RCL A.3.5), 38ᵛ/1–9: Law *Swerian* 1, as Liebermann I.396;
²2A3ʳ s.v. Gliscywa   From RKA, DRc/R1 (Textus Roffensis, *olim* RCL A.3.5), 91ʳ/12–14: Law VI Æthelstan 8,6 (extract), as Liebermann I.180;
²2A5ᵛ   From CCA, lost MS: Land-agreement (1032; extract) between Eadsige, priest (later abp of Canterbury), and Christ Church (= Sawyer 1465), later printed in full by Somner in 1660.1, from which ed. Robertson 1956: 170/21–24 (no. 86);
²2B2ʳ s.v. Legalitas   From RKA, DRc/R1 (Textus Roffensis, *olim* RCL A.3.5), 48ʳ/21–48ᵛ/2: Law III Æthelred 3,1, as Liebermann I.228;
²2B4ʳ s.v. Mancusa   From 1574.1 2E1ʳ: Ælfric's *Grammar*, concluding sentence, as Zupitza 1880: 296;
²2C3ᵛ s.v. Quarentena   From RKA, DRc/R1 (Textus Roffensis, *olim* RCL A.3.5), 38ʳ/19–23: Law *Pax*, as Liebermann I.390;
²2D4ᵛ s.v. Twelfhyndus   From RKA, DRc/R1 (Textus Roffensis, *olim* RCL A.3.5), 90ᵛ/7–10: Law VI Æthelstan 8,2 (extract), as Liebermann I.178;
²2D8ᵛ   From CUL Ff.1.27, p. 202, as stated on 2V3ʳ (= MS 'ex Bibliotheca Publica *Cantabrigiensi*'): *Durham* (as Dobbie 1942: 27), amended

from E3ᵛ (col. 76), as indicated by line 14 ȝðelpolð → Æþelpalð, but other errors are taken over in lines 17 pıſ (*recte* hıſ) and 20 ðe (*recte* ðæɲ), and new errors (?emendations) are added, e.g., line 17 he → þe. Cf. Dekker 2000: 293.

TYPE:

Main text of Selden's preface in a Great Primer Roman (Body 118):
Main historical texts in Haultin's Pica Roman (Body 82) interspersed with Granjon's 2nd Pica Italic 'pendante' (e.g. F3ʳ, 4G3ʳ).

AS4: The Spelmanian Great Primer Anglo-Saxon is combined with the Great Primer Roman: a4ᵛ, b1, b2ᵛ, d1ᵛ.

Special sorts shown:

   12 lower-case sorts: ð, *e*, ꝼ, ȝ, ı, ɲ, ſ, τ, ẏ; þ, ð, p;
   4 capitals: Є, Ꞩ, ꟽ, Ȣ;
   3 others: þ, ꝩ, ꞏj.
 Total: 19 sorts.

²X3ʳ–²2D7ᵛ Glossary

Main text in Granjon's 2nd Pica Italic interspersed with Haultin's Pica Roman.
AS3 with AS2 s (beside AS3 s): The Lambardian Pica Anglo-Saxon (with additional Parkerian s) is combined with Haultin's Pica Roman.

Special sorts shown:

   13 lower-case sorts: ð, e, ꝼ, ȝ, Ꞩ, ı, ɲ, ſ, τ, y; þ, ð, p;
   6 capitals: Æ¹, Æ², Є, ꟽ, Ȣ, Ð;
   3 others: ꝩ, þ, ꞏj.
 Total: 22 sorts.

On 2X4ʳ AS2 s occurs in unſcẏlðıȝ (bottom line) and AS3 s in ſpıɲıȝe (penultimate line).

 Copies seen: All copies seen lack g2:
 [Wing H2094] APL O.11.7; CCA W/E.6.18 (owned by Somner with his annotation on 5C1ʳ); CUL R.2.17–18 (split at 3I5/6), Pet.P.5.17; ECC S12.2.17–8 (g1 misplaced after ²2N3; Abp Sancroft's copy bound in 2 vols, both with gold-tooled contemporary binding with his armorial crest); OBL R.4.74; PO 1652.1 (4V3.4 occurs twice, g1 misplaced after ²2N3; owned by Wm Richardson (d.1775), armorial crest in gold leaf on front cover of 'The Society of Writers to the Signet');
 [Wing H2094aA] OBL Douce A.subt.42.
 Copies also at: Wing H2094: BL, BCL, BUL, CCC, CGC, CJC, CPH, CSJ, TCC, CaCL, ChestC, DCL, EAL, EdUL, HCL, HHC, LBL, LCL, NLS, NMS, NT, OAS, OEC, OEF, OJC, OLC, OMaC, OMC, OQC, OWmC, OWoC, OXC, SoUL, SPC, SUL, WAL, WCC, WCL, WiCL, WoCL, YML, DEWL, DML, NLI, TCD, ULim, GCB; FSL, USLC, NYHS, HHL, IUL, BMC, GC, GSU, KSRS, LCP, MCRS, PUL, SCN, SLC, UAZ, UCLA, UMI, UTA, UVL, YUB; VSL.

Wing H2094aA: CMC, Eton, GML, LHL, LSH, NUL, OBC, OHC, OHM, ONC, KSC, GUB; DDUL, PUL.

Bibliography: Alston III.i.no.1; Baker & Womack 1999: 350–356 (art. on Twysden by Richard Ovenden); Gross/Graves 1975: no. 1124; Bailey & Cambridge 2016; Cronne 1962: 44–45; Dekker 2000: 293; Hetherington 1980: 135–141, 189–208 (sources used by Somner); Howlett 1976 (*Durham*); Jessup 1965; Lucas Doane and Cunningham 1997: 42–47 (Faustina A.v); O'Donnell 2001; Toomer 2009: 1.349–359. GR 54 (Glossary), 531.

1652.2: Selden, John, t Marchamont Needham, *Of the Dominion, or, Ownership of the Sea*, t of *Mare Clausum* (= **1635.1**). London: William Du-Gard, 1652. Wing S2432; ESTC R15125. AS5.

 Context: See **1635.1**. This translation printed by order of the Committee for Foreign Affairs 26 June 1652. The Council ordered 200 copies and a reward of £200 for Ne(e)dham the translator (8 Nov 1652, 3 & 10 Feb 1653). For references see **Bibliography** below.

ASC **(extracts)**

 Collation: 2^0 in 4s: π^2 A^2 a–k^2 B–$3R^4$ [\$3 signed (-A1, Q3, S3, T3, 3M3)] 272 leaves, paginated [i–xlviii], 1–176, 179–274, 279–500, *501–502* (pp. 180, 460–462 not numbered; pp. 48 misnumbered 49, 72 misnumbered 71, 100–101 misnumbered 99–100, 390 misnumbered 400).

SOURCES OF PASSAGES UTILIZING ANGLO-SAXON TYPES:

2K3 (pp. 255–256)	From **1635.1** Y2^v: ASC 897 (as Thorpe 1861: I.175/37–177/5);
2L1^v–2^r (pp. 260–61)	From **1635.1** Y4^v: ASC 1008 (as Thorpe 1861: I.258/26–30);
2L3^v–4^r (pp. 264–5)	From **1635.1** Z2^r: ASC 1012 (as Thorpe 1861: I.268/38–270/4);
2M1^r (p. 267)	From **1635.1** Z3^r: ASC 1052 (as Thorpe 1861: I.312/12–15);
2M2 (pp. 269–270)	From **1635.1** Z4^r: ASC 1014 (as Thorpe 1861: I.274/27–8).

TYPE:

Main text in Ameet Tavernier's Great Primer Roman (Body 117.5) interspersed with Guyot's Great Primer Italic;

AS5: The Wheelockian Great Primer Anglo-Saxon occurs on 2K3, 2L1^v–2^r, 2L3^v–4^r, 2M1^r, 2M2. Special sorts shown:

12 lower-case sorts:	ð, *e*, ꝼ, ᵹ, ı, ꝓ, ꞃ, ꞇ, ẏ; þ, ð, p;
5 capitals:	Æ¹, Є, Ꝧ, Ꞅ, Ð;
2 others:	þ, Ᵹ.
Total:	19 sorts.

 Copies seen: APL DD.III.31 (lacks π); CUL Broughton 25; LFL 18L; OBL Vet.A3.d.163.

Copies also at: BL, CCA, CMC, DWL, EAL, EUL, GlCL, LiCL, LL, LSH, NCL, NLS, NLW, NT, OEC, OWoC, SAC, SUL; FSL, NYPL, NYCU, NYHS, HHL, HUL, GWU, JCB, MUL, NLC, NWU, UCBL, UCLA, USNA, UTA, YUB, UWO; ATL, NLA, SSA.

Bibliography: McKenzie & Bell 2005: 1.313–314, 319, 325–326, 331.

1652.3: Boxhorn, Marcus Zuerius, *Historia Universalis Sacra et Profana, a Christo nato ad annum usque MDCL*. Leiden: Pieter Leffen, 1652.

Collation: 4^0: *–2*^{4} A–6T^4 a–s^4. [16], 1072; [2], 107, [37] p.

Contains the Creed in OE on N3 (pp. 101–102), printed in a Pica Italic showing æ for OE æ, but no other special AS sorts are shown.

Copies seen: CSJ 3.8.19.

Copies also at: TCC, DUL, Eton, LWI, OHM, OQC, OSJ.

1653.1: Verstegan, Richard, *A Restitution of Decayed Intelligence in Antiquities*. 4th edn of 1605.2. London: Thomas Newcomb I for Joshua Kirton, 1653. Wing V269; ESTC R10115.

Collation: 8^0: A–S^8 T^4. [24], 264 [i.e. 262], [10] p.

Words in AS and other Germanic languages appear in Textura with no special sorts.

Copy seen: CUL Syn.7.65.158.

Copies also at: BL, BCL, BLC, TCC, CUW, ERCP, Eton, NLS, OCC, OSA, QMU, QUB, SJS, UBL; FSL, USLC, HHL, HUL, IUL, JCB, KSRL, NLC, PTS, UTA, TUL; CCPL, QCL, UAL.

1653.2: [Boxhorn, Marcus Zuerius], *Metamorphosis Anglorum, sive Mutationes variæ Regum, Regni, Rerumque Angliæ. Opus Historicum et Politicum*. [Leiden: W.C. van der Boxe], 1653.

Collation: 12^0: *^{2} A–Y^{12} Z^2 2A^6. [4], 536 p.

Includes an edition of Selden's *Jani Anglorum* (1610.2) at sigs G10^r–M2^r (pp. 163–267), but the AS words are reproduced in Roman on H2^v, I6^r, and I10^v, with what should be *wergild* on I6^r rendered as 'pepzilo'!

Copy seen: CUL R.6.72 (sig Z misbound between X and Y).

Copies also at: AUL, CSJ, TCC, DUL, Eton, EUL, GUL, LFL, LPL, LSH, LUL, MJRUL, NLS, NT, OEC, OMaC, OMFC, OQC, OSJ, SUL, TCD.

1654.1: Ware, Sir James, *De Hibernia & Antiquitatibus ejus*. London: John Grismond II for John Crooke and Thomas Heath, 1654. Wing W843; ESTC R13244. AS3.

Words

>   **Collation:** 8⁰: A–R⁸ [$4 signed (-A1,2)] 136 leaves, paginated [i–xvi], 1–253, *254–256* (pp. 44, 191 not numbered); p. 62 shows 6 with only rh side imprinted, but printed fully in CUL Hib.7.654.7.

TYPE:

Main text in Arthur Nicholls's Pica Roman (Body 81) interspersed with Nicholls's Pica Italic (e.g. F3; some mixed sorts, e.g. *fh*).

AS3: The Lambardian Pica Anglo-Saxon occurs in combination with Nicholls's Pica Roman in words on D4ʳ (p. 39):

Special sorts shown: 6 lower-case sorts: ð, *e*, ꝼ, ᵹ, ı, ẏ.

>   **Copies seen:** CUL Hib.8.654.2 (with gold-tooled binding in brown calf), Hib.8.654.3 (with engraving by Hollar of 'Hibernia Antiqua' stuck on A5ᵛ), Hib.7.654.3, Hib.7.654.4, Hib.7.654.5, Hib.7.654.6 (lacks A1, R8; owned by James Espinasse); (with no. 6 in p.no. 62 fully printed): Hib.7.654.7.
>
>   **Copies also at:** AUL, BL, BCLNI, BUT, CCA, CGC, CMC, CSJ, TCC, DUL, Eton, KCL, LPL, LSH, MJRUL, MTP, NLW, OBL, OCC, OGF, OJC, OQC, OWmC, OWoC, SCL, StA, WoCL, YML, DOL, NLI, TCD, ULim, PBN, BSB, GUB, MSB; HHL, IUL, BPM, CUofA, GETS, JCB, KSRL, LCP, NLC, PUL, TCH, UCBL, UCLA, YUB.

Bibliography: Empey 2017; Parry 1995: 155–156; Pennington 1982: items 681, 1091 (re. maps by Hollar on D6ᵛ, N8ʳ).

1654.2: *Musarum Oxoniensium Elliofoía sive ob Fœdera, Auspiciis Serenissimi Oliveri Reipub. Ang. Scot. & Hiber. Domini Protectoris.* Oxford: Leonard Litchfield I, 1654. Wing O902; ESTC R203114; Madan 1895–1931: no. 2243; Turner 1948.

>   **Collation:** 4⁰: A–L⁴. [4], 68, 89–104 p.

17C AS verse by Joseph Williamson on K2ʳ printed in Italic with no special sorts.

>   **Copy seen:** CSJ U.20.75(13)
>
>   **Copies also at:** TCC, CUW, DUL, EdUL, HU, KUL, LJM, LSH, LU, LUL, MJRUL, NLS, NLW, NRL, NU, NUL, OAS, OBC, OJC, OMaC, ONC, OSJ, OXC, OU, SHU, UBL, WCF, YUL, TCD.

1655.1: Junius, Franciscus, *Observationes in Willerami Abbatis Francicam Paraphrasin Cantici Canticorum.* Amsterdam: Christoffel Cunrad for Adriaen Vlack, 1655. AS6.

OE Bede, OE Boethius, OE Gospels, Rushworth Gospels, Liber Scintillarum, Words

>   **Collation:** 8⁰: π⁸ A–X⁸ [$5 signed (D3 missigned C3)] 176 leaves, paginated [i–xvi], 1–311, *312–336*.

SOURCES OF PASSAGES UTILIZING ANGLO-SAXON TYPES (selected longer extracts only):

C8ʳ (p. 47)   From OBL Junius 12 (SC 5124 = Junius's own transcript of OBL Bodley 180 (SC 2079; siglum B) collated with Otho A.vi (siglum C, since damaged by fire)), p. 40/25–40: OE Boethius, ch. 30.2 (extract), as Sedgefield 1899: 69/17–32; Godden/Irvine 2009: 305/38–52;

I2ʳ (p. 131)   From 1643.1, 2V2ᵛ/9–11 and 2S2ᵛ/11–26: OE Bede, IV.23 and IV.19 (extracts), as Miller 1890–8: I.2, 336/33–338/1 and 322/17–24;

K1ʳ (p. 145)   From 1643.1 Y4ʳ/23–6: OE Bede, II.20 (extracts), as Miller 1890–8: I.1, 150/27–28;

L4ᵛ (p. 168)   From 1643.1, 2X1ʳ/18–22: OE Bede, IV.24 (extracts), as Miller 1890–8: I.2, 346/1–3;

L5 (pp. 169–70)   From 1571.1, C2ᵛ, L4ʳ: OE Gospels, Mt 5.11–12, 16.13 (extracts), as Liuzza 1994: 14, 34;

L5ᵛ (p. 170)   From (prob) 1644.1, C4ʳ/15–16: Law Alfred, ch. 1.8, as Liebermann I, 48;

From OBL Auct. D.2.19, 6ᵛ (Junius 76 contains Junius's own partial transcript of Auct. D.2.19): Rushworth Gospels, Mt 5.11 (extract), as Tamoto 2013: 12;

L7ᵛ (p. 174)   From 1643.1, 2Q3ᵛ/9–10 and 3B3ʳ/2–5: OE Bede, IV.32 and IV.13 (extracts), as Miller I.2, 380/30–382/1 and 304/9;

M6ʳ (p. 187)   From 1571.1, 2B3ʳ, 2R3ʳ: OE Gospels, Mk 14.30, and Lk 22.34, 60 (extracts), as Liuzza 92 and 149, 151;

M7ᵛ (p. 190)   From 1643.1, 2V3ʳ/1–3: OE Bede, IV.23 (extract), as Miller I.2, 338/24;

O3ᵛ (p. 214)   From OBL Auct. D.2.19, 101ᵛ, 115ʳ: Rushworth Gospels, Lk 11.22, 19.46 (extracts), as Tamoto 2013: 201, 229;

P3 (pp. 229–30)   From OBL Junius 12, p. 29/21–36: OE Boethius, ch. 23 (extract), as Sedgefield 1899: 51/28–52/13; Godden/Irvine 2009: 288/2–289/16.

Q6ʳ (p. 251)   From 1643.1, 2K2ʳ/12–15: OE Bede, III.27 (extract), as Miller I.2, 244/23–24;

From BL, Royal 7 C.iv, 29ʳ/8–10: Liber Scintillarum, ch. 10.27 in Rochais 1957: 41, as Rhodes 1889: 53/1–3.

TYPE:

Main text in Junius's Pica Roman interspersed with his Pica Italic (both cut by Christoffel van Dijck), with the headwords for monosyllabic words (P5ʳ–R1ᵛ) in an English-size Textura (Junius's Pica English).

AS6: The Junian Pica Anglo-Saxon (by van Dijck) occurs in the reader's specimen on π8ᵛ and in combination with Junius's Pica Roman in text on C8ʳ, I2ʳ,

K1r, L4v–5v, L7v, M6r, M7v, O3v, P3, Q6r, and in words or phrases on F8r, I2v, K2r, K6r, L5v, L7v, M3v, M4v, M5v, M8, N3v, N6, N7v, O2r, O3, O4r, O5r, O6v, O7, O8, P1, P2r, P3v, P4, P5r–R1v, R4r, S3v, T2v, T3r, T4, X5r–7v.
Special sorts shown in specimen on π8r:

    11 lower-case sorts: ð, ꝼ, ȝ, ı, ꞃ, ſ, ꞇ, ẏ; þ, ð, ꝥ;
    8 capitals: Ꞃ, ꬲ, Ᵹ, Ꝫ, Ꟁ, S; Þ, Ð;
    1 other: ꝫ.
 Total: 20 sorts.

Special sorts shown in text:

    11 lower-case sorts: ð, ꝼ, ȝ, ı, ꞃ, ſ, ꞇ, ẏ; þ, ð, ꝥ;
    4 capitals: ꬲ, Ᵹ, Ꝫ, S,
    2 others: þ, ꝫ.
 Total: 17 sorts.

 Overall total: 11 + 8 + 2 = 21 sorts.

 Copies seen: CCA W2/X.3.37 (Junius's gift to Somner as recorded by Somner on fo iiv); CUL 2.38.50; MBS P.o.germ.1628.o; OBL Douce.W.92, 8⁰.I.8.Th.BS¹.

 Note 1: OBL MS Junius 75 (SC 5186) is Junius's own copy (sigs A–V only) with his extensive annotations, probably in preparation for a 2nd edition.

 Note 2: LPB PB.1601.TL is Jan van Vliet's copy with his extensive annotations (not seen; reported by Noorwinden 1992: xix, n.33).

 Copies also at: BL, NLS, OAS, OCC, OLC, OQC.

Bibliography: Gumbert 1975.
Note: Junius's commentary is based on:
Merula, Paulus, *Willerami Abbatis in Canticum Canticorum Paraphrasis Gemina: Prior Rhythmis Latinis, Altera Veteri Lingua Francica* (Leiden: ex officina Plantiniana, 1598).
See also:
Bartelmez, Erminnie Hollis (ed.), *The "Expositio in Cantica Canticorum" of Williram von Ebersberg, 1048–1085*, Memoirs of the American Philosophical Society 69 (Philadelphia, 1967).
Facsimile: Ed. Norbert Voorwinden, ESGP 1 (Amsterdam: Rodopi, 1992), slightly enlarged, based on the copy in The Hague, Koninklijke Bibliotheek, KW 1173 F 50.

1655.2: Junius, Franciscus, *Cædmonis Monachi Paraphrasis Poetica*. Amsterdam: Christoffel Cunrad for Adriaen Vlack, 1655. AS 6.

 Note: Re-issue edited by Edward Rowe Mores (pronounced Morris) (1730–78) with new sigs ∴ and P added at the end in 1752, to which plates were added in 1754.

Genesis, Exodus, Daniel, Christ and Satan, Prayer (verse)

Collation: 4⁰: ∴² A–O⁴ [$3 signed (-∴1, O3)] 58 leaves, pp. [i–iv], 1–106, *107–112*.

SOURCES OF PASSAGES UTILIZING ANGLO-SAXON TYPES:

A1ʳ–M2ʳ: From OBL Junius 11, the sole MS witness for all four poems (facsimile by Gollancz 1927, digital facsimile by Muir 2015), paginated by Junius: OE poems *Genesis* (as Doane 2013), *Exodus* (as Lucas 2020), *Daniel* (as Farrell 1974), *Christ and Satan* (as Sleeth 1982), all as Krapp 1931;

M2ʳ–O1ᵛ: From Julius A ii, 136–7ʳ (facsimile by Robinson/ Stanley 1991: 31.2): OE poem *Prayer*, as Dobbie 1942: 94–96.

TYPE:

AS6: The main text is in Junius's 'Pica Saxon' (Oxford University Specimen 1693, d1–2, simulated item by item in Hart 1970: 38–40), i.e. his 'Pica Roman' with special Saxon sorts substituted for particular AS letter-forms. Body size not available as not set solid. Face 80 x 1.8: 2.9. The Pica Roman (which occurs unmixed with Saxon sorts on O2ʳ–3ʳ and in the running titles) corresponds to the Mediaen Romeyn (no. 1) on the widow Elsevier type-specimen (Dreyfus 1963: pl. 12), and both the Pica Roman and the Saxon sorts that go with it are attibutable to Christoffel van Dijck (Lane 1993: 57, commentary on *Kleine Text Curcyf no. 2*).

Special sorts shown in the text:

    11 lower-case sorts: ð, ꝼ, ᵹ, ı, ꝑ, ꞃ, ꞇ, ẏ; þ, ð, ƿ;

    8 capitals: Ꞇ, ꬲ, Ᵹ, Ꝺ, ꟽ, Ꞩ; Ƿ, Ð;

    2 others: þ, ꝫ.

Total: 21 sorts.

Copies: BUL HDa (uncut, lacks ∴); CUL F.9.74; ECC S1.4.26 (Junius's gift to Abp Sancroft); LUB 499.F.20 (acquired in 1690 with Isaac Vossius's books), 1213.B.39 (given by F. van Lelyveld to the Bibliotheek van de Maatschappij der Nederlands Letterkunde); OBL MS Junius 73 (Junius's copy, 'Notae' of 1752 added), Mar 125(2) (Marshall's copy).

CUL U*.5.160 is an unusual copy, being interleaved and having the 'Notæ' and plates of the 1754 re-issue added. On ∴2ʳ (p. [iii]) the signature and catchword have left an impression but were not inked. The interleaved pages show a different watermark.

Copies also at: BL, TCC, CCA CLC.II.C22 (possibly Somner's copy), LCL Hurst B.388, LSA, MJRUL, OBrC, OEC, OEF, OMaC, OQC, OTC, UCL. Only 27 copies are known; for a list (of 25) see Lucas 2000: xlvi–xlix.

Bibliography: Lucas 2000: xxxvii–xlv; Niles 2015: 116–120.

Facsimile: Lucas 2000.

1655.3: Dugdale, Sir William, and Roger Dodsworth, *Monasticon Anglicanum*, vol. I. London: Richard Hodgkinson, 1655. Wing D2484; ESTC R225645. AS 3. **Charters etc.**

    Collation: 2⁰ in 4s: π⁴ a–e⁴ A–7F⁴ [$3 signed (-4H1, 4S3, 6D2; S1 missigned R1, 2E2,3 missigned E2,3, 5I2 missigned 4I2)] 600 leaves, paginated [i–xliv], 1–1151, *1152* (pp. 609–610, 612, 692–694, 946–948, 978 not numbered, pp. 19 misnumbered 11, 183 misnumbered 189, 690 misnumbered 691).

SOURCES OF PASSAGES UTILIZING ANGLO-SAXON TYPES:

D2ʳ (p. 27)   From RKA, DRc/R1 (Textus Roffensis, *olim* RCL A.3.5) 119ʳ: Charter of King Æthelbert to Rochester (entire L + OE) 604 (Sawyer 1; Birch 3);

E3ʳ (p. 37)   From Harley Charter 43 C 1: Charter of King Edward to Winchester (entire L + OE) 908 (Sawyer 376; Birch 620);

K2ᵛ–3ʳ (pp. 76–7)   From Vitellius A.xiii (Register of Chertsey), 20ᵛ–23ʳ: Grant of land to Chertsey Minster (entire L + OE) 672 × 674 (Sawyer 1165; Birch 34); cf. (Tite 2013: 159);

L4ʳ (p. 87)   From Augustus ii, fo 57: Charter of King Eadred to Canterbury Cathedral (entire) 949 (Sawyer 546; Birch 880);

N3 (pp. 101–102)   From Claudius B.vi, 34ᵛ: Charter of King Eadred granting land to Abingdon (entire) 955 (Sawyer 567; Birch 906);

Q2ᵛ (p. 124)   From Tiberius A.xiii, 23ʳ: Charter of King Offa to St Michael's at Bishop's Cleeve (entire) 768 × 779 (Sawyer 141; Birch 246);

Q3ʳ (p. 125)   From Tiberius A.xiii, 47ʳ: Charter of King Beornwulf of Mercia settling a dispute over land at Westbury-on-Trym (entire) 824 (Sawyer 1433; Birch 379);

Q3 (pp. 125–6)   From Tiberius A.xiii, fo 48: Charter of King Offa of Mercia to Worcester (entire) 793 × 796 (Sawyer 146; Birch 273);

R4ᵛ (p. 136)   From Tiberius A.xiii, fo 185: Charter of Wulfstan bp of Wo to Ealdestune (1089; entire) (Hearne, *Hemingi chartularium*, 1723, II.420–421; Pelteret 63);

S2ᵛ–S3ʳ (pp. 140–1)   From PRO Ch.R. 9 Edw. III, no. 49 + PRO Pat.R. 4Edw. IV, pt 3, m.3: Charter of King Edgar to Worcester (entire) 964 (Sawyer 731; Birch 1135);

S4ᵛ–T1ʳ (pp. 144–5)   From (?) a copy ('Autographum Saxonico charactere scriptum' s.xvi/xvii) of Vespasian B.xxiv, 76ᵛ (Dugdale says his source was an Arundel MS, but no such MS has been identified; cf. Tite 2003: 179): 1st grant of privileges by Pope Constantine I to Evesham 709 (entire, Latin text in AS characters following the source MS): as Sayers and Watkiss 2003: §§318–323, pp. 314–318;

Note: The variant readings reflect Vespasian B.xxiv, as Britanniarum ecclesiae (314/27), require (316/17), undique om. (*but* concilio *is not*, 316/18), est om. (318/1), Kenredus rex (318/12);

T1 (pp. 145–6)　　　From Vespasian B.xxiv, fo 64: Charter of King Cenric of Mercia to Evesham (L with names in AS types, entire) 709 (Sawyer 80; Birch 125);

2A2^r (p. 187)　　　From Tiberius E.viii, pt i, fo 218 (s.xvii): Charter of Edward the Confessor to Wells (entire) 1065 (Sawyer 1042; Kemble 816; Keynes 1996^2: 232–238, 257, no. 9);

2B21^v–2^r (pp. 194–5)　　　From a lost MS (?ME) formerly in the King's Remembrancer's Office: Charter of King Æthelstan to Milton (Do) (entire, with L version on p. 196 col 1) 843 for 834 (Sawyer 391; Robertson 23; Birch 738–739);

2C2^v–3^r (pp. 204–5)　　　From (prob) Augustus ii. 6: Charter of King Edgar to Pershore Abbey (large extracts) 972 (Sawyer 786; Birch 1282);

2E1^r (p. 217)　　　From Harley 61 (s.xv), Lieger Booke of Shaftesbury abbey (formerly D'Ewes A214 in Watson 1966: 123), 4^v: Charter of King Æthelred to Shaftesbury (entire, L + OE) 1001 (Sawyer 899; Kemble 706);

2E3 (pp. 221–2)　　　From OBL Auct.D.2.16, fo 1: Leofric's gift to Exeter (entire), as Robertson 1956: App. I, no. 1;

2E4^r–2F1^r (pp. 223–225) From OBL Auct.D.2.16, 8^v–14^r: Æthelstan's gifts to Exeter (entire), as Förster 1943, 63–80;

2K1 (pp. 257–258)　　　From PRO, Ch.R 44 Hen. III, m.1: Charter of King Æthelred to Wherwell Abbey (entire, L + OE) 1002 (Sawyer 904; Kemble 707);

2K1^v–2^v (pp. 258–260)　From Oxford, Christ Church, Eynsham Cart. 7^r: Charter of King Æthelred to Eynsham Abbey (entire, L + OE) 1005 (Sawyer 911; Kemble 714);

2K3^v (p. 262)　　　From Oxford, Christ Church, Eynsham Cart. 9^r: Agreement between Bp Wulfwig and Earl Leofric and Godgifu his wife (entire) 1053 × 1055 (Sawyer 1478; Robertson 115);

2L1 (pp. 265–6)　From Cotton Charter viii.6 (copy of, 1652): Charter of King Eadred to Wulfric (entire without names subscribed) 949 (Sawyer 550; Birch 882);

2L1^v–2^r (pp. 266–7)　From BL Loan MS 30 (Cartulary of Burton Abbey, St) fo 9: Will of Wulfric (entire) 1002 (1004: Sawyer 1536; Whitelock 17);

2L3 (pp. 269–270)　　　From BL Loan MS 30, fos 8–9: Charter of King Æthelred to Burton (entire, L with OE bounds) 1004 (Sawyer 906; Kemble 710);

2M2^v–3^r (pp. 276–7)　　　From Dorchester, Dorset RO, D124 (s.xi): Charter of King Cnut to Orc his thane (entire, including the caption on the back apparently not printed since Dugdale) 1024 (Sawyer 961, Kemble 741);

2M3 (pp. 277–278) From ibid.: Orc's guild at Abbotsbury (entire) 1041 (Kemble 942; Thorpe 1865: 605–608);

2M4ʳ (p. 279) From PRO, Ch.R, 8 Edw. II, m.3, no. 5(1): Writ of Edward theConfessor in favour of his housecarl Usk 1053 × 1058 (Sawyer 1063; Harmer 1);

From PRO, Ch.R, 8 Edw. II, m.3, no. 5(2): Writ of Edward the Confessor in favour of St Peter's, Abbotsbury 1058 × 1066 (Sawyer 1064; Harmer 2; cf. Keynes 1989, esp 235–238);

From PRO, Ch.R. 8 Edw, II, m.3, no. 5(3): Writ of William I in favour of St Peter's, Abbotsbury (Pelteret 26);

2N4ʳ (p. 287) 'Ex historia Mariani Scoti MS in bibliotheca Bodleiana v.3 7 jur.': Charter of King Edmund to Bury St Edmunds (entire) 945 (Sawyer 507, Birch 808);

2X4ᵛ–2Y1ʳ (pp. 352–3) From RKA, DRc/R1 (Textus Roffensis, *olim* RCL A.3.5), fo 143: Charter of King Edmund to Bp Burhric re. land at Malling, K (entire) 942 × 946 (Sawyer 514; Birch 779);

6I3 (pp. 989–990) From a copy made by the dean of the chapel royal at Windsor 1640 in fake OE: privilege granted to Wolverhampton OSB (entire) (Sawyer 1380, t Duignan 1888);

6I4ᵛ (p. 992) From a copy made by the dean of the chapel royal at Windsor 1640 from Harley Charter 43. D 29: Alleged writ of Edward the Confessor (later confirmed by Henry II and Edward I) to Wolverhampton (entire) (Sawyer 1155; Harmer 114).

TYPE:

Main text in Haultin's Pica Roman (Body 82) interspersed with Granjon's 2nd Pica Italic 'Pendante' (e.g. H4ᵛ);

and in words/names on D2ᵛ, D3ʳ, 2N4ᵛ.

Special sorts shown:

12 lower-case sorts: ð, *e*, ꝼ, ȝ, ı, ꝑ, ꞅ, ꞇ, ẏ; þ, ð, ƿ;
9 capitals: Æ¹, Æ², Є, Ꝺ, Ꞥ, S, Ꝑ, Ð, Ƿ;
3 others: þ, ꝛ, ꞁ.

Total: 24 sorts.

Note 1: Upper-case Ꝺ shown for lower-case h on D2, Q2ᵛ, and 2M3; on R4ᵛ Roman upper-case H shown with AS upper-case Ꝺ used lower-case;

Note 2: Roman **M** is preferred to AS **M** on R4ᵛ;

Note 3: AS capital S not shown on K2ᵛ–3ʳ; Roman S shown instead;

Note 4: AS capital Ƿ clear on 2M4ʳ in Ƿillelm (cp. Ɓꞃiꝺꞇꞃi immediately below).

Copies seen: ECC 306.2.56 (lacks π3); TCD G.c.17 (5R2 and 5R3 in reverse order), RR.b.28 (lacks π3; owned by Claudius Gilbert (d.1743)).

Copies also at: BL, BrPL, CCA, CUL, ChC, CCC, CCL, CFM, CGC, CJC, KCC, CPC, CSJ, CSS, TCC, CaCL, DCL, DUL, DWL, EdUL, GlCL, HHC, LBL, LCL, LGI, LHL, LiCL, LIL, LMT, LPL, LUL, MJRUL, MTP, NLS, NLW, NT, NUL, OBL, OAS, OBC, OCC, OEF, OHC, OJC, OLC, OMC, ONC, OQC, OSJ, OStH, OTC, OWoC, OXC, SACL, SCL, SoUL, SPC, WAL, WiCL, WoCL, YML, DEWL, DML, NLI, ULim, PBN, GUB; FSL, USLC, NYCU, UTS, HHL, HUL, IUL, GC, LCP, NLC, SLU, UTA, UVL, YUB, TUL; CTCM.

Bibliography: Corbett 1986; Cronne 1962: 50–52; Maddison *et al.* 1953: no. 3; Parry 1995: 228–236; Pennington 1982 (re. Hollar: see index for references); Urry 1997: xi (on Somner's contribution).

Edition: J. Caley, H. Ellis and B. Bandinel, 6 vols (London, 1817–30).

1655.4: Selden, John, *De Synedriis & Præfecturis Iuridicis Veterum Ebræorum Liber Tertius & Ultimus*, vol. III. For vol. I see **1650.3**; vol. II (1653) shows no Anglo-Saxon. London: James Flesher, 1655, also for Cornelius Bee. Wing S2426(A). AS3.

Words

Collation: 4⁰: A⁴ a–b⁴ c² B–3K⁴ 3L² [$3 signed (-A1,2, c2, 3L2)] 236 leaves, paginated [i–xxviii], 1–441, *442–444*.

TYPE:

Main text in an English-size Roman (Body 92) interspersed with much Arabic and Hebrew.

Uses red to highlight certain items 2Y2ᵛ–3H1ʳ.

AS3: the Lambardian Pica Anglo-Saxon combined with a Pica Roman occurs in words on 2D3ʳ (p. 205).

Special sorts shown: *e*, ᵹ, ꞇ; ð   3 + 1 + 0 = 4 sorts

Copies seen: Wing S2426A: CUL C.5.61, Q*5.57(E); TCD HH.kk.67.

Copies also at: APL, BCL, CPH, CSJ, TCC, LHL, LPL, LRCP, OQC, OTC, OXC, SPC, WAL, KSC, PBN, BSB, MBS, MUC; USLC, HHL, IUL, UCLA.

Bibliography: Toomer 2009: II.763–786.

1655.5: Verstegen, Richard, *A Restitution of Decayed Intelligence*. Re-issue of **1653.1** = 4th edn of **1605.2**. London: Thomas Newcomb I for Joshua Kirton, 1653. Wing V270; ESTC R3529.

Collation: 8⁰: A–S⁸ T⁴. [24], 264 [i.e. 262], [10] p.

Copy seen: CCC.28.143.

Copies also at: BL, CPC, KLL, PBL, LHL, LL, LU, NMS, DCLI, PBN, MBS; FSL, NYCU, HHL, IUL, EmU, NLC, PUL, UCBL, UCLA, UPL, UTA, UVL, YUB, TUL.

1655.6: Grotius, Hugo, *Historia Gotthorum, Vandalorum, & Langobardorum.* Amsterdam: Louis Elzevier, 1655.

    Collation: 8⁰: *⁴ a–i⁸ k² A–3S⁸ 3T⁴. [8], 148, 932, [98] p.

On 2O4ʳ–2P6ᵛ the glossary of proper names occasionally includes AS cognates, but all linguistic forms are printed in Italic with no special sorts.

    Copy seen: CUL Bb*.5.15.

    Copies also at: AUL, BL, KCC, TCC, DUL, EdUL, Eton, GUL, LPL, LSH, LUL, MCS, MJRUL, NLS, NLW, NT, OAS, OCC, OEC, OHM, OMaC, OQC, OSJ, OTI, OWoC, SUL, UBL, WCC.

1656.1: Lambarde, William, *A Perambulation of Kent.* 3rd edn of 1576.2; = 1640?.1 with ±A1. London: [Richard Hodgkinson] for Matthew Walbancke and Daniel Pakeman, 1656. Wing L216; ESTC R40445. AS3 with AS2 s. Identical with 1640?.1 except for substitute title page.

    Copy seen: CUL R.5.57.

    Copies also at: BL, BPL, TCC, DC, GUL, LHL, LSH, NLS, NT, OBL, WCF, WIHM; FSL, HHL, HUL, BEC, JCB, UCLA, YUB.

1656.2: [Nicholas Nicholls (printer), Specimen of Hebrew and Anglo-Saxon Types] [London: Nicholas Nicholls, 1656]. AS7.
Alfredian Boethius, Law 'Geþyncðo' (extracts) = printer's trials

    Collation: Loose sheets.

SOURCES OF PASSAGES UTILIZING ANGLO-SAXON TYPES:

Sheet 2:   From OBL, Junius 12, 39ᵛ/25–40: Alfredian Boethius, xxx.ii, ed. Rawlinson 1698.2, sig. I2ʳ (p. 67), as Sedgefield 1899: 69, Godden/Irvine 2009: I.452 (the prose version on which Metre 17 was based); a line of text is missing between 'þa ryht [æþelo]' and '[s]ædon' (37–8); some transcriptional errors involving þ/ð, e.g., oð ðæt, æþelo *for* MS oð þæt, æðelo, but there are far more such errors in the same passage in **1698.2**;

Sheet 3:   From **1596.2** 2I7ᵛ–8ʳ: AS Law 'Geþyncðo', §§1–7 (om. end of §3 and §4), as Liebermann 1903–16: I.456–458; this passage has been heavily proof-read;

Sheet 6:   From **1596.2** 2I7ᵛ–8ʳ: AS Law 'Geþyncðo', §§1–3 (om. end of §3), as Liebermann 1903–16: I.456.

TYPE:

AS7: The Somnerian Pica Anglo-Saxon is shown in text on sheets 2, 3, 6: Special sorts shown:

> 12 lower-case sorts: ð, *e*, ꝼ, ᵹ, ı, ꝑ, ſ, τ, ẏ; þ, ð, ꝑ;
> 7 capitals: A, Ꞇ, Є, Ᵹ, Ð, S, Đ;
> 4 others: þ, ꝫ, ꝫ, ∴.

Total: 23 sorts.
Copy seen: OBL, University Archives, SEP.P17b(4a).
Bibliography: Berry & Johnson 1935: 2; Morison/Carter 1967: 233–238 (re. Hebrew).

1656.3: Blount, Thomas (1618–79), *Glossographia: or, a Dictionary, Interpreting all such Hard Words, Whether Hebrew, Greek, Latin, Italian, Spanish, French, Teutonick, Belgick, British or Saxon, as are now used in our refined English Tongue ... With Etymologies, Definitions, and Historical Observations on the same*. London: Thomas Newcomb for Humphrey Mosely & George Sawbridge, 1656. Wing B3334. 1st edn.
Note: This being a hard words dictionary there is a preponderance of words of foreign origin.
OE etymologies
Collation: 8⁰: A–2V⁸; [688] p.
Type: Main text in a Long Primer Roman (Body 66) in double columns.
AS2/3: What is apparently a mixture of the Parkerian and Lambardian Pica Anglo-Saxon sorts occurs in the OE etymology given s.v. *Gospel* on S5r. Only 4 lower-case sorts are found: ð, *e*, ᵹ, ſ. With so little to go on the identification must be tentative, especially as this occurrence is two years earlier than the first definite sighting of the Somnerian Pica Anglo-Saxon in **1658.2**. But even there sorts from AS2 and AS3 are mixed in, so the sorts here are most likely a mixture of AS2 and AS3.

OE etymologies, when they occur, are usually cited in the same Textura as is used for headwords, as s.v. *Folkmoote, Gavelkind, Gild, Tithing, Wassail, Wisard*.
   Copy seen: CJL I.5.43 (gift of Revd Lionel Gatford 1715).
   Copies at: BL, CMC, CCA, CaCL, DCL, LGL, LSH, MJRUL, NLW, NT, OBL, OQC, WIHM; NYPL, FSL, HUL, HHL, DDUL, LCP, IUL, NLC, UCBL, UCH, UCLA, UOC, UTA, WMUL, YUB; ATL, OUL, SSA.
   Facsimile: English Linguistics 1500–1800 no. 153 (Menston: Scolar, 1969).
   Bibliography: Alston V.45.

1657.1: Camden, William, *Remaines, Concerning Britain: Their Languages, Empreses, Names, Apparell, Surnames, Artillarie, Allusions, Wise Speeches, Anagrammes, Proverbs, Armories, Poesïes, Monies, Epitaphes*, ed. John Philipot (Somerset Herald) and W[illiam]. D[u-gard]. London: Thomas Warren for Isabella Waterson, then Simon Waterson and Robert Clavell, and also Simon

Miller, 1657. 6th edn of 1605.1 re-set from 5th edn 1636.4. Wing C374A/B/C. Individual sorts only: AS3 ȝ and p (erron for þ).

>Collation: Wing C374B: 4⁰: ᵖA² B–3F⁴ 3G² [$3 signed (+ 2T4; -K3, L3, P3, R3, T3, V3, X3, Y3, 2B3, 2O3, 2P3, 2V3, 3B3; 3D3 missigned 'd d3'; 3G2 missigned 3F2)] 208 leaves, paginated [i–iv], 1–411, *412* (pp. 406 misnumbered 604, 409 misnumbered 332, 410 misnumbered 334, 411 misnumbered 331).

>Wing C374A/C show -ᵖA1 + π² (with π1 the portrait added, and π2 a variant tp), therefore 209 leaves.

>Note: State 2 shown by 3D3 missigned 'dd3' with no space between the two 'd's.

SOURCES OF PASSAGES UTILIZING ANGLO-SAXON TYPES:

D4ʳ (p. 23)   From **1636.1** D4ʳ: Lord's Prayer, with no (*for* **1623.2** do) at line 7;
D4 (pp. 23–4) From **1636.1** D4: Lord's Prayer (with marginal variants from another version) with fwa fwa at line 3, and coftnung at line 7.

TYPE:
Main text in Arthur Nicholls's Pica Roman (Body 81) interspersed with Robert Granjon's 2nd Pica Italic *pendante*.

D4 (pp. 23–24): no special sorts, but æ is correct in the second version of the Lord's Prayer in OE; suprascript translation to the first version in Granjon's 2nd Pica Italic.

AS3: The Lambardian Pica Anglo-Saxon (individual special sorts only) occurs on E4ᵛ (p. 32) in a report on the spelling reform practices advocated by Smith in **1568.3**: 3, p (erron for þ).

Note: A passage from Chaucer's *Nun's Priest's Tale* is printed in Granjon's 2nd Pica Italic with no special sorts on 2S1.

>**Copies seen:** State 1 (with 3D3 missigned 'd d3'): Wing C374A: CUL R.5.35; BL G2925; Wing C374B: TCC X.7.195 (includes tp for C374A in front of that for C374B); State 2 (with 3D3 missigned 'dd3'): Wing C374B: BL 1608/4651; Wing C374C: BL 808.b.3 (lacks D4).

>**Copies also at:** Wing C374A: BrCL, ChC, CSJ, CLL, CUW, DUL, HCL, LiCL, LSH, MTP, NLS, NLW, NT, NUL, OBL, OLC, SPC, UCL; FSL, NYPL, UTS, HHL, HUL, IUL, KSRL, LCP, MUL, NWU, UCH, UCLA, YUB, TUL. Wing C374B: NLS, OBL, QUB; HHL, HUL, IUL, BPM, DSRL, UCLA. Wing 374C: Eton, NLS, OBL, UBL; USLC, UTS, HHL, UVC.

Bibliography: see 1605.1.
Facsimile: Wing C374A (copy used not stated): New York: AMS Press, 1972.

1658.1: Dugdale, Sir William, *The History of St Pauls Cathedral in London*. London: Thomas Warren, 1658. Wing D2482; ESTC R16413. AS3.
Charters

>Collation: 2⁰: A⁴ B–3Y² 3Z⁴ [$2 signed (+A3; -Q2, 2G2, 2P1, 3P2, 3X2; Q1 missigned 2Q1)] 142 leaves, paginated [i–viii], 1–299, *300–306* (pp. nos 137–156, 179–180 not

used, pp. 161–170 assigned to inserted illustrations; pp. 40, 50, 58–59, 110, 115, 175–6 not numbered; pp. 129 misnumbered 126, 174 misnumbered 192, 293–297 misnumbered 263–267).

SOURCES OF PASSAGES UTILIZING ANGLO-SAXON TYPES:

2R1ʳ (p. 185)   From the lost St Paul's MS called 'Liber B' (s.xiii); fragmentary copy survives as OBL Rawlinson B.372 (SC 11709), 20ʳ: Charter of King Æthelstan granting privileges to St Paul's 925 × 939 (Sawyer 452; Birch 735, ultimately from this printing; Kelly 2004: 13);

2R2ʳ (p. 187)   From ibid. 20ᵛ: Æthelflæd's bequest to St Paul's of lands at Laver (E) and Cockhampstead (Hrt) c.1000 (Sawyer 908; Whitelock 1930: no. xxii, ultimately from this printing; Kelly 2004: 23);

2R2ᵛ–2S1ʳ (pp. 188–189)   From ibid. 20ᵛ: Charter of Cnut 1033 × 1035 (Sawyer 992; Kemble 1319, ultimately from this printing; Kelly 2004: 27);

2S1ᵛ (p. 190)   From ibid. 21ᵛ: Writ of Edward the Confessor to St Paul's (Sawyer 1104; Gibbs 1939: no. 1 from Liber A; Kelly 2004: 28);

2T2ᵛ (p. 196)   From London, Guildhall Library, MS 25,501 [Liber A, sive Pilosus, 1241; *olim* St Paul's Cathedral, MS W.D.1], 1ʳ, no. 5: Writ of William I granting the castle and land at Bishop's Stortford (Hrt) to Bp Maurice of London (Pelteret 39; Gibbs 1939: no. 5).

TYPE:

Main text of Appendix in Pierre Haultin's English-size Roman (Body 92).

AS3: The Lambardian Pica Anglo-Saxon (Body 80) combined with a Pica Roman (to be seen on 2E2ʳ, 2F1ʳ) occurs in text as indicated above under Contents, and in words in the errata on 3Z3ʳ. From the second instance onwards the Anglo-Saxon text is leaded so that it occupies more space.

Special sorts used:

12 lower-case sorts:	ð, ꝺ [= ð], e, f, ᵹ, Ꝺ [only in errata], p, r, t, ẏ; Ꝥ [used lc], þ [in æᵹþeþ on 2S1ᵛ], ð, p;
3 capitals:	Æ¹, Ꝼ, ꝺ [used correctly];
2 others:	þ, ꝫ.

Total: 18 sorts.

Copies: CUL Bury 9.2, Keynes D.5.1 (A1 appears after A4), Sel.2.54 (lacks A1; contemporary gold-tooled binding commemorating the author's gift '1657'); ECC 303.3.37 (gift of the countess of Bath, a descendant of Mildmay, College founder, with gold-tooled covers showing her armorial crest); TCD RR.d.27 (lacks A1, 3Z4; owned by Claudius Gilbert).

Copies also at: BL, CCA, CCC, CCL, CFM, CJC, KCC, CMC, CPC, CSJ, TCC, CaCL, DUL, GUL LCL, LHL, LMT, LSH, MOL, NAL, NewCL, NLS, OBL, OBC, OCC, ONC, OSJ, OTC, OWmC, OWoC, OXC, SBT, SJS, SoUL, SPC, SUL, UCL, WAL, WCC, WCF, WCL, WiCL, DML, PBN, GCB, GUB; FSL, USLC, NYPL, NYCU, GTS, UTS, HHL, HUL,

IUL, LCP, NLC, NWU, PUL, SfUL, UCBL, UCH, UCLA, UTA, UVL, YUB, QUK, TUL; ANZ, ATL, OUL, USL, VSL.

Bibliography: Maddison et al. 1953: no. 23; Parry 1995: 236–240; Pennington 1982: items 1016–27, 1029–30, 1392 (see index for other references).

Editions: 2nd edn by Edward Maynard, London: George James for Jonah Bowyer, 1716. Another edn by Henry Ellis, London, 1818.

1658.2: Burton, William, *A Commentary on Antoninus his Itinerary*. London: Thomas Roycroft for Henry and Timothy Twyford, 1658. Wing B6185; ESTC R6432. AS7 (words) with a few sorts from AS2/3.

OE place-names

Collation: 2^0 in 4s: $\pi a^2 \ A^2 \ a^2 \ a^{*2} \ B^2 \ b^2$ (b2 + χ1.2) C–D^2 E–$2N^4$ O–P^2 [$2 signed (-A1, a2, a*2, B2, C2, D2, 2O2, 2P2; πa2 signed '*a*')] 148 [+ 2] leaves, paginated [i–xxiv], 1–266, 267–272.

Note: πa (when all present) is used as a wrapper around sig. A.

TYPE:

Main text in Arthur Nicholls's English-size Roman (Body 92) interspersed with his English-size Italic.

The occurrence of AS7 before Somner's Dictionary (**1659.1**) is notable.

AS7: Nicholas Nicholls's Somnerian Pica Anglo-Saxon occurs in words on L2ᵛ (p. 60), 2C1ᵛ (p. 178), 2D1ʳ (p. 185), 2E3ᵛ (p. 198), 2E4ᵛ (p. 200), 2F3ʳ (p. 205), 2M2ᵛ (p. 252).

Special sorts shown: ð, ȝ, 1, þ, ſ, τ; p; Є.   Total: 7 + 1 = 8 sorts.
Some sorts from AS3 with AS2 s are mixed in:
AS2 s occurs with AS7 on 2E4ᵛ;
AS3: two sorts occur with AS7: e occurs on 2E3ᵛ and 2M2ᵛ (once each), and y on 2E3ᵛ.

Copies seen: With b2χ1.2: APL R.IV.4 (sigs B and b in reverse order; lacks πa1); LFL 8H (lacks πa1); BL 190.a.2 (lacks πa1), G8157 (lacks πa2); gold-tooled binding with arms of George III);

Without b2χ1.2: CUL Fff.73, Gg.4.37 (lacks πa1; gift of John Hackett, bp of Lichfield, 1670; contemporary binding of brown calf with some gold-tooling).

Copies also at: BUL, CCA, CGC, CMC, CQC, CSel, CSJ, TCC, ChestC, DCL, DUL, EdUL, Eton, HHC, LGL, LHL, LMT, LPL, LRS, LSH, LWI, MJRUL, MTP, NLA, NLS, NLW, NMS, NT, NUL, OBL, OBC, OCC, OEC, OMC, OQC, OSJ OTC, OWoC, OXC, SPC, SUL, WCC, WiCL, WIHM, YML, DML, TCD, PBN, GUB; FSL, NYPL, HHL, HUL, IUL, CUofA, DDUL, KSRL, NLC, PUL, SLC, UCH, UCLA, UOC, UTA, UTK, YUB, TUL; NLA, NSW, USL, UWL.

Bibliography: Parry 1995: 262–267; Empey 2017; Pennington 1982: item 1368; Rivet and Smith 1979: 150–182 (re. Antonine Itinerary), 238–509 (re. identification of place-names).

1658.3 Ware, Sir James, *De Hibernia & Antiquitatibus ejus, Disquisitiones. Editio Secunda, Emendatior & quarta parte aucior. Accesserunt Rerum Hibernicarum Regnante Henrico VII, Annales*. London: Evan Tyler for John Crook 1, 1658. 2nd enlarged edn of 1654.1. Wing W844; ESTC R204005. AS3.
Words

    Collation: 8⁰: A–2G⁸ [$4 signed (-A1; 2A3 missigned 2B3; R2ᵛ missigned R3)] 240 leaves, paginated [i–xvi], 1–356, ²[i–vi], ²1–99, ²100⁰102 (p. 48 not numbered; pp. 220 misnumbered 120, 295 misnumbered 195; no. 5 in p. no. 154 imperfectly printed).

TYPE:
Main text in Arthur Nicholls's Pica Roman (Body 81) interspersed with Nicholls's Pica Italic (e.g. F7ᵛ–8).
AS3: The Lambardian Pica Anglo-Saxon occurs in combination with Nicholls's Pica Roman in words only on D6ʳ (p. 43).
Special sorts shown: 6 lower-case sorts: ð, *e*, ꝼ, ᵹ, 1, ẏ.
Note: Shows IR1 in an Irish word on I1ʳ (p. 113): McGuinne 1992: 22.

    Copies seen: CUL Hib.8.658.5, Hib.7.658.2 (2G8 a stub); Hib.8.658.4 shows A1 reversed and bound in after A2.

    Copies also at: APL, BL, DRD, GML, HHC, KCL, LHL, LL, LUL, NLS, NT, OBL, OGF, OLC, OWmC, OXC, SPC, WCC, DEWL, DML, NLI, TCD, ULim, GUB, MBS; FSL, HHL, HUL, IUL, CUofA, KSRL, LCP, NLC, SCN, UCLA, YOB, TUL.

Bibliography: Pennington 1982 (re. Hollar illustrations on A1ᵛ, D8ᵛ, P7ᵛ, V8ᵛ: see index for references); Sharpe & Hoyne 2020: no. 37 on pp. 130–132.

1658.4: Phillips, Edward (Milton's nephew), *The New World of English Words: Or, a General Dictionary*. London: Evan Tyler for Nathaniel Brookes, 1658. Wing P2068; ESTC R14781.

    Collation: 2⁰: (a–b)⁴ (c)⁶ A–2Q⁴ 2R⁶ 2S⁴. [360] p.
Gives the derivation of words as AS, but does not cite the appropriate forms in AS type.

    Copies at: BL, BLC, EdUL, LBL, LSH, LUL, NLS, NLW, NT, OBL, OQC, OStH, SoUL, SUL; FSL, USLC, HHL, HUL, IUL, NLC, UCBL, UCH, UCLA, UTA, UVL, UVC; AUNZ, NLA, OUL.

Bibliography: Kerling 1979: 87–134.
Facsimile: English Linguistics 1500–1800, no. 162 (Menston: Scolar, 1969).

1659.1: Somner, William, *Dictionarium Saxonico-Latino-Anglicum*. Oxford: William Hall for Daniel White (London), 1659. Wing S4663; ESTC R15040. AS7.
Dictionary Citations

    Collation: 2⁰ in 4s: πa⁴ b⁴ (b2 + χ1) A–2V⁴ 2X⁴ (±2X3) 2Y–3T² [$2 signed (+2R3, 2T3; -3L2, 3S2)] 226 leaves, unpaginated until 2X4ʳ (= p. 1), then pp. 1–80, *81–86*

(p. 79 not numbered; pp. 23 misnumbered 26, 59 misnumbered 61, 62 misnumbered 60, 63 misnumbered 66, 66 misnumbered 63).

State 2 shown by pp. 59, 62 numbered correctly.

SOURCES OF PASSAGES UTILIZING ANGLO-SAXON TYPES (longer passages only):

Q2ʳ (s.v. Ḡeðp̄ync) From OBL Junius 15 (SC 5127; Junius's transcript of Tiberius B.i), pp. 12/23–13/7: *Orosius* I.1 (extract), as Bately 1980: 17/6–36 = part of the passage about Ohthere's voyage (Brewer 1952–3);

2Q4r (s.v. unnan) From KNA (*olim* PRO) Patent Roll 43 Henry III membrane 15 (calendared Henry III 5:3; pr. Ellis 1868): ME Proclamation of Henry III (18 Oct 1258), as Dickins & Wilson 1951: 8–9, Mossé 1952: 187–89.

2X4ʳ–3L1ᵛ From BL Royal 15.B.xxii, 5ʳ–70ᵛ: Ælfric's Grammar, as Zupitza 1880, sig. R;

3M1ʳ–3S1ᵛ From OBL Junius 71 (SC 5182), Junius's transcript of APM 47 + BL Add 32246 (facsimile of whole MS in OBL MS Facs.d.76): Pseudo-Ælfric's Vocabulary (as Wright-Wülker 1884: I, cols 106–191, some corrections from APM 47 in Förster 1917; see Ladd 1960).

TYPE:

Dictionary:

Headwords in AS7: Nicholas Nicholls's Somnerian Pica Anglo-Saxon (Body 80) interspersed with text in Arthur Nicholls's Pica Roman and his Pica Italic; Special sorts shown in the specimen on b2ʳ:

    10 lower-case sorts: ð, f, ᵹ, p, ſ, τ, ẏ; þ, ð, ƿ;
    1 capital: Ð;
    2 others: þ, ꝼ.
Total: 13 sorts.

Note: These special sorts are the same selection and in the same order as in Spelman **1639.4**.

ÆLFRIC'S GRAMMAR AND PSEUDO-ÆLFRIC'S VOCABULARY:

AS7: The main text in AS7 is combined with Arthur Nicholls's Pica Roman. Special sorts shown in the AS alphabet on 2X4ᵛ (p. 2):

    12 lower-case sorts: ð, e, f, ᵹ, ı, p, ſ, τ, ẏ; þ, ð, ƿ;
    13 capitals: A, Æ¹, Æ², Є, Ḡ, Ꝺ, K, ꟽ, S, Ƿ (2N2ᵛ), Ð, Ᵹ, W;
    4 others: þ, ꝼ, ꝫ (both on Q2ʳ, 2Y2ᵛ), ȷ̇ (Q2ʳ).
Total: 29 sorts.

Note 1: Square C and the punctus elevatus are not found.

Note 2: Cap Ᵹ, e.g. on 2P3ʳ, 2R3ᵛ–2X1ʳ is square in form; no other capital wynn is found.

Note 3: OBL, OU Archives, SEP.P17b(3), fo 44, 'A bond for restoring ... 177 pound weight of Saxon Letters from Will' Hall', dated 22 Aug 1657, shows that the university lent (?matrices for making) type to Hall for printing 'of a new Saxon Lexicon composed by William Somner' and that Hall paid £45 on deposit for the privilege.

  Copies seen: State 1 (with pp. 59, 62 misnumbered): CUL Bb*.8.43 (C); OBL 3024.c.1 (with annotations by Joseph Bosworth s.xix: cf. 1698.1 copy O.T.Anglo-Sax.d.1–3); State 2 (with pp. 59, 62 correctly numbered): CCA W/R.8.28 (with appendix of 2 leaves in Somner's hand after 2X2); ECC S5.1.32 (Abp Sancroft's copy); MBS 2⁰.L.g.sept.11.c; OBL Douce S.291 (with gold-tooled binding of red morocco, e18c; shows b2χ1 after b4 with map of Britannia Saxonica etched by Michael Burghers), 302.w.1, MS Junius 7 (SC 5119) with annotations by Junius (especially to the Ælfric and pseudo-Ælfric) and uncropped edges.

  Copies also at: BL, BCL, CCC, CMC, CPH, CSJ, TCC, CaCL, DCL, DUL, ECL, LCL, LGL, LHL, LSH, MCS, MJRUL, NCL, NLS, NLW, NT, NUL, OAS, OBC, OBrC, OCC, OEC, OHC, OLC, OQC, OSA, OSJ, OTI, OXC, UBL, WCL, WIHM, WiCL, DML, TCD, PBN, GUB; FSL, USLC, NYPL, NYHS, HHL, HUL, IUL, NLC, UCBL, UCLA, UTA, UVL, YUB, TUL.

Bibliography: Alston III.i.2; Gadd 2013: 436 (M. Kilburn); Hetherington 1980: 141–182, 209–221; Joan 1962; Lutz 1988; Madan 1895–1931: III.106–107, no.2458; Maddison et al. 1953: no. 27; Marckwardt 1947; Niles 2015: 121–123, 139–142; Parry 1995: 185–188; Urry 1997: xiii–xiv; Yerkes 1976–7. GR 55.

Manuscripts:
CCA Lit.E.20–1 (2 vols) contain the full text of this work from the preliminaries to the list of subscribers in Somner's hand; it is marked up by the printer and shows printer's ink from the thumb/fingers on fo 3^r, etc.

CCA Lit.C.9–10 (2 vols) contain the text of this work (not the preliminaries) in Somner's hand; it is a fair copy, but with some additions and corrections.

CCA W/B.5.1 is an interleaved copy of Minsheu's *Emendatio sui Ductoris in Linguas* (1627.1) with extensive lists of AS headwords (apparently a draft for 1659.1); see Lucas 2002.

Facsimile: English Linguistics 1500–1800 no. 247 (Menston: Scolar Press, 1970).

1659.2: Janssonius, Joannes, *Novus Atlas, sive Theatrum Orbis Terrarum*, vol. IV (= Camden's *Britannia*, as in 1607.2). 2nd edn of 1646.3. Amsterdam: Joannes Janssonius, 1659. CAS 4.

ASC (C) and (F), OE proper names

  Collation: 2⁰: *-2*2 A–2A² 2B¹ 2C–2E² 2F¹ 2G–2Q² 2R¹ 2S–3F² 3G¹ 3H–3L² 3M¹ 3N–3O² 3P¹ 3Q–3S² 3T¹ 3V–4E² 4F¹ 4G–4H² 4I¹ 4K–4L² 4M¹ 4N–4O² 4P¹ 4Q–4T² 4V¹ 4X–5E² 5F–5G¹ 5H–5K² 5L¹ 5M² 5N¹ 5O–5Z² 6A¹ 6B–6I² 2A–P² 2Q¹ 2R² 2S¹ [$2 signed (-*1, A2, D2, P2, T2, Y2, 2C2, 2E2, 2G2, 2L2, 2N2, 2S2, 2V2, 2Y2, 3B2, 3D2, 3F2, 3K2, 3N2, 3Q2, 3S2, 3V2, 3Z2, 4B2, 4D2, 4G2, 4H2, 4K2, 4N2, 4Q2, 4S2,

4T2, 4X2, 4Z2, 5B2, 5C2, 5D2, 5H2, 5I2, 5M2, 5O2, 5Q2, 5S2, 5V2, 6B2, 6E2, 6H2, ²A2, ²B2, ²I2, ²K2, ²M2, ²N2, ²O2, ²P2; 4E1 missigned 'Feee')] 268 leaves, paginated [i–viii], 1–364, ²1–50, ²51-2 (pp. 138 misnumbered 238, 269 misnumbered 369, 285–286 misnumbered 385–386, 296 misnumbered 396, 321 misnumbered 312, 326–327 misnumbered 126–127, 342–343 misnumbered 242–243, 353 misnumbered 153, ²29–30 misnumbered 25–26, ²34 misnumbered 36; 55 double-page openings with illustrative maps are not included in the pagination).

SOURCE OF PASSAGE UTILIZING ANGLO-SAXON TYPES:

5Z2ᵛ (p. 336) From **1646.3** 5Z2ᵛ: ASC(C + F) 189/188 (extracts), both as Thorpe 1861: I.14–15.

TYPE: (cf. **1646.3**)

Main text in Pierre Haultin's English-size Roman (Body 94) interspersed with an English-size Italic (Robert Granjon's 3rd English-size Italic at sig. 4G–4X, 5Y–6E, 2I–L).

CAS4: The Dutch Janssonian English-size imitation of the Lambardian Pica Anglo-Saxon used in combination with the English-size Roman:

The specimen on 2*2ʳ shows the following special sorts:

    9 lower-case sorts: ð (with S-like curled ascender), ꝼ, ȝ (= yogh belonging to a roman fount), ꝑ, ꞅ, ꞇ, ẏ; þ, ð̃;

    5 capitals: E, Ꝺ, ꟽ, S, Ð;

    2 others: ꝫ, þ.

Total: 16 sorts.

Note: Also shown is italic *p* for 'vv', Æ for 'æ', swash *Æ*, *fc* for 'X'.

CAS4: The Dutch Janssonian English-size Anglo-Saxon combined with the English-size Roman occurs in the text in words on pp. 11, 47 (retaining erron. p from **1607.2** for **1600.1** þ; inverted 2 used for t), 56, 66, 69, 74 (showing **3** beside AS ȝ, and M inverted), 77–84, 87, 89–93, 95, 97–98, 99 (d used for S; 2 sorts for H/h used lc), 100 (t inverted), 101–102, 105, 107, 108 (retaining from **1607.2** erron. ꟽẏnꞅðeꝑ for **1600.1** mẏnꞅꞇeꝑ), 112–114, 117, 119, 121, 124, 125 (with italic *p* for p), 128–129, 130 (with d for S twice), 131–132, 134 (with inverted t), 138, 140 (with italic *p* for p), 144 (with inverted 2 for t), 145–148, 154–157, 161–162, 167, 172, 180–181, 183 (with 2 sorts for cap M), 185, 187–188, 190, 194 (with inverted 2 for t), 195–196, 200 (with 2 r's and two different inverted 2's for t), 203, 205, 211, 219, 221, 223–224, 228, 230 (with inverted 2 for t), 233, 237, 241–243, 244 (with d used for d and S almost side by side; inverted 2 for t), 246, 248, 250, 253–255, 258, 263, 274, 286, 290–291, 294, 296–297, 298 (with erron. þ and italic p for wynn), 302–303, 304 (with S-like d used as S), 310 (with S-like d and large f), 313 (with italic *p* for p), 315, 317, 321, 338 (with italic *p* for p erron for þ), 342–344, 350, 352. Anglo-Saxon words also occur combined with a Great Primer Roman (= 1666 Janssonius specimen A2ᵛ Text Romeyn no. 2, used also for sig. 3Y) in head-notes set in François Guyot's Great Primer Italic (Body 117; in Janssonius specimen 1666 A2ᵛ as Text Cursijf no. 1), e.g. pp. 77, 128, 187, 290, 338 (best e.g. of use and contrast with setting in English-size), for which some larger sorts were presumably designed, though the sizes are mixed up in use. Large sorts occur side by side smaller ones for r (e.g. on 3R2ᵛ/ab), t (e.g. on 3F1ʳ), p (e.g. small on N2ʳ/b, large on S2ᵛ/a). Perhaps this explanation also accounts for the two h/H's to be seen side by side, e.g., on 2I1ʳ?

Special sorts used in the text:

ð (with S-like curl at the top of the ascender), ꝼ, ȝ, Ꝺ, ꝑ (x2), ꞃ, ꞇ (x2), ẏ; þ, ð, ꝑ (x2);
Ꝼ, Ꝺ, Ꝿ (2, e.g. on 3L2ʳ/b), Ꞅ, Ð;
ȷ̇.

11 (ꝑ, ꞇ, ꝑ x 2) + 5 (Ꝿ x 2) + 1 = 21 sorts

Also uses the 3 'yogh' of the English-size Roman, e.g. on T1ʳ/a (p. 67).

Anglo-Saxon capitals are also used with roman ones in a Latin inscription on 4D2ᵛ/a.

Copies seen: CUL Huntingdon 8.7 (lacks 3Y); ECC S12.2.4 (in contemporary gold-tooled binding with Abp Sancroft's coat-of-arms superimposed); CSJ SL.1.34 (gift of Joseph Thurston); OBL Gough.Gen.top.224.

Bibliography: Keuning 1951: 83–86; Koeman/Krogt 1997: 1:405.4V; Lucas 2018: 233–239; Skelton 1970: no. 66.

Facsimile: Mais 1951 (tp, 2*1ᵛ, and 34 maps only, reduced).

1659.3: Blaeu, Joan I, *Nvevo Atlas del Reyno de Ingalaterra* [sic] (= Atlas Mayor, vol. v = Spanish translation of Camden's *Britannia*, as in 1607.2). Amsterdam: Joan Blaeu I, 1659. CAS3.

ASC (C) and (F) extracts, OE proper names

Collation: 2⁰: π2² *–2*² A–Q² R¹ S–X² Y¹ Z–2P² 2Q¹ 2R–2S² 2T¹ 2V–2Y² 2Z¹ 3A² 3B¹ 3C–3D² 3E¹ 3F–3N² 3O¹ 3P–4C² 4D¹ 4E–4K² 4L¹ 4M–4N² 4O¹ 4P² 4Q¹ 4R–4Y² 4Z¹ 5A–5C² 5D¹ 5E² 5F¹ 5G–5H² 5I¹ 5K–5L² 5M¹ 5N–5O² 5P¹ 5Q–5V² 5X¹ 5Y–5Z² 6A¹ 6B–6C² 6D¹ 6E² 6F¹ 6G–6M² 6N¹ 6O² 6P¹ 6Q–6Y² 6Z¹ 7A² 7B¹ 7C–7F² 7G¹ 7H–7N² 7O¹ 7P–7R² [7S]¹ [$1 signed] 288 leaves, paginated [i–xii], 1–447, 448–450 (pp. 312, 433 not numbered, and the pages showing maps are not included in the pagination; pp. 75 misnumbered 65, 78 misnumbered 68). Because this is a large atlas all the leaves are mounted on guards.

SOURCE OF PASSAGE UTILIZING ANGLO-SAXON TYPES:

7F2ʳ (p. 413)   From 1645.1 7E2ʳ: ASC(C + F) 188/189 (extracts), as Thorpe 1861: 14–15, including erron. ꝼoꞃȝẏpð. Ultimately from 1607.2 4Y4ʳ, including erron. ꝼæ oꝑ ꝼæ with p for þ.

TYPE:

Main text in Robert Granjon's English-size roman (Body 95) interspersed with Granjon's 3rd English-size Italic (e.g. on V2ᵛ–X2ᵛ).

CAS 3: The Blaeu/Voskens English-size Anglo-Saxon occurs in the specimen on 2*2ʳ and is used in combination with the English-size Roman in the text in words on pp. 13, 59, 70, 77 (used with Granjon's English-size Italic), 82, 84–85, 91, 95, 98, 104, 106, 111–114, 116–117, 119, 122, 124, 127–128, 129 (with *recte* Tpuþabpıʒ), 130, 133, 135, 137–138, 143, 145–146, 148–149, 151–152, 155–158, 160–173, 176 (with erron. Ɔepropape for 1607.2 Ɔeprc-pape), 178–82, 185, 187, 193–194, 201, 206–207, 215–216, 219, 221, 225, 228 (with erron. Ðeaʒleʒe for 1607.2 Ðeaðleʒe), 232–234, 240, 244, 246, 250, 260, 263, 265, 267, 271–272, 274 (with erron. d for ð), 277, 282, 287–288, 290, 292, 295, 297, 299–300, 304–307, 316, 328, 336, 350, 356, 359, 361, 363, 369, 371, 373, 380, 385, 387, 389, 395, 417, 422, 424, 425 (with 7 instead of ꝑ x2), 432 (with 7 instead of the ꝑ), 441.

Special sorts shown in the specimen on 2*2ʳ:

    10 lower-case sorts: ð, ꝼ, ʒ, Ð, p, r, τ; þ, δ, p;
    7 capitals: Æ¹, Æ², Ꮛ, Ɔ, Ꞩ, Ð, X;
    2 others: þ, ꝥ.
    Total: 19 sorts.

Note 1: The specimen shows Roman not AS y, and gives the equivalence of Ð as h, hence its inclusion here with the lower-case rather than upper-case letters. Roman H is used as an initial capital in an AS name-element Heopτu on 6V1ʳ.

Special sorts shown in the text:

    11 lower-case sorts: ð, *e* (on 2Y2ʳ only), ꝼ, ʒ, p, r, τ, ẏ; þ, ð, p;
    5 capitals: Ꮛ, Ð (used lc Z2ᵛ), Ɔ, Ꞩ (1st on 2Z1ʳ, used as ð on 3G1ʳ, 6L1ʳ, 6S1ᵛ, 6V2ʳ, 6Z1ʳ), Ð;
    1 other: ꝥ (approximated by 7 towards the end).
    Total: 17 sorts.
    Overall total: 11 + 8 + 3 = 22 sorts.

Note 2: AS e occurs only once, as indicated;

Note 3: The s-sort sometimes shows the top-stroke rolled over tightly, and so extending to the right less than the usual one, as shown on the 1695 specimen: see, e.g., 5Z2ᵛ. Some s-sorts are inferior and may be brought in from another fount (? Hebrew final-position 'tzade'): see, e.g., 2Z1ʳ.

Note 4: Two kinds of sort are shown for y, one with an accent, one with a dot, and y occurs in two sizes, Pica as well as English-size. Pica y with a dot to the left occurs on 2K1ʳ, 2Y1ᵛ, 5A2ᵛ, and with a dot to the centre/right on 2P1ᵛ, 3G2ᵛ, 5A2ᵛ, 5G1ʳ, 6I2ᵛ. Pica y with an accent to the right occurs on 6I2ᵛ. English-size y

with dot to the centre occurs on 5G1ʳ. English-size y with an accent to the right occurs on 2S1ᵛ, 2X1ʳ, 3B1ʳ, 5O2ᵛ, 6I2ᵛ. English-size y with an accent to the centre occurs on 2S1ᵛ; the y and the accent are seriously misaligned on 2Y2ʳ.
Note 5: An opportunity to use capital Æ is missed on 3P2ᵛ.
Note 6: Anglo-Saxon capitals are also used with Roman ones in a Latin inscription on 4S2ᵛ.
> **Copy seen:** LBL Whitaker 32a (with maps and illustrations hand-coloured; 'Blaeu' binding of white vellum on boards with gold-tooled ornament; gift of Stanley H. Burton).

Bibliography: Koeman 1967: I.Bl.60A; Lucas 2018: 229–233; Pettegree & Weduwen 2019: 110–115; Skelton 1970: no. 64; Vervey 1981: 13–16.

1659.4: Janssonius, Joannes, Dutch *Atlas Major*, vols IV–V (or VII–VIII) (= Dutch translation of Camden's *Britannia*, as in 1607.2). Re-issue of 1647.4 with the new date indicated by an added slip pasted over the relevant tp cartouche, split into two: vol. IV (or VII), *, A–2Z4 (S. England, and Wales); and vol. V (or VIII), 3A–4K (N. England + Scotland and Ireland). Amsterdam: Joannes Janssonius, 1659. CAS4.
Contents and TYPE as **1647.4**.
Bibliography: Krogt 1997: 1:436C.

1660.1: Somner, William, *A Treatise of Gavelkind*. London: Robert and William Leybourn for John Crooke and Daniel White, 1660. Wing S4668; ESTC R20010. AS7.
> **Date:** 1660. On A3ᵛ the author states that the book was written 12 years previously. On 2E4ᵛ there is a statement of approval by James Ussher, abp of Armagh, dated 7 Apr 1647.

ASC, OE Bede, Charters, Laws, Wills
> **Collation:** 4⁰: a⁴ A–2F⁴ [$3 signed (-a1,2, A3, 2C3, 2F3)] 120 leaves, paginated [i–xvi], 1–216, *217–224*.

SOURCES OF PASSAGES UTILIZING ANGLO-SAXON TYPES:
C3ʳ (p. 13) From CCA, lost MS (s.xiii?; extant in Stowe Charter 27): Will of Æthelwyrd 958 (excerpts): Sawyer 1506; Birch 1010 + 1011; Robertson 32;
C3ᵛ (p. 14) From Canterbury DC, Reg. A, fo 143, or Reg. E, fo 44 (both s.xiii): Agreement between Abp Eadsige and Æthelric c.1045 (L + excerpt from ME version of OE text): Sawyer 1471; Kemble 773; Robertson 101 (OE only); From Canterbury DC, Reg. A, 141ᵛ, or Reg. E. fo 43 (both s.xiii): Will of Æthelric 961 × 995 (excerpt from ME version of OE text): Sawyer 1501; Kemble 699; Whitelock 16;

F1ᵛ–2ʳ (pp. 34–5)   From Tiberius B.i, 159ʳ, 163ʳ: ASC B 1050 (end), 1055 (near end), passages unique to this MS: Extracts as Thorpe I.312, 326;

F3ʳ (p. 37)   From 1643.1 3P2ʳ: OE Bede, V.22 (phrase) in discussion of OE gecynd;

K1ʳ (p. 65)   From RKA, DRc/R1 (Textus Roffensis, *olim* RCL A.3.5), 32ᵛ/22–4: AS Law 'Walreaf' (Liebermann I.392); only witness;

L2ᵛ (p. 76)   From 1639.4 2M2ᵛ, 1644.1 H2ᵛ: AS Law 'Be Wifmannes Beweddunge' 1/2, 2/3, 3/4, 6 (Liebermann I.442);

L4ᵛ (p. 80)   From 1568.2 2F4ᵛ (or 1639.4 2Y5ᵛ): AS Law II Cnut Prol. (Liebermann I.308); not from 1644.1 which omits ðonne;

M3ᵛ (p. 86)   From 1568.2 2L2ᵛ: AS Law II Cnut 79 (phrase; Liebermann I.366); not from 1644.1 Q3ʳ which has ʒepepoð, and not in 1639.4;

M4ᵛ (p. 88)   From a lost MS: Charter of abp Wulfred to Canterbury 805 × 832 (passage of 10 lines): Sawyer 1622;

N2ᵛ (p. 92)   From 1643.1 3H2ᵛ/34–8: OE Bede, V.13 (extract); texts match;

N3ʳ (p. 93)   From 1639.4 2M2ᵛ (or 1644.1 H2ᵛ): AS Law 'Be Wifmannes Beweddunge' 4 (Liebermann I.442); the reference is to 1639.4;

N3 (pp. 93–4)   From 1568.2 2K3ᵛ, or 1644.1 Q2ʳ: AS Law II Cnut 70,1 (phrase; Liebermann I.356);

P3ᵛ (p. 110)   From 1568.2 2E3ᵛ, or 1644.1 N3ᵛ: AS Law I Cnut 11,1 (phrase; Liebermann I.294)

Q1ʳ (p. 113)   From (1) unknown MS: phrase, as heading to Charter of King Edgar to Ealhhelm his thane 975: Sawyer 802; Birch 1315 (from Add 15350, 74ᵛ), and (2) 1639.4 2S7ʳ: Charter of King Æthelred to Canterbury 1006 for 1001 (phrase from end of witness list referring to Ælfheah, bp of Winchester): Sawyer 914; Kemble 847 (last 4 lines);

Q1ᵛ (p. 114)   From 1568.2 Y1ᵛ: AS Law II Edgar 1,1 (Liebermann I.196); the reference is to 1568.2.

From 1596.2 2I5ʳ: Will of Byrhtric 973 × 987 (phrase): Sawyer 1511; Whitelock 11; (Campbell 1973: no. 35); the reference is to 1596.2;

R1ʳ (p. 121)   From 1568.2 O1ᵛ, or 1644.1 D4ᵛ: AS Law Alfred and Guthrum 2 (Liebermann I.126);

2C2ᵛ–3ʳ (pp. 196–7)   From a lost MS: Marriage agreement between Godwine and Byrhtric, father of bride 1016 × 1020 (apparently entire): Sawyer 1461; Robertson 77 (from 1660.1);

2C3ᵛ–2D2ᵛ (pp. 198–204) From Canterbury DC, Reg. A, fos 142–143 or Reg. E, fo 43 (both s.xiii): Will of Æthelstan Ætheling 1015 (entire): Sawyer 1503; Whitelock 20;

2D3ᵛ (p. 206)   From a lost MS: Writ of Henry I (L + OE, entire): Pelteret 47;

2E2ʳ–3ᵛ (pp. 211–14)   From Canterbury DC, Reg. A, 143ᵛ or Reg.E. fo 44 (both s.xiii): ME version of Will of Wulfgyth (entire): Sawyer 1535; Whitelock 32; see also Lowe 1989;

2E3ᵛ–4ᵛ (pp. 214–216)   From CCA, lost MS: Land-agreement between Eadsige, priest (later abp of Canterbury), and Christ Church 1032: Sawyer 1465; Robertson 86 from **1660.1**.

TYPE:

Main text in Pierre Haultin's English-size Roman (Body 92) interspersed with Robert Granjon's first English-size Italic;

AS7: Nicholas Nicholl's Somnerian Pica Anglo-Saxon combined with a Pica Roman in text as indicated above under Contents, with 20 lines set solid on 2D3ᵛ; and in words on A4ᵛ, B2, B4ʳ, C4ʳ, F1ʳ, F3, L3ᵛ, L4ʳ, Q4ʳ, S2ᵛ, S3ᵛ.

Special sorts shown:

    12 lower-case sorts: ð, e, f, ʒ, ı, p, r, t, ẏ; þ, ð, p;
    13 capitals: A, Æ¹, Æ², L, E, Ɫ, Ð, K, M, S, Đ, Ƿ, W;
    2 others: þ, ꝯ.

Total: 27 sorts.

Copies: CUL Bb*.4.51(E); OBL 4⁰.W.5.Jur., Wood 585¹ (uncropped; lacks 2F).

Copies also at: CaCL, DCL, DUL, EAL, LGL, LHL, LSH, NLS, OAS, RRH, UBL, DML, TCD, BPN; FSL, USLC, NYCU, HHL, HUL, NWU, UCH, UCLA, UMI, UTA, YUB, TUL.

Bibliography: Thirsk 1984: 353.

1661.1: Dugdale, Sir William, and Roger Dodsworth, *Monasticon Anglicanum*, vol. II (vol. I **1655.3**, vol. III **1673.1**). London: Alice Warren, 1661. Wing D2486; ESTC R211977. AS3.

Charters

    Collation: 2⁰ in 4s: π¹ A² *² a–c² B–4R⁴ 4S–4Z² 5A–5Q⁴ 5R⁴ (5R3 + c2) 5S–5V⁴ 5X–5Z² 6A–7A⁴ 7B–7P² [$3 signed (-A2, *2, a2, b2, c2, 2I1, 3B3, 3S1, 3X3, 4E3, 4F2, 4R3, 5R3, 5S2, 7A3; O3 missigned O5, 4A2 missigned 3A2)] 555 leaves, paginated [i–xxii], 1–1057, *1058–1116* (sig. 5R3c1–2 not included in the numeration; pp. nos 71–72, 87–94 used twice, pp. nos 735–736 not used, pp. 363–364, 366, 486–488, 504, 515–516, 520, 571–572, 576–578, 588, 667–668, 710, 774, 778, 782, 829–830, 835–836, 932, 1036, 1050 not numbered, pp. 32 misnumbered 30, 88*bis* misnumbered 98, 131 misnumbered 121, 224 misnumbered 223, 232 misnumbered 233, 276 misnumbered 264, 288 misnumbered 286, 447 misnumbered 451, 617–620 misnumbered 627–630, 633 misnumbered 632, 733 misnumbered 735, 890 misnumbered 900, 900 misnumbered 890, 938 misnumbered 926). 2nd issue: p. 938 correctly numbered.

SOURCES OF PASSAGES UTILIZING ANGLO-SAXON TYPES:

C2ᵛ (p. 12)   From Tiberius C.ix (s.xiii), fos 48–49 + PRO, Cart. ant. R.12, no. 1 (s.xiii): Charter of King Edward the Confessor to Waltham Abbey 1062 (L + OE, entire): Sawyer 1036; Kemble 813; Davies 1957: 35–38, §356;

5X1 (pp. 857–858)   From Harley 436 (s.xiv; formerly owned by the earl of Pembroke), 73ʳ–4ᵛ: Charter of King Athelstan to Wilton Abbey 933 (entire): Sawyer 424; Birch 699; Hoare 1827: 17–18;

5X1ᵛ–5X2ʳ (pp. 858–859)   From Harley 436 (s.xiv), 59ʳ–62ᵛ: Charter of King Athelstan to Wilton Abbey 937 (L + OE, entire): Sawyer 438; Birch 714; Hoare 32–33;

From Harley 436 (s.xiv), 81ᵛ, 83–87: Charter of King Eadwig to Wilton Abbey 955 (entire): Sawyer 582; Birch 917; Hoare 46–47;

5Y1ᵛ–5Z2ʳ (pp. 862–7)   From Harley 436 (s.xiv), fos 78–80: Charter of King Edgar to Wilton Abbey 968 (entire): Sawyer 766; Hoare 12–13;

From Harley 436 (s.xiv), 88ʳ: Charter/Heading of King Edgar to Wilton Abbey 974 (entire): Sawyer 799; Birch 1304; Hoare 49–50;

From Harley 436 (s.xiv), 39ʳ–42ᵛ: Charter of King Æthelred to Wilton Abbey 994 (L + OE, entire): Sawyer 881; Kemble 687; Hoare 22–24;

From Harley 436 (s.xiv), fos 36–39: Charter of King Eadred to Wulfric thane (re. Wilton) 946 (1st part): Sawyer 519; Birch 818; Hoare 21–22.

TYPE:

Main text in Arthur Nicholls's Pica Roman (Body 81) interspersed with a Pica Italic (e.g. on Z1ᵛ, 2G1ʳ–3ʳ).

AS3: The Lambardian Pica Anglo-Saxon occurs in text as listed above under Contents and in words on 5Y1ʳ.

The following sorts occur:

    13 lower-case sorts: ð, ẟ [= ð], е, ꝼ, ᵹ, ƕ, ꞁ, ꞃ, ꞇ, ẏ; ꝑ, đ, ꝓ;
    7 capitals: Æ¹, Є, Ƕ, Ⲙ, Ꝑ, Đ, Ꝓ;
    3 others: þ, ꝫ, ꞏ.
Total: 21 sorts.

Note: Since Ƕ and Ꝑ occur as both upper- and lower-case they are counted only once in calculating the total number of special sorts.

Copies seen: State 1: BL 4786.k.6; CUL Pet.B.9.20; TCD G.c.18 (1st issue: lacks 7P2; 5Y2 misplaced after 5Z2; 5E2/5E3, 6G2/6G3, 6V2/6V3, 6Y2/6Y3 each in reverse order);

State 2: CUL R.1.16, Huntingdon 12.10; ECC 306.2.57 (lacks c2).

Copies also at: BCLW, BUL, CCA, CCC, ChC, CCL, CFM, CGC, KCC, CPC, CPH, CSJ, CSS, TCC, CUZ, CaCL, ChestC, DCL, DUL, EdUL, GlCL, HRC, KNA, LCL, LGI, LGL, LHL, LiCL, LMT, LSH, MJRUL, LS, NLW, NT, NUL, OBL, OCC, OStH, OTC, OWoC,

SBT, SCL, SoUL, SPC, UBL, WCC, WCL, WiCL, YML, DEWL, DML, NLI, ULim, PBN; FSL, NYCU, UTS, HHL, HUL, IUL, CUofA, GC, NLC, UCRL, UTA, UVL, TUL; CTCM.
Bibliography: Maddison *et al.* 1953: no. 5; Pennington 1982 (see index for references).

1661.2: Blount, Thomas (1618–79), *Glossographia: or, a Dictionary, interpreting all such Hard Words of Whatsoever Language, now used in our refined English Tongue; With Etymologies, Definitions, and Historical Observations on the same.* London: Thomas Newcomb for George Sawbridge, 1661. Wing B3335; ESTC R25635. 2nd edn of **1656.3**.
OE etymologies occasionally cited but no Anglo-Saxon types
Collation: 8^0: A–2V^8; [688] p.
Type: Main text in a Long Primer Roman (Body 67) in double columns.
No Anglo-Saxon types but OE etymologies occasionally cited in the same Textura as is used for headwords, as s.v. *Gospel*.
Copy seen: CUL Bb*.5.41(F).
Copies also at: BL, TCC, GML, LBL, LL, NLS, NLW, NT, OBL; TCD, GUB; FSL, HHL, CinU, IUL, NLC, UCBL, UCH, UCLA, UTA, YUB; ATL.
Bibliography: Alston V.49.

1662.1: Ridley, Sir Thomas, expanded edn by John Gregory, *A View of The Civile and Ecclesiasticall Law*. 4th edn of **1634.1**. Oxford: William Hall for John Forrest and Edward Forrest, 1662. Wing R1454, 1454A; ESTC R29320, R220837. AS7.
Laws, Will of Byrhtric
Collation: 8^0: A–2D^8 [$4 signed (-A1,3,4, M4, N4, O3, S3, X3, 2B4)] 216 leaves, paginated [i–xii], 1–397, *398–430* (pp. nos 181–190 not used; p. 195 not numbered; pp. 206 misnumbered 126, 237 misnumbered 137, 240 misnumbered 122, 241 misnumbered 137, 244 misnumbered 144, 245 misnumbered 112, 248 misnumbered 124, 249 misnumbered 123, 251 misnumbered 151, 252 misnumbered 238, 253 misnumbered 235, 256 misnumbered 242, 257 misnumbered 239, 260 misnumbered 246, 261 misnumbered 243, 264 misnumbered 250, 265 misnumbered 247, 268 misnumbered 254, 269 misnumbered 151: attention is drawn to these pagination errors on 2B8^r).
Note: variant states shown at G3 and p. 195 (N3^r):
State 1 G3 missigned F3, p. 195 not numbered; State 2 G3 correctly signed, p. 195 correctly numbered.
SOURCES OF PASSAGES UTILIZING ANGLO-SAXON TYPES:
H2^r (p. 103)   From **1634.1** L3^r: Extracts from Laws I Cnut 16, 17 (Liebermann I, 296), and II Cnut 46.1 (Liebermann I, 344);

N3^v–5^v (pp. 196–200)   From **1634.1** T1^v–2^v: Extracts from Laws Ine 4 (Liebermann I, 90), I Æthelstan Prol. (Liebermann I, 146), I Edmund Prol., 2 (Liebermann I, 184), II Edgar 1, 4 (Liebermann I, 196–198), I Cnut 8 (Liebermann I, 290–292);

Q8^v–R1^r (pp. 254–5)   From **1634.1** 2A1^v: Extracts from Laws I Cnut 3 (Liebermann I, 282), I Cnut 11 (Liebermann I, 294) with reference to the same law at II Edgar 2 (Liebermann I, 196);

R4^v–5^r (pp. 262–3)   From **1634.1** 2A4^v: Extract from Law I Cnut 6 (Liebermann I, 288–90);

S4^v (p. 278)   From **1634.1** 2C1^r: Extracts from Law Ælfred 5 (Liebermann I, 50);

S5^v (p. 280)   From **1634.1** 2C1^v–2^r: Extract from Will of Byrhtric (Birch 1885–93: no. 1132; Whitelock 1930: no. 11; Campbell 1973: no. 35; Sawyer 1511);

S6^r (p. 281)   From **1634.1** 2C2^v: Extract from Law Ælfred 8 (Liebermann I, 54).

TYPE:

Main text in Arthur Nicholls's Pica Roman (Body 80); Notes (in which the OE occurs) in a Long Primer Roman (Body 66) apparently that by van Dijck (Morison/Carter 1967: 136).

AS7: Nicholas Nicholl's Somnerian Pica Anglo-Saxon occurs in text in the Notes (which are set in the Long Primer Roman) combined with Arthur Nicholls's Pica Roman on H2^r, N3^v–5^v, Q8^v–R1^r, R4^v–5^r, S4^v, S5^v, S6^r. The Anglo-Saxon in the Notes therefore stands out because it is set in a larger size than the surrounding Notes.

Special sorts shown:

12 lower-case sorts:	ð, e, f, ᵹ, 1, p, ſ, τ, ẏ; þ, ð, ƿ;
3 capitals:	A, Æ¹, Є;
3 others:	þ, ꝯ, ꝫ.
Total:	18 sorts.

Note: d used for ð on N3^v in Ꝁeint; p used for ƿ; some sorts upside down on R4^v.

Copies seen: Wing R1454, State 1: CUL Pet.L.2.2; OBL Bliss B.82; State 2: APL AA.VI.27;

Wing R1454A showing State 2: CUL H.13.14 (lacks 2D8); OBL Wood 676 (uncropped).

Copies also at: Wing R1454: CGC, TCC, CCA, DUL, EdUL, LUL, OJC, OUP, OWoC, OXC, PBN; FSL, UTS, HUL, IUL, KSRL, UCBL, UCLA, UTA, YUB, TUL, YUC.

Wing R1454A: BL, CMC, CSJ, Eton, GML, NLW; NYPL, UTS, HHL, UCLA.

Bibliography: Madan 1895–1931: III.167, no. 2606.

1662.2 Blaeu, Joan I, *Geographiæ Blavianæ Volumen Quintum, quo Anglia, quæ est Europæ Liber Undecimus, continetur* (= Atlas Maior, vol. V = Camden's *Britannia*, as in 1607.2). 3rd edn of 1645.1, slavishly re-set from 1648.1. Amsterdam: Joan Blaeu I, 1662. CAS3.

ASC (extracts), OE proper names

    Collation: 2⁰: π¹ a–c² A–2B² 2C¹ 2D–2O² 2P¹ 2Q–2S² 2T¹ 2V² 2X¹ 2Y–2Z² 3A¹ 3B–3I² 3K¹ 3L–3T² 3V¹ 3X–3Y² 3Z¹ 4A–4F² 4G¹ 4H–4K² 4L¹ 4M–4R² 4S¹ 4T–4V² 4X¹ 4Y² 4Z¹ 5A–5I² 5K¹ 5L² 5M¹ 5N² 5O¹ 5P–5R² 5S¹ 5T² 5V¹ 5X–5Z² 6A¹ 6B² 6C¹ 6D–6G² 6H¹ 6I–6K² 6L¹ 6M–7B² [$1 signed (+a2, 6X2; -a1, 6X1)] 262 leaves, paginated [i–xiv], 1–400, *401–402* (the pages showing maps are not included in the pagination). Because this is a large atlas all the leaves are mounted on guards.

    Note: As in 1648.1 the page heading on 2Z1ʳ is erron. 'BARK-SHIRE' instead of 'SUSSEX', but the different typesetting can be seen on the same page, where the catchword is 'etiam' for 1648.1 'iam', as well as in the correct numbering of the pages from p. 360 onwards.

SOURCE OF PASSAGES UTILIZING ANGLO-SAXON TYPES:

6Q1ᵛ (p. 370)   From **1648.1** 6Q1ᵛ: ASC(C + F) 188/189 (extracts), as Thorpe 1861: 14–15, including erron. foꞃᵹyþð. Ultimately from 1607.2 4Y4ʳ, including erron. ꞅæ oþ ꞅæ with p for þ, but note the use of AS ſ in all 4 instances of ꞅæ, as opposed to only the first in 1648.1.

TYPE:

Main text in Pierre Haultin's Great Primer Roman (Body 114) interspersed with a Great Primer Italic [the same as that used in 1645.1, 1648.1] (e.g. S2ʳ–T1ᵛ) in two columns;

CAS3: The Blaeu/Voskens English-size Anglo-Saxon occurs in the specimen on b2ʳ and is used in combination with Haultin's Great Primer Roman in the text in words on pp. 13, 52, 63, 74 (combined with the Italic), 76–77, 83, 87, 89, 95, 97, 101–104, 106–107, 109, 112, 114, 116–117, 118 (with Tꞃuþabꞃiᵹ *recte* for 1648.1 Tꞃuþabꞃiᵹ), 119, (122–123), 125–127, 131, 133–134, 136–137, 139–140, 143, 145–146, 148–161, 164 (with erron. Ɱeꞃꞃoþaꞃe from 1648.1), 166–170, 173–175, 181–182, 188, 194–195, 203–204, 207–209, 211–212, 214 (with erron. Ꝺeaᵹleᵹe from 1648.1), 219–221, 226, 230, 232, 236, 245, 247, 249, 251, 255–256, 258, 261, 265, 269–272, 273 (with erron. –ꞃype for 1648.1 –ꞅcype), 276–277, 279–280, 283–284, 286, 288, 291, 300, 307, 317, 321, 324–325, 327, 332–333, 335, 342, 345, 347–348, 349 (with 7 instead of the punctus versus from 1648.1), 354, 373, 377, 379–80 (with 7 instead of the punctus versus x2 from 1648.1), 386 (with 7 instead of punctus versus), 395;

Special sorts shown in specimen on b2ʳ:

        11 lower-case sorts: ð, *e*, ꝼ, ᵹ, ꞃ, ꞅ, ꞇ, ẏ; þ, ð, p;
        8 capitals: Æ¹, Æ², Є, Ꝺ, Ɱ, Ꞅ, Đ, X;
        2 others: þ, ꝯ.
    Total: 21 sorts.

Special sorts shown in the text:
- 11 lower-case sorts: ð, е, f, ʒ, ꝑ, ſ, τ, ẏ; þ, ð, p;
- 5 capitals: Є, Ꝺ (used lc and uc 2N1ʳ), Ϻ, Ƨ (used for lc ð on 3C1ʳ), Đ;
- 1 other: ⅉ (often just an oversized 7).

Total: 17 sorts.

Overall total sorts: 11 + 8 + 3 = 22.

Note 1: Two s-sorts can be seen together on 3S1ʳ (p. 203), 4C2ᵛ (p. 226), 5A1ʳ (p. 277).

Note 2: The y-sort shown, e.g., on 2G1ʳ (p. 103), mostly has an acute accent instead of a dot, but the one with a dot also occurs, e.g., on 2S1ᵛ (p. 136), 2Y2ᵛ (p. 146).

Note 3: AS capitals are also used with Roman ones in a Latin inscription on 4N2ᵛ.

Note 4: When the Blaeu English-size Anglo-Saxon is used in combination with Haultin's English-size Roman (Body 96), as on 5D2ᵛ, the appearance is much improved. An English-size Roman y has been provided with a suprascript acute accent for printing in this size.

Copies seen: BL Maps C.4.c.1 (Shirley T.BLA-10; with tp and maps hand-coloured); CUL Atlas 2.66.5; CSJ SL.1.19 (lacks a1).

Bibliography: Koeman 1967–71: Bl.56; Koeman 1970: 68–70; Lucas 2018: 229–233; Pettegree & Weduwen 2019: 110–115; Skelton 1970: no. 71; Vervey 1981: 13–16.

1662.3: Blaeu, Joan I, *Cinqvième Volvme de la Geographie Blaviane, contenant L'Angleterre, qui fait l'onzième Livre de L'Europe.* (= Atlas Maior, vol. V = French translation by J. Salabert of Camden's *Britannia*, as in 1607.2). 2nd edn of 1645.2 presumably from a copy with handwritten corrections, as indicated by the changes made to the AS readings. Amsterdam: Joan Blaeu I, 1662. CAS3.

Date: Preface dated 1 Jan 1662 (a2ʳ); engraved tp dated 1662. A copy in Paris, Bibliothèque Nationale, is dated 1662 on the typographical tp. Other copies of this typographical tp show the date 1663, presumably a re-issue with only the date changed (Skelton 1970: 117). There is also a re-issue with the typographical tp dated 1667 but otherwise unchanged.

ASC (extracts), OE proper names

Collation: 2⁰: π² *2 2*2 A–2E² 2F¹ 2G–2K² 2L¹ 2M–2O² 2P¹ 2Q² 2R¹ 2S–2Y² 2Z¹ 3A–3G² 3H¹ 3I–3R² 3S¹ 3T² 3V¹ 3X–4H² 4I¹ 4K–4L² 4M¹ 4N² 4O¹ 4P–4T² 4V¹ 4X² 4Y¹ 4Z–5C² 5D¹ 5E² 5F¹ 5G–5N² 5O¹ 5P–6D² [$1 signed (+*2; -*1)] 224 leaves, paginated [i–xii], 1–321, 322–324 (pp. 242, 244, 274, 314 not numbered; pp. 235–236 misnumbered 277–278; the pages showing maps (except 6A1ᵛ) are not included in the pagination). Because this is a large atlas all the leaves are mounted on guards.

SOURCE OF PASSAGE UTILIZING ANGLO-SAXON TYPES:

5V2ʳ (p. 301)   From 1645.2: ASC(C + F) 188/189 (extracts), as Thorpe 1861: 14–15, including erron. ſæ op ſæ with p for þ, and note the use of AS ſ (as opposed to Roman long ſ) in only the first of 4 instances of ſæ; ſoɼʒẏpð is also from 1607.2.

TYPE:

Main text in Pierre Haultin's English-size Roman (but with different capitals; Body 96) interspersed with Robert Granjon's English-size Italic, e.g., on 2Q2ᵛ, in two columns.

CAS3: The Blaeu/Voskens Anglo-Saxon occurs in the specimen on 2*2ʳ and it is used in combination with Haultin's English-size Roman in the text in words on pp. 12, 46, 55, 63 (with 7 used for 1st instance of punctus versus ⁊), 65–66, 70, 74, 76, 81, 83, 86–92, 95, 97, 99, 100 (with Tɼuþabɲɪʒ *recte for* 1645.2 Tɼuþabɲɪʒ), 101, 104, 106–108, 109 (with nepan *recte for* 1645.2 nepan, but Ealðen Ɱẏnðeɲ with omission of ſ), 112, 114, 115 (with *recte* -ſopð), 116–117, 119–120, 122, 124, 127–134, 136–137, 140 (with erron. Ɱeɲſopape for 1607.2 Ɱeɲſc-pape, 1645.2 Ɱeɲſcþape), 142 (with erron. –ſchẏſe for –ſchẏpe taken over from 1645.2), 143–145, 148–150, 155–156, 160, 166, 174, 177–179, 181–183, 187–189, 192 (with 7 instead of 1645.2 ⁊), 194, 196 (with *recte* Ðunceðune- for 1645.2 erron. Ðunðeðune-, but 7 instead of 1645.2 ⁊), 199 (with 7 instead of 1645.2 ⁊), 205, 207–209, 212, 213–214 (with initial d for S in 1645.2 Snoꞇꞇenʒaham-), 216, 220, 223–224 (with *recte* Wɪpeceaſ-ꞇeɲ ſcẏpe for 1645.2 erron. Wɪne-ceap-ven-pcẏʒe), 225–226, 228–231, 233–235, 237, 239, 248, 254, 261, 263, 267 (with erron. Eueɲþɪc- for 1645.2 Eueɲpɪc), 276–277, 281, 284–285, 287, 290;

Anglo-Saxon forms that would be included in a completely faithful rendering of Camden's text are omitted on pp. 269, 270–271, 275, 303, 306, 308, 312, 318.

Special sorts shown in specimen on b2ʳ:

    11 lower-case sorts: ð, *e*, ꝼ, ʒ, p, ſ, ꞇ, ẏ; þ, ð, p;
    8 capitals: Æ¹, Æ², E, Ð, Ɱ, S, X; Ð;
    2 others: þ, ⁊.

Total: 21 sorts.

Special sorts shown in the text:

    11 lower-case sorts: ð, *e*, ꝼ, ʒ, p, ſ, ꞇ, ẏ; þ, ð, p;
    5 capitals: E, Ð (used lc and uc on 2V1ᵛ), Ɱ, S, Ð;
    1 other: ⁊ (e.g., 3I2ᵛ).

Total: 17 sorts;

Overall total sorts: 11 + 8 + 3 = 22.

Note 1: Two s-sorts, one with a short top-stroke hooked downwards, can be seen together on, e.g., 2A2ᵛ (p. 86); regular s (with longer top-stroke going across rather than up) occurs from 2O2ʳ.

Note 2: English-size dotted y from another fount occurs on 2B2ᵛ, 2I1ᵛ; Haultin's English-size y provided with an accent first occurs on 2L1ʳ. On 4G2ᵛ two y-sorts with differently orientated accents occur side by side; presumably there was more than one matrix.

Note 3: Roman H occurs initially in Hẏpɼt (2T1ʳ).

Note 4: Anglo-Saxon capitals are also used with Roman ones in a Latin inscription on 4C1ʳ.

Note 5: The typographical usage of OE is on the whole more accurate in this edition than in the contemporary Latin edition 1662.2, perhaps because the exemplar was more accurate, or because someone knowledgeable checked it. In particular, the typographer shows awareness of the need to use ð not ẟ for lc ð, as is confirmed by the hypercorrection at 4D2. On the other hand the reproduction of Anglo-Saxon forms was progressively abandoned from 5H1ʳ onwards, but this feature is taken over from 1645.2.

> Copies seen: BL 114.h*.5 (1667 re-issue), Maps C.5.b.1 (dated 1663; Shirley T.BLA-1q), both with hand-coloured maps and tp; PAL Vb.27 (engraved tp lacks title label; with hand-coloured maps, tp and illustrations; contemporary Dutch white vellum gold-tooled binding).

Bibliography: Koeman 1967–71: Bl.58; Lucas 2018: 229–233; Pettegree & Weduwen 2019: 110–115; Saunders 1991 (re. Colbert); Skelton 1970: nos 72, 84 (= 1667 re-issue); Vervey 1981¹: 13–16 and n. 19; Vervey 1981²: 201–202.

Facsimile: Amsterdam: Theatrum Orbis Terrarum, 1967 (using the copy in Amsterdam UB originally presented to Jean-Baptiste Colbert, Louis XIV's Controleur Général des Finances).

1662.4: Blaeu, Joan I, *Nvevo Atlas del Reyno de Inglaterra*. (= Atlas Mayor, vol. V = Spanish translation of Camden's *Britannia*, as in 1607.2). 2nd edn re-set from 1659.3. Amsterdam: Joan Blaeu I, 1662. CAS 3.

ASC (extracts), OE proper names

> Collation: As 1659.3 except that sig. 5Y consists of one leaf only (not two as in 1659.3), and so the total number of leaves is reduced by one; pp. 75, 78 numbered correctly, and p. 77 is misnumbered 65.

Note: Because this is a large atlas all the leaves are mounted on guards.

SOURCE OF PASSAGE UTILIZING ANGLO-SAXON TYPES:

7F2ʳ (p. 413)   From 1645.1 7E2ʳ: ASC(C + F) 188/189 (extracts), as Thorpe 1861: 14–15, including erron. ɼorʒẏpð. Ultimately from 1607.2 4Y4ʳ, including erron. ɼæ op ɼæ with p for þ.

TYPE:

Main text in an English-size roman (Body 95) interspersed with Robert Granjon's 3rd English-size Italic (e.g. on V2ᵛ–X2ᵛ).

CAS3: The Blaeu/Voskens English-size Anglo-Saxon occurs in the specimen on 2*2ʳ and is used in combination with the English-size Roman in the text (except for the crude approximations mentioned below) in words on pp. 82, 84–85, 119, 122, 129 (with *recte* Tpuþabpıȝ), 130, 135, 137–138, 143, 145–146, 148–149, 151, 152, 155–158, 160 (with Leſþa for *recte* Leſpa), 161–73, 176 (with erron. Ɯeɲſopaɲe for 1607.2 Ɯeɲſc-paɲe), 178–82, 185, 187, 193–194, 201, 206–207, 215–216, 219, 221, 225, 228 (with erron. Ƕeaȝleȝe for 1607.2 Ƕeaðleȝe), 232–234, 240, 244, 246, 250, 260, 263, 265, 267, 271–272, 274 (with erron. d for S), 277, 282, 287–288, 290, 292, 295, 297, 299–300, 304–307, 316, 328, 336, 350, 356, 359, 361, 363, 369, 371, 373, 380, 385, 387, 389, 395, 417, 422, 424, 425 (with 7 instead of ꝑ x2), 432 (with 7 instead of ꝑ), 441.

Special sorts shown in the specimen on 2*2ʳ:

  10 lower-case sorts: ð, f, ȝ, Ƕ, ɲ, ſ, τ; þ, ð, ꝑ;
  7 capitals: Æ¹, Æ², Ɛ, Ɯ, S, Ð, X;
  2 others: þ, ꝑ.
 Total: 19 sorts.

Note 1: The specimen shows Roman not Anglo-Saxon y, and gives the equivalence of Ƕ as 'h', hence its inclusion here with the lower-case rather than upper-case letters: in the text note (erron.) ƕanτeſcpẏƕ on 2R1ʳ. Roman H is used in an Anglo-Saxon name-element Heoɲτu on 6V1ʳ.

Special sorts shown in text:

  11 lower-case sorts: ð, *e*, f, ȝ, ɲ, ſ, τ, ẏ; þ, ð, ꝑ;
  5 capitals: Ɛ, Ƕ (used lc Z2ᵛ), Ɯ, S (1st on 2Z1ʳ, used as ð on 3G1ʳ), Ð;
  1 other: ꝑ (sometimes approximated by 7).
 Total: 17 sorts;

Overall total: 11 + 8 + 3 = 22 sorts.

Note 2: The typesetter evidently had initial difficulties with the Anglo-Saxon, as on pp. 13, 59, 70, 77 (used with Granjon's English-size Italic), the first occurrences of Anglo-Saxon, r is served by p, t is served by upside-down 2 and s is served by a Hebrew final-position 'tzade', and other crude approximations are resorted to. These difficulties recur on pp. 91, 95, 98, 104, 106, 111–114, 116–117, 124, 127, 128 (with Italic utilized), 133 (where the Hebrew final-position 'tzade' and yet more crude approximations are resorted to).

Note 3: Two y-sorts shown on 2P1ᵛ (p. 130): one has an acute accent (the acuteness of which seems to vary), the other shows a Pica y with a superscript dot to the left of centre, also on 5G1ʳ (3×), and on 6I2ᵛ there occurs a Pica y with a dot over the centre. On 2S1ᵛ, 2X1ʳ, there occurs a variant y with the accent to the right of centre, and on 3I2ᵛ a further variant with the accent to the left of centre. On 3G2ᵛ there occurs an English-size y with a suprascript dot to the left of centre. On 5O2ᵛ there occurs a Pica y with an acute accent to the left of centre. Note 4: Anglo-Saxon capitals are also used with roman ones in a Latin inscription on 4S2ᵛ.

    Copy: BL Maps C.5.c.2 (Shirley T.BLA-1w), with maps and some illustrations hand-coloured.

Bibliography: Koeman 1967: 1.Bl.60B; Lucas 2018: 229–233; Pettegree & Weduwen 2019: 110–115; Skelton 1970: no. 73.

1662.5: Phillips, Edward (Milton's nephew), *The New World of English Words: Or, a General Dictionary.* 2nd edn of **1658.4.** London: Evan Tyler for Nathaniel Brookes, 1658. Wing P2069; ESTC R130.

    Collation: 2⁰: π² a–c⁴ [d]² A–2R⁴ [2S1]. [352] p + 1 leaf of plates.
Words but no AS special sorts.

    Copy seen: OBL A.1.22 Art.

    Copies also at: BL, CUW, DUL, EdUL, HU, KUL, LBL, LJM, LU, LUL, MJRUL, NLW, NRL, NU, NUL, OU, SHU, UBL, YUL, TCD; NYPL, IUL, BJH, NWU, PUL, YUB.

1662.6: Reuter, Johannes [Janis Reiters], *Oratio Dominica XL. Linguarum.* Riga: Heinrich Bessemesser, 1662.

    Collation: 8⁰:)(⁸ ()(1 + 1). 18 p.
Lord's Prayer in Anglo-Saxon printed in Granjon's 3rd English-size Italic on sig.)(5ʳ (version as **1605.1**).

    Copy: See Stanley 1987: 74.

Bibliography: Sharpe & Hoyne 2020: no. 41 on p. 136. See below, **1675.3**.

1663.1: Taylor, Silas, *alias* Domville, *The History of Gavel-Kind.* London: William Wilson for John Starkey, 1663. Wing T553; ESTC R30161. AS3.
AS Laws, *ASC* (extracts)

    Collation: 4⁰: A⁴ a–b⁴ B⁴ (-B1 + χ1.B1) C–Z⁴ 2A² 2B–2D⁴ 2E⁴ (2E3 + χ1) 2F⁴ [$2 signed (-A1, 2A2, 2B1)] 124 leaves, paginated [i–xxvi], 1–180, *181–184*, 185–210, *211–220*.

SOURCES OF PASSAGES UTILIZING ANGLO-SAXON TYPES:
G4ʳ (p. 47)   From **1643.1** C3ʳ: Historiola, supplementing the OE Bede (extract): Miller 1891: I.2, 486/21; the reference is to Wheelock;
K3ᵛ (p. 70)   From (prob) **1568.2** Y4ᵛ: AS Law III Edgar 5,1–2: Liebermann I.202;
Q4ʳ (p. 119)   From **1568.2** O1ᵛ: AS Laws Alfred and Guthrum 2 (extract): Liebermann I.126; the reference is to Lambarde;

From 1568.2 V3ᵛ: AS Law 'Norðleoda laga' 7 (extract): Liebermann I.460; Lambarde's own 'Elizabethan Anglo-Saxon' version;

From 1568.2 C1ᵛ–G3ʳ: AS Laws Ine 6,3, 23,3 (extracts): Liebermann I.92, 100;

Q4ᵛ (p. 120)   From 1635.1 Z2ʳ: ASC 1012 (as Thorpe 1861: I.268/38–270/4); the reference is to Selden;

T3ᵛ (p. 142)   From 1568.2 2D2ᵛ: AS Law I Cnut Prol. (extract): Liebermann I.278;
From 1568.2 2F4ᵛ: AS Law II Cnut Prol.: Liebermann I.308;

T4ʳ (p. 143)   From 1568.2 2K3ᵛ: AS Law II Cnut 70,1: Liebermann I.356;
From 1568.2 2L2ᵛ: AS Law II Cnut 78 (extract): Liebermann I.364.

TYPE:

Main text in Haultin's English-size Roman (Body 92) interspersed with an English-size Italic (as on pp. 58–59).

AS3: The Lambardian Pica Anglo-Saxon is combined with Haultin's Pica Roman (used in the index in sig. 2F) in text as indicated above and in words on E2ʳ, R2ʳ, T3ʳ, 2A1.

Note: Beside ordinary AS3 ð there occurs another sort, which is probably capital 8 with the shoulder broken off; capital 8 is not used, even when there was on opportunity, as on G4ʳ Seaxena.

Special sorts shown:

    14 lower-case sorts: ð, [8], e, f, ᵹ, ƕ, n, r, t, ẏ; p, ð, p, p;
    2 capitals: Є, Ð;
    3 others: ꝺ, þ, ꝼ.
  Total: 19 sorts.

Note: Some of the lower-case sorts are capital in form: p, p.

Copies seen: OBL Wood 585² (uncropped); Lacking 2F: CCA W2/B.2.2, with corrections by Somner (Gough 1780: I.450); Lacking 2F, with 2E3χ1 bound between +χ1.B1: OBL Viner 509, Douce TT 172 (text slightly cropped on D3ᵛ); Lacking 2E3χ1, 2F: OBL 4⁰A2³.Jur.BS; Lacking 2F (but handwritten index ?s.xvii in its place) and with 2E3χ1 bound after 2E4: MBS 4⁰.J.rel.54 (signed James Case, Bury St Edmunds (?s.xviii), stamp of 'Inner Temple' on tp).

Copies also at: BL, BCL, BrCL, BUL, CUL, CSJ, CUW, DUL, EAL, EdCL, GUL, LGL, LHL, LPL, LSH, MTP, NLS, NLW, NT, ONC, OQC, SBT, SoUL, UBL, DKI, DML, NLI, TCD; FSL, USLC, NYCU, HHL, HUL, IUL, AAS, KSRL, NLC, NWU, UCLA, UVL, YUB, QUK, TUL; ATL.

Bibliography: Thirsk 1984: 353.

1663.2: Selden, John, t Marchamont Needham, ed. J[ames] H[owell], *Mare Clavsvm; The Right and Dominion of the Sea*. London: [William Du-Gard] for

Andrew Kembe and Edward Thomas, 1663. Wing S2431; ESTC R15177. Re-issue of **1652.2**. AS5.

 Copy seen: TCC Grylls.1.136.

 Copies also at: BL, ECC, CMC, CPH, LMT, MSL, NLW, NT, OBL, OAS, OGF, OStE, SAC, SoUL, UBL, WoCL, TCD; FSL, USLC, NYHS, NYCU, HHL, HUL, IUL, AAS, DDUL, HCP, ISU, MUL, PUL, UCLA, UMI, YUB, TUL; ANU, ATL, NLA, QSC.

1663.3: Phillips, Edward (Milton's nephew), *The New World of English Words: Or, a General Dictionary*. Re-issue of **1658.4** from 2nd edn **1662.5**. London: no printer stated, for Nathaniel Brookes and William Cartwright, 1663. Wing P2070; ESTC R40102.

 Collation: 2^0: π a–c^4 χ^2 A–2R^4 χ^2 2S^4. 362 p.

 Copy seen: OBL Douce.P.subt.119.

 Copies also at: BL, ECC, CLS, LUL, SUL, SUW, WIHM; HHL, IUL, SLWU, USL, YUB.

1663.4: Alford, alias Griffith, Michael, *Fides Regia Anglicana sive Annales Ecclesiæ Anglicanæ*. 4 vols. Liège: Johannes Mathias Hovius, 1663.

 Collation (vol. III only): 2^0 in 4s: π^2 A–4C^4 4D^2 ^{2}A–2X^6 ^{2}Y^4 ^{2}Z–^{2}2A^6. [4] 580 156 [128] p.

At III.149–51 (sig T3^r–4^r) King Alfred's will in Latin is printed in Italic from **1574.2** E2^v–E4^v (as Edwards 1866: 57–60, 71–5).

 Copy seen: ECC 304.2.52–55 (vol. III lacks 2Q3).

 Copies also at: BL, CGC, CQC, CSJ, TCC, DUL, LFL, MCS, NLS, OJC, OMaC, OQC, OWmC, UBL.

1664.1: Spelman, Sir Henry, ed. Sir William Dugdale, *Glossarium Archaiologicum: continens Latino-Barbara, Peregrina, Obsoleta, & Novatæ significationis Vocabula*. London: Alice Warren, 1664. 2nd edn completed by Dugdale from **1626.1**, the copy of which used by the printer for **1664.1** sigs A1^r–3B2^r is preserved as OBL MS e Musaeo 48 (SC 3733), 5^r–250^v (illus. Moore 1992: pls 48–49); fo 4^r = proof of sig. G1^r. Wing S4925; ESTC R14937. AS3 with occasional AS2 s.

 Context: Dugdale, still a young man, met Spelman in 1637 (Hamper 1827: 9–11) and Spelman encouraged Dugdale by recommending him to Thomas Howard, e of Arundel (Junius's patron), for service of the king in the College of Arms; see also Letter XI (5 June 1637) in Hamper 1827: 166. Dugdale's revision of Spelman's Glossarium was by arrangement with Charles Spelman (Sir Henry's nephew), as seen in Letter CXXXIII (19 June 1662) and the agreement signed 29 Nov 1662, in Hamper 1827: 358–361. In Letter CXXXV (12 Apr 1664) Charles Spelman approves the dedication to himself (Hamper 1827: 363).

Citations as in an Encyclopaedia from Ælfric Grammar, Homily, Alfredian Preface PC, ASC (E), Charters, Gospels, Laws, OE Martyrology, Wills
> Collation: 2⁰ in 4s: π² πA² A² B–4D⁴ [$3 signed (-V3, X3, Y3, Z3, 2A3, 2B3, 2C3, 2D3, 2E3, 4D3; 3Z2 missigned 2Z2)] 294 leaves, paginated [i–xii], 1–576 (pp. 112 misnumbered 108, 141 misnumbered 161, 248 misnumbered 258, 434 misnumbered 435). Note: Second state shown by 3Z2 signed correctly.

SOURCES OF PASSAGES UTILIZING ANGLO-SAXON TYPES:

B2ᵛ (p. 4) From 1626.1 A3ʳ: AS Law Edward and Guthrum 11 (Liebermann I.134), and II Cnut 26 (Liebermann I 328);

C1ᵛ (p. 10) From 1626.1 A6ʳ: AS Law II Cnut 58.1 (Liebermann I.350);

D4ᵛ (p. 24) From 1626.1 C2ᵛ: Mt.20:25 (with ðeoðo corrected to ðeoða);

E4ʳ (p. 31) From 1626.1 C6ᵛ: Prol. to Laws of Alfred and Guthrum (Liebermann I.126);

H1ʳ (p. 49) From 1626.1 E5ʳ: AS Law Edward and Guthrum 9 (Liebermann I.132);

I3ᵛ (p. 62) From 1626.1 G1ʳ: Will of Mantat during reign of Cnut leaving land at Twywell (Nth) to Thorney Abbey, C (extract) = Sawyer 1523;

L3ᵛ (p. 78) From 1626.1 H5ᵛ: AS Law I Cnut 26 (Liebermann I.304);

M1ʳ (p. 81) From 1626.1 I1ʳ: Mt.15.27 (with eaτað retained for eτað);

M1ᵛ (p. 82) From 1626.1 I2ʳ: Mt.23.4 (not 11.4 as stated), Lk 11.46;

M2ʳ (p. 83) From 1626.1 I2ᵛ: Jn.15.2 (with pe for þe);

N2ᵛ (p. 92) From 1626.1 K1ᵛ: AS Law Alfred 3 (Liebermann I.50–51);

N3ᵛ (p. 94) From 1626.1 K3ʳ: William I: London Charter in AS (Pelteret 8; pr. Liebermann 1903–16: I.486, Robertson 1925: 230), extract from §1;

N4ʳ (p. 95) From 1626.1 K3ʳ: ASC E 1066 (as Thorpe I.337);

V4ᵛ (p. 152) From 1626.1 P6ʳ: AS Law Ine 3 (Liebermann I.90);

2D1ʳ (p. 201) From 1626.1 V6ʳ: AS Law Ine 49 (Liebermann I.110);

2D3ᵛ (p. 206) From (prob) 1568.2 C4ᵛ/6–8: AS Law Ine 13,1 (Liebermann I, 94–95);

2E1ʳ (p. 209) From 1626.1 X4ʳ: AS Law II Edmund Prol.2-§1 (Liebermann I.186);

2E1ᵛ (p. 210) From 1626.1 X4ʳ: AS Law II Edmund 7 (Liebermann I.188);

2E1ᵛ (p. 210) From 1626.1 X4ʳ: AS Law Edward Confessor 12.6 (AS proverb extrapolated from L text; Liebermann I.638–639); By he spere or side oððe bær;

2E2ʳ (p. 211) From 1626.1 X5ʳ: just the word finð-fæpelðe from AS Charter Æthelred to Christ Church Canterbury (Sawyer 914; Hart 1966: p. 62, no. 84; Kemble 715);

2G4ʳ (p. 231) From 1626.1 Z6ʳ: Laws Alfred 2 (Liebermann I.48);

2H1ᵛ (p. 234) From 1626.1 2A3ʳ: Mt.5.40; Lk.22.24, also Ps 106.40;

2K3ʳ (p. 253) From 1626.1 2C2ᵛ: Mt.25.27 (extract);

2L1ʳ (p. 257) From 1626.1 2C5ʳ: Law I Cnut 20 (Liebermann I.300);

2L2ʳ (p. 259) From 1626.1 2C6ᵛ: Law Ine 6,3 (Liebermann I.92–93);

2L3ᵛ (p. 262) From 1626.1 2D2ʳ: Law III Edgar 5 (Liebermann I.202–203);

2L4ʳ (p. 263) From 1626.1 2D3ʳ: ASC C 1065 (Thorpe I.332/10);

2M2ᵛ (p. 268) From 1626.1 2D6ʳ: Law II Cnut 61 (Liebermann I 350–351);

2N2ᵛ (p. 276) From 1626.1 2E5ʳ: Ælfric, Easter Day Sermon (Godden 1979: 150/9–10);

From 1626.1 2E5ʳ: Law II Edgar 4 (Liebermann I.198);

2N3ᵛ (p. 278) From 1626.1 2E6ʳ: Law II Cnut 35 (Liebermann I.336–338);

2N3ᵛ (p. 278) From 1626.1 2E6ᵛ: Law I Cnut 20 (Liebermann I.300);

2Q2ʳ (p. 299) From 1626.1 2H1ʳ: Law Edward Confessor 23 (Liebermann I.648);

2Q3ʳ (p. 301) From 1626.1 2H2ᵛ: Law Alfred 61 (Liebermann I.82);

2T4ᵛ (p. 328) From 1626.1 2L1ᵛ: Law Dunsæte 3,2 (Liebermann I.376);

2X1ʳ (p. 337) From 1626.1 2M1ᵛ: Diploma of King Henry I (Pelteret 44);

2Y2ᵛ (p. 348) From 1626.1 2N1ᵛ: Law Dunsæte 3,2 (Liebermann I.376); cf. 2T4ᵛ;

2Z1ʳ (p. 353) From 1626.1 2N5ʳ: OE Martyrology (extract; Rauer 2013: §94b);

Note: The new material not present in 1626.1 begins on 3B2ᵛ (p. 372).

3D1ᵛ (p. 386) From 1571.1 L1ʳ/1, X4ʳ/22–3, 2E2ʳ/4–6: Mt 19.4, Mk 10.6, Lk 2.23;

3D2ʳ (p. 387)   From 1574.2 F2ʳ/35–7: Alfredian Preface to the *Pastoral Care*, as Sweet 1871: 9/1–2;

From 1644.1 Q2ʳ/18: Law II Cnut 71a (Liebermann I.358);

3H1ᵛ–3H2ʳ (pp. 418–419)   From CCC 196, pp. 8/13–17 (with 17c annotation calling attention to the content), 18/13–18 (with 17c annotation 'Majus'), 25/6–9 (with underlining ?s.xvii), 29/17–30/4, 39/14–16, 43/27–44/2, 44/3–8, 56/7–17, 72/4–11 (with s.xvii annotation 'aiðaneꞅ'), 186/8–13, 94/15–95/6, 97/20–3 (with s.xvii annotation 'pẏntꞃeꞅ ꞅꞃuma'), 106/3–19: OE Martyrology (series of extracts mainly about months): Rauer 2013: §§ 58, 73b, 83a, 94, 111a (1st sentence ... mẏð ꞃe lẏꞅte), 116a, 116b (... æꞃtepa liþa), 139, 171, 200 with added sentence re. Sept 'Alfricus nominat hunc mensem Ðæꞃꞅæꞃt monaþ', 217, 221a, 233;

3H4ʳ (p. 423)   From 1644.1 N1ᵛ/38–41: Law I Cnut 3.2 (opening sentence; Liebermann I.282);

3K2ʳ (p. 435)   From 1644.1 P2ᵛ/12–13: Law II Cnut 32/35 (extract; Liebermann I.338);

3M1ᵛ (p. 450)   From 1644.1 G3ʳ/20–1: Law II Æthelstan, epilogue, re. Synod of Grately c.928 (Lambarde's Elizabethan OE, ?t from Quadripartitus, on which see Wormald 1997: 260–262); Liebermann I.166;

3Q2ʳ (p. 483)   From 1571.1 E2ᵛ/18–19: Mt 8.32;

3R2ʳ (p. 491)   From 1644.1 F1ᵛ/39–41: Law Edward and Guthrum 6.1 (Liebermann I.130);

3R3ʳ (p. 493)   From 1571.1 G4ᵛ, S2ᵛ/19, 2H4ᵛ/7–9: Mt 13.11, Mk 4.1, 1Lk 8.10;

From 1643.1 Q2ᵛ/14–15: OE Bede II.i (Miller I.1, 94/22);

3S4ʳ (p. 503)   From RKA, DRc/R1 (Textus Roffensis, *olim* RCL A.3.5), 1ᵛ/3–5: Law Æthelberht of K 16 (Liebermann I.4);

3V2ʳ (p. 515)   From 1571.1 2E1ᵛ/23–4: Lk 2.21;

3V3ᵛ (p. 518)   From CUL Hh.1.10, 93ᵛ: Ælfric, Grammar, postscript, last sentence (Zupitza 296/15);

3V4ʳ (p. 519)   From RKA, DRc/R1 (Textus Roffensis, *olim* RCL MS A.3.5), 144ʳ/5–145ʳ/24: Will of Byrhtric 973 × 987 (Sawyer 1511; extract: Whitelock 11/23);

3Y3ʳ (p. 533)   From 1644.1 M3ʳ/22–3: Law II Æthelred 9, opening phrase (Liebermann I.226);

3Z1ʳ (p. 537)   From 1655.3 2M4ʳ: Writ of William I in favour of St Peter's, Abbotsbury (Pelteret 26);

4C4ᵛ (p. 568)   From CCC 201 (formerly owned by Edward Cradock, Lady Margaret Professor of Divinity Oxford University 1575–94): AS Law

'Geþyncðo' (Liebermann I.456–458), pp. 101–102, the text of which that here matches (apart from palpable errors); cp. **1576.2** 2Z2ᵛ–3ᵛ;

4D1ʳ (p. 569) From ibid., p. 102 (where the four laws follow on from each other): AS Laws 'Norðleoda' (Liebermann I, 458–61), 'Mircna' (Liebermann I 462–463), 'Að 1' (Liebermann I.464–465), the text here matching (apart from palpable errors) that in CCC 201, e.g. 'Arces' for 'Arcebisceopes' at Norðleoda 2; cp.**1568.2** V3ᵛ/7–X1ʳ/11, V4ᵛ/9–X1ʳ;

4D3ʳ (p. 573) From **1644.1** B3ʳ: Law Ine 71 (Liebermann I.120).

TYPE:

Main text in double columns in Pierre Haultin's Pica Roman (Body 82) interspersed with Robert Granjon's 2nd Pica Italic;

AS3: The Lambardian Pica Anglo-Saxon combined with Haultin's Pica Roman occurs as indicated above under Contents and in words (or phrases) on many other pages.

AS2/3: Parkerian s occurs beside Lambardian s, e.g., H1ʳ (p. 49), Parkerian s in ꝼæꞃꞇen, Lambardian s in aðaꞃ.

Special sorts shown:

    10 + [1] lower-case sorts: ð, [ẟ], e, ꝼ, ȝ, p, ꞃ, ꞇ, ẏ; ð, p;
    4 capitals: Æ², Є, Ꝺ (used lc), ẟ;
    3 others: þ, ꞇ, j̇.
    Total: 17 + [1] sorts.

Note 1: ẟ is very commonly used for ð, e.g. on D4ᵛ–E1ʳ, E3ᵛ, H1ʳ (where it is also used correctly for the capital), L3ᵛ, etc. ẟ with the shoulder broken off occurs for ð on H1ʳ in ꞇocpeðene.

Note 2: p is used erroneously for þ in poꞃnıȝ 'Thorney' on I3ᵛ.

Note 3: The AS types are used for Irish names on V3ʳ, V4ʳ (p. 151).

    Copies seen: State 1: CUL Bb*.2.2(B) (gift of George I, 1715) shows 2H1 and 2H4 in reversed order; CCC L.7.12 (gift of Edward Montagu 22 Nov 1664); LFL 18I; OBL 302.y.5.

    State 2 (with 3Z2 signed correctly): ECC S5.1.3 (with addition of **1687.1** sigs a–c after A2; Abp Sancroft's copy with gold-tooled binding of (?)1687 with Sancroft's armorial crest superimposed).

    Copies also at: BL, BCLNI, BCLW, CCA, CME, CSJ, CaCL, ChCL, DCL, DUL, GUL, KNA, LCL, LiCL, LHL, LSE, LSH, NCL, NLS, NLW, NT, OBC, OCC, OJC, OLC, ONC, OQC, OStE, OSJ, OWmC, OWoC, PML, LRS, SAC, SBT, SPC, SUL, UBL, WCF, WCL, WiCL, YML, DML, KSC, ULim, PBN, GCB, BSB; FSL, USLC, NYCU, HHL, HUL, IUL, AAS, NLC, NWU, PTS, UCLA, UOC, UTA, UTK, WCW, WUM, QUK, TUL; NLA, NSW, UNSW, UTL, VUW.

Bibliography: Maddison *et al.* 1953: no. 31. GR 6283.

1664.2: [van Vliet, Jan], *'t Vader Ons in xx Oude Duijtse en Noordse Taelen met d' Uijtleggingen &C.* [Dordrecht: Hendrik and Johann I van Esch], 1664. Re-issued with a new title-page, Breda: Abraham Subbinck, 1666. AS 6.

Precedents: Previous collections of the Lord's Prayer in various languages include Gessner 1555.1, Megiser 1593.1, Freher 1610.6, Mylius 1612.2, Boxhorn 1650.4.

Lord's Prayer, Song of Simeon

Collation: 8⁰: π¹ a⁴ A–C⁸ [$5 signed (-a4)] 29 leaves, paginated [i–x], 1–48. The re-issue adds another leaf after π1.

SOURCES OF PASSAGES UTILIZING ANGLO-SAXON TYPES:

A6ʳ–7ᵛ (pp. 11–14)   From 1643.1 3S4: Lord's Prayer, as Thorpe 1844–6: II.596;
              From 1665.2 B3ᵛ–4ʳ: Lord's Prayer (Mt 6.9–13), as Liuzza 1994: 12;
              From 1665.2 2G3ʳ: Lord's Prayer (Lk 11.2–4), as Liuzza 1994: 125;

A8ʳ (p. 15)   From 1665.2 Z4ᵛ: Song of Simeon (Lk 2.29–32), as Liuzza 1994: 103;

C1 (pp. 33–4)   From 1605.1 C4: Lord's Prayer (Mt 6.9–13; OE gloss somewhat garbled), as Skeat 1871–87: 55.

Note 1: On a4ʳ van Vliet cites 1665.2 as having been printed by the van Esch brothers in 1663; since he was a friend of Junius dealing with the same printers he presumably saw 1665.2 before it was actually published.

Note 2: Van Vliet may have had access to what is now OBL MS Junius 39, containing excerpts from 1610.6, or he may have used the book itself, and also 1650.4.

TYPE:

Main text (Preface and Commentary) in the Junian Pica Roman attributable to Christoffel van Dijck.

AS 6: Christoffel van Dijck's Pica Anglo-Saxon cut for Franciscus Junius occurs in the specimen on A1ʳ and in text on A6, A8ʳ, C1ʳ, and in words in the commentary on A2ᵛ–6ʳ, A7, B2ʳ–3ʳ, B4ᵛ, B5ᵛ–6ʳ, C2ʳ, C3ᵛ–5ʳ.

Special sorts shown in the specimen:

    11 lower-case sorts: ð, ꝼ, ȝ, ı, ꝑ, ſ, ꞇ, ẏ; þ, ð, p;
    8 capitals: Ꞇ, Є, Ᵹ, Ð, Ϻ, 8; Þ, Ð;
    3 others: þ, ꝗ, ꝗ.
  Total: 22 sorts.

Special sorts shown in the text:

    11 lower-case sorts: ð, ꝼ, ȝ, ı, ꝑ, ſ, ꞇ, ẏ; þ, ð, p;
    6 capitals: Ꞇ, Ᵹ, Ð, 8; Þ (erron. for P on B2ᵛ; only instance), Ð;
    3 others: ꝗ, ꝗ, ∴.
  Total: 20 sorts.

Overall total: 11 + 8 + 4 = 23 sorts.

Note: This book also utilizes the Junian Pica Gothic, Runic, Danish, Icelandic, and a Pica Textura (found in the Ploos van Amstel specimen of 1767 as 'Mediaan Duits' no. 2 on sig. C6 and as 'Mediaan Duyts' on sig. F7).
Copies seen: OBL MS Junius 95 (SC 5206); 1666 re-issue: BL 1568/4177.
Copieas also at: LUL, NUL.
Bibliography: Dekker 1997: 36–38; Dekker 1999: 151–158.

1665.1: Gregory, John, *Notes and Observations upon some Passages of Scripture.* London: James Flesher for Richard Royston and Nathaniel Brookes, 1665. 3rd edn of **1646.1.** Wing G1922; ESTC R34214. AS3.
Words
>   **Collation:** 4^0: A^4 a–b^4 B–Y^4 [\$2 signed (+A3; -A1,2)] 96 leaves, paginated [i–xxiv], 1–166, *167–168*.

TYPE:
Main text in a Pica Roman (Body 80) interspersed with Robert Granjon's 2nd Pica Italic *pendante* (with variant *J*).
AS3: The Lambardian Pica Anglo-Saxon occurs in ꞇunᵹal Wƿıꞇeᵹan (with ꞇ for t, i.e 'white star') on V1ᵛ (p. 146), where it is combined with the Pica Roman; Special sorts used:

>   4 + [1] lower-case sorts: e, ᵹ, Ð, ı, ꞇ;
>   1 other: ꞇ.
>   Total: 4 [+1] + 0 + 1 = 6 sorts.

Note: Other special sorts are used for astrological symbols on V2ᵛ.
>   **Copies seen:** BL 3752.aa.13; LFL 4B.
>   **Copies also at:** OBL, GUB; UTS, IUL, UCLA.

Bibliography: see **1646.1.**

1665.2 Junius, Franciscus, and Thomas Marshall, *Quatuor D.N. Jesu Christi Euangeliorum Versiones Perantiquæ Duæ, Gothica scil. et Anglo-Saxonica + Gothicum Glossarium.* Dordrecht: Hendrik and Johann I van Esch, 1665. AS6.
>   **Date:** 1665. Probably in print to be viewed privately by 1663: see **1664.2.**

Gospels, etc.
>   **Collation:** 4^0: π^1 *–2^{*4} A–$4B^4$ 2^*–3^{*4} ^{2}A–$3H^4$ [\$3 signed (-*1, 2*3, 2^*1)] 521 leaves, paginated [i–xviii, 1], 2–565, *566–568*, [²i–xxiv, 1], ²2–431, *432* (pp. 384, ²32, ²416 not numbered).

SOURCES OF PASSAGES UTILIZING ANGLO-SAXON TYPES:
A1ʳ–3B4ʳ (pp. 1–383)   From **1571.1** based on OBL Bodley 441 (B), collated with B and CCC 140 (Cp), CUL Ii.2.11 (A), and OBL Hatton 38 (H): see 3Q1ff. for discussion; OE Gospels, as Liuzza 1994: 3–202;
Other citations include:

3O4ʳ (p. 479) From OBL MS Junius 101 (SC 5212 = Junius's excerpted transcript of Julius A.x, collated with CCC 196), 6ᵛ/26–33: OE Martyrology, as Herzfeld 1900: 198/8–12, Kotzor 1981: II.243/2–6; Rauer 2013: §217b;

²N1ʳ (p. 97) From OBL MS Junius 101 (SC 5212 = Junius's excerpted transcript of Julius A.x, collated with CCC 196), 6ᵛ/23–33: OE Martyrology, as Herzfeld 1900: 198/6–12, Kotzor 1981: II.242/15–243/6; Rauer 2013: §§217a–b;

²T1ʳ (p. 145) From OBL MS Junius 12 (SC 5124 = Junius's transcript of OBL Bodley 180 (SC 2079) collated with Otho A.vi (since damaged by fire)), fos 14d/6–10, 15a/14–15: (a) Alfredian translation of Boethius's *De Consolatione Philosophiae*, XII (extract), as Sedgefield 1899: 26/28–9; and (b) the corresponding verse, *Metres of Boethius* 7.9–16, as Krapp 1932: 160; Godden/Irvine 2009: I.406; both receive 'metrical' pointing;

²X1ᵛ (p. 162) From OBL MS Junius 15 (SC 5127 = Junius's transcript of Tiberius B.i), p. 64/33–35: OE Orosius IV.6 (extract), coll. Sweet 1883: 174/15–17, Bately 1980: 93/31–33;

²2B2ᵛ (p. 196) From OBL MS Junius 66 (SC 5177 = Junius's transcript of Tiberius A.iii, 60ᵛ–64ᵛ), p. 10/19–31: Ælfric's Colloquy (excerpt from continuous OE gloss), as Garmonsway 1939: 187–191;

²2P2ᵛ–3ʳ (pp. 300–1) From OBL MS Junius 12 (SC 5124 = Junius's transcript of OBL Bodley 180 (SC 2079) collated with Otho A.vi (since damaged by fire)), 47ʳ/19–27: Alfredian translation of Boethius's *De Consolatione Philosophiae*, XXXIII.5 (edited extract), as Sedgefield 1899: 80/11–19; Godden/Irvine 2009: I.316/177–85.

Note: On 2*4ᵛ Marshall refers to the following books:

Leland, John, Κυκνειον ασμα. *Cygnea cantio* (Commentarii). London: Reyner Wolfe, 1545 [1543]. STC 15444;

Jonas, Runolphus, *Recentissima antiquissimæ linguæ septentrionalis incunabula, id est grammaticæ Islandicæ rudimenta nunc primum ... edita*. Copenhagen: Peder Hake, 1651;

Wormius, Olaus, RUNER *seu Danica Literatura antiquissima vulgò Gothica dicta luci reddita*. Copenhagen: Melchior Martzan and Georg Holst, 1651 [= 2nd edn, 1st edn 1636];

Spelman, Sir Henry, *Concilia, Decreta, Leges, Constitvtiones, in re Ecclesiarum Orbis Britannici*. London: Richard Badger 1, 1639 = **1639.4**.

TYPE:

AS6: The main text of the OE Gospels is in Christoffel van Dijck's Pica Anglo-Saxon cut for Franciscus Junius combined with van Dijck's Pica Roman on A1ʳ–3B4ʳ, and in citations sporadically on 3C4ʳ–4B4ᵛ and throughout the Gothic Glossary on 2E1ʳ–3H4ʳ.

The AS specimen on 2*4ʳ shows the following special sorts:
  11 lower-case sorts: ð, f, ȝ, ı, p, ſ, τ, ẏ; þ, ð, p;
  9 capitals: Ⱡ, Є, Ⱡ, Ð, ꟽ, 8; Þ, Ð, Þ;
  3 others: ⁊, þ, ∴.
 Total: 23 sorts.

There is also a specimen alphabet set out on 2D3ᵛ with two sizes of ⁊, so showing all 24 sorts.

Note: The Þ used is van Dijck's (and not the same as that in the later OUP specimen, which was cut by van Walpergen).

Special sorts shown in the text:
  11 lower-case sorts: ð, f, ȝ, ı, p, ſ, τ, ẏ; þ, ð, p;
  9 capitals: Ⱡ, Є, Ⱡ, Ð, ꟽ, 8; Þ, Ð, Þ;
  4 others: ⁊, ⁊, þ, ∴.
 Total: 24 sorts.

Note: The Junian Pica Roman (Body 84) attributable to van Dijck occurs in the main text 3C1ʳ–3P2ʳ, 23*1ʳ–4ᵛ; the Junian Pica Italic (Body 84) also attributable to van Dijck occurs sporadically, e.g. 3P2–3; the Junian Pica Gothic occurs in the specimen on 2*4ʳ and in the text on A4ᵛ–E4ʳ, K3ʳ–L3ʳ, L4ʳ–2G2ᵛ, 2H4ʳ–2M4ʳ, 2P4ᵛ–3A4ʳ, and in citations on 3C4ʳ–3P2ʳ, etc., throughout the Gothic Glossary on 2E1ʳ–23F4ʳ, and the alphabet is set out 2A1ʳ–B3ᵛ; the Junian Pica Runic occurs on 2*4ʳ, 3G4ʳ, 3S4ᵛ, 3T2ʳ, 3T3ᵛ, 3T4ᵛ, 3V1ᵛ–2ʳ, 3V3ʳ, 3V4ᵛ, 3X1ʳ (4 lines), 3X3ʳ, and sporadically elsewhere, and the alphabet is set out and discussed 2C1ʳ–D3ʳ; the Junian Pica Icelandic occurs in text on 2E2ᵛ, 2F1ʳ, 2Q2ᵛ, 22A2ᵛ, and in words on 2*4ᵛ, 3F4, 3V3ʳ (3 lines of text), 3X2ʳ, and a specimen 'Frankish' alphabet occurs on 2D3ᵛ; the Junian Pica Danish occurs in words on 3S4ᵛ–3T1ᵛ.

Note 2: A Textura alphabet specimen used for Dutch is set out on 2D4ʳ.

Note 3: Other exotic founts are also used (as well as Hebrew and Greek): Syrian, Arabic, Coptic on 3C4, 3D2ʳ, 3D3, 3D4ᵛ, etc., 3R2–3S1.

 Copies seen: CCA W/I.4.28 (Somner's copy, gift of Edmund Castell 1668); CUL 1.24.4 (author's gift to Fabian Philipps, with corrections in Junius's hand, e.g., on A1ʳ, ²D4ʳ), 1.24.8, Huntingdon 52.12 (owned by Owen Manning 1763), Young 100–101 (2 vols); ECC S1.3.25 (lacks *1ʳ; Abp Sancroft's copy); MBS 4⁰.B.rel.21.ʳ; MRL, Hibernian Bible Society 1665/512 (tp stamped 'A Wood').

 Copies also at: BL, BUL, KCC, CSJ, TCC, CWC, DCL, DUL, EdUL, Eton, GlCL, GUL, KCL, LCL, LPL, LSH, LU, LUL, MCS, MJRUL, NUL, OAS, OBC, OCC, OEC, OEF, OHM, OJC, OLC, OMaC, OQC, OSJ, OTC, OTI, RCL, SPC, SUL, UCL, WCC, WCL, WiCL.

Bibliography: Douglas 1939: 160–162 (re. Philipps); Lucas 1998; Niles 2015: 125–127. GR5861.

Printer's Copy: OLC

Manuscript: OBL Junius 55 (SC 5167 = Junius's transcript of the Gothic Gospels).
Note: OBL Eng.bibl.c.3, p. 51, has a trial/copy tp by Humfrey Wanley, followed by Mt, Mk and Lk (up to ch. 8) copied by him in imitative AS script.

1665.3: Selden, John, *De Iure Naturali & Gentium, iuxta Disciplinam Ebræorum*, ed. Johann Heinrich Boecler. Strassburg: (prob) Georg Andreas Dolhopff for Georg Andreas Dolhopff and Johann Eberhard Zetzner (sumptibus) 1665; variant for Johann Andreas Endter and the heirs of Wolfgang Endter II of Nuremberg (sumptibus) 1665. 2nd edn of **1640.4**. BLG S1862. CAS5.

    Printer: [Strassburg: (prob) Dolhopff, Georg Andreas (1627–1711). Dolhopff married a daughter of the Strassburg publisher Johann Andreas Zetzner, whom he served as a printer from 1662. From 1668 to 1671 Balthasar Joachim Endter worked for them, and the contact between the two businesses (Dolhopff/Zetzner in Strassburg, and Endter in Nuremberg) probably gave rise to the Endter's interest in the book.]

OE Gospels, Law of Alfred (extracts)
    Collation: 4^0: π^2 *–5^{*4} A–$2O^4$ $2P^4$ ($2P1 + \chi1,2,3$) 2Q–$5T^4$ $5V^2$ 5X–$5Z^4$ $6A^2$ [$3 signed (-$3^*$3, 3A3, 6A2)] 482 leaves, paginated [i–xliv], 1–892, *893–920* (pp. 356 misnumbered 346, 361 misnumbered 261, 371 misnumbered 361, 611 misnumbered 613).

SOURCES OF PASSAGES UTILIZING ANGLO-SAXON TYPES:
4F3 (pp. 597–8)   From **1640.4** 4D4ʳ: OE Gospels: Mt 5.31, Lk 1.28, 42, 11.27, Mk 7.26, Jn 4.7, Lk 16.18, Mt 19.10, also two words hýɼ pıɼ from Orosius (as Bately 1980: 148/9n.).
5T2ᵛ (p. 884)   From **1640.4** 5O4ʳ: Preface to Law of Alfred 49.5 (extract), as Liebermann I.44.

TYPE:
The main text is in Pierre Haultin's English-size Roman (Body 96) interspersed with an English-size Italic.
CAS5: A German imitation of AS1 occurs in text as indicated above and in words on 3M2ᵛ (p. 460), 3N1 (pp. 465–466) combined with Haultin's English-size Roman.

Special sorts shown:
    11 lower-case sorts: ð, ꝼ, ᵹ, 1 (once only on sig. 5T2ᵛ), ɲ, ɼ, ꞇ, ẏ; þ, ð, p;
    5 capitals: Æ², Є, Ⱨ, Ⳙ, Ð;
    2 others: þ, ⁊.
    Total: 18 sorts.

Note: The type-specimen book for the Endters [Ernesti 1721] does not include an Anglo-Saxon design.

Copies seen: CUL C.4.5; BL 494.g.3 shows π1 reversed without the 'imprimatur'; TCC F.8.4 (lacks π1).

Copies also at: CSJ, DUL, EUL, GUL, LBL, LSH, MJRUL, NLS, NT, OBL, OHM, OLC, OWmC, OWoC, OXC, SoUL, YUL.

Bibliography: Oldenbourg 1911: 74–75 (re. sale-catalogue of the Endters 1670); Schäfer 2000 (on Dolhopff).

1665.4: Ussher, James, *Veterum Epistolarum Hibernicarum Sylloge*. 2nd edn of 1632.1. Paris: Louis Billaine, 1665.

Collation: 4^0: π^4 e^4 A–L^4 [16], 92 p.

Fragments of AS in 1632.1 rendered in Italic on D2^r, M2^r; fragment of Irish rendered in Roman on G2^r.

Note: Billaine evidently did not have the use of AS sorts at this time; cf. 1678.2.

Copy seen: CUL Hib.5.665.2.

Copies also at: BL, DCL, DUL, NLS, OBL, OEC, OJC, OQC, ORP, UCL.

1665?.1: [Nicholls, Nicholas], [Type-specimen] beginning 'The *Saxon* Alphabet'. [London: Nicholas Nicholls c.1665]. AS7.

Type-specimen: Individual Letter-sorts

Collation: 1^0.

TYPE:

AS7: Nicholas Nicholls's Somnerian Pica Anglo-Saxon.

Special sorts shown:

	10 lower-case sorts:	ð, *e*, f, ᵹ, p, r, t; þ, ð, p;
	5 capitals:	Æ², Є, Ꝺ, Ꟃ, 8;
	2 others:	þ, ꝫ.
Total:	17 sorts.	

Copy seen: BL, Bagford Collection, Harley 5977, no. 200.

Bibliography: Mores 1778/1961: 15, n. 5; Mosley 1984: no. 168. See List of Types.

Facsimile: Mores 1778/1961: lxxv.

1666.1: Dugdale, Sir William, *Origines Juridiciales*. London: Francis and Thomas Warren, 1666. Wing D2488; ESTC R5005. AS3.

Date: 1666, presumably before the Great Fire of London [2–7 Sept], as the printers were apparently ruined by it (although Thomas Warren II began printing again in 1690). 'Imprimatur' on $\pi1^v$ dated 24 May 1666. According to Miller (1948: 300) few copies survived the Great Fire, but several are listed below.

ASC(E) + Lawsuit (extracts)

Collation: 2^0: π^4 A² B–2I⁴ 2K–3G² 3H⁶ ²A–²2G² [\$3 signed (-A2, 2B1, 2G1,2,3, 2I1, 2K2, 2Z1,2, 3A1,2, 3B1, 3F1,2, 3G1, 3H2,3, ²A1, ²2F2, ²2G2; 3H1 missigned 2H1)] 238 leaves, paginated [i–xii], 1–332, *333–344*, 1–115, *116–118* (pp. nos ²95–96 used twice; pp. ²90 misnumbered 88, ²91 misnumbered 85).

State 2 indicated by pp. ²90–91 numbered correctly.

SOURCES OF PASSAGES UTILIZING ANGLO-SAXON TYPES:

C4ʳ (p. 15) From OBL Laud misc 636 (facs. Whitelock 1954), 64ᵛ/8–13: *ASC*(E) 1087 (extract), as Thorpe 1861: 355; Clark 1970: 12/73–9;

F1ᵛ (p. 34) From RKA, DRc/R1 (Textus Roffensis, *olim* RCL A.3.5) (facs. Sawyer 1957–62), 155ᵛ/7–13, or from BL Harley 311 29ᵛ/31–6: Lawsuit (*c*.995) about the estate of Snodland, Kent (Sawyer 1456), Robertson 69/15–20; since Harley 311 (1646) provides an accurate transcript the only clue to which source was used is Dugdale's error of ꞅcıpeꞅ for ꞅcẏpeꞅ-, where the AS ꞃ in Harley 311 is more capable of being mistaken for a p than that in the Textus Roffensis; the words ꞅe Lınᵹe have been substituted for the third word he.

Note: List of AS Laws with MS sources on H3ᵛ (p. 54): Claudius A.viii, D.ii, E.xiv, Cleopatra A.xvi, Nero A.i, Otho A.x, B.xi, Titus A.xxvii, Vitellius A.xiii, E.v.

TYPE:

The main text is in Pierre Haultin's English-size Roman (Body 93.5).

AS3: The Lambardian Pica Anglo-Saxon combined with a Pica Roman (no separate instance in the book) occurs in text as indicated under Contents above. Special sorts shown:

8 + [3] lower-case sorts:	ẟ [shoulder broken off, for ð], *e*, ꞅ, ᵹ, ƕ, ꞃ, ꞅ, ꞇ; ꝧ [used lc], ð, þ;
1 capital:	Є;
1 other:	ꝫ.
Total:	13 sorts.

Copies seen: State 1: ECC S2.1.38 (Abp Sancroft's copy with his armorial crest in gold on the covers); TCD I.ff.37 (lacks π1, 3H3–4). State 2 (with pp. ²90–91 numbered correctly): CCA W/H.5.21 (Somner's copy, 'ex dono dignissimi auctoris' π2ʳ); BL 709.i.4, G11965; CUL J.7.12.

Copies also at: BCL, BrCL, BUL, CNC, TCC, ECL, EdUL, LGI LMT, MJRUL, NLW, OBL, ONC, OQC, OSJ, OWoC, DML; NYCU, HHL, HUL, MUL, PUL, SLC, UCLA, UTA, TUL; SSA.

Bibliography: McKenzie & Bell 2005: 1.586 (4 Jan 1668); Maddison *et al.* 1953: no. 32; Pennington 1982 (see index for references).

1666.2: [van Vliet, Jan], *'t Vader Ons in xx Oude Duijtse en Noordse Taelen met d' Uijtleggingen &C.* Breda: Abraham Subbinck, 1666. Re-issue of **1664.2** with new tp. AS6.

1668.1: Wilkins, John, *An Essay towards a Real Character and a Philosophical Language*. London: no printer stated, for Samuel Gellibrand and John Martin, 1668. Wing W2196; ESTC R21115.

    Collation: 2^0: [A]^2 a–d^2 B–3M^4 3a^4 ^{2}3A–3T^4 (3M4 and ^{2}3T4 blank). [20], 454, [2]; [160] p + 4 leaves illustrations.

Lord's Prayer in many languages including an Anglo-Saxon (called 'Old Saxon') version printed in a Textura with no special sorts on 3K2^r–4^r.

    Copy seen: CUL M.13.30.

    Copies also at: BL, BCL, BrCL, BrPL, BUL, CCA, CCC, CGC, CJC, CMC, CSJ, TCC, CaCL, ChestC, DCL, DRD, DUL, DWL, Eton, GlCL, GML, GUL, HHC, KNA, ILP, LBL, LMT, LSH, MJRUL, NHM, NLS, NLW, NT, OBL, OAS, OBC, OCC, OEC, OEF, OHC, OHM, OJC, OMaC, OMC, OMHS, ONC, OQC, OSJ, OTC, OWmC, OWoC, RLW, LRS, RUL, SCL, SDL, SUL, UBL, UCL, WAL, WCF, WiCL, YML, DML, NLI, TCD, ULim, PBN, GCB, BSB; FSL, USLC, NYPL, NYAM, NYCU, GTS, UTS, HHL, HUL, APS, BMC, HCN, KSRL, LCP, LSU, NLC, NWU, SCN, SLU, UAZ, UCBL, UCH, UCIL, UCLA, UCRL, UMI, UNC, UTA, UTK, UVL, VCU, WMUL, WUM, YUB; ANU, AUNZ, MonUL, NLA, NSW, OUL, QCL, SJTC, SMUL, SSA, UML, UNSW, USL.

Bibliography: Dobson 1968: I.253–62; Hüllen 1999: 250–301; Knappe 2012.

1669.1: Vorst, Johannes, *Observationum in Linguam Vernaculam Specimen*. Köln an der Spree: Georg Schultze, 1669. BLG V613.

    Collation: 12^0: A–D^{12} (lacks D12). [2], 93, [1] p.

Cites OE forms in Granjon's 3rd Pica Italic, *Cicero Currens*, e.g., on A7^v, B11^v, D9^v, and on D10^v–11^r there are two passages from **1655.2** D4^v/15–16 (= *GenA* 1407–1409), and E1^v/4–6 (= *GenA* 1487b–1491a). Translated into German in (J.C. Gottsched's) *Beyträge zur Critischen Historie der deutschen Sprache, Poesie und Beredsamkeit* 7 (Stück 26)/1741, pp. 179–241.

    Copy seen: BL 1568/4147.

    Copy also at: OBL MS Junius 96.

1670.1: Sheringham, Robert, *De Anglorum Gentis Origine Disceptatio*. Cambridge: John Hayes for Edward Story, 1670. Wing S3236; ESTC R14840. AS3. **ASC, OE Bede, Ælfric Homilies (all extracts)**

    Collation: 4^0 in 8s: a–b^8 A–2I^8 [$4 signed (-a1; Q4 missigned R4)] 272 leaves, paginated [i–xxxii], 1–488, *489–510* (pp. nos 95–96 used twice). Note: F4.5 and K8 are cancels.

SOURCES OF PASSAGES UTILIZING ANGLO-SAXON TYPES:

C2^v (p. 36)   From **1643.1** K1^v/17–20: OE Bede I.12 (extract; Miller I.1.52/2–4);

                             From **1643.1** 3V2^r/39–42: ASC 449 (extract), as Thorpe I.20/17–20;

V4ᵛ–5ʳ (pp. 310–311)   From CUL Ii.1.33, 175ᵛ: Ælfric, Homily *De Falsis Diis*, as Pope 1967–8: II.682–3, lines 104–25;
X6ʳ (p. 329)   From (prob) CUL Gg.3.28, 56ᵛ: Ælfric, Homily Feria III de dominica oratione (opening sentence), as Clemoes 1997: 325/3–6;
2A8ᵛ–2B1ʳ (pp. 382–383)   From **1643.1** F1ʳ: ME *Metrical Chronicle* attrib. 'Robert of Gloucester', as Wright 1887, I.15, lines 211–215.

TYPE:

Main text in Pierre Haultin's English-size Roman (Body 93.5) interspersed with Robert Granjon's 3rd English-size Italic (e.g. I2ʳ).

AS3: The Lambardian Pica Anglo-Saxon is set out as an alphabet on M1ʳ, and occurs in text as indicated under Contents above and in words on P6ʳ, R7ᵛ, S2ᵛ, S6ʳ, V8ᵛ, where it is combined with Arthur Nicholls's Pica Roman (Body 82).

Special sorts shown in specimen:

9 [+1] lower-case sorts:	ð, f, ȝ, ꞃ, ꞅ, ꞇ, ẏ; þ, ð, p [= þ with ascender partially broken off];
5 [+2] capitals:	E, L [pres. for Ḷ], Ꝺ, ꟽ; þ [same as lc], Ð, p [= lc 'wynn'];
3 others:	ꝺ, þ, ∴.
Total:	17 [+3] sorts.

Note 1: There is no *e*.

Note 2: The part of the note underneath the AS specimen relating to punctuation derives from Junius, as **1655.1** π8ʳ.

Special sorts shown in the text (with frequent setting errors):

10 [+2] lower-case sorts:	ð, [δ = ð], f, ȝ, ꞃ, ꞅ, ꞇ, ẏ; þ, ð, p [often þ with ascender partially broken off];
3 capitals:	E, Ꝺ, Ð;
2 others:	ꝺ, þ.
Total:	15[+2] sorts.

Note 3: In text capital S is also used for ð, and several letters have the Roman not Anglo-Saxon form.

Note 4: Also contains two Gothic alphabets (woodcuts) on L7ᵛ and L8ᵛ; Gothic text on X2ᵛ, Y5ʳ, Z4ᵛ, and words on S1ʳ; and some Runic letters and text (woodcuts) on O1ʳ, P5, P8, Q3, S4ᵛ, S8, T1ʳ.

Copies seen: ABH 1327; CUL R.11.66, Cam.d.670.13, Adams.7.67.1, Bury.46.8, Pet M.1.13; ECC 321.4.8; TCD HH.kk.65, RR.l.4, Fag.Q.9.28; MBS Brit.488 (bookplate of Johann Conrad Feuerlem).

Copies also at: BL, BCL, BPL, CCC, CMC, CSJ, TCC, DCL, DUL, EAL, ECL, Eton, LCL, LGL, LSH, MJRUL, MTP, NCL, NLS, NLW, NMS, OBL, OAS, OBC, OCC, OHC,

OJC, OMC, OQC, OWmC, OWoC, OXC, UBL, WCL, WIHM, YML, DEWL, DML, NLI, RIA, PBN, GCB, BSB, GUB; FSL, USLC, GTS, UTS, HHL, HUL, IUL, DDUL, KSRL, LCP, NLC, TCH, UCBL, UCLA, UTA, UVL, YUB, TUL; OUL, USL.

Bibliography: Fell 1993: 88–89, 92; Fell 1996: 28–34 (with reduced reproduction of Q3^r = Fig. 1); Parry 1995: 324–325. GR5279.

1670.2: Blount, Thomas (1618–79), *Glossographia, or, a Dictionary, Interpreting all such Hard Words of Whatsoever Language, now used In our refined English Tongue; With Etymologies, Definitions, and Historical Observations on the same.* London: Thomas Newcomb for George Sawbridge, 1661.Wing B3336; ESTC R6021. 3rd edn of **1656.3**, 2nd edn **1661.2**.
OE etymologies occasionally cited but no Anglo-Saxon types
Collation: 8^0: A–2X^8 2Y^4(-2Y4); [16], 144, 155–202, 209–708, [2] p.
Type: Main text in a Long Primer Roman (Body 66) in double columns.
No Anglo-Saxon types but OE etymologies occasionally cited in the same Textura as is used for headwords, as s.v. *Gospel*.

    Copy seen: CUL Bb*.5.33(F).

    Copies also at: BL, BCL, CGC, DUL, LGL, LSH, NAL, NLS, NLW, OBL, OEF, OTI, UCL, WIHM; ULim, BN; USLC, FSL, HUL, IUL, LCP, LSU, MUL, NWU, SCN, SfUL, SLU, UCBL, UCLA, UTA, YUB; TUL; SMUL, UML, USL.

Bibliography: Alston V.50.

1671.1: Gregory, John, *The Works of the Reverend and Learned Mr. John Gregory.* London: Roger Norton II for Richard Royston and Thomas Williams, 1671. 4th edn of **1646.1** based on slavish reprint of 3rd edn **1665.1**. Wing G1914; ESTC R12236. AS7.
Words

    Collation: As **1665.1**.

TYPE:
Main text in Arthur Nicholls's Pica Roman (Body 81.5), interspersed with his Pica Italic.
AS7: The Somnerian Pica Anglo-Saxon occurs in two words on V1^v (p. 146) in combination with Arthur Nicholls's Pica Roman;
Special sort used: ᵹ; for capital T the printer has used a Hebrew sort for ꝥ 'daleth'.
Other special sorts are used for astrological symbols on b4^r and V2^v.

    Copies seen: APL E.VII.1^1; BL 1016.h.16^1; CUL Bury.41.1, Syn.7.67.92.

    Copies also at: BCLNI, KCC, CSJ, DCL, ECL, GML, ILP, LCL, LHL, LiCL, LSH, LUL, MJRUL, NLS, OBL, OAS, OLC, ONC, OQC, OWoC, OXC, SML, UBL, YML, TCD, BSB,

GUB; UTS, HHL, HUL, KSRL, MUL, PUL, SLU, UCLA, UCRL, UMI, WMUL, WUM, YUB.

Bibliography: see 1646.1.

1671.2: Dugdale, Sir William, *Origines Juridiciales*, 2nd edn, re-set page by page from 1666.1. London: Thomas Newcomb 1 for Abel Roper, John Martin, and Henry Herringman, 1671. Wing D2489; ESTC R225633. AS7.

ASC(E) + **Lawsuit (extracts)**

Collation: 2⁰: A–2I⁴ 2K–3I² ²A–²2G² [$3 signed (-Q3, 2B1, 2G1,2,3, 2I1, 2P2, 2R2, 2S2, 2V2, 2Z1,2, 3A1,2, 3B1, 3G1,2, 3I2, 3H2,3, ²A2, ²B2, ²C2, ²D2, ²E2, ²F1, ²G2, ²H2, ²I2, ²K2, ²L2, ²M2, ²N2, ²O2, ²P2, ²Q2, ²R2, ²S2, ²T2, ²V2, ²X2, ²Y2, ²Z2, ²2A2, ²2B2, ²2C2, ²2D2, ²2E2, ²2F2, ²2G2; 3F2 missigned 2F2)] 234 leaves, paginated [i–viii], 1–336, *337–340*, 1–117, *118–120* (pp. 198 misnumbered 200, 243–246 misnumbered 343–346, 277–280 misnumbered 275–278, 282–283 misnumbered 280–281).

SOURCES OF PASSAGES UTILIZING ANGLO-SAXON TYPES:

C4ʳ (p. 15) From **1666.1** C4ʳ: *ASC*(E) 1087 (extract), as Clark 1970: 12/73–79;

F1ᵛ (p. 34) From **1666.1** F1ᵛ: Lawsuit (*c*.995) about the estate of Snodland, K (Sawyer 1456), as Robertson 1956: 69/15–20.

TYPE:

Main text in Arthur Nicholls's English-size Roman (Body 94) interspersed with his English-size Italic.

AS7: Nicholas Nicholls's Somnerian Pica Anglo-Saxon combined with a Long Primer Roman occurs in text as listed above.

Special sorts shown:

9 (+ 1) lower-case sorts:	ð, *e*, ꝼ, ȝ, Ð, ꝑ, ꞃ, ꞇ; þ, ƿ; no ð used;
1 capital:	Є;
1 other:	⁊.

Total: 12 sorts.

Copies seen: BL 21.c.7, G11803; TCD HH.bb.10 (owned by William Palliser); LFL 11H.

Copies also at: BCL, BUL, CGC, KCC, CSJ, CLL, CUW, DCL, DUL, GUL, KNA, LCL, LGI, LLS, LUL, MJRUL, NewCL, NPG, NT, NUL, OBL, OAS, OBC, OCC, OEC, OMaC, OMC, OStE, OWmC, OWoC, OXC, SoUL, SUL, WCF, WiCL, WRL, YML, BSB, GUB; FSL, USLC, NYCU, HHL, HUL, IUL, LCP, NLC, NWU, UCLA, UMI, UNC, UPL, UTA, UTK, WBU, YUB, TUL; AHC, ANU, ATL, QSC, UAL, VSC, VUW.

Bibliography: McKenzie & Bell 2005: II.11 (14 July 1671); Maddison *et al.* 1953: no. 33; Pennington 1982 (see index for references).

1671.3: Skinner, Stephen, *Etymologicon Linguæ Anglicanæ*. London: Thomas Roycroft (typis) for Henry Brome, Robert Clavell, Benjamin Tooke, and Thomas Sawbridge, 1671. Wing S3947; ESTC R7781. AS7.
Edited by Thomas Henshaw from unpublished materials left at Skinner's death in 1667.
Words
    Collation: 2^0 mainly in 4s: [Booklet 1] π^2 a^2 B–D^4 E–V^2 [Booklet 2] 2A–2V^4 2X–2Z^2 [Booklet 3] 3A–3Y^4 3Z^6 [Booklet 4] 4A–5V^4 5X^2 [\$2 signed (+3Z; -a2, V2, 5X2)] 400 leaves, unnumbered.
TYPE:
Main text of Dictionary entries in a Pica Roman (Body 81).
AS7: Nicholas Nicholls's Somnerian Pica Anglo-Saxon combined with the Pica Roman.
Special sorts shown in specimen on V2^v:

	11 lower-case sorts:	ð, *e*, f, ʒ, ı, ꝑ, ſ, τ, ẏ; þ, p;
	5 capitals:	Є, Ƕ, ꟽ, S, Ð;
	2 others:	þ, ꟷ (broad-topped).
Total:	18 sorts.	

Special sorts shown in text 2A3^v–5X1^v:

	12 lower-case sorts:	ð, *e* (1st on 2C3^v), f, ʒ, ı (1st on 2D4^v), ꝑ, ſ, τ, ẏ (1st on 2D1^v); þ (1st on 2E1^v), ð (1st on 2F1^r), p;
	6 capitals:	Æ^2, Є, Ƕ, ꟽ, S, Ð;
	No other sorts.	
Total:	18 sorts.	

Overall total: 20 sorts.

    Copies seen: CUL Bb*.8.41b(B) (with ð written in by hand in the specimen on V2^v), Bb*.8.42b(C), Bury.17.9; CCC L.5.4; LFL 18I.
    Copies also at: BL, BCL, BPL, BSE, BUL, CCA, CGC, CSJ, CTH, TCC, CaCL, CLL, DCL, DRD, DUL, EAL, ECL, EdUL, GUL, HCL, HHC, KBG, KNA, LCL, LHL, LRS, LSH, MJRUL, MTP, NLS, NLW, NT, OBL, OAS, OBC, OCC, OEC, OHC, OJC, OLC, OMaC, ONC, OQC, OSA, OSJ, OStC, OCT, OTI, OWmC, OWoC, OXC RLW, SBT, SML, SoUL, SPC, SUL, UBL, WAL, WCL, WiCL, WIHM, WoCL, YML, RIA, TCD, ULim, BPN, GUB; FSL, USLC, NYHS, UTS, HHL, HUL, IUL, KSRL, LCP, NLC, SCN, SIU, SLU, UCBL, UCDL, UCRL, UMI, UTA, UVL, WUM, YUB, TUL; MTC, NLA, OLS, OUL, SCI, VSL, VUW.
Bibliography: Görlach 2002: 92–93; Kerling 1979: 135–156; Weekley 1931.
Facsimile: Hildesheim: G. Olms, 1970 (slightly reduced) from Münster, Englisches Seminar, XVIII.5366/1.

1671.4: Phillips, Edward (Milton's nephew), *The New World of Words: Or, a Universal English Dictionary*. 3rd edn of **1658.3**. London: no printer stated for Nathaniel Brookes 1671. Wing P2071; ESTC R6416.

    Collation: 2⁰: π⁴ b⁴ χ² A–3A⁴. [396] p.

Words, none printed using special AS sorts.

    Copy seen: BL 741.k.28.

    Copies also at: BHCL, CUW, DAL, DUL, EdUL, GML, HFL, HU, KUL, LBL, LJM, LU, LUL, MCS, NJRUL, MTP, NLS, NLW, NRL, NT, NU, NUL, OBL, OEF, ONC, SHU, YUL, DML, TCD; FSL, USLC, NYPL, HHL, HUL, IUL, AAS, BMC, JCB, NLC, UCH, UCLA, UTA, UVL; ATL.

1672.1: Selden, John, *Titles of Honor* (3rd edn, re-set from **1631.1**). London: Evan Tyler and R. Holt for John Leigh, Thomas Dring, and Thomas Bassett, 1672. Wing S2440, S2440A, S2440B = ESTC R22094, R218681, R221821. AS7.

AS Laws (extracts)+

    Collation: 2⁰ in 4s: π² a⁴ b–c⁶ A–5B⁴ 5C² [$2 signed (+b3, c3; 2C missigned C)] 394 leaves, paginated [i–xxxvi], 1–756 (pp. 388 misnumbered 352, 389 misnumbered 345, 503 misnumbered 502, 516–517 misnumbered 508–9). State 2 indicated by pp. 516–517 numbered correctly.

SOURCES OF PASSAGES UTILIZING ANGLO-SAXON TYPES:

M3ʳ (p. 93)	From **1631.1** O2ʳ: Law Ine Prol. (extract; Liebermann I.88);
3R2ʳ (p. 499)	From **1631.1** 4D3ʳ: OE Bede II.14 (Miller I.1/138/16–17);
3R3ʳ (p. 501)	From **1631.1** 4D4: Law Norðleoda 2–5 (Liebermann I.460);
3R3ᵛ (p. 502)	From **1631.1** 4D4ᵛ: Law II Cnut 58,1–2 (Liebermann I.350);
	From **1631.1** 4E1ʳ: Charter assigning lease of land by Oswald bp of Worcester (Sawyer 1332; Robertson 1939: no. 55, p. 114/3–4);
3R4ʳ (p. 503)	From **1631.1** 4E1ʳ: Extract from glossed Ps 67.27;
	From **1631.1** 4E1ᵛ: Ælfric, Life of St George (Skeat 1881: I.308, lines 5–7 abridged);
3R4ᵛ–3S1ʳ (pp. 504–5)	From **1631.1** 4E2ᵛ: OE Bede v.4 (Miller I.2/394/14–16), also III.2 (Miller 158/7–8);
3S1ʳ (p. 505)	From **1631.1** 4E3ʳ: OE Bede III.14 (Miller I.1/194/4–5);
3S1ᵛ (p. 506)	From **1631.1** 4E3ʳ: ASC D 870 (Thorpe 1861: I.138/17–20);
	From **1631.1** 4E3ᵛ: Diploma of William I supporting the rights of Baldwin abbot of Bury St Edmunds 31 May 1081, extract (Pelteret 28, as Douglas 1932: 50–5, no. 7);
3S2ʳ (p. 507)	From **1631.1** 4E4ʳ: OE Bede II.9 (Miller I.1/122/19);
	From **1631.1** 4E4: ASC D 897, 1013 (Thorpe 1861: I.175/29–32, 270/41);

3S2ᵛ (p. 508)	From 1631.1 4E4ᵛ: Writ of Edward the Confessor 1042 x1066 to St Paul's, London (Sawyer 1104; Gibbs 1939: 9; Harmer 1989: no. 54);
	From 1631.1 4F1ʳ: ASC D 905 (Thorpe 1861: I.181/35–36);
3S3ʳ (p. 509)	From 1631.1 5Z3ᵛ: Ælfric's Glossary: Extract (Zupitza 1880: 300/15; Wright/Wülcker 1883–4: no. 10);
3S3ᵛ (p. 510)	From 1631.1 4F2ʳ: ASC D 886 (Thorpe 1861: I.157/16–18);
3T2ʳ (p. 515)	From 1631.1 4G1ʳ: Law II Cnut 71–1a (Liebermann I.356–358);
	From 1631.1 4G1ʳ: Law 'Geþyncðo' 2 (Liebermann I.456);
3T3ʳ (p. 517)	From 1631.1 4G2: Law II Cnut 71.1–5 (Liebermann I.358);
3V2ʳ (p. 523)	From 1631.1 4H2ʳ: ASC E 1064 (Thorpe 1861: I.331/5–6);
3V2ᵛ (p. 524)	From 1631.1 4H2ᵛ: Law Ine Prol. (extract; Liebermann I.88–9);
4K2ᵛ (p. 628)	From 1631.1 5A2ʳ: Law Ine 10 (extract; Liebermann I.94);
4L2ᵛ (p. 636)	From 1631.1 5B3ʳ: Ælfric, *On the New Testament* (extract; Marsden 2008: 228/877);
4P4ᵛ–4Q1ʳ (pp. 672–673)	From 1631.1 5G4ᵛ: OE Martyrology re St George (Rauer 2013: §67/1–4, 6–13);
4Q1ᵛ (p. 674)	From 1631.1 5H1ʳ: Ælfric, Life of St George (Skeat 1881: I.308, lines 28–29).

TYPE:

Main text in Arthur Nicholls's English-size Roman (Body 95) interspersed with his English-size Italic;

AS7: Nicholas Nicholls's Pica Anglo-Saxon occurs in combination with a Pica Roman as indicated above, also in words on c4ᵛ, c6ʳ, 3Q2ʳ, 3T3ᵛ, 3T4ᵛ, 3V3ʳ, 4F2ᵛ, 4H2ᵛ, 4V2ᵛ, 4V3ᵛ.

Special sorts shown:

	12 lower-case sorts:	ð, *e*, ꝼ, ȝ, ı, ƿ, ſ, τ, ẏ; þ, ð, p;
	8 capitals:	A, Æ¹, Æ², Є, Ⴐ, ᛖ, S, Ð;
	3 others:	þ, ꝫ, ꝭ.
Total:	23 sorts.	

Copies seen: State 1:

Wing S2440: TCD GG.bb.34 (owned by William Palliser?); Wing S2440B: OBL Vet.A3.c.149;

State 2 (with pp. 516–517 correctly numbered):

Wing S2440: BL 605.g.14; CUL Pet.P.4.6 (with addition of 2 leaves containing a list of books printed for John Starkey, fl.1656–89); TCD RR.d.31 (owned by Claude Gilbert), OBL Vet.A3.c.177 (with ±4Z3);

Wing S2440A: CUL O.2.31 (with contemporary gold-tooled binding of brown calf); DML M1.3.11;

Bibliography: see 1631.1.
Edition: N.J. Clark, *Titles of Honor / By John Selden*, Lawbook Exchange, 2006.

1673.1: Dugdale, Sir William, *Monasticon Anglicanum*, vol. III; for vols I and II see 1655.3 and 1661.1. London: Thomas Newcomb I or II for Abel Roper, John Martin, and Henry Herringman, 1673. Wing D2486B. AS7.
Charters
>   **Collation:** 2⁰: A–3B⁴ 3C–3G² ²3A–²3Z⁴ 4A–4B⁴ 4C–4D² [$2 signed (-A1,2, G1, Q1, 3C2, 3D2, 3E2, 3F2, 3G2, 4C2, 4D2; G2 missigned F2)] 306 leaves, paginated [i–viii], 1–394, 1–218 (pp. nos ²120–129 not used; no pp.nos assigned to 3C2; pp. 112–114, 393–394, ²1–2, ²210 not numbered, pp. 119 misnumbered 117, ²113 misnumbered 123).
>   Note: Evidently printed in two booklets with insufficient space allowed for Part I, as indicated by the overlap in signatures at 3A–G.

SOURCES OF PASSAGES UTILIZING ANGLO-SAXON TYPES:

2Q3ᵛ (p. 302)	From 1658.1 2R1ʳ: Charter of King Æthelstan granting privileges to St Paul's (as Birch 1883–99: II.no. 735)
2Q4ʳ (p. 303)	From 1658.1 2R2ʳ: Æthelflæd's bequest to St Paul's of lands at Laver (E) and Cockhampstead (Hrt) (as Whitelock 1930: no. 22);
2Q4ᵛ (p. 304)	From 1658.1 2R2ᵛ–2S1ʳ: Charter of Cnut (as Kemble 1839–48: VI.no.1319);
	From 1658.1 2S1ᵛ: Writ of Edward the Confessor to St Paul's (as Gibbs 1939: no. 1);
2R2ᵛ (p. 308)	From 1658.1 2T2ᵛ: Writ of William I granting the castle and land at Bishop's Stortford (Hrt) to Bp Maurice of London (as Gibbs 1939: no. 5).

TYPE:
Main text in a Pica Roman (Body 81.5) interspersed with Granjon's 2nd Pica Italic 'pendante' (e.g., on B3ʳ, 2Q2ᵛ);
AS7: Nicholas Nicholls's Somnerian Pica Anglo-Saxon occurs in combination with the Pica Roman in text as indicated under Sources above;
Special sorts shown:

>   12 lower-case sorts: ð, *e*, ꞙ, ȝ, Ð, 1, ꝥ, ꞃ, ꞇ, ẏ; þ, ð, p;
>   8 (+1) capitals: A, Æ¹, Æ², Є, Ⱡ, ⱺ, S, W;
>   2 others: þ, ꝯ.

Total: 23 sorts.

Copies seen: APL MM.I.5 (3C2 not shown); ECC 306.2.58 (3C2 (stub) not shown, 3D–3G misplaced after 4B4); TCD G.c.19 (A3 shown before A2, lacks A4; owned by Claudius Gilbert), RR.b.30 (4C1.2 misplaced after 3C1; owned by Claudius Gilbert), Fag.Q.3.15.

Copies also at: Wing S2440: CUL, ChestC, EdUL, KNA, LWI, MJRUL, NCL, PBN; USLC, NYCU, HHL, NLC, TUL; MonUL, QSC.

Wing S2440A: BCL, BCLNI, CUL, CCC, CGC, CMC, TCC, ChestC, DUL, DWL, EdUL, LHL, LL, LSH, LUL, MJRUL, NLS, NLW, OHM, OJC, OXC, SUL, WAL, NUIG, BSB; USLC, NYPL, HHL, HUL, IUL, NWU, PUL, UCBL, UCDL, UCLA, UCSR, YUB, MMU, UVC.

Wing S2440B: DUL, HRC, LPL, MJRUL, NT, OBL, OBC, WRL, DEWL, GUB; FSL, SMU, QUK; UAL.

Bibliography: McKenzie & Bell 2005: 11.9 (1 June 1671), 11.11 (14 July 1671), 11.37 (11 June 1672), 11.79 (19 Jan 1675); Maddison et al. 1953: no. 6; Pennington 1982 (see index for references).

1673.2: Dugdale, Sir William, *Monasticon Anglicanum*, vol. II, re-issue of **1661.1**. London: Alice Warren (typis) for Robert Scott, 1673. Wing D2486A; ESTC R174768.

1673.3: Selden, John, *Uxor Ebraica, seu de Nuptiis et Divortiis ex Jure Civili, id est, Divino & Talmudico, Veterum Ebræorum, Libri Tres*. 2nd edn of **1646.6**. Frankfurt an der Oder: Andreas Beckmann for Jeremias Schrey, 1673. BLG S1858.

Collation: 4^0: 2 pts π^2)(^{4} 2)(^{4}(lacks)(4) 3)(^{2} A–2Y^4 2Z^2 3A–3L^4; pt 2 begins at 3L4, A–2I^4. [18], 136 p, fos 137–144, 145–456, [22], 248, [8] p.

The passages in AS included in Bk II, chs 27 and 29 in **1646.6** are omitted at 2B4^r (p. 199) and 2E3^v (p. 222).

Copies seen: CUL L*.7.9(AA), Hunt.45.18; TCC L.11.4; TCD Fag.Q.3.14 (lacks 2P2).

Copies also at: BL, ChC, EdUL, EUL, GUL, LFL, LL, LPL, LSE, LSH, MCS, MJRUL, OBL, OAS, OBC, OMC, ONC, OXC, RUL, SoUL, UBL, WIHM.

1673.4: Verstegan, Richard, *A Restitution of Decayed Intelligence in Antiquities*. 6th edn of **1605.2**. London: printer not stated, for Samuel Mearne, John Martin and Henry Herringman, 1673. Wing V271; ESTC R9443.

Collation: 8^0: *^{4} A–2B^8 2C^4. [24], 374, [18] p.

Words in AS and other Germanic languages appear in Textura with no special sorts.

Copy seen: CUL R.5.59.

Copies also at: BL, BCL, CCC, GCC, CMC, CSJ, CSS, DAL, EAL, ECL, GML, HCL, LFL, LMT, LSH, MJRUL, NT, NUL, OBL, OJC, OStH, OWoC, OXC, RLW, RUL, SCL, UBL,

WCL, WIHM, TCD, PBN; FSL, HHL, HUL, IUL, GUW, LCP, NLC, PUL, SLU, UCBL, UCLA, UTA, UVL, WBU, YUB, TUL; ANZ, AUNZ.

1674.1: Camden, William, ed. John Philipot (Somerset Herald) and W[illiam] D[u-gard], *Remains, Concerning Britain: their Languages, Names, Surnames, Allusions, Anagramms, Armories, Moneys, Impresses, Apparel, Artillerie, Wise Speeches, Proverbs, Poesies, Epitaphs*, 7th edn of **1605.1** re-set from 6th edn **1657.1**. London: no printer stated, for Charles Harper and John Amery, 1674. Wing C375; ESTC R21833. Individual sorts only: AS7 ȝ and **p**.

Lord's Prayer; Letter-symbols

> **Collation:** 8⁰: A⁴ B–2N⁸ [$4 signed (-A1,2,4); 2C3missigned 2C5] 284 leaves, paginated [i–viii], 1–556, 557–560 (pp. 193–208 (= sig. O) misnumbered 191–206, 375 misnumbered 374).

SOURCES OF PASSAGES IN ANGLO-SAXON TYPES:

C7ᵛ–8ʳ (pp. 30–1)   From **1657.1** D4ʳ: Lord's Prayer, with 'no' at line 7;
C8ʳ (p. 31)   From **1657.1** D4: Lord's Prayer (with marginal variants from another version) with ſwa ſwa at line 3, and coſtnung at line 7.

TYPE:

Main text in Arthur Nicholls's Pica Roman (Body 82) interspersed with Nicholls's Pica Italic (with variant **k**).

C7ᵛ–8ʳ (pp. 30–31): no special sorts, but æ is correct in the second version of the Lord's Prayer in OE; suprascript translation to the first version in Nicholls's Pica Italic.

AS7: The Somnerian Pica Anglo-Saxon (individual special sorts only) occurs on D5ᵛ (p. 42) in a report on the spelling reform practices advocated by Smith in **1568.3: 3**, p (erron for þ).

Note: A passage from Chaucer's *Nun's Priest's Tale* is printed in Nicholls's Pica Italic with no special sorts on 2D8.

> **Copies seen:** CPH K.7.23; BL 292.b.1, 980.e.9 (lacks A1).
>
> **Copies also at:** CSS, CUW, DUL, GUL, HOL, LRS, LSH, LWI, MJRUL, NAL, NLW, NT, OBL, OAS, OCC, OJC, OStC, OXC, SDC, SUL, UCL, WAL, YML, NLI, TCD, ULim, PBN, GUB; FSL, HHL, HUL, IUL, DDUL, NLC, NWU, PUL, SLC, SLU, UCBL, UCH, UCLA, UMI, UPL, UTA, UTK, WMUL, YUB, TUL; UAL, USL.

Bibliography: see **1605.1**.

1674.2: Ray, John, *A Collection of English Words*. London: Henry Brugis for Thomas Burrell, 1674. Wing R388; ESTC 236812. For 2nd edn see **1691.3**.

> **Collation:** 8⁰: A–K⁸ L⁴. [16], 77, 76–142, 173–178, [2], p.

AS words, along with those from other languages, are cited in Italic type with no special sorts.
>Copy seen: CUL Pp*.4.32(F).
>Copies also at: BL, LPL; IUL.

Bibliography: Keynes 1951: no. 23.

1674.3: Blount, Thomas (1618–79)], *Glossographia: or, a Dictionary, interpreting the Hard Words of Whatsoever Language, now used in our refined English Tongue; With Etymologies, Definitions, and Historical Observations on the same.* London: Thomas Newcomb for Robert Boulter, 1674. Wing B3337; ESTC R15304. 4th edn of **1656.3**, 2nd edn **1661.2**, 3rd edn **1670.2**.
OE etymologies occasionally cited but no Anglo-Saxon types
Collation: 8^0: A–2Y^8, 2Z^4 (2O3 missigned 2P3; pp 206, 478–479 misnumbered 226, 479–478 respectively); [16], 688, 687–706, [4] p.
Type: Main text in a Long Primer Roman (Body 67) in double columns.
No Anglo-Saxon types but OE etymologies occasionally cited in the same Textura as is used for headwords, as s.v. *Gospel*.
>Copy seen: CUL U.6.91.
>Copies also at: BL, CGC, LCL, LL, NLW, NT, NUL, OBC, OBL, SDL, UBL; NYPL, HHL, HUL, GUW, IMI, IUL, MUL, NLM, UCBL, UCLA, UPL, USNA, UTA, YUB, UWO; ATL, OUL, USL.

Bibliography: Alston V.51.

1675.1: Ridley, Sir Thomas, expanded edn by John Gregory, *A View of The Civile and Ecclesiasticall Law*, 5th edn of **1634.1** slavish reprint of 4th edn **1662.1**. Oxford: Henry Hall for Richard Davis, 1675. Wing R1456, R1457 = ESTC R29321, R7470. AS7.
Laws, Will of Byrhtric
>**Collation:** 8^0: A–2D^8 [$4 signed (-A1, F4, M4, N4, 2B3)] 216 leaves, paginated [i–xii], 1–396, *397–430* (pp. nos 181–190 not used).

SOURCES OF PASSAGES UTILIZING ANGLO-SAXON TYPES: as **1662.1**.
TYPE:
Main text in a Pica Roman (Body 81.5); Notes (in which the OE passages occur) in a Long Primer Roman (Body 67).
AS7: Nicholas Nicholls's Somnerian Pica Anglo-Saxon occurs in text combined with the Pica Roman on H2^r (p. 103), N3^v–5^v (pp. 196–200), Q8^v–R1^r (pp. 254–255), R4^v–5^r (pp. 262–263), S4^v (p. 278), S5^v (p. 280), S6^r (p. 281). Special sorts shown:

>11 lower-case sorts: ð, f, ᵹ, ı, p, ſ, τ, ẏ; þ, ð, ƿ;
>4 capitals: A, Æ¹, Є, Ð;

3 others: þ, ꝫ, ꝛ.
Total: 18 sorts.
Note: As in 1662.1 ð used for 8 on N3ᵛ in 8eınꞇ.
> **Copies seen:** Wing R1456: CUL H.11.72, CC.4.44; Wing R1457: CUL Broughton 190, Huntingdon 60.1; APL AA.V.35 (lacks 2D8).
> **Copies also at:** Wing R1456: BL, CJC, CSJ, DWL, LPL, OBL, OJC, YML, KSC, TCD, ULim, PBN, GUB; HHL, HUL, IUL, NWU, PUL, UCH, UMI, YUB.
> Wing R1457: BL, TCC, DUL, EAL, EdUL, LPL, LSH, NLS, NLW, OBL, OAS, OHC, OPH, WCL, DKI, GUB; FLS, UTS, HHL, HUL, KSRL, UCBL, UCDL, UCLA, WMUL, YUB.

Bibliography: Wing R1456: Madan 1895–1931: III.317, no. 3074.
Wing R1457: Madan 1895–1931: III.337, no. 3119.

1675.2: Janssonius, Joannes, *Atlas Major*, vols V–VI, split re-issue of **1659.2** (*Novus Atlas*, vol. IV, with Latin text of Camden's *Britannia*, as in **1607.2**). Amsterdam: Joannes Janssonius II van Waesberge, [1675]. CAS4.
> **Edition:** The setting of the text is identical with **1659.2**, split into two: vol. V, A–4R (Southern England, and Wales); and vol. VI, 4S–6I + ²A–S (Northern England + Scotland and Ireland), or, in a copy in a private collection (called OxonPC by Krogt 1997), vol. V, A–4C, vol. VI, 4D–6I + ²A–S. The Vienna copy is dated 1646, so it is possible that it is made up of sheets from the 1st edn **1646.3**, of which the **1659.2** edn is a slavish re-setting.
> **Copies:** None seen; as listed by Krogt 1997, one in MBS, one in VON, and one in 'OxonPC'. Information on that in 'OxonPC' kindly supplied by the private owner (vol. V dated 1659, vol. VI dated 1662, in contemporary Dutch gold-tooled white vellum binding).

Bibliography: Krogt 1997: 1:406.5–6.

1675.3: Reuter, Johannes, *Oratio Dominica XL. Linguarum.* 2nd edn of **1662.6**. Rostock: Johann Keil, 1665. Facsimile ed. B. Jégers (Copenhagen: Imanta, 1954).
> **Collation:** 8⁰:)(⁸. [16] p.

Lord's Prayer in Anglo-Saxon printed in a Pica Italic with no special sorts on)(5ʳ.
> **Copy seen:** facsimile only.

1676.1: Speed, John, *The Theatre of the Empire of Great Britaine Presenting an Exact Geography of the Kingdomes of England, Scotland, Ireland, and the Iles adjoyning, with the Shires, Hundreds, Citys and Shire Townes, within the Kingdome of England.* London: no printer stated for Thomas Basset and Richard Chiswell 1676. 5th edn of **1611.1**. Wing S4886; ESTC R13825. AS2/3.

OE proper names

Collation: 2⁰: ¶², A–3V², [Addition 3 ✻² ⁺ ², 5 unsigned bifolia], 3X–4E², [Addition ¶¹, A–2E²], 4F–4H² [$1 signed (+ B2, C2, 4G2;—¶1, A1)]. 156 leaves [+ additions of 14 and 56 leaves], foliated (always on the text side) [i–viii], 1–94, 99–126, 131–132, 137–146, *147–152* (fo nos 19–20 not used), paginated 95–98, 127–130, 133–136 (pp. 95–96, 127–128, 130, 133–134 not numbered).

Note 1: The text is printed back to back with the maps, and the map pages, being always a double-page opening on the reverse side of text pages, receive no numbers.

Note 2: This make-up (apart from the additions) mirrors that of earlier editions, as 1614.1.

TYPE: The size varies according to the amount of text in relation to the amount of space available.

The preferred type is a Pica Roman (as on L1ʳ)   Body 82   Face 80 × 1.6: 2.5
but the following also occur:
an English-size Roman (as on I1ʳ)   Body 95   Face 90 × 2.4: 3.1
a Long Primer Roman (as on Y1ʳ, 2K1ʳ)   Body 65   Face 60 × 1.4: 2.0
Italics of the same size as the main text are used to highlight names, etc.

AS 2/3: Two Anglo-Saxon Pica designs are used mixed together in county names. They occur with main text in English-size (as on I1ʳ), with Pica (as on L1ʳ), and with Long Primer (as on Y1ʳ and 2K1ʳ).

AS2: The Parkerian Pica Anglo-Saxon.
Special sorts shown: ð, ꝼ, ı, ꝑ, ſ, ꞇ, þ; Æ, &.   7 + 2
AS3: The Lambardian Pica Anglo-Saxon.
Special sorts shown: h (= ꝺ), ꝑ, ẏ, ð.   4

Anglo-Saxon **i** is used (once), but not **g**. The setting is prone to errors, as **f** for **r**, **r** for **s**, **s** for **r**, **ð** for **d**.

Copies seen: CUL Qq*.1.280(AA); Hanson.bb.43; Ely.a.188 (lacks ¶1).
Copies also at: APL, BL, BrCL, CGC, CSJ, TCC, CLL, DCL, EdUL, GNM, HHC, LHL, LSA, LSH, MJRUL, NLS, NLW, NT, OBL, OBrC, OGF, OMaC, OMC, OQC, OXC, RCL, SUL, WIHM, DEWL, DML, NLI, TCD, PBN, GUB; NYPL, NYHS, NYCU, HHL, HUL, IUL, BMC, JCB, NLC, UTA, UVL, YUB; VSL.

Bibliography: Skelton 1970: no. 92.

1676.2: Sammes, Aylett, *Britannia Antiqua Illustrata*. London: Thomas Roycroft, 1676. Wing S535; ESTC R19100. AS7.

Ælfric homilies, Laws, ASC (A), OE Bede (all extracts)

Collation: 2⁰ in 4s: π¹ A⁴ B² C–4F⁴ [$2 signed (-3N2)] 299 leaves, paginated [i–x], 1–582, *583–588* (pp. 140, 144, 184, 206, 228, 446, 455, 468–470, 520, 526, 532, 548, 553, 560 not numbered; pp. 127 misnumbered 129, 285 misnumbered 275, 437 misnumbered 447).

SOURCES OF PASSAGES UTILIZING ANGLO-SAXON TYPES:

3H3ʳ (p. 417)   From 1644.2 K1ᵛ/17–20: OE Bede I.15 (Miller 52/2–4, 8–9);
                From 1644.2 3V2ʳ/38–41: ASC (A) 449 (Thorpe 1861: I.20/18–21);
3M2ᵛ (p. 448)   From 1670.1 V4ᵛ–5ʳ: Ælfric, Homily *De Falsis Diis*, as Pope 1967–8: II.682–683, lines 104–125;
3N4ʳ (p. 459)   From 1670.1 X6ʳ: Ælfric, Homily Feria III de dominica oratione (opening sentence), as Clemoes 1997: 325/3–6;
3X1ᵛ (p. 518)   From 1639.4 Q1 (10, 12): Laws Wihtræd, §§9, 11 (Liebermann I.13), with MnE t;
4D3ʳ–4E3ᵛ (pp. 56–78)   From 1644.2 A1ʳ–B3ᵛ: Laws of Ine (in full with MnE t; Liebermann I.89–123);

TYPE:

Main text in Arthur Nicholls's English-size Roman (Body 93) interspersed with his English-size Italic (mixed with Great Primer capitals, e.g. P4ʳ).

A Paragon Roman (Body 132) is used for the Letters of Pope Gregory on 3Q2ʳ–3S3ʳ.

AS7: Nicholas Nicholls's Somnerian Pica Anglo-Saxon occurs in the specimen on 3G3ᵛ (p. 410) and in text as indicated above under Contents.

Special sorts shown in the specimen:

    11 lower-case sorts: ð, *e*, f, ᵹ, ı, ɲ, ſ, τ; þ, ð, ƿ;
    6 + 1 capitals: Æ², Ł [see Note 1 below], Ɛ, Ƕ, Ϻ, S, Ð; lower-case 'wynn' is shown also as a capital;
    2 + 1 others: ᚼ, þ; a semi-colon is used in place of the punctus versus.

Total: 19 + 2 sorts.

Note 1: The Ł is not the same as that shown by the James foundry, does not occur in text, and is probably an E with the central arm broken off.

Note 2: The lower-case y shows no dot, so is not included here as a special sort.

Note 3: The statement in English 'An imperfect Sentence the *English Saxons* marked with a single point ᛫ [actually a punctus versus] a full period with three, placed thus (∴)', which occurs at the bottom, derives from the Latin statement in Junius 1655.1 π8ʳ.

Special sorts shown in text in combination with Arthur Nicholls's Pica Roman (which is used for parallel English translation on 4D3ʳ–4E3ᵛ);

Special sorts shown in text:

    12 lower-case sorts: ð, *e*, f, ᵹ, ı, ɲ, ſ, τ; ẏ; þ, ð, ƿ;
    6 capitals: Æ², Ɛ, Ƕ, Ϻ, S, Ð;
    2 other: þ, ᚼ.

Total: 20 sorts.

Note 4: An arabic 7 is used for 'and' until 4D3ʳ (Laws of Ine), when ꝛ takes over. On 3X1ᵛ a Hebrew letter Daleth (?) is used.

Note 5: On 3G3ᵛ there are also a Runic and a Gothic character-set (both woodcuts); Runic also occurs in text or words on 3H1ʳ, 3K4, 3L1ᵛ, 3L2ʳ, 3L3ʳ, 3L4ᵛ, 3M2ʳ, 3M3ʳ.

Old Norse is printed in a Textura on 3K2, 3L3ᵛ–4ʳ, 3O4ʳ; Welsh is printed in a Textura on 3V2ʳ.

> Copies seen: APL Q.III.1; CUL N.13.15; ECC 310.2.30 (lacks illustration after A4); TCD RR.b.36, W.a.25; LFL 18H (illustration after A4 bound in upside down); MBS Res/2⁰Brit.85 (signed 'William Evans').
>
> Copies also at: BL, BCL, BPL, BUL, CCA, CCC, CMC, CSJ, CTH, TCC, CLL, CUW, DUL, ECL, GlCL, GUL, HCL, LCL, LHL, LSH, MJRUL, NAL, NCL, NLS, NLW, NMS, NT, NUL, OBL, OBC, OCC, OEC, OHC, OJC, OLC, OMC, ONC, OQC, OSJ, OSL, OStE, OWoC, PML, SDL, SoUL, SUL, UBL, WiCL, DML, DRCS, NLI, PBN, BSB, GUB; FSL, NYPL, HHL, HUL, IUL, AAS, ISU, LCP, MUL, NLC, NWU, PTS, UCH, UCLA, UCRL, UNC, UTA, UVL, YUB, QUK, TUL, UVC; NSW, SSA, USL, UWA, VPL.

Bibliography: Fell 1993: 88–89, 92; Fell 1996: 29–34; Parry 1995: 313–324. GR5280.

1676.3: Langhorne, Daniel (–1681), *An Introduction to the History of England: Comprising the Principal Affairs of this Land, from its first Planting to the Coming of the English Saxons.* London: for Charles Harper & John Avery, 1676. Wing L395; ESTC R13965. AS7.

Collation: 8⁰: π² B–O⁸; [4], 200, [8] p.

ME *Metrical Chronicle* attrib. 'Robert of Gloucester' (extract)

SOURCE OF PASSAGE UTILIZING ANGLO-SAXON TYPES:

B5v (p 10)   From **1643.1** Fır: ME *Metrical Chronicle* attrib. 'Robert of Gloucester', as Wright 1887, I.15, 37, lines 211–215, 505;

Type:

Main text in Pica Roman (Body 83)

AS7: The Somnerian Pica Anglo-Saxon combined with the Pica Roman is shown in the passage cited above.

Special sorts shown: 10 lower-case sorts: ð, e, f, ᵹ, ꞃ, ſ, τ, þ, ð, p;
                      3 capitals: E, Ð, Đ;
                      1 other: þ.
          Total: 14 sorts.

> Copy seen: CUL Syn.7.67.106.
>
> Copies also at: BL, CSJ, CUW, DUL, ECL, EdUL, LHL, NLS, OAS, OBL, SPC; GUB; FLS, HHL, HUL, UCH, UCLA, YUB.

1677.1: La Bigne, Margarinus de, *Maxima Bibliotheca Veterum Patrum, ex Antiquorum Scriptorum Ecclesiasticorum*, ed. Philippe Despont. Lyon: Anisson, 1677. Revised reprint of **1644.3**.

    Collation: (vol. xiii only) 2⁰ in 6s: π² A–3R⁶. [4], 755, [1] p.

Vol XIII includes Nicolaus Serarius's *Epistolæ S. Bonifacii* (**1618.2**), where the OE verse *Proverb from Winfred's Time* (Dobbie 1942: 57) occurs in Epistola lxi. It is taken over here on H4ʳ (p. 91) in a Pica Italic (with no special sorts) quoted as prose in a Latin prose letter itself printed in a Pica Roman.

    Copies seen: CUL 3.4.13, BL 464.f.13.

1678.1: Spelman, John, and Sir Henry, ed. Christopher Wase and Obadiah Walker, *Ælfredi Magni Anglorum Regis Invicissimi Vita*. Oxford: Sheldonian Theatre, 1678. Wing S4934; ESTC R4024 (note also T161493). AS7.

    Context: This edition is a Latin translation (probably by Wase) of the original written in English; the English version was subsequently edited by Hearne in 1709. According to Wood writing in 1679 a complaint was made in parliament against the printing of 'popish' books (including this one) at the Oxford Theatre: Wood, ed. Clark 1892: II.449.

    Note 1: The dedication hails Charles II as the true natural heir of King Alfred (A2r), thus prioritizing his Anglo-Saxon heritage. The editor, Obadiah Walker, was master of University College Oxford, which was thought (wrongly) to have been founded by King Alfred.

    Note 2: OUP bought the copyright from Spelman's executors 11 Nov 1672.

ASC, Laws, PPC (extracts), *Promissio Regis*

    Collation: 2⁰: A⁴ b² c² d² B–V² X–2R⁴ 2S–2V² [$3 signed (-A3, b2, c2, E2, 2N3, 2O3, 2P3, 2Q3, 2R3)] 136 leaves, paginated [i–xl], 1–220, *221–232* (pp. 186–189, 192–193, 218, 220 not numbered).

    Variant state indicated by b1 unsigned (CUL Qq*.2.134).

    Note: Between sigs b and c (in MBS copy after d2; in APL copy spread through sigs b–d) seven leaves of illustrations (versos blank), some by Burghers, are inserted.

SOURCES OF PASSAGES UTILIZING ANGLO-SAXON TYPES:

Except as otherwise indicated these instances of Old English occur in the Notes, printed in a Pica Roman, rather than the Great Primer of the main text.

O2ʳ (p. 35)	From **1643.1** 3Z4ᵛ: ASC 878 (extract), as Thorpe 1861: 148–149; the form Ƿeꞇmoꞃ is distinctive;
O2ᵛ (p. 36)	From **1568.2** O1ᵛ: Law Alfred and Guthrum 1, as Liebermann I.126;
X1ᵛ (p. 62)	From OBL Junius 60 (SC 5171; Junius's transcript from Vitellius A.vii (this part now destroyed by the 1731 fire)), fo 2: *Promissio Regis* with two sections on royal duties, as Stubbs 1874: 355–357, Wright and Halliwell 1841–3: II.194;

	the oath as Liebermann I.214; there is another text in Cleopatra B.xiii, 56ʳ/1–57ʳ/17, but, *pace* Stubbs, there is no collation in Junius 60; coll. Clayton 2008: 148–149; cf. **1689.3**, c1ᵛ–2ʳ.
Y1ʳ (p. 69)	From **1568.2** M3ᵛ: Law Alfred 41, as Liebermann I.74;
2B3ᵛ (p. 98)	From OBL Digby A.4 (SC 1605), art.12, 97ʳ/1–8: ME verse *Poema Morale* 1–4, as Marcus 1934: 169;
2F1ʳ (p. 125)	From **1666.1** C4ʳ: ASC(E) 108[7] (extract), as Thorpe 1861: 355; Clark 1970: 12/73–79
2O3ʳ–4ʳ (pp. 193–5)	From **1574.2** E2ᵛ–E4ᵛ: Latin version of King Alfred's will (Sawyer 1507; ed. Edwards 1866: 57–60, 71–75) in roman type;
2O4ᵛ–2P1ʳ (pp. 196–197)	From **1574.2** F1ʳ–2ʳ: OE prose preface to the Alfredian translation of Pope Gregory's *Pastoral Care* (as Sweet 1871–2: 2–9) with parallel Latin text from **1574.2** F3ʳ–4ᵛ in rh column; correction of Parker's reading ᵹɲetunᵹ to ᵹɲetun (line 1) is noted;
2P1ᵛ (p. 198)	From **1574.2** F2ᵛ: OE verse preface to the Alfredian *Pastoral Care*, as Dobbie 1942: 110, with parallel Latin text in rh column from **1574.2** F4ᵛ;
2P2 (pp. 199–200)	From **1643.1** C3ʳ–4ʳ: WS Genealogical Regnal List, with parallel Latin translation in rh column, as Dumville 1986: 21–25, Miller 1890–98: 486–488;
2Q1ʳ–2ᵛ (pp. 205–8)	From OBL Junius 15 (SC 5127; Junius's transcript of Tiberius B.i), pp. 9/28–13/9: *Orosius* I.1 (extract) as Bately 1980: 13/29–18/2, the passage about Ohthere and Wulfstan's voyages (Brewer 1952–3) in lh column with parallel Latin text in rh column.

TYPE:

Main text in a Great Primer Roman (leaded) interspersed with a Great Primer Italic.

Notes in Arthur Nicholl's Pica Roman (Body 81) interspersed with Granjon's Pica Italic 'pendante'.

AS7: Nicholas Nicholls's Somnerian Pica Anglo-Saxon used in combination with Arthur Nicholl's Pica Roman as indicated above under Contents and in words on E2ᵛ, O1ᵛ, X3ᵛ, Y3ᵛ, Y4ᵛ, 2B3ᵛ, 2E1–4 (in brackets in main text).

Special sorts shown:

	11 lower-case sorts:	ð, f, ᵹ, ı, ꝑ, ſ, τ, ẏ; þ, ð, p;
	10 + 1 capitals:	A, Æ¹, Æ², Є, Ŀ, Ð, Ϣ, S, Ð, Ƿ, W (on 2P2ʳ);
	3 + 1 others:	⁊, þ, ∴ ; also uses a raised dot on 2P2 and 2Q1–2.
Total:	24 + 2 sorts.	

AS5: Wheelockian English-size Anglo-Saxon E is used sporadically in combination with AS7 Pica on 2P2^r, 2Q1^v, 2Q2.

Copies seen: APL R.III.2; CUL Qq*.2.134 (2L3 ordered before 2L2; annot. with AS on F1^v and collation with Cleopatra B.xiii on X1^v), R.1.29 (large paper; gift of George I), R.1.35; LFL 18I; MBS Res/2⁰Brit.96.

Copies also at: BL, BCL, BUL, CCA, CCC, CGC, CMC, CPH, CSJ, TCC, CaCL, DCL, DUL, EdUL, GlCL, GML, LBL, LCL, LHL, LiCL, LMT, LSH, MJRUL, MTP, NAL, NLS, NLW, NT, OBL, OAS, OBC, OCC, OJC, OLC, OLMH, OMC, ONC, OQC, OSJ, StE, OTC, OWmC, OWoC, RCL, SCL, SML, SPC, SUL, UBL, WAL, WCF, WCL, WIHM, WoCL, DML, KSC, TCD, ULim, PBN, GCB, GUB; FSL, USLC, NYPL, HHL, HUL, IUL, JCB, KSRL, LCP, NLC, NWU, SLC, UCBL, UCLA, UOC, UTA, UTK, UVL, YUB, TUL; ASP, NLA, NSW, SSA, USL, VSL.

Bibliography: Carter 1975: 112–113; Fairer 1986: 807; Hagedorn 1997: 92–93; Keynes 1999: 254–256; Madan 1895–1931: III.no. 3197; Stanley 1987: 412–413; Wood 1892: II.449.

Note: *DNB* XX.538 refers to Obadiah Walker, *Versio Latina et Annotationes ad Alfredi Magni Vitam Joannis Spelman* (Oxford, 1678), fol., but I have been unable to locate such a separate work either as a printed book or as a manuscript.

Manuscript: OBL e.Mus.75 (English autograph; SC 3696); OBL Ballard 55 (a copy *c.*1660; SC 10841); OBL Rawlinson D.324 (prepared for the press by Hearne (1709); SC 15363).

1678.2: Du Fresne, Charles, Lord Du Cange, *Glossarium ad Scriptores Mediæ & Infirmæ Latinitatis.* Paris: Gabriel Martin for Louis Billaine (impensis), 1678. CAS6.

Words

Collation: [see also vol. III, i4^v]. 2⁰ in 4s:
[vol. I] π^2 $^2\pi^2$ $^\pi$A–H^4 $^\pi$I^6 $^\pi$K–R^4 A–V^4 X^4 (±X2.3) Y–4R^4 [$3 signed (+I4; -D3)] 418 leaves, paginated [I–VIII], i–lxxviii, in columns lxxvii–cc, 1–1372, *1373–1376* (col nos clxxxvii–cxc used twice; cols cxcix–cc not numbered; cols clxxxviii misnumbered clxxxiii, 101 misnumbered 01, 541–542 misnumbered 537–538, 975 misnumbered 675, 1341 misnumbered 341);
Note 1: State 2 shown by I4 unsigned; State 3 shown by col 101 numbered correctly.
[vol. II] π^2 ¶A–¶3D^4 ¶3E^6 A–2R^4 2S^4 (2S1 + χ1) 2T–3C^4 3D^6 [$3 signed (+¶3E4, 3D4; ¶F3 missigned F3, ¶2R3 missigned ¶2Q3)] 410 leaves, in columns [i–viii], 1–824, 1–808 (cols ^{2}655–656 misnumbered 656–657, ^{2}688 misnumbered 988);
Note 2: State 2 shown by cols ^{2}655–6 numbered correctly.
[vol. III] π^2 A–5D^4 5E^6 $^2\pi^2$ ($^2\pi^2$ + χ1–6) a–i^4 [$3 signed (+ 5E4)] 430 (+ 6) leaves, in columns [i–viii], 1–1560, then paginated [i–iv], 1–72 (col nos 1153–1154 not used; col nos 1239–1240 used twice).

SOURCES OF PASSAGES UTILIZING ANGLO-SAXON TYPES:
Dictionary entries showing use of Selden 1623.3, 1672.1, Somner 1659.1, 1660.1, Spelman 1626.1, 1664.1, and others.

TYPE:
Main text of Glossarium in Pierre Haultin's Pica Roman (Body 84) interspersed with Granjon's Pica Italic 'pendante' (e.g. 2Z1); nb. 2 Qs, e.g. on II.110 = G4ʳ.

CAS6: Du Cangian Pica Anglo-Saxon occurs in a specimen on πR4ʳ Illustration 48 and in words combined with Haultin's Pica Roman on [vol. I] cols 7, 39, 41, 53, 106–108, 139, 148, 177, 183, 186–187, 283, 313, 338, 348, 351, 366–368, 377, 385, 432–433, 508, 521, 550, 557, 561, 567, 575, 577, 586, 588, 590–591, 594, 602, 609, 621, 623, 627, 635636, 638, 647, 655, 690, 744, 746, 808, 825, 830, 850, 868, 910, 979, 982, 985, 999, 1009, 1026, 1033, 1117, 1172, 1202, 1215–1216, 1247, 1265–1267, 1270, 1332–1333.

Special sorts shown in specimen: ð, ꝼ, ȝ, þ, ꞃ, ꞇ, ẏ; ð, p.   9 lower-case sorts.

[vol. II] CAS6 occurs in words combined with Haultin's Pica Roman in ¶A- on cols 4, 6, 46, 61–62, 68, 138–139, 178, 180, 183, 222–223, 261, 269, 312, 317, 331, 335–336, 343, 351–353, 361–362, 365, 369–371, 378, 389–390, 423, 436–437, 445, 448–449, 452–453, 460, 462–464, 471, 474–476, 481–482, 491, 517–518, 539, 544–546, 562, 566, 585–586, 595–596, 600, 602–603, 605, 615–616, 618–619, 621–625, 633, 645, 678, 685, 691–693, 695–696, 698, 710, 716, 729, 732, 744–749, 751, 770, 772, 801–802, 804, 810, 813–814, 816–818, A- cols 6, 8, 22–23, 55, 94, 200, 205–207, 212–214, 220–221, 223, 238, 243, 247, 252, 264, 280, 300, 302, 305–308, 327–328, 339, 367, 375, 377, 422, 499, 512, 515, 554, 566, 581, 675–676, 679, 697, 715, 730, 749, 774;

[vol. III] CAS6 occurs in words combined with Haultin's Pica Roman on cols 6, 24, 41–42, 46, 50, 59, 67, 70, 78, 118, 120–121, 123, 129, 133, 146, 174, 193, 205, 239, 264, 285–286, 305, 319, 371, 432–433, 441, 461, 473, 501, 604, 610–611, 709, 721, 732–734, 743, 749, 756, 758, 848–849, 874, 876, 878, 883, 913, 921–922, 925, 932, 946, 968, 973, 976, 978–980, 987, 996, 1006, 1012, 1021, 1024, 1033, 1112, 1117–1118, 1121, 1126, 1158, 1167, 1169, 1189, 1195, 1200, 1203, 1214, 1218, 1224, 1229, 1246, 1344, 1346, 1355, 1360–1361, 1370, 1378, 1386, 1389, 1392, 1394–1395, 1397–1398, 1400–1406, 1410; on 2D4ᵛ (col 432) it occurs in a catchword.

> Copies seen: CUL Aa*.7.5–7; ECC S11.1.2–4 (Abp Sancroft's copy with his armorial crest gold-tooled on the covers); TCD Q.b.1–3 (vol. I lacks 4R4; gift of Thomas Herbert, e of Pembroke (d.1733)), ss.bb.16–18 (stub of vol. I sig. X2.3 cancel present; vol. II sig. 2S1χ1 misplaced after 2S3; owned by Richard Lapp (then Vicar of Kinsale, subsequently archdeacon of Cork 1688–90) who had it from the library of Sir John Percival 1686, and given by Claudius Gilbert); LFL 30E (vol. I).
>
> Vol I: 1st state (with col 101 misnumbered 01) shown by LFL 30E (owned by Nicholas Stratford, bp of Chester, d.1707); TCD Q.b.1, ss.bb.16; 2nd state (with I4

unsigned) shown by LFL 30E; 3rd state (with correct number 101) shown by CUL Aa*.7.5; ECC S11.1.2;

Vol II: 1st state (with cols ²655–656 misnumbered 656–657) shown by TCD Q.b.2; 2nd state (with correct numbering) shown by CUL Aa*.7.6; ECC S11.1.4; TCD ss.bb.17.

Copies also at: AUL, BL, ChC, CJC, CSJ, CTH, DCL, DUL, EdUL, ERCP, Eton, KCL, KNA, LBL, LRS, MCS, MJRUL, NLS, NT, OBL, OAS, OBC, OCC, OHC, OJC, OLC, OMaC, OMC, ONC, OSJ, OSP, OTI, OXC, SAC, SLC, SPC, UBL, SUW, WCC, WCF, WCL, YML.

Bibliography: Considine 2008.
Editions: G.A.L. Henschel, 7 vols (Paris, 1840–50), rev. Léopold Favre, 10 vols (Niort, 1883–7), available on-line.

1678.3: Phillips, Edward (Milton's nephew), *The New World of Words: Or, a Universal English Dictionary*. 4th edn of **1658.3.** London: William Rawlins II for Obadiah Blagrave, 1678, also for Robert Harford, 1678. Wing P2072, P2072A; ESTC R8254, R217309.

Collation: 2⁰: π¹ A² a⁴ b² ²A⁴ B–3F⁴. [436] p.

Words with no use of special AS sorts.

Copy seen: Wing P2072A: CSJ L.7.1.

Copies also at: Wing P 2072: BL, CUL, CLL, GUL, LBL, LSH, NLW, NT, OBL, OStC, OWmC, PBN; FLS, NYPL, HUL, IUL, EmU, LCP, UCLA, YUB, TUL. ATL, OUL.

Wing P2072A: EdUL, GUL, NOW, NUL, OBL, OLC, YML; HHL, HUL, KSRL, MUL, UCLA, UTA, YUB, QUK.

1679.1: Thwaites, Edward, *Heptateuchus Anglo-Saxonicus, una cum Fragmentis V. & N. Testamenti Anglo-Saxonicis.* Oxford: Sheldonian Theatre, [1679], prospectus printed but not published; see **1698.1.** AS6.

OE Heptateuch (specimen)

Collation: 4⁰: apparently a single half-sheet with 2nd leaf signed A, but the leaves have been cut down to 163 × 105 mm and 162 × 109 mm respectively and pasted into a scrap-book collection.

SOURCE OF PASSAGE UTILIZING ANGLO-SAXON TYPES:

A1ʳ   From OBL, Laud misc.509, 3ʳ: OE Genesis 1.1–14, as Crawford 1969: 81; Marsden 2008: 8–9.

TYPE:

AS6: Main text in Christoffel van Dijck's Pica Anglo-Saxon cut for Franciscus Junius combined with Junius's Pica Roman (also cut by van Dijck)
Special sorts shown:

	11 lower-case sorts:	ð, f, ᵹ, ı, ꝑ, ſ, τ, ẏ; þ, ð, ꝓ;
	2 capitals:	Ꝼ, ẞ;
	3 others:	þ, ⁊, ∴
Total:	16 sorts.	

Copy seen: BL, Bagford Collection, Harley 5929, nos 358–359.
Bibliography: see 1698.1.

1679.2: Selden, John, *De Synedriis & Præfecturis Iuridicis Veterum Ebræorum Libri Tres. Editio ultima priori correctior.* Amsterdam: Hendrick and Dirk Boom I and widow of Joannes van Someren, 1679. Bks I–III, Bk I = 2nd edn of 1650.3, Bk III = 2nd edn of 1655.4. CAS3.

Extracts from Ælfric, OE Bede, Canons of Edgar, Gospels

Collation: 4⁰: *–²*⁴ A–2Z⁴ ²A–3I⁴ a–2m⁴ [$3 signed (-*1,2, ²A1, a1; B3 missigned E3; 2a2–3 missigned a1–3, 2b2 missigned b2)] 552 leaves, paginated [i–xvi], 1–361, *362–368*, ²[1–2], ²3–428, ²*429–440*, ³[1–2], ³3–266, ³256–280 (pp. 256 misnumbered 254; ²8 misnumbered 2; ²368 misnumbered 370; ³253 misnumbered 353).

SOURCES OF PASSAGES UTILIZING ANGLO-SAXON TYPES:

T3ʳ (p. 149)   From 1650.3 2N3ʳ: Ælfric, CH2.xxiv, as Godden 1979: 226/162;
    From 1650.3 2N3ʳ: Mt 18.17 (extract), as Liuzza 1994: 37;

T4ᵛ (p. 152)   From 1650.3 2O2ʳ: Mt 18.17 (extract), as Liuzza 1994: 37;

X4ʳ (p. 167)   From 1650.3 2R3ʳ: OE Bede, III.22 (word amanſumoðe), as Miller 1890–8: I.228/11; other forms presumably reconstructed from it;

2N2ʳ (p. 283)   From 1650.3 3V3ʳ: Phrase beᵹeondan ſæ extracted from 'Directions for a Confessor' (*olim* Canons of Edgar), as Fowler 1965: 20/113;

2T2ᵛ–3ᵛ (pp. 332–4)   From 1650.3 4H2ᵛ: Nowell, *Vocabularium Saxonicum*, svv. Ealdor, Ealdorman, Ealdorburh (Marckwardt 1952: 59–60);
    From 1650.3 4H3ʳ: re: S. George Ealdorman in Cappadocia;
    From 1650.3 4H3ʳ: OE Bede, III.8 (phrase mið hiſ Ealdorhlcneſſe), as Miller 1890–8: I.172/8;
    From 1650.3 4H3ʳ: Wulfstan's Canons of Edgar 2 (extrapolated phrase ẏldpan ⁊ ẏldpum), as Fowler 1972: 2; other phrases (Ealdpum ⁊ Ealdpaſ; Ealdpmannum) not traced;
    From 1650.3 4H3ʳ: Mt.16.21 (phrase), as Liuzza 1994: 34; Mk 10.33 (phrases, adapted), as Liuzza 1994: 83; Mt 27.12, 20 (phrase), as Liuzza 1994: 58, 59;
    From 1650.3 4H3ᵛ: Mk 8.31, 11.27, 14.43 (phrases), as Liuzza 1994: 79, 86, 92; Lk 22.52 (phrase), as Liuzza 1994: 150; Lk 22.66 (phrases), as Liuzza 1994: 151.

Note: Quotations from the ME Romance *Gamelyn* occur on ²2Y4ᵛ–²2Z1ʳ in the Textura type: see Beadle 1992.

TYPE:

Main text in the Pica Roman attributable to Christoffel van Dijck (= Mediaen Romeyn 1 on the Widow Elsevier specimen, Body 83) interspersed with the Pica Italic (also attributable to van Dijck, e.g., 2C2 = Mediaen Cursijf 2 on the Widow Elsevier specimen), and Arabic, Greek, Hebrew, Syriac, Textura (e.g., X4ᵛ).

CAS3: The Blaeu/Voskens English-size Anglo-Saxon combined with the Pica Roman occurs in the text as indicated above under Contents and in words on p4ᵛ (p. ³120 = **1655.4** 2D3ʳ).

Special sorts shown:

        10 lower-case sorts: *e*, ꝼ, ᵹ, ı, ꝓ, ſ, ꞇ, ẏ; þ, p;

        3 capitals: Ꝼ, Ꝧ, 8 (used for ð);

        2 others: ꝥ (used for þ), ꝫ.

  Total: 15 sorts.

The Anglo-Saxon is on an English-size body, so the lines with Anglo-Saxon in them take up more space.

    Copies seen: CUL 2.25.57 (signed Joannes Workman); TCD KK.ff.34 (p. 2 not numbered; Claudius Gilbert's copy); HH.ee.29, Fag.D.4.6.

    Copies also at: BL, BUW, TCC, ChCL, CUW, DUL, EdUL, HU, KUL, LBL, LFL, LJM, LQL, LUL, MJRUL, NLS, NUL, OBL, OHM, OJC, OMC, ONC, OQC, OXC, SUL, UBL, UCL, WCL, WIHM, WoCL, YUL.

Bibliography: see 1650.3.

1680.1: Selden, John, *The History of Tythes*. [London]: no printer stated; tp says 1618, but *recte* 1680; slavishly re-set from **1618.1**. STC 22173; Wing S2428A; ESTC S117082. AS7.

    Context: According to Wood, *Athenae Oxonienses* (ed. Bliss) III.369 'The said book or History was reprinted in 1680 in qu⟨arto⟩ with the old date put to it, at which time the press and fanatical party were too much at liberty, occasiond by the popish plot. Whereupon Dr. Thom. Comber answerd it in a book entit. An Historical Vindication of the Divine Right of Tithes, &c. Lond. 1681 qu⟨arto⟩', presumably Wing C5472 = ESTC R12545.

Extracts from ASC, Laws, Canon of Edgar *Be Dædbetan*

    Collation: 4⁰: a–e⁴ A–3K⁴ ²a–f⁴ [$3 signed (-a1,3, e3, C3, Y3, Z3, 2A3, 2D3, 2E3, 2F3, 2G3, 2H3, 2I3, 2K3, 2P3, ²c3)] 268 leaves, paginated [i–vi], I–XXII, *XXIII–XXXIV*, 1–491, *492–496* (p. 343 misnumbered 334).

SOURCES OF PASSAGES UTILIZING ANGLO-SAXON TYPES: as **1618.1**.

TYPE:

Main text in Pierre Haultin's English-size Roman (Body 93) interspersed with Robert Granjon's 3rd English-size Italic;

AS7: Nicholas Nicholls's Somnerian Pica Anglo-Saxon (leaded to Body 98) occurs in combination with a Pica Roman on e1^v, e2^r, 2C2^r (p. 203), 2C2^v (p. 204), 2D3 (pp. 213–214), 2D4^r (p. 215), 2E1^r (p. 217), 2E1^v–2^v (pp. 218–220), 2E3^v (p. 222), 2E4^r (p. 223), 2F1 (pp. 225–226), 2I3^r (p. 253), 2K1^v (p. 258), 2K2^r (p. 259), 2L4^v (p. 272), 2M2^v (p. 276), 3F2^v (p. 412).

Special sorts shown:

      11 lower-case sorts: ð, ꞃ, ᵹ, ı, ꝑ, ſ, τ, ẏ; þ, ð, p;
      4 capitals: Æ², Ð, Ꝺ, Ȝ;
      2 others: þ, ꝫ.

  Total: 17 sorts.

Note 1: Some problems encountered by the compositor are indicated: **p** occurs for AS **r** in *ðuph* on 2D3^r; for the punctus versus the compositor has used an apostrophe followed by a small 7 on 2D4^r, and subsequently a semi-colon is used.

Note 2: AS **e** is not used in the exemplar, **1618.1**.

    Copies seen: CCC 1.7.8; OBL Vet.A3.e.1039.

    Copies also at: BL, BUT, CUL, CDC, CaCL, DRD, GML, LCL, NLS, NLW, OMFC, SPC, StA, SUL, WCC, WiCL, DML, TCD, BSB; NYCC, UTS, HHL, HUL, IUL, CUofA, HLC, KSRL, MUL, PST, WMUL; UML.

Bibliography: see **1618.1**.

1680.2: Dugdale, Sir William, *Origines Juridiciales*, 3rd edn of **1666.1**, mainly a re-issue of **1671.2**. London: [Thomas Newcomb I or II] for Christopher Wilkinson, Thomas Dring II and Charles Harper, 1680. Wing D2490; ESTC R5556. AS7.

ASC(E) + **Lawsuit (extracts)**, as **1671.2**

Bibliography: Maddison *et al.* 1953: no. 34.

1680.3: Lüdecke, Thomas, *Orationis Dominicæ Versiones præter Authenticam ferè Centum ... magnam partem ex ære ad editionem à Barnimô Hagiô traditæ*. Berlin: Christoph Runge II, 1680. BLG L1075.

    Collation: 4°: a–b⁴ A–H⁴. [16], 64 p.

The Lord's Prayer in OE (citing Freher **1610.6**, headed 'SAXONICA Antiqua') occurs on F2^r printed in a Great Primer Textura (Body 116) with no special sorts, and on F2^v there is space for the 'ANGLO-SAXONICA' text with the 'Lectio' below (citing Reuter **1662.6**, Wilkins **1668.1**), printed in an English-size Italic with no special sorts.

Copy seen: CUL XVI.11.40.

Copies also at: BL, CSJ, KCL, MCS, OBL, OJC.

1681.1: Du Fresne, Charles, Lord Du Cange, *Glossarium ad Scriptores Mediæ & Infimæ* [sic] *Latinitatis*. Frankfurt: Balthasar Christopher Wust (typis) for Johann David Zunner, 1681. BLG D859; VD17: 3:006761T and 7:629767W. CAS6. **Words**

    Collation: [cf. also collation taken over from 1678.2 in vol. II, i4ᵛ]

    2⁰ in 4s: [vol. I] π⁴ [π1 + χ1] πA—H⁴ πI⁶ πK—P⁴ A–4R⁴ ¶A–¶3D⁴ ¶3E⁶ [$3 signed (+πI4, ¶3E4; -D3; πE2 missigned E3)] 616 (+1) leaves, paginated [i–xii] 1–76, then in columns 77–172, 1–1372, *1373–1376*, ²1–824 (cols 662 misnumbered 621, 877 misnumbered 77, col ²337 shows 1st 3 suprascript);

    [vol. II] π¹ A–3C⁴ 3D⁶ ²π² ²A–5A⁴ ²5B⁶ ²5C–D⁴ (²5D4 + χ10) ³π² a–i⁴ [$3 signed (+ 3D4, ²5B4; -²Y4)] 629 (+10) leaves, in columns [i–iv], 1–808, ² [i–viii], ²1–1552, then paginated ³[i–iv], ³1–72 (col nos ²1441–1448 not used; cols ²866 misnumbered 869, ²1255–1258 misnumbered 1253–1256, ²1328 misnumbered 132 with 3 inverted, ²1462 misnumbered 5862).

TYPE:

Main text of Glossarium in Pierre Haultin's Pica Roman (Body 83.5) interspersed with Granjon's Pica Italic 'pendante'.

CAS6: The Du Cangian Pica Anglo-Saxon as in 1678.2 occurs in a specimen on πP4ᵛ and in words combined with Haultin's Pica Roman in the same sig. and column locations as 1678.2, from which it is re-set page by page.

    Copies: CUL Ely a.177–9 (in 3 vols), Pet.B.9.4–6 (in 3 vols); TCD FF.bb.6–7.

    Copies also at: BL, CQC, TCC, DUL, GlCL, ICS, OSL, OStE, OWoC, SML.

Bibliography: see 1678.2.

1681.2: Mabillon, Jean, *De Re Diplomatica Libri VI*. Paris: Jean-Baptiste Coignard I for Louis Billaine, 1681.

    Collation: 2⁰: a⁴ e⁴ A–2V⁴ 2X–3D² 3E²(+χ2) 3F–4C² 4D*² 4D–5B⁴ 5C–5I². [16], 634, [26] p.

Engraving of AS script with alphabet on 2Y2ʳ.

    Copy seen: CUL Mm.1.21.

    Copies also at: AUL, BL, CCA, CQC, CSJ, TCC, DUL, ECL, EdUL, Eton, GUL, KCL, LBL, LiCL, LSH, MCS, MJRUL, NLS, NT, OBL, OAS, OJC, OMaC, OMC, ONC, OQC, OSJ, OTC, RUL, UBL, WCF, WoCL, WIHM.

1681.3: Selden, John, *Jani Anglorum*. London: for T[homas] D[ring] II (impensis), 1681. Wing S2429 (Wing 2429A with variant tp: Thomas Braddyll (typis) for sale at the shop of Thomas Benskin). ESTC R16039 and R183689. 2nd edn of 1610.2 but with editorial changes matching 1653.2 (e.g., F9ᵛ), and the AS words are reproduced in Roman on A7ʳ, C4ᵛ, and F9ᵛ, with what should be *wergild* on C4ᵛ rendered as 'pepzilo', as in 1653.2.

> Collation: 12⁰: A–F¹² G⁶. [2], 3–153, [1] p.
> Copy seen: CUL R.6.68.
> Copies also at: Wing S2429: BL, TCC, LPL, MTP, TCD, PBN; USLC, HHL, HUL, LCP, UCLA, YUB.
> Wing S2429A: CGC; YUB.

1681.4: Blount, Thomas (1618–79)], *Glossographia: or, a Dictionary, interpreting the Hard Words of Whatsoever Language, now used in our refined English Tongue; With Etymologies, Definitions, and Historical Observations on the same.* London: Thomas Newcomb for Thomas Flesher, 1681.Wing B3338. 5th edn of 1656.3, 2nd edn 1661.2, 3rd edn 1670.2, 4th edn 1674.3.
OE etymologies occasionally cited but no Anglo-Saxon types
Collation: 8⁰: A–2Y⁸ 2Z⁴; [16], 712 p.
Type: Main text in a Long Primer Roman (Body 67) in double columns.
No Anglo-Saxon types but OE etymologies occasionally cited in the same Textura as is used for headwords, as s.v. *Gospel*.

> Copy seen: CUL XV.17.2.
> Copies also at: APL, BL, TCC, CUW, CaCL, ChestC, DUL, EdUL, LSH, NLW, NT, OBL, OWoC, OXC, QUB, SBT; NYPL, FSL, HHL, APS, DDUL, IUL, JCB, KSRL, NLC, PUL, SCN, SLC, SLU, UCBL, UCH, UCLA, UOC, UTA, YUB, TUL, UVC; ATL, NLA, OUL, UNSW.

Bibliography: Alston V.52.

1682.1: Dugdale, Sir William, and Roger Dodsworth, *Monasticon Anglicanum*, vol. I, slavish repr. of 1655.3. [London: Thomas Newcomb II] for Christopher Wilkinson, Thomas Dring, and Charles Harper (impensis), 1682. Wing D2485; ESTC R1439. AS7.
Charters etc.

> Collation: 2⁰: π² (π1 + χ1) a–c⁴ A–3V⁴ 3X⁴⁺¹ (3X2 + χ1) 3Y–7F⁴ 7G–7H² [$2 signed (+A3, Q3, 2Y3, 3A3, 3F3, 4I3, 6D3, 6F3, 6G3, 6I3, 6P3, 6Q3, 6R3; -4H1, 6D2, 7G2, 7H2; 2E2 missigned E2, 2G2 missigned G2, 4R2 missigned 3R2, 4Y1 missigned 3Y1; 3X2χ1 signed 3X2)] 594 + 2 leaves, paginated [i–xxxii], 1–1159, *1160* (pp. nos 531–532 occur twice; pp. 609–610, 612, 692–694, 946–948, 978, 1152 not numbered, p. 690 misnumbered 691).

SOURCES OF PASSAGES UTILIZING ANGLO-SAXON TYPES:
As 1655.3 (whence all come directly).
TYPE:
Main text in Arthur Nicholls's Pica Roman (Body 81.5) interspersed with a Pica Italic (e.g. H4ᵛ p. 64).
AS7: Nicholas Nicholls's Somnerian Pica Anglo-Saxon is used in combination with Arthur Nicholls's Pica Roman:
Special sorts shown:
	12 lower-case sorts:	ð, e, f, ȝ, ı, p, ſ, τ, ẏ; þ, ð, p;
	7 capitals:	Æ¹, Æ², E, Ð, M, S, Ð;
	3 others:	þ, ꝗ, ꝭ.
Total:	22 sorts.	

Note 1: Several sorts are not used, as A, L, Ll.
Note 2: Ð used occasionally lc, e.g., K3ʳ perðalf. On 2A2ʳ capital Roman H is used with capital AS Ð used lower-case, e.g. Hpitðicumb.
Note 3: On N3ʳ roman Æ, E, M are used sporadically instead of AS Æ, E, M.
Note 4: On Q2ᵛ roman W is used instead of AS p; lc p is used on 2M4ʳ where uc p is used in 1655.3.

Copies seen: BL 4786.k.6, G11795, 209.g.5 (gold-tooled binding with arms of George III); TCC L.11.3 (π1χ1 reversed); TCD Fag.Q.3.13; MBS Res/2⁰H.mon.58 (lacks π1χ1 and π2, gold-tooled contemporary binding, formerly belonged to monastery Wessofontani).
Copies also at: CCC, CGC, ChC, CPH, ChestC, CLL, DUL, KNA, LGL, LPL, LSH, NLS, NT, OBL, OBC, OEC, OXC, RCL, RLW, SBT, SCL, SPC, UBL, WCC, WCL, WRL, PBN; HHL, IUL, IBUL, MUL, UCLA, UCRL, UTA, WCW, TUL, UWO.

Bibliography: Maddison *et al.* 1953: no. 4.

1682.2: [Cooke, Edward] (of Middle Temple), *Argumentum Anti-Normannicum*. London: John Darby, for Matthew Keinton, Jonathan Robinson, and Samuel Sprint, 1682. Wing C5998A and C5998B = ESTC R1971 and R35619. AS7.
Charters
Collation: 8⁰: π² A⁴ B–K⁸ L⁶ M⁴ [$4 signed (-A3,4, M3,4)] 88 leaves, paginated [1–12], i–clxiv (p. clvi not numbered).
SOURCES OF PASSAGES UTILIZING ANGLO-SAXON TYPES:
F8ᵛ (p. lxxx)   From 1658.1 2T2ᵛ: Writ of William I granting the castle and land at Bishop's Stortford (Hrt) to Bp Maurice of London (opening formula), as Gibbs 1939: no. 5 (Pelteret 39);
G1ʳ (p. lxxxi)   From London, PRO, Cartae Antiquae, Roll 9 (*olim* 1), m.1, no. 13 (s.xiii): Writ of King William I confirming rights to St Augustine's Canterbury already granted by Edward the Confessor, opening formula (Pelteret 6).

TYPE:

Main text in Arthur Nicholls's English-size Roman (Body 94); Appendix in a Pica Roman (Body 82).

AS7: Nicholas Nicholls's Somnerian Pica Anglo-Saxon occurs in text combined with the Pica Roman as listed above under Contents.

Special sorts shown:

   9 lower-case sorts: ð, *e*, ꝼ, ȝ, ı, ꝥ, ſ, ꞇ; þ;
   3 capitals: Є, Ꝼ, Ð;
   1 other: ꜠.
 Total: 13 sorts.

Copies seen: Wing C5998A: CUL R.11.68; Wing C5998B: CSJ H.10.29 (given by Peter Gunning, bp of Ely, 1684).

Copies also at: Wing C5998A: ECC, LIL, NLS, OBL, OQC, TCD; USLC, UTS, HUL, BA, MUL, NLC, UCLA, UPL.

Wing C5998B: BL, BUL, CMC, CaCL, DUL, EAL, KNA, LGL, LHL, NLW, NT, OBL, OAS, OQC, OXC, UBL, WCC, DML, PBN; FSL, NYPL, UTS, HHL, HUL, IUL, LCP, NLC, NWU, PUL, SLC, UCLA, UTA, WMUL, YUB, QUK, TUL.

Bibliography: Zook 1999: 82.

1682.3: Selden, John, *The Reverse or Back-Face of the English Janus*, trans. Adam Littleton (alias Redman Westcot) from *Jani Anglorum* (1610.2). [London:] no printer stated, for Thomas Bassett and Richard Chiswell, 1682. Re-issued in 1683.4. Wing S2436. AS7.

Words

 Collation: 2⁰ in 4s: A⁴ (a)–(c)⁴ B–Q⁴ R⁶ [$2 signed (+R3; -A1)] 82 leaves, paginated [i–xxxii], 1–131, *132* (pp. 46, 100, 104 not numbered; p. 103 misnumbered 102).

TYPE:

Main text in an English-size Roman (Body 93) interspersed with Robert Granjon's 3rd English-size Italic (with mostly larger capitals in another design). AS7: The Somnerian Pica Anglo-Saxon occurs in combination with a Pica Roman on B4ᵛ (one word; p. 8), F2ᵛ (one word; p. 36), G2ᵛ–3ʳ (words only, p. 94) showing the following seven sorts:

   6 lower-case sorts: ð, *e*, ȝ, ꝥ, ſ; p;
   1 capital: Ꝏ.
 Total: 7 sorts.

Note 1: As in **1610.2** Roman i, W [and sometimes e] are preferred where AS sorts could have been used appropriately.

Note 2: An extract from the beginning of the Laws of Ine (as Liebermann I.88–) occurs in an English-size Textura on N3ʳ.

 Copy seen: CUL J.9.6; see also **1683.4**.

Copies also at: BL, CCA, DAL, DUL, ECL, GUL, LGI, NLS, NLW, OXC, SAC, WCL, YML, DEWL, DKI, NLI, TCD, ULim; NYPL, HUL, PHS, PUL, UCH, UCLA, UTA, YUB; MonUL, OUL.
Bibliography: see 1610.2.

1682.4: Morhof, Daniel Georg, *Unterricht von der teutschen Sprache und Poesie, deren Ursprung, Fortgang und Lehrsassen*. Kiel: Joachim Reumann for Johann Sebastien Riecheln 1682, 2nd edn Lübeck & Frankfurt for Johann Biedemeyer 1700. No AS type.
Words, often quoted from Skinner 1671.3.
Collation: 1682.4: 8^0: [8], 907 [i.e. 807], [1] p.
1700 edn: 8^0: [20], 728, [2], 510, [2] p.
SOURCES OF PASSAGES UTILIZING ANGLO-SAXON TYPE: None: see Type below.
Type:
Main text in a German Pica Fraktur.
Anglo-Saxon words occur occasionally in a Pica Italic, as *metan* on p. 65 of the 1700 edition.
   Copies: 1682.4: BL 628.a.10.(1); Oxford Taylorian Inst: ARCH.80.G1682.
   1700 edn: BL 1064.e.7; OBalliolC AL 0152g24.
   Copies also at: QUB, LSH.
   Facsimile: Boetius, Henning (ed.), *Daniel Georg Morhofens Unterricht von der teutschen Sprache und Poesie* (Bad Homburg: Gehlen 1969) = 1700 edn.
Bibliography: Stanley 1987: 70.

1683.1: Dugdale, Sir William, and Roger Dodsworth, *Monasticon Anglicanum*, vol. I, re-issue of 1682.1 with new tp. 1st edn 1655.3. [London: Thomas Newcomb II], sold by Robert Scott, 1683. Not found in Wing or ESTC, NUC 150/601. AS7.
Charters
As 1682.1.
   Copy seen: APL MM.I.4 (lacks 3X2χ1).

1683.2: Dugdale, Sir William, *Monasticon Anglicanum*, vol. III, re-issue of 1673.1 with new tp. London: Thomas Newcomb I or II, sold by Robert Scott, 1683. Wing D2486C; ESTC R225644. AS7.
Charters
As 1673.1.
   Copy seen: TCC L.11.5.

Copies also at: CCC, EdUL; NYCU, HHL.

1683.3: Selden, John, *Tracts written by John Selden of the Inner-Temple: The First Entituled Jani Anglorum Facies Altera*, t Adam Littleton (alias Redman Westcot), re-issue of **1682.3** = *Reverse of the English Janus*, t of *Jani Anglorum* (1610.2). [London:] no printer stated, for Thomas Bassett and Richard Chiswell 1682, variant to be sold at the shop of Robert Clavell. Wing S2441 and S2441A. AS7.
Words
As 1682.3.

Copies seen: S2441: CUL Acton.a.25.66, Adams.3.68.3; LFL 18I; S2441A (with variant tp): TCC M.15.26.

Copies also at: S2441: BL, CCA, KCC, CMC, CSJ, TCC, CUW, DAL, DWL, EAL, LHL, MTP, NLS, OBL, OBC, OJC, OXC, PBL, UBL, WCL, TCD, PBN, BSB; FSL, NYCU, NYHS, HHL, HUL, KSRL, LCP, MUL, NLC, NWU, PTS, UCLA, WCW, TUL; OUL, USL.
S2441A: BL, CUL, CCA, DAL, DUL, ECL, GUL, LBL, LL, LSH, MTP, NLS, NLW, NT, OBL, OBC, OEF, OHM, OMC, OQC, OWoC, OXC, PUY, QUB, SAC, SUL, UBL, WCL, YML, DML; FSL, NYPL, UTS, HHL, HUL, DDUL, PTS, UCH, UCLA, UTA, YUB, OUL, USL.

Bibliography: see 1610.2.

1683.4: Browne, Sir Thomas, *Certain Miscellany Tracts*, ed. Thomas Tenison. London: no printer stated, for Charles Mearne 1683. Wing B5151; ESTC R25304.
Collation: 8°: A^4 B–P^8. [8], 215, [9] p.
On K6^v–L1^r (pp. 140–5) there are six passages of what purport to be equivalent AS versions of the corresponding 17c English, but only some words have been archaized and the 17c grammar is intact; no special sorts are used.

Copy seen: CUL Keynes.C.5.8.

Copies also at: BL, KCC, CCA, NCM, OBL, OBC; UTS, HUL, NLM, UMI, YUB, MUM.

1684.1: Gregory, John, *The Works of the Reverend and Learned Mr. John Gregorie* (5th edn of **1646.1**, 4th edn **1671.1**). Pt I = *Notes ... upon ... Scripture*. London: Mary Clark for Richard Royston, Benjamin Tooke I and Thomas Sawbridge, 1684. Wing G1924; ESTC R12193. AS7.
Words
Collation: 4°: π^4 a–b^4 B–Z^4 [$2 signed] 100 leaves, paginated [i–xxiv], 1–175, *176* (p. 172 not numbered).
TYPE:
Main text in a Pica Roman (Body 81) interspersed with a Pica Italic.

AS7: The Somnerian Pica Anglo-Saxon occurs on V4ʳ (p. 151) in two words in combination with the Pica Roman;
Special sorts shown: ᵹ, ꝺ (used erron. for ꞇ).
Note: Other special sorts are used for astrological symbols on b4ʳ and X1ʳ.
> Copies seen: CUL Bassingbourne 181 (Pt I after Pt II, with tp of combined parts (π1) removed to front of book), Syn.7.68.129 (Pt I after Pt II, lacks tp of Pt I (π2), and π4 before π3); ECC 323.4.65¹ (π2 occurs after b4).
> Copies also at: BL, BCLW, BPL, CCC, CGC, CMC, CSJ, TCC, CUW, ChestC, DUL, EdCL, LPL, MJRUL, NLS, NewCL, NT, OBL, OHC, OWmC, OXC, UBL, WCL, DML, BSB; FSL, NYPL, HHL, IUL, DDUL, GETS, LCP, NLC, SLU, UCBL, UCLA, UTA, YUB; OUL.

Bibliography: see 1646.1.

1684.2: Spelman, Sir Henry (written 1614), *Of The Law-Terms: A Discourse.* [London:] no printer stated, for Matthew Gillyflower, 1684. Wing S4929. AS7. Another edition (better) in **1698.3**, item (4).

Laws

Collation: 8⁰: π² B–F⁸ G⁴ [$4 signed (-G1,2)] 46 leaves, paginated [i–iv], 1–88.

SOURCES OF PASSAGES UTILIZING ANGLO-SAXON TYPES:

C3ʳ (p. 21)	From Lambarde 1568.2 C2ᵛ: Law Ine 3 (Liebermann I.90);
C3ᵛ (p. 22)	From Lambarde 1568.2 Q3ᵛ: Law Edward and Guthrum 9 (Liebermann I.132);
C4ᵛ (p. 24)	From Lambarde 1568.2 2E4ᵛ: Law I Cnut 17 (Liebermann I.296);
F5ʳ (p. 73)	From Lambarde 1568.2 2B4ᵛ: Law II Æthelred 8.3 (Liebermann I.224);

TYPE:
Main text in a Pica Roman (Body 81) interspersed with a Pica Italic.
AS7: Nicholas Nicholls's Somnerian Pica Anglo-Saxon is used in combination with the Pica Roman in text as indicated above under Contents and in words on D4ᵛ.
Special sorts shown:

11 lower-case sorts:	ð, e, f, ᵹ, ı, p, r, ꞇ, ẏ; þ, ꝑ;
1 other:	ꝺ.

Total: 12 sorts.
Copy seen: CUL J.12.66.
> Copies also at: BL, BCL, CSJ, EAL, EdUL, GUL, KLL, LHL, LPL, LSH, OBL, OQC, OWoC, OXC, DKI, DML, PBN, BSB; FSL, USLC, NYCU, HHL, DDUL, MUL, NLC, SLC, UCLA.

Bibliography: Van Norden 1949–50: 132 and n. 8.

1684.3: Junius, Franciscus, and Thomas Marshall, *Quatuor D.N. Jesu Christi Euangeliorum Versiones Perantiquæ Duæ, Gothica scil. et Anglo-Saxonica + Gothicum Glossarium*. Amsterdam: Johannes Janssonius II van Waesberge, 1684. Re-issue of 1665.2 with new tp to each part. AS 6.

Gospels, etc.

> Collation: As 1665.2 except that it shows ±*1, and sig. 2* is signed † and shows ±†1.

Anglo-Saxon and Type as 1665.2 (part 2).

> Copies seen: Both parts together: QUB Percy 57. Part 1 = Gothic/Anglo-Saxon Gospels only: OBL N.T.Goth.e.2; Part 2 = Gothic Glossary only: OBL Gough Sax.lit.152, 301.e.42.
>
> Copies also at: BL, BUL, CUL, CSJ, GUL, LBL, MCS, MJRUL, NLS, NT, NUL, OEF, ORP, OSJ, OTI, QUB, RUL, UBL, UCL, WoCL, TCD.

Bibliography: see 1665.2.

1684.4: Foxe, John (ed.), *The Second Volume of the Ecclesiasticall History, containing the Acts and Monuments of Martyrs*. 9th edn of 1570.1 (2nd edn) reset from 8th edn 1641.2. London: no printer stated, for the Stationers' Co., 1684. Wing F2036; ESTC R3576. AS 7.

Extracts from 1566.1, 1567.1 *taken from* 1641.2

> Collation (vol. II, including preliminary, books 7 and 8 only): 2⁰ in 6s: π¹ A–2Z⁶ [$3 signed] 277 leaves, paginated [i–ii], 1–551, 552 (pp. 159 misnumbered 153, 379 misnumbered 387).
>
> Note: a single leaf illustration has been added after 2Q6.

SOURCES OF PASSAGES UTILIZING ANGLO-SAXON TYPES:

These passages are from 1641.2 re-set line by line with spasmodic AS sorts:

2I2ᵛ/b/18–34 (p. 376)   From 1641.2 2P1ᵛ/a/18–36: Ælfric's letter to Wulfsige III, extracts (Fehr 1914: §§135–142);

2I2ᵛ/b/65–2I3ʳ/a/51 (pp. 376–377)   From 1641.2 2P1ᵛ/b/1–2P2ʳ/a/6: Ælfric's second letter to Wulfstan, extracts (Fehr 1914: §§86–95, 97–109);

2I3ᵛ/a/68–2I4ᵛ/b/17 (pp. 378–380)   From 1641.2 2P2ᵛ/a/64–2P4ʳ/b/31: Ælfric's *Sermo de Sacrificio in die Pascae*, same omissions as 1570.1 (Godden 1979: XV);

These passages are from 1641.2 re-set page by page without AS sorts:

2I2ᵛ/a/63–6 (p. 376)   From 1641.2 2P1ʳ/b: Ælfric's 'Excusatio Dictantis' (opening statement) at the end of his homily *Depositio S. Martin* (Godden 1979: XXXIV);

2I2ᵛ/a/74–7 (p. 376)   From 1641.2 2P1ʳ/b: Ælfric's *Grammar*, opening statement from OE Preface (cf. Zupitza 1880: 2);

This passage is from 1641.2 re-set in Pica Italic page by page without AS sorts:

2L5ᵛ/b/77–81 (p. 406)   From **1641.2** 2S1ᵛ/a/47–51: ASC (E), annal for 1129 (Clark 1954: 51).

TYPE:

Main text set in double columns in a Pica Roman (Body 82) interspersed with a Pica Italic (e.g. on 2K4–6 = Mediaan Cursijf no. 2 on Widow Elzevier sheet TSF 1.12, but with variants k, Q).

AS7: Nicholas Nicholls's Somnerian Pica Anglo-Saxon combined with the Pica Roman occurs in the text as indicated above under Contents.

Special sorts shown in the specimen on 2I3ᵛ:

   12 lower-case sorts: ð, e, f, ȝ, ı, ƿ, ſ, τ, ẏ; þ, ð, p;
   3 capitals: Æ², S, Ð;
   1 other: ꝫ.
 Total: 16 sorts.

Special sorts shown in the text:

   11 lower-case sorts: ð, f, ȝ, ı, ƿ, ſ, τ, ẏ; þ, ð, p;
   6 capitals: Æ², Ꞓ, Ð, ꟽ, S, Ð;
   2 others: þ, ꝫ.
 Total: 19 sorts.

 Overall Total: 20 sorts.

Note: Despite its availability, as shown in the specimen, lower-case e is not used in the text, because in **1570.1**, the first edition with these passages, the AS type used did not include a special sort for e, and successive editions have been set from the preceeding one.

 Copies seen: CUL P.1.2, Pet.S.3.10.

 Copies also at: APL, BL, BCL, BCLW, CCA, KCC, TCC, CUW, DWL, ECL, EdUL, Eton, GlCL, GUL, LCL, LHL, LSH, MJRUL, MTP, NCCL, NCL, NT, NUL, OBL, OBrC, OCC, OHM, OLMH, OMFC, OQC, ORP, OStE, OTC, OWoC, PML, RCL, RLW, SDL, WAL, WCL, YML, DEWL, DML, NLI, TCD, ULim, PBN, GUB; FSL, NYPL, NYHS, NYCU, UTS, HHL, HUL, IUL, BMC, GC, HCP, JCB, LCP, MA, PHS, SCN, SLU, UCBL, UCLA, UCRL, UMI, UTA, WMUL, YUB, TUL; ANZ, ATL, CML, DKC, MTC, QCL, QML, SSA, VPL.

Bibliography: see **1570.1**.

1684.5: Paris, Matthew, ed. William Watts, *Vitæ Duorum Offarum sive Offanorum, Merciorum Regum*, 2nd edn of **1639.3**. London: no printer stated, for Anne Mearne, Thomas Dring II, Benjamin Tooke I, Thomas Sawbridge, and George Wells, 1684 (part 2 dated 1683). Wing P359, 2nd part; ESTC R25517. AS7.
Words

 Collation: 2⁰: π*⁶ 6N–7R⁴ *⁹ [$2 signed (+ π*3,5, 6V3, 7H3; -π*1,2, 7E2; π*5 mis-signed π*4)] 136 leaves, paginated [i–xii], 961–1175, *1176*, 1177–1212 (pp. nos 1041–

1048 used twice; pp. 1075–1077 not numbered; pp. 1000 misnumbered 1001, 1002–1007 misnumbered 102–1027, 1089 misnumbered 1091, 1093 misnumbered 1013, 1143 misnumbered 1140). Note: Sig.* comprises double leaves.

TYPE:

Anglo-Saxon sorts occur only in the Glossary. Remarks are therefore confined to this part of the book.

Main text in a Long Primer Roman (Body 67).

AS7: The Somnerian Pica Anglo-Saxon combined with a Pica Roman occurs in words on *2ʳ, *6ᵛ, *7ʳ.

Special sorts shown: ð, *e*, ʒ, ı, þ, ꞇ, ẏ.   7 + 0 + 0 = 7 sorts

> Copies seen: CUL Bury 15.3; TCD P.b.2, Fag.Q.2.29 (π*4 misplaced after π*6, with contemporary white vellum blind-stamped binding); LPL KA130 (Wing P359A, with matter from Part I ('Adversaria in Historia Matthæi Parisiensis') bound in between 7R4 and *1).
>
> Copies also at: BL, BPL, CMC, TCC, ChCL, DUL, ECL, EdUL, LGL, NCL, NLS, NLW, NT, OBL, OAS, OHM, OQC, OSJ, OWoC, OXC, SCL, UBL, WAL, WCC, WCL, WIHM, DML, KSC, NLI, BSB; NYHS, HHL, HUL, IUL, BMC, MCRS, NLC, UCBL, UCLA, UTA, UTK, YUB, UVC.

Bibliography: see **1639.3**.

1684.6: Browne, Sir Thomas, *Certain Miscellany Tracts*, ed. Thomas Tenison. London: no printer stated, for Charles Mearne and Henry Bonwicke, 1684. Re-issue of **1683.3** with new tp. Wing B5152; ESTC R9918. No AS sorts.

> Copy seen: CUL Syn.7.68.58.
>
> Copies also at: BL, CPC, CSJ, TCC, CUZ, CLL, CUW, DUL, ERCP, Eton, GML, GRCP, GUL, IPL, LHL, LPL, LRCS, LSH, MJRUL, MTP, NCL, NHS, NLW, OBL, OAS, OBC, OEF, OQC, OStH, OWmC, WCC, WCF, WIHM, DML, KSC, GUB; FSL, USLC, NYPL, NYAM, HHL, HUL, IUL, HLC, KSRL, LCP, NLC, NLM, NWU, PUL, UCBL, UCH, UCLA, UTA, UVL, YUB, NLO, TUL.

1685.1: Howell, William, *An Institution of General History* (Vol III, Part IV only). London: [? Mary Clarke or Elizabeth Flesher (née Bee) for] Miles Flesher II for Mary Howell (née Ashfield), 1685. Wing H3139; ESTC R23475. AS7.

ASC, Asser, OE Bede, Laws (extracts)

> Collation: 2⁰ in 4s: πA⁴ B–3N⁴ 3O–3P² [$2 signed (2E2 missigned E2)] 240 leaves, paginated [i–viii], 1–464, 465–72 (pp. 94 misnumbered 95, 161 misnumbered 153, 168 misnumbered 160, 180–181 misnumbered 190–191, 303 misnumbered 304).

SOURCES OF PASSAGES UTILIZING ANGLO-SAXON TYPES:

	Prob used 1644.2 (= 1643.1 and 1644.1 combined); transcriptional errors are frequent.
N4^r (p. 95)	From 1643.1 3V2^v–3^r: ASC 477, 485, 495, as Thorpe I.22, 24–25; errors in transcription include peum for Ƿealum.
R2^r (p. 123)	From 1639.2 3C4^r: ref. to OE Bede I.15 and IV.16 re. form of 'Jutes';
S2^r (p. 131)	From 1643.1 3V2^r: ASC 449 (extract), as Thorpe I.18–20; From 1643.1 K1^r: OE Bede I.15, as Miller 1890–8: I.50/17–22; reference is made to Wheelock's edn;
T1^r (p. 137)	From 1643.1 R4^r: OE Bede II.5 (opening words), as Miller 1890–8: 108/21–22; From 1643.1 3X3^v: ASC 686, as Thorpe I.62;
T2^v (p. 140)	From 1643.1 3V2^r: ASC 491, as Thorpe I.24;
Y2^r (p. 163)	From 1643.1 3Y2^v: ASC 777, as Thorpe I.92;
Y3^v (p. 166)	From 1643.1 3Y4^r: ASC 825 (and ref. to 823), as Thorpe I.112 (110);
Z2^r (p. 171)	From 1643.1 3V4^r: ASC 568, as Thorpe I.32;
Z3^r (p. 173)	From 1643.1 3X1^r: ASC 611 and 614, as Thorpe I.38;
Z4^r (p. 175)	From 1643.1 3X2^r: ASC 648, as Thorpe I.48;
2A3^r (p. 181)	From 1643.1 3Y1^r: ASC 755 (extract), as Thorpe I.84;
2A3^v (p. 182)	From 1643.1 3Y2^v–3^r: ASC 787 (lacks 1st sentence), as Thorpe I.96;
2B1^v (p. 186)	From 1643.1 3Y3^v: ASC 823 (beginning), 827 (beginning), as Thorpe I.110, 112;
2B2^r (p. 187)	From 1643.1 3Y4^v: ASC 832, 835, as Thorpe I.114, 116; From 1643.1 C1^r: Preface to OE Bede (extract), as Miller 1890–8: 2/2–3;
2B3^r (p. 189)	From 1643.1 3Y4^v: ASC 836 (end), as Thorpe I.118;
2B3^v (p. 190)	From 1643.1 3Y4^v: ASC 837–8, 851 (beginning), as Thorpe I.118, 120; From 1574.2 A1^v ('Asser. p. 2. Edit. Parkeriana qua nos utimur, Saxonicis characteribus quibus Asserius ipse librum scripsit.'): Latin text of Asser's *Life of Alfred* (ch. 3), as Stevenson 1959: 4–5;
2B4^r (p. 191)	From 1574.2 A2^r: Latin text of Asser's *Life of Alfred* (extract), as Stevenson 1959: ch. 9/11–12;
2B4^v (p. 192)	From 1643.1 3Z2^r: ASC 860 (extracts), as Thorpe I.128–30;
2C1^r (p. 193)	From 1643.1 3Z2^v: ASC 866 (end), 867 (beginning), as Thorpe I.130;

2C1ᵛ (p. 194)	From 1574.2 B1ʳ: Latin text of Asser's *Life of Alfred* (extracts), as Stevenson 1959: ch. 30/1–5, 16–20;
2C2ʳ (p. 195)	From 1643.1 3Z2ᵛ: ASC 870 (beginning), as Thorpe I.134; From 1574.2 B1ᵛ: Latin text of Asser's *Life of Alfred* (extracts), as Stevenson 1959: ch. 37/3–4;
2C2ᵛ (p. 196)	From 1643.1 3Z3ᵛ: ASC 871 (extract), as Thorpe I.140;
2C3ʳ (p. 197)	From 1574.2 A1ʳ, B1ʳ: Latin text of Asser's *Life of Alfred* (extracts), as Stevenson 1959: chs 1/1–5, 29/4–6;
2C3ᵛ (p. 198)	From 1574.2 B3: Latin text of Asser's *Life of Alfred* (extracts), as Stevenson 1959: chs 47/8–9, 49/19–26; From 1643.1 3Z4ʳ: ASC 875 (extract), as Thorpe I.144;
2C4ʳ (p. 199)	From 1574.2 B3ᵛ: Latin text of Asser's *Life of Alfred* (extracts), as Stevenson 1959: ch. 50c/5–7, 19, ch. 52/4–6;
2C4ᵛ (p. 200)	From 1644.1 E2ᵛ: Laws of Alfred and Guthrum §1, with Lambarde's headings for §§2, 3, 4, as Liebermann I.126–128.
2D1ʳ (p. 201)	From 1643.1 4A1ʳ: ASC 882 (beginning), as Thorpe I.150; From 1574.2 C1ʳ: Latin text of Asser's *Life of Alfred* (extract), as Stevenson 1959: ch. 63/2–4; Howell follows 1574.2 Ine ſe [*recte* Meuse] but explains 'Ine' as Rhine;
2D1ᵛ (p. 202)	From 1643.1 4A4: ASC 894 (extracts), as Thorpe I.170;
2D2ʳ (p. 203)	From 1643.1 4B1ᵛ–2ʳ: ASC 897 (extracts), 901 (extract), as Thorpe I.176– 178;
2D3ʳ (p. 205)	From 1574.2 E1ʳ: Latin text of Asser's *Life of Alfred* (extract), as Stevenson 1959: ch. 104/7–9;
2D4ʳ (p. 207)	From 1574.2 C4ᵛ: Latin text of Asser's *Life of Alfred* (extract), as Stevenson 1959: ch. 80/18–19 ;
2D4ᵛ (p. 208)	From 1574.2 E2ᵛ, E3ʳ: Latin text of King Alfred's will (extracts), as Edwards 1866: 57/12–16, 59/5–9;
2E1ʳ (p. 209)	From 1643.1 4B2ᵛ: ASC 904–5 (extracts), as Thorpe I.180;
2E1ᵛ (p. 210)	From 1643.1 4B3: ASC 913 (beginning), as Thorpe I.186;
2E3ᵛ (p. 214)	From 1643.1 4C1ʳ: ASC 921 (extracts), as Thorpe I.194–5;
2F2ᵛ (p. 220)	From 1643.1 4C3ʳ: ASC 942–3 (extracts, including *5Boroughs* 5b–8a, as Dobbie 1942), as Thorpe I.208–10;
2F3ʳ (p. 221)	From 1643.1 4C3ᵛ: ASC 946 (end), as Thorpe I.212;
2F4ᵛ (p. 224)	From 1643.1 4C4ʳ: ASC 973 (extract = *Coronation of Edgar* 3–8a, om.5b–7a, as Dobbie 1942), as Thorpe I.224;
2N4ᵛ (p. 280)	From 1644.1 G2ʳ: Law II Æthelstan 20 (Lambarde's heading), as Liebermann I.160;
2O3ᵛ (p. 286)	From 1644.1 D4ʳ: Law Alfred 41 (beginning), as Liebermann I.74;

2P2ᵛ–2V3ʳ (pp. 291–333)   From **1644.1**: a summary account of AS Laws with many citations;

On 2N2ᵛ there are references to 'Spelman. Glossar.' (prob **1664.1**), Selden's 'Titles of Honour' (prob **1672.1**), Somner's 'Glossar.' (prob **1659.1**).

TYPE:

Main text in Pierre Haultin's English-size Roman (Body 94) interspersed with an English-size Italic.

AS7: Nicholas Nicholls's Somnerian Pica Anglo-Saxon combined with (prob) Arthur Nicholls's Pica Roman (g appears on N4ʳ in oƒʄlogon) occurs in text in the right-hand margins as indicated above under Contents and in words on P1ʳ, V4ʳ, 2A1ʳ, 2E2ʳ, 2F1ʳ, 2F3ᵛ, 2H3ʳ, 2N2ᵛ, 2N3, 2O1ᵛ, 2O2ᵛ, 2O3ʳ, 2O4ʳ, 2P2ʳ.

Transcribed from AS5, the Wheelockian Great Primer Anglo-Saxon, so AS7 A not used and there were some problems in transcribing the Wheelockian AS t: 2-shaped r appears sporadically in place of AS ꞇ, e.g. on N4ʳ; cap T rendered as E on 2C4ᵛ; ð rendered as ð; ᛫ (punctus versus) rendered as i to give ȝeꞃohꞇoni on 2A3ᵛ.

Special sorts used:

    12 lower-case sorts: ð, *e*, ꝼ, ȝ, ı, ꝑ, ꞃ, ꞇ, ẏ; þ, ð, p;

    7 capitals: Æ² (1st on 2B4ᵛ), Є (1st on 2B2ʳ), Ǝ (Gk E with rh openings closed off, and used upside down as cap B on 2B1ᵛ), Ð, Ɱ, Ƨ, Đ;

    3 others: ꝶ, þ, ᛫ (1st on 2B2ʳ).

Total: 22 sorts.

Copies seen: CUL Gg.2.16, O.7.4(OS), O.7.7(OS); ECC S12.2.13 (Abp Sancroft's copy); LFL 14H (lacks πA1).

Copies also at: BL, CCA, KCC, CPH, CSJ, TCC, DCL, DUL, EdUL, ILP, LHL, NCL, NLS, OBL, OHM, OLC, OMC, ONC, OQC, OSJ, OStE, OXC, SML, StA, WAL, WCF, WiCL, YML, DML, ULim, GUB; USLC, NYHS, HHL, IUL, BCB, BJH, LSU, PSL, UCLA.

1685.2: Selden, John, *Fleta seu Commentarius Juris Anglicani* + Selden's *Dissertatio*, 2nd edn, slavish re-setting of **1647.2**, State 2. London: Samuel Roycroft for Henry Twyford, Thomas Basset, John Place II and Samuel Keble, 1685. Wing F1291; ESTC R37347. AS7.

ASC (extract)

    Collation: 4⁰: A–4B⁴ [$2 signed (-A1)] 284 leaves, paginated [i–viii], 1–553, 554–556 (pp. nos 63–64 used twice; pp. 59 misnumbered 95, 85 misnumbered 58, 483 misnumbered 384).

SOURCE OF PASSAGE UTILIZING ANGLO-SAXON TYPES:

3Q2ᵛ (p. 480)   From **1647.2** 3Q2ᵛ: *Anglo-Saxon Chronicle* 435, recte 409 (opening statement), as Thorpe 1861: I.16/27–30.
TYPE:
Main text of Dissertatio in Pierre Haultin's English-size Roman (Body 92) interspersed with Arthur Nicholls's English-size Italic (with Great Primer capitals).
AS7: Nicholas Nicholls's Somnerian Pica Anglo-Saxon occurs in text as indicated above combined with Haultin's English-size Roman.
Special sorts shown: lower-case: ð, *e*, ꝼ, 1, p, ſ, τ; þ; other: ꝛ.   8 + 0 + 1 = 9 sorts.

> Copies seen: TCC P.8.70 (gift of Sir Thomas Sclater (†1736); after p. 552 there are two blank pages unnumbered); TCD NN.gg.55 (lacks 4B4).

> Copies also at: APL, BL, BUL, CSJ, EdUL, HOL, HRC, LGI, LHL, LIL, LPL, LSE, NLW, NT, OBL, OCC, OJC, OMC, ONC, OSJ, OXC, PML, UBL, UCL, WCL, WoCL, NUIG, ULim, BSB; FSL, USLC, NYCU, HHL, HUL, IUL, KSRL, LCP, MUL, PUL, SCN, UCBL, UNC, UPL, WMUL, TUL; CDLS, OLS, QSC, UML.

Bibliography: see 1647.2.

1686.1: Parr, Richard, *The Life of the Most Reverend Father in God, James Usher, Late Lord Arch-bishop of Armagh, Primate and Metropolitan of all Ireland. With a Collection of Three Hundred Letters between the said Lord Primate and most of the Eminent Persons for Piety and Learning in his time, both in England and beyond the Seas*. London: printed for Nathaniel Ranew, 1686. Wing P548; ESTC R1496. AS7.

Latin words

> Collation: 2⁰: [A]⁴ B–O⁴ P² 2A–2I² *–4*² 3A–3L⁴ 3M² 4A–4Z² ²4A–4T⁴ 4U² 5A–5G² χ¹. [8], 103, [5], 33, [19], 92, 301–624, 28, [2] p., 1 leaf illustrations.

SOURCE OF PASSAGE UTILIZING ANGLO-SAXON TYPES:
4L2 (pp. 551–2)   From a lost MS containing a letter from Gerald Langbaine to Ussher dated 21 June 1650 (Boran 2015: no. 561): Latin passage and captions to runic alphabet taken by Langbaine from OBL Auct.F.4.32 (SC 2176), 20ʳ;
TYPE:
AS7 occurs as indicated showing the following lower-case special sorts:
e, ꝼ, ᵹ, 1, p, ſ, τ + capital Є.
The Irish Moxon types (1680–) occur in one Irish word, as noted by McGuinne 1992: 53.

> Copies seen: CUL U.7.19, Acton.a.8.27.

> Copies also at: APL, BL, BCLNI, BCLW, BPL, BrPL, BUT, CCA, CCC, CMC, CSJ, TCC, CaCL, ChestC, DCL, DRD, DUL, ECL, EdUL, Eton, GlCL, GML, HRC, LBL, LHL, LHU, LiCL, LMT, MTP, MJRUL, NAL, NLW, NT, OBL, OAS, OBC, OCC, OGF, OHM, OJC, OMC, ONC, OQC, OSJ OStE, OWoC, SAC, SCL, SDL, SML, SoUL, SPC, SUL, TCL, UBL, WAL, WCC, WCF, WCL, WiCL, WoCL, YML, DEWL, DML, NLI, TCD,

ULim, PBN, BSB, GUB; FSL, NYPL, UTS, HHL, HUL, IUL, CUofA, KSRL, LCP, MUL, NLC, NWU, PFL, PTS, UCBL, UCH, UCLA, UCRL, UTA, UTK, WMUL, YUB, TUL, UVC; ATL, AUNZ, DKC, FUL, MonUL, MTC, NLA, OUL, QCL, USL, VUW.
Bibliography: Sharpe & Hoyne 2020: no. 55 on pp. 173–174.

1686.2: Browne, Sir Thomas, *The Works of the Learned Sr Thomas Brown*, including as Part IV *Certain Miscellany Tracts*, ed. Thomas Tenison. London: no printer stated, for Thomas Basset, Richard Chiswell, Thomas Sawbridge, Charles Mearne, and Charles Brome, 1686. Repr. of **1683.3/1684.5**. Wing B5150; ESTC R19807. No AS sorts.
   Copy seen: CUL Syn.3.68.7.
   Copies also at: BL, BCL, BPL, ChC, CFM, CJC, CMC, CNC, CSel, CSJ, CTH, TCC, DUL, EAL, ECL, EdUL, ERCP, Eton, GUL, LiCL, LPL, LRCO, LRCS, LSE, MJRUL, NAL, NCCL, NCL, NLS, NLW, NT, OBL, OCC, OJC, OLMH, OMaC, OMC, ONC, OPC, OSC, OSJ, OSL, OXC, PML, RLW, SAC, SBT, SDC, StA, WAL, WCF, WCL, WoCL, DML, TCD, PBN, BSB, GUB; FSL, NYPL, NYAM, NYCU, HHL, HUL, IUL, BMC, CLM, EmU, HCP, ILF, JCB, LCP, NLC, NLM, NWU, PTS, SCN, UCH, UCLA, UCRL, UOC, UTA, UTK, UVL, VCU, WCAI, WMUL, WUM, YUB, TUL; ATL, MonUL, MULNZ, NLA, NSW, SJTC, SSA, UML, USL, VSL.

1687.1: Spelman, Sir Henry, completed by Sir William Dugdale, ed. Sir James Astry, *Glossarium Archaeologicum*, 3rd edn of **1626.1**, slavish reprint of 2nd edn **1664.1**. London: Thomas Braddyll for George Pawlett and William Freeman, 1687. Wing S4926; ESTC R10264. AS7.
Citations, as in an Encyclopaedia
   Collation: 2⁰ in 4s: π² A² a–d² B–4D⁴ [$2 signed (-A1, a2, b2, c2, d2)] 300 leaves, paginated [i–xxiv], 1–576 (pp. 110 misnumbered 100, 554 misnumbered 559, 559 misnumbered 554).
SOURCES OF PASSAGES UTILIZING ANGLO-SAXON TYPES:
Since the book is a slavish reprint of **1664.1** the passages of OE and references are the same, being taken over from that earlier edition. The most extensive text is on 4C4ᵛ–4D1ʳ.
TYPE:
Main text in a Pica Roman (Body 82) interspersed with a Pica Italic.
AS7: Nicholas Nicholls's Somnerian Pica Anglo-Saxon occurs in the specimen on d2ᵛ and is combined with the Pica Roman in words and passages.
Special sorts shown in specimen:
12 lower-case sorts:	ð, e, f, ȝ, ᴆ, ı, p, r, ẏ; þ, ð, ƿ;
5 capitals:	Æ², Є, ᴍ, S, Ð;
2 others:	þ, ɼ.
Total: 19 sorts.	

Special sorts shown in text:

  13 lower-case sorts: ð, *e*, ꝼ, ȝ, Ꝺ, ı, p, ſ, ꞇ, ẏ; þ, ð, p;
  6 capitals: Æ¹, Æ², Є, Ꟙ, 8, Ð;
  2 others: þ, ⁊.
Total: 21 sorts.

Note 1: 8 used for ð on M1ʳ s.v. *Beudum*.
Note 2: þ used for þ on 3Z1 s.vv. *Thanus, Thrimsa*.
Note 3: Punctus versus, e.g. on 4D1ʳ/b/12, is a 7 with a suprascript dot, much too large.

  Copies seen: APL N.II.14; CUL Syn.2.68.10; MBS 2⁰.L.lat.134 (binding of white vellum on boards, blind-stamped).

  Copies also at: BL, BCL, CCA, CSJ, TCC, ChCL, DUL, ECL, EdUL, HHC, HRC, LHU, NLS, NLW, NT, NUL, OBL, OAS, OBC, OCC, OEC, OEF, OHC, OMC, OSL, OWoC, SCL, SML, UBL, WAL, WoCL, YML, DML, NLI, PBN, BSB, GUB; FSL, NYCU, UTS, HHL, HUL, IUL, DDUL, GC, ISU, KSRL, SCN, SIU, SLU, UCLA, UMI, UTA, WMUL, YUB; ATL,

Bibliography: see 1664.1.

1687.2: Ussher, James, *Britannicarum Ecclesiarum Antiquitates*, 2nd edn of 1639.2. London: no printer stated, for Benjamin Tooke, 1687. Wing U160; ESTC R9506. AS7.

ASC, **prose Guthlac, Martyrology, Saints (resting place)**

  Collation: 2⁰: A⁴ a⁴ B–3S⁴ 3T–4F² [A–3S: $2 signed (+A3; -A1,2); 3T–4F: $1 signed (3T1, 3V1, 3X1 missigned 1T, 1V, 1X respectively)] 282 leaves, paginated [i–xvi], 1–509, *510–514*, ²507–514, 515–548, *549–550* (pp. nos 137–144, 337–338 not used; p. 504 not numbered; pp. 43–46 misnumbered 63–66, 132–133 misnumbered 140–141, 247 misnumbered 427, 258 misnumbered 250, 263 misnumbered 255, 304 misnumbered 288, 500 misnumbered 400, 505 misnumbered 405).

SOURCES OF PASSAGES UTILIZING ANGLO-SAXON TYPES:

D2ᵛ (p. 20)	From **1639.2** E2ᵛ: ASC (F) 167, as Thorpe 1861: 1.15, Baker 2000: 11;
F1ʳ (p. 33)	From **1639.2** H3ʳ: OE prose Life of St Guthlac (Gonser 1909: 113, ch. 3, line 2/3), featuring the names ȝꞃanꞇe ea, ȝꞃanꞇe ceaſꞇeꞃ;
2D1ʳ (p. 209)	From **1639.2** 3C4ʳ: Contrasting the forms Geatum/Iotum 'Jutes' between OE Bede I.15 (Miller 1890: I.1.52/4) and ASC (E) 449 (Thorpe 1861: I.21/14);
3B3ʳ (p. 383)	From **1639.2** 4Z2ᵛ: OE Martyrology at 17 Mar (Rauer 2013: §44/2);

3M3ʳ (p. 463)   From **1639.2** 5V3ʳ: re. the resting place of SS Aidan and Patrick at Glastonbury (Liebermann, *Heiligen*, 1889: II.37 on p. 17);

3M4ᵛ (p. 466)   From **1639.2** 5X2ʳ: ASC (E) 430, as Thorpe 1861: I.19;

TYPE:

Main text in Pica Roman (Body 82) interspersed with a Pica Italic (e.g. on 2V3ᵛ). AS7: Nicholas Nicholls's Somnerian Pica Anglo-Saxon is combined with the Pica Roman.

Special sorts shown:

    9 lower-case sorts: ð, *e*, ꝼ, ᵹ, ı, ꝥ, ſ, ꞇ, ẏ;
    2 capitals: Ꟃ, Ð;
    1 other: ꝫ.

  Total: 12 sorts.

Note: Roman **w** is used instead of AS p, e.g., on D2ᵛ.

Note 2: AS types are used for Irish on 3K4ᵛ, 3M1ᵛ, 3N3ʳ.

    Copies seen: ABH 1582; APL C.III.9¹; CUL 6.23.11, Huntingdon.26.1, Pet.Q.4.19; CCC D.4.4¹.

    Copies also at: BL, BCL, BPL, BUL, CCA, CGC, CJC, CNC, CSJ, ChestC, ChCL, DUL, DWL, ECL, Eton, GlCL, GML, CUL, HHC, LCL, LHL, LPL, LSH, MJRUL, MTP, NLS, NLW, OBL, OBC, OCC, OHC, OHM, OJC, OMC, ONC, OQC, OStE, PML, SAC, SDL, SSPC, WAL, WCC, WCL, WoCL, YML, DCLI, DML, KSC, NLI, TCD, PBN, BSB, GUB; FSL, NYPL, NYCU, UTS, HUL, IUL, DDUL, SCP, NLC, PFL, SLU, UCLA, UCRL, UVL, YUB, TUL; AUNZ, SCI, FUL.

Bibliography: see **1639.2**.

1687.3: Ussher, James, *A Discourse of the Religion Anciently Professed by the Irish and Brittish*, 3rd (claims to be 4th) edn, re-set from **1631.2** (2nd edn), 1st edn **1622.2**. London: no printer stated, for Benjamin Tooke, 1687. Wing U170; ESTC R19057. AS7 (phrase).

Alfredian Preface to the Pastoral Care (extract)

    Collation: 4⁰: A–O⁴ [$2 signed (-A1, O2)] 56 leaves, paginated [i–viii], 1–99, *100–104*.

SOURCE OF PASSAGE IN ANGLO-SAXON TYPES:

F1ʳ (p. 33)   From **1631.2** D6ᵛ: *Preface* to the Alfredian *Pastoral Care*, 3-word extract (Sweet 1871: I.6/22); the ultimate source in **1622.2** is indicated by the **j** in 'mjnum' taking over Irish **i**.

TYPE:

Main text in Arthur Nicholls's Pica Roman (Body 81.5) interspersed with his Pica Italic.

AS7: Nicholas Nicholls's Somnerian Pica Anglo-Saxon occurs in combination with Arthur Nicholls's Pica Roman in a phrase as indicated above;
Special sorts used: ꝇ, ꝑ, s; Ꝺ (used on its side for ꞇ).
Total: 4 sorts.
Copies seen: APL JJ.IV.83²; CUL Hib.7.687.6, F.10.27², Hunt.62.5².
Copies also at: BL, BCLNI, CCC, CSJ, CUW, Eton, LHL, LPL, LSH, MCS, NLW, OBL, OCC, OHC, OWoC, QUB, SPC, UBL, WAL, DML, NLI, TCD, GUB; FSL, UTS, HHL, CUofA, LCP, NLC, UCLA, UTA, TUL, UWO.
Bibliography: see 1622.2.

1687?.1: [Oxford University Press] [Type-specimen] beginning 'A B C:'. [Oxford: Sheldonian Theatre, c.1687]. Wing F621A. AS7.
Printer's specimen with OE Lord's Prayer
    Collation: 8⁰: π a⁸ π b⁴ [none signed] 12 leaves, unnumbered.
SOURCE OF PASSAGE UTILIZING ANGLO-SAXON TYPES:
π b1ʳ   From 1664.2, A6ʳ: Lord's Prayer, Mt 6.9–13 (as in 1665.2, B3ᵛ–4ʳ).
TYPE: various specimens.
AS7: Nicholas Nicholls's Somnerian Pica Anglo-Saxon occurs in the specimen on π b1ʳ with the Lord's Prayer in OE:
Special sorts shown:

	12 lower-case sorts:	ð, ꝇ (end of last word only), ꝼ, ʒ, 1, ꝑ, ſ, ꞇ, ẏ; þ, ð, p;
	9 capitals:	A, Ɛ, Ꞡ, Ꝺ, K, ꟽ, S, Ð, W;
	5 others:	þ, ꝫ, ꝯ, ꞉, Ɛ
Total:	26 sorts.	

    Copy seen: OXC D.124(3ˣ).
Bibliography: Morison/Carter 1967: 229 (by John Simmons); Mosley 1984: no. 169.
Facsimile: Morison/Carter 1967: pl. 11.

1688.1: Anon., *No Antiquity for Transubstantiation, Plainly Proved from the Judgment of the Most Learned Men that lived in Time of the Saxons*. London: no printer stated, 1688. Wing N1174; ESTC R4612.
    Collation: 4⁰: A–E⁴. [2], xiv, [2], 24 p.
Contains translation of Ælfric's Easter Sermon, Ælfric's Letter to Wulfsige (extract), Ælfric's Letter to Wulfstan, and other short items from 1566.1 on C2ʳ–E4ᵛ (pp. 3–24). No AS sorts.
    Copy seen: BL 3936.3.2.

Copies also at: BULW, CUW, DUL, EdUL, HU, KLL, KUL, LBL, LHU, LU, MJRUL, NLW, NRL, NU, NUL, OBL, OEC, SHU, StA, YUL, TCD; UTS, YUB.

1688.2: [Patrick, John], *A Full View of the Doctrines and Practices of the Ancient Church relating to the Eucharist*. London: no printer stated for Richard Chiswell, 1688. Wing P729; ESTC R13660.

Collation: 4^0: π^4 a^4 B–$2C^4$ $2D^2$. [16], 202, [2] p.
Contains summary translation of Ælfric's Easter Sermon, Ælfric's Letter to Wulfsige (extract), Ælfric's Letter to Wulfstan from 1566.1 in ch. 16 on $2A3^v$–$2B3^v$ (pp. 182–90). No AS sorts.

Copy seen: CUL 8.23.58⁶ (lacks 2D2).

Copies also at: BL, BCLW, BStE, CSJ, TCC, CaCL, DUL, DWL, Eton, GUL, ILP, LFL, LHL, LiCL, LUL, NLS, NT, OBL, OAS, OBrC, OCC, OEC, OJC, OMaC, OMC, ONC, RLW, SDL, UBL, WCC, WCF, WCL, DML, TCD, ULim; FSL, UTS, HHL, HUL, IUL, DDUL, LCP, NLC, PUL, RBS, UCLA, UTA, YUB; MonUL, NLA.

1689.1: [Skinner, Stephen], *Gazophylacium Anglicanum*, rev. Richard Hogarth. London: Elizabeth Holt and William Horton for Randall Taylor, 1689. Wing G426; ESTC R388. AS7.
Words

Collation: 8^0: A–$2A^8$ $2B^6$ ^22A–$^22K^8$ $^22L^2$ [\$4 signed (-A1,2, ²2L2)] 282 leaves, not paginated.

TYPE:
Headwords in a Long Primer Textura. Main text in a Long Primer Roman (Body 67).
AS7: Nicholas Nicholls's Somnerian Pica Anglo-Saxon appears in the specimen on $A8^v$ and on most pages of the text in words in various entries as deemed appropriate, where it is combined with Arthur Nicholls's Pica Roman (with some English-size sorts mixed in).

Special sorts shown on specimen on $A8^v$:

    12 lower-case sorts: ð, *e*, f, ȝ, 1, p, ſ, τ, ẏ; þ, ð, p;
    10 capitals: A, Æ¹, Æ², Є, Ꮧ, K, ꟽ, S, Ð, W;
    1 other: ꞇ.
  Total: 23 sorts.

Special sorts shown in text of Dictionary:

    11 lower-case sorts: ð, *e*, f, ȝ, 1, p, ſ, τ, ẏ; ð, p;
    10 capitals: A, Æ¹, Æ², Є, Ꮧ, K, ꟽ, S, Ð, W;
    1 other: þ (erron. s.v. 𝕭irth);
  Total: 22 sorts.

Overal total: 24 sorts.

Note 1: þ/Þ not found—uses mostly ð, or, if capital, Ð, th on e.g. C4ʳ in Bæth s.v. 𝔅𝔞𝔱𝔥.

Note 2: variant sorts:

Some letters have been re-cut and the new version appears beside the original one: the re-cut lower-case g is flat-topped and has a larger bowl; re-cut d shows the ascender having less hook-over at the top. For examples see, e.g., C8ʳ, re-cut d in Beoðan s.v. 𝔅𝔦𝔡 beside usual d s.v. 𝔅𝔦𝔡 *Guests*; C6ʳ, re-cut g s.v. 𝔅𝔢𝔤𝔲𝔦𝔩𝔢 beside usual g s.v. 𝔅𝔢𝔢𝔰𝔱𝔦𝔫𝔤𝔰; C6ʳ, flat-topped t s.v. 𝔅𝔢𝔤𝔢𝔱 beside usual t s.v. 𝔅𝔢𝔢𝔱𝔩𝔢.

Note 3: No ð with shortened ascender found.

Note 4: A distinctive capital G (from another roman fount, not AS7) is sometimes used in OE words, e.g. K8ᵛ s.v. 𝔊𝔞𝔟𝔢𝔩.

> **Copies seen:** LFL 4B; BL 1480.aa.27; CUL Adv.c.98.10 (interleaved with larger paper; owned by Walter White 1800, Sir Percy Thompson).
>
> **Copies also at:** TCC, DUL, DWL, GML, GUL, LPL, LSH, NLS, NLW, OBL, OQC, OTC, OXC, SBT, SUL, KSC, GUB; FSL, USLC, HHL, HUL, IUL, NLC, NLM, SCN, UCH, UCLA, UTA, YUB; UAL, VSL.

Bibliography: Görlach 2002: 78–81, 92; Starnes and Noyes 1946: 64–68.

Facsimile: English Linguistics 1500–1800 no. 166 (Menston: Scolar Press, 1969).

1689.2: [Cooke, Edward] (of Middle Temple), *A Seasonable Treatise*. London: J[ohn] D[arby], for Jonathan Robinson, 1689. Wing C6001; ESTC R7506. Re-issue of 1682.2 with new tp. AS7.

Charters, as 1682.2.1

> Copy seen: CUL Ll.8.63.
>
> Copies also at: BL, TCC, LSH, NLS, NT; NYPL, NLC.

1689.3: Hickes, George, *Institutiones Grammaticæ Anglo-Saxonicæ, et Moeso-Gothicæ*, with subsidiaries by Runólfur Jónsson and Edward Bernard. Oxford: Sheldonian Theatre, 'typis Junianis', 1689. Wing H1851; ESTC R8123 (also ESTC R473686). AS6; tp AS7.

Bede, Promissio Regis, Words, List of Manuscripts

> **Context:** Following the publication of an Anglo-Saxon dictionary by Somner 1659.1, this book offers the first published Anglo-Saxon grammar, as well as an Icelandic grammar and dictionary and a study of foreign words in English. It was meant to lay a firm foundation for the study of Anglo-Saxon and Germanic studies relating to English. It also offers the first published catalogue

of manuscript and printed sources for Anglo-Saxon and related languages; many of the manuscripts listed had not long been at the Bodleian, the Hatton manuscripts having arrived in 1671, and Junius's in 1677; this list, impressive as it is, was superceded by Wanley's catalogue in Hickes 1703/5.1. Together with Somner's dictionary the grammatical part of this book became the basis for virtually all study of Old English for the next 200 years.

Collation: 4^0: π^4 b–c^4 d^2 A–2T^4 2V^2 (2V2 + χ1) [$2 signed (+A3; -P2, 2V2)] 184 + 1 leaves, paginated [i–xxviii], 1–114, *115–120*, 1–182, *183–220*.

SOURCES OF PASSAGES UTILIZING ANGLO-SAXON TYPES (longer passages only):

π2^r (tp)	From 1643.1 3S2^v/26–8: OE Bede V.22 (Miller I.2.480/30) extract;
c1^v–2^r	From Junius 60 (copy by Junius of Vitellius A.vii, since damaged by fire) fo 2: OE Promissio Regis (Liebermann I.214 = §1 only; coll. Clayton 2008: 148–9; cf. 1678.1, X1^v);

Note: There is a transcript with English translation of this text by Humfrey Wanley (1672–1726) in OBL Eng.bibl.c.3 (SC 33184), p. 47. It could be directly based on Vitellius A.vii but is more probably based on Hickes's printed text. There is a note on p. 4 'All that is contein'd in this volume was written by Mr Humfrey Wanley in the time of his apprenticeship at Coventry, and since that given to me by himself on June 22nd 1697. William Elstob', quoted by Keynes 1996: 151, n. 87. Wanley was recruited to the Bodleian in 1695.

2I3^r–2P3^v Lists of printed sources and manuscripts (including contents) by collection (for AS manuscripts cf. Gneuss 1996) and/or language.

2I3^r (p. 133) *Libri Moeso-Gothici*:

1. Uppsala, Universitetsbibliotek, DG 1: Codex Argenteus 'Gothic Gospels' (formerly owned by Isaac Vossius; cf. no. 38 below): http://urn.kb.se/resolve?urn=urn:nbn:se:alvin:portal:record-60279;
2. OBL, Junius 98 (SC 5209): printed book, Bonaventura Vulcanius, *De literis & lingua Getarum, sive Gothorum* (Leiden, 1597);

2I3^v (p. 134) *Libri Angl.Sax. Excusi* List of printed sources:

3. Parker/Foxe Gospels 1571.1,
4. Junius/Marshall Gospels 1665.2,
5. Spelman's Psalter 1640.3,
6. Lisle's Ælfric on the Old and New Testaments 1638.1,
7. Parker/Joscelyn's Testimonie of Antiquity 1566.2,
8. Foxe's Book of Martyrs 1570.1,
9. Wheelock's OE Bede and ASC 1643.1 and 1643.2,

	10.	Lambard's Archaionomia 1568.2,
	11.	Somner's Dictionary 1659.1,
	12.	Dugdale's Monasticon Anglicanum 1655.3,
	13.	Spelman's Alfredi Magni Vita 1678.1,
	14.	Selden's Eadmer 1623.3,
	15.	Junius's Cædmon 1655.2.

2I4^r–2L3^v (pp. 135–50)   List of manuscripts (and printed sources) in Oxford:

2I4^r (p. 135)	16.	Laud misc.509 (SC 1042), 120^v–41^v: 'Pentateuchum' (only this part cited);
	17.	Laud misc.201 (SC 852): Lisle's Saxon-English Psalter (s.xvii);
	18.	Laud misc.482 (SC 1054): 'Canones Poenitentiales';
	19.	Laud misc.661 (SC 1201): 'Chronicon Saxonicum' to 915; transcript 1565;
	20.	Laud misc.636 (SC 1003): Chronicon Saxonicum = Peterborough Chron.;
	21.	Bodley 441 (SC 2382): Gospels, gives contents and notes used for 1571.1;
2I4^r–2K1^r	22.	Bodley 343 (SC 2406): Homilies, lists 62 items;
2K1^{rv}	23.	Bodley 340 (SC 2404): Homilies, lists 31 items;
2K1^v (p. 138)	24.	Bodley 34 (SC 1883): eME 'Katharine group', 'Semi-saxonicè'
	25.	Selden supra 62 (SC 3450): Dictionariolum Saxonico-Anglicum by Richard James 1620–30, prob a transcript of James 41 (SC 3878);
	26.	Hatton 20 (SC 4113): Alfredian t of Gregory's Pastoral Care;
	27.	Hatton 76 (SC 4125): Alfredian t of Gregory's Dialogues;
2K2^r (p. 139)	28.	James 42 (SC 3879): Glossarium Saxonico-Latinum (c.1600);
	29.	Auct.D.2.19 (SC 3946): Rushworth/McRegol Gospels;
	30.	Hatton 38 (SC 4090): Gospels s.xii/xiii;

Inter Codd. Junianos

	31.	Junius 11 (SC 5123); 'Cædmonis Paraphrasis Poetica Genesios' = OE poems, *Genesis, Exodus, Daniel, Christ and Satan*;
2K2^{rv}	32.	Hatton 113/114 (SC 5210/5134; olim Junius 22): Homilies, lists 39 items;
	33.	Hatton 115 (SC 5135; olim Junius 23): Homilies, lists 24 items;
2K2^v–3^r	34.	Hatton 116 (SC 5136; olim Junius 24): Homilies, lists 21 items;
2K3^r–4^v	35.	Junius 121 (SC 5232): Codex Canonum & Constituionum Ecclesiæ Anglicanæ, with 134 items listed;

2K4ᵛ (p. 144) 36. Junius 1 (SC 5113): eME Ormulum, semi-*Saxonicè*;

37. (?) Junius 115a–b (SC 5226): Glossarii v Linguarum Septentrionalium Gothicæ, Anglo-Saxonicæ, Francicæ, Islandicæ, Runicæ, by Junius;

Apographa Juniana 'Junius's Transcripts' [Items 67 and 85–6 are original MSS]

38. Junius 55 (SC 5167): Codex Argentei Apographum, the Gothic Gospels, then in the possession of Junius's nephew, Isaac Vossius, and sold by him to de la Gardie who gave it to Uppsala, now no. 1 above;

39. Junius 107 (SC 5218): Hymni Veteris Ecclesiæ, with AS interlinear gloss;

40. Junius 52 (SC 5164): Regula Benedicti, Æthelwoldus, etc.

41. Junius 12 (SC 5124): Boëthius, De Consolatione Philosophiæ in OE;

42. Junius 38 (SC 5150): Wulfstani archiepiscopi Paraenesis;

43. Junius 100 (SC 5211): Incertus Autor de Sanctis in Anglia sepultis;

44. Unidentified: Adami status post lapsum;

45. (?) Junius 108 (SC 5219): Hymnarium v. Anglosaxonicæ F. Junii inpræfatione ad suum Gl. Goth;

46. Junius 48 (SC 5160): De duodecim Abusis secundum Cyprianum;

2L1ʳ (p. 145) 47. Junius 47 (SC 5159): Hexamaeron, from Hatton 115, coll. Hatton 116;

48. Junius 39 (SC 5151): Decalogue, Lord's Prayer, Creed with notes by Markward Freher (cf. Junius 64 (SC 5175));

49. Junius 76 (SC 5187): Excerpts from Lindisfarne and Rushworth Gospels in L with OE glosses;

50. Junius 69 (SC 5180): Commentitia ipsius Domini epistola de coelo dilapsa;

51. Junius 74 (SC 5185): Nicodemi Pseudo-Evangelium;

52. Unidentified: 'Sancti in Anglia sepulti' = (?)no. 43;

53. Junius 70 (SC 5181): OE Alfredian Soliloquies of St Augustine;

54. Junius 61 (SC 5172): Quaestiones ... inter Adrianum et Ritheum;

55. Junius 59 (SC 5170): De peccatorum medicina;

56. Junius 63 (SC 5174): Modus confitendi;

57. Junius 104 (SC 5215): Interogationes Sigewulfi presbiteri;

58. Junius 60 (SC 5171): OE *Promissio regis*;

518   CATALOGUE OF EARLY PRINTED BOOKS CONTAINING ANGLO-SAXON

	59. Junius 15 (SC 5127): Orosius from Tiberius B.i, coll. Lauderdale;
	60. Junius 44 (SC 5156): De observatione lunae et quae cavenda;
2L1ᵛ (p. 146)	61. Junius 41 (SC 5153): De primo die seculi;
	62. Junius 65 (SC 5176): OE excerpts re. Christian duties from Nero A.i, fos 71, 100;
	63. Junius 101 (SC 5212): Calendarial notes headed 'Menologium';
	64. Unidentified: Fragmentum Epistolæ ab Ælfrico Episcopo script, ad jam nunc ordinatos. Descript. ex Cod. MS Collegii Benedict. Cant. [CCC 201] p. 31. Partem descripsit Junius, reliquam Londinum revocatus non potuit absolvere. Item, Officium hominis Christiani. Descript. ex perantiquis membranis Isaaci Vossii.
	65. Junius 71 (SC 5182): Ælfrici præsulis Glossarium (via Rubens);
	66. Junius 26 (SC 5138): Nowell's Dictionarium Saxonicum MS;
	67. Junius 43 (SC 5155): printed book, Joannes Meursius, *Roma luxurians, sive, De luxu Romanorum, liber singularis* (Copenhagen, 1631), with notes 'De somniorum diversitate' by Junius from Tiberius A.iii, pp. 70, 80;
	68. Junius 27 (SC 5139): Latin Psalter with interlinear OE translation, s.x;
	69. Junius 102 (SC 5213): Wulfstan, 5 Sermons coll. from Nero A.i, CCC 201, and Hatton 113/14;
	70. Junius 62 (SC 5173): Wynflæd's agreement 990 x 992 (Sawyer 1454) and Charter of King Cnut to Bury St Edmunds 1021 x 1023 (Sawyer 980);
	71. Junius 67 (SC 5178): ASC (C), 'Abingdon', beginning;
	72. (?) Digby 4 (SC 1605), fo 97, Moralium Præceptorum Fragmentum = eME *Poema Morale*;
	73. Junius 40 (SC 5152): Excerpta ex Libro Scintillarum (Defensor of Ligugé);
	74. Junius 103 (SC 5214): Evangelica Dano-Saxonice (i.e. ON) + 'Exorcismi sacri ad reddendos agros fertiles', both from Caligula A.vii;
	75. Junius 77 (SC 5188): Latin-OE glossary by Junius + Onomasticon;
	76. Junius 53 (SC 5165): Alfredian version of Gregory's Pastoral Care;
	77. Junius 72 (SC 5183): Ælfric's Glossary from Julius A.ii;

2L2ʳ (p. 147)	78.	Junius 105 (SC 5216): OE *Judith* (poem) from Vitellius A.xv;
	79.	Junius 85–6 (SC 5196–7): Homilies in 2 volumes, s.xi;
	80.	Junius 66 (SC 5177): Monachicum Colloquium inter Discipulum & Magistrum Latino-Saxonicum from Tiberius A.iii;
	81.	Unidentified: Chronici Veteris fragmentum longam Regum Saxonum seriem aliquo- usque pertrahens = (?) no.71;
	82.	Junius 58 (SC 5169): OE Liber medicinalis;
	83.	Fell 8–18 (SC 8696–8706): Dictionarium Septentrionale in 5 languages, Junius's materials prepared for publication by Fell, but not printed;

Inter Codd. Dugdal. In Musæo Ashmoleano 'Dugdale MSS in Ashmolean'

84. Dugdale 29 (SC 6519): Dugdale's Dictionarium *Saxonico-Lat* 1644;

In Bibl. Coll. D. Johannis Bapt. 'In St John's College Library'

85. St John's 154: Ælfric's Grammar s.xi;
86. St John's 194: Gospels in Latin; AS Charter (Sawyer 1636) s.xii.

Libros Impress. manu Junii emendatos 'Printed books annotated by Junius'

87. Junius 10 (SC 5122): Wheelock, OE Bede + ASC **1643.1** + Laws **1644.1**;

2L2ᵛ (p. 148)	88.	Junius 18 (SC 5130): Selden, Eadmer **1623.3**;
	89.	Junius 33 (SC 5145): Spelman, Psalter **1640.3**;
	90.	Junius 54 (SC 5166): *The xiii Bukes of Eneados of ... Virgill translatet ... bi ... Gawin Douglas* (London 1553; STC 24797);
	91.	Junius 9 (SC 5121): *The Workes of ... Geffrey Chaucer*, ed. Thomas Speght (London 1598; STC 5077/8);
	92.	Junius 73 (SC 5184): Junius, Cædmon **1655.2** (= no. 15);
	93.	Junius 7 (SC 5119): Somner, Dictionary **1659.1** (= no. 11);

Libet etiam Catalogum Codd. Bodl. *claudere cum*

94. Exeter coll. PGWD 64(1): printed book, Hugues Menard (ed.), *Diui Gregorii ... magni liber sacramentorum*, (Paris, Dionysius Moreau, 1642). 'Literis Anglo-Saxonicis totum exaratum est', but not so;
95. Junius 6 (SC 5118): Dictionarium veteris linguae anglicanae (Chaucer);
96. Junius 82 (SC 5193): printed book, *Karoli magni et Ludouici pii ... capitula* (Paris, 1640);
97. Bodley 579 (SC 2675): Leofric Missal (France s.ix/x) with AS additions;

(p. 149)		98.	Auct. F.4.32 (SC 2176): Includes AS Invention of the Cross;
		99.	Bodley 342 (SC 2405): Homilies, with 41 items listed;
(p. 150)		100.	Bodley 865 (SC 2737): Capitula of Theodulf, with 15 chapters listed.

2L3ᵛ–2N3ᵛ (pp. 150–66)   List of MSS (and printed sources) in Cambridge:

(p. 150)	CUL	101.	Kk.3.18, OE Bede;
		102.	Ii.2.4, Alfredian Pastoral Care;
		103.	Ii.2.11, OE Gospels;
		104.	Ff.1.23, Psalms L + OE;
(p. 151)		105.	Ii.4.6, Homilies, with 35 items detailed;
		106.	Hh.1.10, Ælfric's Grammar;
		107.	Unidentified: 'Annales *Saxonici*', perhaps a Brut chronicle such as Hh.vi.9 or Kk.i.12;
(p. 152)		108.	Gg.3.28, Ælfric, Homilies, with 105 items detailed;
(p. 155)		109.	Ii.1.33, Homilies & Lives of Saints, with 52 items detailed.
(p. 156)	TCC	110.	B.15.34, Homilies, with 28 items detailed;
(p. 157)		111.	R.4.26, ME *Metrical Chronicle* attrib. 'Robert of Gloucester' (not B.14.52, *pace* Gneuss);
		112.	R.5.22, Bede s.xiv, Alfredian Pastoral Care s.xi, Vitae Sanctorum s.xii;
		113.	R.9.17, Ælfric's Grammar s.xi/xii;
		114.	R.17.1, Eadwine Psalter, L + OE, s.xii.
	CCC	115.	57, Benedictine Rule, L + some OE glosses;
		116.	196, OE Martyrology;
		117.	70, AS & later English Laws, s.xiv;
		118.	190, Archbishop Wulfstan's Commonplace-book;
		119.	449, Ælfric's Grammar;
		120.	12, Alfredian Pastoral Care;
		121.	41, OE Bede;
(p. 158)		122.	144, Corpus Glossary;
		123.	140, WS Gospels;
		124.	162, Homilies, with 51 items detailed;
(p. 159)		125.	178, Homilies, with 31 items details; Benedictine Rule;
(p. 160)		126.	188, Homilies, with 45 items detailed;
(p. 161)		127.	198, Homilies, with 63 items detailed;
(p. 162)		128.	302, Homilies, with 32 items detailed;
(p. 163)		129.	322, Alfredian version of Gregory's *Dialogues*;
		130.	173, AS Parker Chronicle (A);
		131.	191, Rule of Chrodegang, L + OE

		132.	421, Homilies, with 15 items detailed;
		133.	419, Homilies, with 15 items detailed;
(p. 164)		134.	402, *Ancrene Wisse* 'written in Saxon Characters';
		135.	422, Red Book of Darley, with *Solomon and Saturn* (verse dialogues) and a Missal with OE annotations;
		136.	303, Homilies, 67 items detailed;
(p. 166)		137.	201, Capitula of Theodulf (45 chs), with 37 items detailed;
		138.	383, AS Laws;
		139.	367 (pt II), Homilies;
		140.	101, AS and later Charters, s.xvi;
		141.	391, L Psalms, Canticles etc, with OE prayers and prognostics;
		142.	307 (pt I), Felix of Crowland, Vita S. Guthlaci (L) s.ix;
		143.	183, Bede, Vitae S. Cuthberti (L) with OE glosses;
		144.	(?) 'Dictionarium *Saxonico-Latinum*. Sed pluteum, in quo disponitur hoc MS Catalogus mihi missus non designat'. Gneuss suggests a copy of Somner 1659.1; Hickes clearly thought it to be a manuscript, but the Corpus Glossary is no. 122 above.
2N3ᵛ–4ʳ (pp. 166–7)			List of MSS in Royal collection (in St James's Palace):
	BL	145.	Royal 7.C.xii: Ælfric, Homilies;
		146.	Royal 1.A.xiv: WS Gospels;
		147.	Royal 7.C.iv: Defensor of Ligugé, Liber Scintillarum with OE gloss;
		148.	Royal 12.D.xvii: Liber Medicinalis, used by Somner;
		149.	Royal 2.B.v: L Psalter and Canticles glossed in OE, used by Lisle for his unpublished edition (no. 17 above);
		150.	Royal 15.B.xxii: Ælfric's Grammar, said to have been used by Somner for his edition in 1659.1.
2N4ʳ (p. 167)			MS in Bibliotheca Lauderdaliana (Duke of Lauderdale):
	BL	151.	Additional 47967: OE Orosius.
2N4ʳ–2O1ʳ (pp. 167–9)			MS in Rochester Cathedral:
	RKA	152.	DRc/R1 (Textus Roffensis, *olim* Rochester Cathedral Library MS A.3.5).
2O1ʳ–2O2ʳ (pp. 169–71)			List of MSS in Worcester Cathedral:
	OBL	153.	Dugdale 12 (SC 6502), pp. 502–5: Catalogue of 92 Charters (cf. Gneuss);
	BL	154.	Harley 4660: 15 Charters s.xvii (cf. Gneuss).
2O2ʳ–2ᵛ (pp. 171–2)			List of MSS in Lambeth Palace:

		155.	427: Psalter with OE gloss, etc. with 9 items listed (used by Lisle for his unpublished edition, no. 16 above);
		156.	489: Homilies with 5 items listed;
		157.	487: Homilies semi-Sax, s.xiii, with 20 items listed;

202ᵛ–204ᵛ (pp. 172–6)   List of MSS in Cotton Library:

    BL   158. Julius A.ii (A.1): Ælfric's Grammar, to be distinguished from the pseudo-Ælfric Grammar printed by Somner 1659.1, Adrian & Ritheus;

    159. Julius A.vi: Hymns and Canticles with OE gloss;

    160. Julius A.ix (A.10): Lives of Saints, etc., s.xiii;

    161. Julius E.vii: Homilies, including Ælfric, Lives of Saints;

    162. Cleopatra B.xiii: Homilies, s.xiv;

    163. Tiberius A.vi (A.5): ASC (B);

    164. Tiberius A.iii: Benedictine Rule & Regularis Concordia, both with OE gloss;

    165. Tiberius B.i: OE Orosius, ASC (C);

    166. Tiberius B.iv: ASC (D);

    167. Tiberius B.v: Bede, De Temporibus (incomplete), Marvels of the East;

(p. 174)   168. Tiberius B.xi (B.8) + Otho B.ii: Alfredian Pastoral Care (but *recte* Otho B.ii belongs with Otho B.x);

    169. Tiberius C.vi: Psalter with OE gloss;

    170. Caligula A.vii: OS *Heliand* etc.;

    171. Caligula A.xiv: Lives of Saints (Martin, Thomas, Mildred);

    172. Caligula A.xv: Computistica, etc.;

    173. Claudius B.iv: OE prose Hexateuch (confused with Junius's *Cædmon* 1655.2);

    174. Claudius D.iii: Benedictine Rule L + OE, s.xiii;

    175. Nero A.i: Ecclesiastical Institutes, Laws, Wulfstan *Sermo Lupi*;

    176. Galba A.xiv: Prayers, Hymns, etc.;

    177. Otho A.viii (Ker 168): Life of St Machutus;

    178. Otho A.x: Laws of Æthelred (fragment);

    179. Otho B.x (B.40): Homilies, Hexaemeron, Lives of Saints;

(p. 175)   180. Otho B.xi: OE Bede;

    181. Otho A.viii (Ker 169): Oratio Gregorii Papae with OE gloss:

    182. Otho B.ii: Alfredian Pastoral Care;

    183. Otho C.i: WS Gospels, Gregory's Dialogues, Vitas Patrum, etc.;

    184. Vitellius A.vii: Promissio regis;

185. Vitellius A.xv: Augustine, Soliloquies, Gospel of Nicodemus, Letter of Alexander, Fragmentum de Juditha (note absence of awareness of *Beowulf*);
186. Vitellius C.v: Homilies;
187. Vitellius D.vii: Nowell's transcripts, s.xvi, of Ælfric, Preface, Letters, also Charters;
188. Vitellius C.iii: Herbarium;
189. Vitellius D.xvii: Homilies for Saints' days (Vita S. *Alphagi*);
190. Vitellius E.xviii: Psalter with OE gloss;
191. Vitellius D.xx: Situation of Durham, with poem *Durham*;
192. Vespasian D.vi: Hymn, Ps 50, glosses;
193. Vespasian D.xiv: Homilies (many by Ælfric), incl. de sacerdotum nuptiis;
194. Vespasian D.xx: Confessional Prayer (= modus confitendi);
195. Vespasian D.xxi: prose life of Guthlac;
196. Titus A.iv: Benedictine Rule, L + OE;
197. Titus D.xxvii: Ælfric's version of Bede's *De Temporibus*

(p. 176) 198. Domitian viii: ASC (F);
199. Domitian A.ix: Miscellany including fragment from an AS Chronicle, s.xv;
200. Cleopatra A.iii: Glossarium Latino-Saxonicum;
201. Tiberius A.xiii: Worcester cartularies;
202. Nero E.i: Homilies, Saints' Lives, AS Charters (these being items 129–30 in Smith 1696: 60);
203. Otho A.vi: Alfredian version of Boethius's Consolation of Philosophy;

2O4^v–2P1^r (pp. 176–7) List of MSS in Canterbury Cathedral '*inter Apographa Guil. Somneri*' [cf. Woodruff 1911: 42–51]:
204. B.4: Miscellany including item 11 'Gesta Servatoris nostri';
205. C.3: Miscellany including 'Cædmonis in Genesin Paraphrasio', Orosius + ASC;
206. E.2: Canuti Regis Leges;
207. E.1: Miscellany including many charters.

2P1^r–1^v (p. 177): Libri Francici, including those of Junius;

OBL 208. Junius 80 (SC 5191): printed book, Matthias Flacius Illyricus (ed.), *Otfridi Evangeliorum Liber* (Basle, 1571);
209. Junius 79 (SC 5190): printed book, Paulus Merula (ed.), *Willerami Abbatis in Canticum Canticorum Paraphrasis Gemina: Prior Rhythmis Latinis, Altera Veteri Lingua*

Francica (Leiden, ex officina Plantiniana, 1598), on which was based Junius **1655.1**.

210. Junius 13 (SC 5125): Tatian's Harmony of the Gospels L + OHG + Gothic;
211. Junius 21 (SC 5133): printed book, Gherard van der Schueren, *Vocabulari[us] q⟨ui⟩ intitulatur Teuthonista* (Cologne, 1477);
212. Junius 42 (SC 5154): Junius's notes on no. 210;
213. Junius 17 (SC 5129): Junius's transcript of no. 208;
214. Junius 16 (SC 5128): *Annalied*, eMHG poem about Anna II, abp of Cologne;
215. Junius 116a–f (SC 5227–8): Glossarium Theotisco-Latinum cum Notis;

(p. 178) 216. Missing (SC 5221): Hymni aliquot Francici interlineate ex membranis *Vossianis*;

217. Junius 20 (SC 5132): printed book, Melchior Goldast, *Alamannicarum Rerum Scriptores aliquot Vetusti* (Frankfurt-am-Main, 1606);
218. Junius 25 (SC 5137): 'Murbach Hymnal';

2P1ᵛ (p. 178) Libri Frisici apud Junius;

OBL 219. Junius 78 (SC 5189): Frisian legal and theological collections;
220. Junius 111 (SC 5222): printed book, Sibrandus Siccama (ed.), *Lex Frisionum* (Franeker, 1617);
221. Junius 109 (SC 5220): printed book, Frisian statutes, *Dat landriucht der Fresena* [Holland, 1483/88];
222. Junius 49 (SC 5161): Extracts from 3 MSS of Frisian laws collated with previous item;

2P2ʳ (p. 179) Libri Runici, cimbro-Gothici, Islandici, &c;

223. TCO (2), WCO: printed book, Ole Worm, [*Runir*], *seu Danica literature antiquissima* (Copenhagen, Melchior Martzan & Georg Holst, 1651);

OBL 224. Junius 8 (SC 5119): printed book, Ole Worm, *Danicorum monumentorum libri sex* (Copenhagen, 1643);
225. Junius 14 (SC 5126): printed book, Ole Worm, *Fasti Danici* (Copenhagen, 1643);
226. Douce V subst.10: printed book, Olaus Verelius, *Manuductio compendiosa ad Runographiam Scandicam antiquam* (Uppsala, 1675);
227. fol. THETA 572: printed book, Olaus Verelius (ed.), *Hervarar Saga* (Uppsala, 1672);

	228. ECO, UCO: printed book, Olaus Vereleus & Johannes Scheffer (eds), *Gothrici & Rolfi Westrogothiae regum historia lingua antiqua gothica conscripta* [Hrólfs saga Gautrekssonar] (Uppsala, Henricus Curio, 1664);
	229. Unidentified: 'Excerpta quædam ex Olao Wormio per Fr. Junium ... MS';
OBL	230. Junius 120 (SC 5231): Gothicae Runae seu linguae septentrionalis ... dictionaries, the MS of Gudmund Andresson's *Lexicon-Islandicum* (Copenhagen, 1683);
2P2^r–2P3^v (pp. 179–82)	Libri à Domino Gabriele de la Gardie, given to Uppsala Universitets-bibliotek 1669, catalogued by Celsius 1745 from de la Gardie's own account (UUB U 65 ac: Jan 1669), which was evidently also used by Hickes as both lists show the same order and (nearly always) wording; further details of several of the MSS in Gödel 1892: 1–24. [Magnus Gabriel de la Gardie (1622–86), Chancellor of Sweden].
UUB	231. DG 3: *Konungasagurne* (Historia Regum), destroyed by fire 1702;
(p. 180)	232. DG 4: Fragmentum Historiae Olai Tryggonii, Norvegiæ Regis (*Ólafssaga Tryggvasonar*), MS, pr. ed. by Olaus Vereleus (Uppsala, 1665);
	233. DG 5: Drama Ἐρωτικόν, Pamphilus och Galathea, Æðra och Hugrecki;
	234. DG 6: Historia de quodam Eli (*Elissaga ok Rosamundu*), in linguam Normannicam;
	235. DG 7: Variæ Britannorum fabulæ (*Strengleikar eða Ljóðabók*);
	236. DG 8: Regis Magni Hagensons Lex Frostoniensis (Frosteitings lag = Norsk lagbok = Konung Magnús Lagabœtirs landslag) + Historia S. Olai minoris (*Ólafssaga ins helga*) [St Olaf II, k of Norway (1015–28)]: http://urn.kb.se/resolve?urn=urn:n bn:se:alvin:portal:record-54183;
	237. DG 9: Corpus Juris Islandici (Islands Lagbok);
	238. DG 10: Grettla (Historia Gretteri Asmundi, *Grettissaga*);
	239. DG 11: Edda Snorra Sturlusonar (Uppsala Edda) & Skalda, MS of pr. ed. by Peder Hansen Resen (Copenhagen, 1665): Edda Snorra Sturlusonar; http://urn.kb.se/resolve?urn=urn:n bn:se:alvin:portal:record-54179;
(p. 181)	240. DG 12: Pars aliqua de Brittlinga Sagu, Icelandic + L, plus 'Lang fadga taal, om nackura Danmarkur og Noregz. Konga'

(*Hákonarsaga Hárekssonar*: account of Danish kings and bishops);

241. DG 13: De Chronico Norvagico (and other antiquities) from the letters of Arngrímr Jónsson to Ole Worm (s.xvii);
242. DG 14: Kn´ytlingasaga (on kings of Denmark and Norway) 1640;
243. DG 15: Historia de quodam Haquinio (*Hákonarsaga Hárekssonar*);
244. DG 17: Speculum Regale eða Konungs-skuggsjá (Icelandic);
245. DG 18: Speculum Regale eða Konungs-skuggsjá (Danish version by Stephan Hansen Stephanius 1643);
246. DG 19: Riddara Christian Frijs Drapa;
247. DG 20: Liber quidam Rhythmicus (Danske Riimkronike);
248. DG 21: Annales Groenlandiæ (986–1473) s.xvii;
249. DG 27: Chronologia Islandico-Latina [but focused on popes and (holy) Roman emperors] 740–1295;
250. DG 41: Hosue Lausnar wijsur Eigelz Schalla Grimsonar (Hǫfuðlausn);
251. DG 46: Corpus Legum Selandiæ (Selandz Lowbog. mad Birckeratten);
252. DG 55: Glossarium priscæ linguæ Danicæ 1636, by Olaus Magnus (Olaf Mansson 1490–1557);
253. DG 64: Libri decem Alexandreidos;
254. Unidentified, probably a copy of Södermannlagen, possibly UUB B 17 or B 56, but the gårdsratt (manor law) is the wrong one (cf. Schlyter 1827–77: IV.xxvii–xxviii, xxx);
255. Unidentified, probably a copy of Södermannlagen, possibly UUB B 10, B 15, or B 17 I (cf. Schlyter 1827–77: IV.xvi, xxix, xxx);
256. Unidentified;
257. Unidentified;
258. UUB C 20, Lexicon Latino-Suethicum, the only known medieval MS;
259. DG 44: Skånelagen (see Schlyter 1827–77: IX.xli–xliii; Brøndum-Nielsen [1920–]61: I.lxiii);
260. DG 46 i: Skånelagen or Skånske Lov (Brøndum-Nielsen [1920–]61: I.lxiii);
261. DG 46 ii: Eriks Sjællandske Lov (Brøndum-Nielsen [1920–]61: v.xiii);
262. Unidentified printed book containing prec. 1578;

263. Unidentified, probably either UUB H 122 or H 129 (Brøndum-Nielsen [1920–]61: II.xxx).

Note: There are many brief quotations of incipits etc in the Catalogue.

TYPE:

Main text in the Junian Pica Roman (attributable to Christoffel van Dijck; Body 83) interspersed with the Junian Pica Italic (also attributable to Christoffel van Dijck).

AS6: Christoffel van Dijck's Pica Anglo-Saxon cut for Franciscus Junius (except that the capital ᛦ used by OUP was cut by Peter de Walpergen, fl.1676–1702) occurs in the specimen on A1^r, in text as listed above under Contents, and in words (etc.) on b3^v, b4, c1^r, c4^r, A1^v–4^v, B1^v–4^r, C2^r–3^r, C4^v–F3^r, F4^r–H1^r, H2, I1^r–2^v, I4^v–K2^v, K3^v–L4^r, M1^r–3^v, M4^v–N1^r, N3^r, N4^v–O2^v, O3^v–4^r, P1, 2E1^r–2I1^v, 2I4^r, 2K1^v–2^r, 2K3^r–4^v, 2L2^v, 2L3^v–4^r, 2M3^v, 2N2, 2N4^r–2O1^v, 2P1^r, 2P4^r, 2Q3^r–2V1^v.

Special sorts shown in the specimen:

    11 lower-case sorts: ð, ꝼ, ȝ, ı, p, ſ, τ, ẏ; þ, ð, p;
    9 capitals: Ꝉ, Є, Ᵹ, Ꝺ, Ϻ, 8; Þ, Ð, ᛦ.

Total: 20 sorts.

Special sorts shown in text and words:

    11 lower-case sorts: ð, ꝼ, ȝ, ı, p, ſ, τ, ẏ; þ, ð, p;
    9 capitals: Ꝉ, Є, Ᵹ, Ꝺ, Ϻ, 8; Þ, Ð, ᛦ;
    1 other: þ.

Total: 21 sorts.

Other special type-designs:

1. The Junian Gothic occurs in specimen on A1^r, text and words on b3, b4, c1, d2^v, A1^v–3^v, A4^v–B1^r, B2^v–F4^r, G1^r–2^r, G3^r–H1^v, H2^v–K1^r, K2^r–3^r, K4^r, L1^v, L3^v–N1^r, N2^r–O4^r, P1, 2E1^r–2I1^v, 2P4^r, 2Q3^r–2V1^v.

2. The Junian Runic occurs in specimen on N1^v, and words on C4^r, D1^r, D3^v, D4^v, E4^v, F1^r–3^r, G2^v, G3^v, K3^v, L3^v–4^r.

3. The Junian Icelandic occurs in words on C2^v (used also in the margin for Welsh!), D1^r (used in the margin for OHG!), F2^r, F3^v (OHG), G4^r, N4^v–P1^v, Q1^r–2I2^v, 2P2^r–3^v.

This fount includes capital Þ cut by Peter de Walpergen at Oxford to add to the Junian fount (Lucas 1998: 187 and notes 51, 53).

4. The so-called 'Pica English' (a textura also probably cut by Walpergen; Lucas 1998: 186), which occurs with the Junian type-designs on the OUP 1693 Specimen, also occurs, e.g. D2^v, K1^r.

AS7: On the title-page, π2^r, the AS quotation from Bede shows the Somnerian Pica Anglo-Saxon: ð, ı, p, ſ, τ, ẏ; ð, p; Ϻ; þ, ꝫ.   8 + 1 + 2 = 11 sorts.

Note: Bernard's *Tabula Alphabetorum*, engraved by Michael Burghers, includes Anglo-Saxon (AD 500), together with Gothic, Runic and historical Latin scripts. The Anglo-Saxon section includes the following:

        9 lower-case designs: ð, f, ʒ, p, ſ, τ; þ, ð, ƿ;
        7 capitals: L, E, Ᵹ, Ꝺ, Ϻ; Þ, Ð.

Copies seen: Lacking 2V2χ1: CUL Bb*.2.24(D); ECC 302.5.10; TCD ss.ee.34 (owned by Claudius Gilbert), II.k.53 (owned by Sir William Palliser, 1830–82); OBL 4⁰.Sigma.370 (π1–P1 only, heavily annotated by Samuel Squire, archdeacon of Bath, b.1715).

With 2V2χ1: BL C.28.i.1 (with the original dedication to Sancroft printed but not published; and with annotations by Hickes, perhaps with a view to revision); Sancroft's own copy (with the handwritten full dedication cut in the printed version for political reasons), which he received as dedicatee, survives as OBL MS Tanner 317, not with his books in ECC.

Copies also at: BUL, CCC, CGC, KCC, CSJ, TCC, DCL, DUL, EdCL, GlCL, GML, LiCL, LPL, LSH, NLS, NLW, NT, NUL, OEF, OHC, OJC, OLMH, OMaC, OQC, ORP, OSJ, OStE, OTC, OTI, OWmC, SAC, UBL, UCL, WCC, YML, DML, NUIG, RIA, ULim, PBN, GUB; FSL, USLC, NYCU, UTS, HHL, HUL, IUL, DDUL, KSRL, LCP, NLC, UCBL, UCLA, UTA, UVL, YUB, TUL; NLA, NSW.

Bibliography: Alston III.i.6; Carter 1975: 119–120; Gadd 2013: 438, 439, 538–539; Gneuss 1996; Harris 1998: 22; Harris 1992: 24–27, 39–45; Hughes 1982; Lucas 1998: 186; Niles 2015: 123–125; Ruano-García 2015: 29–30 (on northern dialect words added by Hickes to Jónsson).

Facsimile (of OBL Tanner 317): English Linguistics 1500–1800, no. 277 (Menston: Scolar, 1971).

Manuscript: BL, Harley 3317, (a) fos 3–19 and (b) 20–29. (a) A MS copy (or draft?) in the hand of Humfrey Wanley with his signature of ownership dated 15 Oct 1691 on what is apparently a trial tp. On fo 19ᵛ there is a list of 'Libri Anglo-Saxonici Excusi' in Wanley's hand: it is the same as that in **1689.3** except for the additions of **1689.3** itself plus **1692.1**, Gibson's edition of the ASC. (b) A list in Wanley's hand of 'Libri Anglo-Saxonici', i.e. manuscripts, showing the same order of libraries as in **1689.3**, but dated 'finis' 11 Nov 1691, also after the publication of **1689.3**. Cf. Harris 1992: 85.

1690.1: Ussher, James, ed. Henry Wharton (chaplain to abp Sancroft), *Historia Dogmatica Controversiæ inter Orthodoxos & Pontificios de Scripturis et Sacris Vernaculis*. London: R[obert] R[oberts] (typis) for Richard Chiswell (impensis), 1690. Wing U179; ESTC R23577. AS7.
Ælfric, etc.

Collation: 4⁰: A⁴ a⁴ B–3P⁴ [$2 signed (+A3; -A2, 2R1)] 248 leaves, paginated [i–xvi], *1–2*, 3–468, *469–480* (pp. 279–280, 304–306 not numbered).

SOURCES OF PASSAGES UTILIZING ANGLO-SAXON TYPES:

R4ᵛ (p. 128) From (?) CCC 101, p. 55 'ex Collectionibus Josselini': Ælfric, Preface to Genesis, opening paragraph (as Crawford 1969: 76; Marsden 2008: 3);

From 1643.1 H1ʳ/30–3: Ælfric, CH I.20, Feria IIII de fide catholica, opening statement (Clemoes 1997: 335/2–3);

From 1639.4 3A6ᵛ: Ælfric's Letter to Wulfsige, bp of Sherborne 992–1001/2, as Fehr 1914: §§61–62;

S2ʳ (p. 131) From 1639.4 2Y4ʳ: Laws I Cnut 21, 22 (... rihtne geleafan), as Liebermann I. 302;

3C1ʳ (p. 377) From 1639.4 3A6ᵛ (§23): Ælfric's Letter to Wulfsige, bp of Sherborne 992–1001/2, as Fehr 1914: §§61–63;

From 1659.1 2X4ʳ/38: Ælfric's Grammar (extract; Zupitza 1889: 3/9);

3C1ᵛ (p. 378) From 1643.1 2A2ᵛ: Ælfric, CH1, Dominica I in Adventu (phrase extract), as Clemoes 1997: XXXIX, 522/75;

From 1643.1 2A2ᵛ: Ælfric, CH2, Assumptio Sanctae Mariae Virginis (phrase extract), as Godden 1979: XXIX, 259/119;

From BL Royal 7 C.iv, 96ʳ/11 (gloss above): Liber Scintillarum, (phrase extract glossing Rochais 1957 ch. 81/18), as Rhodes 1889: 219/12;

3C2ʳ (p. 379) From 1638.1 K4ᵛ/3–4: Ælfric on Old and New Testament (extract);

3C2ᵛ–3D1ᵛ (pp. 380–6) From OBL Laud misc.509, fos 1–3, coll. CUL Ii.1.33, CCC 101 (s.xvi): Ælfric, Preface to Genesis (entire), as Crawford 1969: 76–80, Marsden 2008: 3–7;

3D1ᵛ–2ʳ (pp. 386–7) From 1643.1 2A3ʳ/24, 2A3ᵛ/15–18: OE translation of Alcuin's *De virtutibus et vitiis* (§ De scripturarum lectione, extracts), as Warner 1917: 94/1–26;

3D3ʳ (p. 389) From Caligula A.vii, 11ʳ/1–3, 34ʳ/9–18: Old Saxon poem *Heliand* 1–5, 1150–6, as Behaghel/Taeger 1984: 4, 42;

3N1ʳ (p. 457) From 1639.4 3C3ʳ, §20: OE and L versions (extract) of the Capitula of Theodulf of Orléans (c.760–821), OE and L as Sauer 1978: 304–403;

3O1ʳ (p. 465) Refers to 1571.1, 1665.2 (very complimentary about Junius).

TYPE:

Main text in Pierre Haultin's English-size Roman (Body 93) interspersed with an English-size Italic (e.g. F1ʳ–2ᵛ).

AS7: The Somnerian Pica Anglo-Saxon occurs in text as indicated above under Contents and in words on a4ᵛ combined with a Pica Roman (a few words on 3C4ʳ = p. 383).

Special sorts shown:

    12 lower-case sorts: ð, *e*, f, ᵹ, ı, ƿ, ſ, τ, ẏ; þ, ð, ꝥ;
    4 capitals: Ꝫ, Ꝧ, Ꝏ, Ð;
    3 others: þ, ꝉ, ∴

 Total: 19 sorts.

Note: Roman d and e often used in place of AS ð and e. Capitals are used sparingly.

  Copies seen: APL C.v.6; ECC 328.2.56; TCD KK.ff.27 (owned by Claudius Gilbert).
  Copies also at: BL, BCLW, BUT, CUL, CPH, CSJ, CTH, TCC, DCL, DRD, DUL, EdUL, LCL, LHL, MJRUL, MTP, NLS, NLW, NT, OBL, OBC, OHC, OJC, OLC, OMC, ONC, OQC, OSJ, OTC, OXC, RLW, SAC, SML, SPC, UBL, WCC, WCF, WCL, WiCL, WoCL, YML; FSL, NYCU, UTS, HUL, DDUL, KSRL, MUL, PFL, PTS, UTA, YUB.

Bibliography: GR 5228.

1690.2: Benson, Thomas, *Thesaurus Linguæ Anglo-Saxonicæ* (prospectus printed but not published). Oxford: Sheldonian Theatre, 1690. Wing S4667. AS6.
Words
  Collation: 4⁰: single half-sheet with 2nd leaf signed A.
TYPE:
AS6: The main text (the beginning of the dictionary at letter A) shows Christoffel van Dijck's Pica Anglo-Saxon cut for Franciscus Junius, with Latin glosses in the Junian Pica Italic (also cut by van Dijck).
Special sorts shown:
    10 lower-case sorts. ð, f, ᵹ, ı, ƿ, ſ, τ, ẏ; þ, ꝥ.
Note: A1ʳ/23 shows þ in abroþen, whereas in 1701.1 the same word appears as abroðen.
  Copy seen: OBL Rawlinson D.377, fos 80–81.
Bibliography: Alston III.i.8; Carter 1975: 414; Foster 1891–2: I.109 (for Benson); Macray 1893: col 212; Nichols 1812: IV.141–142.

1691.1: Wharton, Henry, *Anglia Sacra*, vol. I. London: no printer stated, for Richard Chiswell (impensis), 1691. Wing W1560; ESTC R4174. AS7.

ASC, OE Bede, Charter (phrases)

Collation: 2⁰ in 4s: π² A² a⁴ b–e⁴ f² g⁴ B–5L⁴ [$2 signed (-A2, f2, 3E2, 3O2; 2E2 missigned E2, 2G2 missigned 2G1)] 438 leaves, paginated [i–iv], v–lviii, *lix–lx*, 1–805, *806–816* (pp. 177–178, 327–328, 395–396, 467–468, 551–552, 591–592, 690 not numbered).

SOURCES OF PASSAGES UTILIZING ANGLO-SAXON TYPES:

2A4ʳ (p. 183)   From **1643.1** F4ᵛ/10–14: OE Bede, I.7 (extract), as Miller 1890-8: I.1.34/26–27;

2E1ᵛ (p. 210)   From an unidentified source: statement by Edwin, a monk, of how Frithestan made Birnstan his successor as bp of Winchester (931): 'Ic Æadwin moncæn on ealden ministræ, &c.'; cp. Sawyer 1428, Harmer 113;

2V4ᵛ (p. 336)   From RKA, DRc/R1 (Textus Roffensis, *olim* RCL A.3.5), 171ʳ/4–14: Writ of William I to Herfast, bp of Thetford *post* 1077 (entire; Pelteret 25);

5H3ᵛ (p. 790)   From **1644.1** 4C3ᵛ/8–9: *ASC* 946, as Thorpe 1861: I.212 (the phrase seofeþe healf ger).

TYPE:

Main text in an English-size Roman. A Pica Roman (Body 82) is used for notes below the text from 2D1ʳ to 3B4ᵛ, interspersed with Robert Granjon's Pica Italic 'pendante', e.g., on 2X4ᵛ–2Y1ʳ.

AS7: Nicholas Nicholls's Somnerian Pica Anglo-Saxon occurs in text as listed above combined with the Pica Roman.

Special sorts shown:

   12 lower-case sorts: ð, *e*, ꝼ, ᵹ, 1, p, ſ, τ, ẏ; þ, ð, p;
   1 capital: K;
   2 others: þ, ⁊ (large);
 Total: 15 sorts.

Note 1: Uses Roman **d** for AS ð, and 7 for ⁊ on 2A4ʳ, and occasional roman **d** on 2V4ᵛ.

Note 2: On 2V4ᵛ capital **K** is unusual in having a j-like descender on the stem.

Copies seen: CUL 5.2.42, Pet.R.4.16; ECC 310.4.23; TCD MM.d.26 ((shows ±a3) owned by Claudius Gilbert), MBS 2⁰.H.eccl.359-1 (binding of white vellum on boards, blind-stamped); LFL 20I.

OBL MS Rawlinson D.730 (SC 13502 = Richard Chiswell's papers) contains a copy of the imprimatur on fo 68ʳ (Moore 1992: 61).

Copies also at: APL, BL, BCL, BCLW, BUL, BULW, BUT, CCA, CCC, CFM, CJC, CNC, CPH, CSel, CSJ, CTH, TCC, ChCL, DCL, DRD, DUL, ECL, EdUL, Eton, GlCL, GML, CUL, HCL, HHC, LCL, LGL, LHL, LHU, LiCL, MJRUL, MTP, NAL, NCL, NLS, NT, NUL, OAS, OBC, OCC, OEC, OHC, OJC, OKC, OLC, OMaC, OMC, ONC, OQC, OSA,

OSJ, StH, OWmC, OWoC, RCL, RLW, SAC, SCL, SML, SPC, UBL, WAL, WCC, WCF, WCL, WiCL, WoCL, YML, DEWL, DML, NLI, ULim, PBN, GUB; USLC, NYPL, NYCU, UTS, HHL, HUL, IUL, ACA, HCP, KSRL, NLC, SLU, UCBL, UCH, UCLA, UMI, UTA, UVL, YUB, QUK, TUL; UTL, UWL.

Bibliography: Douglas 1939: 183–191; Gross/Graves 1975: no. 1125, Hardy 1862–71: no. 21. GR5183.

1691.2: Gale, Thomas, *Historiae Britannicae, Saxonicae, Anglo-Danicae, Scriptores XV*. Oxford: Sheldonian Theatre, 1691. Wing G154; ESTC R200686. AS7.

BDS, **Charters**

Collation: 2^0: *2 (*1 + c1) a–b⁴ A–5C⁴ ²–⁵5C⁴ ⁶5C² 5D–5O² [$3 signed (-*2, A1, G1, M2, P2, S2, Z1, 2O1, 3B3, 3D3, 3V2, 4T3, 4Z3, 5C3, 5F2; 4F2 missigned 'Pfff 2')] 430 (+1) leaves, paginated [i–xxii, 1–2], 3–796, *797–840* (pp. 8, 48–50, 91–92, 140, 176–178, 288–290, 336, 382–384, 524, 551–552, 563–564, 700–702, 733–734, 756–758 not numbered; [State 1: pp. 27–30 (1st) misnumbered 19–22, 33–40 misnumbered 25–32, 41–48 misnumbered 33–39, *40*, 51–52 misnumbered 40–41, 53–54 misnumbered 45–46, 56 misnumbered 48], 88 misnumbered 78, 217–224 misnumbered 218–225, 296 misnumbered 300, 339 misnumbered 342, 342 misnumbered 339, 457 misnumbered 157, 517–518 misnumbered 516–517).

State 1 shows sigs B–D numbered ²1–8, 9–24; State 2 shows sig. A numbered [1–2], 3–7, *8*, sigs B–C numbered 9–24; B3 signed B2; Both states show sig. E numbered 25–32.

SOURCES OF PASSAGES UTILIZING ANGLO-SAXON TYPES:

T4ᵛ (p. 152)	From TCC R.7.28, fo 14: *Bede's Death Song* (WS version, as Dobbie 1942: 108); for this version of the text see Dobbie 1937: 90;
3S4ᵛ (p. 512)	From TCC O.2.1, fo 79: Writ of King Edward appointing Wulfric abbot of Ely 1055 × 1065 (entire; Sawyer 1100; Harmer 47);
3T3ᵛ (p. 518)	From (prob) TCC O.2.41, pp. 81–86: Charter of King Edgar to Ely 970 (entire, L with AS names; Sawyer 779; Birch 1266);
3T4ʳ (p. 519)	From TCC O.2.41, pp. 86–88: Charter of King Edgar to Ely 970 (entire, L + OE; Sawyer 780; Birch 1268);
3T4ᵛ–3V1ʳ (pp. 520–1)	From TCC O.2.41, pp. 88–92: Charter of King Edgar to Ely 970 (entire, L + OE; Sawyer 781; Birch 1269);
3V1 (pp. 521–522)	From TCC O.2.41, pp. 92–95: Charter of King Æthelred to Ely 1004 (entire, L + OE; Sawyer 907; Kemble 711 (L only));
3V1ᵛ–2ʳ (pp. 522–3)	From TCC O.2.41, pp. 95–98: Charter of King Cnut to Ely re. land at Wood Ditton 1022 (entire, L + OE; Sawyer 958; Kemble 734);

TYPE:

Main text in Arthur Nicholls's English-size Roman (Body 93) interspersed with an English-size Italic (e.g. on 2A2–3).

AS7: Nicholas Nicholls's Somnerian Pica Anglo-Saxon occurs combined with a Pica Roman in text as indicated above.

Special sorts shown:

    12 lower-case sorts: ð, *e*, ꝼ, ᵹ, ı, ꞃ, ſ, τ, ẏ; þ, ð, p;

    12 capitals: A, Æ¹, Æ², Є, Ⱡ, Ð, ꝳ, K, 8, Ð, Ᵹ (on 3T3ᵛ, 3V2ʳ), ital. *W*;

    3 others: þ (on 3T4ᵛ), ꝗ, ∴.

Total: 27 sorts.

Copies seen: State 1: CUL X.9.33 (shows *1χ1 before *1), R.8.37, Acton.a.25.180 (shows *2 after a4); TCD W.b.15. State 2: APL O.11.11 (lacks *1.2, but *1χ1 present; B2.3 in reverse order); LFL 13G (lacks (*1χ1).

Copies also at: AUL, BL, BCL, BCLW, BUL, CCA, CCC, ChC, CGC, CJC, KCC, CMC, CSJ, TCC, ChestC, DCL, ECL, HRC, LBL, LCL, LHL, LMT, LPL, LSH, NLS, NLW, OBL, OAS, OBC, OCC, OEC, OHC, OJC, OMC, ONC, OQC, OSJ, OWoC, OXC, RCL, SDL, SPC, UBL, WCL, WIHM, YML, DEWL, DML, NLI, PBN, GCB, GUB, MBS; FSL, HHL, HUL, CUofA, HCP, LCP, TCH, UCBL, UCH, UCLA, UMI, UTA, YUB, QUK; UML, VSL, VUW.

Bibliography: Carter 1975: 227–228, 417.

1691.3: Ray, John, *A Collection of English Words* (2nd edn of **1674.2**). London: no printer stated, for Christopher Wilkinson, 1691. Wing R389; ESTC R14631. AS7.

 Note: Ray drew on information from William Nicolson (James 1956: 74). On Ray see Derham 1760, Gunther 1928.

Words

 Collation: 12⁰: A–K¹² [$5 signed (-A1,2)] 120 leaves, paginated [i–xxiv], 1–211, *212–216* (pp. 46 misnumbered 47, 47 misnumbered 46).

TYPE:

Main text in a Pica Roman (Body 81) interspersed with a Pica Italic.

AS7: Nicholas Nicholls's Somnerian Pica Anglo-Saxon occurs in combination with the Pica Roman in words on A10ᵛ, B12ʳ (p. 23), G10ʳ–H4ᵛ (pp. 139–52), H7 (pp. 157–158).

Special sorts shown:

    11 lower-case sorts: ð, ꝼ, ᵹ, ı, ꞃ, ſ, τ, ẏ; þ, ð, p;

    2 capitals: Ⱡ, Є.

Total: 13 sorts.

Copy seen: CUL Dd*.5.5(F)¹.

Copies also at: BL, BUL, CCA, CMC, CME, CSJ, TCC, DUL, ERCP, GUL, LBL, LPL, LSH, NHM, NLS, NLW, OBL, OAS, OMaC, OQC, OXC, OMHS, RUL, UBL, WIHM, TCD, PBN, BSB; FSL, NYPL, HHL, HUL, IUL, BMC, DDUL, KSRL, LCP, NLC, PUL, UCLA, UPL, YUB, TUL; ADL.

Bibliography: Considine 2017: 109–113; Dobson 1968: I.188–189; Gladstone 2012; Keynes 1951: 41–43, no. 24.

Facsimile: English Linguistics 1500–1800 no. 145 (Menston: Scolar, 1969), from OBL Douce.R.14.

Edition: W.W. Skeat. London: Trübner, for the English Dialect Society, 1874.

1691.4: (?)Drummond, William, *Polemo-Middinia*, and James V of Scotland (attrib.), *Christs Kirk*, ed. Edmund Gibson. Oxford: Sheldonian Theatre, 1691. Wing D2204; ESTC R25046. AS6.

Words

Collation: 4°: a^4 b^2 A–C^4 [\$2 signed (+A3; -a1)] 18 leaves, paginated [i–xii], 1–22, 23–24.

TYPE:

Main text of Drummond's *Polemo-Middinia* in the Pica Roman attributable to Christoffel van Dijck and given to OUP by Junius (Body 83) interspersed with Junius's Pica Italic (also cut by van Dijck), and *Christs Kirk* in Peter de Walpergen's Pica Textura (Body 82.5) that appears with the types given by Junius on the OUP specimens **1693.2**, **1695.2**.

AS6: Christoffel van Dijck's Junian Pica Anglo-Saxon combined with the Junian Pica Roman occurs in words in the text of the notes on A1^r, A2, A3^v–B1^r, B2^r–C3^r, showing the following special sorts:

   10 lower-case sorts: ð, ꝼ, ᵹ, ı, þ, ſ, τ, ẏ; ð, p;
   2 capitals: Ꞇ, Ꝫ.
  Total: 12 sorts.

The notes also utilize the Junian Pica Gothic, Pica Icelandic and Pica Runic, as well as the Pica Roman, Pica Italic and (Walpergen's) Pica Textura; consequently, albeit on a smaller scale, they are as visually remarkable as the combination of these designs in **1689.3**.

Copy seen: CUL Bb*.9.5^{15}(D) (signed 'Thom. Tanner.' on a1^r).

Copies also at: AUL, BL, BUL, CCC, CGC, CSJ, TCC, DUL, EdUL, GML, HHC, LPL, LSH, OBL, OAS, OBC, OCC, OMaC, OQC, OSJ, OXC, SPC, PBN, FSL, NYPL, HHL, HUL, IUL, DDUL, KSRL, NLC, UCLA, UTA, YUB, TUL.

Bibliography: Sykes 1926: 9.

1692.1: Gibson, Edmund, *Chronicon Saxonicum*. Oxford: Sheldonian Theatre, 1692. Wing A3185; ESTC R1430. AS6; tp AS7.
ASC

    Collation: 4⁰: π a² b⁴ (b4 + χ1.2) A–2V⁴ [$2 signed] 178 + 2 leaves, paginated [i–xii], 1–244, 245–280, [1–2], 3–64 (p. ²62 misnumbered 64).

SOURCE OF PASSAGE UTILIZING ANGLO-SAXON TYPES:

A1ʳ–2H2ᵛ (pp. 1–244)   From Tiberius A.vi, 115ᵛ–164, Domitian A.viii, fos 30–70, and OBL Laud misc. 636, 1–91ᵛ (sole authority for prologue description of Britain): ASC (conflated text based on C, E and F), as Thorpe 1861: 1.3–385;

TYPE:

AS6: The main text is in Junian Pica Anglo-Saxon cut by Christoffel van Dijck, and is combined with Junius's Pica Roman (also by van Dijck), in which the Latin text is set. Words in AS also occur in the regulæ on 2N2ʳ–2T3ᵛ.

Special sorts shown on the specimen on 2N1ᵛ:

    11 lower-case sorts: ð, f, ȝ, ı, p, ꞃ, τ, ẏ; þ, ð, p;
    9 capitals: Ꞇ, Є, Ᵹ, Ꝺ, ₥, 8; Ƿ, Ð, Ꝼ.
  Total: 20 sorts.

Special sorts shown in the text:

    11 lower-case sorts;   ð, f, ȝ, ı, p, ꞃ, τ, ẏ; þ, ð, p;
    8 capitals: Ꞇ, Є, Ᵹ, Ꝺ, ₥, 8; Ð, Ꝼ;
    2 others: þ, ꝫ.
  Total: 21 sorts.

Overall total: 22 sorts.

Note 1: Capital Ƿ is apparently not used in the text, Ð being preferred; in the place-name index on 2S3ʳ Th- is used.

Note 2: The capital Ꝼ is the one by Walpergen added at OUP.

AS7: The motto on the tp is in the Somnerian Pica Anglo-Saxon cut by Nicholas Nicholls combined with the Junian Pica Roman (attributable to van Dijck); Special sorts shown:

    10 lower-case sorts: ð, e, f, ȝ, ı, p, τ, ẏ; þ, ð;
    1 capital: Æ²;
    2 others: þ, ∴ (triple point).
  Total: 13 sorts.

Copies seen: APL R.v.10 (b4χ1–2 occurs after 2N4); CUL Gg.5.48 (b4χ1–2 occurs after 2N4); CCC SC.5.23 (b4χ1–2 occurs after 2M4); LFL 6H; OBL 4⁰.C.114.Art, Gough Sax.lit.93 (SC 18324; A1ʳ–2T3ᵛ only; interleaved with handwritten MnE translation by Gough, also notes).

Copies also at: AUL, BL, BCLW, BrPL, BUT, CCA, KCC, CMC, CPH, CSel, CSJ, TCC, CaCL, CUW, DCL, DUL, ECL, EdUL, GlCL, GML, GUL, HHC, LHL, LMT, MJRUL,

NCL, NLS, NLW, NUL, OBC, OCC, OEC, OHC, OJC, OMC, ONC, OQC, OSA, OSJ, OTC, OTI, OXC, SML, SPC, UBL, UCL, UUM, WAL, WCC, WCL, WoCL, YML, DEWL, DML, NLI, NUIG, TCD, ULim, GCB, BSB, GUB, MPHL; FSL, USLC, NYHS, NYCU, HHL, HUL, IUL, BPM, GETS, KSRL, LCP, NLC, OSU, PTS, SCN, UCBL, UCIL, UCLA, UCRL, UTA, UTK, UVL, YUB, MMU, QUK, TUL; ANZ, SJTC, USL.

The copy of this book at Blickling (NT) contains annotations by Edward Lhuyd.
Bibliography: Carter 1975: 419; Earle and Plummer 1892–9: II.cxxiv–cxxv, cxxix–cxxxi; Fairer 1986: 811; Gadd 2013: 438 (M. Kilburn); Keynes 2014: 161–162 (on map at b4χ1ᵛ–2ʳ); Levine 1991: 330–331; Niles 2015: 132–134; Sykes 1926: 10–11; [Walker] 1813: II.54 (Gibson to Charlett 2 Jan 1720 on his thoughts on revision).

1692.2: Jonson, Ben, *The English Grammar*, 2nd edn of 1640.2, in *The Works of Ben Jonson*. London: Thomas Hodgkin for Henry Herringman, Edward Brewster II, Thomas Bassett, Richard Chiswell, Matthew Wotton, and George Conyers, 1692. Wing J1006; ESTC R15282. AS7.
OE letter symbols
  Collation (adapted from Greg): 2⁰ in 4s: [Booklet 1] A⁶ B–2L⁴ [Booklet 2] 2O–3B⁴ 3C² [Booklet 3] 3E–5B⁴ 5C² [$2 signed (+A3; -A1,2, 3N1; R2 missigned R1, 4Z1 missigned 5A1)] 366 leaves, paginated [i–xii], 1–264, 281–382, 393–744, *745–748* (pp. nos 375–376 not used; pp. 369–371 misnumbered 369–370, 412 misnumbered 406, 413 misnumbered 403, 540–541 misnumbered 538–539, 699 misnumbered 669); double columns. Note: Greg reports G1 unsigned, but it is signed in all copies examined here.
TYPE (*English Grammar* only):
Main English text in a Pica Roman (Body 82); L text in a Pica Italic (Body 82).
AS7: Nicholas Nicholls's Somnerian Pica Anglo-Saxon:
Roman (not Italic as in 1640.2) þ and ð shown on 4R3ʳ (p. 677).
  Copies seen: APL I.I.11; CUL Y.7.10, Brett-Smith.a.9 (with blind-stamped binding).
  Copies also at: BL, BCL, BUL, ChC, KCC, CMC, CSJ, TCC, EdUL, LHU, LSH, MJRUL, NLS, NT, OBL, OAS, OEF, OMC, OWoC, OXC, SJS, SoUL, UBL, NUIG, TCD, PBN, BSB; FSL, USLC, NYHS, NYCU, HHL, HUL, BMC, DDUL, GSU, KSU, MCRS, NLC, NWU, PUL, SCN, SCU, SLU, UCH, UPL, USNA, UTA, UTK, WMil, WMUL.
Bibliography: Alston I.no. 10; Greg III.1082–1084.

1693.1: Somner, William, ed. James Brome, preface by White Kennet, notes by Edmund Gibson, *A Treatise of the Roman Ports and Forts in Kent*. Oxford: Sheldonian Theatre for (S4669A only) George West, John Crosley & Henry Clements, 1693. Wing S4669 and S4669A. ESTC R19864 and R222413. AS7.
Charter, ASC (extracts), Law

Collation: 8⁰: a⁶ b–h⁸ i⁴ A–H⁸ I² [$4 signed (-a1,2,4, i3,4, E4, H3, I2; a3 missigned a4, H4 missigned I4)] 132 leaves, paginated [i–xii], 1–118, *119–120*, ²1–117, ²*118–32*.

SOURCES OF PASSAGES UTILIZING ANGLO-SAXON TYPES:

A5ᵛ (p. 210)	From RKA, DRc/R1 (Textus Roffensis), 5ʳ/2–4: Laws of Hlothære and Eadric 16 (Liebermann I.11), extract, abridged;
B8ᵛ (p. 232)	From CCA, MS Lit.E.1, 4ᵛ/7–8 (s.xvii): ASC(D) 1052 (extract), as Thorpe 1861: I.312/b/20–21;
C5ᵛ (p. 242)	From CCA, Chart Ant. C 1279 (Red Book 7): Grant of land by Egbert to Ætheric 845 for 830 (extract with some text garbled; Sawyer 282; Birch 396);
C6ʳ (p. 243)	From CCA, MS Lit.C.8, 56ʳ/3–4 (s.xvii): ASC(C) 893 (= 895) (extract), as Thorpe: I.162/a/24–25;
E4ᵛ–5ʳ (pp. 272–3)	From 1660.1 2E3ᵛ–4ᵛ: Grant of land by Eadsige, priest, bp of St Martin's nr Canterbury, to Christ Church 1032 (Sawyer 1465), as Robertson 1956: no. 86.
F1ʳ (p. 281)	From CCA, MS Lit.C.8, 47ʳ/11 ASC(C) 669 (extract), as Thorpe: I.56/b/11–14.

TYPE:

Main text in an English-size Roman (Body 93).

AS7: Nicholas Nicholls's Somnerian Pica Anglo-Saxon occurs in text as detailed above under Contents and in words on d1ᵛ, g5ʳ, h8ʳ, A1ᵛ, A2ᵛ, A4ᵛ, A5ʳ, A6ʳ, B1ʳ, B2ʳ, B8ʳ, C3ʳ, C8, D1ʳ, D3ᵛ, D7, D8ᵛ, E1ᵛ, E2ʳ, E3ᵛ, E4ʳ, F1ᵛ, F7ᵛ, G3ᵛ.

Special sorts shown:

11 lower-case sorts:	ð, ꝼ, ȝ, ı, ƿ, ſ, τ, ẏ; þ, ð, p;
9 (+1) capitals:	A, Æ¹, Æ², L, Є, Ⴚ, Ꝺ, 8, Ð, W;
2 others:	þ, ⁊.

Total: 22 (+1) sorts.

Copies seen: APL O.VII.22 (lacks a1); CCA W2/B.2.9; CUL Adams.7.69.7, Pet.M.2.8, Hunt.60.14 (from the library of White Kennett), R.12.4 (lacks a1); ECC 321.5.48; OBL 8⁰.C.155.Linc., Tanner 917, Wood 218², Douce ss.8 (lacks a1), Gough Kent 66 (lacks a1). S4669A with variant tp: OBL Gough Kent 63 (lacks a1).

Copies also at: S4669: BL, CCC, CMC, CQC, CSJ, TCC, CaCL, DUL, Eton, LPL, MJRUL, NLS, NLW, NT, OCC, OEF, OHC, OJC, OQC, OSL, OStE, OTC, SML, SPC, StA, UBL, WAL, WCF, YML, DEWL, TCD, BSB, GUB; NYPL, HHL, HUL, IUL, DDUL, HTC, JCB, KSRL, NLC, NWU, PUL, UCBL, UCLA, UTA, UTK, YUB, QUK, TUL; VSL, WCS.

Bibliography: Bennett 1957: 160–161; Carter 1975: 422; Sykes 1926: 14.

Manuscript: CCA Lit.C.7, fos 20–36, is a copy of the text of this book in Somner's hand with some corrections, but without the content of the footnotes; the marks on fo 20ʳ suggest that it was used by the printer.

1693.2: [Oxford University Press], *A Specimen of the Several Sorts of Letter given to the University by Dr. John Fell*. Oxford: Sheldonian Theatre, 1693. Wing F622; ESTC R33320. Type-specimen AS6, AS7.

Printer's Specimen with OE Lord's Prayer

Collation: 8^0 in 4s: π^2 a^4 b–c^4 d^2 $^2d^4$ U^8 [$1 signed (+U2,3)] 28 leaves, unnumbered.

SOURCES OF PASSAGES UTILIZING ANGLO-SAXON TYPES:

c4^r From 1664.2, A6^r: Lord's Prayer, Mt 6.9–13 (as in 1665.2, B3^v–4^r)

d2^r From 1664.2, A6^r: Lord's Prayer, Mt 6.9–13 (as in 1665.2, B3^v–4^r)

TYPE: various specimens.

AS6: Christoffel van Dijck's Junian Pica Anglo-Saxon occurs in the specimen on d2^r with the Lord's Prayer in OE:

Special sorts shown:

	11 lower-case sorts:	ð, ꝼ, ᵹ, ı, ꝑ, ꞃ, ꞇ, ẏ; þ, ð, ƿ;
	8 capitals:	Ꞇ, Ɛ, Ꝉ, Ꝺ, ꝳ, S, Ð, Ƿ;
	2 others:	ꝫ, ∴.
Total:	21 sorts.	

AS7: Nicholas Nicholls's Somnerian Pica Anglo-Saxon occurs in the specimen on c4^r with the Lord's Prayer in OE:

Special sorts shown:

	12 lower-case sorts:	ð, *e* (in line 3 þe), ꝼ, ᵹ, ı, ꝑ, ꞃ, ꞇ, ẏ; þ (in line 3 þe), ð, ƿ;
	11 capitals:	A, Æ^2, Ɛ, Ǝ, Ꝉ, Ꝺ, K, ꝳ, S, Ð, *W*;
	4 others:	þ, ꝫ, ꝫ, ∴.
Total:	27 sorts.	

Note: K is shown in both the lower-case and upper-case alphabet; *W* is shown instead of *Ƿ*.

Copies seen: CUL Broxbourne c.39 (lacks sig. U); TCC V.15.22^2 (U8 blank); LFL T12 (lacks sig. U).

Copies also at: CMC, LPL, NLW, OBL; GUB; NYCU, UCLA.

Bibliography: Berry & Johnson 1935: 6; Carter 1975: 421; Morison 1967: 229–230 (by John Simmons); Mosley 1984: no. 170.

Facsimile: *A Specimen of the Several Sorts of Letter given to the University by Dr. John Fell Oxford, 1693*, London, Tregaskis, 1928. For simulations see Hart 1970: 8–40c.

1695.1: [Oxford University Press], *A Specimen of the Several Sorts of Letter given to the University by Dr. John Fell*. Oxford: Sheldonian Theatre, 1695. Wing F623(A) ESTC R32025. Type-specimen AS6, AS7.

Printer's Specimen with OE Lord's Prayer

Collation: 8^0 in 4s: π^2 a–e^4 (e2 + χ1,2) [$2 signed] 22 + 2 leaves, unnumbered.

Note: Issue 2 shows the additions to sig. e.

SOURCES OF PASSAGES UTILIZING ANGLO-SAXON TYPE:

d2ʳ From 1664.2, A6ʳ: Lord's Prayer, Mt 6.9–13 (as in 1665.2, B3ᵛ–4ʳ)
e2ʳ From 1664.2, A6ʳ: Lord's Prayer, Mt 6.9–13 (as in 1665.2, B3ᵛ–4ʳ)

TYPE: various specimens.

AS6: The Junian Pica Anglo-Saxon cut by Christoffel van Dijck occurs in the specimen on e2ʳ with the Lord's Prayer in OE:

Special sorts shown:

11 lower-case sorts:	ð, ꝼ, ᵹ, ɩ, ꞃ, ſ, ꞇ, ẏ; þ, ð, p;
8 capitals:	Ⱡ, Ԑ, Ᵹ, Ꝺ, ꟽ, Ꞅ, Đ, Ⅴ;
2 others:	ꝫ, ∴.
Total:	21 sorts.

Note 1: The Ⅴ (Wynn) was cut by Peter de Walpergen at Oxford and added to the Junian fount.

AS7: Nicholas Nicholls's Somnerian Pica Anglo-Saxon occurs in the specimen on d2ʳ with the Lord's Prayer in OE:

Special sorts shown:

12 lower-case sorts:	ð, *e* (in line 3 þe), ꝼ, ᵹ, ɩ, ꞃ, ſ, ꞇ, ẏ; þ (in line 3 þe), ð, p;
11 capitals:	A, Æ², Ԑ, Ꞓ, Ᵹ, Ꝺ, K, ꟽ, Ꞅ, Đ, W;
4 others:	þ, ꝫ, ꝫ, ∴.
Total:	27 sorts.

Note 2: K is shown in both the lower-case and the upper-case alphabet; W is shown instead of Ⅴ.

Copies seen: Issue 1: CUL Broxbourne d.46; Issue 2 (with 2 leaves added in sig. e): BL Bagford collection, Harley 5929, nos 160, 164, 166, 170, 175, 179, 184, 187, 193, 196, 201, 205, 208, 211, 215, 218, 222, 226, 231, 235, 238, 242, 246, 251 (with the leaves cut up and pasted into a scrap-book collection); TCC X.32.12[11]; OUP Archives, Specimen no. 10.

Copies also at: Wing F623: LPL, , OBL, OAS, OWoC, OXC; HHL, BA, YUB.

Wing F623A: OBL, OAS, OXC, PBN; NLC, PPL.

Bibliography: Berry & Johnson 1935: 6–7; Carter 1975: 426–427; Morison 1967: 230–231 (by John Simmons); Mosley 1984: no. 171; Simmons 1959: nos 48–49.

Facsimile: For simulations see Hart 1970: 44–63.

1695.2: Kennett, White, *Parochial Antiquities attempted in the History of Ambrosden, Burcester, and other adjacent parts in the Counties of Oxford and Bucks.* Oxford: Sheldonian Theatre, 1695. Wing K302; ESTC R25441. AS7.

AS Charter (spurious?)

Collation: 4⁰: a–b⁴ A–5O⁴ [$2 signed] 432 leaves, paginated [i–xvi], 1–703, 704–850 (pp. nos 553–554 not used).

SOURCE OF PASSAGE UTILIZING ANGLO-SAXON TYPES:

G1ᵛ (p. 50)   From OBL James 24 (17c transcript in semi-imitative AS script), pp. 54/39–55/3: Writ of Edward the Confessor declaring gift of the estate at Islip (O) where he was born to Westminster Abbey (Sawyer 1148; Harmer 104).

Note: Printing this writ in AS type, and occasionally modifying the spelling, e.g., ð for th, Ⱳ (Walpergen's) for W, enhances its apparent authenticity beyond that in the transcript.

TYPE:

Main text in the Oxonian English-size Roman (Body 92) interspersed with the Oxonian English-size Italic (e.g. 3P1ᵛ);

AS7: Nicholas Nicholls's Somnerian Pica Anglo-Saxon occurs in combination with a Pica Roman (Body 80; as on 4O3ᵛ–4ʳ) in text as indicated above and in words on D2ᵛ, E3ʳ, S1ᵛ, 3C1ʳ, 4Z3, 5B2ʳ, 5B3ʳ, 5B4ʳ, 5C1, 5C2ᵛ, 5D2ʳ, 5D3–4, 5E1ᵛ, 5E2ᵛ, 5E3ʳ, 5F2–3, 5F4ʳ, 5G1–2ʳ, 5G3–4, 5H1–5I1, 5I2ᵛ, 5I3ᵛ–5K1ʳ, 5K2ᵛ–3ʳ, 5K4, 5L1, 5L3ʳ, 5L4ᵛ, 5M1–2ʳ, 5M4, 5N1ᵛ, 5N2–3, 5N4ᵛ–5O2ʳ, 5O3–4.

Special sorts shown:

	12 lower-case sorts:	ð, ℯ, ꝼ, ȝ, ı, ꝓ, ꞃ, ꞇ, ẏ; þ, ð, p;
	7 (+1) capitals:	Ⱡ, Ɛ, Ɫ, Ⱳ, 8, Ð, Ⱳ (= Walpergen's), W (on 5K4ᵛ);
	3 others:	þ, ⁊, ⁊.
Total:	23 sorts.	

Note 1: Junius's Pica Gothic occurs on E3ʳ, 5C2ᵛ, 5G3, 5G4ᵛ.

Note 2: Junius's Pica Icelandic occurs on E3ʳ, 5G4ᵛ, 5H1ᵛ, 5I4ʳ, 5K1ʳ, 5K2ᵛ, 5M4ʳ (used for Danish), 5O3ᵛ.

Copies seen: APL R.v.6 (with contemporary blind-stamped binding of brown calf); CUL Ll.14.3, Pet.v.3.42; OBL Gough.Eccl.top.67b and Don.d.56 (both with author's additions and notes), Douce K.114.

Copies also at: BL, BCL, CCA, CMC, TCC, ChCL, ECL, LCL, LHL, LPL, LSH, NLS, NLW, NT, OAS, OCC, OEC, OJC, OQC, OSA, OSH, OStE, OTC, OxHC, UBL, WCC, WCL, WoCL, YML, DEWL, TCD, PBN; USLC, HHL, HUL, IUL, JCB, KSRL, NLC, UCBL, UCH, UCIL, UCLA, UMI, UTA, YUB, QUK; UML, VSL.

Bibliography: Bennett 1957: 161–3; Carter 1975: 229, 426.

1695.3: Camden, William, *Camden's Britannia, newly translated into English, with large additions and improvements*, ed. Edmund Gibson. London: Freeman Collins for Abel Swalle and Awnsham and John Churchill 1695. Based on the

6th edn of Camden's *Britannia* (1607.2) and the earlier translation by Philemon Holland (1610.5, 2nd edn 1637.1). Wing C359; ESTC R12882. AS7.

OE proper names

   Context: There was a proposal to reprint this book by subscription (Wing C373; ESTC R176553):
   Swalle, Abel, *Proposals for Printing by Subscription, Cambden's Britannia, English* [London, 1692/3] (OBL (Vet.) 2597 b.1), and *New Proposals for Printing by subscription, Cambden's Britannia, English*, London, 20 Apr 1693 (OBL Wood 658 (806); McKenzie & Bell 2005: III.150; ESTC R3261), the second raising the price from 26s to 32s on account of the expense of the maps. Subsequently (6 July 1693) a warrant was issued to Abel Swall & Awnsham Churchill to publish the edition (McKenzie & Bell 2005: III.154).

   Collation: 2^0 in 4s: π^2 πA^2 πa–g^2 πB–N^4 πO^2 A–$3F^4$ 3G–$3H^6$ 3I–$3M^4$ 3N–$4N^2$ a–l^2 [\$1 signed πA πa–g πO 3N–l; \$2 signed πB–πN A–2P 3K–3M; \$1,3 signed 2Q–3I with 3 signed *2Q etc, except that 2X3 is signed 2X, and 3G5 3H5 signed **3G **3H] 374 leaves, mostly in columns, part paginated, pp. [i–xxxvi], cols i–cxcvi, *cxcvii–cc*, 1–832, pp. 833–848, cols 849–1116, *1117–1118*, pp. *1119–1162* (col nos 1055–1056 used twice, cols 877–882 not numbered, cols xcv—xcvi misnumbered cxv—cxvi, cols 697–8 mislabelled p. 697).

   What are described here as gatherings 2Q–3I may be made up of 2 or 3 contiguous (i.e. not integrated) sheets: for discussion see Walters and Emery 1977: 125–128.

   Sigs a–l could be described as a separate Booklet. Note: Leaves with illustrations are additional.

SOURCES OF PASSAGES UTILIZING ANGLO-SAXON TYPES:

2N3^r (col. 570)   From **1692.1** M4^r (p. 95/27–29): ASC (ed. Gibson) 894, as Thorpe 1861: I.170a/26–28;

3A2 (cols 742–3)   From **1643.1** V4^r (p. 143): OE Bede (ed. Wheelock) II, 13 (end), as Miller 1890–8: I.136/25, 138/15 and II/134 (variant reading from CCC MS 41);

3G3^v (p. 838)   From **1607.2** 4Y4^r: ASC(C + F) 189/188 (extracts), both as Thorpe 1861: I.14–15;

3G5^r/a (p. 841)   From **1571.1** Q4^v (p. 120): Mk 1.8, as Liuzza 1994: 63.

Note: Gibson corrects Camden's OE, e.g., on 2C3^v.

TYPE:

Main text in double columns in a Pica Roman (Body 82) interspersed with a Pica Italic (Body 81, e.g. on E1–4).

AS7: Nicholas Nicholls's Somnerian Pica Anglo-Saxon combined with the Pica Roman occurs in the text as indicated above and in words on cols xxix, clxxi, clxxiv, clxxxiii, 1, 5–6, 13, 25, 30, 43–45, 47–48, 50, 57, 59, 62, 69, 73, 85, 87–88, 91, 98–99, 101–102, 105, 112–113, 117–118, 120, 131, 134, 137, 139–140, 142, 145, 149–150, 153, 159–160, 165, 167–168, 173, 175–176, 179–180, 185–187, 190, 192–193, 196–197, 200, 202, 204, 210–211, 231, 233–234, 236, 238, 240, 245–246, 251, 255–256, 267–268, 277, 280, 283, 294, 296, 309–310, 339, 341, 347, 350–351, 365–368, 371, 383, 385, 388, 395, 401, 403, 409, 411, 419, 425, 427, 429, 439, 455, 457, 459, 463, 471, 473–474, 481–482, 489, 491, 501, 510, 513, 515, 519, 521, 524–525, 527, 529, 534, 537, 539, 544, 546, 551–553, 556–557, 565–566, 568, 576, 603, 631, 681, 705, 707, 710–711, 713, 715, 717, 738, 741, 749–750, 762, 765, 774–775, 778–779, 783 ('the likeness of the Saxon p, p, and ſ'), 787, 796, pp. 842/b, 847, cols 853–854, 858–860, 1050, 1106.

Special sorts shown:

13 lower-case sorts:	ð, *e*, ꝼ, ȝ, h, ɩ, ꝑ, ſ, τ, ẏ; þ, ð, p;
7 capitals:	Æ², Є, Ŀ, Ⅿ, 8, Ð, Ƿ;
1 other:	þ (on p. 487).
Total:	21 sorts.

New sorts:

On A1ʳ where there is a new lower-case **h** (also used as a capital, e.g., on 2D1ᵛ, 2D3ʳ and 2F4ʳ). On F2ʳ some sorts appear with a flat top, as **t**, and **g**; all on col 570;

On K3ʳ (col 153) there is an **ð** with a shorter ascender, probably broken off;

On B1ʳ there is a **d** which is like **S** with a shorter top stroke, used as capital S on 2L3ᵛ, but this S-like **d** and **S** are different in the length of the top stroke, which is probably broken off on the shorter one, as can be seen on πM3ᵛ;

Note 1: AS capitals are also used with Roman ones in a Latin inscription on 2F4ʳ (col 462).

Note 2: The Gothic and Runic sorts shown on 3G5ʳ are larger than those of Junius (and Voskens), although still made to fit in with Pica type. Icelandic þ is the one cut by Walpergen that appears on the OUP specimen.

Copies seen: CUL R.7.1 (shows πf–πg after πO; 2A4 torn off at the bottom; lacks map after 2P4);

State 2 (with cols xcv–xcvi numbered correctly): CUL Pet.B.7.9, R.1.13 (on thick paper, chain 29 mm; lacks map after πg2), Hanson.bb.21 (lacks maps after Z4 and 2A4); LFL Case B2 (π1ᵛ portrait of Camden, π2ʳ title cut out and remounted on replacement leaves; lacks 2X3).

Copies also at: BL, BCL, BCLNI, BCLW, BPL, CCA, ChC, CCL, CGC, CJC, KCC, CMC, CNC, CPC, CSC, CSJ, CTH, CfCL, ChCL, CLL, DCL, DRD, DUL, DWL, ECL, EdUL, GlCL, GML, CUL, HCL, IMC, LCL, LHL, LiCL, LMT, LRS, LSH, MJRUL, NHM, NLS, NLW, NT, OBL, OBC, OLMH, OMC, ONC, ONuC, OQC, ORS, OSA, OSJ, OSL, OStE,

OWmC, OWoC, OXC, OxHS, PrPL, SCL, SML, UBL, UUM, WCC, WCL, WoCL, DML, NLI, TCD, ULim, PBN, BSB, GUB; FSL, NYPL, HHL, HUL, IUL, AAS, HCP, LCP, MCRS, NLC, NMU, NWU, UCBL, UCH, UCLA, UNC, UTA, UVL, YUB, TUL, UVC; AML, ATL, OUL, SSA, TML, UML, UNSW, USL, VSL, VUW.

Bibliography: Ellis 1843: 214–235 (letters from Gibson to Charlett on the paper for the edition and to whom it should be dedicated); Keynes 2014: 163 (on map of AS Britain at πI2; Levine 1991: 327–336; McKenzie & Bell 2005: III.176–177 (11 Sept 1694 re possible inclusion of additions by N. Johnston); Mayhew 2000: 239–261; Moore 1992: 18; Parry 1995: ch. 12; Skelton 1970: no. 117; Sykes 1926: 16–19; Walters and Emery 1977; and see Facsimile, pp. 9–11. See also bibliographies to 1586.1, 1607.2, etc,

Facsimile: intr. S. Piggott, with a bibliographical note by G. Walters (Newton Abbott, 1971).

Manuscript (Printer's Copy): Cardiff, Central Library, MS 4.172 (sigs 2O3^r/1–2X2^v/40).

1695.4: Selden, John, *De Iure Naturale et Gentium*, ed. Johann Heinrich Boeckler. Wittenberg: Johann Michael Goderitsch, for Jeremias Schrey at Frankfurt-an-der-Oder and Leipzig, 1695. 3rd edn of 1640.4, being a slavish re-setting of 1665.3 (2nd edn). BLG S1863; VD17: 14:019946V. CAS7.

Note: According to VD17 and BLG this book is apparently the only one published by Schrey that purports to have been issued in Leipzig as well as Frankfurt-an-der-Oder

OE Gospels, Law of Alfred (extracts)

Collation: 4°: π²)(² *–5*⁴ A–2O⁴ 2P⁴ (2P1 + χ1,2,3,4,5,6) 2Q–5T⁴ 5V² 5X–5Z⁴ 6A² [$3 signed (-3*3, 3A3, 6A2)] 484 leaves, paginated [i–xlviii], 1–892, 893–920 (p. 692 not numbered; p. 85 misnumbered 83).

SOURCES OF PASSAGES UTILIZING ANGLO-SAXON TYPES:

4F3 (pp. 597–8)   From 1665.3 4F3: OE Gospels: Mt.5.31, Lk.1.28, 42, 11.27, Mk.7.26, Jn.4.7, Lk.16.18, Mt.19.10; also OE Orosius VI.xxx, two words hýꞅ piꞃ for L 'concubina' (as Bately 1980: 148/9n.).

5T2^v (p. 884)   From 1665.3 5T2^v: Preface to Law of Alfred 49.5 (extract; Liebermann I.44).

TYPE:

Main text in a Pica Roman (Body 84) interspersed with a Pica Italic (e.g., 4I1^r). CAS7: The Wittenberg 1695 imitation of CAS5 occurs in text as indicated above and in words on 3M2^v (p. 460), 3N1 (pp. 465–466) combined with the Pica Roman.

Evidence of wooden sorts supplementing metal ones is that the instances of the same sort do not match each other, e.g., **g** on p. 460.

Special sorts shown:

  11 lower-case sorts: ð (also uses a fractur ð), ꝼ (also uses fractur ꝼ), ᵹ, ı, ꝥ, ſ, τ, ẏ; þ, ð, ƿ (also uses fractur ƿ);
  7 capitals: Æ, Є, Ꝺ (but see below), ꝳ, Ƿ, Ð;
  2 others: þ, ꝛ.
 Total: 18 sorts.

Note 1: H, e.g., top of 3N1ᵛ (p. 466), is from another fount (sim to 1636.3)
Note 2: M may also be from another fount.

 Copies: BL 494.g.4 (lacks sigs)(1.2; P3 present twice); TCD HH.ff.38, Fag.O.5.4 (2P𝛘1,2,3,4,5,6 misplaced after 2N4); LFL 54E (lacks π1, 2P𝛘1,2,3,4,5,6; bookplate of William S. Goddard (1757–1845)); OBL Hebrew & Jewish Studies Mont 58I2.

Bibliography: see 1640.4.

1695.5: Heirs of Joan Blaeu I (= Joan II and Pieter Blaeu), *Proeve der drukkerye*, Amsterdam, Heirs Joan Blaeu, 1695. Type-specimen (auction catalogue). CAS3.
Letter-sorts

 Collation: 4⁰: A–D⁴ [$3 signed (-A1)], unnumbered. Recto side only.

TYPE:

CAS3: The Pica Anglo-Saxon (misleadingly called 'Auguſtyn') shown in the specimen on D1ʳ was almost certainly cut by one of the Voskens half-brothers, Bartholomaeus Voskens the Elder (1613/16–69) or Reinier/Reinhard Voskens (1621–c.1670), as they were the two punchcutting members of the family who were active in the early 1640s; since Dirk Voskens took over the Blaeu business in 1678 it is not, however, absolutely impossible that he inherited this work from another punchcutter, and not all the Blaeu punches and matrices went to Voskens (Enschedé 1978: 115). The Anglo-Saxon fount occurs also on the Widow Voskens specimen 1700?.2.

[80] x 2: 2.8 (but x 3.0); the Body is calculated from the 4-line specimen in 1700?.2.

Special sorts shown:

  10 lower-case sorts: ð, ℯ, ꝼ, ᵹ, ꝥ, ſ, τ; þ, ð, ƿ;
  8 capitals: Æ¹, Æ², Є, Ꝺ, ꝳ, S, Ð, X;
  2 others: þ, ꝛ.
 Total: 20 sorts.

Note: Since the designs include both lower-case ℯ (with its tongue sticking out) and upper-case X, they may have been modelled on both the Parkerian Great Primer Anglo-Saxon (X) and the Lambardian or possibly the Somnerian Pica Anglo-Saxon (ℯ). Note also the design of S, which has virtually no turn-over to the right for the top stroke, so aiding confusion with **d** (if this confusion had not already occurred at the design stage).

 Copy seen: LUB Letterproeven 744D, no. 33 (A3 before A2, C4 after D1).
Bibliography: Hellinga 1962: 1.125; Kleerkooper and van Stockum 1914–16: II.1171–1172; Lane 2004: no. 138.

1695.6: Selden, John, *Uxor Ebraica, seu de Nuptiis et Divortiis ex Iure Civili, id est, Divino & Talmudico, Veterum Ebræorum, Libri Tres.* 3rd edn of **1646.6**, slavishly re-set page by page from the 2nd edn **1673.3**, which omitted the passages of Anglo-Saxon for want of special sorts. Wittenberg: Johann Michael Goderitsch, for Jeremias Schrey at Frankfurt-an-der-Oder 1695. BLG S1859. The passages in AS included in Bk II, chs 27 and 29 in **1646.6** are omitted at 2B4^r (p. 199) and 2E3^v (p. 222).

 Copy seen: BL 4034.f.30.
 Copies also at: ChC, NT, OBL Hebrew & Jewish Studies Library.

1696.1: Selden, John, *Tituli Honorum Autore Clarissimo & Eruditissimo Antiqvario Joanne Seldeno, Interioris Templi, Armigero. Juxta Editionem Tertiam Londinenßem Anni 1672. Cui Accessisse Dicuntur Seldeni Emendationes & Additamenta Latine Vertit Notasque Addidit,* ed. Simon Johann Arnold. Latin t of **Titles of Honor**, 3rd edn **1672.1**. Wittenberg: Johann Michael Goderitsch, for Jeremias Schrey and the heirs of Heinrich Johann Meyer at Frankfurt-an-der-Oder, 1696. BLG S1865; VD17: 1:009620S. CAS7.
Bede, ASC, Martyrology, Psalms, Ælfric: Grammar, On NT, LS; Charters, Laws (extracts)

 Collation: 4°: π²)o($^{2+1}$ *–3*⁴ A–2N⁴ ²A–²5C⁴ ²5D² [$3 signed (-3*2, K2, 2G3, ²K2, ²5B3, ²5D2; 2D3 missigned D3, ²3M3 missigned 3m2, 24M3 missigned 4m2)] 547 leaves, paginated [i–xxxiv], *1*, 2–288, ²*1*, ²2–690, ²*691–766*, except that ²193–200 are foliated (pp. nos ²305–306 not used; pp. 17–64 misnumbered 27–74, 212 misnumbered 221, ²186–187 misnumbered 136–137, ²190–191 misnumbered 140–141, fo ²197 misnumbered 397, fo ²200 misnumbered 101, pp. ²280 misnumbered 780, ²487–488 misnumbered 587–588).

SOURCES OF PASSAGES UTILIZING ANGLO-SAXON TYPES:
R1^v (p. 130)   None: not taken over from **1672.1** M3^r;
²2U1 (pp. ²339–40)   From **1672.1** 3R2^r: OE Bede II.14 (Miller I.1/138/16–17);
²2U2^v (p. ²342)   From **1672.1** 3R3^r: Law Norðleoda 2–5 (Liebermann I.460);
        From **1672.1** 3R3^v: Law II Cnut 58,1–2 (Liebermann I.350);
²2U3^v (p. ²344)   From **1672.1** 3R3^v: Charter (Sawyer 1332);
²2U3^v (p. ²344)   From **1672.1** 3R4^r: Extract from glossed Ps 67.27;

²2U3ᵛ (p. ²344)	From 1672.1 3R4ʳ: Ælfric, Life of St George (Skeat 1881: I.308, lines 5–7 abridged);
²2U4ᵛ–22X1ʳ (pp. ²346–7)	From 1672.1 3R4ᵛ–3S1ʳ: OE Bede v.4 (Miller I.2/394/14–16), also III.2 (Miller 158/7–8);
²2X1ʳ (p. ²347)	From 1672.1 3S1ʳ: OE Bede III.14 (Miller I.1/194/4–5);
²2X1ᵛ (p. ²348)	From 1672.1 3S1ᵛ: ASC D 870 (Thorpe 1861: I.138/17–20);
²2X2ʳ (p. ²349)	From 1672.1 3S1ᵛ: Diploma of William I 1081, extract (Pelteret 28);
²2X3ʳ (p. ²351)	From 1672.1 3S2ʳ: OE Bede II.9 (Miller I.1/122/19);
²2X3ʳ (p. ²351)	From 1672.1 3S2ʳ: ASC D 897, 1013 (Thorpe 1861: I.175/29–32, 270/41);
²2X3ᵛ (p. ²352)	From 1672.1 3S2ᵛ: (1) Writ of Edward the Confessor 1042 × 1066 (Sawyer 1104); (2) ASC D 905 (Thorpe 1861: I.181/35–36);
²2X4ʳ (p. ²353)	From 1672.1 3S3ʳ: Ælfric's Glossary: Extract (Zupitza 1880: 300/15);
²2Y1ʳ (p. ²355)	From 1672.1 3S3ᵛ: ASC D 886 (Thorpe 1861: I.157/16–18);
²2Y4ᵛ (p. ²362)	From 1672.1 3T2ʳ: Law II Cnut 71–1a (Liebermann I.356–358); Law 'Geþyncðo' 2 (Liebermann I.456);
²2Z2ʳ (p. ²365)	From 1672.1 3T3ʳ: Law II Cnut 71.1–5 (Liebermann I.358);
²3A2ᵛ (p. ²374)	From 1672.1 3V2ʳ: ASC E 1064 (Thorpe 1861: I.331/5–6);
²3A3ʳ (p. ²375)	From 1672.1 3V2ᵛ: Law Ine Prol. (extract; Liebermann I.88–89);
²3S3ᵛ (p. ²512)	From 1672.1 4K2ᵛ: Law Ine 10 (extract; Liebermann I.94);
²3T4ʳ (p. ²521)	From 1672.1 4L2ᵛ: Ælfric, On the New Testament (extract; Marsden 2008: 228/877);
²4C1 (pp. ²571–572)	From 1672.1 4P4ᵛ–4Q1ʳ: OE Martyrology re St George (Rauer 2013: §67/1–4, 6–13);
²4C2ʳ (p. ²573)	From 1672.1 4Q1ᵛ: Ælfric, Life of St George (Skeat 1881: I.308, lines 28–9).

TYPE:

Main text in a Pica Roman (Body 84) interspersed with a Pica Italic (e.g. 2N2ᵛ–3ᵛ). CAS7: The Wittenberg Pica Anglo-Saxon imitation of CAS5 occurs in text as indicated under Contents above and in words (with the Pica Roman) on sigs ²2S4ʳ, ²2Z2ᵛ, ²3A3ᵛ, ²3A4ʳ, ²3N3ᵛ, ²4H4ʳ, ²4I1ʳ, ²4T2ʳ, ²4T4ʳ.

Evidence of wooden sorts supplementing metal ones is that the instances of the same sort do not match each other, but the quality of matching is better in this book than in 1695.4, so it looks as though there was an attempt to either improve or supercede the wooden sorts.

Special sorts shown:

8 (+1) lower-case sorts: ð, f, ȝ, ƿ, ſ, τ; þ, ð, p (= Fraktur p);
5 (+1) capitals: E (from another fount), Ð (Ð + Fraktur H both on ²2U2ᵛ), Ϻ, Ƨ, Đ;
2 others: Þ, ꝫ.

Total: 15 (+2) sorts.

Copies seen: BL 9915.a.19; OBL Vet. D3 e.118.
Copies also at: AUL, NLS.

Bibliography: see 1672.1.

1696.2: Selden, John, *De Synedriis & Praefecturis Iuridicis Veterum Ebraeorum Libri Tres. Editio novissima indicibus copiosissimis locupletata.* 3rd edn re-set from 1679.3. Wittenberg: Johann Michael Goderitsch, for Jeremias Schrey and the heirs of Heinrich Johann Meyer at Frankfurt-an-der-Oder, 1696. BLG S1864; VD17: 14:019942Q. CAS7.

Extracts from Ælfric, OE Bede, Canons of Edgar, Gospels

Collation: 4⁰:)(⁴ *-2*⁴ A-8M⁴ a-g⁴ [$3 signed (-)(1,2, *2, 2*3, C3, 3N1, 6P3, 8B3; 2U3 missigned U3, 5U2 missigned 5U3)] 732 leaves, paginated [i–xxiv], 1–1383, *1384*1440 (pp. 458, 465–467, 1021, 1367 not numbered; the page number 473 appears as 'Fol. 7.'; pp. 58–59 misnumbered 57–58, 62–63 misnumbered 61–62, 217 misnumbered 117, 314 misnumbered 114, 366–367 misnumbered 364–365, 550 misnumbered 50, 685 misnumbered 585, 688 misnumbered 588, 1029 misnumbered 102, 1206 misnumbered 1106, 1232 misnumbered 1332, 1236 misnumbered 1136, 1246 misnumbered 1146, 1248 misnumbered 1249, 1273 misnumbered 1173, 1280 misnumbered 1380, 1297 misnumbered 1197, 1298 misnumbered 1398, 1307 misnumbered 1207, 1343 misnumbered 3343, 1368 misnumbered 1367, 1369 misnumbered 1368).

Note: 2*4 is not present in any of the copies seen and the catchword on 2*3ᵛ coordinates with A1ʳ.

SOURCES OF PASSAGES UTILIZING ANGLO-SAXON TYPES:

2A4ᵛ (p. 192)   From 1679.2 T3ʳ: Ælfric, CH2.xxiv (extract), as Godden 1979: 226/162;
   From 1679.2 T3ʳ: Mt 18.17 (extract), as Liuzza 1994: 37;

2B2ᵛ (p. 195)   From 1679.2 T4ᵛ: Mt 18.17 (extract), as Liuzza 1994: 37;

2D3ᵛ (p. 214)   From 1679.2 X4ʳ: OE Bede III.22 (word amanſumoðe), as Miller 1890–8: I.228/11; other forms presumably reconstructed from it;

2Y4ʳ (p. 359)   From 1679.2 2N2ʳ: Phrase beȝeonðan Ƨæ extracted from 'Directions for a Confessor' (*olim* Canons of Edgar), as Fowler 1965: 20/113;

3G2ᵛ–3ᵛ (pp. 420–2)   From 1679.2 2T2ᵛ–3ᵛ: Nowell, *Vocabularium Saxonicum*, svv. Ealdor, Ealdorman, Ealdorburh (Marckwardt 1952: 59–60); re: S. George Ealdorman in Cappadocia; OE Bede III.8 (phrase mid his Ealdorlicnesse), as Miller 1890–8: I.172/8; Wulfstan's Canons of Edgar 2 (extrapolated phrase yldran ʒ yldrum), as Fowler 1972: 2; other phrases (Ealdrum ʒ Ealdras; Ealdorman-num) not traced; Mt.16.21 (phrase), as Liuzza 1994: 34; Mk 10.33 (phrases, adapted), as Liuzza 1994: 83; Mt 27.12, 20 (phrase), as Liuzza 1994: 58, 59; Mk 8.31, 11.27, 14.43 (phrases), as Liuzza 1994: 79, 86, 92; Lk 22.52 (phrase), as Liuzza 1994: 150; Lk 22.66 (phrases), as Liuzza 1994: 151.

Note: Quotations from the ME Romance *Gamelyn* occur on 6B1ᵛ–2ʳ in the Textura type.

TYPE:

Main text in a Pica Roman (Body 84) interspersed with a Pica Italic (e.g., 2I4–2K1), Arabic, Greek, Hebrew, Syriac and a Fractur.

CAS7: The Goderitsch 'Pica' Anglo-Saxon combined with the Pica Roman occurs in text as indicated above and in words on 7M1ʳ (p. 1193). Metal sorts are supplemented by wooden ones.

Special sorts shown in text:

    11 lower-case sorts: ð, *e*, f, ʒ, ı, p, r, t, ẏ; þ, ƿ;
    1 (+1) capitals: Є, 𝔐 (= Fractur);
    1 (+1) others: ꝥ (used for þ), ꜧ (= upside-down Roman capital L);

    Total: 13 + 2 sorts.

Copies seen: BL 4034.f.29 (2M misplaced after 2P, 6P1,2 after 6P3,4); CUL Bensly.5.g.43; TCD HH.ff.41; OBL Hebrew & Jewish Studies Mont 58Ba8[3].

Copies also at: AUL, TCC, GUL, NLS, UBL, YML.

Bibliography: see 1650.3.

1696.3: Ussher, James, *Veterum Epistolarum Hibernicarum Sylloge*. 3rd edn of 1632.1 probably re-set from 1665.4. Hessen-Nassau: Johann Nikolaus Andreae, 1696. BLG U153. Fragments of AS in 1632.1 rendered in Italic on E2ᵛ, Q2ʳ; fragment of Irish rendered in Roman on I3ʳ.

    Collation: 4⁰:)(⁴ 2)(⁴ A–P⁴ Q²; [16], 124 p.

    Copy seen: CUL Hib.7.696.4

    Copies also at: BL, DUL, LL, OBL.

1696.4: Phillips, Edward (Milton's nephew), *The New World of Words: Or, a Universal English Dictionary.* 5th edn of **1658.3**. London: no printer stated, for Richard Bentley, Joshua Phillips, Henry Rhodes, and John Taylor, 1696. Wing P2073; ESTC R24462.

    Collation: 2⁰: π⁴ A–I⁴ K⁶ 2A–2L⁴ 3A–3I⁴ 3K² 4A–4I⁴ 4K⁶ 5A–5H⁴ 5I². [498] p.
    Copy seen: CUL XVI.3.39.
    Copies also at: BL, BCL, CGC, DUL, EdUL, KNA, LUL, MJRUL, NAL, NLS, OBL, OSJ, UBL, RIA, PBN; HHL, HUL, IUL, KSRL, LCP, LSU, MCRS, SLU, UCBL, UCH, UCLA, UMI, UTA, UTK, TUL; ATL, OUL, USL.

1698.1: Thwaites, Edward, *Heptateuchus, Liber Job, et Evangelium Nicodemi, ... Judith.* Oxford: Sheldonian Theatre, 1698; for prospectus see **1679.1**. Wing B2198; ESTC R4371. AS6.

OE Heptateuch, Ælfric's homily on Job, Gospel of Nicodemus, Judith (poem)
    Collation: 4⁰: π¹⁺⁴ (π1 prec. by χ1) A–X⁴ 2A–2D⁴ [$2 signed] 105 leaves, paginated (excluding frontispiece) [i–viii], 1–168, ²1–32.
SOURCES OF PASSAGES UTILIZING ANGLO-SAXON TYPES:

π4ᵛ	From OBL Laud misc.509 (SC 942), 122ᵛ–30ᵛ: Ælfric, *On the Old Testament* (9 brief excerpts), previously printed by Lisle **1623.1**, as Crawford 1969: 21, 28, 31, 32, 33–34, 47, Marsden 2008: 204, 207, 209–210, 216;
	Note: π4ᵛ/16 ʒeppıtu] MS and Lisle bec;
A1ʳ–2ᵛ (pp. 1–4)	From OBL, Laud misc.509, 1ʳ–3ʳ: Ælfric's *Preface to Genesis*, as Crawford 1969: 76–80, Marsden 2008: 3–7;
A3ʳ–X1ʳ (pp. 5–161)	From OBL, Laud misc.509, 3ʳ–113ᵛ: OE Heptateuch, i.e. Genesis, Exodus, Leviticus, Numbers, Deuteronomy, Joshua, Judges, as Crawford 1969: 81–414, Marsden 2008: 8–198.
X1ʳ–3ʳ (pp. 161–3)	From OBL, Laud misc.509, 113ᵛ–15ᵛ: Epilogue to OE Heptateuch, as Crawford 1969: 414–417, Marsden 2008: 198–200.
X2ᵛ–4ᵛ (pp. 164–8)	From OBL Laud misc.381 (SC 956), 154ʳ–9ʳ, transcript (with t) by Lisle of CUL Gg.3.28, 223ᵛ/3–226ʳ/18: Ælfric, CH ser.2, Dominica I in mense Septembri, quando legitur Job, as Godden 1979: 260–267, lines 7–225; in Gg.3.28 the beginning (ðu⟨m⟩ peþ) and end (heahfæðeþe) of the text copied in Laud misc.381 is underlined in ink and there is a line down the outer margin of the pages of the intervening text; Thwaites's statement (π4ʳ) that Lisle copied this text from a Cotton MS must be erroneous;

2A1ʳ–2C2ᵛ (pp. 1–20) From OBL Junius 74 (SC 5185), 1ʳ–11ʳ (transcript by Junius of CUL Ii.2.11, 173ᵛ–93ʳ, collated with BL Vitellius A.xv, pt.1, 60ʳ–86ᵛ): OE Gospel of Nicodemus, as Hulme 1898: 471–515, Cross 1996: 139–247.

2C3ʳ–2D1ᵛ (pp. 21–6) From OBL Junius 105, pp.1–12: *Judith*, as Dobbie 1953: 99–109, Griffith 1998: 97–107.

TYPE:

AS6: Main OE texts in Junius's Pica Anglo-Saxon combined with a Pica Roman (on π4ᵛ).

Special sorts shown:

        11 lower-case sorts: ð, ꝼ, ᵹ, ı, ꞃ, ſ, ꞇ, ẏ; þ, ð, ꝑ;
        9 capitals: Ꞇ, Ε, Ᵹ, Ꝺ, ꝳ, &; Þ, Ð, Ƿ;
        4 others: þ, ꝏ, ꝏ, ∴.
   Total: 24 sorts.

Note 1: Capital Ƿ is the one in the OUP specimen cut by Walpergen, e.g. V1ʳ/25. Note 2: The different sized Tironian signs for 'and' can be seen, e.g., on D4ʳ, penultimate line.

    Copies seen: CUL 1.24.7¹; OBL Douce BB.438. OBL O.T.Anglo-Sax.d.1/1–3 showing the imprimatur of 27 Dec 1697 on π1ᵛ, is Joseph Bosworth's copy, the whole partially annotated and interleaved with printed biblical text stuck on the additional leaves (excluding the *Evangelium Nicodemi*) and handwritten verse line numbers to *Judith* with reference to the printed edition by Grein 1857: I.120–9, and to the partial translation by Turner 1823 edn(?): (III.303–7). Cf. **1659.1**, copy OBL 3024.c.1 (with annotations by Joseph Bosworth s.xix).

    Copies also at: APL, AUL, BL, BUL, CCA, CCC, CMC, CSJ, TCC, CaCL, CLL, DCL, DUL, ECL, EdUL, GUL, HHC, LSH, NCL, OCC, OEC, OEF, OJC, IKC, OMC, OQC, OSJ, OTC, OWoC, SCL, SDL, UBL, WCF, WoCL, DML, TCD, ULim, GUB, MBS; FSL, USLC, NYPL, NYHS, NYCU, HHL, HUL, IUL, NLC, UCBL, UTA, UTK, UVL, YUB, TUL; USL.

Bibliography: Carter 1975: 432; Gadd 2013: 439–440 (M. Kilburn); Harris 1992: 69–70, 198–199 (re. Charlett's attempt to suppress the dedication to Hickes); Lucas 1997: 381 (re. *Judith*); Money 1998: 125–128 (re. Charlett's attempt to suppress the dedication to Hickes); Murphy 1980–81 (re. Thwaites); Nichols 1812: IV.141–149 (re. Thwaites); Niles 2015: 129–132. GR 5229.

    Note: Wing B2197A and CLC B2198- record an earlier date of publication (1696) only in Lincoln Cathedral Library, but it is not included in the catalogue by Hurst 1982 and the Librarian informs me that it is not there.

1698.2: Rawlinson, Christopher, *An. Manl. Sever. Boethi Conſolationis Philosophiæ Libri v. Anglo-Saxonice Redditi ab Alfredo.* Oxford: Sheldonian Theatre, 1698. Wing B3429; ESTC R8772. AS6.

Author: (sumptibus) Rawlinson, Christopher (1677–1733); according to Sir Henry Ellis, Rawlinson was much assisted by Edward Thwaites (Nichols 1812: IV.146).

Note: Rawlinson's family coat-of-arms with three escallops, two and one, separated by two horizontal fesses appears on the tp: see Tashjian et al 1990: 195.

Alfredian translation of Boethius

Collation: 4⁰: π¹ a⁴ b² A–2B⁴ [$2 signed (-a1)] 107 leaves, paginated [i–xiv], 1–198, *199–200*.

SOURCES OF PASSAGES UTILIZING ANGLO-SAXON TYPES:

a4ᵛ–T3ʳ (pp. [x–xiv], 1–149)	From OBL Junius 12 (SC 5124 = Junius's transcript of OBL Bodley 180 (SC 2079) collated with Otho A.vi (since damaged by fire)), 1ʳ–89ᵛ: Alfredian translation of Boethius's *De Consolatione Philosophiae*, as Sedgefield 1899; Godden/Irvine 2009.
a4ᵛ (bottom)	From Junius 12 (copied from Otho A.vi), fo iiib: proem to *Meters of Boethius*, printed as prose with metrical pointing, as Krapp 1932: 153, Godden/Irvine 2009: 384.
T3ᵛ–2B3ᵛ (pp. 150–98)	From Junius 12 (copied from Otho A.vi), integral to the text of the whole work: *Meters of Boethius*, printed as verse half-lines, as Krapp 1932: 153–203, Godden/Irvine 2009: 384–539.

Note: Junius 12 contains the L printed text of Boethius's *De Consolatione Philosophiae*, ed. Theodorus Sitzman (Hanau, 'typis' heirs of Andreas Wechel (Frankfurt-am-Main), 'apud' Claude de Marne and the heirs of Johann Aubry 1, 1607 (BLG B1686; USTC 2118652)) cut and pasted into strips.

TYPE:

AS6: The main OE texts are in Christoffel van Dijck's Pica Anglo-Saxon cut for Franciscus Junius (except that the capital Ƿ used by OUP was cut by Peter de Walpergen) combined with the Junian Pica Roman (also cut by van Dijck). Special sorts shown:

        11 lower-case sorts: ð, f, ᵹ, ı, ꝑ, ſ, τ, ẏ; þ, ð, ꝑ;
        9 capitals: L, Є, Ꞡ, Ꝺ, ꟽ, 8; Þ, Ð, Ƿ;
        4 others: þ, ɉ, ɉ, ∴ .
   Total: 24 sorts.

Note 1: The different sized Tironian signs for 'and' can be seen together, e.g., on M3ʳ, lines 1–2.

Note 2: Capital Ƿ is the one cut by Walpergen in the OUP specimen, e.g. V1ʳ/25.

Copies seen: CUL 1.24.7²; MBS A.lat.b.81.m (lacks π1; binding of brown calf gold-tooled with shield of Biblioteca Palatina); OBL Douce BB.445.

Copies also at: APL, BL, BCL, BCLNI, CCA, KCC, CMC, CSJ, CTH, TCC, DCL, DUL, ECL, GML, HHC, LHL, LiCL, MJRUL, NewCL, NLS, NLW, NUL, OBrC, OEF, OJC, OMaC, OMC, OQC, OSA, OSJ, OTI, OWmC, OXC, UBL, DKI, GUB; FSL, USLC, NYCU, UTS, HHL, HUL, IUL, DDUL, GCL, GSU, LCP, NLC, SCN, UCLA, UMI, UPL, UTA, UVL, YUB, TUL; USL.

Bibliography: Carter 1975: 430–431; Fairer 1986: 813–814; Nichols 1812: IV.146; Niles 2015: 128–129.

1698.3: Spelman, Sir Henry, ed. Edmund Gibson, *Reliquiæ Spelmannianæ*. Oxford: Sheldonian Theatre, for Awnsham and John Churchill, 1698. Wing S4930; R22617. AS7.

Set by the compositor John Rance (Simpson 1935: 171)

Laws and Charters

Collation: 2^0 in 4s: π^{1+2} a–c^4 d^2 (d1 + χ1) A–$2B^4$ (2B4 + χ1) 2C–$2E^4$ $2F^2$ [$3 signed (-d2, R3, 2F2)] 133 leaves, paginated [i–xxxiv], 1–214, *215–228* (pp. 47–48, 56, 66–68, 105–106, 133–134, 163–164, 187–188, 201–202 not numbered).

SOURCES OF PASSAGES UTILIZING ANGLO-SAXON TYPES:

Note: Citations from **1568.2** could be from the edition by Wheelock in **1644.1**.

Item (1):

B4ᵛ (p. 16) From **1596.2** 2I7ᵛ: Law 'Geþyncðo' 2 (Liebermann I.456); Spelman cites p. 502 (*recte* 500);

C2ʳ (p. 19) From 'lost' Cartulary of Abbotsbury: Charter of Egbert 958 granting land in Do and 3 *perticæ* at 'Lonk' (?Looke (Farm) in Puncknowle, Do) to 'Alur[ed]' thane (Keynes 1989: 226–227); From BL Add 82931 (*olim* Earl of Macclesfield MS 24.g.9), 'Liber de Hyda', 33ʳ/b: Charter of Æthelred II granting land at Manningford Abbots (W) to Æthelwold, bp of Winchester (Sawyer 865, as Edwards 1866: 232): L text + 1st 3 words of OE;

D3ʳ (p. 29) From **1568.2** 2L1ᵛ: Law II Cnut 74 (Liebermann I.360); omission of ne before naðeꞃ is distinctive of Lambarde's text;

D4 (pp. 31–2) From **1568.2** 2L2ᵛ: Law II Cnut 78 (Liebermann I.364); Lambarde's æꞇ ðam ꝼẏꞃꝺunᵹ ꞇoꝼoꞃan is distinctive;

Item (4): The passages in Item 4 are apparently not from **1684.2**.

K3ʳ (p. 77) From **1568.2** C2ᵛ: Law Ine 3 (Liebermann I.90);

K3ᵛ (p. 78) From **1568.2** Q3ᵛ: Law Edward and Guthrum 9 (Liebermann I.132); ꞇocƿeꝺon not from **1684.2** ꞇocƿeꝺene; From **1568.2** 2E4ᵛ: Law I Cnut 17 (Liebermann I.296); om. ⁊ lencꞇen ꝺaᵹum. (incl. **1684.2**) after ẏmbꞃen ꝺaᵹum. and ends aᵹan ꞅẏ oꝼeꞃ ꞇƿelꝼ-ꞇa ꝺæᵹ:· which is not in in **1684.2**.

M4ᵛ (p. 96)   From 1568.2 2B4ᵛ: Law II Æthelred 8.3 (Liebermann I.224);
Item (6):
R1ᵛ (p. 130)   From 1568.2 M3ᵛ: Law Alfred 41 (Liebermann I.74);
R2ʳ (p. 131)   From 1568.2 2G4ᵛ: Law II Cnut 18.1 (Liebermann I.320).
TYPE:
Main text in an English-size Roman.
AS7: Nicholas Nicholls's Somnerian Pica Anglo-Saxon occurs in combination with a Pica Roman (presumably the modified Garamont of Morison and Carter 1967: 133) in the text as listed above and in words on B2ʳ, C1ᵛ, E3ʳ, G2ᵛ, L3ʳ.
Special sorts shown:

   11 lower-case sorts: ð, ꝼ, ʒ, ı, ꝥ, ſ, ꞇ, ẏ; þ, ð, ƿ;
   4 capitals: Æ, Є, Ⱦ, Ð;
   3 others: þ, ꞇ, ∴ .
 Total 18 sorts.

Copies seen: CUL J.7.22 (Q2/3 in reverse order); LFL 18I.
Copies also at: BL, BUL, CCC, CMC, CSJ, TCC, ChCL, CLL, DCL, DUL, EAL, EdUL, GML, HHC, HRC, LHL, LHU, LIL, LSH, MTP, NLS, NLW, NPG, NT, OBL, OBC, OCC, OJC, OLC, OLMH, OMaC, OMC, ONC, OQC, OStE, OWoC, RLW, SDL, SPC, UBL, WAL, WCL, WRL, YML, DEWL, DKI, DML, NLI, TCD, ULim, PBN; FSL, NYHS, NYCU, UTS, HHL, HUL, IUL, GCL, KSRL, LCP, NLC, NWU, UCBL, UCLA, UCSR, UMI, UTA, YUB, QUK; AUNZ, OUL, SSA, UAL, USL, VSC.
Bibliography: Carter 1975: 229–230, 432; Cronne 1962: 44; Parry 1995: 177–179; Simpson 1935: 162–163; Sykes 1926: 21–22.
Manuscripts: Item (1) in Harvard Law School MS 2062 (author's draft) and OBL e.Mus.79, a fair copy (SC 3694) as noted by Keynes 1989: 224–225; Item (4) in OBL e.Mus.107 (autograph) on which see Van Norden 1949–50: 132–133.

1699.1: Elstob, William, *Hormesta Pauli Orosii* (prospectus printed but not published). Oxford: Sheldonian Theatre, 1699. Wing O465A. AS6.
Orosius
 Collation: 4⁰: π1, π2. 2 leaves, separately mounted, π2 paginated 1–2.
SOURCE OF PASSAGE UTILIZING ANGLO-SAXON TYPES:
π2 (pp. 1–2) From OBL Junius 15 (SC 5127), transcript of Tiberius B.i by Junius collated by Marshall with what is now BL Add 47967, the Tollemache Orosius (ed. Campbell, EEMF 3) formerly owned by the duke of Lauderdale: OE Orosius, Bk I, ch. 1 (beginning; ed. from Add 47967 by Bately 1980: 8/11–9/32).
Note 1: Elstob made his own transcript of Junius's, which is now Oxford, Trinity College D.92, on deposit in OBL;
Note 2: Bately 1980: xxv, n. 2, claims that Joscelyn transcribed a passage from Book I, ch. i, in Vitellius D.vii, but no such passage is to be found there.

TYPE:

AS6: Main OE text in the Junian Pica Anglo-Saxon cut by Christoffel van Dijck combined with the Junian Pica Roman also by van Dijck.

Special sorts shown:

   11 lower-case sorts: ð, ꝼ, ȝ, ı, ꝑ, ſ, τ, ẏ; þ, ð, p;
   8 capitals: Ꞃ, Є, Ᵹ, Ꝺ, Є, Ꞩ; Ð, Ƒ;
   4 others: þ, ꞏ, ꞏ, ∶.
 Total: 23 sorts.

Note 1: No capital p is shown.

Note 2: The uc Ƒ shown is that cut by Walpergen, which appears on the OUP specimen 1693.2.

Copy seen: BL Lansdowne 373, fos 86–87.

Bibliography: Campbell 1953: 24; Carter 1975: 432; Fairer 1986: 822; Nichols 1812: IV.112–140 (re. the Elstobs).

1699.2 Benson, Thomas, *Thesaurus Linguæ Anglo-Saxonicæ Dictionario Gul. Somneri, Quoad numerum vocum, aucior* (prospectus printed but not published), published as *Vocabularium Anglo-Saxonicum* 1701.1. Wing S4667A; ESTC R233449. AS6.

Words

 Collation: 4°: single half-sheet with 2nd leaf signed A. In the BL copy the leaves have been cut down to 181 × 108 mm and 174 × 107 mm respectively and pasted into a scrap-book collection.

TYPE:

AS6: Main text (the beginning of the dictionary at letter A) showing Christoffel van Dijck's Pica Anglo-Saxon cut for Franciscus Junius, with Latin glosses in the Junian Pica Italic (also cut by van Dijck).

Special sorts shown:

   10 lower-case sorts: ð, ꝼ, ȝ, ı, ꝑ, ſ, τ, ẏ; þ, p.

Note 1: As in 1690.2 A1ʳ/23 shows þ in abroþen, whereas in 1701.1 the same word appears as abroðen.

Note 2: The 1701.1 full edition utilized AS8, the Oxford University Small Pica Anglo-Saxon newly cut by Peter de Walpergen.

 Copies: BL, Bagford Collection, Harley 5929, nos 355–356; OBL Rawlinson D.377, fos 80–81 (where the unevenly inked imprint has led to it being erroneously assigned the date 1690, as noted by Fairer 1986: 813, n. 6).

Bibliography: Alston III.i.8; Carter 1975: 414; Foster 1891–2: I.109 (for Benson); Macray 1893: col 212; Nichols 1812: IV.141–142.

1700.1: Motte, Benjamin, *Oratio Dominica*. London: [sigs B and C Sheldonian Theatre, Oxford, the rest (?)Mary Clarke (Motte's mother-in-law) for] Benjamin Motte for Daniel Brown and William Keblewhite, 1700. Wing M2944; ESTC R15295. AS7.

Printer: Stated on A4^r to be Benjamin Motte, who, besides being the compiler, was a bookseller/publisher.

Lord's Prayer

Collation: 4⁰: A⁴ a⁴ B–I⁴ [$2 signed (+B3; -A2)] 40 leaves, paginated [i–viii], 1–72 (p. 70 unnumbered, pp. 71–72 misnumbered 70–71).

Earlier State: Main text ends on I2^v, I3 (pp. 69–70 both numbered) contains PATER in umpteen languages, I4 presumed blank.

SOURCES OF PASSAGES UTILIZING ANGLO-SAXON TYPES:

G3^r (p. 53)   From **1665.2** B3^v–4^r (Mt 6.9–13): Lord's Prayer (from the Junius Gospels);

G3^v (p. 54)   From **1662.6**)(5^r, and **1668.1** 3K2^r–4^r (the so-called 'Old Saxon' version): Lord's Prayer (altera vetustior).

TYPE:

Since the book illustrates over 100 linguistic versions of the Lord's Prayer it is a typographical historian's paradise, especially for 'exotic' type-designs; most, not, for example, Chinese on D3^r (woodcut pictograms), utilize metal types. There is no one main text type.

AS7: Nicholas Nicholls's Somnerian Pica Anglo-Saxon occurs in text as listed above, where it is combined with a Pica Roman.

Special sorts shown:

    12 lower-case sorts: ð, e (G3^v), ꝼ, ᵹ, ı, ƿ, ꞃ, ꞇ, ẏ; þ, ð, ꝑ;

    3 capitals: A, Ᵹ, Ꝥ;

    1 other: ⁊.

  Total: 16 sorts.

Gothic (C3^r), Runic (C3^v), and Icelandic (C4^r) all occur in the types left by Junius to Oxford University; the Icelandic variety includes the Þ (capital 'Thorn') cut for the University by Walpergen (Lucas 1998: 187).

Note: In this book Irish is distinguished from Anglo-Saxon by printing the Lord's Prayer in Moxon's Irish type-design of 1685 (McGuinne 1992: 54) on H1^r.

Copies seen: CCC B.9.28 (lacks I3; gift of S.S. Lewis 1891); OBL Douce.O.160, C.17.26.Linc.

Earlier State (lacks I4): CUL Bb*.10.22(E), Broxbourne.c.61; LFL T763⁶ (lacks A1); PO 1700.1.

Copies also at: BL, BLH, CJC, CMC, CWC, DCL, DRD, EdUL, HCL, NLS, NLW, NT, OXC, DML, RIA, GUB; FSL, HHL, HUL, NLC, UCLA, UTA, UWO.

Bibliography: Birrell & Garnett 1928: no. 79; Carter 1975: 436; Sharpe & Hoyne 2020: no. 58 on p. 178.

1700.2: (corporate) University of Oxford, *Exequiæ Desideratissimo Principi Gulielmo Glocestriæ Duci.* Oxford: Sheldonian Theatre, 1701. Wing O885; ESTC R6065. AS6.
AS compositions s.xvii by Elstob and Wanley
  Collation: 2⁰: A–2O² [$1 signed (-A1; +A2, F2, G2, H2, I2, K2, P2, Q2, R2, S2, T2, V2, X2, 2C2, 2E2, 2H2; A2 missigned 'A')] 74 leaves, unnumbered.
SOURCES OF PASSAGES UTILIZING ANGLO-SAXON TYPES:
P1ʳ   AS 'verse' composition by William Elstob (1673–1715);
2I2ᵛ   AS 'verse' composition by Humfrey Wanley (1672–1726).
TYPE:
Main Latin text in Nicholas Nicholls's Great Primer Roman (Body 117), but several other special/exotic types are used for specific purposes.
AS6: The Junian Pica Anglo-Saxon combined with Arthur Nicholls's Pica Roman occurs in (generally non-alliterating) 'verse' text on P1ʳ and 2I2ᵛ printed in half-lines;
Special sorts shown:
            11 lower-case sorts: ð, f, ᵹ, ı, p, ɼ, τ, ẏ; þ, ð, ƿ;
            8 capitals: L, Є, Ŀ, Ƕ, Ɱ, S, Ð, Ƿ;
            4 others: þ, ꝫ, ꝭ, ∴ .
  Total: 23 sorts.
Note 1: The capital Ƿ ('Wynn') is that cut for OUP by Walpergen;
Note 2: Junius's Pica Runic also occurs in text on P1ʳ.
  Copy seen: CUL Keynes P.7.10.
  Copies also at: BL, CCC, CMC, CSJ, TCC, LCL, LHL, LUL, MJRUL, OBL, OAS, OCC, OJC, OQC, OWoC, OXC, SCL, WAL, WCF, YML; FSL, HHL, HUL, CUI, GUW, KSRL, UCLA, WMW, YUB.
Bibliography: Carter 1975: 436; Fairer 1986: 815; Murphy 1982: 28–33 (on other attempts at OE verse by Elstob preserved in MS).

1700.3: Phillips, Edward (Milton's nephew), *The New World of Words: Or, a Universal English Dictionary.* 6th edn of **1658.3**. London: no printer stated, for Joshua Phillips and Henry Rhodes, 1700. Wing P2074; ESTC R181772.
  Collation: 2⁰: π⁴ A–I⁴ K⁴⁺² 2A–2L⁴ 3A–3L⁴ 3K² 4A–4I⁴ 4K⁶ 5A–5H⁴ 5I² [406] p.
No AS.
  Copy seen: CGC A.16.20.

Copies also at: CUW, DUL, EdUL, HU, KUL, LJM, MJRUL, NLW, NRL, NU, OBL, SHU, YUL, TCD; IUL, UTA, WCM.

1700.4 Hickes, George, 'A Letter from Dr George Hickes, dated May the 22d, 1700, to Dr Sloane, concerning the Saxon Antiquity, mentioned N. 247 [p. 441] of these Transactions [by W. Musgrave, 1698]. With an account of his Book now in the Press at Oxford', *Philosophical Transactions of the Royal Society*, 22 (1700), no. 260, pp. 464–469.

Ælfred Jewel
Text/Inscription of Ælfred Jewel (recently then discovered in Somerset, as reported by Musgrave) given on p. 466 as 'AELFRED MEC HETT GEWYRCAN' (*recte* HEHT). No Anglo-Saxon types, but something resembling a square C has been improvised.
Bibliography: Hinton 1974: 29–48; Okasha 1971: 48–49.

1700?.1: Thwaites, Edward, [Alfredian translation of Pope Gregory's *Pastoral Care*]. [Oxford: Sheldonian Theatre, *c*.1700], printed specimen not published. AS6.

Alfredian Pastoral Care (beginning)
    Collation: 4⁰: single half-sheet with inner side printed and verso of 1st leaf signed A; inner pages paginated 1–2.
SOURCE OF PASSAGE UTILIZING ANGLO-SAXON TYPES:
A1ᵛ–2ʳ (pp. 1–2)   From Junius 53 (SC 5165), pp. 12–14/1, a transcript of Tiberius B.xi (since virtually destroyed by fire) coll Hatton 20 and Otho B.ii (since damaged by fire): Alfredian *Pastoral Care*, as Sweet 1871: I.22–4 (= Gregory's letter to Giovanni II (the Roman) bp of Ravenna and the beginning of ch. 1).
Note: The Latin text is included at the back of Junius 53; the relevant portion is on sig.3L1ᵛ–2ʳ (pp. 890–891).
    Note: MS Junius 91 is a copy of *Gregorii Magni episcopi Romani De Cura Pastorali liber verè aureus*, ed. Jeremiah Stephens, London, Thomas Harper for Philemon Stephens and Christopher Meredith, 1629 (STC 12348), but this is not the same text as is included in Junius 53.
TYPE:
AS6: Main text in Junian Pica Anglo-Saxon, cut by Christofel van Dijck, combined with Junius's Pica Roman (also by van Dijck), in which the Latin text is set.

Special sorts shown:

  11 lower-case sorts: ð, ꝼ, ᵹ, ı, ꝑ, ꞃ, ꞇ, ẏ; þ, ð, p;
  2 capitals: Ð, Ð;
  3 others: þ, ꝫ, ∴ .
 Total: 16 sorts.

Copy seen: OBL Rawlinson D. 377, fos 86–87.

Note: on A2^r there is a handwritten note (s.xviii) saying 'This a specimen of an Edition of Gregory which | Mr Thwaites designed'.

Bibliography: Carter 1975: 435; Macray 1893: col. 212; Nichols 1812: IV.141–149 (re. Thwaites).

1700?.2 (ante1714): Widow Dirck Voskens (Alida/Aaltje d.1714), *Proef van Letteren die te bekomen zyn, by de Weduwe van Dirk Voskens en Zonen, Lettergieters op de Bloemgragt tot Amsterdam.* Amsterdam: Widow Dirck Voskens, c.1700. Type-specimen CAS3.

Letter-sorts, OE Bede

 Collation: 2⁰: single sheet printed on recto only.

SOURCE OF PASSAGE UTILIZING ANGLO-SAXON TYPE:

From 1643.1 G1^r (p. 33/38): OE Bede, I.7 (extract), as Miller 1890–8: 1.36/33 to 38/2; in 1643.1 G1^r line 38 is the first long line (as opposed to half-page-width column line) on p. 33.

TYPE:

CAS3: The Pica Anglo-Saxon, which first occurs in 1645.1 and already in a specimen in 1695.5, was almost certainly cut by one of the Voskens half-brothers, Bartholomeus (1613/16–69) and Reinier (1621–c.1670), as they were the two punchcutting members of the family who were active in the early 1640s. [80] x 2: 2.8; the Body is calculated from this 4-line specimen.

Special sorts shown:

  11 lower-case sorts: ð, *e*, ꝼ, ᵹ, ı, ꝑ, ꞃ, ꞇ; þ, ð, p;
  2 capitals: 8 (used as ð), Ð;
  2 others: þ, ꝫ.
 Total: 15 sorts.

Copy seen: LUB R 63.8 (4), no. 90, R 63.8 (2) A (between 65 & 66).

Bibliography: Hellinga 1962: 126 and pl. 160; Lane 2004, no. 11, who assigns it to 1707.

1701.1: Benson, Thomas, *Vocabularium Anglo-Saxonicum Lexico Gul. Somneri magna parte aucius.* Oxford: Sheldonian Theatre for Samuel Smith and Benjamin Walford, 1701. ESTC T101265; 18cCat 1763B1. AS8.

Note: Benson was a protegé of William Nicolson and subsequently married his daughter, Mary, and had a career in the Church.
Words
Collation: 4⁰: π¹ a² A–Z⁴ 2A² [$2 signed (-a1)] 1 + 96 leaves, unnumbered.
TYPE:
AS8: Main text in the Small Pica Anglo-Saxon (Face 66 x 1.5: 2.4) by Peter de Walpergen (fl. Oxford 1676–1703†) combined with Christoffel van Dijck's Small Pica Roman (Body 69; McKitterick 1977: 70, no. 225 Descendiaen Romeyn), with Latin glosses in van Dijck's Small Pica Italic (Face 66 x 1.3: 2.00; Hart 1970: 26). Special sorts shown:
      11 lower-case sorts: ð, f, ȝ, ı, p, ſ, ꞇ, ẏ; þ, ð, p;
Note: AS capitals are not used even at the price of using Th- and W- for some words; the only capitals cut were Ð and Ƿ (later additions, see 1703/05.1), but they are not shown in this book. Walpergen died in 1703, and it is probable that he was still working on this fount when he died.
Copies seen: CUL Bb*.5.2(D), Bury.28.4; LFL 103E (π reversed); OBL Gough Sax.lit.175 (π reversed, with additions in the hand of Humfrey Wanley, and 18c gold-tooled binding of brown calf).
Copies also at: BL, BCL, BUL, CCA, CCC, ChC, CSJ, TCC, DCL, DUL, DWL, EdUL, Eton, GUL, HHC, KCL, LBL, LHL, LPL, LSH, LUL, MCL, MCS, MJRUL, NLS, NLW, NT, NUL, OEC, OMaC, OQC, OSA, OWmC, OWoC, SBP, UBL, UCL, YML, BSB, GUB; FSL, USLC, NYPL, NYCU, HHL, HUL, APS, AZU, BCB, BJH, CHPL, CUI, CWR, DDUL, DenPL, IBUL, ISU, LCP, LSUM NLC, NWU, PFL, PUL, RNJ, RUH, SfUL, TCH, TNO, UCBL, UCH, UCLA, UCRL, UDN, UMI, UTK, UVL, WCW, YUB, MMUL, TUL, UW.
Bibliography: 1699.2 (prospectus); Alston III.i.9; Fairer 1986: 813; Bankert 2012: 419; Carter 1975: 438.

1701.2: Elstob, William, [Wulfstan] *Sermo Lupi Episcopi, Saxonice Latinam interpretationem notasque adjecit* (printed but not published, later incorporated in 1703/5.1). Oxford: Sheldonian Theatre, 1701. AS6.
Wulfstan, Pseudo-Wulfstan, Law
Collation: 2⁰: ‡2B² [‡2C]² ‡2D² [‡2B2 and ‡2D1 signed] 6 leaves, paginated [i], 1–11.
SOURCES OF PASSAGES UTILIZING ANGLO-SAXON TYPES:
‡2B2ʳ–‡2D1ᵛ (pp. 2–9)   From MSS I (Nero A.i, 110ʳ–15ʳ), C (CCC 201, pp. 82–6), and E (Hatton 113, 84ᵛ–90ᵛ): Wulfstan, *Sermo Lupi ad Anglos*, as Bethurum 1957: 267–75, Whitelock 1963: 47–67;
‡2D2 (pp. 10–11)   From MSS E (Hatton 113, 91ᵛ–3ᵛ), and C (CCC 201, pp. 28–9), coll. K (Tiberius A.iii, 90ᵛ–91ʳ), §5 (from

	K alone): Pseudo-Wulfstan, *Be mistlican gelimpan*, as Napier 1883: 169–75, nos 35 and 36 (= K; §5 = pp. 174/5–175/7);
‡2D2ᵛ (p. 11)	From CCC 201, p. 30: Edict of Æthelred on Penitence, 'Ðis man geredde', as Liebermann I.262 (VIIa Atr); Napier 1883: 180–181, no. 39.

TYPE:

Main text in double columns, with OE in lh column and Latin translation in rh column, and textual variants and commentary at the bottom of the page.
AS6: the Junian Pica Anglo-Saxon cut by Christoffel van Dijck combined with the Junian Pica Roman (also by van Dijck) is used for the OE text;
Special sorts shown:

	11 lower-case sorts:	ð, f, ʒ, ı, ꝑ, ɼ, ꞇ, ẏ; þ, ð, ꝑ;
	8 (+1) capitals:	Ꞇ, Є, Ᵹ, Ꝺ, Ϻ, Ꞩ, Ð, Ꝑ (Junius, on ‡2D2ʳ), Ⲡ (Walpergen, on ‡2C2ʳ);
	4 others:	þ, ꝗ, ꝗ, ∴ .
Total:	23 (+1) sorts.	

Note: There is no capital ꝑ.

Copy seen: RUL, Stenton Collection 270.071 (from Madden sale 1867, lot 539).
Bibliography: All except tp and Burghers's engraving subsequently incorporated in 1703/5.1 (Hickes's *Thesaurus*), pt.III.ii, sig. ‡2B1ᵛ–‡2D2ᵛ (all signed; pp. 98–108). GR 6500.

1702.1: Madox, Thomas, *Formulare Anglicanum or, A Collection Of Ancient 𝕮𝖍𝖆𝖗𝖙𝖊𝖗𝖘 and 𝕴𝖓𝖘𝖙𝖗𝖚𝖒𝖊𝖓𝖙𝖘 of divers kinds, taken from the Originals, placed under several Heads, and deduced (in a Series according to the Order of Time) from the Norman Conquest to the End of the Reign of King Henry the VIII*. No printer stated, for Jacob Tonson and Robert Knaplock, 1702. ESTC T97067, also T97560 (large paper). AS7.
Documents: Charters etc.

Collation: 2⁰: π² ᵖb–ᵖc² a–h² i² (i2 = stub on which double-leaf illustration mounted; i2 + χ1 = stub on which double-leaf illustration mounted) B–5Y² (3I2 not present, no break in text) [$1 signed] 250 leaves, paginated [i–xii], i–xxiv, *xxxv–xxxviii*, 1–441, *442–52* (pp. nos 210–211 not used; pp. 246–247 misnumbered 236–7).

Note: Illustration on i2χ1 shows specimens of handwriting found in charters from the time of William the Conqueror.

SOURCES OF PASSAGES UTILIZING ANGLO-SAXON TYPES:

CATALOGUE OF EARLY PRINTED BOOKS CONTAINING ANGLO-SAXON 561

B1ʳ (p. 1, no. i)   From Augustus ii, fo 81 (BM Facs iv.40): Writ of Edward the Confessor confirming grant of land at Wormley (Hrt) to Westminster Abbey 1057 × 1066 (Sawyer 1134, as Harmer 90);

K2ᵛ (p. 36, no. lx)   From a lost MS formerly at Westminster Abbey: Writ of Edward the Confessor confirming gift of land at Wennington (E) to Westminster Abbey 1042 × 1044 (Sawyer 1117, as Harmer 73);

V1ʳ (p. 73, no. cxxxv)   From CCC 111, p. 95 (item 41): Record of a lease of land at Charlcombe (So) to William Hoset in return for which he was to serve in war at the king's summons 1066 × 1084, as Hunt 1893: no. 33 (cf. Pelteret 30);

2Y2ʳ (p. 175, no. cclxxxiii)   From a lost MS formerly at Westminster Abbey: Charter of King Edgar granting land at Hampstead (Mx) to Mangoda, his loyal *minister* 978 for (?)974 (Sawyer 805; OE bounds, as Birch 1309);

2Y2ᵛ (p. 176, no. cclxxxiv)   From Augustus ii, fo 35 (BM Facs iv.28): Account of the purchase of land at Offham (K) by Godric of Bourne from his sister Eadgifu 1044 × 1048 (Sawyer 1473, as Robertson 103);

3P1ᵛ (p. 238, no. cccxcv)   From Augustus ii, fo 34 (BM Facs iv.33): Bequest by Thurstan of land at Wimbish (E) to Christ Church, Canterbury 1042 × 1043 (Sawyer 1530, as Whitelock 30);

4E1ᵛ (p. 290, no. ccccxci)   From Augustus ii, fo 80 (BM Facs iv.29): Writ of King Edward declaring that Abbot Leofstan and the brethren in Bury St Edmunds are to have sake and soke over all their own men both inside and outside the borough 1044 × 1065 (Sawyer 1071, as Harmer 11);

5N2ᵛ (p. 416, no. dccl)   From CCC 140, 1ʳ (Ker no. 35, art. 2): Manumission stating that Edric has bought the freedom of a woman and her daughter, as Earle 1888: 269, no. 7;

5N2ᵛ (p. 416, no. dccli)   From CCC 140, 1ʳ (Ker no. 35, art. 2): Manumission stating that two 'scot' villains Ælfric and Ægelric have been freed for the abbot of Bath's soul, as Earle 1888: 269, no. 11;

5N2ᵛ (p. 416, no. dcclii)   From CCC 140, 1ʳ (Ker no. 35, art. 2): Manumission stating that Ælfwig 'se red' has bought his own freedom from Abbot Ælfsige of Bath (†1087), as Earle 1888: 269, no. 6;

5P1ʳ (p. 421, no. dcclxvi)   From a lost MS formerly at Westminster Abbey: Will of Leofwine, son of Wulfstan 998 (Sawyer 1522, as Napier and Stevenson 1895: no. 9).

TYPE:
Main text in a Pica Roman (Body 83) interspersed with a Pica Italic.
AS7: Nicholas Nicholls's Somnerian Pica Anglo-Saxon combined with the Pica Roman occurs in text as indicated above and in words on 2a1ᵛ.
Special sorts shown:

    13 lower-case sorts: ð, *e* (on 4E1ᵛ), f, ᵹ, Ꝺ, h (on V1ʳ), ı, p, ſ, t, ẏ; þ, ð̄, ꝑ;
    4 capitals: Æ², Є, ꟿ, Ð;
    3 others: þ̄, ꝫ, ꝭ.
  Total: 20 sorts.

Note 1: S with the top right stroke broken off used as ð on 2a1ᵛ;
Note 2: Some sorts are different from standard AS7, especially g and t with flat top strokes, and ð with shorter ascender and bar without serifs, and d like capital S with the top right stroke broken off but with a smaller bowl, but also one with a larger bowl, also new h on V1ʳ.

Copies seen: CUL J.7.19 (given by the author); CCC I.6.18 (given by the author).
Copies also at: T97067: BL, BromCL, BUL, CCA, CJC, CTH, CaCL, CLL, DCL, DCoL, EAL, EdUL, HOL, KCL, LBL, LCBL, LL, LRCS, LSH, LUL, MCS, MJRUL, NCL, NewCL, NLS, NT, OAS, OEC, OKC, OMC, ONC, OOC, OSJ, OWoC, QUB, RUL, SAN, StA, SUL, UBL, UKC, WAL, YML, YUL, DKI, NLI, NUIG, RIA, ULim, PBS, GUB; UTS, HHL, HUL, IUL, BPM, CUI, DDUL, EmU, KSRL, NLC, PUL, SLC, UCBL, UCH, UCLA, UCRL, UMI, UTA, UWS, YUC.

T97560: BL, BCL, BriCL, ECC, TCC, Eton, LHL, LPL, NT, OHC, OTC, SHC, WSS, TCD; FSL, NYCU, UTS, BJH, PFL, TCH, UPL, QBN, UW; ANZ, BSC.

Bibliography: Keynes 1994: 171; Levine 1991: 368–373.

1703.1: Wake, William, *The State of the Church and Clergy of England in their Councils, Synods, Convocations, Conventions, and other* 𝔓𝔲𝔟𝔩𝔦𝔠𝔨 𝔄𝔰𝔰𝔢𝔪𝔟𝔩𝔦𝔢𝔰, *historically deduced from the Conversion of the Saxons, to the Present Times*. No printer stated, for Richard Sare, 1703. ESTC T98005. AS7.
Words + L Letter

Collation: 2⁰: π², [a]–[e]² πA–B⁴ πC² (πC2 not present) B–3E⁴ 3F–3I² 3K–4L⁴ 4M–4N² (4N2 not present) ²A–²S² ²T² (²T2 + χ1) ²V–²2E² ²2F² (²2F2 not present) ²2G²–²2P² [$2 signed πA–C B–4N (-πC2, 3F2, 3G2, 3H2, 3I2, 4M2, 4N2); $1 signed [a]–[e] ²A–²2P (²2C missigned 2D)] 410 +1 leaves, paginated [i–xxiv], i–xviii, *xix–xx*, 1–622, *623–624*, ²1–247, ²*248–250* (²T2c1 numbered ²77–78*bis*; pp. nos ²100–199, ²215216 not used; pp. nos ²239–240 used twice; pp. 123, 126 misnumbered 128, 123, 233–234 misnumbered 231–232, 328 misnumbered 326, 482 misnumbered 428, 511 misnumbered 411, 579, 582 misnumbered 575, 570).

SOURCE OF PASSAGE UTILIZING ANGLO-SAXON TYPES:
Y1ʳ (p. 161)   From OBL Hatton 113, iiʳ/1–20: Latin letter summoning bp Wulfstan of Worcester to the Council of Winchester 1070 (Ker 331, art. 79, noted by Wanley in 1703/5.1 II.G1ᵛ, ed. Darlington 1928: 189–90);

TYPE:
Main text in Arthur Nicholls's Pica Roman (Body 82) interspersed with a Pica Italic.
AS7: Nicholas Nicholls's Somnerian Pica Anglo-Saxon combined with Arthur Nicholls's Pica Roman occurs in Latin text as indicated above and in OE words on T2ʳ:

Special sorts shown:

    7 lower-case sorts: ð, *e*, ᵹ, ꝑ, ꞃ, ꞇ; ꝑ;
    3 capitals: Є, Ϻ; Ð;
Total: 10 sorts.

Note: In Latin only the following are shown: ᵹ, ꞇ; Є, Ϻ.

Copies seen: CUL Adv.a.73.1 (with πA–C before [a]–[e]; additions/corrections by the author, and notes by Thomas Baker (1656–1740); additional errata slip pasted on ²2P1ᵛ), Pet.R.4.13 (with πA–C before [a]–[e]); CCC D.4.20 (additional errata slip pasted on ²2P2ᵛ); DML G3.2.4 (?earlier state: shows addenda on ²2P2ʳ with no catchword, and a list of books sold by Richard Sare and A. and J. Churchill on ²2P2ᵛ; blind-stamped contemporary binding in brown calf).

Copies also at: APL, BL, CCA, ECC, CJC, CMC, CSJ, TCC, DCL, DRD, DWL, EdUL, Eton, GUL, HHC, HOL, LBL, LFL, LHL, LPL, LSE, MJRUL, MTP, NCL, NewCL, NLPS, NLS, NUL, OBL, OAS, OBrC, OCC, OEC, OJC, OMaC, OMC, ONC, OOC, OQC, OPH, OStE, OTC, OUC, OWmC, OWoC, PML, RLW, RUL, ShCL, SML, StA, SUB, UBL, WAL, WCF, WFM, YML, DKI, TCD, ULim, GUB, MBS; NYCU, UTS, HHL, HUL, ACA, BCB, CRDS, EmU, GETS, IBUL, KSRL, LSU, NLC, PUL, RLV, SLWU, TCH, UCBL, UCH, UCLA, UMI, UOC, UPL, UTA, UVL, WMW, YUB, TUL.

Bibliography: Darlington 1928; Ramsay 1995: 384 (use of Canterbury archives); Sykes 1926: 28–30.

Facsimile (copy used not stated): Farnborough: Gregg, 1967 (lacks additional errata slip).

1703.2: Somner, William, *The Antiquities of Canterbury*, ed. Nicolas Batteley. No printer stated, for Robert Knaplock, 1703. 2nd edn of **1640.1**. ESTC T147218. AS2/3.

Legal Agreement

Collation: 2^0: [Part 1] $^{1-3}\pi^2$ a–b^2 B–$3D^2$ *A–X^2 [Part 2] $^4\pi^2$ ^{2}A–^{2}2Y^2 $2Z_1$ ^{3}A–$^3R_2$ $^3S^1$ *Y^2 [b2 + χ_1 G2 + χ_1 ^{2}A2 (stub) + χ_2 ^{2}C1 + χ_3 ^{2}C2 + χ_1 ^{2}E1 + χ_2 ^{2}G2 + χ_1 ^{2}I1 + χ_1 ^{2}I2 + χ_4 ^{2}K1 + χ_5 ^{2}Z1 + χ_2; $1 signed (-3D1 ^{2}A1)] 279 + 25 leaves, paginated [i–xxii], 1–192 [excluding additional pages], *193–196*, *1–80, *81–84*, ^{2}[i–viii], ^{2}1–178 [excluding additional pages], ^{3}1–70, ^{3}71–74; *pp. 49 misnumbered 50, 52 misnumbered 49, 78 misnumbered 87, ^{2}p. 168 misnumbered 164, ^{3}p. 23 not numbered. Illustrations on added leaves.

SOURCES OF PASSAGES UTILIZING ANGLO-SAXON TYPES:

$2Z1^v$ (p. 178)   From **1640.1** $2Z2^v$: BL Stowe Charter 30 (Sawyer 1215);
$2Z2^r$ (p. 179)   From **1640.1** $2Z3^r$: Agreement, Christ Church and Merchant Guild (Pelteret 90). Ed. Urry 1967: 385 from **1640.1**.

TYPE:

Main text in the 'Fell' Pica Roman (Body 84 Face 80 × 2: 3) interspersed with the complementary Pica Italic both cut by Walpergen *c*.1687 and shown on the OUP Specimen 1693 (Hart 1970: 25) and see Morison 1967: 248.

   Note: The bookseller/publisher Robert Knaplock (fl. London, 1696–1737†) was the brother of Ralph Knaplock, who in turn was partner of Jacob Tonson in 1697 (*Register of Company of Stationers* III (1917) 475). Tonson was freed by Thomas Bassett in 1678, Basset being one of the publishers of **1676.1**, the last book to use the Parkerian/Lambardian Pica Anglo-Saxon before this one. This tenuous connection is a possible explanation of how Knaplock and his printer came to have the use of these special type-designs, which had not been used for 27 years.

AS 2/3: The Parkerian Pica Anglo-Saxon mixed with some Lambardian Pica Anglo-Saxon sorts (**d, e, h**) occurs in text on $2Z1^v$–2^r, in words on $B1^r$ (p. 1) and $Y1^r$ (p. 81), and capitals used in a Latin inscription on $P2^r$ (p. 55). Body 83 Face 80 x 1.8: 2.9.

Special sorts shown:

	13 lower-case sorts:	ð, *e*, ꝼ, ȝ, h, ı, p, ꞃ, τ, ẏ; þ, ð, p;
	5 capitals:	Æ^2, Є, Ꝺ, S, Ð;
	1 other:	ꝧ.
Total:	19 sorts.	

Note 1: Lower-case **d** is the Lambardian **S**-like design but with the top arm broken or cut off.
Note 2: Lower-case AS **h** occurs only once, on 2Z1^v, and is the Lambardian **h** with the feet filed off.
Note 3: Ð occurs only in Latin on P2^r.

Copy seen: CUL L*.7.9(AA).

Copies also at: APL, BL, BAL, BCL, BUL, CCA, ECC, CGC, CPH, CQC, CSJ, TCC, DCL, HRC, KNA, LCL, LHL, LL, LPL, LU, MCS, MJRUL, NAL, NCL, NLW, NT, OBL, OAS, OHC, OMaC, OMC, OPH, OQC, OSJ, OStE, OTC, OWoC, OXC, UBL, WAL, WiCL, YML, DEWL, TCD, GUB; FSL, NYPL, NYCU, BAM, BCCH, CPL, MHC, NLC, RUH, UCBL, UCH, UCSB, USMA, UWS, QUK, UCC.

Bibliography: Urry 1977: v–xxiv.

Facsimile (reduced, 88%): Urry, William (introd.), *The Antiquities of Canterbury by William Somner*, Wakefield, EF Publishing, 1977. Omits main tp and whole of Part 2 except for illustrations.

1703/5.1: Hickes, George, William Elstob, Sir Andrew Fountaine, Runólfur Jónsson, & Humfrey Wanley, *Antiquæ Literaturæ Septentrionalis* [*Thesaurus*] *Libri Duo*. Oxford: Sheldonian Theatre, 1703/1705. ESTC N49869 and T108393. AS6, AS8.

Editor: In his diary for 6 Oct 1705 Thomas Hearne (1678–1735) noted that 'M^r. Wanley writ the Preface to the Catalogue of Septentrional MSS. in English, wch was afterwards translated into Latin by M^r. Thwaites, or else his Pupils, who supervis'd and corrected the whole Catalogue, & order'd it as he pleas'd' (Hearne 1885: 52). While this remark applies to Booklet 5, and sigs $^†a1^r$–$^†d1^v$ in particular, Thwaites's letters indicate that his roll was indeed supervisory, as Hearne stated. Thwaites's letter to Wanley of 3 July 1702 asks Wanley to send more copy (presumably of Booklet 5) and wants to know if Wanley has sent the specimen drawings of letters to Peter van Walpergen so that he can get on with cutting them (Harris 1992: 372). Cf. also Harris 1992: 68–69, and see further under TYPE below. For the practicalities of printing the work see Bennett 1948.

Date: 1703–5. Booklet 1: portrait of Hickes by White dated 1703; specimen of Codex Argenteus by Burghers dated 12 Apr 1703 [*b2χ*1]; Hickes's preface to Adam Otley dated 10 June 1703 [*m*1^v]; Hickes's preface to Sir John Pakington dated 10 June 1703 [*q*1^v]. Booklet 2: Hickes's preface to William Nicolson dated 1 May 1703 [*b*1^v]. Booklet 3: Hickes's preface to Roger Sheldon dated 24 Apr 1703 [*a*2^v]. Booklet 4: Hickes's dedicatory letter to Charlwood Lawton dated 14 Dec 1702 [‡*a*2^v]; Hickes's Præfatio Epistolaris to Bartholomew Shower dated 13 Aug 1701 [‡2R2^r]; Hickes' letter to Fountaine dated 29 Sept 1704 [‡3A2^v]. Booklet 5: Wanley's dedication to

Robert Harley dated 18 Aug 1704 [†d1ᵛ]. See also under Type below, AS8. There is a prospectus dated 22 Jan 1700 signed 'W[illiam] B[owyer]' 1 saying 'I here send you a short Account of Dr. Hicks's Book, now in the Press at Oxford' (Feather 1976: no. 21). Sigs ‡2B2ʳ–‡2D2ᵛ of Booklet 4 previously printed as 1701.2.

Ælfric, ASC, *Brunanburh*, *Cædmon's Hymn*, *Durham*, *Exodus*, Finnsburg fragment, *Genesis A*, *Gloria I*, Gospel of Nicodemus, *Judith*, OE Martyrology, *Maxims I & II*, *Menologium*, *Meters of Boethius*, Wulfstan, Charters, Laws, Manumissions etc.,

Facsimiles of Alphabets, List of Manuscripts, Middle English

Collation: 2⁰:

Booklet 1: π¹+² †–3†² a–q² (b2 + χ1) A–3N² (2N2 + χ1–4; 2T2 + χ1–2; 2X2 + χ1) [$2 signed (-3†2, n2, 3N2)] 159 + 8 leaves, numbered pp. [*1–18*], i–l (pp. nos xxxiii–xxxiv not used; pp. xlix–l not numbered);

Booklet 2: a–b² A–2E² [$2 signed (-a1, 2E2)] 60 leaves, numbered [i–viii], 1–111 (p. 112 not numbered);

Booklet 3: a² *A–*Z² (*A2 + χ1–6) [$2 signed (-a2)] 48 + 6 leaves, numbered [i–iv], 1–92;

Booklet 4: ‡a–b² ‡A–‡3A² (‡S + χ1–2; ‡2R + χ1–2; ‡2T + χ1–10) [$2 signed (-‡2T2), ‡A1 missigned A1, ‡K2 missigned K2, ‡L1 missigned L1, ‡N2 missigned N2] 98 + 14 leaves, numbered [i–viii], 1–188 (pp. 160, 168, 186 not numbered);

Booklet 5: π¹ †a–d² †A–4M² †4N¹ [$2 signed, †4I2 missigned I2, †4N2 not present] 172 leaves, numbered pp. [i–xviii], 1–326 (pp. 292 and 316 misnumbered 293 and 314 respectively);

Booklet 6: A–O² [$2 signed (-A1)] 28 leaves, unnumbered.

Altogether: 565 + 28 leaves.

SOURCES OF PASSAGES UTILIZING ANGLO-SAXON TYPES:

Booklet 1 (Praefatio to whole work addressed to Adam Ottley written by Wanley in English and t into L by Thwaites according to Hearne):

b2χ1ʳ	Various facsimiles (numbered I, II, V, VI, VIII, IX), the first at least attributable to Humfrey Wanley (note to b2ᵛ), engraved by Burghers 12 Apr 1703, including three lines from UUB DG1 (Codex Argenteus, Gothic Gospels) and a picture of St Luke from Lichfield, Gospels of St Chad;
d2ʳ	From CTH 1, 78ʳ: Writ of William I 1067 (Pelteret 6; cf. **1682.2**: G1ʳ);
d2ᵛ	From lost Cotton Charter: Writ of William I to William, bp of London 1067 (Pelteret 33);
d2ᵛ	From Cotton Charter VII.1: Charter of Henry I 1107 (Pelteret 46);

*d*2ᵛ	From Harley Charter 111 B.49: Charter of Henry II 1155 × 1161 (Pelteret 51);
*e*1ʳ	From Faustina A.x: Ælfric's Grammar (brief extracts from §xxiii);
*f*1ʳ	From Cotton Charter VIII.37: Record of a dispute between Athelstan bp of Hereford and Wulfstan re. land at Inkberrow (Wo) 1010 × 1023 (Sawyer 1460);
*f*1ᵛ–2ʳ	From Cotton Charter VIII.38: Will of Wynflæd 950 (Sawyer 1539);
	Præfatio to Grammatica Anglo-Saxonica addressed to John Pakington
*o*2ᵛ–*p*1ʳ	From (?) Cotton Augustus ii.6: King Edgar to Pershore Abbey (extract; Sawyer 786);
*p*1	From a lost MS: Bounds of Salwarpe and Waresley (Wo) (Sawyer 1597);
*p*1ᵛ	From Tiberius A.xiii, fo 100: Charter of bp Oswald re. land at Evenlode (Sawyer 1325);
	A1ʳ–3N2ʳ Institutiones Grammaticæ Anglo-Saxonica: many words and brief citations; Ch. 22 on Anglo-Norman and 'Semi-Saxon' (early Middle English): pp. 134–77
A2ʳ (p. 3)	Facsimiles of alphabets by Wanley engraved by Burghers from Nero D.iv, Bodley 441, Tiberius B.xi (drawn by John Sturt (?): see Keynes 2003: 194, n. 84), Hatton 20, Hatton 115, Hatton 113, Bodley 180, Junius 1 (ME *Ormulum*), Hatton 114, Hatton 38, Hatton 116, UUB DG 1 (Gothic Gospels), Gothic and Greek; see Keynes 1996: 152, n. 93. Facsimiles from some of the same manuscripts occur in Wanley's 'Book of Specimens', now Longleat House MS 345, as Nero D.iv on fo 121 (*ex informatione* Simon Keynes)
V1ᵛ (p. 78)	Facsimiles and alphabet from Digby 63 (Computistica; also 'Book of Specimens' fo 80) and Hatton 20;
2L1ᵛ (in fn)	From OBL Laud misc.636: ASC (E) extract from entry for 449 (Thorpe 1861: I.21);
2L2ʳ (p. 136)	Facsimile of Anglo-Saxon and Runic alphabet (in parallel) from Otho B.x, fo '165' (Ker 179)
2L2ᵛ	Facsimile of Runic alphabet from Domitian ix, fo 11 (Ker 151)
	From WCL, Liber Albus I (s.xiii), 14ʳ: Writ of Edward the Confessor to bp Giso (Sawyer 1116; Harmer 69/1–5);

2M1ʳ	From Cotton Charter VIII.15: Writ of William I to bp Walchelin (Pelteret 32);
2M2	From Harley 4660 (s.xvii), 8ᵛ or from lost original: Charter of King Edgar to Ealdormann Beorhtnoth 964 (Sawyer 726);
2M2ᵛ	From Harley 4660 (s.xvii), 9ʳ or from lost original: Lease of land at Moreton (Wo) by abp Oswald 990 (Sawyer 1363);
2M2ᵛ–2N1ʳ	From Harley 4660 (s.xvii), 9ᵛ or from lost original: Lease of land at Bentley in Holt (Wo) by abp Wulfstan 1017 (Sawyer 1384);
2N1ʳ	From Cotton Charter VII.13: Writ of Edward the Confessor 1041 × 1066 (Sawyer 1141; Harmer 97);
2N1ᵛ (p. 142)	From Harley 4660 (s.xvii), 10ʳ or from lost original: Lease of land at Hill and Moor (Wo) by bp Ealdred 1046 × 1053 (Sawyer 1406);
2N1ᵛ–2ʳ	Notice of Alfred Jewel with three drawings (see 1700.4 and Keynes 1992);
2N2ᵛ (in fn.)	From OBL Laud misc.636, 62ᵛ: ASC (E) 1085/6 (extracts; as Thorpe 1861: 353/2–14, 355/20–23; Clarke 1958: 8/23–9/38, 12/95–8);
2N2χ1–2	Facsimiles made by Burghers or Spofforth from specimens almost certainly by Wanley, 'Specimina scripturæ Gallico-Romanæ': Examples of Norman/French/Celtic writing (for Wanley's own account of his prospective 'Book of Specimens' see Heyworth 1989: 67–71, for Wanley as facsimilist see Keynes 1996: 126–129, and Parkes 1997: 127):—
2N2χ1ʳ	OBL Auct.F.4.32 (SC 2176), 1ʳ (s.x³): St Dunstan prostrate before Christ (Wormald 1952: pl. 1); discussed on 2N2ᵛ;
2N2χ1ᵛ	Fig. I: WCL, Liber Albus I, 14ʳ (s.xiii): Writ of Edward the Confessor confirming bp Giso in his diocese (text on 2S1ʳ); Keynes 1996²: 255, no. 1;

Fig. II: Kew, National Archives, E.31/2, Domesday Book, text (sample) and reconstructed alphabets (see Keynes 1996: 152, n. 95);

Fig. A: OBL Junius 121, 4ʳ, Decrees of Council of Winchester 1076;
Fig. B: MS lost from Worcester Cathedral (s.xi/xii), L record of Wulfstan II's attainment of bishopric of Worcester, copied s.xvii in Harley 4660, 11ᵛ–12ʳ (Pelteret 147); text on 2X2;

2N2χ1ᵛ–2N2χ2ʳ Fig. C: MS lost from Norwich Cathedral (s.xii¹), Foundation Charter of Norwich Cathedral Priory (1101),

	reconstructed alphabetical sequence of capitals, and episcopal signatories from witness list (see note below);
	2N2χ2ʳ Fig. D: OXC, Eynsham Cartulary (s.xii), 7ʳ, beginning of foundation charter (Sawyer 911; pr. Salter 1907–8: 1.19);
	Figs IV–V: TCC B.14.39 (s.xiii), 24ʳ, ME & F prayer to Christ (*IMEV* 1949; Brown 1932: no. 15); 56ᵛ, F collect for St Nicholas;
	Figs VI–VII: LPL 487 (s.xiii), 3ʳ, Beginning of ME sermon for Quadragessima Sunday (Morris 1868: 11); 23ᵛ, excerpt from ME 'Pater Noster' (Morris 1868: 63, lines 145–72);
	Fig. VIII: blank space, image not supplied from Titus D.v;
	Fig. [IX]: TCC B.14.39 (s.xiii), 83ʳ, L epitaph for Robert (?Grosseteste);
2P1ʳ	From CUL Ii.2.11, 182ʳ, 184ᵛ: Gospel of Nicodemus (extracts from §§ XV.2 and XVII.3, as Cross 1996: 185–187, 199);
2P1ʳ	From Durham, Prior's Kitchen, D&C Muniments 2.1, Pontificalium no. 9 (transcript supplied by William Nicolson): Writ of bp Flambard granting land to Durham Cathedral 1106 × 1128 (Pelteret 64);
2R1ʳ	From OSJ 194 (s.xii), 2ᵛ: Grant of land to Christ Church Canterbury by King Æthelred 979 (Sawyer 1636);
2R2	From Cotton Charter VII.6 (s.xii): Writ of Edward the Confessor confirming gift of land at Chalkhill (Mx) to Westminster Abbey 1044 × 1051 (Sawyer 1121; Harmer 77);
2R2ᵛ	From WCL, Liber Albus I, 14ʳ (s.xiii): Writ of Edward the Confessor to bp Giso (Sawyer 1116; Harmer 69; Keynes 1996²: 255–260, no. 7), cf. above 2L2ᵛ;
2R2ᵛ–2S1ʳ	From WCL, Liber Albus I, 14ʳ (s.xiii): Writ of Edward the Confessor confirming grant of property to bp Giso (Sawyer 1111; Harmer 64; Keynes 1996²: no. 1);
2S1ʳ	From WCL, Liber Albus I, 14ʳ (s.xiii): Writ of Edward the Confessor confirming bp Giso in his diocese 1061 × 1066 (Sawyer 1112; Harmer 65; Keynes 1996²: no. 3), facsimile copy on 2N2χ1ᵛ;
2S1ʳ	From WCL, Liber Albus I, 17ᵛ (s.xiii): Writ of Edward the Confessor granting land to bp Giso 1061 × 1066 (Sawyer 1115; Harmer 68; Keynes 1996²: no. 8);
2S1ᵛ	From WCL, Liber Albus I, 17ᵛ (s.xiii): Writ of Queen Edith granting land to bp Giso 1066 × 1075 (Sawyer 1241; Harmer 72; Keynes 1996²: no. 15);

2S1^v	From WCL, Liber Albus I, 14^r (s.xiii): Writ of King Harold granting rights to bp Giso 1066 (Sawyer 1163; Harmer 71; Keynes 1996^2: no. 11);
2S1^v	From WCL, Liber Albus I, 17^v–18^r (s.xiii): Writ of Edward the Confessor to bp Giso concerning the discharge of his obligations on land at Chew (So) 1061 × 1066 (Sawyer 1113; Harmer 66; Keynes 1996^2: no. 4);
2S1^v (in fn)	From WCL, Liber Albus II, 21^v–2^r (s.xv/xvi): Writ of Edward the Confessor to bp Giso regarding the rate of discharge 1061 × 1066 (Sawyer 1114; Harmer 67);
2S2	From WCL, Liber Albus I, 18^r (s.xiii): Writ of Queen Edith granting land at Milverton (So) to bp Giso 1061 × 1066 (Sawyer 1240; Harmer 70; Keynes 1996^2: no. 10);
2S2^v (p. 168)	From WCL, Liber Albus I, 18^r (s.xiii): Writ of William I to William de Courseulles-sur-Mêr 1076 × 1083 (Pelteret 29; Keynes 1996^2: no. 18);
2S2χ1	Facsimiles made by Burghers from more specimens by Wanley of French/Celtic writing: OBL Auct. F.4.32 (s.x^3): 20^r, Runic alphabet, 22^r 'Incipit paruum experimentum de luna', 23^r 'Incipiunt pauca excerpta de mensuris calculi', 24^r 'Incipiunt pauca testimonia de prophetarum libris', 28^v 'Incipit lectio prima Geneseos'
2V1^r	From lost Worcester original of Harley 4660, 3^r (s.xvii): Charter of Æthelred k of Mercia to bp Oftfor of Worcester 691 × 699 (Sawyer 77);
2V2^v–2X1^r	From lost Worcester original of Harley 4660, 6^v (s.xvii): Memorandum about k Ceolwulf's request for land from bp Heahberht 822 × 823 (Sawyer 1432);
2X1^v	From lost Worcester original of Harley 4660, 4^v (s.xvii): Familia at Worcester to bp Wærferth 892 (Sawyer 1416);
2X1^v–2^r	From lost Worcester original of Harley 4660, 8^r (s.xvii): bp Wilfrid to Worcester about a grant of land 922 (Sawyer 1289).
2X2^v (p. 176)	Facsimiles of Bodley 426 (SC 2327; Philippus presbyter on Job); Hatton 93 (SC 4081; exposition of the mass)
2X2χ1	Facsimile of papal consecration of Wells cathedral, from Cathedral Charter 2 (s.xi, Keynes 1996^2: no. 2); discussed on p. 177. Ch. 23 on Anglo-Saxon poetry (usually printed in half-lines or verses): pp. 177–221

2Y1ʳ	From Otho A.vi (since damaged by fire), coll. in Junius 12: *Meters of Boethius* 3 (Krapp 1932: 156; Godden/Irvine 2009: 1.388);
2Y1ᵛ	From Otho A.vi, 68ʳ: *Meters of Boethius* 20, 210b–224a (Krapp 1932: 183; Godden/Irvine 2009: 1.469);
2Y1ᵛ–2ʳ	From Vitellius D.xx (damaged in 1731 fire), former fo 20ᵛ: *Durham* (coll. Dobbie 1942: 27);
2Y2	From Junius 121, fo 42: *Gloria I* 1–50 (Dobbie 1942: 74–76);
2Y2ᵛ	From Junius 11, p. 166: *Exodus* 447–458, 506–514 (Krapp 1931: 103–104, 105; Lucas 2020: 132, 141);
2Y2ᵛ	From Vitellius A.xv, fo 207: *Judith* 199–222 (Dobbie 1953: 104–105; Griffith 1997: 102–103);
2Z1	From Tiberius B.iv (ASC D, 937), 49ʳ–50ʳ: *Brunanburh* (Dobbie 1942: 16–20; Campbell 1938: 93–95);
2Z1ᵛ	From Otho A.vi (since damaged by fire), copied in Junius 12: *Meters of Boethius* 6 (Krapp 1932: 159–160; Godden/Irvine 2009: 1.400–401);
2Z1ᵛ–2ʳ	From Junius 11, pp. 137–141: *Genesis A* 2850–2922 (Krapp 1931: 84–86, Doane 1978: 217–221);
2Z2ʳ	From Otho A.vi (since damaged by fire), copied in Junius 12: *Meters of Boethius* 2 (Krapp 1932: 155–156; Godden/Irvine 2009: 1.386–387);
2Z2ᵛ	From Otho A.vi (since damaged by fire), copied in Junius 12: *Meters of Boethius* 9 (Krapp 1932: 163–165; Godden/Irvine 2009: 1.419–421);
2Z2ᵛ–3A1ʳ	From Junius 11, pp. 75–8: *Genesis A* 1555–96 (Krapp 1931: 48–49; Doane 1978: 155–157);
3A1ʳ	From Otho A.vi (since damaged by fire), copied in Junius 12: *Meters of Boethius* 4 (Krapp 1932: 156–158; Godden/Irvine 2009: 1.389–390);
3A1	From CCC 173 (ASC A, 975), 28ᵛ–29ʳ: *Death of Edgar* (Dobbie 1942: 22–24);
3A1ᵛ–2ᵛ	§IX discusses OE metre, with some verse half-line examples
3A2ʳ	From CUL Kk.3.18 (OE Bede), 72ᵛ: *Cædmon's Hymn* (Dobbie 1942: 106);
3A2ʳ	From Junius 11, p. 162: *Exodus* 389–396 (Krapp 1931: 102; Lucas 2020: 125–126);
3A2ʳ	From Junius 11, pp. 141–142: *Genesis A* 2923–2931 (Krapp 1931: 86; Doane 1978: 221);

3A2ᵛ	From Junius 11, p. 83: *Genesis A* 1752–1756 (Krapp 1931: 53–54; Doane 1978: 163);
3A2ᵛ	From Junius 11, p. 1: *Genesis A* 1–5 (Krapp 1931: 3; Doane 1978: 109);
3B1ʳ	From Junius 11, p. 60: *Genesis A* 1203–1213 (Krapp 1931: 38; Doane 1978: 137);
3B1ʳ	§XI contains nine examples of individual OE verses containing five syllables
3B1ʳ–2ᵛ	From Caligula A.vii: Quotations from Old Saxon
3B2ᵛ–3C1ʳ	From LPL 487 (leaf now lost): *Finnsburg Fragment* (Dobbie 1942: 3–4; Fry 1974: 31–36; Tolkien/Bliss 1982: 19–20);
3C1ʳ–3C2ʳ	Quotations from Old Norse
3C2ᵛ–3D1ʳ	Quotations from eME, ME and MnE
3D1ᵛ	From Vitellius A.xv, 203ʳ: *Judith* 41–54 (Dobbie 1953: 100; Griffith 1997: 98);
3E2ʳ–3F2ʳ	From Tiberius B.i, 112ʳ–114ᵛ: *Menologium* (Dobbie 1942: 49–55; Karasawa 2015: 74–84);
3F2	From Tiberius B.i, 115ʳᵛ: *Maxims II* (Dobbie 1942: 55–57);
3G1ʳ–3K1ʳ	Notes on *Menologium* and *Maxims II* including quotations from OE texts of which the following are the longer ones
3I2	From Julius A.x: OE *Martyrology* (prose) 27 Mar, 23 Apr, 15 May (Rauer 2013: §§58, 67, 88 (excerpts))
3I2ᵛ	From (?) Nero A.i, fo 63 (Joscelyn's transcript of CCC 173): Law Alfred 43 (Liebermann, I.78);
3I2ᵛ	From (?) Nero A.i, 42ʳ: Law II Edgar 5–5.1 (Liebermann, I.198);
3I2ᵛ–3K1ʳ	From (?) Nero A.i, 8ʳ–10ʳ: Law I Cnut 14–17.3 (Liebermann, I.294–298);
3K1ʳ	From ECL 3501, 90ʳ–91ᵛ: *Maxims I* 71–143 printed as prose (Krapp & Dobbie 1936: 159–161; Muir 1994: I.254–257).
3K1ᵛ–3N2ʳ	Ch. 24 on 'Poetica Semi-Saxonica' = eME poetry.

Note to 2N2χ1ᵛ–2N2χ2ʳ Fig. C: The excerpt from the witness list is preceeded by the phrase 'Nomina Archiepiscoporum et episcoporum' before 'Ego Anselmus'. The only document I have found that includes this phrase is Dodwell 1974: no. 3 on pp. 2–4 (= Davis 2010: 706), the Charter of Henry I (1101), recorded in Norwich Record Office DCN 40/3 (= Registrum III, 49ʳ–51ᵛ), which is apparently a later copy (s.xv/xvi) of an earlier original. Hickes's text on 2O1ʳ (p. 145) refers to the 'elegantissima charta originali fundationis ecclesiae Norwicensis' accessed with the help of Thomas Tanner (Chancellor of Norwich 1700–). The document is printed by C. Reyner, *Apostolatus Benedictorum in Anglia* (Douai, 1626), tract ii, §6, pp. 146–147, cited in the revised version of Dugdale's *Monasticon* (1823 IV.16–17, no. 5), but not found in earlier editions. Reyner gives the source as from Norwich cathedral priory (Nordouicensi coenobio), which could have been DCN 40/3 or an earlier original. It seems likely that Wanley (if it was him) had access to such an earlier version with Tanner's help.

Booklet 2 deals with Old High German grammar.

A2ʳ   Alphabetical facsimiles of German scripts, including from Caligula A.vii (also in Wanley's 'Book of Specimens', fo 119) and Junius 25 (cf. Heyworth 1989: 108, Letter 55)

Booklet 3 deals with Old Norse.

*A2χ1ʳ–2ᵛ   Alphabetical facsimiles of Runic letters from various sources, including Junius 1, Domitian A.ix, ECL 3507, Oxford, St John's 17, Otho B.x, Otho C.v, p. 41 (also in Wanley's 'Book of Facsimiles', 138ᵛ)

*A2χ2ᵛ–3ᵛ   Facsimiles of ECL 3507 (Exeter Book); Runic alphabets from Caligula A.xv, Galba A.ii and Galba A.iii

Booklet 4 contains the Præfatio Epistolaris addressed to Bartholomew Shower:

‡A1ᵛ–2ʳ   From HCL P.i.2, fo 134 (s.xi): Record of dispute concerning land in He 1016 × 1035 (Sawyer 1462);

‡A2ᵛ–‡B1ʳ   From Augustus ii.15 (s.x/xi): Record of a dispute between Wynflæd and Leofwine 990 × 992 (Sawyer 1454);

‡B1ᵛ   From ECL 2519 (s.xi): Charter of Æthelstan 925 × 939 granting land to Exeter Minster (Sawyer 386);

‡B1ᵛ   From ECL 2517 (s.xi): Charter of Æthelstan 925 × 939 granting land to Exeter Minster (Sawyer 389);

‡B1ᵛ–2ʳ   From ECL 2521 (s.xi): Charter of Edgar 967 granting land to Wulfnoth Rumuncant (Sawyer 755);

‡C1ʳ   From HCL P.i.2, fo 135 (s.xi): Record of purchase of land by Leofwine, br of Leofflæd, from Eadric 1043 × 1046 (Sawyer 1469; also cited sig. ‡2E2ᵛ);

‡C1ʳ   From CCC 140/111, p. 8: Manumission from the time of Ælfsige abbot of Bath 1075–87 (Earle 1888: 268, §1);

‡C1ʳ (note)   From 1568.2 M3ᵛ: Law Alfred 1.41 (Liebermann I.74);

‡C1ᵛ   From CCC 140/111, p. 8: Manumissions from the time of Ælfsige abbot of Bath 1075–87 (Earle 1888: 268–9, §§4, 2, 3, 5);

‡C1ᵛ   From CCC 286, 74ᵛ: Grant by Ealhburg to Canterbury St Augustine's (Harmer 1914: 6);

‡C1ᵛ	From CCC 286, fo 77 (s.x): Agreement between Wulfric, abbot of Canterbury St Augustine's, and Ealdred concerning land (Sawyer 1455);
‡C1ᵛ	From Bodley 155 (SC 1974), 196ᵛ: Essex Charter re. land at Stifford (E) c.1090 (Hart 1971: no. 106);
‡C2ʳ	From Lichfield CL, Gospels of St Chad, p. 4: Record of Lawsuit (Ker no. 123; Earle 1888: 236–237) + other minor items;
‡C2ᵛ–‡D1ʳ	From Bodley 579, fo 1: Manumissions from Exeter (Earle 1888: 253–254, §§5, 4, 3, 1, 2; Orchard 2002: II.1–2);
‡D1ʳ	From Bodley 579, 377ᵛ: Manumission from Exeter (Earle 1888: 256–7; Orchard 2002: II.514);
‡D2ʳ	From ECL 3501, 4ᵛ: Manumissions from Exeter (Earle 1888: 258–264, §§2, 1; for these preliminaries to the Exeter Book see Chambers/Förster/Flower 1933: 47–54);
‡D2ʳ	From ECL 3501, 6ʳ: Manumission from Exeter (Earle 1888: 262–263);
‡D2ʳ	From ECL 3501, 6ʳ: Manumission from Exeter (Earle 1888: 261–262)
‡D2ʳ	From ECL 3501, 4ʳ: Manumission from Exeter (Earle 1888: 258);
‡D2ʳ	From ECL 3501, 4ᵛ: Manumission from Exeter (Earle 1888: 259–260);
‡D2	From ECL 3501, 4ʳ: Manumissions from Exeter (Earle 1888: 257–258);
‡D2ᵛ	From ECL 3501, 5ᵛ: Manumission from Exeter (Earle 1888: 260–261);
‡D2ᵛ (note)	From (?) ECL 2702 (s.xi): Edward joins dioceses of D & Co to make a united bishopric at Exeter (Sawyer 1021);
‡E1ᵛ	From ECL 3501, 4ᵛ: Manumission from Exeter (Earle 1888: 259);
‡E1ᵛ	From ECL 3501, 5ʳ: Exeter, permission to ring bells (Earle 1888: 260);
‡E1ᵛ–‡E2ʳ	From ECL 3501, 7ʳ: List of Guild-members, Exeter (Earle 1888: 264–266; Thorpe 1865 608–609);
‡E2	From CCC 111 (with 140), pp. 55–56: From the Cartulary of Bath priory (Hunt 1893: 3–4; Thorpe 1865: 615–617);
‡E2ᵛ–‡F1ʳ	From Tiberius B.v, fo 75: Ely, guild regulations (Thorpe 1865: 610–613):
‡F1	From Tiberius B.v, fo 75: Exeter, notice of guild assembly (Thorpe 1865: 613–614):

‡F1ᵛ	From CCC 140, fo 1: Ten manumissions and an agreement made by the prior of Bath (Earle 1888: 269–271);
‡F2ʳ	From CCC 111 (with 140), p. 8: Five manumissions issued under Abbot Ælfsige of Bath 1065–87 (Hunt 1893: lxxvi–lxxvii; Earle 1888: 268–269).
‡F2ᵛ	From (prob) Faustina A.x, 6ᵛ/9–10: Ælfric's Grammar (Zupitza 1880: 14/21–15/1);
‡F2ᵛ	From **1692.1**, C2ᵛ: ASC (E) 560 (extract as Thorpe 1861: 31);
‡G2ᵛ (note)	From Tiberius B.v, 76ᵛ: List of Freeholders (Pelteret 1986: 472–473);
‡H1	From Augustus ii, fo 34 (s.xi, BM Facs iv.33): Bequest by Thurstan of land at Wimbish (E) to Christ Church, Canterbury 1042 × 1043 (Sawyer 1530; Whitelock 30);
‡H1ᵛ	From Augustus ii, fo 35 (s.xi, BM Facs iv.28): Account of the purchase of land at Offham (K) by Godric of Bourne from his sister Eadgifu 1044 × 1048 (Sawyer 1473; Robertson 103);
‡H2ᵛ	From RKA, DRc/R1 (Textus Roffensis, *olim* RCL A.3.5), fo 48: Law III Æthelred 3.1 (Liebermann I.228);
‡H2ᵛ	From CCC 383. p. 83: Law Alfred & Guthrum 3 (Liebermann I.126);
‡L2ʳ	From RKA, DRc/R1 (Textus Roffensis, *olim* RCL A.3.5), fos 155–156: Resolution of a dispute between Godwine bp of Rochester and Leofwine son of Ælfeah (Sawyer 1456; Robertson 69);
‡L2ᵛ (note)	From an unknown source: Unidentified (?)Edict 'And þ ilce gedo eac ða biscopas heora gedwilcra. ⁊ eac mine Ealdormanna. ⁊ gereafa ⁊ ic wille þ mine biscopas. ⁊ gereafa ðæs demað eallum ðe hio gehyrsumian gebyrað'.
‡M1ʳ	From Nero A.i, 21ᵛ–22ʳ: Law II Cnut 19, 19.1–2 (Liebermann I.320–322);
‡N2ʳ	From RKA, DRc/R1 (Textus Roffensis, *olim* RCL A.3.5), fos 144–145: Will of Byrhtric 973 × 987 (Sawyer 1511; Whitelock 11);
‡O1ᵛ	From CCC 111 (with 140), pp. 88–90 (s.xii): Will of Wulfwaru 984 × 1016 (Sawyer 1538; Whitelock 116);
‡O1	From Augustus ii, fo 42: Will of Badanoth Beotting 845 × 853 (Sawyer 1510; Robertson 6);
‡O2ʳ	From Augustus ii, fo 64: Will of Abba, reeve 833 × 839 (Sawyer 1482; Harmer 2);

‡P1ᵛ–2ʳ	From RKA, DRc/R1 (Textus Roffensis, *olim* RCL A.3.5), fos 147–148: Ælfeah reports on the estate at Wouldham (K) 960 × 988 (Sawyer 1458, Robertson 41);
‡P2ᵛ	From Claudius B.vi, fo 102 (s.xiii): Will of Ælfric, abp 1003 × 1004 (Sawyer 1488; Whitelock 18);
‡R1ʳ	From (?) Harley 358, 44ᵛ–45ʳ (s.xvi): Cnut grants privileges to Bury St Edmunds abbey 1021 × 1023 (Sawyer 980);
‡R1ʳ	From (?) BL Add 14847, 32ᵛ (s.xiii): Writ of William I to Æthelmær 1066 × 1070 (Pelteret 19);
‡S1ᵛ	From Somers Ch. 18 (lost): Marriage agreement by Wulfric on marrying the sister of abp Wulfstan 1014 × 1016 (Sawyer 1459; Robertson 76), also printed below more fully on ‡T2ᵛ and in Booklet 5, 4G1ᵛ–2ʳ, no. 18;
‡S1χ1–2	Facsimiles prob by Wanley, attrib to the engraver Sutton Nicholls, of (Tab B) signs of the cross in various charters, (Tab C) spurious charter of William I (1080–6; Davis 1913: 286, Bates 1998: 115) to Durham from (?) DCL Muniments 1.1. Reg.9 (s.xii²), (Tab D) from a lost MS (s.xii) charter of Æthelbald k of Mercia 716 (Sawyer 82) said to be spurious by Hickes on ‡T2ʳ; ‡S1χ1ʳ is blank, prob intended for Tab A, which is lacking;
‡T2ᵛ	Fuller version of preceding item;
‡V1	From ECL 2528 (s.xi): Diploma of William I to Leofric bp of Exeter 1069 (Pelteret 17);
‡V2ᵛ–‡X1ʳ	From Somers Ch. 6 (lost): Resolution of dispute over swine-pasture at Leigh (Wo) 825 (Sawyer 1437; Robertson 5);
‡Z1ʳ–2ᵛ	From 1568.2 with notes of MS readings by de Laet from RKA, DRc/R1 (Textus Roffensis, *olim* RCL A.3.5), fos 1–3: Laws Æthelberht (Liebermann, I.3–8);
‡Z2ᵛ–‡2A1ʳ	From 1568.2 with notes of MS readings by de Laet from RKA, DRc/R1 (Textus Roffensis, *olim* RCL A.3.5), 3ᵛ–5: Laws Hlothære and Eadric (Liebermann, I.9–11);
‡2B2ʳ–‡2D1ᵛ	From 1701.2: Wulfstan, *Sermo Lupi ad Anglos* (Bethurum 1957: 267–275, Whitelock 1963: 47–67) from MSS I (Nero A.i, 110ʳ–15ʳ), C (CCC 201, pp. 82–86), and E (Hatton 113, 84ᵛ–90ᵛ);
‡2D2	From 1701.2: Ps-Wulfstan, *Be mistlican gelimpan* (Napier 1883: 169–175, nos 35 and 36 (= K; §5 = pp. 174/5–175/7) from MSS E (Hatton 113, 91ᵛ–3ᵛ), and C (CCC 201, pp. 28–29), coll. K (Tiberius A.iii, 90ᵛ–91ʳ), §5 from K alone);

‡2D2ᵛ	From 1701.2: Edict of Æthelred on Penitence, 'Ðis man geredde' (Liebermann I.262 (VIIa Atr); Napier 1883: 180–1, no. 39), from CCC 201, p. 30;
‡2E1ʳ	From Otho B.ii (damaged in 1731 fire), 350ᵛ (now lost): Hidage for Defence (Robertson 1956 App. II, no. 1);
‡2E1ᵛ	From RKA, DRc/R1 (Textus Roffensis, *olim* RCL A.3.5), 39ᵛ, & 1568.2 V4ᵛ/9–X1ʳ (2 versions): Mircna Laga (Liebermann I.462);
‡2E1ᵛ	From 1568.2, V3ᵛ: Law Norðleoda §1 (Lambarde v Athelstan, where his Elizabethan AS is distinctive; Liebermann I.458);
‡2E2ᵛ	Another citation of Sawyer 1469 as on ‡C1ʳ.
‡2E2ᵛ–2F1ʳ	From RKA, DRc/R1 (Textus Roffensis, *olim* RCL A.3.5), 38ᵛ: Law Swerian (Liebermann, I.396–398);
‡2F1ʳ	From RKA, DRc/R1 (Textus Roffensis, *olim* RCL A.3.5), 39ᵛ: Law Að (Liebermann, I.464);
‡2F1ʳ	From RKA, DRc/R1 (Textus Roffensis, *olim* RCL A.3.5), fo 93: Law Geþyncðo (Liebermann, I.456–458);
‡2F1ᵛ	From RKA, DRc/R1 (Textus Roffensis, *olim* RCL A.3.5), 38ʳ: Law Pax (Liebermann, I.390);
‡2F1ᵛ–2ʳ	From RKA, DRc/R1 (Textus Roffensis, *olim* RCL A.3.5), fos 162–163: Land-dispute at Bromley (K) s.x² (Sawyer 1457; Robertson 59);
‡2F2ʳ–2G1ʳ	From CCC 201, pp. 147–9: English kings (Liebermann, I.1–9);
‡2G1ʳ–2H1ʳ	From CCC 201, pp. 149–51: English saints (Liebermann, I.9–19);
‡2H2ʳ–2O2ʳ	*Historia Hialmari Regis Biarmlandiæ atque Thulemarkiæ*: Runic ON text ed. Johan Peringskiöld of Stockholm (on whom see below Booklet 5, 4I1ᵛ–4L1ʳ);
‡2R1χ1	Facsimile of Charter of K Edgar to Worcester 964 from Harley 7513 (s.xii¹) discussed ‡Y1ᵛ–2ʳ (Sawyer 731).

Booklet 5:

†A1ʳ–†2C2ʳ (pp. 1–103)		List of manuscripts in OBL:
†A1ʳ–†C1ʳ	1.	Bodley 342, listing 46 homilies;
†C1ʳ–†D1ᵛ	2.	Bodley 340, listing 32 homilies (nos XIV–XV not used);
†D2ʳ–†G1ʳ (p. 15)	3.	Bodley 343, listing 82 homilies;
†G1ᵛ–†H1ᵛ (p. 26)	4.	Hatton 113 (formerly Junius 99), listing 32 homilies;
†H2ʳ–†I2ᵛ (p. 31)	5.	Hatton 114 (formerly Junius 22), listing 42 homilies;
†I2ᵛ–†K2ᵛ (p. 36)	6.	Hatton 115 (formerly Junius 23), listing 39 homilies &c.;
†K2ᵛ–†L2ʳ (p. 40)	7.	Hatton 116 (formerly Junius 24), listing 28 homilies;

†L2ᵛ–†M1ʳ (p. 44)	8.	Junius 85–86, listing 8 homilies &c.;
†M1ʳ–†P2ʳ	9.	Junius 121, Ecclesiastical Institutes &c., listing 145 items;
†P2ʳ–†Q2ʳ (p. 59)	10.	Junius 1, ME *Ormulum* (s.xi/xii), listing 30 divisions;
†Q2ʳ (p. 63)	11.	Auct. F.4.32, 10ʳ–18ᵛ, Invention of the Holy Cross;
†Q2ᵛ	12.	Bodley 180, Alfredian tr of Boethius (s.xii);
†Q2ᵛ	13.	Bodley 441, WS Gospels;
†Q2ᵛ–†R1ʳ	14.	Laud misc. 636, ASC (E);
†R1ʳ–2ʳ (p. 65)	15.	Laud misc. 482, Penitential &c., listing 12 items;
†R2ʳ–†S1ʳ	16.	Laud misc. 509, Pentateuch &c., listing 11 items (see also 256);
†S1ᵛ–2ʳ (p. 71)	17.	Hatton 20, Alfredian Pastoral Care, listing 5 items;
†S2ʳ–†T2ᵛ	18.	Hatton 76, Gregory's Dialogues in OE, Herbarium, listing 4 main items with sub-headings;
†T2ᵛ (p. 76)	19.	Junius 27, Glossed Psalter;
†T2ᵛ	20.	Hatton 38, WS Gospels (s.xii/xiii);
†V1ʳ	21.	Junius 11, 'Cædmon' poems;
†V1ʳ–2ʳ	22.	Bodley 865, 89ʳ–112ᵛ, OE version of Capitula of Theodulf, listing 20 items;
†V2	23.	Bodley 34 (s.xiii^in) ME Lives of SS Katherine, Margaret, Juliana &c.;
†V2ᵛ–†X1ʳ (p. 80)	24.	Auct. D.2.16, Leofric's & Æthelstan's gifts to Exeter;
†X1	25.	Auct. D.2.19, MacRegol/Rushworth Gospels with OE Gloss;
†X1ᵛ–2ʳ	26.	Bodley 579, List of Sureties, Inscription, Manumissions &c;
†X2ʳ	27.	Bodley 572, Rubrics, Crypograms, Glosses;
†X2ʳ	28.	Digby 4 (SC 1605), fo 97, ME *Poema Morale*;
†X2	29.	Bodley 163 (SC 2016), L Bede (CH fo 152ᵛ), L/OE Charm;
†X2ᵛ (p. 84)	30.	Auct. D.2.14 (SC 2698) L Gospels;
†X2ᵛ	31.	Bodley 730 (SC 2709), 144ʳ–7ᵛ, L/OE glossaries (excerpts);

The following MSS are transcripts by Junius (unless otherwise stated):

†X2ᵛ	32.	Laud misc. 661 (SC 1202), ASC to 977 transcribed from Tiberius A.vi, + WS Genealogy from Tiberius A.iii, fo 175;
†X2ᵛ–†Y1ʳ	33.	e Mus. 106 (SC 3627), Ælfric's Grammar transcribed by Gerard Langbaine (1608/9–58; *ODNB*);

†Y1r	34.	Junius 12, OE Boethius;
†Y1r	35.	Junius 15, OE Orosius;
†Y1	36.	Junius 38, Extracts from CCC 201;
†Y1v	37.	Junius 39, OE Decalogue;
†Y1v–2r	38.	Junius 40, Theological commonplaces in OE attributed to Defensor of Ligugé, *Liber Scintillarum*;
†Y2r	39.	Junius 41, Pieces from Tiberius A.iii;
†Y2v	40.	Junius 43, printed book, Joannes Meursius, *Roma luxurians, sive, De luxu Romanorum, liber singularis* (Copenhagen, 1631), with notes 'De somniorum diversitate' added by Junius from Tiberius A.iii, pp. 70, 80;
†Y2v	41.	Junius 45, Junius's notes from OE MSS, Julius A.iii, Junius 85–86, CCC 201;
†Y2v–†Z1v	42.	Junius 44, 'De observatione lunae et quae cavenda' in OE from Tiberius A.iii and Hatton 115;
†Z1v–2r (p. 90)	43.	Junius 47, *Hexameron*, from Hatton 115, 116;
†Z2r	44.	Junius 50, Lindisfarne Gospels (extracts) from Nero D.iv;
†Z2	45.	Junius 52, *Benedictine Rule* in OE, &c.;
†Z2v	46.	Junius 53, OE *Pastoral Care*, from Tiberius B.xi;
†Z2v	47.	Junius 58, OE Liber medicinalis, from Hatton 76;
†2A1r (p. 93)	48.	Junius 59, OE De peccatorum medicina, from Tiberius A.iii;
†2A1r	49.	Junius 60, OE *Promissio Regis* from Vitellius A.vii;
†2A1r	50.	Junius 61, *Adrian & Ritheus*, from Julius A.ii;
†2A1r	51.	Junius 62, Wynflæd's agreement and Charter of King Cnut to Bury, from Augustus ii;
†2A1	52.	Junius 63, Modus confitendi, L + OE, from Tiberius A.iii;
†2A1v–2r	53.	Junius 65, OE excerpts re. Christian duties, from Nero A.i, fos 71, 100;
†2A2r (p. 95)	54.	Junius 66, OE Master/Pupil dialogue, from Tiberius A.iii;
†2A2r	55.	Junius 67, ASC (C) (beginning) from Tiberius B.i;
†2A2r	56.	Junius 68, 'Admonitio', from Hatton 76;
†2A2	57.	Junius 69, 'ipsius Domini epistola de coelo dilapsa', from CCC 140, Tiberius A.iii;

†2A2ᵛ	58.	Junius 70, St Augustine, *Soliloquies*, OE, from Vitellius A.xv;
†2A2ᵛ	59.	Junius 71, Ælfrici præsulis Glossarium (via Rubens), from what is now APM 47 + BL Add 32246;
†2A2ᵛ	60.	Junius 72, Ælfric's Glossary, from Julius A.ii;
†2A2ᵛ–†2B1ʳ	61.	Junius 74, Nicodemi Pseudo-Evangelium, from CUL Ii.2.11;
†2B1	62.	Junius 102, Wulfstan, 5 Sermons coll. from Nero A.i, CCC 201, and Hatton 113/14;
†2B1ᵛ (p.98)	63.	Junius 103, Evangelica Dano-Saxonice (i.e. ON) + 'Exorcismi sacri ad reddendos agros fertiles', both from Caligula A.vii;
†2B1ᵛ	64.	Junius 104, Interogationes Sigewulfi presbiteri, from Hatton 115/116;
†2B1ᵛ	65.	Junius 105, *Judith*, from Vitellius A.xv;
†2B1ᵛ–2ʳ	66.	Junius 107, Hymni Veteris Ecclesiæ, with AS interlinear gloss, from Vespasian D.xii, Julius A.vi, Tiberius A.iii;
†2B2ʳ	67.	Junius 108, Junius's preface to Gothic Gospels;
†2B2ʳ (p. 99)	68.	Junius 46, cited as 109, Gregory's *Dialogues* in OE from Hatton 76 + Regularis Concordia (excerpts) from Tiberius A.iii.
†2B2ʳ–†2C2ʳ		Other Transcripts (s.xvi/xvii), some prepared for publication:
†2B2	69.	Laud misc.381, William Lisle's Hexateuch, from Claudius B.iv;
†2B2ᵛ–†2C1ʳ	70.	Laud misc.201, William Lisle's Saxon-English Psalter;
†2C1ʳ	71.	Bodley 33, Joscelyn's Dictionariolum Saxonico-Latinum, transcript by John Parker *c.*1600;
†2C1ʳ	72.	James 41, Dictionariolum Saxonico-Anglicum by Richard James 1620–30 + James 42, Glossarium Saxonico-Latinum (*c.*1600);
†2C1ʳ	73.	Selden supra 62, OE miscellany by Richard James;
†2C1ᵛ (p. 102)	74.	Selden supra 63, Nowell's Dictionarium Saxonico-Anglicum;
†2C1ᵛ	75.	Junius 26, Junius's transcript of no. 74;
†2C1ᵛ	76.	Junius 37, Memoranda by Junius;
†2C1ᵛ	77.	Junius 76, Junius's transcript of excerpts from Lindisfarne and MacRegol/Rushworth Gospels;

†2C1v	78.	Junius 77, L-OE Glossary augmented from others by Junius;
†2C1v	79.	Junius 112, L-OE Dictionary compiled by Junius;
†2C1v	80-1.	Junius 2-3, OE-L Dictionary by Junius, noting also Fell 8-18: Dictionarium Septentrionale in 5 languages, Junius's materials prepared for publication by Fell, but not printed;
†2C1v	82.	Junius 4-5, Junius's Etymologicon Linguae Anglicanae, later printed by Lye 1743;
†2C1v	83.	Marshall 78, brief AS Grammar by Thomas Marshall;

Printed Books annotated by Junius:

†2C1v (p. 102)	84.	Junius 9, *The Workes of ... Geffrey Chaucer*, ed. Thomas Speght (London 1598; STC 5077/8);
†2C1v	85.	Junius 7, Somner's Dictionary 1659.1;
†2C2r	86.	Junius 10, Wheelock's OE Bede and ASC 1643.1 and 1643.2;
†2C2r	87.	Junius 18, Selden's Eadmer 1623.3;
†2C2r	88.	Junius 32, *Hortus Vocabularum* (Westminster, Wynkyn de Worde 1500; STC13829);
†2C2r	89.	Junius 54, *The xiii Bukes of Eneados of ... Virgill translatet ... bi ... Gawin Douglas* (London 1553; STC 24797);
†2C2r	90.	Junius 73, Junius's Cædmon 1655.2;
†2C2r	91.	Junius 92, *Regula S. Benedicti*, ed. Baudoin Moreau (Douai 1611), interlined with OE version from Tiberius A.iii by Junius;
†2C2r	92.	Junius 33, Spelman's Psalter 1640.3;
†2C2r	93.	Marshall 223 (*olim* 72), Ælfric, *Saxon Treatise concerning the Old and New Testament*, ed. Lisle 1623.1, annotated by Junius;
†2C2r–†2D1r		Manuscripts (and printed sources) in Other Oxford Libraries: *In Bibliotheca Ashmoliana*
†2C2		94. Ashmole 328, Byrhtferth's Manual;
†2C2v (p. 104)		95. Dugdale 29: Dugdale's Dictionarium *Saxonico-Anglicum* 1644;
†2C2v		Printed books in the Ashmole collection:
	96.	Lambard's *Archaionomia* 1568.2;
	97.	Parker/Foxe *Gospels* 1571.1;

	98.	Lambard's *Perambulation of Kent* wrongly assigned to 1623 but *recte* 1576.2 or 1596.1;
	99.	Parker/Joscelyn's *Testimonie of Antiquity*, ed. Lisle 1623.1;
	100.	Spelman's *Concilia* 1639.4;
	101.	Spelman's Psalter 1640.3;
	102.	Wheelock's OE Bede 1643.1, &c.

In St John's College Library

†2C2ᵛ–†2D1ʳ   103.   OSJ 154, Ælfric's Grammar &c.
†2D1ʳ   104.   OSJ 194, 2ʳᵛ, Charter of K Æthelred 979 (Sawyer 1636).

In All Souls College Library

†2D1ʳ   105.   OAS 38, 1ʳ–12ᵛ, Ælfric's Grammar (part); see below, 176;

In Corpus Christi College Library

†2D1ʳ   106.   OCC 279, part ii, OE Bede (incomplete);

In the treasury of Christ Church

†2D1ʳ   107.   Eynsham Cartulary, 7ʳ, K Æthelred to Eynsham Abbey 1005;

†2D1ᵛ–†2X1ʳ (pp. 106–173) List of manuscripts in Cambridge (for Wanley's handwritten descriptions of Cambridge MSS made in 1699 see Harley 7055, fos 125–147):

In the Library of Corpus Christi College

†2D1ᵛ (p. 106)   108.   CCC 146, Adjurations headed Ðalrunᵹ;
†2D1ʳ–†2E1ʳ   109.   CCC 196, OE Martyrology;
†2E1ʳ   110.   CCC 23, Prudentius, glossed;
†2E1ʳ (p. 109)   111.   CCC 44, Canterbury Pontifical;
†2E1   112.   CCC 265, 'Wulfstan's Commonplace Book', Directions for a Confessor, Law IV Edgar, &c.;
†2E1ᵛ   113.   CCC 391, Prayers, Prognostics &c.;
†2E1ᵛ   114.   CCC 326, *Aldhelm* (OE poem), Glosses to his *De laude virginitatis*;
†2E1ᵛ–†2F1ʳ   115.   CCC 190, Notes & Glosses, Ecclesiastical Institutes &c.;
†2F1ʳ (p. 113)   116.   CCC 449, Ælfric's Grammar;
†2F1ᵛ   117.   CCC 12, Alfredian version of Gregory's *Cura Pastoralis*;
†2F1ᵛ–2ʳ   118.   CCC 41, OE Bede, Homilies, &c.;
†2F2   119.   CCC 144, Corpus Glossary;

†2F2ᵛ (p. 116)	120.	CCC 140, Gospels, Manumissions, Homily (see also 136);
†2F2ᵛ–†2G2ᵛ	121.	CCC 162, Homilies;
†2G2ᵛ–†2H2ʳ	122.	CCC 178, Homilies, Rule of St Benedict;
†2H2ʳ–†2I1ʳ	123.	CCC 188, Homilies;
†2I1ʳ–2ᵛ (p. 125)	124.	CCC 198, Homilies;
†2I2ᵛ–†2K1ᵛ	125.	CCC 302, Homilies;
†2K1ᵛ (p. 130)	126.	CCC 322, OE version of Gregory's *Dialogues*;
†2K1ᵛ	127.	CCC 173, ASC (A), Laws, Glosses to Sedulius;
†2K1ᵛ–2ʳ	128.	CCC 191, Rule of Chrodegang L + OE;
†2K2 (p. 131)	129.	CCC 421, Homilies;
†2K2ᵛ–†2L1ʳ	130.	CCC 419, Homilies;
†2L1ʳ–†2M1ʳ	131.	CCC 303, Homilies;
†2M1ʳ–†2O2ᵛ (p. 137)	132.	CCC 201, *Regularis Concordia*, Bede *De die judicii*, Homilies, Laws &c.;
†2O2ᵛ	133.	CCC 96 (s.xv, annot. s.xvi), Chronicon attrib. John Brompton;
†2P1ʳ (p. 149)	134.	CCC 402, eME *Ancrene Wisse*;
†2P1ʳ	135.	CCC 422, Red Book of Darley, with *Solomon and Saturn* (verse dialogues) and a Missal with OE annotations;
†2P1	136.	CCC 140 + 111, Gospels, Homily, Manumissions (Pelteret 70–86); see also 120;
†2P1ᵛ–2ʳ	137.	CCC 101 (s.xvi), Charters, OE Genesis (with Ælfric's Preface from no. 149 below);
†2P2ʳ (p. 151)	138.	CCC 214, Boethius, with OE glosses (part);
†2P2ʳ	139.	CCC 278 (s.xiv) ME Psalter, with specimen Ps 65 'Jubilate';
†2P2ʳ	140.	CCC 444, ME *Genesis and Exodus*;
†2P2ʳ	141.	CCC 286, Grants to St Augustine's Canterbury added s.x to s.xvi, Gospels;
		In Cambridge University Library
†2P2ᵛ (p. 152)	142.	CUL Hh.1.10, Ælfric, *Glossary* (incomplete);
†2P2ᵛ	143.	CUL Ff.1.23, Psalms with continuous OE gloss + canticles;
†2P2ᵛ	144.	CUL Ii.2.11, WS Gospels &c.;
†2Q1ʳ	145.	CUL Kk.3.18, OE Bede;
†2Q1ʳ (p. 153)	146.	CUL Ii.2.4, Alfredian version of Gregory's *Pastoral Care*;

†2Q1r–†2R2v	147.	CUL Gg.3.28, Ælfric, Homilies, Preface + 43 + 51 listed &c.;
†2R2v–†2S1v (p. 160)	148.	CUL Ii.4.6, Homilies, listing 36 items;
†2S1v–†2T1r	149.	CUL Ii.1.33, Homilies & Saints' Lives, listing 44 items.

In Trinity College Library

†2T1v–2r (p. 166)	150.	TCC B.15.34, Homilies, listing 28 items;
†2T2r	151.	TCC R.9.8 (s.xvi) given by Thomas Neville, Ælfric's Grammar;
†2T2	152.	TCC R.9.17, Ælfric's Grammar + Distichs of Cato;
†2T2v (p. 168)	153.	TCC R.5.22, OE Pastoral Care;
†2T2v	154.	TCC B.15.33, Isidore, *Etymologiæ* (s.ix), annotated by Stephen Batman (s.xvi);
†2T2v–†2V1r	155.	TCC R.17.1, Eadwine's Psalter with OE gloss;
†2V1r–2v	156.	TCC B.14.52 (s.xiii), 12c homilies, listing 35 items;

In Trinity Hall Library

†2V2v–†2X1r	157.	CTH 1 (s.xv¹), Thomas of Elmham, *Historia Abbatiæ S. Augustini Cantuariensis*, citing Elmham's list of 8 books sent 'a Gregorio ad Augustinum': see Hardwick 1858: xxv–xxvii; Emms 2004. Possible candidates for some of these books now are BL Vespasian A.i (Vespasian Psalter), CCC 286 (Gospels of St Augustine), and CCC 197B + Otto C.v (Cambridge-London Gospels), but there was a fire in St Augustine's in 1168 which probably caused considerable destruction.
†2X1v–†2Z1v (pp. 174–82)		List of manuscripts in the Royal Library at St James's Palace
†2X1v–2v	165.	Royal 7 C.xii, Homilies, listing 41 items;
†2X2v–†2Y2v (p. 175)	166.	Royal 12 D.xvii, Medicinal recipies, listing 88 + 67 + 76 items;
†2Y2v–†2Z1r (p. 179)	167.	Royal 7 C.iv, Continuous OE gloss to Defensor of Liguge's *Liber Scintillarum*;
†2Z1r (p. 181)	168.	Royal 1 B.vii, L Gospels with OE manumission added;
†2Z1r	169.	Royal 1 A.xiv, WS Gospels;
†2Z1	170.	Royal 1 D.ix, L Gospels with OE documents added;

†2Z1ᵛ (p. 182)	171.	Royal 2 B.v, L Psalter with continuous OE gloss, prayers &c.;
†2Z1ᵛ	172.	Royal 15 B.xxii, Ælfric's Grammar;
†2Z1ᵛ	173.	Royal 5 E.xi, Glosses to Aldhelm, *De laude virginitatis* (prose);
†2Z1ᵛ	174.	Royal 6 A.vi, Glosses to Aldhelm, *De laude virginitatis* (prose);
†2Z1ᵛ	175.	Royal 6 B.vii, Glosses to Aldhelm, *De laude virginitatis* (prose);
†2Z1ᵛ	176.	Royal 12 G.xii, Ælfric's Grammar (part); see also above, 105;
2Z2ʳ–3X1ʳ (pp. 183–265)		List of manuscripts in the Cotton Library at Westminster
2Z2ʳ	177.	Julius A.ii, Ælfric's Grammar/Glossary, Adrian & Ritheus, &c.;
2Z2ʳ–3A1ʳ	178.	Julius A.vi, Continuous OE gloss to 100 hymns & 27 canticles;
3A1ʳ (p. 185)	179.	Julius A.x, OE *Martyrology* (incomplete);
3A1	180.	Julius C.ii (s.xvii), Laws;
3A1ᵛ–3B1ᵛ	181.	Julius E.vii, Homilies & Saints' Lives, listing 48 items;
3B1ᵛ (p. 190)	182.	Caligula A.xiv (incomplete), Saints' Lives;
3B1ᵛ–3C1ʳ	183.	Otho B.x, Homilies & Saints' Lives, listing 33 items;
3C1ʳ–3D2ʳ	184.	Tiberius A.iii, Continuous OE gloss to Benedictine Rule, Prayers, Homilies &c., listing 69 main items;
3D2ʳ–3E1ʳ (p. 199)	185.	Faustina A.ix, Homilies, listing 38 items;
3E1	186.	Cleopatra B.xiii, Homilies, Promissio Regis, &c.;
3E1ᵛ–3F1ᵛ (p. 202)	187.	Vespasian D.xiv, Homilies &c., listing 56 items;
3F1ᵛ–2ᵛ	188.	Vitellius D.xvii, Homilies for Saints' Days, listing 60 items;
3F2ᵛ–3G2ʳ (p. 208)	189.	Vitellius C.v, Homilies, listing 65 items;
3G2 (p. 211)	190.	Otho C.i, ws Gospels, Vitas Patrum, &c., listing 9 parts;
3G2ᵛ–3H2ʳ	191.	Nero A.i, Laws, Ecclesiastical Institutes &c., listing 36 items;
3H2ʳ–3I1ʳ	192.	Tiberius B.v, De temporibus, *Marvels of the East*, List of bishops, &c.;

3I1ʳ (p. 217)	193.	Vitellius C.iii, Glosses to a herbarium &c., listing 8 items;
3I1ʳ	194.	Tiberius B.xi, Alfredian version of Gregory's Pastoral Care;
3I1ʳ	195.	Otho B.ii, Alfredian version of Gregory's Pastoral Care;
3I1ʳ	196.	Otho A.vi, Alfredian version of Boethius;
3I1	197.	Claudius D.iii (s.xiii), Benedictine Rule L + OE, &c.;
3I1ᵛ	198.	Titus A.iv, L + OE Benedictine Rule;
3I1ᵛ–2ʳ	199.	Vitellius A.xv, pts I & II, the Beowulf MS, listing 10 items;
3I2ʳ (p. 219)	200.	Otho B.xi, OE Bede, ASC (A²), Laws, &c., listing 14 items;
3I2ʳ	201.	Tiberius B.i, OE Orosius, *Menologium*, ASC (C) &c.;
3I2	202.	Tiberius A.vi, ASC (B), &c.;
3I2ᵛ	203.	Tiberius B.iv, ASC (D), &c.;
3I2ᵛ	204.	Domitian viii, ASC;
3I2ᵛ–3K1ʳ	205.	Tiberius C.i, Names of the Winds, Homilies, Prayers &c.;
3K1 (p. 221)	206.	Vespasian A.i, L Psalter with continuous OE gloss &c.;
3K1ᵛ–2ᵛ	207.	Vitellius E.xviii, L Psalter with continuous OE gloss &c.;
3K2ᵛ	208.	Tiberius C.vi, L Psalter with continuous OE gloss, Homily &c.;
3K2ᵛ	209.	Julius C.vi (s.xvi), Leland, various collected excerpts;
3K2ᵛ–3L1ʳ	210.	Tiberius A.vii, Prosper, *Versus ad coniugem*, OE gloss (2 leaves);
3L1ʳ (p. 225)	211.	Tiberius C.iii (s.xiv), L Bede (attrib) prob Giraldus Cambrensis;
3L1ʳ	212.	Caligula A.vii, OS *Heliand*, OE Charm;
3L1	213.	Claudius A.iii, Metrical inscription *Halgungboc* (entire, sole witness), Laws (VI Atr.) &c.;
3L1ᵛ	214.	Claudius A.viii, 74ʳ–75ᵛ L charters with OE by Joscelyn (s.xvi);

3L1ᵛ–2ʳ	215.	Claudius C.ix (s.xii), William of Malmesbury, Charters &c.;
3L2ᵛ (p. 228)	216.	Nero A.xiv (s.xiii), (eME) *Ancrene Riwle*, Prayers, Creed &c.;
3L2ᵛ–3M1ʳ	217.	Caligula A.ix (s.xiii), (eME) *Laȝamon's Brut, Owl and the Nightingale* &c.;
3M1	218.	Nero E.i, L Saints' Lives, Laws IV Edgar &c.;
3M1ᵛ–2ʳ	219.	Nero C.iii (s.xv), Nicholas Upton *De studio militari*, documents &c.;
3M2ʳ (p. 231)	220.	Galba A.ii, L sermons, OE computus, recipes, runes;
3M2ʳ	221.	Galba A.xiv, Prayers, recipes, listing 12 items;
3M2ʳ	222.	Galba A.xix (s.xii), ME *Proverbs of Alfred* (fragments);
3M2ᵛ	223.	Otho A.viii, Life of St Machutus, L Prayer with continuous OE gloss;
3M2ᵛ	224.	Otho A.x, Law IX Atr;
3M2ᵛ–3N1ʳ	225.	Otho A.xii, Charm, *Battle of Maldon*;
3N1ʳ (p. 233)	226.	Otho A.xiii, Homilies, listing 13 items;
3N1	227.	Caligula A.xv, Computistica listing 31 items, *De temporibus anni*;
3N1ᵛ	228.	Otho A.xviii, Homily on St Laurence (fragment);
3N1ᵛ	229.	Galba E.ii (s.xiii), Cartulary of St Benet's, Holme;
3N1ᵛ–3O1ʳ	230.	Claudius B.vi (s.xiii), Cartulary of Abingdon Abbey, listing 112 items;
3O1ʳ (p. 237)	231.	Otho C.xiii (s.xiii), (eME) *Laȝamon's Brut*;
3O1	232.	Otho C.xvi (s.xvi/xvii), Cartulary of St John's, Beverley;
3O1ᵛ	233.	Otho B.ix, L Gospels, with OE manumissions &c. in blank spaces;
3O1ᵛ	234.	Otho C.xv, Homily on Lent (fragment of 1 folio);
3O1ᵛ	235.	Vitellius C.ix (s.xvii), Charters, AS glossary &c.;
3O1ᵛ	236.	Otho E.i, Glossary;
3O1ᵛ–2ʳ	237.	Cleopatra A.iii, Glossaries;
3O2ʳ (p. 239)	238–9.	Titus A.xv–xvi (s.xvi), Joscelyn's OE Dictionary;
3O2ʳ	240.	Domitian ix, Chronicle (fragment), OE Bede (extracts), Rune names;
3O2ʳ	241.	Vitellius A.xii, Runic alphabets, Lord's Prayer &c.;

3O2ʳ	242.	Vitellius E.v (s.xvi), Charters with OE bounds;
3O2	243.	Vitellius D.vii (s.xvi), Transcripts by Joscelyn;
3O2ᵛ	244.	Vitellius D.xx, *Durham* (OE poem);
3P1ʳ	245.	Vitellius A.vii, OE *Promissio Regis*, Forms of Exorcism &c.;
3P1ʳ	246.	Vitellius A.xiii (s.xiii), Chertsey cartulary &c.;
3P1ʳ	247.	Vitellius C.viii, Prayers, Ælfric De temporibus &c.;
3P1	248.	Vespasian A.v (s.xvi), Transcripts by Lambarde and Nowell;
3P1ᵛ (p. 242)	249.	Vespasian A.ix (s.xvi), Transcripts by Joscelyn;
3P1ᵛ	250.	Vespasian A.xxii (s.xiv), Ælfric Homilies I.1 &c.;
3P1ᵛ	251.	Vespasian A.xv (s.xvi), Transcripts by Joscelyn;
3P1ᵛ–2ʳ	252.	Vespasian B.xxiv (s.xii), Evesham cartulary;
3P2ʳ	253.	Vespasian D.vi, Glosses, *Kentish Hymn*, Psalm 50 &c.;
3P2ʳ	254.	Vespasian D.xv, Title to penitentials;
3P2ʳ–3Q1ʳ	255.	Vespasian D.xii, Continuous gloss to hymns & canticles;
3Q1ʳ (p. 245)	256.	Vespasian D.xxi (with 16 above), OE t of Felix, *Vita Guthlaci*;
3Q1ʳ	257.	Cleopatra C.viii, Titles & glosses to Prudentius *Psychomachia*;
3Q1ᵛ	258.	Vespasian D.xx, L Penitential + OE Prayer;
3Q1ᵛ	259.	Vespasian E.vi (s.xvii), L-OHG Glossary (excerpts) copied by F. Lindenbrog;
3Q1ᵛ	260.	Vespasian E.viii (s.xvii), Vocabularium Saxonico-Latinum by W. Camden &c.;
3Q1ᵛ–2ʳ	261.	Faustina A.iii (s.xiii), Charters re. Westminster Abbey;
3Q2ʳ (p. 247)	262.	Titus D.xviii (s.xiii), (eME) *Wohunge of ure Lauerd, Hali Meiðhad* &c.;
3Q2	263–4.	Titus D.xxvi–xxvii, private devotions, confraternity rules, Ælfric *De Temporibus*, Prognostications &c.;
3Q2ᵛ	265.	Domitian xv (s.xv), 98ᵛ, Charter of Edgar to Ely;
3Q2ᵛ	266.	Domitian xviii (s.xvi/xvii), Runic inscription, ASC excerpts copied by Nowell;

3Q2ᵛ	267.	Domitian i, Glosses to Isidore, Bede, Recipe, Book-list &c.;
3Q2ᵛ	268.	Cleopatra C.vi (s.xiv), ME version of Simon of Gent, *Regula*;
3Q2ᵛ	269.	Cleopatra B.vi (s.xiv), 201ᵛ, Prayers, Creed &c.;
3Q2ᵛ–3R1ʳ	270.	Caligula A.xi (s.xv), ME *Chronicle* (RGlouc), *Piers Plowman*;
3R1 (p. 249)	271.	Domitian vii, OE documents in *Liber Vitae Dunelmensis*;
3R1ᵛ–3S1ʳ	272.	Nero D.iv, Continuous gloss to Lindisfarne Gospels, 30 items;
3S1 (p. 253)	273.	Claudius B.iv, OE Hexateuch, listing 6 items;
3S1ᵛ–3T1ᵛ	274.	Tiberius A.xiii, Worcester Cartulary, OE homily &c., 138 items;
3T1ᵛ–3V2ʳ (p. 258)	275.	Augustus ii, Charters (see Sawyer 1958: 50–51);
3V2ʳ–3X1ʳ	276.	Cotton Charters (see Sawyer 1958: 54).
3X1ᵛ–3Y1ʳ (pp. 266–9)		List of manuscripts in Lambeth Palace Library
3X1ᵛ	277.	LPL 489, Homilies, listing 8 items;
3X1ᵛ–2ᵛ	278.	LPL 487, (eME) Homilies &c., listing 19 items;
3X2ᵛ–3Y1ʳ	279.	LPL 427, Continuous gloss to Psalms & Canticles, Prayer &c.;
3Y1ʳ	279a.	Formerly in LPL 427: *Finnsburh Fragment* see Booklet 1, 3B2ᵛ;
3Y1ʳ	280.	LPL 204, Gregory's *Dialogues* (L) with occasional OE glosses.
3Y1ᵛ–2ᵛ (pp. 270–2)		List of manuscripts in Canterbury Cathedral Library
3Y2ᵛ	281.	CCA Register A (s.xv), Charters;
	282.	CCA Register B (s.xv), Charters;
	283.	CCA Lit.E 2 (Nowell, s.xvi), Laws of Cnut from Harley 55 (332 below) coll. CCC 383;
	284.	CCA W2/X.2.18, Somner's copy of **1568.2** with his annotations;
	285.	CCA Lit.B 4, item 10 (s.xvi), Laws of Alfred;
(p. 271)	286.	CCA Lit.E 1 (Nowell, s.xvi), ASC (D) 1043–79 (Lutz 1982: 327–329, n. 92) &c.;
	287.	CCA Lit.B 4, item 11 (s.xvi), Ps.Nicodemus;
	288.	CCA Lit.C 8 (s.xvii), ASC (C);
	289.	CCA Lit.C9–10 (cf. Lit.E 20–1), Somner's autograph of **1659.1**;

	290.	CCA Lit.C 5 (s.xvii), 'Cædmon' poems &c.;
	291.	CCA Lit.C 3, item 4 (s.xvii), Medicinalis Anglicus (from 166 above);
	292.	CCA Lit.C 3, item 2 (s.xvii), Orosius (from 201 above);
	293.	CCA Lit.C 4 (s.xvii), Pentateuch (from 273 above);
	294.	CCA Lit.C 6 (s.xvii), Laws Henry I;
	295.	CCA Lit.C 3, item 5 (s.xvii), Extracts from sermons published by Gerardus Vossius 1645;
(p. 272)	296.	CCA W/R.8.24 (Somner's copy of 1639.4 with his annotations);
	297.	CCA W/E.6.20 (Somner's copy of 1644.2 with his annotations);
	298.	CCA W/B.2.23 (Somners copy of 1640.3);
	299.	CCA W2/X.3.12 (Somner's copy of 1650.1 with his annotations);
	300.	CCA Chart. Ant. T 37, grant of land at Topsham to Exeter;
	301.	CCA Lit.D 2 (s.xvi), Latin-English dictionary, with OE by Somner;
	302.	CCA W/B.5.1 (Somner's interleaved copy of 1627.3 with a draft version of his dictionary = 1659.1)
3Z1^r–2^v (pp. 273–6)		Manuscript in Rochester Cathedral Library
3Z1^r–2^v –	303.	RKA, DRc/R1 (*olim* Rochester Cathedral Library A.3.5) Textus Roffensis;
4A1 (pp. 277–8)		List of manuscripts in possession of Dr George Hickes
4A1	304.	BL, Harley 436 (s.xiv), Wilton Cartulary;
4A1^v	305.	BL, Harley 438 (s.xvi), Rule of Chrodegang (Lucas 2003: 349–356);
4A2^r–4B1^v (pp. 279–82)		List of manuscripts in Exeter Cathedral Library
4A2^r–4B1^r –	306.	ECL 3501, The Exeter Book, listing 58 items;
4B1^r –	307.	ECL 3507, Hrabanus Maurus, Isidore, with OE glosses, runes;
4B1	308.	ECL 2518–2519 et al., Exeter charters, listing 13 items.
4B2 (pp. 283–4)		Manuscript possessed by Thomas Thynne, Viscount Weymouth (1640–1714; ODNB)

CATALOGUE OF EARLY PRINTED BOOKS CONTAINING ANGLO-SAXON 591

4B2	309.	Marquis of Bath, Longleat, 39 (s.xiv), Glastonbury Cartulary, listing 34 items;
4C1ʳ (p. 285)		Charters in Wells Cathedral Library
4C1ʳ	310.	WCL Liber Albus I (s.xiii), Wells Cartulary, listing 10 items;
4C1ᵛ–2ᵛ (pp. 286–288)		List of manuscripts possessed by John Moore (1646–1714; *ODNB*), bp of Norwich later Ely
4C1ᵛ–2ʳ	311.	CUL Ff.2.33 (s.xiii), Bury St Edmund's Cartulary, 48 items;
4C2	312.	CUL Kk.5.16, the Moore Bede, *Cædmon's Hymn*, glosses;
4D1ʳ (p. 289)		Manuscript possessed by Thomas Cartwright of Aynho (Nth)
	313.	BL, Faustina A.x, Ælfric's Grammar, Benedictine Rule &c.;
4D1		Manuscript in Litchfield Cathedral Library
	314.	Lich 1, St Chad Gospels (L), containing document in OE.
4D2ʳ–4E1ᵛ (pp. 291–294)		List of manuscripts in the Arundel/Norfolk Collection (given to the Royal Society in 1667 by Henry Howard, subsequently 6th duke of Norfolk, and then to the British Museum in 1831)
4D2	315.	BL, Arundel 60, Continuous gloss to Psalter, Canticles &c.;
4D2ᵛ–4E1ᵛ	316.	BL, Arundel 155, L Psalter, Continuous gloss to Prayers;
4E2ʳ–4F1ᵛ (pp. 295–298)		List of manuscripts in Durham Cathedral Library
4E2ʳ–4F1ᵛ	317.	DCL A.IV.19, 'Durham Ritual', with continuous OE gloss &c.;
4F1ᵛ	318.	DCL A.II.17, L Gospels, with OE annotations;
4F1ᵛ	319.	DCL B.IV.24, Benedictine Rule (L + OE) &c.;
4F1ᵛ	320.	Durham, Prior's Kitchen, D&C Muniments 2.1, Pontificalium no. 9 (Pelteret 64); see also Booklet 1, 2P1.
4F2ʳ–4G1ᵛ (pp. 299–301)		Catalogue of Worcester Charters
4F2	321.	OBL Dugdale 12 (s.xvii), list of 92 charters at Worcester;

4F2ᵛ–4G1ʳ	322.	Lost MS with 17 + 2 items seen by Hickes in Worcester, much of it transcribed in Harley 4660 (s.xvii): see Booklet 1, 2V1ʳ–2X2ᵛ;
4G1ʳ–2ᵛ (pp. 301–3)		Catalogue of Charters brought together by John Somers (1651–1716; *ODNB*), 1st Baron Evesham, now lost
	323.	24 charters including Sawyer 76, 117, 147 &c: cf Keynes 2008: 59, n. 73.
4G2ʳ (p. 303)		Catalogue of Westminster Charters
	324.	(?) BL Faustina A.iii (s.xiii), listing 9 items.
4G2ʳ (p. 303)		Manuscript possessed by John Battely (1646–1708; *ODNB*), archdeacon of Canterbury, brother of Nicolas (editor of 1703.2)
	325.	BL Harley 761, Latin-OE Dictionary by Wheelock (et al.).
4G2ʳ (p. 303)		Manuscript possessed by John Maitland (1616–82; *ODNB*), duke of Lauderdale
	326.	BL Additional 47967, OE Orosius.
4G2ᵛ–4H1ʳ (pp. 304–5)		Manuscripts possessed by Robert Burscough (1651–1709; *ODNB*), Rector of Totnes
	327.	BL Harley 585, Herbarium (Ps.Apuleius) + Medicina de quadrupedibus + metrical charms;
4H1ʳ	328.	Unidentified transcripts from Ælfric, Easter homily (II.15), Ælfric, Letters on Canons, Laws II–IV Eg, Abt (from Julius C.ii, itself a transcript by Francis Tate *c*.1589), Ælfric, Preface to Grammar.
4H1ʳ (p. 305)		Manuscript at Lincoln Cathedral
	329.	LCL 298, no. 2, 2 adjacent leaves from an OE Hexateuch &c.;
4H1ʳ (p. 305)		Manuscript at the Library of the College of Arms
	330.	Waiting Room, Charter (Sawyer 1026);
4H1ʳ (p. 305)		Manuscript possessed by Ralph Thoresby (1658–1725; *ODNB*), antiquary of Leeds
	331.	Lost Transcripts by Laurence Nowell *c*.1565 from Higden's *Polychronicon*, Westminster Abbey charters, OE Orosius &c: see Thoresby 1715: 531, no. 118, summarized by Flower 1935: 53, 55.

4H1ᵛ–4I1ʳ (pp. 306–9)		Manuscripts possessed by Sir Simonds D'Ewes (1602–50; *ODNB*), on whose library see Watson 1966
4H1ᵛ	332.	BL Harley 55, Recipes, Laws II, III Edgar, I, II Cnut &c.;
4H1ᵛ	333.	BL Harley 107, Ælfric's Grammar;
4H1ᵛ–2ʳ	334.	BL Harley 61 (s.xv), Shaftesbury Cartulary;
4H2ʳ	335.	BL Harley Ch. 43 C 6, Edgar to bp Æthelwold 975 (Sawyer 801);
4H2ʳ	336.	BL Harley Ch. 43 C 2, Edgar to Cenwulf 961 (Sawyer 697);
4H2ʳ	337.	BL Harley 552 (s.xvi), Benedictine Rule, Regularis Concordia from Tiberius A.iii &c.;
4H2	338.	BL Harley 596 (s.xvii), Charters from Rochester and Winchester;
4H2ᵛ (p. 308)	339.	(?) BL Harley 358, 604 (s.xv–xvii) Charters re. foundations of religious houses, cathedrals &c., (cf. Watson 1966: 32);
4H2ᵛ	340.	(?) BL Harley 2044, charter transcripts from the College of Arms;
4H2ᵛ	341.	BL Harley 589, art. 47, Ælfric's Grammar, edn by D'Ewes;
4H2ᵛ	342.	BL Harley 258 (s.xvii), Transcripts from MSS in OBL, BL Cotton, OXC, OCC, Textus Roffensis;
4H2ᵛ	343.	BL Harley 66 (s.xvi), Transcripts from cartularies of St Albans, Westminster abbeys &c.;
4H2ᵛ	344.	BL Harley 596 (s.xvii), Transcripts of AS Laws;
4H2ᵛ	345.	BL Harley 533 (s.xvii), Transcript of Simeon of Durham; 129ᵛ–30ᵛ, OE poem *Durham* by D'Ewes from Vitellius D.xx;
4H2ᵛ	346.	BL Harley 7567, 45ʳ–6ᵛ, Junius's transcript (s.xvii) of OE poem *Durham* (Fry 1992: 86–90);
4H2ᵛ	347.	(?) BL Harley 3449 (s.xvii), OE Gospels extracts;
4H2ᵛ	348.	BL Harley 307, printed book **1644.1** with annotations by Junius;
4H2ᵛ	349.	BL Harley 526, OE glosses to Bede's *Vita Cuthberti*;
4I1ʳ (p. 309)	350.	BL Harley 76, Gospels (incomplete), Charters and Papal Bull re. Bury St Edmunds Abbey.

4I1ʳ		Charters in keeping of William Petyt (1640–1707; *ODNB*), Keeper of the Tower Records, housed in the White Tower
	351.	PRO C 53 (Charter Rolls) and C 66 (Patent Rolls), with references to those pertaining to Abbotsbury, Beverley, Canterbury (abp), Canterbury St Augustine's, Durham, York, Bury St Edmund's, Ely, St Benet of Holme (Nf), St Paul's (London). Ottery St Mary, St Frideswide's (Oxford), Ramsey, Wherwell (Ha), Worcester, Winchester, Wolverhampton;
4I1ʳ		Charters in possession of Robert Harley (1661–1724; *ODNB*) 352. Unidentified copy of Hereford CL, P.i.2, fo 134 (Sawyer 1462), with cross-reference to Booklet 4, ‡Y1ᵛ.
4I1ᵛ–4L1ʳ		Scandinavian MSS noticed briefly by Hermannsson 1929: 79. Johan Peringskiöld was secretary to the Antikvitetesarkiv, now part of the Royal Library in Stockholm, and sent a list of MS items there (Harris 1992: 61). Collation may be attempted of the items listed here with Gödel 1897–1900, but the information available from this list and from Gödel requires supplementation to make certain identification of the items listed with those extant in the Royal Library at Stockholm.

TYPE: This is a large sophisticated book using many typefaces building on the typographic success of 1689.3.

Main text in Junius's Pica Roman (Body 89) interspersed with Junius's Pica Italic, both cut by Christoffel van Dijck.

AS6: Junius's Pica Anglo-Saxon, also by van Dijck, is used throughout the book and is the principal AS type design used, found as indicated above. Junius's 'Pica Saxon' (Oxford University Specimen 1693, d1–2, simulated item by item in Hart 1970: 38–40), is his 'Pica Roman' with special Saxon sorts substituted for particular AS letter-forms (except that the square capital Ƥ used by OUP was cut by Peter de Walpergen). Face 80 x 1.8: 2.9.

Special sorts shown in the specimen in Booklet 2, A1ʳ:

    11 lower-case sorts: ð, f, ȝ, ı, ɲ, ɼ, τ, ẏ; þ, ð, p;
    10 capitals: Ɫ, Ꮄ, Ɠ, Ꭰ, Ꭼ, 8; Þ, Ð, Ᵽ, Ƥ;
 Total: 21 sorts.

Special sorts shown in the text:

    11 lower-case sorts: ð, f, ȝ, ı, ꞃ, ꞅ, ꞇ, ẏ; þ, ð, ƿ;

    9 capitals: Ⱡ, Ɇ, Ᵹ, Ƕ, Ɱ, Ꞅ; Ð, Þ, Ƿ (no capital Ƿ found);

    5 others: þ, ꝥ, ꝉ, ꝭ, ∴.

Total: 25 sorts.

Overall total: 26 sorts.

Note 1: Two capital wynn's are found, that cut by van Dijck and the square one cut by de Walpergen. As well as in the specimen, both appear, e.g., in Booklet 1, 3A1ʳ.

Note 2: Two sizes of tyronian sign are found used without distinctive function. Both are found, e.g., in Booklet 4, ‡2G2ʳ.

AS8: The Small Pica Anglo-Saxon cut for Oxford University Press by Peter de Walpergen (fl. Oxford 1676–1703†). Found in Booklet 5, †2D1ᵛ–†4I1ʳ (Wanley's catalogue of AS manuscripts after Oxford, which is in the larger Pica), where it is combined with Christoffel van Dijck's Small Pica Roman (Body 69; Face 66 x 1.5: 2.4; McKitterick 1977: 70, no. 225 Descendiaen Romeyn), interspersed with van Dijck's Small Pica Italic (Body 68.5; Face 66 x 1.3: 2.00; Hart 1970: 26). Also occasionally interspersed with a Small Pica Textura used for MnE citations (Body 67).

Special sorts shown:

    11 lower-case sorts: ð, f, ȝ, ı, ꞃ, ꞅ, ꞇ, ẏ; þ, ð, ƿ;

    2 capitals: Ð, Ƿ;

    2 small capitals: ᴆ, ᴡ;

    2 others: þ, ꝥ.

Total: 17 sorts.

In 1701.1 no capitals are found, and that is also the case in Booklet 5 up to †2V, where Th- is used instead of Ð, and W- instead of Ƿ. However, after the libraries in Oxford and Cambridge have been dealt with, the section on other libraries (starting with those in the Royal collection) begins on †2X1ᵛ, where Ƿ makes its first appearance, and Ð first appears on †2X2ʳ. The abbreviation þ also makes its first appearance on †2X2ᵛ. These three extra sorts also appear in Booklet 6, Index VI, G1ʳ–M1ᵛ (Wanley's index to authors and works cited in Booklet 5), Ð notably in lemma on L2 and Ƿ notably in lemma on M1. Small capital Ð first appears on †2Z1ᵛ in the name ÆÐELSTAN, and small capital ᴡ first appears on †3A1ᵛ in the name ÆÐELPERD. It seems probable that the five extra sorts became available during the printing of Booklet 5, i.e. Walpergen was making new sorts as the printing of the book progressed; see note above under **Editor**. In this case the dating of Booklet 6 to 1703 and of Booklet 5 to

1705 must be notional, as Walpergen's death in 1703 would have rendered him incapable of adding new sorts as late as 1705. In any case indexes are usually made after the composition of the material they index, so in reality Booklet 6 should probably be dated 1705. There is also the probability that the printing of such a large book had already begun before 1703, as 1701.2 comprises Booklet 4, sigs ‡2B1ᵛ–‡2D2ᵛ of 1703/05.1 all signed as for the larger book published subsequently; the date of its dedication is 13 Aug 1701, the same as Hickes's Præfatio Epistolaris to Bartholomew Shower signaled above under **Date**. For evidence that printing had started as early as 1698 see Harris 1992: 100–105.

Note: AS8 sorts are also used occasionally in L and F, as on †2T2ᵛ, probably in imitation of insular minuscule script.

Other special type-designs:

1. The Junian Gothic occurs in specimen on Booklet 2, A1ʳ, and in text and words especially in Booklet 2, e.g., A1ʳ–Z2ʳ, passim. Note that the capital B matches that in the specimen of 1664.2, and not that in 1695.1.

2. The Junian Runic occurs in Booklet 1, e.g., on 3G1ʳ.

3. The Junian Icelandic occurs in Booklet 1, e.g., on 3C1ᵛ, and in Booklet 3, passim. This fount includes capital Þ cut by Peter de Walpergen at Oxford to add to the Junian fount (Lucas 1998: 187 and notes 51, 53).

4. The so-called 'Pica English' (a textura probably cut by Walpergen; Lucas 1998: 186), which occurs with the Junian type-designs on the OUP 1693 Specimen, occurs, e.g., in Booklet 1, 3N1ʳ–2ʳ, and in Booklet 4, †2B2.

> Copies: CUL XV.2.19–20 (catchword at Booklet 1, h1ʳ shows final t dropped), Bb*.1.4–5(AA), Pet.C.12.23–24, Huntingdon 17.7–9 (3 vols, vol. I = Booklets 1–2, II = Booklets 5–6, III = Booklets 3–4).
>
> Copies also at: N49869: APL, ECC, CMC, CaCL, GUL, KCL, KNA, LHL, NCL, NT, OAS, OBC, OBrC, OCC, OEC, OOC, OSA, OSJ, OStE, OTC, OWoC, UBL, YML, ULim, AUB; HUL, BJH, UCLA, UMI, WCM.
>
> T108393: AUL, BL, BCL, BUL, ChC, CCC, ECC, CJC, CMC, CSJ, TCC, DCL, DRD, DUL, EAL, EdUL, Eton, GUL, HCL, HHC, HU, KCL, KNA, LHL, LSH, LUL, MJRUL, NewCL, NLPS, NLS, NT, NUL, OBL, OAM, OAS, OBC, OCC, OEC, OHC, OHM, OJC, OLC, OMC, ONC, OQC, OSL, StE, OStH, OTC, OWmC, OWoC, OXC, PMAG, QUB, RUL, SBP, StA, WAL, WCF, WRL, YUL, NLI, TCD, PBS, BSB, GUB; USLC, NYPL, NYHS, NYCU, HHL, IUL, BMC, CUI, CWR, IBUL, ISU, KSRL, LCLP, LCP, LSU, NLC, OSU, RNJ, RUH, SfUL, SUNY, TCH, TNO, UAF, UCBL, UCH, UCLA, UND, UOC, UPL, URNY, UTA, UVL, WUM, YUB, MMU, QUK, VCC; NLA, UTL, VSL, VUW; UWJ.

Bibliography: Baker & Womack 1999: 394–400 (art. on Wanley by C.A. Simmons); Bennett J.A.W. 1948; Bennett G.v. 1957: 18–19; Carter 1975: 446;

Fairer 1986: 816–819; Feather 1984: 50; Gadd 2013: 441 (M. Kilburn); Gatch in Damico 1998: 45–57 (on Wanley); Harris 1983; Harris 1992: 45–107; Harris, in Damico 1998: 19–32 (on Hickes); Lerer 2001; Levine 1991: 353–367; Niles 2015: 147–158, 176–182. For documentation relating to this work see Harris 1992: 438–446.

Facsimile: Anglistica & Americana 64, Hildesheim, Georg Olms, 1970. Uses copy in Hannover, Niedersächsische Landesbibliothek, Lg 10 000, with defective pages taken from Wolfenbüttel, Herzog August Bibliothek, Kb 2⁰ 47. The order of booklets (and sub-booklet) has been rearranged: 4, 1 (supplementary), 5, 6, 1, 2, 3. Size reduced.

1705.1: Hickes, George & William Elstob, *Several Letters which passed between Dr George Hickes and a Popish Priest upon occasion of a Young Gentlewoman's Departing from the Church of England to that of Rome*. William Bowyer I for Richard Sare, 1705. 18cCat 2027H15. ESTC T88124. AS7.

OS Heliand (epithets for BVM), Ælfric, Homily (extract), Benedictine Office
  Collation: 8⁰: A⁸, b–c⁸ B–Y⁸ 2A–2E⁸ [$4 signed (-A1, Q1)] 232 leaves, paginated [i–xlviii], 1–336, *337–416* (pp. 225–226 not numbered).

SOURCES OF PASSAGES UTILIZING ANGLO-SAXON TYPES:

b3ʳ–4ʳ   Collected from Caligula A.vii: OS *Heliand*, list of epithets applied to BVM: Ɯunelica maʒaꞇ. Thia Daviðeꞅ ðohꞇoꞃ ... Iðiꞅ unpemma.

b7ᵛ   From (prob) OBL Junius 121, 160ʳ: end of Ælfric's Homily (II.29) on the Assumption of the BVM (Godden 1979: 259/134–137); there is nothing to distinguish the text from that of CUL MS Gg.3.28;

2B4ʳ–2E6ᵛ   From Junius 121, 42ʳ–55ᵛ: *Benedictine Office* (Ure 1957: 81–102), with verse passages printed in half-lines.

TYPE:
Main text in a Pica Roman (Body 82.5).
AS7: Nicholas Nicholls's Somnerian Pica Anglo-Saxon occurs in combination with the Pica Roman in text as indicated above under Contents and in words on E7ᵛ (p. 62), E8ʳ (p. 63), also sporadically for Latin text on 2C2ʳ–2E5ʳ.
Special sorts shown:
   11 lower-case sorts: ð, ꝼ, ʒ, ı, ꞃ, ꞅ, ꞇ, ẏ; þ, ð̄, ꝑ;
   11 capitals: A, Æ², Ꞇ, Є, Ꞇ̄, Ꝺ, K, Ɯ, 8; Ð, Ꝼ;
   3 others: þ̄, ꝫ, Ꝫ;
   Total: 25 sorts.
Note 1: Capital Æ¹ and Ƿ are not used.
Note 2: Lower-case ẏ shows the dot to the right.

Note 3: Gothic and Runic sorts are shown in woodcuts on 2B6^r.
   Copies: APL E.VII.14; CUL F.4.14.
   Copies also at: AUL, BL, ECC, CPC, CQC, CSJ, DCL, Eton, EUL, LBL, LFL, LHL, LPL, NewCL, NLS, NT, OBL, OCC, OEF, OMaC, ONC, OPH, OSA, OStE, OWoC, OXC, RUL, UBL, YML, TCD, ULim; FSL, GTS, UTS, HHL, HUL, GCL, IBUL, KSRL, PST, UCLA, UCSB, UTA, TUL; OUL, XCU.

Bibliography: Nichols 1812: I.2–488 (re. Bowyer). GR 6261.

PART 3

List of Punchcutters and Printers, Bibliography
(Medieval MSS, Post-Medieval MSS, Printed Books)

∴

List of Punchcutters

Le Bé, Guillaume I (Paris, 1523/4–98)

A younger colleague of Claude Garamont, he was trained in punchcutting at the Estienne press in the early 1540s. In Paris he helped build up a core collection of punches and matrices by Garamont, Granjon, Haultin and others. This collection became the basis for the main Paris typefoundry lasting through four generations of Le Bés and two of Fourniers up to the beginning of the nineteenth century. Possibly the punchcutter of the Anglo-Saxon designs in the Smithian Great Primer Anglo-Saxon Phonetic Special Sorts (CAS1: Paris, 1568.3). Vervliet 2010: 44–45.

Le Bé, Guillaume III (Paris 1610?–85)

While principally a typefounder, he sometimes turned his hand to punchcutting. He is possibly the punchcutter of the Du Cangian Pica Anglo-Saxon (Paris 1678.2): CAS6.

Dijck, Christoffel van (c.1603–69, fl. Amsterdam 1640–69)

The finest punchcutter of his time, the son of a Dutch Reformed Church minister, he was born at Dexheim (Germany) near the city of Frankenthal established by Dutch Protestant refugees in 1562 and famous for its goldsmiths, to one of whom Christoffel was apprenticed, probably when his father died in 1621. At some point in the next few years Christoffel used his skills learnt as a goldsmith to start cutting punches. In 1623, when Frankenthal was ceded to Spain by treaty, many of the goldsmiths there migrated back to Amsterdam, where Christoffel is recorded from 1640. He set up his own typefoundry in 1647. He supplied type to the printing houses of Blaeu in Amsterdam and Elzevier in Leiden and by 1658 had a virtual monopoly of the supply of quality types in the Netherlands. He cut the Junian Pica Anglo-Saxon (AS6) first seen in 1655.1 and 1655.2 and Junius uses it in combination with van Dijck's Pica Roman. The distinctive shape of punches left by Junius to Oxford University matches that of other punches known to have been cut by van Dijck (see Illustration 32). Cf. Part I, ch. 4 pp. 127–137. Lane 2012.

Guyot, François (fl. Antwerp 1539–68, London 1568, d.1570)

Typecaster to Christophe Plantin in Antwerp, Guyot was a skilful punchcutter and matrix-maker. He stayed in John Day's house in London in 1568 and through Day several of his type-designs were introduced into England. He may have cut special sorts for John Hart the spelling reformer, but it seems unlikely that he cut Anglo-Saxon sorts for Day (AS1, AS2). His second son Gabriel Guyot stayed with Day in 1576. His associate Charles Tressel settled in London. Cf. Part I, ch. 2, pp. 38–39. Briels 1974: 292–300 (François + Gabriel).

Haultin, Pierre (c.1510–78, fl. Geneva and Lyon 1550–65, Paris 1565–70, La Rochelle 1571–8)

Haultin, from the Le Mans area of France, was a quality punchcutter who as a staunch Protestant was persecuted from time to time. In La Rochelle from 1571 onwards he was in a safe haven watched over by Marguerite of Angoulême, sister of François I. His type-designs spread all over Italy as well as France, Switzerland and England. He is the possible punchcutter of the Parkerian Great Primer Anglo-Saxon (AS1: London, **1566.1**) and of the Parkerian Pica Anglo-Saxon (AS2: London, **1576.1**). Both designs first appear combined with Romans by Haultin and are well matched with them. Haultin's nephew Jérôme was based in London from 1568 and could have acted as intermediary between Day in London and Pierre Haultin in France. He was available in Paris at the time when the Smithian Great Primer Anglo-Saxon special sorts were cut. Desgraves 1960; Jimenes 2017; Vervliet 2010: 42–43. Cf. Part I, ch. 2, pp. 40–41.

Hoogenacker, Arent Corsz[oon] van (Leiden c.1579–1636)

A competent punchcutter with his own typefoundry, he is the only known candidate for cutting the Dutch Elsevierian English-size Anglo-Saxon (CAS2.2) and the Dutch Mairian English-size Anglo-Saxon (CAS2.3), both produced somewhat hastily in 1636 for the pirated printing of Selden's *Mare Clausum* (**1636.1, 1636.2**). Enschedé 1978: 66–67; Lane 1995; Lucas 2001.

Köblin, Balthasar (Konstanz c.1654–c.1680)

A punchcutter known to have cut non-Latin types, his distance from Strasbourg makes him a long shot for the cutting of the Strassburg English-size Anglo-Saxon of **1665.3** (CAS5).

Malherbe Des Portes, Mathieu (Paris c.1659–c.1726)

A cutter of punches and dies for coins and medals who turned his hand to occasional punchcutting for typefounders; he is best known for the 'Cicero la Police' cut for the typefounder Pierre Cot c.1700. Possibly too young to have cut the Du Cangian Pica Anglo-Saxon (Paris **1678.2**): CAS6.

Nicholls, Arthur (fl. London 1632–40)

Probably the best English punchcutter of the first half of the seventeenth century, nothing is known of his background. He is the only punchcutter known who could have cut the Spelmannian Great Primer Anglo-Saxon for Spelman's *Concilia* **1639.4** (AS4). He may also have cut the Wheelockian Great Primer Anglo-Saxon, which was cut in London by early 1640 and though no doubt made in anticipation of Wheelock's *Bede* **1643.1**, first appears in **1641.3**. Father of Nicholas Nicholls. Lane 1991.

Nicholls, Nicholas (fl. London 1637–71†)

Son of Arthur Nicholls, who evidently brought his son up in the trade. His skill as a punchcutter was not quite as great as his father's. The specimen **1665?.1** attributed to Nicholas is the earliest surviving English type-specimen and includes the design of AS7, the Somnerian Pica Anglo-Saxon called 'English'-size cut in anticipation of Somner's *Dictionarium* **1659.1**, though it first appeared in **1658.2**. Reed/Johnson 1952: 163–167.

Voskens, Bartholomaeus the Elder (Amsterdam 1613/16–1669) and Reinier/Reinhard Voskens (Amsterdam 1621–c.1670), half-brothers

Members of a distinguished family of punchcutters and typefounders, one of them probably cut the designs for the Dutch Blaeu/Voskens Pica Anglo-Saxon that first appears in 1645.1 (CAS3). It later occurs in the Heirs of Joan Blaeu type-specimen of 1695.5, as well as on the Widow (of Dirk) Voskens type-specimen 1700?.2(ante1714). Lane 2004: 50–59.

Walpergen, Peter van (fl. Oxford 1676–1703†)

A Dutch punchcutter who had worked in Jakarta with Hendrick Voskens, Walpergen was recruited by Thomas Marshall, collaborator with Junius on 1665.2, to work for the nascent Oxford University Press being set up by John Fell. Walpergen cut several type-designs for the university press. In particular he cut the Oxford University Press Small Pica Anglo-Saxon (AS8) used for parts of Wanley's catalogue of Anglo-Saxon manuscripts in Hickes's Thesaurus (1703/5.1). He was apparently still working on this design when he died in 1703.

List of Printers and Booksellers also Draughtsmen/Engravers

This list includes all books containing Anglo-Saxon types listed in the Catalogue. In accordance with the conventions of the series persons of the same name, often father and son, are distinguished by the appropriate roman number after their name, as John Day I, providing the same information as the convention in STC and Wing of distinguishing them by the appropriate arabic number.

1 England

1.1 London

Amery, John, bookseller, fl.1668–96, *Dict. 1668–1725* 5, Mellot no. 58, Wing IV.13–14.
1674.1 (for).

Aspley, William, bookseller, fl.1599–1640†, STC III.6–7.
1637.1 (for).

Badger, Richard I, fl. as bookseller 1614–29, printer 1629–41†, STC III.8, Mellot no. 173, Wing IV.48.
1639.4, 1640.3.

Bassett, Thomas, bookseller, fl.1658–99, *Dict. 1641–67* 16, Mellot no. 297, Wing IV.67–70, *BME* 57.
1672.1 (for), **1676.1** (for), **1685.2** (for), **1692.2** (for).

Beale, John, printer, fl.1611–43†, STC III.16, Wing IV.73.
Took over the copyrights of William Hall 1614.
1611.2, 1621.1, 1623.4, 1626.1.

Bee, Cornelius, bookseller, fl.1634–72†, STC III.17, *Dict. 1641–67* 19, Wing IV.76.
Father of Elizabeth Flesher.
1639.3 (for), **1644.1** (*impensis*, for), **1644.2** (for), **1650.3** (for), **1652.1** (*impensis*, for), **1655.4** (for).

Bishop, George, bookseller, fl.1566–1611†, STC III.22.
1590.1 (for), **1594.2** (for), **1600.1** (for).

Bishop, George (fl.1562–1611†), and John Norton 1, bookseller, fl.1586–1612†, STC III.126–127, Mellot no. 535, BME 83–84.
1607.2 (*impensis,* for), **1610.5** (for).

Bishop, Richard, printer, fl.1636–58, STC III.22, Wing IV.101–102.
Succeeded to the printing business of William Stansby (Greg 1967: 100); brother-in-law of Miles Flesher I.
[**1640.3** (sig. B)], **1640.4**, **1646.6**.

Bollifant (*alias* Carpenter), Edmund (of Eliot's Court Press), printer, fl.1585–1602†, STC III.25.
1596.2, (?)**1600.1**.

Bowyer, William I, printer, (1663–1737; ODNB), *Dict. 1668–1725* 44–45, Wing IV.121.
Apprentice to Miles Flesher II, freed 1686.
[**1703/5.1**], **1705.1**.

Braddyll, Thomas, printer, fl.1679–1704, Mellot no. 734, Wing IV.122–123.
Apprentice to Thomas Roycroft, freed 1679.
1687.1.

Bradwood, Melchisidec (of Eliot's Court Press), printer, fl.1602–18, STC III.28.
[**1617.1**, sigs A–S].

Brewster, Edward II, bookseller, fl.1653–99, Wing IV.126–128.
1692.2 (for).

Brome, Henry, bookseller, fl.1656–81†, Mellot no. 820, Wing IV.133–136.
1671.3 (for).

Brown, Daniel, bookseller, fl.1672–1729, Wing IV.145–146.
1700.1 (for).

Browne, John I, bookseller, fl.1598–1622†, STC III.30.
1612.1 (for), **1613.1** (for).

LIST OF PRINTERS AND BOOKSELLERS

Browne, John II, bookseller, fl.1612–34, STC III.30.
1617.1 (for), **1625.1** (for).

Busby, John II, bookseller, fl.1607–31†, STC III.33.
1612.1 (for), **1613.1** (for).

Bynneman, Henry, printer, fl.1566–83†, DLB 37–40, STC III.35, Barnard & Bell 1991, Eccles 1957, Handover 1960: 27–34, Mellot no. 923.
His printing business passed to Eliot's Court Press.
An inventory of his goods dated 3 May 1583 includes various matrices, but AS is not specified (Eccles 1957: 83–84, items 45–52).
1568.1, 1581.1, 1582.1.

Carpenter, Edmund, see Bollifant.

Chiswell, Richard (1639–1711; ODNB), bookseller, fl.1667–1711, *Dict. 1641–67* 45–46, Mellot no. 1152, Wing IV.190–195, Brennan 1980, Moore 1992: 53–64, BME 143–144.
Son-in-law of Richard Royston.
1676.1 (for), **1690.1** (*impensis*, for), **1691.1** (*impensis*, for), **1692.2** (for).

Churchill, Awnsham and John, booksellers, fl.1691–1700, *Dict. 1668–1725* 69–70, Mellot nos 1166–1167, Wing IV.195–198.
Brothers in partnership.
1695.3 (for), **1698.3** (for).

Clarke, Mary, printer, fl.1678–1705†, *Dict. 1668–1725* 72, Mellot no. 1176, Wing IV.208–209.
Daughter of Richard Cotes, mother-in-law of Benjamin Motte.
1684.1, [**?1700.1**].

Clavell, Robert, bookseller, fl.1657–1711, *Dict. 1641–67* 47, Mellot no. 1182, Wing IV.210–213.
Apprentice to Richard Royston, freed 1657.
1657.1 (for), **1671.3** (for).

Collins, Freeman, printer, fl.1679–1713†, *Dict. 1668–1725* 78, Mellot no. 1241, Wing IV.227–228.
Apprentice to Thomas Newcomb 1, freed 1676.
1695.3.

Conyers, George, bookseller, fl.1683–1712, *Dict. 1668–1725* 80, Wing IV.232–233.
1692.2 (for).

Cotes, Richard, printer, fl.1627–53†, STC III.46, *Dict. 1641–67* 53, Wing IV.239–42.
Brother of Thomas Cotes, who was apprentice to William Jaggard, freed 1606, and succeeded to the printing materials of William's son, Isaac.
Father of Mary Clarke.
1650.2.

Cotes, Thomas, printer, fl.1627–41†, STC III.46, *Dict. 1641–67* 53, Wing IV.242.
Brother of Richard Cotes, see above.
[1632.2].

Crooke, Andrew I, bookseller, fl.1632–74†, STC III.48, *Dict. 1641–67* 56–57, Mellot no. 1390, Wing IV.250–252.
Brother of John Crooke.
1637.1 (for).

Crooke, John I, bookseller, fl.1637–69†, STC III.48, *Dict. 1641–67* 57, Mellot no. 1393, Wing IV.255–257.
Brother of Andrew Crooke I; (?)brother-in-law of Benjamin Tooke.
1654.1 (for), **1660.1** (for).

Darby, John I, printer, fl.1662–1707†, *Dict. 1641–67* 61, *Dict. 1668–1725* 97, Wing IV.280–282.
1682.2, 1689.2.

Dawson, John I, printer, fl.1613–34?†, STC III.50, *Dict. 1557–1640* 85.
1632.2.

Dawson, John II, printer, son of prec., fl.1637–48, STC III.50–1, *Dict. 1641–67* 63, Wing IV.291.
1639.1, [1640.2].

Day, John I (1522–84†), printer, fl.1546?–84, STC III.51–52, DLB 78–93, Oastler 1975, Fairfield 1972, King 2001.
John Wolfe (fl.1579–1601†) was apprenticed to John Day I from 1562 for seven years, and an assignee of Day's son Richard, who also ceased printing in 1584.
1566.1, 1566.2, 1568.2, 1570.1, 1571.1, 1572.1, 1574.1, 1574.2, 1576.1, 1583.1.

LIST OF PRINTERS AND BOOKSELLERS

Denham, Henry, printer, fl.1563–90?, STC III.53–4, DLB 94–6.
His printing materials were partly taken over by Peter Short.
1596.1 (begun by).

Dring, Thomas II, bookseller, fl.1665–95†, *Dict. 1668–1725* 107, Wing IV.305–306.
1672.1 (for), **1682.1** (*impensis*, for), **1684.5** (*impensis*, for).

Du-Gard, William, printer, fl.1644–62†, DLB 97–101, *Dict. 1641–67* 67–68, Mellot no. 1808, Wing IV.307–308.
1652.2, [**1663.2**].

East, Thomas, see Snodham.

Eglesfield, Francis, bookseller, fl.1641–91, STC III.57–8, *Dict. 1641–67* 69–70, Wing IV.315–316.
1638.1 (for).

Eld, George, printer, fl.1600–24†, DLB 114–8, STC III.58.
Took Miles Flesher I as partner 1617.
1605.1.

Eliot's Court Press, printing syndicate based in Eliot's Court in Little Old Bailey, fl.1584–1680, DLB 119–123, STC III.58–59, Plomer 1922, 1923.
Succeeded to the printing business of Henry Bynneman (†1583).
[**1586.1**], [**1587.1**], [**1590.1**], [**1594.2**], [**1596.2**], [**1600.1**], [**1607.2**], [**1610.3**, ?sig.5G], [**1610.5**], [**1617.1**, sigs A–S].
See also Bollifant, Bradwood, Griffin, Haviland.

Flesher, Elizabeth, printer, fl.1671–89, *Dict. 1668–1725* 118, Wing IV.339–340.
Daughter of Cornelius Bee, widow of James Flesher and step-mother of Miles Flesher II.
[**1685.1**].

Flesher, James, printer, fl.1649–70†, *Dict. 1641–67* 75–76, Mellot no. 2019, Wing IV.340–342.
Son of Miles Flesher I; husband of Elizabeth Flesher; father of Miles Flesher II.
1650.1, **1650.3**, **1652.1**, **1655.4**, **1665.1**.

Flesher, Miles I, printer, fl.1617–64†, STC III.65, *Dict. 1641–67* 76, Mellot no. 2020, Wing IV.343–344.

Features in the will of John Haviland (of Eliot's Court Press; †1638): Plomer 1922: 182; brother-in-law of Richard Bishop; father of James Flesher.
1639.3, [1646.2], 1647.1, 1647.2.

Flesher, Miles II, bookseller, fl.1679–88†, Wing IV.344–345.
Son of James Flesher.
1685.1 [for].

Freeman, William, bookseller, fl.1682–1713, *Dict. 1668–1725* 122, Mellot no. 2079, Wing IV.353.
Apprentice to Thomas Dring II; freed 1681.
1687.1 (for).

Gillyflower, Matthew, bookseller, fl.1672–1702, *Dict. 1668–1725* 128, Wing IV.374–375.
Apprentice to Andrew Crooke I; freed 1666.
1684.2 (for).

Griffin, Edward II (of Eliot's Court Press), printer, fl.1637–52†, STC III.72, *Dict. 1641–67* 86, Mellot no. 2315, Wing IV.393–394.
1638.1.

Grismond, John II, printer, fl.1641–66†, *Dict. 1641–67* 87, Wing IV.396–398.
Apprentice to Miles Flesher I, freed 1641.
1654.1.

Hall, William, printer, fl.1598–1614, *Dict. 1557–1640* 121, STC III.75.
Copyrights taken over by John Beale 1614.
1611.1, 1611.2.

Harper, Charles, bookseller, fl.1667–1709, *Dict. 1668–1725* 144, Mellot no. 2452, Wing IV.424–425.
1674.1 (for), **1682.1** (*impensis*, for).

Haviland, John (of Eliot's Court Press), printer, fl.1621–38†, STC III.79–80.
1623.1, 1625.1, 1626.2, 1627.1.

Heath, Thomas, bookseller, fl.1651–69, *Dict. 1641–67* 95, Wing IV.438–439.
1654.1 (for).

Hebb, Andrew, bookseller, fl.1625–48†, STC III.81, *Dict. 1641–67* 95, Wing IV.439.
1637.1 (for).

Helme, John, bookseller, fl.1607–16†, STC III.81.
1610.2 (for), **1612.1** (for), **1613.1** (for), **1614.3** (for).

Herringman, Henry, bookseller and publisher, 1628–1704, *Dict. 1641–67* 96–97, Wing IV.443–446, Miller 1948; assignments (copyrights) bought by Jacob Tonson.
Apprentice to Abel Roper I, freed 1652.
1671.2 (for), **1673.1** (for), **1692.2** (for).

Hodgkin, Thomas, printer, fl.1676–1724†, *Dict. 1668–1725* 158, Wing IV.460–461.
Apprentice to Richard Hodgkinson, freed 1662; business partner of William Horton 1686, 1689.
1692.2.

Hodgkinson, Richard, printer, fl.1624–75†, STC III.84, *Dict. 1641–67* 99, Wing IV.461–462.
One of the printers named in the Star Chamber act of 1637. Shared a printing house with Thomas Badger, son of Richard Badger I, c.1637–40.
1640?.1, **1655.3**, **[1656.1]**.

Holt, Elizabeth, printer, fl.1689–1703†, *Dict. 1668–1725* 160, Wing IV.463.
Widow of Ralph Holt; business partner of William Horton 1689.
1689.1.

Holt, Ralph, printer, fl.1670–88†, *Dict. 1668–1725* 160, Wing IV.464.
1672.1.

Horton, William, printer, fl.1684–1702†, *Dict. 1668–1725* 162, Wing IV.470.
Business partner of Ralph Holt 1688, Elizabeth Holt 1689, Thomas Hodgkin 1686, 1689.
1689.1.

Howell, Mary (née Ashfield), widow of the author William Howell, fl.1685, Wing IV.472.
1685.1 (for), but cf. Miles Flesher II.

Humble, George, bookseller, 1572–1640†, ODNB, *Dict 1557–1640* 146, STC III.86–87, BME 335–336.
Nephew of John Sudbury. Father of William Humble.
1611.1 (for), **1611.2** (for), **1623.4** (for), **1627.2** (for), **1632.1** (for).

Humble, William (1612–86), bookseller, fl.1640–59, *Dict. 1641–67* 102, Wing IV.474, BME 336.
Elder son of George Humble, to whose business he succeeded in 1640. He inherited the rights, plates and presumably the special AS sorts that applied to Speed's *Theatre* 1611.1 etc., all of which he sold in 1659 to William Garrett, who in turn sold them to Roger Rea.

Islip, Adam, printer, fl.1591–1639†, Mellot no. 2719, STC III.88–89.
Acquired in 1594 part of the printing material of John Wolfe (fl.1579–1601), who was apprenticed to John Day I from 1562 for seven years (cf. Windet, John).
1607.1, [**1610.1**], [**1614.1**], [?**1619.1**], **1631.3**.

Jaggard, William, printer, fl.1594–1623†, DLB 138–145, STC III.90–91.
1608.1 (*typis*), **1610.4**, **1619.2**.

Jugge, Richard, fl. as bookseller 1545?–58, printer 1559–77†, STC III.95–96.
1567.1.

Keble, Samuel, bookseller, fl.1675–1715(?), *Dict. 1668–1725* 176–7, Mellot no. 2819, Wing IV.509.
Apprentice to William Lee II from 1667.
1685.2 (for).

Keblewhite, William, bookseller, fl.1694–1702, *Dict. 1668–1725* 177, Wing IV.510.
1700.1 (for).

Keinton, Matthew, bookseller, fl.1655–84, *Dict. 1668–1725* 177, Wing IV.510.
1682.2 (for).

Kembe, Andrew, bookseller, fl.1632–65, STC III.96, *Dict. 1641–67* 109, Wing IV.511.
Brother-in-law of Christopher Meredith.
1663.2 (for).

Kingston, Felix, printer, fl.1597–1653†, STC III.99–100, *Dict. 1641–67* 109–10, Wing IV.517–518.
[1610.3, sigs 4A–4V], **1631.3, 1637.1.**

Knaplock, Robert, bookseller/publisher, fl.1696–1737†, *Dict. 1668–1725* 180, Wing IV.520.
Apprentice to Richard Simpson, freed 1689.
1702.1 (for), **1703.2** (for).

Latham, George I, bookseller, fl.1620–58†, STC III.103, *Dict. 1641–67* 113–114, Wing IV.532.
Son-in-law of Matthew Lownes.
1637.1 (for).

Lee, William II (called William Lee I by Wing IV.540–541), bookseller, fl.1620–58(?+), STC III.104–105, *Dict. 1641–67* 113–114.
Associate of Daniel Pakeman; father of John Leigh.
1647.2 (for).

Legat, John I, printer, fl.1586–1620† (in Cambridge 1588–1610), STC III.105; also McKitterick 1992: 109–133, *TCBS*, 3 (1959), 96–103.
A printer to Cambridge University 1588–1620; father of John Legat II; father-in-law of Simon Waterson.
1614.2.

Legat, John II, printer, fl.1620–58†, STC III.105–6, *Dict. 1641–67* 116, Wing IV.543–544; also *The Library*, VI.11 (1989), 1–9.
Son of John Legat I. brother-in-law of Simon Waterson,
1637.1, 1640.1.

Leigh, John, bookseller, fl.1670–86†, *Dict. 1668–1725* 187, Wing IV.544.
Son of William Lee II.
1672.1 (for).

Leybourn, Robert and William, printers, fl. in partnership 1651–61, *Dict. 1641–67* 116–117, Wing IV.547–549.
Robert was apprentice to William Stansby, freed 1618; William was his son.
1660.1.

Lownes, Humphrey I, fl. as bookseller 1590–1603 and printer 1604–30†, DLB 170–176, STC III.109.
Brother of Matthew Lownes; in partnership with Robert Young from 1627.
[1610.3], [1612.1], 1613.1.

Lownes, Matthew, bookseller, fl.1595–1625†, STC III.109–110.
Brother of Humphrey Lownes I; father-in-law of George Latham.
1612.1 (for), 1613.1 (for).

Martin, John, bookseller, fl.1649–80†, *Dict. 1641–67* 123, Mellot no. 3438, Wing IV.597–599.
1671.2 (for), 1673.1.

Mathewes, Augustine, printer, fl.1619–38, STC III.116.
1622.1.

Mearne, Anne, bookseller, fl. 1682–93, *Dict. 1668–1725* 202, Wing IV.604.
Widow of Samuel Mearne.
1684.5 (*impensis*, for).

Meighen, Richard, bookseller, fl.1614–42?†, STC III.117, *Dict. 1641–67* 126–127, Wing IV.606.
Associate of Daniel Pakeman.
1635.1 (for).

Meredith, Christopher, bookseller, fl.1625–53†, in partnership with Philemon Stephens I 1625–42, STC III.118, *Dict. 1641–67* 127, Wing IV.607–608.
Brother-in-law of Andrew Kembe, who inherited his copyrights.
1639.4 (*impensis*, for).

Middleton, Henry, printer, fl.1567–87†, STC III.119.
Associate of Thomas East, whose printing material he shared 1567–72.
1576.2.

Miller, Simon, bookseller, fl.1654–88, *Dict. 1641–67* 129, Wing IV.617–618.
Apprentice to Andrew Crooke I, freed 1654.
1657.1 (for).

Motte, Benjamin (fl.1687–1738†; ODNB), bookseller, *Dict. 1668–1725* 212–213, Mellot no. 3680, Wing IV.632.

Apprentice to Ellen Cotes, widow of Richard Cotes, freed 1675; son-in-law of Mary Clarke.
1700.1 [for].

Newbery, Ralph, publisher and bookseller, fl.1560–1604†, STC III.124.
1576.2 (for), 1581.1 (for), 1582.1 (for), 1586.1 (per), 1587.1 (per), 1588.1 [for], 1591.1 [for], 1592.1 [for], 1594.1 [for].
Newbery was a bookseller, who had books printed for him, sometimes without recording the name of the printer while claiming the credit himself. The use of AS2 in 1588.1 can hardly be from any source but the Eliot's Court Press, with whom Newbery was already in association for 1586.1 and 1587.1. Newbery had ornamental printer's devices that occur in books printed for him, so he may also have supervised the use of other printer's materials, such as Anglo-Saxon printing types. He worked both with Middleton (1576.2) and Bynneman (1581.1, 1582.1) whose materials went to the Eliot's Court Press.

Newcomb, Thomas I, printer to the king, fl.1648–81†, *Dict. 1641–67* 136–7, Mellot no. 3736, Wing IV.646–650.
Apprentice to Gregory Dexter (emigrated 1644), freed by Richard Cotes 1648; father of Thomas Newcomb II.
1671.2.

Newcomb, Thomas I or II
1656.3, 1673.1, [1680.2].

Newcomb, Thomas II, printer to the king, fl.1672–91†, Mellot no. 3737, Wing IV.649–652.
Son of Thomas Newcomb I.
[1682.1], [1683.1], [1683.2].

Nicholls, Nicholas, typefounder, fl. 1637–71†, see Index of Punchcutters.
Son of Arthur Nicholls.
1656.2, 1665?.1.

Norton, Bonham, stationer, fl.1594–1635†, STC III.125–6, *Dict. 1557–1640* 201–203, Mellot no. 3768.
Cousin of John Norton I, cousin-in-law of Joyce Norton.
1599.1.

Norton, John I (fl.1586–1612), bookseller, STC III.126–127, *Dict. 1557–1640* 203–205, *BME* 497.
Husband of Joyce Norton, cousin of Bonham Norton.
1607.2.

Norton, John II (John 1 in Wing IV.663), printer, fl.1621–40†, STC III.127, *Dict. 1641–67* 138.
Probably nephew of John Norton I; apprentice to Adam Islip, freed 1616. His widow became Alice Warren, q.v.

Norton, Joyce, publisher, fl.1632–8, STC III.127, *Dict. 1557–1640* 205.
Widow of John Norton I, who was a cousin of Bonham Norton; associate of Richard Whitaker.
1637.1 (for [assigned]).

Norton, Roger II, printer, fl.1658–99, Wing IV.664–666.
Grandson of Bonham Norton.
1671.1.

Okes, Nicholas, printer, fl.1606–45†, DLB 193–198, STC III.129–130, Blayney 1982: 20–30, 292–313.
1623.2.

Pakeman, Daniel, bookseller, fl.1631–64†, STC III.132, *Dict. 1641–67* 143, Wing IV.687–688.
Associate of William Lee II, and of Richard Meighen.
1640?.1 (for), **1647.2** (for), **1656.1** (for).

Pawlett, George, bookseller, fl.1684–90†, *Dict. 1668–1725* 233, Wing IV.704–705.
1687.1 (for).

Place, John II, bookseller, fl.1675–1704†, Wing IV.715.
1685.2 (for).

Rea, Roger the Elder and Roger the Younger, fl.1650–62–?1668, *Dict. 1641–67* 153, Wing IV.746, *BME* 546.
1650/?1665.1 (for).

Roberts, Robert, printer, fl.1676–1701†, *Dict. 1668–1725* 255, Wing IV.757–758.
1690.1 (typis).

LIST OF PRINTERS AND BOOKSELLERS

Robinson, Jonathan, bookseller, fl.1665–1711, *Dict. 1668–1725* 256, Wing IV.759–761.
1682.2 (for), **1689.2** (for).

Roper, Abel I, bookseller, fl. 1641–80†, *Dict. 1641–67* 157, Wing IV.767–768.
Apprentice to Henry Seile, freed 1637.
1671.2 (for), **1673.1** (for).

Roycroft, Samuel, printer, fl.1678–1717†, Wing IV.772–774.
Son of Thomas Roycroft.
1685.2.

Roycroft, Thomas, printer, fl.1650–77†, *Dict. 1641–67* 158, Mellot no. 4357, Wing IV.774.
Father of Samuel Roycroft; King's Printer for Oriental Languages; his printing house was destroyed in the Great Fire of London 1666.
1658.2, **1671.3** (*typis*), **1676.1.**

Royston, Richard, bookseller, fl.1627–86†, DLB 219–230, STC III.148, *Dict. 1641–67* 158–159, Wing IV.776–781.
Father-in-law of Richard Chiswell.
1650.2 (for), **1671.1** (for), **1684.1** (for).

Sare, Richard, bookseller, fl.1681–1724†, *Dict. 1668–1725* 261–262, Wing IV.792–793.
Apprentice to John Place, freed 1684.
1703.1 (for), **1705.1.**

Sawbridge, Thomas, bookseller, fl.1667–92†, *Dict. 1668–1725* 263, Wing IV.797–799.
1671.3 (for), **1684.1** (for), **1684.5** (*impensis*, for).

Scott, Robert, bookseller and publisher, fl.1661–99, *Dict. 1668–1725* 264–265, Mellot no. 4502, Wing IV.800–801, also Nichols 1812: I.423–424.
1673.2 (for), **1683.1** (sold by), **1683.2** (sold by).

Seile, Henry I, bookseller, fl.1619–61†, STC III.151, *Dict. 1641–67* 162, Wing IV.802–803.
1623.1 (for).

Short, Peter, printer, fl.1590–1603†, DLB 239–243, STC III.154, Yamada 1989.
Assignee of Richard Day, fl.1579–84 (son of John Day I), for which see Greg & Boswell 1930: 30; succeeded to part of the printing material of Henry Denham (fl.1563–90), for which see Greg & Boswell 1930: 51, 55. His widow, Elizabeth, married Humphrey Lownes I.
1596.1.

Simmons, Mary, printer fl.1656–67, and Samuel, her (step-)son, printer, (fl.1666–78). Widow and son of Matthew Simmons, fl.1635–54†, *Dict. 1641–67* 164–165, Wing IV.810, 814–815.
1650/?1665.1.

Smith, Samuel II, bookseller, fl.1681–1703, *Dict. 1668–1725* 276, Wing IV.828–830. Associate of Benjamin Walford. Apprentice to Samuel Gellibrand, freed 1682.
1701.1 *impensis*.

Snodham, Thomas, printer, fl.1609–25†, STC III.157–158.
Apprentice to Thomas East, to whose printing material he succeeded. East in turn had succeeded to some of the printing material of John Day I *c*.1585; cf. Windet.
1610.2, 1616.1.

Sprint, Samuel, bookseller, fl.1669–1707†, *Dict. 1668–1725* 279–280, Wing IV.839–840.
1682.2 (for).

Stansby, William, printer and bookseller, fl.1597–1638†, DLB 266–274, STC III.160–161, Bland 1998, Bracken 1985.
Succeeded to the printing business of John Windet in 1609/10; his business passed to Richard Bishop.
1614.3, 1617.1 (prelims and sigs T–2Z), [1618.1], 1623.3, 1631.1, 1635.1.

Starkey, John, bookseller, *c*.1630–90, *Dict. 1668–1725* 280, Wing IV.842–844.
1663.1 (for).

Stationers' Co., DLB 275–91, STC III.161–164, Wing IV.844–854.
Granted a charter by Mary I in 1557 and became a liveried London company in 1560. Acquired copyrights from 1584. From 1604 imprints 'for' the Company

were assigned to one of the Company's English, Latin (1616–27) or Irish stock (1618–39) ventures.
1607.1 (for), **1610.1** (for), **1610.3** (for), **1614.1** (for), **1619.1** (for), **1641.2** (for), **1684.4** (for).

Stephens, Philemon I, bookseller, fl.1622–65†, STC III.164–165, *Dict. 1641–67* 172, Wing IV.856–857.
Brother of Jeremiah Stephens, the author, who assisted Sir Henry Spelman. In partnership with Christopher Meredith 1625–41.
1639.4 (*impensis*, for), **1646.2** (for), **1647.1** (for).

Sudbury, John, bookseller, fl.1600?–18?, *Dict 1557–1640* 259, STC III.165, *BME* 641–642.
Uncle to George Humble.
1611.1 (for), **1611.2** (for).

Swalle, Abel, bookseller, fl.1679–99, *Dict. 1641–67* 174, Mellot no. 4687, Wing IV.862–863.
1684.5 (for), **1695.3** (for).

Thomas, Edward, bookseller, fl.1654–82†, *Dict. 1641–67* 176, Wing IV.880–882.
1663.2 (for).

Tonson, Jacob I, bookseller and publisher (1656–1736), *Dict. 1668–1725* 189–190, Wing IV.893–895, Bernard 2019.
Apprentice to Thomas Basset, freed 1678. Associate of Robert Knaplock. Brother of Richard Tonson (fl.1675–90) who was apprentice to Elizabeth Walbancke, freed 1676.
1702.1 (for).

Tooke, Benjamin I, bookseller and publisher, fl.1669–1716†, *Dict. 1668–1725* 293, Wing IV.896–900, also Nichols 1812: IX.167.
Apprentice to John Crooke I, freed 1666.
1671.3 (for), **1684.1** (for), **1684.5** (*impensis*, for), **1687.2** (for), **1687.3** (for).

Twyford, Henry, bookseller, fl.1640–89, STC III.172, *Dict. 1641–67* 183, Wing IV.905–907.
Apprentice to William Lee II, freed 1640; ?kinsman of Timothy Twyford.
1685.2 (for).

Twyford, Henry and Timothy, booksellers, fl.1657–70, *Dict. 1641–67* 183, Wing IV.905–908.
Timothy was apprentice to Henry (not his father), freed 1656.
1658.2 (for).

Tyler, Evan, printer, fl. Edinburgh, Leith and London 1640–82†, STC III.172, *Dict. 1641–67* 184, Mellot no. 4811, Wing IV.908–912.
Apprentice to Robert Young, freed 1639.
1672.1.

Walbancke, Matthew, bookseller, fl.1618–60, STC III.175, *Dict. 1641–67* 186, Wing IV.935–936.
1647.2 (for), **1656.1** (for).

Walford, Benjamin, bookseller, fl.1689–1710, *Dict. 1668–1725* 298–299, Wing IV.936–937.
Associate of Samuel Smith. Apprentice to Robert Scott, freed 1686.
1701.1 *impensis*.

Warren, Alice, née Law, printer, fl.1659–65†, *Dict. 1641–67* 188, Wing IV.942–943.
Widow 1st of John Norton II (†1640; Wing's John Norton 1), then of Thomas Warren I. (Step-)mother of Francis Warren and Thomas Warren II.
1661.1, **1664.1**, [**1673.2** (*typis*)].

Warren, Francis, printer, fl.1666, *Dict. 1641–67* 188–189, Wing IV.943.
Son of Thomas Warren I, freed 1664, (step-)son of Alice Warren, brother of Thomas Warren II; his printing material destroyed in the Great Fire of London 1666.
1666.1.

Warren, Thomas I, bookseller (1638–) and printer, fl.1645–59†, STC III.177, *Dict. 1641–67* 189, Wing IV.943–944.
Married, Alice, widow of John Norton II; father of Francis and Thomas Warren II.
1657.1, **1658.1**.

Warren, Thomas II, printer, fl. 1666, 1690–1714†, *Dict. 1641–67* 188–189, Wing IV.944.

LIST OF PRINTERS AND BOOKSELLERS

Son of Thomas Warren I, freed 1666, (step-)son of Alice Warren, brother of Francis Warren; his printing material destroyed in the Great Fire of London 1666, but he began again in 1690.
1666.1.

Waterson, Isabella, bookseller, fl.1657, Wing IV.945.
Widow of John Waterson (†1656), (step-)mother of Simon Waterson II.
1657.1 (for).

Waterson, Simon I, bookseller, fl.1584–1635†, STC III.178.
Father of John Waterson; son-in-law of John Legat I.
1605.1 (for), **1614.2** (for), **1623.2** (for).

Waterson, Simon II, bookseller, fl.1653–7, *Dict. 1641–67* 189, Wing IV.945.
Son of John Waterson.
1657.1 (for).

Wells, George, bookseller, fl.1675–87†, *Dict. 1668–1725* 306–7, Wing IV.951.
1684.5 (*impensis*, for).

Whitaker, Richard, bookseller, fl.1619–48†, STC III.181, *Dict. 1641–67* 192, Wing IV.955–956.
1631.1 (for), **1637.1** (for).

White, Daniel, bookseller, fl.1658–60, *Dict. 1641–67* 192, Wing IV.956.
1659.1 (for), **1660.1** (for).

Wight, Thomas, bookseller (1590–) and printer, fl.1597–1605, STC III.183.
1599.1, 1602.1.

Wilkinson, Christopher, bookseller, fl.1668–93, *Dict. 1668–1725* 315–316, Wing IV.970–971.
1682.1 (*impensis*, for), **1691.3** (for).

Williams, Thomas II, bookseller, fl.1648–79, *Dict. 1668–1725* 317, Wing IV.975–976.
1671.1 (for).

Wilson, William, printer, fl.1645–65†, *Dict. 1641–67* 196, Mellot no. 5134, Wing IV.980–981.
1663.1.

Windet, John, printer, fl.1584–1610†, DLB 319–325, STC III.184–185, Mellot no. 5137, Bland 1999.
Succeeded in 1593 to part of the printing material of John Wolfe (fl.1579–1601; DLB 326–329), who was apprenticed to John Day I from 1562 for seven years, and was appointed executor to Wolfe 22 April 1601; cf. Snodham. Succeeded by William Stansby.
[1596.1] (sig.G), [1598.2].

Wotton, Matthew, bookseller, fl.1683–1725, *Dict. 1668–1725* 321, Mellot no. 5161, Wing IV.985–986.
Apprentice to Charles Harper, freed 1685; associate of George Conyers.
1692.2 (for).

Young, Robert, printer, fl.1624–43†, STC III.193, *Dict. 1641–67* 199, Wing IV.1000.
Apprentice to Humphrey Lownes I, freed 1612, in partnership 1627–30, associate of Richard Badger 1640, also of Miles Flesher I and John Haviland.
1631.2, 1631.3, 1637.1, 1641.1.

1.2   Cambridge

Daniel, Roger (1593?–1667†), bookseller and printer in London 1620?–29?, 1650–66, Printer to Cambridge University 1632–50, fl.1620–67†, STC III.49, *Dict. 1641–67* 60–61, Wing IV.278–280, McKitterick 1992: 168–193, 296–306.
1641.3, 1643.1, 1644.1, 1644.2.

Hayes, John, printer, fl. London 1655–67, Cambridge 1670–1705†, Printer to Cambridge University 1669–1705, *Dict. 1641–67* 94, Mellot no. 2476, Wing IV.434–437, McKitterick 1992: 342–362; his London business was ruined by the Great Fire 1666.
1670.1.

Story, Edward, bookseller, fl.1653–77, †1692/3, *Dict. 1641–67* 172, Wing IV.858.
1670.1 (for).

1.3   Oxford

Davis, Richard, bookseller, fl.1646–90, *Dict. 1641–67* 62, Wing IV.284–286.
1675.1 (for).

Forrest, Edward II, bookseller, fl. 1646–85, *Dict. 1641–67* 77, Wing IV.347–348.
Son of Edward Forrest I (fl.1625–57?+; STC III.66), from whom the son is often not distinguishable; in partnership with John Forrest.
1646.1 (for), **1662.1** (for).

Forrest, John, bookseller, fl. 1655–72, *Dict. 1641–67* 77, Wing IV.348.
?Kinsman of Edward Forrest I and II, with whom he was in partnership.
1662.1 (for).

Hall, Henry I, printer, fl.1642–80, Printer to Oxford University 1644–69, *Dict. 1641–67* 88, Wing IV.412–415.
Apprentice to William Turner, freed by him and Miles Flesher I 1640; acquired Turner's printing materials after 1643. Father of William Hall II; there was also a son Henry II, who was freed by patrimony 1661, but it is not clear whether he became a printer in his own right.
1646.1, 1675.1.

Hall, William II (called William I by Wing IV.415–6), printer, fl.1657–72, Printer to Oxford University 1662, *Dict. 1641–67* 89.
Son of Henry Hall I; a son, William III, was an apprentice typefounder in Fell's press 1672–9 (Carter 1975: 196).
1659.1, 1662.1.

Sheldonian Theatre [= nascent Oxford University Press], fl.1665–, Wing IV.678–681.
1678.1, 1687?.1 (type-specimen), 1689.3 (*typis Junianis*), 1690.2, 1691.2, 1691.4, 1692.1, 1693.1, 1693.2 (type-specimen), 1695.1 (type-specimen), 1695.2, 1698.1 (*typis Junianis*), 1698.2 (*typis Junianis*), 1698.3, 1699.1, [1700.1 (sigs B, C)], 1700.2, [1700?.1], 1701.1, 1701.2, 1703/5.1.

Turner, William, bookseller and printer, fl.1624–43†, Printer to Oxford University 1624–40, *Dict. 1641–67* 182, Wing IV.905.
On his death his printing materials were bought by Henry Hall I.
1634.1, [1639.1].

2 Ireland

2.1 *Dublin*

Stationers' Society, fl.1618–41, STC III.164, Wing IV.854–855, Pollard 2000: 541–544.
1622.2, 1632.1, 1639.2.

3 Netherlands

3.1 *Amsterdam*

Blaeu, Joan I (1596–1673), printer, fl.1630–73, Mellot no. 541, Pettegree & Weduwen 2019: 110–115; Vervey 1981a; his printing works were destroyed by fire 1672.
1645.1, 1648.1, 1648.2, 1659.3, 1662.2, 1662.3, 1662.4.

Blaeu, Heirs of Joan I, fl.1679–1703, Mellot no. 540.
1695.5 (type-specimen).

Boom, Dirk I and Hendrick, printers, fl.1669–80, Mellot nos 627–628.
1679.2.

Cunrad, Christoffel, printer, fl.1650–84, Mellot no. 1409.
1655.1, 1655.2.

Janssonius, Joannes [= Jan Jansson] (1596–1664), printer, fl.1613–64, Mellot no. 2747; Pettegree & Weduwen 2019: 114, 269, 276.
1646.3, 1646.4, 1647.3, 1659.2.

Janssonius van Waesberge, Johannes II, printer, fl.1675–1706, Ledeboer 1869, Mellot no. 2749.
[1684.3].

Someren, widow of Joannes van, printer, fl.1678–1703, Mellot no. 4914.
1679.2.

Voskens, Widow of Dirk (†1691), son of Bartholomeus (*c.*1612–1669), nephew of Renier (Reinhard), punchcutters and typefounders, McMurtrie 1924, Mori 1923.
1700?.2(ante1714) (type-specimen sale catalogue).

3.2 *Breda*
Subbinck, Abraham, printer, fl.1652–66.
[1664.2].

3.3 *Dordrecht*
Esch, Hendrick and Johann I van, printers, fl. in partnership 1659–77, Mellot nos 4883–4884.
[1664.2], 1665.2, [1684.3].

3.4 *The Hague*

Vlack, Adriaen, bookseller (and printer), fl. London 1633–42, Paris 1643–8, Delft 1651, The Hague, 1651–66; Mellot no. 5042, Kossman 1937: 440–443 (books printed), Miller 1979.
1655.1 (for), **1655.2** (for).

3.5 *Leiden*

Elzevier, Bonaventura and Abraham, printers in partnership, fl.1620–53, Copinger 1927.
1636.1.

Elzevier, Johan and Daniel, printers and booksellers, fl.1652–55, Mellot nos 1872 and 1870; Pettegree & Weduwen 2019: 269, 275, 278–80.
1652.1 (for).

Maire, Johan and Theodore, printers, Johan fl.1603–57, Johan and Theodore (Dirk) in partnership 1636, Mellot no. 3329.
1636.2.

Unidentified printer (possibly Janssonius, Amsterdam)
1636.3.

4 France

4.1 *Paris*

Billaine, Louis, bookseller, fl.1652–81†, Renouard, *Répertoire*, p. 39, Mellot no. 508.
1678.2 (*impensis*, for).

Estienne, Robert the Younger, printer, fl.1556–70.
1568.3.

Martin, Gabriel I, printer, fl.1670–92†, Renouard, *Répertoire*, p. 307, Mellot no. 3435.
1678.2 (*typis*).

4.2   Strasbourg (Became French 1681): See 5.4 Below

5   Germany

5.1   Frankfurt-am-Main
Wust, Balthasar Christoph I, printer, fl.1658–1700, BLG v.345–346.
1681.1 (typis).

Zunner, Johann David II, bookseller, fl.1666–1700, BLG v.348, Mellot no. 5198.
1681.1 (for).

5.2   Frankfurt-an-der-Oder
Meyer, Heinrich Johann, heirs of, booksellers, fl.1691–9 (also at Wittenberg from 1698), BLG v.306.
1696.1 (*sumptibus*, for), **1696.2** (*impensis*, for).

Schrey, Jeremias, bookseller, fl.1673–98, BLG v.328.
1695.4 (for), **1696.1** (*sumptibus*, for), **1696.2** (*impensis*, for).

5.3   Nuremberg
Endter, Johann Andreas (fl.1652–70), and the heirs of Wolfgang Endter II (fl.1657–79), booksellers, BLG v.264–265; Mellot no. 1885; Reske 2007: 731–733.
1665.3 (*sumptibus*, for).

5.4   Strassburg, Became Strasbourg (France) 1681
Dolhopff, Georg Andreas (1627–1711), printer and bookseller, fl.1662–1711, BLG v.261, Mellot no. 1710; Schäfer 2000; Reske 2007: 906. Son-in-law of Johan Eberhard Zetzner.
1665.3 (*sumptibus*, for).

Zetzner, Johann Eberhard (†1705), bookseller, fl.1664–80, BLG v.346, Mellot no. 5189.
1665.3 (*sumptibus*, for).

5.5   Wittenberg
Goderitsch, Johann Michael, printer, fl.1687–1706(?), BLG v.274; Reske 2007: 1015.
1695.4, 1696.1, 1696.2 (*literis*).

No Printer Stated
1636.3, 1641.2, 1665.3, 1674.1, 1680.1, 1682.3, 1683.4, 1684.2, 1684.4, 1687.2, 1687.3, 1691.1, 1691.3, 1702.1, 1703.1.

6   List of Draughtsmen/Engravers (Based in London unless Otherwise Stated)

Böcklin, Johann Christoph, 1657–1709, Leipzig, Wittenberg.
1696.1.

Burghers, Michael, 1648–1727, *ODNB*; *BME* 118–119.
1678.1, 1689.3, 1691.2, 1692.1, 1693.1, 1695.2, 1698.1, 1698.2, 1701.1(?), 1701.2, 1703/5.1.

Clein/Cleyn, Francis, 1582–1658, draughtsman, *ODNB*.
1652.1.

le Clerc, Sébastien, 1637–1714, Paris.
1678.2.

F., I.F., unidentified, fl. Strasbourg 1665
1665.3.

Haffner, Melchior, elder and younger fl. Augsburg, Frankfurt-am-Main, Ulm 1681–1704.
1681.2.

Hole, William, fl.1601–24, *ODNB*; *BME* 324–325.
1607.2, 1610.5, 1612.1, 1637.1, 1644.1.

Hollar, Wenceslaus, 1607–77, *ODNB*; *BME* 325–327.
1655.3, 1658.1, 1658.2, 1658.3, 1661.1, 1671.2, 1673.1, 1682.1, 1683.1.

Hondius, Jodocus (Joost van Hondt), 1563–1612, *ODNB*; *BME* 328–329.
1611.1, 1614.1, 1616.1, 1627.1, 1632.1, 1645.1, 1645.2, 1646.5, 1650/?1665.1, 1659.3, 1662.2, 1662.3, 1662.4, 1676.1.

Kip, William, fl.c.1585–1618, *ODNB*; *BME* 373–374.
1607.2, 1610.5.

Loggan, David, 1634–92, *ODNB*; *BME* 432–433.
1666.1, 1671.2.

Lombart, Pierre, *c.*1613–82, *ODNB*; *BME* 413.
1652.1.

Lyne, Richard, fl.*c.*1570–*c.*1600, *ODNB*; *BME* 420–421.
1574.1, 1576.2, 1596.2 (woodblock after **1576.2**).

Moll, Herman, 1634–1732, *ODNB*; *BME* 456–458.
1702.1.

Morden, Robert, fl.1669–1701, *ODNB*; *BME* 462–464.
1695.3.

Nicholls, Sutton, 1668–1729, *ODNB*; *BME* 490–492.
1695.3, 1703/5.1.

Nolin, Jean-Baptiste, Paris 1657–1708, Le Blanc 1970–1: 101, draughtsman
1678.2.

Norden, John, *c.*1547–1625, *ODNB*; *BME* 494–495.
1610.5, 1611.1.

Ortelius, Abraham, 1527–98, *ODNB*.
1637.1 (added in CUL Syn.2.63.1).

Owen, George, 1552–1613, *ODNB*, surveyor.
1607.2.

Rhodes, B., fl.1703–5.
1703/5.1.

Rogers, William, fl.1584–1619, *ODNB*; *BME* 565–566.
1600.1.

Sandvoort, Abraham Dirksz, 1624–*c.*1665, Dordrecht.
1665.2.

Savage, John, fl.1683–1701, *BME* 583–584.
1702.1.

Saxton, Christopher, 1542?–1610?, *ODNB*; *BME* 585.
1611.1.

Schweitzer/Schwytzer, Christoph(er), fl.1611–16, wood-engraver.
1611.1, 1614.1, 1616.1.

Speed, John, 1552?–1629, *ODNB*; *BME* 623–625; mainly re-worked maps by others.
1611.1, 1614.1, 1616.1, 1627.1, 1632.1, 1637.1 (added in CUL Syn.2.63.1), **1645.1, 1645.2, 1646.3** (copied), **1646.4** (copied), **1646.5, 1647.3** (copied), **1647.4** (copied), **1647.5, 1648.1, 1648.2, 1650/?1665.1, 1659.3, 1659.4, 1662.2, 1662.3, 1662.4, 1676.1.**

Spofforth, Robert, fl.1700–7, *BME* 625.
1703/5.1.

Sturt, John, 1657–1730, *ODNB*; *BME* 640–641.
1695.3.

Vaughan, Robert, *c.*1597–1663, *BME* 684–685.
1655.3.

Vertue, George, 1684–1756, *ODNB*; *BME* 686–687.
1703/5.1.

White, Robert, 1646–1703, *ODNB*; *BME* 716–717.
1672.1, 1676.1, 1683.3, 1687.1, 1695.3, 1698.3, 1703/5.1.

Bibliography

Medieval Manuscripts

MS   Ker   Gneuss   ASMMF   Printed Book

The last column in this list includes all printed books containing Anglo-Saxon text (from the relevant manuscripts) printed with special sorts. Italic references to classification numbers in this book indicate that the manuscript is referred to in that entry, but not necessarily as a source for the Anglo-Saxon material in the printed book. Those listed, catalogued or facsimiled in **1689.3** and **1703/5.1** appear with the abbreviation *cat* (= catalogued) or *facs* (facsimiled) after the classification number followed by the manuscript number in the list, as 1689.3*cat*1 means item 1 in the list of manuscripts found in **1689.3**. When the manuscript is cited as well as appearing in the catalogue the reference appears in the form 1689.3 + *cat*1. Facsimiles (probably originating with Wanley) engraved by Burghers and others are referred to in the form 1703/5.1*facs*1/3, which means Booklet 1, p. 3. Lost and unidentified manuscripts are not included.

Cambridge University Library

MS	Ker	Gneuss	ASMMF	Printed Book
Add 3020				*1626.1*
Ff.1.23	13	4	93	1640.3, 1689.3*cat*104, 1703/5.1*cat*143
Ff.1.27	14	–	94	1652.1
Ff.2.33 (s.xiii, Bury St Edmunds Cartulary)				1703/5.1*cat*311
Gg.3.28	15	11	95	1639.4, 1643.1, 1670.1, 1689.3*cat*108, 1703/5.1*cat*147
Hh.1.10	17	13	97	1566.1, 1568.1, 1639.4, 1689.3*cat*106, 1703/5.1*cat*142
Ii.1.33	18	–	98	1643.1, 1670.1, 1689.3*cat*109, 1690.1, 1703/5.1*cat*149
Ii.2.4	19	14	99	*1568.1*; 1574.2, 1689.3*cat*102, 1703/5.1*cat*146
Ii.2.11	20	15	100	*1566.1*; 1571.1, 1689.3*cat*103, 1703/5.1 + *cat*44
Ii.4.6	21	18	101	1566.1, 1643.1, 1689.3*cat*105, 1703/5.1*cat*148
Kk.3.18	23	22	103	*1568.1*, 1643.1, 1689.3*cat*101, 1703/5.1 + *cat*45
Kk.5.16	25	25	105	1703/5.1*cat*312

Cambridge, Corpus Christi College

12	30	37	23	1568.1, 1689.3*cat*120, 1703/5.1*cat*117
23	31	38	24	1703/5.1*cat*110
41	32	39	25	1568.1, 1643.1, 1689.3*cat*121, 1703/5.1*cat*118
44	33	40	26	1703/5.1*cat*111
57	34	41	27	1689.3*cat*115
70 (s.xiv, AS + later English laws)				1689.3*cat*117
96 (s.xv, annot s.xvi, Chronicon attrib John Brompton)				1703/5.1*cat*133
101				*1566.1*, 1689.3*cat*140, 1703/5.1*cat*137
140 + 111	35	44	29/30	*1566.1*; 1571.1, 1689.3*cat*123 1702.1, 1703/5.1 + *cat*120 + *cat*136
144	36	45	31	1689.3*cat*122, 1703/5.1*cat*119
146	37	46	32	1703/5.1*cat*108
162	38/41	50	33	1643.1, 1689.3*cat*124, 1703/5.1*cat*121
173	39/40	52/3	34	1566.1, *1568.1*, *1574.1*, 1643.1, 1689.3*cat*130, 1703/5.1 + *cat*127
178	41	54/55	35	1689.3*cat*125, 1703/5.1*cat*122
183	42	56	36	1689.3*cat*143
188	43	58	37	1689.3*cat*126, 1703/5.1*cat*123
190	45	59	38	1566.1, 1567.1, 1639.4. 1689.3*cat*118 1703/5.1*cat*115
191	46	60	39	1567.1, 1643.1, 1689.3*cat*131, 1703/5.1*cat*128
196	47	62	40	1626.1, 1631.1, 1664.1, 1689.3*cat*116 1703/5.1*cat*109
198	48	64	41	1566.1, 1643.1, 1689.3*cat*127, 1703/5.1*cat*124
201	49/50	65/6	42	*1568.2*, *1572.1*, 1639.2, 1639.4, 1664.1, 1701.2, 1689.3*cat*137, 1703/5.1 + *cat*132
214	51	68	43	1703/5.1*cat*138

265	53	73	45	1566.1, 1703/5.1*cat*112
278 (s.xiv, ME Psalter)				1703/5.1*cat*139
279				1567.1
286	55	83	47	1703/5.1 + *cat*141
302	56	86	48	1689.3*cat*128, 1703/5.1*cat*125
303	57	–	49	1689.3*cat*136, 1703/5.1*cat*131
307 (L)	–	88	–	1689.3*cat*142
322	60	92	52	1689.3*cat*129, 1703/5.1*cat*126
326	61	93	53	1703/5.1*cat*114
367	63	100	54	1689.3*cat*139
383	65	102	55	*1566.1*, 1568.2, *1581.1*, 1639.4, 1689.3*cat*138, 1703/5.1
391	67	104	57	1689.3*cat*141, 1703/5.1*cat*113
402 (s.xii, *Ancrene Wisse*, 'written in Saxon characters')				1689.3*cat*134, 1703/5.1*cat*134
419	68	108	58	*1572.1*, 1643.1, 1689.3*cat*133, 1703/5.1*cat*130
421	68/69	109	59	1689.3*cat*132, 1703/5.1*cat*129
422	70	110/111	60	1689.3*cat*135, 1703/5.1*cat*135
444 (s.xiv, ME *Genesis and Exodus*)				1703/5.1*cat*140
449	71	115	61	1689.3*cat*119, 1703/5.1*cat*116

Cambridge, Trinity College

B.14.39 (s.xiii)				1703/5.1 + *facs*1/144
B.14.52 (s.xiii, 12c homilies)				1703/5.1*cat*56
B.15.33	–	176	–	1703/5.1*cat*54
B.15.34	86	177	80	1643.1, 1689.3*cat*110, 1703/5.1*cat*50
O.2.1	93	–	87	1691.2
O.2.41 (s.xii)				1691.2
R.4.26 (ME)				1643.1, 1689.3*cat*111
R.5.22	87	180	81	?1574.2, 1689.3*cat*112, 1703/5.1*cat*53
R.7.28	88	–	82	1691.2
R.9.8 (s.xvi, Ælfric's Grammar, given by Neville)				1703/5.1*cat*51
R.9.17	89	182	83	1689.3*cat*113, 1703/5.1*cat*52
R.17.1	91	–	85	1640.3, 1689.3*cat*114, 1703/5.1*cat*55

Cambridge, Trinity Hall

1 (Elmham, s.xv)   1703/5.1 + *cat*157

Canterbury Cathedral Archives

Chart. Ant. C 1279	1693.1
Chart. Ant. T 37	1703/5.1*cat*300
Reg. A (s.xiii/xv)	1660.1, 1703/5.1*cat*281
Reg. B (s.xv)	1703/5.1*cat*282
Reg. E (s.xiii)	1660.1

Dorchester Record Office

D124 (s.xi)   1655.3

Durham, Dean and Chapter (= Cathedral Library)

A.II.17	105	220	118	1703/5.1*cat*318
A.IV.19	106	224	119	1703/5.1*cat*317
B.IV.24	109	248	122	1703/5.1*cat*319

Prior's Kitchen, Muniments 2.1, Pontificalium 9 (s.xi/xii)1703/5.1 + *cat*320

Exeter, Cathedral Library

2517 (s.xi)				1703/5.1
2518 (s.xi)				1703/5.1*cat*308
2519 (s.xi)				1703/5.1 + *cat*308
2521 (s.xi)				1703/5.1
2528 (s.xi)				1703/5.1
2702 (s.xi)				1703/5.1
3501	20/116	15/257	130	1566.1, 1703/5.1 + *cat*306
3507	116	258	131	1703/5.1*cat*307 + *facs*3/4

Hereford Cathedral Library

P.i.2 (s.xi)   1703/5.1

Kew, National Archives (*formerly London, Public Record Office*)

C 53 (Charter Rolls)	1703/5.1*cat*351
C 66 (Patent Rolls)	1703/5.1*cat*351
Cart. ant. R.9 (s.xiii)	1682.2
Cart. ant. R.12 (s.xiii)	1661.1
Ch.R. 8 Edw. II	1655.3
Ch.R. 9 Edw. III	1655.3
Ch.R. 44 Hen. III	1655.3
Domesday Book	1703/5.1*facs*1/144
Pat.R. 4 Edw. IV	1655.3

Lichfield Cathedral Library

Gospels of St Chad	123	269	159	1703/5.1 + *cat*314

Lincoln Cathedral Library

298 (2)	125	276	161	1703/5.1*cat*329

London, British Library

Additional Manuscripts

Add 14847 (s.xiii)				*1703/5.1*
Add 47967	133	300	171	1689.3*cat*151, 1703/5.1*cat*326
Add 82931 (*olim* Earl of Macclesfield, MS 24.g.9)				1574.1, 1574.2
'Liber de Hyda' (s.xv),				1639.4, 1698.3
Arundel 60	134	304	174	1640.3, 1703/5.1*cat*315
Arundel 155	135	306	175	1703/5.1*cat*316

Cotton MSS

Augustus ii				1631.1, 1655.3, 1702.1, 1703/5.1 + *cat*275
Caligula A.vii (OS)	137	308	177	1689.3*cat*170, 1690.1, 1703/5.1 + *cat*212, 1703/5.1*facs*2/3, 1705.1
Caligula A.ix (s.xiii, eME *Laʒamon's Brut, Owl & Nightingale*)				1576.2, 1703/5.1*cat*217

Caligula A.xi (s.xv, ME *Chronicle* (RGlouc), *Piers Plowman*)				1703/5.1*cat*270
Caligula A.xiv	138	309/10	178	1689.3*cat*171, 1703/5.1*cat*182
Caligula A.xv	139	311	179	1689.3*cat*172, 1703/5.1*cat*227 1703/5.1*facs*3/4
Claudius A.iii	141/185	313/4	181	1618.1, 1639.4, 1689.3*cat*200, 1703/5.1*cat*213
Claudius A.viii (s.xvi, L charters with OE by Joscelyn)				1703/5.1*cat*214
Claudius B.iv	142	315	182	1689.3*cat*173, 1703/5.1*cat*273
Claudius B.vi (s.xiii, Cartulary of Abingdon Abbey)				1618.1, 1655.3, 1703/5.1 + *cat*230
Claudius C.ix (s.xii, William of Malmesbury, charters, etc)				1703/5.1*cat*215
Claudius D.ii (s.xvi)				1568.2
Claudius D.iii (Benedictine Rule, L + OE, s.xiii)			183	1689.3*cat*174, 1703/5.1*cat*197
Cleopatra A.iii	143	319/20	184	1703/5.1*cat*237
Cleopatra B.vi (s.xiv, f. 201ᵛ, Prayers, Creed &c)				1703/5.1*cat*269
Cleopatra B.xiii	144	322/3	185	1566.1, 1689.3*cat*162, 1703/5.1*cat*186
Cleopatra C.vi (s.xiv, ME version of Simon of Gent, *Regula*)				1703/5.1*cat*268
Cleopatra C.viii	145	324	186	1703/5.1*cat*257
Domitian i	146	326	187	1703/5.1*cat*267
Domitian vii	147	327	188	1703/5.1*cat*271
Domitian viii	148	328	189	1607.2, 1639.2, 1689.3*cat*198, 1692.1, 1703/5.1*cat*204
Domitian ix (s.xv, Miscellany including fragments from ASC)				1689.3*cat*199, 1703/5.1*cat*240, 1703/5.1*facs*1/136
Domitian xv (s.xv, charter of Edgar to Ely on f. 98ᵛ)				1703/5.1*cat*265
Domitian xviii (s.xvi/xvii, transcripts by Nowell, ASC &c)				1703/5.1*cat*266
Faustina A.iii (s.xiii, charters re Westminster Abbey)				1703/5.1*cat*261(?324)
Faustina A.v	152	–	191	1618.1, 1652.1
Faustina A ix	153	–	192	1566.1, 1703/5.1*cat*185
Faustina A.x	154	331	193	1703/5.1 + *cat*313
Faustina B.iii	155	332	194	1623.3
Galba A.ii + iii	156	–	196	1703/5.1*cat*220, 1703/5.1*facs*3/4
Galba A.xiv	157	333	197	1689.3*cat*176, 1703/5.1*cat*221
Galba A.xix (s.xii, ME *Proverbs of Alfred*)				1703/5.1*cat*222

Galba E.ii (s.xiii, Cartulary of St Benet's, Holme)				1703/5.1*cat*229
Julius A.ii	158/9	335/6	198	1655.2, 1689.3*cat*158, 1703/5.1*cat*177
Julius A.vi	160	337	199	1689.3*cat*159, 1703/5.1*cat*178
Julius A.ix (Lives of Saints, s.xiii)				1689.3*cat*160
Julius A.x	161	338	200	1703/5.1 + *cat*179
Julius C.ii (s.xvii, Laws)				1703/5.1*cat*180
Julius C.vi (s.xvi, Leland)				1703/5.1*cat*209
Julius C.vii				1631.1
Julius E.vii	162	339	201	1631.1, 1689.3*cat*161, 1703/5.1*cat*181
Nero A.i	163/4	340/1	202	1566.1; 1568.2, 1618.1, 1689.3*cat*175, 1701.2, 1703/5.1 + *cat*191
Nero A.xiv (s.xiii, eME *Ancrene Riwle*, Prayers, Creed, etc)				1703/5.1*cat*216
Nero C.iii (s.xv, Nicholas Upton, *De studio militari*, etc)				1703/5.1*cat*219
Nero D.iv	165	343	206	1605.1, 1652.1, 1703/5.1*cat*272 1703/5.1*facs*1/3
Nero E.i	166 (+ 29)	344/5	207	1689.3*cat*202, 1703/5.1*cat*218
Otho A.vi	167	347	208	1655.1,1689.3*cat*203, 1703/5.1 + *cat*196
Otho A.viii	168/9	348	209	1689.3*cat*177/181, 1703/5.1*cat*223
Otho A.x	170	349	210	1689.3*cat*178, 1703/5.1*cat*224
Otho A.xii	171/2 (burnt)	350	211	1574.2, 1703/5.1*cat*225
Otho A.xiii	173	351	212	1703/5.1*cat*226
Otho A.xviii	174	352	213	1703/5.1*cat*228
Otho B.ii	175	353	214	1689.3*cat*168/182, 1703/5.1 + *cat*195
Otho B.ix	176	354	215	1703/5.1*cat*233
Otho B.x	180	356	216	1643.1, 1689.3*cat*179, 1703/5.1*cat*183
Orho B.xi	180	357	217	1618.1, 1623.1, 1631.1, 1639.2, 1643.1, 1689.3*cat*180, 1703/5.1*cat*200
Otho C.i	181	358	218	1571.1, 1689.3*cat*183, 1703/5.1*cat*190
Otho C.xiii (s.xiii, eME *Laʒamon's Brut*)				1703/5.1*cat*231

Otho C.xv	183	–	220	1703/5.1cat234
Otho C.xvi (s.xvi/xvii, Cartulary of St John's, Beverley)				1703/5.1cat232
Otho E.i	184	360	221	1703/5.1cat236
Tiberius A.iii	186	363	223	1689.3cat164, 1701.2, 1703/5.1cat184
Tiberius A.iii ff. 174–7	155	363	223	1623.3
Tiberius A.vi	188	364	224	*1623.3*. 1639.4, 1643.1, 1689.3cat163, 1692.1, 1703/5.1cat202
Tiberius A.vii	189	365	225	1703/5.1cat210
Tiberius A.xiii	190	366	226	1631.1, 1639.4, 1655.3, 1689.3cat201, 1703/5.1 + *cat274*
Tiberius B.i	191	370	227	*1576.3, 1589.1, 1598.1, 1623.3, 1635.1, 1640.4, 1660.1,* 1689.3cat165, 1703/5.1 + *cat201*
Tiberius B.iv	192	372	228	1568.1, 1631.1, 1635.1, 1689.3cat166, 1703/5.1 + *cat203*
Tiberius B.v	22 + 193/4	21 + 373/4	229	1689.3cat167, 1703/5.1 + *cat192*
Tiberius B.xi	195 (burnt)	375	230	*1622.2*, 1689.3cat168, 1703/5.1cat194, 1703/5.1*facs1/3*
Tiberius C.i	196/7	376	231	1703/5.1cat205
Tiberius C.iii (s.xiv L Bede (attrib) but prob Giraldus Cambrensis)				1703/5.1cat211
Tiberius C.vi	199	378	233	1689.3cat169, 1703/5.1cat208
Tiberius C.ix (s.xiii)				1661.1
Tiberius E.viii (s.xvii)				1655.3
Titus A.iv	200	379	235	1689.3cat196, 1703/5.1cat198
Titus A.xv–xvi (s.xvi, Joscelyn's OE Dictionary)				1703/5.1cat238–9
Titus D.xviii (s.xiii, eME *Wohynge of ure Lauerd, Hali Meiðhad*)				1703/5.1cat262
Titus D.xxvi–xxvii	202	380	237	1689.3cat197, 1703/5.1cat263–4
Vespasian A.i	203	381	238	1631.1, 1703/5.1cat206
Vespasian A.v (s.xvi, transcripts by Nowell and Lambarde)				1703/5.1cat248
Vespasian A.ix (s.xvi, transcripts by Joscelyn)				1703/5.1cat249
Vespasian A.xv (s.xvi, transcripts by Joscelyn)				1703/5.1cat251
Vespasian A.xxii (s.xiv(?), Ælfric, Homilies I.1 &c)				1703/5.1cat250

Vespasian B.xxiv (s.xii, Evesham cartulary)				1655.3, 1703/5.1*cat*252
Vespasian D.vi	207	389/90	243	1689.3*cat*192, 1703/5.1*cat*253
Vespasian D.xii	208	391	244	1703/5.1*cat*255
Vespasian D.xiv	209	392	245	1566.1, 1689.3*cat*193, 1703/5.1*cat*187
Vespasian D.xv	211	393	246	1703/5.1*cat*254
Vespasian D.xx	212	395	247	1689.3*cat*194, 1703/5.1*cat*258
Vespasian D.xxi	344	657	248	1639.2, 1689.3*cat*195, 1703/5.1*cat*256
Vespasian E.vi (s.xvii, L-OHG glossary copied by F. Lindenbrog)				1703/5.1*cat*259
Vespasian E.viii (s.xvii, Vocab Sax-Lat by Camden)				1703/5.1*cat*260
Vitellius A.vii	213	397	249	1689.3*cat*184, 1703/5.1*cat*245
Vitellius A.xii	214	398	250	1703/5.1*cat*241
Vitellius A.xiii (s.xiii, Chertsey cartulary &c)				1655.3, 1703/5.1*cat*246
Vitellius A.xv, pt 2	216	399	251	1689.3*cat*185, 1703/5.1 + *cat*199
Vitellius C.iii	218/9	402	253	1689.3*cat*188, 1703/5.1*cat*193
Vitellius C.v	220	403	254	1689.3*cat*186, 1703/5.1*cat*189
Vitellius C.viii	83/221	173/404	255	1703/5.1*cat*247
Vitellius C.ix (s.xvii, Charters, AS glossary &c)				1703/5.1*cat*235
Vitellius D.vii (s.xvi, transcripts by Joscelyn)				1703/5.1*cat*243
Vitellius D.xvii	222	406	256	1689.3*cat*189, 1703/5.1*cat*188
Vitellius D.xx	223	–	257	1689.3*cat*191, 1703/5.1 + *cat*244
Vitellius E.v (s.xvi, Charters with OE bounds)				1703/5.1*cat*242
Vitellius E.xviii	224	407	258	1689.3*cat*190, 1703/5.1*cat*207
Cotton Charters				1703/5.1*cat*276
Cotton Charter VII.1				1703/5.1
Cotton Charter VII.6				1703/5.1
Cotton Charter VII.13				1703/5.1
Cotton Charter VIII.15				1703/5.1
Cotton Charter VIII.37				1703/5.1
Cotton Charter VIII.38				1703/5.1

Harley MSS

Harley 55, ff.5–13	226	412	260	1568.2, 1703/5.1*cat*332
Harley 61 (s.xv)				1655.3
Harley 76	–	413	–	1703/5.1*cat*360

Harley 107	227	414	261	1703/5.1*cat*333
Harley 436 (s.xiv)				1661.1, 1703/5.1*cat*304
Harley 526	230	419/20	264	1703/5.1*cat*349
Harley 585	31	421	265	1703/5.1*cat*327
Harley Charter 43				1655.3, 1703/5.1*cat*335/6
Harley Charter 111 B.49				1703/5.1
Royal 1.A.xiv	245	–	285	1689.3*cat*46, 1703/5.1*cat*169
Royal 1.B.vii	246	445	281	1703/5.1*cat*168
Royal 1.D.ix	247	447	282	1703/5.1*cat*170
Royal 2.B.v	249	451	284	1689.3*cat*149, 1703/5.1*cat*171
Royal 5.E.xi	252	458	286	1703/5.1*cat*173
Royal 6.A.vi	254	464	288	1703/5.1*cat*174
Royal 6.B.vii	255	466	289	1703/5.1*cat*175
Royal 7.C.iv	256	70	290	1655.1, 1690.1, 1689.3*cat*147, 1703/5.1*cat*167
Royal 7.C.xii	257	471/2	291	1689.3*cat*145, 1703/5.1*cat*165
Royal 12.D.xvii	264	479	298	1689.3*cat*148, 1703/5.1*cat*166
Royal 12.G.xii	265	480	299	1703/5.1*cat*176
Royal 15.B.xxii	269	494	303	*1568.1*, 1659.1, 1689.3*cat*50, 1703/5.1*cat*172
Stowe 2	271	499	306	1640.3
Stowe 944	274	500	309	*1574.2*
Stowe Charter 30				1640.1
Loan MS 30 (Cartulary of Burton Abbey)				1655.3

London, College of Arms

Waiting Room (Charter, Sawyer 1026)	1703/5.1*cat*330

London, Guildhall Library

MS 25,501 (*olim* St Paul's W.D.1, 'Liber A')	1658.1

London, Lambeth Palace Library

204	277	510	313	1703/5.1*cat*280
427	280/281	517/8	316	1689.3*cat*155, 1703/5.1*cat*279/a
487	282	–	317	1689.3*cat*157, 1703/5.1 + *cat*278, 1703/5.1*facs*1/144
489	283	520	318	1689.3*cat*156, 1703/5.1*cat*277

BIBLIOGRAPHY

London, St Paul's

'Liber B' (lost)   1658.1
See also London, Guildhall

Longleat House, Marquis of Bath

39 (s.xiv, Glastonbury Cartulary)   1703/5.1*cat*309

Manchester, John Rylands University Library

Lat.420 (L)   1626.1

Oxford, Bodleian Library (SC no. in brackets)

Ashmole 328 (6882 + 7420)	288	526	337	1703/5.1*cat*94
Auct.D.2.14 (2698)	290	529	339	1703/5.1*cat*30
Auct.D.2.16 (2719)	291	530	340	1655.3, 1703/5.1*cat*24
Auct.D.2.19 (3946)	292	531	341	1655.1, 1689.3*cat*29, 1703/5.1*cat*25
Auct F.4.32 (2176)	297	538	346	1689.3*cat*98, 1703/5.1*cat*11, 1703/5.1*facs*1/144 + 168
Bodley 34 (1883; 'semi-Saxonicé: eME 'Katharine group')				1689.3*cat*24, 1703/5.1*cat*23
Bodley 155 (1974)	303	554	352	1703/5.1
Bodley 163 (2016)	304	555	353	1703/5.1*cat*29
Bodley 180 (2079)	305	–	354	1655.1, 1703/5.1*cat*12, 1703/5.1*facs*1/3
Bodley 340 (2404)	309	569	358	1689.3*cat*23, 1703/5.1*cat*2
Bodley 342 (2405)	309	569	358	1689.3*cat*99, 1703/5.1*cat*1
Bodley 343 (2406)	310	–	359	*1572.1*, 1689.3*cat*22, 1703/5.1*cat*3

Bodley 426 (2327)	–	576	–	1703/5.1*facs*1/176
Bodley 441 (2382)	312	577	361	1571.1, 1689.3*cat*21, 1703/5.1*cat*13, 1703/5.1*facs*1/3
Bodley 572 (2026)	313	583	362	1703/5.1*cat*27
Bodley 579 (2675)	315	585	364	1689.3*cat*97, 1703/5.1 + *cat*26
Bodley 730 (2709)	317	–	366	1703/5.1*cat*31
Bodley 865 (2737)	318	608	367	1689.3*cat*100, 1703/5.1*cat*22
Digby 4 (1605; s.xii, eME *Poema Morale*)				1678.1, 1689.3*cat*72, 1703/5.1*cat*28
Digby 63 (1664)	319	611	369	1703/5.1*facs*1/78
Hatton 20 (4113)	324	626	377	*1568.1*, 1689.3*cat*26, 1703/5.1*cat*17, 1703/5.1*facs*1/3 + 78
Junius 25 (5137; Murbach Hymnal)				1703/5.1*facs*2/3
Junius 27 (5139)	335	641	389	1689.3*cat*68
Hatton 38 (4090; Gospels, s.xii/xiii)				1689.3*cat*30, 1703/5.1*cat*20, 1703/5.1*facs*1/3
Hatton 76 (4125)	328	632–4	382	1689.3*cat*27, 1703/5.1*cat*18
Hatton 93 (4081)	329/30	635/6	383	1703/5.1*facs*1/176
Hatton 113 (5210)	331	638	384a	1701.2, 1689.3*cat*32, 1703.1, 1703/5.1*cat*4, 1703/5.1*facs*1/3
Hatton 114 (5134)	331	638	384b	1689.3*cat*32, 1703/5.1*cat*5, 1703/5.1*facs*1/3
Hatton 115 (5135)	332	639	385	1689.3*cat*33, 1703/5.1*cat*6, 1703/5.1*facs*1/3
Hatton 116 (5136)	333	–	386	1689.3*cat*34, 1703/5.1*cat*7, 1703/5.1*facs*1/3
Junius 1 (5113; semi-Saxonicé, eME *Orrmulum*)			387	1689.3*cat*36, 1703/5.1*cat*10, 1703/5.1*facs*1/3
Junius 11 (5123)	334	640	388	1655.2, 1689.3*cat*31, 1703/5.1 + *cat*21

Junius 27 (5139)	335	641	389	1703/5.1*cat*19
Junius 85–6 (5196–7)	336/7	642/3	390	1689.3*cat*79, 1703/5.1*cat*8
Junius 121 (5232)	338	644	391	1566.1, 1689.3*cat*35, 1703/5.1 + *cat*9, 1703/5.1*facs*1/144, 1705.1
Laud misc.482 (1054)	343	656	398	1689.3*cat*18, 1703/5.1*cat*15
Laud misc.509 (1042)	657 344		399	1623.1, 1679.1, 1689.3*cat*16, 1690.1, 1698.1, 1703/5.1*cat*16
Laud misc.636 (1003)	346	–	401	1566.1, 1567.1, 1626.1, 1631.1, 1639.2, 1639.4, 1666.1, 1692.1, 1689.3*cat*20, 1703/5.1 + *cat*14

Oxford, All Souls College

38	265	480	335	1703/5.1*cat*105

Oxford, Christ Church

Eynsham Cartulary	1655.3, 1703/5.1*cat*107, 1703/5.1*facs*1/144

Oxford, Corpus Christi College

279	354	673	412	1703/5.1*cat*106

Oxford, St John's College

17	360	683	418	1703/5.1*facs*3/4
154	362	686	420	1689.3*cat*85, 1703/5.1*cat*103
194 (s.xii, L Gospels, AS Charter: Sawyer 1636)				1689.3*cat*86, 1703/5.1 + *cat*104

Strood, Rochester, Medway Archives and Local Study Centre

DRc/R1 (Textus Roffensis) (*olim* RCL A.3.5)	373	–	441	1568.2, 1576.2, 1639.4, 1652.1, 1655.3, 1660.1, 1664.1, 1666.1, 1689.3*cat*152, 1690.1, 1691.1, 1693.1, 1703/5.1 + *cat*303

Uppsala, Universitetsbibliotek

DG 1 (s.vi), Codex Argenteus, Gothic Gospels   1689.3*cat*1, 1703/5.1*facs*1/3

Wells Cathedral Library

Liber Albus I (s.xiii)   1703/5.1 + *cat*310, 1703/5.1*facs*1/144 + 176

Liber Albus II (s.xv/xvi)   1703/5.1

Post-Medieval Manuscripts

Cambridge, Corpus Christi College

70 + 258, Parkerian copy of Claudius D.ii	1568.2
100 (Parkerian)	1574.2
101 (Joscelyn)	1690.1,
111 (s.xvi)	1702.1

Canterbury, Christ Church Cathedral Archives and Library

Lit.B.2 (Nowell)	1568.2
Lit.B.4 (Somner's transcripts incl. Gesta servatoris nostri)	1689.3*cat*204, 1703/5.1*cat*285 + 287
Lit.C.3 (Somner's transcripts incl. Cædmon, Orosius, *ASC*)	1689.3*cat*205, 1703/5.1*cat*291/2/5
Lit.C.4 (s.xvii, Pentateuch from Claudius B.iv)	1703/5.1*cat*293
Lit.C.5 (s.xvii, Cædmon poems &c)	1703/5.1*cat*290
Lit.C.6 (s.xvii, Laws Henry I)	1703/5.1*cat*294
Lit.C.8 (s.xvii, *ASC* C)	1693.1, 1703/5.1*cat*288
Lit.C.9–10 (pr book, Somner's autograph of 1659.1)	1703/5.1*cat*289
Lit.D.2 (s.xvi, Latin-English dictionary with OE by Somner)	1703/5.1*cat*301
Lit.E.1 (Nowell, *ASC* D, Somner's transcripts incl. many charters)	1689.3*cat*207, 1693.1, 1703/5.1*cat*286
Lit.E.2 (Nowell, Laws Cnut from Harley 55 coll CCC 383)	1568.2, 1689.3*cat*206, 1703/5.1*cat*283

W2/X.2.18 (pr book, Somner's copy of **1568.2** + annotations)   1703/5.1*cat*284

W2/X.3.12 (pr book, Somner's copy of **1650.1** + annotations)   1703/5.1*cat*299

W/B.2.23 (pr book, Somner's copy of **1640.3**)   1703/5.1*cat*298

W/B.5.1 (pr book, Somner's copy of **1627.3** with draft of **1659.1**)   1703/5.1*cat*302

W/E.6.20 (pr book, Somner's copy of **1644.2** + annotations)   1703/5.1*cat*297

W/R.8.24 (pr book, Somner's copy of **1639.4** + annotations)   1703/5.1*cat*296

Lawrence KS, Kenneth Spencer Research Library

MS E107, ff. 38–54, 207–10, apparently marked by the printer   **1639.4**

London, British Library

Add 35333 (art. 5: Wheelock)   **1639.4**
Add 43703 (Nowell)   **1568.2, 1643.1**
Add 43704 (Nowell)   **1568.1**

Cotton MSS
Vitellius D.vii (Joscelyn)   **1566.1, 1567.1, 1639.2, 1689.3***cat*187

Dept of Printed Books
Henry Davis Gift M30 (Nowell)   **1568.2**
Harley 66 (s.xvi, transcripts of cartularies St Albans/Westminster)   1703/5.1*cat*343
Harley 258 (s.xvii, transcripts from various MSS)   1703/5.1*cat*342
Harley 307 (pr book **1644.1** with annotations by Junius)   1703/5.1*cat*348
Harley 311 (copy of Textus Roffensis, 1646)   **1666.1**
Harley 358 (s.xvi)   1703/5.1 + *cat*339?
Harley 438 (s.xvii, Rule of Chrodegang: Lucas 2003: 349–56)   1703/5.1*cat*305
Harley 440 (copy of CCC 191 by William Retchford)   **1643.1**

Harley 533 (s.xvii, transcript by D'Ewes from Vitellius D.xx)	1703/5.1*cat*345
Harley 552 (s.xvi, Benedictine Rule &c from Tiberius A.iii)	1703/5.1*cat*337
Harley 589 (s.xvii, Ælfric's Grammar ed D'Ewes)	1703/5.1*cat*341
Harley 596 (s.xvii, Charters from Rochester & Winchester)	1703/5.1*cat*338/344
Harley 604 (s.xvii, foundation charters)	1703/5.1*cat*339?
Harley 761 (s.xvii, L-OE dictionary by Wheelock et al)	1703/5.1*cat*325
Harley 2044 (charter transcripts from College of Arms)	1703/5.1*cat*340?
Harley 3449 (s.xvii, OE Gospels extracts)	1703/5.1*cat*347?
Harley 4660 (charters transcribed by William Hopkins, s.xvii)	1689.3*cat*154, 1703/5.1
Harley 7567 (s.xvii, Junius's transcript of *Durham*)	1703/5.1*cat*346
Lansdowne 717	1574.2?

Norwich, Norfolk Record Office

7197 (s.xvii; papers of Sir Henry Spelman)	1626.1

Oxford, Bodleian Library (SC *no. in brackets*)

Bodley 33 (27647; Joscelyn's AS dictionary, transcribed J. Parker)	1703/5.1*cat*71
Douce V subst.10 (pr book, Vereleus, *Ad Runographiam*, 1675)	1689.3*cat*226
Dugdale 12 (6502; catalogue of 92 charters, s.xvii)	1689.3*cat*153, 1703/5.1*cat*321
Dugdale 29 (6519; Dugdale's Dictionarium *Saxonico-Lat* 1644)	1689.3*cat*84, 1703/5.1*cat*95
e Mus. 106 (3627; Ælfric's Grammar transcribed by Langbaine)	1703/5.1*cat*33
Eng.bibl.c.3 (33184; Wanley's notebook 1690–4)	*1689.3*
Fell 8–18 (8696–8706; Junius's Dictionarium Septentrionale in 5 Languages prepared for publication by Fell	1689.3*cat*83
fol. THETA 572 (pr book, Vereleus, *Herverar Saga*, 1672)	1689.3*cat*227

BIBLIOGRAPHY 647

James 24 (s.xvii)	1695.2
James 41 (3878; Dictionariolum Saxonico-Anglicum 1620–30)	1703/5.1*cat*72
James 42 (3879: Glossarium Saxonico-Latinum, c.1600)	1689.3*cat*28
Junius 2–3 (5114/5; OE-L dictionary by Junius, noting Fell 8–18)	1703/5.1*cat*80–1
Junius 4–5 (5116/7; Junius's Etymologicon Anglicanæ)	1703/5.1*cat*82
Junius 6 (5118; Dictionarium veteris linguae anglicanae: Chaucer)	1689.3*cat*95
Junius 7 (5119; pr book, J's copy of Somner's dictionary 1659.1)	1689.3*cat*93, 1703/5.1*cat*85
Junius 8 (5119; pr book, Worm, *Dan monumentorum*,1643)	1689.3*cat*224
Junius 9 (5121; pr book, J's copy of Speght's Chaucer)	1689.3*cat*91, 1703/5.1*cat*84
Junius 10 (5122; pr books, J's copy of 1643.1 & 1644.1)	1689.3*cat*87, 1703/5.1*cat*86
Junius 12 (5124; copy of Bodley 180, coll. Otho A.vi)	1655.1, 1656.2, 1665.2, 1698.2, 1689.3*cat*41, 1703/5.1 + *cat*34
Junius 13 (5125; pr book, Tatian's Gospel Harmony)	1689.3*cat*210
Junius 14 (5126; pr book, Worm, *Fasti Danici*, 1643)	1689.3*cat*225
Junius 15 (5127; copy of Tiberius B.i)	1659.1, 1665.2, 1678.1, 1689.3*cat*59, 1699.1, 1703/5.1*cat*35
Junius 16 (5128; Junius's transcript of *Annalied*, eMHG poem)	1689.3*cat*214
Junius 17 (5129; Junius's transcript of Junius 80)	1689.3*cat*213
Junius 18 (5130; pr book, J's copy of 1623.3)	1689.3*cat*88, 1703/5.1*cat*87
Junius 20 (5132; pr book, Melchior Goldast, 1606)	1689.3*cat*217
Junius 21 (5133; pr book, Gherard van der Schueren, 1477)	1689.3*cat*211
Junius 25 (5137; 'Murbach Hymnal')	1689.3*cat*218
Junius 26 (5138; Nowell's Dictionarium Saxonicum)	1689.3*cat*66, 1703/5.1*cat*75
Junius 32 (5144; *Hortus Vocabularum* 1500)	1703/5.1*cat*88
Junius 33 (5145; pr book, J's copy of 1640.3)	1689.3*cat*89, 1703/5.1*cat*92
Junius 37 (5149; Memoranda by Junius)	1703/5.1*cat*76
Junius 38 (5150; Wulfstani archiepiscopi Paraenesis)	1689.3*cat*42, 1703/5.1*cat*36
Junius 39 (5151; Decalogue etc)	1689.3*cat*48, 1703/5.1*cat*37
Junius 40 (5152; Defensor of Ligugé, *Liber Scintillarum*, excerpts)	1689.3*cat*73, 1703/5.1*cat*38

Junius 41 (5153; De primo die seculi)   1689.3*cat*61, 1703/5.1*cat*39
Junius 42 (5154; Junius's notes on Junius 13)   1689.3*cat*212
Junius 43 (5155; pr book, with Junius's notes from Tiberius A.iii)   1689.3*cat*67, 1703/5.1*cat*40
Junius 44 (5156; De observatione lunae et quae cavenda)   1689.3*cat*60, 1703/5.1*cat*42
Junius 45 (5157; Junius's notes from Julius A.iii, CCC 201, etc)   1703/5.1*cat*41
Junius 46 (5158; transcripts from Hatton 76 & Tiberius A.iii)   1703/5.1*cat*66
Junius 47 (5159; Hexaméron, from Hatton 115, coll. 116)   1689.3*cat*47, 1703/5.1*cat*43
Junius 48 (5160; De duodecim abusis secundum Cyprianum)   1689.3*cat*46
Junius 49 (5161; extracts from MSS coll Junius 109)   1689.3*cat*222
Junius 50 (5162; Junius's transcript of extracts from Nero D.iv)   1703/5.1*cat*44
Junius 52 (5164; Regula Benedicti etc)   1689.3*cat*40, 1703/5.1*cat*45
Junius 53 (5165; copy of Tiberius B.xi, coll Hatton 20 & Otho B.ii)   1689.3*cat*76, 1700?.1, 1703/5.1*cat*46
Junius 54 (5166; pr book, J's copy of STC 24797)   1689.3*cat*90, 1703/5.1*cat*89
Junius 55 (5167; copy of Codex Argenteus)   1689.3*cat*38
Junius 58 (5169; OE Liber medicinalis)   1689.3*cat*82, 1703/5.1*cat*47
Junius 59 (5170; De peccatorum medicina)   1689.3*cat*55, 1703/5.1*cat*48
Junius 60 (5171; copy of Vitellius A.vii)   1679.1, 1689.3 + *cat*58 1703/5.1*cat*49
Junius 61 (5172; Quæstiones ... inter Adrianum et Ritheum)   1689.3*cat*54, 1703/5.1*cat*50
Junius 62 (5173; transcripts of Sawyer 980 and 1454)   1689.3*cat*70, 1703/5.1*cat*51
Junius 63 (5174; Modus confitendi)   1689.3*cat*56, 1703/5.1*cat*52
Junius 65 (5176; OE excerpts from Nero A.i, ff. 71, 100)   1689.3*cat*62, 1703/5.1*cat*53
Junius 66 (5177; copy of Tiberius A.iii)   1665.2, 1689.3*cat*80, 1703/5.1*cat*54
Junius 67 (5178; transcript of ASC (C), beginning)   1689.3*cat*71, 1703/5.1*cat*55
Junius 68 (5179; 'Admonitio' from Hatton 76)   1703/5.1*cat*56
Junius 69 (5180; Commentitia ... epistola de coelo dilapsa)   1689.3*cat*50, 1703/5.1*cat*57
Junius 70 (5181; OE Alfredian Soliloquies by St Augustine)   1689.3*cat*53, 1703/5.1*cat*58

Junius 71 (5182; Ælfrici præsulis Glossarium, via Rubens)   1659.1, 1689.3*cat*65, 1703/5.1*cat*59

Junius 72 (5183; Ælfric's Glossary from Julius A.ii)   1689.3*cat*77, 1703/5.1*cat*60

Junius 73 (5184; pr book, J's own copy of his 1655.2)   1689.3*cat*92, 1703/5.1*cat*90

Junius 74 (5185; copy of CUL Ii.2.11, coll. Vitellius A.xv, pt 1)   1698.1, 1689.3*cat*51, 1703/5.1*cat*61

Junius 76 (5187; copy of Auct.D.2.19)   1655.1, 1689.3*cat*49, 1703/5.1*cat*77

Junius 77 (5188; Latin-OE glossary by Junius)   1689.3*cat*75, 1703/5.1*cat*78

Junius 78 (5189; Frisian legal and theological collections)   1689.3*cat*219

Junius 79 (5190; pr book, Merula, *Willeram*, basis for 1655.1)   1689.3*cat*209

Junius 80 (5191; pr book, *Otfridi Evangeliorum Liber*, 1571)   1689.3*cat*208

Junius 82 (5193; pr book, Karoli magni ... capitula, 1640)   1689.3*cat*96

Junius 92 (5203; pr book, *Regula S. Benedicti*, 1611)   1703/5.1*cat*91

Junius 98 (5209; pr book, Bonaventura Vulcanius)   1689.3*cat*2

Junius 100 (5211; De sanctis in Anglia sepultis)   1689.3*cat*43

Junius 101 (5212; copy of Julius A.x, coll. CCC 196)   1665.2, 1689.3*cat*63

Junius 102 (5213; Wulfstan sermons coll. Nero A.i etc)   1689.3*cat*69, 1703/5.1*cat*62

Junius 103 (5214; Extracts from Caligula A.vii)   1689.3*cat*74, 1703/5.1*cat*63

Junius 104 (5215; Interogationes Sigewulfi presbiteri)   1689.3*cat*57, 1703/5.1*cat*64

Junius 105 (copy of Vitellius A.xv, *Judith*)   1689.3*cat*78, 1698.1, 1703/5.1*cat*65

Junius 107 (5218; Hymns with AS gloss)   1689.3*cat*39, 1703/5.1*cat*66

Junius 108 (?) (5219; Junius's preface to Gothic Gospels)   1689.3*cat*45, 1703/5.1*cat*67

Junius 109 (5220; pr book, *Dat Landriucht der Fresena*, 1483/8)   1689.3*cat*221

Junius 111 (5222; pr book, *Lex Frisionum*, 1617)   1689.3*cat*220

Junius 112 (5223; L-OE dictionary compiled by Junius)   1703/5.1*cat*79

Junius 115a–b (?) (5226; Glossarium by Junius)   1689.3*cat*37

Junius 116a–f (5227–8; Glossarium Theotisco-Latinum)   1689.3*cat*215

Junius 120 (5231; MS of Andresson's *Lexicon-Islandicum*, 1683)   1689.3*cat*230

Laud misc.201 (852; Lisle's Saxon-English Psalter, s.xvii) — 1689.3cat17, 1703/5.1cat70

Laud misc.381 (956; Lisle's transcript of CUL Gg.3.28) — 1698.1, 1703/5.1cat69

Laud misc.661 (1201; 1565 transcript of AS chronicle to 915) — 1689.3cat19, 1703/5.1cat32

Marshall 78 (8660; sketch of AS grammar) — 1703/5.1cat83

Marshall 223 (8658; **1623.1** annotated by Junius) — 1703/5.1cat93

Selden supra 62 (3450; Richard James, OE miscellany, 1620–30) — 1689.3cat25, 1703/5.1cat73

Selden supra 63 (3451; Nowell, Dictionarium Sax-Ang) — 1650.3, 1703/5.1cat74

Oxford, Exeter College

PGWD 64(1) (pr book, Gregory, *Liber Sacramentorum*, 1642) — 1689.3cat94

– (pr book, Vereleus, *Hrólfs saga Gautrekssonar*, 1664) — 1689.3cat228

Oxford, Trinity College

92   William Elstob, transcript of OE Orosius from Junius 15, based on Tiberius B.i — 1699.1

–   (pr book, Worm, *Runir*, 1651) — 1689.3cat223

San Marino, California, Henry E. Huntington Library

HM 26341 (Nowell) — 1568.2

Uppsala, Universitetsbibliotek

C 20	Lexicon Latino-Suethicum	1689.3cat258
DG 3	*Konungasagurne*, destroyed by fire 1702	1689.3cat231
DG 4	*Ólafssaga Tryggvasonar*, MS, pr Vereleus 1665	1689.3cat232
DG 5	Drama, Pamphilus och Galathea	1689.3cat233
DG 6	*Elissaga ok Rosamundu*, in linguam Normannicam	1689.3cat234
DG 7	*Strengleikar eda Ljódabók*	1689.3cat235
DG 8	Frostleitings lag + *Ólafssaga ins helga*	1689.3cat236

DG 9	Islands Lagbok	1689.3cat237
DG 10	*Grettissaga*	1689.3cat238
DG 11	Edda Snorra Sturlusonar, MS of ed. Resen, 1665	1689.3cat239
DG 12	Pars de Brittlinga Sagu + *Hákonarsaga Hárekssonar*	1689.3cat240
DG 13	De Chronico Narvagico from letters of Jónsson to Worm	1689.3cat241
DG 14	Knýtlingasaga 1640	1689.3cat242
DG 15	Hákonarsaga Hárekssonar	1689.3cat243
DG 17	Speculum Regale (Icelandic)	1689.3cat244
DG 18	Speculum Regale (Danish)	1689.3cat245
DG 19	Riddara Christian Fríjs Drapa	1689.3cat246
DG 20	Danske Riimkronike	1689.3cat247
DG 21	Annales Groenlandiæ (986–1473), s.xvii	1689.3cat248
DG 27	Chronologia Islandico-Latina 740–1295	1689.3cat249
DG 41	Hofudlausn	1689.3cat250
DG 44	Skanelagen	1689.3cat259
DG 46	i Skanelagen or Skanske Lov	1689.3cat260
DG 46	ii Corpus Legum Selandiæ, Eriks Sjællandske Lov	1689.3cat251/261
DG 55	Glossarium Danicæ 1636 by Olaf Mansson 1490–1557	1689.3cat252
DG 64	Libri decem Alexandreidos	1689.3cat253

Printed Books

Abercrombie, David, 'Extending the Roman Alphabet: Some Orthographic Experiments of the Past Four Centuries', in *Towards a History of Phonetics*, ed. R.E. Asher & J.A. Henderson, Edinburgh: Edinburgh University Press, 1981, pp. 206–224.

Adams, Eleanor N., 'An Early Example of the Use of "Anglo-Saxon" Type', *The Athenæum*, 4340 (1910[2]), p. 821. [1567.1].

Adams, Eleanor N., *Old English Scholarship in England from 1566–1800*, Yale Studies in English 55 (New Haven: Yale University Press, 1917).

Aldhelm, see Ehwald.

Aldrich, Keith, Philipp & Raina Fehl, *Franciscus Junius, The Literature of Classical Art*, 2 vols, California Studies in the History of Art 22 (Berkeley: University of California Press, 1991).

Allison, A.F. & D.M. Rogers, *The Contemporary Printed Literature of the English Counter-Reformation between 1558 and 1640*, 2 vols (Aldershot: Scolar, 1989–94).

Alston, R.C., *A Bibliography of the English Language from the Invention of Printing to the Year 1800*, 10 vols (Leeds: Arnold, 1965–73). [1640.2].

Amert, Kay, 'Origins of the French Old-Style: The Roman and Italic Types of Simon de Colines', *Printing History*, 14 (1992), pp. 17–40.

Anderson, Donald M., *The Art of Written Forms: The Theory and Practice of Calligraphy* (New York: Dover, 1969).

Arber, Edward, *A Transcript of the Register of the Company of Stationers of London 1554–1640*, 4 vols (London: Arber, 1875–7, vol. 5, Birmingham: Arber, 1894).

Arber, Edward, *The Term Catalogues 1668–1709 A.D.*, 3 vols (London: Arber, 1903–6). [1684.2].

Armstrong, Elizabeth, 'The Publication of the Royal Edicts and Ordinances under Charles IX: The Destiny of Robert (II) Estienne as King's Printer', *Proceedings of the Huguenot Society*, 19.2 (1953–4), pp. 41–59. [1568.3].

Assmann, Bruno, *Angelsächsische Homilien und Heiligenleben*, Bibliothek der angelsächsischen Prosa 3 (Kassel: Wigand, 1889). [1566.1].

Assmann, Bruno, 'Übersetzung von Alcuin's De Virtutibus et Vitiis Liber. Ad Widonem Comitem', *Anglia*, 11 (1889), pp. 371–391. [1643.1].

Atkins, Ivor, 'The Origin of the Later Part of the Saxon Chronicle known as D', *English Historical Review*, 55 (1940), pp. 8–26.

Atkins, Ivor & N.R. Ker, *'Catalogus Librorum Manuscriptorum Bibliothecae Wigorniensis' made in 1622–1623 by Patrick Young, Librarian to King James I* (Cambridge: Cambridge University Press, 1944).

Axel-Nilsson, Christian, *Type Studies: The Norstedt Collection of Matrices in the Typefoundry of the Royal Printing Office, A History and Catalogue* (Stockholm: Norstedts Tryckeri, 1983).

Baddeley, Susan, *L'Orthographe française au temps de la Réforme* (Geneva: Droz, 1993).

Bailey, R.N. & E. Cambridge, 'Dating the Old English Poem *Durham*', *Medium Ævum*, 85 (2016), pp. 1–14. [1652.1].

Baines, Phil & Andrew Haslam, *Type & Typography* (London: Laurence King, 2005).

Baker, John H., *English Legal Manuscripts in the United States of America: A Descriptive List, Part II Early Modern and Modern Periods (1558–1902)* (London: Selden Society, 1990). [1626.1].

Baker, Peter S., *The Anglo-Saxon Chronicle: A Collaborative Edition: volume 8: MS F* (Cambridge: Brewer, 2000). [1607.2].

Baker, William & Kenneth Womack (eds), *Pre-Nineteenth-Century British Book Collectors and Bibliographers*, Dictionary of Literary Biography 213 (Detroit: Gale, 1999). [Parker, Selden, Twysden, Ussher, Wanley]

Balsamo Luigi & Alberto Tinto, *Origini del Corsivo nella Tipografia Italiana del Cinquecento*, Documenti sulle Arti del Libro 6 (Milan: Edizioni Il Polifilio, 1967).

Bankert, Dabney A., 'Oxford, Bodleian Library, MS Rawlinson C.887: An Unpublished Seventeenth-Century Anglo-Saxon Glossary by Nathaniel Spinckes', *The Library*, VII.13 (2012), pp. 400–422. [1701.1].

Barker, Nicolas, 'The Aldine Roman in Paris, 1530–1534', *The Library*, V.29 (1974), pp. 5–20.

Barker, Nicolas, *Aldus Manutius and the Development of Greek Script & Type in the Fifteenth Century* (New York: Fordham University Press, 1992 edn).

[Barker, Nicolas], 'The History of Printing Types', *The Book Collector*, 48 (1999), pp. 493–511.

Barnard, John & Maureen Bell, 'The Inventory of Henry Bynneman (1583) A Preliminary Survey', *Publishing History*, 29 (1991), pp. 5–46.

Barratt, D.M., 'The Library of John Selden and its Later History', *Bodleian Library Record*, 3 (1950–51), pp. 128–42, 208–13, 256–74.

Bately, Janet, 'John Joscelyn and the Laws of the Anglo-Saxon Kings', in *Words, Texts and Manuscripts: Studies in Anglo-Saxon Culture Presented to Helmut Gneuss on the Occasion of his Sixty-Fifth Birthday*, ed. M. Korhammer with the assistance of K. Reichl & H. Sauer (Cambridge: Cambridge University Press, 1992), pp. 435–66. [1568.2].

Bately, Janet, *The Old English Orosius*, EETS ss 6 (London: Oxford University Press, 1980). [1640.4, 1665.2].

Bates, David, *Regesta Regum Anglo-Normannorum* (Oxford: Clarendon Press, 1998). [1703/5.1].

[Le Bé, Guillaume II], *Sixteenth-Century French Typefounders: The Le Bé Memorandum*, ed. Harry Carter, Documents Typographiques Français III (Paris: for A. Jammes, 1967).

Le Bé-Moretus Collection of Specimen Fragments c.1599: see Dreyfus.

Beadle, Richard, '"I wol nat telle it yit": John Selden and a Lost Version of the *Cook's Tale*', in *Chaucer to Shakespeare: Essays in Honour of Shinsuke Ando*, ed. T. Takamiya & R. Beadle (Cambridge: Brewer, 1992), pp. 55–66.

Beadle, Richard, 'Macro MS 5: A Historical Reconstruction', *Transactions of the Cambridge Bibliographical Society*, XVI.1 (2016), pp. 35–77.

Behaghel, Otto, *Heliand und Genesis*, 9th edn rev. B. Taeger (Tübingen: Niemeyer, 1984). [1690.1].

Bennett, G.V., *White Kennett 1660–1728 Bishop of Peterborough* (London: SPCK, 1957). [1693.1].

Bennett, J.A.W., 'Hickes's *Thesaurus*: A Study in Oxford Book-Production', *English Studies 1948* = *English Studies*, 1 (1948), pp. 27–45. [1703/5.1].

Berkhout, Carl, 'Laurence Nowell (1530–ca.1570)', in *Medieval Scholarship: Biographical Studies on the Formation of a Discipline*, vol. 2: Literature and Philology, ed. H. Damico, with D. Fennema & K. Lenz (New York: Garland, 1998), pp. 3–17. [1568.2].

Berkhout, Carl, 'William Lambarde and Old English', *Notes and Queries*, 246 (2000), 414–420. [1568.2, 1568.3, 1576.2, 1605.1].

Berkhout, Carl T. & Milton McC. Gatch, *Anglo-Saxon Scholarship: The First Three Centuries* (Boston MA: G.K. Hall, 1982).

Berkowitz, David S., *John Selden's Formative Years: Politics and Society in Early Seventeenth-Century England* (Washington DC: Folger Shakespeare Library, 1988). [1618.1, 1635.1].

Bernard, Stephen, *The Letters of Jacob Tonson in Bodleian MS. Eng. lett. c. 129* (Oxford: Oxford Bibliographical Society, 2019).

Berry, W. Turner & A.F. Johnson, *Catalogue of Specimens of Printing Types by English and Scottish Printers and Founders 1665–1830* (London: Oxford University Press, 1935).

Birch, Walter de Gray, *Cartularium Saxonicum: A Collection of Charters relating to Anglo-Saxon History*, 4 vols (London: Whiting & Co., 1883–99). [1639.4, 1640.1].

Birrell & Garnett, *Catalogue of I Typefounders' Specimens II Books printed in Founts of Historic Importance III Works on Typefounding Printing & Bibliography offered for sale* (London: Birrell & Garnett Ltd, 1928).

Bischoff, Bernhard, *Latin Palaeography: Antiquity and the Middle Ages*, t D. Ó Cróinín & D. Ganz (Cambridge: Cambridge University Press, 1990).

Bischoff, Bernhard, *Manuscripts and Libraries in the Age of Charlemagne*, t M. Gorman (Cambridge: Cambridge University Press, 1994).

Bishop, T.A.M., *English Caroline Minuscule* (Oxford: Clarendon Press, 1971).

Le Blanc, Charles, *Manuel de l'Amateur d'Estampes, contenant un dictionnaire des graveurs de toutes les nations*, 2 vols (Amsterdam: Hissink, 1970–1). [J-B. Nolin].

Bland, Mark, 'William Stansby and the Production of *The Workes of Beniamin Jonson*, 1615–16', *The Library*, VI.20 (1998), pp. 1–33.

Bland, Mark B., 'John Windet and the Transformation of the Book Trade, 1584–1610', *Papers of the Bibliographical Society of America*, 107 (2013), pp. 151–92.

Blayney, P.W.M., *The Texts of King Lear and their Origins*, vol. I, *Nicholas Okes and the First Quarto* (Cambridge: Cambridge University Press, 1982). [1610.4].

Blomefield, F., & C. Parkin, *An Essay towards a Topographical History of the County of Norfolk*, 11 vols (London: W. Bulmer for W. Miller, 1805–10), supplemented by an Index Nominum by John N. Chadwick (King's Lynn: J.N. Chadwick, 1862).

Boissevain, Jeremy, *Friends of Friends: Networks, Manipulators and Coalitions* (Oxford: Blackwell, 1974).

Boon, G.C., 'Camden and the *Britannia*', *Archaeologia Cambrensis*, 136 (1987), pp. 1–19. [1586.1, 1610.5].

Boran, Elizabethanne, with (Latin and Greek translations by) David Money, *The Correspondence of James Ussher 1600–1656*, 3 vols (Dublin: Irish Manuscripts Commission, 2015).

Bozzolo, Carla, Dominique Coq, Denis Muzerelle & Enzio Ornato, 'Page Savante, Page Vulgaire: Étude Comparative de la Mise en Page des Livres en Latin et en Français écrits ou imprimés en France au xve Siècle', in *La Présentation du Livre*, ed. E. Baumgartner & N. Boulestreau (Paris x—Nanterre: 1987), pp. 122–133.

Bracken, James K., 'William Stansby's Early Career', *Studies in Bibliography*, 38 (1985), pp. 214–216.

Bracken, James K., & Joel Silver (eds), *The British Literary Book Trade, 1475–1700*, Dictionary of Literary Biography 170 (Detroit: Gale, 1996). [= DLB] [Printers].

Brackmann, Rebecca, *The Elizabethan Invention of Anglo-Saxon England: Laurence Nowell, William Lambarde, and the Study of Old English*, Studies in Renaissance Literature 30 (Cambridge: Brewer, 2012).

Bradshaw Collection, see Sayle.

Branden, Lode van den, Elly Cockx-Indestege, Frans Sillis, *Bio-Bibliografie van Cornelis Kiliaan* (Nieuwkoop: De Graaf, 1978).

Bremmer, Rolf H. Jr (ed.), *Franciscus Junius and his Circle* (Amsterdam: Rodopi, 1998).

Bremmer, Rolf H. Jr, 'The Anglo-Saxon Pantheon according to Richard Verstegen (1605)', in Graham, *Recovery*, pp. 141–172. [1605.2].

Bremmer, Rolf H. Jr, '"Mine is bigger than Yours": The Anglo-Saxon Collections of Johannes de Laet (1581–1649) and Sir Simonds D'Ewes (1602–1650)', in *Anglo-Saxon Books and their Readers*, ed. T.N. Hall & D. Scragg (Kalamazoo: Medieval Institute, 2008), pp. 136–74, [1640.3].

Brennan, Michael, 'A Volume of Richard Chiswell's Papers', *The Library*, VI.2 (1980), pp. 218–219.

Breuker, Philippus H. 'On the course of Franciscus Junius' Germanic Studies with special Reference to Frisian', in *Aspects of Old Frisian Philology*, ed. R.H. Bremmer Jr, G. van der Meer & O. Vries, Amsterdamer Beiträge zur Älteren Germanistik 31/32 (Amsterdam, 1990), pp. 42–68, repr. in Bremmer, *Junius and his Circle*, pp. 129–57.

Brewer, D.S., 'Sixteenth, Seventeenth and Eighteenth Century References to the Voyage of Ohthere (Ohtheriana IV)', *Anglia*, 71 (1952–3), pp. 202–211. [1589.1, 1598.1].

Briels, J.G.C.A., *Zuidnederlandse Boekdrukkers en Boekverkopers in Republiek der Verenigde Nederlanden omstreeks 1570–1630*, Bibliotheca Bibliographica Neerlandica 6 (Nieuwkoop: De Graaf, 1974). [François Guyot; Gabriel Guyot].

Bromwich, John, 'The First Book printed in Anglo-Saxon Type', *Transactions of the Cambridge Bibliographical Society*, III.4 (1962), pp. 265–291. [1566.1, 1566.2].

Brøndum-Nielsen, Johs (gen. ed.), *Danmarks gamle landskabslove med kirkelovene*, 9 vols (København: Gyldendal, [1920–]61). [1689.3].

Brook, G.L. & R.F. Leslie, *Lagamon: Brut*, EETS os 250/277 (London: Oxford University Press, 1963/1978). [1576.2, 1596.2].

Brook, V.J.K., *A Life of Archbishop Parker* (Oxford: Clarendon Press, 1962).

Brooke, Christopher, *A History of Gonville and Caius College* (Woodbridge: Boydell, 1985). [1568.1, 1574.1].

Brown, Carleton, *English Lyrics of the XIIIth Century* (Oxford: Clarendon Press, 1932). [1703/5.1].

Bruce, John, & Thomas T. Perowne, *Correspondence of Matthew Parker, D.D. Archbishop of Canterbury*, Parker Society (Cambridge: Cambridge University Press, 1853).

Burlington Fine Arts Club Exhibition of Bookbindings (London: Burlington Fine Arts Club, 1891). [Case L, no. 30 = 1574.1].

Butt, J., 'The Facilities for Antiquarian Study in the Seventeenth Century', *Essays and Studies*, 24 (1938[1939]), pp. 64–79. [1618.1].

Cameron, A.F., 'Middle English in Old English Manuscripts', in *Chaucer and Middle English Studies in honour of Rossell Hope Robbins*, ed. B. Rowland (London: Allen & Unwin, 1974), pp. 218–229.

Campbell, A., *The Battle of Brunanburh* (London: Heinemann, 1938). [1643.1].

Campbell, A., *Charters of Rochester*, Anglo-Saxon Charters 1 (London: Oxford University Press, 1973). [1576.2].

Carley, James P., 'Books seen by Samuel Ward 'in Bibliotheca Regia', circa 1614', *British Library Journal*, 16 (1990), pp. 89–98.

Carley, James P. & Colin G.C. Tite (eds), *Books and Collectors 1200–1700: Essays presented to Andrew Watson* (London: British Library, 1997).

Carter, Harry, *The Fell Types: What has been done in and about them* (New York: Oxford University Press, 1968).

Carter, Harry, *A View of Early Typography up to about 1600* (Oxford: Clarendon Press, 1969a).

Carter, Harry, *The Type Specimen of Delacolonge (Lyons 1773)* (Amsterdam: Van Gendt, 1969b).

Carter, Harry, 'Huguenot Typography', *Proceedings of the Huguenot Society of London*, 21 (1970), pp. 532–544.

Carter, Harry, *A History of the Oxford University Press Volume 1 ... to the year 1780* (all published) (Oxford: Clarendon Press, 1975).

Carter, Harry, see also Le Bé, Morison.

C[arter], H. & J.S.G. S[immons], *A Specimen of Types cast at the University Press, Oxford, in matrices believed to have been bought at Leyden in 1637* (Oxford: Oxford University Press, 1957).

Carter, Matthew, 'Theories of Letterform Construction. Part 1', *Printing History*, 14 (1992), pp. 3–16.

Casamassima, Emanuele, 'I Disegni di Caratteri di Ludovico degli Arrighi Vicentino (notizie 1510–1527)', *Gutenberg-Jahrbuch* 1963, pp. 24–36.
Casamassima, Emanuele, 'Ancora su Ludovico degli Arrighi Vicentino (notizie 1510–1527) Risulati di una "Recognitio"', *Gutenberg-Jahrbuch* 1965, pp. 35–42.
Catach, Nina, *L'Orthographe française à l'époque de la Renaissance* (Geneva: Droz, 1968).
Catto, Jeremy, 'Andrew Horn: Law and History in Fourteenth-Century England', in *The Writing of History in the Middle Ages: Essays Presented to Richard William Southern*, ed. R.H.C. Davis, & J.M. Wallace-Hadrill (Oxford: Oxford University Press, 1981), pp. 367–391.
Celsius, O.O. (Olof Olofsson), *Bibliothecae Upsaliensis Historia*, Uppsala, 1745; repr. with Swedish translation by Sten Hedberg with commentary by G. Hornwall (Uppsala, Acta Bibliothecae R. Universitatis Upsaliensis 17, 1971). [1689.3].
Chambers, R.W., Max Förster & Robin Flower, *The Exeter Book of Old English Poetry* (London: Percy Lund, Humphries & Co., 1933). [1703/5.1].
Christianson, Paul, 'Young John Selden and the Ancient Constitution, ca. 1610–18', *Proceedings of the American Philosophical Society*, 128 (1984), pp. 271–315. [1610.2, 1612.1, 1614.3, 1618.1].
Clapp, S.L.C., 'The Beginnings of Subscription Publication', *Modern Philology*, 29 (1931–2), pp. 199–224. [1617.1].
Clark, John W., *Historiola Collegii Corporis Christi by John Josselin*, Cambridge Antiquarian Society Octavo Publications XVII (Cambridge: Cambridge Antiquarian Society, 1880). [CCC].
Clayton, Mary, 'The Old English *Promissio Regis*', *Anglo-Saxon England*, 37 (2008), pp. 91–150. [1689.3].
Clement, Richard W., 'The Discovery of Anglo-Saxon England: An Exhibition drawn from the Holdings of the Kenneth Spencer Research Library University of Kansas Lawrence, Kansas, U.S.A. March–May 1989', *Old English Newsletter*, 22.2 (Binghamton, 1989), Appendix B.
Clement, Richard W., 'The Beginnings of Printing in Anglo-Saxon, 1565–1630', *Publications of the Bibliographical Society of America*, 91 (1997), pp. 192–244.
Clemoes, Peter, *Ælfric's Catholic Homilies: The First Series: Text*, Early English Text Society, Supplementary Series 17 (Oxford: Oxford University Press, 1997).
Clough, James & Chiara Scattolin, *Alphabets of Wood: Luigi Melchiori & the History of Italian Wood Types* (Cornuda: Tipoteca Italiana, 2014).
Cockayne, T. Oswald, *Leechdoms, Wortcunning, and Starcraft of Early England*, Rolls Series 35, 3 vols (London: Longmans, Green, Reader, and Dyer, 1864–6). [1623.3].
Collier, Wendy E.J., 'A Thirteenth-Century User of Anglo-Saxon Manuscripts', *Bulletin of the John Rylands University Library of Manchester*, 79 (1997), pp. 149–165.

Conner, Patrick W., *Anglo-Saxon Exeter: A Tenth-Century Cultural History* (Woodbridge: Boydell, 1993).

Considine, John P., 'Post-classical heritages: Du Cange and his world', in idem, *Dictionaries in Early Modern Europe: Lexicography and the Making of Heritage* (Cambridge: Cambridge University Press, 2008), pp. 250–287. [1678.2].

Considine, John P., *Small Dictionaries and Curiosity* (Oxford: Oxford University Press, 2017). [1691.1].

Cooper, Charles H. & Thompson Cooper, *Athenae Cantabrigienses*, 2 vols (Cambridge: Deighton, Bell & Co., 1858–61).

Copinger, H.B., *The Elzevier Press* (London: Grafton, 1927). [1636.1].

Corbett, Margery, 'The Title-Page and Illustrations to the *Monasticon Anglicanum* 1655–1673', *The Antiquaries' Journal* (1986), pp. 102–109. [1655.3].

Corbett, Margery & Ronald W. Lightbown, *The Comely Frontispiece: The Emblematic Title-Page in England 1550–1660* (London: Routledge & Kegan Paul, 1979), pp. 153–161. [1612.1].

Crawford, A. & A.P. Jones, 'The Early Typography of Printed Welsh', *The Library*, VI.3 (1981), pp. 217–231.

Crawford, Earl of [James Ludovic Lindsay], *Bibliotheca Lindesiana*, 4 vols (Aberdeen: Aberdeen University Press, 1910). [1572.1].

Crawford, S.J., *The Old English Version of the Heptateuch, Ælfric's Treatise on the Old and New Testament and his Preface to Genesis*, EETS, o.s. 160 (London: Oxford University Press, rev. edn 1969). [1623.1, 1690.1].

Crick, Julia, 'Historical Literacy in the Archive: Post-Conquest Imitative Copies of Pre-Conquest Charters and Some French Comparanda', in M. Brett & D.A. Woodman (eds), *The Long Twelfth-Century View of the Anglo-Saxon Past*, (Farnham: Ashgate, 2015), pp. 159–190.

Crick, Julia & Alexandra Walsham (eds), *The Uses of Script and Print, 1300–1700* (Cambridge: Cambridge University Press, 2004).

Cromartie, Alan, *Sir Matthew Hale 1609–1676: Law, Religion and Natural Philosophy* (Cambridge: Cambridge University Press, 1995). [1635.1].

Cronne, Henry A., 'The Study and Use of Charters by English Scholars in the Seventeenth Century: Sir Henry Spelman and Sir William Dugdale'. In *English Historical Scholarship in the Sixteenth and Seventeenth Centuries*, ed. L. Fox, Dugdale Society (London: Oxford University Press, 1956). [1626.1].

Cronne, Henry A., 'Charter Scholarship in England', *University of Birmingham Historical Journal*, 8 (1962), pp. 26–61.

Cross, J.E., *Two Old English Apocrypha and their Manuscript Source: The Gospel of Nichodemus and The Avenging of the Saviour*, with contributions by D. Brearley,

J. Crick, T. Hall & A. Orchard (Cambridge: Cambridge University Press, 1996), pp. 139–247. [1703/5.1].

Damico, Helen, with Donald Fennema & Karmen Lenz, *Medieval Scholarhsip: Vol. 2, Literature and Philology* (New York: Garland, 1998). [Nowell, Hickes, Wanley].

Dammery, Richard, 'Editing the Anglo-Saxon Laws: Felix Liebermann and Beyond', in *The Editing of Old English*, ed. D.G. Scragg & P.E. Szarmach (Woodbridge: Brewer, 1994), pp. 251–261. [1568.2].

Danielsson, Bror, *John Hart's Works on English Orthography and Pronunciation (1551, 1569, 1570)*, 2 vols, Acta Universitatis Stockholmiensis; Stockholm Studies in English 5, 11 (Stockholm: Almqvist & Wiksell, 1955–63).

Darlington, Reginald R., *The* Vita Wulfstani *of William of Malmesbury*, Camden Soc. III.xl (London: Royal Historical Society, 1928). [1703.1].

Darlow, T.H. & H.F. Moule, *Historical Catalogue of Printed Editions of The English Bible 1525–1961*, rev. A.S. Herbert (London: British and Foreign Bible Society, 1968).

Davenport, Cyril, *Royal English Bookbindings* (London: Seeley, 1896). [1572.1].

Davies, J. Conway, 'A Recovered Manuscript of Symeon of Durham', *Durham University Journal*, 44 (1950–51), pp. 22–8.

Davies, J. Conway, *Cartæ Antiquæ [Wiltunense]*, n.s. 33 (London: Pipe Roll Society, 1957). [1661.1].

Davis, G.R.C., *Medieval Cartularies of Great Britain and Ireland*, rev. C. Breay, H. Harrison & D.M. Smith (London: British Library, 2010).

Davis, H.W.C., *Regesta Regum Anglo-Normannorum 1066–1154*, 4 vols (Oxford: Clarendon Press, 1913–69); vol. 2 entitled *Regesta Henrici Primi 1100–1135*, ed. C. Johnson & H.A. Cronne, 1956. [1572.1, 1703/5.1].

Davis, Herbert & Harry Carter, ed., *Mechanick Exercises on the whole Art of Printing (1683–4) by Joseph Moxon* (London: Oxford University Press, 1962 edn).

Dekker, Kees, '"Vide Kilian ...": The Role of Kiliaan's *Etymologicum* in Old English Studies between 1650 and 1665', *Anglia*, 114 (1996), pp. 514–43.

Dekker, Kees, 'Jan van Vliet (1622–1666) and the Study of Old English in the Low Countries', in *The Middle Ages after the Middle Ages in the English-speaking World*, ed. M-F. Alamichel & D. Brewer (Cambridge: Brewer, 1997), pp. 27–42.

Dekker, Kees, 'The Old Frisian Studies of Jan van Vliet (1622–1666) and Thomas Marshall (1621–1685)', *Amsterdamer Beiträge zur Älteren Germanistik*, 49 (1998), pp. 113–138. [1626.1].

Dekker, Kees, *The Origins of Old Germanic Studies in the Low Countries*, Brill's Studies in Intellectual History 92 (Leiden: Brill, 1999). [1664.2].

Dekker, Kees, 'Francis Junius (1591–1677): Copyist or Editor?', *Anglo-Saxon England*, 29 (2000), pp. 279–296. [1652.1].

DeMolen, Richard L., 'The Library of William Camden', *Proceedings of the American Philosophical Society*, 128 (1984), pp. 327–409.

Denholm-Young, Noel, 'Who wrote *Fleta*?', in *Collected Papers of N. Denholm-Young* (Cardiff: University of Wales Press, 1969), pp. 187–198. [1647.2].

Derham, William, *Select Remains of the Learned John Ray M.A. and F.R.S. with his Life* (London: George Scott, 1760). [1691.3].

Desgraves, Louis, *Les Haultin 1571–1623*, L'Imprimerie à La Rochelle 2 (Geneva: Droz, 1960).

Dewar, Mary, *Sir Thomas Smith A Tudor Intellectual in Office* (London: Athlone Press, 1964). [1568.3].

Dickins, Bruce, 'William L'Isle the Saxonist and Three XVIIth Century Remainder-Issues', *English and Germanic Studies*, 1 (1947–8), pp.53–55. [1638.1].

Dickins, Bruce, 'The Irish Broadside of 1571', *Transactions of the Cambridge Bibliographical Society*, I.1 (1949), pp. 48–60. [1574.2].

Dickins, Bruce, *The Genealogical Preface to the Anglo-Saxon Chronicle*, Department of Anglo-Saxon Occasional Papers 2 (Cambridge, 1952).

Doane, A.N., *Genesis A, A New Edition* (Madison: University of Wisconsin Press, 1978), rev. edn, Medieval and Renaissance Texts and Studies 435 (Tempe AZ, 2013).

Dobbie, Elliot Van Kirk, *The Manuscripts of Cædmon's Hymn and Bede's Death Song, With a Critical Text of the 'Epistola Cuthberti de obitu Bedae'* (New York: Columbia University Press, 1937). [1652.1].

Dobbie, Elliot Van Kirk, *The Anglo-Saxon Minor Poems*, ASPR 6 (New York: Columbia University Press, 1942). [1574.2, 1652.1, 1655.2].

Dobson, E.J., *English Pronunciation 1500–1700* (Oxford: Clarendon Press, 1968 edn). [1568.3].

Dodwell, Barbara, *The Charters of Norwich Cathedral Priory*, 2 vols, Pipe Roll Society 78 & 84 (London, 1974 & 1985). [1703/5.1].

Douglas, D.C., *Feudal Documents from the Abbey of Bury St. Edmunds*, Records of the Social and Economic History of England and Wales 8 (London: Oxford University Press, 1932). [1631.1].

Douglas, David C., *English Scholars* (London: Cape, 1939). [1691.1].

Doyle, A.I., '*Bede's Death Song* in Durham Cathedral Library, MS. A.IV.36', in *Symeon of Durham*, ed. D. Rollason (Stamford: Shaun Tyas, 1998), pp. 157–60.

Drage, Elaine, 'Bishop Leofric and the Exeter Cathedral Chapter, 1050–1072: A Reassessment of the Evidence', Unpubl. D.Phil. thesis, Oxford University, 1978.

Dreyfus, John G., *Type Specimen Facsimiles*, I (London: Bowes and Bowes, 1963); vol. II, annotated by Hendrik D.L. Vervliet & Harry Carter (London: Bowes & Bowes, 1972) reproduces Plantin 1567 and c.1585 plus the Le Bé-Moretus Specimen c.1599.

Dugdale: see Hamper.

Duignan, W.H., *The Charter of Wulfrún to the Monastery at "Hamtun" (Wolverhampton)* (Wolverhampton: J. Steen & Co., 1888). [1655.3].

Dumville, David N., 'The Sixteenth-Century History of Two Cambridge Books from Sawley', *Transactions of the Cambridge Bibliographical Society*, 7:4 (1980), 427–444, repr. in idem, *Histories and Pseudo-Histories of the Insular Middle Ages*, (Aldershot: Variorum, 1990).

Dumville, David [N.], 'The West Saxon Genealogical Regnal List: Manuscripts and Text', *Anglia*, 104 (1986), pp. 1–32. [1643.1, 1678.1].

Dumville, David N., 'On the Dating of Some Late Anglo-Saxon Liturgical Manuscripts', *Transactions of the Cambridge Bibliographical Society*, 10 (1991), pp. 40–57.

Dumville, David [N.], *Facsimile of MS. F: The Domitian Bilingual*, The Anglo-Saxon Chronicle A Collaborative Edition (Cambridge: Brewer, 1995).

Dumville, David [N.] and Michael Lapidge, *The Annals of St Neots with Vita Prima Sancti Neoti*, The Anglo-Saxon Chronicle A Collaborative Edition 17 (Cambridge: Brewer, 1985).

Dunkin, Paul S., 'Foxe's *Acts and Monuments*, 1570, and Single-Page Imposition', *The Library*, v.2 (1947–48), pp.159–170. [1570.1].

Earle, John, *A Hand-Book to the Land-Charters, and other Saxonic Documents* (Oxford: Clarendon Press, 1888). [1702.1, 1703/5.1].

Earle, John, & Charles Plummer, *Two of the Saxon Chronicles Parallel*, 2 vols (Oxford: Clarendon Press, 1892–9). [1692.1].

Eccles, Mark, 'Bynneman's Books', *The Library*, v.12 (1957), pp. 81–92. [1568.1].

Echard, Siân, *Printing the Middle Ages* (Philadelphia PA, University of Pennsylvania Press, 2008).

Edwards, B.J.N., *William Camden: his Britannia and some Roman Inscriptions* (Maryport: Senhouse Roman Museum, 1998). [1586.1].

Edwards, Edward, *Liber Monasterii de Hyda*, RS 45 (London: Longmans, Green, Reader, and Dyer, 1866). [1574.1, 1574.2, 1639.4].

Edwards, Edward, *Lives of the Founders of the British Museum*, 2 vols (London: Trübner, 1870). [vol. II, pp. 670–85 (= Bk III, ch. v) on Thomas Grenville (1755–1846)].

Eisenstein, Elizabeth L., *The Printing Press as an Agent of Change. Communication and Cultural Transformations in Early-Modern Europe* (Cambridge: Cambridge University Press, 1979).

Ellis, Henry, *Original Letters of Eminent Literary Men of the Sixteenth, Seventeenth, and Eighteenth Centuries*, Camden Soc. I.23 (London: J.B. Nichols, 1843). [1600.1, 1607.2, 1695.3].

Elmham, Thomas of, see Hardwick.

Elrington, Charles R., *The Whole Works of the most Rev. James Ussher*, 17 vols (Dublin: Hodges, Smith & Co., 1847–64). See also Boran.

Emden, A.B., *A Biographical Register of the University of Oxford A.D. 1501 to 1540* (Oxford: Clarendon Press, 1974).

Emms, Richard, 'St Augustine's Abbey, Canterbury, and the "First Books at the Whole English Church"', in *The Church and the Book*, ed. R.N. Swanson (Woodbridge: Brewer, 2004), pp. 32–45. [1703–5.1].

Empey, Mark, '"A real credit to Ireland, and to Dublin": the Scholarly Achievements of Sir James Ware', in *Dublin: Renaissance City of Literature*, ed. C. Gribben & K. Miller (Manchester: University Press, 2017), pp. 119–138. [1654.1, 1658.3].

Enschedé, Charles, t and rev. Harry Carter, *Typefoundries in the Netherlands from the Fifteenth to the Nineteenth Century by Charles Enschedé*, ed. L. Hellinga (Haarlem: Stichting Museum Enschedé, 1978).

Ernesti, J.H.G., *Die wol-eingerichtete Buchdruckerey* [of the Endters at Nürnberg] (Nürnberg: Johann Andrea Endters seel. Sohn und Erben, 1721, 2nd edn 1733). [1665.3].

Eros, John F., 'A 17th-Century Demonstration of Language Relationship: Meric Casaubon on English and Greek', *Historiographica Linguistica* 3 (1976), pp. 1–13. [1650.1].

Evans, Joan, *A History of the Society of Antiquaries*, (Oxford: Oxford University Press, 1956).

Evans, Ruth, 'An Anonymous Old English Homily for Holy Saturday', *Leeds Studies in English*, n.s.12 (1981), pp. 129–153. [1643.1].

Evenden, Elizabeth, *Patents, Pictures and Patronage: John Day and the Tudor Book Trade* (Aldershot: Ashgate, 2008).

Evenden, Elizabeth, & Thomas S. Freeman, *Religion and the Book in early Modern England: the Making of Foxe's Book of Martyrs* (Cambridge: Cambridge University Press, 2011). [1570.1].

Ehwald, Rudolf, *Aldhelmi Opera*, MGH auct. ant. 15 (Berlin: Weidmann, 1919). [1632.3].

Fairbank, Alfred & Bruce Dickins, *The Italic Hand in Tudor Cambridge*, Cambridge Bibliographical Society Monograph 5 (London: Bowes & Bowes, 1962).

Fairer, David, 'Anglo-Saxon Studies', ch. 29 in *The History of the University of Oxford*, gen. ed. T.H. Aston, vol. v, *The Eighteenth Century*, ed. L.S. Sutherland & L.G. Mitchell (Oxford: Clarendon Press, 1986). [1678.1, 1692.1].

Fairfield, Leslie P. 'The Mysterious Press of "Michael Wood" (1553–1554)', *The Library*, v.27 (1972), pp. 220–232. [= John Day 1].

Feather, John, *Book Prospectuses before 1801 in the John Johnson Collection, Bodleian Library, Oxford: A Catalogue with Microfiches* (Oxford: Oxford Microform Publications for the Bodleian Library, 1976).

Feather, John, *English Book Prospectuses An Illustrated History* (Newton PA: Bird & Bull Press, and Minneapolis: Daedalus Press, 1984). [1617.1].

Feather, John, *A History of British Publishing* (London: Routledge, 1991 edn).

Febvre, Lucien, & Henri-Jean Martin, *The Coming of the Book: The Impact of Printing 1450–1800*, t D. Gerard, ed. G. Nowell-Smith & D. Wootton (London: NLB, 1976). First published in French as *L'Apparition du Livre* in 1958.

Fehr, Bernhard, *Die Hirtenbriefe Ælfrics*, Bibliothek der angelsächsischen Prosa 9 (Hamburg: H. Grand, 1914), repr. suppl. P. Clemoes (Darmstadt: Wissenschaftliche Buchgesellschaft, 1966). [1566.1, 1570.1].

Feliciano, Felice (c.1460), *Alphabetum Romanum*, ed. G. Mardersteig, t R.H. Boothroyd (Verona: Officina Bodoni, 1960).

Fell, Christine, 'Norse Studies, Then Now and Hereafter', in *Viking Revaluations*, ed. A. Faulkes & R. Perkins (London: Viking Society for Northern Research, University College, 1993), pp. 85–99. [1670.1, 1676.1].

Fell, Christine, 'The First Publication of Old Norse Literature in England and its Relation to its Sources', in *The Waking of Angantyr: the Scandinavian Past in European Culture*, ed. E. Roesdahl & P.M. Sørensen, Acta Jutlandica 71:1, Humanities series 70 (Aarhus: Aarhus University Press, c.1996). [1670.1, 1676.1].

Ferguson, F.S., *Additions to 'Title-Page Borders 1485–1640'* (London: Bibliographical Society, 1936).

Ferguson, W. Craig, *Pica Roman Type in Elizabethan England* (Aldershot: Scolar, 1989).

Finberg, Herbert P.R., *The Early Charters of the West Midlands*, Studies in Early English History 2 (Leicester: Leicester University Press, 1961). [1639.4].

Finberg, H.P.R., *The Early Charters of Wessex*, Studies in English History 3 (Leicester: Leicester University Press, 1964). [1639.4].

Fine Bindings 1500–1700 from Oxford Libraries: Catalogue of an Exhibition (Oxford: Bodleian Library, 1968). [1566.1, 1643.1].

Fisher, Matthew, *Scribal Authorship and the Writing of History in Medieval England* (Columbus: Ohio State University Press, 2010).

Flower, Robin, 'Laurence Nowell and the Discovery of England in Tudor Times', *Proceedings of the British Academy*, 21 (1935), pp. 47–73. [1703/5.1].

Foot, Mirjam M., *The Henry Davis Gift: A Collection of Bookbindings*, 2 vols (London: British Library, 1978–83). [1570.1, 1574.1, 1583.1].

Foot, Mirjam M., *Studies in the History of Bookbinding* (Aldershot: Scolar, 1993). [1570.1].

Ford, Alan, *James Ussher: Theology, History, and Politics in early-modern Ireland and England* (Oxford: University Press, 2007). [1622.2, 1631.2, 1632.3, 1639.2, 1665.4, 1687.2, 1687.3, 1690.1, 1696.3].

Forster, H., 'The Rise and Fall of the Cambridge Muses (1603–1763)', *Transactions of the Cambridge Bibliographical Society*, 8 (1982), pp. 141–172. [1641.3].

Förster, Max, *Zur Geschichte des Reliquienkultus in Altengland*, Sitzungsberichte der Bayerischen Akademie der Wissenschaften, Philosophisch-Historische Abteilung, Heft 8 (München, 1943). [1655.3].

Foster, Joseph, *Alumni Oxonienses 1500–1714*, 4 vols (Oxford: Parker, 1891–2). [1690.2, 1699.2].

Fournier, Pierre Simon, le jeune, *Modèles des Caracteres de l'Imprimerie* (Paris: Fournier, 1742); facsimile intr. J. Mosley (London: Eugrammia Press, 1965). [CAS6].

Fowler, Roger, 'A Late Old English Handbook for the Use of a Confessor', *Anglia*, 83 (1965), pp. 1–34. [1639.4, 1650.3, 1679.2, 1696.2].

Fowler, Roger, *Wulfstan's Canons of Edgar*, EETS os 266 (London: Oxford University Press, 1972). [1639.4, 1650.3, 1679.2, 1696.2].

Fox, Cyril & Bruce Dickins, *The Early Cultures of North-West Europe*, H.M. Chadwick Memorial Studies (Cambridge: Cambridge University Press, 1950). [1703/5.1].

Fox, Levi, *English Historical Scholarship in the Sixteenth and Seventeenth Centuries*, Dugdale Society (London: Oxford University Press, 1956).

Foys, Martin K., *Virtually Anglo-Saxon: Old Media, New Media, and Early Medieval Studies in the Late Age of Print* (Gainsville: University Press of Florida, 2007).

Franzen, Allen J., *Desire for Origins: New Language, Old English, and Teaching the Tradition* (New Brunswick: Rutgers University Press, 1990).

Franzen, Christine, *The Tremulous Hand of Worcester: A Study of Old English in the Thirteenth Century* (Oxford: Clarendon Press, 1991).

Fry, Donald K., 'A newly Discovered Version of the Old English Poem *Durham*', in *Old English and New*, ed. J.H. Hall, N. Doane & D. Ringler (New York: Garland, 1992), pp. 83–96. [1703–5.1].

Fuks, L. & R.G. Fuks-Mansfeld, *Hebrew Typography in the Northern Netherlands 1585–1815*, 2 vols (Leiden: Brill, 1984–7). [1636.2].

Fuller, Thomas, *The History of the University of Cambridge, from the Conquest to the year 1634*, ed. M. Prickett & T. Wright (Cambridge: J. & J.J. Deighton, 1840). [1574.1].

Fussner, F. Smith, *The Historical Revolution: English Historical Writing and Thought 1580–1640* (London: Routledge & Paul, 1962). [1586.1, 1618.1].

Gadd, Ian, *The History of Oxford University Press, Volume I: Beginnings to 1780* (Oxford: Oxford University Press, 2013).

Gale, J.S., *John Joscelyn's Notebook: A Study of the Contents and Sources of B.L., Cotton MS. Vitellius D. vii*, unpubl. M.Phil. thesis, University of Nottingham, 1978.

Gardner, William B., 'George Hickes and his "Thesaurus"', *Notes and Queries*, 200 (1955), pp. 196–199. [1703/5.1].

Garfield, Simon, *Just My Type: A Book about Fonts* (London: Profile, 2010).

Gaskell, Philip, *A New Introduction to Bibliography* (Oxford: Clarendon Press, 1972). [1568.1].

Gaskell, Philip, 'A Nomenclature for the Letter-forms of Roman Type', *The Library*, v.29 (1974), pp. 42–51.

Gessner, Christian F., *Die so nöthig als nützliche Buchdruckerkunst und Schriftgiesserey*, 2 vols (Leipzig: Gessner, 1740, repr. Hannover, 1981). [CAS 5].

Gibson, Margaret, T.A. Heslop & Richard W. Pfaff (eds), *The Eadwine Psalter: Text, Image, and Monastic Culture in Twelfth-Century Canterbury*, Publications of the Modern Humanities Research Association 14 (London, 1992).

Gillespie, Raymond, 'Irish Printing in the Early Seventeenth Century', *Journal of Irish Economic and Social History*, 15 (1988), pp. 81–88.

Gladstone, Jo, '*New World of English Words*: John Ray, FRS, the Dialect Protagonist, in the Context of his Times (1658–1691)', in J. Considine (ed.), *The Seventeenth Century*, Ashgate Critical Essays on Early English Lexicographers 4 (Farnham: Ashgate, 2012), 261–299. [1691.3]

Gneuss, Helmut, 'Der älteste Katalog der angelsächsischen Handschriften und seine Nachfolger', in idem, *Books and Libraries in Early England* (Aldershot: Variorum, 1996). [1689.3].

Gneuss, Helmut, 'Humfrey Wanley borrows Books in Cambridge', *Transactions of the Cambridge Bibliographical Society*, 12.2 (2001), pp. 145–160.

Gneuss, Helmut, *Handlist of Anglo-Saxon Manuscripts: A List of Manuscripts and Manuscript Fragments Written or Owned in England up to 1100*, Medieval and Renaissance Texts and Studies 241 (Tempe, AZ, 2001). This list supercedes idem, 'A Preliminary List of Manuscripts written or owned in England up to 1100', *Anglo-Saxon England*, 9 (1981), pp. 1–60. Superceded by next.

Gneuss, Helmut & Michael Lapidge, *Anglo-Saxon Manuscripts: A Bibliographical Handlist of Manuscripts and Manuscript Fragments written or owned in England up to 1100* (Toronto: University of Toronto Press, 2014). Supercedes prec.

Godden, Malcolm, *Ælfric's Catholic Homilies*, EETS ss 5 (London: Oxford University Press, 1979). [1566.1, 1570.1].

Godden, Malcolm & Susan Irvine, *The Old English Boethius*, 2 vols (Oxford: Oxford University Press, 2009). [1655.1].

Gödel, Vilhelm, *Katalog öfver Upsala Universitets Biblioteks fornisländska och fornorska Handskrifter*, Skrifter utgifna af Humanistiska vetenskapssamfundet i Upsala, II.1 (Uppsala: Almqvist & Wiksell, 1892). [1689.3].

Gödel, Vilhelm, *Katalog öfver Kongl. Bibliotekets Fornisländska och Fornnorska Handskrifter* (Stockholm: P.A. Norstedt, 1897–1900). [1703/5.1].

Goines, David L., *A Constructed Roman Alphabet: A Geometric Analysis of the Greek and Roman Capitals and of the Arabic Numerals* (Boston: D.R. Godine, 1982).

Goldschmidt, E. Ph., *Medieval Texts and their First Appearance in Print* (London: Bibliographical Society, 1943).

Gollancz, Israel, *The Cædmon Manuscript of Anglo-Saxon Biblical Poetry, Junius XI in the Bodleian Library* (London: Oxford University Press, 1927). [1655.2].

Gonser, Paul, *Das angelsächsische Prosa-Leben des hl. Guthlac*, Anglistische Forschungen 27 (Heidelberg: Winter, 1909). [1639.2].

Görlach, Manfred, *Explorations in English Historical Linguistics*, ch. 2: 'English Etymology 1617–1882' (Heidelberg: Winter, 2002), pp. 71–136. [1671.3, 1689.1].

Gough, Richard, *British Topography: Or, an Historical Account what has been done for illustrating the Topographical Antiquities of Great Britain and Ireland* (London; for T. Payne & Son, &J. Nichols, 1780). [1663.1].

Graham, Timothy, 'A Parkerian Transcript of the List of Bishop Leofric's Procurements for Exeter Cathedral: Matthew Parker, The Exeter Book, and Cambridge University Library MS Ii.2.11', *Transactions of the Cambridge Bibliographical Society*, X.4 (1994), pp. 421–59.

Graham, Timothy, 'Abraham Wheelock's Use of CCCC MS 41 (Old English Bede) and the Borrowing of Manuscripts from the Library of Corpus Christi College', *Cambridge Bibliographical Society Newsletter* (Summer 1997a), pp. 10–16.

Graham, Timothy, 'The Beginnings of Old English Studies: Evidence from the Manuscripts of Matthew Parker', in Sato 1997b, pp. 29–50.

Graham, Timothy, 'Robert Talbot's "Old Saxonice Bede": Cambridge University Library, MS Kk.3.18 and the "Alphabetum Norwagicum" of British Library, Cotton MSS, Domitian A.ix', in Carley & Tite, *Books and Collectors* (1997c), pp. 295–316.

Graham, Timothy, 'Early Modern Users of Claudius B.iv: Robert Talbot and William L'Isle', in *The Old English Hexateuch*, ed. R. Barnhouse & B.C. Withers, Medieval Institute Publications (Kalamazoo MI: Western Michigan University, 2000a), pp. 287–293. [1623.1].

Graham, Timothy (ed.), *The Recovery of Old English: Anglo-Saxon Studies in the Sixteenth and Seventeenth Centuries*, Medieval Institute Publications (Kalamazoo MI: Western Michigan University, 2000b).

Graham, Timothy, 'Anglo-Saxon Studies: Sixteenth to Eighteenth Centuries', in *A Companion to Anglo-Saxon Literature*, ed. P. Pulsiano & E. Treharne (Oxford: Blackwell, 2001), pp. 415–433.

Gransden, Antonia, 'Antiquarian Studies in Fifteenth-Century England', *The Antiquaries Journal*, 60 (1980), pp. 75–97.

Grant, R.J.S., 'A Note on *The Seasons for Fasting*', *Review of English Studies*, n.s. 23 (1972), pp. 302–304. [1643.1].

Greg, W.W., *English Literary Autographs 1550–1650*, 3 pts + supplement (London: Oxford University Press, 1925–32). [1605.1].

Greg, W.W., *A Bibliography of the English Printed Drama to the Restoration*, 3 vols (London: Bibliographical Society, 1939–57). [1640.2].

Greg, W.W., *A Companion to Arber* (Oxford: Clarendon Press, 1967).

Greg, W.W. and E. Boswell, *Records of the Court of the Stationers' Company 1576 to 1602—from Register B* (London: Bibliographical Society, 1930). [1596.1].

Grein, C.W.M., *Bibliothek der angelsächsischen Poesie* (Göttingen: Wigand, 1857). [1698.1].

Gross, Charles, ed. E.B. Graves, *A Bibliography of English History to 1485* (Oxford: Clarendon Press, 1975).

Gruys, J.A., & C. de Wolf, *Thesaurus 1473–1800: Dutch Printers and Booksellers With places and years of activity*, Bibliotheca Bibliographica Neerlandica 28 (Nieuwkoop: De Graaf, 1989).

Gumbert, J.P., 'The *Willeram* Goes to Print', *Quaerendo*, 5 (1975), pp. 205–217. [1655.1].

Gunther, Robert W. T., *Further Correspondence of John Ray* (London: Ray Society, 1928). [1691.3].

Haddan, A.W. & W. Stubbs, *Councils and Ecclesiastical Documents*, 3 vols (Oxford: Clarendon Press, 1869–73). [1567.1].

Hagedorn, Suzanne C., 'Matthew Parker and Asser's *Ælfredi Regis Res Gestæ*', *Princeton University Library Chronicle*, 51 (1989), pp. 74–90. [1574.2].

Hagedorn, Suzanne C., 'Received Wisdom: The Reception History of Alfred's Preface to the Pastoral Care', in A.J. Frantzen & J.D. Niles (eds), *Anglo-Saxonism and Construction of Social Identity* (Gainsville: University Press of Florida, 1997), pp. 86–107. [1678.1].

Haller, William, *Foxe's Book of Martyrs and the Elect Nation* (London: Cape, 1967). [1570.1, 1571.1].

Hamper, William, *The Life, Diary, and Correspondence of Sir William Dugdale, Knight, sometime Garter principal King of Arms* (London: Harding, Lepard & Co., 1827). [1664.1].

Handover, P.M., *Printing in London from 1476 to Modern Times* (London: Allen & Unwin, 1960). [Henry Bynneman].

Hardwick, Charles, *Historia Monasterii S. Augustini Cantuariensis by Thomas of Elmham*, RS 8 (London: Longman, Brown, Green, Longmans, and Roberts, 1858). [1703–5.1].

Hardy, Thomas Duffus, *Descriptive Catalogue of Materials relating to the History of Great Britain and Ireland (to 1327)*, 3 vols, RS 26 (London: Longman, Green, Longman, and Roberts, 1862–71).

Hargreaves, Geoffrey D., 'Florentine Script, Paduan Script, and Roman Type', *Gutenberg-Jahrbuch*, 67 (1992), pp. 15–34.

Harmer, F.E., *Select English Historical Documents of the Ninth and Tenth Centuries* (Cambridge: Cambridge University Press, 1914). [1574.2, 1652.1, 1703/5.1].

Harmer, F.E., *Anglo-Saxon Writs* (Manchester: Manchester University Press, 1952; repr. Stamford: Paul Watkins, 1989). [1695.2, 1702.1].

Harms, Hans, *Themen alter Karten* (Oldenburg: Völker, 1979). [1636.2].

Harris, Oliver D., 'William Camden, Philemon Holland and the 1610 Translation of *Britannia*', *The Antiquaries Journal*, 95 (2015), pp. 279–303. [1610.5].

Harris, R.L., 'George Hickes, White Kennet, and the Inception of the *Thesaurus Linguarum Septentrionalium*', *Bodleian Library Record*, 11 (1983), pp. 169–86. [1703/5.1].

Harris, Richard L., *A Chorus of Grammars: The Correspondence of George Hickes and his Collaborators on* Thesaurus linguarum septentrionalium, Publications of the Dictionary of Old English 4 (Toronto: Pontifical Institute of Mediaeval Studies, 1992). [1703/5.1].

Harris, Richard L., 'George Hickes (1642–1715)', in *Medieval Scholarship: Biographical Studies on the Formation of a Discipline*, vol. 2: Literature and Philology, ed. H. Damico, with D. Fennema & K. Lenz (New York: Garland, 1998), pp. 19–32. [1689.3, 1703/5.1].

Harrison, Julian, 'William Camden and the F-text of the *Anglo-Saxon Chronicle*', *Notes and Queries*, 252 (2007), pp. 222–224. [1607.2].

Harsley, Fred, *Eadwine's Canterbury Psalter*, EETS os 92 (London: Trübner, 1889). [1640.3].

Hart, C.R., *The Early Charters of Eastern England*, Studies in Early English History 5 (Leicester: Leicester University Press, 1966). [1639.4].

Hart, Cyril R., *The Early Charters of Essex*, Department of English Local History Occasional Papers, ser. 1, no. 10 (Leicester: Leicester University Press, 1971). [1703/5.1].

Hart, C.R., *The Early Charters of Northern England and the North Midlands*, Studies in Early English History 6 (Leicester: Leicester University Press, 1975).

Hart, Horace, *Notes on a Century of Typography at the University Press Oxford 1693–1794*, ed. H. Carter (Oxford: Clarendon Press, 1970). [1567.1, 1693.2, 1695.1].

Hazeltine, Harold D., 'Selden as Legal Historian: A Comment in Criticism and Appreciation', in *Festschrift Heinrich Brunner zum Siebzigsten Geburtstag*, dargetracht von Schülern und Verehren (Weimar: Böhlau, 1910), pp. 579–630.

Hearne, Thomas, *Hemingi Chartularium Ecclesiæ Wigorniensis*, 2 vols (Oxford: Sheldonian Theatre, 1723). [1655.3].

Hearne, Thomas, *Chronicon, sive Annales Prioratus de Dunstaple, una cum excerptis e chartulario ejusdem prioratus* (Oxford: Sheldonian Theatre, 1733).

Hearne, Thomas, *Remarks and Collections of Thomas Hearne*, vol. I, ed. C.E. Doble, Oxford Historical Society Publications II (Oxford, 1885). [1703/5.1].

Helgerson, Richard, *Forms of Nationhood: The Elizabethan Writing of England* (Chicago: Chicago University Press, 1992). [1612.1].

Hellinga, Lotte, A. Duke, J. Harskamp & T. Hermans, *The Bookshop of the World: The Role of the Low Countries in the Book-Trade 1473–1941* ('t Goy-Houten: Hes & de Graaf, 2001).

Hellinga, Lotte & J.B. Trapp, *The Cambridge History of the Book in Britain, vol. III, 1400–1557* (Cambridge: Cambridge University Press, 1999).

Hellinga, Wytze Gs., *Copy and Print in the Netherlands: An Atlas of Historical Bibliography* (Amsterdam: Federatie der Werkgeversorganisatiën in het Boekdrukkersbedrijf, 1962).

Herendeen, Wyman H., *William Camden* (Woodbridge: Boydell, 2007). [1586.1].

Hermannsson, Halldór, *Icelandic Manuscripts*, Islandica 19 (Ithaca: Cornell University Library, 1929). [1703/5.1].

Hetherington, M. Sue, 'Sir Simonds D'Ewes and Method in Old English Lexicography', *Texas Studies in Language and Literature*, 17 (1975), pp. 75–92.

Hetherington, M. Sue, *The Beginnings of Old English Lexicography* (Spicewood TX, privately printed, 1980). [1650.1, 1652.1, 1659.1].

Heyworth, P.L., *Letters of Humfrey Wanley Palaeographer, Anglo-Saxonist, Librarian 1672–1726* (Oxford: Clarendon Press, 1989).

Hill, Betty, 'Trinity College Cambridge MS. B.14.52, and William Patten', *Transactions of the Cambridge Bibliographical Society*, IV.3 (1966), pp. 192–200. [1566.1].

Hind, Arthur M., *Engraving in England in the Sixteenth & Seventeenth Centuries: A Descriptive Catalogue with Introductions*, 3 vols, vol. III completed by M. Corbett & M. Norton (Cambridge: Cambridge University Press, 1952–64). [1612.1, 1613.1].

Hines, John, *The Scandinavian Character of Anglian England in the Pre-Viking Period*, British Archaeological Records, British series 124 (Oxford: BAR, 1984).

Hinton, David A., *A Catalogue of the Anglo-Saxon Ornamental Metalwork, 700–100: in the Department of Antiquities, Ashmolean Museum* (Oxford: Clarendon Press, 1974). [1700.4]

Hoare, Richard C., et al., *Registrum Wiltunense, Saxonicum et Latinum* (London: typis Nicholsianis, 1827). [1661.1].

Hobson, G.D., *Bindings in Cambridge Libraries* (Cambridge: Cambridge University Press, 1929). [1623.1].

Holthausen, Ferdinand, 'Ein altenglisches Gedicht über die Fastenzeiten', *Anglia*, 71 (1952–3), pp. 191–201. [1643.1].

Hombergen, Jan, 'Some Remarks on the Spelman Psalter', *Amsterdamer Beiträge zur älteren Germanistik*, 19 (1983), 105–137. [1640.3].

Howe, E., 'The Le Bé Family: Typefounders, Printers, Paper Merchants, Engravers and Writing Masters, 1525–1730', *Signature*, 8 (1938), pp. 1–27.

Howlett, D.R., 'Two Old English Encomia', *English Studies*, 57 (1976), 289–93. [1652.1].

Hughes, L., 'Sir Thomas Smith: Elizabethan Author and Book Collector', in *The Book Trade in Early Modern England: Practices, Perceptions, Connections*, ed. J. Hinks & V. Gardner (New Castle DE: Oak Knoll Press, & London: British Library, 2014,) pp. 87–105. [1568.3].

Hughes, Shaun F.D., 'The Anglo-Saxon Grammars of George Hickes and Elizabeth Elstob', in Berkhout and Gatch, *Anglo-Saxon Scholarship*, pp. 119–147. [1689.3].

Huisstede, P. van, & J.P.J. Brandhorst, *Dutch Printer's Devices 15th–17th Century: A Catalogue* (Nieuwkoop: De Graaf, 1999). [1636.3].

Hüllen, Werner, *English Dictionaries 800–1700: The Topical Tradition* (Oxford: Clarendon Press, 1999). [1668.1]

Hunt, William, *Two Chartularies of the Priory of St. Peter at Bath*, Somerset Record Society Publications 7 (London: Harrison & sons, 1893). [1702.1, 1703/5.1].

Hunter, Michael, 'The Facsimiles in Thomas Elmham's History of St. Augustine's, Canterbury', *The Library*, v.28 (1973), pp. 215–220.

Hurst, Clive, *Catalogue of the Wren Library of Lincoln Cathedral: Books printed before 1801* (Cambridge: Cambridge University Press, 2005). [1698.1].

Ingram, James, *An Inaugural Lecture on the Utility of Anglo-Saxon Literature* (Oxford: Oxford University Press, 1807).

Isaac, Frank, 'Elizabethan Roman and Italic Types', *The Library*, IV.14 (1933), pp. 85–100, 212–228. [1566.1, 1568.1, 1568.2].

Isaac, Frank, *English & Scottish Printing Types 1535–58 * 1552–58*, Bibliographical Society Facsimiles and Illustrations iii (London: Oxford University Press, 1932).

Isaac, Frank, *English Printers' Types of the Sixteenth Century* (London: Oxford University Press, 1936). [1567.1].

Jackson, William A., *Records of the Court of the Stationers' Company 1602 to 1640* (London: Bibliographical Society, 1957). [1610.3].

James, Montague R., *A Descriptive Catalogue of the Manuscripts in the Library of Corpus Christi College Cambridge*, 2 vols (Cambridge: Cambridge University Press, 1912).

James, Montague R., *The Canterbury Psalter* (London: P. Lund, Humphries & Co., 1935).

Jane, L.C., *Asser's Life of King Alfred: Translated with Inroduction and Notes*, King's Classics (London: Chatto & Windus, 1908). [1574.2].

Jayne, Sears, & Francis R. Johnson, *The Lumley Library: The Catalogue of 1609* (London: British Museum, 1956). [1568.2, 1572.1, 1574.1, 1574.2].

Jessup, Frank W., *Sir Roger Twysden, 1597–1672* (London: Cresset Press, 1965). [1652.1].

Jeudwine, Wynne, *Art and Style in Printed Books: Six Centuries of Typography, Decoration & Illustration*, vol. I, *The Fifteenth and Sixteenth Centuries* (London: privately printed, 1979).

Jimenes, Rémi, 'Reconsidering Pierre Haultin's Early Career: Roots, Training, Beginnings (1546–1550)', *The Library*, VII.18 (2017), pp. 62–80.

Joan, M., r.s.m., 'Minsheu's *Guide into the Tongues* and Somner's *Dictionarium*', *Mediaeval Studies*, 24 (1962), pp. 375–377. [1617.1, 1659.1].

Johnson, A.F., *Type Designs: Their History and Development* (London: Grafton, 1934a; 2nd edn 1959; 3rd edn London: Deutsch, 1966).

Johnson, A.F., *A Catalogue of Engraved and Etched English Title-Pages down to the death of William Faithorne, 1691* (London: Bibliographical Society, 1934b).

Johnson, A.F., 'Sources of Roman and Italic Types used by English Printers in the Sixteenth Century', *The Library*, IV.17 (1937), pp. 70–82.

Johnson, A.F., 'The Italic Types of Robert Granjon', *The Library*, IV.21 (1941), pp. 291–308, also in his *Selected Essays*, ed. Muir, pp. 260–71.

Johnson, A.F., *Selected Essays on Books and Printing*, ed. P.H. Muir (Amsterdam: Van Gendt, 1970).

Johnson, A.F., 'Some Types Used by Paolo Manuzio', in his *Selected Essays*, ed. Muir, pp. 255–259. [1572.1].

Johnson, A.F. & Stanley Morison, 'The Chancery Types of Italy and France', *The Fleuron*, 3 (1924), pp. 23–51.

Johnson, John & Strickland Gibson, *Print and Privilege at Oxford to the year 1700*, Oxford Bibliographical Society 7 (Oxford: Oxford University Press, 1946).

Juel-Jensen, Bent, 'Bibliography of the Early Editions of the Writings of Michael Drayton', in *The Works of Michael Drayton*, ed. J.W. Hebel, 5 vols (Oxford: Blackwell, 1961), V, 265–306. [1612.1, 1613.1, 1622.1].

Karasawa, Kazutomo, *The Old English Metrical Calendar (Menologium)* (Cambridge: Brewer, 2015). [1703/5.1].

Keleman, Erick, 'A Reexamination of the Date of A Testimonie of Antiquitie, One of the First Books Printed in Anglo-Saxon Types', *American Notes and Queries*, 10.4 (1997), pp. 3–10. [1566.1].

Kelley, Donald R., *Foundations of Modern Historical Scholarship: Language, Law, and History in the French Renaissance* (New York: Columbia University Press, 1970). [1614.3].

Kelly, Rob R., *American Wood Type 1828–1900: Notes on the Evolution of Decorated and Large Types and Comments on Related Trades of the Period* (New York: Van Nostrand Reinhold Co., 1969 repr. New York: Da Capo Press, 1977).

Kelly, S.E., *Charters of St Paul's, London*, Anglo-Saxon Charters 10 (Oxford: Oxford University Press, 2004). [1658.1].

Kemble, John M., *Codex Diplomaticus Aevi Saxonici*, 6 vols (London: English Historical Society, 1839–48). [1639.4].

Kendrick, T.D., *British Antiquity* (London: Methuen, 1950). [1605.1].

Kendrick, T.D., T.J. Brown, R.L.S. Bruce-Mitford, H. Roosen-Runge, A.S.C. Ross, E.G. Stanley, A.E. Werner, *Evangeliorum Quattuor Codex Lindisfarnensis Musei Britannici Codex Cottonianus Nero D. IV*, 2 vols (Oltun & Lausanne: Urs Graf, 1956). [1605.1, 1652.1].

Ker, N.R., *Catalogue of Manuscripts containing Anglo-Saxon* (Oxford: Clarendon Press, 1957, rev. edn 1991).

Ker, N.R., *Medieval Libraries of Great Britain: A List of Surviving Books* (London: Royal Historical Society, 1964 edn, and *Supplement*, ed. A.G. Watson, 1987).

Ker, N. R., 'Hemming's Cartulary: a description of the two Worcester Cartularies in Cotton Tiberius A xiii', in *Studies in Medieval History presented to Frederick Maurice Powicke*, ed. R. W. Hunt, W. A. Pantin, R. W. Southern (Oxford: Clarendon Press, 1948), repr in Ker's *Books, Collectors and Libraries*, ed. Andrew G. Watson (London: Hambledon, 1985), 31–59.

Ker, N.R., 'Medieval Manuscripts from Norwich Cathedral Priory', *Transactions of the Cambridge Bibliographical Society*, 1.1 (1949), pp. 1–28. [Robert Talbot].

Ker, N.R., *The Pastoral Care: King Alfred's Translation of St. Gregory's Regula Pastoralis (MS Hatton 20 in the Bodleian Library at Oxford, MS Cotton Tiberius B.xi in the British Museum, MS Anhang 19 in the Landesbibliothek at Kassel)*, EEMF 6 (Copenhagen: Rosenkilde & Bagger, 1956). [1568.1].

Kerling, Johan, *Chaucer in Early English Dictionaries: The Old-Word Tradition in English Lexicography down to 1721 and Speght's Chaucer Glossaries* (Leiden: University Press, 1979). [1617.1, 1658.4, 1671.3]

Keuning, J., 'The Novus Atlas of Johannes Janssonius', *Imago Mundi*, 8 (1951), pp. 71–98. [1646.3, 1659.2].

Keynes, Geoffrey, *John Ray, 1627–1705: A Bibliography 1660–1970* (London: Faber, 1951; repr. Amsterdam: Van Heusden, 1976). [1674.2, 1691.3].

Keynes, Simon, 'The Lost Cartulary of Abbotsbury', *Anglo-Saxon England*, 18 (1989), pp. 207–243. [1655.3].

Keynes, Simon, 'The Discovery and First Publication of the Alfred Jewel', *Somerset Archaeology and Natural History*, 136 (1992), pp. 1–8. [1703/5.1].

Keynes, Simon, 'The "Dunstan B" Charters', *Anglo-Saxon England*, 23 (1994), pp. 165–193. [1702.1].

Keynes, Simon, 'The Reconstruction of a Burnt Cottonian Manuscript: The Case of Cotton MS. Otho A.1', *The British Library Journal*, 22 (1996a), pp. 113–160. [1689.3, 1703/5.1].

Keynes, Simon, 'Giso, Bishop of Wells (1061–88)', *Anglo-Norman Studies*, 19 (1996b), pp. 203–271. [1655.3, 1703/5.1].

Keynes, Simon, *The Liber Vitae of the New Minster and Hyde Abbey Winchester British Library Stowe 944*, EEMF 26 (Copenhagen: Rosenkilde & Bagger, 1996c). [1574.1, 1574.2].

Keynes, Simon, 'The Cult of King Alfred', *Anglo-Saxon England*, 28 (1999), pp. 225–356. [1678.1].

Keynes, Simon, 'The Power of the Written Word: Alfredian England 871–899', in *Alfred the Great*, ed. T. Reuter (Aldershot: Ashgate, 2003), pp. 175–197. [1703/5.1].

Keynes, Simon, 'Anglo-Saxon Charters: Lost and Found', in *Myth, Rulership, Church and Charters: Essays in Honour of Nicholas Brooks*, ed. J. Barrow & A. Wareham (Aldershot: Ashgate, 2008), pp. 45–66. [1703/5.1].

Keynes, Simon, 'Mapping the Anglo-Saxon Past', in *Towns and Topography: Essays in Memory of David H. Hill*, ed. G.R. Owen-Crocker & S.D. Thompson (Oxford: Oxbow, 2014), pp. 147–170. [1568.2].

Kiessling, Nicolas, *The Library of Anthony Wood* (Oxford: Oxford Bibliographical Society, 2002). [1566.2].

Kimmens, Andrew C., *The Stowe Psalter*, Toronto OE Series 3 (Toronto: University of Toronto Press, 1979). [1640.3].

Kinane, Vincent & Anne Walsh (eds), *Essays on the History of Trinity College Library, Dublin* (Dublin: Four Courts Press, 2000).

King, John N., '"The Light of Printing": William Tyndale, John Foxe, John Day, and Early Modern Print Culture', *Renaissance Quarterly*, 54 (2001), pp. 52–85.

King, John N., *Foxe's Book of Martyrs and Early Modern Print Culture* (Cambridge: Cambridge University Press, 2006). [1570.1].

Kirk, R.E.G. & Ernest F. Kirk, *Returns of Aliens dwelling in the City and Suburbs of London from the Reign of Henry VIII to that of James I*, 4 vols, Publications of the Huguenot Society of London 10 (Aberdeen: Aberdeen University Press, 1900–8).

Kleerkooper, M.M., & W.P. van Stockum Jr, *De Boekhandel te Amsterdam voornamelijk in de 17ᵉ Eeuw*, 2 vols (The Hague: Nijhoff, 1914–16). [1695.5].

Kleist, Aaron J., 'Monks, Marriage, and Manuscripts: Matthew Parker's Manipulation (?) of Ælfric of Eynsham', *Journal of English and Germanic Philology*, 105 (2006), pp. 312–327. [1567.1].

Kleist, Aaron J., 'Matthew Parker, Old English, and the Defense of Priestly Marriage', in *Anglo-Saxon Books and their Readers: Essays in Celebration of Helmut Gneuss's 'Handlist of Anglo-Saxon Manuscripts'*, ed. T.N. Hall & D. Scragg (Kalamazoo: Medieval Institute, 2008), pp. 106–133. [1567.1].

Knappe, Gabriele, 'Theory meets Empiricism: English Lexis in John Wilkins' Philosophical Language and the Role of William Lloyd', in J. Considine (ed.), *The Seventeenth Century*, Ashgate Critical Essays on Early English Lexicographers 4 (Farnham: Ashgate, 2012), 301–321. [1668.1]

Koeman, Cornelis, *Joan Blaeu and his Grand Atlas* (Amsterdam: Theatrum Orbis Terrarum, 1970). [1645.1, 1648.1, 1648.2, 1659.3, 1662.2, 1662.3, 1662.4].

Koeman, Cornelis, *Atlantes Neerlandici: Bibliography of Terrestrial, Maritime and Celestial Atlases and Pilot Books, published in the Netherlands up to 1880*, 5 vols (Amsterdam: Theatrum Orbis Terrarum, 1967–71). [1645.1, 1646.3, 1646.4, 1647.3, 1648.1, 1648.2, 1659.2, 1659.3, 1662.2, 1662.3, 1662.4] See also Krogt.

Kornexl, Lucia, *Die 'Regularis Concordia' und ihre altenglische Interlinearversion* (Munich: Fink, 1993). [1623.3].

Korsten, Frans, 'The Elzeviers and England', in *The Bookshop of the World: The Role of the Low Countries in the Book-Trade 1473–1941*, ed. L. Hellinga, A. Duke, J. Harskamp, T. Hermans ('t Goy-Houten: Hes & de Graaf, 2001), pp. 131–143. [1635.1].

Kossmann, E.F., *De Boekhandel te 's-Gravenhage tot het Eind van de 18de Eeuw*, Bijdragen tot de Geschiedenis van den Nederlandschen Boekhandel 13 (The Hague: Nijhoff, 1937), pp. 435–453. [Adriaen Vlack].

Kotzor, Günter, *Das altenglische Martyrologium*, 2 vols (Munich: Bayerische Akademie der Wissenschaften, Philosophisch-Historische Klasse 67–68, 1981). [1626.1].

Krapp, George P., *The Junius Manuscript*, ASPR 1 (New York: Columbia University Press, 1931). [1655.2].

Krapp, George P., *The Paris Psalter and the Meters of Boethius*, ASPR V (New York: Columbia University Press, 1932). [1703/5.1].

Krogt, Peter van der, *Koeman's Atlantes Neerlandici* ('t Goy-Houten: HES, 1997–2010). [1645.1, 1646.3, 1646.4, 1647.3, 1648.1, 1648.2, 1659.2, 1659.3, 1662.2, 1662.3, 1662.4].

Kunst, C., 'William Camden's *Britannia*: History and Historiography', in *Ancient History and the Antiquarian: Essays in Memory of Arnaldo Momigliano*, ed. M.H. Crawford & C.R. Ligota, Warburg Institute Colloquia 2 (London: Warburg Institute, 1995), pp. 117–131. [1586.1].

Lambarde, William, *Dictionarium Angliae Topographicum & Historicum: An alphabetical description of the chief places in England and Wales* (London: for Fletcher Gyles, 1730).

Lane, John A., 'Arthur Nicholls and his Greek Type for the King's Printing House', *The Library*, VI.13 (1991), pp. 297–322. [1634.1].

Lane, John A., 'Identifying Typefaces', *The Library*, VI.14 (1992), pp. 357–365. [1566.1, 1576.1].

Lane, John A., *The Enschedé Type Specimens of 1768 & 1773: A Facsimile with an Introduction and Notes*, The Enschedé Font Foundry (Haarlem: Stichting Museum Enschedé, 1993).

Lane, John A. 'Arent Corsz Hogenacker (ca. 1579–1636): An Account of his Typefoundry and a Note on his Types', *Quaerendo*, 25 (1995), pp. 83–113, 163–191.

Lane, John A., *Early Type-Specimens in the Plantin-Moretus Museum* (London: British Library, 2004). [1700?.1].

Lane, John A., *The Diaspora of Armenian Printing 1512–2012* (Amsterdam and Yerevan: University of Amsterdam, 2012). [van Dijck].

Lane, John A., 'Peter de Walpergen His Training & Later Work in Oxford', in *Dutch Types used in the English Book of Common Prayer*, ed. Christopher G. Manson & Seth Rash (Baltimore MD: Hill Press, 2014 (= 2020)), pp. 7–20. [Walpergen; AS8].

Langefeld, Brigitte, *The Old English Version of the Enlarged Rule of Chrodegang*, Münchner Universitätsschriften Texte und Untersuchungen zur englischen Philologie 26 (Frankfurt-am-Main: Lang, 2003). [1567.1].

Lapidge, Michael & Michael Herren, *Aldhelm The Prose Works* (Ipswich: Brewer, 1979). [1632.3].

Ledeboer, A.M., *Het Geslacht Van Waesberghe ...* (The Hague, 1869).

Lerer, Seth, 'Old English and its Afterlife', in *The Cambridge History of Medieval English Literature*, ed. D. Wallace (Cambridge: Cambridge University Press, 1999).

Lerer, Seth, 'The Anglo-Saxon Pindar: Old English Scholarship and Augustan Criticism in George Hickes's *Thesaurus*', *Modern Philology*, 99 (2001), pp. 26–65. [1703/05.1].

Levine, Joseph M., *The Battle of the Books: History and Literature in the Augustan Age* (Ithaca & London: Cornell University Press, 1991). [1692.1, 1695.3, 1702.1, 1703/5.1].

Levison, Wilhelm, *England and the Continent in the Eighth Century* (Oxford: Clarendon Press, 1946).

Levy, F.J., 'The Making of Camden's *Britannia*', *Bibliothèque d'Humanisme et Renaissance*, 26 (1964), pp. 70–98. [1586.1].

Levy, F.J., *Tudor Historical Thought* (San Marino CA: Huntington Library, 1967). [1586.1, 1607.2].

Liebermann, F., *Die Gesetze der Angelsachsen*, 3 vols (Halle: Niemeyer, 1903–16). [1566.1, 1568.2, 1574.1].

Liebermann, F., *Die Heiligen Englands* (Hannover: Hahn, 1889). [1639.2].

Liebermann, Felix, 'Notes on the Textus Roffensis', *Archaeologia Cantiana* 23 (1898), pp. 101–112. [1576.1].

Likhachev, see Simmons.

Liuzza, R.M., *The Old English Version of the Gospels*, 2 vols, EETS os 304 & 314 (Oxford, Oxford University Press, 1994/2000). [1571.1].

Liuzza, R.M., *Anglo-Saxon Prognostics* (Cambridge: Brewer, 2011). [1623.3].

Lowe, E.A., *Codices Latini Antiquiores, part II, Great Britain and Ireland* (Oxford: Clarendon Press, 1935).

Lowe, Kathryn A., '"As Fre as Thowt"?: Some Medieval Copies and Translations of Old English Wills', *English Manuscript Studies 1100–1700*, 4 (1993), pp. 1–23.

Loyn, H.R., *A Wulfstan Manuscript containing Institutes, Laws and Homilies: British Museum Cotton Nero A.I*, EEMF 17 (Copenhagen: Rosenkilde & Bagger, 1971). [1566.1].

Lucas, Peter J., *Exodus* (London: Methuen, 1977), 2nd edn (Exeter University Press, 1994), 3rd edn (Liverpool University Press, 2020). [1655.2].

Lucas, Peter J., 'A Testimonye of Verye Ancient Tyme? Some Manuscript Models for the Parkerian Anglo-Saxon Type-Designs', in *Of the Making of Books: Medieval Manuscripts, their Scribes and Readers: Essays presented to M.B. Parkes*, ed. P.R. Robinson & R. Zim (Aldershot: Scolar, 1997), pp. 147–188.

Lucas, Peter J., 'Junius, his Printers and his Types: An Interim Report', in *Franciscus Junius and his Circle*, ed. R.H. Bremmer Jr (Amsterdam: Rodopi, 1998), pp. 177–197. [1655.1, 1655.2].

Lucas, Peter J., 'Parker, Lambarde, and the Provision of Special Sorts for Printing Anglo-Saxon in the Sixteenth Century', *Journal of the Printing Historical Society*, 28 (1999), pp. 41–69.

Lucas, Peter J., 'Sixteenth-Century English Spelling Reformers and the Printers in Continental Perspective: Sir Thomas Smith and John Hart', *The Library*, VII.1 (2000a), pp. 3–21.

Lucas, Peter J., 'Scribal Imitation of Earlier Handwriting: "Bastard Saxon" and its Impact', in M-C. Hubert, E. Poulle, M.H. Smith (eds), *Le Statut du Scripteur au Moyen Age:*

Actes du XIIe Colloque Scientifique du Comité International de Paléographie Latine (Cluny, 17–20 Juillet 1998), Matériaux pour l'Histoire publiés par l'École des Chartes 2 (Paris, 2000b), pp. 151–160.

Lucas, Peter J., *Franciscus Junius's Cædmonis Monachi Paraphrasis Poetica Genesios...*, Early Studies in Germanic Philology 3 (Amsterdam: Rodopi, 2000c). Re-issued as e-book (Leiden: Brill, 2021): https://doi.org/10.1163/9789004455948 [1655.2].

Lucas, Peter J., 'Cotton MS Domitian A.viii, the F-version of the *Anglo-Saxon Chronicle*, and William Camden', *Notes and Queries*, 247 (2001a), pp. 98–99. [1607.2].

Lucas, Peter J., 'Printing Anglo-Saxon in Holland and John Selden's *Mare Clausum seu de Dominio Maris*', *Quaerendo*, 31 (2001b), pp. 120–136. [1635.1, 1636.1, 1636.2, 1636.3].

Lucas, Peter J., 'John Minsheu, Polymath and Poseur: Old English in an Early Seventeenth-Century Dictionary', in *Of Dyuersitie & Chaunge of Langage: Essays presented to Manfred Görlach on the occasion of his 65th birthday*, ed. K. Lenz & R. Möhlig (Heidelberg: Winter, 2002), pp. 144–156. [1617.1].

Lucas, Peter J., 'From Politics to Practicalities: Printing Anglo-Saxon in the Context of Seventeenth-Century Scholarship', *The Library*, VII.4 (2003), pp. 28–48.

Lucas, Peter J., 'Abraham Whelock and the Presentation of Anglo-Saxon: From Manuscript To Print', in *Beatus Vir: Studies in Early English and Norse Manuscripts in Memory of Phillip Pulsiano*, ed. A.N. Doane & K. Wolf, Arizona Center for Medieval and Renaissance Studies 319 (Tempe AZ, 2006), pp. 383–439.

Lucas, Peter J., 'The Earliest Modern Anglo-Saxon Grammar: Sir Henry Spelman, Abraham Wheelock and William Retchford', *Anglo-Saxon England*, 45 (2016a), pp. 379–417.

Lucas, Peter J., *Corpus Christi College, Cambridge II: MSS 12, 144, 162, 178, 188, 198, 265, 285, 322, 326, 449*, ASMMF 25, MRTS 497 (Tempe AZ, 2016b).

Lucas, Peter J., 'William Camden, Seventeenth-Century Atlases of the British Isles and the Printing of Anglo-Saxon', *The Antiquaries Journal*, 98 (2018), 219–244.

Lucas, Peter J., 'A Conspectus of Letters to and from Sir Henry Spelman (1563/4–1641)', *The Antiquaries Journal*, 102 (2022), 370–388 + on-line supplement: doi:10.1017/S00035815220000026.

Lucas, Peter J., Alger N. Doane & I.C. Cunningham, *Latin Manuscripts with Anglo-Saxon Glosses*, ASMMF 5, MRTS 175 (Tempe AZ, 1997). [1652.1].

Lucas, Peter J., Timothy Graham, R.J.S. Grant, & Elaine M. Treharne, *Corpus Christi College, Cambridge I: MSS 41, 57, 191, 302, 303, 367, 383, 422*, ASMMF 11, MRTS 265 (Tempe AZ, 2003).

Lucas, Peter J. & Jonathan Wilcox, *Manuscripts Relating to Dunstan, Ælfric, and Wulfstan; the "Eadwine Psalter" Group*, ASMMF 16, MRTS 343 (Tempe AZ, 2008).

Lucas, Peter J. & Angela M. Lucas, *Manuscripts in France*, ASMMF 18, MRTS 381 (Tempe AZ, 2012).

Lutz, Angelika, 'Zur Rekonstruktion der Version G der angelsächsichen Chronik', *Anglia*, 95 (1977), pp. 1–19. [1643.1].

Lutz, Angelika, 'Das Studium der angelsächsischen Chronik im 16. Jahrhundert: Nowell und Joscelyn', *Anglia*, 100 (1982), pp. 301–356.

Lutz, Angelika, 'Zur Entstehungsgeschichte von William Somner's *Dictionarium Saxonico-Latino-Anglicum*', *Anglia*, 106 (1988), pp. 1–25. [1659.1].

Lutz, Angelika, 'The Study of the Anglo-Saxon Chronicle in the Seventeenth Century and the Establishment of Old English Studies in the Universities', in Graham, *Recovery*, pp. 1–82.

Madan, Falconer, *Oxford Books. A Bibliography of Printed Works Relating to the University and City of Oxford or Printed or Published There*, 3 vols (Oxford: Clarendon Press, 1895–1931). [1568.1, 1634.1, 1636.4, 1646.1, 1654.2, 1659.1].

Madan, Falconer, *A Brief Account of the University Press at Oxford with Illustrations together with a Chart of Oxford Printing* (Oxford: Clarendon Press, 1908).

Maddison, Francis, Dorothy Styles & Anthony Wood, *Sir William Dugdale 1605–1686: A list of his Printed Works and of his Portraits with Notes on his Life and the Manuscript Sources* (Warwick: L. Edgar Stephens for the Records and Museum Committee, Warks Co. Co., 1953). [1655.3, 1658.1, 1659.1, 1661.1, 1664.1, 1666.1, 1671.2, 1673.1, 1680.2, 1682.1].

Mais, S.P.B., *Britannia 1651–1951* (London & New York, 1951). [1646.3, 1659.2].

Marckwardt, Albert H., *Laurence Nowell's Vocabularium Saxonicum* (Ann Arbor: University of Michigan Press, 1952). [1650.3].

Marcus, Hans, *Das Frühmittelenglische "Poema Morale"*, Palaestra 194 (Leipzig: Mayer & Müller, 1934). [1678.1].

Mardersteig, Giovanni, 'Aldo Manuzio e i Caratteri di Francesco Griffo da Bologna', in *Studi di Bibliografia e di Storia in onore di Tamaro de Marinis*, 4 vols ([Verona: Stamperia Valdonega], 1964), III.105–147.

de la Mare, A.C., *The Handwriting of Italian Humanists* (Oxford: for the Association Internationale de Bibliophilie, 1973).

Marez Oyens, F.B. de, 'Jan Janssen as Counterfeiter and Pirate', *Quaerendo*, 9 (1979), pp. 350–352. [Janssonius].

Marsden, Richard, *The Old English Heptateuch and Ælfric's Libellus de Veteri Testamento et Novo*, EETS os 330 (Oxford: Oxford University Press, 2008). [1672.1, 1696.1].

Martin, Henri-Jean, *The History and Power of Writing*, t L.G. Cochrane (Chicago: University of Chicago Press, 1995). First published as *Histoire et Pouvoirs de l'Écrit*, 1988.

Martin, John (Librarian to the Duke of Bedford), *Bibliographical Catalogue of Books Privately Printed* (London: J. & A. Arch, Payne & Foss, J. Rodwell, 1834). [1572.1].

May, A., 'Making "Real" Type: Virtue Regained', *Printing Historical Society Bulletin*, 32 (1992), pp. 4–8.

Mayhew, Robert, 'Edmund Gibson's Editions of *Britannia*: Dynastic Chorography and the Particularist Politics of Precedent, 1695–1722', *Historical Research*, 73 (2000), pp. 239–261. [1695.3].

McGuinne, Dermot, *Irish Type Design* (Blackrock, Co. Dublin: Irish Academic Press, 1992). [1574.2].

McKenzie, D.F. & Maureen Bell, *A Chronology and Calendar of Documents relating to the London Book Trade, 1641–1700*, 3 vols (Oxford: Oxford University Press, 2005).

McKerrow, R.B., 'Some Notes on the Letters i, j, u, and v in Sixteenth Century Printing', *The Library*, III.1 (1910), pp. 239–259.

McKerrow, R.B., *Printers' & Publishers' Devices in England & Scotland 1485–1640*, Bibliographical Society Illustrated Monographs xvi (London: Bibliographical Society, 1949). [1568.1].

McKerrow, R.B., & F.S. Ferguson, *Title-Page Borders used in England & Scotland 1485–1640*, Bibliographical Society Illustrated Monographs xxi (London: Bibliographical Society, 1932); see also Ferguson 1936. [1570.1, 1572.1, 1574.1].

McKisack, May, *Medieval History in the Tudor Age* (Oxford: Clarendon Press, 1971). [1568.1].

McKitterick, David J., 'A Type-Specimen of Christoffel van Dijck?', *Quaerendo*, 7 (1977), pp. 66–75.

McKitterick, David J., *The Library of Sir Thomas Knyvett of Ashwellthorpe c.1539–1618*, CUL Historical Bibliography Series 3 (Cambridge: Cambridge University Press, 1978). [1571.1].

McKitterick, David, *Four Hundred Years of University Printing and Publishing in Cambridge 1584–1984. Catalogue of the Exhibition in The University Library Cambridge* (Cambridge: Cambridge University Press, 1984).

McKitterick, David J., 'The Eadwine Psalter Rediscovered' in *The Eadwine Psalter: Text, Image, and Monastic Culture in Twelfth-Century Canterbury*, ed. M. Gibson, T.A. Heslop & R.W. Pfaff (London: Modern Humanities Research Association, 1992a). [1640.3].

McKitterick, David J., *A History of Cambridge University Press, Volume 1, Printing and the Book Trade in Cambridge 1534–1698* (Cambridge: Cambridge University Press, 1992b). [Daniel].

McKitterick, David J., 'From Camden to Cambridge: Sir Robert Cotton's Roman Inscriptions, and their Subsequent Treatment', in Wright, *Sir Robert Cotton*, pp. 105–128. [1586.1].

McKitterick, David J., '"Not in STC": Opportunities and Challenges in the ESTC', *The Library*, VI.2 (2005), pp. 178–194.

McLean, Ruari (ed.), *Typographers on Type: An Illustrated Anthology from William Morris to the Present Day* (London: Lund Humphries, 1995).

McMurtrie, D.C., 'The Brothers Voskens and their Successors', *The Inland Printer* (Chicago), Oct. 1924, pp. 59–66. [1645.1].

McPherson, David, *Ben Jonson's Library and Marginalia*, Studies in Philology Texts and Studies 71 (Chapel Hill: University of North Carolina Press, 1974). [1640.2].

Mendyk, Stan A.E., *'Speculum Britanniae': Regional Study, Antiquarianism, and Science in Britain to 1700* (Toronto: University of Toronto Press, 1989). [1576.2, 1586.1].

Méron, J., *Orthotypographie: Recherches Bibliographiques* (Paris, 2002).

Millar, Eric G., *The Lindisfarne Gospels* (London: Trustees of the British Museum, 1923). [1652.1].

Miller, C. William, 'Henry Herringman, Restoration Bookseller-Publisher', *Papers of the Bibliographical Society of America*, 42 (1948), pp. 292–306. [1666.1].

Miller, Leo, 'Milton and Vlacq', *Papers of the Bibliographical Society of America*, 73 (1979), pp. 145–207. [Adriaen Vlack].

Miller, T., *The Old English Version of Bede's Ecclesiastical History of the English People*, EETS o.s. 95–6, 110–11 (London: Kegan Paul, Trench, Trübner, 1890–8). [1568.1, 1623.1, 1643.1].

Money, D.K., *The English Horace: Anthony Alsop and the Tradition of British Latin Verse* (Oxford: Oxford University Press, 1998). [1698.1].

Moore, J.K., *Primary Materials Relating to Copy and Print in English Books of the Sixteenth and Seventeenth Centuries*, Oxford Bibliographical Society Occasional Publications 24 (Oxford, 1992). [1626.1, 1639.4, 1691.1, 1695.3].

Moreland, Carl & David Bannister, *Christie's Collectors Guides: Antique Maps* (Oxford: Phaidon Christie's, 1989 [= 3rd] edn). [1646.3].

Mores, Edward Rowe, *A Dissertation upon English Typographical Founders and Founderies (1778)*, ed. H. Carter & C. Ricks (Oxford: Oxford Bibliographical Society, 1961). [1567.1, 1752.1, 1754.1].

Mori, Gustav, *Die Schriftgießer Bartholomäus Voskens in Hamburg und Reinhard Voskens in Frankfurt a. M.* (Frankfurt-am-Main: B. Krebs, [1923]).

Mori, Gustav, *Frankfurter Schriftproben aus dem 16. bis 18. Jahrhundert*, introd. R. Diehl (Frankfurt-am-Main: Stempel, 1955).

Morison, Stanley, *Type Designs of the Past and Present* (London: Fleuron, 1926).

Morison, Stanley, *On Type Designs*, ed. P.M. Handover (London: Benn, 1962).

Morison, Stanley, *Politics and Script*, Lyell Lectures 1957 ed. N. Barker (Oxford: Clarendon Press, 1972).

Morison, Stanley, *Selected Essays in the History of Letter-Forms in Manuscript and Print*, ed. D. McKitterick, 2 vols (Cambridge: Cambridge University Press, 1981).

Morison, Stanley, *Early Italian Writing-Books Renaissance to Baroque*, ed. N. Barker (London: British Library, 1990).

Morison, Stanley & Harry Carter, *John Fell—The University Press and the Fell Types* (Oxford: Clarendon Press, 1967).

Morris, Richard, *Old English Homilies and Homiletic Treatises*, EETS OS 29 (London: Kegan Paul Trübner, 1868). [1703/5.1].

Morton-Smith, M.B., *Catalogues of Books offered for sale by M.B. Morton-Smith*, Shanley Green, (?)1957.

Mosley, James, *British Type Specimens before 1831: A Hand-List*, Oxford Bibliographical Society Occasional Publications 14 (Oxford, 1984). [1567.1].

Mosley, James, 'French Academicians and Modern Typography: Designing new Types in the 1690s', *Typography Papers* (University of Reading), 2 (1997), pp. 5–29. [CAS6].

Mosley, James, 'Type Specimens of the Imprimerie royale 1643–1828', *Bulletin du Bibliophile*, n.s. 1 (2002), pp. 70–99. [CAS6].

Muir, Bernard J., *The Exeter Anthology of Old English Poetry: An Edition of Exeter Dean and Chapter MS 3501* (Exeter: University of Exeter Press, 1994). [1703/5.1].

Muir, Bernard J. & N.A. Sparks, *A Digital Facsimile of Bodleian Library, MS Laud misc. 636, "The Peterborough Chronicle"*, Bodleian Digital Texts 4 (Oxford, 2015).

Munby, A.N.L., 'The Gifts of Elizabethan Printers to the Library of King's College, Cambridge', *The Library*, v.2 (1948), pp. 224–232. [1574.1, 1574.2].

Munby, A.N.L. & Lenora Coral, *British Book Sale Catalogues 1676–1800: A Union List*, (London: Mansell, 1977).

Murphy, Michael, 'Abraham Wheloc's Edition of Bede's *History* in Old English', *Studia Neophilologica*, 39 (1967), pp. 46–59. [1643.1].

Murphy, Michael, 'John Foxe, Martyrologist and "Editor" of Old English', *ES*, 49 (1968), pp. 516–523. [1571.1].

Murphy, Michael, 'Scholars at Play: A Short History of Composing in Old English', *Old English Newsletter*, 15.2 (1982), pp. 26–36. [1641.3, 1700.2].

Murphy, Michael & Edward Barrett, 'Abraham Wheelock, Arabist and Saxonist', *Biography*, 8 (1982), pp. 163–185. [1643.1].

Napier, Arthur S., *The Old English Versions of the enlarged Rule of Chrodegang*, EETS OS 150 (London: Kegan Paul, Trench, Trübner, 1916). [1567.1].

Nativel, Colette, *Franciscus Junius, De Pictura Veterum libri tres (Roterodami, 1694): Édition, traduction et commentaire du livre I*, Travaux du Grand Siècle 3 (Geneva: Droz, 1996).

Nelson, Stan, 'Cutting Anglo-Saxon Sorts', *Fine Print*, 12 (1986), pp. 228–229.

Newcombe, D., 'A Finding List of Extant Sixteenth- and Seventeenth-Century Editions of John Foxe's *Acts and Monuments*', in D. Loades (ed.), *John Foxe and the English Reformation* (Aldershot: Scolar, 1997), Appendix, pp. 306–30. [1570.1].

Newdigate, Bernard H., *Michael Drayton and his Circle* (Oxford: Shakespeare Head Press for Blackwell, 1941). [esp ch. 14 re the present ch. 6].

Nichols, John, *Bibliotheca Topographica Britannica*, 8 vols (London: John Nichols, 1780–90). [AS5].

Nichols, John, *Literary Anecdotes of the Eighteenth Century*, 9 vols (London: John Nichols, 1812; repr. New York, 1966).

Niles, John D., *The Idea of Anglo-Saxon England 1066–1901: Remembering, Forgetting, Deciphering, and Renewing the Past* (Chichester: Wiley Blackwell, 2015).

Nixon, H.M., 'Elizabethan Gold-Tooled Bindings', in *Essays in Honour of Victor Scholderer*, ed. D.E. Rhodes, Mainz, 1970, pp. 219–70. [1570.1, 1572.1, 1574.1].

Nixon, Howard M. & Mirjam M. Foot, *The History of Decorated Bookbinding in England* (Oxford: Clarendon Press, 1992). [1572.1, 1643.1].

Norden, Linda Van, 'Peiresc and the English Scholars', *Huntington Library Quarterly*, 12 (1948–9), pp. 369–389. [1626.1].

Norden, Linda Van, 'Sir Henry Spelman on the Chronology of the Elizabethan College of Antiquaries', *Huntington Library Quarterly*, 13 (1949–50), pp. 131–160. [1698.3].

Nurse, Bernard, 'The 1610 Edition of Camden's *Britannia*', *The Antiquaries Journal*, 73 (1993), pp. 158–160. [1610.5].

O'Donnell, Daniel P., 'Junius's Knowledge of the Old English Poem *Durham*', *Anglo-Saxon England*, 30 (2001), pp. 231–245. [1652.1].

Oastler, C.L., *John Day, the Elizabethan Printer*, Oxford Bibliographical Society Occasional Publications 10 (Oxford, 1975).

Oates, John C.T., *Abraham Wheelock (1593–1653) Orientalist: Anglo-Saxonist, & University Librarian*, Sandars Lectures in Bibliography, Cambridge, 1966 (unpubl. typescript at CUL Cam.b.966.2; contents mostly included in next). [1640.3].

Oates, J.C.T., *Cambridge University Library: A History. From the Beginnings to the Copyright Act of Queen Anne* (Cambridge: Cambridge University Press, 1986). [1640.3, 1641.3, 1643.1, 1644.1].

Ó'Cuív, Brian, *Abidil Gaoidheilge & Caiticiosma: Seán Ó Cearnaigh's Irish Primer of Religion published in 1571* (Dublin: Institute for Advanced Studies, 1994). [IR1]

Ogg, David, *Ioannis Seldeni: Ad Fletam Dissertatio*, Cambridge Studies in English Legal History (Cambridge: Cambridge University Press, 1925). [1647.2, 1685.?].

Okasha, Elisabeth, *Hand-List of Anglo-Saxon Non-Runic Inscriptions* (Cambridge: University Press, 1971). [1700.4]

Oldenbourg, Friedrich, *Die Endter Eine Nürnberger Buchhändlerfamilie (1590–1740)* (Munich & Berlin: R. Oldenbourg, 1911). [1665.3].

Oliver, Leslie M., 'Single-Page Imposition in Foxe's *Acts and Monuments*, 1570', *The Library*, v.1 (1946–47), pp. 49–56. [1570.1].

Olocco, Riccardo, 'A New Method of Analysing Printed Type', *Journal of the Printing Historical Society* III.5 (2020), pp. 191–222.

Orchard, Nicholas, *The Leofric Missal*, 2 vols, Henry Bradshaw Society 113–14 (Woodbridge: Boydell, 2002). [1703/5.1].

Ordnance Survey, *Facsimiles of Anglo-Saxon Manuscripts*, 3 vols (Southampton: Ordnance Survey, 1878–84). [1574.2].

Osley, A.S., 'The Origins of Italic Type', in *Calligraphy and Palaeography: Essays presented to Alfred Fairbank on his 70th Birthday*, ed. A.S. Osley (London: Faber & Faber, 1965), pp. 107–120.

Ould, Martyn, *Printing at the University Press, Oxford 1660–1780*, 2 vols (Seaton: Old School Press, 2016–18).

Page, R.I., 'Anglo-Saxon Texts in Early Modern Transcripts', *Transactions of the Cambridge Bibliographical Society*, VI.2 (1973), pp. 69–85.

Page, R.I., 'A Sixteenth-Century Runic Manuscript', in *Studies in Honour of René Derolez*, ed. A.M. Simon-Vandenbergen (Gent: Rijksuniversiteit Seminarie voor Engelse en Oud-Germaanse Taalkunde, 1987), pp. 384–390; repr in Page's *Runes and Runic Inscriptions*, ed. D. Parsons (Woodbridge: Boydell, 1995), pp. 289–294.

Page, R.I., 'The Sixteenth-Century Reception of Alfred the Great's Letter to his Bishops', *Anglia*, 110 (1992), pp. 36–64. [1568.1, 1574.2].

Page, R.I., *Matthew Parker and his Books* (Kalamazoo MI: Western Michigan University, 1993). [1567.1].

Parker, M., K. Melis and H.D.L. Vervliet, "Typographica Plantiniana": II. Early Inventories of Punches, Matrices, and Moulds, in the Plantin-Moretus Archives', *De Gulden Passer*, 38 (1960), pp. 1–139.

Parkes, M.B., 'Archaizing Hands in English Manuscripts', in Carley and Tite 1997: pp. 101–141.

Parry, Graham, *The Trophies of Time: English Antiquarians of the Seventeenth Century* (Oxford: Oxford University Press, 1995). [1586.1, 1605.1, 1610.2, 1612.1, 1614.3, 1618.1, 1622.2, 1626.1, 1632.1, 1639.2, 1640.1, 1641.1, 1646.2, 1654.1, 1655.3, 1658.1, 1658.2, 1659.1, 1670.1, 1676.1, 1695.3, 1698.3].

Parry, Graham, 'An Incipient Medievalist in the Seventeenth Century: William Somner of Canterbury', *Studies in Medievalism*, 9 (1997), pp. 58–65. [1640.1].

Pelteret, D.A.E., 'Two Old English Lists of Serfs', *Mediæval Studies*, 48 (1986), pp. 470–513. [1703/5.1].

Pelteret, David A.E., *Catalogue of English Post-Conquest Vernacular Documents* (Woodbridge: Boydell, 1990). [1566.1, 1572.1, 1605.2, 1626.1, 1631.1, 1640.1, 1655.3, 1658.1, 1660.1, 1664.1, 1672.1, 1682.2, 1691.1, 1696.1, 1702.1, 1703.2, 1703/5.1].

Pennington, Richard, *A Descriptive Catalogue of the Etched Work of Wenceslaus Hollar 1607–1677* (Cambridge: Cambridge University Press, 1982). [1655.3, 1661.1].

Pettegree, Andrew & Arthur der Weduwen, *The Bookshop of the World: Making and Trading Books in the Dutch Golden Age* (London: Yale University Press, 2019).

Piggott, Stuart, 'William Camden and the *Britannia*', *Proceeedings of the British Academy*, 37 (1951), pp. 199–217. [1586.1, 1587.1, 1590.1, 1594.2, 1600.1, 1607.2, 1610.5, 1695.3].

Plantin, Christophe, [*Index sive Specimen characterum C. Plantini*], type-specimen issued from Antwerp, 1567, facsimile intro. D.C. McMurtrie (New York, 1924). See also Dreyfus.

Plantin, Christophe, *An Account of Calligraphy and Printing in the Sixteenth Century*, t R. Nash, intro. S. Morison (New York: Liturgical Arts Society, 1949).

Plomer, Henry R., 'Henry Bynneman, Printer, 1566–83', *The Library*, I.9 (1908), pp. 225–244. [1568.1].

Plomer, Henry R., 'The Eliot's Court Printing House, 1584–1674', *The Library*, IV.2 (1922), pp. 175–184. [1594.2].

Plomer, Henry R., 'Eliot's Court Press: Decorative Blocks and Initials', *The Library*, IV.3 (1923), pp. 194–209. [1594.2].

Plomer, Henry R., *English Printers' Ornaments* (London: Grafton, 1924).

Plomer, Henry R., 'The 1574 Edition of Dr. John Caius's *De Antiquitate Cantebrigiensis Academiæ Libri Duo*', *The Library*, IV.7 (1927), pp. 253–268. [1574.1].

Pocock, J.G.A., *The Ancient Constitution and the Feudal Law* (Cambridge: Cambridge University Press, 1987). [1626.1].

Pohl, Benjamin, 'The (Un)Making of a History Book: Revisiting the Earliest Manuscripts of Eadmer of Canterbury's *Historia novorum in Anglia*', *The Library*, VII.20 (2019), pp. 340–370. [1623.3].

Pollard, Graham & Albert Ehrman, *The Distribution of Books by Catalogue from the Invention of Printing to A.D. 1800 based on material in the Broxbourne Library* (Cambridge: for the Roxburghe Club, 1965). [1617.1].

Pollard, M., *A Dictionary of the Members of the Dublin Book Trade 1550–1800* (London: Bibliographical Society, 2000).

Pope, John C., *Homilies of Ælfric: A Supplementary Collection*, EETS os 259–60 (London: Oxford University Press, 1967–8). [1643.1].

Powicke, F.M., 'Sir Henry Spelman and the *Concilia*', *Proceedings of the British Academy*, 16 (1930), pp. 345–379. Repr in *Studies in History*, ed. L. Sutherland (London: Oxford University Press, 1966). [1639.4].

Powicke, [F.]M., 'William Camden', *English Studies 1948*, pp. 67–84. [1586.1].

Pulsiano, Phillip, 'The Scribes and Old English Gloss of the Eadwine's Canterbury Psalter', in *Proceedings of the Patristic, Mediaeval and Renaissance Conference* (Villanova University, Augustinian Historical Institute), 14 (1989), pp. 223–60.

Pulsiano, Phillip, *Anglo-Saxon Manuscripts in Microfiche Facsimile*, vol. 2, *Psalters I*, Medieval & Renaissance Text & Studies 137 (Binghamton NY, 1994).

Pummer, H., 'Johannes Janssonius. Buchdrucker und Buchhändler der Königin', *Nordisk Tidskrift för Bok- und Biblioteksväsen*, 69 (1982), pp. 33–48.

Putnam, B.H., 'The Earliest Form of Lambard's 'Eirenarcha' and a Kent Wage Assessment of 1563', *English Historical Review*, 41 (1926), pp. 260–273. [1581.1].

Ramsay, Nigel, 'The Cathedral Archives and Library', in *A History of Canterbury Cathedral*, ed. P. Collinson, N. Ramsay & M. Sparks, Oxford, 1995, ch. viii, pp. 341–407. [1703.1].

Rauer, Christine, *The Old English Martyrology* (Cambridge: Boydell & Brewer, 2013). [1626.1, 1631.1, 1664.1].

Reed, Talbot Baines, *A History of the old English Letter Foundries*, rev. A.F. Johnson (London: Faber & Faber, 1952).

Renouard, Philippe, 'Les Fondeurs de Caractères Parisiens et leur Clientèle de Province à la fin du xviie siècle', *Bulletin du Bibliophile* (1900), pp. 3–16, 79–86. [CAS 6].

Renouard, Philippe, *Répertoire des Imprimeurs Parisiens Libraires et Fondeurs de Caractères en exercice à Paris au XVIIe siècle* (Nogent le Roi: Libr. des Arts et Métiers-Éditions, 1995). Facsimile reprint of Renouard's corrected proofs (1898), as the original edition was never published. [1678.2].

Reske, Christoph, *Die Buchdrucker des 16. und 17. Jahrhunderts im deutschen Sprachgebiet* (Wiesbaden: Harrassowitz, 2007).

Reyner, Clement, *Apostolatus Benedictinorum in Anglia* (Douai: Ex officinâ Lavrentii Kellami, 1626). [1703/5.1].

Rhodes, E.W., *Defensor's Liber Scintillarum*, EETS os 93 (London: Trübner, 1889). [1655.1, 1690.1].

Ricci, Seymour de, *English Collectors of Books and Manuscripts 1530–1930 and their Marks of Ownership* (Cambridge: Cambridge University Press, 1930).

Rice, M.E., '"Old English", and an Intriguing Etymology: Two Observations upon Philemon Holland's Translation of Camden's "Britannia"', *Notes and Queries*, 211 (1966), pp. 375–376. [1610.5].

Rissanen, Matti, 'Middle English Translations of Old English Charters in the *Liber Monasterii de Hyda*: A case of Historical Error Analysis', in *Linguistics across Historical and Geographical Boundaries: in Honour of Jacek Fisiak on the Occasion of his Fiftieth Birthday*, ed. Dieter Kastovsky & A. Szwedek, 2 vols (Berlin: Mouton de Gruyter, 1986), I.591–603.

Rivet, A.L.F. and Colin Smith, *The Place-Names of Roman Britain* (London: Batsford, 1979). [1658.2].

Roberts, E.S., *The Works of John Caius, M.D.* (Cambridge: Cambridge University Press, 1912). [1568.1, 1574.1].

Robertson, A.J., *The Laws of the Kings of England from Edmund to Henry I*, Cambridge, 1925, repr. New York, AMS, 1974.

Robertson, A.J., *Anglo-Saxon Charters* (Cambridge: Cambridge University Press, 1939, rev. 1956). [1655.3, 1702.1].

Robinson, Fred C., 'Syntactical Glosses in Latin Manuscripts of Anglo-Saxon Provenance', *Speculum*, 48 (1973), pp. 443–475.

Robinson, Fred C. & E.G. Stanley, *Old English Verse Texts from many Sources: A Comprehensive Collection*, EEMF xxiii (Copenhagen: Rosenkilde & Bagger, 1991). [1605.5, 1655.2].

Rochais, H.M., *Liber Scintillarum*, CCSL 117.1 (Turnhout: Brepols, 1957). [1655.1, 1690.1].

Rockett, William, 'Historical Typography and British History in Camden's *Britannia*', *Renaissance and Reformation*, 26 (1990), pp. 71–80. [1586.1].

Rockett, William, 'The Structural Plan of Camden's *Britannia*', *Sixteenth Century Journal*, 26 (1995), pp. 829–841. [1586.1].

Roebuck, Thomas, 'Edmund Gibson's 1695 Britannia and Late-Seventeenth-Century British Antiquarian Scholarship', *Erudition and the Republic of Letters*, 5 (2020), 427–481. [1695.3].

Rollason, David, *Symeon of Durham: Libellvs de Exordio atqve procvrsv istivs, hoc est Dvnhelmensis, Ecclesie, Tract on the Origins and Progress of this the Church of Durham* (Oxford: Clarendon Press, 2000).

van Romburgh, Sophie, *"For my worthy freind [sic] Mr. Franciscus Junius": an edition of the correspondence of Francis Junius F.F. (1591–1677)* (Leiden: Brill, 2004).

Ronalds, Craig & Margaret Clunies Ross, '*Thureth*: A Neglected Old English Poem and its History in Anglo-Saxon Scholarship', *Notes and Queries*, 246 (2001), pp. 359–370. [1639.4].

Rooses, Max, *Correspondance de Christophe Plantin*, 9 vols, Uitgaven der Antwerpsche Bibliophilen 12, 15, 26, 29–34 (Antwerp: Buschmann, 1883–1920; repr. Neudeln, Liechtenstein, 1968).

Roper, Geoffrey, 'Arabic Printing and Publishing in England before 1820', *British Society for Middle Eastern Studies Bulletin*, 12 (1985), pp. 12–32.

Roper, Geoffrey, 'Persian Printing and Publishing in England in the 17th Century', in *Iran and Iranian Studies: Essays in Honor of Iraj Afshar*, ed. K. Eslami (Princeton NJ: Zagros, 1998), pp. 316–328.

Rosier, James L., 'The Sources of John Joscelyn's Old English-Latin Dictionary', *Anglia*, 78 (1960), pp. 28–39.

Rosier, James L., 'The Sources and Methods of Minsheu's *Guide into the Tongues*', *Philological Quarterly*, 40 (1961), pp. 68–76. [1617.1].

Rowse, A.L., *Four Caroline Portraits* (London: Duckworth, 1993).

Ruano-García, Javier, 'Northern Ascriptions in MS Lansdowne 1033 [by White Kennett]: George Hickes's *Dictionariolum Islandicum* in Focus', *Historiographia Linguistica*, 42 (2015), pp. 21–38. [1689.3].

Rymer, Thomas, *Foedera, Conventiones, Litterae, et cujuscunque generis Acta Publica, inter Reges Angliae et alios quosvis Imperatores, Reges, Pontifices...*, vols 1–17 (London: A. & J. Churchill, 1704–35). [1572.1].

Salter, H.R., *Eynsham Cartulary*, 2 vols, Oxford Historical Society 49, 51 (Oxford: Clarendon Press, 1907–8). [1703/5.1].

Sanders, Vivienne, 'The Household of Archbishop Parker and the Influencing of Public Opinion', *Journal of Ecclesiastical History*, 34 (1983), pp. 534–547.

Sato, Shuji, *Back to the Manuscripts*, Occasional Papers 1 (Tokyo: Centre for Medieval English Studies, 1997).

Sauer, Hans, *Theodulfi Capitula in England: Die altenglischen Übersetzung, zusammen mit dem lateinischen Text*, Münchener Universitäts-Schriften 8 (München: Fink, 1978). [1639.4, 1643.1].

Sauer, Hans, 'Knowledge of Old English in the Middle English period', in R. Hickey and S. Puppel (eds), *Language History and Linguistic Modelling*, 2 vols (Berlin: Mouton de Gruyter, 1997), I.791–814.

Saunders, Stewart, 'Public Administration and the Library of Jean-Baptiste Colbert', *Libraries & Culture*, 26 (1991), pp. 283–300. [1662.3].

Sawyer, Peter [H.], *Textus Roffensis: Rochester Cathedral Library Manuscript A.3.5*, 2 vols, EEMF vii, xi (Copenhagen: Rosenkilde & Bagger, 1957–62). [1576.1, 1664.1].

Sawyer, Peter H., *Anglo-Saxon Charters: An Annotated List and Bibliography*, Royal Historical Society Guides and Handbooks 8 (London, 1968). [1574.1, 1574.2, 1576.1]. Supplementary information is available on-line at http://www.esawyer.org.uk.

Sayers, Jane E. & Leslie Watkiss, *Thomas of Marlborough: History of the Abbey of Evesham*, Oxford Medieval Texts (Oxford: Clarendon Press, 2003). [1655.3].

[Sayle, Charles E.,] *A Catalogue of the Bradshaw Collection of Irish Books in the University Library Cambridge*, 3 vols (Cambridge: Cambridge University Library, 1916). [1622.2, 1632.1, 1639.2].

Schäfer, Jürgen, 'John Minsheu: Scholar or Charlatan?', *Renaissance Quarterly*, 26 (1973), pp. 23–35. [1617.1].

Schäfer, W.E., 'Georg Andreas Dollhopf(f), ein Straßburger Verleger', *Simpliciana: Schriften der Grimmelshausen-Gesellschaft*, 22 (2000), pp. 343–361. [1665.3].

Schipper, Jacob, *König Alfreds Übersetzung von Bedas Kirchengeschichte*, Bibliothek der angelsächsischen Prosa 4 (Leipzig: Wigand, 1899). [1568.1].

Schreiber, Fred, *The Estiennes: An Annotated Catalogue of 300 Highlights of their various Presses* (New York: E.K. Schreiber, 1982). [1568.3].

Schröer, Arnold, *Die angelsächsischen Prosarbeitungen der Benediktinerregel*, Bibliothek der angelsächsischen Prosa 2 (Kassel, 1885–8, repr. with afterword by H. Gneuss, Darmstadt: Wissenschaftliche Buchgesellschaft, 1964).

Sclater, William, *The Crowne of Righteousnes* (London: John Grismond for John Clarke 1, 1654) (Wing S916).

Scragg, D.G. & C. Weinberg, *Literary Appropriations of the Anglo-Saxons from the Thirteenth to the Twentieth Centuries* (Cambridge: Cambridge University Press, 2000).

Seaton, Ethel, *Literary Relations of England and Scandinavia in the Seventeenth Century* (Oxford: Clarendon Press, 1935).

Seaton, Ethel, 'John Selden in Contact with Scandinavia', *Saga-Book of the Viking Society*, 12 (1937–45), pp. 261–271. [1635.1].

Sedgefield, Walter J., *King Alfred's Old English Version of Boethius De Consolatione Philosophiae* (Oxford: Clarendon Press, 1899).

Sharpe, Kevin, 'The Earl of Arundel, His Circle and the Opposition to the Duke of Buckingham, 1618–1628', in idem, *Faction and Parliament: Essays on Early Stuart History* (Oxford: Clarendon Press, 1978), pp. 209–244. [Junius].

Sharpe, Richard & Mícheál Hoyne, *Clóliosta, Printing in the Irish Language, 1571–1871: An Attempt at Narrative Bibliography* (Dublin: School of Celtic Studies, Dublin Institute for Advanced Studies, 2020). [IR1].

Shawcross, John T., 'An Allusion to "The Church Militant" in Howell's *An Institution of General History*', *George Herbert Journal*, 6 (1983), at p. 49. [1685.1].

Sherman, William [H.], *Used Books: Marking Readers in Renaissance England* (Philadelphia: University of Pennsylvania Press, 2008).

Shirley, Rodney W., *Early Printed Maps of the British Isles, 1477–1650* (London: Map Collectors' Circle, 1991 edn). [1574.1, 1576.2, 1596.2, 1600.1, 1607.2, 1610.5, 1611.1, 1614.1, 1616.1, 1623.2, 1627.1, 1631.1, 1632.1, 1636.2, 1637.1, 1644.1, 1645.1, 1645.2, 1646.3, 1646.4, 1646.5, 1647.3, 1647.4, 1647.5, 1648.2, 1650/?1665.1].

Shirley, Rodney W., *Maps in the Atlases of the British Library* (London: British Library, 2004). [1645.1, 1646.3, 1646.4, 1647.3, 1648.1, 1648.2, 1662.2, 1662.3, 1662.4].

Simmons, J.S.G., 'Specimens of Printing Types before 1850 in the Typographical Library at the University Press, Oxford', *The Book Collector*, 8 (1959), pp. 397–410. [1695.1].

Simmons, J.S.G. & Bé van Ginneken-van de Kasteele, *Likhachev's Watermarks: An English-Language Version*, 2 vols, Monumenta Chartæ Papyraceæ Historiam Illustrantia 15 (Amsterdam: Paper Publications Society, 1994). [1600.1].

Simpson, Percy, *Proof-Reading in the Sixteenth Seventeenth and Eighteenth Centuries* (London: Oxford University Press, 1935, repr. 1970). [1698.3].

Sisam, Kenneth, *Studies in the History of Old English Literature* (Oxford: Clarendon Press, 1953). [1568.2].

Skeat, Walter W., *The Holy Gospels in Anglo-Saxon, Northumbrian, and Old Mercian Versions, synoptically arranged, with Collations exhibiting all the Readings of all the MSS.* (Cambridge: Cambridge University Press, 1871–87). [1605.1].

Skeat, Walter W., *Ælfric's Lives of Saints*, EETS os 76, 82, 94, 114 (London: Kegan Paul, Trench, 1881–1900). [1643.1].

Skelton, R.A., *County Atlases of the British Isles 1579–1850: A Bibliography* (vol. I 1579–1703) (London: Carta, 1970). [1607.2, 1610.5, 1611.1, 1612.1, 1613.1, 1622.1, 1637.1, 1646.3, 1659.2, 1695.3].

von Slagle, Geoffrey, 'A Note on Early Welsh Orthography', *The Library*, VI.5 (1983), pp. 254–256.

Smeijers, Fred, *Counterpunch: Making Type in the Sixteenth Century, Designing Typefaces Now* (London: Hyphen, 1996).

Smith, Margaret M., 'The Design Relationship between the Manuscript and the Incunable', in *A Millenium of the Book: Production, Design & Illustration in Manuscript & Print 900–1900*, ed. R. Myers & M. Harris (Winchester: St Paul's Bibliographies, & Delaware: Oak Knoll Press, 1994), pp. 23–43.

Smyth, Alfred P., *The Medieval Life of King Alfred the Great: A Translation and Commentary on the Text Attributed to Asser* (Basingstoke: Palgrave, 2002). [1574.2].

Solopova, Elizabeth, 'From Bede to Wyclif: The Knowledge of Old English within the Context of Late Middle English Biblical Translation and Beyond', *RES*, ns 71 (2019), pp. 805–827.

Sparkes, Nicholas A., 'Finding Matthew Parker in Manuscripts of the *Anglo-Saxon Chronicle*', *Publications of the Bibliographical Society of America*, 108 (2014), pp. 107–111.

Spelman, John, *The Life of Ælfred the Great*, ed. T. Hearne (Oxford: Sheldonian Theatre, 1709). [1678.1].

Springell, Francis C., *Connoisseur & Diplomat. The Earl of Arundel's Embassy to Germany in 1636 as recounted in William Crowne's Diary, the Earl's letters and contemporary sources with a catalogue of the topographical drawings made on the jouney by Wenceslaus Hollar* (London: Maggs Bros, 1963). [Arundel, patron of Junius].

Stanley, Eric G., *A Collection of Papers with emphasis on Old English Literature*, Publications of the DOE 3 (Toronto: Pontifical Institute of Mediaeval Studies, 1987). [1678.1].

Stanley, E.G., 'Old English = "Anglo-Saxon": the modern sense for the language anticipated by Archbishop Matthew Parker in 1567, and by John Strype in 1711, Camden's use in *Remaines* (1605) for the Anglo-Saxon people noted; together with notes on how *OED* treats such terms', *Notes and Queries*, 240 (1995), pp. 168–173, suppl. p. 437. [1567.1].

Star Chamber, *A Decree of Starre-Chamber, concerning Printing made the eleventh day of July last past* (London: Robert Barker & assignees of John Bill 1, 1637); STC 7757.

Starnes, DeWitt T. & Gertrude E. Noyes, *The English Dictionary from Cawdrey to Johnson 1604–1755* (Chapel Hill: University of North Carolina Press, 1946). [1689.1].

Steiner, Roger J., *Two Centuries of Spanish and Engish Bilingual Lexicography (1590–1800)*, Janua Linguarum, ser. pract. 108 (The Hague: Mouton, 1970). [1617.1].

Stevenson, William H., *Asser's Life of King Alfred*, with an article on recent work by D. Whitelock (Oxford: Clarendon Press, 1959). [1574.2].

Strongman, Sheila, 'John Parker's Manuscripts: An Edition of the Lists in Lambeth Palace MS 737', *Transactions of the Cambridge Bibliographical Society*, VII.1 (1977), pp. 1–27. [1567.1].

Strype, John, *The Life and Acts of Matthew Parker* (London: for John Wyat, 1711; repr. in 3 vols, Oxford: Clarendon Press, 1821). [1566.1, 1567.1, 1568.1].

Stubbs, William, *Memorials of Saint Dunstan Archbishop of Canterbury*, RS 63 (London: Longman, 1874). [1678.1].

Summit, Jennifer, *Memory's Library: Medieval Books in Early Modern England* (Chicago: University of Chicago Press, 2008).

Sweeney, Tony, *Ireland and the Printed Word: A Short Descriptive Catalogue of Early Books ... Printed: 1475–1700* (Dublin: Éamonn de Búrca, 1997).

Sweet, Henry, *King Alfred's Orosius*, EETS os 79 (London: Trübner, 1883). [1640.4, 1665.2].

Sweet, Henry, *King Alfred's West-Saxon Version of Gregory's 'Pastoral Care'*, EETS os 45 and 50 (London: Trübner, 1871–2). [1574.2, 1664.1].

Sweet, Henry, *The Oldest English Texts*, EETS os 83 (London: Trübner, 1885). [1640.3].

Sykes, Norman, *Edmund Gibson Bishop of London 1669–1748: A Study in Politics & Religion in the Eighteenth Century* (London: Oxford University Press, 1926). [1692.1, 1693.1, 1695.3, 1698.3].

Tamoto, Kenichi, *The Macregol Gospels or The Rushworth Gospels* (Amsterdam: Benjamins, 2013). [1655.1].

Taylor, E.G.R., *Late Tudor and Early Stuart Geography 1583–1650* (London: Methuen, 1934; repr. New York: Octagon, 1968). [1586.1, 1607.2].

Taylor, Simon, *The Anglo-Saxon Chronicle: A Collaborative Edition, Volume 4, MS B* (Cambridge: Brewer, 1983).

Temple, Elzbieta, *Anglo-Saxon Manuscripts 900–1066*, Survey of Manuscripts illuminated in the British Isles 2 (London: Harvey Miller, 1976). [1640.3].

Thirsk, Joan, *The Rural Economy of England* (London: Hambledon, 1984). [1660.1, 1663.1].

Thompson, Edward M., *An Introduction to Greek and Latin Palaeography* (Oxford: Clarendon Press, 1912).

Thompson, W. Meredith, *Þe Wohunge of ure Lauerd*, EETS os 241 (London: Oxford University Press, 1958). [1703/5.1].

Thoresby, Ralph, *Ducatus Leodiensis: or, the Topography of the Ancient and Populous Town and Parish of Leedes* (London: for Maurice Atkins, 1715). [1703/5.1].

Thorpe, Benjamin, *Ancient Laws and Institutes of England*, 2 vols (London: Eyre & Spottiswoode, 1840). [1618.1, 1639.4, 1644.1].

Thorpe, Benjamin, *The Homilies of the Anglo-Saxon Church*, 2 vols (London: Ælfric Society, 1844–6). [1605.1, 1643.1].

Thorpe, Benjamin, *The Anglo-Saxon Chronicle according to the several original authorities*, 2 vols, RS 23 (London: Longman, Green, Longman & Roberts, 1861). [1568.1, 1607.2, 1618.1, 1623.3, 1631.1, 1635.1, 1636.1, 1636.2, 1636.3, 1637.1, 1639.2, 1639.4, 1643.1, 1645.1, 1645.2, 1646.3, 1646.4, 1647.2, 1647.5, 1648.1, 1648.2, 1652.1, 1652.2, 1659.2, 1659.3, 1662.2, 1662.3, 1662.4, 1663.1, 1666.1, 1672.1, 1676.2, 1678.1, 1685.2, 1687.2, 1691.1, 1692.1, 1693.1, 1695.3, 1696.1, 1703/5.1].

Thorpe, Benjamin, *Diplomatarium Anglicanum aevi Saxonici* (London, 1865). [1618.1, 1655.3, 1703/5.1].

Tinto, Alberto, 'I Tipi della Stamperia del Popolo Romano', *Gutenberg-Jahrbuch* (1967), pp. 26–38.

Tite, Colin G.C., *The Early Records of Sir Robert Cotton's Library: Formation, Cataloguing, Use* (London: British Library, 2003).

Tolkien, J.R.R., *Finn and Hengest: The Fragment and the Episode*, ed. Alan Bliss (London: Harper Collins, 1982). [1703/5.1].

Toomer, G.J., *Eastern Wisedome and Learning: The Study of Arabic in Seventeenth-Century England* (Oxford: Clarendon Press, 1996). [1635.1].

Toomer, G.J., 'Selden's *Historie of Tithes*: Genesis, Publication, Aftermath', *Huntington Library Quarterly*, 65 (2002), pp. 345–378. [1618.1].

Toomer, G.J., *John Selden: A Life in Scholarship*, 2 vols (Oxford: Oxford University Press, 2009).

Treadwell, Michael, 'The Grover Typefoundry', *Journal of the Printing Historical Society*, 15 (1980/81), pp. 36–53.

Turner, Alberta, 'Another Seventeenth-Century Anglo-Saxon Poem', *Modern Language Quarterly*, 9 (1948), pp. 389–393. [1654.2].

Turner, Gerard L'E., *Elizabethan Instrument Makers* (Oxford: Oxford University Press, 2000). Contains an appendix 'Description of a Digital Capture Technique for Engraved Characters on Brass', by M.St J. Turner, pp. 289–93.

Turner, Sharon, *The History of the Anglo-Saxons*, 4th edn (London: Longman, Hurst, Rees, Orme, & Brown, 1823). [1698.1].

Twomey, Juliet S., 'Whence Jenson. A Search for the Origins of Roman Type', *Fine Print*, 15 (1989), pp. 134–141.

Twyman, Michael, 'The Graphic Presentation of Language', *Information Design Journal*, 3 (1982), pp. 2–22.

Type Specimen Facsimiles, see Dreyfus.

Ullman, B.L., *Ancient Writing and its Influence* (London: Harrap, 1932; repr. Cambridge MA, 1969).

Ullman, B.L., *The Origin and Development of Humanistic Script*, Storia e Letteratura 79 (Rome: Edizioni de Storia e Letteratura, 1960).

Urry, William, *Canterbury under the Angevin Kings* (London: Athlone Press, 1967). [1640.1].

Urry, William, Introduction [on William Somner] to facsimile reprint of 2nd edn of 1640.1, q.v., 1977.

Utley, Francis L., 'Two Seventeenth-Century Anglo-Saxon Poems', *Modern Language Quarterly*, 3 (1942), pp. 243–261. [1641.3].

Vaciago, P., 'Old English Glosses to Latin Texts: A Bibliographical Handlist', *Medioevo e Rinascimento*, 4 (1993), pp. 1–67.

Vervey, H. de la F., 'Dr. Joan Blaeu and his Sons', *Quaerendo*, 11 (1981a), pp. 5–23. [1645.1, 1645.2, 1648.1, 1648.2, 1659.3, 1662.2, 1662.3].

Vervey, H. de la F., 'The Glory of the Blaeu Atlas and the "Master Colourist"', *Quaerendo*, 11 (1981b), pp. 197–229. [1645.1, 1645.2, 1648.1, 1648.2, 1659.3, 1662.2, 1662.3].

Vervliet, H.D.L., *The Type Specimen of The Vatican Press 1628* (Amsterdam: Herzberger, 1967). [1568.2, 1572.1].

Vervliet, H.D.L., *Sixteenth-Century Printing Types of the Low Countries* (Amsterdam: Herzberger, 1968).

Vervliet, H.D.L., 'The Italics of Robert Granjon', *Typography Papers* (Reading), 3 (1998), pp. 5–59.

Vervliet, H.D.L., 'Roman Types by Robert Granjon', *De Gulden Passer*, 76–77 (1998–9), pp. 5–76.

Vervliet, H.D.L., 'Les Italiques de Corps Gros-Romain de la Renaissance Française', *Bulletin du Bibliophile*, 1 (1999), pp. 5–45. [1568.3].

Vervliet, H.D.L., 'Printing Types of Pierre Haultin (ca. 1510–87)', *Quaerendo*, 30 (2000), pp. 87–129, 173–227.

Vervliet, H.D.L., 'Early Paris Italics 1512–1549', *Journal of the Printing Historical Society*, n.s. 8 (2005), pp. 5–55.

Vervliet, Hendrik D.L., *French Renaissance Printing Types: A Conspectus* (London: Bibliographical Society & Printing Historical Society, 2010).

Vervliet, H.D.L., 'The combinable type-ornaments of Robert Granjon 1564–1568', *Journal of the Printing Historical Society*, n.s. 22 (2015), pp. 25–61.

Verzeichnis der im deutschen Sprachbereich erschienenen Drucke des xvi. Jahrhunderts, Herausgegeben von der Bayerischen Staatsbibliothek in München in Verbindung mit der Herzog August Bibliothek in Wolfenbüttel, 14 vols (Stuttgart: Hiersemann, 1983–97). VD 16.

Veyrin-Forrer, Jeanne, 'Le "Cicero la Police" et Mathieu Malherbe Des Portes', *Bulletin de la Librairie Ancienne et Moderne*, 51 (1971), pp. 207–14, repr. in idem, *La Lettre et le Texte* (Paris: École normale supérieure de jeunes filles, 1987), pp. 81–87. At CUL CCC.52.441 there is a copy with summary notes in the hand of J. Dreyfus. [CAS6].

Veyrin-Forrer, Jeanne & André Jammes, *Les Premiers Caractères de l'Imprimerie Royale. Étude sur un spécimen inconnu de 1643*, Documents Typographiques Français II (Paris: Jammes, 1958). [1566.1, 1567.1, 1568.1, 1568.2, 1570.1, 1571.1, 1574.1, 1574.2].

Vine, Angus E., *In Defiance of Time: Antiquarian Writing in Early Modern England* (Oxford: University Press, 2010). [ch. 3 1610.5; ch. 6 1612.1].

Vine, Angus, 'Copiousness, Conjecture and Collaboration in William Camden's *Britannia*', *Renaissance Studies*, 28 (2014), pp. 225–241. [1587.1 + all other edns].

Voet, Leon, *The Golden Compasses*, 2 vols (Amsterdam: Van Gendt, 1969–72).

Wakeman, Geoffrey, 'The Design of Day's Saxon', *The Library*, v.22 (1967), pp. 283–298. [1574.1].

[Walker, John], *Letters Written by Eminent Persons in the Seventeenth and Eighteenth Centuries ... Lives of Eminent Men, by John Aubrey*, 2 vols (vol. II in 2 parts) (London: Longman, Hurst, Rees, Orme & Brown, 1813). [1692.1].

Walters, Gwyn & Frank Emery, 'Edward Lhuyd, Edmund Gibson and the Printing of Camden's *Britannia* 1695', *The Library*, v.32 (1977), pp. 109–137. [1695.3].

Warner, George, *The Libelle of Englyshe Polycye: A Poem on the Use of Sea Power 1436* (Oxford: Clarendon Press, 1926). [1635.1].

Warner, Rubie D-N., *Early English Homilies from the Twelfth Century MS. Vesp. D.xiv*, EETS os 152 (London: Kegan Paul, Trench, Trübner, 1917). [1643.1].

Warnicke, Retha M., *William Lambarde, Elizabethan Antiquary 1536–1601* (Chichester: Phillimore, 1973). [1568.2].

Watson, Andrew G., *The Library of Sir Simonds D'Ewes* (London: British Museum, 1966). [1655.3]. See also Ker, *Medieval Libraries*.

Watts, V., 'English Place-Names in the Sixteenth Century: The Search for Identity', in *Sixteenth-Century Identities*, ed. A.J. Piesse (Manchester: Manchester University Press, 2001). [1586.1].

Weekley, Ernest, 'Our Early Etymologists', *Quarterly Review*, 257, (1931), pp. 63–72. [1671.3].

Whitelock, Dorothy, *Anglo-Saxon Wills* (Cambridge: Cambridge University Press, 1930). [1574.1, 1576.1, 1655.3, 1660.1, 1702.1].

Whitelock, Dorothy, *The Peterborough Chronicle (The Bodleian Manuscript Laud Misc. 636)*, EEMF 4 (Copenhagen: Rosenkilde & Bagger, 1954). [1566.1; 1567.1 +].

Whitelock, Dorothy, 'The Old English Bede', *Proceedings of the British Academy*, 48 (1962), pp. 57–90. [1643.1].

Whitelock, Dorothy, [*Wulfstan:*] *Sermo Lupi ad Anglos* (London: Methuen 1963 edn). [1572.1].

Whitelock, Dorothy, 'The List of Chapter-Headings in the Old English Bede', in *Old English Studies in Honour of John C. Pope*, ed. R.B. Burlin & E.B. Irving Jr (Toronto: University of Toronto Press, 1974), pp. 263–284. [1643.1].

Wilkins, David, *Concilia Magnae Britanniae et Hiberniae*, 4 vols (London: William Bowyer for Robert Gosling (*sumptibus*), 1737).

Williams, F.B., 'Scholarly Publication in Shakespeare's Day', in *Joseph Quincy Adams Memorial Studies*, ed. J.G. McManaway, G.E. Dawson & E.E. Willoughby (Washington DC: Folger Shakespeare Library, 1948), pp. 755–773. [1617.1].

Willis, Robert & John W. Clark, *The Architectural History of the University of Cambridge and of the Colleges of Cambridge and Eton*, 4 vols (Cambridge: Cambridge University Press, 1866). [1572.1].

Wishart, D., 'Exotics at OUP', *Matrix*, 21 (2001), pp. 62–84.

Wood, Anthony à, *The Life and Times of Anthony Wood, Antiquary, of Oxford 1632–1695, Described by Himself*, ed. A. Clark, vol. II, Oxford Historical Society 21 (Oxford: Clarenon Press, 1892). [1678.1] See also Kiessling.

Woodruff, C. Eveleigh, *A Catalogue of the Manuscript Books* [in Canterbury Cathedral Library] (Canterbury: Cross & Jackman, 1911).

Woolf, D.R., *The Idea of History in Early Stuart England: Erudition, Ideology, and 'The Light of Truth' from the Accession of James I to the Civil War* (Toronto: University of Toronto Press, 1990). [1614.3, 1631.1].

Wormald, Francis & C.E. Wright, *The English Library before 1700* (London: Athlone Press, 1958). [1607.2].

Wormald, Patrick, 'Quadripartitus', in *Law and Government in Medieval England and Normandy: Essays in Honour of Sir James Holt*, ed. G. Garnett & J. Hudson (Cambridge: Cambridge University Press, 1994), pp. 111–147. [1568.2].

Wormald, Patrick, 'The Lambarde Problem: Eighty Years On', in *Alfred the Wise: Studies in Honour of Janet Bately on the occasion of her sixty-fifth birthday*, ed. J. Roberts, J.L. Nelson with M. Godden (Woodbridge: Brewer, 1997), pp. 237–275. [1568.2].

Worman, Ernest J., *Alien Members of the Book-Trade during the Tudor Period* (London: Blades, East & Blades, 1906).

Wright, C.E. 'The Dispersal of the Monastic Libraries and the Beginnings of Anglo-Saxon Studies. Matthew Parker and his Circle: A Preliminary Study', *Transactions of the Cambridge Bibliographical Society*, I.3 (1951), pp. 208–237.

Wright, C.J. (ed.), *Sir Robert Cotton as Collector: Essays of an early Stuart Courtier and his Legacy* (London: British Library, 1997).

Wright, David H., *The Vespasian Psalter: British Museum Cotton Vespasian A.I*, EEMF 14 (Copenhagen: Rosenkilde & Bagger, 1967). [1640.1].

Wright, Thomas & James O. Halliwell, *Reliquiæ Antiquæ: Scraps from Ancient Manuscripts illustrating chiefly Early English Literature and the English Language*, 2 vols (London: William Pickering, 1841–3). [1678.1].

Wright, Thomas & Richard Wülcker, *Anglo-Saxon and Old-English Vocabularies*, 2nd edn, 2 vols in 1 (London: Trübner, 1883–4). [Ælfric's Glossary, no. 10: 1631.1].

Wright, William A., *The Metrical Chronicle of Robert of Gloucester*, 2 vols, RS 86 (London: Eyre & Spottiswoode for HMSO, 1887). [1643.1, 1670.1].

Yamada, Akihiro, *Peter Short: An Elizabethan Printer* (Tokyo: Meisei University, 1989). [1596.1].

Yerkes, David, 'Dugdale's Dictionary and Somner's *Dictionarium*', *English Language Notes*, 14 (1976–7), pp. 110–112. [1659.1].

Zachrisson, Bror, *Studies in the Legibility of Printed Text*, Stockholm Studies in Educational Psychology 11 (Stockholm: Almqvist & Wiksell, 1965).

Zook, Melinda S., *Radical Whigs and Conspiratorial Politics in Late Stuart England* ([Philadelphia]: Pennsylvania Stae University Press, 1999). [1682.2].

Zupitza, Julius, *Ælfrics Grammatik und Glossar*, Sammlung englischer Denkmäler 1 (Berlin: Weidmann, 1880; repr. with preface by H. Gneuss, 1966). [1568.1].

General Index

References are to pages in Part 1 and to catalogue numbers in Part 2. The index is supplemented by the Bibliography, which, under Manuscripts, lists which printed books they are cited in, by the List of Punchcutters and the List of Type-Designs, where instances of each Anglo-Saxon design are supplied, and by the List of Printers and Booksellers, where books produced by or for the people in these trades are listed. Readers looking for specific OE works should find them here but are advised to check also via the manuscript(s) in which they occur.

Abba, reeve, will of (833 × 839)   1703/5.1
Ælfric, abp of Canterbury (995–1005), will of 1703/5.1
Ælfric of Eynsham (c.955–c.1010), AS homilist: *Catholic Homilies*   107–108, 1643.1, 1650.3, 1670.1, 1676.2, 1679.2, 1690.1, 1696.2, 1698.1, 1705.1; *Colloquy* 1665.2, 1684.3; *Excusatio Dictantis* 1566.1/2, 1570.1, 1576.1, 1583.1, 1596.1, 1610.3, 1631.3, 1641.2, 1684.4; *Grammar* 4, 1566.1/2, 1568.1, 1570.1, 1574.1, 1576.1, 1583.1, 1596.1, 1610.3, 1631.3, 1639.4, 1641.2, 1652.1, 1659.1, 1664.1, 1684.4, 1690.1, 1696.1, 1703/5.1; *Glossary* 4, 1631.1, 1672.1; Pseudo-Ælfric's *Vocabulary* 1659.1; (Other) *Homilies* 1643.1, 1670.1, 1676.2; *Letter to Sigeferth* 1566.1/2, 1621.1, 1623.1, 1638.1, 1643.1; *Letter to Sigeweard* 1623.1, 1631.1, 1638.1, 1672.1, 1690.1, 1696.1, 1698.1; *Letter to Wulfsige* III 1566.1/2, 1570.1, 1576.1, 1583.1, 1596.1, 1610.3, 1623.1, 1631.3, 1638.1, 1639.4, 1641.2, 1643.1, 1644.1, 1684.4, 1688.1 (t), 1690.1; *First Latin Letter to Wulfstan* 1567.1; *Second Letter to Wulfstan* 11; Latin text 1566.1/2, 1570.1, 1576.1, 1583.1, 1596.1, 1610.3, 1623.1, 1631.3, 1641.2, 1643.1, 1684.4, 1688.1 (t); *Lives of the Saints* 1631.1, 1643.1, 1650.3, 1672.1, 1679.2, 1696.1; *Preface to Genesis* 1690.1, 1698.1; *Sermo de Sacrificio in die Pascae* (CH II.15) 15, 103, 1566.1/2, 1576.1, 1583.1, 1596.1, 1610.3, 1623.1, 1624.1 (t), 1626.1, 1631.3, 1638.1, 1641.2, 1664.1, 1684.4, 1688.1 (t)

Æthelberht, k of Kent (560–616)   5; charter of   1655.3, 1682.1, 1683.1
Æthelflæd, bequest to St Paul's (c.1000) 1658.1, 1673.1, 1683.2
Æthelmær (d.1015), ealdormann, son of Æthelweard, will of   1574.1
Æthelred, k of Mercia (675–704), charter of 1703/5.1
Æthelred (k 978–1016), charter of   1639.4, 1655.3, 1660.1, 1661.1, 1664.1, 1682.1, 1683.1, 1691.2, 1703/5.1; edict of 1701.2, 1703/5.1
Æthelric, will of (961 × 995)   1660.1
Æthelstan (k 927–39), charter of   1618.1 (spurious), 1655.3, 1658.1, 1661.1, 1673.1, 1682.1, 1683.1, 1683.2, 1703/5.1
Æthelstan ætheling (d.1014), son of K Æthelred, will of   1660.1
Æthelweard (d.998), ealdormann, father of Æthelmær, L *Chronicle* by   1601.1
Æthelwyrd, will of (958)   1660.1
Alcuin (c.735–804), scholar: *De virtutibus et vitiis*, OE t of   1643.1, 1690.1
Aldgate, London, Holy Trinity Priory, cartulary of   5
Alford (alias Griffith), Michael (1587–1652), Jesuit ecclesiastical historian   1663.4
Alfred (k 886–899), will of   1574.1, 1574.2, 1663.4, 1678.1; works considered Alfredian: *Pastoral Care*   1568.1, 1574.1, 1574.2, 1597.1, 1602.2, 1603.1, 1622.2, 1631.2, 1664.1, 1678.1, 1687.3. 1700?.1.
See also Boethius
Alfred Jewel   1700.4, 1703/5.1
Anglo-Saxon, punches for   24; assembling types for   25

Anglo-Saxon Chronicle 7, 42, 44, 1567.1, 1568.1, 1570.1, 1574.1, 1576.1, 1583.1, 1596.1, 1607.2, 1610.3, 1618.1, 1623.1, 1623.3, 1626.1, 1631.3, 1635.1, 1636.1, 1636.2, 1636.3, 1637.1, 1639.2, 1641.2, 1643.1, 1645.1, 1645.2, 1646.3, 1646.4, 1647.2, 1647.5, 1648.1, 1648.2, 1652.1, 1652.2, 1659.2, 1659.3, 1660.1, 1662.2, 1662.3, 1662.4, 1663.1, 1664.1, 1666.1, 1670.1, 1671.2, 1672.1, 1675.2, 1676.2, 1678.1, 1680.1, 1680.2, 1684.4, 1685.1, 1685.2, 1687.2, 1691.1, 1692.1 (edn), 1693.1, 1695.3, 1696.1, 1703/5.1

Antiquaries, Elizabethan Society of 181

Arabic types 88–89

d'Armillier, Hubert, former apprentice of Granjon, in London by 1553 38

Arnold, Richard (d.1521), historian of London 1503.1

Arrighi, Lodovico degli (fl. Vicenza 1510–27), Italian printer/publisher 69–70

Arundel. *See* Howard

Asser, bp of Sherborne (c.895–909) 17; *Life of King Alfred* 1574.2, use of 1685.1; for other works *see* Parker

Badanoth Beotting, will of (845 × 853) 1703/5.1

Badger, Richard I (1585–1641), printer 59, 79, 88, 201, 205

Bale, John (1495–1563), antiquary 5, 19

Basque, New Testament printed in 18

Basset, Thomas (fl.1658–96), publisher 77, 202

Bath priory, cartulary of 1703/5.1

Battely, Nicolas (1648–1704), editor of Somner's *Antiquities* 78, 1703.2

Le Bé, Guillaume I (1523/4–98), punchcutter at Paris 148–149

Le Bé, Guillaume III (1610?–85), typefounder at Paris 172, 206

Beale, John (fl.1611–43†), printer 76, 78, 200–201

Bede, Venerable (d.635), OE version of *Historia Ecclesiastica* 1568.1, 1574.1, 1614.4, 1618.1, 1623.1, 1631.1, 1638.1, 1639.2, 1643.1, 1650.3, 1650.4, 1652.1, 1655.1, 1660.1, 1663.1, 1670.1, 1672.1, 1676.2, 1679.2, 1685.1, 1687.2, 1689.3, 1691.1, 1695.3, 1696.1, 1696.2, 1700?.2(ante1714). *See also* Wheelock

Bede's Death Song, OE poem 10, 1652.1, 1691.2

Bembo, Pietro (1470–1547), Italian poet 103

Benedictine Office, OE prose 1705.1

Benson, Thomas (b.1678/9), Oxford Saxonist turned cleric: *Vocabularium Anglo-Saxonicum* (1701.1) 97, 140, 207; prospectus (1690.2) 138, 207, (1699.2) 207

van Beerninck, Anna, widow of Daniel Elsevier, type-specimen issued by (1681) 131

Beornwulf, k of Mercia (823–25), charter of 1655.3, 1682.1, 1683.1

Bible, OE 1679.1 (Genesis), 1698.1 (Heptateuch)

La Bigne, Margarinus de (1546–90), theologian 1618.5, 1644.3, 1677.1

Billaine, Louis (fl. Paris 1652–81†), publisher 169, 205

Bishop, George (d.1611), printer 75, 79

Bishop, Richard (fl.1631–53), printer 57, 87, 89, 92, 191, 193

Blaeu, Joan (1596–1673), Dutch printer of atlases 143, 183, 200, 1645.1, 1645.2, 1646.5, 1647.5, 1648.1, 1648.2, 1659.3, 1662.3, 1662.4; heirs of, type-specimen (1695.5) 158, 200

Blount, Thomas (1618–79), lexicographer 1656.3, 1661.2, 1670.2, 1674.3, 1681.4

Boethius (c.480–524), administrator and philosopher at Ravenna: *De Consolatione Philosophiæ* t into OE = OE Boethius 1655.1, 1656.2, 1665.2, 1684.3, 1698.2 (edn), 1703/5.1 (*Meters*)

Boleyn, Anne, 2nd wife of Henry VIII 18

Bollifant (*alias* Carpenter), Edmund (fl.1584–1602), printer at Eliot's Court Press 75, 196

Boniface (Winfred), St (675–754), English missionary in Holland & Germany 1605.5, 1618.5

Bontius, William (Willem de Bondt; d.1646), Leiden professor of Law 149

Book of Common Prayer 22–23

Boom, Hendrick & Dirk I (fl.1669–80), printers at Amsterdam 159, 201
Boswell, Sir William (d.1650), English ambassador at The Hague 200
Boxhorn, Marcus Zuerius (1602–53), Leiden philologist 142: *Apologia pro Navigationibus Hollandorum* (1633) 149; *Historia Universalis* 1652.3; *Metamorphosis Anglorum* 1653.2; *Prima Religionis Christianæ Rudimenta* 1650.5
Bradwood, Melchisidec (fl.1602–18), printer at Eliot's Court Press 194
Browne, Samuel (fl.1641–65), bookseller & negotiator 86
Browne, Sir Thomas (1605–82), polymath author 1683.4, 1684.6, 1686.2
Brunanburh, OE poem 1703/5.1
Bullokar, William (c.1531–1609), orthoepist: *Short Introduction* 36
Burghley. *See* Cecil
Burton, William (1609–57), antiquary: *Commentary on Antoninus his Itinerary* (1658.2) 84, 202
Bynneman, Henry (d.1583), printer 41, 82–83, 194
Byrhtric, will of (973 × 987) 1576.2, 1596.2, 1634.1, 1640?.1, 1660.1, 1662.1, 1664.1, 1675.1, 1703/5.1

Cædmon's Hymn, OE poem 1703/5.1
Caius, John (1510–73), historian: *De Antiquitate Cantabrigiensis Academiæ* (1568.1) 176, 1574.1
Cambridge, St Sepulchre's church 93
Cambridge University, AS lectureship at 93, 183; University Librarian 93; *Irenodia Cantabrigiensis* (celebratory verses) (1641.3) 97
Camden, William (1551–1623), antiquarian author 143, 176, 181–182: *Britannia* (1586.1) 75, 157, (1587.1) 75, (1590.1) 75, (1594.2) 75, 182, (1600.1) 75, 182, (1607.2) 77, 159, 159, 176, 183, 201, (1610.5) 78, 1637.1, 1695.3; *Remains* (1605.1) 144–145

du Cange, Charles de Fresne, sieur (1610–88), Latin lexicographer (1678.2, 1681.1) 144, 169–172, 183, 205–206
Canterbury Cathedral, charters relating to 1655.3, 1660.1, 1682.1, 1683.1, 1693.1, 1703/5.1
Carew, Richard (1555–1620), antiquary 181
Casaubon, Meric (1599–1671), scholar: *Quatuor* (1650.1) 79
Caxton, William (d.1492), printer 15
Cecil, Sir William (later Lord Burghley) 8, 11, 36, 183, 194
Cenric (*recte* Coenred), k of Mercia (c.675–709), charter of 1655.3, 1682.1, 1683.1
Ceolwulf I, k of Mercia (821–23), request for land by 1703/5.1
Charles I, k (1625–49) 23, 128, 148
Charters, AS (listed by Sawyer (S) or Pelteret (P) number):
S1 1655.3, 1682.1, S77 1703/5.1, S80 1655.3, 1682.1, S141 1655.3, 1682.1, S146 1655.3, 1682.1, S282 1693.1, S376 1655.3, 1682.1, S386 1703/5.1, S389 1703/5.1, S391 1655.3, 1682.1, S424 1661.1, S438 1661.1, S451, 1618.1, S452 1655.3, 1658.1, 1673.1, 1682.1, S507 1655.3, 1682.1, S514 1655.3, 1682.1, S519 1661.1, S546 1655.3, 1682.1, S550 1655.3, 1682.1, S567 1655.3, 1682.1, S582 1661.1, S726 1703/5.1, S731 1632.3, 1644.4, 1655.3, 1682.1, 1703/5.1, S745 1639.4, S755 1703/5.1, S766 1661.1, S779 1691.2, S780 1691.2, S781 1691.2, S786 1655.3, 1682.1, 1703/5.1, S802 1660.1, S805 1702.1, S865 1698.3, S881 1661.1, S899 1655.3, 1682.1, S904 1655.3, 1682.1, S906 1655.3, 1682.1, S907 1691.2, S908 1655.3, 1658.1, 1673.1, 1682.1, S911 1655.3, 1682.1, S914 1626.1, 1639.4, 1660.1, 1664.1, S958 1691.2, S961 1655.3, 1682.1, S980 1703/5.1, S992 1655.3, 1658.1, 1673.1, 1682.1, S1021 1703/5.1, S1036 1661.1, S1042 1655.3, 1682.1, S1063 1655.3, 1682.1, S1064 1655.3, 1682.1, S1071 1702.1, S1100 1691.2, S1104 1631.1, 1655.3, 1658.1, 1672.1, 1673.1, 1682.1, 1696.1, S1111 1703/5.1, S1112 1703/5.1, S1113 1703/5.1, S1114 1703/5.1, S1115 1703/5.1,

Charters, AS (cont.)
S1116 1703/5.1, S1117 1702.1, S1121 1703/5.1, S1134 1702.1, S1141 1703/5.1, S1148 1695.2, S1149 1598.2, S1155 1655.3, 1682.1, S1163 1703/5.1, S1165 1655.3, 1682.1, S1215 1640.1, 1703.2, S1240 1703/5.1, S1241 1703/5.1, S1246 1631.4, S1289 1703/5.1, S1325 1703/5.1, S1332 1631.1, 1672.1, 1696.1, S1363 1703/5.1, S1380 1655.3, 1682.1, S1384 1703/5.1, S1406 1703/5.1, S1416 1703/5.1, S1431 1639.4, S1432 1703/5.1, S1433 1639.4, 1655.3, 1682.1, S1437 1703/5.1, S1454 1703/5.1, S1455 1703/5.1, S1456 1666.1, 1671.2, 1680.2, 1703/5.1, S1457 1703/5.1, S1458 1703/5.1, S1459 1703/5.1, S1460 1703/5.1, S1461 1660.1, S1462 1703/5.1, S1465 1652.1, 1660.1, 1693.1, S1469 1703/5.1, S1471 1660.1, S1473 1702.1, 1703/5.1, S1478 1655.3, 1682.1, S1482 1703/5.1, S1488 1703/5.1, S1501 1660.1, S1503 1660.1, S1506 1660.1, S1507 1574.1, 1574.2, 1663.4, 1678.1; S1510 1703/5.1, S1511 1576.2, 1596.2, 1634.1, 1640?.1, 1660.1, 1662.1, 1664.1, 1675.1, 1703/5.1, S1522 1702.1, S1523 1664.1, S1530 1702.1, 1703/5.1, S1535 1660.1, S1536 1655.3, 1682.1, S1538 1703/5.1, S1539 1703/5.1, S1597 1703/5.1, S1622 1660.1, S1636 1703/5.1; P6 1682.2, 1703/5.1, P8 1503.1, 1577.1, 1626.1, 1640?.1, 1664.1, P17 1703/5.1, P19 1703/5.1, P25 1691.1, P26 1655.3, 1664.1, 1682.1, P28 1631.1, 1672.1, 1696.1, P29 1703/5.1, P30 1702.1, P32 1703/5.1, P33 1703/5.1, P39 1655.3, 1658.1, 1673.1, 1682.1, 1682.2, P44 1572.1, 1605.2, 1626.1, 1664.1, P46 1703/5.1, P47 1660.1, P51 1703/5.1, P64 1703/5.1, P90 1640.1, 1703.2, P147 1703/5.1

Chaucer, Geoffrey (d.1400), poet, *Canterbury Tales* 15

Chertsey Minster, grant of land to 1655.3, 1682.1, 1683.1

Chiswell, Richard (fl.1667–1711), publisher 77, 196

Christ and Satan, OE poem 1655.2

Christina, (1626–89), q of Sweden 161

Chrodegang, Rule of in AS 1567.1, 1643.1

Church in England 14–15, 183

Cnut, k (1016–35), charter of 1655.3, 1658.1, 1673.1, 1682.1, 1683.1, 1683.2, 1691.2

Coke, Sir Edward (1552–1634), lawyer 1644.4

Commonwealth in England (1649–60) 23

Cooke, Edward (fl.s.xvii[mid]), lawyer 1682.2, 1689.2

Corsz[oon] van Hoogenacker, Arent (fl. Leiden 1579–1636), punchcutter 86, 156–157, 198

Cot, Pierre (fl. Paris c.1700), typefounder 172, 206

Cotes, Richard (fl.1627–53†), printer 89, 199

Cotton, Sir Robert (1571–1631), founder of the Cottonian library 179, 181

Cotton, Sir Thomas (1594–1662), heir to the Cottonian library 104, 106

Creed in OE 1566.1/2, 1609.1, 1610.6, 1623.1, 1638.1, 1650.5, 1652.3

Crosaigh, Pilip Mac Cuinn, Irish poet 20, 197

Daniel, OE poem 1655.2

Daniel, Roger (1593?–1667; fl. London 1620–29, 1650–66; Printer to Cambridge University 1632–50) 94–96, 195, 199–200

Daniel, William (d.1628), t of *Book of Common Prayer* into Irish 21

Dawson, John (fl.1613–34?†), printer 76, 82, 196

Day, John (1522–84), printer 13–15, 29, 34, 39, 41, 55–56, 60, 72, 80, 191, 193; for works printed *see* Foxe, Lambarde, Parker

Death of Edgar, OE poem 1703/5.1

Denham, Henry, printer 37, 41

D'Ewes, Sir Symonds (1602–50), antiquary & politician 93–94, 179, 199

van Dijck, Christoffel (c.1603–69), Dutch punchcutter 128–131, 138–140, 157, 201–202, 207, 210, 212

Dodsworth, Roger (1585–1654), antiquary collaborator with Dugdale 1655.3, 1661.1, 1682.1, 1683.1

Dolhopff, Georg Andreas (fl. Strassburg 1662–1711), printer 168, 205

Drayton, Michael (1563–1631), poet: *Poly-Olbion* 78, 1612.1, 1613.1

Drummond, William (1585–1649), Scottish poet 1691.4

Du-Gard William (1606–62), printer & editor 98, 1674.1

Dugdale, Sir William (1605–86), antiquarian
  scholar   179, 204; *Monasticon
  Anglicanum*   (1655.3, 1661.1) 79, 179,
  184, 1682.1, 1683.1, 1683.2; *Originales
  Juridiciales*   (1666.1) 79, 179;
  St Pauls   (1658.1) 79, 179.
  See also Spelman H.
Durham Cathedral, charter relating to
  1703/5.1
Durham, OE poem   1652.1, 1703/5.1

Eadred, k (923–55), charter of   1655.3, 1661.1,
  1682.1, 1683.1
Eadwig, k (955–59), charter of   1661.1
Edgar, k 943–75, canons of (*Directions for a
  Confessor*)   1618.1; (*Be Dædbœtan*)
  1680.1; (*Be Dædbœtan*)   1639.4, 1643.1,
  1644.1, 1650.3, 1679.2, 1696.2; charter
  of 1632.3, 1639.4, 1655.3, 1660.1, 1661.1,
  1682.1, 1683.1, 1691.2, 1702.1, 1703/5.1.
  See also Death
Edith, q (1045–66), writ of   1703/5.1
Edmund I, k (920/1–46), charter of   1655.3,
  1682.1, 1683.1
Edward the Confessor, k (1042–66), charter of
  5, 56, 1655.3, 1661.1; writ of 1598.2,
  1631.1, 1655.3, 1658.1, 1672.1, 1673.1,
  1682.1, 1682.1, 1683.1, 1683.2, 1691.2,
  1695.2, 1696.1, 1702.1, 1703/5.1; laws of
  1644.1
Edward the Elder, k (c.874–924), charter of
  1655.3, 1682.1, 1683.1
Egbert, k (802–39), charter of   1698.3
Eliot's Court Press (fl.1584–1680), printing
  syndicate   73–74, 77–78, 83, 87, 182,
  194,196
Elizabeth I, q (1558–1603) 10, 18;
  t *The Miroir of the Synnefull Soule*   19;
  Queen Elizabeth's Irish Types (IR1)
  20–21, 197–198
Elmham, Thomas, *History of St Augustine's,
  Canterbury*   5, 8
Elsevier, Daniel (d.1680), Dutch printer/
  publisher   131
Elstob, William (1674?–1715), Oxford
  Saxonist   180, 1705.1; *Orosius*   1699.1;
  Sermo Lupi (1701.2) 180; AS 'verse'
  composition by   1700.2.
  See also Hickes, *Thesaurus*

Ely, guild regulations at   1703/5.1
Elzevier, Bonaventura and Abraham I
  (fl.1620–53), printers at Leiden   149, 152,
  154–156
Endter, Balthasar Joachim & Johann Andreas
  (fl. Nuremberg 1652–79), publishers   169,
  205
Erpenius (van Erpe), Thomas (1584–1624),
  Arabist at Leiden   86
Estienne, Robert II, printer at Paris   35, 193
Evesham abbey, grant of privileges to
  1655.3, 1682.1, 1683.1
Exeter, unified bishopric at   1703/5.1;
  cathedral, list of books given by bp Leofric
  to   1566.1/2, 1623.1, 1638.1, 1655.3, 1682.1,
  1683.1; Æthelstan's gift to 1655.3, 1682.1,
  1683.1; script characteristic of
  115–116, 125–126
Exodus, OE poem   1655.2, 1703/5.1

Figgins, Vincent (1766–1844), typefounder
  203
Finnsburg Fragment, OE poem   1703/5.1
Flesher, James (fl.1649–70†), printer, son of
  next   79, 80, 89, 195–197, 199
Flesher, Miles I (fl.1617–64†), printer   87,
  89, 199
Fournier, Pierre Simon, le jeune (1712–68),
  punchcutter & typefounder in Paris   170,
  206
Fox, Luke (1586–1635), explorer   1635.2
Foxe, John (d.1587), author   22; *Book of
  Martyrs*   (1571.1) 109*n*, (1576.1) 25, 56,
  60–61, 73, (1583.1) 55, (1596.1) 56,
  (1610.3) 77, (1631.3) 77, 1684.4;
  AS *Gospels*   (1571.1) 29, 35, 176
Franckton, John, printer in Dublin   21
Freher, Marquard (1565–1614), German
  professor at Heidelberg   1609.1, 1610.6
Fresne. *See* du Cange

Gale, Thomas (1636–1702), antiquarian
  1691.2
Garamont, Claude (1480–1561),
  punchcutter   36, 56, 69, 103, 148, 209–211
Garrett, William (fl.1659), businessman   75
Genealogical Regnal List, WS   1643.1, 1678.1,
  and *see* MS Tiberius A.iii.
Genesis, OE poem   1655.2, 1669.1, 1703/5.1

Gessner, Christian Friedrich (1701–56),
    typefounder & printer 169, 205
Gessner, Conrad (1516–65), Swiss
    bibliographer & philologist 1555.1
Geþyncðo, AS law 66, 1576.2, 1596.2, 1608.1,
    1610.4, 1614.4, 1619.2, 1631.1, 1640?.1,
    1656.2, 1664.1, 1672.1, 1698.3, 1703/5.1
Gibson, Edmund (1669–1748), bp of Lincoln,
    then London, Oxford Saxonist 180,
    1691.4 (ed.), 1695.3 (ed.), 1698.3 (ed.);
        Chronicon Saxonicum (1692.1) 180
Gil, Alexander (1565–1635), orthoepist
    1621.1
Gilbert, Sir Humphrey (c.1539–83), explorer
    1576.3
Gloria I, OE poem 1703/5.1
Glover, Robert (1544–88), Somerset Herald:
    Nobilitas Politica (1608.1) 78
Goderitsch, Johann Michael (fl. Wittenberg
    1687–96), printer 25, 172–175, 206
Gospel of Nicodemus, OE 1698.1, 1703/5.1
Gospels in OE 1571.1, 1613.3 (Jn), 1623.1
    (Mt), 1626.1 (various), 1640.4 (various),
    1646.7 (Jn), 1650.3 (various), 1655.1
    (various), 1664.1 (various), 1665.2,
    1665.3 (various), 1679.2 (various),
    1684.3, 1695.3 (Mt), 1695.4, 1696.2 (Mt)
Gospels of St Chad 1703/5.1
Granjon, Robert, punchcutter 20, 38, 161,
    210–213
Greaves, John (1602–52), Savilian Professor of
    Astronomy at Oxford University 86,
    89; *Discourse on the Romane Foot* 87
Gregory, John (1607–46), author & editor
    82, 89; *Notes and Observations* (1650.2)
    89, 1646.2, 1665.1, 1671.1, 1684.1.
    See also Ridley
Griffin, Edward II (fl.1637–52†), printer at
    Eliot's Court Press 75, 79, 196
Griffo, Francesco (1450–1518), Italian
    punchcutter 103
Grimm, Jacob (1785–1863), Germanic
    philologist 26
Grismond, John II (f.1641–66†), printer 195
Grotius, Hugo (1583–1645), scholar at
    Leiden 127, 182, 1655.6;
        De Mari Libero (1633) 149

Grover, Thomas (c.1630–75), took over
    Nicholls typefoundry 1672, types passed to
    James 97, 200
Guild, William (1586–1657), Scottish
    theologian 1624.1
Guillaume de Branteghem (d.1543), Belgian
    ecclesiastical author: *La Vie de Nostre
    Seigneur* 69
Guthlac, OE prose 1639.2, 1687.2
Guyot, François, punchcutter 34, 37, 156,
    186, 203, 205
Guyot, Gabriel, son of prec 37

Hail Mary, prayer in OE 1613.3, 1646.7
Hakluyt, Richard (1553–1616), travel writer
    1589.1
Halgungboc, OE verse inscription 1639.4
Hall, Henry (fl. Oxford 1642–80), printer,
    father of William Hall II 89, 201
Hall, William (fl.1598–1614), printer 77, 188,
    194, 196
Hall, William II (fl. Oxford 1657–72), Printer
    of Oxford University 1662 85–86, 204
Hamon, Pierre (1530–69), writing-master to
    Charles IX of France 193
Harold, k (1066), writ of 1703/5.1
Hart, John, Chester Herald (1567–74),
    orthoepist: *Orthographie* 35–36, 40, 41;
        Methode 35–36, 40
Haultin, Jérôme, nephew of next,
    typefounder in London 21, 40, 194, 198
Haultin, Pierre, punchcutter 18, 21, 38, 60,
    79–80, 191, 193–194, 198, 209
Haviland, John (fl.1621–38), printer at Eliot's
    Court Press 74, 79, 196–197
Hayes, John (printer to Cambridge University
    1669–1705†) 78, 195
Hearne, Thomas (1678–1735), antiquarian
    scholar and diarist 140, 208; *Chronica
    Prioratus de Dunstable* (1733) 204
Heinsius, Daniel (1580–1655), Dutch scholar
    & poet 183
Heliand, continental Old Saxon poem
    1690.1, 1703/5.1, 1705.1
Henry I, k (1100–35), charter of 1572.1,
    1605.2, 1626.1, 1703/5.1; writ of 1660.1;
    diploma of 1664.1

GENERAL INDEX

Henry II, k (1154–89), charter of 1703/5.1
Henry III, k (1216–72), Proclamation of (1258) 1659.1
Henry VIII, k (1509–47) 6, 14, 18
Henshaw, Thomas (1618–70), editor of Skinner 1671.3
Hickes, George (1642–1715) 136, 170, 184, 1700.4, 1705.1; *Institutiones Grammaticae* (1689.3) 134–136, 180; *Thesaurus* (1703/5.1) 140, 180, 184, 207–208
Hodgkinson, Richard (fl.1624–75†), printer 78–79, 197
Holdsworth, Richard (1590–1649), Cambridge academic 1641.3
Holinshed, Raphael (1529–80), English chronicler 1577.1
Holland, printing AS in 144, 149–166
Holland, Philemon (1552–1637), translator 1610.5
Homilies, AS, anonymous 1643.1
Hondius, Jodocus (Joost de Hondt, 1563–1612), engraver of maps 75–76, 160
Horne, Robert, dean of Durham (1568) 10
Howard, Thomas (1585–1646), earl of Arundel, patron of Junius 127, 179
Howell, William (fl. s.xvii³), historian 1685.1
Humble, George (fl.1611–32), nephew of John Sudbury, publisher 75, 171, 194, 196
Humble, William (fl.1640–59), son of prec 75

Ingulf (d.1109), attrib., *Historia Croylandensis* 1601.1
Irish, printing of 16, 20
Islip, Adam (fl.1591–1639†), printer 79–81, 194, 196

Jaggard, William (fl.1594–1623†), printer 79, 83, 197
James I, k (1603–25) 23, 87, 128, 177, 181
James V, k of Scotland (1513–42), poetic patron 1614.4
James, John, typefounder (catalogue 1782) 97, 200, 203
Janssonius, Joannis (1588–1664), son-in-law of Hondius, entrepreneur/printer of atlases based in Amsterdam 25, 139, 160–166, 183, 201; type-specimen of (1666) 148, 201; atlases (1646.3) 160–161, **1646.4**, 1647.3, 1647.4, 1659.2, 1659.4, **1675.2**
Janssonius van Waesbergen, Johannes II (fl.1675–1706), son-in-law of prec 160
Jean I de Tournes (1504–64), French printer 69
Jeanne d'Albret, q of Navarre (1555–72) 18
Jonson, Ben (1572–1637), playwright 1640.2, 1692.2
Jordan, Raimon (fl.1178–95), troubadour from Toulouse 1597.1
Joscelyn, John (1529–1603), Abp Parker's Latin Secretary 8n, 11–13, 45–46, 51–54, 125. *See also* Parker
Judith, OE poem 1698.1, 1703/5.1
Jugge, Richard (d.1577), printer 41
Junius, Franciscus (1545–1602), theologian, father of next 127; *Animadversiones* (1608 edn) 128
Junius, Franciscus (1591–1677), scholar of Germanic 23, 27, 87, 98, 127–136, 157, 179–182, 184, 201–203; his printing utensils 128, 184, 210, 212; *Cædmonis Paraphrasis Poetica* (1655.2) 127, 179, 184; *Observationes in Willerami Paraphrasin* (1655.1) 127, 180, 184; *De Pictura Veterum* (1637) 132; with Thomas Marshall *Gothic Gospels* (1665.2) 129, 133–134, 180, **1684.3**
Junius, Joannes Casimirus (1582–1624), half-brother of prec 128

Kearney, John (1545–87?), t of Catechism into Irish 17, 21, 198
Kearney, William (fl. s.xvi³/⁴), printer at Dublin 17, 20, 21
Kennett, White (1660–1728), antiquarian bishop 1695.2
Kiliaan (van Kiel), Cornelis (1528–1607), Dutch lexicographer 1599.2, 1605.4, 1613.2, 1623.5, 1623.6, 1632.4, 1642.1
Kingston, Felix (fl.1597–1653†), printer 78, 194
Knaplock, Robert (fl.1696–1737†), publisher 77, 196; Robert, his brother 77
Köblin, Balthasar (fl. Konstanz c.1654–80), punchcutter 169, 205

La Rochelle, protestant safe-haven 18, 191
de Laet, Johannes (1581–1649), Dutch geographer interested in AS 200
Laȝamon's *Brut* (c.1190), eME verse chronicle 1576.2, 1596.2
Lambarde, William (1536–1601), antiquarian author 65, 181, 183; *Archaionomia* (1568.2) 11, 29, 31, 65, 176, 181, 173.
    See also Wheelock; *Eirenarcha* (1581.1) 65, 67, 73, (1582.1) 73, (1588.1) 75, (1591.1) 75, (1592.1) 75, (1594.1) 75, (1599.1) 75, (1602.1) 75, (1607.1) 79, (1610.1) 80, (1614.2) 80, (1619.1) 80; *Perambulation of Kent* (1576.2) 25, 60, 63–66, 73, 83, 176, 203, (1596.2) 79, (1640?.1) 80
Langbaine, Gerald (1609–58), Keeper of Oxford University Archives, Provost of Queen's College 84–87, 204
Langhorne, Daniel (d.1681), historian 1676.3
Lautizio de Bartolomeo dei Rotelli (fl. Perugia s.xvi[1]), goldsmith & punchcutter 69
Laws, AS 1566.1/2 (1 Cnut), 1568.2, 1574.1 (Alfred), 1581.1 (Ine), 1582.1 (Ine), 1588.1 (Ine), 1591.1 (Ine), 1592.1 (Ine), 1594.1 (Ine), 1599.1 (Ine), 1602.1 (Ine), 1607.1 (Ine), 1610.1 (Ine), 1610.2 (Ine), 1612.1 (Ine), 1613.1 (Ine), 1614.2 (Ine), 1614.4 (assorted), 1618.1 (assorted), 1619.1 (Ine), 1622.1 (Ine), 1623.1 (1 Cnut), 1623.3 (Æthelstan, Edgar, 1626.1 (assorted), 1631.1 (various), 1634.1 (various), 1638.1 (Cnut), 1639.1 (Cnut), 1639.4 (assorted), 1640.4 (Alfred), 1641.1 (Cnut), 1643.1 (various), 1644.1, 1646.6 (various), 1652.1 (various), 1653.2 (Ine), 1655.1 (Alfred), 1660.1 (various), 1662.1 (various), 1663.1 (various), 1664.1 (various), 1665.3 (Alfred), 1672.1 (various), 1675.1 (various), 1676.2 (Ine, Wihtræd), 1678.1 (Alfred), 1680.1 (various), 1684.2, 1685.1 (various), 1690.1 (various), 1693.1 (Hloþhære), 1695.3 (Alfred), 1696.1 (various), 1698.3 (various), 1703/5.1 (various). *See also Geþyncðo*

Legal agreements, AS 1640.1, 1652.1, 1655.3, 1660.1, 1666.1, 1671.2, 1680.2, 1682.1, 1683.1, 1693.1, 1702.1, 1703.2, 1703/5.1
Legat, John II (fl. 1620–58†), printer 195
Leiden University 127
Leland, John (c.1503–52), antiquary 5
Leofric, bp of Exeter (1046–72), scriptorium of 115. *See also* Exeter
Leofwine, will of (998) 1702.1
L'Estrange, Hamon (1583–1654), son of Sir Nicholas (d.1591/2), ward of Sir Henry Spelman 177
Libelle of Englyshe Policye, ME poem 1635.1
Liber Scintillarum, L florilegium of biblical and patristic quotations by Defensor of Ligugé, t into OE 1655.1, 1690.1
Lindisfarne Gospels, L with OE gloss 1652.1
Lisle, William (1569–1637), antiquarian scholar 76, 181; *Divers Ancient Monuments* (1638.1) 76, 80; *Saxon Treatise* (1623.1) 80
Lord's Prayer in OE 1555.1, 1566.1/2, 1593.1, 1605.1, 1609.1, 1610.6, 1612.2, 1613.1, 1614.3, 1623.1, 1623.4, 1629.1, 1634.4, 1638.1, 1646.7, 1650.5, 1657.1, 1662.6, 1664.2, 1668.1, 1674.1, 1675.3, 1680.3, 1687?.1, 1693.2, 1695.1, 1700.1
Lownes, Humphrey I (fl.1590–1630), publisher and printer 78, 194
Lüdecke, Thomas (fl.1680), compiler 1680.3
Lupus of Ferrières, scholar s.ix 55
Luther, Johan Erasmus (1642–83), typefounder at Frankfurt 150
Lyly, Peter, (fl.1550–80) Registrar of the Consistory Court at Canterbury, specialist in archaic script 9

Mabillon, Jean (1632–1707), palaeographer 1681.2
Madox, Thomas (1666–1727), legal historian 1702.1
Maire, Johan & Dirk (Theodore) (fl. in partnership 1636), printers at Leiden 149, 154, 156
Malherbe Des Ports, Mathieu (c.1659–c.1726), occasional punchcutter at Paris 170, 206
Mantat, anchorite, will of (1017 × 1035) 1664.1

Manuscripts. *See also* Bibliography, and the lists in 1689.3 and 1703/5.1
  Cambridge, Corpus Christi College
    41: 105, 110, 112; 100: 9; 111: 6; 138: 7, 42, 108, 110, 112; 140: 43n, 108, 110, 112, 114n; 162: 103, 106, 108, 114n, 123; 173: 45, 47, 98–99, 105, 110–112, 120, 123; 178: 9; 188: 108, 110, 112, 121, 123; 190: 13, 44, 48n, 47, 53n, 107, 111–114, 115, 124–125; 191: 107, 110, 112, 116; 198: 44–47, 107, 110, 112; 201: 107, 110, 112, 116, 120–121, 125; 265: 13, 44, 48n, 47, 193; 279: 107, 111, 113; 318: 108, 110, 112; 379: 6; 383: 6, 107, 110, 112; 419: 107, 110, 112, 116–117, 125; 449: 13; 488: 8n; 583: 8
  Cambridge, St John's College   27: 110, 113
  Cambridge, Sidney Sussex College
    102: 105, 110
  Cambridge, Trinity College B.15.34   107, 110, 113, 116, 118, 120–121; R.4.26: 107, 110, 113; R.5.16: 109, 111, 113; R.5.22: 105, 110, 113; R.7.28: 9; R.17.1: 108, 111, 113, 181
  Cambridge, Trinity Hall   1: 5, 107, 111, 113, 125
  Cambridge, University Library Dd.3.12
    108n, 109n; Ff.1.23: 108, 111–112; Ff.1.27: 108, 110, 112, 124–125; Ff.1.28: 107, 110, 112; Gg.3.28: 107–108, 110, 112, 120–121, 125; Hh.1.10: 6, 48, 47, 108, 109n, 110, 112, 116; Ii.1.33: 107, 110, 112, 112n; Ii.2.4: 108, 109n, 110, 112, 115–116; Ii.2.11: 44–45, 47, 108, 109–112, 116; Ii.4.6: 45n, 107, 110, 112; Kk.3.18: 6, 48n, 105, 110, 112, 125
  Durham, Cathedral Library A.IV.36
    9–10
  Exeter, Cathedral Library   3501: 44, 47
  Glasgow, University Library Hunter
    215: 5
  London, British Library, Additional
    6395: 200; Add 25384: 107n; Add 34600: 104n; Add 34652: 47, 105–106, 109n; Add 35333: 107n; Add 43703: 106n; Arundel 60: 181; Cotton Claudius B.iv 6–7; Cleopatra B.xiii 44–45, 47; Domitian vii 6; Faustina A.ix 44–45, 47; Faustina A.x 109n; Julius F.vi 104n;
    Nero A.i 6, 44, 47; Nero C.iii 44; Otho B.xi 44–45, 47, 104–106, 110, 113; Otho C.i 45n; Tiberius A.iii 105–106, 110, 113; Tiberius A.vi 45, 47, 105; Tiberius A.xiii 45n; Tiberius B.i 6, 7, 17, 44–46, 47, 193; Tiberius B.iv 45, 47; Tiberius C.ii 104–105, 110, 113, 120–122, 125; Vespasian D.xiv 6, 44, 47, 53, 193; Vitellius D.vii 11–12, 52; Harley 8: 106n; Harley 686: 110n; Harley 761 109n; Royal 1.A.xiv 109n; Stowe 2: 181
  Lambeth Palace   1370: 192
  Oxford, Bodleian Library, Ashmole
    854: 204; Ballard 4: 202; Bodley 441: 6, 45n; Cherry 36: 19n; Hatton 38: 45n; Hatton 113: 48, 49–51, 53, 193; Hatton 114: 45n, 48, 50; Junius 66: 106n; Junius 121: 12, 44–45–49, 67; Laud misc 201: 181; Laud misc. 482: 45n; Laud misc. 636: 44–45, 47, 138
  Corpus Christi College   197: 16
  Westminster Abbey   30: 62
  Worcester Cathedral   F.124: 4
  Facsimiles of   1703/5.1
Manutius, Aldus (1449–1515), Italian printer   103
Marguerite of Angloulême (1492–1549), q of Navarre, authoress of *Le Miroir de l'Ame Pecheresse*   18
Martin, Gabriel (fl. Paris 1652–81†), printer   169, 205
Martyrology, OE   **1626.1**, **1631.1**, **1639.2**, **1664.1**, **1665.2**, **1672.1**, **1684.3**, **1687.2**, **1696.1**, 1703/5.1
Mary I, q (1553–58)   19
Marshall, Thomas (1621–85), Rector of Lincoln College Oxford 132: with Franciscus Junius *Gothic Gospels* (**1665.2**) 129, 133–134, **1684.3**
Maxims II, OE poem   1703/5.1
Megiser, Hieronymus (c.1554–1618/19), German polymath linguist   **1593.1**
Menologium, OE poem   1703/5.1
Middle English, printing of   15
Middleton (Nf), vicar of   93
Middleton, Henry (fl.1567–87), printer   58, 65, 75, 194

Milles, Thomas (c.1550–1627), nephew of Robert Glover, author & editor   79; *Catalogue of Honor*   (1610.4) 79; *Treasurie*   (1619.2) 79
Minsheu, John (1560–1627), lexicographer: *Ductor in Linguas*   (1617.1) 56, 75, 81 (1625.1, 1626.2) 75
Mores, Edward Rowe (1731–78), antiquarian   97
Morhof, Daniel Georg (1639–91), literary historian   1682.4
Motte, Benjamin (d.1710), publisher   1700.1
Mylius (van der Mijle), Abraham (1563–1637), linguist   1612.2

Needham, Marchamont (1620–78), t of Selden's *Mare Clausum*   98, 1652.2, 1663.2
Neobar, Conrad (d.1540), printer in Paris   69
Newbery, Ralph (fl.1560–1604), publisher/entrepreneur   60–62, 65, 72–75, 194
Nicholls, Arthur (fl.1632–40), punchcutter & typefounder   82, 97, 199–200, 202–204, 209–210, 212
Nicholls, Nicholas (fl.1637–71†), son of prec, punchcutter & typefounder   82, 85, 87, 97, 136, 200, 202–204, 209; *Specimen of Anglo-Saxon types* (1656.2) 85; *The Saxon Alphabet* (1665?.1) 85
Norman Yoke of dictatorial kingship   23
Normandy, dukes of, law tract concerning   1568.2, 1644.1
Norstedt collection of matrices, Stockholm   148
Norton, Bonham (1565–1635), printer   75
Norton, John (fl.1621–45), printer   78
Nowell, Laurence (1530–(?)70), antiquary   11, 183; *Vocabularium Saxonicum* (s.xvi⁴)   1650.3, 1679.2, 1696.2

Offa, k of Mercia   757–96, charter of 1655.3, 1682.1, 1683.1
Orc, thane of King Cnut, his guild at Abbotsbury (1041)   1655.3, 1682.1, 1683.1
Orosius, OE   1640.4, 1698.3; Ohtere's voyage   1576.3, 1589.1, 1598.1, 1635.2, 1659.1, 1665.2, 1678.1, 1684.3

Oxford University: *Musarum Oxoniensium ... Foedera* (celebratory verses)   1654.2; *Exequiæ* (celebratory verses)   1700.2
Oxford University Press, nascent at Sheldonian Theatre   83, 202; receives Junius's printing utensils   128, 131–132, 184, 210, 212; Small Pica AS type-design   138–141, 207–208

Padua, location for transfer of roman letter-design from manuscript to print   1460/1470: 103
Paris, Matthew (1200–59), chronicler   88; *Vitæ Duorum Offarum*, ed. Watts (1639.3) 89, 1644.5, 1684.5
Parker, John (1548–1618), son of next   197
Parker, Matthew, abp of Canterbury (1559–75)   3–4, 8, 11, 14, 21–22, 29, 34, 42, 52–55, 60, 65–66, 125, 136, 184, 197; works produced under his auspices: *A Testimonie of Antiquitie* (1566.1) 11–13, 15, 25, 29–30, 39–40, 41, 45, 176, 183, 237–243; *Ælfredi regis res gestæ* (1574.2) 17, 29, 33, 36, 176; *De Antiquitate Britannicæ* (1572.1) 53, 176; *Defence of Priestes Mariages* (1567.1) 176
Parr, Richard (fl.s.xvii⁴), biographer of Ussher   1686.1
Pasquier de Louhans, Estienne, (fl. France s.xvi^mid), translator   69
Patrick, John (fl. s.xvii⁴), author   1688.2
Peringskiöld, Johan (1654–1720), secretary to the Antikvitetesarkiv, Stockholm   1703/5.1
Philipot, John (1588–1645), Somerset Herald   1674.1
Phillips, Edward (1630–96), lexicographer (Milton's nephew)   1658.4, 1662.5, 1663.3, 1671.4, 1678.3, 1696.4, 1700.3
Plantin, Christophe (1520–89), printer in Antwerp   37, 69
Poema Morale, ME poem   1678.1
Prayers, OE   1643.1; *Prayer*, OE poem 1655.1. *See also* Lord's Prayer
Prognostication, OE   1623.3
Promissio Regis, OE   1678.1, 1689.3
Proper names, OE   1586.1, 1587.1, 1590.1, 1594.2, 1596.3, 1600.1, 1607.2, 1610.5,

Proper names, OE (*cont.*)
1611.1, 1614.1, 1616.1, 1616.2, 1623.2, 1623.5, 1626.3, 1627.1, 1627.2, 1627.3, 1632.1, 1632.2, 1632.3, 1637.1, 1639.5, 1645.1, 1645.2, 1646.3, 1646.4, 1647.4, 1647.5, 1648.1, 1648.2, 1650/?1665.1, 1655.6, 1657.1, 1658.2, 1659.2, 1659.3, 1662.2, 1662.3, 1662.4, 1675.2, 1676.1, 1695.3, 1696.3; cf. Words

Proverb from Winfred's Time, OE verse 1605.5, 1618.5, 1644.3, 1677.1

Psalter, L, t into French and printed in Gascon 18

Psalter, OE 1626.1, 1631.1, 1640.3, 1672.1, 1696.1

Rawlinson, Christopher (1677–1733), Oxford Saxonist 173: *Boethi Consolationis Philosophiæ Libri V* (1698.2) 180, 203

Ray, John (1627–1705), naturalist 1674.2, 1691.3

Rea, Roger, the Elder (d.1665) and the Younger (fl.1650–62–?68), publishers 76–77, 196

Recorde, Robert (c.1512–58), antiquary 7

Regularis Concordia (c.973), document of Benedictine Reform 1623.3

Retchford, William (fl.1635–65), AS verse by 1641.3

Reuter, Johannes (Janis Reiters) (1632–95), translator 1662.6

Ridley, Sir Thomas (fl. s.xvii²) legal writer: *View of ... Law*, ed Gregory (1634.1), 81 (1639.1) 82, (1662.1) 86, (1675.1) 86

Robert of Gloucester's Chronicle, ME metrical work (s.xiii⁴) 1643.1, 1670.1, 1676.3

Rochester bridge, charter relating to construction 1576.2, 1596.2, 1640?.1

Roycroft, Thomas (fl.1650–77†), printer 84, 197, 202

Runic ON, *Historia Hialmari Regis* 1703/5.1

Rushworth Gospels (OBL Auct. D.2.19) 1655.1

Saints, resting place of, OE account 1639.2, 1687.3

Sammes, Aylett (c.1636–79), antiquary 1676.2

de Sanlecque, Jacques II (1612–59), punchcutter at Paris 170, 205

Savile, Sir Henry (1549–1622), scholar 1596.3, 1601.1

Scaliger, Joseph Justus (1540–1609), scholar at Leiden 127

Schrey, Jeremias (fl. Frankfurt-an-der-Oder 1673–98), publisher 172–175, 206

Scottish Gaelic, first book printed in (1567) 20

Scripts, AS engraved 1681.2; caroline and insular 16–17; Secretary (s.xvi) 192; hierarchy of 114

Script reform 55

Seasons for Fasting, OE verse 1643.1

Selden, John (1584–1654), scholar and polymath 23, 27, 57–59, 80, 87, 127, 136, 143, 179, 182–183, 205: *Dissertatio ad Fletam* (1647.2) 89, **1685.2**; *Eadmeri Historiæ* (1623.3) 57, 179; *Historie of Tithes* (1618.1 etc) 59, 81, 179; *De Iure Naturali* (1640.4) 57, 167, 179, 205 (1665.3) 167–168, 174, 205, 207, (1695.4) 174, 206; *Jani Anglorum* (1610.2) 80; *Mare Clausum* (1635.1) 57–58, 143, 148–157, 179; t Nedham (1652.1, 1663.2) 94; Dutch pirated editions (1636.1) 149, 152, 154–157, (1636.2) 149, 154–157, (1636.3) 149–150, 154–157; *De Synedriis* (1650.3, 1655.4) 89, 179, (1679.2) 160, 174, 207, (1696.2) 174–175, 206; *Titles of Honor* (1614.4) 59, 80, (1631.1) 57, 179; *Tituli Honorum* (1696.1) 172–174, 206; *Uxor Ebraica* (1646.6) 57, (1673.3) 172. See also Twysden

Serarius, Nicolaus (1555–1609), editor of letters by Boniface 1605.5, 1618.5

Shakespeare, William (1564–1616), playwright, 1st folio edn of works (1623) 182

Sheringham, Robert (1602–78), historian: *De Anglorum Gentis Origine Disceptatio* (1670.1) 79, 83

Short, Peter (d.1603), printer 56

Sibthorp, Sir Christopher (d.1632), English lawyer based in Ireland 1622.2

Simeon, Song of (Lk 2.29–32) 1664.2

Simmons, Mary (fl.1656–67) & Samuel (fl.1665–78), printers   76, 196
Skinner, Stephen (1623–67), lexicographer   1671.3, 1689.1
Smith, Sir Thomas (1513–77), Secretary of State (1548–9, 1572–6), orthoepist 138–142: *De recta & emendata Linguæ anglicæ scriptione, Dialogus* (1568.3) 35, 144–148, 193
Snodham, Thomas (fl.1609–25†), printer   76, 80, 195–196
van Someren. *See* Boom
Somner, William (1598–1669), as lexicographer   (1659.1) 11, 82–83, 85, 87, 97, 127, 136–138, 143–144, 179, 183, 202–204; *Antiquities of Canterbury* (1640.1) 78, 179, (1703.2) 77; *Roman Ports and Forts* (1693.1) 179; *Treatise of Gavelkind* (1660.1) 179. Supplied glossary to Twysden *Scriptores*   80, 179, 181
Speed, John (1552–1629), cartographer   76, 182, 621: *Theatre of the Empire*   (1611.1) 76, 157, 178, (1614.1) 76, L edn   (1616.1) 76, (1627.1, 1632.1) 76, (1650/?1665.1) 76, (1676.1) 77; *History of Great Britaine*   (1611.2) 76
Spelman, Sir Henry (1563/4–1641), statesman and antiquarian   59, 87–88, 82–94, 96, 98, 103–104, 107, 109, 127, 143, 177–179, 181–183, 200, 202, **1684.2, 1698.3**; *Archaismus Graphicus*   88, 183; *Archæologus*   (1626.1) 78, 88–89, 178, 183; *Glossarium Archaiologicum*, ed Dugdale   (1664.1) 80, 88, 144, 179, 183, **1687.1**; *Concilia*   (1639.4) 78, 88, 90–91, 97, 107, 178, 183, 205; *Larger Treatise concerning Tithes*   (1647.1) 89; *De Sepultura*   (1641.1) 89; *Tithes too Hot*   (1646.2) 89
Spelman, Sir John, son of prec (d.1643): *Alfredi Regis ... Vita*, ed. Walker   (1678.1) 98; *Psalterium*   (1640.3) 59, 78, 109, 178, 181
Spelman, Roger, nephew of Sir Henry   182
Stansby, William (fl.1597–1638), printer   56–57, 80–81, 87, 167, 191, 193–194, 205

Stephens, Jeremy (1592–1665), vicar of Wootton, Northants, scholar, assistant to Sir Henry Spelman   178
Stow, John, antiquarian author 174: *Survey of London*   (1598.2) 56
Sudbury, John (fl.1610–15), uncle of George Humble, publisher   76, 194, 196
Symeon of Durham, work by   9

Talbot, Alethia, heiress of e of Shrewsbury, m Thomas Howard   182
Talbot, Elizabeth, heiress of e of Shrewsbury, m Henry Gray, e of Kent, patroness of Selden   182
Talbot, Mary, heiress of e of Shrewsbury, m William Herbert, e of Pembroke, dedicatee of Selden's *Eadmer*   182
Talbot, Robert (c.1505–58), prebendary of Norwich, antiquary   6, 8
Tavernier, Ameet (1522–70), Belgian punchcutter   88, 209, 212
Taylor, Silas (1624–78), antiquarian author: *History of Gavelkind*   (1663.1) 79
Ten Commandments, as   1566.1/2, 1610.6, 1623.1, 1638.1, 1650.5
Testimonie of Antiquitie. See Parker
Theodulf of Orléans (c.760–821), Capitula of, oe & l   **1639.4, 1643.1, 1690.1**
Thomas de Axbridge   5, 8
Thwaites, Edward (1678–1711), Anglo-Saxonist   138, 140–141, 180, 208; *Heptateuchus*   (1698.1) 180; *Pastoral Care*   1700?.1
Thynne, Francis (1544–1608), antiquary   181
Tonson, Jacob (1635–1736), publisher   77
Tory, Geoffrey (1480–1533), French calligraphic artist   103, 192
Tremulous Hand of Worcester (s.xiii)   4, 9, 52
Tressel, Charles, son of Adriaen, 'graver of letters' in London   39
Trissino, Gian Giorgio (1475–1550), Italian author interested in spelling-reform   68
Turner, William (printer to Oxford University 1624–40)   82, 195
Twysden, Sir Roger (1597–1672), historian & politician 172: *Historiæ Anglicanæ Scriptores x*, ed Selden   (1652.1) 80, 89, 179, 181

Tyler, Evan (fl.1652–83), printer   195
Type, how made   24
Type designs   190–213
Types, Textura and Roman   15

Ussher, James (1581–1656), abp of Armagh   84, 106, 176–177, **1690.1**; *Britannicarum Ecclesiarum Antiquitates*   (**1639.2**) 84, 177, **1687.2**; *Discourse*   (**1631.2**) 78, **1687.3**; *Religion Anciently Professed by the Irish*   (**1622.2**) 177; *Veterum Epistolarum Hibernicarum Sylloge* (**1632.3**) 84, 177, **1665.4**, **1696.3**. *See also* Parr

Verstegan (Rowlands), Richard (c.1550–1640), Anglo-Dutch antiquary   **1605.3**, **1613.3**, **1628.1**, **1634.2**, **1646.7**, **1653.1**, **1655.5**
van Vliet, Jan (1620–66), scholar pupil of Junius   131, **1664.2**, **1662.2**
Vorst, Johannes (1623–76), German protestant theologian   **1669.1**
Voskens, Bartholomeus (1613/16–69) & Reinier (1621–c.1670), punchcutters at Amsterdam   131, 157, 200
Voskens, widow of Dirk (d.1691), type-specimen of (**1700?.2(ante1714)**)   157–158, 200–201
Vossius, Gerardus Joannes (1577–1649), scholar at Leiden, husband of Junius's sister Elisabeth   127, **1645.2**
Vredius (de Wree), Olivarius (1596–1652), neo-Latin poet   **1650.4**
Vulcanius (de Smet), Bonaventura (1538–1614), Flemish humanist   **1597.1**

Wake, William (1657–1737), abp of Canterbury (1716–37)   **1703.1**
Walker, Obadiah (1616–99), historian, Master of University College Oxford   98. *See also* Spelman, John
van Walpergen, Peter (fl. Oxford 1676–1703†), punchcutter to OUP   138, 140–141, 201–202, 207–208, 213
Wanley, Humfrey (1672–1726), palaeographer   138, 140–141, 180, 208; as 'verse' composition by **1700.2**; for *Thesaurus* (**1703/5.1**) *see* Hickes

Ward, Samuel (1572–1642), Master of Sidney Sussex College Cambridge   104
Ware, Sir James (1594–1666), antiquarian historian   **1654.1**, **1658.3**
Warren, Alice (fl.1659–65†), printer   79–80, 195, 197
Warren, Francis (fl. 1666), son of Thomas I, brother of Thomas II, printer   79, 195
Warren, Thomas I & II (fl.1645–59†; 1666), printers   79, 195
Watts, William (c.1590–1649), editor   89. *See also* Paris, Matthew
Weever, John (1576–1632), antiquary   **1631.4**
Welsh, printing of   (1567) 20, (1592) 27
Wharton, Henry (1664–95), ecclesiastical author   **1690.1**, **1691.1**
Wheelock, Abraham (1593–1653), Spelman's Lecturer in Anglo-Saxon at Cambridge University, also Professor of Arabic   23, 59, 87, 93–127, 178, 183, 205; *Anglo-Saxon Chronicle* (ed.)   (**1643.1** + **1644.2**) 94, 97, 178, 183; *Archaionomia*   (**1644.1**) 78, 94, 100, 102, 178, 183; Bede's *Ecclesiastical History* (ed.)   (**1643.1**) 94–97, 104–105, 107, 178, 183, 205. *See also* Bede. AS verse by   **1641.3**
Wight, Thomas (fl.1597–1603), printer   75, 196
Wilkins, John (1614–72), polymath natural philosopher   **1668.1**
William I, (k 1066–87); writ of   **1503.1**, **1577.1**, **1655.3**, **1658.1**, **1664.1**, **1673.1**, **1682.1**, **1682.2**, **1683.1**, **1683.2**, **1689.2**, **1691.1**, **1703/5.1**; charter of **1576.2**, **1596.2**, **1626.1**, **1640?.1**, **1664.1**, diploma of **1631.1**, **1672.1**, **1696.1**, **1703/5.1**; laws of   **1644.1**
Williamson, Sir Joseph (1633–1701) 17C AS verse by   **1654.2**
Wilson, William (1645–65†), printer   79, 195
Winchester, charters relating to   **1655.3**
Windet, John (fl.1584–1610), printer   56, 191
Wolfe, John (fl.1579–1601), printer   56
Wolverhampton, St Mary's church (later St Peter's), privileges granted to   **1655.3**, **1682.1**, **1683.1**

Wooden sorts, used instead of metal type 25–26
Worcester, charters relating to 1639.4, 1655.3, 1682.1, 1683.1, 1703/5.1; charter assigning lease of land by Oswald, bp of (d.992) 1631.1, 1672.1, 1696.1, 1703/5.1
Words, OE 1599.2, 1605.3, 1605.4, 1607.3, 1610.2, 1611.2, 1612.1, 1613.2, 1617.1, 1617.2, 1622.1, 1623.6, 1625.1, 1626.2, 1632.3, 1632.4, 1639.3, 1642.1, 1644.5, 1645.3, 1646.1, 1646.2, 1647.1, 1650.1, 1650.2, 1653.1, 1653.2, 1654.1, 1655.4, 1656.3, 1658.3, 1658.4, 1659.1, 1661.2, 1662.5, 1663.3, 1665.1, 1665.4, 1669.1, 1670.2, 1671.1, 1671.3, 1671.4, 1673.4, 1674.2, 1674.3, 1678.2, 1678.3, 1681.1, 1681.3, 1681.4, 1682.3, 1682.4, 1683.3, 1683.4, 1684.1, 1684.5, 1686.1, 1689.1, 1690.2, 1691.3, 1691.4, 1696.4, 1699.2, 1700.3, 1701.1, 1703.1
Cf. Proper names

Worm, Olé (1588–1654), Danish antiquary 178
Wrist-band, AS with scroll-work 120–121
Wulfgyth, will of (1042 × 1053) 1660.1
Wulfric, will of (1002) 1655.3, 1682.1, 1683.1
Wulfstan I, bp of Worcester, abp of York (d.1023), sermon by 1572.1, 1605.2, 1643.1, 1701.2, 1703/5.1; sermon attrib to 1701.2, 1703/5.1
Wulfstan II, bp of Worcester (d.1095) 52
Wust, Balthasar Christoph I (fl. Frankfurt-am-Main 1658–1700), printer 172, 206
Wynflæd, will of (950) 1703/5.1

Young, Robert (fl.1624–43†), printer 79, 194–195, 205

Zetzner, Johann Andreas (fl. Strassburg 1664–80), publisher 168, 205
Zunner, Johann David II (fl. Frankfurt-am-Main 1666–1700), publisher 172, 206